THE OXFORD HANDBOOK OF
ARTS AND CULTURAL MANAGEMENT

THE OXFORD HANDBOOK OF

ARTS AND CULTURAL MANAGEMENT

Edited by
YUHA JUNG,
NEVILLE VAKHARIA,
and
MARILENA VECCO

OXFORD
UNIVERSITY PRESS

OXFORD
UNIVERSITY PRESS

Oxford University Press is a department of the University of Oxford. It furthers
the University's objective of excellence in research, scholarship, and education
by publishing worldwide. Oxford is a registered trade mark of Oxford University
Press in the UK and certain other countries.

Published in the United States of America by Oxford University Press
198 Madison Avenue, New York, NY 10016, United States of America.

© Oxford University Press 2024

All rights reserved. No part of this publication may be reproduced, stored in
a retrieval system, or transmitted, in any form or by any means, without the
prior permission in writing of Oxford University Press, or as expressly permitted
by law, by license, or under terms agreed with the appropriate reproduction
rights organization. Inquiries concerning reproduction outside the scope of the
above should be sent to the Rights Department, Oxford University Press, at the
address above.

You must not circulate this work in any other form
and you must impose this same condition on any acquirer.

Library of Congress Cataloging-in-Publication Data
Names: Jung, Yuha, author. | Vakharia, Neville, author. | Vecco, Marilena, author.
Title: The Oxford handbook of arts and cultural management / edited by Yuha
Jung, Neville Vakharia, and Marilena Vecco Other titles: Oxford handbooks
Description: New York : Oxford University Press, [2024] |
Series: Oxford handbooks series | Includes index. |
Identifiers: LCCN 2023034051 (print) | LCCN 2023034052 (ebook) |
ISBN 9780197621615 (hardback) | ISBN 9780197621622 (epub) | ISBN 9780197621646
Subjects: LCSH: Arts—Management. | Cultural property—Protection.
Classification: LCC NX760 .J86 2024 (print) | LCC NX760 (ebook) |
DDC 706—dc23/eng/20231206
LC record available at https://lccn.loc.gov/2023034051
LC ebook record available at https://lccn.loc.gov/2023034052

DOI: 10.1093/oxfordhb/9780197621615.001.0001

Printed by Integrated Books International, United States of America

Contents

About the Editors xi
List of Contributors xiii

PART I. INTRODUCTION TO ARTS AND CULTURAL MANAGEMENT

1. Introduction to *The Oxford Handbook of Arts and Cultural Management*: Where We Are and Where We Are Heading 3
   YUHA JUNG, NEVILLE VAKHARIA, AND MARILENA VECCO

2. The Contingencies of an Academic Field: Arts Management Research in Canada 23
   JONATHAN PAQUETTE AND JULIE BÉRUBÉ

3. Analyzing the Cultural and Creative Industries Ecosystem under the Lens of Complex Adaptive Systems: Beyond the Sector 41
   LEONARDO MAZZONI, STEFANIA OLIVA, AND LUCIANA LAZZERETTI

4. Methods and Methodologies in Arts and Cultural Management Research: A Review and Research Agenda 59
   RUTH RENTSCHLER AND JIAXIN LIU

PART II. THEORIES IN ARTS AND CULTURAL MANAGEMENT RESEARCH

5. A Social Value Judgment Model of Corporate Governance in Performing Arts Organizations 79
   ROY SUDDABY, PETER SHERER, DIEGO CORAIOLA, AND KARL SCHWONIK

6. Open Systems Theory in Arts Management 101
   YUHA JUNG AND TRAVIS NEWTON

7. Framing Nonprofit Arts and Culture Sectors through
   Economic Theory   119
   BRUCE A. SEAMAN

8. Mapping Theories in Arts and Cultural Management Research   141
   KATE KEENEY AND YUHA JUNG

PART III. CULTURAL POLICIES, DIPLOMACY, CULTURAL PLANNING, AND LEGAL CONCERNS

9. Mapping Cultural Policy: Cultural Bureaucracy as Concept,
   Norm, and Analytical Tool   163
   CAROLE ROSENSTEIN

10. The Future of Cultural Diplomacy: From Digital to Algorithmic   183
    NATALIA GRINCHEVA

11. Cultural Planning and a "Community Turn" in the Arts:
    Maximizing Cultural Resources for Social Impact   203
    TOM BORRUP

12. Copyright as an Engine for Creativity: A Critical Appraisal
    of Contemporary Developments in Intermediaries' Liability
    Regulation   221
    MIRA BURRI

13. The Role of Heritage Communities in Cultural Heritage
    Management: An International Law Perspective   239
    SIMONA PINTON

PART IV. LEADERSHIP AND GOVERNANCE IN ARTS AND CULTURAL ORGANIZATIONS

14. Ethics in Cultural Leadership: Relationships of Value   263
    JONATHAN PRICE

15. Shared Leadership and the Evolution of Festivals:
    What Can Be Learned?   283
    JOSEPHINE CAUST AND KIM GOODWIN

16. The Death of white Supremacy Culture in the US Creative Sector and Implications for Arts Management: A Critical Race Theory View   299
   Quanice Floyd and Antonio C. Cuyler

17. An Explorative Study on State-Owned Museum Performance in Italy: The Interplay between the Director's Characteristics and Board Diversity   315
   Paola Dubini and Alberto Monti

PART V. MANAGEMENT STRUCTURES AND STRATEGIES FOR ARTS AND CULTURAL ORGANIZATIONS

18. Event Co-Creation: A Participatory Perspective on Arts and Cultural Management   349
   Leonore van den Ende

19. Knowledge Management in Arts and Cultural Organizations: A Conceptual Framework for Organizational Performance   371
   Neville Vakharia

20. Project Management for Cultural Events: Toward a Systemic Approach   393
   Lucio Argano

21. A New Future for Cultural Union Workers?   411
   Rachel Shane and Josh Austin

PART VI. MARKETING FOR ARTS AND CULTURAL ORGANIZATIONS

22. Games and Museums: A Novel Approach to Attracting and Retaining Audiences   437
   Marta Pizzetti and Giulia Miniero

23. The Relationship between Marketing and Fundraising for Arts and Cultural Organizations   457
   Hyunjung Lee, Kyoungnam Ha, and Youngseon Kim

24. Creation and Consumption Experience of Cultural Value in
    Contemporary Art 481
    IAN FILLIS, BORAM LEE, AND IAN FRASER

25. Servicescape Concept in the Cultural and Creative Sectors 497
    CHRISTIAN JULMI

PART VII. FINANCING AND FUNDRAISING FOR ARTS AND CULTURAL ORGANIZATIONS

26. An International Perspective on Arts and Cultural Funding:
    Private, Public, and Hybrid Models 523
    YI LIN AND HUIHUI LUO

27. Contemporary Findings on Individual Donations and
    Fundraising Strategies 545
    JENNIFER WIGGINS

28. Tax Incentives for Arts and Cultural Organizations 575
    SIGRID HEMELS

29. Non-Fungible Tokens and Nonprofit Management: Participation,
    Revenue Generation, and Strategic Planning 593
    HEATHER R. NOLIN AND AMY C. WHITAKER

PART VIII. AUDIENCE DEVELOPMENT: PARTICIPATION, ENGAGEMENT, AND EVALUATION

30. Improving Accessibility and Inclusion in the Performing Arts for
    People with Disabilities: Moving Beyond a "Checking-the-Boxes"
    Approach 623
    ALLISON AMIDEI AND ELENA SV FLYS

31. Performance Evaluation in the Arts: A Multidisciplinary Review
    and a New Pragmatic Research Agenda 641
    FRANCESCO CHIARAVALLOTI

32. Evaluating Cultural Value: The Quintessential Wicked Problem 663
    BEN WALMSLEY

33. Measuring Customer Multisensory Experience in Live Music 681
    Manuel Cuadrado-García, Juan D. Montoro-Pons,
    and Claudia E. Goyes-Yepez

PART IX. ENTREPRENEURSHIP AND INTRAPRENEURSHIP IN ARTS AND CULTURAL ORGANIZATIONS

34. Entrepreneurship in Culture: Concepts, Perspectives, Success Factors 703
    Elmar D. Konrad and Marilena Vecco

35. Engaged Dissent: Entrepreneurship and Critique in the Institutional Practice of Three Contemporary Artists 723
    Adrienne Callander

36. Assessing the Business Model of Creative and Cultural Organizations Participating in the European Capital of Culture Program 743
    Giovanni Schiuma, Daniela Carlucci, Francesco Santarsiero, and Rosaria Lagrutta

37. Cultural Firms' Performance from a Regional Development Perspective: Evidence from Europe 761
    Andrej Srakar and Marilena Vecco

PART X. FUTURE DIRECTIONS FOR ARTS AND CULTURAL MANAGEMENT

38. The Globalized and Changing Landscape of the Arts: The Era of Post-Pandemic and Civil Unrest 785
    Pier Luigi Sacco

39. Aligning Arts Research with Practitioner Needs: Beyond Generalizations 805
    Sunil Iyengar

Index 823

About the Editors

Yuha Jung is Associate Professor of Arts Administration at the University of Kentucky. Her research focuses on systems theory and cultural diversity in arts and culture organizations. Her work is interdisciplinary in nature and includes museum studies, arts management, historic preservation, and the law. She has published various peer-reviewed articles, coedited the book *Systems Thinking in Museums* (2017), and wrote the monograph *Transforming Museum Management* (2022). She is a 2023 recipient of the National Endowment for the Humanities Research and Development Grant. She holds an MA, MPA, and PhD. She expects to receive a JD in 2024.

Neville Vakharia is Associate Dean for Research and Planning as well as an Associate Professor in the graduate Arts Administration and Museum Leadership program at Drexel University. He teaches management, strategic planning, and entrepreneurship, and his research centers on the integration of technology, information, and knowledge to foster sustainable, resilient, and relevant organizations and communities. He holds a BS in materials engineering, an MS in arts administration, and a PhD in information science. His work has been published internationally, and he has received public and private funding to develop new tools and resources that benefit the cultural and social sectors.

Marilena Vecco is Full Professor of Economics and Entrepreneurship at Burgundy Business School and Professor Associate at the Marcoux Chair in Arts Management at HEC Montréal. She holds a PhD in economic sciences from the University of Paris I and a PhD in economics of institutions and creativity from the University of Turin. From 2011 to 2016 she was Assistant Professor in Cultural Entrepreneurship at Erasmus University Rotterdam. Her research centers on cultural economics and entrepreneurship with a particular focus on cultural heritage and art markets. She has researched and consulted for several public and private organizations, including the OECD, World Bank, and European Commission.

Contributors

Allison Amidei, University of North Carolina–Charlotte

Lucio Argano, Catholic University of the Sacred Heart

Josh Austin, University of Kentucky

Julie Bérubé, University of Quebec in Outaouais

Tom Borrup, University of Minnesota

Mira Burri, University of Lucerne

Adrienne Callander, University of Arkansas

Daniela Carlucci, University of Basilicata

Josephine Caust, University of Melbourne

Francesco Chiaravalloti, University of Amsterdam

Diego Coraiola, University of Victoria

Manuel Cuadrado-García, University of Valencia

Antonio C. Cuyler, University of Michigan

Paola Dubini, Bocconi University

Ian Fillis, Liverpool John Moores University

Quanice Floyd, Drexel University

Elena SV Flys, TAI School of the Arts

Ian Fraser, University of Stirling

Kim Goodwin, University of Melbourne

Claudia E. Goyes-Yepez, independent scholar

Natalia Grincheva, University of Melbourne

Kyoungnam Ha, Pacific Lutheran University

Sigrid Hemels, Erasmus University Rotterdam; Lund University

Sunil Iyengar, National Endowment for the Arts

Christian Julmi, University of Hagen

Yuha Jung, University of Kentucky

Kate Keeney, University of Maryland

Youngseon Kim, Central Connecticut State University

Elmar D. Konrad, University of Applied Sciences Mainz

Rosaria Lagrutta, University of Basilicata

Luciana Lazzeretti, University of Florence

Boram Lee, University of South Australia

Hyunjung Lee, University of Hartford

Jiaxin Liu, University of South Australia

Huihui Luo, Shanghai Jiao Tong University

Leonardo Mazzoni, University of Padova

Giulia Miniero, Franklin University Switzerland

Alberto Monti, University of Genova

Juan D. Montoro-Pons, University of Valencia

Travis Newton, Le Moyne College

Heather R. Nolin, independent researcher

Stefania Oliva, University of Florence

Jonathan Paquette, University of Ottawa

Simona Pinton, University of Padova

Marta Pizzetti, emlyon business school

Jonathan Price, University of Leeds

Ruth Rentschler, University of South Australia

Carole Rosenstein, George Mason University

Pier Luigi Sacco, University of Chieti–Pescara

Francesco Santarsiero, University of Basilicata

Giovanni Schiuma, Libera Università Mediterranea - LUM "Giuseppe Degennaro"

Karl Schwonik, University of Calgary

Bruce A. Seaman, Georgia State University

Rachel Shane, University of Kentucky

Peter Sherer, University of Calgary

Andrej Srakar, University of Ljubljana

Roy Suddaby, University of Victoria

Neville Vakharia, Drexel University

Leonore van den Ende, Vrije University Amsterdam

Marilena Vecco, Burgundy Business School; HEC Montréal

Ben Walmsley, University of Leeds

Amy C. Whitaker, New York University

Jennifer Wiggins, Kent State University

Yi Lin, Peking University

PART I
INTRODUCTION TO ARTS AND CULTURAL MANAGEMENT

CHAPTER 1

INTRODUCTION TO *THE OXFORD HANDBOOK OF ARTS AND CULTURAL MANAGEMENT*

Where We Are and Where We Are Heading

YUHA JUNG, NEVILLE VAKHARIA, AND MARILENA VECCO

The Oxford Handbook of Arts and Cultural Management surveys the current state of research in arts and cultural management and suggests directions for future work. The handbook is focused on research and theory, with a theoretical and empirical approach to the field's larger issues and to emerging research that would support its transformation. By presenting the state of the field, this book helps define future research directions for emerging and experienced scholars while also serving as a first-line pedagogical tool for faculty and students. It updates existing, outdated anthologies with a fresh, forward-looking, up-to-date take on the field's research and future directions. It supports the writing of new works and contributions to the development of new knowledge. Moreover, by commissioning scholastic, empirical, and theoretical chapters from perspectives that are emerging and cutting-edge, it contributes to moving the field's research forward.

We deliberately chose the term "arts and cultural management" in an effort to be inclusive of the different terms and global trends used to describe the field. While "cultural management" has been a preferred term in recent years (DeVereaux 2019), "arts administration," "arts management," "cultural management," and "cultural administration" are used interchangeably in different geographical contexts, and all are used throughout the handbook.

Introduction to the Field

Arts and cultural management is a field, not a single discipline. By definition, a field encompasses and is associated with diverse disciplines. It is interdisciplinary in that different scholars from two or more disciplines study different aspects of arts, and researchers do not have to be limited to the research design, theory, and methodology of one discipline only (Aboelela et al. 2007). Arts and cultural management scholars write from different disciplines, perspectives, and epistemologies (Paquette 2019; Jung 2017). In other words, researchers from such related but distinct fields and disciplines as public administration, business administration, heritage studies, legal studies, nonprofit management, economics, and other social sciences can be found studying arts and cultural organizations and their environments while utilizing a broad range of qualitative, quantitative, and mixed methodologies.

While this diverse, interdisciplinary range of practices and the associated complexity provide positive benefits to the field, much of this work is overlooked due to its disparate sources and approaches, found across disciplines and fields of scholarship with various venues of outputs. Because it is a relatively young field with only about five decades of academic research and higher education training programs (Rosewall and Shane 2018), there is an imbalance in research areas and theorizing about arts and cultural organizations (Paquette 2019). For example, some subtopics such as marketing and leadership are more heavily discussed and represented in arts and cultural management literature (Paquette 2019), while research on programming, accounting, and evaluation are less represented. Therefore, within arts and cultural management, there is a crucial need for a curated, high-quality, first-line resource for advanced students and scholars. Moreover, the field of arts and cultural management needs a unified understanding of frequently encountered topic areas and concepts and more critical materials that could be easily accessible by students and emerging academics.

Significance of the Book and Target Audiences

A singular, organized resource, with potential to be updated periodically, would increase the reach and pedagogical impact of the field's work. This handbook addresses those needs, providing a collection of empirical, theoretical, and methodological chapters surveying research in arts and cultural management from a global perspective. It focuses on rigorous and in-depth contributions by both leading and emerging scholars from diverse backgrounds and locations. The handbook introduces and presents diverse theories and methodologies to inform readers about the application of these concepts to arts and cultural management, providing an important step toward advancing new research in the field.

It is an opportune moment to have this book for the field. More countries recognize the impact that cultural and creative industries may have on their economy as well as their role in the well-being and sustainability of society. Additionally, the number of arts and cultural management programs worldwide has increased over time. In particular, there is significant growth in the number of graduate programs, including relevant Ph.D. programs, where students can explore arts management issues, challenges, and gaps in practice and research.

Therefore, the primary audiences for this handbook are graduate students, professors, and scholars. It can be used as a text and reference book and as a pedagogical tool for faculty and students in arts and cultural management graduate programs across the globe. Examples of specific courses that could benefit from this book include those addressing research surveys, marketing and fundraising, management, leadership and governance, and audience engagement, in departments and programs focused on arts and cultural management, management, and other related fields such as museum studies, heritage management, and public administration. Additionally, both emerging and established scholars can use this handbook to familiarize themselves with the current state and knowledge of arts and cultural management research and to help develop their future research directions.

The field is maturing, which is reflected in the depth of knowledge creation and research output that is seeking an increased theoretical and empirical grounding compared to what was previously a more practitioner-based approach. By extension, there is a need for more rigorous empirical research and theory for emerging scholars in graduate and Ph.D. programs internationally. The book also plays a role in envisioning new future scenarios for arts and cultural organizational research as the field emerges from a post-pandemic world and seeks to support a more equitable, sustainable, and just society.

Conceptualization of the Field over Time

While arts and cultural management is something people have done for centuries, its establishment in the 1960s as a field of studies in a modern sense means the academic history of the field is relatively short (Paquette and Redaelli 2015; Shane 2017). For example, in the United States, Yale University and Florida State University had their first postgraduate programs in 1966 (Shane 2017). The United Kingdom saw its first formal academic program in arts management in 1976 at City University in London (Pick 2020). Australia started its first arts and cultural management master's program in 1979 at the University of South Australia (then the South Australian Institute of Technology).

Germany established an arts and cultural management course of studies in 1987 at the Hamburg University of Music and Theatre, while Singapore launched its first BA in Arts Management in 1993 at the LASALLE College of the Arts. The number of degree programs in arts and cultural management has also grown significantly in Europe, Asia, and South Africa, making arts management part of higher education curricula (Shane 2017).

Several journals have been founded in the field, including the *Journal of Arts Management, Law, and Society* in 1968 (JAMLS n.d.), *Journal of Cultural Economics* in 1977 (Evard and Colbert 2000), *International Journal of Cultural Policy* in 1994 (Evard and Colbert 2000), *International Journal of Arts Management* in 1998 (IJAM n.d.), and *European Journal of Cultural Management and Policy* in 2011 (ENCATC n.d. a), and relevant research is found in more than twenty journals, including the five listed here (see Keeney and Jung, this volume). Additionally, there have been several field-specific conferences established, such as Social Theory, Politics, and the Arts in the 1970s, the International Association of Arts and Cultural Management (AIMAC) in 1991 (Evard and Colbert 2000), and ENCATC in 1992 (ENCATC n.d. b).

The relative newness of arts and cultural management meant scholars had to conceptualize and consider whether it was a discipline, subdiscipline, field, or something else entirely. Dorn (1992), in his article entitled "Arts Administration: A Field of Dreams?," questioned the legitimacy of arts administration (a term more frequently used in the United States) as a discipline within higher education institutions. Evard and Colbert (2000) said that with the number of specialized journals and conferences growing, it was becoming a distinctive subdiscipline. Rentschler and Shilbury (2008) identified it as an emerging academic discipline and suggested ideas for developing a rating system for its journals as an effort toward more professionalization. In this context, Cuyler (2014) identified needs for more specific field research agendas and faculty research preparedness in order to train future arts management researchers and to move toward more professionalization of the field, shed the negative perception of the field as something soft and not rigorous, and develop a comprehensive body of knowledge. Based on Miller's (2001, 2) understanding of cultural management as "a tendency across disciplines," DeVereaux (2019, 5) suggested that thinking about cultural management as a "tendency" would be fitting because "it has attracted an eclectic mix of researchers and practitioners trained, variously, as sociologists, political scientists, educators, artists, philosophers, curators, theatre managers, and others interested in the same general area of practice and inquiry."

In the last decade or so there has been greater consensus that it is more firmly established as a recognized field of study. In mapping the graduate curriculum of arts management in the United States, Varela (2013) found that arts management graduate curricula across the country were mostly consistent. This is one example of the field's professionalization, and one that will likely continue moving forward.

The Oxford Handbook of Arts and Cultural Management marks and reaffirms such continuing establishment, providing field's research and directions for emerging and established scholars. In Chapter 2 of this *Handbook*, Paquette and Bérubé conceptualize arts and cultural management as a field, not a discipline, based on analysis of research output measures (associations and learned societies, publications and journals, available research funding, and research chairs) of Canadian arts and cultural management faculty. Previous works have viewed the fact that arts and cultural management does not fit into a traditional disciplinary mold as a weakness (Dorn 1992), but it is time to shed that viewpoint and see it instead in a different light. Instead of seeing this as a weakness, let us rather embrace it as a strength and even leverage it.

Mapping the Authors of *The Oxford Handbook of Arts and Cultural Management*

As mentioned previously, the field of arts and cultural management is fluid and dynamic, characterized by the crossing of disciplinary boundaries—an advantage in facing today's multifaceted circumstances. To gain a comprehensive understanding of the complex, dynamic, and intertwined challenges that cannot be addressed by a sole entity, organization, or discipline (Bronstein 2003) and to develop the most suitable solutions, perspectives from different disciplines should be integrated (Cummings and Kiesler 2005). In this vein, Jung (2017) argued that the arts and cultural management field's multidisciplinarity and interdisciplinarity are strengths. This field-based approach provides a critical context to study various parts of the larger cultural and creative industry ecosystem, including actors, relationships, and structures. These approaches are extremely relevant, as they allow us to fully understand the complexity of art and cultural phenomena, which otherwise would be overlooked or only partially understood. As the interdisciplinary nature of the field is developed through organic networks based on the needs and interests of arts and cultural communities (Paquette and Redaelli 2015), it allows organizations and entities to address the difficult challenges in a way that is grounded in the needs of the communities they serve.

One way the interdisciplinary qualities of the field are evident is in the disciplinary diversity among the contributing authors to this volume. We mapped the contributing authors' gender, profession, number of publications and citations, disciplinary homes, research subfields, terminal degree disciplines, time since their terminal degree completion, and their current locations. Kaitlyn Hardiman, an editorial assistant for this handbook and a Ph.D. student in the Department of Arts Administration at the University of Kentucky, helped collect this mapping data and created some of the figures used in this section. For ease and simplicity of analysis, we opted to use word clouds to present some of the aggregate information, specifically for contributing authors' current academic units, research subfields, and terminal degree fields and disciplines. In this visual tool the most-repeated words are displayed larger and the least-repeated words are displayed smaller, visually illustrating the amount of repetition in words.

FIGURE 1.1 Contributing authors' current academic units.

The gender (the authors acknowledge that the concept of gender is fluid and cannot be presented in black and white terms. It is based on cursory representation of authors' genders and may not accurately reflect how they self identify) makeup of authors is a bit imbalanced: 44 percent female and 56 percent male (out of about seventy contributing authors), which presents a slightly higher representation of male scholars. Most authors hold faculty positions in higher education institutions, with 80 percent of the authors being professors and the rest being students, consultants, higher education administrators, practitioners, research center directors, and research fellows. The authors' average number of publications is forty-five, and their lifetime citations are 677 as of February 2023.

Figure 1.1 shows the contributing authors' current academic units. Most chapter authors' academic units include "management," "entrepreneurship," "business," "marketing," "arts administration," or "culture" in their unit titles. Figure 1.2 represents the contributing authors' research areas and subfields, which mostly center around art, culture, cultural policy, and cultural entrepreneurship. Figure 1.3 represents the most frequent terminal degrees of the contributing authors. Most of them have degrees in or related to marketing, arts administration, business administration, management, and economics.

The graph in Figure 1.4 shows the number of years since the contributing authors' terminal degree completion. As the graph indicates, the career lengths are quite diverse, as the authors range from emerging scholars to much more experienced researchers. While some authors have just begun their research journey and are still pursuing their terminal degrees, others have spent more than thirty years conducting research in arts and cultural management. On average, authors contributing to this handbook have over fourteen years of experience since attaining their terminal degrees, with the

FIGURE 1.2 Contributing authors' research subfields.

FIGURE 1.3 Contributing authors' terminal degree fields and disciplines.

largest number of authors having six to ten years of experience. This broad diversity of emerging and veteran scholars provides a unique combination of fresh perspectives on emerging concepts and seasoned approaches to long-standing issues of importance to arts and cultural management.

As shown in the map (see Figure 1.5), most contributing authors are currently located in North America, Western Europe, and Australia. However, their current locations do not necessarily represent their racial, ethnic, and national origin. For example, Yuha Jung, one of the editors of the handbook, was born and grew up in South Korea and currently works at the University of Kentucky in the United States. Geographic representation, however, shows that there is a clear representational issue in the arts and cultural management scholarship presented by this handbook. Additionally, the lack of

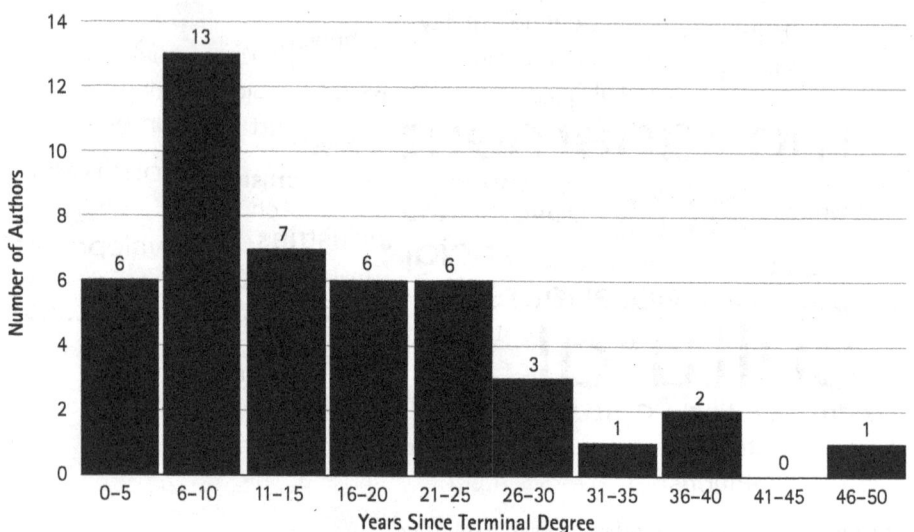

FIGURE 1.4 Years since authors' terminal degree completion.

FIGURE 1.5 Current geographical location of contributing authors.

representation from other parts of the world does not mean that researchers in those regions do not do arts and cultural management research. This is discussed as one of the major limitations of this handbook and one that we hope to be able to address in future editions. Further limitations, including this issue, are discussed at the end of the chapter.

Arts and cultural management as a field is now firmly established with increasing legitimacy, but disproportionately so, especially in terms of geographic location. The field is facing more challenges, but these challenges also generate significant opportunities for us to broaden and deepen research impact and relevance by addressing societal challenges and becoming agents of change. We can utilize our complex and diverse network of perspectives, methodologies, and theories to further our field's research and education, thereby leveraging those strengths to expand the field's reach and network to be much more collaborative and inclusive of diverse voices and perspectives.

How the Book Is Organized

The book is divided into ten sections, covering the main topics studied under the umbrella of arts and cultural management. These sections, which are briefly described in the section that follows, are:

1. Introduction to Arts and Cultural Management
2. Theories in Arts and Cultural Management Research
3. Cultural Policies, Diplomacy, Cultural Planning, and Legal Concerns
4. Leadership and Governance in Arts and Cultural Organizations
5. Management Structures and Strategies for Arts and Cultural Organizations
6. Marketing for Arts and Cultural Organizations
7. Financing and Fundraising for Arts and Cultural Organizations
8. Audience Development: Participation, Engagement, and Evaluation
9. Entrepreneurship and Intrapreneurship in Arts and Cultural Organizations
10. Future Directions for Arts and Cultural Management

Each section includes four to five chapters with the last section having two. These chapters are not meant to be exhaustive in covering possible topics and perspectives within each section. Rather, to provide variety, each section includes samples from the field surveying current and novel research and themes, emerging and challenging themes, and future directions.

Introduction to Arts and Cultural Management

The aim of this introductory section is to contextualize arts and cultural management research as a field of study. It describes the field in terms of theories, research methods, and methodologies, highlighting strengths and challenges in research design, data collection methods, and analysis.

Arts and cultural management can be defined as a heterogeneous field, distinctly different from a discipline. While a discipline is linked to specific types of education and certifications, a field is not confined to these constraints and allows for the acceptance and use of different research traditions, theories, and methodologies in a variety of contexts and conditions (Abbott 1988; Blok et al. 2019). While this broader perspective can create challenges in studying the field as a whole, a field-based approach creates the necessary context to study the actors, relationships, and structures that are part of the larger cultural and creative industry ecosystem.

The study of arts and cultural management can draw from varied ontologies and epistemologies, each with its own research methods and methodologies. Scholars in this field approach their work from both complementary and contradictory worldviews, with varying units of analysis spanning individuals to organizations to sectors to entire geographic regions. Given this, the research methods and methodologies used by these scholars vary greatly and are evolving to capture new types of data, information, and knowledge.

As the study of arts and cultural management continues to gain legitimacy, it must play a dual role. It must continue to undertake field-building efforts to establish itself through dedicated, reputable publishing outlets, through engagement in communities of practice, and by building a solid body of research that demonstrates the breadth and depth of our field. Additionally, the study of arts and cultural management must be part of the broader conversations happening outside of our field, influencing other fields and disciplines by sharing what is common with them while demonstrating what is unique. It is only through this combination of field-building and field integration that the research community's impact can be maximized.

Theories in Arts and Cultural Management Research

Arts and cultural management draws from interdisciplinary theories that are widely used in the fields of business administration, public and nonprofit management, organization science, sociology, and more. Yet researchers have identified that there is very little theorizing of arts organizations going on in the field of arts and cultural management (Paquette 2019). More research is needed to shed light on theories used in arts and cultural management research and to identify theoretical contributions by their disciplinary origins and use. The transferability of theories and their application to the arts and cultural management field can still be considered limited compared to other domains such as cultural economics.

As the body of research in arts and cultural management begins to mature, newer research approaches are emerging that utilize a broader set of theories to support more impactful research. The complexity of arts and cultural organizations and the dynamic environments in which they operate require a more nuanced theoretical lens.

As arts and cultural organizations seek to create relevant experiences and maintain artistic excellence, theories focused on social value, for example, can be applied to study this dichotomy. To understand how arts and cultural organizations can best support increasingly diverse communities, the use of systems theories provides the necessary context to assess how internal actions drive external results. Economic theories can be applied to arts and cultural management research, particularly when this research combines the positive and normative elements of these theories.

The chapters in this section demonstrate how the application of a broader set of theories is highly relevant to arts and cultural management research, helping to move the field forward and providing valuable theoretical grounding and applications for education and practice.

Cultural Policies, Diplomacy, Cultural Planning, and Legal Concerns

"Cultural policy," "cultural diplomacy," and "cultural planning" are distinct but interrelated terms, and each must be contextualized within the political boundaries and legal and governmental structures that serve as the unit of analysis. While this contextualization can create challenges in generalizing research in these areas, this research is crucial for understanding how arts and cultural organizations can adapt to changes in the political, social, economic, technological, and legal landscape, which is becoming more and more challenging. The chapters in this section address several critical topics including equitable cultural heritage preservation, new forms of creating and distributing art, and emerging legal implications for creative works, while also identifying future research needs.

Cultural policy has only recently emerged as a growing component of public policy (Bennett 2004; van der Ploeg 2006), fostering debate over artistic and cultural production and consumption. This opens significant opportunities to study cultural policy as enacted through various government policy agendas while also mapping its evolution. These opportunities for research range from how communities can advocate for and promote policies that preserve cultural heritage to the need for cultural policies that protect new forms of artistic expression and intellectual property. Similarly, cultural diplomacy research provides fertile ground to explore new artistic and cultural practices through differing diplomatic channels, actors, digital technologies, and legal constructs. Finally, cultural planning research has studied how governments and communities can mobilize resources to address civic and social concerns, with new opportunities to advance equity-based approaches in the arts.

Understanding how arts and cultural management research links to broader policy, diplomacy, and planning efforts can support the case for the role of arts and culture in society while also providing new research opportunities linked to contemporary societal issues.

Leadership and Governance in Arts and Cultural Organizations

The study of effective leadership and governance in arts and cultural organizations has long focused on identifying the important functions of senior leadership and governing boards (Turbide and Laurin 2014). These studies emphasized the knowledge, skills, and abilities that drive success and organizational effectiveness. However, rapid changes in our social, political, and ethical landscapes have created new challenges for those who must lead and govern these organizations. The chapters in this section cover a range of contemporary issues facing the leaders and governing bodies of arts and cultural organizations.

These new dilemmas, contemporary threats, and opportunities vary from the artistic works their organizations present and the objects they display to their active role in addressing past injustices and beyond. Increased public awareness and perception of these social and ethical matters have pressured organizations to cease being neutral and to take a stance on social and political matters. Leadership must dynamically address these issues while also maintaining the stability of their organization and its governance, a challenge and struggle for many organizations.

In response to these environmental shifts, organizational structures must also shift. Structures that feature a singular, visionary leader or dual co-leaders must be revisited. New approaches to leadership structures expand the circle of leaders in organizations, utilizing each leader's specialized skills and creating a collaborative leadership structure that can be more than the sum of its parts. The governance implications of a multileader organization must also be considered, in that the governing body must now develop processes to work with decentralized leadership structures.

The COVID-19 pandemic and social justice movements throughout the world have brought about a need to rethink not only the role of leadership and governance but also, and more importantly, the role that arts and cultural organizations can play in addressing these issues. A new type of leader and new approaches to governance will ensure the relevance and sustainability of the field in the future.

Management Structures and Strategies for Arts and Cultural Organizations

Arts and cultural organizations must operate in the most effective and efficient manner in order to accomplish their goals and fulfil their missions. Management practices and approaches that bolster operational capacity and stakeholder engagement must be deliberately and intentionally implemented. The chapters in this section address critical management approaches that are essential to organizational success in an evolving and dynamic environment.

As arts and cultural organizations seek to engage audiences and other stakeholders in programmatic efforts, the concepts of co-creation and co-production have emerged, in which organizations actively include outside participants in the development and delivery of their programs and offerings (Luonila and Jyrämä 2020). However, successful co-creation and co-production efforts require new management approaches and strategies that rethink traditional spectatorship models.

Key to achieving operational effectiveness in arts and cultural organizations is the need to strategically use data, information, and knowledge as an organizational asset. Knowledge management is a critical function for arts and cultural managers. It is a holistic, sociotechnical concept that involves people, processes, and technology (Desouza and Paquette 2011). In an increasingly data-informed, knowledge-driven society, managers must have access to institutionalized knowledge to make decisions, understand their stakeholders, and drive organizational performance.

As the work of arts and cultural organizations becomes more complex, managers are expected to undertake multiple functions and tasks within their organizations. The theories and frameworks of project management could provide managers with strategies to improve efficiency and effectiveness (Van der Wagen and White 2015; Cserhàti and Szabo 2014). Arts and cultural managers can benefit from the successful use and application of these strategies in other fields to address the increasingly complex tasks and functions they face. Similarly, the management of an organization's human resources now requires a more complex understanding of collective action and organized labor efforts, whereby the needs of employees must be prioritized as a key part of service to an organization's mission.

As managers seek to improve how they manage their internal stakeholders while deepening engagement with and relevance to external stakeholders, the concepts of cocreation, knowledge management, and project management provide valuable insights into structures and strategies for organizational effectiveness and performance.

Marketing for Arts and Cultural Organizations

Because arts and cultural organizations seek to connect with new audiences and visitors, traditional marketing theories and approaches alone cannot succeed in engaging the next generation of arts and cultural patrons. Managers of arts and cultural organizations must undertake innovative marketing and engagement strategies that reach people in new ways while providing novel program experiences. The chapters in this section contribute to various marketing and engagement strategies that explore inventive means to reach and engage.

Digital experiences such as gamification and virtual reality are emerging in the delivery of arts and cultural programs, primarily in response to the expectations of consumers and because of their appeal to younger audiences (Piccialli and Chianese 2017; Zollo et al. 2022). Digital engagement strategies can be effective but are also risky, and they must be linked to programmatic outcomes to avoid becoming costly efforts with little return. Arts and cultural managers who create meaningful, authentic digital experiences can expand their audiences, both on-site and online.

While marketing approaches are often viewed as a means by which earned revenue is generated, it is important to understand marketing's relationship with fundraising and the generation of contributed revenue. Yet many organizations treat these two functions independently, often to the detriment of each. Newer approaches using relationship marketing strategies, in which marketing is viewed as a holistic function of the entire organization, can support donor retention and expansion of an organization's donor base. This broader perspective on marketing can support efforts that increase both earned and contributed revenues, thereby supporting arts and cultural organizations' sustainability.

Marketing is also a powerful tool in creating value for an artistic product, providing context to consumers of art, and linking the artwork to the artist's vision. Taken more broadly, marketing can be a tool for the social construction of value, validating both the artist and the artwork. The deliberative construction of an environment in which art is experienced can affect how consumers engage with artworks. The creation of novel, hybrid environments for arts experiences is an emerging area of study and practice.

Incorporating updated marketing approaches that appeal to changing consumer behaviors and tastes is a critical management function. There are many lines of research inquiry to pursue in these nascent areas, with immediate implications for arts and cultural organizations.

Financing and Fundraising for Arts and Cultural Organizations

While differences in public funding policies, business models, and revenue streams exist, there is always a need for consistent, reliable, and growing sources of funds to support an organization's mission and vision. The chapters in this section describe how changes in individual, institutional, and governmental support practices have created a new environment that requires the diversification of sources and revenue.

Reaching a diverse base of individual donors has become an increasingly important strategy for arts and cultural organizations, particularly after the Great Recession of 2007–2009, when public funding sources waned (Rosenstein et al. 2013). Simultaneously, crowdfunding platforms grew in prominence, providing access to new supporters and serving as an important source of sustaining revenue for many organizations. However, these donors are seeking more of a connection to the organizations they support (Sneddon, Evers, and Lee 2020; Kottasz 2004), and managers of arts and cultural organizations must find new ways to engage these donors in their work. Beyond individual donor motivations, it is also vital that organizations deeply understand how market forces and reputation affect their base of public and private support.

The recent development and use of blockchain technologies and associated non-fungible tokens (NFTs) have opened up another potential source of funding with direct applicability for arts and cultural organizations (Valeonti et al. 2021). While this emerging technology is already in use in selected cases within arts and cultural organizations, as it becomes more commonplace leaders must be aware of the associated benefits and risks. Further, with the emergence of new technologies, national and international policy efforts must evolve to balance protecting the rights of artistic creators with allowing for innovative ways to adapt and distribute artistic products.

At the governmental level, cultural policy and tax legislation serve as the fundamental means by which public funds are distributed to arts and cultural organizations. While cultural policy varies greatly by country, arts and cultural leaders must understand their role as policy advocates, making the case for support by demonstrating the instrumental and intrinsic impacts of their organization's work. This new landscape of financing and fundraising requires stronger, more relevant connections between arts and cultural organizations and the people and institutions that support them.

Audience Development: Participation, Engagement, and Evaluation

Today's arts and cultural organizations seek more than transactional engagements with their audiences. They are now expected to demonstrate their public value, showing how they contribute to some greater common good in communities and society (Moore 1995; Scott 2016). This broader, more normative role requires new leadership and marketing strategies and measures of success. Programs and offerings must serve increasingly diverse audiences and communities while also leveraging digital engagement strategies and experiential, multisensory approaches. Finally, these programs and offerings must be accessible to individuals who face physical and cognitive barriers to traditional means of engagement.

As arts and cultural organizations explore ways to increase their public value and relevance, their methods of evaluation must also evolve. Traditional strategies that focused solely on attendance figures, visitation levels, and earned revenues are no longer sufficient for assessing organizational performance. These traditional evaluative approaches simply reflect back on an organization's programs and offerings and do not provide the depth and breadth needed for understanding the true impact of an organization's work. Ideally, evaluative efforts should drive positive change within the organization and those served by it. Thus, evaluation becomes increasingly more challenging when the broader concepts of value are included. Today's approaches to evaluation must take into account the determinants and outcomes of public value as well as the effectiveness of experiential and aesthetic dimensions of arts and cultural offerings. The chapters in this section elucidate critical approaches to enhance arts and cultural participation, engagement, and evaluation from a values-based perspective.

Entrepreneurship and Intrapreneurship in Arts and Cultural Organizations

With increasing recognition of the importance of arts and culture to economic development, the concepts and principles of entrepreneurship provide a useful means by which to study how artists, organizations, and the creative industries can thrive. The chapters in this section address a broad range of entrepreneurial principles, from the traditional view of entrepreneurship as the creation of new ventures to entrepreneurship within existing structures, known as intrapreneurship.

Even in established organizations, applying the principles of entrepreneurship and entrepreneurial thinking can enhance the organization's culture and the overall success of the enterprise. By leveraging and adapting frameworks from outside the creative sector, empirical studies of entrepreneurial activity are now possible, bringing the cultural and creative industries into the broader entrepreneurship literature.

Artists working within institutions can apply their own agency to disrupt traditional approaches and break down institutional barriers. The artist as intrapreneur must often oppose isomorphic pressures to maintain the status quo while also negotiating the social networks within the organization in order to achieve their vision and transform institutional norms.

From a sector-wide perspective, entrepreneurial activity can be affected by the external economic conditions that support or hinder it. Small organizations can act entrepreneurially to leverage larger external opportunities, often driven by governmental policy, that can strengthen their value propositions, enhance their visibility, and strengthen relationships with stakeholders. Similarly, understanding the regional economic conditions that support entrepreneurial activity and its effect on the performance of cultural firms provides insights into the effects of public policy decisions and their relationship to decisions made by firms.

As the study of entrepreneurship and intrapreneurship in arts and cultural organizations continues to grow and mature, new perspectives that link to extant theories and literature are needed, while new theories unique to artists, arts organizations, and creative industries must also emerge.

Future Directions for Arts and Cultural Management

The shock of the COVID-19 pandemic and widespread civil unrest accelerated an evolution of the arts and cultural field. The concluding chapters of the book highlight the broader role of the arts in society and the implications for future directions in research.

Even before the global pandemic, the arts and cultural landscape had been characterized by the impact of a new cycle of globalization. This transition has been expedited by new technologies such as immersive media, artificial intelligence, and decentralized currencies, which created novel possibilities in terms of production, distribution, and consumption that were not feasible even two decades ago. Bottom-up forms of production are now highly relevant in a post-pandemic world, contributing to social cohesion, inclusion, democratization of culture, and the enhancement of resilience and sustainability by addressing well-being, mental health, and social issues.

With increasing recognition of the role of arts and culture in an era of rapid change, there is a growing need for coordinated research efforts among funding agencies, researchers, and practitioners. This holistic approach can support the creation of broader research agendas that allow for the collection of timely data, support strong research methods and methodologies, and take into account the multidimensional and complex nature of cultural phenomena.

Limitations and What's Next

While the handbook covers a variety of topics and research areas in the arts and cultural management, the authors' current locations and academic institutions represent mostly North America, Western Europe, and Australia. We followed the invitation model to recruit authors and commission chapters, which means that we were limited by our educational background, networks, and journals we can read (i.e., those written in English) in identifying whom to invite. Most authors are coming from English-speaking countries, and we only invited authors who write in English. This limited the geographical scope of the scholarship. Additionally, while the editors did their best to include as many topic areas as possible, the authors' final work determined what could be included. We hope to overcome some of these limitations in future editions. In Chapter 38 of this *Handbook*, Pier Luigi Sacco states, "The West is demographically declining, whereas the global South is rising, and even though financial resources, and thus production capacity, are still mostly concentrated in the West, global audiences are increasingly non-Western. There is therefore a clear competitive push toward broadening the spectrum of content away from Western-centrism" (790). This quote not only advocates for inclusivity and accessibility of arts and cultural management scholarship for equity perspectives but also frames it as an economically beneficial thing to do. We no longer have an excuse to not be inclusive. The editors will strive to be more inclusive of global perspectives in the future editions of *The Oxford Handbook of Arts and Cultural Management*.

The study of arts and cultural management is at a critical juncture. Significant opportunities exist to both broaden and deepen research approaches for increased impact and relevance. With growing recognition that arts and culture must take on a larger role in addressing societal challenges, researchers must also recognize their critical role as agents of change. The future of arts and cultural management research must be one of interdisciplinarity, collaboration with practitioners, and integration with broader fields of study. Our field requires this, and our true impact as scholars demands this.

References

Abbott, Andrew. 1988. *The System of Professions: An Essay on the Division of Expert Labour*. Chicago: University of Chicago Press.

Aboelela, Sally W., Elaine Larson, Suzanne Bakken, Olveen Carrasquillo, Allan Formicola, Sherry A. Glied, Janet Haas, and Kristine M. Gebbie. 2007. "Defining Interdisciplinary

Research: Conclusions from a Critical Review of the Literature." *Health Services Research* 42, no. 1p1: 329–346. https://doi.org/10.1111/j.1475-6773.2006.00621.x.

Bennett, Oliver. 2004. "Review Essay: The Torn Halves of Cultural Policy Research." *International Journal of Cultural Policy* 10, no. 2: 237–248.

Blok, Anders, Maria D. Lindstrøm, Marie L. Meilvang, and Inge K. Pedersen. 2019. "Ecologies of Boundaries: Modes of Boundary Work in Professional Proto-jurisdictions." *Symbolic Interaction* 42, no. 4: 588–617.

Bronstein, Laura R. 2003. "A Model for Interdisciplinary Collaboration." *Social Work* 48, no. 3: 297–306. https://doi.org/10.1093/sw/48.3.297.

Cserháti, Gabriella, and Lajos Szabó. 2014. "The Relationship Between Success Criteria and Success Factors in Organisational Event Projects." *International Journal of Project Management* 32, no. 4: 61–624.

Cummings, Jonathon, and Sara Kiesler. 2005. "Collaborative Research Across Disciplinary and Organizational Boundaries." *Social Studies of Science* 35, no. 5: 703–722. https://doi.org/10.1177/0306312705055535.

Cuyler, Antonio C. 2014. "Critical Issues for Research in Arts Management." *ENCATC Journal of Cultural Management and Policy* 4, no. 1: 9–13.

Desouza, Kevin, and Scott Paquette. 2011. *Knowledge Management: An Introduction*. New York: Neal-Schuman.

DeVereaux, Constance. 2019. "Cultural Management as a Field." In *Arts and Cultural Management*, edited by Constance DeVereaux, 3–12. New York: Routledge.

Dorn, Charles M. 1992. "Arts Administration: A Field of Dreams?" *Journal of Arts Management, Law, and Society* 22, no. 3: 241–251. https://doi.org/10.1080/10632921.1992.9944406.

ENCATC. n.d. a. "ENCATC Journal." Accessed March 28, 2023. https://www.encatc.org/en/resources/journal/.

ENCATC. n.d. b. "History." Accessed March 28, 2023. https://www.encatc.org/en/about-us/history/.

Evard, Yves, and François Colbert. 2000. "Arts Management: A New Discipline Entering the Millennium?" *International Journal of Arts Management* 2, no. 2 (Winter 2000): 4–13. https://www.jstor.org/stable/41064684/.

IJAM. n.d. "International Journal of Arts Management." Accessed March 28, 2023. https://www.sdabocconi.it/en/international-journal-arts-management.

JAMLS. n.d. "Journal Information." Accessed March 28, 2023. https://www.tandfonline.com/action/journalInformation?journalCode%3Dvjam20/.

Jung, Yuha. 2017. "Threading and Mapping Theories in the Field of Arts Administration: Thematic Discussion of Theories and Their Interdisciplinarity." *Journal of Arts Management, Law, and Society* 47, no. 1: 3–16. https://doi.org/10.1080/10632921.2016.1241970.

Kottasz, Rita. 2004. "How Should Charitable Organisations Motivate Young Professionals to Give Philanthropically?" *International Journal of Nonprofit and Voluntary Sector Marketing* 9, no. 1: 9–27.

Luonila, Mervi, and Annukka Jyrämä. 2020. "Does Co-Production Build on Co-Creation or Does Co-Creation Result in Co-Producing?" *Arts and the Market* 10, no. 1: 1–17. https://doi.org/10.1108/AAM-04-2019-0014.

Miller, Toby. 2001. "What It Is and What It Isn't: Cultural Studies Meets Graduate-Student Labor." *Yale Journal of Law and the Humanities* 13, no. 1: 69.

Moore, Mark H. 1995. *Creating Public Value: Strategic Management in Government*. Cambridge, MA: Harvard University Press.

Paquette, Jonathan. 2019. "Organizational Theories in Arts Management Research." *Journal of Arts Management, Law, and Society* 49, no. 4: 221–223. https://doi.org/10.1080/10632921.2019.1631033.

Paquette, Jonathan, and Eleonora Redaelli. 2015. *Arts Management and Cultural Policy Research*. London: Palgrave Macmillan.

Piccialli, Francesco, and Angelo Chianese. 2017. "A Location-Based IoT Platform Supporting the Cultural Heritage Domain." *Concurrency and Computation: Practice and Experience* 29, no. 11: e4091.

Pick, Martyn. 2020. "John Pick Obituary." *Guardian*, March 2, 2020. https://www.theguardian.com/culture/2020/mar/02/john-pick-obituary.

Rentschler, Ruth, and David Shilbury. 2008. "Academic Assessment of Arts Management Journals: A Multidimensional Rating Survey." *International Journal of Arts Management* 10, no. 3: 60–71. http://www.jstor.org/stable/41064964.

Rosenstein, Carole, Vanessa Riley, Natalia Rocha, and Tyler Boenecke. 2013. "The Distribution and Policy Implications of US State Government General Operating Support to the Arts and Culture: Lessons from the Great Recession." *Cultural Trends* 22, no. 3–4: 180–191.

Rosewall, Ellen, and Rachel Shane. 2018. "Preface." In *Arts and Cultural Management: Critical and Primary Sources*, edited by Ellen Rosewall and Rachel Shane, xiii–xv. New York: Bloomsbury Academic.

Scott, Carol A., ed. 2016. *Museums and Public Value: Creating Sustainable Futures*. London: Routledge.

Shane, Rachel. 2017. "Editor-in-Chief's Introduction." *Journal of Arts Management, Law, and Society* 47, no. 1: 1–2. https://doi.org/10.1080/10632921.2017.1289766.

Sneddon, Joanne N., Uwana Evers, and Julie A. Lee. 2020. "Personal Values and Choice of Charitable Cause: An Exploration of Donors' Giving Behavior." *Nonprofit and Voluntary Sector Quarterly* 49, no. 4: 803–826.

Turbide, Johanne, and Claude Laurin. 2014. "Governance in the Arts and Culture Nonprofit Sector: Vigilance or Indifference?" *Administrative Sciences* 4, no. 4: 413–431.

Valeonti, Foteini, Antonis Bikakis, Melissa Terras, Chris Speed, Andrew Hudson-Smith, and Konstantinos Chalkias. 2021. "Crypto Collectibles, Museum Funding and OpenGLAM: Challenges, Opportunities and the Potential of Non-Fungible Tokens (NFTs)." *Applied Sciences* 11, no. 21: 9931.

van der Ploeg, Frederick. 2006. "The Making of Cultural Policy: A European Perspective." In *Handbook of the Economics of Art and Culture*, vol. 1, edited by Victor A. Ginsburg and David Throsby, 1183–1221. Amsterdam: Elsevier. https://doi.org/10.1016/S1574-0676(06)01034-9.

Van der Wagen, Lynn, and Lauren White. 2015. *Human Resource Management for the Event Industry*. 2nd ed. Abingdon, UK: Routledge.

Varela, Ximena. 2013. "Core Consensus, Strategic Variations: Mapping Arts Management Graduate Education in the United States." *Journal of Arts Management, Law, and Society* 43, no. 2: 74–87. https://doi.org/10.1080/10632921.2013.78156.

Zollo, Lamberto, Riccardo Rialti, Anna Marrucci, and Cristiano Ciappei. 2022. "How Do Museums Foster Loyalty in Tech-Savvy Visitors? The Role of Social Media and Digital Experience." *Current Issues in Tourism* 25, no. 18: 2991–3008.

CHAPTER 2

THE CONTINGENCIES OF AN ACADEMIC FIELD

Arts Management Research in Canada

JONATHAN PAQUETTE AND JULIE BÉRUBÉ

Introduction

The disciplinary model is the dominant structure of academic research. In ways similar to professions, disciplines encompass practices that are transmitted through education, training, certifications, and socialization (Larson 1977; Abbott 1988; Blok et al. 2019). While several new interdisciplinary programs of study have emerged in universities in recent decades, the disciplinary model remains dominant. Biology, chemistry, sociology, political science, anthropology, and physics, among other disciplines, remain important references for the organization of academic research. The disciplinary model in universities (Clark 1987; Abbott 2001; Lamont 2009; Jacobs 2014) has been, and continues to be, an important way of structuring education and research, and an essential way of distributing organizational resources (such as public funding) and symbolic capital (such as recognition by peers) (Abbott 2005). The model of academies (e.g., the Académie des sciences morales et politiques in France and the Royal Swedish Academy of Sciences) offers a good example of the kind of institutions that grant a certain disciplinary and merit-based recognition.

Outside of academia, the medical profession, engineering, nursing, law, and architecture are good examples of fully integrated disciplines (Abbott and Meerabeau 2020). These professions are archetypes of both professionalization and disciplinarity (Evetts 2003, 2013; Fournier 1999); they claim authority not only over a body of knowledge and an object of study but also over a body of practices (Brock, Powell, and Hinings 1999). Through this authority, professions have successfully established their collective goals by means of external recognition and have solidified autonomy over the regulation of professionals within their fields (Larson 1977; Paradeise 1988; Tripier, Dubar, and Boussard 2013;

Champy 2015). As such, these professions occupy a unique place in academic research, as preoccupations with application and professional practice mesh well with the various agents who contribute to the protection of practice and disciplinary knowledge.

Conceptual parallels between professions and disciplines—and the extension of these parallels to fields of study—can offer fruitful material for developing an understanding of arts management and its place in academia. Much like professions, disciplines are institutions that insist on the reproduction and auto-regulation of their membership. This insistence on reproduction and auto-regulation implies values, norms, and an ethos that circulates among the members, who adhere to the discipline and, by extension, subject themselves to imposed processes in order to gain full membership, including training, examinations, and contests (Freidson 2001; Zahra and Newey 2009). According to Tight (2020, 422–423), disciplines have a number of core characteristics: an object of study, a "body of accumulated specialist knowledge," core theories and concepts, specific terminologies, specific methods, and an institutional anchorage or "manifestation"—the last of which includes degrees, journals, and academic institutions.

By contrast, fields do not rely on institutions that can select, socialize, and regulate their members—at least not in ways that are as authoritative as those found in disciplines. Like occupations or semi-professions (Etzioni 1969), one can enter a field from a variety of different paths and evolve through unpredictable social and organizational trajectories. While fields may include components that can bring them closer to disciplines at times—or sometimes certain agents and institutions may contribute to the construction of a disciplinary project—fields tend to be heterogeneous and hetero-regulated; they depend on resources (financial, material, organizational, and symbolic) that are loosely coupled. In these respects, arts management can be said to be an academic field (Devereaux 2009; Ebewo and Sirayi 2009)—albeit one that is perhaps on rocky footing, especially given the fact that there are very few opportunities for doctoral training that opens space for the interdisciplinary discussions necessary to socialize new members in the field.

While one can say that there is an accumulated body of knowledge on arts management—most of which is consigned to a few textbooks and journals—and while there are some educational programs and conferences, arts management does not rely strictly on a core object of study. In many ways, cultural policy and creative industries are common objects of study that intersect with arts management, though they are not necessarily or definitively "arts management" subjects. And, of course, there are debates and notions that help to socialize entrants to the field of arts management (e.g., the debate between cultural democracy and democratization of culture).[1] However, arts management is largely a field that borrows concepts and notions from others—it is a "borrower's field" (Brindle and Devereaux 2011, 5). Given its borrowing nature and lack of core object of study—not to mention the fact that it does not fit the academic model of disciplines and disciplinary organizations—it is evident from the outset that arts management is faced with a number of unique research challenges, opportunities, and contingencies. However, to what extent are these research contingencies similar to those of other research fields?

Building on an institutionalist framework for understanding academic work and fields, this chapter documents the contingencies of arts management research in Canada. There are no arts management PhD programs in Canada, making it an interesting case for understanding the heterogeneity of research in a field. While there are dozens of graduate programs in arts management across Canada, there are no arts management doctoral degrees to be had. Unless they have obtained their degrees abroad, Canadian researchers evolving in the field often have degrees from business schools, communication studies programs, or political science fields (the last of which are commonly coupled with a specialization in public policy). In other words, there are no doctoral programs in arts management to socialize new entrants into the field, and very few mechanisms to regulate entrants and auto-regulate academic work among peers, at least not domestically, making Canadian arts management a very heterogeneous field. The Canadian case is not unique in this sense, as a lack of field-oriented doctoral degrees is common in many other countries. However, the linguistic conditions of Canada, with the coexistence of two official languages and linguistic communities, bring to salience different spaces and institutions for research dissemination. Culturally and institutionally, as a case study, Canada has many commonalities with Britain, Australia, and the United States, but its French-speaking community also experiences challenges encountered by many researchers who conduct their research in a language other than English and, ultimately, in academic spaces that have a different audience, a different reach, and different needs.

In this chapter, the objective is to understand fields from an institutional perspective by focusing on the possibilities available to those who navigate and conduct their careers in arts management. As such, this chapter does not offer an analysis or stratification of research practices in Canada, nor does it attempt to determine the symbolic capital of the field (Bourdieu 1976, 1991) versus other fields or established disciplines. Rather, the objective of this chapter is to understand both the dynamics of national institutions that practice arts management research and the financial and symbolic capital that is effectively available to and accumulable by researchers in the field who work in Canadian universities.

To this end, four parameters are studied: associations and learned societies, publications and journals, available research funding, and research chairs. This chapter concludes with observations on the conditions of research in the field and reflections on the methodological challenges unique to the study of arts management as a field of research.

Associations and Learned Societies

Associations and learned societies are often among the general elements surveyed to assess the characteristics of a discipline or the vitality of a field. In the field of arts management, the Canadian Association of Arts Administration Educators (CAAAE) is one of the most important associations. Founded in 1983, the CAAAE focuses its efforts on education, pedagogy, and arts management program development. More specifically, the CAAAE's work focuses on exchanging best practices, strengthening the curriculum in arts management and arts education programs, and providing advocacy for arts management education in colleges and universities. Membership in the CAAAE is institutional, comprising twelve institutions and the faculty/researchers that facilitate their undergraduate and graduate programs. In this respect, the CAAAE's actions and purpose echo those of its American counterpart, the Association of Arts Administration Educators (AAAE). It should be noted, however, that, while the CAAAE represents well-established researchers in Canadian arts management, the dissemination of knowledge is not its aim and main purpose.

While associations are important vectors for advocacy, learned societies are important catalysts for research diffusion and meetings between peers (Pérez-Cabañero and Cuadrado-Garcia 2011). In Canada, however, there is no national or even regional learned society whose focus is on arts management or whose membership is based on researchers' status in the field. This means there are no annual or regularly scheduled arts management research conferences in Canada.

Considering this lack of a national and/or regional research-focused learned society for arts management, the question can be raised as to how arts management expertise circulates in Canada and to what extent it meshes with disciplinary platforms for research dissemination. In order to answer this question, annual conferences and their programs—in English and French—were studied over a ten-year period. Going through the most important and regular (annual, biannual) conference programs, we surveyed the presence of arts management, cultural management, and cultural policy research topics based on keywords and abstracts and tried to identify whether any of these themes were not simply part of panels but had a prominent place in the program (such as full-day or main conference theme, or keynote speech).

In English, the programs of three disciplinary associations—the Administrative Sciences Association of Canada (ASAC), the Canadian Political Science Association (CPSA), and the Canadian Communication Association (CCA)—were surveyed. Most of the associations surveyed organize annual congresses in collaboration with the Federation for the Humanities and Social Sciences (FHSS) of Canada. A closer look at past conferences reveals that arts management themes are virtually absent from disciplinary conferences during the period 2011–2021. Expanding the analysis to include cultural policy themes marginally increases the presence of arts-management-related research at these conferences. For the CPSA, since 2017 special panels have been organized on culture and global trades and on local cultural policies, with little attention devoted to management or organizational matters. For the CCA, cultural policy work is consistently presented every year at its conferences, albeit in small numbers (two to five papers out of approximately two hundred presentations per edition). Therefore, these national and disciplinary conferences do not appear to be where Canadian scholars from the field disseminate their English-language work.

Switching focus to French-language disciplinary conferences reveals a slightly different portrait. For instance, the Association francophone pour le savoir, a federation of French-speaking institutions and learned societies founded as the Association canadienne-française pour l'avancement des sciences (ACFAS) in 1923, actively promotes scientific culture in Canada and organizes an annual conference where researchers and organizations can submit proposals for workshops and colloquiums. ACFAS follows a traditional disciplinary model to organize its different sections, with five main knowledge domains (health sciences; natural sciences, mathematics, and engineering; letters, arts, and human sciences; social sciences; and education), each divided in terms of disciplines and objects of study (e.g., economy, labor, and markets; organizations and management; media, communications, and information sciences; etc.). Over the years, ACFAS has also provided room for interdisciplinary colloquiums and workshops. At first glance, single-paper presentations on arts management in the disciplinary sections of ACFAS compare to what is found in English-speaking associations. For social sciences, humanities, education sciences, and management, the average number of papers presented yearly ranges between three and eleven for the period surveyed. The presence of arts management papers at the conference, however, is marginal, and the inclusion of cultural policy papers does not increase the numbers. That being said, where the situation differs is with special thematic colloquiums. Over the period studied, there has been, at minimum, one arts-management-focused or arts-management-leaning special colloquium per year—for instance, "Artistic Work and the Economy of Creation in Sociology" in 2013, "Creativity Under Constraint in Sociology" in 2014, "Management of Arts and Culture in Business" in 2016, and "Philanthropy and Social Innovation" in 2018, organized by researchers in cultural management, are all examples of art management research activities organized during ACFAS's yearly congress.

Similarly, a survey of the Société québécoise de sciences politiques (SQSP) conference programs reveals a pattern of arts-management-related projects that converges with what can be observed at ACFAS—albeit with SQSP the focus tends to be more on the side of cultural policy. While SQSP is an association of organizations and individuals belonging to a variety of disciplines, a deeper look at its programs reveals that French-speaking researchers in Canada—and more specifically Québec—rarely present their work in individual sessions or in regular panels, but use the conference as an opportunity to organize special days or special themed activities centered around cultural policy.

What is evident from these examples is that very few nationally defined spaces in Canada offer arts management researchers opportunities to present their work. Instead, these researchers must often look to international venues to find spaces that are definitively arts management in nature and scope. Consequently, Canadian arts management researchers have become intimately familiar with the Association internationale de management de l'art et de la culture (AIMAC), an international conference founded in 1991 at the HEC-Montréal Business School (Evard and Colbert 2000). Given its focus on arts and cultural management, AIMAC is a natural venue for Canadian arts management scholars, as are other international conferences such as the International

Conference on Cultural Policy Research (ICCPR) and Social Theory, Politics and the Arts (STP&A).

With PhDs—and initial socialization to scientific work—in marketing, public policy, sociology, political science, economics, and organizational theory, it appears that Canadian researchers working in arts management do not necessarily see or privilege their own national/regional disciplinary conferences as the natural outlets for their academic work. This is in no small part because arts management research events in Canada often do not follow an annual pattern and are only periodically organized. As shall be discussed later in this chapter, the research funding picture for arts management seems to indicate that when periodic arts management research events are organized in Canada, it is usually as an alternative to international conferences or the prevailing Canadian disciplinary model of conferences.

Publications

Academic publications are one of the most important indicators of research activity and vitality of fields. The questions to consider are where Canadian authors publish on arts management, what main themes and subthemes they tend to focus on, and how they fare in the field in terms of research outputs compared to researchers based in institutions outside Canada. In order to answer this question, SciVal—a bibliometric database prepared by Elsevier—was used. Given the database's functionalities, this section also brings to salience international comparisons and patterns of international cooperation involving researchers based in Canadian institutions. This chapter also brings forward data from other research repositories that are more inclusive of French-language publications in Canada. In addition, building on the most-published Canadian authors in the field—a criterion that, we argue, is indicative of a persistence of and association with field-related research—we tried to understand where else they find suitable outlets to publish their works beyond major journals in the field, such as the *International Journal of Arts Management* and the *Journal of Arts Management, Law and Society*, and whether we can identify some patterns. In this case, we used the ranking produced in SciVal and researched the total publication output of these researchers in Scopus, another database surveying academic publications.

First, publications authored by at least one Canadian researcher and published in the *International Journal of Arts Management* or the *Journal of Arts Management, Law and Society*—two academic journals primarily focused on arts management—were surveyed. From 2012 to 2022, a total of 55 publications were written (or co-written) by Canadian authors, which makes Canadian researchers the third-most-published group in these journals after Americans (125 papers) and the French (72 papers). At first glance, 45.5 percent of publications involving a Canadian author were made through international collaborations (ten papers co-authored with French researchers and six with American researchers), while 14.6 percent resulted from national collaborations;

36.4 percent had a single author. More than half of these papers were published by HEC-Montréal-affiliated authors, and one out of five was published by researchers affiliated with the University of Ottawa. The most common research keywords in this pool of publications were "art," "cultural policy," "Québec," "personnel," "artist," and "business models." By contrast, from the American-authored publications, the most prominent keywords were "art," "arts management," "nonprofit," and "organizations." In terms of international collaborations, only thirteen papers (or 10 percent) of American-authored publications involved international collaborators. Of the papers authored by French researchers, 37.5 percent were produced in collaboration with researchers from other countries. The most prominent keywords used to index the research output of French authors included "museums," "arts," "business models," "visitors," and "cultural industries."

While the above examples represent but a small pool of work, they are, nevertheless, indicative of a collaborative (and thematic) pattern in the works published by these journals. To extend the pool of available work and to further understanding of publication patterns, the publications of three additional journals were considered: the *International Journal of Cultural Policy*, *Cultural Trends*, the *Journal of Cultural Economics*, and *Poetics*. With these new journals included, the total number of published works between 2012 and 2022 related to arts management increased to 1,894. American authors were the most-published in this group, with 419 publications (see Table 2.1), followed by authors from the United Kingdom, with 403 publications. Canadian authors ranked fifth, with 116 publications, just behind Australian (145) and French (133) authors. Canadian authors were the most likely to collaborate with international authors on publications (39 percent of their output), as compared to French (37 percent), Australian (27 percent), American (17 percent), and UK (17 percent) authors. In terms of themes within this international pool, cultural policy, art, culture, museums, artists, and creative industries are the most prominent. A closer look at Canadian papers specifically brings forth the following keywords: "art," "cultural policy," "culture," "Canada," "Québec," "artist," and "policy."

Table 2.1. Published Works in Five Major Journals in the Field (2012–2022)

Country of academic affiliation	Total number of outputs	Proportion of international co-authorship in published works
United States	419	17%
United Kingdom	403	17%
Australia	145	27%
France	133	37%
Canada	116	39%

Two observations can be made at this point. First, based on the most prominent keywords, it appears that Canadian authors see international journals as publication outlets where case studies on Canada or Québec can be disseminated—an observation that runs counter to the commonly held belief that international journals are uninterested in material that discusses domestic (that is, solely Canadian) policies and issues. This pattern seems to be sustained beyond the *International Journal of Arts Management*—which could be seen as the most sympathetic to Canadian material of the sample of journals assessed, in large part because of where it is edited and its history with HEC-Montréal. Second, Canadian authors have a pattern of international collaborations with American and French authors. Delving further into the research output, we see that these collaborations tend to bring Canadian materials (organizations, policies, and artists) into comparative perspective.

Beyond these commonly known outlets, where else do Canadian authors publish their work on arts management and, by extension, the commonly associated theme of cultural policy? To answer this question, a sample of the fifty Canadian researchers most published in the abovementioned journals was taken to assess their research outputs in other outlets. The first observation that can be made is that there is no other single journal that appears to be a common publication outlet. When we investigated other academic journals where these authors have published, we found that only two of the authors have published in the same journal. This suggests that there are no other national or international journals that serve as natural, common alternatives to the six journals that were assessed.

The fifty authors sampled have published one or more pieces in 220 journals indexed in the Scopus bibliographic database. These authors have mostly published in sociology journals (34), followed by marketing (28), economics (27), political science (22), psychology (21), general management studies and organizational studies (20), geography and urban studies (19), communication studies (13), cultural studies (9), and, more marginally, information studies, education sciences, and computer sciences journals. This diversity of discipline may suggest a pattern of accidental publishing behavior, whereby someone published in an arts management journal without having a research program consistent with the discipline, even in its broadest definition. However, given the small pool of authors (fifty), and based on the field knowledge in Canada, the authors that appear on the list clearly have arts-management-focused research programs. It is more probable that arts management research crosses disciplinary boundaries and can be relatively well framed in other contexts. This is commonly seen in communication studies, management, organizational studies, public administration, and public policy publications, and a cursory look at publication abstracts reveals as much. Alternatively, arts management researchers may tend to publish in the disciplines in which they were socialized and received their doctoral degrees and may occasionally have a second research area of focus. This is noticeable in some publication patterns, where researchers who are frequently published in arts management are also frequently published in sociology, general marketing, or psychology. Finally, the strong representation of marketing studies journals (28 out of 220 journals) may be largely due to the fact that graduate arts management education in Canada owes a lot to marketing, with the graduate education most closely associated with arts management being the marketing degree offered by HEC-Montréal (Colbert 2017)—which itself may be a Canadian singularity.

Similarly, an important Canadian characteristic that is perhaps not well captured in SciVal and Scopus databases is its French-English bilingualism. To correct this gap, research was conducted in the Persée database, a French counterpart to the Erudit.org journals database. The Persée database mostly indexes journals from Canada, though a few from France and Belgium are also captured. While the Persée database does not allow for a focused search on researcher affiliations, it remains a useful tool for determining where and how arts management research circulates in French-language journals. The keyword "arts management" is associated with papers published in *Téoros* (a tourism studies journal), *La revue d'études théâtrales* (theater studies), *Ethnologies, anthropologies et sociétés* (ethnography), *Politiques et sociétés* (political science), and *Management international* (generalist management studies).

Another pattern that is not perceptible in SciVal or Scopus databases is in relation to publications in transfer journals, or journals with a broader audience that includes professionals. This is the case with journals like *Liaison* and *L'annuaire théâtral*. Similarly, another outlet for arts management publications that are not covered by bibliometric databases is that of "cultural journals" or "revues culturelles," which are cultural journals that have an essayistic nature but are not double-blind peer-reviewed. Journals such as *ETC* and *La vie des arts*, from the 1980s, likely saw in their pages the first French-language publications of arts management research in Canada—years before the creation of the *International Journal of Arts Management* in 1998. Other types of publications, such as HEC's French-language case studies, have also been important contributors to the field of arts management in Canada.

In sum, arts management research diffused by authors affiliated with Canadian institutions tends to be produced in large proportion through international collaborations. In international journals, authors affiliated with a Canadian institution tend to publish not conceptual papers but Canadian case studies, often in comparative perspective. Because of the limited publication outlets available to them, Canadian authors tend to publish their work in journals related to the discipline in which they were trained or obtained their PhD. This suggests that arts management research output circulates in outlets other than those most associated with the field. Arts management research also circulates in French-language journals, with many of the field's debates emanating from cultural journals and transfer journals that date back to the 1980s.

Public Funding for Research

Funding is another area in which the dynamics of an academic field can be understood. In Canada, there exists an extensive system of governmental research funding, where the federal and provincial governments play an important part in supporting research development through grants to universities to support research infrastructures, as well as through a grant system that directly funds researchers and their research projects.

At the federal level, the Canadian government developed a system of national research funding that echoes the creation of the Canada Council for the Arts in 1957. Along with the National Sciences and Engineering Council of Canada (NSERC) and the Canadian Institutes of Health Research (CIHR), the Social Sciences and Humanities Research Council of Canada (SSHRC) is one of three federal granting agencies that fund research projects by Canadian researchers based on merit and peer evaluations. SSHRC's purview includes arts management research projects.

SSHRC offers a host of different grants, some of which are targeted to MA, PhD, and postdoctoral researchers, while others cover faculty research. Programs such as "Knowledge" and "Insight Development" fund researchers' core projects through grants that can reach up to $500,000 CAD over a period of three to five years. Similarly, the standard grant, dedicated to the support of independent and fundamental research, is a multiyear grant that typically lasts three to five years, with a funding range of $15,000 to $50,000 CAD a year. Other programs offer support for partnership development with community stakeholders, for organizing events, and for supporting research dissemination. Grants are distributed through funding competitions where candidates submit project proposals to SSHRC, to be evaluated by a panel of disciplinary experts. While the panels evaluating proposals are often interdisciplinary, SSHRC imposes many restrictions and tends to redirect submissions to discipline-based panels whenever possible. SSHRC is, arguably, one of the most important and prestigious sources of research funding in Canada. Not only is SSHRC a source of funding, but it is an important source of symbolic capital; receiving an SSHRC award reinforces a researcher's legitimacy. This source of distinction in Canadian academia is not so much linked to the amount received (which is mostly in a fixed range) but is rather a function of whether a researcher is "fundable" and is able to win grants and awards.

For the purpose of this chapter, efforts were made to understand how arts management research fares in terms of funding received through SSHRC. A survey of SSHRC's funding database was an important methodological challenge, since arts management is considered a field and not a discipline. To search the SSHRC database, three clusters of subthemes germane to the field—in both English and French—were created: (1) a core arts management cluster, which aggregates the following research descriptors: "arts management," "cultural management," "cultural administration," "arts organizations," "artists and management," "artists and organization," and "cultural organizations"; (2) a cultural policy cluster; and (3) a creative industries cluster. The SSHRC database indexes projects that received funding between 1998 and 2022; for the purposes of this exercise, the full range of the period was used to identify the number of grants related to the three clusters received over that period and the type of competitions that attracted the most funding.

In the arts management funding cluster, the research funding received from SSHRC between 1998 and 2022 is modest (see Table 2.2). Out of the fifty-four grants distributed to arts management projects, twenty-three were awarded through the "talent"

Table 2.2. SSHRC Research Funding in the Arts Management Cluster (1998–2022)

Type of funding	Number of grants	Proportion of total grants offered
Funding for student research (including one postdoctoral grant)	23	42.5%
Standard research grants	8	15%
Community partnership programs	6	10.5%
Other funding (literature reviews, events organization)	17	32%

grants, which are funds to support the research of master's and doctoral candidates. Six projects received funding through community partnership grants, and eight were awarded through standard research grants (a grant developed to support research excellence in the field). The remaining seventeen grants were obtained through special targeted funding opportunities, most of which came in the form of requests for literature reviews or in support of events or workshops. Given the modest number of standard grants identified with this cluster of data, a search and analysis of frequently published Canadian researchers in the field of arts management was subsequently conducted. However, this added layer of analysis only uncovered three additional arts-management-related grants, all of which were awarded in support of a conference (and, consequently, were left out of Table 2.2).

The creative industries cluster of funded projects, on the other hand, provides a somewhat different picture. A total of 103 grants were distributed to support creative industries projects between 1998 and 2022 (see Table 2.3). Of the total number of projects funded, forty-four were standard research grants and forty-one were grants for graduate students. Only five community partnership projects were funded; the remaining thirteen grants were awarded to support literature reviews, events, and workshops. The main difference between this cluster of funded projects and the arts management cluster is that more standard research grants were awarded in support of fieldwork and fundamental research in the field.

Finally, there were a total of 169 grants awarded in the cultural policy research cluster. Of these grants, the majority (ninety-one) were awarded to MA and PhD students and postdoctoral researchers (see Table 2.4). Standard research grants constituted approximately a third of funded projects related to cultural policy (fifty-four). Fourteen grants were awarded to community partnership projects, and ten were awarded under other funding, primarily linked to workshops on cultural policy research.

While the sample above constitutes a small number of grants—approximately 330 in total—it reflects the small size of the Canadian arts management research community, a community that, even when broadly including creative industries and cultural policy

Table 2.3. SSHRC Research Funding in the Creative Industries Cluster (1998–2022)

Type of funding	Number of grants	Proportion of total grants offered
Funding for student research (including four postdoctoral grants)	41	40%
Standard research grants	44	43%
Community partnership programs	5	4.5%
Other funding (literature reviews, events organization)	13	12.5%

Table 2.4. SSHRC Research Funding in the Cultural Policy Cluster (1998–2022)

Type of funding	Number of grants	Proportion of total grants offered
Funding for student research (including 11 postdoctoral grants)	91	54%
Standard research grants	54	32%
Community partnership programs	14	8%
Other funding (literature reviews, events organization)	10	6%

projects, remains small in comparison to other fields. Despite the small numbers, there are a couple of observations that can be made about how Canadian arts management researchers operate. First, over the past two decades, an average of ten students per year received funding for an arts management, creative industries, and/or cultural policy project. To put this observation into perspective, in 2020–2021 alone, SSHRC granted 1,513 graduate bursaries (MA and PhD); among these were 163 in political science, 81 in philosophy, 83 in communication studies, 45 in management studies, and 42 in criminology. Comparing the arts management average of ten students per year to these results would be unfair; however, comparing them to the yearly results of political science subdisciplines, for instance, brings a better perspective to the numbers. Of the 163 total political science graduate student projects funded by SSHRC in 2020–2021, 25 belonged to the subdiscipline of international relations, 11 to political theory and political philosophy, 11 to comparative politics, and 11 to public policy. Some subdisciplines, such as local government or political history, received no grants in 2020–2021. Contrasting these numbers with those of the aggregate provides a better sense of the recognition arts management graduate students' projects receive from SSHRC.

A similar exercise can be used when it comes to the funding available to researchers through the standard grants stream. Between 1998 and 2022, a total of 106 standard grants were awarded for works in arts management, creative industries, and cultural policy—which represents a yearly average of approximately four grants in the field. Using the competition year of 2020–2021 as a baseline, by comparison, out of 2,681 applications, SSHRC awarded 153 standard grants to management and business studies faculties, 88 to political science faculties, 44 to philosophy faculties, and 38 to communication studies faculties. Once again, it is worth noting that these numbers reflect grants based on discipline, which probably makes it unfair to compare them against arts-management-related projects. However, delving into political science subdisciplines provides a better comparison: in 2020–2021, funding was provided for twenty-five projects in international relations, fourteen in comparative politics, seven in public policy, six in electoral studies, and five in political thought, with the rest divided among other subdisciplines. Compared to these numbers, the field of arts management appears to fare reasonably well and receive a decent level of recognition from SSHRC.

Hence, if the focus is placed strictly on the arts management cluster, the number of funded projects would be rather small (possibly distressingly so for researchers in the field). What explains this relative lack of arts management research funding (less than one project funded per year over the past two decades) from the federal agency? One explanation could have to do with the necessity of funding: how much funding is needed to conduct arts management research? Many well-published authors in the field have received little to no funding from SSHRC; however, they were still able to conduct research and use their existing relationships to carry out important case studies. Alternatively, there are other, nonfederal sources of funding available to researchers who focus strictly on arts management. For instance, after the government of Canada, Québec has the most extensive funding agency in the country. The Fonds de recherche du Québec science et culture (FRQSC) funds Québec-based academics in many fields, including arts management. Researchers from HEC-Montréal and the Institut national de recherche scientifique (INRS)—which have the largest cluster of cultural policy researchers in Canada—together receive an average of two to three research grants per year through the FRQSC funds for arts management projects. Similarly, Mitacs—a not-for-profit association created in 1999 and funded through federal and provincial governments—has funded 116 projects and case studies associated with arts organizations. While the Mitacs awards do not bring much symbolic prestige to researchers, they do offer funds that can help strengthen researchers' links with arts organizations and help transfer knowledge to practice.

Additionally, government and private sector research funding (through research contracts) are common sources of revenue in Canadian universities. Looking at Statistics Canada's data on research revenues, the federal government's contracts represent approximately 14 percent of research funds available to the average Canadian university, while provincial contracts represent an average of 12.6 percent (Statistics Canada 2022). At the Université du Québec Network, for instance, contracts from the provincial government can provide in excess of 25 percent of the research funding gathered by researchers. As for private funding, the ranges are between 10 percent and 13 percent of the available research funding at Canadian universities. It is very likely that arts management researchers seek funds from some of these alternative sources. Looking at the funding patterns at INRS, and considering the importance of the Ministère de la culture et des communications in Québec and the Department of Canadian Heritage at the federal level, it is highly probable that these funding sources play an important role in research projects in arts management. Despite being less prestigious, these sources of funding can be important sustainers of arts management research in Canada.

Research Chairs

Research chairs play an important part in the development of research. More specifically, research chairs are essential for the development of new areas of research and for the consolidation of fields. We documented the existing chairs by building on our knowledge of the field in Canada and also by looking into databases of federally and provincially funded research chairs. Ideas about research chairs, their funding, and their purpose differ greatly in different national contexts. In Canada, privately funded research chairs are not the norm. In the humanities and social sciences, privately funded chairs are offered very modest funding. Universities and the federal government are the most important actors when it comes to developing research chairs. Research chairs typically involve a reduction of teaching loads for chairholders so that they can concentrate on research activities. Most of the chairs in Canada also involve regular yearly funding. These vary between programs. For instance, the Program of Canadian Research Chairs, funded by the federal government, guarantees chairholders annual funding of $100,000 to 200,000 CAD per year for fieldwork, research dissemination, and/or lab material, on renewable terms of five to seven years.

One of the most important research chairs when it comes to arts management in Canada is undoubtedly the Carmelle and Rémi Marcoux Research Chair on Arts Management, housed at HEC Montréal. This research chair, originally held by François Colbert and which received over $1 million CAD in 1991, is undoubtedly a beacon of arts management research in Canada, and an institution around which the field has developed over the years (Rentschler and Shilbury 2008). It benefits from a generous private source of funding, something rare for a social sciences and humanities research chair in Canada. This chair, like many research chairs, acts as an important community hub, offering fundamental institutional support around which professors and students can develop relationships. Research chairs often organize events, publish material, and have the capacity to speak for the field to governments and decision-makers because of their visibility. The Carmelle and Rémi Marcoux Research Chair, in particular, is an important component of the history of research in arts management in Canada.

While there is probably no other research chair in Canada that is more explicitly devoted to arts management than the Carmelle and Rémi Marcoux Research Chair, many others belong to a broader conception of arts management research. Some research chairs have been created by universities to promote the study of cultural policy and arts organizations. For instance, in 1998 at INRS, the Chaire Fernand-Dumont sur la culture was created in honor of the famous Québécois sociologist of culture Fernand Dumont. This research chair focuses on arts organizations, cultural ecosystems, cultural policy, and the relationships between territories and culture. Under this research chair sit ten researchers, making it one of the most research-intensive chairs of its kind in Canada when it comes to the study of culture. Similarly, the International Francophonie Research Chair on Cultural Heritage Policy, created in 2019 at the University of Ottawa, is another chair created to study arts and heritage organizations, focusing on the French-speaking world from a comparative perspective.

In addition to community-supported or university-funded research chairs, there are research chairs that belong to important networks and bring visibility to cultural research in Canada. The UNESCO chairs program in Canada, for instance, offers thirty-one research chairs, two of which are relevant to the study of culture: the UNESCO chair on the urban landscape at the Université de Montréal is focused on conservation, while the UNESCO chair on diversity of cultural expression, housed at the Université Laval in Québec city, focuses on law and cultural expressions in the arts. While the former is strictly focused on heritage, the latter documents the complex situation and the hardships of arts organizations in the global context and the strategies developed to support a diversity of artistic expression. Although the UNESCO chair network typically offers modest support for its chairholders, both chairs have been able to qualify for funding offered to research chairs by Québec's research councils, giving them additional resources to conduct their missions.

Finally, when it comes to academic prestige, the most important research chairs in Canada belong to the Canada Research Chairs (CRC) program, a special governmental fund developed in 2000 with the intention of curtailing what was referred to as the "brain drain" (the exodus of high-level Canadian academics). Since its inception, the CRC program has evolved to include objectives more closely aligned with governmental priorities in science. Two CRCs are devoted to pressing issues in cultural policy. One is held by Sarah Bannerman at McMaster University and is concerned with the evolution and governance of communication and media policies in Canada. The other is held by Jonathan Roberge at INRS and focuses on arts organizations and policies in the digital environment; in particular, it documents issues such as the discoverability of cultural content online, with an eye toward the representation of Québec and French cultural items in the digital world. Other research chairs are concerned with cultural and creative industries in Canada: the Chair in Cultural Economy (Deborah Leslie, University of Toronto), the Chair in Creative Innovation and Leadership (David Gauntlett, Toronto Metropolitan University), and the Chair in Arts, Culture and Global Relations (Sarah Smith, Western University). These research chairs fit with national priorities but are designed around the personalities and orientations of their chairholders. In this sense, these chairs represent an important opportunity for creating a space for arts and cultural management research.

Conclusions

Studying a field and understanding its dynamics can come with important methodological challenges. This chapter provides some insights that may inform future research on the dynamics of the field of arts management. The main methodological difficulty for understanding arts management—and arts management research in particular—has to do with the predominance of the disciplinary structures of academic work and institutions. Disciplines tend to benefit from a more robust position in universities, whereas interdisciplinary programs are often shared between departments or faculties. Beyond its often precarious place in university structures, arts management frequently suffers from the disciplinary organization of research grants. In Canada, the major national granting agencies are organized under a disciplinary model. This represents a challenge for assessing the nature and type of funding that arts management researchers can get; however, this is not just a methodological challenge but also a challenge for researchers who need to strategize and navigate the conventions of a field or a discipline to secure funding. Understanding publication patterns beyond the well-known publication outlets of the field also constitutes an important methodological challenge. This chapter has proposed a number of strategies for responding to these challenges, though future work may want to include career strategy analyses with researchers.

This chapter highlights the importance of international spaces for research diffusion to Canada-based researchers in arts management. International conferences and journals offer the most obvious spaces to circulate academic work on arts management. From a Canadian perspective, arts management is an international research field, and this is evident in the proportion of international publications by Canadian authors. While there is a domestic "life" for Canadian arts management authors—a number of local spaces for research dissemination—these tend to be sporadic and associated with very specific themes. There are no permanent domestic journals or conference spaces for Canadian researchers. Moreover, there do not seem to be any prominent alternative outlets to the major international journal in the field for academics associated with Canadian universities. Looking at the output of the most published Canadian researchers in the most prominent journals of the field, there is no strong pattern—disciplinary or otherwise—to their publication choices. This suggests that Canadian academics likely circulate their research in non-arts-management disciplinary journals and adopt a mixed publication strategy, with a mixed adherence to field or discipline. This strategy, however, is not evident in the main conference venues. When it comes to funding, arts management does not fare as well as research funded on germane topics such as cultural policy or creative industries. Nonetheless, the aggregate of the three interrelated objects of the field shows funding patterns that do not compare well to disciplines but compare favorably to the funding patterns of subdisciplines. Finally, research chairs have played an important part in the intellectual life of arts management in Canada. Research chairs have had a seminal effect on the field of arts management, dating back to the early 1990s. More recently, the introduction of new chairs has complemented the field with new research themes—often explored over periods that can last a decade—especially if funded by the Canada Research Chairs program. Research chairs in Canada retain a collaborative nature; they attract resources and constitute a nodal point for an academic community.

Note

1. Cultural democracy and the democratization of culture refer to two distinct rationales, or views on the accessibility of culture in cultural policy. Cultural democracy can be said to be—historically and philosophically—an answer to the democratization of culture, an approach that emphasized the economic and geographic accessibility of culture, without challenging cultural hierarchies and while taking the canons of great (elite) culture for granted. Cultural democracy is a cultural policy whose principles aim to promote cultural programming that is more inclusive of popular culture. Challenges to cultural hierarchy are inherent to cultural democracy. For more information on this important debate, see DiMaggio and Useem 1978; Donnat 1991; Evrard 1997; Mulcahy 2006; and Hadley 2021.

References

Abbott, Andrew. 1988. *The System of Professions: An Essay on the Division of Expert Labour*. Chicago: University of Chicago Press.
Abbott, Andrew. 2001. *Chaos of Disciplines*. Chicago: University of Chicago Press.
Abbott, Andrew. 2005. "Linked Ecologies: States and Universities as Environments for Professions." *Sociological Theory* 23, no. 3: 245–274.
Abbott, Pamela, and Liz Meerabeau. 2020. *The Sociology of the Caring Professions*. London: Routledge.
Blok, Anders, Maria D. Lindstrøm, Marie L. Meilvang, and Inge K. Pedersen. 2019. "Ecologies of Boundaries: Modes of Boundary Work in Professional Proto-Jurisdictions." *Symbolic Interaction* 42, no. 4: 588–617.
Bourdieu, Pierre. 1976. "Le champ scientifique." *Actes de la recherche en sciences sociales* 2, no. 2: 88–104.
Bourdieu, Pierre. 1991. "Le champ littéraire." *Actes de la recherche en sciences sociales* 89 no. 1: 3–46.
Brindle, Meg, and Constance DeVereaux. 2011. *The Arts Management Handbook: New Directions for Students and Practitioners*. New York: M. E. Sharpe
Brock, David M., Michael J. Powell, and C. R. Hinings. 1999. *Restructuring the Professional Organization: Accounting, Healthcare and Law*. London: Routledge.
Champy, Florent. 2015. *Nouvelle théorie sociologique des professions*. Paris: Presses Universitaires de France.
Clark, Burton R. 1987. *The Academic Profession: National, Disciplinary, and Institutional Settings*. Berkeley: University of California Press.
Colbert, François. 2017. "A Brief History of Arts Marketing Thought in North America." *Journal of Arts Management, Law, and Society* 47, no. 3: 167–177.
DeVereaux, Constance. 2009. "Arts and Cultural Management: The State of the Field: Introduction." *Journal of Arts Management, Law, and Society* 38, no. 4: 235–238.

DiMaggio, Paul, and Useem, Michael. 1978. "Cultural Democracy in a Period of Cultural Expansion: The Social Composition of Arts Audiences in the United States." *Social Problems* 26, no. 2: 179–197.

Donnat, Olivier. 1991. "Démocratisation culturelle: la fin d'un mythe." *Esprit* 170, nos. 3–4: 65–82.

Ebewo, Patrick, and Mziwoxolo Henderson Sirayi. 2009. "The Concept of Arts/Cultural Management: A Critical Reflection." *Journal of Arts Management, Law, and Society* 38, no. 4: 281–295.

Etzioni, Amitai. 1969. *The Semi-Professions and Their Organization*. New York: Free Press.

Evard, Yves, and François Colbert. 2000. "Arts Management: A New Discipline Entering the Millennium?." *International Journal of Arts Management* 2, no. 2: 4–13.

Evrard, Yves. 1997. "Democratizing Culture or Cultural Democracy?" *Journal of Arts Management, Law, and Society* 27, no. 3: 167–175.

Evetts, Julia. 2003. "The Sociological Analysis of Professionalism: Occupational Change in the Modern World." *International Sociology* 18, no 2: 395–415.

Evetts, Julia. 2013. "Professionalism: Value and Ideology." *Current Sociology* 61, nos. 5–6: 778–796.

Fournier, Valérie. 1999. "The Appeal to 'Professionalism' as a Disciplinary Mechanism." *Sociological Review* 47, no. 2: 280–307.

Freidson, Eliot L. 2001. *Professionalism, the Third Logic: On the Practice of Knowledge*. Chicago: University of Chicago Press.

Hadley, Steven. 2021. "Democratic Cultural Policy." In *Audience Development and Cultural Policy*, edited by Steven Hadley, 25–56. London: Palgrave Macmillan.

Jacobs, Jerry A. 2014. *In Defense of Disciplines: Interdisciplinarity and Specialization in the Research University*. Chicago: University of Chicago Press.

Lamont, Michèle. 2009. *How Professors Think: Inside the Curious World of Academic Judgment*. Cambridge, MA: Harvard University Press.

Larson, Magali Sarfatti. 1977. *The Rise of Professionalism*. Berkeley: University of California Press.

Mulcahy, Kevin V. 2006. "Cultural Policy: Definitions and Theoretical Approaches." *Journal of Arts Management, Law, and Society* 35, no. 4: 319–330.

Paradeise, Catherine. 1988. "Les professions comme marchés du travail fermés." *Sociologie et sociétés* 20, no. 2: 9–21.

Pérez-Cabañero, Carmen, and Manuel Cuadrado-García. 2011. "Evolution of Arts and Cultural Management Research over the First Ten AIMAC Conferences (1991–2009)." *International Journal of Arts Management* 13, no. 3: 56–68.

Rentschler, Ruth, and David Shilbury. 2008. "Academic Assessment of Arts Management Journals: A Multidimensional Rating Survey." *International Journal of Arts Management* 10, no. 3: 60–71.

Statistics Canada. 2022. "Revenue of Universities by Type of Revenues and Funds." Accessed December 12, 2022. DOI: https://doi.org/10.25318/3710002601-eng.

Tight, Malcolm. 2020. "Higher Education: Discipline or Field of Study?" *Tertiary Education Management* 26, no. 4: 415–428.

Tripier, Pierre, Claude Dubar, and Valérie Boussard. 2013. *Sociologie des professions*. Paris: Armand Colin.

Zahra, Shaker A., and Lance R. Newey. 2009. "Maximizing the Impact of Organization Science: Theory-Building at the Intersection of Disciplines and/or Fields." *Journal of Management Studies* 46, no. 6: 1059–1075.

CHAPTER 3

ANALYZING THE CULTURAL AND CREATIVE INDUSTRIES ECOSYSTEM UNDER THE LENS OF COMPLEX ADAPTIVE SYSTEMS

Beyond the Sector

LEONARDO MAZZONI, STEFANIA OLIVA,
AND LUCIANA LAZZERETTI

Introduction

OVER the last decades, the cultural and creative sectors have been the focus of an increasing number of analyses that have investigated their ability to generate economic value (Howkins 2002; Cooke and Lazzeretti 2008), their influence on the performance of other sectors and the wider economy (Innocenti and Lazzeretti 2019), and their centrality to policy regarding the development of regions and cities (Scott 2006; Pratt 2008; Vecco 2009).

Recently, a new challenge in the debate on the role of the cultural and creative sectors in the economy and society is represented by the advent of information and communication technologies. The digital revolution brings with it new opportunities for the development of the cultural and creative sectors in terms of new professional skills, entrepreneurship, new ways of experiencing cultural heritage, and new communication channels for cultural and creative products (Massi, Vecco, and Lin 2021). Moreover, the economic crisis triggered by the pandemic has shown the increased dependence of creative activities on intangible, digital, and knowledge-based factors, despite traditional industrial aspects and cultural resources (Cruz and Teixeira 2021).

Considering this increasing interest in CCIs, several taxonomies have been proposed to capture and measure the different activities and organizations that are part of this unit of analysis. However, although these taxonomies have been modified and expanded to include multiple typologies of activity, current definitions still fail to capture the changing nature of this object of study, especially when considering a historical perspective.

Previous studies suggest that an evolutionary perspective based on complexity thinking can help define a broader theoretical framework for studying the cultural and creative economy, one able to detect connections with labor markets, communities, and other social aspects (Jung 2011; Comunian 2019). This opens the door to an ecosystem approach to the study of cultural and creative organizations (De Bernard, Comunian, and Gross 2021).

In order to enlarge this debate, this chapter applies the complex adaptive system approach for identifying the actors, relationships, properties, and structures of the CCI ecosystem. This lens of analysis can help clarify how the concept of CCIs has changed over time and propose a new instrument for mapping relationships and dynamics of CCIs, as an alternative to existing approaches mainly based on industrial specializations.

Therefore, the research question that drives the analysis is: "What is the most suitable approach to define and analyze CCIs?" The discussion finds its roots in the model of culture-economy-society-technology that describes the phases in the evolutionary path of the relationship between culture, economy, society, and technologies and how it has been transformed by the current digital revolution.

The chapter is structured as follows. The next section synthesizes the literature on CCIs in terms of taxonomies proposed for the classification of the activities that pertain to the sector, identifying the limitations of such an approach and discussing how scholars integrate it with the potential offered by the ecological approach. The next section opens the discussion on complexity thinking, which originated from an (eco) system approach. It introduces the definition and characteristics of a complex adaptive system and discusses how the cultural and creative sector can be interpreted through a systemic approach and an evolutionary viewpoint. Finally, the conclusion discusses the possible merits of this approach and offers insight for driving future research.

An Overview of the Taxonomies of Cultural and Creative Industries: From Mapping Document to Ecological Approach

Over the last decades, several studies have discussed how the literature on the cultural and creative economy has evolved (Chen and Chen 2014; Gong and Hassink 2017;

Lazzeretti et al. 2018). Jason Potts collected the key contributions in a book on the economics of creative industries (Potts 2016). Despite these efforts, there is still inconsistency about what can be considered under the umbrella of "cultural and creative activities." This inconsistency only increases when the debate concerns the definition of CCIs. Several approaches have been proposed over the years.

As Cunningham (2002) points out, cultural industries were initially studied by applying neoclassical economics to the arts, looking at the initiatives of government at the national level. Since the 1980s, the growth of new organizational models and networks of organizations increasingly oriented toward creativity has spurred a shift from the model of "public art" toward new models based on the "new economy" and increasingly studied with a managerial approach.

In the policy dimension, although the term "creative industries" was used for the first time in Australia in 1994 with the report "Creative Nation: Commonwealth Cultural Policy" (Boix et al. 2013), the debate on CCIs has become central since the first decade of the 2000s thanks to the work of the Department of Culture, Media and Sports (DCMS) in the United Kingdom. DCMS produced two reports in 1998 and 2001, proposing a mapping document (DCMS 2001) that could be seen as the first attempt to classify CCIs. In this regard, DCMS (2001, 5) defined CCIs as "industries which have their origin in individual creativity, skill and talent and which have a potential for wealth and job creation through the generation and exploitation of intellectual property."

This mapping document represents the first attempt to classify CCIs with definite borders. It aims to provide support for governments in developing cultural and creative policies, especially considering the fuzziness and uncertainty around the stakeholders involved in the production and consumption of such goods/services (Cunningham et al. 2008). Indeed, according to well-known scholars (Throsby 2001; Jeffcutt and Pratt 2002; Caves 2003), the unique characteristics of products and performances, the huge variety in the purchasing behaviors of customers and the capacity to generate commercial revenue by selling "expressive value" included in symbolic, aesthetic, social, and authentic means are distinctive traits that justified the introduction of a new industrial taxonomy.

Starting with the contribution by DMCS, there have been several tentative efforts to define the CCI concept. An interesting approach is the concentric circle model proposed by Throsby (2001), based on the idea of the cultural value intrinsically rooted in cultural goods. According to the model, the higher the cultural content of a good or service, the closer it will be to the center of the model, represented by the core creative arts. The greater the importance of the commercial content of the good or service, the more it moves away from the core creative arts toward the outer circles.

In a similar vein, the World Intellectual Property Organization (WIPO 2003) proposed a method for estimating CCIs' impact on the economy based on copyright. The model includes those industries involved directly or indirectly in the creation, manufacture, production, broadcast, and distribution of copyrighted works. Three categories are identified: core copyright industries, interdependent copyright industries and "partial copyright industries." The first are industries that are fully dependent on copyrighted material, while the second are engaged in the production, manufacture, and sale of enabling equipment for the production or distribution of cultural products and services. Finally, partial copyright industries are those in which a portion of their activities is related to copyrighted work and other protected subjects and may involve creation, production, manufacturing, performance, broadcasting, communication, exhibition, distribution, or sales.

Another taxonomy is proposed by UNESCO and divides CCIs into two categories: industries in core cultural domains and industries in expanded cultural domains (UNESCO 2005). According to this taxonomy, cultural industries are defined as a set of activities that produce and distribute cultural goods or services, considering specific attributes, uses, or purposes, able to embody or convey cultural expressions, irrespective of the commercial value they may have.

A different taxonomy is offered by Americans for the Arts (2005), which identifies arts-centric businesses as organizations that operate in sectors related to the production and distribution of the arts. This taxonomy, however, does not take into account aspects relating to technology and communication.

Finally, the symbolic text model focuses on "high arts" versus "popular culture dichotomy," identifying the cultural sectors the activities able to communicate and distribute symbolic text or messages (Throsby 2008).

Other approaches have been applied to study CCIs. UNCTAD (2010) divides creative industries using a smile curve model and positions traditional cultural activities in the upstream part and the activities closer to market in the downstream part, adopting a taxonomy that includes four main groups: heritage, arts, media, and functional creations. The first two represent to some extent the source of creativity, while the other two are more oriented toward communication and marketing.

The KEA report (2006) on the creative and cultural sector offers another example of CCI taxonomy. It considers the cultural sector to be composed of non-industrial sectors and an industrial sector, while the creative sector is constituted by creative industries and activities and related industries in which culture plays a pivotal role as a creative input (KEA 2006).

A diverse approach is that of the Work Foundation, which holds that the central core is not "the arts" but instead "all forms of 'original product.' " Rather than using "creative" as the distinguishing feature of this sector, the model instead uses "expressive value" (O'Connor 2010).

Scholars have contributed other voices to the debate. For instance, Lazzeretti, Boix, and Capone (2008), benchmarking between Italy and Spain and between France and the United Kingdom (Boix et al. 2013), proposed a distinction between traditional creative industries (publishing, architecture, engineering, music, film, and performing arts) and nontraditional creative industries (R&D, software and computer service, and advertising). Lazzeretti and Capone (2015) employed a new approach called "narrow and broad" to quantify CCIs, where the narrow range includes the traditional CCIs and the broad range adds two categories, tourism and heritage-related activities.

Despite the numerous definitions proposed, the debate remains open, and recent literature has raised numerous criticisms. Classifying the CCIs based on an industrial approach leads to grouping together types of activities that have extremely different characteristics, production models, outputs, and markets. This makes it difficult to compare different sectors (Gong and Hassink 2017). Such an approach results in fragmented research, because individual research projects focus on specific objects and lack a way to connect different scales and dimensions (Comunian 2019). Furthermore, a model mainly based on industrial specialization, resource agglomeration, and localized knowledge spillovers is not able to capture the opportunity discovery system created by the interaction and interdependence between creative and noncreative agents (Autio et al. 2018).

Numerous researchers have attempted to widen the CCI debate, considering other actors and elements, such as cultural and creative clusters and districts (Santagata 2006; Lazzeretti 2008), creative cities (Hall 2000; Landry 2012), or creative classes (Florida 2012). Such approaches have the merit of overcoming sectoral specialization and offering a more comprehensive description of CCIs. However, these approaches still remain partial, being applied only to specific components and unable to express a holistic dimension.

As a consequence of these criticisms, in the last decade alternative approaches have emerged, based on two key points (Florida 2012):

1. The concept of a creative economy presents blurred boundaries. Thus no single definition can be applied because of the concept's instability and the presence of subjective criteria of classification.
2. A wider diffusion of new theoretical frameworks, with units of analysis that focus on ecology, systems, and networks.

Scholars have recently stressed how culture and creativity are evolving "organisms" that nurture workers and consumers. They represent a connective social structure that results from the formal and informal interactions of many actors, thanks to geographical or cognitive proximities (Markusen 2011; Holden 2015). Accordingly, Sterback (2014) claims that the notion of creative ecology configures a new model where creativity and culture are embedded "within a holistic worldview" that "reveals interdependencies with economic, social, cultural and environmental systems" (Sterback 2014, 4). Another important contribution comes from Howkins (2010), who proposes the idea of a biological ecosystem as a framework to inquire about human creativity (see also Stankevičiene et al. 2011). Howkins (2010, 11) defines creative ecology as "a niche where diverse individuals express themselves in a systemic and adaptive way, using ideas to produce new ideas," and proposes four aspects of creative ecologies: diversity, change, learning, and adapting. These consequential phases identify the ecological pattern: variety is the origin of change, which is the vehicle that pushes the human race to imitate and learn until the last stage, where species collaborate and compete and only the resilient ones survive (Stankevičiene et al. 2011).

From this perspective, new taxonomies that aim to look at economic agents' consumption and production in a wide and extensive logic have emerged. For example, Markusen proposes an ecological framework focused on the interrelation among people (cultural workers, supporters, participants), businesses and organizations (arts nonprofits, cultural firms, public art agencies), and places (cultural regions, cities, neighborhoods). Markusen's work (2011) emphasizes the leading role of nonprofit entities in the ecology of California.

Holden (2015) identifies three spheres of culture, each of which is permeable to the others: publicly funded culture (supported by the state or by philanthropists), commercial culture (which operates through the market), and homemade culture (amateur and voluntary, such as video and music uploaded on social networks or other internet platforms). According to Holden, what matters are the roles that organizations and people can play to make a difference. He identifies four archetypes: guardians, connectors, platforms, and nomads. Guardians take care of tangible and intangible cultural assets (museums, libraries, archives, performing arts such as theater). Connectors are producers and entrepreneurs (whether individuals or institutions such as museums) that harvest money and use it to create fertile ground for artists and cultural activities. Platforms are venues, galleries, community halls, clubs, streets, and websites. Nomads are the viewers, listeners, and readers (the demand side of culture).

Sterback proposes a definition of "roles" in order to identify the contributions of various organisms. Roles recognize a set of behaviors, attitudes, and activities. Six types of functions (roles) are proposed: communicators, connectors, creators, disruptors, enablers, and providers (Sterback 2014). Communicators are those that explain and show creative processes and products. Connectors establish relationships among members of the ecosystem. Creators are those in charge of thinking about and realizing creative products and ideas. Disruptors represent the obstacles inside an ecosystem (lobbyists, hostile audiences, media, etc.). Enablers make possible the ideas of artists and organize the context where performances take place. Providers are the supplier of resources and services. Sterback adds also the category of domestic creatives, who are privately creative through cooking, fashion, gardening, or craftmaking.

The main shift seen with this ecological paradigm is the conviction that "infrastructures and industry" are less useful as organizing concepts than "relationships and processes" (Sterback 2014) and that new demand and consumption patterns, as well as new value creation modes, have reshaped the debate around cultural and creative activities (NESTA 2009).

More recently, De Bernard, Comunian, and Gross (2021) have revised the literature on cultural and creative ecologies and ecosystems, which they define as a complex adaptive system that can become the object of analysis by multiple disciplines. Such an approach allows us to consider organizations, activities, and dynamics that fall under the broad umbrella of culture and creativity, and study them through a variety of approaches and methodologies.

These new perspectives depart from the vertical perspective that characterizes the definition of culture and creativity based on industrial specializations, recognizing that components, actors, and dimensions, as well as the logics of consumption and production, can be multiple and belong to different sectors. Moreover, the components of these activities act in an interdependent way and are capable of influencing each other. It follows that the logic of specialization is too narrow to capture the wide possibilities for the development of cultural and creative activities.

Complexity Thinking and the Evolution of Cultural and Creative Activities

As the previous section demonstrates, the introduction of notions such as creative ecology (Markusen 2011) or ecology of culture (Holden 2015) marks the starting point of a rethinking of the production of economic value, its modalities, and its connections. UNIDO (2014) discusses the concept of the creative ecosystem in a way that takes account of more than just geographical proximity. Potts et al. (2008) argue that the theoretical conception of cultural and creative activities should move toward a market-based interpretation because (1) the economic environment in which they have developed is a service-oriented economy and (2) complexity thinking has widely diffused in economics and managerial sciences.

Concerning the first point, the consequence of this market-based perspective is a tangible phenomenon, looking at the emerging zones of cities and the birth new firms, whose first resource has become service-oriented creativity, in other words creativity as the main resource for innovation. Thanks to the presence of entrenched networks of people and artifacts, reactive to this kind of model and diffused by widespread digital media, underline the possibility to scale up to the global level (Wen and Li 2014). In this scenario, design, architecture, fashion, and software are examples of creative activities that are becoming the central hub, substituting for the cultural core that characterized the emergence of the CCI paradigm (Potts et al. 2008).

The second point, regarding the diffusion of complexity thinking, deserves a deeper look as well as an analysis of its disruptive character. Martin and Sunley (2007) looked at the impact complexity thinking has had on economics and concluded that at that time it had not yet reached the level of a theoretical paradigm, even though it had introduced fundamental elements for the study of economic systems. Nearly fifteen years later, Hidalgo (2021) offered a clear-cut map of the more recent contributions that network science, in particular the notions of relatedness and economic complexity, has made to the understanding of socioeconomic phenomena. Even though complexity thinking is still in its infancy as it concerns economics and management, this is a clear sign that something has changed.

What exactly is a complex system? Martin and Sunley (2007, 577) wrote that "a system is complex when it comprises non-linear interactions between its parts, such that an understanding of the system is not possible through a simple reduction to its component elements." Moreover, they reported seven generic properties that complex systems should have:

1. *Distributed nature.* Complex systems are multiscalar networks diffused with the entrenchment of actors and relationships.
2. *Openness.* Complex systems have blurry boundaries that continuously interact with the external environment.
3. *Nonlinear dynamics. Two* Complex systems do not follow the same script, and they show feedback and interactions among their subsystems.
4. *Limited functional decomposability.* Complex systems can be decomposed into subsystems, but the validity of this division is uncertain and dynamic in time.
5. *Emergence and self-organization.* New orders emerge as agents and structures interact in many different ways.
6. *Adaptive behavior.* Complex systems and their components critically react to the changing conditions of the system and the external environment.
7. *Nondeterminism and nontractability.* The functions and shapes of complex systems cannot be predetermined.

These seven properties help to characterize the notion of a complex system, despite the difficulties in defining a precise theoretical framework and appropriate units of analysis. The strong tendency to analyze complexity using network science (Hidalgo 2021) indicates that researchers are moving toward a focus on dynamism rather than stability, toward connections of products and services rather than single products, toward change rather than equilibrium, toward multiscalar phenomena rather than linear feedback

The Increasing Complexity of the Cultural and Creative Industries Ecosystem: An Evolutionary Overview

Cultural economics has a long tradition that goes from the initial studies of "art" to a wider meaning of "culture" (Rizzo and Mignosa 2013). In the first phase, cultural economics has applied economic analysis to performative arts, cultural heritage, and cultural industries. The discipline was born in the mid-1960s when some economic studies began to deal with the economic role of the state in financing the arts (Throsby 1994). In this scenario, cultural heritage is considered a stock of resources to be preserved (Rizzo and Throsby 2006).

With the advent of policies for economic regeneration starting from cultural resources, artistic heritage becomes an asset for the economic development of cities and regions and is considered a factor of production. The focus is on cultural clusters and districts (Cinti 2007; Lazzeretti 2008). The discipline of arts and cultural management begins to emerge where the objectives of cultural institutions are expressed in terms of efficiency, cost per user, and audience diversity (Holden 2004).

With the advent of studies on the creative economy (Florida 2002, 2012; Landry 2012), the focus becomes the creative process, and culture is no longer considered a mere factor of production but is thought of as a "creative capacity" (Lazzeretti 2012a). In such a scenario, the importance of innovative processes developed in creative places increases.

In recent years, a number of scholars have begun to develop a critical approach to the study of cities' and regions' development paths driven by CCIs. Florida (2017) recognized that the emergence of the creative class has produced gentrification and the growth of inequality in major cities. This new phase is also interlinked with the emergence of globalization, the economic crisis of 2008, and climate change. Such considerations lead to a rethinking of the societal function of cultural heritage (Lazzeretti 2012b). The importance of local communities and the risk of loss of identity of places emerge in this context.

A new challenge for the cultural and creative sector is represented by the digital revolution, in the new phase of technological enhancement of culture (Lazzeretti 2021). The disruptive advent of digital technology in production, consumption, and everyday life activities and relationships has completely reshaped cultural and creative activities. Cultural consumption such as cinema is now juxtaposed with the provision of movies and series on multiple platforms (Parnell 2021). The possibility of exploring art galleries directly from home would not be possible without reliable and diffuse IT infrastructure. In addition, the idea generation process has been influenced by digital means, such as the exchange and sharing of information through cloud-computing-based services. In this scenario, the complexity of cultural and creative activities has magnified not by the IT revolution per se but for the enabling character of this transformation. Baskerville, Myers, and Yoo (2020) described the ontological reversal of information systems that have shifted from "mirrors" to "creator" factors. The consequences impact specific aspects of business models—namely, organizations' relationships with customers, suppliers, and competitors. Let's consider the evolution of two big companies, Apple and Netflix.

In the case of Apple, the sharp demarcation between utilitarian and non-utilitarian products has been blurred (Lampel and Germain 2016), showing the emergence of design, marketing, and communication as cultural elements. People mostly acquire Apple products for these reasons, despite the products' powerful performance. In the case of Netflix, the quality of the cultural products it offers is the product of a huge study based on big data, carried out across a period of years with matrix completion techniques (looking at co-occurrence of preferences across billions of users' profiles). In this case, culture is central and IT is used as an enhancement tool.

Creative and cultural activities have become intrinsically dependent on IT, generating large profits for companies able to outdo their competitors (Hearn, Roodhouse, and Blakey 2007; Lampel and Germain 2016). Customers have become co-creators of content, and thus the ultimate target of companies that can personalize content based on algorithms (Vargo and Lusch 2004). As suggested by Boudreau and Lakhani (2013, 67), "the crowd has become a fixed institution available on demand," and IT makes possible activity that is individual-customer-centric.

Platforms meant as service provision tools emerge as new organizational forms, transaction facilitators, innovative building blocks, and hybrid forms of those (Gawer 2021). These infrastructures have become catalysts of multiple potential outcomes. And instead of competing directly with each other, they often engage in "coopetition" (for example, the same user can access both Amazon Prime and Netflix, rather than having to choose just one) (Hearn, Roodhouse, and Blakey 2007).

The disruptive emergence of a business-to-consumer (B2C) logic has progressively eroded the power of intermediaries in cultural consumption (e.g., experts and cultural institutions), provoking the birth of an "economy of prescribers, who are active third parties operating in parallel with procedures and consumers" (Benghozi and Paris 2016, 76). New technologies and virtual environments, such as the metaverse, blockchain, and NFTs, are creating exponentially larger numbers of applications for cultural and creative products. They have already enlarged the offerings of traditional cultural organizations such as museums, which have started to replicate some of their masterpieces digitally. Even creative industries such as fashion have entered the virtual environment by digitizing iconic products or creating new virtual collections.

In a nutshell, we are seeing the emergence of a new order—a sort of metaphysical creative cluster, where a new value-creating system, one based on the (supposed) power of individuals and characterized by hyperchoices and hyperofferings enabled by IT, influences the production and consumption of culture (Warren and Fuller 2009; Benghozi and Paris 2016; Landoni et al. 2020).

This paradigm shift has in turn influenced the relationship between culture and creativity and the concepts of community, territory, and society. While there are positives— for example, during the pandemic the virtual projection of territories and people made communication possible even as people had to isolate—the negative side is evident as well. As underlined by Lazzeretti (2020), imagination (and all the neurological processes linked to it) is the main element that separates humans from machines. Furthermore, the need to rethink the rights of artists in the new digital environment is urgent, especially given that IT monopolies are becoming more and more consolidated.

A Novel Approach for Mapping Cultural and Creative Activities

The considerations described so far show the evolution of the organizations, actors, and elements that are part of the creative and cultural activities.

Starting from the model proposed by Lazzeretti (2020) that identifies five phases in the relationship between culture, economy, society, and technology, and applying the concept of complex adaptive systems, we can tentatively identify specific actors and resources that have characterized each phase (Table 3.1).

Table 3.1. The Five Phases of Evolution of Culture, Economy, Society, and Technology Stylised Through an Ecosystem Approach

	Driver	Key actors	Key resources	Geographic focus	Typology of relationships
1. Conservation	Conservation	Central governments; museums	Cultural heritage	National	Closed
2. Economic enhancement of culture	Local development	Local institutions; museums; service firms; customers; cultural districts	Cultural heritage; market	Regional	Open in closed systems (e.g., within cultural districts)
3. Cultural enhancement of the economy	Innovation	Creative class; emergence of creative sectors and clusters (e.g., fashion, design, architecture)	Cultural heritage; applied technology; branding strategies	City	Open in closed but globally connected systems (metropolitan cities)
4. Social enhancement of culture	Grand challenges (overtourism; sustainability; well-being)	Local communities; nonprofit organizations	Cultural heritage; social values (identity and authenticity)	Local communities	Open in "small worlds"
5. Technological enhancement of culture	Digital transformation (ontological reverse of IT)	IT developers; amateurs; individuals; virtual communities	Software; cultural heritage; social media	Global networks	Globally open

Source: Authors' elaboration based on Lazzeretti 2020.

Table 3.1, borrowing from the ecosystem approach and in particular the framework of complex adaptive system, explains the evolution of the cultural and creative environment. In particular, it shows the key actors and resources, the geographical setting, and the typology of relationships. It is interesting to note that if in the first phase the focus was on the national level and the conservation of cultural heritage, over the years the activities related to different types of enhancement (cultural, economic, social, technological) have assumed a priority role, as have the actors who drive different phases of this enhancement. This goes hand in hand with the change in the definition of CCIs, which increasingly incorporates aspects not directly connected with those activities typically considered the "core of the arts." At this stage, the multiscalar nature of the system is still minimal, as is its openness.

Furthermore, while the geographical setting becomes more and more strict—from the national to the community level, up to the networks of individuals (even if in a global context)—the number of relationships that exist between actors increases, making the ecosystem wider. This has triggered an inverse relationship between the dimension of the unit of analysis of cultural and creative activities and the ecosystem dimension. While the first has shrunk over time, the second has increased, showing how important it is to carefully think through the multiscalar and evolutionary networks that propagate from individual companies to creative amateurs. Despite an evident fragmentation, the inclusion of an increasingly wider number of connections again underline how the ecosystem approach is a promising framework to furtherly explore. What seems still to be missing is an upward and downward logical path analysis able to organize the elements in relation to potential outcomes (Stam and van der Ven 2021). Particularly interesting are the reciprocal links between the emergence of a creative outcome and the effects on the creative environment—an analytical perspective difficult to capture with traditional approaches.

Figure 3.1 traces a possible way to develop and to integrate the elements of Table 3.1 into a theoretical framework that depicts the creative outcome as a result of a mix between structure and agency, where cultural and creative actors shape (and are shaped by) the creative environment.

In line with Wurth, Stam, and Spigel (2021), the recent attention dedicated to entrepreneurship as a new form (the creation of new ventures) with a new function (the discovery of new opportunities) should be explored and contextualized for the unique characteristics that make cultural and creative activities different from ordinary products and services, especially in terms of the link to aggregated societal value.

A new research agenda on the topic should provide a theoretical and empirical framework to:

1. Identify the set of elements able to explain the prevalence of cultural and creative activities and their historical path creation trajectory. What elements and conditions explain the emergence of this pattern. How does the general level of socioeconomic development influence it?

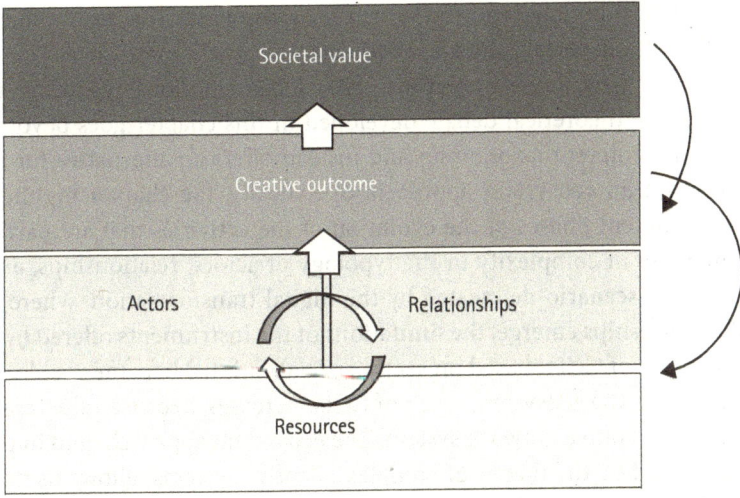

FIGURE 3.1 Creative activities: Path creation.
Source: Authors' elaboration based on Stam and van der Ven 2021.

2. Define the typologies of the value of cultural and creative activities. In this case, the definition of productive entrepreneurship adopted by Stam and Van der Ven (2021) and by Wurth, Stam, and Spigel (2021) should be adapted to the capacity of cultural and creative activities to generate societal value and contribute to societal building (entrepreneurship as a way to identify the possible existence of promising channels). This implies a different operationalization of cultural and creative high potential new venture (what are the distinctive features to be included in such a definition?), overcoming a perspective solely based on "hunting" for rare emblematic cases (such as Cirque du Soleil) and instead searching for new paradigms that can come from specific combinations of endowment conditions.

Conclusion

This chapter aimed to explore the different classifications of CCIs proposed over time and whether an ecosystem approach may be considered a new representation of the relationships and dynamics of CCIs as an alternative to those based on industrial specializations.

By analyzing the existing literature, the chapter identifies the limitations of taxonomies of CCIs based on an industrial approach. A significant point in the debate over the classification of CCIs has to do with the blurriness of the definition used and the impossibility of finding a unique object of analysis; instead, the object may change depending on the context and purpose of the analysis. This is related to the multiple meanings of cultural heritage and the value they assume, starting from different geographical, cultural, and social contexts (Vecco 2010).

Although there have been numerous critical contributions regarding the definition of CCIs, the theoretical debate developed in this chapter goes beyond simply summarizing the different taxonomies and instead offers an alternative for the study of CCIs based on an ecosystem approach. Specifically, the chapter highlights how, retracing the different phases of the evolution of the activities that are part of CCIs, we see an increase in complexity in the typology of actors, relationships, and global reach. In the new scenario delineated by the digital transformation, where different actors and relationships emerge, the limitations of the instruments offered by the classical classifications of CCIs (based on sector specializations) become visible. With the digital shift, in fact, the ecosystem reach of CCIs increases, because value-creating capacity is embedded into a network system. The ecosystem approach, and in particular the insights offered by the theory of complex adaptive systems, allows us not only to identify actors and activities that are part of the ecosystem but to map the relationships between them. This approach drives new opportunities for analyzing the different network relationships that emerge in the new phase of technological enhancement of culture (Lazzeretti 2020). Moreover, it helps to understand how cultural and creative organizations contribute to creating their environment as they and the components of that environment mutually interact and react to changes in the external environment and internal conditions.

Literature on ecosystems in CCIs is still in infancy, despite some contributions that have applied this approach to entrepreneurial activity in the cultural and creative sectors (Chandna and Salimath 2020; Loots et al. 2021). However, a broad approach based on CCIs as a complex adaptive system is still an underresearched topic. This chapter represents a first attempt to go in this direction, to find new tools for studying the digital transformation in CCIs.

Further contributions to the ecosystem lens on cultural and creative activities should start to conceive and empirically test new frameworks to analyze the mechanisms that link the conditions and resources of a context to the development of a well-structured system of cultural and creative activities. The identification of adequate entrepreneurial forms and functions could be a way to move past an analysis solely based on industrial specializations and instead explore the emergence of the phenomenon; furthermore, it could suggest policy tools that could be applied in order to generate specific interventions and programs (see Stam and Van der Ven 2021).

Acknowledgements

This work was supported by CHANGES, PNRR, Mission 4, PE5, NextGenEU (CUP B53C22004010006).

REFERENCES

Americans for the Arts. 2005. *Creative Industries 2005: The Congressional Report*. Washington, DC: Americans for the Arts.

Autio, Erkko, Satish Nambisan, Llewellyn D. W. Thomas, and Mike Wright. 2018. "Digital Affordances, Spatial Affordances, and the Genesis of Entrepreneurial Ecosystems." *Strategic Entrepreneurship Journal* 12, no. 1: 72–95.

Baskerville, Richard L., Michael D. Myers, and Youngjin Yoo. 2020. "Digital First: The Ontological Reversal and New Challenges for Information Systems Research." *Management Information Systems Quarterly* 44, no. 2: 509–523. https://doi.org/10.25300/MISQ/2020/14418.

Benghozi, Pierre-Jean, and Thomas Paris. 2016. "The Cultural Economy in the Digital Age: A Revolution in Intermediation?" *City, Culture and Society* 7, no. 2: 75–80. https://doi.org/10.1016/j.ccs.2015.12.005.

Boix, Rafael, Luciana Lazzeretti, Francesco Capone, and Daniel Sanchez-Serra. 2013. "The Geography of Creative Industries in Europe: Comparing France, Great Britain, Italy and Spain." In *Creative Industries and Innovation in Europe: Concepts, Measures and Comparative Case Studies*, edited by Luciana Lazzeretti, 23–44. London: Routledge.

Boudreau, Kevin J., and Karim R. Lakhani. 2013. "Using the Crowd as an Innovation Partner." *Harvard Business Review* 91, no. 4: 60–69.

Caves, Richard E. 2003. "Contracts Between Art and Commerce." *Journal of Economic Perspectives* 17, no. 2: 73–83. https://doi.org/10.1257/089533003765888430.

Chandna, Vallari, and Manjula S. Salimath. 2020. "When Technology Shapes Community in the Cultural and Craft Industries: Understanding Virtual Entrepreneurship in Online Ecosystems." *Technovation* 92: 102042. https://doi.org/10.1016/j.technovation.2018.06.005.

Chen, Chin-Yu, and Jwu-Jenq Chen. 2014. "The Intellectual Structure of Creative Industries Studies in 2003–2012: Invisible Taiwan." *Business Economics* 404: 40–440. https://doi.org/10.7763/JOEBM.2014.V2.93.

Cinti, Tommaso. 2007. *Musei e territorio: le dinamiche relazionali nel cluster museale di Firenze*. Vol. 7. Rome: Carocci.

Comunian, Roberta. 2019. "Complexity Thinking as a Coordinating Theoretical Framework for Creative Industries Research." In *A Research Agenda for Creative Industries*, edited by Stuart Cunningham and Terrt Flew, 39–57. Cheltenham, UK: Edward Elgar. https://doi.org/10.4337/9781788118583.00010.

Cooke, Philip, and Luciana Lazzeretti. 2008. *Creative Cities, Cultural Clusters and Local Economic Development*. Cheltenham, UK: Edward Elgar. https://doi.org/10.4337/9781847209948.

Cruz, Sara C. Santos, and Aurora A. C. Teixeira. 2021. "Spatial Analysis of New Firm Formation in Creative Industries Before and During the World Economic Crisis." *Annals of Regional Science* 67, no. 2: 385–413. https://doi.org/10.1007/s00168-021-01052-3.

Cunningham, Stuart. 2002. "From Cultural to Creative Industries: Theory, Industry and Policy Implications." *Media International Australia* 102, no. 1: 54–65. https://doi.org/10.1177/1329878X0210200107.

Cunningham, Stuart, John Banks, and Jason Potts. 2008. "Cultural Economy: The Shape of the Field." In *The Cultural Economy. The Cultures and Globalization Series 2*, edited by H. K. Anheier and Y. R. Isar, 15–26. London: SAGE Publications Ltd.

DCMS. 2001. *Classifying and Measuring the Creative Industries*. London: Department for Culture, Media, and Sport.
De Bernard, Manfredi, Roberta Comunian, and Jonathan Gross. 2021. "Cultural and Creative Ecosystems: A Review of Theories and Methods, Towards a New Research Agenda." *Cultural Trends* 31, no. 4: 1–22. https://doi.org/10.1080/09548963.2021.2004073.
Florida, Richard. 2002. *The Rise of the Creative Class: And How It's Transforming Work, Leisure, Community and Everyday Life*. New York: Basic Books.
Florida, Richard. 2012. *The Rise of the Creative Class Revisited*. New York: Basic Books.
Florida, Richard. 2017. *The New Urban Crisis: How Our Cities Are Increasing Inequality, Deepening Segregation, and Failing the Middle Class—and What We Can Do About It*. London: Hachette UK.
Gawer, Annabelle. 2021. "Digital Platforms and Ecosystems: Remarks on the Dominant Organizational Forms of the Digital Age." *Innovation* 24, no. 1: 1–15. https://doi.org/10.1080/14479338.2021.1965888.
Gong, Huiwen, and Robert Hassink. 2017. "Exploring the Clustering of Creative Industries." *European Planning Studies* 25, no. 4: 583–600. https://doi.org/10.1080/09654313.2017.1289154.
Hall, Peter. 2000. "Creative Cities and Economic Development." *Urban Studies* 37, no. 4: 639–649.
Hearn, Greg, Simon Roodhouse, and Julie Blakey. 2007. "From Value Chain to Value Creating Ecology: Implications for Creative Industries Development Policy." *International Journal of Cultural Policy* 13, no. 4: 419–436. https://doi.org/10.1080/10286630701683367.
Hidalgo, César A. 2021. "Economic Complexity Theory and Applications." *Nature Reviews Physics* 3, no. 2: 92–113. https://doi.org/10.1038/s42254-020-00275-1.
Holden, John. 2004. *Creating Cultural Value: How Culture Has Become a Tool of Government Policy*. London: Demos.
Holden, John. 2015. *The Ecology of Culture*. Swindon, UK: Arts and Humanities Research Council.
Howkins, John. 2002. *The Creative Economy: How People Make Money from Ideas*. London: Penguin.
Howkins, John. 2010. Creative Ecologies. New Brunswick, London: Transaction Publishers.
Innocenti, Niccolò, and Luciana Lazzeretti. 2019. "Do the Creative Industries Support Growth and Innovation in the Wider Economy? Industry Relatedness and Employment Growth in Italy." *Industry and Innovation* 26, no. 10: 1152–1173. https://doi.org/10.1080/13662716.2018.1561360.
Jeffcutt, Paul, and Andrew Pratt. 2002. "Managing Creativity in the Cultural Industries." *Creativity and Innovation Management* 11, no. 4: 225–233. https://doi.org/10.1111/1467-8691.00254.
Jung, Yuha. 2011. "The Art Museum Ecosystem: A New Alternative Model." *Museum Management and Curatorship* 26, no. 4: 321–338. https://doi.org/10.1080/09647775.2011.603927.
KEA. 2006. *The Economy of Culture in Europe: Study Prepared for the European Commission*. Brussels: Directorate-General for Education and Culture.
Lampel, Joseph, and Olivier Germain. 2016. "Creative Industries as Hubs of New Organizational and Business Practices." *Journal of Business Research* 69, no. 7: 2327–2333. https://doi.org/10.1016/j.jbusres.2015.10.001.
Landoni, Paolo, Claudio Dell'era, Federico Frattini, Antonio Petruzzelli, Roberto Verganti, and Luca Manelli. 2020. "Business Model Innovation in Cultural and Creative Industries: Insights from Three Leading Mobile Gaming Firms." *Technovation* 92–93: 102084. https://doi.org/10.1016/j.technovation.2019.102084.
Landry, Charles. 2012. *The Creative City: A Toolkit for Urban Innovators*. Sterling, VA: Earthscan. https://doi.org/10.4324/9781849772945.

Lazzeretti, Luciana. 2008. "The Cultural Districtualization Model." In *Creative Cities, Cultural Clusters and Local Development*, edited by Philip Cooke and Luciana Lazzeretti, 93–120. Cheltenham, UK: Edward Elgar.

Lazzeretti, Luciana. 2012a. *Cluster creativi per i beni culturali. L'esperienza toscana delle tecnologie per il restauro e la valorizzazione*. Florence: Firenze University Press. https://doi.org/10.36253/978-88-6655-124-9.

Lazzeretti, Luciana. 2012b. "The Resurge of the 'Societal Function of Cultural Heritage': An Introduction." *City, Culture and Society* 4, no. 3: 229–233. https://doi.org/10.1016/j.ccs.2012.12.003.

Lazzeretti, Luciana. 2020. "What Is the Role of Culture Facing the Digital Revolution Challenge? Some Reflections for a Research Agenda." *European Planning Studies* 30, no. 9: 1–21. https://doi.org/10.1080/09654313.2020.1836133.

Lazzeretti, Luciana. 2021. *L'ascesa della società algoritmica ed il ruolo strategico della cultura*. Milan: Franco Angeli.

Lazzeretti, Luciana, Rafael Boix, and Francesco Capone. 2008. "Do Creative Industries Cluster? Mapping Creative Local Production Systems in Italy and Spain." *Industry and Innovation* 15, no. 5: 549–567. https://doi.org/10.1080/13662710802374161.

Lazzeretti, Luciana, and Francesco Capone. 2015. "Narrow or Broad Definition of Cultural and Creative Industries: Evidence from Tuscany, Italy." *International Journal of Cultural and Creative Industries* 2, no. 2: 4–19.

Lazzeretti, Luciana, Francesco Capone, and Niccolò Innocenti, 2018. "The Rise of Cultural and Creative Industries in Creative Economy Research: A Bibliometric Analysis." In *Creative Industries and Entrepreneurship*, 13–34. Edward Elgar Publishing.

Loots, Ellen, Miguel Neiva, Luis Carvalho, and Mariangela Lavanga. 2021. "The Entrepreneurial Ecosystem of Cultural and Creative Industries in Porto: A Sub-Ecosystem Approach." *Growth and Change* 52, no. 2: 641–662. https://doi.org/10.1111/grow.12434.

Markusen, Anne. 2011. *California's Arts and Cultural Ecology*. San Francisco: James Irvine Foundation.

Martin, Ron, and Peter Sunley. 2007. "Complexity Thinking and Evolutionary Economic Geography." *Journal of Economic Geography* 7, no. 5: 573–601. https://doi.org/10.1093/jeg/lbm019.

Massi, Marta, Marilena Vecco, and Yi Lin. 2021. *Digital Transformation in the Cultural and Creative Industries*. London: Routledge. https://doi.org/10.4324/9780429329852.

NESTA. 2009. *Culture of Innovation: An Economic Analysis of Innovation in Arts and Cultural Organisations*. London: National Endowment for Science, Technology, and the Arts.

O'Connor, Justin. 2010. *The Cultural and Creative Industries: A Literature Review*. Newcastle, UK: Creativity, Culture and Education.

Parnell, Claire. 2021. "Mapping the Entertainment Ecosystem of Wattpad: Platforms, Publishing and Adaptation." *Convergence* 27, no. 2: 524–538. https://doi.org/10.1177/1354856520970141.

Potts, Jason, Stuart Cunningham, John Hartley, and Paul Ormerod. 2008. "Social Network Markets: A New Definition of the Creative Industries." *Journal of Cultural Economics* 32: 167–185.

Potts, Jason. 2016. *The Economics of Creative Industries*. Cheltenham, UK: Edward Elgar. https://doi.org/10.4337/9781785361517.

Pratt, Andy. C., 2008. Creative Cities: The Cultural Industries and the Creative Class. *Geografiska annaler: Series B, Human Geography* 90, no. 2: 107–117.

Rizzo, Ilde, and Anna Mignosa. 2013. *Handbook on the Economics of Cultural Heritage*. Cheltenham, UK: Edward Elgar. https://doi.org/10.1007/s10824-008-9066-y.

Rizzo, Ilde, and David Throsby. 2006. "Cultural Heritage: Economic Analysis and Public Policy." In *Handbook of the Economics of Art and Culture*, vol. 1, edited by Victor Ginsburgh and David Throsby, 983–1016. Amsterdam: Elsevier. https://doi.org/10.1016/S1574-0676(06)01028-3.

Santagata, Walter. 2006. "Cultural Districts and Their Role in Developed and Developing Countries." In *Handbook of the Economics of Art and Culture*, vol. 1, edited by Victor Ginsburgh and David Throsby, 1101–1119. Amsterdam: Elsevier. https://doi.org/10.1016/S1574-0676(06)01031-3.

Scott, Allen J. 2006. "Creative Cities: Conceptual Issues and Policy Questions." *Journal of Urban Affairs* 28, no. 1: 1–17. https://doi.org/10.1111/j.0735-2166.2006.00256.x.

Stam, Erik, and Andrew Van de Ven. 2021. "Entrepreneurial Ecosystem Elements." *Small Business Economics* 56, no. 2: 809–832. https://doi.org/10.1007/s11187-019-00270-6.

Stankevičienė, Jelena, Rasa Levickaitė, Monika Braškutė, and Elinga Norelkaitė. 2011. "Creative Ecologies: Developing and Managing New Concepts of Creative Economy." *Business, Management and Economics Engineering* 9, no. 2: 277–294. https://doi.org/10.3846/bme.2011.19.

Sterback, Elise. 2014. *Creative Ecology: A New Model for Resilience in Creative Communities*. Auckland: Creative Coalition.

Throsby, David. 1994. "The Production and Consumption of the Arts: A View of Cultural Economics." *Journal of Economic Literature* 32, no. 1: 1–29.

Throsby, David. 2001. *Economics and Culture*. Cambridge: Cambridge University Press.

Throsby, David. 2008. "Modelling the Cultural Industries." *International Journal of Cultural Policy* 14, no. 3: 217–232. https://doi.org/10.1080/10286630802281772.

UNCTAD. 2010. *Creative Economy Report*. Geneva: United Nations Conference on Trade and Development.

UNESCO. 2005. *The Convention on the Protection and Promotion of the Diversity of Cultural Expressions*. Paris: United Nations Educational, Scientific and Cultural Organization.

UNIDO. 2014. "The Creative Ecosystem: Facilitating the Development of Creative Industries." Working Paper 08/2014, Research, Statistics, and Industrial Policy Branch, United Nations Industrial Development Organization, Vienna.

Vargo, Stephen L., and Robert F. Lusch. 2004. "Evolving to a New Dominant Logic for Marketing." *The Service-Dominant Logic of Marketing* 68, no. 1: 21–46. https://doi.org/10.1509/jmkg.68.1.1.24036.

Vecco, Marilena. 2009. "Creative and Cultural Industries and Cities." *International Journal of Sustainable Development* 12, nos. 2–4: 192–209. https://doi.org/10.1504/IJSD.2009.032777.

Vecco, Marilena. 2010. "A Definition of Cultural Heritage: From the Tangible to the Intangible." *Journal of Cultural Heritage* 11, no. 3: 321–324. https://doi.org/10.1016/j.culher.2010.01.006.

Warren, Lorraine, and Ted Fuller. 2009. "Methodological Issues Arising from Research into the Emergence of Enterprise in the Creative Industries." Brighton: British Academy of Management Conference.

Wen, Wen, and Henry Siling Li. 2014. "Future Forming: A Rethink on the Creative Economy." *Cultural Science Journal* 7, no. 1: 68–82. https://doi.org/10.5334/csci.64.

WIPO. 2003. *Guide on Surveying the Economic Contribution of the Copyright-Based Industries*. Geneva: World Intellectual Property Organization.

Wurth, Bernd, Erik Stam, and Ben Spigel. 2021. "Toward an Entrepreneurial Ecosystem Research Program." *Entrepreneurship Theory and Practice* 46, no. 3: 1042258721998948. https://doi.org/10.1177/1042258721998948.

CHAPTER 4

METHODS AND METHODOLOGIES IN ARTS AND CULTURAL MANAGEMENT RESEARCH

A Review and Research Agenda

RUTH RENTSCHLER AND JIAXIN LIU

Introduction

This chapter examines the development of methods and methodologies in arts and cultural management (ACM) research by undertaking a selective review of the literature (Colbert and St-James 2014). Methods entail the rationale for the research approach and the lens through which analysis occurs. Methodologies support the methods chosen. They provide the perspective for the study, dictated by the worldview to be used in it (Creswell and Creswell 2018). ACM is a concept spawned by general business studies (e.g., in management, sociology, economics, and policy). We examine *International Journal of Arts Management*, *International Journal of Cultural Policy*, *Journal of Arts Management, Law and Society*, *Journal of Cultural Economics*, and *Poetics* from 1969 to 2022, identifying legitimacy changes over time. The selection criteria entailed journals in existence for more than twenty years and with a journal impact factor greater than 1.2. We extend analysis by scrutinizing in-text citations and references in these journals, leading to a diverse literature base for analysis. From this analysis, three different worlds appear (Colbert and St-James 2014; Dharmani, Das, and Prashar 2021): arts management, cultural economics, and cultural policy.

In doing so, this study seeks to overcome the view that there is one true and abiding set of methods and methodologies. What was deemed innovative as a research method or methodology in 1969 is quite different from what is deemed creative in 2022. For example, Edelstein's (1970) article on arts governance provided personal insights as a practitioner that were novel for the time. However, in 2022, scholars are studying vlogs, TripAdvisor views of graffiti tours, and NFTs (Patrickson 2021; Reason 2022; Seok, Joo, and Nam 2020), asking in no uncertain terms about their purpose (Floridi 2014; Nadini et al. 2021). Recognition of the breadth of the field and the debt it owes to other disciplines is important as a means of overcoming "academic absolutism" (Gray 2010), the view that there is one best way to undertake research. Our approach opens up debate on what *can* be, rather than focusing on what *is* or *should be* in terms of research methods and methodologies. Therefore, gaining greater awareness of the ontological, epistemological, and methodological approaches of other disciplines allows for insights into how they influenced the development of ACM research methods and methodologies, demonstrating imagination, inventiveness, and innovation. Against this brief background, this study asks the question: How, why, and what are the dominant methods and methodologies employed in the different disciplines that legitimize the field under investigation over time?

The rest of this chapter is structured as follows. The next section defines ACM. Second, we examine legitimacy, relating it to the development of ACM methods and methodologies in a contested field of competing disciplines at various stages of evolution. Third, we review the ACM field from 1969 until 2022, highlighting disciplines and approaches taken ontologically, epistemologically, and methodologically. The chapter concludes by highlighting the strengths and weaknesses of each discipline in research approaches, pointing to future research opportunities in relation to methods and methodologies.

Defining Arts and Cultural Management

ACM is a contested term with no clearly accepted definition. ACM has been defined in several ways, including from a functional perspective and from a critical perspective (e.g., Chong 2010; Evard and Colbert 2000; Rentschler and Shilbury 2008). Functional definitions posit that arts management is akin to planning, leading, organizing, and monitoring, while critical definitions align themselves with the school of thought that sees the arts as providing aesthetic experiences for audiences through management discourse (Araújo, Davel, and Rentschler 2020). The critical school seeks to overcome the reliance on generalist theories of management being applied willy-nilly to the arts without taking heed of their singularities. The reasons for this disparity are that (1) some in the arts have been inclined to reject managerial approaches, while (2) while others value collaboration over competition, (3) still others are just opening their eyes to ACM through education or leadership training programs, and (4) another group may belong to related but distinct fields of endeavor, such as management, sociology, economics and policy, each of which has its own journals, such as *Poetics* (founded in 1971), *Journal of Cultural Economics* (founded in 1977), and *International Journal of Cultural Policy* (founded in 1993). The *International Journal of Arts Management* was founded after these other journals, in 1998. The *Journal of Arts Management, Law and Society* (founded in 1969 as *Performing Arts Review*, with a name change to *Journal of Arts Management and Law* in 1982 and to its current name in 1993) was the first journal established in the field, but as a journal for the performing arts; only later did it take on arts management. We follow DeVereaux (2019) in defining ACM as a distinguishable phenomenon treated as "an identifiable, consumable and value-laden public good" (89) for the benefit of society and its people. Our definition of ACM includes understanding of the value of the arts for artists and audiences, disseminated through arts managerial knowledge in praxis (compare with Rentschler and Shilbury 2008; Veal and Burton 2014). There is no doubt that the arts are shaped by "intellectual achievement" that reflects the "systems and beliefs of society" (Fillis 2011, 13). Thus, our ACM definition acknowledges its foundations in other disciplines, while recognizing development that draws on sociology, economics, and policy as well as from the general business literature plus the arts and culture literature (e.g., creativity, culture, and community).

Legitimizing the Field of Arts and Cultural Management

Legitimacy is the generalized perception that actions are desirable, proper, or appropriate within a socially constructed field (Suchman 1995), "manipulat[ing] and deploy[ing] evocative symbols in order to obtain societal support" (Suchman 1995, 572). Legitimacy can be an asset or resource possessed by individuals (Rentschler, Fillis, and Lee 2022), dependent on a history of events (Suchman 1995). Fields develop through perceived legitimacy, embedded in a broader understanding of how it is gained, maintained, and sustained. Gaining legitimacy occurs in a new line of activity where there is a need to win acceptance for the field. After legitimacy has been conferred on a field by others, the maintenance of that legitimacy occurs when a field is taken for granted (Suchman 1995). Proactively sustaining legitimacy extends Suchman's (1995) legitimacy types, ensuring that past successes open doors for future development. Legitimacy theory provides a perspective on how ACM can overcome the "liability of newness" to take its place among preexisting and taken-for-granted fields (Suchman 1995). Astonishingly, journals in the fine arts recorded early research on art as an investment, the US art market, the business of art, and urban planning (e.g., Timothea 1901; Moody 1913; Stuart 1917; Robertson 1918). These articles used a narrative and descriptive approach to tell the story of art, weaving in discussion of other matters that years later have gained legitimacy in ACM research. From such early articles in the art historical *Fine Arts Journal*, it took just over fifty years for the first

ACM journal to be founded (*Performing Arts Review*, in 1969), illustrating the slow emergence of a legitimate field of research.

Approach

In order to identify key shifts regarding methods and methodologies, the authors used a systematic but selective means of searching the literature. Methodology provides the philosophy (e.g., *Weltanschauung*), with methods providing the tools (e.g., observation, interview, survey, big data), together supporting the study approach. Figure 4.1 shows why and how the literature was identified, how articles from the literature were screened, and which articles were included and or excluded.

First, we ran a search for the keyword "arts," "cultural," and "management" in the journal titles to identify journals in the ACM field. Next, we selected journals that had been extant for at least twenty years and that have an impact factor above 1.2. Initially, all articles in five main ACM journals were retrieved every five years. The rationale for selecting five-year intervals was that organizational strategy is usually developed on a five-year basis in most businesses (Rentschler and Geursen 2004); hence it is a period of time in which change can be identified. Next, the total number of articles was reviewed, excluding those that were not investigatory articles (e.g., editorials, book reviews, organization profiles). Then references for each article were scrutinized to identify more articles for analysis beyond the scope of the five journals. This resulted in a total of 589 articles for examination. The disciplinary context of the journals in which those articles were found encompassed management, sociology, economics, and policy.

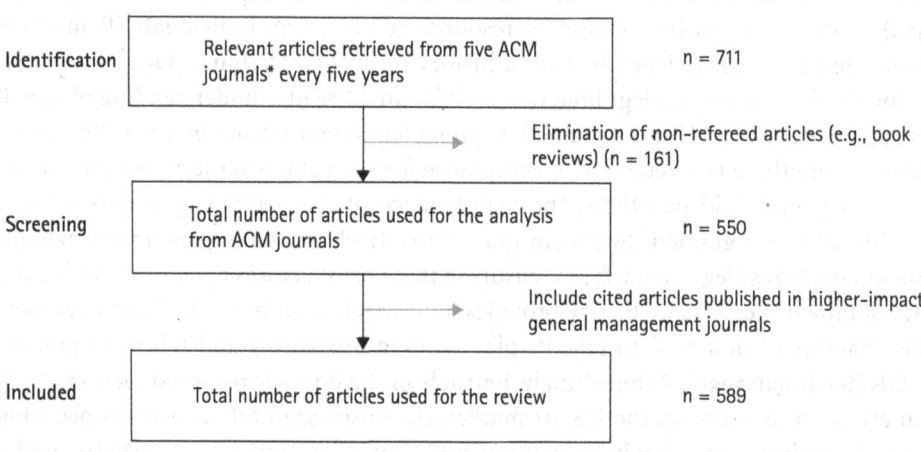

*Journal of Arts Management, Law & Society; Poetics; International Journal of Cultural Policy; International Journal of Arts Management; Journal of Cultural Economics

FIGURE 4.1 Search procedure for relevant ACM articles.

This chapter does not attempt to assess the sophistication of the ACM research methods and methodologies examined. However, it does provide a baseline about ACM research methods and methodologies by focusing on three broad paradigms identified by Gray (2010): realist, interpretivist, and positivist. The realist paradigm is defined as a richly detailed description of social worlds, highlighting personal worldviews, opinions, and deep, rich sociological research (e.g., Davis 1969; DiMaggio 1997; Zolberg 1981). The interpretivist paradigm explores the processes by which social worlds and their experiences are socially constructed. Anthropological and phenomenological approaches could fall into this category. Both realism and interpretivism use small numbers of participants, as in the approach known as "deep hanging out" (Walmsley 2018), although the interpretivist paradigm can also use larger participant numbers (e.g., Pitts and Price 2022). There is sometimes an oscillation between these two poles, with each methodological approach enriching the other (Holstein and Gubrium 2011). Ontologically, realism and interpretivism rely on the interaction between researcher and research participants, influencing the interpretation of findings. Epistemologically, realists and interpretivists contend that knowledge is developed interdependently, with insights from both researcher and research participant co-creating the outcome.

The positivist approach is defined as dependent on the hypothetico-deductive method to verify a priori hypotheses. Examples could include self-report surveys to assess behavioral, physiological, and psychological aspects of audience experiences (Au, Zuo, and Yam 2022). Epistemologically, positivists contend that knowledge is developed independently of and with no influence from the insights of either the researcher or the research participant (Park, Konge, and Artino 2020). Ontologically, it relies on there being one true reality that can be understood, identified, and measured.

Arts and Cultural Management Research Methods and Methodologies

ACM research is undertaken from different perspectives, often dependent on the discipline of origin, that can be classified as realist, interpretivist, or positivist (Gray 2010), which parallels legitimacy as sought, gained, and sustained, illustrated as the field developed. Realist research sees the researcher undertaking studies embedded in the field, often as a participant-observer or even as a member of a particular group that is the focus of study. Many early studies in ACM had a sociological bent or were undertaken by sociologists (e.g., Becker 1976; DiMaggio 1997). Interpretivist studies are undertaken broadly by audience researchers (e.g., Reason 2022; Verdaasdonk 2005), cultural policy researchers, and others—for instance, in evaluating cultural policies (e.g., Vecco and Srakar 2020) or assessing the validity of their typologies (e.g., Srakar and Vecco 2021). Researchers adopting an interpretivist stance seek to use observation, narratives, interviews, content, or a combination of these as a means of understanding the researcher worldview, sometimes in combination with case studies and or historical studies. Positivist research is broadly undertaken by cultural economists. Positivists use surveys and large secondary data sets to identify patterns and longitudinal transactions in the ACM field (e.g., Mei and Moses 2005; Franklin, Lee, and Rentschler 2021), although one-shot surveys also abound (e.g., Höllen, Lengfeld, and Konrad 2020). Researchers in ACM have challenged the dominant paradigm of positivist disciplines, extending the body of knowledge in ACM as the field moves through the stages of gaining, maintaining, and sustaining legitimacy.

Table 4.1 illustrates how legitimacy was gained, maintained, and sustained.

In the first phase of ACM evolution, scholars were seeking to establish a field, have it recognized, and borrow classic management, sociological, and economic theories that were functional in perspective and apply them to ACM (e.g., DiMaggio 1987; Jeffri 1988). Often these scholars were giants of the field, on whose shoulders we stand. The picture painted by ACM researchers is of supplementing mainstream theories (Buffkins 1981; Ettinger and Hutchens 1989), reiterating general management thought, and seeking to gain legitimacy for applying that body of knowledge to the ACM field.

In the second phase, legitimacy had been carved out, at least in part, by the founding giants, enabling those who followed to develop significant empirical studies, both

Table 4.1. Arts and Cultural Management Evolution

Period	Gaining legitimacy Functional (1960s–1980s)	Maintaining legitimacy Technical (1980s–2000)	Sustaining legitimacy Aesthetic (2001–2022)
Point of view	Practical viewpoint	Empirical viewpoint	Critical viewpoint
Perspective	Classic management theory	Arts management theory	Integrated theories
Picture	A supplement to general management A terrain for the dissemination of managerial thought A soft, undisciplined field A developing profession that needs to create a body of knowledge	An emerging discipline situated at the intersection of a theoretical domain (management) and a field (the arts) A field that has a significant difference to other business fields A subdiscipline belonging to management disciplines	A critical tendency across disciplines A field characterized by fragmented knowledge involving multiple actors An uncertain progeny of management, but as likely to come from other fields (e.g., sociology, economics, policy)
Publications	Buffkins 1981; DiMaggio 1987; Jeffri 1988; Ettinger and Hutchens 1989; Dorn 1992	Evard and Colbert 2000; Rentschler and Shilbury 2008; Chong 2010; Kirchberg and Zembylas 2010; Wei 2011	Miller 2001; Kirchner and Rentschler 2015; Paquette and Redaelli 2015; DeVereaux 2019; Araújo, Davel, and Rentschler 2020

quantitative and qualitative, often using descriptive statistics (e.g., DiMaggio 1987), in an emerging discipline at the intersection of a theoretical domain (management) and a field (the arts). The field of the arts is argued to be considerably different from the field of management (Evard and Colbert 2000), but theoretically there is little differentiation within ACM theory at this stage of evolution (Wei 2011); it continues to borrow from management, sociology, economics, and policy (e.g., Kirchberg and Zembylas 2010; Towse 2010; Throsby 2010; Bell 2015).

In the third phase of evolution, a critical viewpoint starts to emerge in ACM theory (Araújo, Davel, and Rentschler 2020; Chong 2010), arguing that the functional perspective is limited because it overlooks the artistic core of the field. At this point the ACM field has been mapped and the terrain acknowledged as legitimate. Not only do international conferences in the arts include ACM topics, but also mainstream management and marketing conferences (e.g., those sponsored by the European Academy of Management) include tracks on it. Mainstream journals no longer consider ACM an anomaly; it is seen as pertinent by some of the highest-quality journals in the world (e.g., Adler 2011). ACM has come of age, a development that is reflected in the sophistication of studies in the field. For example, new research methods have emerged, such as longitudinal studies using annual reports as data (Alexander 2018; Rentschler, Fillis, and Lee 2022); big-data studies mapping the NFT revolution in the arts, collectibles, and gaming (Nadini et al. 2021); and meta-studies examining the online consumption of cultural goods (Tyrowicz, Krawczyk, and Hardy 2020), and demand in the performing arts (Legoux et al. 2014).

Gaining Legitimacy

A field seeking to gain legitimacy "requires a diverse arsenal of techniques" (Suchman 1995, 586) applied over time, uncovering knowledge in the field. Just as early ACM definitions hark back to the stems from which the field developed (management, sociology, economics, and policy), so the methods and methodologies of ACM research emerged from a similar fractured past as the discipline sought legitimacy. Within management, the notion of ACM has important ancestors that draw insights from traditions that focused on processes of production, such as those around "culture industries" (Adorno 1991; Peterson 1997) or art worlds (Becker 1976), and on distinction, class, and taste (Bourdieu 1984). These sociologists have been influential in later ACM research as well (e.g., Lee, Fillis, and Fraser 2022; Rentschler, Lee, and Fillis 2021).

Early ACM research from the 1970s, with a North American focus, was often but not always sociological in nature and largely qualitative (narrative or conceptual), mostly at the micro level of the individual or the meso level of the institution (e.g., Zolberg 1981). Nonetheless, standardized and rationalized methods of undertaking research were evident early on in some studies. For example, there were landmark and groundbreaking quantitative studies using descriptive statistics, mapping arts leaders in an emerging field (e.g., DiMaggio 1987) about whom scholars had previously known nothing.

Similarly, early studies took a leap into the unknown to undertake studies on arts board directors and their characteristics; Abzug et al.'s (1993) seminal sociological article on boards of directors in Boston and Cleveland in the United States noted that "we have almost no systematically-collected baseline data" (272) on arts board directors.

Such was the state of play in the early days of ACM research. These early methods and methodologies shed light on art worlds (comprising networks of artists, critics, audiences, philanthropists, and sponsors) whose workings were largely unknown to scholars or to the public who attended their productions or exhibitions. Early sociologists were followed by later scholars from a range of fields who developed notions of culture as produced and manufactured, crafted or sculpted, revealing systems and explaining perceptions of artistry, sometimes governance, management, and audiences (e.g., Edelstein 1970; Mintzberg 1987; Taubman 1969).

In the early years, studies made a theoretical contribution in general terms entailing a narrative storyline that revealed the mechanisms by which events and activities played out over time. Some such studies do not use data at all but are personal reflections (e.g., Edelstein 1970; Kraus 1985). This can be challenging but is a form of research that is preferred by philosophers and some sociologists (e.g., Adorno 1991). The benefit of adopting empirical research is that it can drive the collection of data, while theoretical contributions without data provide a philosophical foundation for future studies.

There was considerable ontological debate about how, why, and what should be studied and what means of study should be undertaken in order to tell the story. However, there is no single recipe for developing methods and methodologies that are deeply informative and richly illuminating while also conceptually strong and theoretically advanced. With contrasting traditions of scholarship, it depends on the scholars' *Weltanschauung* as to whether one type of storytelling was considered more appropriate than another. Different methods and methodologies can produce understandings of the world based on lived experience or understandings based on generalized representations of the world as seen from above or outside. Storytelling captures temporality, human emotion, meaning, and plot (Cloutier and Langley 2020). However, abstract, generalized representations identify hypotheses, variables, developing relations between constructs in terms of correlation, and units of analysis (Towse and Hernández 2020). Data can generate empirical pathways, offering an explanatory reference point from the outside of the world being studied (Cloutier and Langley 2020).

In sum, from the 1960s to the 1980s, methods and methodologies in ACM gained legitimacy by adopting traditional research approaches from established fields. Mimicry allows ACM and its methods and methodologies to "overcome the liability of newness" (Singh, Tucker, and House 1986) and "increase their otherwise limited chances of survival" (March 2013). Traditional research approaches (e.g., conceptual, case study, interview, survey; see Durham 1977; Hafner 1980; Nielsen, Nielsen, and McQueen 1975; Smith 1969) were dominant in early studies, often with a focus on North America and on museums and the performing arts.

Maintaining Legitimacy

ACM maintained legitimacy by expanding to more rigorous studies and seeking to theorize the field (e.g., Curry 1982; Griffin 2008; Kawashima 1997). Thus, a broader scope of studies was employed, along with unconventional methods and methodologies, to overcome the lack of empirical data on a particular issue (e.g., Belk and Andreasen 1982). In the 1980s and the 1990s, Adorno's "cultural industry" became the "creative industries" through government policy in a range of countries—the United Kingdom, New Zealand, and Australia, to name a few. There was a move beyond the North American focus. The discourse had changed to include the role of government through the introduction of new public management, bringing neoliberalism into the lexicon (McGuigan 2005; Volkerling 2000). The change in name to "cultural industries" paralleled a change in the focus of ACM research away from the product and toward the audience. It was realized by scholars and practitioners alike that little was known about many aspects of ACM—for example, about artists and arts audiences. Many assumptions proved to be wrong. Answers to questions such as "Why do artists need a 'real' job?," "Who is my audience?," and "Who is my market?" spawned a range of quantitative artist and audience studies supported by arts councils in various countries (e.g., Close 1998; Throsby and Thompson 1994).

Starting in 2000, the scope of quantitative ACM studies expanded from an audience-centric perspective to an industrial orientation, and soon after that to an integrative perspective. Statistical, econometrical, and numerical analyses were conducted to reveal hidden patterns and perceptions in responses to questionnaires (e.g., Barnett and Díaz-Andreu 2005), surveys (e.g., Höllen, Lengfeld, and Konrad 2020), secondary statistical data (e.g., Mei and Moses 2005; Vecco and Srakar 2020), and meta-literature (e.g., Noonan 2003). Broader sources of data offer a reference point for theorizing, tapping into quotes that provide evidence for arguments, gazing into people's lived experiences, and telling why and how choices are made and decisions taken in specific instances in time (Cloutier and Langley 2020).

In sum, from the 1980s to 2000, ACM methods and methodologies maintained legitimacy by integrating with other fields. Legitimacy that is desirable, proper or appropriate occurred between individual and collective evaluators (Walker, Thomas, and Zelditch 1986; Zelditch 2001; Tyler 2006). While early studies focused on museums and the performing arts, using conceptual studies, case studies, and surveys (e.g., Zolberg 1981; DiMaggio 1987; Frey 1998), over time there was a shift to broader studies on new themes such as audiences and artists.

Sustaining Legitimacy

In the twenty-first century, ACM sustained legitimacy by developing reviews of the field (e.g., Colbert and St-James 2014; Evard and Colbert 2000; Kirchner and Rentschler 2015;

Rentschler, Fillis, and Lee 2022), turning to digital research opportunities (De la Vega et al. 2019; Floridi 2014; Nadini et al. 2021), and embracing innovative approaches to research, whether ethnographic (Bell and Vachhani 2020; vom Lehn 2006), biographical (Fillis 2011), or historical (Jones et al. 2016; Rentschler, Fillis, and Lee 2022). Studies continued to broaden as the field developed, moving from a North American focus to include Europe, Africa, and Asia (e.g., Aróstegui, Arturo, and Rius-Ulldemolins 2022; Cattaneo and Snowball 2019; Reynolds, Tonks, and MacNeill 2017; Zhang and Courty 2021). For example, China is but one Asian country brought into the field of study (Huo 2016; Zhang 2019).

Studies have been undertaken on organizational space (e.g., Vecco and Srakar 2020) and the industrial stage (e.g., Dharmani, Das, and Prashar 2021), using digital analysis, online tools, and big-data methods and methodologies (Floridi 2014; Nadini et al. 2021). By adopting creative and innovative approaches (Behrens et al. 2020; Reason 2022), ACM continued to broaden its influence methodologically in order to sustain its legitimacy (Zimmerman and Zeitz 2002), continuing to see studies published in mainstream management journals (Rodner et al. 2020). Creative methodologies were nonetheless "an uneasy catch all" (355) of approaches from as wide a span as drawing and vlogging to YouTube videos and analyzing images from photography. Innovative approaches (e.g., content analysis, meta-analysis, historical analysis, and digital analysis) built on the lacunae in the literature. Examining data longitudinally, such as content analysis in annual reports and other documents (e.g., Rentschler 2006; Rentschler, Lee, and Subramaniam 2021; Rentschler, Subramaniam, and Martin 2019), biographical research techniques (e.g., Oakley 2010; Shilbury, Ferkins, and Smythe 2013), and online research methods (e.g., Cleland, Adair, and Parry 2022; Hall, Voranau, and Rentschler 2020), is essential in times of global pandemics that limit access to data subjects but is also pertinent to the more general need to pivot to new ways of conducting research, especially during periods of extreme disruption. Such expansion contributes to the broadening and rethinking in ACM research by providing alternative approaches to data collection and analysis (Fillis 2015; Rentschler, Lee, and Subramaniam 2021). The approach also addresses ontological matters as it uncovers a distinct form of knowledge (Cleland, Adair, and Parry 2022; Fillis 2015). Uncovering data not accessible by other means, such as surveys, can complement existing knowledge by revealing unknown influences that shape ACM research development.

In sum, in order to sustain legitimacy in the digital era, ACM research methods and methodologies continued to be innovative in a broader sphere of endeavor, as the concept of an arts and culture industry took on new meaning. For example, in big-data studies (e.g., Almeida, Lima, and Gatto 2019; Nadini et al. 2021; Wuepper and Patry 2017) mathematicians and neuroscientists have joined forces with blockchain technologists and computer scientists to employ novel techniques in order to expand what little knowledge currently exists on art, collectibles, games development, NFTs, and cryptocurrency (Zhang 2019). And general management journals now accept ACM scholarship as a legitimate field of study (Rodner et al. 2020).

Conclusions

A substantial body of ACM studies has developed, with its methods and methodologies evolving over the period of this selective review. ACM insights have not only developed the field but also influenced general business publications, enriching both. Working from legitimacy theory, we identified how early scholars employed realist, interpretivist, or positivist methods and methodologies (e.g., to explore the origins and consequences of class in exposure to the arts), as well as the emergence of studies with a social science focus when investigating the characteristics of arts managers (e.g., DiMaggio 1987; Rentschler 2001) with Bourdiesian theory (e.g., DiMaggio and Useem 1978). Later on, with the expansion of the ACM field into a multidisciplinary one with a variety of foci (O'Reilly 2011; Colbert and St-James 2014), with its own literature and emergent journals (Rentschler and Shilbury 2008), scholars sought more depth and richness from empirical studies on ACM, as well as a greater understanding of the methods and methodologies that may inhibit or enable ACM research. Such development overcame criticism of being myopic (e.g., Bennett 2004; Gray 2010) in its research approaches.

By examining methods and methodologies over fifty years, it is evident that there has been significant work in the field over time (Table 4.2). An analysis of the differences within and between disciplines, and of the co-evolutionary approach of those disciplines, uncovered important ontological and epistemological patterns in relation to what is studied, how it is studied, and why it is studied, as Table 4.2 illustrates. ACM has built upon related disciplines such as management, sociology, economics, and policy. Yet it has also developed its own significant fields of research, which have entered the general business field as well. Hence, the influence is not one-way.

Table 4.2. Characteristics of ACM Research Methods and Methodologies Over Time (1960–2022)

Gaining legitimacy (1960s–1980s)	Maintaining legitimacy (1980s–2000)	Sustaining legitimacy (2001–2022)
Identifying the field	Scoping the field	Developing the field
Narrative and realist	Narrative and empirical	Narrative, empirical (interpretive and positivist), digital
Sociological and economic studies	Social science studies	Interdisciplinary studies
Qualitative	Qualitative and quantitative	Big data, digital data embracing interdisciplinary insights
Separation from the object of study	Closeness to the object of study	Insider and outsider studies
Historical studies	Contemporary studies	Micro, meso, macro, and meta-studies

Future Research Directions

The opportunity for further theory-building remains open to scholars who can build on the work of earlier traditions, striving for new insights and perspectives that have so far remained problematic or elusive due to a broader focus. First, from a theoretical perspective, we recommend that future scholars review our typology in regard to debates in ACM. Specifically, there is a need for further studies on the legitimacy of the field. Insights may aid understanding of how, and why a field can gain, maintain, and sustain legitimacy. There is further theoretical integration of literature from management, sociology, economics, and policy, along with other fields.

Second, from a methodological perspective, there is a need for longitudinal studies, integrative perspectives, and meta-research. There are complementarities between approaches that remain little explored, so scholars working in teams across disciplines and across nations can combine their distinctive perspectives (e.g., King and Schramme 2019). More studies are utilizing complex interactions between different methods and methodologies, becoming more cross-disciplinary and providing richer and deeper insights and analysis. Furthermore, historical studies are becoming more sophisticated and examining longer time periods, giving insights into new domains that previously have been overlooked. These historical studies can be supported by increasingly rich data from literature and practice, as well as numerical and statistical data that have become newly accessible with the development of technology. For example, big-data studies (e.g., Nadini et al. 2021; Wuepper and Patry 2017), using novel techniques and cross-disciplinary teams of scholars, will expand what is known about the field and investigate such new topics as digital objects.

Third, from an empirical perspective, there is an opportunity to expand on systematic literature reviews, of which there are few in ACM and related domains such as the creative industries or cultural tourism (e.g., Khlystova, Kalyuzhnova, and Belitski 2022; O'Connor 2010). Systematic literature reviews are only now starting to appear (Dharmani et al. 2021), having been largely ignored in ACM research methods and methodologies to this point. This could take the field forward into new territory, with teams of scholars with complementary skill sets (e.g., internationalism, big data, mapping skills, virtual reality; see, for example, King and Schramme 2019), working together to provide rich insights into the field. What literature reviews do exist tend to be nascent, limited, and often focused on technical aspects (Nadini et al. 2021) rather than ACM.

Thus, much remains to be done. Pressing questions include: How and why have ACM research methods and methodologies changed? How is the field moving forward in times of disruptive change and global crisis in the creative industries? What are the prospects for synthesis between different methods and methodologies in an emerging field of endeavor, and how might they be taken forward? How do we reveal deeper and detailed contexts in ACM using online and meta-data? What are the transformations in arts organizations and the creative and cultural industries in the digital era (Floridi 2014)? While these are vast research areas, they have tended to be less examined in the

ACM field, although there are exceptions—investigations have been done regarding specific regions, such as Asia and the Pacific Rim (e.g., Caust 2015; Ren and Zhu 2017; Rentschler, Lee and Fillis 2021), pushing the debate to become more heterogeneous. However, there is much work to be done.

References

Abzug, Rikki, Paul DiMaggio, Bradford H. Gray, Michael Useem, and Chul Hee Kang. 1993. "Variations in Trusteeship: Cases from Boston and Cleveland, 1925–1985." *Voluntas* 4, no. 3: 271–300.

Adler, Nancy J. 2011. "Leading Beautifully: The Creative Economy and Beyond." *Journal of Management Inquiry* 20, no. 3: 208–221.

Adorno, Theodor W. 1991. *The Culture Industry: Selected Essays on Mass Culture*. London: Routledge.

Alexander, Victoria D. 2018. "Heteronomy in the Arts Field: State Funding and British Arts Organizations." *British Journal of Sociology* 69, no. 1: 23–43.

Almeida, Carla Cristina Rosa de, João Policarpo Rodrigues Lima, and Maria Fernanda Freire Gatto. 2019. "Expenditure on Cultural Events: Preferences or Opportunities? An Analysis of Brazilian Consumer Data." *Journal of Cultural Economics* 44, no. 3: 451–480.

Araújo, Bianca, Eduardo Davel, and Ruth Rentschler. 2020. "Aesthetic Consumption in Managing Art-Driven Organizations: An Autoethnographic Inquiry." *Organizational Aesthetics* 9, no. 3: 63–84.

Aróstegui, Rubio, Juan Arturo, and Joaquim Rius-Ulldemolins. 2022. "Opera Houses: From Democratization to Plutocratic Control? Lyric Production, Economic Management, and Elite Control in the Main Spanish Opera Houses during the Period of Austerity (2009–2018)." *International Journal of Cultural Policy* 28, no. 3: 359–378.

Au, Wing Tung, Zhumeng Zuo, and Paton Pak Chun Yam. 2022. "Quantitative Measure of Audience Experience." In *Routledge Companion to Audiences in the Performing Arts*, edited by Matthew Reason, Lynne Conner, Katya Johanson, and Ben Walmsley, 326–342. London: Routledge.

Barnett, Tertia, and Margarita Díaz-Andreu. 2005. "Knowledge Capture and Transfer in Rock Art Studies: Results of a Questionnaire on Rock Art Decay in Britain." *Conservation and Management of Archaeological Sites* 7, no. 1: 35–48.

Becker, Howard S. 1976. "Art Worlds and Social Types." *American Behavioral Scientist* 19, no. 6: 703–718.

Behrens, Ronny, Natasha Zhang Foutz, Michael Franklin, Jannis Funk, Fernanda Gutierrez-Navratil, Julian Hofmann, and Ulrike Leibfried. 2020. "Leveraging Analytics to Produce Compelling and Profitable Film Content." *Journal of Cultural Economics* 45, no. 2: 171–211.

Bell, David. 2015. *Cultural Policy: Key Ideas in Media and Cultural Studies*. London: Routledge.

Bell, Emma, and Sheena J. Vachhani. 2020. "Relational Encounters and Vital Materiality in the Practice of Craft Work." *Organization Studies* 41, no. 5: 681–701.

Belk, Russell W., and Alan Andreasen. 1982. "The Effects of Family Life Cycle on Arts Patronage." *International Journal of Cultural Policy* 6 (December): 25–35.

Bennett, Oliver. 2004. "Review Essay: The Torn Halves of Cultural Policy Research." *International Journal of Cultural Policy* 10, no. 2: 237–248.

Bourdieu, Pierre. 1984. *Distinction: A Social Critique of the Judgement of Taste.* Cambridge, MA: Harvard University Press.

Buffkins, Archie. 1981. Memo to Dr. Martha A. Turnage. John F. Kennedy Center for the Performing Arts, Washington, DC, May 4, 1981.

Cattaneo, Nicolette, and Jen Snowball. 2019. "South Africa's Trade in Cultural Goods and Service with a Focus on Cultural Trade with BRICS Partners." *International Journal of Cultural Policy* 25, no. 5: 582–601.

Caust, Josephine. 2015. *Arts and Cultural Leadership in Asia.* Routledge Advances in Asia-Pacific Studies. London: Taylor and Francis.

Chong, Derrick. 2010. *Arts Management.* 2nd ed. London: Routledge.

Cleland, Jamie, Daryl Adair, and Keith Parry. 2022. "Fair Go? Indigenous Rugby League Players and the Racial Exclusion of the Australian National Anthem." *Communication and Sport* 10, no. 1: 74–96.

Close, Helen. 1998. *Who's My Market? A Guide to Researching Audiences and Visitors in the Arts.* Sydney: Australia Council for the Arts.

Cloutier, Charlotte, and Ann Langley. 2020. "What Makes a Process Theoretical Contribution?" *Organization Theory* (online). https://doi.org/10.1177/2631787720902473.

Colbert, François, and Yannik St-James. 2014. "Research in Arts Marketing: Evolution and Future Directions." *Psychology and Marketing* 31, no. 8: 566–575.

Creswell, John W., and J. David Creswell. 2018. *Research Design: Qualitative, Quantitative, and Mixed Methods Approaches.* 5th ed. Thousand Oaks, CA: SAGE.

Curry, David J. 1982. "Marketing Research and Management Decisions." *Journal of Arts Management and Law* 12, no. 1: 42–58.

Davis, Clive J. 1969. "They're Not All 'My Fair Lady.'" *Performing Arts Review* 1, no. 1: 11–17.

De la Vega, Pablo, Sara Suarez-Fernández, David Boto-García, and Juan Prieto-Rodríguez. 2019. "Playing a Play: Online and Live Performing Arts Consumers Profiles and the Role of Supply Constraints." *Journal of Cultural Economics* 44, no. 3: 425–450.

DeVereaux, Constance. 2019. *Arts and Cultural Management: Sense and Sensibilities in the State of the Field.* Milton, UK: Routledge.

Dharmani, Pranav, Satyasiba Das, and Sanjeev Prashar. 2021. "A Bibliometric Analysis of Creative Industries: Current Trends and Future Directions." *Journal of Business Research* 135: 252–267.

DiMaggio, Paul. 1987. "Managers of the Arts: Careers and Opinions of Senior Administrators of US Art Museums, Symphony Orchestras, Resident Theaters, and Local Arts Agencies." Research Division report #20. National Endowment for the Arts, Washington DC.

DiMaggio, Paul. 1997. "Culture and Cognition." *Annual Review of Sociology* 23, no. 1: 263–287.

DiMaggio, Paul, and Michael Useem. 1978. "Social Class and Arts Consumption: The Origins and Consequences of Class Differences in Exposure to the Arts in America." *Theory and Society* 5, no. 2: 141–161.

Dorn, Charles M. 1992. "Arts Administration: A Field of Dreams?" *Journal of Arts Management, Law, and Society* 22, no. 3: 241–251.

Durham, Floyd. 1977. "An Exploration of Some of the Causes of a Developing Painter's Colony in Fort Worth, Texas." *Journal of Cultural Economics* 1, no. 1: 25–34.

Edelstein, Leonard. 1970. "Regional Theater Board of Directors." *Performing Arts Review* 1, no. 3: 437–444.

Ettinger, Linda F., and James Hutchens. 1989. "Preparing Arts Administrators of the Future: The Need for Interprofessional Education." *Arts Education Policy Review* 90, no. 4: 32–36.

Evard, Yves, and François Colbert. 2000. "Arts Management: A New Discipline Entering the Millennium?" *International Journal of Arts Management* 2, no. 2: 4–13.

Fillis, Ian. 2011. "The Evolution and Development of Arts Marketing Research." *Arts Marketing: An International Journal* 1, no. 1: 11–25.

Fillis, Ian. 2015. "Biographical Research as a Methodology for Understanding Entrepreneurial Marketing." *International Journal of Entrepreneurial Behaviour and Research* 21, no. 3: 429–447.

Floridi, Luciano. 2014. *The Fourth Revolution: How the Infosphere Is Reshaping Human Reality*. Oxford: Oxford University Press.

Franklin, Adrian, Boram Lee, and Ruth Rentschler. 2021. "The Adelaide Festival and the Development of Arts in Adelaide." *Journal of Urban Affairs* 44, nos. 4–5: 588–613.

Frey, Bruno. 1998. "Superstar Museums: An Economic Analysis." *Journal of Cultural Economics* 22: 113–125.

Gray, Clive. 2010. "Analysing Cultural Policy: Incorrigibly Plural or Ontologically Incompatible?" *International Journal of Cultural Policy* 16, no. 2: 215–230.

Griffin, Des. 2008. "Advancing Museums." *Museum Management and Curatorship* 23, no. 1: 43–61.

Hafner, Theodore. 1980. "A Theory of International Communications—From Helsinki to Camp David to SALT II." *Performing Arts Review* 10, no. 2: 136–148.

Hall, Grant, Raman Voranau, and Ruth Rentschler. 2020. "Digital Workers, Well-being and Networking: The Case of Transformational Festivals and the Importance of Co-creation." In *Digitalization in the Cultural and Creative Sectors: Production, Consumption and Entrepreneurship in the Digital and Sharing Economy*, edited by Massi, Marta, Marilena Vecco, and Yi Lin, 224–244. Routledge.

Höllen, Max, Christian Lengfeld, and Elmar D. Konrad. 2020. "Business Success for Creative and Cultural Entrepreneurs: Influences of Individual- and Firm-Related Factors on Revenue and Satisfaction." *International Journal of Arts Management* 22, no. 2: 52–65.

Holstein, James A., and Jaber F. Gubrium. 2011. "The Constructionist Analytics of Interpretive Practice." In *The SAGE Handbook of Qualitative Research*, edited by Norman K. Denzin and Yvonna S. Lincoln, 341–358. Thousand Oaks, CA: SAGE Publications.

Huo, Zhengxin. 2016. "Legal Protection of Cultural Heritage in China: A Challenge to Keep History Alive." *International Journal of Cultural Policy* 22, no. 4: 497–515.

Jeffri, Joan. 1988. "Notes from the Artplex: Research Issues in Arts Administration." *Journal of Arts Management and Law* 18, no. 1: 5–12.

Jones, Candace, Silviya Svejenova, Jesper Strandgaard Pedersen, and Barbara Townley. 2016. "Misfits, Mavericks and Mainstreams: Drivers of Innovation in the Creative Industries." *Organization Studies* 37, no. 6: 751–768.

Kawashima, Nobuko. 1997. "Theorising Decentralisation in Cultural Policy: Concepts, Values, and Strategies." *European Journal of Cultural Policy* 3, no. 2: 341–359.

Khlystova, Olena, Yelena Kalyuzhnova, and Maksim Belitski. 2022. "The Impact of the COVID-19 Pandemic on the Creative Industries: A Literature Review and Future Research Agenda." *Journal of Business Research* 139: 1192–1210.

King, Ian W., and Annick Schramme. 2019. *Cultural Governance in a Global Context: An International Perspective on Art Organizations*. Palgrave Studies in Business, Arts and Humanities. Cham, Switzerland: Springer International Publishing.

Kirchberg, Volker, and Tasos Zembylas. 2010. "Arts Management: A Sociological Inquiry." *Journal of Arts Management, Law, and Society* 40, no. 1: 1–5.

Kirchner, Theresa A., and Ruth Rentschler. 2015. "External Impact of Arts Management Research: An Extended Analysis." *International Journal of Arts Management* 17, no. 3: 46–67.

Kraus, M. Williams. 1985. "The Untrained Audience for the Performing Arts." *Performing Arts Review* 19, no.1: 102–107.

Lee, Boram, Ian Fillis, and Ian Fraser. 2022. "To Sell or Not to Sell? Pricing Strategies of Newly-Graduated Artists." *Journal of Business Research* 145: 595–604.

Legoux, Renaud, François Carrillat, Benjamin Boeuf, and Jessica Darveau. 2014. "A Meta-Analysis of Demand and Income Elasticity in the Performing Arts." Paper presented at the 2014 ACEI Conference, Montreal.

March, James G. 2013. *Handbook of Organizations*. Routledge Library Editions. London: Taylor and Francis.

McGuigan, Jim. 2005. "Neo-Liberalism, Culture, and Policy." *International Journal of Cultural Policy* 11, no. 3: 229–241.

Miller, Toby. 2001. "What It Is and What It Isn't: Cultural Studies Meets Graduate-Student Labor." *Yale Journal of Law and the Humanities* 13, no. 1: 69–94.

Mintzberg, Henry. 1987. "Crafting Strategy." *Harvard Business Review* 65, no. 4: 66–77.

Mei, Jianping, and Michael Moses. 2005. "Vested Interest and Biased Price Estimates: Evidence from an Auction Market." *Journal of Finance* 60, no. 5: 2409–2435.

Moody, Walter D. 1913. "'The Chicago Plan': To Make Chicago Beautiful, Healthful and Convenient." *Fine Arts Journal* 29, no. 3: 560–574.

Nadini, Matthieu, Laura Alessandretti, Flavio Di Giacinto, Mauro Martino, Luca Maria Aiello, and Andrea Baronchelli. 2021. "Mapping the NFT Revolution: Market Trends, Trade Networks, and Visual Features." *Scientific Reports* 11, no. 1: 20902–20913.

Nielsen, Richard P., Angela B. Nielsen, and Charles McQueen. 1975. "Attendance Types of Performing Arts Events and Explanations for Attendance and Non-Attendance." *Performing Arts Review* 6, no. 1: 43–69.

Noonan, Douglas S. 2003. "Contingent Valuation and Cultural Resources: A Meta-Analytic Review of the Literature." *Journal of Cultural Economics* 27, no. 3/4: 159–176.

Oakley, Ann. 2010. "The Social Science of Biographical Life-Writing: Some Methodological and Ethical Issues." *International Journal of Social Research Methodology* 13, no. 5: 425–439.

O'Connor, Justin. 2010. *The Cultural and Creative Industries: A Literature Review*. 2nd ed. Newcastle upon Tyne, UK: Creativity, Culture and Education.

O'Reilly, Daragh. 2011. "Mapping the Arts Marketing Literature." *Arts Marketing: An International Journal* 1, no. 1: 26–38.

Paquette, Jonathan, and Eleonora Redaelli. 2015. *Arts Management and Cultural Policy Research*. London: Palgrave Macmillan.

Park, Yoon Soon, Lars Konge, and Anthony R. Artino. 2020. "The Positivism Paradigm of Research." *Academic Medicine* 95, no. 5: 690–694.

Patrickson, Bronwin. 2021. "What Do Blockchain Technologies Imply for Digital Creative Industries?" *Creativity and Innovation Management* 30, no. 3: 585–595.

Peterson, Richard A. 1997. "Creating Country Music: Fabricating Authenticity." *Annual Review of Sociology* 30: 311–334.

Pitts, Stephanie E., and Sarah M. Price. 2022. "The Benefits and Challenges of Large-Scale Qualitative Research." In *Routledge Companion to Audiences in the Performing Arts*, edited by Matthew Reason, Lynne Connor, Katya Johanson, and Ben Walmsley, 343–354. London: Routledge.

Reason, Matthew. 2022. "Creative Methods and Audience Research: Affordances and Racial Potential." In *Companion to Audiences in the Performing Arts*, edited by Matthew Reason, Lynne Conner, Katya Johanson, and Ben Walmsly, 355–373. London: Routledge.

Ren, Shuang, and Ying Zhu. 2017. "Candle in the Wind: Arts and Cultural Leadership Within the Process of Market-Oriented Economic Reform in China." *Journal of General Management* 42, no. 4: 80–89.

Rentschler, Ruth. 2001. "Is Creativity a Matter for Cultural Leaders?" *International Journal of Arts Management* 3, no. 3: 13–24.

Rentschler, Ruth. 2006. "Women's Art as Indicator of Social Change." *Australian Cultural History* 24: 115–134.

Rentschler, Ruth, Ian Fillis, and Boram Lee. 2022. "Artists Versus Arts Council: A Longitudinal Analysis of Brand Legitimacy." *Poetics* 92, part A: art. 101623.

Rentschler, Ruth, and Gus Geursen. 2004. "Entrepreneurship, Marketing and Leadership in Non-Profit Performing Arts Organisations." *Journal of Research in Marketing and Entrepreneurship* 6, no. 1: 44–51.

Rentschler, Ruth, Boram Lee, and Ian Fillis. 2021. "Towards an Integrative Framework for Arts Governance." *International Journal of Arts Management* 24, no. 1: 17–31.

Rentschler, Ruth, Boram Lee, and Nava Subramaniam. 2021. "Calculative Practices and Socio-political Tensions: A Historical Analysis of Entertainment, Arts and Accounting in a Government Agency." *Accounting History* 26, no. 1: 80–101.

Rentschler, Ruth, and David Shilbury. 2008. "Academic Assessment of Arts Management Journals: A Multidimensional Rating Survey." *International Journal of Arts Management* 10, no. 3: 60–71.

Rentschler, Ruth, Nava Subramaniam, and Brian Martin. 2019. "A Longitudinal Study of Aboriginal Images in Annual Reports: Evidence from an Arts Council." *Accounting and Finance* 59, no. 3: 1591–1620.

Reynolds, Sarah, Ann Tonks, and Kate MacNeill. 2017. "Collaborate Leadership in the Arts as a Unique Form of Dual Leadership." *Journal of Arts Management, Law, and Society* 47, no. 2: 89–104.

Robertson, Lionel. 1918. "Venice and the United Stated in Business and in Art." *Fine Arts Journal* 36, no. 10: 18–23.

Rodner, Victoria, Thomas J. Roulet, Finola Kerrigan, and Dirk vom Lehn. 2020. "Making Space for Art: A Spatial Perspective of Disruptive and Defensive Institutional Work in Venezuela's Art World." *Academy of Management Journal* 63, no. 4: 1054–1081.

Seok, Hwayoon, Yeajin Joo, and Yoonjae Nam. 2020. "An Analysis of the Sustainable Tourism Value of Graffiti Tours Through Social Media: Focusing on TripAdvisor Reviews of Graffiti Tours in Bogota, Colombia." *Sustainability* 12, no. 11: 4426–4445.

Shilbury, David, Lesley Ferkins, and Liz Smythe. 2013. "Sport Governance Encounters: Insights from Lived Experiences." *Sport Management Review* 16, no. 3: 349–363.

Singh, Jitendra V., David J. Tucker, and Robert J. House. 1986. "Organizational Legitimacy and the Liability of Newness." *Administrative Science Quarterly* 31, no. 2: 171–193.

Smith, George Alan. 1969. "Arts Administrators Need and Potential in New York State: A Study for the New York State Council on the Arts." *Performing Arts Review* 1, no. 1: 127–190.

Srakar, Andrej, and Marilena Vecco. 2021. "Assessing the Validity of Cultural Policy Typologies for Central-Eastern European Countries." *International Journal of Cultural Policy* 27, no. 2: 218–232.

Stuart, Evelyn. 1917. "Contemporary American Art as an Investment." *Fine Arts Journal* 35, no. 4: 243–257.

Suchman, Mark C. 1995. "Managing Legitimacy: Strategic and Institutional Approaches." *Academy of Management Review* 20, no. 3: 571–610.

Taubman, Joseph. 1969. "Performing Arts Management and Administration." *Performing Arts Review* 1, no. 1: 31–50.

Throsby, C. David. 2010. *The Economics of Cultural Policy*. Cambridge: Cambridge University Press.

Throsby, C. David, and Beverley J. Thompson. 1994. *But What Do You Do for a Living? A New Economic Study of Australian Artists*. Strawberry Hills, NSW: Australia Council.
Timothea. 1901. "In Chicago Art Galleries." *Fine Arts Journal* 12, no. 1: 22–23.
Towse, Ruth. 2010. *A Textbook of Cultural Economics*. Cambridge: Cambridge University Press.
Towse, Ruth, and Trilce Navarrete Hernández. 2020. *Handbook of Cultural Economics*. 3rd ed. Cheltenham, UK: Edward Elgar.
Tyler, Tom R. 2006. "Psychological Perspectives on Legitimacy and Legitimation." *Annual Review of Psychology* 57, no. 1: 375–400.
Tyrowicz, Joanna, Michal Krawczyk, and Wojciech Hardy. 2020. "Friends or Foes? A Meta-analysis of the Relationship Between 'Online Piracy' and the Sales of Cultural Goods." *Information Economics and Policy* 53: 100879–100896.
Veal, Anthony James, and Christine Burton. 2014. *Research Methods for Arts and Event Management*. Harlow, UK: Pearson Education.
Vecco, Marilena, and Andrej Srakar. 2020. "Direct, Indirect and Cross-Lagged: The Effects of Cultural Policy on Nascent Cultural Entrepreneurship." *International Journal of Arts Management* 22, no. 2: 66–82.
Verdaasdonk, Dorothee. 2005. "Moviegoing Frequency Among Dutch Consumers: Interaction Between Audiences and Market Factors." *International Journal of Arts Management* 7, no. 2: 55–65.
Volkerling, Micheal. 2000. "The Necessity of Utopia: Lessons from the Culture of Economics." *International Journal of Cultural Policy* 2000, no. 1: 29–47.
vom Lehn, Dirk. 2006. "Embodying Experience: A Video-Based Examination of Visitors' Conduct and Interaction in Museums." *European Journal of Marketing* 40, nos. 11–12: 1340–1359.
Walker, Henry A., George M. Thomas, and Morris Zelditch Jr. 1986. "Legitimation, Endorsement, and Stability." *Social Forces* 64, no. 3: 620–643.
Walmsley, Ben. 2018. "Deep Hanging Out in the Arts: An Anthropological Approach to Capturing Cultural Value." *International Journal of Cultural Policy* 24, no. 2: 272–291.
Wei, Tan. 2011. "About Discipline Attributes of Arts Management and Related Issues." *Art and Design* 2: 193–194.
Wuepper, Dabid, and Marc Patry. 2017. "The World Heritage List: Which Sites Promote the Brand? A Big Data Spatial Econometrics Approach." *International Journal of Cultural Economics* 41: 1–21.
Zelditch, Morris. 2001. "Processes of Legitimation: Recent Developments and New Directions." *Social Psychology Quarterly* 64, no. 1: 4–17.
Zhang, Fenghua, and Pascal Courty. 2021. "The China Museum Visit Boom: Government or Demand Driven?" *Journal of Cultural Economics* 46, no. 1: 135–163.
Zhang, Jian. 2019. "Artwork Securitization: A Chinese Style of Artwork Investment." *International Journal of Cultural Policy* 25, no. 2: 171–187.
Zimmerman, Monica A., and Gerald J. Zeitz. 2002. "Beyond Survival: Achieving New Venture Growth by Building Legitimacy." *Academy of Management Review* 27, no. 3: 414–431.
Zolberg, Vera L. 1981. "Conflicting Visions in American Art Museums." *Theory and Society* 10, no. 1: 103–125.

PART II
THEORIES IN ARTS AND CULTURAL MANAGEMENT RESEARCH

CHAPTER 5

A SOCIAL VALUE JUDGMENT MODEL OF CORPORATE GOVERNANCE IN PERFORMING ARTS ORGANIZATIONS

ROY SUDDABY, PETER SHERER, DIEGO CORAIOLA, AND KARL SCHWONIK

THERE are unique challenges in creating effective governance structures for performing arts organizations. Most of these challenges derive from the inherent hybridity of arts organizations, which typically pursue two missions that often conflict: artistic excellence and economic accountability. The conflict is often reflected in microcosm by two roles found in performing arts organizations, roles that also often conflict: the artistic director and the executive director. The artistic director is tasked with the creation and execution of the aesthetic mandate of the organization. The executive director, similar to a corporate CEO, manages the day-to-day business operations of the organization. When the individuals who fill this role work well together, the organization succeeds. However, when they do not work well together, the organization suffers.

The tricky task of balancing these roles typically falls to the board of directors, the main oversight body of most performing arts organizations in the United States and Canada. Board members in performing arts organizations serve many functions. They may be recruited to the board because of their technical expertise—for example, accountants, lawyers, and marketers. Alternatively, board members may be recruited because of their connections with important external stakeholders—for example, politicians, corporate executives, philanthropists, and celebrity performers.

As a result, boards of performing arts organizations are very different from both corporate boards and the boards of other nonprofits, tending to be larger, more diverse, and often more conflicted. Conflicts arise because, despite best efforts to achieve balance in the competing missions of an arts organization, the balance is often tilted in favor of the business mission of the organization. The executive director often has more of a direct reporting line to the board, and performance indicators tend to privilege business functions because it is often easier to measure attendance than aesthetic quality or public enrichment (Reid and Karambayya 2009; Voogt 2006).

Critics of the corporate governance practices of performing arts organizations argue that the conflict between the artistic and economic missions of performing arts organizations is incommensurable and typically favors the business mission of the organization, even when the relationship between the artistic director and the executive director is positive (Peterson 1986; Galli 2011). As Yvette Nolan, a playwright, director, and prominent board member of provincial and national arts organizations in Canada, observes, because the model of corporate governance by boards was borrowed from the corporation in order to appease regulators, donors, and taxpayers who increasingly demand more accountability from public sector and nonprofit entities, the model will always privilege business over artistic interests:

> I have been the artistic director of a theatre company and worked closely with my chair to make our theatre better, stronger, and more functional. But still I do not believe in the structure. In fact, twenty-five years of working in theatre has served to convince me that the board of directors is actually a fiction. There is no there there.
>
> (Nolan 2020, 1)

Nolan's quote captures the essential tension that differentiates performing arts organizations from both corporations and other nonprofits. They must balance the inherently conflicting demands for artistic and aesthetic excellence that are unique to performing arts with competing demands to conform to the structure, economic accountability, and governance practices of businesses.

How do performing arts organizations achieve balance between artistic and business interests in their governance structure? More critically, what should the decision criteria be when economic and aesthetic tensions conflict? The answers to these questions rest in understanding that the purpose of the board of directors in a performing arts organization is not the same as in corporations or other nonprofits. In those organizations the board serves to ensure that managers do not act in self-interest. In performing arts organizations, as we demonstrate below, the board serves to balance the competing tensions to be legitimate (to appear to be economically responsible) and to be authentic (to be aesthetically creative).

In order to do so, however, we must gain some theoretical perspective on how and why corporate models of governance evolved this way in performing arts organizations. We address the first question by drawing from neo-institutional theory, a theory of organizations based on the premise that many of the practices adopted by organizations under the guise of rationality and efficiency are predicated instead on culturally derived assumptions of what efficiency *should* be. We address the second question by applying concepts of *social value judgment theory*, an extension of institutional theory, to common corporate governance decisions. As we demonstrate, decisions about corporate governance are determined largely by claims of *legitimacy* or *authenticity* made to distinctly different audiences with distinct assumptions of worth. The priority given to each is determined by contextual conditions that give greater salience to different audiences.

Social Value Judgments

The adoption of models of governance from other categories of organizations is a form of institutional isomorphism, a concept derived from institutional theory that suggests that organizations often adopt structures, processes, and practices not because they actually improve the performance of an organization but rather because they make the organization appear similar to other, more legitimate forms of organization (Meyer and Rowan 1977; DiMaggio and Powell 1983). Standards of legitimacy come from different sources. Governments may impose rules for arts organizations that must be complied with in order to be eligible for funding. Professional advisors, business consultants, or large institutional actors such as the National Endowment for the Arts often articulate "best practices" of governance for arts organizations that are not coercive but are influential because they establish standards or norms of governance used by high-status arts organizations. Alternatively, arts organizations simply copy characteristics of other arts organizations that they perceive to have an outstanding reputation or that are considered high-status exemplars.

Why do arts organizations copy practices from non-arts organizations? The answer lies in an emerging theory of organizational behavior termed social value judgments (Parsons 1960; Rindova, Pollock, and Hayward 2006; Bitektine 2011). The theory argues that organizations are subject to an array of different forms of social evaluation by different audiences. As a result, they must interpret and evaluate a complex array of social pressures from these audiences and allocate a degree of salience to each audience in order to make sense of the often-conflicting signals of appropriate or inappropriate behavior. The pressures conflict because different audiences have different value systems (Coleman 1990), institutional logics (Thornton and Ocasio 2008), and orders of worth (Boltanski and Thévenot 2006). Social evaluations are processes of judgment that determine the willingness of different audiences to engage in the exchange of resources with a firm (Pollock et al. 2019).

Different audiences—regulators, corporate donors, private philanthropists, critics, and consumers of the arts—each attach a different degree of value to the various practices of performing arts organizations. Regulators, for example, value compliance with legal expectations more than artistic creativity. Critics and elite audiences, by contrast, may value compliance with the artistic canon more than the general populace (DiMaggio and Useem 1983). Corporate donors may value the number of consumers of an arts organization more than do private philanthropists, who in turn may accord greater value to the social status of those consumers. Performing arts organizations must assess the salience of each social signal sent by these various audiences. Critically, the constitution of the board of directors and their mandate must be adjusted to reflect the various social signals sent by these different audiences.

Researchers have identified a broad range of social value judgments. Some of these—status (Washington and Zajac 2005; Podolny 2010), reputation (Bitektine 2011; Kilduff and Krackhardt 1994), identity (Brickson 2005; Ashforth, Rogers, and Corley 2011), and legitimacy (Suddaby, Bitektine, and Haack 2017; Suchman 1995)—have been the focus of decades of empirical research. Others—authenticity (Carroll and Wheaton 2009) and celebrity (Zavyalova, Pfarrer, and Reger 2017)—are emergent areas of increased empirical attention. While each of these categories of social value judgment plays an important role in the constitution and perceived effectiveness of performing arts boards, we focus attention on the two types of value judgments that most directly capture the core competing tensions of performing arts organizations: legitimacy and authenticity. These two constructs were chosen because they best capture the inherent tension between artistic excellence and economic stability that characterizes most performing arts organizations. As we elaborate below, while the constructs focus attention on different categories of stakeholders, when the legitimacy and authenticity needs of the organization are addressed in board composition, they have a generative effect on both the artistic and economic performance of the organization.

Legitimacy

Legitimacy is a category of social judgment that confers a perception of appropriateness and acceptability of an entity or a practice by a particular audience based on a shared system of values, norms, and beliefs (Suchman 1995; Suddaby, Bitektine, and Haack 2017). The concept has deep historical roots in the social sciences, where scholars sought to explain how institutional actors (sovereigns, governments, and other rulers) gained authority and submission from the populations they ruled. German sociologist Max Weber observed that submission to an order was not exclusively the result of coercion but instead was determined by the willingness of the population "to submit to an order," which "always in some sense implies a belief in the legitimate authority of the source imposing it" (Weber 1964, 132). A critical element of this definition of legitimacy is that it is a form of power granted to an entity by an audience, rather than forcibly wrested from it. That is, legitimacy is a form of social judgment conferred exogenously rather than cultivated endogenously.

Organizational theories of legitimacy accept this assumption but have focused considerable attention on the institutional and strategic practices by which perceptions of legitimacy can be managed (Suchman 1995; Oliver 1991). Legitimacy is understood to be a resource that can be cultivated by (1) strategies in the material world, by altering the types and degree of dependence on its constituens (Pfeffer and Salancik 1978); (2) strategies in the symbolic world, by appearing to conform to prevailing norms of constituents by sending the right signals (Ashforth and Gibbs 1990); and (3) taking efforts to change prevailing norms (Hirsch and Andrews 1983. The capacity to manage legitimacy is enhanced when entities reject the assumption that they are subject to universal norms and replace it with the observation that they are subject to the social value judgments of multiple audiences (Suddaby, Bitektine, and Haack 2017). When the norms of diverse audiences are not universal, the ability of an entity to manage perceptions of legitimacy is enhanced, despite the endogenous nature of legitimacy as a power that is exogenously conferred.

AUTHENTICITY

Authenticity is a category of social judgment in which an entity or product is deemed to be "real," "genuine," or "true." Authenticity is a polysemous construct whose meaning is often dependent upon the context in which it is used. Two distinct and somewhat contradictory definitions of authenticity appear in the literature. In sociology and management research, authenticity is viewed as a social construction that is "not a 'real' thing or something that can be objectively determined but rather [is] a socially constructed phenomenon [by which] certain specific aspects of a product, performance, place or producer somehow get deified and treated as authentic by audiences in a particular social context" (Carroll and Wheaton 2009, 256). In this view, authenticity is, somewhat ironically, a claim to reality that is not itself real.

In philosophy and art theory, however, authenticity is an objective claim to reality that may take one of two forms. The first, *nominal authenticity*, is based in history and is a claim of provenance—in other words, that a work of art is not a forgery or a piece of music or literature is not plagiarized (Dutton 2004). The second, *expressive authenticity*, is derived from existential philosophy and refers to the act of being true to one's own personal creative muse—"faithfulness to the performer's own self, original, not derivative" (Kivy 1995, 7)—while contributing to the living critical tradition of a corpus of literature or music or a genre of art (Dutton 2004).

In contrast to legitimacy, nominal and expressive authenticity is largely endogenously determined. While outsiders—audiences and critics—are important to determining what is or is not authentic, they are not determinative of authenticity in and of themselves but rather serve as custodians or monitors whose discretion is limited to ensuring that the artists' creativity contributes to but does not violate the historically determined tradition of the art form. Existentialism and art theory hold that artistic authenticity is "achieved only when an artwork expresses the authentic values of its maker, especially when those values are shared by the artist's immediate community" (Dutton 2004, 271).

Authenticity and Legitimacy in Corporate Governance of Performing Arts Organizations

The distinctions between legitimacy and authenticity form the foundation of the inherent conflict between economy and artistry that fuels the governance challenges in performing arts organizations. Executive directors are largely concerned with managing the external legitimacy of the performing arts organizations, while artistic directors are almost exclusively focused on maintaining its internal authenticity. Important issues and conflict arise from these differences. The primary audience for achieving authenticity, for example, is relatively small, cohesive, and elite, composed almost exclusively of professional critics, academics, elite consumers, and other (peer) artists. The primary audience for legitimacy, by contrast, is very heterogeneous and consists of regulators, mass-market consumers, and community constituents, or corporate and private donors.

As we elaborate in the balance of this section, however, the distinctions between legitimacy and authenticity provide clues that help address the inherent conflict between economy and artistry in governing performing arts organizations. In our discussion we focus on three critical questions that are central to good governance in the performing arts: What social evaluation factors guide board composition? What priority is given to economy or artistry in decision-making? How do social value judgments determine which resources will be acquired and deployed by the organization?

Board Composition

The relationship between board composition and organizational performance has received substantial theoretical (Hillman and Dalziel 2003; Lynall, Golden, and Hillman 2003) and empirical (Hillman, Canella, and Paetzold 2000) attention, particularly in the for-profit sector. Considerably less attention has been paid to this relationship in the nonprofit sector, and even less research has examined the relationship between board composition and performance in the arts sector (however, see Cornforth 2001; Dalziel, Gentry, and Bowerman 2011; Dubini and Monti 2018 as important exceptions). Despite the extensive empirical attention given to understanding this relationship, the results are mixed and often contradictory. One clear conclusion has emerged from this research: effective boards should be diverse in their demographic characteristics and in their expertise and disciplinary backgrounds (Carter, Simkins, and Simpson 2003).

While this empirical insight is consistent in both the for-profit and nonprofit sectors, researchers struggle to find a consistent theory that explains the precise way in which diversity influences effective governance or, indeed, what precisely diversity means.

Instead, a variety of theoretical explanations are used to explain the need for heterogeneity in board member characteristics. Four main theories are typically used: agency theory, resource dependence theory, institutional theory, and social network theory (Lynall, Golden, and Hillman 2003). The heterogeneity of theories is needed to account for the varied functions that most boards actually perform. Agency theory explains how boards manage internal relationships, particularly how they conduct oversight of managers (Fama and Jensen 1983). Resource dependency theory—and its extension to stakeholder theory (Sherer and Leblebici 2015)—explains how boards manage external relationships with key stakeholders, through which the firm accesses material resources (Pfeffer and Salancik 1978). Institutional theory explains how firms manage the legitimacy demands of their external environments (Suchman 1995; Zajac and Westphal 1996). Social network theory describes how firms manage their external sources of information (Gulati and Gargiulo 1999). Apart from the suggestion that these different theories gain greater salience at different stages of an organization's life cycle (Lynall, Golden, and Hillman 2003), there is no coherent theoretical explanation that accounts for the variety of functions that an effective board must play.

The lack of clarity arises, in part, because the bulk of this research has occurred in for-profit organizations, where the role of material resources and economic competition dominates. Some clarity arises when we view the various roles on boards of performing arts organizations, where the demands from the economic and social symbolic environments are somewhat more balanced. In their analysis of the relationship between board composition and organizational performance in Italian opera houses, Dubini and Monti (2018) organize board diversity into four main roles: controllers, other specialists, influential people, and cultural managers.

Controllers manage compliance with the expectations of outside sources of revenue and normative expectations of how to manage that revenue (finance experts, auditors, and management consultants), consistent with the assumptions of agency theory. *Other specialists* are disciplinary experts in areas adjacent to the core financial function of the organization (such as lawyers and marketing experts), consistent with the predictions of agency theory. *Influential people* are board members who maintain information flows from even more peripheral stakeholders of the firm and help manage the status and reputation of the organization, consistent with social network theory. *Cultural managers* are experts in the specific arts sector and manage the creativity of the organization's performances and the relationship between the organization and cultural elites.

Viewed through the theoretical lens of social judgment theory, Dubini and Monti's (2018) typology describes a mix of competencies at the board level that reflects the hybrid demands placed on performing arts organizations by the material/economic environment and the social/symbolic environment. Given this, the typology can be condensed into two types, each of which is devoted to managing two competing social value judgments—legitimacy and authenticity. Controllers and other specialists focus largely on those stakeholders that provide material/economic resources for the firm: financial capital, material resources, and so on. Influential people and cultural managers focus largely on those stakeholders that provide social/symbolic resources for the firm:

status, reputation, and so on. That is, controllers and other specialists address the firm's need for legitimacy, while influential people and cultural managers address the firm's need for authenticity.

The foregoing theory, therefore, suggests that, all things being equal, a well-functioning performing arts organization will structure its board with a view to balancing the competing objectives of gaining both corporate legitimacy and performative authenticity. This is our first proposition:

> **Proposition 1a:** A well-functioning performing arts organization will have an equal number of board members who occupy the roles of controllers or other specialists, whose primary mandate is to ensure legitimacy, and board members who occupy the roles of influential people or cultural managers, whose primary mandate is to ensure authenticity.

A critical question, however, is under what conditions should the proportions of board members be different from an equal split between those who reflect the organization's need for legitimacy and those reflecting its need for authenticity? For example, in their formative years many performing arts organizations seek to establish a reputation as an elite or avant-garde producer of art. As a result, the organization will value creativity and authenticity in its core products as opposed to faithful reproduction of performances required to achieve mass-market legitimacy. In such cases, critics are more salient stakeholders than, for example, mass-market consumers. We would expect, in such cases, the board structure to reflect this strategic objective.

> **Proposition 1b:** Where performing arts organizations are interested in establishing their reputation for artistic excellence, the organization will have a disproportionate number of board members who occupy the role of influential people or cultural managers whose primary mandate is to ensure authenticity.

The reverse would be true for arts organizations that seek economic stability rather than artistic creativity.

> **Proposition 1c:** Where performing arts organizations are interested in establishing a stable mass-market audience, the organization will have a disproportionate number of board members who occupy the role of controllers or other specialists whose primary mandate is to ensure legitimacy.

Decision-Making

The relationship between board composition and strategic decision-making in for-profit organizations has received substantial attention in management theory (Forbes and Milliken 1999) and research (Ruigrok, Peck, and Keller 2006; Bathala and Rao 1995). Considerably less attention is paid to understanding this relationship in performing arts organizations, although there is an emerging body of research that analyzes how strategic decision-making in the performing arts differs from such decision-making in other organizations (Cray, Inglis, and Freeman 2007; Assassi 2007; Kong 2008). This research has generated a number of empirical findings that demonstrate how the boards of performing arts organizations differ from boards in other types of organizations in how they exercise their oversight role over management and, more particularly, their role in strategic decision-making.

For example, prior research suggests that boards of directors of performing arts organizations often make operational rather than strategic decisions (Cray and Inglis 2011). Moreover, performing arts boards tend to make more internally focused decisions (i.e., on human resource issues) than externally focused decisions. In a study of participants in decisions made in Canadian arts organizations, Cray and Inglis (2011) found that in a sample of fifty-seven strategic decisions made by fourteen performing arts organizations, the board of directors participated in twelve of those strategic decisions in their organizations.[1] The administrative director, by contrast, participated in only seven of those decisions, and the artistic director was restricted to five decisions. Perhaps most striking is the observation that while performing arts organizations are acutely sensitive to the need to assess performance on both economic and aesthetic features, in practice they emphasize economic and financial measures (Turbide and Laurin 2009).

Why do performing arts boards engage on low-level decisions that in most other organizations would be made by managers? The answer becomes clearer when we view corporate governance in performing arts organizations through the theoretical lens of social value judgments. In the corporate world, the board largely acts as an intermediary between management and shareholders, who often have different interests in how the resources of the organization should be allocated and distributed (Jensen and Meckling 1976). Despite their differences, however, shareholders and managers in corporations share common assumptions of economic rationality, efficiency, and accountability as the primary logic to apply to strategic decisions (Thornton and Ocasio 2008).

In the world of performing arts, on the other hand, the role of the board is quite different. Rather than monitoring the propensity of managers to act in self-interest, arts boards serve as an intermediary between the organization and a diverse variety of stakeholders or audiences, both internal and external, each with different standards of social evaluation. Some of these audiences push the arts organization toward standards of conformity that rest on the same assumptions of economic rationality, efficiency, and accountability found in corporations. That is, they apply social evaluation standards of legitimacy. Government funding agencies, foundations, regulators, and professional associations are the most likely audiences to demand legitimacy. Other audiences, however, push the arts organization toward standards of conformity that rest on assumptions of aesthetic or artistic excellence. Critics, for example, may require a symphony to perform works that demonstrate adherence to a cultural canon. And musicians may push to perform pieces that demand a high degree of technical proficiency. However, it is entirely possible that neither of these standards will fill the performance venue with paying consumers. These audiences privilege authenticity over legitimacy.

In contrast to for-profits or even other nonprofit organizations, the tension between needs for authenticity and needs for legitimacy tends to permeate all sorts of decisions in a performing arts organization. Many decisions that are ostensibly operational in nature may hold tremendous potential to compromise the artistic integrity of the organization. Consider, for example, the surplus meaning attached to personnel decisions in arts organizations. Hiring a violinist in a symphony involves some purely technical and rational considerations, including the violinist's skill, experience, and expected salary, and some considerations that are judgments of aesthetic taste, such as the candidate's experience in the appropriate canon (Allmendinger and Hackman 1996) and the potential of her reputation to enhance or diminish the organization's status with critics (Glynn and Lounsbury 2005).

Viewed through a social value judgment lens, thus, it becomes clear why boards of performing arts organizations engage in a broader range of decisions than corporations (Cray and Inglis 2011), many of which are largely operational rather than strategic decisions (Vakharia et al. 2018) and which focus on reconciling the tension between the demands of aesthetic artistry and the demands for economic efficiency and accountability (Reid and Karambayya 2009). The high degree of engagement in decisions by boards of arts organizations is likely attributable to the competing demands for managerial legitimacy and artistic authenticity.

Proposition 2a: In a well-functioning performing arts organization, the primary role of the board of directors is to reconcile competing demands of authenticity and legitimacy.

An extension of the application of a social value judgment lens to the nature of decision-making in performing arts organizations suggests that, under most conditions, boards will attempt to balance the tensions between legitimacy and authenticity in the firm. However, there may be some contexts in which the demands for one form of social evaluation will outweigh others. Status is one such context. Prior research reveals that the consumption of art is related to social class (Bourdieu Pierre 1983 DiMaggio and Useem 1983). Similarly, class distinctions exist between different categories of performing arts, some of which are considered "highbrow" or high-status, and others of which are considered "popular" or low-status (Shrum 1991). Moreover, status orders are created within each of these categories, in which some performing arts organizations in a given category, say symphonies, are considered high-status and others are considered low-status. In the 1950s, critics identified five US symphonies as elite: the "Big Five" included New York, Boston, Chicago, Philadelphia, and Cleveland (Gilbert 1994; Hart 1973).

A growing body of research suggests that high-status orchestras behave quite differently than lower-status orchestras. They are slower to hire female musicians (Guitierrez 2021), are more likely to innovate both in repertoire of performances and in organizational structure (Kremp 2010), and are highly dependent upon corporate support for their financial stability (Scherer 2007) These somewhat disconnected empirical observations suggest that status and reputation may play an important role in determining the relative salience of legitimacy and authenticity claims in the strategic decision-making processes of performing arts organizations. That is, it may be that high-status arts organizations may not seek to simply balance claims of authenticity and legitimacy, but may allocate a higher preference for one category of social evaluations over another.

However, we must be careful to not conflate status and reputation. While they appear to be similar constructs, prior research demonstrates that status and reputation are distinct and derive from different social processes. In a study of competitive intercollegiate athletics, Washington and Zajac (2005) demonstrate that reputation is a social value judgment conferred on an organization because of its performance—its success in achieving its core mission. Status, by contrast, "refers more to the unearned ascription of social rank" (Washington and Zajac 2005, 282). Status, therefore, may result from something other than technical prowess. It is a historical accretion of social position derived from social judgments that are independent of performance. The elite status of the Big Five symphony orchestras in the United States may be the result of their founding date and age or their location in prominent US cities rather than any superior claim to aesthetic excellence. The New York Philharmonic, thus, may be considered a high-status symphony because of its long history, its elite patrons, its media coverage, and its location in a world-class city, independent of its technical skill.

This observation has implications for how the boards of high-status performing arts organizations weigh the relative importance of authenticity and legitimacy claims when making strategic decisions. If we assume that reputation is based on an arts organization's ability to excel at aesthetic performance and artistic integrity (in other words, attributes that define claims of authenticity), we can therefore also assume that the boards of organizations seeking to establish a strong reputation will prioritize aesthetic interests over legitimacy interests in making strategic decisions. This prioritization is more likely to be pursued by an aspirational organization than by an established one. Such organizations are more likely to adopt a narrow focus on select audiences, such as critics or internal professionals, whose understanding of the standards of aesthetic performance and artistic integrity are clearly established. In the language of social value judgment theory, non-elites that aspire to establish their reputation will do so by narrowly pursuing aesthetic recognition.

Proposition 2b: Non-elite performing arts organizations are more likely to prioritize authenticity over legitimacy in strategic decisions.

Elite performing arts organizations, by contrast, will be more concerned with preserving their elite status. As a result, they will be more attentive to a wider variety of audiences and their demands for legitimacy.

Proposition 2c: Elite performing arts organizations are more likely to prioritize legitimacy over authenticity in strategic decisions.

Resource Acquisition and Deployment

Like most nonprofits, performing arts organizations engage in a diverse array of resource acquisition efforts in order to fund their core mission. Prior research demonstrates that the activities used to generate financial support fall into four main categories: obtaining government grants, attracting private philanthropic donations, attracting corporate philanthropic donations, and generating commercial revenue from performances or educational programs (DiMaggio 1987; Sherer, Suddaby and Rozsa de Coquet 2019). Prior research also suggests that most performing arts organizations manage the risks associated with each revenue source by diversifying their resource acquisition into a portfolio that draws relatively equally from each category (Froelich 1999). Viewed through the lens of resource dependence theory (Pfeffer and Salancik 1978), adopting a portfolio approach to resource acquisition is a rational approach to managing risky resource dependencies (Gronbjerg 1993; Powell and Friedkin 1986).

Viewed through the lens of social value judgments, however, there are important differences that arise between self-generated commercial income, on one hand, and the three sources of philanthropic income (government, corporations, and private donors), on the other. The latter three sources of funding, each of which originates from dominant institutional actors, tend to place considerable degrees of isomorphic constraint on the arts organizations that succeed in getting funding. For example, substantial prior research shows that government funding tends to encourage program proliferation and mission drift in nonprofits (Bernstein 1991; Kramer 1985). Additional research suggests that government funding encourages nonprofits to mimic their funders by adopting more bureaucratic governance structures (Frumpkin and Galaskiewicz 2004). Corporate funding, similarly, makes performing arts organizations more risk-averse in their performative repertoire. Martorella (1977) observes that corporate funding correlates with the adoption of relatively safe popular titles in US opera houses. Heilbrun (2000) and Pierce (2000), similarly, attribute increased isomorphism in operatic repertoires to the growth of corporate funding in the United States. In a comprehensive analysis of performing arts organizations in Canada, Sherer, Suddaby, and Rozsa de Coquet (2019) observed that firms that depend on private and corporate philanthropy or government funding tended to be less innovative in their artistic mission than firms that rely on self-generated commercial funding.

It is not particularly surprising that external funding reduces innovation and encourages isomorphism, both in performing repertoire and in organizational structure. Viewed through the lens of social judgment theory, corporate, private, and individual funders place demands of external legitimacy on a performing arts organization. These demands can only be achieved by becoming isomorphic—not with the external environment, as might be predicted by institutional theory (DiMaggio and Powell 1983), but with the major source of resources from the external environment, as predicted by resource dependence theory (Pfeffer and Salancik 1978).

Proposition 3a: Performing arts organizations that derive the majority of their resources from private, public, or government philanthropy are more likely to adopt practices and structures that privilege legitimacy claims over authenticity claims.

Self-generated revenue, by contrast, may grant performing arts organizations a degree of autonomy from external stakeholders such as government, private, and corporate donors. There are, however, limits to the freedom granted by earned revenue. Customers are an audience that—like government, private, and corporate audiences—imposes a form of social value judgment on performing arts organizations. While elite audiences may reinforce the aesthetic integrity and artistic values of the arts organization, mass-market audiences may impose performance demands on an arts organization that are inconsistent with aesthetic excellence (Peterson 1992; DiMaggio and Useem 1983; Alexander 2018). Consistent with the observation that performing arts organizations do best financially by achieving a balanced portfolio of resources (Suddaby, Sherer, and Rosza de Coquet 2020), it is also likely the case that they are more likely to gain artistic and aesthetic freedom when they have a balanced portfolio of resources.

Proposition 3b: Performing arts organizations that derive resources from a mixed portfolio of self-generated commercial revenue, corporate philanthropy, private philanthropy, and government subsidy are more likely to adopt practices and structures that privilege authenticity claims over legitimacy claims.

Summary and Conclusion

The intent of this chapter is to demonstrate the power of viewing governance issues in performing arts organizations through the lens of social judgment theory. Prior research on governance in arts organizations has tended to adopt one of three theoretical lenses: agency theory (Radbourne 2003; Reid and Turbide 2012), resource dependence/stakeholder theory (Turbide and Laurin 2009, 2014; Parmer, Freeman, Harrison, Wicks, Purnell and de Colle 2010), or institutional theory (Amans, Mazars-Chapelon, and Villesèque-Dubus 2015; Knardal 2020). Agency theory focuses attention on the need to monitor and control the self-interest of management vis-à-vis shareholders, a relationship that applies to for-profit corporations but offers little insight into the governance practices of a typical performing arts organization. Resource dependence theory and institutional theory, by contrast, each draw attention to the need to understand how performing arts organizations signal economic and operational competence to external stakeholders—government regulators, donors, and philanthropic foundations. Each theory makes a useful contribution to understanding some limited aspects of what performing arts organizations actually do.

However, all three theories fail to capture the unique character and identity of performing arts organizations that, in addition to appearing economically and operationally competent to some stakeholders, must also signal artistic creativity and aesthetic integrity internally to their performers and externally to critics and audiences. That is, while prior theories help us understand how performing arts organizations achieve legitimacy, *they fail to explain how these organizations simultaneously achieve both legitimacy and authenticity*. Because of this, as the earlier quote by Nolan discloses, most performing arts executives begrudgingly adopt the ceremonial signals of legitimacy but are fully aware that in so doing they run the risk of compromising the authenticity of the organization by engaging in practices that satisfy stakeholders but avoid artistic risk. The paradox of governance in performing arts organizations is how to manage the essential tension between competing social judgments of legitimacy and authenticity by different "audiences."

This paper offers a theoretical framework and a set of constructs by which we can begin to more fully articulate and analyze this essential tension. There is a growing understanding among researchers who study performing arts organizations of the inadequacy of existing theories, typically borrowed from other disciplines, to offer a comprehensive explanation for why boards of directors in performing arts organizations are different. Considerable effort has been devoted to trying to bring together the relevant bits from existing theories to create an integrated framework of organizational governance for performing arts (Rentschler, Lee, and Fillis 2021; Besharov and Smith 2014). Integrative frameworks drawn from the private sector or even from the nonprofit sector fail to account for the unique competitive challenges in the field of cultural production (Bourdieu 1983), where aesthetic value and judgment, elite taste and critique, and literary and artistic authority are as influential in decision-making as the need to appear to be operationally efficient and financially stable.

Performing arts organizations do compete in the "real" world for economic capital, material resources, and human capital. However, they also must compete in the cultural world for social symbolic resources like status, reputation, identity, legitimacy, and authenticity. Our main contribution is the overarching observation that, just as performing arts organizations do best financially by achieving a balanced portfolio of resources (Sherer, Peter D., Roy Suddaby, and Mary Rozsa de Coquet 2019), so too do they succeed artistically when they are able to balance their need to demonstrate legitimacy with their need to signal authenticity. We have focused on the board of directors in performing arts organizations because we see this as the primary mechanism by which competing claims of legitimacy and authenticity are reconciled. However, the tension arises in many other facets of performing arts, particularly in the day-to-day interactions and negotiations between executive directors and artistic directors. We clearly need empirical work to help us understand the practices and strategies that make these relationships succeed or fail. Viewing these relationships through the lens of social value judgments, we believe that conflicts can be successfully "blended" (Glynn and Lounsbury 2005) by acquiring an understanding that many forms of social judgment we tend to see as synonymous—legitimacy and authenticity, or status and reputation—are premised on some important conceptual differences. Understanding these differences is the first step to reconciling them.

We have also focused somewhat exclusively on two broad constructs drawn from social judgment theory: legitimacy and authenticity. These two constructs were chosen because they best capture the inherent tension between artistic excellence and economic stability that characterizes most performing arts organizations. However, there is considerable opportunity to extend both the range of application and the nuance of interpretation of these constructs by elaborating precisely how they can improve both the artistic integrity and the economic performance of arts organizations.

Much of the work needed to elaborate the role of legitimacy and authenticity in improving both economic and artistic performance can be accomplished through focused empirical research. A logical first step, as described in our first set of propositions (1a, 1b, and 1c), would be to reexamine the construct of board diversity through the lens of social judgment theory. Prior empirical research on board diversity has tended to operationalize diversity based on well-established categories of gender, race, age, and related demographic variables. Few studies, however, have operationalized board diversity on behavioral or role characteristics, and none, with the possible exception of the study by Dubini and Monti (2018), have operationalized diversity based on the degree to which a board member attends to questions of artistic authenticity versus economic legitimacy. In fact, the distinction between different types of social value judgment orientation was not the primary focus of Dubini and Monti's (2018) study. We have simply retrospectively reconstructed their categories of "controllers," "influential people," and so on around the defining elements of authenticity and legitimacy.

A number of important questions about board diversity emerge when viewed through the lens of social judgment theory. Do highly creative, cutting-edge organizations have a disproportionate number of board members with a predisposition toward authenticity? Do arts organizations that pursue largely commercial success, by contrast, have a disproportionate number of board members with a predisposition toward legitimacy? Clearly, this type of research could be conducted quantitatively by assessing the dispositions of individual board members. While we do not yet have validated scales for these assessments, researchers have made considerable advances in this direction (Schoon 2022; Tost 2011).

Our second set of propositions draws attention to the ways in which the tension between legitimacy and authenticity is resolved in making strategic decisions at the board level. In contrast to the first set of propositions, which views legitimacy and authenticity judgments as a property of individual personalities or roles, these propositions view legitimacy and authenticity as processes that unfold in negotiated interpersonal actions at the board level. As a result, much of this research will be qualitative in nature. Studying these processes will require a degree of either direct observation (ethnographic studies) or retrospective reconstruction by the participants (interviews). There are very few ethnographic studies of board interactions in either for-profit or nonprofit organizations. This is perhaps unsurprising because of the sensitive nature of the decisions made at the level of the board. That said, there are some powerful examples of ethnographic studies of board governance in action (i.e., Golden-Biddle and Rao 1997; Samra-Fredericks 2000) that could easily be applied to an analysis of how the tension between legitimacy and authenticity is negotiated. Similarly, while there are few studies of the use of interviews to retrospectively reconstruct strategic decision-making processes at the board level, the study by Cray and Inglis (2011) discussed above serves as an exemplar of how this type of research might be best conducted.

Perhaps the most interesting aspect of social value judgments in the governance of arts organizations that remains unexplored is the collectively held assumptions regarding status orders in different arts communities. While we have overt ranking systems that reflect status order assumptions in for-profit businesses, such as the Fortune 500 (Podolny 2010), or in educational systems, such as the *Business Week* rankings of business schools (Elsbach and Kramer 1996), there is little empirical research that explores the explicit or implicit status orders of arts organizations and how status order affects access to material resources. This is somewhat surprising given the profound role of critics, professionals whose primary function is to make value judgments on arts organizations (Glynn and Lounsbury 2005).

A critical but underappreciated dimension of performing arts organizations is their need to justify their existence to different audiences, each of which applies vastly different and often opposing logics of taste or worth (Boltanski and Thévenot 2006) in how they judge the organization. These overlooked elements of social judgment have been largely absent from most theoretical and empirical analyses of the performing arts. We have sketched an outline of how social judgment theory may help bring aesthetics and artistry back into how we assess governance practices in arts organizations. Our hope is that this is the beginning of a more rigorous and comprehensive approach to theorizing organizations in the performing arts.

NOTE

1. The types of strategic decisions and the frequency of their occurrence in the sample (in parentheses) are: human relations (16), image (8), organizational structure (8), product (7), building (7), funding (5), strategic plan (2), location (1), quality (1), staying alive (1), and technology (1).

REFERENCES

Alexander, Victoria D. 2018. "Heteronomy in the Arts Field: State Funding and British Arts Organizations." *British Journal of Sociology* 69, no. 1: 23–43.

Allmendinger, Jutta and J. Richard Hackman. 1996. "Organizations in changing environments: the case of East German Symphony Orchestras." *Administrative Science Quarterly*, 41, 337–389.

Amans, Pascale, Agnès Mazars-Chapelon, and Fabienne Villesèque-Dubus. 2015. "Budgeting in Institutional Complexity: The Case of Performing Arts Organizations." *Management Accounting Research* 27: 47–66.

Ashforth, Blake E., and Barrie W. Gibbs. 1990. "The Double-Edge of Organizational Legitimation." *Organization Science* 1, no. 2: 177–194.

Ashforth, Blake E., Kristie M. Rogers, and Kevin G. Corley. 2011. "Identity in organizations: Exploring cross-level dynamics." *Organization Science* 22, no. 5: 1144–1156.

Assassi, Isabelle. 2007. "The Programming Strategies and Relationships of Theatres: An Analysis Based on the French Experience." *International Journal of Arts Management* 9, no. 3: 50–64.

Bathala, Chenchuramaiah T., and Ramesh P. Rao. 1995. "The Determinants of Board Composition: An Agency Theory Perspective." *Managerial and Decision Economics* 16, no. 1: 59–69.

Bernstein, Susan R. 1991. "Contracted Services: Issues for the Nonprofit Agency Manager." *Nonprofit and Voluntary Sector Quarterly* 20: 429–443.

Besharov, Marya L., and Wendy K. Smith. 2014. "Multiple Institutional Logics in Organizations: Explaining Their Varied Nature and Implications." *Academy of Management Review* 39, no. 3: 364–381.

Bitektine, Alex. 2011. "Toward a Theory of Social Judgments of Organizations: The Case of Legitimacy, Reputation, and Status." *Academy of Management Review* 36, no. 1: 151–179.

Boltanski, Luc, and Laurent Thévenot. 2006. *On Justification: Economies of Worth*. Princeton, NJ: Princeton University Press.

Bourdieu, Pierre. 1983. *The Field of Cultural Production*. New York: Columbia University Press.

Brickson, Shelley L. 2005. "Organizational identity orientation: Forging a link between organizational identity and organizations' relations with stakeholders." *Administrative Science Quarterly* 50, no. 4: 576–609.

Carroll, Glen R., and Dennis R. Wheaton. 2009. "The Organizational Construction of Authenticity: An Examination of Contemporary Food and Dining in the US." *Research in Organizational Behavior* 29: 255–282.

Carter, D. A., B. J. Simkins, and W. G. Simpson. 2003. "Corporate Governance, Board Diversity, and Firm Value." *Financial Review* 38, no. 1: 33–53.

Coleman, James S. 1990. "Commentary: Social institutions and social theory." *American Sociological Review* 55, no. 3: 333–339.

Cornforth, Chris. 2001. "What Makes Boards Effective? An Examination of the Relationships Between Board Inputs, Structures, Processes and Effectiveness in Nonprofit Organisations." *Corporate Governance: An International Review* 9, no. 3: 217–227.

Cray, David, and Loretta Inglis. 2011. "Strategic Decision Making in Arts Organizations." *Journal of Arts Management, Law, and Society* 41, no. 2: 84–102.

Cray, David, Loretta Inglis, and Susan Freeman. 2007. "Managing the Arts: Leadership and Decision Making Under Dual Rationalities." *Journal of Arts Management, Law, and Society* 36, no. 4: 295–313.

Dalziel, Thomas, Richard J. Gentry, and Michael Bowerman. 2011. "An Integrated Agency-Resource Dependence View of the Influence of Directors' Human and Relational Capital on Firms' R&D Spending." *Journal of Management Studies* 48, no. 6: 1217–1242.

de Voogt, Alex. 2006. "Dual Leadership as a Problem-Solving Tool in Arts Organizations." *International Journal of Arts Management* 9, no. 1: 17–22.

DiMaggio, Paul. 1987. *Managers of the Arts: Careers and Opinions of Senior Administrators of US Art Museums, Symphony Orchestras, Resident Theaters, and Local Arts Agencies*. Research Division Report #20. Washington, DC: Seven Locks Press.

DiMaggio, Paul J., and Walter W. Powell. 1983. "The Iron Cage Revisited: Institutional Isomorphism and Collective Rationality in Organizational Fields." *American Sociological Review* 48, no. 2: 147–160.

DiMaggio, Paul, and Michael Useem. 1983. "Cultural Democracy in a Period of Cultural Expansion: The Social Composition of Arts Audiences in the United States." *Social Problems* 26, no. 2: 179–197.

Dubini, Paola, and Alberto Monti. 2018. "Board Composition and Organizational Performance in the Cultural Sector: The Case of Italian Opera Houses." *International Journal of Arts Management* 20, no. 2: 56–70.

Dutton, Denis. 2004. "Authenticity in Art." In *Oxford Handbook of Aesthetics*, edited by Jerrold Levinson. Oxford: Oxford University Press. 258–274

Elsbach, Kimberly D., and Roderick M. Kramer. 1996. "Members' Responses to Organizational Identity Threats: Encountering and Countering the *Business Week* Rankings." *Administrative Science Quarterly* 41, no. 3: 442–476.

Fama, Eugene F., and Michael C. Jensen. 1983. "Separation of Ownership and Control." *Journal of Law and Economics* 26, no. 2: 301–325.

Forbes, Daniel P., and Frances J. Milliken. 1999. "Cognition and Corporate Governance: Understanding Boards of Directors as Strategic Decision-Making Groups." *Academy of Management Review* 24, no. 3: 489–505.

Froelich, Karen A. 1999. "Diversification of Revenue Strategies: Evolving Resource Dependence in Nonprofit Organizations." *Nonprofit and Voluntary Sector Quarterly* 28, no. 3: 246–268.

Frumkin, Peter, and Joseph Galaskiewicz. 2004. "Institutional Isomorphism and Public Sector Organizations." *Journal of Public Administration Research and Theory* 14, no. 3: 283–307.

Galli, Jaime D. 2011. "Organizational Management in the Non-Profit Performing Arts: Exploring New Models of Structure, Management and Leadership." Master's thesis, University of Oregon. https://scholarsbank.uoregon.edu/xmlui/bitstream/handle/1794/11210/Galli_research.pdf?sequence=1.

Gilbert, Ann C. 1994. "Women in the Big Five Orchestras: An Exploratory Study of the Factors Affecting Career Development." PhD dissertation, University of Akron.

Glynn, Mary Ann, and Mike Lounsbury. 2005. "From the Critics' Corner: Logic Blending, Discursive Change and Authenticity in a Cultural Production System." *Journal of Management Studies* 42, no. 5: 1031–1055.

Golden-Biddle, Karen, and Hayagreeva Rao. 1997. "Breaches in the Boardroom: Organizational Identity and Conflicts of Commitment in a Nonprofit Organization." *Organization Science* 8, no. 6: 593–611.

Gronbjerg, Kirsten A. 1993. *Understanding Nonprofit Funding: Managing Revenues in Social Services and Community Development Organizations.* San Francisco: Jossey-Bass.

Gulati, Ranjay, and Martin Gargiulo. 1999. "Where Do Interorganizational Networks Come From?" *American Journal of Sociology* 104, no. 5: 1439–1493.

Gutierrez, Sheena. 2021. "Gender Bias Among the Big Five Orchestras—As Illustrated in Hiring Practices of Women Instrumentalists." PhD dissertation, University of Miami.

Hart, Phillip. 1973. Orpheus in the New World. W.W. Norton, New York.

Heilbrun, James. 2000. "Explaining the Repertory of Opera Companies in the United States." Paper presented at the XIth International Conference on Cultural Economics, University of St. Thomas, Minneapolis.

Hillman, Amy J., Albert. A. Canella, and Ramona L. Paetzold. 2000. "The Resource Dependency Role of Corporate Governance Directors: Strategic Adaptation of Board Composition in Response to Environmental Change." *Journal of Management Studies* 37, no. 2: 235–256.

Hillman, Amy J., and Thomas Dalziel. 2003. "Boards of Directors and Firm Performance: Integrating Agency and Resource Dependence Perspectives." *Academy of Management Review* 28, no. 3: 383–396.

Hirsch, Paul, and John A. Y. Andrews. 1983. "Ambushes, Shootouts, and Knights of the Roundtable: The Language of Corporate Takeovers." pp. 145–55 in *Organizational Symbolism*, edited by Louis R. Pondy, Peter J. Frost, Gareth Morgan, and Thomas C. Dandridge. Greenwich, Conn.: JAI

Jensen, Michael C., and William H. Meckling. 1976. "Theory of the Firm: Managerial Behavior, Agency Costs and Ownership Structure." *Journal of Financial Economics* 3, no. 4: 305–360.

Kilduff, Martin, and David Krackhardt. 1994. "Bringing the individual back in: A structural analysis of the internal market for reputation in organizations." *Academy of Management Journal* 37, no. 1: 87–108.

Kivy, Peter. 1995. *Authenticities: Philosophical Reflections on Musical Performance*. Ithaca: Cornell University Press.

Knardal, Per S. 2020. "Orchestrating Institutional Complexity and Performance Management in the Performing Arts." *Financial Accountability and Management* 36, no. 3: 300–318.

Kong, Eric. 2008. "The Development of Strategic Management in the Nonprofit Context: Intellectual Capital in Social Service Nonprofit Organizations." *International Journal of Management Reviews* 10, no. 3: 281–299.

Kramer, Roderick M. 1985. "The Future of the Voluntary Sector in a Mixed Economy." *Journal of Applied Behavioral Science* 21: 377–391.

Kremp, Pierre-Antoine. 2010. "Innovation and Selection: Symphony Orchestras and the Construction of the Musical Canon in the United States (1879–1959)." *Social Forces* 88, no. 3: 1051–1082.

Lynall, Matthew D., Brian R. Golden, and Amy J. Hillman. 2003. "Board Composition from Adolescence to Maturity: A Multitheoretic View." *Academy of Management Review* 28, no. 3: 416–431.

Martorella, Roseanne. 1977. "The Relationship Between Box Office and Repertoire: A Case Study of Opera." *Sociological Quarterly* 18, no. 3: 354–366.

Meyer, John W., and Brian Rowan. 1977. "Institutionalized organizations: Formal structure as myth and ceremony." *American Journal of Sociology* 83, no. 2: 340–363.

Nolan, Yvette. 2020. "Governance Structures for Theatres, by Theatres." Mass Culture/Mobilisation Culturelle, September 28, 2020. https://massculture.ca/2020/09/governance-structures-for-theatres-by-theatres-by-yvette-nolan/.

Oliver, Christine. 1991. "Strategic Responses to Institutional Processes." *Academy of Management Review* 16, no. 1: 145–179.

Parmer, Bidhan L., R. Edward Freeman, Jeffrey S. Harrison, Andrew C. Wicks, Lauren Purnell, and Simone de Colle. 2010. "Stakeholder Theory: The State of the Art." *The Academy of Management Annals*, 4, no. 1: 403–445.

Parsons, Talcott. 1960. *Structure and Process in Modern Societies*. Glencoe, IL: Free Press.

Peterson, Richard A. 1986. "From Impressario to Arts Administrator: Formal Accountability in Nonprofit Cultural Organizations." In *Nonprofit Enterprise in the Arts: Studies in Mission and Constraint*, edited by P. J. DiMaggio, 161–183. New York: Oxford University Press.

Peterson, Richard A. 1992. "Understanding Audience Segmentation: From Elite and Mass to Omnivore and Univore." *Poetics* 21, no. 4: 243–258.

Pfeffer, Jeffrey, and Gerald R. Salancik. 1978. *The External Control of Organizations: A Resource Dependence Perspective*. New York: Harper & Row.

Pierce, J. Lamar. 2000. "Programmatic Risk-Taking by American Opera Companies." *Journal of Cultural Economics* 24: 45–63.

Podolny, Joel M. 2010. *Status Signals*. Princeton, NJ: Princeton University Press.

Pollock, Timothy G., Kisha Lashley, Violina P. Rindova, and Jung-Hoon Han. 2019. "Which of these things are not like the others? Comparing the rational, emotional, and moral aspects of reputation, status, celebrity, and stigma." *Academy of Management Annals* 13, no. 2: 444–478.

Powell, Walter W., and Rebecca Friedkin. 1986. "Politics and Programs: Organizational Factors in Public Television Decision Making." In *Nonprofit Enterprise in the Arts*, edited by P. DiMaggio, 245–278. New York: Oxford University Press.

Radbourne, Jennifer. 2003. "Performing on Boards: The Link Between Governance and Corporate Reputation in Nonprofit Arts Boards." *Corporate Reputation Review* 6, no. 3: 212–222.

Reid, Wendy. and Rekha Karambayya. 2009. "Impact of Dual Executive Leadership Dynamics in Creative Organizations." *Human Relations* 62, no. 7: 1073–1112.

Reid, Wendy, and Johanne Turbide. 2012. "Board/Staff Relationships in a Growth Crisis: Implications for Nonprofit Governance." *Nonprofit and Voluntary Sector Quarterly* 41, no. 1: 82–99.

Rentschler, Ruth, Boram Lee, and Ian Fillis. 2021. "Towards an Integrative Framework for Arts Governance." *International Journal of Arts Management* 24, no. 1: 17–31.

Rindova, Violina P., Timothy G. Pollock, and Matthew L. A. Hayward. 2006. "Celebrity Firms: The Social Construction of Market Popularity." *Academy of Management Review* 31: 50–71.

Ruigrok, Winfried, Simon I. Peck, and Hansueli Keller. 2006. "Board Characteristics and Involvement in Strategic Decision Making: Evidence from Swiss Companies." *Journal of Management Studies* 43, no. 5: 1201–1226.

Samra-Fredericks, Dalvir. 2000. "An Analysis of the Behavioural Dynamics of Corporate Governance—a Talk-Based Ethnography of a UK Manufacturing 'Board-in-Action.'" *Corporate Governance: An International Review* 8, no. 4: 311–326.

Scherer, Frederic M. 2007. "Corporate Structure and the Financial Support of US Symphony Orchestras." Working paper, Harvard University.

Schoon, Eric W. 2022. "Operationalizing Legitimacy." *American Sociological Review* 87, no. 3: 478–503.

Sherer, Peter D., and Huseyin Leblebici. 2015. "Governance in professional service firms: From structural and cultural to legal normative views." pp. 189–212 in Laura Empson, Daniel Muzio, Joseph P. Broschak and Bob Hinings (Editors), *The Oxford Handbook of Professional Service Firms*, London, UK: Oxford University Press.

Sherer, Peter D., Roy Suddaby, and Mary Rozsa de Coquet. 2019. "Does Resource Diversity Confer Organizational Autonomy in Arts Organizations? Extending Resource Dependence Theory." *Journal of Arts Management, Law, and Society* 49, no. 4: 224–241.

Shrum, Wesley. 1991. "Critics and Publics: Cultural Mediation in Highbrow and Popular Performing Arts." *American Journal of Sociology* 97, no. 2: 347–375.

Suchman, Mark C. 1995. "Managing Legitimacy: Strategic and Institutional Approaches." *Academy of Management Review* 20, no. 3: 571–610.

Suddaby, Roy, Alex Bitektine, and Patrick Haack. 2017. "Legitimacy." *Academy of Management Annals* 11, no. 1: 451–478.

Thornton, Patricia H., and William Ocasio. 2008. "Institutional logics." pp. 99–128 in Royston Greenwood, Christine Oliver, Kerstin Sahlin and Roy Suddaby (Editors), *The Sage Handbook of Organizational Institutionalism*, London: Sage.

Tost, Leigh Plunkett. 2011. "An Integrative Model of Legitimacy Judgments." *Academy of Management Review* 36, no. 4: 686–710.

Turbide, Johanne, and Claude Laurin. 2009. "Performance Measurement in the Arts Sector: The Case of the Performing Arts." *International Journal of Arts Management* 11, no. 2: 56–70.

Turbide, Johanne, and Claude Laurin. 2014. "Governance in the Arts and Culture Nonprofit Sector: Vigilance or Indifference?" *Administrative Sciences* 4, no. 4: 413–432.

Vakharia, Neville, Marilena Vecco, Andrej Srakar, and Divya Janardhan. 2018. "Knowledge Centricity and Organizational Performance: An Empirical Study of the Performing Arts." *Journal of Knowledge Management*, no. 22: 1124–1152.

Washington, Marvin, and Edward J. Zajac. 2005. "Status Evolution and Competition: Theory and Evidence." *Academy of Management Journal* 48, no. 2: 282–296.

Weber, Max. 1964. *The Theory of Social and Economic Organization*. Translated by Talcott Parsons. New York: Free Press.

Zajac, Edward J., and James D. Westphal. 1996. "Who Shall Succeed? How CEO/Board Preferences and Power Affect the Choice of New CEOs." *Academy of Management Journal* 39, no. 1: 64–90.

Zavyalova, Anastasiya, Michael D. Pfarrer, and Rhonda K. Reger. 2017. "Celebrity and infamy? The consequences of media narratives about organizational identity." *Academy of Management Review* 42, no. 3: 461–480.

CHAPTER 6

OPEN SYSTEMS THEORY IN ARTS MANAGEMENT

YUHA JUNG AND TRAVIS NEWTON

Introduction

OPEN systems theory sees an organization as an integral part of its environment, and the environment in turn is a necessary and inescapable component of organizational existence. An organization's internal actors and systems, parts and elements of the environment, and the larger ecosystem are interconnected and interdependent, mutually affecting one another in a multidirectional way (Jung 2022). Open systems theory is more like a worldview, or a paradigm, as Ludwig von Bertalanffy (1972) categorizes it, rather than a narrow theory confined to a single discipline. The most important aspect of open systems theory is that it views the environment as an essential element, one that is inescapable, necessary, and interdependent, and which therefore should not be ignored when seeking to understand organizations (Scott and Davis 2007); this quality sets it apart from other theories that may acknowledge the environment but do not fully embrace it. In the time of COVID-19 recovery and waves of civil movements, organizations need to focus more on their environment, uncertainties of the environment, and lack of information, all of which require nimble and flexible decision-making structures and processes. These circumstances require organizational practices to be more resilient and boundaries to be more permeable—characteristics that open systems theory could support.

This theory is fitting for the arts and cultural sector given the environmental changes and challenges that many arts and cultural organizations face. The ability to be adaptable and flexible is a necessity for survival, especially with a changing financial landscape, including governmental funding changes for arts and culture (Rohter 2012; Nonprofit Finance Fund 2013) and rapid environmental change caused by years of the ongoing pandemic and recovery. Open systems theory offers lessons for organizations to be more flexible, compassionate, and strategic in the face of a constantly changing environment because of its unique emphasis on an understanding of the environment as a necessary component of any system or organization, making open systems theory ideal to apply in order to foster a deeper connection with an organization's constituents and larger communities.

We focus on open systems theory as the primary example of a theory where the environment is a necessary element, not just something that is important. In other words, the premise of this theory is that an organization as a system cannot exist without its environment (Macy 1991). The open systems perspective has the potential to become a more prominent foundational theory in arts and cultural management research because this theory has wide interconnections with other types of organizational theoretical thought (e.g., structural contingency theories, resource dependence theory, and population ecology theory) used in related fields, such as public administration and nonprofit management (Shafritz, Ott, and Jang 2016). Additionally, it already has been used in the field of arts and cultural management, although the extent of its use has been limited, which is further discussed later. This chapter argues that adopting an open systems theory perspective that includes environmental interactions as necessary and interdependent components of organizations can further benefit the study and management of arts organizations, especially in the areas of community engagement as well as diversity, equity, and inclusion (DEI) practices.

The first two sections of this chapter provide a general understanding of systems theory and its relationship to organizational theory. To draw connections between open systems theory and arts and cultural management research, we began with a targeted literature review (Herrick and Pratt 2012), focusing on one area in depth: open systems theory and its related theories as found in arts and cultural management research. The review was conducted by searching abstracts with key terms, such as "systems theory" and "systems thinking," in eighteen arts and cultural management–related journals over the past two decades.[1] While eighteen is not a small number of journals to search through, it is certainly not an exhaustive list and does not include journals that are focused on general organization theories or management research. The list of journals was chosen based on their relevance to arts and cultural research based on previous publications (Chang and Wyszomirski 2015; Rentschler and Shilbury 2008).

By looking at the threads of systems theory perspective in organization theories (which are fundamental to studying arts and cultural organizations) and arts and cultural research, this chapter aims to present what systems theory is, how it has been used in organizational theories as well as arts and cultural research, and why and how it can be further applied. This chapter specifically presents (1) an overview of the theory, including the origins, structure, and characteristics of open systems theory and examples of systems thinking; (2) related organization theories that adopt or are influenced by open systems perspectives; (3) specific examples of arts and cultural management studies that fall under or are closely related to open systems theory applied at the macro and micro levels; and (4) the rationale and further potential for utilizing the theory in the field's research, especially in the areas of community engagement and DEI practices, making deeper connections between arts organizations and their communities. By doing so, the authors hope to establish it as a broad and overarching foundational theory for the field of arts and cultural management due to its relevance to important, current issues of arts and cultural management.

Open Systems Theory, Structure, and Thinking

Before discussing the details of the theory, it is important to define some of the relevant terms. Systems are almost always thought of as open. "Closed system by its definition does not have a place in systems thinking; there is rarely a closed system in the world," as almost all systems exist in relation to their environment (Jung and Love 2017, 8). This is why "systems theory" and "open systems theory" are often used interchangeably in the literature (Jung and Vakharia 2019). Additionally, the relationship between "systems theory" and "systems thinking," terms that are also sometimes used interchangeably, warrants a distinction. Systems thinking is a practical application of systems theory, with the aim of understanding and working with systems (Arnold and Wade 2015); it can be considered as almost like a learned skill or mind orientation, when one applies open systems theory to real-life situations and problems (Jung and Vakharia 2019). Examples of systems thinking skills are systems intelligence (Törmänen, Hämäläinen, and Saarinen 2016) and system leadership (Senge, Hamilton, and Kania 2015; Saarinen and Hämäläinen 2004). This section discusses the origin of systems theory, the qualities of open systems theory as they are related to openness to the environment, the transformative nature of open systems, and applicational examples of systems theory.

Origins of Systems Theory

Tracing its origins to the 1930s and the development of systems theory by Ludwig von Bertalanffy (1933), open systems theory emphasizes the importance of "throughput of resources from the environment" (Scott and Davis 2007, 93). The external environment is viewed not simply as a factor to be considered among many but rather as an essential and integral component. Von Bertalanffy's systems theory finds its origins in Western philosophy, including Aristotle's statement that "the whole is more than the sum of its parts" (1972, 407). Von Bertalanffy was a biologist, and his initial exploration of systems was related more to organisms, but he later suggested that replacing "organisms" with "organized entities" forming the basis of systems theory as it relates to organizations (1972, 410).

A similar line of thinking is also found in Eastern philosophy in the Buddhist concept of mutual causality (Macy 1991; Jung 2022). Mutual causality defines relationships among parts to have *dynamic interdependence*—affecting each other in a mutual manner, not unidirectionally, as is often assumed in scientific, positivist causal relationships. In Buddhism, this inescapable mutual causal relationship among parts is described as *paticca samuppada*, or dependent co-arising (Macy 1991). Naess (1973) explains how this mutual belonging is everywhere, inescapable, and fundamental among all parts of any system, social or natural.

Systems Concepts Based on the Level of Environmental Engagement

Scott and Davis (2007) discuss the concept of system variety by making the case that organizations, as systems, change over time, and interaction with the environment is essential for the functioning of an open system. Further, the source of system variety is the environment: "from an open system point of view, there is a close connection between the condition of the environment and the characteristics of the systems within it" (Scott and Davis 2007, 95). Based on the relationship with other factors in their environments, there are many different types and levels of systems, such as mechanistic systems, organic systems, and social systems.

Boulding (1956) identified and articulated nine different levels of systems: (1) frameworks, (2) clockworks, (3) cybernetic systems, (4) open systems, (5) blueprinted-growth systems, (6) internal-image systems, (7) symbol-processing systems, (8) social systems, and (9) transcendental systems. The first three levels are physical (mechanistic) systems, and levels 4–6 represent biological (organic) systems. Levels 7 and 8 represent human and social systems, while level 9 represents the possibility of a new system not yet envisioned that could be developed in the future. These levels are introduced in order of complexity. In other words, as a system moves from 1 to 8 (from mechanic to social systems), it becomes more complex, more loosely connected, more dependent on other parts, more capable of self-maintenance and renewal, more able to grow and change, and more open to the environment (Scott and Davis 2007).

In mechanistic systems (e.g., a machine), the parts behave in a certain order that is highly constrained and limited, while in organic systems (e.g., a plant or animal), the parts are more interdependent and less constrained, with more flexibility and adaptability for change. In social systems, like organizations, the independent parts are loosely connected, with fewer constraints and limitations; they can be characterized as complex and flexible, capable of independent actions while being interdependent (Ashby 1952; Buckley 1967). These flexible, moving parts make it possible for organizations to more easily adapt to their external environment.

Because open systems fully acknowledge the interaction between organizations and their external environment, they can maintain themselves based on feedback and throughput of resources from the environment (Scott and Davis 2007). When a system cannot transform or change itself based on throughput from the environment, it is not considered an open system, and it is not able to maintain its own survival or sustain itself. Organic, human, and social systems have this ability to maintain themselves and are therefore open systems. From this perspective, the environment is an essential part of a system, not something to be managed, controlled, or avoided.

Transformative Nature of Open Systems

The transformation of organizations through interactions with their environments can be explained by the processes of morphostasis, which "tend to preserve or maintain a system's given form, structure, or state," such as circulation and respiration in biological systems and socialization and control activities in social systems (Scott and Davis 2007, 95). Additionally, morphogenesis is the process of changing the system, such as learning, growing, and differentiating (Scott and Davis 2007). Therefore, while open systems maintain and stabilize themselves through certain mechanisms (morphostasis), they differentiate themselves from others and become more elaborate in structure (morphogenesis) by learning to adapt to change in relation to their external environment. As the parts of social organizations are more loosely connected than the parts of mechanical or biological systems, they have the potential to transform or change their structural characteristics over time, something that can serve as an advantage (Scott and Davis 2007).

It is precisely the close and inescapable interconnections and interdependencies between organizations and their environment that can help to transform organizations. Different parts of systems and their environments form nested, networked structures. Such structures are a type of hierarchy that is more like a rhizome—a networked root structure that does not have top or bottom—than like a traditional top-down structure (Macy 1991). This structure helps open social systems to be flexible and adaptable and to maintain or renew themselves through a positive feedback function (Macy 1991). "This feedback mechanism of an open system receives inputs from the external environment and transforms them into useful output for their environment by its internal throughput process" (Jung 2022, 21). A feedback function can work in a negative way, where organizations accept only the input that is already considered valuable to the internal system and ignore contradictory inputs, therefore maintaining the status quo rather than making relevant changes (Jung 2022). When they do not pay attention to external changes in their environment (e.g., information, resources, people, audiences, wider communities, multiple perspectives, and politics), organizations cannot transform or renew themselves in order to be relevant (Jung 2022).

Systems Thinking Skills: Systems Intelligence and System Leadership

Systems thinking, as discussed above, is a practical application of systems theory, which includes skills like systems intelligence (SI) (Törmänen, Hämäläinen, and

Saarinen 2016) and system leadership (Senge, Hamilton, and Kania 2015; Saarinen and Hämäläinen 2004). These systems thinking skills are especially useful in making practical changes to organizations (e.g., restructuring departments within an organization in relation to internal needs and external demands) as well as transforming them at the micro level (e.g., individual actors within an organization making behavioral changes in relation to other actors' behaviors and changing needs of the organization). Based on Peter Senge's (1990) concept of systems thinking and Goleman's (1998) concept of emotional intelligence, Saarinen and Hämäläinen (2004) first developed and defined SI. SI is a micro-level conscious mental capacity to fuel action in response to other actors' thinking and behavior within a complex environment (Saarinen and Hämäläinen 2004). In exercising SI, actors use interactive feedback systems to observe and manage their own behavior, affect the behavior of others through their own actions, and try to improve the larger environment together through mutual mental and behavioral changes (Törmänen, Hämäläinen, and Saarinen 2016). SI intends to alter an actor's way of thinking in order to change micro-behaviors, therefore affecting the whole system in a sustainable way (Sasaki 2017).

While all actors in a system can embrace systems intelligence to make transformative changes to their system, it can be most effective when applied at the leadership level. When a leader values and develops systems intelligence in managing an organization, they can create an internal system that is more open to diverse perspectives, essentially triggering the positive feedback function mentioned earlier (Macy 1991). In other words, through leadership's application of SI, a system or organization can be more receptive to diverse perspectives of internal and external actors, which in turn can challenge deeply ingrained mental models of actors, creating an environment where meaningful changes are more likely to happen and diverse ideas are more likely to be heard (Senge, Hamilton, and Kania 2015). Systems-intelligent leaders see their organization and actors as part of a larger social ecosystem (Saarinen and Hämäläinen 2004).

Threads of Open Systems Theory in Organization Theories

While open systems theory is relatively new to arts and cultural management, for decades it has been a steady influence in and connector of work in organizational theory, utilized in such fields as business administration, public administration, and nonprofit management (Jung and Love 2017; Jung and Vakharia 2019). More specifically, it has been one of the main threads in many different schools of organization theory, including structural organization theories, cybernetics, structural contingency theories, and theories concerning environments (e.g., resource dependence theory, population ecology theory, and neo-institutional theory).

Generally, open systems theory falls under the umbrella of *structural organization theories*. Early structural organization theories were concerned with relationships among the parts within an organization, such as positions, groups of positions (e.g., units and departments), and processes. In other words, they focused on how the structural design of an organization affects the coordination and control of specialized units and departmentalization (Shafritz, Ott, and Jang 2016, 170). While modern structural theories pay attention to external environmental forces, such as different markets, cultures, regulatory environments, technologies, competitions, and the economy (Shafritz, Ott, and Jang 2016, 169–170), these components are often described as something that an organization has to *deal with* rather than to *work with*. The open systems perspective added the external environment and its parts as important *structural* components, influencing theories of organizations to consider how outside factors are related to organizations (Scott 2003) and shifting the focus of analysis from internal systems of organizations to "external dynamics of organizational competition, interaction, and interdependency" (Shafritz, Ott, and Jang 2016, 340).

A second theory that influenced the open concept of systems and therefore legitimating the inclusion of the environment as an organizational "part" is *cybernetics*. The most important aspect of cybernetics (Wiener 1948) relevant to systems theory and an open perspective on organizations is the idea of self-regulation. Self-regulation is like a thermostat, which regulates the temperature based on the feedback it is receiving from external elements (i.e., temperature sensors) and is constantly adjusting in order to keep the temperature at the desired level. Cybernetic systems include "biological, social, or technological systems that can identify problems, do something about them, and receive feedback to adjust themselves" (Shafritz, Ott, and Jang 2016, 341). Therefore, this theoretical view is deeply concerned with monitoring external and environmental changes in order to control what is happening internally.

Another example of organization theory based on an open systems perspective is *structural contingency theory*, based on work by Burns and Stalker (1961), which heavily considers the external environment of an organization. Burns and Stalker believed that there is not a single best way to structure organizations, as organizations adapt to their environments. Therefore, a successful organizational structure is often determined by its environment. For example, when organizations operate within a stable environment, more of a mechanistic form (controlled and compartmentalized) would be appropriate to achieve greater efficiency; when they operate in a fast-changing environment, an organic structure (decentralized and networked) is more appropriate, as it can allow greater flexibility for innovation and adaptation (Burns and Stalker 1961; Lawrence and Lorsch 1967). "Contingency theory embraces the idea that different levels of environmental uncertainty favor different organizational forms" (Hatch 2018, 83). Therefore, perceiving and understanding the environmental characteristics in terms of level of complexity (the number and diversity of elements within the environment) and rate of change (how rapidly an environment changes) become important in forming organizational structure (Hatch 2018). However, uncertainty cannot be avoided completely because it is inherent in any environment due to political, economic, legal, or other forces (e.g., a firm's competitive situation, impact of new technology, or volatility of the market) (Hatch 2018).

The general principle of open systems theory that emphasizes the essential element of systems environments is also found in theories that consider organizational boundaries in relation to their environment. *Resource dependence theory*, explained by Pfeffer and Salancik (1978), can help determine organizational boundaries by analyzing how the environment determines the power distribution of organizations and how that affects organizational reach. Resource dependence theory views environments as necessary for organizational survival, as organizations exchange resources in them, and organizations' ability to handle resource-related uncertainties in their environment give them power (Pfeffer and Salancik 1978). In other words, "the more resources an organization controls, the greater its influence within its inter-organizational network" (Hatch 2018, 80).

Population or *organizational ecology theory* focuses more on environmental analysis than resource dependence theory does (Hatch 2018). Just like a biological ecology, where the most adaptable organisms survive, an organizational environment or ecology would select for those competitors that best adapt to the environment (Hannan and Freeman 1977; Carroll 1984). A population ecology approach can be useful to address macro aspects of organizational ecology, such as governmental or regulatory agents' practices and public policy, than to study an individual organization (Hatch 2018).

While the emphasis of organizational ecology theory is more on environmental analysis, *neo-institutional theory* is more aligned with resource dependence theory and is interested in the interconnections between organizations and their environment. Neo-institutional theory pays close attention to the notion that organizations gain social legitimacy through acceptance by society and adherence to social norms (e.g., what are considered appropriate ways to organize) (Hatch 2018). DiMaggio and Powell (1983) were advocates of this view, arguing that organizations compete for political power and institutional legitimacy as well as resources and market shares.

Of the aforementioned organization theories, those that are influenced by or closely connected to an open systems perspective are more widely used in the field of arts and cultural management, even though their connection to open systems theory is often implicit rather than explicit.

OPEN SYSTEMS THEORY IN ARTS AND CULTURAL MANAGEMENT

While the application of open systems theory to the study of arts and cultural organizations is presently rather limited, there is some movement toward using it for organizational management and research in the museum field, a subsector of arts and culture (Fopp 1997; Jung 2011; Latham and Simmons 2014; Jung and Love 2017). Additionally, by understanding open systems theory as a worldview or paradigmatic concept (Von Bertalanffy 1972), one can identify more uses of systems theory in an arts and cultural context. However, the following examples are not meant to be exhaustive; rather, they show how systems theory or closely related organization theories can be used to study arts and cultural management. When examining how open systems theory is used in an arts and cultural context, one can consider the level of application, whether macro or micro. Macro-level discussions are focused on the relationship between organizations and their environment or on how the environment influences multiple organizations or an industry. Micro-level applications are more focused on interdepartmental relationships and how individuals' mental models and actions affect the rest of their organization in relation to their external environment.

Macro-Level Application

An example of macro-level application of open systems theory is the work of Jung and Vakharia (2019), who suggest that open systems theory could be useful as arts and cultural organizations, as a sector, adapt their structure to improve their financial and nonfinancial performance. By taking an open systems approach that includes the impact of the external environment, they shed light not only on internal operations but also on how the organization engages with its broader community, not simply as a resource provider but as a partner. They suggest that in order to conduct a more holistic and thorough self-evaluation of organizational effectiveness that factors in the environmental influence, arts and cultural organizations can look beyond easy-to-measure financial data and focus on establishing nonfinancial metrics, such as degree and extent of community engagement, that could be helpful to the entire industry.

Gallagher (2020) uses organizational ecology theory to understand how the entrepreneurial climate of a city impacts the sustainability of arts and cultural organizations, offering an interesting perspective on the limited use of open systems theory to analyze the position of arts and cultural organizations within their environment. Gallagher references the work of Florida and others who have focused on the one-way benefit the arts can provide to economic development efforts, with limited (if any) consideration of how external conditions influence the operations of organizations. Gallagher's work extends to organizational ecology theory, making the case that geography plays a major role in the level of entrepreneurial activity in a given region or state. While Gallagher does not specifically point out her work as being related to open systems theory, her overall theoretical view, with its focus on the external environment, is aligned with the open systems perspective.

Resource dependence theory, a subtheory of the larger open systems theory cluster, is a lens through which to view how organizations manage their external relationships. Resource dependence theory is already common in arts and cultural research. For example, Sherer, Suddaby, and de Coquet (2019) helpfully reinforce the long-understood concept of resource diversification as an important component of successful arts management. This suggests that resource dependence theory is useful to arts organizations that wish to gain or maintain autonomy and "aesthetic freedom" while managing their dependence on external providers of key resources.

Micro-Level Application

Micro-level application of open systems theory to arts and culture is more concerned with interaction among actors and units within a system in relation to the external environment. Jung reinforces the importance of actors and smaller units to a well-functioning open system: "A person as a system of itself is part of an organization, a social system. An organization is a part of its larger community, which is part of a larger society, country, and the rest of the world" (Jung 2022, 20).

As an example of micro-level application of open systems, Kuesters (2010) used Luhmann's (1977) systems theory to examine how arts managers' roles mix artistic and financial management, drawing on Luhmann's concept of de-differentiation (societal or paradigmatic shift or meshing of boundaries between different units within the system).

Another example of micro-level application is Jung's (2022) open systems theory, based on an empirical longitudinal ethnographic study of an art museum. Observing and studying one museum over an eight-year span, Jung (2022) refined her theory of open systems, specifically contextualized for museum management. She applied different levels of analysis, including individual, departmental, organizational, and environmental, to analyze an art museum's change or inaction over time and what that reveals about how the museum has coexisted with its community. Jung (2022) emphasizes the importance of the open systems feedback loop function within the museum system, either negative or positive, resulting in either inaction or transformational change toward meaningful community engagement.

The final example of micro-level application of open systems perspective is Keeney and Jung (2018)'s systems intelligence and system leadership discussion. Keeney and Jung conducted an empirical study analyzing qualifications in arts and cultural leadership job advertisements and found that the qualities most in demand in arts and cultural leaders are closely related to systems intelligence, such as abilities to see connections between the organization and its community and to build relationships with various subcommunities and entities of that community.

OPEN SYSTEMS THEORY FOR COMMUNITY ENGAGEMENT AND DEI ISSUES

Open systems theory explains how an organization is necessarily part of its larger environment and that what the organization does internally necessarily influences its service provisions (e.g., exhibitions, performances, and programs) consumed by its community. As explained above, organizations as social systems are loosely connected by their independent, moving parts, making organizations adaptable to external environments; external environments, in turn, can influence organizations' internal structures. Open systems theory can explain how the internal structure and culture of an organization are reflected in what it creates and presents to the community, illuminating that "organizations cannot exist in isolation from their communities" (Jung 2022, 1). For example, when workers in a cultural organization do not work well together as a team and bring limited perspectives that do not represent the needs and interests of the larger community, the organization's programming would reflect both the internal work dysfunction and the mental models of the workers (i.e., ingrained ways of thinking about and doing things). This may result in the creation of programs that are not relevant to nor inclusive of most of the local community, attracting only a small proportion of the community that shares the mental models of the workers. This can lead to a conclusion that the organization is connected to one small section of the community while ignoring many other subcommunities. This is what Jung (2022) found in her research: her subject museum strived to attract diverse community members, but did so without reflecting diverse communities' perspectives and inputs; in the end it ended up attracting more people like existing museum visitors (e.g., white, highly educated, and wealthy).

The need to work with diverse communities is especially important for nonprofit or public arts and cultural organizations that have multiple purposes (mission, artistic vision, educational goals, and financial sustainability), seeking both to serve their communities and to generate something beneficial for society. The US nonprofit structure, as an example, provides a certain type of organization—that is, 501(c)(3) public benefiting organizations—with the benefits of federal income tax exemption for themselves and tax deductions for their donors (additionally, most states will honor that exemption status in regard to state income tax, property tax, and other excise taxes) (Brennen et al. 2021). These benefits act like built-in government subsidies mandating arts and cultural organizations to provide goods and services that are beneficial to the wider communities they are part of (Jung and Vakharia 2019; Jung 2018). In countries where arts and cultural organizations are primarily funded by the government, this argument for serving diverse populations becomes even stronger.

Yet most arts organizations, because of their origin, have been more concerned with serving the elite members of society. For example, the origins and practices of the Louvre and the Boston Symphony Orchestra in the nineteenth century provide a deep understanding of the creation of a system upon which mainstream arts and cultural organizations continue to operate today. The Louvre, in Paris, opened its doors to the public in 1793. While the general population was allowed to visit the museum, the motivation was to promote national power and wealth rather than to provide education or other services to the public, who were largely deemed unable to understand the high culture displayed at the museum (McClellan 2003). Likewise, on the establishment of the Museum of Fine Arts and the Boston Symphony Orchestra, DiMaggio points out that "these institutions were to provide a framework, in the visual arts and music, respectively, for the definition of high art, for its segregation from popular forms and for the elaboration of an etiquette of appropriation" (1982, 40). While both the Louvre and Boston Symphony were open to the public in a narrow sense, their establishment was meant to preserve and present the social status of a few. This is still felt in today's arts and cultural world. For example, the makeup of visual and performing arts audiences is whiter, older, more educated, and wealthier than the overall population (Farrell and Medvedeva 2010; Silber and Triplett 2015; Stein 2020).

It is interesting to note, however, that although institutions like the Boston Symphony Orchestra were founded in order to create and preserve culture for the elite, there was still a recognized need to engage with the broader population. As DiMaggio points out, "A secret or thoroughly esoteric culture could not have served to legitimate the status of American elites; it would be necessary to share it, at least partially" (1982, 48). This observation refers to the fact that Boston's elites needed the masses to legitimize and appreciate their efforts to support classical music. Therefore, even the creation of a system to enshrine high culture in the United States depended upon, interacted with, and fed off its environment, thus making it an open system.

Systems theory has the potential to change how people look at arts and cultural management research and practice and expand what arts and cultural organizations can be to broader audiences, especially when those organizations embrace the transformative power of open systems (morphogenesis, or the positive feedback function of learning, growing, and differentiating) (Macy 1991; Scott and Davis 2007). Open systems theory can help both the people who work in organizations and the researchers who study those organizations see the multiple connections that exist, especially those they were not aware of, and can help them recognize and utilize positive feedback—that is, when they receive new input from the external environment that contradicts internal practice and spurs organizations to make lasting internal and structural changes.

Understanding and studying arts and cultural organizations from the open systems perspective, therefore, can help shed light on the importance of genuine community engagement as well as DEI practices, encouraging arts and cultural organizations to pay attention to community inputs that have traditionally been ignored. Many arts and cultural organizations use the term "community engagement" to describe their programming, but the term's definition is just beginning to be codified in the literature. Borwick (2012, 14) defines community engagement as "a process whereby institutions enter into mutually beneficial relationships with other organizations, informal community groups, or individuals," making it clear that this process not only interacts with the external environment, but depends upon it. This view is reinforced by Taylor (2020, 5), who frames community engagement as "extending expectations beyond that of tacit viewer and art object to a mutually beneficial, ongoing relationship." Based upon the definitions offered by Borwick and Taylor, it is clear that a primary characteristic of community engagement involves intentional, ongoing, reciprocal, and participatory interaction with the environment—elements that are also components of open systems theory (Katz and Kahn 1966). As previously mentioned, Jung and Vakharia (2019) suggest that open systems theory could be useful as arts and cultural organizations adapt their structure to improve their financial and nonfinancial performance, with community engagement being cited as one potential area of nonfinancial performance to be better understood and assessed. Open systems theory adds important context and value to any work that aims to illuminate the process of community engagement.

The holistic and inclusive nature of open systems theory, and a management system based on it, can improve arts organizations' practice in DEI areas by reinforcing active listening and reflection on the input from diverse perspectives within and outside the walls of organizations. When this inclusive philosophy is adopted, organizations and scholars studying them can see people and communities as integrated components of the organizational system, rather than treating them as isolated entities. In this process, organizations would be more likely to listen to their diverse communities' changing needs, interests, and perspectives and create artistic and educational programs that are relevant to their local communities (Jung 2022; Jung and Vakharia 2019). When coupled with systems thinking skills adopted at the micro level of organizational practice, the impact could be much larger. For example, leaders with more systems intelligence—the ability to see the various connections and interdependent realities of many parts both internal and external to the organization—can help create culture and structure within the organization that encourage actors to see how their thinking affects the actions of others. Both actors and leaders can be more observant of and sympathetic to the needs and interests of their audiences and communities, adopting systemic ways to meet those external needs rather than focusing narrowly on the needs of their traditional audiences. By changing their culture and structure, arts and cultural organizations can become more open to multiple voices and perspectives.

One limitation of open systems theory is that it lacks a more critical and postmodern perspective, such as that found in critical systems theory or feminist systems theory. Critical systems theory criticizes the lack of acknowledgment of power differences among people within a system and the difficulty of implementing a truly democratic process of decision-making when there is a power imbalance (Bausch 2001; Flood and Jackson 1991). Without addressing the power imbalance issues and biases and preconceived notions that people bring to the table, an open systems perspective can be less practical. Feminist systems theory emphasizes the importance of including marginalized voices and seeking impactful social change, and it questions the normative approach of systems theory that comes with sexist and racist ideologies (Stephens 2013). To be mindful of and reflect on these normative ideologies, researchers must approach their subjects with multiple methodologies and perspectives that will lead to social impact (Stephens, Jacobson, and King 2010). However, application of these critical perspectives is still not prevalent in the arts and cultural research. The necessity for such perspectives needs to be more strongly emphasized, given the current elitist orientation of the arts and the heightened societal pressure on them to be more inclusive and equitable.

What is also lacking is the empirical, large-scale research that applies systems theory to arts and cultural organizations. This is due to the general lack of empirical research on organizational structures and their relationship to external factors in the arts and culture, compared to this type of research conducted in other industries (Jung and Vakharia 2019). This presents an opportunity for arts and cultural management researchers to be more deliberate in testing existing and new variables that consider both internal and external factors of arts and cultural management using open systems theory.

Conclusion

The heart of the open systems perspective is the deep connection between parts of a system, such as actors, units, and organizations, and their external environments. Its deep inclusivity of varied perspectives inside and outside the system distinguishes it from other, more compartmentalized theoretical approaches. The origins of the open systems perspective are found in both Eastern and Western broad philosophical traditions, demonstrating the immanent nature of open systems perspective. The way open systems theory has influenced prominent organization theories, some of which have already been used in the field of arts and cultural management research, albeit in a limited way, suggests that the theory could be more readily adopted in arts and cultural management research.

For arts organizations, the mutual exchange of thoughts, ideas, needs, and concerns between the organization and its community can help organizations pursue deeper engagement with the communities they serve. Its broad application and ability to be applied to both macro and micro levels make the theory versatile, justifying the argument that the theory should be one of the foundational theories of arts and cultural management. Given arts organizations' symbiotic relationship with their diverse communities and societal environment (or their stated desire to develop such a relationship), open systems characteristics are fundamental to a well-functioning arts organization. Indeed, there are examples within the arts and cultural management literature that clearly align with open systems theory but do not necessarily call it out by name. Further, arts and cultural organizations generally have an outward-facing orientation, focusing on serving their communities. Recently, more organizations have begun to move toward involving their communities as active participants and co-creators, rather than simply as passive observers (Jeanneret and Brown 2017). Open systems theory is a useful lens through which to not only conceptualize these efforts but also strengthen, support, and sustain them.

Note

1. The list of journals examined includes *Artivate*; *Arts & Health*; *Cultural Trends*; *Curator*; *European Journal of Cultural Management and Policy*; *International Journal of Arts Management*; *International Journal of Cultural Policy*; *International Journal of Nonprofit*

and *Voluntary Sector Marketing; International Journal of the Inclusive Museum; Journal of Arts Management, Law, and Society; Journal of Cultural Economics; Journal of Urban Affairs; Museum Management and Curatorship; Nonprofit and Voluntary Sector Quarterly; Nonprofit Management & Leadership; Poetics; Public Administration Review; Urban Affairs Review;* and *Voluntas.*

References

Arnold, Ross D., and Jon P. Wade. 2015. "A Definition of Systems Thinking: A Systems Approach." *Procedia Computer Science* 44: 669–678.

Ashby, W. Ross. 1952. *A Design for a Brain*. New York: John Wiley.

Bausch, Kenneth C. 2001. *The Emerging Consensus in Social Systems Theory*. New York: Kluwer Academic/Plenum.

Boulding, Kenneth E. 1956. "General Systems Theory: The Skeleton of Science." *Management Science* 2, no. 3: 197–208.

Brennen, David A., Darryll K. Jones, Beverly I. Moran, and Steven J. Willis. 2021. *The Tax Law of Charities and Other Exempt Organizations*. Durham, NC: Carolina Academic Press.

Borwick, Doug. 2012. *Building Communities, Not Audiences: The Future of the Arts in the United States* Winston-Salem, NC: ArtsEngaged.

Buckley, Walter. 1967. *Sociology and Modern Systems Theory*. Upper Saddle River, NJ: Prentice Hall.

Burns, Tom, and George M. Stalker. 1961. *The Management of Innovation*. London: Tavistock.

Carroll, Glenn R. 1984. "Organizational Ecology." *Annual Review of Sociology* 10, no. 1: 71–93.

Chang, Woong Jo, and Margaret Wyszomirski. 2015. "What Is Arts Entrepreneurship? Tracking the Development of Its Definition in Scholarly Journals." *Artivate* 4, no. 2: 11–31. https://www.jstor.org/stable/10.34053/artivate.4.2.0011.

DiMaggio, Paul. 1982. "Cultural Entrepreneurship in Nineteenth-Century Boston: The Creation of an Organizational Base for High Culture in America." *Media, Culture and Society* 4, no. 1: 33–50.

DiMaggio, Paul, and W. W. Powell. 1983. "The Iron Cage Revisited: Institutional Isomorphism and Collective Rationality in Organizational Fields." *American Sociological Review* 48, no. 2: 147–160.

Farrell, Betty, and Maria Medvedeva. 2010. *Demographic Transformation and the Future of Museums*. Washington, DC: American Association of Museums.

Flood, Robert L., and Michael C. Jackson, eds. 1991. *Critical Systems Thinking: Directed Readings*. Chichester, UK: Wiley.

Fopp, Michael. 1997. *Managing Museums and Galleries*. London: Routledge.

Gallagher, B. Kathleen. 2020. "The Roots of Great Innovation: Entrepreneurial Climate and the Sustainability of Arts and Culture Organizations." *Artivate* 9, no. 1: 67–81.

Goleman, Daniel. 1998. *Working with Emotional Intelligence*. New York: Bantam.

Hannan, Michael T., and John H. Freeman. 1977. "The Population Ecology of Organizations." *American Journal of Sociology* 91, no. 5: 481–510.

Hatch, Mary J. 2018. *Organization Theory: Modern, Symbolic, and Postmodern Perspectives*. Oxford: Oxford University Press.

Herrick, Charles, and Joanna Pratt. 2012. "Sustainability in the Water Sector: Enabling Lasting Change Through Leadership and Cultural Transformation." *Nature and Culture* 7, no. 3: 285–313. https://doi.org/10.3167/nc.2012.070303.

Jeanneret, Neryl, and Robert Brown. 2017. "Research, Practice, and Policy Connections: The ArtPlay Case Study." *Arts Education Policy Review*, no. 1, 37–50.

Jung, Yuha. 2011. "The Art Museum Ecosystem: A New Alternative Model." *Museum Management and Curatorship* 26, no. 4: 321–338.

Jung, Yuha. 2018. "Economic Discussion of Conflict Between Public Education Policies and Common Good Arts in the United States." *Journal of Arts Management, Law, and Society* 48, no. 2: 98–107. doi: 10.1080/10632921.2017.1303412.

Jung, Yuha. 2022. *Transforming Museum Management: Evidence-based Change Through Open Systems Theory*. London: Routledge/Taylor & Francis.

Jung, Yuha, and Ann Rowson Love, eds. 2017. *Systems Thinking in Museums: Theory and Practice*. Lanham, MD: Rowman and Littlefield.

Jung, Yuha, and Neville Vakharia. 2019. "Open Systems Theory for Arts and Cultural Organizations: Linking Structure and Performance." *Journal of Arts Management, Law, and Society* 49, no. 4: 257–273.

Katz, Daniel, and Robert L. Kahn. 1966. *The Social Psychology of Organizations*. New York: John Wiley & Sons.

Keeney, Kate Preston, and Yuha Jung. 2018. "Global Arts Leadership: An Exploration of Professional Standards and Demands in Arts Management." *Journal of Arts Management, Law, and Society* 48, no. 4: 227–242.

Kuesters, Ivonne. 2010. "Arts Managers as Liaisons Between Finance and Art: A Qualitative Study Inspired by the Theory of Functional Differentiation." *Journal of Arts Management, Law, and Society* 40, no. 1: 43–57.

Latham, Kiersten, and John Simmons. 2014. *Foundations of Museum Studies: Evolving Systems of Knowledge*. Westport, CT: Libraries Unlimited.

Lawrence, Paul R., and Jay W. Lorsch. 1967. "Differentiation and Integration in Complex Organizations." *Administrative Science Quarterly* 12, no. 1: 1–30.

Luhmann, Niklas. 1977. "Differentiation of Society." *Canadian Journal of Sociology* 2, no. 1:29–53.

Macy, Joanna. 1991. *Mutual Causality in Buddhism and General Systems Theory: The Dharma of Natural Systems*. Albany: State University of New York Press.

McClellan, Andrew. 2003. "A Brief History of Art Museum Public." In *Art and Its Publics: Museum Studies at the Millennium*, edited by Andrew McClellan, 1–50. Oxford: Blackwell.

Naess, Arne. 1973. "The Shallow and the Deep, Long-Range Ecology Movement. A Summary." *Inquiry* 16, no. 1-4: 95–100.

Nonprofit Finance Fund. 2013. "Nonprofit Finance Fund Survey of 5900+ Nonprofits: Organizations Innovating and Adapting to New Reality." March 25, 2013. https://www.prnewswire.com/news-releases/nonprofit-finance-fund-survey-of-5900-nonprofits-organizations-innovating-and-adapting-to-new-reality-199837941.html.

Pfeffer, Jeffrey, and Gerald R. Salancik. 1978. *The External Control of Organizations: A Resource Dependence Perspective*. New York: Harper and Row.

Rentschler, Ruth, and David Shilbury. 2008. "Academic Assessment of Arts Management Journals: A Multidimensional Rating Survey." *International Journal of Arts Management* 10, no. 3: 60–71. https://www.jstor.org/stable/41064964.

Rohter Larry. 2012. "In Europe, Where Art Is Life, Ax Falls on Public Financing." *New York Times*, March 25, 2012. https://www.nytimes.com/2012/03/25/world/europe/the-euro-crisis-is-hurting-cultural-groups.html.

Saarinen, Esa, and Raimo Hämäläinen. 2004. "Systems Intelligence: Connecting Engineering Thinking with Human Sensitivity." In *Systems Intelligence: Discovering a Hidden Competence* in *Human Action and Organizational Life*, edited by Esa Saarinen and Raimo Hämäläinen, 9–37. Helsinki: Helsinki University of Technology.

Sasaki, Yasuo. 2017. "A Note on Systems Intelligence in Knowledge Management." *The Learning Organization* 24, no. 4: 236–244.

Scott, W. Richard. 2003. *Organizations: Rational, Natural, and Open Systems*, 5th ed. Upper Saddle River, NJ: Prentice Hall.

Scott, W. Richard, and Gerald F. Davis. 2007. "Organizations as Open Systems." In *Organizations and Organizing: Rational, Natural and Open Systems Perspectives*, 87–106. New York: Routledge.

Senge, Peter. 1990. *The Fifth Discipline: The Art and Practice of the Learning Organization*. New York: Doubleday.

Senge, Peter, Hal Hamilton, and John Kania. 2015. "The Dawn of System Leadership." *Stanford Social Innovation Review* 13, no. 1: 27–33. https://ssir.org/articles/entry/the_dawn_of_system_leadership.

Shafritz, Jay M., J. Steven Ott, and Yong Suk Jang. 2016. *Classics of Organization Theory*, 8th ed. Boston, MA: Cengage Learning.

Sherer, Peter D., Roy Suddaby, and Mary Rozsa de Coquet. 2019. "Does Resource Diversity Confer Organizational Autonomy in Arts Organizations? Extending Resource Dependence Theory." *Journal of Arts Management, Law, and Society* 49, no. 4: 224–241.

Silber, Bohne, and Tim Triplett. 2015. *A Decade of Arts Engagement: Findings from the Survey of Public Participation in the Arts, 2002-2012*. Washington, DC: National Endowment for the Arts. https://www.arts.gov/sites/default/files/2012-sppa-feb2015.pdf.

Stein, Tobie S. 2020. "Racial and Ethnic Diversity in the Performing Arts Workforce." In *Racial and Ethnic Diversity in the Performing Arts Workforce*, 1–27. London and New York: Routledge.

Stephens, Anne. 2013. *Ecofeminism and Systems Thinking*. New York: Routledge.

Stephens, Anne, Chris Jacobson, and Christine King. 2010. "Towards a Feminist-Systems Theory." *Systemic Practice and Action Research* 23, no. 5: 371–386.

Taylor, Johanna K. 2020. *The Art Museum Redefined: Power, Opportunity and Community Engagement*. Cham, Switzerland: Palgrave Macmillan.

Törmänen, Juha, Raimo Hämäläinen, and Esa Saarinen. 2016. "Systems Intelligence Inventory." *The Learning Organization* 23, no. 4: 218–231.

von Bertalanffy, Ludwig. 1933. *Modern Theories of Development: An Introduction to Theoretical Biology*. Oxford: Oxford University Press.

von Bertalanffy, Ludwig. 1972. "The History and Status of General Systems Theory." *Academy of Management Journal* 15, no. 4: 23–29.

Wiener, Norbert. 1948. *Cybernetics*, Cambridge, MA: MIT Press.

CHAPTER 7

FRAMING NONPROFIT ARTS AND CULTURE SECTORS THROUGH ECONOMIC THEORY

BRUCE A. SEAMAN

INTRODUCTION

SOME observers of cultural economics have not been sanguine about its ability to adequately guide cultural policy or provide useful insights to cultural managers. One might identify three primary strains of this skepticism: (1) discordant values between economics and the cultural sector; (2) inherent limitations of a rationality-focused, constrained optimization, market equilibrium, allocative efficiency, and price-mechanism-based conventional economics; and (3) a unique susceptibility of the cultural sector to the ongoing and expanding digital technological revolution that presents further challenges to the standard tools of economics. The purpose of this chapter is to examine some of these issues and provide evidence that cultural economics as a field has been admirably open to a broader vision of economics that recognizes not only the contributions of other social science fields but also the importance of non-neoclassical strains of economic analysis. Further improvements in blending standard economics with these other perspectives are needed, but there does not seem to be a compelling case for an entirely new economics to make cultural economics relevant and useful.

Throsby (1994), Hutter (1996), Frey (2000, see chapters 1 and 2), Blaug (2001), Seaman (2009), Klamer (2016a, 2016b), and Cameron (2019a, 2019b) identify important strengths and weaknesses of economic applications to the cultural sector. In 2021, Throsby focused attention on a largely favorable assessment of those contributions to the study of creative industries, cultural heritage, and economic development, while also acknowledging the importance of the economic analysis of consumer behavior and demand, the transformative digital economy, artistic labor markets, and urban and regional issues.[1] In addition to broader methodological issues, and factors affecting arts and culture demand and participation, the narrower focus of this chapter is on evaluating market definition and competitive and market power issues related to substitution versus complementary relationships (e.g., does the television broadcast of arts performances suppress or stimulate attendance at live events? How much do sports compete with the arts?) within the cultural sector, and static and dynamic pricing strategies that can be used by cultural organizations. And it documents selected research efforts that go beyond a narrow vision of economics.

How Serious Are the Strains between Economics and Culture?

The distinction between economic and cultural values can be exaggerated (Hutter and Frey 2010), but that distinction (Throsby 2001; Choi et al. 2007), and the distinction between various *instrumental* values and *intrinsic* values (McCarthy et al. 2004) might limit the ability of economists to communicate with policymakers and cultural players. In fact, Klamer (2016a, 2016b) calls for a dramatic change to a "value-based approach to cultural economics" to rescue it from what he fears is near irrelevancy to the science of economics, the art world, and cultural policymakers. While that agenda is not entirely clear, he favorably cites research including the "nonstandard" concepts of cultural and social capital, play, happiness, and the creative commons (Klamer 2016a, 368). It might also be linked to efforts to explore the relationship between aesthetics and economics (Mossetto 1993) and to evaluations of how experimental aesthetics can clarify the complex ways that people interact with works of art (Locher 2014). Angelini and Castellani (2019) applaud Klamer's recommendation and identify cultural value as including social, spiritual, historical, symbolic, and aesthetic components. But they concede that the relationship between economic and cultural value remains an open question. Cultural value could be encompassed within economic value, could be separate but with a positive effect on economic value, or could be fundamentally distinct from economic value (Angelini and Castellani 2019).

The relative modesty of many cultural economists has multiple causes. Cowen (1998) issued a sobering warning in his "Why Everything Has Changed: The Recent Revolution in Cultural Economics," with more focus on the revolution in culture than in the tools of cultural economics, but expressed alarm about the difficulty of keeping cultural economics relevant in the face of such transformations, mostly linked to technology. Cameron (2019a) acknowledges ongoing improvements in the technical sophistication of cultural economics, but concedes it remains largely an application of conventional tools of economic analysis to somewhat unconventional issues, without avoiding the methodological weaknesses of key tools like econometrics (e.g., limited capacity to test for falsification of assumptions, research design, and conclusions, but possibly also the deficient stress on economic significance versus statistical significance, which is highly sensitive to sample size). For both Cowen and Cameron, these concerns regarding the limitations of economic analysis seem to persist even in the face of the widely admired promise shown by, for example, the insightful application of economic concepts to the often unique and changing contractual relationships historically found in the cultural sector (Caves 2000).

Cameron (2019a) further laments the lack of evidence that cultural economics research has had "any large global impact in recent times" (Cameron 2019b, 22). More dramatically, the entire enterprise of trying to improve this research and its relevance is viewed by sociologist Pratt (2020) as "beyond [the] grasp" of those applying cultural economics due to transformations in the creative economy such as the widespread replacement of firms by serial projects, the reality of extensive self-employment instead of "continuous labor markets," and the role of digitalization creating "platform monopolies," not merely as market distortions but as substitutes for markets (186). Pratt argues that only a wholesale shift to heterodox economics along with the common refrain to expand the insights of other social sciences and the humanities can save cultural economics from irrelevancy. As argued by Caust (2003), "core cultural values" need to be reasserted into cultural policymaking to save it from the economists and marketers who have "captured" it to champion a "market driven" rather than an "arts driven" agenda.

Complaints About the Weaknesses of Cultural Economics Are Sometimes Misplaced

But what does it mean to champion heterodox economics and inject core cultural values into the analysis? One problem is that heterodoxy seems to encompass an impossibly wide range of alternatives, including perspectives as diametrically opposed as Austrian and Marxian economics, and can incorporate institutional, social, and evolutionary economics, as well as a special focus on feminist and ecological perspectives. And continual heterodox demands for a more interdisciplinary approach with fields like sociology, whose actual boundary lines with economics can be opaque (Gibbons 2005), seem almost tiresome and even uninformed. Indeed, it is commonplace to acknowledge that economics overlaps with other social science fields beyond sociology (e.g., political science, anthropology, psychology) and business fields such as marketing, strategic management, finance, and decision sciences. The pages of the *Journal of Cultural Economics* and other cultural and cultural policy journals have certainly never been limited to research applying only the narrowest of economic methods. However, as with the rest of the field of economics, there has been a notable increase in the focus on technically sophisticated methods, especially in empirical analysis, arguably at the expense of innovations in conceptual creativity and a focus on addressing the real challenges facing the cultural sector.

Yet criticisms can easily miss the mark. As Throsby observed in his 2021 keynote remarks at the twenty-first biennial conference of the Association for Cultural Economics International, characterizations of cultural economists as philistines who have focused solely on the non-unique and more measurable economic impacts such as jobs, income, and regional output typically envision only a parody version of economic analysis that ignores the many criticisms by cultural economists themselves of such often inflated claims (Snowball 2008). Hardly striking a defensive tone, Cowen (1998) goes further and offers an unapologetic defense of how capitalist market economies and commercialization itself have enhanced more than threatened the development of highbrow culture, as well as disseminating popular culture. This generally optimistic assessment of the impact of relentless market forces (including digitalization) on at least for-profit sectors of culture is shared by Waldfogel (2017), who links digitalization to a "golden age" for music, movies, books, and television. In this view (Waldfogel 2017), the ongoing reduced fixed costs of producing, distributing, and advertising such products as well as the consumer benefits of increased product variety have outweighed any loss of intellectual property revenue linked to piracy (which itself has generally been reduced by streaming services that generate revenue).

The Unique Contributions of Behavioral Economics Can Be Easily Exaggerated

Coate and Hoffman (2022) highlight the previous research in cultural economics that incorporates insights from behavioral economics such as experiments, psychometrics, and psychophysiology, which address the realities of emotional response, bodily and mood changes, social contagion and the quest for popularity, and variations in psychological and language attributes of different ethnic groups. But they concede that many of their examples that have applied a "behavioral lens" are not new even if the contributions of other fields, especially psychology, "have not been paid their due" and given sufficient credit for adding key insights into economic decision-making (Coate and Hoffman 2022, 20). Their ultimate conclusion is restrained: that cultural economics has an opportunity to grow by "acknowledging and embracing behavioral economics" (Coate and Hoffman 2022, 20), so even for those not convinced by its potential, it is worth examining such opportunities.

To more clearly assess the importance of behavioral economics, it is also important to be sensitive to the way the term "behavioral" can be used. For example, when Ateca-Amestoy and Prieto-Rodriguez (2013) evaluate the forecasting ability of behavioral models of arts participation (attending jazz concerts or visiting museums and art galleries) they do not rely on any insightful concepts from psychology applied to behavioral economics. Instead, they evaluate the forecasting ability of latent class count regression models to determine if the estimated causal relationships between standard independent variables and arts participation for the in-sample population can be extrapolated to the forecasted behavior of the out-of-sample population. They find that such predicted extrapolation is successful, but this technical point is not a good example of the unique and valuable insights behavioral economics can provide regarding anomalous behavioral patterns and the limits to rational decision-making and information processing.

It is wise to celebrate but remain cautious about the research benefits of the seemingly "irrational" decisions highlighted in behavioral economics, since some of those valuable insights (such as the systematic tendency to weight expected losses more heavily than equal expected gains) that challenge standard utility or income maximization models are variations on much older themes. Leibenstein (1950) surveyed the history of the non-additivity problem in consumer demand theory (i.e., the degree to which market demand is the simple sum of individual demands) focusing on fashions, bandwagon and snob effects (being more or less likely to buy something because others are doing so), social taboos, and Veblen conspicuous consumption effects (the purchase of expensive goods and services to publicly display one's wealth rather than for their consumption benefits), tracing some of these insights to as early as before 1834. And the asymmetry in valuation caused by the endowment effect (an important behavioral economics insight about the tendency to require more compensation for losing something you own than you would be willing to pay to acquire it in the first place) is important, but asymmetries in valuation are also common in microeconomic theory. Standard utility theory distinguishes compensating variations in income from equivalent variations in income and except for special cases, those will not be equal. That is, the additional income needed to compensate for a bad outcome (e.g., a price increase, or by extension losing a piece of art you currently own) is generally higher than the income one would pay to achieve a good outcome (avoiding the price increase, or by extension, obtaining a piece of art you do not currently own).

In summary, there is no denying that the application of insights from psychology that have led to the rise of behavioral economics and a rethinking of the very meaning of rational behavior have great potential in examining consumer and supplier decisions in the cultural sector, where motives are generally assumed to be more complex than mere utility or income maximization models can capture. But as further illustrated below, cultural economics did not have to await the rise of behavioral economics and an enhanced focus on the complexity of psychological and social influences on behavior to incorporate some of those insights into its research.

For example, performing arts attendance and demand studies have long incorporated various lifestyle determinants, as well as racial, peer group, and spousal effects (the role played by friends, colleagues, spouses, and significant others in determining one's participation in the arts), gender, and, less often, sexual orientation factors into empirical studies without linking them explicitly to a behavioral economics or core values foundation. In fact, Andreasen and Belk (1980) argued that lifestyle, attitudes, and socialization can be more reliable predictors of attendance than demographic and socioeconomic factors. They identify the dimensions of optimism, hedonism, traditionalism, passivity/homebody, inner-directedness, self-sufficiency, and "eclecticism" among important traits affecting arts attendance. "Qualitative" audience surveys over three different types of performances, interdisciplinary motivational scaling methods, and factor analysis are used by Swanson, Davis, and Zhao (2008) to examine differential motivations for attending arts performances, finding that aesthetic, educational, recreational, and self-esteem motivations are most closely linked to regular attendees, while the only occasional audience was motivated more by escapism. In contrast to sports studies, social interaction was not an important motive (Swanson, Davis, and Zhao 2008).

But the skepticism about the payoff from new approaches to cultural economics expressed above is not inconsistent with supporting more aggressive incorporation of behavioral economics and insights from psychology and other social sciences. Other important improvements include the further exploitation of larger and more reliable databases and, as recommended by Cameron (2019b), the adoption of meta-analysis quantitative techniques as well as more qualitative methods. Furthermore, applying insights from happiness studies is also growing in the arts but still faces the common challenge of isolating directional causal relationships (Hand 2018; Wheatley and Bickerton 2017, 2019). An example of the application of happiness research to arts and sports activities is discussed later in this chapter.

THE COMPETITION PROBLEM IN ECONOMICS

Dramatic digital technological changes present challenges and opportunities to providers of cultural services, and highlight an issue that has rarely been central in cultural economics: how competitive is the provision of cultural goods and services, and how prone is that economic sector to artificially created market power?[2]

The ability of economic analysis to address this question is complicated by a long-standing methodological dispute regarding the meaning of competition and market efficiency that long predates cultural economics. It is generally acknowledged that economics giants like Adam Smith, Alfred Marshall, and Joseph Schumpeter discussed the merits of dynamic, creatively destructive, and process competition quite differently than the long-run purely competitive equilibrium and static allocational efficiency focus of microeconomic theory (e.g., Nelson and Winter 1977; Rothbard 2012). Issues like market definition may have less meaning in the kinds of dynamic settings that the digital age has further enhanced. Audretsch, Baumol, and Burke (2001) introduce a series of papers devoted to "competition policy in dynamic markets" that highlight the inadequacies of static economic models and the traditional preoccupation with price competition. They explain how the evolution of the economic analysis of dynamic competition has adopted key elements of the Austrian emphasis on a limited supply of entrepreneurial resources and the importance of incentives in generating welfare-enhancing product and process innovation, even if accompanied by pockets of temporary market power.

CULTURAL EXAMPLES OF MARKET TESTS OF COMPLEMENTARITY VERSUS COMPETITIVE SUBSTITUTION

Both United States and European antitrust enforcers have adopted the SSNIP test (small but significant nontransitory increase in price) or hypothetical monopolist test as a standard conceptualization of market analysis. Although this approach is well grounded in the economic theory of the relationship between market power and price, the mechanics and data requirements can render it difficult to implement compared to more qualitative and descriptive metrics (e.g., similarity of product characteristics and cost; similarity of distribution systems and of customers targeted). It becomes especially problematic in zero or ambiguous price environments, or when other forms of competition such as consumer information and attention cost or product quality and variety are especially important and might justify adapting the "small but significant" framework to those alternative metrics rather than to prices (Mandrescu 2018).

Important market definition tests might focus on the relative movements over time in the quantities sold or market shares of competing candidates for the relevant market. An important example from the for-profit cultural sector is whether there is a separate "theatrical movie market" in contrast to a "home/mobile entertainment market" (including both physical—e.g., CD/DVD, and alternative digital dimensions). Rather than a complex SSNIP analysis of pricing power, one might search for direct versus inverse quantity relationships over time. One such analysis argues that since the theatrical market for films has had steady box office revenue (not including pandemic effects) whereas digital home entertainment has increased each year while physical forms of home entertainment have declined each year, one should view digital and physical home entertainment options as one market and theatrical film attendance as a separate market (Marciszewski 2020).

Another example where economic theory provides ambiguous predictions is whether the increasingly prevalent live broadcasting of music, dance, and theatrical performances by prominent arts organizations has a positive (complementary) or negative (substitution) impact on local live arts performance attendance. Theoretically, it is unclear whether such external live high-quality broadcasts promote or cannibalize local live theater attendance. In a "quasi-field experiment," it was found that the Royal National Theatre's live theater broadcasts to cinemas in the United Kingdom seems to have increased the size of audiences inside that theater itself (Bakhshi and Throsby 2014).

In a significant extension using the very large Audience Finder database of 16 million box office transactions across fifty-four performing arts organizations, Bakhshi and Whitby (2014) examined whether attendance at other theaters (not just the Royal National Theatre) had also increased in the wake of such live theater broadcasts from London. Recognizing that endogeneity bias could skew the results since those local theaters that would opt for National Theatre Live likely already had favorable demographics for high local audience attendance, they focused on the change over time in the geographic distribution in ticket sales. Their findings were generally consistent with the demand stimulation (complementarity) theory rather than the cannibalization (substitution) theory. On average, local areas within a three-kilometer radius of a cinema showing Royal National Theatre broadcasts witnessed a 5 percent increase in local theater attendance over the following twelve months. However, this beneficial effect was driven by London-area theaters, which experienced an average 6.4 percent attendance increase. Outside London, there was no measurable effect in either direction.

The relationship between live performing arts attendance and the availability of similar online content was a burgeoning issue prior to COVID-19. In contrast to the substantial literature exploring the effect of file-sharing and piracy (and to a lesser extent legal streaming) on the sale of for-profit recordings and live attendance at for-profit concerts, there is less currently known about the effect of online consumption and attendance at live performing arts events and visits to museums. This relatively young literature has generally identified either no major negative effects or that the complementary effects of digital options on live performance and museum attendance outweigh substitution relationships across varying settings in different countries. Using a survey of internet users in France and Brittany, Nguyen, Dejean, and Moreau (2014) explored the effects of legal streaming of music (e.g., Spotify, YouTube, and Deezer) on both offline music sales (e.g., CD's) and attendance at live concerts. They distinguished among three different types of music: international and national stars, local musical talent, and classical music, and found (unlike most studies of file-sharing) that streaming did not adversely affect offline music CD sales, and actually increased attendance at concerts of international and national star music artists. There was no such boost in attendance at performances by local musicians or at classical music concerts, but also no notable negative effects, a result they properly report with caution inasmuch as they surmise that the lack of visibility of classical and local-artist music on streaming sites is a major reason for that result.

Evrard and Krebs (2018) examine the real versus virtual experience in the case of the Louvre and find complementarity between those two dimensions of the overall cultural experience, and conclude that for all types of consumers, there is "no equivalence between the digital experience and the visit to a museum" (358). De la Vega et al. (2020) identify an important case using Spanish data where complementarity between online consumption and live attendance at theater, ballet, opera, Spanish operetta, and classical music performances seems to outweigh the competitive substitution threat. They note that high prices for live performances along with an absence of available supply options in some regions can limit the attendance of current performing arts consumers and allow them to meet a kind of excess demand for live performance by turning to online options, a complementary effect supported by their empirical evidence for various musical performing art forms. De la Vega et al. (2020) find that this effect is not as prevalent for theater-goers who are less likely to watch a play online, where "partial" consumption with more flexible time commitments is less of an option. A major issue has been whether online accessibility, even if complementary to in-person live attendance, can expand audiences for the performing arts in contrast to further reinforcing existing socioeconomic inequalities in highbrow performing arts consumption. They recognize that since the complementarities they find seem to be especially prevalent for those who were already performing arts patrons, the degree of new audience creation may be limited, but can be stimulated by a more creative use of online communication to advertise more accessible prices, new productions, and the unique benefits of an in-person arts experience.

Ateca-Amestoy and Castiglione (2022) uncover more nuanced interactions between digital and live museum and art gallery engagement when distinguishing between hand-held and mobile devices in contrast to desktop internet access. Using the 2012 USA Survey of Public Participation in the Arts, they find strong complementarity between live visual arts visits and hand-held/mobile device internet exposure, but non-mobile internet consumption does not affect on-site visits. They also find that live visual arts attendance has become even more feminized and linked to income, urban residency and higher education and occupations requiring more education (with education having the strongest effect on all forms of access, a result that has been found in participation, attendance studies over decades). Among their recommendations for museum/art gallery managements is to further improve their physical displays and consider implementing some form of on-line fees for their on-line collections to safeguard revenues.

A creative nonprice market test was applied to the museum sector in Italy (galleries and museums but also monuments, archeological areas, and parks). Cellini, Cuccia, and Lisi (2020) investigated 2015 museum census data from the Italian Statistics Institute to determine whether various museum services (a total of thirty-seven) provided by private and government museums linked to enhancing accessibility (e.g., more flexible opening times including evenings and special events), the quality of a museum visit (e.g., brochures, audio guides, tour guides, childcare options) and the availability of internet services are sensitive to the provision of such services by potentially competing neighboring museums (within the same province). Finding such regional sensitivity confirms the expected reality that while individual museums will clearly be differentiated with a varying product mix of collection, conservation, research, and exhibition activities, it is unlikely that museum managers would view their individual institutions as so unique that such spatial effects could be totally ignored.

However, Cellini, Cuccia, and Lisi (2020) recognized that even if such spatial influences on service provision are found, it is unclear whether the primary reason is (1) a "strategic interdependence" regarding the competition for visitors, (2) peer pressure among museum managers who are concerned about their personal and institutional reputations, or (3) other factors. The econometric model they use controls for many independent variables, and separate subsample estimations are made regarding private and government (public) museums, but the key focus is on the public or private "spatial lag" variable (to capture "neighborhood effects"), constructed as the average number of services provided by other museums in the same province. Although the subsample estimations do not address the neighborhood effects of private on public or public on private museums, the most striking result is no evidence of spatial interdependency among private museums, but a positive and highly statistically significant spatial effect on public museums. Of special interest is the intriguing suggestion by Cellini, Cuccia, and Lisi (2020) that this asymmetry in neighborhood effects offers little support for a theory of traditional market competition among museums, since they surmise that if such competition were to exist it would be especially evident among private museums, where by contrast neighborhood interdependency is in fact absent in their data. Relying in part on the institutional setting of public museums in Italy, they suggest that the greater sensitivity of public museums to spatial effects from other museums is more reflective of peer and reputational (scientific and social recognition) pressure among public museum managers rather than competitive interdependence across regions.

The Broader Market for Leisure Activities versus a Market for the Arts: Theory and Evidence

In their analysis of the decision to allocate leisure time between active engagement in sports and cultural activities, Hallman et al. (2017) cite modeling innovations originally made by Gary Becker. Both the Becker (1965) and Stigler and Becker (1977) versions of consumer theory are linked to household production, and they make the important distinction between Z ultimate commodities (with "culture" as a possible Z commodity) that enter the utility function and X market goods and services that enter the household production function (e.g., tickets to a play), along with t (time) and "embodied human capital" (H) as productive inputs, subject to a full income budget constraint that is exhausted by money spending and opportunity cost of time spending. It was motivated to avoid relying on "taste variations" as a default explanation of behavior, instead deriving a wider variety of constraint variations linked to shadow relative price and full income differences. But even the Hallman et al. (2017) study does not focus on important concepts from the Becker consumer household production model such as "cross marginal productivity" effects between the X market goods across various art forms or between broader categories like sports and the arts, or time spent in sports and various arts activities, or the possible endogenous effect of arts, sports, or other leisure activities on embodied human capital. Such productivity effects could reduce the shadow price of Z culture so as to generate substitution and real income effects that increase the consumption of the ultimate commodity Z culture and increase the utilization of both X arts and X sports market goods (and time on both activities) devoted to producing that additional quantity of culture. This important contribution to consumer choice theory has never been fully exploited in the cultural economics literature.

The Lancaster product characteristics analysis (1966) has also been compared to Bourdieu (1989) in examining cultural products and "social space," but with only bullfights and circuses as the alternative to arts activities (Sintas and Álvarez 2002). Lévy-Garboua and Montmarquette (2011) do not focus on sports versus the arts, but their taste-cultivation model is consistent with a negative relationship between the consumption of popular culture and the kind of highbrow artistic consumption that tends to rise with the accumulation of "specific consumption capital." Those examples only hint at substitution relationships that would justify broader markets in order to better understand competitive interactions in the nonprofit arts. Suggesting instead quite narrow markets, McKenzie and Shin (2020) observe that some demand studies have recently emphasized the role of information asymmetry and the discounting of other cultures by native consumers, along with superstar theories and the increasing availability of micro-level data on sales transactions to focus on single highly differentiated cultural products, at least in the for-profit cultural industries.

Fernandez-Blanco and Prieto-Rodriguez (2001) examined those attending live sports events, attending the cinema, and listening to music using Spanish data. They conclude that sports "do not compete against the consumption of music or cinema" (using a bivariate probit estimation of a three-equation system, generating positive error covariances among all three activities). Those authors used the same approach to address whether popular and classical music listeners substantially overlap (Prieto-Rodriguez and Fernandez-Blanco 2000), and also found evidence of what might be called complementarity inasmuch as those listening to classical music are also highly likely to listen to popular music. But unfortunately, as with sports versus the arts, there is no clear causal connection that, for example, makes classical music listening more productive at appreciating popular music, and their conclusion is fully consistent with the simple idea that people who enjoy live entertainment and social events tend to consume all types of such events/attractions (such people are often called omnivores). That is, they identify a common background and "innate taste for music" such that "if you are a music fan, you listen to both classical and popular music" (Prieto-Rodriguez and Fernandez-Blanco 2000,155).

By contrast, Montgomery and Robinson (2006) expressed skepticism about such complementary relationships related to arts and sports activities and found more mixed evidence using data from the United States Performing Arts Research Coalition. They use a model similar to Fernandez-Blanco and Prieto-Rodriguez (2001) but with continuous (natural log of number of times attended) rather than binary probit (attend or not attend) modeling, and examine attendance at performing arts events (e.g., orchestra, opera, theater, dance), sports (amateur and professional), and popular events (e.g., comedy, rock concert, clubs, movies). When they generate the error covariances between equations for percentage of attendance (attendance share) at various events, controlling for both total attendance and attendee demographic characteristics, their results are quite varied (and different from the case of total attendance): (1) within the performing arts group, covariances are positive and significant, suggesting complements; (2) other covariances are negative, suggesting substitutes, but they are not particularly strong between performing arts and the two sports categories. The strongest substitution relationship was between sports and movies, and movies also have the strongest substitution relationship with performing arts events and with popular events. This is consistent with Sanchez, Elliott, and Simmons (2016, 3848) who found a "large and robust negative effect of mega-sports events on cinema admissions."

The relationship between cultural consumption and other popular entertainment options like video games is addressed by Borowiecki and Prieto-Rodriguez (2015). That study exhibits two challenges in drawing firm conclusions about substitution versus complementary relationships affecting the nonprofit arts: (1) as they observe, reliable pricing data are typically not available to estimate traditional cross price elasticities between video games and other cultural options; and (2) the significance for nonprofit arts managers of their complementarity finding that the probability of game playing increases with the consumption of other cultural goods is weakened by "other cultural goods," focusing on listening to music or watching television, both very common activities popular among the younger and less well educated demographic group that they link to high levels of video game playing. A more optimistic finding for the arts may be that the probability of video game playing also increases with active activities such as writing and visual arts production.

In another allocation of time analysis, Muñiz, Rodriguez, and Suárez (2011) utilized data from the Time Use Survey in Spain. As with the Hallman et al. (2017) study using longitudinal data from the German Socio-Economic Panel that found largely a complementary relationship between active engagement in arts and active engagement in sports activities, they did not limit their analysis to "passive" consumption activities, but also focused on active cultural and sports types of participation. For example, time spent on sports activity (hours/day) was defined as active (walking, playing football, going to the gym, fishing, and swimming; it also included dancing, which appears as an active cultural activity as well), and passive (attending sporting events). And time spent on cultural participation was also active (painting, sculpture, ceramics, graphics, pottery, making movies, singing, dancing, playing musical instruments, writing prose or poetry), and passive (attending cultural events). This study uses constant elasticity of substitution (CES) utility functions along with many demographic control variables, and assumes the opportunity cost of time is the same between sports and the arts, but does not utilize explicit price data. As is common in this literature, the positive correlation between the residuals in the sports and arts equations are utilized from their bivariate probit estimations, as both probability of participation and amount of time allocated, to suggest a complementary relationship.

How does this 2011 Spanish study compare to the Hallman et al. 2017 German analysis? Sports and arts participation is measured by Hallman et al. based on answers to the panel survey questions about the frequency of active participation and sports, and art or musical activities.

Sports and cultural participation as dependent variables are estimated simultaneously using a bivariate probit model, with many demographic control variables, including "satisfaction with current life," on a 1–10 scale. Again, there are no price variables. They claim that their model is at least consistent with Becker household production optimization subject to money and time constraints. Their results indicate that the types of activities are interrelated, with correlation of the errors of both equations consistent with modest complementarity. A positive relationship is found between human capital and sports and cultural participation, but as usual, this is measured as "exogenous education" with no explicit interdependency between cultural consumption capital and sports consumption capital, as would be suggested by the Becker model.

Existing Incorporation of Intrinsic Benefits Linked to Happiness Research

As noted at the outset, when identifying potential limitations of the application of economics to culture one of the criticisms of cultural economics is that insufficient attention is paid to the intrinsic benefits of the arts, values and emotions, and the increasingly large literature on "happiness research." Happiness research has not yet had a strong explicit impact on cultural economics, despite Frey and Stutzer (2002) identifying its potential contributions to the broader field of economics. Happiness can be distinguished from the concept of psychic income as it affects artist or athlete labor supply decisions (with psychic income potentially providing an important alternative to money income). In fact, a number of papers have addressed this issue with relevance to the arts and cultural sectors. For example, Downward and Rascuite (2011) ask whether sport makes people happy, previewing how this question could be adapted to arts and culture. Two helpful overview treatments with implications for arts and culture research are Throsby's *Economics and Culture* (2001) and Ateca-Amestoy's "Leisure and Subjective Well-Being" (2011).

Research integrating arts, culture, and sport with a focus on subjective well-being is being done by Wheatly and Bickerton (2017, 2019), working in economics, statistics, and management. A prior review of the quality of life and well-being in culture and sport was provided by Galloway et al. (2006). Wheatly and Bickerton (2017) utilize data from wave 2 (2010–2011) of the United Kingdom Household Longitudinal Study (a multitopic longitudinal survey of forty thousand households selected in 2008). Included are arts activities (51.5 percent report engaging at least once in the past year), arts events (67.9 percent, with concerts and cinema cited most often), museums (34.8 percent), libraries (31.4 percent), archives (4.1 percent), historical sites (57.7 percent), moderate-intensity sports (58.8 percent, with 31.5 percent engaging weekly), and mild-intensity sports (55.4 percent, with 21.1 percent engaging weekly).

Mean satisfaction levels for those engaging or not engaging in the various activities (on a Likert scale of 1–7) are derived for the criteria "satisfied with life," "satisfied with the amount of leisure time," and "satisfied with job," and also for "general happiness" (measured on a 1–4 Likert scale). They report ANOVA-significant (1 percent) differences in mean satisfaction "with life" linked to engaging or not engaging in various segments within arts and culture. Generally, the relative mean satisfaction levels are similar whether for "satisfied with life," "satisfied with amount of leisure time," "satisfied with job," or "general happiness." The results for the key activities are reported, with the first number being the happiness index score for those engaging in the activity and the second number applicable to those not engaging in that activity. For arts activities the index scores were 4.86 and 4.67; for arts events, 4.80 and 4.86 (meaning that life satisfaction was reduced by engagement); library scores were 4.89 and 4.78; archives, 4.98 and 4.81; museums, 4.86 and 4.79; and historical sites, 4.85 and 4.76. ANOVA-significant (1%) differences in mean life satisfaction linked to engaging or not engaging in sports can be compared with those cited above for the arts and culture as follows: moderate-intensity sport, 4.79 compared to 4.87 (that is, a life satisfaction reduction when engaged); mild-intensity sport, 4.82 and 4.81, suggesting almost no effect of engagement. But it is noteworthy that satisfaction with the amount of leisure time is greater among those engaging in both moderate- and mild-intensity sport compared to those not engaging at all, and both of those sports activities have a positive effect on general happiness. It is also striking that differences between those engaging or not engaging in both sports and all of the arts categories are statistically *insignificant* with regard to job satisfaction. At least regarding life satisfaction, these results provide modest evidence favoring the arts activities, but the sports categories involved more strenuous direct activity in contrast to some of the arts activities that were more clearly spectator-focused rather than involving direct participation, making direct comparisons more difficult. And differences using the measures other than life satisfaction seem limited.

This type of research does not prove that economists are devoting sufficient attention to this less traditional kind of analysis, but it belies the criticism that economists doing research related to arts and culture are uninterested or unengaged in these issues. The limited evidence cited suggests that satisfaction with arts and cultural activities compared reasonably well to those in sports, although those comparisons do *not* apply to more passive consumer-oriented participation in the arts compared to sport, which would be of more interest to nonprofit arts and cultural organizations assessing any potential competitive threat from the sports sector for leisure/entertainment spending.

Benefits Linked to Child Development, Education, and Health: Mozart Effects and Pelé Effects

Economists also have not ignored the role that arts/culture and sport might play in producing "better" (not just happier) people. This can also include the effects on a spirit of cooperation, discipline, and work habits. Conversely, some studies address the damage that can be caused by arts and sports due to excessive emotional pressure, injuries, and excessive competitive zeal. Arts enthusiasts have long hoped that there were indeed favorable feedback effects from the study of music (or even just listening to it) and broader educational outcomes, but evidence of this so-called Mozart effect can be hard to generate. By extending the argument to participation in sports, a Pelé effect (named in honor of the Brazilian football legend) might be identified.

Cabane, Hille, and Lechner (2016) find some support for both effects using the German Socio-Economic Panel Study (SOEP) by investigating the effects of adolescents' participation in music and sports. The survey asks whether respondents play a musical instrument or pursue singing seriously, followed by questions regarding what type, whether alone or in a group, starting age, and whether they take music lessons outside of school. Similar general questions are asked about sport: "Do you play sports?" followed by asking about the most important sport played, where it is played, starting age, and how often they participate in organized sports competitions. There are also questions related to educational achievements and plans, and cognitive (measured by standardized tests) and noncognitive skills (from the SOEP youth questionnaire linked to five personality traits: conscientiousness, openness, extroversion, neuroticism, and agreeableness). Educational success is measured with respondent's school type and whether university study is envisioned, and recent school grades are provided in mathematics, German, and a foreign language. Health measures and school attendance information are also available.

There are many interesting findings in Cabane, Hille, and Lechner (2016) that suggest additional payoffs from expanding this kind of research, but one key comparative result is that playing music fosters better educational outcomes compared to doing sports, particularly for girls and for children from more highly educated families. However, doing sports is especially good at improving subjective perceptions of health (no evidence is provided about objective measures). Doing both music and sport was the surest route to educational success, suggesting some complementarity in effectiveness between the arts and sports. That these results were reported in the journal *Labour Economics* is consistent with the argument that economists have not been ignoring these broader "intrinsic" benefits of cultural activities, and that such research is available to those specializing in cultural economics.

Prices May Not Be Critical for Market Definition but Pricing Strategies Remain Important

Static price discrimination of various types, including de facto tying contracts between fixed and variable charges, are common in the arts. They have been extensively studied for the for-profit popular music concert industry, but with insights for nonprofit arts managers as well (Courty and Pagliero 2014). Rushton (2015) provides a comprehensive analysis of the many pricing strategies that can be employed in the arts, including the nonprofit performing arts, museums, and festivals. Baldin et al. (2018) provide a sophisticated analysis of the interrelationship between price variations across seating sections and the allocation of seats to such sections, and how those choices vary with the competing goals of revenue maximization and attendance maximization.

Dynamic pricing is not yet widely used in the nonprofit arts world but has the potential to be a useful additional pricing tool in the nonprofit sector, even if not as valuable as for many for-profit organizations, including sports franchises (Seaman 2018). It has been used in situations where temporal demand differences are important, and buyers can be segmented based on whether they can pre-commit to buy early or must (or may choose to) wait to buy closer to the time when goods and services are rendered. The two primary dynamic pricing approaches are (1) peak-load pricing (or time-of-use pricing) and (2) yield management, which essentially prices a perishable commodity like airline seats, hotel rooms, and more recently entertainment venue seats based on the changing available unfilled capacity over time, typically relative to a benchmark of expected unfilled capacity, such that if there are more unfilled seats or rooms than projected by some target number of days prior to them "perishing," prices are reduced (and prices are increased if there are fewer available).

Dynamic pricing can effectively supplement the various forms of static price discrimination and has become relatively common in American sports. Pricing varies with such short-run supply and demand factors such as team opponent, weather conditions, and recent performance of the home team (Paul and Weinbach 2013). But such strategies have not yet been as common with sports organizations outside the United States, with a study of FC Bayern Munich's possible adoption of dynamic pricing suggesting large potential revenue gains if it were adopted (Kemper and Breuer 2016).

More sophisticated pricing strategies are also increasingly being attempted by arts organizations, such as the Chicago Symphony Orchestra, Sydney Opera House, Goodman Theatre in Chicago, and the Center Theatre Group in Los Angeles. The Chicago Symphony Orchestra (CSO) experience has been especially dramatic, exploiting both static and dynamic pricing strategies, as described in detail by Ravanas (2008). He reports that the CSO notably increased its percentage of subscription sales and renewals, reduced marketing expenses, and reduced the number of unfilled seats by re-evaluating its pricing related to seat location, types of programming, times of day, days of the week, season of the year, and time of purchase. It increased its seating price categories from thirteen to twenty based on concentric squares around the center of the main seating area (and significantly increased average price in some sections while reducing it in others). After evaluating its past ticketing experiences over seventy years of programming, it also increased average price for some programs and reduced them for others, while also increasing the variability of its prices between matinees and evenings, midweek and weekend, and seasons of the year and holidays. Especially related to more dynamic strategies, it increased the incentives for subscribers to buy early and in greater quantities relative to single ticket sales, and, focusing on yield management, it increased the frequency with which it reevaluated its entire pricing scales so as to better adjust to either higher-than-expected or lower-than-expected seat sales.

Ravanas (2008) also describes various challenges and internal opposition the CSO faced in implementing these strategies. Nonprofit arts organizations especially can struggle with conflicting objectives that make it more difficult to adopt dynamic pricing strategies that focus on revenue generation rather than audience-building or artistic objectives (Labaronne and Slembeck 2015). Therefore, such aggressive pricing approaches confront complex implementation problems as well as managerial resistance despite their potential for generating critical revenue in markets challenged by the external shocks of ever-changing technologies and even pandemics.

Conclusion

Cultural economists seem to be especially aware of the limitations of standard theoretical tools (e.g., utility and profit maximization, price as the key allocation of resource mechanism, and market equilibrium) and sophisticated empirical models (e.g., distinguishing causality from correlation, economic versus statistical significance, and the challenges in falsifying hypotheses). But even when giving a fair hearing to calls for significant methodological improvements and greatly improved data quality, the review in this chapter of the research that is being done (and in some cases has been done for a long time) suggests a less pessimistic assessment of how much dramatic reform of cultural economics research is needed. Key parts of the criticisms about an undue stress on quantitative versus qualitative and value issues, a failure to adapt standard models to incorporate behavioral, psychological, and sociological determinants of behavior, and failures to adequately account for the dramatic consumption, production, and organizational changes created by the digital revolution are being addressed, even if inadequately, and it is important not to continually bash a straw-man version of what economics is and what economists do. The contributions of an enlightened and flexible version of economic analysis to the issues confronting arts and culture decision-makers continue to be valuable even in the absence of the methodological revolution that some both inside and outside of cultural economics champion.

Notes

1. His keynote presentation to the virtual 21st Biannual Conference of the Association of Cultural Economics International 2021 was titled "The Relevance of Cultural Economics for Cultural Policy." He also documented the topics most commonly addressed since 2001 in key cultural economics and cultural policy academic journals, with the *Journal of Cultural Economics* focused upon demand and consumer behavior, markets and finance, supply and firm behavior, international trade, and cultural/artistic labor topics, but with notable

increases from 2011 to 2020 in papers addressing heritage and urban/city issues. *Cultural Trends* frequently publishes research on demand, consumer behavior, and labor topics, but also on creative industries, policy reviews, and cultural institutions. The *International Journal of Cultural Policy* focuses on creative industries, but also urban and regional issues and heritage (with substantial increases in the past ten years in those three areas), as well as cultural diplomacy and cultural policy theory and practice.
2. This is different from just presuming local market power and using essentially monopoly models without much analysis of competitive forces to analyze the behavior of nonprofit arts organizations; see Seaman (2004).

References

Andreasen, A., and R. W. Belk. 1980. "Predictors of Attendance at the Performing Arts." *Journal of Consumer Research* 7: 112–120.

Angelini, Francesco, and Massimiliano Castellani. 2019. "Cultural and Economic Value: A Critical Review." *Journal of Cultural Economics* 43, no. 2: 173–188. https://doi.org/10.1007/s10824-018-9334-4.

Ateca-Amestoy, Victoria M. 2011. "Leisure and Subjective Well-Being." In *Handbook on the Economics of Leisure*, edited by Samuel Cameron, 52–78. Cheltenham, UK: Edward Elgar.

Ateca-Amestoy, Victoria M., and Juan Prieto-Rodriguez. 2013. "Forecasting Accuracy of Behavioural Models for Participation in the Arts." *European Journal of Operational Research* 229, no. 1: 124–131.

Ateca-Amestoy, Victoria, and Concetta Castiglione. 2022. "Live and Digital Engagement with the Visual Arts." *Journal of Cultural Economics*. Published online December 26, 2022. https://doi.org/10.1007/s10824-022-09466-3.

Audretsch, David B., William J. Baumol, and Andrew E. Burke. 2001. "Competition Policy in Dynamic Markets." *International Journal of Industrial Organization* 19: 613–634.

Baldin, Andrea, Trine Bille, Andrea Ellero, and Daniela Favaretto. 2018. "Revenue and Attendance Simultaneous Optimization in Performing Arts Organizations." *Journal of Cultural Economics* 42, no. 4: 677–700. https://doi.org/10.1007/s10824-018-9323-7.

Bakhshi, Hasan, and David Throsby. 2014. "Digital Complements or Substitutes? A Quasi-Field Experiment from the Royal National Theatre." *Journal of Cultural Economics* 38, no 1:1–18. doi:10.1007/s10824-013-9201-2.

Bakhshi, Hasan, and Andrew Whitby. 2014. "Estimating the Impact of Live Simulcast on Theatre Attendance: An Application to London's National Theatre." NESTA Working Paper 14/04, June. www.nesta.org.uk/wp14-04.

Baumol, William J., and William G. Bowen. 1965. "On the Performing Arts: The Anatomy of Their Economic Problems." *American Economic Review* 50, no. 2: 495–502.

Baumol, William J., and William G. Bowen. 1966. *Performing Arts: The Economic Dilemma*. New York: Twentieth Century Fund.

Becker, Gary S. 1965. "A Theory of the Allocation of Time." *Economic Journal* 75: 493–517.

Blaug, Mark. (Ed.) 1976. *The Economics of the Arts: Selected Readings*. London and Boulder CO: Westview Press and Martin Robertson.

Blaug, Mark. 2001. "Where Are We Now in Cultural Economics?" *Journal of Economic Surveys* 15, no. 2: 123–143.

Borowiecki, Karol J., and Juan Prieto-Rodriguez. 2015. "Video Games Playing: A Substitute for Cultural Consumption?" *Journal of Cultural Economics* 39, no. 3: 239–258. doi: 10.1007/s10824-014-9229-y.

Bourdieu, Pierre. 1989. "Social Space and Symbolic Power." *Sociological Theory* 7, no 1: 14–25.

Cabane, Charlotte, Adrian Hille, and Michael Lechner. 2016. "Mozart or Pelé: The Effects of Adolescents' Participation in Music and Sports." *Labour Economics* 41: 90–103. https://doi.org/10.1016/j.labeco.2016.05.012.

Cameron, Samuel. 2019a. "Contemporary Challenges to Cultural Economics." In *A Research Agenda for Cultural Economics*, edited by Samuel Cameron, 21–40. Cheltenham, UK: Edward Elgar. doi: 10.4337/9781788112314.

Cameron, Samuel. 2019b. "What Is the Agenda for Cultural Economics?" In *A Research Agenda for Cultural Economics*, edited by Samuel Cameron, 166–174. Cheltenham, UK: Edward Elgar. doi: 10.4337/9781788112314.

Caust, Jo. 2003. "Policy Making: How Arts Policy Has Been 'Captured' by the Economists and the Marketers." *International Journal of Cultural Policy* 9, no. 1: 51–63. doi: 10.1080/1028663032000089723.

Caves, Richard E. 2000. *Creative Industries: Contracts Between Art and Commerce*. Cambridge, MA: Harvard University Press.

Cellini, Roberto, Tiziana Cuccia, and Domenico Lisi. 2020. "Spatial Dependence in Museum Services: An Analysis of the Italian Case." *Journal of Cultural Economics* 44, no. 4: 535–562. https://doi.org/10.1007/s10824-019-09373-0.

Choi, Andy S., Franco Papandrea, and Jeff Bennett. 2007. "Assessing Cultural Values: Developing an Attitudinal Scale." *Journal of Cultural Economics* 31, no. 4: 311–335. doi: 10.1007/s10824-007-9045-8.

Coate, Bronwyn, and Robert Hoffman. 2022. "The Behavioral Economics of Culture." *Journal of Cultural Economics* 46: 3–26. https://doi.org/10.1007/s10824-021-09419-2.

Courty, Pascal, and Mario Pagliero. 2014. "The Pricing of Art and the Art of Pricing; Pricing Styles in the Concert Industry." In *Handbooks in Economics: Art and Culture*, vol. 2, edited by Victor A. Ginsburgh and David Throsby, 299–356. Amsterdam: Elsevier B.V.

Cowen, Tyler. 1998. *In Praise of Commercial Culture*. Cambridge, MA: Harvard University Press.

De la Vega, Pablo, Sara Suarez-Fernández, David-Boto-Garcia, and Juan Prieto-Rodríguez. 2020. "Playing a Play: Online and Live Performing Arts Consumers Profiles and the Role of Supply Constraints." *Journal of Cultural Economics* 44, no. 3: 425–450. https://doi.org/10.1007/s10824-019-09367-y.

Downward, Paul, and Simona Rasciute. 2011. "Does Sport Make You Happy? An Analysis of the Well-Being Derived from Sports Participation." *International Review of Applied Economics* 25, no. 3: 331–348. doi:10/1080/02192171.2019.511168.

Evrard, Yves, and Anne Krebs. 2018. "The Authenticity of the Museum Experience in the Digital Age: The Case of the Louvre." *Journal of Cultural Economics* 42, no. 3: 353–363. https://doi.org/10.1077/s10824-017-9209-x.

Fernández-Blanco, Victor. and Juan Prieto-Rodríguez. 2001. "Are Live Sports Substitutes for Cultural Consumption? Some Evidence from the Spanish Case." In *Economia do Desporto*, edited by Muradalli Ibrahimo, Zorro Mendes, and Fernando Tenreiro. Lisbon: Editora Vulgata.

Frey, Bruno. 2000. *Arts and Economics: Analysis and Cultural Policy*. Berlin: Springer-Verlag.

Frey, Bruno, and Alois Stutzer. 2002. "What Can Economists Learn from Happiness Research?" *Journal of Economic Literature* 40: 402–435.

Galloway, S., D. Bell, C. Hamilton, and A. Scullion. 2006. *Quality of Life and Well-Being: Measuring the Benefits of Culture and Sport: Literature Review and Think-Piece*. Edinburgh: Analytical Services Division, Scottish Executive Education Department.

Gibbons, Robert. 2005. "What Is Economic Sociology and Should Any Economist Care?" *Journal of Economic Perspectives* 19, no. 1: 3–7.

Hallman, Kirstin, Christina Muñiz Artime, Christoph Breuer, Sören Dallmeyer, and Magnus Metz. 2017. "Leisure Participation: Modeling the Decision to Engage in Sports and Culture." *Journal of Cultural Economics* 41, no. 4: 467–487.

Hand, Chris. 2018. "Do the Arts Make You Happy? A Quintile Regression Approach." *Journal of Cultural Economics* 42, no. 2: 271–286. https://doi.org/10.1007/s10824-017-9302-4.

Hutter, Michael. 1996. "The Impact of Cultural Economics on Economic Theory." *Journal of Cultural Economics* 20, no. 2: 263–268.

Hutter, Michael, and Bruno S. Frey. 2010. "On the Influence of Cultural Value on Economic Value." *Revue d'Economie Politique* 120, no. 1: 35–46. doi: 10.3917/redp.201.0035.

Kemper, Christoph, and Christoph Breuer. 2016. "How Efficient Is Dynamic Pricing for Sports Events? Designing a Dynamic Pricing Model for Bayern Munich." *International Journal of Sport Finance* 11: 4–25.

Klamer, Arjo. 2016a. "The Value-Based Approach to Cultural Economics." *Journal of Cultural Economics* 40, no. 4: 365–373.

Klamer, Arjo. 2016b. *Doing the Right Thing: A Value Based Economy*. Hilversum, Netherlands: SEC.

Labaronne, Leticia, and Tilman Slembeck. 2015. "Dynamic Pricing in Nonprofit Performing Arts." *International Journal of Nonprofit and Voluntary Sector Marketing* 20: 140–154.

Lancaster, Kelvin J. 1966. "A New Approach to Consumer Theory." *Journal of Political Economy* 74, no 2: 132–157. https://doi.org/10.1086/259131.

Leibenstein, Harvey. 1950. "Bandwagon, Snob and Veblen Effects in the Theory of Consumers' Demand." *Quarterly Journal of Economics* 64, no. 2: 183–207.

Levy-Garboua, Louis, and Claude Montmarquette. 2011. "Demand." In *A Handbook of Cultural Economics*, 2nd ed., edited by Ruth Towse, 177–189. Cheltenham, UK: Edward Elgar.

Locher, Paul J. 2014. "Contemporary Experimental Aesthetics: Procedures and Findings." In *Handbooks in Economics: Art and Culture*, vol. 2, edited by Victor A. Ginsburgh and David Throsby, 49–80. Amsterdam: Elsevier B.V.

Mandrescu, Daniel. 2018. "The SSNIP Test and Zero Pricing Strategies: Considerations for Online Platforms." *European Data Protection Review* 4: 244–257.

Marciszewski, Mark. 2020. "The Paramount Decrees and Block Booking: Why Block Booking Would Still Be a Threat to Competition in the Modern Film Industry." *Vermont Law Review* 45: 227–285.

McCarthy, Kevin F., Elizabeth H. Ondaaje, Laura Zakaras, and Arthur Brooks. 2004. *Gifts of the Muse: Reframing the Debate About the Benefits of the Arts*. Santa Monica, CA: RAND.

McKenzie, Jordi, and Sunny Y. Shin. 2020. "Demand." In *A Handbook of Cultural Economics*, 3rd ed., edited by Ruth Towse and Trilce Navarrete Hernández, 216–227. Cheltenham, UK: Edward Elgar. doi: 10.4337/978788975803.

Montgomery, Sarah S., and Michel D. Robinson. 2006. "Take Me Out to the Opera: Are Sports and Arts Complements? Evidence from the Performing Arts Research Coalition Data." *International Journal of Arts Management* 8, no. 2: 24–37.

Mossetto, Gianfranco. 1993. *Aesthetics and Economics*. Boston: Kluwer.

Muñiz, Christina, Plácido Rodriguez, and Maria J. Suárez. 2011. "The Allocation of Time to Sports and Cultural Activities: An Analysis of Individual Decisions." *International Journal of Sport Finance* 6: 245–264.

Nelson, Richard R., and Sidney G. Winter. 1977. "Simulation of Schumpeterian Competition." *American Economic Review* 67, no. 1: 271–276.

Nguyen, Godefroy Dang, Sylvain Dejean, and François Moreau. 2014. "On the Complementarity Between Online and Offline Music Consumption: The Case of Free Streaming." *Journal of Cultural Economics* 38, no. 4: 315–330. doi:10.1007/s10824-013-9208-8.

Paul, Rodney, and Andrew Weinbach. 2013. "Determinants of Dynamic Pricing Premiums in Major League Baseball." *Sport Marketing Quarterly* 22: 152–165.

Peacock, Alan. 1969. "Welfare Economics and Public Subsidies for the Arts." *Manchester School of Economic and Social Studies* 37, no. 4: 323–335.

Pratt, Andy C. 2020. "Review of S. Cameron (ed.): *A Research Agenda for Cultural Economics*." *Journal of Cultural Economics* 44, no. 1: 185–187. https://doi.org/10.1007/s10824-020-09383-3.

Prieto-Rodríguez, Juan, and Victor Fernández-Blanco. 2000. "Are Popular and Classical Music Listeners the Same People?" *Journal of Cultural Economics* 24, no. 2: 147–164.

Ravanas, Philippe. 2008. "Company Profile: Hitting a High Note: The Chicago Symphony Reverses a Decade of Decline with New Programs, New Services and New Prices." *International Journal of Arts Management* 10, no. 2 68–78.

Rothbard, Murray N. 2012. "Competition and the Economists." *Quarterly Journal of Austrian Economics* 15, no. 4: 396–409.

Rushton, Michel. 2015. *Strategic Pricing for the Arts*. London: Routledge. https://doi.org/10.4324/9781315883144.

Sanchez, Sofia Izquierdo, Caroline Elliott, and Robert Simmons. 2016. "Substitution Between Leisure Activities: A Quasi-Natural Experiment Using Sports Viewing and Cinema Attendance." *Applied Economics* 48, no. 40: 3848–3860. doi: 10.1080/00036846.2016.1145353.

Seaman, Bruce A. 2004. "Competition and the Non-Profit Arts; The Lost Industrial Organization Agenda." *Journal of Cultural Economics* 28, no. 1: 167–193.

Seaman, Bruce A. 2009. "Cultural Economics: State of the Arts and Perspectives." *Estudios de Economía Aplicada* 27, no. 1: 7–32.

Seaman, Bruce A. 2018. "Static and Dynamic Pricing Strategies; How Unique for Nonprofits?" In *Handbook of Research on Nonprofit Economics and Management*, 2nd ed., edited by Bruce A. Seaman and Dennis R. Young, 199–224. Cheltenham, UK: Edward Elgar. doi:10.4337/9781785363528.

Sintas, Jordi, and Ercilia Álvarez. 2002. "The Consumption of Cultural Products: An Analysis of the Spanish Social Space." *Journal of Cultural Economics* 26, no. 2: 115–138.

Snowball, Jeanette D. 2008. *Measuring the Value of Culture: Methods and Examples in Cultural Economics*. Berlin, Heidelberg: Springer Verlag.

Stigler, George, and Gary Becker. 1977. "De Gustibus Non Est Disputandum." *American Economic Review* 67: 76–90. http://www.jstor.org/stable/1807222.

Swanson, Scott R., J. Charlene Davis, and Yushan Zhao. 2008. "Art for Arts Sake? An Examination of Motives for Arts Performance Attendance." *Nonprofit and Voluntary Sector Quarterly* 37, no. 2: 300–323.

Throsby, David. C. 1994. "The Production and Consumption of the Arts: A View of Cultural Economics." *Journal of Economic Literature* 32, no. 1: 1–29.

Throsby, David 2001. *Economics and Culture*. Cambridge: Cambridge University Press.

Throsby, David C., and Glenn A. Withers. 1979. *The Economics of the Performing Arts*. London: Edward Arnold.

Waldfogel, Joel. 2017. "How Digitalization Has Created a Golden Age of Music, Movies, Books and Television." *Journal of Economic Perspectives* 31, no. 3: 195–214. doi: 10.1257/jep.31.3.195.

Wheatley, Daniel, and Craig Bickerton. 2017. "Subjective Well-Being and Engagement in Arts, Culture and Sport." *Journal of Cultural Economics* 41, no. 1: 23–45. doi:10.1007/s10824-016-9270-0.

Wheatley, Daniel, and Craig Bickerton. 2019. "Measuring Changes in Subjective Well-Being from Engagement in the Arts, Culture and Sport." *Journal of Cultural Economics* 43, no. 3: 421–442. https://doi.org/10.1007/s10824-019-9342-7.

CHAPTER 8

MAPPING THEORIES IN ARTS AND CULTURAL MANAGEMENT RESEARCH

KATE KEENEY AND YUHA JUNG

Introduction

A relatively new academic discipline, arts management is truly interdisciplinary—informed by multiple existing fields including the arts, management, and sociology, to name a few. Paquette and Redaelli (2015) make a further distinction, defining arts management cultural policy as transdisciplinary through the integration of academic knowledge via practitioners, policymakers, researchers, and communities. In an investigation of how the arts management discipline has evolved over time, Evard and Colbert (2000) note that it is the practice of arts and arts' close relationship to society that distinguish arts management as its own subdiscipline situated within the theoretical structure of management. The authors further argue that, "while still a part of management, arts management has also, over the years, evolved into a specific body of knowledge, placing it in a class of its own" (Evard and Colbert 2000, 9). Therefore, while we refer to the field of arts and culture management as a singular form, there is an implication of plurality, as the field is made up of interdisciplinary, interconnected fields of study. This research employs a targeted literature review and analysis to extend understanding of theoretical application in arts management research and suggest broader theoretical adoption in arts management education and practice.

Although there are many indications that arts management has grown to be a clear discipline (or at least a subdiscipline), the field continues to rely on a wide array of theoretical knowledge that has been borrowed from other fields (Paquette 2019). Additionally, Paquette and Redaelli (2015, 10) note that arts management discourse "does not have a strong enough system of meanings to be able to develop communicative rhetoric that reaches the research paper format," which is an indication of a defined discipline. This position leaves scholars and practitioners with questions and an uncertain grounding as theory develops outside of the arts management discipline. If indeed the study of arts management is reliant on blending theory and practice, what theories should be understood and how have they developed over time? Theory-based evidence formed through repeated observations and empirical research allows organizations to predict new issues and be confident in addressing them. Such evidence is especially important given the changing practice and pressures on arts organizations caused by the global pandemic, economic downturn, and civil unrest. In response to these external pressures, many arts organizations are eager to adopt related structural and systemic changes. Therefore, the application of theories in research advocated in this paper has potential to influence practice in a positive and meaningful way.

Not only is theory-based evidence needed in practice, but also this knowledge is essential in arts management education. Arts management education developed from the management field in the 1960s (Paquette and Redaelli 2015) and has grown with professional organizations and numerous graduate and undergraduate programs primarily in the United States and Europe. If we use the field's US-based curriculum standards as one point of reference (AAAE 2014, 2018), it is apparent that theoretical knowledge is presented in the understanding of the creative process and in the study of leadership and management in the organizational context. According to these standards, leadership and organizational management are two of the few pronounced theoretical concepts that should be mastered by both undergraduate and graduate students. A growing interest in arts management doctoral education is another signal for this demand and maturation of the academic field. Related doctoral programs show the interdisciplinary nature of the discipline and are affiliated with programs in public affairs, education, and cultural policy.

Framed by Bourdieu's theory of practice (1990, 1993), we employ a systematic literature review (SLR) to understand the interdisciplinary theoretical contributions to arts management research. This SLR expands upon theoretical mapping work by Jung (2017). In the present research, the authors reviewed 36 academic journals of interest and ultimately found evidence of theory in arts management research in a sample of 19 journals and 297 articles. The SLR method provides research objectivity in that it is replicable and gives evidence regarding which theories are commonly used in arts management research and how they are used. We acknowledge that any academic conversation is evolving and dependent upon dispositions (i.e., how different theories are used and duplicated) of those who participate in the field's conversation (Bourdieu 1990, 1993).

Findings shine light on the theoretical foundation of arts management, including what theoretical knowledge most informs the field and what may be missing. We make connections among theories that are dominant in the field and expose gaps in understanding that may inform our approaches in arts management education and practice.

Conceptual Framework

Bourdieu's theory of practice (1990, 1993) implies that agents operate based on their tacit practical logic and embodied learning that influence and are influenced by their context or field rather than based on explicit or economic rationality (Hatch 2018). The important concepts of Bourdieu's theory are *habitus, field, capital,* and *practice.*

According to Bourdieu (1990), the *habitus*—a system of dispositions and ways of being in relation to others and the environments—is often taken for granted and is internal to each field. Drawing on ideas by French sociologist and anthropologist Marcel Mauss (1982), who thought learned habits are shaped by the culture they are part of, Bourdieu defined a habitus as a way actors internalize the social order, which becomes visible when one practices within the field. Insiders, or field members, can maintain a field and its hierarchies without noticing their own involvement, thus making intentional and transformative change difficult (Bourdieu 1990). Applying this concept to arts management and this research, one can conceive of habitus as a shared set of dispositions internal to the members of the field. The ways in which scholars repeatedly apply theories, or entertain certain subfields but not others, are part of our habitus.

Bourdieu (1990) defines a *field*, such as an academic field or a class, as a structure of hierarchical relationships based on different forms of *capital*. For example, the arts management field is structured by cultural capital (e.g., educational qualifications); the social field, by social capital (e.g., leading to honors and titles through networks and use of connections); the academic field, by academic capital; the economic field, by economic capital; and the list goes on (Hatch 2018). Thus, the field of arts management as an academic field or discipline is structured by academic capital that is specific to arts management. For example, academic capital may be defined by field members' potential and possibilities for success, such as their education, knowledge, and publication records. Like the way in which cultural capital is "embodied in styles of speech, gesture, dress, and physical appearance" (Hatch 2018, 139) arts management academic capital is reflected in the ways we do research, write, publish, and network. For example, knowledge of certain theories as capital influences how we study certain phenomena. Capital explains the continuing process of reproducing social orders (Bourdieu 1986).

Bourdieu (1990) explained a *practice*—the embodiment of shared rules, values, and processes—as repeatable actions informed by shared knowledge among actors in a field. Practice requires active exercising to achieve a desired outcome, whether it is to gain a skill, knowledge, or expertise, often requiring one to embody continuous practice (e.g., absorbing knowledge about and techniques of playing an instrument in the process of mastering it). When each field interacts with other fields, class and power established within each field interact with those in other fields in determining who has enough power to influence not only their own field but also other fields as well (Bourdieu 1990). People who have power are reluctant to give up their power, finding ways to reinforce their dominance in a given field or fields and not wanting to change the social structure they benefit from. Because of this tendency, often change is incremental rather than revolutionary, though a field is transformable (Bourdieu 1990; Hatch 2018).

While the relationship among habitus, practice, field, and capital cannot be reduced to a simple formula that would fit all situations, Bourdieu (1984) suggests the following equation for understanding: [(habitus)(capital)] + field = practice (Smith 2020). To apply it to theory use in the arts and cultural management field, and borrowing the understanding of Maton (2014), the interconnections between scholars' dispositions (habitus, such as how certain theories are used in the field) and their position in the field (capital, such as education, prestige of one's academic position, understanding of certain theories and knowledge, and publication record) can determine what kind of theories are duplicated and more widely used in the practice of arts management research given the current social state of the field (which is growing and interdisciplinary in nature).

Therefore, to understand the practice of the arts management field, it is necessary to identify and map habitus (theoretical dispositions) that have been shaped by arts and cultural management academic capital over time, reproducing the social and academic orders. By focusing on mapping of habitus (i.e., use-patterns of theories of arts and cultural management research), we can explore the tacit understanding of how our field operates and influences researchers' behaviors (e.g., use of certain theories while not utilizing others).

THEORETICAL MAPPING IN ARTS MANAGEMENT

The precursor of the current work is Jung's (2017) theoretical mapping in arts management. This paper examined theories used in one arts management journal, the *Journal of Arts Management, Law, and Society*, between 1990 and 2014. Jung (2017) used a systematic literature review and qualitative content analysis to identify, recognize, and connect theories that are represented in this specific journal. One contribution of the paper was to demonstrate that arts management scholars bring theories from many different disciplinary areas and that they work fluently in related areas such as public administration and business administration.

Discussion on theory use in arts management exists but is often limited to one area of theories or general progression of research including theories. Paquette and Redaelli (2015) discuss theories and concepts that are relevant to managerial considerations in arts management and include organizational thinking about larger, environmental aspects of complexity and interconnectedness in organization theories. For example, they discuss the open-systems conception (e.g., Lawrence and Lorsch 1967), new institutional theory (Powell and DiMaggio 1991), and theorization of power within the organizational context (e.g., Pfeffer 1981). Yet Paquette and Redaelli (2015) mainly discuss *organizational theories*, as opposed to the broader mapping of all relevant theories, which is the focus of the current research.

Rosewall and Shane (2018) edited a four-volume anthology designed to address critical current and past topics and theoretical models based on existing publications. Although not a mapping project, the compilation provides foundational or influential work in shaping arts and cultural management research. The anthology covers four critical developmental areas: leadership and governance, cultural policy, resource development, and participation and engagement. While the volume includes theoretical and conceptual articles, the focus is the field's progression of research topics and ideas.

The present mapping research is distinguishable from the two examples above in that it covers a wide variety of disciplinary theories, not just organizational theories, and focuses on theory development and progression. Therefore, it contributes to existing theoretical knowledge in two ways. We focus only on theories used in arts and cultural management (distinguishing this project from Rosewall and Shane's 2018 work) drawn from multiple academic journals (adding to Jung's 2017 work). This approach allows us to factor in the interdisciplinary nature of the field(s) and expands theoretical findings beyond organization and policy related theories (Paquette and Redaelli 2015).

Research Methods

Traditional literature reviews are "used to manage the diversity of knowledge for a specific academic inquiry," yet are criticized as introducing bias by the researcher (Tranfield, Denyer, and Smart 2003, 208). Systematic literature reviews (SLRs) differ in that they are systematic, transparent, and replicable (Tranfield, Denyer, and Smart 2003). Given the interdisciplinary and evolving nature of arts management scholarship, the SLR allows researchers to map the field, both historically and looking forward. This SLR was completed in spring 2021.

Search Criteria and Data Extraction

The first step in our research process was to identify arts-management-related scholarship defined by academic journals. We relied in part on previous publications (Chang and Wyszomirski 2015; Rentschler and Shilbury 2008) as well as our existing knowledge of related academic journals to determine a pool of journals that represented the diverse disciplines that inform the field, including museum management, creativity and business, nonprofit management, urban planning, and public administration. We developed an initial pool of thirty-six journals of interest.

After establishing a pool of journals, we then systematically collected data by using keyword searches to review and sort through abstracts. We searched all journal articles that were available to us digitally through our respective institutional libraries. For arts-and-culture-related journals, we searched abstracts for "theor*" (to obtain "theory," "theories," "theoretical," "theorizing," etc.). For journals from other disciplines, we expanded the search to include "art*" and "cultur*." Once we had completed the keyword search, we reviewed each abstract to determine its suitability for this research on theoretical applications in arts management scholarship. After reviewing the abstracts for appropriateness, we narrowed the sample to 312 articles from nineteen journals. Seventeen journals that we had originally included in the search sample were eliminated, as they did not contain abstracts with the keyword search criteria. We did not include book reviews, nor did we include all uses of the word "theory" and related words. For example, while we reviewed statements such as that a particular research project "advances theory" or "presents a theoretical framework," we did not always include them due to lack of a mention of the specific theories used. We collected identifying characteristics for each article and stored these data in Microsoft Excel.

Coding Approach and Process

We used abductive logic, based on an existing inventory (Ferraro and Beunza 2018), to develop a codebook. The codebook was based on Jung's (2017) categorization of nine major groups of theories that emerged from arts management scholarship: art, legal, sociology, psychology, policy, political, management and organization, marketing, and economic theories. After a review of our sample and the initial coding process, we expanded the codebook to fourteen theory categories. The five additional theory categories were pedagogy/education, museology, philosophy, critical theory, and communication. We coded each article for theories used, sometimes finding as many as four unique theories. After the coding process, we eliminated some articles that were originally included in the sample from the keyword search. For example, some abstracts include the term "theor*" but do not expand upon a specific theory in the research. After the coding process, we had 297 articles in the sample. We completed coding individually, after which we discussed results and reviewed each other's codes. When there was disagreement, we discussed the assigned code(s) and came to consensus.

Although systematic literature reviews are replicable (Tranfield, Denyer, and Smart 2003), we acknowledge that authors' contributions to the search parameters and coding procedures introduce subjectivity to the qualitative research process (Strauss and Corbin 1990). In short, research is a value-laden process (Glaser and Strauss 1967). We acknowledge the possibilities of a single theory meeting the definition of more than one major theory category. For example, agency theory—which explains the relationship or transaction between a principal and an agent—is an economic principle that is foundational to the interdisciplinary fields of management, organizations, and public administration (Kessler 2013). Additionally, the SLR process shed light on issues related to the definitions of a discipline versus a theory. For example, is museology a discipline or a theory? For this research, we selected a single theory code for each theory that best fit the application in the arts management context and used this coding scheme consistently throughout the research. Lastly, we were presented with the application of both theorists and theories in extant literature. We note that theorists (e.g., Pierre Bourdieu,

Karl Marx, etc.) are different from theories. However, for this mapping exercise we treated them similarly, as arts management scholars apply a theory or the work of a theorist in similar ways in the research process.

This research method was limited by the materials available to us in digital form through our academic libraries. Additionally, the SLR was limited to keyword searches performed in journal abstracts. This approach was based on other SLRs (Batory and Svensson 2019) but is not the only way to map scholarship. These findings lead to a general understanding of theories used in arts management research and could serve as a basis to develop pedagogical tools.

Results and Analysis

Results reveal that numerous disciplines and related theories contribute to arts management scholarship. Although the interdisciplinary nature of arts management scholarship is not surprising, this close inspection not only offers knowledge about what theories are dominant but also may explain the lack of "theorizing" that Paquette (2019) has observed. The arts management field is built upon a patchwork of existing knowledge ranging from economic to aesthetic. If we only look at confined arts management academic spaces (e.g., arts management or administration journals), the scope and use of theories used in the field may seem narrower than they are. This traditional theoretical foundation explains aspects of the nature of art creation, artists, arts organizations, and artistic value but presents challenges for researchers who are working to track and advance theories in the field. Importantly, these findings extend beyond "arts management journals" to understand the current, idiosyncratic social state of the field that is growing and interdisciplinary in nature.

Table 8.1 presents the summary findings of dominant theories in arts management scholarship and establishes a form of habitus that is central to the field. Habitus, which is often taken for granted, is internal to each field and only becomes visible when it is actually practiced (how theories are used) (Bourdieu 1990). Through exploring dispositions of the field in its growing and interdisciplinary state, we reveal the dominant theories used and the patterns of use in different subfields. By understanding the members' capital in terms of how and what they publish in what subfields, we can understand a more accurate and wider view of theoretical dispositions and how they have been duplicated while leaving gaps in some areas, thus reproducing social and academic orders within our field.

Dominant Theories in Arts Management Scholarship

Sociological theories were the most-cited theories from this sample (78). Sociology emerged as a dominant theory because of the common use of Bourdieu's theories, such

Table 8.1. Dominant Theories in Arts Management Scholarship

Theory codes and subcodes	No. of articles	Definition	Example theories and theorists from research sample	Dominant journals (at least 2 or more articles)
Sociology	78	Theoretical assumptions and normative concerns about the world and those in it, including individuals, societies, processes, and institutions (Hurst 2018).	Actor-network theory; Henri Lefebvre; identity theory; institutional logics theory; Karl Marx; network theory; social constructionism; Pierre Bourdieu's cultural production; intersectionality; sociology of religion	*Poetics*; *Journal of Arts Management, Law, and Society*; *Museum Management and Curatorship*; *International Journal of the Inclusive Museum*; *International Journal of Cultural Policy*; *International Journal of Arts Management*; *European Journal of Cultural Management and Policy*; *Curator*; *Cultural Trends*; *City and Community*, *Arts and Health*
Economics	62	Theories that predict the behavior of consumers (irrational or rational) and the way they make use of scarce resources (Richardson 2003). Market for and economic value of the arts.	Agency theory; central place theory; economic cluster theory; game theory; resource dependency theory; Richard Florida; superstars	*Cultural Trends*; *International Journal of Arts Management*; *International Journal of Cultural Policy*; *Journal of Cultural Economics*; *Museum Management and Curatorship*; *Nonprofit and Voluntary Sector Quarterly*
Management: Leadership (3) Marketing (10)	33	Theories that explain motivating, influencing, or leading individuals or groups informally or formally (Kessler 2013).	Branding theory; leadership theories; new public management; relationship marketing; stakeholder theory	*Curator*; *International Journal of Arts Management*; *International Journal of Cultural Policy*; *International Journal of Nonprofit and Voluntary Sector Marketing*; *Journal of Arts Management, Law, and Society*; *Museum Management and Curatorship*; *Nonprofit and Voluntary Sector Quarterly*
Organizations	29	The impact of organizations on the behavior of those within them and vice versa. The impact of organizations on social systems and the environment and vice versa (Pfeffer 1997).	Competing values framework; institutional theory; neo-institutional theory; open systems theory; organizational ecology	*International Journal of Arts Management*; *International Journal of Cultural Policy*; *International Journal of the Inclusive Museum*; *Journal of Arts Management, Law, and Society*; *Museum Management and Curatorship*

Category	#	Description	Theories/Concepts	Journals
Policy/Political Legal (2) Includes political philosophy, political theory and thought, public administration theory	27	Theories that explain democracy, justice, legitimacy. The nature and purpose of the state and roles of public organizations and actors (Frederickson et al. 2015; Shapiro 2002).	Cultural theory; public governance theories; advocacy coalitions; multiple streams framework; theories of hegemony; theories of democracy and participation	*Artivate*; *European Journal of Cultural Management and Policy*; *International Journal of Cultural Policy*; *Journal of Arts Management, Law, and Society*
Pedagogy/Education	19	The observation of teachers and students in learning environments and the process of learning or knowledge production (Ladson-Billings 1995). Overlaps with psychology and processes of cognitive development.	Constructivism; contextual learning; curriculum theories; John Dewey; situated learning; theory of exploration; theory of knowledge	*Curator*; *International Journal of the Inclusive Museum*; *Museum Management and Curatorship*
Psychology	19	Theories and science of the mind and behavior, including the behaviors of individuals or groups (APA n.d.). Behavioral and human science (Pérez-Álvarez 2018)	Behavioral psychology; experiential learning; identity construction; narrative theory; recovery theory; social cognitive learning; social learning theory	*Artivate*; *Arts in Health*; *Curator*; *International Journal of Arts Management*; *Journal of Arts Management, Law, and Society*; *Museum Management and Curatorship*
Museology	18	Museum studies research. The changing social role of museums and museum values (Brown and Mairesse 2018).	Collections management theories; ideas-people-objects model (IPO); new museology; museum sound theory	*Curator*; *International Journal of the Inclusive Museum*; *Museum Management and Curatorship*
Philosophy	17	Arguments and thought processes that examine, analyze, and clarify concepts, including beliefs, reality, morality, and existence (Warburton 2013).	John Dewey, Jürgen Habermas, Michel Foucault; meta-ethics and normative ethics	*Curator*; *International Journal of Cultural Policy*; *Museum Management and Curatorship*
Critical Theory	11	Theories that offer a departure, critique, or "emancipation" from traditional theory and knowledge (Macdonald 2017; Delgado and Stefancic 2017).	Critical; feminist; queer; race	*International Journal of the Inclusive Museum*; *Museum Management and Curatorship*

(continued)

Table 8.1. Continued

Theory codes and subcodes	No. of articles	Definition	Example theories and theorists from research sample	Dominant journals (at least 2 or more articles)
Entrepreneurship	11	Theories that explain the ways in which innovative people and organizations develop new products and services. The environments and contexts that promote entrepreneurship (Baker and Welter 2020).	Effectuation theory	Artivate
Communication	8	Theories that aid in understanding the process of communication (one-way, two-way, etc.) (van Ruler 2018; Littlejohn and Foss 2008).	Communication and design theory; dialogic theory; linguistics	Curator; International Journal of the Inclusive Museum; Museum Management and Curatorship
Art	5	Philosophical theories of what art is. The function and value of art to people and societies. The aims and means of art (Berger 2000).	Aesthetics; instrumentalism; literary theory	Cultural Trends; Journal of Arts Management, Law, and Society; Museum Management and Curatorship
Other	6	N/A	Archival theory; conservation theory; ecology theory; service-design-related theories; theology	

Note: Authors relied on previous research (including Jung 2017) and the SLR to develop fourteen theory categories. Subcodes are included in the total number of articles.

as the theory of cultural production (Bourdieu 1993). Additionally, sociology emerged as a common secondary code, indicating that authors relied on sociology and other theoretical disciplines (economics, entrepreneurship, critical theory, organizations, etc.) to advance research. The expansive domain of sociology heavily informs multiple disciplines, including management and artistic expression. The reliance on sociology reflects the established field of cultural sociology (Dewey 1959; Bourdieu 1984, 1986, 1990, 1993) and early arts management scholarship, most notably the work of Paul DiMaggio (1976, 1983, 1988). Sociology's influence on the field raises questions about the common alignment of arts management education with management and business. Although management is informed by sociology, most often through organizational theory, the management discipline is devoid of concepts related to cultural sociology, for example.

The second-most-common theoretical area was economics (62). Importantly, and as we expand upon later in the chapter, the prevalence of economic theories is explained in part by a single journal, *Journal of Cultural Economics*. Of the sixty-two economics-related articles, almost half (25) came from this source. Additionally, economic theory was common in several of the journals that emphasized nonprofit and public management (without an arts focus) and in journals with a focus on cultural policy. Jung (2017) reported on authors' academic associations in her discussion of articles inclusive of economic theory. Here, some scholars were associated with departments of economics and cultural economics outside of the United States. This connection appears less common across arts management curricula, as cultural economics is not an explicit competency at the undergraduate or graduate level in the United States (AAAE 2014, 2018). However, any discussion of cultural policy and public funding—considered foundational knowledge—is dependent upon an understanding of the economic implications of public subsidy in any context. A foundational work that underscores the influence of economic theory on the field is Baumol and Bowen's *Performing Arts: The Economic Dilemma* (1966).

In a rough tie for third place were management (33), organizations (29), and policy/political legal (27), with more or less equivalent levels of prominence in the sample. Again, organizational and managerial theories overlap, especially in the application of organizational management—a common theme in arts management education (Jung 2017). Given the prevalence of both, and the numerous theories applied in the present research, we separated management and organizations into two distinct theory categories. In delineating this separation, we coded leadership and marketing theory, among others, as management. Codes for organizational theory include theories that connect organizations as systems. Recent calls for arts organizations to be more attentive to their communities and their external environments suggest heightened importance of better connecting organizational theory to management and practice.

We organized the next most prevalent theoretical category as a combination of political theory and philosophy, policy, and legal theories (27). We recognize that these disciplines are unique, but they relate in terms of application in arts management scholarship. Of this sample, there was emphasis on cultural policy, including the appropriate role of the state and processes of support for the arts. Legal theories were the least prevalent (2).

Less prominent theories include pedagogy/education (19), psychology (19), museology (18), philosophy (17), critical theory (11), communication (8), art (6), and others (5). Five of these theory categories are additions to Jung's 2017 mapping effort: pedagogy/education, museology, philosophy, communication, and critical theory. Pedagogical theory is not normally considered a core component of arts management knowledge, so this was a surprising and informative result. Knowing more about how people process and obtain knowledge is very relevant to the work of arts organizations, many of which express a commitment to education and/or enlightenment. There is some overlap between the pedagogy/education and psychology codes (thirty-eight total codes), specifically as it relates to the process of learning. Given the presence of theories related to education, pedagogy/education and psychology, and the ways in which people learn about and from the arts, may be a future focus for arts management scholarship and education.

Museology is also worth expanding upon as a term that is used indiscriminately as both a theory and a discipline. All coded articles came from museum-specific journals, which indicates that museology as a theory is adopted mostly by the visual arts field. Still, museology is defined as museum studies research (Brown and Mairesse 2018), which is lacking when compared to accepted notions of theoretical work (Asher 1984). Other museum- and visual-arts-related theories in this category include collections management theories and new museology, among others.

Critical theory is another category that deserves attention given the rise in importance of issues related to racism and systematic exclusion, pronounced by social justice movements including MeToo and Black Lives Matter. This category includes critical, feminist, queer, and race theory. Several codes are attributed to a single publication, *the International Journal of the Inclusive Museum*. These findings suggest that these theories should be given a "home" in more permanent scholarly journals and in arts management education.

However interdisciplinary and dispersed the uses of theories may seem, this embodied practice of repeatedly used theories in certain subfields and not in others is part of our habitus, shaping and being shaped by the repeated practice of field members. For example, some members' positions in sociology and economics that are more established than those in the interrelated field of arts and culture management come with increased positional academic capital and influence.

Theoretical Contributions Influenced by Academic Journal

As may be expected, the focus of the academic journal is a predictor of the theories used by contributing authors. For example, the presence of economic theories (the second most common theories in the sample) is explained by the *Journal of Cultural Economics*—a journal that has a clear theoretical focus. This journal is well established and advances the subdiscipline of cultural economics in a sophisticated way, continuously reinforcing the need and new production of related research.

The presence of psychology codes is explained in part by the journal *Arts and Health*, in which research aligns with psychological effects of the arts on physical and mental health. The use of entrepreneurship theory is almost exclusively found in the journal *Artivate*. All but one pedagogy/education code and all uses of communication theory were from articles in museum-focused journals (*Curator, International Journal of the Inclusive Museum, Museum Management and Curatorship*). Table 8.2 sorts the findings by academic journal and shows which journal has a singular theoretical focus versus a wider range of theoretical contributions. Journals with a single or narrow theoretical focus, such as *Artivate, City and Community*, and *International Journal of Nonprofit and Voluntary Sector Marketing*, are indicated by one or two dominant codes. These findings underscore the importance of considering a range of related journals to understand the theoretical makeup of the field.

Table 8.2. Prominent Theories by Academic Journal

Journal name and available online publication date	No. of articles	Dominant codes	Minor codes
International Journal of Cultural Policy (1997)	39	Sociology; (18) policy/political (10); economics (7)	Management; organizations; philosophy
Journal of Arts Management, Law, and Society (1992)	38	Economics (9); policy/political (8); sociology (8)	Management; organizations
Museum Management and Curatorship (1995)	35	Management (5); museology (7)	Communication; critical theory; economics; organizations; pedagogy/education; philosophy; psychology; sociology
Curator (1997)	31	Pedagogy/education (10); museology (7)	Critical theory; psychology; sociology
Journal of Cultural Economics (1997)	28	Economics (25)	Sociology
International Journal of Arts Management (1998)	24	Organizations (9); management (7)	Economics; sociology
International Journal of the Inclusive Museum (2011)	24	Sociology (6); pedagogy/education (5)	Critical theory; communication; management; museology; policy/political
Cultural Trends (1989)	14	Sociology (6)	Art; economics; psychology
Artivate (2012)	11	Entrepreneurship (10)	Economics; policy/political; psychology;
Poetics (1971)	11	Sociology (11)	Economics
European Journal of Cultural Management and Policy (2011)	7	Policy/political (3); sociology (3)	

(*continued*)

Table 8.2. Continued

Journal name and available online publication date	No. of articles	Dominant codes	Minor codes
Arts and Health (2009)	6	Psychology (3); sociology (3)	
Nonprofit and Voluntary Sector Quarterly (1999)	5	Economics (3); management (2)	
International Journal of Nonprofit and Voluntary Sector Marketing (2001)	3	Management/marketing (3)	
City and Community (2002)	2	Sociology (2)	
Nonprofit Management and Leadership (1997)	2	Organizations (1); sociology (1)	
Voluntas (1990)	2	Management (1); sociology (1)	
Public Administration Review (1965)	1	Economics (1)	
Urban Affairs Review (1997)	1	Economics (1)	

Other findings pertain to the evolution of theoretical interests overtime. Roughly two-thirds of the articles in the sample of nearly three hundred articles were published in 2010 or later. Therefore, we closely examined articles in the last ten years of publication to find evidence of new or emerging theoretical interests. Prior to 2010, there was only one instance of critical theory (2009). Communication theories were found in articles published in 2011 (in museum-focused journals). Entrepreneurship appeared in articles published in 2015 and later (mostly in *Artivate*). Although there were a few uses of both museology and pedagogy/education theories, the application of these has increased since 2010. Future research is needed to show exactly how the field is shifting theoretically over time.

While change can be slow in a field where its habits and values are reproduced based on its social order, changes do happen, however incremental they may be. Due to change in external social conditions, such as heightened attention to social injustice, the members of the field change how they practice by utilizing different theoretical dispositions that are not traditionally used. Additionally, the establishment of new journals, such as *Artivate*, encourages the use of new theoretical dispositions by its members.

Discussion and Conclusions

This research underscores the importance of examining and adopting interdisciplinary approaches in arts management scholarship and education. Results show that the field is growing theoretically, including embracing theoretical viewpoints that have not been applied before from outside or related disciplines and advancing new theories specific to arts management. With these data in hand, we return to Paquette's (2019) call to legitimize organizational theory in arts management. Although organizational theory is just one of many contributions to the field, this research suggests wide interdisciplinary theoretical use with few contributions from arts management theory per se. As interdisciplinary scholars, arts and culture management researchers come from multiple disciplines and publish research in a similar fashion. There is no dearth of theory use, but the patterns observed in this chapter indicate that theoretical applications stem from different subfields or related fields, which makes it difficult to assess them together. Yet this could be an advantage, giving researchers or field members a broad foundation on which to theorize in ways specific to arts organizations and management, with less constraint regarding what theory to apply to their specific studies.

Despite an expansion of the use of theory in the last decade, Bourdieu's (1990) theory of practice offers one explanation for the prevalence of some theories over others in arts management scholarship. Practice must be actively exercised and embodied to achieve a desired outcome. Likewise, to contribute to the arts management discipline, researchers build upon the work of one another, thus leading to an echo chamber, or the reproduction of theories where ideas and beliefs are reinforced by a community of scholars (Bourdieu 1986, 1990). Popular and more dominant theories are more likely to be used and promoted than others from more marginalized, smaller, or niche fields. Additionally, there is more incentive to follow an established path (e.g., use of better-known and established theories) in members' professional academic advancement, reinforcing certain academic capital of the field(s).

Although there are some drawbacks of reinforcing similar ideas in all contexts, an important outcome of peer-reviewed academic research is that through the process the field—or scholarly community—identifies what is foundational. If indeed arts management was born from management (Paquette 2019; Paquette and Redaelli 2015), this research shows that today's field relies upon a solid foundation of interdisciplinary knowledge. We continue to build upon sociology, management, and organizational theories in scholarship and education. Economic theory is an equally important contributor, but the findings from this sample cannot be divorced from the impact of a single journal focused on cultural economics which contributes to the findings from this research sample.

Figure 8.1 offers a way to conceptualize theoretical foundations (shown at the base of the pyramid) and emerging theoretical applications that will be instrumental to arts management research moving forward. The figure is based on the SLR described in this chapter as well as the authors' knowledge of how similar theories may be grouped together for application in the arts management context.

Arts management has clear foundations in sociology, management and organizations, and economics, which together provide a fundamental theoretical focus. Beyond this foundation, however, the application of theory is wide-ranging. These findings may be interpreted as a disadvantage or advantage for the field moving forward. Bourdieu's contributions (1990, 1993) suggest that common theoretical application is explained by

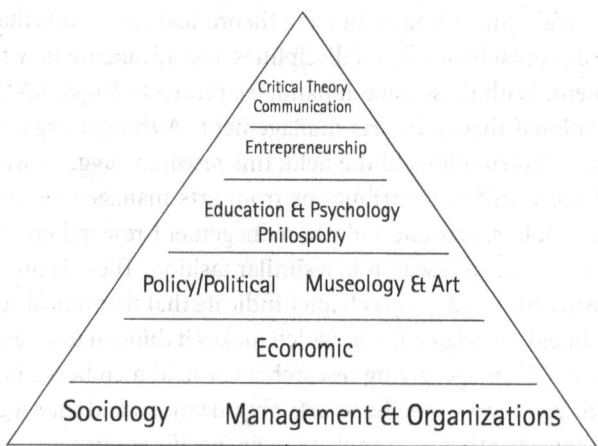

FIGURE 8.1 Conceptual map of theoretical use in arts management research.

members' reproduction of that application and/or the specific academic journals that inhabit a field. These traditional theoretical foundations are important but should not limit theoretical advancement. Another concern is that without a theoretical focus, arts management becomes a moving target—or, worse, atheoretical. On the other hand, by embracing new knowledge, arts management is equipped to adjust to new climates and realities. An essential role of researchers is to disrupt existing knowledge or social orders. We would expect nothing less of quality arts management research. The scattered and interdisciplinary pattern and use of theories of the field, as discussed above, indicates that the field's habitus could be seen as more fluid and transformable. For example, we can expect more use of critical and postmodern theories as arts organizations navigate the global pandemic and address pressing structural social issues.

Still, given the limited production of arts management research, we are slow to make revolutionary (as opposed to incremental) change to keep up with the pace of environmental change. Bourdieu (1993) suggests that members of a field can either "preserve" or "transform" existing structures. As discussed, this may be explained because people who have power—who are considered to produce dominant theories and are part of dominant and more powerful fields, often with more resources—are reluctant to give up their power. Rather, they find ways to reinforce their dominance in each field or fields, and they do not want to change the social structure from which they benefit. These tendencies cannot be divorced from the traditional processes tied to academic research production and publication as well as promotion and tenure. In a way interdisciplinarity is a solution to the problems that arise from reliance on one dominant field or voice, and we should embrace it more comfortably moving forward.

In a practice-oriented field like arts management, theory-based evidence is essential to the design and management of arts organizations in a changing world, and in organizational environments that are often resistant to change. The power of prediction, often found in theory, gives confidence to arts managers who are experimenting with organizational forms and practices. One of the most important contributions of arts management research may be to upend the status quo in arts management practice and education. These findings will inform future arts management research and education, including curriculum, standards, and teaching materials.

REFERENCES

AAAE. 2014. *Standards for Arts Administration Graduate Program Curricula: A Living Document*. Association of Arts Administration Educators.

AAAE. 2018. *Standards for Arts Administration Undergraduate Curricula: A Living Document*. Association of Arts Administration Educators.

APA. n.d. *Glossary of Psychological Terms*. American Psychological Association. Accessed July 24, 2021. http://www.apa.org/research/action/glossary.aspx.

Asher, Herbert B. 1984. *Theory-Building and Data Analysis in the Social Sciences*. Knoxville: University of Tennessee Press.

Baker, Ted, and Friederike Welter. 2020. *Contextualizing Entrepreneurship Theory*. London: Routledge.

Batory, Agnes, and Sara Svensson. 2019. "The Fuzzy Concept of Collaborative Governance: A Systematic Review of the State of the Art." *Central European Journal of Public Policy* 13, no. 2: 28–39. https://doi.org/10.2478/cejpp-2019-0008.

Baumol, William, and William Bowen. 1966. *Performing Arts: The Economic Dilemma*. London: Twentieth Century Fund.

Berger, Karol. 2000. *A Theory of Art*. Oxford: Oxford University Press.

Bourdieu, Pierre. 1984. *Distinction: A Social Critique of the Judgement of Taste*. Translated by Richard Nice. Cambridge, MA: Harvard University Press.

Bourdieu, Pierre. 1986. "The Forms of Capital." In *Handbook of Theory and Research for the Sociology of Education*, edited by J. Richardson, 241–258. New York: Greenwood. https://www.marxists.org/reference/subject/philosophy/works/fr/bourdieu-forms-capital.htm.

Bourdieu, Pierre. 1990. *The Logic of Practice*. Cambridge: Polity Press. First published 1980.

Bourdieu, Pierre. 1993. *The Field of Cultural Production*. Cambridge: Polity Press.

Brown, Karen, and François Mairesse. 2018. "The Definition of the Museum Through Its Social Role." *Curator* 61, no. 4: 525–539. https://doi.org/10.1111/cura.12276.

Chang, Woong Jo, and Margaret Wyszomirski. 2015. "What Is Arts Entrepreneurship? Tracking the Development of Its Definition in Scholarly Journals." *Artivate* 4, no. 2: 11–31. https://www.jstor.org/stable/10.34053/artivate.4.2.0011.

Delgado, Richard, and Jean Stefancic. 2017. *Critical Race Theory: An Introduction*. 3rd ed. New York: New York University Press.

Dewey, John. 1959. *Art as Experience*. New York: Capricorn Books.

Dimaggio, Paul. 1983. "Cultural Policy Studies: What They Are and Why We Need Them." *Journal of Arts Management and Law* 13, no. 1: 241–248. https://doi.org/10.1080/07335113.1983.9942100.

DiMaggio, Paul. 1988. *Managers of the Arts: Careers and Opinions of Senior Administrators of U.S. Art Museums, Symphony Orchestras, Resident Theatres, and Local Arts Agencies*, 2nd ed. Washington, DC: Seven Locks Press.

DiMaggio, Paul, and Paul M. Hirsch. 1976. "Production Organizations in the Arts." *American Behavioral Scientist* 19, no. 6: 735–752. https://doi.org/10.1177/000276427601900605.

Evard, Yves, and François Colbert. 2000. "Arts Management: A New Discipline Entering the Millennium?" *International Journal of Arts Management* 2, no. 2: 4–13. https://www.jstor.org/stable/41064684.

Ferraro, Fabrizio, and Daniel Beunza. 2018. "Creating Common Ground: A Communicative Action Model of Dialogue in Shareholder Engagement." *Organization Science* 29, no. 6: 1187–1207. https://doi.org/10.1287/orsc.2018.1226.

Frederickson, H. George, Kevin B. Smith, Christopher Larimer, and Michael J. Licari. 2015. *The Public Administration Theory Primer*, 3rd ed. Boulder, CO: Westview Press.

Glaser, Barney G., and Anselm Strauss. 1967. *The Discovery of Grounded Theory: Strategies for Qualitative Research*. Chicago: Aldine.

Hatch, Mary J. 2018. *Organization Theory: Modern, Symbolic, and Postmodern Perspectives*. Oxford: Oxford University Press.

Hurst, Allison L. 2018. *Classical Sociological Theory and Foundations of American Sociology*. Corvallis: Oregon State University. https://open.oregonstate.education/sociologicaltheory/.

Jung, Yuha. 2017. "Threading and Mapping Theories in the Field of Arts Administration: Thematic Discussion of Theories and Their Interdisciplinarity." *Journal of Arts Management, Law, and Society* 47, no. 1: 3–16. https://doi.org/10.1080/10632921.2016.1241970.

Kessler, Eric H. 2013. *Encyclopedia of Management Theory*. Thousand Oaks, CA: SAGE.

Ladson-Billings, Gloria. 1995. "Toward a Theory of Culturally Relevant Pedagogy." *American Educational Research Journal* 32, no. 3: 465–491. https://doi.org/10.2307/1163320.

Lawrence, Paul, and Jay Lorsch. 1967. "Differentiation and Integration in Complex Organizations." *Administrative Science Quarterly* 12, no. 1: 1–47.

Littlejohn, Stephen, and Karen Foss. 2008. *Theories of Human Communication*, 9th ed. Belmont, CA: Thomson Wadsworth.

Macdonald, Bradley J. 2017. "Traditional and Critical Theory Today: Toward a Critical Political Science." *New Political Science* 39, no. 4: 511–522. https://doi.org/10.1080/07393148.2017.1378857.

Maton, Karl. 2014. "Habitus." In *Pierre Bourdieu: Key Concepts*, edited by Michael Grenfell, 48–64. Abingdon, UK: Routledge.

Mauss, Marcel. 1982. "Deconstructing Organizational Taboos: The Suppression of Gender Conflict in Organizations." *Organization Science* 1, no. 4: 339–359. https://doi.org/10.1287/orsc.1.4.339.

Paquette, Jonathan. 2019. "Organizational Theories in Arts Management Research." *Journal of Arts Management, Law, and Society* 49, no. 4: 221–223. https://doi.org/10.1080/10632921.2019.1631033.

Paquette, Jonathan, and Eleonora Redaelli. 2015. *Arts Management and Cultural Policy Research*. Basingstoke, UK: Palgrave Macmillan.

Pérez-Álvarez, Marino. 2018. "Psychology as a Science of Subject and Comportment, Beyond the Mind and Behavior." *Integrative Psychological and Behavioral Science* 52, no. 1: 25–51. https://doi.org/10.1007/s12124-017-9408-4.

Pfeffer, Jeffrey. 1981. *Power in Organizations*. Marshfield, MA: Pitman.

Pfeffer, Jeffrey. 1997. *New Directions for Organization Theory: Problems and Prospects*. Oxford: Oxford University Press.

Powell, Walter, and Paul DiMaggio. 1991. *The New Institutionalism in Organizational Analysis*. Chicago: University of Chicago Press.

Rentschler, Ruth, and David Shilbury. 2008. "Academic Assessment of Arts Management Journals: A Multidimensional Rating Survey." *International Journal of Arts Management* 10, no. 3: 60–71. https://www.jstor.org/stable/41064964.

Richardson, G. B. 2003. *Economic Theory*. London: Routledge. https://doi.org/10.4324/9781315016429.

Roswell, Ellen, and Rachel Shane. 2018. *Arts and Cultural Management: Critical and Primary Sources*. New York: Bloomsbury.

Shapiro, Ian. 2002. "Problems, Methods, and Theories in the Study of Politics, or What's Wrong with Political Science and What to Do About It." *Political Theory* 30, no. 4: 596–619. doi:10.1177/0090591702030004008.

Smith, Mark K. 2020. "Pierre Bourdieu on Education: Habitus, Capital, and Field. Reproduction in the Practice of Education, the Encyclopaedia of Pedagogy and Informal Education." Infed.org. https://infed.org/mobi/pierre-bourdieu-habitus-capital-and-field-exploring-reproduction-in-the-practice-of-education.

Strauss, Anselm, and Juliet Corbin. 1990. *Basics of Qualitative Research: Grounded Theory Procedures and Techniques*. Thousand Oaks, CA: SAGE.

Tranfield, David, David Denyer, and Palminder Smart. 2003. "Towards a Methodology for Developing Evidence-Informed Management Knowledge by Means of Systematic Review." *British Journal of Management* 14, no. 3: 207–222. https://doi.org/10.1111/1467-8551.00375.

van Ruler, Betteke. 2018. "Communication Theory: An Underrated Pillar on Which Strategic Communication Rests." *International Journal of Strategic Communication* 12, no.4: 367–381. https://doi.org/10.1080/1553118X.2018.1452240.

Warburton, Nigel. 2013. *Philosophy*, 5th ed. Abingdon, UK: Taylor & Francis.

PART III

CULTURAL POLICIES, DIPLOMACY, CULTURAL PLANNING, AND LEGAL CONCERNS

CHAPTER 9

MAPPING CULTURAL POLICY

Cultural Bureaucracy as Concept, Norm, and Analytical Tool

CAROLE ROSENSTEIN

MAPPING has been a prime mode of engagement in cultural policy since the field's inception in the mid-1960s, when planning began for UNESCO's 1967 Monaco Roundtable on Cultural Action and Policy. Much of the work undertaken during preliminary planning, advisory, and expert meetings, as well as the work of the Monaco Roundtable itself, concentrated on beginning to conceive and articulate a shared understanding of universal human needs in regard to culture. That work was fundamental because policies are meant to address needs, so a clear understanding of cultural need is required to provide the underlying rationale for cultural policy and cultural policy development. At the 1970 UNESCO Intergovernmental Conference on Institutional, Administrative and Financial Aspects of Cultural Policies, then-Director-General René Maheu put the matter this way:

> The Universal Declaration of Human Rights, adopted by the United Nations in 1948, declares that: "Everyone has the right freely to participate in the cultural life of the community." It is not certain that the full significance of this text, proclaiming a new human right, the right to culture, was entirely appreciated at the time. If everyone, as an essential part of his dignity as a man, has the right to share in the cultural heritage and cultural activities of the community — or rather of the different communities to which men belong (and that of course includes the ultimate community—mankind)—it follows that the authorities responsible for these communities have a duty, so far as their resources permit, to provide him with the means for such participation.... Everyone, accordingly, has the right to culture, as he has the right to education and the right to work. This, as I have said, means that so far as possible the public authorities should provide him with the means to exercise this right. This is the basis and first purpose of cultural policy.
>
> (Quoted in Girard and Gentil 1983, 182–183)

At the same time that they believed in and hoped to build consensus around the notion that certain universal cultural needs exist and can be subject to an accounting, roundtable organizers also emphasized that different nations would address those needs in distinctive ways and that part of UNESCO's work in cultural policy development would be to acknowledge that diversity and aid in preserving it.

In service to those commitments, Monaco planners requested reports on cultural policy in twenty-two nations, and one of the key actions taken following the roundtable was sponsorship of the seventy-seven volumes of the *National Studies of Cultural Policy* series published by UNESCO from 1969 to 1987. As the earliest draft reports were delivered, they quickly revealed a considerable problem: authors were being asked to describe something—a national cultural policy—that as yet remained only loosely defined and certainly was not familiar. Lacking a clear conceptual foundation, the reports were highly variable and did not meet organizer expectations (Silva 2015). Initially, the Monaco Roundtable had been conceived as a forum to discuss how nations cultivate and regulate artistic expression, but even the initial planning meetings made apparent that a narrow or explicit focus on the arts could not provide a stable platform for international discussion, cooperation, and action. Cold War rhetoric and cultural diplomacy programs had explicitly used the treatment of artists and artistic expression to draw a bright line between East and West, and a focus on government action toward the arts immediately resulted in tension and conflict.

Instead, the emerging cultural policy program at UNESCO shifted its focus to a new idea: *cultural development*.[1] And how was this new idea to be understood? Over the following three decades, it came to be conceived as the progressive movement of states toward more efficient and effective means of addressing the cultural needs of their populations. The national studies of cultural policy and the national profiles subsequently produced for Council of Europe cultural policy programs should be understood in reference to this concept. These profiles are not primarily descriptive; rather, they are oriented toward measurement, assessment, and development, and intended to push in a direction understood as a progression, moving from "less developed" to "more developed." The profiles were designed to fit the practical purpose of comparing how well a nation was meeting universal cultural needs and nudging nations around the world toward further cultural development through cultural policy.[2] To aid the production of comparable profiles, authors were presented with a template for describing a national cultural policy. Its first item: "Describe the principles which guide the administrative structure and the methods of financing cultural activities in the country" (quoted in Silva 2016).[3]

THE FRENCH MODEL

The emergence, character, and influence of the concept of cultural development and its expression in the national cultural policy profiles cannot be fully appreciated without identifying them as the work of cultural policy impresario Augustin Girard, operating in the various institutional settings where he played leading roles. Girard was director of research and statistics at the French Ministry of Culture from 1963 to 1993, a frequent consultant, delegate, and rapporteur for UNESCO cultural policy programs and meetings, and leader of the Cultural Development Program and the program of cultural policy review at the Council of Europe from 1970 through the 1980s. Working in these roles, he was the progenitor of comparative cultural policy and also led the development of the existing archive of documentation of actual national cultural policies that forms much of the body of knowledge in the field. Girard's work deserves a whole monograph of its own (indeed, it has one: see Martin 2013); here, I want to emphasize just one very important aspect—the way Girard used the concept of cultural development to link "progress" in cultural policy to a national cultural bureaucracy structured by a centralized cultural agency, a model clearly inspired by the French Ministry of Culture. According to Martin (2013, 17), Girard, through his work with UNESCO and the Council of Europe, oversaw a period when "we can really, fully, without vainglory or hyperbole, speak of the influence of the 'French model' well beyond the borders of France" (translation added).

France's stake in establishing and disseminating a French model of cultural policy was much higher than might immediately be apparent. Pendergast (1976) argues that in the postwar period, the French viewed their power to influence East-West relations and their own former colonies as residing primarily in their role as a global cultural arbiter. France worked to cement that role at UNESCO, which may be viewed as "a multinational expression of a historical French governmental impulse towards the institutionalization of culture" (Pendergast 1976, 474; and see Vestheim 2019). In this context, it is important to note that the cultural policy program was developed after the French power base at UNESCO was threatened by a 1965 consolidation and attendant budget reduction of line items for areas where the French had retained the greatest conceptual and administrative control—culture, social science, and the humanities.

UNESCO "adopted [Girard's] formula to introduce into cultural action the scientific spirit of experimentation" (Moulinier 1990, 4, translation added). Two reports authored by Girard bookend the first phase of the UNESCO cultural policy program. In both, Girard articulates the French Model and advocates for its efficiency and effectiveness. In *Cultural Policy: A Preliminary Study* (1969), he writes:[4]

> A great many States . . . have become, or are becoming, aware of *the need to place all cultural services under a single department*. The acknowledged advantages of this are as follows: 1. The possibility of coordinating, at the national level, measures which are regarded at the local level as parts of a whole . . . 2. The possibility of arriving at a general conception of cultural action which will give consistency and continuity to what were once disparate and intermittent measures and will therefore lead to a better use of public funds. 3. The possibility of establishing priorities, in keeping with the aims of democratization, with a view to decentralizing cultural activities. A centralization phase is necessary as a preliminary to pressing for genuine

decentralization. 4. The possibility of giving cultural affairs adequate moral and political authority at governmental level.

(UNESCO 1969, 37, emphasis added)

In *Cultural Development* (1983), Girard's synthetic review of the program's work to date, he adds budgetary authority, evaluation, and international cooperation to the central agency's remit:

> The central authorities are responsible for taking stock of the needs arising as a result of developments in society and the policy of the government; they must determine the ultimate aims to be embraced by the nation, decide on priority objectives and allocate the requisite resources; they have the task of establishing the machinery for analysing needs and keeping check of results, embarking on and supporting new experiments in areas as yet unexplored; lastly, they alone can promote the international co-operation essential for progress. Passing on culture, on the other hand, is fundamentally the responsibility of the local authorities. If it is undertaken by the central authorities the result is over-centralization, with all the accompanying disadvantages: concentration of activities in the capital, use of a limited number of companies and artists, red tape. The central authorities should reduce direct management to the minimum.
>
> (Girard 1983, 181–182)

Using the concept of cultural development, Girard established the French Model not just as an example of how a cultural policy system might be structured but rather as a norm. A good place to see how this worked is in the report and proceedings for the review of cultural policy in Italy produced for the Council of Europe program of cultural policy review. Girard served as chair of the Examiners' Group for the Italy review, which took place in 1994–1995.[5] The review calls for greater centralization of Italian cultural bureaucracy at the national level:

> Clearly it is important for the government at any time, and particularly in stringent economic times, to have some overall cultural vision both for the sake of the quality of its citizens and also (especially in Italy) for one of the country's chief assets. This does not necessarily mean that a single, unified ministry is the only, or even the most appropriate, means of getting to that point. It does, however, strongly suggest that there should be meaningful dialogue, coordination and some common denominator between the numerous ministries and departments of state which have a stake in cultural policy.... We believe that the key to developing a strong and appropriate modern role for central government lies in the following:
>
> - High-level coordinated national policy
> - Cooperative public strategy with clear objectives
> - Setting minimum standards of operation
> - Decentralization of defined and agreed functions

- Control of implementation of legal provisions
- Evaluation of results

(Gordon 1995, 21, 25)

In his own published discussion of the review, Girard advocates in a more assertive way Italy's "need for a strong central authority" (1996, 57) that sets policy, controls budgets, allocates responsibilities to subnational and local levels, and evaluates the activities of subordinate agencies and institutions.[6]

During formal examination of the report at Strasbourg, Girard "requested a more detailed discussion on the important issue of a possible single cultural ministry in Italy and current links between the various ministries" (Gordon 1995, 120). In reply, Antonio Paolucci, the Italian minister for cultural heritage and author of the national report on Italy prepared for the Examiners' Group, answered:

> In response to the earlier questions from the French delegation, the Minister stressed the inherent dilemma in the relationship between culture as heritage, on the one hand, and culture as tourism, on the other. [The Italian cultural bureaucracy included a national agency for Heritage and another, separate national agency for Tourism.] It is incontestable that in cities like Florence and Venice tourism could be a destructive force owing largely to lack of variety or imagination in itineraries. He agreed that it was very important for better working links to be established between his Ministry and other relevant bodies. Whilst he would welcome improved cooperation, *he did not believe an imposed "solution" would be capable of achieving what was hoped for.* Everyone already had too much to do, and *the answer lay in establishing a practical link from the bottom up.*
>
> (Reported in Gordon 1995, 122, emphasis added)

This exchange illustrates how Paolucci was made to argue against the French Model as a norm, to explain how Italy could achieve "progress" without adopting that particular form of governmentality. The objective of promulgating this norm was to "modernize" "cultural administration," "evaluation techniques," "institutions," and "procedures" (Girard 1996). This would mean "overcoming contradictions" such as those between "the traditional fragmentation of authority and strategic co-ordination" and between "traditional bureaucratic practices and modern management methods" (Girard 1996, 57).

The French Model as a Norm

The example of the Italian cultural policy review is just one among many that illustrate the international reach of the French Model as a norm. In Senegal over the period from 1966 to 1970, the French used bilateral funding instruments to push for the transformation of a merged Department of Education and Culture into an autonomous and expanded Culture

Ministry, coinciding with the planning and execution of UNESCO's 1969 meeting in Dakar, "Problems of Cultural Policy in Africa," a key venue for advancing the Francafrique regime (Cohen 2021, 35; and see Desportes 2020). In the framework for monitoring the success of the 2005 Convention on the Protection and Promotion of the Diversity of Cultural Expressions (an instrument spearheaded by France and the Francophone world), the mere existence of a Ministry of Culture is counted as an indicator of the capacity to fulfill a principal goal: to "support sustainable systems of governance for culture" (Anheier 2015, 36).[7] The list could go on and on. The power of this norm and the institutional processes through which it was promulgated cannot be overstated. In their study of global cultural policy isomorphism, Alasuutari and Kangas (2020, 8) find that

> some countries had ministries dedicated to culture already in the 1940s; following the example of the Soviet Union, several socialist states also established them. Among Western countries, having established its ministry of culture in 1960, France was a predecessor and active in promoting the idea of such a governmental structure to other states. According to our count, by 2018, 164 countries have established a ministry of culture.[8] . . . [T]here were certainly other motives behind states establishing a ministry of culture, but the UNESCO program obviously affected the trend. Except for the states in which cultural policy is handled at a sub-state level, *all the countries that produced a national report have established a ministry of culture, typically synchronously with the report.* . . . UNESCO's advocacy was surely not the only reason for instituting a culture ministry but taking part in its program by producing a national report seemed to increase the likelihood that such a ministry is instituted.
>
> (Emphasis added)

If, as Miller and Yudice contend, "national cultural policies are a privileged terrain of hegemony" (2002, 8), then the French Model is a hegemony of hegemonies.

There are a number of reasons why it is important to recognize that the French Model serves as a norm in cultural policy. First, it is easy to misunderstand the diffusion of the French Model if we fail to identify it as a norm. Norms present as natural and ahistorical. One of the most important things that we miss when looking from the normative point of view is the way norms have been intentionally constituted and disseminated, often for particular purposes. Further, norms are evaluative; they define what is "normal" and what is "abnormal." In this way, norms are a tool of power used to demean and suppress what is not-normative, to disappear it, to justify interfering with it. The history discussed here shows that the French Model has diffused throughout the world not because it is "modern" or "rational" and therefore somehow inevitable, nor because it is a "Gold Standard" (cf. Dubois 2016), but instead because specific actors and institutions have used their power, resources, and influence to promulgate it for particular political ends.

Second, norms make poor analytical tools. A norm operates like a lens to shape our view of the world; whatever does not fit the norm often is rendered illegible. When we look at the world from a normative point of view, it is too easy to miss what the norm does not recognize. Undertaking the study of cultural policies around the world requires being able to identify all of the different sorts of practices and arrangements that make up the possible universe, and a powerful norm can get in the way of doing that. Ultimately, the diffusion of a norm can make comparison seem unnecessary. Why compare at all when, around the world today, it appears that the adoption of a ministry of culture is nearly universal? But are we to conclude that, for example, the contemporary UK system (see Figure 9.1) parallels the French system (see Figure 9.2) simply because both include a central ministry? How are these ministries integrated into their

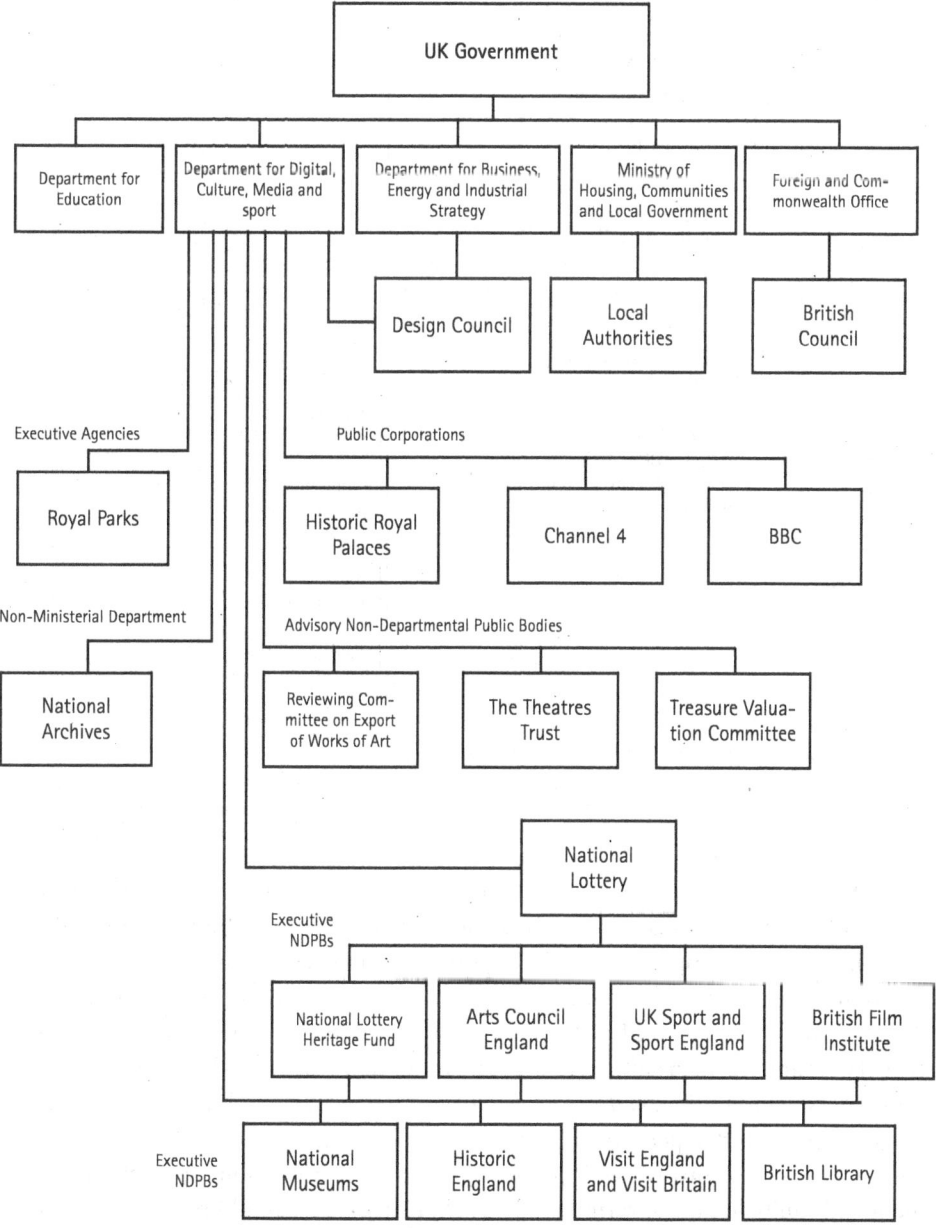

FIGURE 9.1 Organizational organigram: United Kingdom.

Source: Council of Europe/ERICarts, "Compendium of Cultural Policies and Trends," 20th ed., 2020. Country profile: United Kingdom (Rod Fisher).

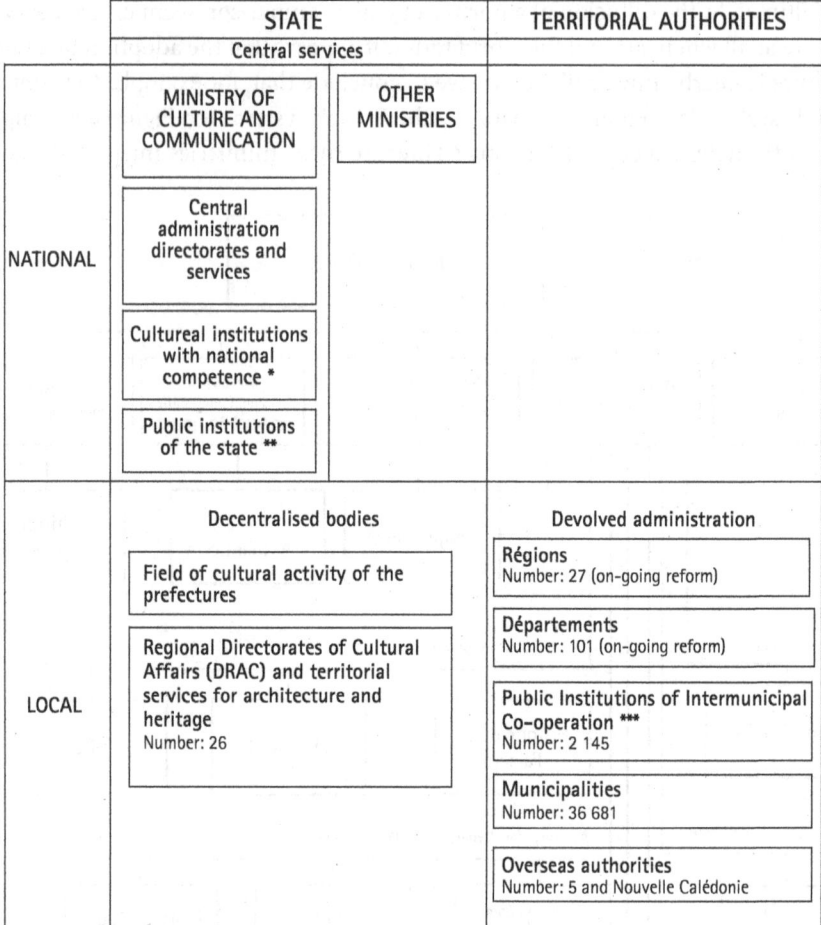

FIGURE 9.2 Organizational organigram: France.
Source: Council of Europe/ERICarts, "Compendium of Cultural Policies and Trends in Europe," 18th ed., 2017. Country profile: France (Thomas Perrin, Jean-Cédric Delvainquière, and Jean-Michel Guy).

respective national cultural policy systems? What is it that they actually do? Only deep and contextualized comparative study can tell us (Belfiore 2004; Rindzeviciute 2021).

Contemporary comparative cultural policy research demands a refreshed analytical framework and a shared terminology for describing cultural policy systems fully delinked from the French Model as a norm. The evidence that new tools are needed is clear. For example, when cultural policies are examined to see how they contribute to *cultural diversity* rather than *cultural development*, "the one overarching recommendation that emerges . . . is that permanent and holistic collaborative frameworks for the governance of culture that involve multiple government ministries, multiple levels of government and multiple non-governmental stakeholder groups should become customary" (Portoles 2017, 51). This shift in perspective results in the map shown in Figure 9.3, one that is enlightening but surely would prove difficult to use for systematic, replicable

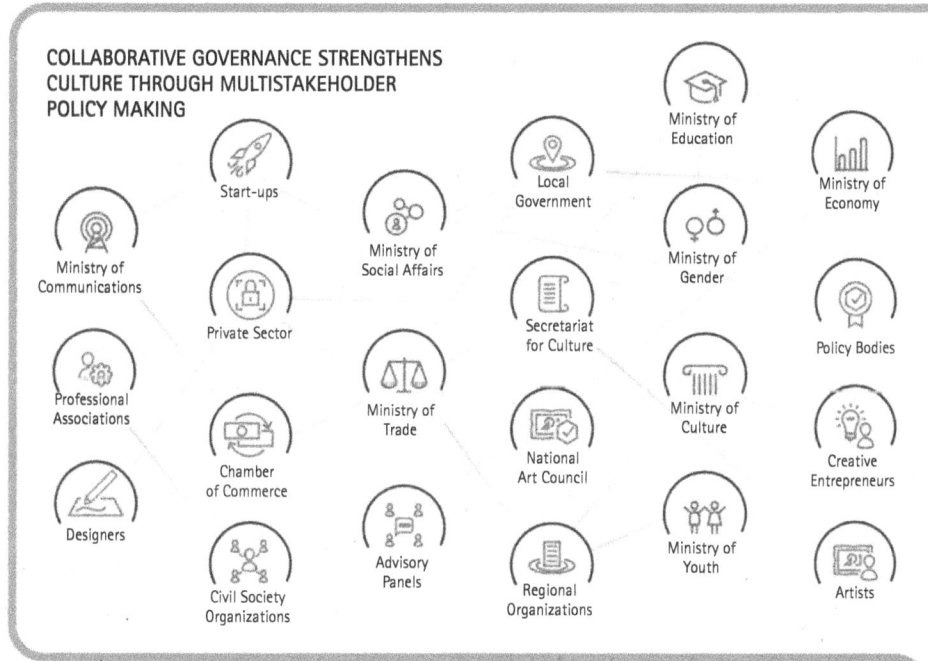

FIGURE 9.3 Collaborative governance strengthens culture through multistakeholder policymaking.
Source: Portoles (2017, 52). © UNESCO 2017. Available under Attribution-ShareAlike 3.0 IGO (https://creativecommons.org/licenses/by-sa/3.0/igo/).

comparison. Without a refreshed approach, there is a further danger of disappearing cultural policy as a distinctive domain of analysis altogether. In their recent study of state action regarding the arts and culture during the COVID-19 pandemic, Betzler et al. (2021) only passingly consider cultural policy, instead focusing their explanations on other "contextual" factors such as GDP, debt ratio, deregulation, and political orientation. Recent, critical research suggests that existing comparative frameworks are proving incapable of explaining different outcomes: Rius-Ulldemolins, Pizzi, and Arostegui (2019) could not explain differences in levels of overall government cultural expenditure using common cultural policy types; Srakar and Vecco (2021) could not use them to explain differences in size of the cultural economy or participation levels.

A New Analytical Approach

To begin this refresh, a good place to start is right where the comparative project itself started: mapping. Good mapping is important for cultural policymakers and administrators working within a system since a clear understanding of the administrative structure and how it works is essential for strategy, policymaking, evaluation, and advocacy. Good mapping is useful for applied comparative cultural policy as well. If we

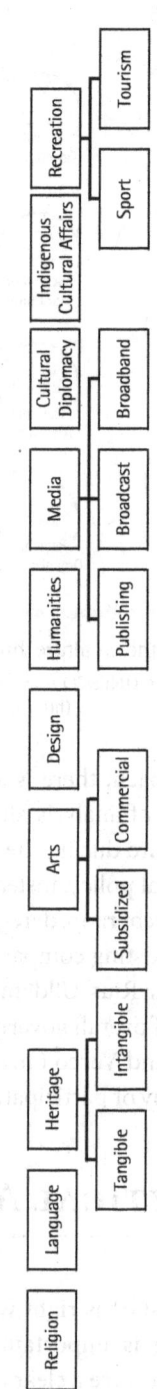

FIGURE 9.4 The cultural policy domain.

no longer take for granted that the French Model is the most efficient and effective way to structure cultural policy in every situation, that opens the way for significant testing and evaluation of a variety of cultural policy approaches. For example, although the democratization of culture has been the primary stated goal of French cultural policy for the past fifty years, it appears that the French have been unable to significantly change the demographic composition of audiences for the subsidized arts (Dubois 2016). Perhaps other ways of organizing cultural policy have had more success? Going forward, good mapping also will be a basic prerequisite for comparative cultural policy research that is oriented toward explanation. The far-reaching diffusion of the French Model as a norm means that an historical moment when we could find some "native" and untouched national cultural policy system now has passed, if it ever existed. A new natural history of cultural policy is required. Moreover, good mapping is a foundation for identifying cases, surfacing differences that may prove determinative in showing causation. As is true of all comparative study that seeks to explain difference, the first challenge is to be able to choose cases that control for a set of carefully defined attributes (Ragin 2014). By applying key analytical categories and descriptors, mapping enables the effective choice of cases. Comparative cultural policy research will not be able to do this well until it moves away from normative thinking. Of course, it may turn out that the proposition that administrative structures have any explanatory value at all also is a product of the normativity of the French Model. If that is the case, it is likely that mapping ultimately will prove to be of little value for understanding causation.

A revised approach to cultural policy mapping that adequately recognizes and then works both to reveal the powerful influence of the French Model as a norm and to balance accommodation and resistance to that norm would be primarily inductive and should be much more careful to distinguish between normative and descriptive characterizations. The mapping exercise begins by drawing a boundary (Schuster 1987) that encompasses the ways in which governments have understood culture. Note that this exercise is different from one that seeks to define culture in the abstract and then tries to trace government actions affecting that domain. In other words, here we are concerned to map what Ahearne (2009) terms *explicit* or *nominal* cultural policies, not *implicit* ones (though it may be useful to note which areas are made explicit and which remain implicit). Figure 9.4 shows what the boundaries of the cultural policy domain look like when drawn using an inclusive approach that considers how governments seem to be expressing a notion of culture through their governance. Already, this approach refreshes outdated thinking: the resulting domain is neither narrowly focused on "the arts" nor is it "anthropological"; it might best be characterized as sociological.[9]

Although every one of the components of this cultural policy domain will be affected by government policies or actions of one sort or another, there is no place where we could map every one of these components onto a corresponding government agency, department, office, or program. All of them certainly will not be considered the responsibility of one centralized agency (though the Nazi Ministry of Propaganda came pretty close). They all may, however, be subject to a dominant or overarching policy orientation such as religious orthodoxy or state control of markets, where one exists. Figure 9.5 shows how national-level administration of the cultural policy domain is structured in the United States. There is no formal administration of religion, language, or sport. Media, tourism, and the creative industries fall under the authority of the Department of Commerce. With the exception of cultural diplomacy, all of the other components of the cultural policy domain fall under the authority of the Department of the Interior or are administered by executive agencies that are provided oversight by congressional Subcommittees on the Interior (this latter group is indicated by dash-surround cells).

While the Departments of Interior, State, and Commerce all engage in policymaking and administration within the cultural policy domain, policies related to cultural activities in the for-profit sector and those related to media are not considered cultural policy in the United States, and this classification is prime, trumping other orders. So, for example, even though it is a quasi-governmental body and not a for-profit entity, the Corporation for Public Broadcasting is provided oversight by congressional Commerce Committees because it is considered a part of the media. And, again following the lines of this fundamental divide, COVID relief for arts and cultural businesses was delivered in the form of loans through the Small Business Administration, while relief for state and local and nonprofit arts and cultural organizations was delivered in the form of grants through the National Endowment for the Arts (NEA), National Endowment for the Humanities (NEH), and Institute of Museum and Library Services (IMLS).

What remains after parceling off the media-related territory, then, encompasses the cultural policy realm in the United States: heritage, the subsidized arts, the humanities, and cultural diplomacy (see Figure 9.6). Mapping cultural administration within this realm reveals three key attributes of the cultural policy system (see Figure 9.7).

First, this system includes two very different modes of administration. One is relatively typical public administration. Heritage and cultural diplomacy are straightforwardly a part of the public sector. Agencies in these areas create policy and implement relevant regulation, provide direct public services, and deliver grants to support activities in their areas of responsibility. They hold cultural patrimony in care for the public. They are accountable to standard administrative rules and procedures. In other words, they behave like a typical public agency. On the other hand, administration of the subsidized arts and the humanities is only partially undertaken in this typical way. The artistic patrimony, for example, is in large part held and administered by quasi-governmental entities such as the National Gallery of Art. The status of the Smithsonian Institution as a part of government is purposely and persistently vague. These quasi-governmental entities provide direct services in the arts and humanities to the public. Further, NEA, NEH, and IMLS, while a regular part of government, do not engage in policymaking or regulation but instead serve in a comparatively limited role, primarily as grantmakers (and sometimes as conveners).

Second, in the area of arts and humanities policy, this system replaces the clear lines of authority institutionalized in department-to-agency relationships with special instruments that allow for flexible coordination and communication across the various entities. Some connections are instituted at the same time as clearly defined lines

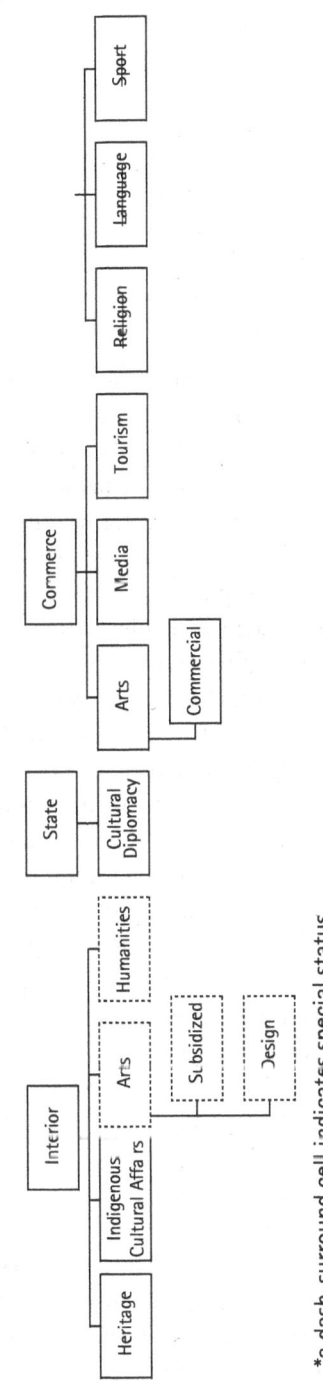

*a dash-surround cell indicates special status

FIGURE 9.5 National-level administration of the cultural policy domain in the United States.

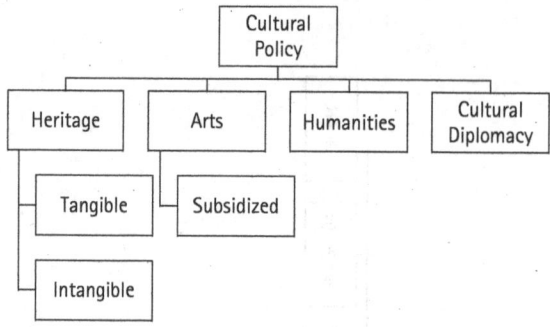

FIGURE 9.6 The cultural policy realm in the United States.

of authority are resisted. Whereas the Department of the Interior/National Park Service has authority over the broad array of heritage activities in various agencies, offices, and programs, each of the cultural venues and agencies in the arts and humanities has some degree of executive power and none are a part of any formal, acting body that ties them together. In other words, the national system for administering arts and humanities policy in the United States is relatively fragmented compared to the national system for administering heritage and cultural diplomacy policy, which is relatively concentrated. In fact, we might say that this structure enables coherent policymaking for heritage and cultural diplomacy and resists coherent policymaking for the arts and humanities. The National Foundation on Arts and Humanities exists today, in large part, merely as the residual mechanism through which the NEA and NEH were established; it has no authority over them and currently is not used in a way that reflects its encompassing role within this structure (see Figure 9.7). The relationship of the Smithsonian to the Kennedy Center and the National Gallery of Art is similar. Some US presidents have used the National Foundation's Federal Council on the Arts and Humanities in something like a policymaking role, but primarily for interagency convening or cooperation. Beginning in the 1980s, that role was taken over by the President's Committee for the Arts and Humanities (PCAH). (That entity collapsed during the Trump administration, but calls for its revival already have been put forward.) Both the Federal Council and the PCAH have coordinated nearly the whole of the second, agency-level tier of this map (see Figure 9.8), along with other cultural offices and programs in federal government, representing a significant if ephemeral area of concentration at the federal level (Rosenstein 2018).

Third, a key attribute of this mapping is that it does not capture a major source of government spending on culture in the United States—namely, tax expenditure entailed by tax deduction for donations to nonprofit heritage, arts, and cultural organizations and by tax exemption for the capital gains from the investments made by foundations and wealthier nonprofit heritage, arts, and cultural organizations. Although they obviously are crucial to the administration of the cultural policy realm in the United States, the policies that govern tax expenditure are not considered cultural policies.

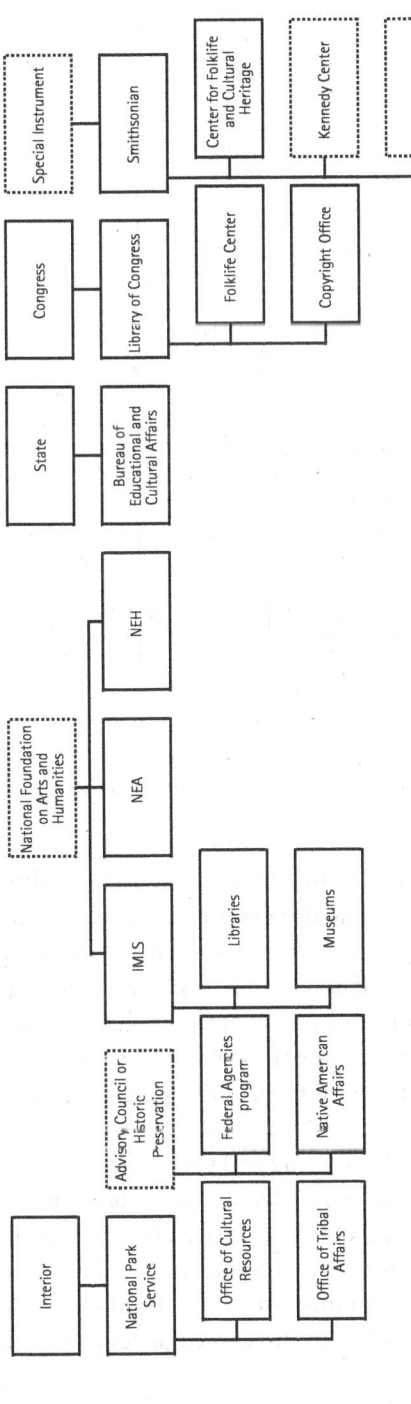

*a dash-surround cell indicates special status

FIGURE 9.7 National-level administration of the cultural policy realm in the United States (including national public sector cultural institutions).

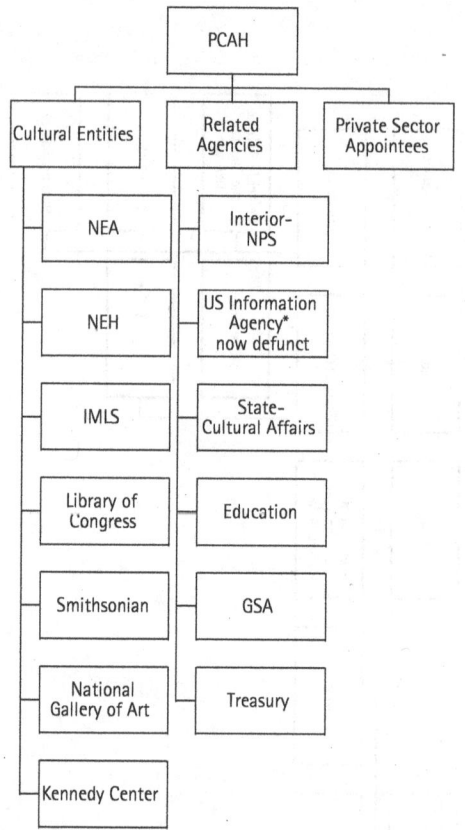

FIGURE 9.8 Composition of the President's Committee on the Arts and Humanities, as enacted.

The claim, frequently made, that the United States lacks a cultural policy, then, is true in the sense that there is in the United States no understanding that one policy regime—a cultural policy regime—encompasses government action toward media, the creative industries, culture and foreign affairs, heritage, and the subsidized arts and humanities.[10] At the same time, based on this mapping exercise, it might be argued that an alternative claim also is true: that the United States has in fact *three* cultural policy regimes: one for media, one for heritage, and one for the subsidized arts and humanities. One is a regulator oriented toward markets, one is a steward oriented toward patrimony, and one is a handmaid oriented toward fostering and presenting creative work and humanistic scholarship. These should be acknowledged as separate cultural policy regimes in that they are viewed as fulfilling quite distinct goals, organized in different organizational forms, administered in very different ways, and only very rarely are they considered together or brought together in administrative or political practice. This picture belies the characterization of cultural policy in the United States as essentially grounded in the principle that one should beware of centralization and of a predominant role for the State in the direct management of cultural institutions, because of the danger of cultural action being reduced to uniformity and lest the controversial element in art be neutralized; those who support this approach prefer to limit State intervention to financial assistance, free from any conditions.

(UNESCO 1970, 11)

While that characterization holds true for policy in the subsidized arts and humanities, it is not true of other US cultural policy. It is a characterization that takes normative assumptions for granted and does not reflect realities on the ground.

The United States has no cultural policy and it has three cultural policies. It is useful to be able to hold both of these truths in our minds because at the same time that the challenges the cultural sector might face will certainly cross, combine, or overlap these areas, the ways in which government will address those challenges are likely to be quite different depending on which defined policy stream they are viewed as rightly belonging to. Further, it is useful to know the principles and repertoires of each stream because governments and politicians are likely to borrow across streams when lines are blurred. So, for example, during the Culture Wars, when Congress wished to regulate expression at the NEA, it borrowed concepts and practices from the Federal Communications Commission, the only federal agency invested with the legitimate authority to regulate expression.

Conclusion

A map of the administrative structure for culture is not a picture of a cultural policy system. It is, instead, a tool for beginning to understand that system. Essential components will be missing from such maps: institutionalized attitudes toward the arts and culture, traditions of governance, powerful legal frameworks, key historical moments in cultural policy development, the status of artists and culture-bearers and their communities, et cetera. And these mappings will miss cultural policy that is not recognized as cultural policy in the local context. Recognizing that the "map is not the territory" is enormously helpful in a context where the French Model is a norm, since that norm lends great weight to administrative structure and invests a highly institutionalized and highly centralized structure with efficiency and effectiveness.[11] Finally, it is useful to be able to say, "Well, when looked at in the French way, we appear to have no cultural policy, but we think of culture, in the context of governance, in our own way." In some places, that local conceptualization of culture in the context of governance may even rise to embody a distinct *cultural policy archetype* (Rosenstein 2021).

A helpful suggestion for those setting off into mapping is to remember that this exercise is in itself a tool of policy and to proceed with care, perhaps with an intention toward contributing to a *humble theory* (and perhaps a humble sort of policy) wherein "we begin to think in the act of describing and see particulars in the act of comparing" (Noyes 2008, 41, quoted in Foster 2015, 9). Ultimately, the first objective of mapping should be to enable people to orient themselves and navigate within a system so that they can understand and act. Those people may be policymakers or cultural administrators or artists or culture-bearers or scholars or activists. One thing they definitely will want to know is: where in this system does authority lie? In that regard, a mapping exercise that concludes "we have no cultural policy" really is not at all helpful. In fact, that conclusion would misapprehend how comparison can be useful. Comparison can help to reveal what is hidden in one context by recognizing it in another. However, when comparisons are wielded with blind normativity, they will prove poor tools for scholars and actors alike.

Notes

1. This reflects a familiar pattern in France's approach to UNESCO as a platform to further its international and bilateral influence; in disputes between the Cold War powers, France "remained aloof from political considerations" and focused on "work of a purely technical nature" (Seydoux, quoted in Pendergast 1976, 466).
2. Whether they ever achieved that goal is open to question. Gordon (2001, 18) argues: "One of the fundamental difficulties of the series . . . is that it is virtually impossible to make any objective assessment of 'cultural needs,' let alone one that identifies common standards. The reviews cannot evaluate the cultural life of a given country, but only make some attempt at assessing the effectiveness of the cultural policy of the public authorities. Quite apart from the problems of definition (e.g., of 'national' and 'culture'), we immediately encounter the dilemmas of what can reasonably be included in public policy—much of culture being commercially provided—and the reality that different aspects of cultural policy (whether overtly or by default) are usually located in a variety of different departments of government at national level."
3. Given the significance that the French Model would take on, it is ironic that the contribution *Some Aspects of French Cultural Policy* (authored by Augustin Girard) explicitly shuns the task of mapping the French cultural bureaucracy and its direct actions: "This study explains the new French concept of what the State can do for culture. It is not, accordingly, a detailed description of what the Ministry of Culture or other interested agencies are doing, but an explanation of measures selected to show how France's cultural policy is being carried out" (1970, 8).
4. Girard is not identified as the author of this report but is acknowledged as having "drafted" it.
5. Christopher Gordon (UK) served as rapporteur for the Italy review and so is identified as the author of the report.
6. In a footnote to his sole-authored article, Girard admits that "the views expressed in this report are not necessarily shared by the rapporteur or the other members of the group and all the more so because I have omitted some of the Group's conclusions and put forward some of my personal opinions" (1996, 64).
7. "Goal 1: Support Sustainable Systems of Governance for Culture" . . . "Means of verification:

- Existence of a ministry of culture or a cultural secretariat with a ministerial status
- Existence of a 'culture committee' in a main national legislature (e.g., parliament)
- Existence of inter-ministerial cooperation mechanisms" (Anheier 2015, 36).

8. This represents a great deal of growth since the 1980s. See Bustamante 2015.
9. In that it is composed of institutions or fields and not learned and shared beliefs and values. Many of the expressive forms that might in the past have been considered cultural in the "anthropological" sense now would be classified as intangible cultural heritage.
10. Those who are familiar with the US literature will note that this interpretation is directly at odds with the premises of Cherbo and Wyszomirski (2000).
11. Scholars of the invention and implementation of lists to govern intangible cultural heritage are particularly insightful on the normative aspect of cultural policy instruments (see, e.g., Kirschenblatt-Gimblett 2004; Hafstein 2009; Bendix, Eggert, and Peselman 2013; Foster and Gilman 2015).

REFERENCES

Alasuutari, Pertti, and Anita Kangas. 2020. "The Global Spread of the Concept of Cultural Policy." *Poetics* 82: 1–13.

Anheier, Helmut. 2015. "Toward a Monitoring Framework." In *Re/Shaping Cultural Policies, 2015*, edited by Yudhishthir Raj Ishar, 31–43. Paris: UNESCO.

Ahearne, Jeremy. 2009. "Cultural Policy Explicit and Implicit: A Distinction and Some Uses," *International Journal of Cultural Policy* 15, no. 2: 141–153.

Belfiore, Eleonora. 2004. "The Methodological Challenge of Cross-National Research: Comparing Cultural Policy in Britain and Italy." Working Paper No. 8, Centre for Cultural Policy Studies, University of Warwick.

Bendix, Regina, Aditya Eggert, and Arnika Peselman, eds. 2013. *Heritage Regimes and the State*. Gottingen: Gottingen University Press.

Betzler, Diana, Ellen Loots, Marek Prokupek, Lenia Marques, and Petja Grafanauer. 2021. "COVID-19 and the Arts and Cultural Sector: Investigating Countries' Contextual Factors and Early Policy Measures." *International Journal of Cultural Policy* 27, no. 6: 796–814.

Bustamante, Mauricio. 2015. "Les politiques culturelles dans le monde: Comparaisons et circulations de modèles nationaux d'action culturelle dans les années 1980." *Le Seuil* 206–207, no. 1: 156–173.

Cherbo, Joni, and Margaret Wyzsomirski. 2000. "Mapping the Public Life of the Arts in America." In *The Public Life of the Arts in America*, edited by Joni Cherbo and Margaret Wyzsomirski, 3–21. New Brunswick, NJ: Rutgers University Press.

Cohen, Joshua. 2021. "African Socialist Cultural Policy: Senegal Under Senghor." *African Arts* 54, no. 3: 28–37.

Desportes, Coline. 2020. "Picasso en nigritie: L'exposition 'Picasso' à Dakar (1972), l'occasion d'une relecture stratégique du primitivisme par Léopold Sédar Senghor." In *Deborder la Negritude: Arts, Politique et Société à Dakar*, edited by Mamadou Diouf and Maureen Murphy, 35–50. Dijon: Presses du Réel.

Dubois, Vincent. 2016. "The 'French Model' and Its 'Crisis': Ambitions, Ambiguities and Challenges of a Cultural Policy." *Debats: Journal on Culture, Power and Society* 130, no. 2: 81–97.

Foster, Michael Dylan. 2015. "UNESCO on the Ground." In *UNESCO on the Ground*, edited by Michael Dylan Foster and Lisa Gilman, 1–16. Bloomington: Indiana University Press.

Foster, Michael Dylan, and Lisa Gilman, eds. 2015. *UNESCO on the Ground*. Bloomington: Indiana University Press.

Girard, Augustin. 1996. "For a Cultural Revival of Italy: A Report on the Council of Europe Review of Italian Cultural Policy." *International Journal of Cultural Policy* 3, no. 1: 55–64.

Girard, Augustin, and Geneviève Gentil. 1983. *Cultural Development: Experiences and Policies*. Paris: UNESCO.

Gordon, Christopher. 1995. *Cultural Policy in Italy*. Strasbourg: Culture Committee of the Council of Europe.

Gordon, Christopher. 2001. *European Perspectives on Cultural Policy: Cultural Policy Reviews*. Paris: UNESCO.

Hafstein, Vladimar. 2009. "Intangible Heritage as a List: From Masterpieces to Representation." In *Intangible Heritage*, edited by Laurajane Smith and Natsuko Akagawa, 93–111. London: Routledge.

Kirshenblatt-Gimblett, Barbara. 2004. "Intangible Heritage as Metacultural Production." *Museum International* 56, nos. 1–2: 52–65.

Martin, Laurent. 2013. *L'enjeu culturel: La reflexion international sur les politiques culturelles, 1963–1993*. Paris: History Committee of the Ministry of Culture and Communication.

Miller, Toby, and George Yudice. 2002. *Cultural Policy*. London: Sage.

Moulinier, Pierre. 1990. *Programme de l'UNESCO en matière de développement culturel: Presentation des travaux realisés depuis 1960*. Paris: UNESCO.

Noyes, Dorothy. 2008. "Humble Theory." *Journal of Folklore Research* 45, no. 1: 37–43.

Pendergast, William. 1976. "UNESCO and French Cultural Relations, 1945–1970." *International Organization* 30, no. 3: 453–483.

Portoles, Jordi Balta. 2017. "Toward More Collaborative Cultural Governance." In *Re/Shaping Cultural Policies, 2018*, edited by Yudhishthir Raj Ishar, 35–52. Paris: UNESCO.

Ragin, Charles. 2014. *The Comparative Method: Moving Beyond Qualitative and Quantitative Strategies*. Berkeley, CA: University of California Press.

Rindzeviciute, Egle. 2021. "Transforming Cultural Policy in Eastern Europe: The Endless Frontier." *International Journal of Cultural Policy* 27, no. 2: 149–162.

Rius-Ulldemolins, Joaquim, Alejandro Pizzi, and Juan Arturo Rubio Arostegui. 2019. "European Models of Cultural Policy: Towards European Convergence in Public Spending and Cultural Participation?" *Journal of European Integration* 41, no. 8: 1045–1067.

Rosenstein, Carole. 2018. *Understanding Cultural Policy*. London: Routledge.

Rosenstein, Carole. 2021. "Cultural Policy Archetypes: The Bathwater and the Baby." *International Journal of Cultural Policy* 27, no. 1: 16–29.

Schuster, J. Mark. 1987. "Making Compromises to Make Comparisons in Cross-National Arts Policy Research." *Journal of Cultural Economics* 11, no. 2: 1–36.

Silva, Gabriela Toledo. 2015. "UNESCO and the Coining of Cultural Policy." Paper presented at the 10th International Conference in Interpretive Policy Analysis.

Silva, Gabriela Toledo. 2016. "UNESCO Monographs in the Making of Cultural Policy." *Cadernos gestão pública e cidadania* 21, no. 70: 190–208.

Srakar, Andrej, and Marilena Vecco. 2021. "Assessing the Validity of Cultural Policy Typologies for Central-Eastern European Countries." *International Journal of Cultural Policy* 27, no. 2: 218–232.

UNESCO. 1969. *Cultural Policy: A Preliminary Study*. Paris: UNESCO.

UNESCO. 1970. *Some Aspects of French Cultural Policy*. Paris: UNESCO.

Vestheim, Geir. 2019. "UNESCO Cultural Policies 1966–1972—The Founding Years of 'New Cultural Policy.'" *Nordic Journal of Cultural Policy* 22, no. 1: 174–195.

CHAPTER 10

THE FUTURE OF CULTURAL DIPLOMACY
From Digital to Algorithmic

NATALIA GRINCHEVA

INTRODUCTION

This chapter conceptualizes changes in arts management practices from the perspective of cultural diplomacy. Understood as a form of cross-cultural communication between countries to improve international relations, cultural diplomacy has always played a unique role in building bridges across borders by connecting artists, cultural communities, and organizations (Schneider 2003). The intangible form of these human-to-human connections has been instrumental in establishing and maintaining long-term and mutually beneficial relationships and trust, which strengthen economic and political alliances and improve cooperation among nation-states (Schneider 2003).

Traditionally, cultural diplomacy has been defined as a government-led cultural or artistic exchange activity with a strong foreign policy agenda and objectives (Clarke 2016). Recently, though, cultural diplomacy has significantly expanded its meaning (Grincheva 2019a). Specifically, a new stream of diplomacy scholarship places the key emphasis not necessarily on diplomatic actors such as governments but on the desirable outcomes of diplomatic activities (Goff 2013). Stressing mutual understanding, respect, peace, and stability between countries as fundamental purposes of cultural diplomacy, the latter understanding of this concept emphasizes the role of nonstate actors in achieving these goals (Kelley 2014). This chapter draws on this expanded understanding of cultural diplomacy and specifically focuses on the conceptualization of emerging activities that engage a wide range of different state and nonstate actors, including cultural organizations, communities, and artists.

The chapter also pays close attention to the new practices of cultural diplomacy in the twenty-first century, empowered by the rapid rise of digital communication and mixed-realities technologies. New media, internet, and mobile communications have drastically increased the scope and intensity of global data connectivity. This digital disruption has transformed the ways in which cultural diplomacy is conducted and understood by governments, arts communities, cultural institutions, and societies. In the digital age, arts diplomacy has acquired new actors, tools, channels, and management strategies. Visual enhancements and algorithms, global networks, big data, artificial intelligence (AI), and virtual and augmented reality (VR and AR) increasingly automate, augment, and complicate cultural diplomacy activities.

This chapter explores, conceptualizes, and illustrates how new media technologies and data practices recalibrate the context in which cultural diplomacy operates by reshaping the medium of artistic communication, empowering new actors and equipping them with new tools to establish, deliver, maintain, and assess their global communication campaigns. The chapter identifies and describes three key aspects of cultural diplomacy transformations in the new conditions of increased digitalization: *virtualization*, *algorithmization*, and *datafication*. Virtualization is the process of creating a simulated or virtual computing environment to significantly expand or augment physical environments to pursue different goals, from designing new, more intense human experiences to simply replacing analog spaces for resource optimization (Portnoy 2016). Algorithmization refers to the processes of employing AI and machine learning to automate different tasks, from delivering public services to making strategic decisions that manage, control, or nudge human behavior in everyday life (Schuilenburg and Peeters 2020). Finally, datafication is understood in this chapter as a process through which social interaction acquires a new digital or online dimension, generating quantified data that allows for real-time tracking and predictive analysis (Schäfer and van Es 2017).

Exploring the most recent cultural diplomacy activities, reflected through institutional and government reports and press releases, the chapter offers a bird's-eye view of current global arts practices to critically reflect on the new dimension of cultural diplomacy. It specifically builds on extensive research across the gray literature (primary sources published by governments, cultural institutions, or civil society actors) to identify and explore the most recent activities carried out within the framework of international cultural exchange programs and cultural sharing projects.

The emerging practices of cultural diplomacy reflect significant transformations of diplomatic activities through digitalization and datafication processes, which have been further amplified in the past few years due to the global COVID-19 pandemic (Grincheva 2021). The analysis draws on digital diplomacy and critical digital culture scholarship to conceptualize the complex processes of virtualization, algorithmization, and datafication as applied to three aspects of diplomacy: cultural sharing or national projection, cultural exchanges, and impact evaluations.

The following section opens the chapter by exploring how VR, AR, and metaverse technologies have offered new virtual avenues for cultural sharing while delivering new cultural experiences to contemporary audiences. The next part explores the power of algorithms and AI to stretch cross-cultural communications and exchanges beyond the human-to-human realm. Finally, the chapter explores opportunities for enhancing cultural diplomacy evaluations through the employment of data analytics that can offer new insights into the value and impact of international arts activities. The chapter concludes by discussing the implications of cultural diplomacy transformations for arts management practices.

SHARING CULTURES: VIRTUALIZATION

Sharing national culture, values, and traditions across borders, or national projection, has always been an important dimension of cultural diplomacy (Grincheva 2020). National projection aims to create a positive image of the nation in the minds of foreigners, in order to promote and support national political and economic policies and secure states' interest in the international arena. Known in the twentieth century also as nation-branding, the paradigm of national projection has a long history, with the most illustrative examples from the nineteenth century, when universal expositions, later known as world expos, started to take place in Europe (Anholt 2007). These expositions offered countries a dedicated platform for demonstrating artistic excellence and cultural achievements. They helped construct national representations to "create a favorable national image abroad, form or strengthen national and ideological alliances, [and] set international or domestic agendas to facilitate culture transfer" (Kaiser 2004, 46).

National projection activities across borders amplified even further with the rise and development of the most prominent and oldest European institutions of cultural promotion, such as the Goethe Institute, British Council, Dante Alighieri Society, Alliance Française, and others (Paschalidis 2009). From the 1870s, these institutions opened in many foreign countries and developed rich cultural programming and resources for international audiences, facilitating language education and cultural exchange. For example, to date the British Council has established a global presence in over a hundred countries and boasts to reach almost a billion people through seventy-six million direct interactions, while engaging seventy-five thousand arts organizations and artists worldwide (British Council 2019). These engagements help establish fruitful international connections, building trust and cultural understanding, while increasing trade and investment flows (British Council 2019).

However, in the past two centuries, cultural sharing via cultural diplomacy programming was basically confined to the physical world, in which governments' strategic foreign policy objectives, economic infrastructures, and direct state support of arts institutions and cultural communities defined the physical mobilities of artists and circulation of cultural content across borders. In the twenty-first century, though, the rise of new media technologies and the internet provided new channels for communication with global audiences, increased the speed of information transfer, and expanded the scope and diversity of international audiences (Bjola and Holmes 2015). Digitalization of culture established more advanced channels for promotion and sharing of heritage artifacts, music, films, performance, and visual or literary arts, which acquired a new form, "disembodied from their point of origin or production," to circulate in "a space that has no particular territorial inscription" (Poster 2006, 25). The internet enabled "planetary transmissions of cultural objects" that can easily cross cultural and geographic boundaries (Poster 2006, 25). From the perspective of cultural diplomacy, digitized cultural objects and various virtual artistic practices or manifestations have strong power to influence people's perceptions of other cultures and traditions through the processes of digital consumption and interaction (Roberts and Lascity 2019). For example, the global impact of American pop culture that travels to different parts of the world via various channels, including digital, is universally recognized (Nye 2004) and even conceptualized in such phenomena as Hollywood diplomacy (Chung 2020), jazz diplomacy (Saito 2019), and more recently hip-hop and rap diplomacies (Dunkel and Nitzsche 2018) and digital museum diplomacy (Grincheva 2020), to name but a few.

The digital environment that is increasingly shaping educational, cultural, communication, and political dimensions of contemporary society has become an arena of cross-cultural struggle for promoting national cultural contents that ideologically construct the perceptions of global audiences. As a result, the digitization of culture has become an important part of foreign policies and strategies that regulate cultural content production, circulation, and trade while shaping protocols of how global audiences access and interact with cultures in the virtual realm (Wong 2021). Not surprisingly, many governments have invested considerable resources to digitize their national heritage and cultural resources to enter and successfully compete in a highly saturated global media space (UNESCO 2021). What started with the mere mass digitization of heritage collections and building an online representation of major arts institutions has resulted in the virtualization of cultural diplomacy, a complex process that increasingly is operating beyond physical reality.

Virtualization of contemporary social life and communications is a highly dynamic and continuous process that creates new forms of cultural mobility, intensifies human experiences of interactions with cultural content, and establishes new avenues for cultural sharing across borders. To borrow from Henri Lefebvre's (1996) terminology, the new virtual spaces of cross-cultural communication, enabled by AR, VR, and gaming technologies, can be understood as a "lived space," a "space of play" coexisting with "spaces of exchange and circulation, political space and cultural space" (172). Especially since early 2020, under the pressure of the pandemic, which disrupted international cultural exchanges in the physical realm, cultural institutions have established new practices in virtual reality, enhancing audiences' cultural engagement. For instance, while a museum has long been conceptualized as an "imaginary space" (Malraux 1967), the "distributed nature" of museums (Smith Bautista and Balsamo 2013) was amplified even further when they were pushed by the pandemic to operate as hybrid institutions existing between physical and virtual worlds.

In 2020 Cuseum launched a new AR mobile app, Museum from Home, that allowed audiences across countries to experience artworks from the comfort of their homes (Cuseum 2020). Users could virtually place paintings and other objects from various museums' collections onto their walls and interact with them. Cuseum also collaborated with the Massachusetts Institute of Technology to conduct research on perceptions of art through augmented and virtual realities. This research challenged assumptions about how people experience art, something discussed by Walter Benjamin (1935) in *The Work of Art in the Age of Mechanical Reproduction*. While Benjamin argued that reproduced copies lose their authenticity and aura, the research, by contrast, suggested "the human brain doesn't really differentiate between digitally reproduced artworks and their originals" (Sinha, Cornell, and Nathan 2020, 5). These insights suggest that virtual reality offers unprecedented opportunities for museum diplomacy, which has always thrived by projecting and sharing national culture and heritage on the world stage. Enhanced through augmented reality, museum diplomacy can now reach people on their mobile phones, creating more targeted, personalized, and intimate experiences for the consumption of and interaction with cultural content.

Creating these new virtual spaces as platforms of cultural diplomacy enables two key dynamics in which cultural actors and governments are increasingly involved. On the one hand, these dynamics are based on a "partial deterritorialization" as they push the boundaries of virtual cross-cultural exchanges; on the other hand, they increasingly "territorialize cyberspace" (Herrera 2009, 88). For example, the establishment of cultural embassies and the implementation of cultural events and projects in a virtual world or massively multiplayer online computer-simulated environments, like Second Life, started early in the twenty-first century. In May 2007, the Republic of Maldives opened the first "virtual embassy" on Second Life's Diplomacy Island (DiploFoundation 2007). However, greater media attention and international acclaim were achieved by the independent Swedish Institute, which, supported by the Swedish Foreign Ministry, established the Swedish embassy in Second Life, also in 2007 (Second House of Sweden 2013). From 2007 till 2012, the embassy successfully ran major international cultural events, including a Raoul Wallenberg exhibition in collaboration with the Jewish Museum in Stockholm and the Open Archive in Budapest, a film festival featuring Swedish and Indonesian cinematography, and a Swedish pop concert for Brazilian audiences, to name but a few. With Swedish lessons for beginners, conferences, and public celebrations of international holidays such as World Book Day, the Swedish Institute established meaningful connections with Second Life communities, offering innovative contributions to the country's cultural sharing and nation-branding efforts (Stevens 2015).

Most recently, technologies for creating world-like, large-group online environments designed for real-time interactivity among participants visually represented by personalized avatars have significantly advanced with the emergence of new metaverse technologies. The term "metaverse" was first coined by Neal Stephenson (1992) in his highly influential science fiction novel *Snow Crash*; recently, the concept of the metaverse as a shared online space that incorporates 3D graphics, either on a screen or in VR, has gained traction. In June 2021, Mark Zuckerberg announced new initiatives to transform his mega-popular social media platform Facebook into a metaverse called Horizon, while Microsoft also confirmed plans for building new metaverse applications along with AR hardware HoloLens (Sparkes 2021).

Apart from large corporations embarking on the development of metaverse platforms to engage global audiences, some national governments have been very proactive in tapping new opportunities. For example, South Korea, which is the world's fourth-largest gaming market, worth more than $16.6 billion, announced ambitious plans to build the first nationwide metaverse (Lee, Park, and Lee 2020). In May 2021, South Korea's Ministry of Science and Information and Communications Technology announced that the country has launched an industry alliance, composed of seventeen major IT companies, to bolster the development of the national metaverse ecosystem (Government of Korea 2021). The implications of this government initiative for cultural diplomacy, especially from the perspective of nation-branding, are promising. In the past three decades the government's investments and efforts in going global by wielding its cultural soft power have produced phenomenal growth in the global popularity of Korean culture, known as Hallyu or the Korean Wave (Kim 2021). Despite the coronavirus restrictions that began in 2020, the number of global Hallyu fans topped 100 million, while the total number of fan clubs rose to 104,770,000 in 109 countries worldwide (Korean Foundation 2020).

Most recently, Korean Wave programming opened up a new channel through virtualization. During the challenging times of the pandemic, when travel was restricted, K-pop groups established new practices of interacting with their global fans in virtual spaces through different metaverse platforms. These offered exciting opportunities for audiences not only to virtually meet their idols but also to engage with the cultural content through co-creation and participatory activities. Hybe, the company behind popular musical groups such as BTS and Tomorrow X Together, launched Weverse, a global fandom platform for VR communication with fans, which also functions as a market space for cultural products from music to cosmetics (Weverse 2021). SK Telecom, the largest South Korean wireless telecommunications operator, with more than 27 million subscribers, launched its K-Pop Metaverse Project, which created a social world for global fans to experience Hallyu on a new level (SK Telecom 2021).

The metaverse VR technology not only enables socialization in a game space but also allows users to modify virtual environments by "inhabiting" them (Stevens 2015, 233). Virtualization of social activities has significant implications for cultural diplomacy. It offers new opportunities to create highly multicultural and multilingual spaces, in which members' geographical proximity is no longer relevant. Instead, these spaces are built on the premise of cultural affinity, curiosity, interest, solidarity, and identity sharing. As a result, technologies shape human cultural experiences and perceptions of shared spaces, redefining their ontological, functional, and cultural conceptualization (Jaskuła 2012). An increasingly virtual space of cultural consumption and interaction loses its dependence on local, contextual, and physical limitations. On the one hand, the process of virtualization has "[shrunk] the world by bridging gaps between hard-to-reach regions and populations otherwise left 'behind'" (Alhashimi 2021). On the other hand, it created new restrictions, gray zones, and access gaps differentiating between "haves" and "have-nots." First, one should not forget that the digital realm is subject to regulations and laws, which are defined by complex processes in the geopolitical climate. Information wars, internet governance and digital censorship, creative media trade regulations, and sanctions continuously shape the global media landscape, producing complex political cartography of zones of access and limitations (Bjola and Holmes 2015).

Furthermore, the digital divide widens the gap between the developing and developed worlds, exacerbating gender, cultural, and social inequalities. For instance, the average gender digital divide is estimated at 23 percent across developing countries (Rowntree 2019). In 2019, almost half of the world population remained offline, with the majority of unconnected people living in the least-developed countries (United Nations 2019). Digital access amplifies cultural, financial, and skills-related barriers. Even living in a country with broadband coverage does not guarantee access, as residents have to own hardware to connect and need the relevant digital literacy skills, knowledge, and language proficiency to meaningfully consume the majority of the content available online, not to mention producing and sharing their own content (Alhashimi 2021).

These inequalities significantly limit the geography of global audiences that could be reached through virtual cultural diplomacy activities, while also preventing cultural actors from more disadvantaged areas from entering and competing in a global media space. This situation highlights that while virtualization of cultural diplomacy increasingly benefits powerful actors on the world stage, it remains an untapped potential for many arts and cultural organizations in countries with fewer resources and less-developed digital infrastructures; such countries lag behind in terms of national cultural promotion in the virtual realm. However, cultural diplomacy is not only about sharing one's own culture; it is also about establishing trustful relationships based on direct human-to-human interactions (Mulcahy 1999). The next section illuminates how the algorithmization of global communications reshapes cross-cultural contact in the twenty-first century.

Relation-Building: Algorithmization

The cultural relations dimension of cultural diplomacy presupposes interaction between parties, providing an "infrastructure" for mutual influence. The constructivist approach in international relations conceptualizes people's social and cultural identities as situated "within a specific, socially constructed world," in which actors collectively create meanings and understandings of themselves and others (Wendt 1992, 398). However, traditional meanings can be reconstructed and identities can be "invent[ed] de novo" (Wendt 1992, 398). Such a reconstruction occurs in "the presence of new social situations that cannot be managed in terms of pre-existing self-conceptions," when people are confronted with new social environments and engage in close interaction with members of different societies (Wendt 1992, 398). These "situations" have been strategically created through various diplomatic exchange programs, which play an important role in building mutually beneficial relationships between countries.

The predominant model of this type of communication is a two-way interactive dialogue that provides an arena for contested ideas and beliefs to be discussed and negotiated among participants from different traditions and backgrounds (Melissen 2005; Snow and Taylor 2009). The core principle behind these diplomatic activities is the claim that bringing together people from different countries helps to achieve mutual understanding, because through personal connections program participants can learn about one another's differences and commonalities and negotiate common values (Parkinson 1977). In past decades, this direct communication among cultural diplomacy participants was heavily dependent on state-sponsored programs, which strategically selected prominent scientists, artists, or athletes to travel abroad to serve as cultural ambassadors. For example, during the Cold War between the United States and the Soviet Union, in order to promote equal rights and democracy the American government financially supported jazz bands that were composed of mostly African American artists. However, "the musicians themselves realized the irony of representing a country that discriminated against blacks at home" (Brown 2006, 81). In dance as well, in spite of the criticism in American society of "choreographers like Martha Graham for works that revolved around the theme of sexuality," the government consistently promoted her company as an example of the unique freedom of individual artists in the United States (Prevots 2001, 3).

With the development of digital technologies, a cross-cultural dialogue that was happening mostly at a high level or that was controlled via diplomatic initiatives was significantly democratized, making ordinary people active participants in online discussions. For example, Seib (2012), in *Real-Time Diplomacy*, identified and analyzed new patterns and modes of instant communication among various players in the international arena. The book especially illuminated the power of ordinary citizens to participate in global informational flows, bypassing governmental institutions and challenging traditional political actors to react to these constant and direct interventions into the informational exchange (Seib 2012). In the twenty-first century, the cultural relations paradigm dominated political rhetoric, claiming that it had become the most appropriate form of diplomatic communication across borders (Hocking et al. 2012). This dialogic model of global online communications stressed the importance of engaging foreign audiences, making people important participants in cross-cultural negotiations, seeking their feedback, and building trust (Jora 2013).

In pursuit of these goals, in the first two decades of the twenty-first century many cultural institutions established an active presence on social media and built interactive platforms for participatory online activities (Grincheva 2020). For example, in the period 2009–2013 Tate Modern implemented its turbinegeneration project, which was designed exclusively as an online environment to connect schools, galleries, and artists from different countries for the co-creation and exchange of contemporary artworks, cultures, and ideas. The network offered a dedicated space for the turbinegeneration community to establish international partnerships between art schools and artists across countries for the co-creation and celebration of contemporary art. In 2010, the project was awarded UNESCO patronage "to demonstrate the organisation's support of an exceptional activity" that "fosters cultural diversity and initiates international dialogue" (Tate 2010); it was also supported by the British Council and ministries of culture in target countries. Over a period of just five years the turbinegeneration online platform became involved in interactive partnerships with schools, artists, educators, and art organizations in more than fifty countries, from Brazil to India (Tate 2013).

While relations established and maintained on social media are "characterized by volatility, mobility and fluidity," they provide "ample opportunities for experience mediation," affecting participants on emotional and cognitive levels and in this way reshaping one another's identities (Jaskuła 2012, 84). Online cultural spaces—facilitated by dedicated cultural institutions—proved to serve as important platforms for learning foreign languages and cultures, demystifying cultural stereotypes, increasing participants' intercultural competences, initiating a cross-cultural dialogue, and establishing trustful support networks and communities (Grincheva 2020), with strong implications for cultural diplomacy. In an age of rapid AI developments, however, this online communication is no longer solely controlled by human beings. Instead, the circulation of content, personal connections and networking is increasingly defined and shaped by the algorithms of service providers' platforms, leading to algorithmization of contemporary communications and social interactions. As Lee and Larsen (2019, 1) noted, "In the name of efficiency, objectivity, or sheer wonderment algorithms are becoming increasingly intertwined with society and culture."

The pervasiveness of algorithmization is especially evident in online communications, where human efforts to deliver information are increasingly replaced by chatbots. Chatbots are algorithms designed to react to online conversations, imitating a dialogue between people (Dahiya 2017). For example, cultural and heritage institutions increasingly use chatbots to sustain live conversations online, answer frequently asked questions, guide visitors to the physical site, or help them to find useful information on topics from ticketing to collections search. Furthermore, as reflected in both tech corporate and government reports, AI is used in creative industries for artistic content creation and targeted distribution, preservation of languages and heritage, and virtual travel (Thornton 2019; Caramiaux 2020).

For example, in 2020 Europeana—the largest digital heritage aggregator in Europe, connecting three thousand institutions and featuring online over fifty million cultural and scientific artifacts—implemented the Culture Chatbot Generic Services project. It developed a chatbot platform and several different versions of chatbots analyzing the use-cases of museums to explore the value of AI and algorithms for sharing cultural heritage across borders (Katz 2020). During the project museums experimented with chatbot technologies and designed a variety of applications that proved to be very helpful in facilitating a more productive cultural exchange via digital heritage collections. With these new algorithmic "helpers," an encounter with another culture could happen at any time without necessarily involving contact with a human being. However, it is indeed premature to judge the capacity of a chatbot to sustain an engaging cross-cultural dialogue that can change a person's perception of another culture.

One cannot deny that the efficiency of AI and robotics when working with large corpora of cultural data and information is much greater than that of a human being. Manovich (2018) stressed that in the future AI will play a larger part in professional cultural production, as it is better at processing large data sets and seeing connections that may not be obvious for a human. For example, Elizabeth Merritt, director of the American Alliance of Museums' Center for the Future of Museums, pointed out that AI applications offer unprecedented opportunities for cultural institutions to increase the accessibility of cultural content while engaging audiences on a new emotional level (Merritt 2017). AI-enabled applications that digitally "resurrect" historical figures, artists, and thought leaders based on archival material and footage enable communication not only across spaces and cultures but also across time. "Chatbots of historical figures, primed by published writings, archives and oral histories[,] could engage with visitors . . . to put history in the hands [of] anyone who owns a smart phone" (Merritt 2017).

The Dalí Museum in the United States went even further than creating a mere mobile chatbot: it employed the power of AI to design a digital version of the greatest master of Surrealism, Salvador Dalí, which can interact with visitors in live conversations to share the artist's life and work (Richardson 2019). The museum used its archives containing hundreds of interviews, quotes, and existing footage from the artist to train an AI algorithm to respond to verbal and nonverbal cues in a human's conversation to recreate Dalí's personality and even imitate his facial and bodily expressions (Dalí Museum 2021). The AI generates up to 190,512 possible combinations of dialogic scripts that allow each visitor to have a unique personal conversation with the artist and even take a selfie at the end of the experience (Dalí Museum 2021). Dalí Lives is a powerful educational tool that enables a more intimate and personalized experience of communication between visitors and artists by simulating one-on-one engagement with a historical figure (Mihailova 2021).

The Dalí Museum's 2019–2020 impact report demonstrated the power of this AI experience to attract a large number of visitors—almost four hundred thousand onsite and eleven million online (Dalí Museum 2020). According to the museum's director, Hank Hine, the success of Dalí Lives can be explained by a unique sense of kinship that the exhibit produces in visitors, consequently engendering a deeper emotional involvement with the art. "This virtual attraction is designed to evoke a sense of immediacy, closeness, and personalization; the digital avatar welcomes museum-goers in a conversational style, maintaining an impression of friendly, almost conspiratorial rapport throughout the experience" (Mihailova 2021, 884). Indeed, while the time gap between audiences and a historical figure might be quite substantial, having a historical figure "standing before visitors in a life-sized kiosk does help bring him into the context of modern life" (Lee 2019).

However, algorithmic modeling of historical figures, no matter how accurate it could be, is still subject to AI bias. As Mihailova (2021) points out, "The digitally reconstructed Dalí in Florida is an algorithmic aggregate of—and also a contemporary addition to—the sum total of the painter's celebrity image," shaped by "the longstanding commercialization and commodification of his image on a global scale" (886). Innovations in algorithmic historical cultural memory stewardship could offer cultural diplomacy exciting opportunities to engage people across borders in new ways, but the question remains whether machines can deliver the same depth, meaning, and quality of communication as human beings. While AI's potential to generate new opportunities in arts creation, cultural production, and promotions is well recognized (Manovich 2018; Zylinska 2020), there are growing concerns about job losses due to automation and about widening inequalities (Alhashimi 2021). Furthermore, technologies can be utilized either for good or for bad; one should not underestimate the negative implications of algorithmization, especially in mass communication, where it can even disrupt cultural diplomacy activities.

In fact, AI and algorithms offer new disinformation and propaganda tools, like bots and fake news, that significantly disrupt the flow of global information exchanges, accelerating anxiety, negative sentiment, and cross-cultural misunderstanding among online participants (Bjola and Holmes 2015). In the domain of arts and culture, for instance, algorithms have the power to shape cultural consumption preferences and tastes by serving as information gatekeepers on social networks (Manovich 2018). Whether provided by transnational tech corporations or by governments, social networks have in the past several years turned into spaces of digital surveillance, where algorithms build up users' profiles by compiling the traces they leave in online environments when they consume content, participate in activities, and interact with people. Algorithms govern the news, opinions, and friends, shaping the social world of people. They are powerful enough to accelerate the cultural and political fragmentation of society, in many cases exacerbating the differences between cultural communities (Riordan 2019). The use of algorithms in social media and online search engines poses serious challenges for cultural diplomacy that aims to create peaceful bridges across borders for building mutual trust and cooperation.

Social media algorithms reinforce echo chambers and increase the fragmentation of social and political debates online, making it much harder for cultural practitioners to engage with foreign publics, especially targeted groups (Riordan 2019). The fact that algorithms ensure that online users receive only content that they already favor minimizes the chances of cross-cultural exposure to new languages, cultural offerings, and activities, only reinforcing prejudices against other cultures. The implication for arts organizations and cultural institutions is that their global reach shrinks to populations that have already developed some sort of cultural affinity and familiarity with their content. "While there may be value in reinforcing the views of those who agree with us, public diplomacy must surely attempt to convince those whose views are different" (Riordan 2019, 100). In this way, algorithmization of digital platforms as avenues of cultural diplomacy can challenge institutional and government efforts to create long-term trustworthy relationships across borders.

As this section has illustrated, AI can both offer exciting opportunities for cross-cultural communication across time and space and have negative implications for diplomacy. However, it also reinforces the process of datafication, which creates the conditions for a more rigorous assessment of diplomatic impact, something that has long been an Achilles heel of public diplomacy (Sevin 2017). The next section aims to unpack the effects of datafication on cultural diplomacy impact assessments.

Impact Evaluations: Datafication

While being a central concern of national governments, which have always sought to convincingly justify their international cultural outreach investments, impact evaluations of cultural diplomacy activities have remained a challenging task (Banks 2011). The long-term nature of cultural diplomacy's possible impacts, the elusiveness of its direct effects on people, and the vagueness of its specific outcomes in relation to foreign policy goals explain why evaluating cultural diplomacy presents such methodological difficulty. In the past, the majority of cultural diplomacy actors relied heavily on descriptive accounts of diplomatic outputs, anecdotal evidence, and the sharing of best practices in the field to demonstrate the value of their activities on the global stage. However, in academic scholarship, these methods have been criticized for their tendency to mislead the impact analysis by presenting information in a very positivist way (Pamment 2014). On the other hand, qualitative approaches that rely on interviews and focus groups of cultural diplomacy programs' participants have proven to be very expensive, time-consuming, and resource-dependent.

However, with the rise of the internet and mobile communications, datafication processes have considerably enriched diplomatic evaluation activities, offering new methods to measure global public engagement, track opinion formation, and assess attention span (Bjola, Cassidy, and Manor 2020). "Data is often described as a critical resource of modern society, or even the oil of the new economy" (Jacobson, Höne, and Kurbalija 2018). Approximately one million people access the internet each day (World Economic Forum 2020). Moreover, the number of mobile phones increased from two billion in 2006 to five billion by the end of 2020 (Statista 2020). The rapid rise of smart cities and the Internet of Things around the globe intensified the generation of data at unprecedented rates (Alhashimi 2021). This amount of data, though, overwhelms the capacity of a human being to effectively analyze it in order to see and employ patterns or trends. The quantity and complexity of this data require innovative digital tools and mechanisms of monitoring, tracking, and analyzing previously invisible activities. The use of data in policymaking transforms decision-making processes as well as the communication of policies to the masses (Giest 2017).

Data analytics, network analysis, and other computation methods have become widely employed in public-policy modeling in recent decades (Kohlhammer et al. 2012). Particularly in the age of big data, ubiquitous computing, crowdsourcing, and open data, public-policy modeling aims to make sense of such huge amounts of information and to condense it specifically for the decision-making process. Jacobson, Höne, and Kurbalija (2018) produced a think-tank report on data diplomacy, which they defined as a three-dimensional framework. It understands big data as (1) a tool for policymaking,

(2) an important component of current diplomatic agendas, and (3) a factor that changes the very environment in which diplomacy operates, influencing geopolitical and geoeconomic positions of states. For example, in December 2021, US commerce secretary Gina M. Raimondo and UK secretary of state for digital, culture, media, and sport Nadine Dorries signed a statement of their governments' shared commitment to deepen the "UK-U.S. data partnership to realize a more peaceful and prosperous future by promoting the trustworthy use and exchange of data across borders" (DCMS 2021). The agreement aims to stabilize bilateral data flows, increase data interoperability, and ensure international data standards, in order to shape the global data environment and support mutually beneficial collaborations on global challenges and opportunities (DCMS 2021).

In the domain of arts and culture, big data collected on audiences increasingly informs the evaluation of arts activities to support decision-making processes, becoming "a source of national, indeed international, obsession" (Gilmore, Arvanitis, and Albert 2018, 13). National arts councils in countries across the globe stressed the value of big data in cultural policymaking—for example, to improve the allocation of public monies, increase the effectiveness of arts organizations in satisfying audiences, and develop new business strategies (Crossick and Kaszynska 2016). The recent attention given to big data and its potential to revolutionize everyday practices of arts management has informed new arts management practices, which increasingly rely on big-data collection and analysis (Gilmore, Arvanitis, and Albert 2018). For example, the Smarter London Together Strategy of the Greater London Authority (GLA) stresses the importance of mapping the city's cultural infrastructure across all boroughs by benchmarking cultural venues and their supporting ecosystems to facilitate strategic economic and cultural planning, including cultural tourism activities that have important implications for nation-branding and diplomacy. The Cultural Infrastructure Map developed by the GLA geovisualizes cultural assets alongside useful contextual data, such as transport networks and population growth, to offer a detailed snapshot of information (Mayor of London 2020). The map makes it possible to correlate different sets of data, such as transport, planning, audience, and demographics, that are specific to a particular geographic area, enabling the tracking of cultural activity, the measurement of cultural assets, and the coordination of human flows to monitor traffic and ensure public safety.

Recently, geovisualization approaches in mapping cultural activities have also been employed in cultural and creative industries research to categorize the size, economic significance, and growth patterns of creative industries, looking at the geographic distribution of global cultural production chains and cultural consumption with an accompanying analysis of "cluster effects" (Duxbury, Garrett-Petts, and Longley 2018). Going beyond global economics, the political implications of cultural activities taking place on the global stage have been addressed through both academic scholarship (Manovich 2020; Grincheva 2018) and professional experimentation in cultural mapping (Culture Counts 2021). In 2018, for instance, researchers from the University of Melbourne collaborated with the Australian Centre for the Moving Image to produce an experimental web application, Museum Soft Power Map, that can measure and map the soft power of museums. The research was instrumental in unlocking the power of big data generated by contemporary museums on-site and online to tell meaningful stories about their local, regional, and global audiences, connections, engagements, and diplomatic implications (Grincheva 2019b, 2022).

The strategic aggregation and analysis of big data generated by audiences in online, mobile, and even offline environments also provided promising perspectives for cultural diplomacy evaluations, especially for understanding patterns in public discourses in order to tailor messages and measure the effectiveness of communication campaigns (Riordan 2019). For example, digital tools have increasingly been used in evaluating public diplomacy activities, especially on social networks. As self-recording tools, social media allow the tracking, aggregation, and analysis of data, exposing public perceptions and even tracing shifts in opinions over time (Ji 2017, 80). For example, Ying (2017) proposed conducting a "web-ecological" analysis of internet-based sources by exploring online conversations among users as well as their engagements with specific political or cultural ideas through the production, sharing, circulation, and consumption of multimedia content. These methods draw on computer science, including data mining and sentiment analysis techniques, for measuring audience valence (Ying 2017; Bjola, Cassidy, and Manor 2020). These data analysis tools offer new opportunities for cultural actors to measure the extent to which foreign audiences engage with, disseminate, repurpose, and interact with cultural content, and they also provide a means to assess how positive or negative these interactions are.

While computational methods significantly increase the scope of data that could be effectively analyzed in a short time, this analysis comes with limitations and biases that should be properly acknowledged. First, quantitative data usually gives an impression of extreme objectivity, which is misleading, as the algorithms reflect the cognitive biases and epistemological prejudices of their designers (Kitchin 2014). Second, these data-intensive metrics offer only limited insights into the impacts of cultural diplomacy; qualitative methods, storytelling, and analysis of "thick" data also need to be employed to complement data analytics (Grincheva 2022). Third, algorithms employed for data analysis can be hacked by a hostile intelligence service to manipulate the policy decision-making of those dependent on its output (Riordan 2019). Finally, one should acknowledge that in certain cases data aggregation and collection violate privacy, freedom of expression, and human rights in the digital age. The notion of "data being the new gold," especially in its use for commercial purposes by platform providers and transnational tech corporations, raises important issues about data privacy, surveillance, and public security. Similarly, the use of technology for data surveillance, particularly in authoritarian states, endangers political freedom and rights to privacy of digital citizens (Wong 2021).

In the cultural community, these questions have become vital, especially since the beginning of the COVID-19 pandemic, when many cultural organizations and arts communities became dependent on online service providers for sharing their activities and keeping meaningful connections with their audiences. For example, during the AI Week event organized by the EU National Institutes for Culture in late 2020, a strong concern was expressed by cultural institutions and artistic groups. They advocated for the creation of digital civic spaces that are not controlled by big tech conglomerates, which already monopolize the global communication space. The co-founder of the Superrr Lab, Elisa Lindinger, warned that a public digital sphere created with the public's interest at heart does not exist at the moment. She advocated for implementing a universal declaration of digital human rights and called for the design of new digital civic spaces that are in the hands of artists and cultural communities (Brodigan 2020). Relying heavily on establishing peaceful and trustful relationships across countries, cultural actors need to properly address these concerns and find a middle ground between data surveillance and impact analysis that is increasingly informed by data collected on global audiences.

As this chapter demonstrates, new media technology and the processes it facilitates, such as virtualization, algorithmization, and datafication, can catalyze positive or negative trends in cultural diplomacy. Digital tools and platforms are not a panacea to improve cross-cultural communication. While they have great potential, they also heavily rely on actors' strategies and specific uses that can either enhance human connections across borders or downplay the efforts of cultural communities to establish a meaningful and mutually beneficial dialogue.

Implications and Conclusions

The disruptions of physical interactions and travel under the pressure of national lockdowns and border closure during the COVID-19 pandemic clearly demonstrated that it is no longer possible or even economically feasible for 3.6 billion people, half of the world's population, to live offline (United Nations 2020). Furthermore, during the crisis, the volume of digital cultural production and its global consumption rate dramatically increased (UNESCO 2020), paving more reliable avenues for digital communication and even diplomacy. Livestreaming, VR and AR tours, and metaverse immersive experiences have reinforced the role of digital technologies in delivering cultural content to global audiences and providing meaningful platforms for cross-cultural communications. This chapter has conceptualized complex processes of cultural diplomacy metamorphosis in the twenty-first century, identifying such important trends as virtualization, algorithmization, and datafication. It has illustrated the increasing penetration of digital technologies in the cultural practices that are designed for international outreach and engagements.

Several decades ago, cultural diplomacy required careful planning and organizational skills from international art managers to successfully navigate global routes; this required that they understand the geopolitical climate, border regulations, and visa and legal issues. Today, sharing cultural content, creating international cultural communities, and bringing artists together in the virtual realm also require strong arts management competences. However, contemporary diplomatic practices increasingly demand greater digital and data literacy in order to productively cross digital boundaries, circulate cultural content in the global media space, and establish meaningful avenues for digital interactive communications with international audiences. "The new space of human presence combines elements of reality and virtuality and becomes . . . the basis for the emergence of new forms of mobility of an unprecedented structure, roles, functions, or intensity" (Jaskuła 2012, 81). These new digital flows of human, cultural, and economic capital present new opportunities for international cultural relations and at the same time engender new forms of risk.

The negative implications of virtualization, algorithmization, and datafication discussed earlier alert us that new digital tools, platforms, and policies must be designed, implemented, and regulated with core participants in mind in order for those digital elements to live up to their potential as catalysts for cross-cultural understanding, trust, and respect. In the digital age, international arts managers must be equipped with foundational critical digital and data knowledge and skills to overcome digital access barriers and inequalities, properly acknowledge digital content creators' rights, address issues of data privacy and surveillance, and create safe public spaces for trustful communications. Furthermore, the rapid development of new technologies, which give audiences self-broadcasting tools and advanced communication opportunities across physical and virtual realities, highlights the importance of multistakeholder cooperation. Because cultural diplomacy in the digital age is becoming more multilayered, multidirectional, and dispersed among many actors, international arts managers have to find ways to encourage democratic governance of digital technologies, with a clear understanding of the roles and responsibilities of the public, private, and civic sectors.

Art managers need strong digital competences in order to design accessible virtual spaces, regulate online communication, and engage in responsible data analysis, with the goal of ensuring the fair use of digital technologies among involved stakeholders and communities, while mitigating risks. These questions about the multiple actors in contemporary cultural diplomacy in the virtual domain deserve a much broader and deeper discussion. New research should explore how digital technologies democratize cultural diplomacy activities, advancing the new role of public and civil society actors (such as independent artists, cultural communities, and arts organizations) as important "cultural ambassadors" in the digital media space. Finally, future research on the use of AI in cultural diplomacy should scrutinize the perspectives shared in this chapter about the power of algorithmization to introduce nonhuman actors into the realm of cross-cultural communications.

References

Alhashimi, Hana. 2021. "Future of Digital Cooperation." In *The Future of Diplomacy After COVID-19: Multilateralism and the Global Pandemic*, edited by Hana Alhashimi, Andres Fiallo, Toni-Shae Freckleton, Mona Ali Khalil, Mulachela Vahd, and Jonathan Viera, 86–117. London: Routledge.

Anholt, Simon. 2007. *Competitive Identity: The New Brand Management for Nations, Cities and Regions*. New York: Palgrave Macmillan.

Banks, Rober. 2011. *A Resource Guide to Public Diplomacy Evaluation*. Los Angeles: Figueroa Press.

Benjamin, Walter. [1935] 2008. *The Work of Art in the Age of Mechanical Reproduction*. Translated by J. A. Underwood. Harlow, UK: Penguin Books.

Bjola, Corneliu, Jennifer Cassidy, and Ilan Manor. 2020. "Digital Public Diplomacy." In *Routledge Handbook of Public Diplomacy*, edited by Nancy Snow and Nicholas J. Cull, 361–369, London: Routledge.

Bjola, Corneliu, and Marcus Holmes. 2015. *Digital Diplomacy: Theory and Practice*. London: Routledge.

British Council. 2019. "Annual Report 2019–20." https://bit.ly/3DYcFdF.

Brodigan, Dearbhla. 2020. "EUNIC DX/AI Week." European Union National Institutes of Culture. https://bit.ly/33BFBfg.

Brown, John. 2006. "Arts Diplomacy: The Neglected Aspect of Cultural Diplomacy." In *America's Dialogue with the World*, edited by William P. Kiehl, 71–90. Washington, DC: Public Diplomacy Council, School of Media and Public Affairs, George Washington University.

Caramiaux, Baptiste. 2020. "The Use of Artificial Intelligence in the Cultural and Creative Sectors." European Parliament. https://bit.ly/33DH191.

Chung, Hye Seung. 2020. *Hollywood Diplomacy: Film Regulation, Foreign Relations, and East Asian Representations*. New Brunswick, NJ: Rutgers University Press.

Clarke, David. 2016. "Theorising the Role of Cultural Products in Cultural Diplomacy from a Cultural Studies Perspective." *International Journal of Cultural Policy* 22, no. 2: 147–163.

Crossick, Geoffrey, and Patrycja Kaszynska. 2016. "Understanding the Value of Arts and Culture: The AHRC Cultural Value Project." Arts and Humanities Research Council. https://bit.ly/328YeXk.

Culture Counts. 2021. "About." https://culturecounts.cc/company.

Cuseum. 2020. "AR Museum from Home." https://cuseum.com/ar-museum-from-home.

Dahiya, Menal. 2017. "A Tool of Conversation: Chatbot." *International Journal of Computer Sciences and Engineering* 5, no. 5: 158–161.

Dalí Museum. 2020. "Impact Report 2019–20." https://bit.ly/3q2dvkW.

Dalí Museum. 2021. "Dalí Lives." https://bit.ly/3GPXepX.

DCMS. 2021. "Deepening Data Partnerships." Department for Digital, Culture, Media, and Sport, United Kingdom. https://bit.ly/3mcLVAi.

DiploFoundation. 2007. "22 May 2007: Maldives Unveils World's First Virtual Embassy." https://bit.ly/3oYygOU.

Dunkel, Mario, and Sina A. Nitzsche. 2018. *Popular Music and Public Diplomacy: Transnational and Transdisciplinary Perspectives*. Bielefeld: Transcript Verlag.

Duxbury, Nancy, W. F. Garrett-Petts, and Alys Longley. 2018. *Artistic Approaches to Cultural Mapping: Activating Imaginaries and Means of Knowing*. London: Routledge.

Giest, Sarah. 2017. "Big Data for Policymaking: Fad or Fasttrack?" *Policy Science* 50: 367–382.

Gilmore, Abigail, Kostas Arvanitis, and Alexandra Albert. 2018. "Never Mind the Quality, Feel the Width." In *Big Data in the Arts and Humanities*, edited by Giovanni Schiuma and Daniela Carlucci, 29–43, New York: Auerbach Publications.

Goff, Patricia. 2013. "Cultural Diplomacy." In *The Oxford Handbook of Modern Diplomacy*, edited by Andrew Cooper, Jorge Heine, and Ramesh Thakur, 419–435, Oxford: Oxford University Press.

Government of Korea. 2021. "Ministry of Science and ICT: News." https://bit.ly/3JJEWtf.
Grincheva, Natalia. 2018. "Mapping Museum Soft Power: Adding Geo-visualization to the Methodological Framework." *Digital Scholarship in the Humanities* 34, no. 4: 730–751.
Grincheva, Natalia. 2019a. *Global Trends in Museum Diplomacy*. London: Routledge.
Grincheva, Natalia. 2019b. "The Form and Content of 'Digital Spatiality': Mapping Soft Power of DreamWorks Animation in Asia." *Asiascape: Digital Asia* 6, no. 1: 58–83.
Grincheva, Natalia. 2020. *Museum Diplomacy in the Digital Age*. London: Routledge.
Grincheva, Natalia. 2021. "Cultural Diplomacy Under the 'Digital Lockdown': Pandemic Challenges and Opportunities in Museum Diplomacy." *Place Branding and Public Diplomacy* 18, no. 1: 8–11.
Grincheva, Natalia. 2022. "Beyond the Scorecard Diplomacy: From Soft Power Rankings to Deep Mapping Explorations." *Convergence* 28, no. 1: 70–91.
Herrera, Geoffrey. 2009. "Cyberspace and Sovereignty: Thoughts on Physical Space and Digital Space." In *Power and Security in the Information Age: Investigating the Role of the State in Cyberspace*, edited by Myriam D. Cavelty, Victor Mauer, and Sai F. Krishna-Hensel, 69–97, Aldershot, UK: Ashgate.
Hocking, Brian, Jan Melissen, Shaun Riordan, and Paul Sharp. 2012. "Integrative Diplomacy in the 21st Century." Netherlands Institute of International Relations "Clingendael."
Jacobson, Barbara, Katherina Höne, and Jovan Kurbalija. 2018. *Data Diplomacy: Updating Diplomacy to the Big Data Era*. Geneva: DiploFoundation.
Jaskuła, Sylwia. 2012. "New Forms of Mobility in the World of Virtualization and Mediatization of Cultures." *Politeja* 20, no. 1: 73–90.
Ji, Li. 2017. "Measuring soft power." In *Routledge Handbook of Soft Power*, edited by Chitty, Naren, Ji, Li, Rawnsley, Gary D. and Craig Hayden, 75–92, London: Routledge.
Jora, Lucian. 2013. "New Practices and Trends in Cultural Diplomacy." *Political Science and International Relations* 10, no. 1: 43–52.
Kaiser, Wolfram. 2004. "The Great Derby Race." In *Culture and International History*, edited by Jessica Gienow-Hecht and Frank Schumacher, 47–59. New York: Berghahn Books.
Katz, Pavel. 2020. "Interacting with the Culture Chatbot." Europeana. https://bit.ly/31VlDM7.
Kelley, Rob. 2014. *Agency Change: Diplomatic Action Beyond the State*. Lanham, MD: Rowman & Littlefield.
Kim, Youna, ed. 2021. *The Soft Power of the Korean Wave*. London: Routledge.
Kitchin, Rob. 2014. *The Data Revolution: Big Data, Open Data, Data Infrastructures and Their Consequences*. London: Sage.
Kohlhammer, Jorn, Kawa Nazemi, Tobias Ruppert, and Dirk Burkhardt. 2012. "Toward Visualization in Policy Modeling." *IEEE Computer Graphics and Applications* 32, no. 5: 84–89.
Korean Foundation. 2020. "Global Hallyu Trends." https://bit.ly/3yuRgIb.
Lee, Dami. 2019. "Deepfake Salvador Dalí Takes Selfies with Museum Visitors." The Verge, May 10, 2019. https://bit.ly/3DXOHzv.
Lee, Francis, and Lotta Bjorklund Larsen. 2019. "How Should We Theorize Algorithms? Five Ideal Types in Analyzing Algorithmic Normativities." *Big Data and Society* 1, no. 2: 1–6.
Lee, Jinju, Jin Suk Park, and Jeonghwan Lee. 2020. "The Impact of Multimarket Competition on Innovation Strategy: Evidence from the Korean Mobile Game Industry." *Journal of Open Innovation and Technology Market: Complex* 6, no. 14: 2–15.
Lefebvre, Henri. 1996. *Writings on Cities*. Oxford, UK: Blackwell.
Malraux, André. 1967. *The Psychology of Art: Museum Without Walls*. London: Secker and Warburg.

Manovich, Lev. 2018. *AI Aesthetics*. Moscow: Strelka Press.

Manovich, Lev. 2020. *Cultural Analytics*. Cambridge, MA: MIT Press.

Mayor of London. 2020. "Cultural Infrastructure Map." https://bit.ly/32bduRd.

Melissen, Jan. 2005. *The New Public Diplomacy: Soft Power in International Relations*. New York: Palgrave Macmillan.

Merritt, Elizabeth. 2017. "AI and the Future of History." American Alliance of Museums. https://bit.ly/3F42lm3.

Mihailova, Mihaela. 2021. "To Dally with Dalí: Deepfake (Inter)faces in the Art Museum." *Convergence* 27, no. 4: 882–898.

Mulcahy, Kevin. 1999. "Cultural Diplomacy and the Exchange Programs: 1938–1978." *Journal of Arts Management, Law and Society* 29, no. 1: 7–28.

Nye, Joseph. 2004. *Soft Power: The Means to Success in World Politics*. New York: Public Affairs.

Pamment, James. 2014. "Articulating Influence: Toward a Research Agenda for Interpreting the Evaluation of Soft Power, Public Diplomacy and Nation Brands." *Public Relations Review* 40: 50–59.

Parkinson, F. 1977. *The Philosophy of International Relations: A Study in the History of Thought*. Beverly Hills, CA: Sage Publications.

Paschalidis, Gregory. 2009. "Exporting National Culture: Histories of Cultural Institutes Abroad." *International Journal of Cultural Policy* 15, no. 3: 275–289.

Portnoy, Matthew. 2016. *Virtualization: Essentials*. London: Routledge.

Poster, Mark. 2006. *Information Please*. Durham, NC: Duke University Press.

Prevots, Naima. 2001. *Dance for Exports: Cultural Diplomacy and the Cold War*. Middletown, CT: Wesleyan University Press.

Richardson, Jim. 2019. "Art Meets Artificial Intelligence as Museum Resurrects Salvador Dalí." Museum Next, February 14, 2019. https://bit.ly/3GN7oHN.

Riordan, Shaun. 2019. *Cyberdiplomacy: Managing Security and Governance Online*. Cambridge, UK: Polity.

Roberts, Candice D., and Myles Ethan Lascity. 2019. *Consumer Identities: Agency, Media and Digital Culture*. Bristol, UK: Intellect Books.

Rowntree, Oliver. 2019. "Connected Women: The Mobile Gender Gap Report 2019." GSM Association. https://bit.ly/3pTV7uo.

Saito, Yoshiomi. 2019. *The Global Politics of Jazz in the Twentieth Century: Cultural Diplomacy and "American Music."* London: Routledge.

Schäfer, Mirko Tobias, and Karin van Es. 2017. *The Datafied Society: Studying Culture Through Data*. Amsterdam: Amsterdam University Press.

Schneider, Cynthia. 2003. "Diplomacy That Works: Best Practices in Cultural Diplomacy." Center for Arts and Culture.

Schuilenburg, Marc, and Rik Peeters. 2020. *The Algorithmic Society: Technology, Power, and Knowledge*. New York: Routledge.

Second House of Sweden. 2013. "Second House of Sweden 2007–2012." https://secondhouseofsweden.wordpress.com/.

Seib, Philip. 2012. *Real-Time Diplomacy: Politics and Power in the Social Media Era*. London: Palgrave Macmillan.

Sevin, Efe. 2017. "A Multi-Layered Approach to Public Diplomacy Evaluation: Pathways of Connection." *Politics and Policy* 45, no. 5: 879–901.

Sinha, Pawan, Molly Cornell, and Lauren Nathan. 2020. "Neurological Perceptions of Art Through Augmented and Virtual Reality." Cuseum. https://bit.ly/3s6sRrb.

SK Telecom. 2021. "Introduce Metaverse." https://www.sktelecom.com/en/view/introduce/metaverse.do.

Smith Bautista, Susana, and Anne Balsamo. 2013. "Understanding the Distributed Museum: Mapping the Spaces of Museology in Contemporary Culture." In *Museums and Higher Education Working Together*, edited by Jos Boys and Anne Boddington, 89–105. London: Routledge.

Snow, Nancy, and Philip Taylor, eds. 2009. *Routledge Handbook of Public Diplomacy*. New York: Routledge.

Sparkes, Matthew. 2021. "What Is a Metaverse." *New Scientist* 251, no. 3348: 28. https://doi.org/10.1016/S0262-4079(21)01450-0.

Statista. 2020. "Worldwide Forecast of Mobile Users." https://bit.ly/3q0RB1f.

Stephenson, Neal. 1992. *Snow Crash*. New York: Random House.

Stevens, Tim. 2015. "Security and Surveillance in Virtual Worlds: Who Is Watching the Warlocks and Why?" *International Political Sociology* 1, no. 9: 230–247.

Tate. 2010. "The Unilever Series: turbinegeneration Is Awarded UNESCO Patronage." Press release, November 16, 2010. https://bit.ly/2MCoy2f.

Tate. 2013. "The Unilever Series: turbinegeneration." https://bit.ly/2K5SOk2.

Thornton, Alex. 2019. "How AI Is Changing Arts and Culture." Microsoft. https://bit.ly/325gYHd.

UNESCO. 2020. "Culture and COVID-19: Impact and Response Tracker." https://bit.ly/3iQLN74.

UNESCO. 2021. "Policy Monitoring Platform: Digital Environment." https://bit.ly/32aEvGm.

United Nations. 2019. "Global Sustainable Development Report." https://bit.ly/3m4n7uf.

United Nations. 2020. "The Age of Global Interdependence. Secretary-General's High-Level Panel on Digital Cooperation." https://bit.ly/3mbybpu.

Weverse. 2021. "About." https://about.weverse.io/en.html.

Wendt, Alexander. 1992. *Social Theory of International Politics*. Cambridge, UK: Cambridge University Press.

Wong, Pak Nung. 2021. *Techno-Geopolitics: US-China Tech War and the Practice of Digital Statecraft*. London: Routledge.

World Economic Forum. 2020. "Global Risks Report 2020." https://bit.ly/3F6Cs4K.

Ying, Jiang. 2017. "Social Media and E-Diplomacy: Scanning Embassies on Weibo." In *Routledge Handbook of Soft Power*, edited by Chitty, N., Ji, L., Rawnsley, C., and Hayden, C., 122–137, London: Routledge.

Zylinska, Joanna. 2020. *AI Art*. Open Humanities Press.

CHAPTER 11

CULTURAL PLANNING AND A "COMMUNITY TURN" IN THE ARTS

Maximizing Cultural Resources for Social Impact

TOM BORRUP

The formal practice of cultural planning, which originated in the 1970s, is not widely understood and is relatively unknown outside municipal or local arts agencies. Especially in the United States, where the research described in this chapter was conducted, cultural planning in its early years demonstrated an ability to build cooperation among nonprofit arts organizations and to elevate their collective capacity to attract public and private sector funding. I join other scholars and practitioners who argue its contributions can be far greater (Bianchini 1999; Ghilardi 2001; Mercer 2006; Montgomery 1990). More recently cultural planning has demonstrated it can mobilize cultural resources to a variety of civic and social concerns. These include racial and cultural equity, affordable housing, transportation, health, local economies, and community vitality, among others.

In Canada, where cultural planning embraces a broader definition of culture and a more engaged role for the sector in civic affairs, Baeker (2010, vi), a Canadian cultural planner, defined the practice thus:

> Cultural planning is about harnessing the assets of a community; celebrating the unique resources, such as heritage properties, natural assets, and community spirit; revitalizing downtown cores that too often have deteriorated; honouring and respecting the unique contributions of our artists and artisans; creating diverse and safe neighborhoods; raising the bar for urban design; protecting our green spaces and becoming better stewards of our environment; and the many other elements that make up a community moving forward confidently in the 21st century.

Since the beginnings of formal practice in the United States, cultural planning grew under the influence of the country's mostly market-driven, predominantly white nonprofit arts sector (Dreeszen 1994; Stevenson 2014). Research described here shows that because of these influences, the practice has not engaged or helped build the full spectrum of cultural resources of communities, and only in isolated cases in the United States has it begun to extend its community impacts. By and large, however, and somewhat ironically, advancing cultural equity is not among the impacts reported.

During most of its forty years of practice, usually under the sponsorship of municipal arts agencies looking to advance the interests of arts organizations, cultural planning has served to advance the work of dominant cultural institutions. Organizations such as symphony orchestras, ballets, art museums, and professional theaters carry out charitable missions to provide cultural programs yet remain overwhelmingly white or Eurocentric in their cultural makeup and orientation, increasingly out of sync with the cities in which they operate.

Partly because of its limited scope, cultural planning grew but did not become as ubiquitous as early advocates anticipated. Cultural planning has often served what I call a *circle-the-wagons* strategy—using the metaphor of white American colonists in the 1800s employing their covered wagons in battles with Native people trying to discourage encroachment on their lands. Cultural planning acted as one defense of the cultural sector against those who would attack, censor, or eliminate the arts from public sector budgets. However, those circled wagons also excluded cultural groups and practices outside of established Eurocentric arts organizations and art forms.

Another Look at Cultural Planning

A survey of United States cultural plans during the second decade of the twenty-first century, described in this chapter, reflects the intentions of some cultural plans to advance equity and diversity but with nominal success. The survey was conducted in 2017 by this author (Borrup 2018) in collaboration with Americans for the Arts and in consultation with Craig Dreeszen, who completed a parallel survey in 1994 (Dreeszen 1994). The online survey was sent to just over two hundred local arts agencies, all members of Americans for the Arts, that reported in a 2015 survey they had completed or updated a cultural plan within the past ten years. The online survey comprised thirty-five questions, many with a multitude of categories and options, including open-ended responses. A total of fifty agencies completed the survey, representing cities of various sizes and similar to the respondents to the 1994 Dreeszen survey. The 2017 survey included many of the same questions asked twenty-three years earlier, with the intent to examine changes over time to cultural planning practices, characteristics of plans, planning intentions, and subsequent community outcomes as reported by the agencies leading, or significantly involved in, these cultural plans.

The survey and comparison provide both a detailed snapshot of more recent practice and a longitudinal look at changes since the 1980s and early 1990s. Specifically, these data illuminate the purpose, process, and outcomes of cultural planning from the perspectives of local arts agencies.

While a wider *community turn* in the arts (Dreeszen 1994) and in cultural planning was in evidence, it represents a slow turn. The full cultural resources of communities are generally not recognized, let alone afforded additional funding or consideration. In conclusion, I cite five limitations that need to be addressed for cultural planning—and for the arts and culture sector—to continue the community turn and to more fully serve their communities.

Roots of Cultural Planning

Tracing the origins of any profession or practice is never a straight line, nor are its beginnings simply attributable to any one person, organization, or event. Practitioners, advocates, scholars, observers, and others on multiple continents have contributed to the evolution of cultural planning, although general agreement places its origins as a formal practice in the United States.

Both Dreeszen (1994, 1998) and Ghilardi (2001) traced the roots of cultural planning to the late nineteenth-century City Beautiful movement, the 1930s Works Progress Administration (WPA) in the United States, and the community arts movement of the 1940s. American community arts activist Maryo Gard Ewell (2000) pointed further back to the Village Improvement movement in Massachusetts in 1853 for its efforts to plant trees, pave streets and sidewalks, and secure recreational facilities and other social amenities. Leavitt (1980) likewise detailed civic improvement groups in various cities in the United States led by women in the late nineteenth century that addressed issues including parks and playgrounds, street lighting, tree planting, libraries, and sidewalks, as well as civic pride. In terms of methods, Dreeszen pointed out that cultural planning shares antecedents in city planning practices formalized during the mid-twentieth century such as participatory neighborhood-level planning to address local amenities, opportunities for youth, tourism, local economic growth, and organizing for collective action, among other local concerns (see Rohe 2009).

The formal practice, as currently understood, is widely considered to have emerged in the late 1970s and through the 1980s in the United States. Ewell related that in 1975 she worked for the Arts Council of Greater New Haven, where "we did a cultural plan and called it that. I think that this may have been one of the very first plans." However, Ewell affirmed that, like most of the early cultural plans, "it was first and foremost an arts plan that asked: 'How can arts organizations and individual artists work together to both protect our sector, secure new venues, and collectively attract more audiences, money, and stature?'" (personal communication, February 27, 2020).

Jones (1993), Landry (2000), Ghilardi (2001), and Stevenson (2014) all credit American Robert McNulty for advocating new thinking about cultural policy and planning beginning in the mid-1970s. Founder of Partners for Livable Places (later Partners for Livable Communities), a Washington, DC, advocacy, research, and publishing nonprofit, McNulty expanded on the standard intrinsic value proposition (that art is simply good for you) advanced by most arts institutions and advocates.

In an early 1980s report, McNulty described that many cities involved in his organization since 1975 "identified some aspect of cultural planning as a focus for their local projects" (1983, 55). In the same report, he recounted a 1976 conference when he was employed by the National Endowment for the Arts (NEA) and his conversations with Los Angeles–based city planner and professor Harvey Perloff about examining cultural amenities. A 1978 NEA grant to a group led by Perloff helped fund this plan. Perloff's (1979) resulting treatise on how the City of Los Angeles should address the arts may not constitute the origins of the practice, but the 1979 plan has been recognized by various scholars as the first formal cultural plan. Perhaps because Perloff was a highly regarded city planner, this early plan was more outwardly focused than the 1975 New Haven plan described by Ewell, as well as most plans over the subsequent twenty years. Further, it was explicitly adopted into formal city and county plans, unlike a majority of subsequent plans (Dreeszen 1994). In the 1980s, the scope of cultural plans narrowed to become more internally focused, conducted by, for, and about the institutional arts sector. While Perloff prescribed a relatively broad role for the arts, his plan did not invoke a broader definition of culture as did some later plans, particularly in Australia and Canada (Baeker 2010; Dowling 1997; Mercer 2006; Stevenson 2014). This focus on arts (versus culture) perhaps set the stage for the planning process to divert attention to the needs of the formal arts sector rather than advocate ways to serve and connect the growing diversity of people and cultural resources of cities.

Purposes of Cultural Planning

With the exponential growth of the formal nonprofit arts sector in the United States beginning in the 1950s, public sector support remained scarce (Kreidler 1996). Arts advocates in the United States looked to other Western democracies where governments provided all or a majority of financial support to cultural institutions, and they sought ways to leverage greater subsidies from all levels of government. Cultural planning in the United States was therefore focused on garnering greater public sector support, as well as increasing funding from the private sector.

In his 1994 doctoral dissertation, which remains, in my view, the most significant study on cultural planning in the United States, Dreeszen (1994), a cultural planning practitioner, observed that new or increased financial resources for the arts tended to follow the completion of a cultural plan. His findings further encouraged arts agencies to focus the primary purpose of planning on leveraging new or increased funding. Local arts agencies that commissioned plans often sought to elevate their positions as leaders within their jurisdictional territory as well (Dreeszen 1994). These are not, in themselves, negative or inappropriate goals. They are simply limited and limiting. While expanding the funding base of established arts organizations and local arts agencies has merit, the greater value they can bring to a range of community concerns is infrequently addressed.

For local governments, in the United States and other parts of the world, cultural planning remains the primary tool for policy-setting in the cultural arena and the best opportunity to gain a more complete understanding of their cultural resources. In the hands of public or private nonprofit arts agencies, whose primary constituencies are nonprofit arts institutions, this centered cultural planning as a self-perpetuating advocacy tool is often little more than coordinated arts marketing and fundraising.

Various international scholars critiqued this orientation. Kunzmann (2004) called such plans "unhelpful and tiresome culture-related shopping lists" (399), while Kovacs (2011) wrote, "the placement of cultural planning in an arts-centered department only reinforces the narrow understandings of what culture and cultural planning are all about" (332). Cultural planning, argued Mercer (2006), "cannot be generated from the self-satisfied and enclosed position which holds that art is good for people and the community" (6).

During the first dozen years of formal cultural planning in the United States, Dreeszen (1994) found that practitioners did not articulate what they meant by culture, yet their plans focused on formal Western arts practices and nonprofits. This limited the scope of what activities and organizations were considered in the planning process. Dreeszen (1994, 243) observed:

> With some notable exceptions, most cultural planning centers upon the interests of arts organizations, arts audiences, and artists. Some plans focus on the arts and assert no pretensions to transform communities. Others purport to plan for the entire community but are concerned with that community mostly for its potential support of the arts.

Cultural planning evolved differently in the United States than in other parts of the world, most significantly because of the cultural sector's dominant market-driven and philanthropic underpinnings, in contrast with most other countries. It also remains a strictly local option, whereas in some countries local governments are required to produce cultural plans, much as they are required to produce master plans addressing infrastructure, transportation, and housing.

While cultural plans that serve as strategic plans for the nonprofit cultural sector have merit for those included in them, cultural planning has only begun to evolve into a more inclusive process that makes visible and addresses the diverse needs of people, their many cultures, their ways of living together, and their collective well-being. At the same time, with more nuanced knowledge of the people in a community, the cultural dimensions of local policy across a spectrum of municipal concerns become more meaningful and can move communities forward in more just and inclusive ways.

The focus of cultural plans often comes more from the practices and biases of consultants hired to prepare them and from templates shared among local agencies to specify the type of plan they want to commission (Stevenson 2014) than from the unique assets and interests of individual communities. Recommendations in most plans are extralegal in that they call for voluntary actions or collaborations among local actors. They sometimes recommend municipal policies related to such factors as public funding, agency capacity-building, public art programs, regulations pertaining to activities in public spaces, and provisions for creative districts or artist live-work spaces.

Seeing More from Cultural Planning

In a retrospective on the broad impacts of the practice in Australia, Dowling (1997) observes that "the theory of cultural planning begins with a fluid and broad definition of culture" (23). Such an approach was advocated by Mercer (2006), a fellow Australian, among others. In practice, however, most cultural planning remains narrowly focused, using a material and Western definition of cultural practices—namely, "the arts." Some early practitioners and scholars, including Bianchini (2004) and Montgomery (1990), along with Mercer and a group of arts and city planning leaders who convened in San Antonio in 1979 (Porter 1980), felt it could be more.

These writers argue that cultural planning holds promise as a novel and complementary approach to municipal planning and policy-setting, what Kovacs (2011) describes as "an ethical corrective to physical planning" (322). Putting this a different way, Ghilardi (2001) wrote, "cultural planning is not the 'planning of culture,' but a cultural (anthropological) approach to urban planning and policy" (125). Whether an ethical corrective or an anthropological approach, cultural planning practices have the potential to add value by informing city planning of the variety of ways of life and ways of living together among increasingly diverse populations.

As an early practitioner and leading thinker, Mercer (2006) saw cultural planning as part of a larger strategy. He argues that "it has to make connections with physical and town planning, with economic and industrial development objectives, with social justice initiatives, with recreational planning, with housing and public works" (6).

Just a year prior to Dreeszen's (1994) study, planning professor Bernie Jones (1993) summarized typical cultural plan goals as:

1. Enhancing community image and promoting economic development
2. Promoting cooperation among cultural organizations
3. Calling for development of cultural facilities
4. Identifying financial resource needs and improving organizational management
5. Enhancing arts marketing and promotion
6. Increasing quantity, quality, and diversity of arts programs

7. Advocating arts education
8. Supporting individual artists

These represent a more nuanced but still internal-sector focus in contrast to the Perloff plan for Los Angeles. Nearly thirty years later, the above remain common elements in cultural plans that continue to focus on the formal, nonprofit cultural sector's needs and aspirations. However, because cultural planning is practiced in a variety of ways, some plans have served wider community-centered purposes. Dreeszen (1994) cited plans in four cities as outliers that addressed wider community concerns and were "not typical of cultural planning documented in this study." He speculated that these plans may "represent the next generation of the practice" (244).

The Borrup (2018) study found that plans fall on a spectrum of purposes. The spectrum does not represent a consistent progression, nor are the items mutually exclusive. From most narrowly focused to most comprehensive, they are:

1. Sustain or increase funding and favorable policies for formal arts activities and organizations
2. Enhance the capacity of arts and cultural organizations to act collectively to advance their individual and common missions
3. Adopt municipal codes and regulations to accommodate more formal and informal cultural practices in public and other regulated spaces
4. Identify and build on distinct cultural assets and community identity, typically for tourism marketing and product branding
5. Animate public spaces and/or civic processes through creative and culturally attuned design, activities, and public art
6. Expand the range of people and cultural practices included in the identity of a community and/or resource and space allocations
7. Employ cultural assets to address economic and/or neighborhood development or other social or educational challenges
8. Determine complex community-wide challenges and devise strategies that bring cultural resources to bear to advance a community vision and/or to address challenges
9. Analyze and strategically leverage unique and diverse cultural characteristics, resources, and activities of both people and places to inform and serve an array of municipal issues and policies such as transit, housing, recreation, health, and education

THE COMMUNITY TURN

According to Wyatt, MacDowall, and Mulligan (2013), "Since late in the twentieth century, the relationship between art-making and community-making has been transformed by a surge of new or renewed interest in the idea of community across all art forms" (82). Is such a turn-to-community that Wyatt, MacDowall, and Mulligan observed affirmed or energized by the practice of cultural planning? Are more arts and culture agencies and local cultural sectors turning their focus outward to impact their communities in multiple ways? Understanding more about the directions and outcomes of cultural planning may help city planners better see how cultural sector aspirations and impacts are addressed through cultural planning and where their work may intersect. Data in this chapter explore whether cultural planning has shown itself catalytic in local policy-setting and organizing the sector to apply its capacities to address a more diverse range of community needs.

Cultural Planning at 40 (Borrup 2018) found that cultural planning continues to produce a turn to community (albeit a slow turn), observed by Dreeszen (1994) twenty-three years earlier:

> The larger-than-the-arts community involvement in cultural planning accelerates what would otherwise be a gradual shift in emphasis from arts development to also embrace community development. Planning sometimes helps achieve a better balance between these dual objectives. It may be during cultural planning that the potential for reciprocity may be understood and the arts and larger communities appreciate what each may do for the other. (Dreeszen 1994, 91)

While some communities continue to circle their arts wagons, the 2018 study affirmed that cultural plans—like most plans—are aspirational and do produce a variety of outcomes even when they fall short of achieving all their goals. These findings look at cultural planning in the United States as of 2017 with direct comparisons to Dreeszen's research twenty-three years earlier. Findings indicate that cultural planning practice and plans across the United States demonstrated changes in approaches and topical concerns in some areas, while in others there was surprisingly little change. The scope of issues addressed, and expectations community leaders had for planning versus outcomes they reported, illustrate some of the most significant changes. However, progress in the outcomes of cultural planning fell especially short in two significant areas: integration of cultural planning with city planning and expanding inclusion of and resources for "underrepresented communities"—meaning communities of color and immigrant communities, populations that collectively represent majorities in many United States cities.

One of the most consistent outcomes of cultural planning in the United States has been its effectiveness at helping arts and cultural organizations, agencies, and sometimes individual artists organize as a sector to act collectively on their own behalf (Borrup 2018). In some cases, cultural planning helps local cultural sectors learn how they can contribute to their communities in ways that extend or go beyond their traditional arts and culture programs. This is often through participation in economic development, tourism, education, public space improvement, and other areas of interest to local governments.

Variations in cultural planning from place to place and over time put its purposes on a spectrum that ranges from reinforcing dominant institutional cultural practices to identifying and equitably weaving the capacities and cultural assets of communities into a broad complement of civic concerns. While most cultural planning in the United States falls closer to the former, a trend has emerged toward expanded definitions of culture and toward the cultural sector serving as a partner to address broader community goals.

EXPECTATIONS VERSUS OUTCOMES

Reasons for entering into cultural planning were the subject of a series of questions in the early part of the survey conducted in 2017 (Borrup 2018). Parallel questions toward the end of the survey related to outcomes or changes respondents observed. In most cases, what respondents indicated they expected from cultural planning was greater than the outcomes they reported. In all but one of twenty-two topical areas, expectations exceeded subsequent outcomes by an average of 18 percent. In comparison with results from a survey asking the same questions by Dreeszen in 1994, the *types* of expectations and outcomes changed significantly.

The highest positive outcome reported in 2017 was in building connections among cultural organizations and activities. Eighty-eight percent hoped to achieve this result, with 84 percent rating this as a positive outcome, one of the most consistent expectation-to-outcome showings.

As seen in Figure 11.1, the widest variation between expectation and outcome in the 2017 survey was in finding new financial resources for the arts and cultural work, where 90 percent rated this as a goal against 46 percent who reported it as an actual outcome. This leaves 44 percent who were disappointed in this regard. Were expectations inordinately raised about the potential outcome of cultural planning to produce new resources, or did cultural planning take on a more expanded meaning, where cities and cultural agencies came to appreciate that it can achieve more than just expanding their budgets?

In other outcomes, 80 percent indicated in the 2017 survey they entered planning hoping to better organize the cultural community to advocate on its own behalf, and 72 percent reported they achieved more capacity for advocacy after planning. In 1994, Dreeszen found that 59 percent entered planning with this expectation, compared with only 19 percent who indicated favorable outcomes in capacity for collective advocacy. This affirms that cultural planning, after a couple of decades of work, has emerged as an efficient vehicle for sector organizing.

An area with one of the lower expectations was assessing the need for and viability of new cultural facilities, with 42 percent expecting progress in that area, and the same percentage indicating affirmative results. Dreeszen (1994) reported that only 12 percent in his 1994 survey entered planning with that expectation, yet 58 percent indicated new facilities

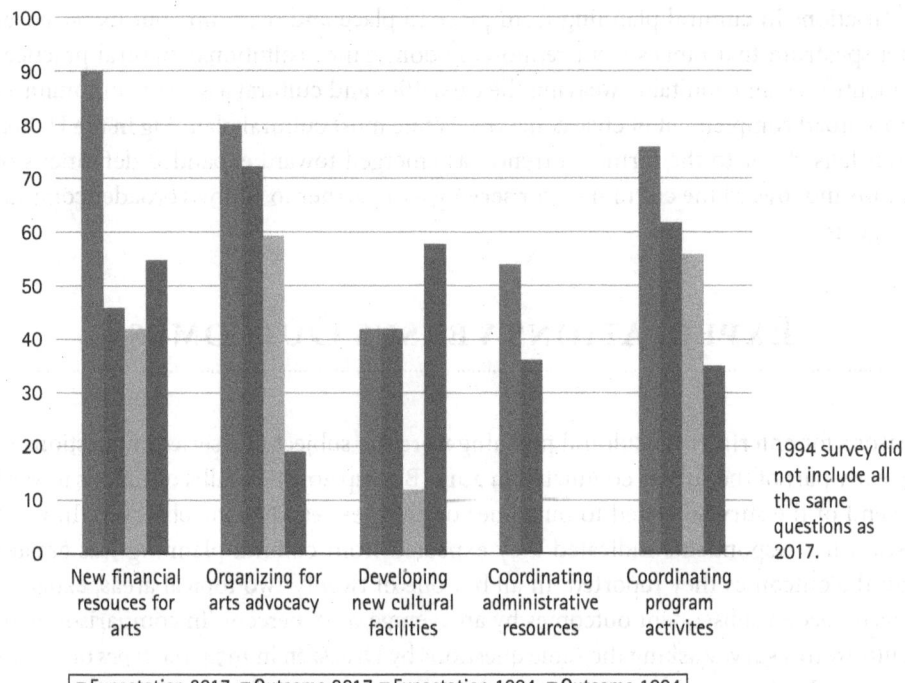

FIGURE 11.1 Survey comparisons of reported expectations to outcomes internal to the sector.

as an outcome. This was one of two areas where Dreeszen found outcomes rated higher than expectations. The other, mentioned above, was in finding new financial resources. These suggest that cultural planning during the 1980s and early 1990s was, as Dreeszen concluded, mostly centered on the interests of arts organizations and arts audiences.

Advancing Community Needs

As seen in Figure 11.2, the most highly rated reason cited for conducting a cultural plan in the 2017 survey, by 94 percent of respondents, was to enable the cultural sector to make greater community impacts. The kinds of impacts were not specified. High expectations in their responses indicate their desire to contribute outwardly to the community, rather than an inward focus on benefits planning brings to the sector. Considerably fewer—76 percent—reported that greater community impact resulted from their plan, and 18 percent reported that impact had not changed.

The second-highest positive outcome was in learning new ways arts and culture can bring value to the community, with 82 percent hoping for this result, against 80 percent reporting gains in this area, a consistent expectation-to-outcome showing. In the earlier study (Dreeszen 1994), only 19 percent reported learning new ways to bring value to the

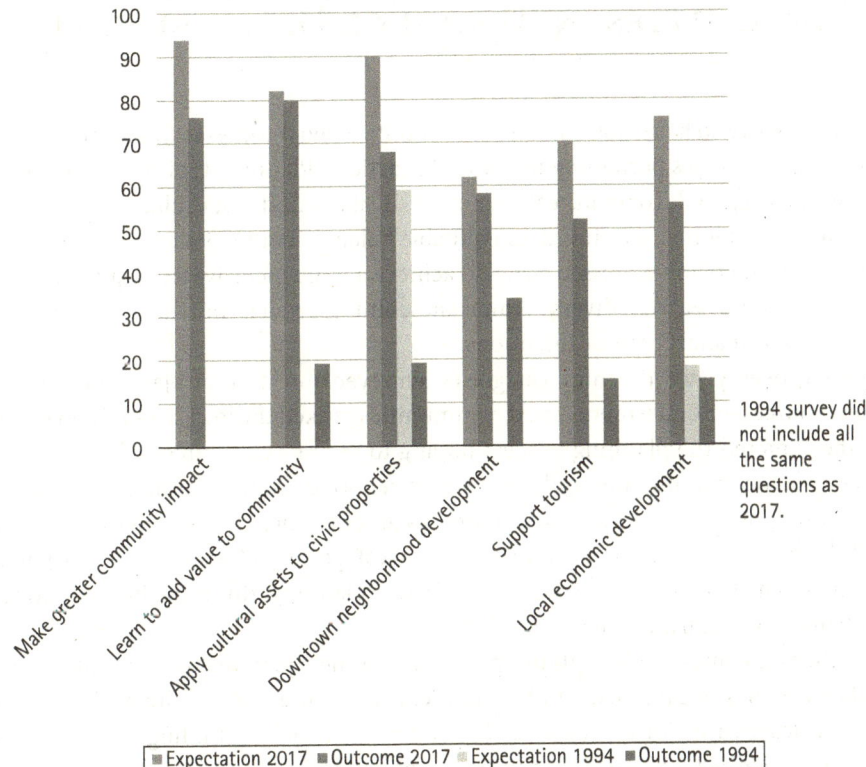

FIGURE 11.2 Survey comparisons of reported expectations to outcomes external to the sector.

community as an outcome, a dramatic change in the nature of expectations between the two time periods.

In the 2017 data, tied with finding new financial resources as the second-highest expectation was identifying strategies to apply cultural resources to civic priorities. In this case, 90 percent anticipated this from planning, while 68 percent indicated improvement in applying cultural resources to civic concerns. This compares with only 19 percent who indicated it as an outcome in 1994 and represents the most dramatic change between the two study periods.

The contrast in reported outcomes between the 1994 and 2017 surveys reflects considerably different priorities. The most significant single outcome reported in 1994 was new financial resources generated for the arts. The second most significant was bolstering education and youth development, followed closely by new cultural facilities. In 2017, these were among the lowest-outcome areas. Instead, the 2017 survey revealed that building connections within the cultural sector, learning new ways to add value to communities, better organizing the cultural community for greater community impact, and better organizing for advocacy were the top outcomes. This indicates changing conditions and expectations in the arts sector and a shift in the purpose of cultural planning. It provides evidence of a community turn, predicted by Dreeszen (1994).

Inequities in Resource Distribution

There are haves and have-nots in every community when it comes to financial resources, facilities, and policies pertaining to cultural practices. Planning typically favors one or more groups of people (or cultures) over others. Data indicate that cultural planning has not done a good job of arriving at an equitable balance. Findings show that many who sponsor cultural plans expressed a goal to achieve a more inclusive and equitable distribution of resources across diverse ethnic and cultural groups (Borrup 2018). However, outcomes fell far short of these intentions.

Among twenty-two outcome categories surveyed for cultural plans, allocation of more resources for underrepresented communities ranked the lowest. While 70 percent said they entered the planning process hoping to see more resources allocated to underrepresented communities, only 26 percent reported "somewhat more" and a mere 4 percent reported allocating "much more" as an outcome. This represents the largest divide between expectations and outcomes of all categories in the study. With 58 percent reporting that allocations were the same as before planning, this is the highest rating of "no change" out of all outcome categories.

In other outcomes, under half (48 percent) said their plan included specific actions to address issues of diversity, equity, and inclusion in the cultural life of the community. This leaves a majority who said they did not, a shocking finding for the cultural sector in the United States in a twenty-first-century context. In a related question about the removal of barriers to create more cultural participation, 82 percent entered cultural planning expecting to remove barriers, with 52 percent reporting progress subsequent to planning. The spread of 30 percent between expectation and outcome is nearly double the average variation between expectations and outcomes in all areas surveyed. This indicates a high level of disappointment or inability to achieve progress in this area.

Limitations of Cultural Planning

Overall, the 2017 survey (Borrup 2018) showed cultural planning to be aspirational—as it should be—and that the cultural sector began to address a growing range of civic concerns. However, as the data above indicate, efforts related to diversity, equity, and inclusion produced the lowest results. Based on these findings, a literature review, and firsthand experience in cultural planning, I distilled five forces or phenomena that have limited cultural planning in its ability to maximize cultural resources for social impact.

"Culture"

The first limitation relates to a narrow use and understanding of "culture." A kind of gravity within the nonprofit arts sector pulls toward a default definition promoted by formal arts institutions and agencies that have kept cultural planning within their orbit. Some scholars (Mercer 2006; Mills 2003; Stevenson 2005; Landry 2008) describe this phenomenon in their arguments for how the promise of cultural planning has been sidetracked by sector self-interest.

Community leaders of all stripes tend to default to "opera-house culture" (Wagner 1975)—the standard cluster of Eurocentric activities, organizational models, and aesthetic values that constitute formal arts institutions and practices. I call this *gravitational pull*. Of course, in a day-to-day community context, gravitating to what is familiar or part of established ways is an understandable phenomenon. People can only begin with what they know and potentially move a step or two to expand on the familiar, what American futurist Steven Johnson (2010, 23) describes as the "adjacent possible."

The sway local arts agencies have over cultural planning and its outcomes puts such planning in the service of securing resources and elevating the agencies' capacities to produce and deliver arts and cultural experiences. While not an unworthy undertaking, it discounts a wider range of cultural needs and potential the sector can bring to a community. With culture locked in a Eurocentric understanding of the arts, this excludes many people and denies social systems and civic infrastructure the benefits of a deeper understanding of their diverse communities and their own cultural biases.

Scarcity Mindset

Another important way to understand culture is through the lens of either abundance or scarcity (Borrup 2021; Martin 1996; Turner and Rojek 2001). Is culture a bottomless well of traditions, and is creativity found in every corner of daily life, something to be continually explored, enjoyed, and fostered? Or is culture a finite cache of aesthetic treasures, and creativity a set of high-powered practices closely held by elite institutions and highly trained artists? This second mindset is grounded in the scarcity or deficit-based mindset or approach predominant in most cultural work, and limits cultural planning.

Seeing culture as either scarce or abundant is essential in understanding the difference between the colonial and exploitive capacities of culture versus its ability to empower and connect. In thinking about where culture resides, what creativity means, and who engages in traditional and creative practices, it is critical to consider this difference. Young (2008, 71) asserts that it is important for culture "to be found and explored everywhere and not viewed as a scarce commodity." Whether implicitly or explicitly practiced, the scarcity mindset creates a hierarchy that stratifies cultural forms and practices, valuing some and devaluing others, and thus sets up or reinforces inequitable power-based relationships.

As part of a colonialist or missionary concept of bringing the benefits of culture or enlightenment to the "uncultured" masses, the scarcity mindset denies the value of some cultures compared to others. Abundance acknowledges and celebrates culture and creativity as ubiquitous and present in the lives and identities of all people. Cultural planning can and should acknowledge the abundance of cultures in communities and strategize ways to appreciate and constructively engage, connect, and support them to generate productive relationship-building.

Professional Silos

The third limitation has to do with professional silos. Most cultural planners emerge from arts sector professions and have limited preparation for their work. Bianchini (1999, 200) argues that narrow training in arts administration is

> inadequate for cultural planners, who also need to know about political economy and urban sociology, about how cities work (as societies, economies, polities, and eco-systems, as well as cultural milieux) and of course about physical planning itself, otherwise they cannot influence it.

Bianchini's comments, while over two decades old at the time of this writing, remain pertinent. There continue to be limited opportunities in the academic arena for preparing cultural planners and little change among agencies hiring planning consultants.

The recent study (Borrup 2018), described above, reveals that only 41 percent of the consultants employed to assist cities in cultural planning consider it to be their primary area of expertise. The next largest group of cultural planning consultants, at 23 percent, specialize in nonprofit arts management or strategic planning. Others bring skills in marketing or economic development. Only a handful of individual university-level courses in cultural planning are offered in the United States. Most cultural planners are self-taught and self-defined. Some bring long associations with large institutions, while others have been more associated with community-based creative practices. Most bring a narrow approach to culture.

In the United States, as well as globally, there is no organized *field* of cultural planning and no formal recognition of the profession, as in credentials or licensing. There is little training and no professional associations or publications for cultural planners. There are no standards of practice or formally recognized methods. Instead, there is a "marketplace" in which municipal or cultural agency "buyers" issue requests for proposals or qualifications and to which independent consultants or firms respond as "suppliers" with a variety of skills to compete for contracts. In a few cases, cultural agency staff produce plans as a service to their municipal or institutional constituencies. The profession itself needs to organize, and academic institutions need to become partners in providing more preparation for planners.

Outsiders at an Inside Job

Cultural planning grew as an interest-group organizing effort among arts nonprofits and arts advocacy organizations. With the exception of some major institutions, those in the cultural sector tend to feel socially marginalized. Political attacks against artists and arts organizations in the 1990s in the United States, for instance, added to a sense of being under siege. The field is frequently found at the bottom of professional pay scales. As in any industry or professional sector that feels itself to be on the outside, banding together proved effective to influence public policy, the media, and private-sector power brokers, including philanthropies. Cultural plans typically include a multitude of goals that the arts and cultural sector understands are best achieved through collective action. This required the proverbial "herding cats," as arts organizations and artists sometimes don't get along. On a local level they have often been in competition with one another for limited charitable support and for audiences.

To its credit, within a few decades cultural planning helped many once-fractured arts and cultural communities learn to work better together. In the more recent survey on cultural planning (Borrup 2018), among the highest reported outcomes was organizing for sector advocacy. In essence, cultural planning represents field organizing. The origins or DNA of cultural planning emerged from a sense of marginalization and the need to organize. Cultural planning has demonstrated it can foster a sense of collective empowerment yet can position the sector in opposition to or in competition with other professions or sectors. The arts and cultural sector needs to fully consider itself a potent member of its larger community, with an interest in lifting all boats.

Women's Work or Real Work?

Leavitt (1980) traced the significant impacts women made in city planning during the late nineteenth century, well before it became a recognized profession. She argued that women helped shape the practice and wrote, "Women's role in civic improvement committees paralleled and, in some cases, paved the way for early planning efforts" (188). Nonetheless, Leavitt asserted, most of the work achieved by a multitude of middle-class, voluntary women's clubs was characterized by city fathers as extensions of housework: "Whereas men had license to address any element of city planning, women's roles were more narrowly determined" (191).

The arts and cultural sector is dominated by women, except in the most senior institutional positions. A study by Americans for the Arts (2018) affirmed that white women dominate the field, with 78 percent of the staff of public and private arts agencies identifying as cisgender female, and 82 percent are white. For this and other reasons, the sector has struggled for recognition in the halls of power. Given that the origins of cultural planning come significantly from the efforts of women, is it any wonder it has remained marginalized within municipal policy?

The daily practice of art (outside the *business* of art) has also been considered a feminine pursuit born of leisure and frivolity, providing little more than diversion from important economic and civic matters. Creative practices typically produce decorative features to embellish the substance of built infrastructure, public spaces, and the interiors of homes—the traditional domain of women. Creative practices and behaviors, if not frivolous and ignorable, are otherwise considered disruptive. Artists have a reputation as troublemakers, best appreciated in the safety of museums that reflect on their contributions after they are dead. Cultural planning needs to assert its significance as central and meaningful in all dimensions of civic concerns.

Conclusions

If cities and communities of all sizes are going to become more just and equitable and if they're going to welcome and accommodate more diverse populations, cities must gain a deeper understanding of the cultures or ways of life of the different people that make them up. Cultural planning, at its best, can help to engage, mobilize, and maximize a fuller spectrum of cultural resources and help advance equity in new ways.

If the arts and culture sector continues to employ cultural planning as defensive positioning with the primary purpose of leveraging resources for the ongoing operations of established institutions, it restricts the potential of cultural planning and becomes a force for stagnation and furtherance of inequity. As a result, cultural divisions and xenophobia will continue to grow. Cities will be ill-equipped to understand and address human needs and major challenges as effectively or equitably as they could and must.

Plans are aspirational by nature; the findings presented above suggest that cultural planning can propel a community turn (Dreeszen 1994; Wyatt, MacDowall, and Mulligan 2013), having the effect, Dreeszen suggested, of accelerating "a gradual shift in emphasis for arts development to also embrace community development" (91). Some changes in the practice of cultural planning are evident from a comparison of the 1994 and 2018 studies. The aspirations and outcomes expressed by cultural agencies can be reasonably extended to their local cultural sectors, as players in those sectors tend to be significantly invested in cultural planning processes.

Significant gaps remain in terms of movement toward cultural equity, building relationships with the practice of city planning, and providing professional development for those involved in the practice itself. While thinking around culture has progressed somewhat in cultural planning, the sector has grown most in adopting instrumental applications of arts and culture in other dimensions of community life, such as economic, place-based, and youth development.

Aspirations of cultural planning have moved from an emphasis on serving the internal needs of the nonprofit cultural sector to better understanding how the sector can address or contribute to a multitude of concerns in their communities. As such, cultural planning does appear to fulfill a leadership role in maximizing cultural resources for social impact. However, this turn has lagged the sector's stated goals and proven a very slow one. The practice brings together the cultural sector on a local level and helps it express and codify its optimistic intentions. It can and has begun to construct strategies to help local arts agencies and cultural sectors find ways to maximize the wider cultural assets in their communities as well as take a more central role in key civic issues. It can do more.

References

Americans for the Arts. 2018. "Local Arts Agency Salaries 2018: A Report About Salaries and Compensation in the Local Arts Agency Field." https://www.americansforthearts.org/

by-program/networks-and-councils/local-arts-network/facts-and-figures/local-arts-agency-salaries-2018.

Baeker, Greg. 2010. *Rediscovering the Wealth of Places: A Municipal Cultural Planning Handbook for Canadian Communities*. St. Thomas, ON: Municipal World.

Bianchini, Franco. 1999. "Cultural Planning and Time Planning: The Relationship Between Culture and Urban Planning." In *Social Town Planning*, edited by C. Greed, 195–202. London: Routledge.

Bianchini, Franco. 2004. "A Crisis in Urban Creativity? Reflections on the Cultural Impacts of Globalisation, and on the Potential of Urban Cultural Policies." Paper presented at the international symposium "The Age of the City: The Challenges for Creative Cities," February 7–10, Osaka, Japan. http://www.artfactories.net/IMG/pdf/crisis_urban_creatvity.pdf.

Borrup, Tom. 2018. "Cultural Planning at 40: A Look at the Practice and Its Progress." https://www.americansforthearts.org/by-program/reports-and-data/legislation-policy/naappd/cultural-planning-at-40-a-look-at-the-practice-and-its-progress.

Borrup, Tom. 2021. *The Power of Culture in City Planning*. New York: Routledge.

Dowling, Robyn. 1997. "Planning for Culture in Urban Australia." *Australian Geographical Studies* 35, no. 1: 23–31. https://doi.org/10.1111/1467-8470.00004.

Dreeszen, Craig. A. 1994. "Reimagining Community: Community Arts and Cultural Planning in America." PhD diss., University of Massachusetts.

Dreeszen, Craig A. 1998. *Community Cultural Planning: A Guidebook for Community Leaders*. Washington, DC: Americans for the Arts.

Ewell, Maryo. 2000. "Community Arts Councils: Historical Perspective." *Culture Work: A Periodic Broadside for Arts and Culture Workers* 5, no. 1: 1–23. https://scholarsbank.uoregon.edu/xmlui/bitstream/handle/1794/346/CultureWork_Vol5_No1.pdf?sequence=1&isAllowed=y.

Ghilardi, Lia. 2001. "Cultural Planning and Cultural Diversity." In *Differing Diversities: Transversal Study on the Theme of Cultural Policy and Cultural Diversity*, edited by T. Bennett, 123–134. Strasbourg: Council of Europe.

Johnson, Steven. 2010. *Where Good Ideas Come From: The Natural History of Innovation*. New York: Riverhead Books.

Jones, Bernie. 1993. "Current Directions in Cultural Planning." *Landscape and Urban Planning* 26, nos. 1–4: 89–97. https://doi.org/10.1016/0169-2046(93)90009-3.

Kovacs, Jason F. 2011. "Cultural Planning in Ontario, Canada: Arts Policy or More?" *International Journal of Cultural Policy* 17, no. 3: 321–340. https://doi.org/10.1080/10286632.2010.487152.

Kreidler, John. 1996. "Leverage Lost: The Nonprofit Arts in the Post-Ford Era." *Journal of Arts Management, Law, and Society* 26, no. 2: 79–101.

Kunzmann, Klaus R. 2004. "Culture, Creativity and Spatial Planning." *Town Planning Review* 75, no. 4: 383–404.

Landry, Charles. 2000. *The Creative City: A Toolkit for Urban Innovators*. Oxford: Earthscan.

Landry, Charles. 2008. *The Creative City: A Toolkit for Urban Innovators*, rev. ed. Oxford: Earthscan.

Leavitt, Jacqueline. 1980. "Planning and Women, Women in Planning." PhD diss., Columbia University.

Martin, Jane R. 1996. "There's Too Much to Teach: Cultural Wealth in an Age of Scarcity." *Educational Researcher* 25, no. 2: 4–10, 16.

Mercer, Colin. 2006. "Cultural Planning for Urban Development and Creative Cities." http://www.kulturplan-oresund.dk/pdf/Shanghai_cultural_planning_paper.pdf.

Mills, Deborah. 2003. "Cultural Planning—Policy Task, Not Tool." *Artwork Magazine* 55: 7–11.
Montgomery, John. 1990. "Cities and the Art of Cultural Planning." *Planning Practice and Research* 5, no. 3: 17–24. https://doi.org/10.1080/02697459008722772.
Partners for Livable Places. 1983. *Toward Livable Communities: A Report on Partners for Livable Places 1975–1982*. Washington, DC: Partners for Livable Places.
Perloff, Harvey S. 1979. "Using the Arts to Improve Life in the City." *Journal of Cultural Economics* 3, no. 2: 1–21. https://doi.org/10.1007/BF02427550.
Porter, R. (Ed.). (1980). *The Arts and City Planning*. New York, NY: American Council for the Arts.
Rohe, William. M. 2009. "From Local to Global: One Hundred Years of Neighborhood Planning." *Journal of the American Planning Association* 75, no. 2: 209–230. https://doi.org/10.1080/01944360902751077.
Stevenson, Deborah. 2005. "Cultural Planning in Australia: Texts and Contexts." *Journal of Arts Management, Law, and Society* 35, no. 1: 36–48.
Stevenson, Deborah. 2014. *Cities of Culture: A Global Perspective*. London: Routledge.
Turner, Bryan S., and Chris Rojek. 2001. *Society and Culture: Scarcity and Solidarity*. London: Safe.
Wagner, Roy. 1975. *The Invention of Culture*. Chicago: University of Chicago Press.
Wyatt, Danielle, Lachlan MacDowall, and Martin Mulligan. 2013. "Critical Introduction: The Turn to Community in the Arts." *Journal of Arts and Communities* 5, nos. 2–3: 81–91. https://doi.org/10.1386/jaac.5.2-3.81_1.
Young, Greg. 2008. *Reshaping Planning with Culture*. London: Routledge. https://doi.org/10.4324/9781315605647.

CHAPTER 12

COPYRIGHT AS AN ENGINE FOR CREATIVITY

A Critical Appraisal of Contemporary Developments in Intermediaries' Liability Regulation

MIRA BURRI

INTRODUCTION

Copyright as an Engine for Creativity

CREATIVITY unfolds and is expressed in diverse forms in a certain legal environment. Law can enable or hinder creativity depending on its design. Copyright law can be particularly critical in this regard, since it, as a subset of intellectual property (IP) protection, has its primary justification in serving the essential function of fostering creativity and the development of the arts.[1] Copyright is there to incentivize creative workers to engage in their creative activities by granting them a temporary monopoly over their works,[2] thereby constraining the otherwise possible free riding associated with information goods, which tend to be non-rivalrous and non-excludable (Landes and Posner 2003). Copyright has a broad scope and can protect a wide range of literary, artistic, and scientific creations, such as novels, poems, plays, films, musical compositions, choreographs, paintings, drawings, photographs, and sculpture. Copyright protects the expression of ideas but not the ideas themselves; neither are facts copyrightable. To qualify for protection, there is a threshold of originality that must be passed. In most countries, however, the work of authorship need not be novel, be ingenious, or have aesthetic merit in order to satisfy the originality requirement (Judge and Gervais 2009). For example, the US Supreme Court defined originality as requiring only that the work be independently created by the author and that it possesses "at least some minimal degree of creativity" (Gervais 2002).[3] Beyond this minimal threshold, to be protected under copyright, no other formalities, such as registration, are typically required upon the creation of the work or in some countries, such as the United States and Canada, upon the additional fixation in a tangible form; there is in this sense a sort of automatism in the granting of copyright protection. Copyright is understood as a package of rights—it encompasses economic and moral rights. The latter seek to protect the integrity and reputation of the creator of the copyrighted work but are not enshrined to the same extent in all jurisdictions (Rigamonti 2006; US Copyright Office 2019). Economic rights include the right of reproduction of the work and its adaptation, translation, public performance, and communication to the public, and those rights last for at least fifty years (but increasingly now seventy years) following the death of the author. Afterward, the work falls into the public domain and creators and licensees can no longer control the distribution and use of the work. This broad, flexible, adaptable, and uncostly type of protection has worked well in local and global markets, and copyright has become an indivisible part of modern legal systems, equipped with sophisticated registration, management, and enforcement mechanisms (Cohen et al. 2019) as well as a level of international harmonization (Goldstein and Hugenholtz 2019).

Copyright is not a perfect tool, however, and the exclusionary control granted to copyright holders does come with certain inefficiencies—on the one hand, and in a static sense, it reduces access to works by users unwilling or unable to pay the higher price charged by rights holders; on the other hand, and in a dynamic sense, copyright protection may impede future creativity by restricting access to a creative work for follow-up creators and hindering dissemination of information (Landes and Posner 2003; Benkler 2006). This trade-off is at the heart of copyright, and copyright law must in principle ensure that there is a balance between the benefits of incentivizing creative work and the costs for society (Fisher 1988; Benkler 2000; Boyle 2000; Cohen 2000). For this purpose, copyright is not an absolute right and includes a variety of exceptions and limitations that provide different opportunities to access and use copyrighted works without the permission of the rights holder and without remuneration—for instance, for parody, news reporting, education, and research. The approaches differ across jurisdictions, with only minimum harmonization given by the international legal framework through the "three-step-test" under Article 13 of the Agreement on Trade-Related Aspects of Intellectual Property Rights (TRIPS) (Geiger, Gervais, and Senftleben 2014).

Regardless of the approach adopted, lawmakers and courts have struggled to attain and preserve copyright's balance; indeed, often the costs for individual borrowers of creative content or for the society as a whole have not been duly taken into account (Balganesh 2009). Different strands of criticism have been formulated in this context over the years—for instance, with regard to the flawed concept of the author as a genius (Woodmansee and Jaszi 1994; Lange 2003; Cohen 2007; Moglen 2002), the related uncertainties and misconceptions about what drives creativity in practice (Kwall 2006; Lunceford and Lunceford 2008; Fisher 2010; Simon 2011), including the underlying incentives theory of copyright and the link to the support of artists' livelihood (Shih Ray Ku, Sun, and Fan 2009; Leenheer Zimmerman 2011; diCola 2013), or the inadequate tools for protecting traditional culture expressions (Brown 1998; Graber 2007; Burri

2020). In spite of this continued criticism, the incentives theory, coupled with predominant neoliberal thinking and effective lobbying by the so-called "copyright industries,"[4] led to a constant expansion of copyright law and the rights granted to copyright holders, stronger enforcement mechanisms, and a corresponding narrowing of copyright's exceptions and limitations, with deep implications for free speech and for individual and collaborative creative processes.[5] This development has been compounded by technological transformation, driven particularly by digitization.

Digitization as a Trigger for Change

Digitization is the ability to express all information (be it audio, text, or still or moving images) as binary digits; it frees information from the tangible medium and makes it networkable and easy to manipulate (including the making of perfect copies of the original). Digitization has also allowed computers to talk a common language (Grimmelmann 2021). As of the 1980s, on top of these technological foundations, a range of new information processing and transmission technologies developed rapidly (Benkler 2006; van Oranje-Nassau et al. 2008). An important consequence of these has been the exponential growth of information offerings available to the consumer; the affordances for "permissionless innovation"[6]; the restructuring of the markets for creative goods and services due to a large decrease in the fixed costs of production, distribution, and advertising of cultural goods (Waldfogel 2017); and the empowerment of users to actively participate in creative processes (Benkler 2006; Cowen 2008). These technological transformations and the multiple societal implications they triggered had important consequences for copyright law (Peukert 2019). This chapter looks only at a subset of these consequences and explores in more detail the emergence of digital platforms as key actors in copyright management and enforcement and the regulatory frameworks that address them, taking the recent EU copyright reform as a case study. The chapter seeks to enquire into the effects of these regulatory initiatives on creative processes.

CHANGED COPYRIGHT ENFORCEMENT FRAMEWORKS: DIGITAL INTERMEDIARIES AS KEY ACTORS

From Analog to Digital

When the international copyright regime was created back in the nineteenth century, the relevant technology that permitted multiplication and distribution of copyrighted works was the printing press. The internet came a century later, so neither the 1886 Berne Convention for the Protection of Literary and Artistic Works nor even the 1995

TRIPS Agreement contains any specific rules for digital technologies, except for the fact that TRIPS extended the scope of copyright protection to explicitly cover computer programs and databases. The international community was quick, however, to acknowledge the far-reaching effects of digitization, both as a powerful tool to create and distribute content and as a potential enhancer of copyright infringement (Schmitz 2015). Policymakers were confronted yet again with the fundamental question underlying copyright: how to secure effective protection of the copyright holders' package of rights while at the same time allowing the public to access and use works and engage in creative activities (Travis 2008). With the adoption of the WIPO Copyright Treaty in 1996, the international community moved toward designing some solutions for digital copyright; however, these were cautiously formulated and left room for different implementation approaches, as in the 1990s the internet was still quite young—many of the applications we use today were either in their infancy or yet unknown, and the pervasive societal embeddedness of the digital medium was at a very early stage (Okediji 2009). A critical development in the post–WIPO Copyright Treaty environment, one that this chapter discusses, is the increased role of internet intermediaries as new actors in the field of copyright enforcement (Jougleux 2017). As rights holders were "faced with a major enforcement failure" (Elkin-Koren 2014, 33), it appeared appropriate that intermediaries carry some of the burden and costs associated with copyright enforcement, especially as they are technically capable of monitoring, filtering, and disabling infringing materials. At the same time, this liability ought not to be too burdensome, since this would hamper growth and innovation (Elkin-Koren 2014; Kuczerawy 2020). Systems for intermediary governance that emerged can largely be split into two groups. First, there are horizontal systems that install rules for all types of intermediaries' liability, be it with regard to hate speech, misleading information, or trademark or copyright infringements, as the European Union does through the 2000 E-Commerce Directive.[7] The second type, as embodied in Section 512 of the 1998 US Digital Millennium Copyright Act (DMCA),[8] specifically targets copyright violations (Sag 2018; Angelopoulos 2020; Spindler 2020). Both systems seek to strike a balance between the different interests involved by creating certain conditional "safe harbors" and a "notice and takedown" procedure as mechanisms to mitigate the risk of legal liability for internet intermediaries while providing copyright holders with ways to have their content removed online.[9] The safe harbor model has evolved over the years, and as the role of intermediaries in the digital space increased (Jougleux 2017), there has been a discrete trend toward heightened responsibilities (de Beer and Clemme 2009; Frosio and Mendis 2020; Mac Síthigh 2020). The recent EU copyright reform is an expression of this trend, marking a significant step toward rendering intermediaries active "gatekeepers" of content shared by their users (Frosio and Mendis 2020, 547; Jougleux 2017; Spoerri 2019). Legislative changes have also been accompanied by technological measures undertaken by platforms (largely in response to pressure from rights holders) that go beyond the legally prescribed measures to include monitoring and filtering mechanisms that tackle infringing content (Elkin-Koren 2014; Hinze 2019; Frosio 2020), with YouTube's Content ID being perhaps the most illustrative example in this context. Although such applications may offer efficient tools to deal with the allegedly vast amount of infringing content (Penney 2019), they come with negative implications, in particular with regard to non-infringing uses of copyrighted works (either under the limitations and exceptions or for works having fallen into the public domain) and can be linked to chilling effects on creativity (Guzman 2015; Bridy 2016; Frosio 2017a; Kulk 2018)—a topic that this chapter discusses later in more detail based on insights from the EU copyright reform.

The EU Copyright Reform as a Case Study

The European Parliament approved in April 2019 the final text of the Directive on Copyright in the Digital Single Market (CDSM), marking the end of a lengthy and highly contentious legislative process. This brought about a substantial change in EU copyright law (Shapiro and Hansson 2019; Bridy 2020), associated with a broader EU initiative—the 2015 Digital Single Market Strategy—to update its legal framework and make it fit for the digital age (European Commission 2015). Apart from the "meta" trigger of the reform, in terms of intermediaries' liability regulation the major concern among policymakers was the so-called "value gap" (European Commission 2016a). The term has to do with the changed conditions in the markets for online content and describes the (alleged) imbalance between the revenues platform providers generate from the use of copyright-protected content uploaded by their users and the revenues rights holders obtain (Frosio 2018a).[10] The problem was linked to the existing EU safe harbor regime, as this does not incentivize platforms to enter into licensing agreements or otherwise provide for conditions more accommodating for rights holders (Angelopoulos 2017; Frosio 2018a). From the EU perspective, the problem was only more acute, as most dominant platforms are US-based and the revenues rarely stay in the EU (European Commission 2016b). The new regime, embodied in Article 17 of the CDSM, addressed this value gap by effectively changing the intermediaries' liability conditionalities.

New Platform Liability Regime

The new EU liability regime follows a two-level approach. On the one hand, it prescribes direct liability for a specific category of platforms, the "online content-sharing service providers" (OCSSPs).[11] On the other hand, it specifies distinct ways to "escape" this liability burden through either licensing or an enhanced "notice and staydown" approach (Senftleben 2020). Under the licensing approach, Article 17(1) of the CDSM demands authorization from the rights holders and mentions licensing, including collective or statutory licensing, as a way to receive such authorization (Quintais et al. 2019; Trapova 2020). Whereas it appears reasonable that Article 17(1) encourages rights clearance initiatives, and whereas this may be feasible under certain circumstances (e.g., with known rights holders or through collecting societies), it confronts the platform with a cumbersome obligation that can hardly be met (Senftleben 2020; Samuelson 2020), as it is almost impossible to imagine that a platform can obtain *all* the necessary licenses for *all* the works uploaded by its users (Angelopoulos and Quintais 2019; Grisse 2019; Reda 2020). As noted earlier, the acquisition of copyright does not demand formalities, and there is nothing like a global or even national register for protected works that can be consulted. Even if the platform is able to identify and contact a rights holder, it may encounter other difficulties, notably the likelihood of striking licensing agreements under fair terms (Grisse 2019; Husovec and Quintais 2021a) and whether these can be all-embracing umbrella licenses. Discrepancies in this context may trigger the use of algorithmic tools, as platforms would need to differentiate between content with a license and such without, as well as lead to reliance on licensing agreements that focus on mainstream works rather than providing access to the wide variety of content uploaded by users with different social, cultural, and ethnic backgrounds (Senftleben 2020). Given the difficulties in meeting the requirements of Article 17(1) of the CDSM, it has been assumed that platforms will heavily rely on the second option (Angelopoulos and Quintais 2019; Quintais 2020).

Under the enhanced "notice and staydown" approach, platforms must meet three cumulative conditions to avoid direct liability. OCSSPs must demonstrate that they have (1) made best efforts to obtain an authorization; (2) made, in accordance with high industry standards of professional diligence, best efforts to ensure the unavailability of works for which the rights holders have provided the relevant and necessary information; and (3) acted expeditiously, upon receiving a sufficiently substantiated notice from the rights holders, to disable access to, or to remove from their websites, the notified works, and made best efforts to prevent their future uploads. With regard to condition (1), there is uncertainty around its proper implementation, and different scenarios—each with certain downsides—have been outlined (Grisse 2019; Husovec 2019; Metzger and Senftleben 2020). Particularly discussed in this context has been the question of whether the duties of the OCSSPs would amount to a monitoring obligation for all uploaded content and therewith clash with the existing ban on general monitoring that EU law prescribes, with users' rights to the protection of personal data and freedom of expression, and with the freedom of platforms to conduct business.[12] The remaining conditions specified by Article 17(4) are more straightforward, but while similar to the conventional "notice and takedown" regime, they come with substantial additional duties, in that the provider must proactively make best efforts to ensure the unavailability of notified works and to make sure that these are not reuploaded. This creates a new "staydown" obligation, which triggers an ongoing duty for the intermediary to prevent the same infringement in the future (Metzger and Senftleben 2020; Kuczerawy 2020). Here again, automatic content recognition technologies, also referred to as "upload filters" (Frosio and Mendis 2020; Senftleben 2020; Samuelson 2020), appear the plausible way to fulfill the staydown obligation (Spindler 2019; Bridy 2020) as well as trigger again the question of whether general monitoring occurs (Shapiro and Hansson 2019; Kuczerawy 2019, 2020). Overall, the new liability rules mark a distinct "shift from a regime in which the law is enforced after a violation of law has taken place (ex post) to a system where technology ensures that violations do not even occur in the first place (ex ante)" (Mongnani 2020, 3; Frosio 2018a) and one that leads to an "institutionalized algorithmic enforcement" (Senftleben 2020, 327 and passim). Both developments open an array of questions with regard to users' rights, transparency, due process, and overall creativity online.

PLATFORM-DEPENDENT ENFORCEMENT AND THE RISKS FOR CREATIVITY ONLINE

Intermediaries' enforcement of copyright is likely to stay as an essential element of contemporary legal systems. Yet its design is malleable, and when enshrined in law it can have massive implications for creativity and for cultural production, distribution, and consumption. The preceding analysis of the new EU intermediaries' liability regime reveals that there may be a few cracks in the system. First, platform-dependent copyright enforcement is illustrative not only of the employment of technology but also of the shift toward its privatization (Gray and Suzo 2020). In contrast to conventional law enforcement, which involves detection, prosecution, adjudication, and punishment through different authorities with various institutionalized checks and balances, such digital enforcement combines all of those functions, and focuses primarily on detection and prevention executed within a small number of mega-platforms that are private businesses and profit-oriented by their very nature (Perel and Elkin-Koren 2016). It is these platforms that encode the legal provisions into their content recognition technologies, and this process inevitably involves decisions regarding legal interpretation and may be influenced by a variety of conscious as well as unconscious considerations (Perel and Elkin-Koren 2016; Burk 2019; Mongnani 2020; Yu 2020), with a considerable potential for bias built into the code that favors the platform's interests and discriminates against certain persons or groups (Tóth 2019). The lack of public oversight only exacerbates this situation. Due to the sheer volume of content removals, with numbers in the billions (Erickson and Kretschmer 2020), tracing which content is permitted or removed and under what conditions is virtually impossible (Perel and Elkin-Koren 2016). Especially in the case of ex ante algorithmic enforcement, the possibility of correcting errors is limited, which in turn reduces the public's ability to intervene (Mongnani 2020). Public oversight is further hampered by the fact that the underlying algorithms are often proprietary and protected as trade secrets (Tóth 2019). This is linked to one of the key issues in the general discourse on the use of algorithms—their inherent opacity as "black boxes" (Perel and Elkin-Koren 2017; Mongnani 2020).

The second issue has to do with licensing as one of the viable ways to escape direct intermediary liability and thereby solve the digital copyright dilemmas. In this context, while the value gap may be a valid (although not yet fully substantiated) claim and while the new rules have clearly improved the bargaining position of rights holders vis-à-vis providers, there is doubt that this treatment is equal; in fact, the law may have given preferential treatment to big rights holders (Husovec and Quintais 2021b). There are various aspects to this concern. Some are linked to the financial resources needed to implement content recognition technologies; others have to do with the stronger positioning of larger players vis-à-vis platforms when compared to that of smaller and individual rights holders. So, for instance, the new "best efforts" obligation encourages OCSSPs to deal proactively with the players that have the most resources, and unless smaller rights holders are organized in collecting societies and these are allowed to negotiate, they are clearly disadvantaged when compared to bigger players. In the same vein, smaller players' bargaining position is quite different and might render fairness illusory if negotiations do occur. At the same time, larger players can extract more revenue from OCSSPs (also through monetization of prefiltering systems, such as Content ID) without the need to enter into collective deals and restructure their business practices (Sag 2018; Peukert 2019; Husovec and Quintais 2021b). The market power of internet intermediaries themselves cannot be underestimated and can seriously undermine the appropriability of creators (Handke 2015). All this translates into (multiple) competitive disadvantages for smaller providers (Spoerri 2019; Husovec and Quintais 2021b). There are also substantial disadvantages in terms of making use of the available copyright limitations and exceptions, and the therewith linked processes of filtering and staydown that platforms must implement. For one, less professionalized creators are more likely to rely on these exceptions and less likely to hold licenses for online exploitation of other people's work beyond these exceptions; moreover, in case of disputes, smaller players may not have the means to object and to substantiate their arguments. Coupled with the unfortunate negotiating position of smaller players, when OCSSPs engage in making their "best efforts" in the authorization of copyrighted works, it is then likely that works of large rights holders remain more available for subsequent noncommercial reuse by other creators across different OCSSPs (Husovec and Quintais 2021b), which raises serious questions with regard to cultural production and diversity. Furthermore, in terms of the actual use of the copyright's exceptions and limitations, while it can be argued that technology is merely a tool that can be implemented for a number of different uses (both restricting and enabling access to content), it may be that content recognition technologies are able to filter out identical or matching content but are not mature enough to differentiate an unlawful use from one covered by the copyright exceptions and limitations (Lester and Pachamanova 2017; Tóth 2019; Burk 2019). To distinguish parody, transformative use, or critical review from the infringing use of copyrighted material requires the ability to recognize context, and while context-aware decision-making is relatively easy for humans, this is not necessarily the case for algorithms (Sag 2018). Even works in the public domain may be a challenge for algorithms (Spoerri 2019; Geiger, Frosio, and Izymenko 2020). In addition, one has to keep in mind that the development or licensing of content recognition technologies, as well as their maintenance, requires substantial resources (Spoerri 2019). It is known, for instance, that Google, as the owner of YouTube, invested over $100 million in its Content ID (Sawers 2018). Given that platforms are profit-oriented and not all of them are as affluent as Google, it is likely that they implement less sophisticated cost-effective content recognition systems, and this comes with the risk that such systems would lead to excessive blocking (so-called "overblocking") as a result of false positive results, ultimately removing (much) more content than the law actually demands (Keller 2015; Montagnani and Trapova 2019; Garstka 2020). While blocking "where there is the slightest doubt as to its lawfulness"[13] may be tempting for an intermediary when faced with the risk of liability (Husovec 2018; Senftleben 2020), its effects can be pernicious not only in terms of impairing users' right to freedom of expression (in both its active and passive dimensions) but also in its broader societal impact, diminishing content diversity (Perel and Elkin-Koren 2016) and discriminating between types of content and genres (e.g., hurting hip-hop artists more than musicians in other genres) (Lester and Pachamanova 2017). Creativity also is at risk due to the underlying "chilling effects" (Garstka 2020; Frosio and Mendis 2020), since the lack of transparency in content recognition systems makes it impossible for creators to understand how to use the platform legally, ultimately resulting in self-censorship (Tóth 2019).

It is fair to note that the EU regime does include certain safeguards, but there are multiple uncertainties regarding whether and how efficiently they can curb the negative effects of (algorithmic-driven) content restriction decisions and enforcement (Schwemer 2020). The first mitigation path will be to focus on enabling, as much as possible, authorization under Article 17(1) of the CDSM by installing legal mechanisms for broad licensing that adequately engage all stakeholders and cover most content (Quintais et al. 2019; Spindler 2019), possibly also employing copyright compensation systems for online use (Handke 2020) as well as smart contracts down the road (Peukert 2019). The second avenue is to provide robust protection of user rights and real implementation of the copyright exceptions and limitations. The CDSM permits such an approach: next to the directive's generic obligation that it "shall in no way affect legitimate uses," Article 17(7) harmonizes and makes mandatory the specific exceptions covering quotation, criticism, review, and use for the purpose of caricature, parody, or pastiche. This is a change to the existing regime under Article 5(3) of the Information Society Directive (which is incoherently implemented by the different EU member states) and explicitly endorses a set of user rights, overriding contractual obligations, and technological protection measures (Quintais et al. 2019; Husovec and Quintais 2021b).[14] Yet there is skepticism as to how this set of rights would actually work in practice (Husovec and Quintais 2021b), and the implementation in the EU member states reveals different approaches—so, for instance, while Italy and Spain subscribe to a "filter first" approach with only ex post protection of user rights, Austria and Germany have included ex ante user rights safeguards that, based on certain quantitative criteria, carve out permitted uses and prevent automatic blocking, demanding manual review by rights holders and ensuring online availability until the dispute's resolution (Keller 2022). The latter approach is also the one recommended by the European Commission in its guidance on Article 17 of the CDSM, which seeks to limit fully automated filtering to manifestly infringing uploads and instructs national implementations to demand the blocking of other content only after human review by rights holders (European Commission 2021).

Fortunately, a more human-rights-oriented approach with regard to intermediaries' liability has also been recently endorsed by the Court of Justice of the European Union (CJEU),[15] importantly in the case where Poland sought the annulment of the "staydown" part of Article 17 of the CDSM, as its "preventive control" mechanisms would "undermine the essence of the right of freedom of expression and information and do not comply with the requirement that limitations imposed on that right be proportional and necessary."[16] In this CJEU judgment, while Article 17 of the CDSM "survived" and the court considered the limitation on freedom of expression justified in relation to the legitimate objective of ensuring a high level of protection for rights holders,[17] it instructed the EU member states to implement Article 17 in such a way as to strike a fair balance between the various fundamental rights, and it instructed that authorities and courts should not interpret in a manner "which would be in conflict with those fundamental rights or with the other general principles of EU law, such as the principle of proportionality."[18]

Concluding Remarks

Intermediary liability in copyright law as a legal design seeks to balance three goals—first, to prevent copyright infringement; second, to protect internet users' lawful speech and activity online; and third, to support innovation and competition in online services. Any reform in the liability regime essentially changes the balance between these objectives and may potentially harm the parties involved (Keller 2020). This inquiry into the recent European copyright reform and in particular the analysis of the new regime of Article 17 have revealed a distinct shift toward stricter liability and responsibility for certain internet intermediaries, one that departs from the standard "notice and takedown" regime as previously applied in the EU and in other jurisdictions (Frosio 2018b; Curto 2020; Ginsburg 2020) and which may under different scenarios involve proactive monitoring obligations as well as automated enforcement. While the benefits for rights holders may be evident and the attempt to close the value gap valid, the overall balance of rights may be skewed in a direction that ultimately hurts creativity rather than fosters it. One can only hope that the directive's implementation in the EU member states will mitigate these risks and create a regulatory environment where the balance between the different stakes is properly safeguarded and the conditions for online creativity work for the benefit of all, not merely for coordinated industry interests (Geller 2000; Patry 2009; Travis 2015) that aim for "'zero risk' as regards possible infringements of their rights."[19] The regulatory environment remains dynamic in general as well as in the concrete area of EU copyright law with the forthcoming Digital Services Act (European Commission 2020; Peukert et al. 2022), and we are bound to see both experimentation at the national level and judicial proceedings. This can be directly linked to the extent to which the new regulatory initiatives will affect the balance of the relationship between the interested parties on the ground and to the extent to which the affected parties and the inherent struggles that we have (such as among major labels, smaller and independent creators, and tech companies) will shape the implementation of the CDSM and ultimately whether or not the directive will change the situation for those in need of it (Kjus and Jacobsen 2022). It will be particularly important in this context to enhance the literacy of the involved creative workers, who should understand the implications of creating content across various media and the impact of copyright, including the management of rights across different platforms (Kjus 2021). In addition to these increased demands for literacy, there is a discrete need for smaller and amateur creators to join forces and seek to address some of the imbalances between large and smaller rights holders that the CDSM triggers (Husovec and Quintais 2021b; Kjus and Jacobsen 2022). In this sense, it should be evident that copyright is not a topic to be solely explored by legal scholarship but one that has profound implications for creative processes and should be embedded in arts and management and cultural policy research (Kjus and Jacobsen 2022).

Notes

1. Next to this primary utilitarian, incentive-driven theory, there are other theories on the rationales for copyright protection, in particular the personhood and the fairness doctrines (Sganga 2018, 17–87).
2. US Constitution, at Article I, § 8, cl. 8 (authorizing Congress "To promote the Progress of Science and useful Arts, by securing for limited Times to Authors and Inventors the exclusive Right to their respective Writings and Discoveries").
3. *Feist Publications v. Rural Telephone Service Co.*, 499 U.S. 340 (1991).
4. The "core" copyright industries include books, music, motion pictures, radio and television broadcasting, computer software, newspapers, video games, and periodicals and journals (Stoner and Dutra 2020). On lobbying in IP (Sell 2003; Netanel 2007).
5. Vaidhyanathan notes in this regard: "Copyright in recent years has certainly become too strong for its own good. It protects more content and outlaws more acts than ever before. It stifles creativity and hampers the discovery and sharing of culture and knowledge" (Vaidhyanathan 2003; 2007, 1210; Lessig 2004).
6. This phrase is attributed to Vint Cerf, one of the fathers of the Internet (Zittrain 2008; Chesbrough and Van Alstyne 2015).
7. Directive 2000/31/EC of the European Parliament and of the Council of 8 June 2000 on certain legal aspects of information society services, in particular electronic commerce, in the Internal Market, OJ L [2000] 178/1 (hereinafter E-Commerce Directive).
8. Digital Millennium Copyright Act (DMCA) § 103, 17 U.S.C. § 1201 (2006) (hereinafter DMCA).
9. There are variations of the safe harbor regime. Besides the notice and takedown procedure, the best-known procedures are the "notice and notice" and "notice and staydown." While similar in the triggering by a notification, they differ in the required intermediary's response and ultimately, in the resulting balance of interests (Angelopoulos and Smet 2016; Hinze 2019).
10. Some authors doubt that such a value gap exists (Frosio 2017b; Bridy 2020).
11. OCSSP is "a provider of an information society service of which the main or one of the main purposes is to store and give the public access to a large amount of

copyright-protected works or other protected subject matter uploaded by its users, which it organizes and promotes for profit-making purposes." Certain providers, such as non-profit online encyclopedias, open-source software-developing and sharing platforms, and business-to-business cloud services, are excluded. Article 2(6) CDSM.
12. Article 17(8) CDSM; Article 15 E-Commerce Directive and existing case-law (Case C-70/10, *Scarlet SA v. SABAM*, ECLI:EU:C:2011:771; Case C-360/10, *SABAM v. Netlog NV*, ECLI:EU:C:2012:85); Case C-484/14, *Mc Fadden v. Sony Music Entertainment Germany GmbH*, ECLI:EU:C:2016:689).
13. Case C-401/19, *Republic of Poland v. European Parliament and Council of the European Union*, Opinion of Advocate General Saugmandsgaard Øe, 15 July 2021, ECLI:EU:C:2021:613, para. 172 (emphasis in the original) (hereinafter Opinion AG Øe).
14. Directive 2001/29/EC of the European Parliament and of the Council of 22 May 2001 on the harmonization of certain aspects of copyright and related rights in the information society, OJ L (2001) 167/10.
15. Joined Cases C-682/18 and C-683/18, *Peterson v. Google and YouTube and Elsevier v. Cyando*, Judgment of 22 June 2021, EU:C:2021:503.
16. Case C-401/19, *Republic of Poland v. European Parliament and Council of the European Union*, Judgment of 26 April 2022, ECLI:EU:C:2022:297.
17. Case C-401/19, *Republic of Poland v. European Parliament and Council of the European Union*, Judgment of 26 April 2022, ECLI:EU:C:2022:297, at paras. 69; 84 et seq.
18. Case C-401/19, *Republic of Poland v. European Parliament and Council of the European Union*, Judgment of 26 April 2022, ECLI:EU:C:2022:297, at para. 99.
19. Opinion AG Øe, para. 216.

References

Angelopoulos, Christina. 2017. "On Online Platforms and the Commission's New Proposal for a Directive on Copyright in the Digital Single Market." Working paper. https://papers.ssrn.com/sol3/papers.cfm?abstract_id=2947800

Angelopoulos, Christina. 2020. "Harmonizing Intermediary Copyright Liability in the EU: A Summary." In *The Oxford Handbook of Online Intermediary Liability*, edited by Giancarlo F. Frosio, 315–334. Oxford: Oxford University Press.

Angelopoulos, Christina, and João Pedro Quintais. 2019. "Fixing Copyright Reform: A Better Solution to Online Infringement." *Journal of Intellectual Property, Information Technology and Electronic Commerce Law* 10: 147–172.

Angelopoulos, Christina, and Stijn Smet. 2016. "Notice-and-Fair-Balance: How to Reach a Compromise Between Fundamental Rights in European Intermediary Liability." *Journal of Media Law* 8: 266–301.

Balganesh, Shyamkrishna. 2009. "Foreseeability and Copyright Incentives." *Harvard Law Review* 122: 1572–1633.

Benkler, Yochai. 2000. "An Unhurried View of Private Ordering in Information Transactions." *Vanderbilt Law Review* 53: 2063–2080.

Benkler, Yochai. 2006. *The Wealth of Networks: How Social Production Transforms Markets and Freedom*. New Haven, CT: Yale University Press.

Boyle, James. 2000. "Cruel, Mean, or Lavish? Economic Analysis, Price Discrimination and Digital Intellectual Property." *Vanderbilt Law Review* 53: 2007–2039.

Bridy, Annemarie. 2016. "Copyright's Digital Deputies: DMCA-Plus Enforcement by Internet Intermediaries." In *Research Handbook on Electronic Commerce Law*, edited by John A. Rothchild, 185–208. Cheltenham, UK: Edward Elgar.

Bridy, Annemarie. 2020. "The Price of Closing the 'Value Gap': How the Music Industry Hacked EU Copyright Reform." *Vanderbilt Journal of Entertainment and Technology Law* 22: 323–358.

Brown, Michael F. 1998. "Can Culture Be Copyrighted?" *Current Anthropology* 39: 193–206.

Burk, Dan L. 2019. "Algorithmic Fair Use." *University of Chicago Law Review* 86: 283–307.

Burri, Mira. 2020. "Cultural Heritage and Intellectual Property." In *Oxford Handbook on International Cultural Heritage Law*, edited by Francesco Francioni and Ana F. Vrdoljak, 459–482. Oxford: Oxford University Press.

Chesbrough, Henry, and Marshall Van Alstyne. 2015. "Permissionless Innovation." *Communications of the ACM* 58: 24–26.

Cohen, Julie E. 2000. "Copyright and the Perfect Curve." *Vanderbilt Law Review* 53: 1799–1819.

Cohen, Julie E. 2007. "Creativity and Culture in Copyright Theory." *UC Davis Law Review* 40: 1151–1205.

Cohen, Julie E., Lydia Pallas Loren, Ruth L. Okediji, and Maureen A. O'Rourke. 2019. *Copyright in a Global Information Economy*, 4th ed. New York: Wolters Kluwer.

Cowen, Tyler. 2008. "Why Everything Has Changed: The Recent Revolution in Cultural Economics." *Journal of Cultural Economics* 32: 261–273.

Curto, Natalia E. 2020. "EU Directive on Copyright in the Digital Single Market and ISP Liability: What's Next at International Level?" *Journal of Law, Technology and the Internet* 11: 84–110.

de Beer, Jeremy, and Christopher D. Clemmer. 2009. "Global Trends in Online Copyright Enforcement: A Non-Neutral Role for Network Intermediaries?" *Jurimetrics* 49: 375–409.

diCola, Peter. 2013. "Money from Music: Survey Evidence on Musicians' Revenue and Lessons About Copyright Incentives." *Arizona Law Review* 55: 301–370.

Elkin-Koren, Niva. 2014. "After Twenty Years: Revisiting Copyright Liability of Online Intermediaries." In *The Evolution and Equilibrium of Copyright in the Digital Age*, edited by Susy Frankel and Daniel Gervais, 29–51. Cambridge: Cambridge University Press.

Erickson, Kristofer, and Martin Kretschmer. 2020. "Empirical Approaches to Intermediary Liability." In *The Oxford Handbook of Online Intermediary Liability*, edited by Giancarlo Frosio, 104–121. Oxford: Oxford University Press.

European Commission. 2015. "A Digital Single Market Strategy for Europe." COM(2015) 192 final.

European Commission. 2016a. "Proposal for a Directive of the European Parliament and of the Council on Copyright in the Digital Single Market." COM(2016) 593 final.

European Commission. 2016b." Online Platforms and the Digital Single Market: Opportunities and Challenges for Europe." COM(2016) 288 final.

European Commission. 2020. "Proposal for a Regulation of the European Parliament and of the Council on a Single Market for Digital Services (Digital Services Act) and Amending Directive 2000/31/EC." COM(2020) 825 final.

European Commission. 2021. "Guidance on Article 17 of Directive 2019/790 on Copyright in the Digital Single Market." COM(2021) 288 final.

Fisher, William W. 1988. "Reconstructing the Fair Use Doctrine." *Harvard Law Review* 101: 1661–1795.

Fisher, William W. 2010. "The Implications for Law of User Innovation." *Minnesota Law Review* 94: 1417–1477.

Frosio, Giancarlo F. 2017a. "The Death of 'No Monitoring Obligations.'" *Journal of Intellectual Property, Information Technology and Electronic Commerce Law* 8: 199–215.

Frosio, Giancarlo F. 2017b. "Reforming Intermediary Liability in the Platform Economy: A European Digital Single Market Strategy." *Northwestern University Law Review* 111: 19–46.

Frosio, Giancarlo F. 2018a. "To Filter, or Not to Filter?" *Cardozo Arts and Entertainment Law Journal* 36: 331–368.

Frosio, Giancarlo F. 2018b. "Why Keep a Dog and Bark Yourself? From Intermediary Liability to Responsibility." *International Journal of Law and Information Technology* 26: 1–33.

Frosio, Giancarlo F. 2020. "Algorithmic Enforcement Online." In *Intellectual Property and Human Rights*, 4th ed., edited by Paul Torremans, 709–744. Alphen aan den Rijn: Kluwer Law International.

Frosio, Giancarlo F., and Sunimal Mendis. 2020. "Monitoring and Filtering: European Reform or Global Trend?" In *The Oxford Handbook of Online Intermediary Liability*, edited by Giancarlo F. Frosio, 344–565. Oxford: Oxford University Press.

Garstka, Krzysztof. 2020. "Guiding the Blind Bloodhounds: How to Mitigate the Risks Art. 17 of Directive 2019/790 Poses to the Freedom of Expression." In *Intellectual Property and Human Rights*, 4th ed., edited by Paul Torremans. Alphen aan den Rijn: Kluwer Law International.

Geiger, Christophe, Giancarlo Frosio, and Elena Izymenko. 2020. "Intermediary Liability and Fundamental Rights." In *The Oxford Handbook of Online Intermediary Liability*, edited by Giancarlo F. Frosio, 138–153. Oxford: Oxford University Press.

Geiger, Christophe, Daniel Gervais, and Martin Senftleben. 2014. "The Three-Step Test Revisited: How to Use the Test's Flexibility in National Copyright Law." *American University International Law Review* 29: 581–626.

Geller, Paul Edward. 2000. "Copyright History and the Future: What's Culture Got to Do with It?" *Journal of the Copyright Society of the U.S.A.* 47: 209–264.

Gervais, Daniel. 2002. "Feist Goes Global: A Comparative Analysis of the Notion of Originality in Copyright Law" *Journal of the Copyright Society of the U.S.A.* 49: 949–981.

Ginsburg, Jane C. 2020. "A United States Perspective on Digital Single Market Directive Art. 17." In *EU Copyright Law: A Commentary*, 2nd ed., edited by Irini Stamatoudi and Paul Torremans, 782–797. Cheltenham, UK: Edward Elgar.

Goldstein, Paul, and P. Bernt Hugenholtz. 2019. *International Copyright: Principles, Law, and Practice*, 4th ed. Oxford: Oxford University Press.

Graber, Christoph Beat. 2007. "Traditional Cultural Expressions in a Matrix of Copyright, Cultural Diversity and Human Rights." In *New Directions in Copyright Law*, vol. 5, edited by Fiona Macmillan, 45–71. Cheltenham, UK: Edward Elgar.

Gray, Joanne E., and Nicolas P. Suzor. 2020. "Playing with Machines: Using Machine Learning to Understand Automated Copyright Enforcement at Scale." *Big Data and Society* 7: 1–13.

Grimmelmann, James. 2021. *Internet Law*, 11th ed. Oregon City, OR: Semaphore Press.

Grisse, Karina. 2019. "After the Storm—Examining the Final Version of Article 17 of the New Directive (EU) 2019/790." *Journal of Intellectual Property Law and Practice* 14: 887–899.

Guzman, Frank. 2015. "The Tension Between Derivative Works Online Protected by Fair Use and the Takedown Provisions of the Online Copyright Infringement Liability Limitation Act." *Northwestern Journal of Technology and Intellectual Property* 13: 181–196.

Handke, Christian. 2015. "Digitization and Competition in Copyright Industries: One Step Forward and Two Steps Back?" *Homo Oeconomicus* 32: 209–234.

Handke, Christian. 2020. "Compensation Systems for Online Use." In *Digital Peripheries: The Online Circulation of Audiovisual Content from the Small Market Perspective*, edited by Petr Szczepanik, Pavel Zahrádka, Jakub Macek, and Paul Stepan, 261–272. Berlin: Springer.

Hinze, Gwenith Alicia. 2019. "A Tale of Two Legal Regimes: An Empirical Investigation into How Copyright Law Shapes Online Service Providers' Practices and How Online Service Providers Navigate Differences in U.S. and EU Copyright Liability Standards." PhD diss., University of California, Berkeley.

Husovec, Martin. 2018. "The Promises of Algorithmic Copyright Enforcement: Takedown or Staydown? Which Is Superior? And Why?" *Columbia Journal of Law and the Arts* 42: 53–84.

Husovec, Martin. 2019. "How Europe Wants to Redefine Global Online Copyright Enforcement." TILEC Discussion Paper no. 2019-16.

Husovec, Martin, and João Pedro Quintais. 2021a. "How to License Article 17? Exploring the Implementation Options for the New EU Rules on Content-Sharing Platforms." *GRUR International* 70: 325–348.

Husovec, Martin, and João Pedro Quintais. 2021b. "Too Small to Matter? On the Copyright Directive's Bias in Favour of Big Right-Holders." In *Global Intellectual Property Protection and New Constitutionalism: Hedging Exclusive Rights*, edited by Tuomas Mylly and Jonathan Griffiths, 219–237. Oxford: Oxford University Press.

Jougleux, Philippe. 2017. "The Role of Internet Intermediaries in Copyright Law Online Enforcement." In *EU Internet Law in the Digital Era: Regulation and Enforcement*, edited by Tatiana-Eleni Synodinou, Philippe Jougleux, Christiana Markou, and Thalia Prastitou, 183–198. Berlin: Springer.

Judge, Elizabeth F., and Daniel Gervais. 2009. "Of Silos and Constellations: Comparing Notions of Originality in Copyright Law." *Cardozo Arts and Entertainment Law Journal* 27: 375–408.

Keller, Daphne. 2015. "Empirical Evidence of 'Over-Removal' by Internet Companies Under Intermediary Liability Laws." *Stanford Center for Internet and Society Blog*. http://cyberlaw.stanford.edu/blog/2015/10/empirical-evidence-over-removal-internet-companies-under-intermediary-liability-laws.

Keller, Daphne. 2020. "How Other Countries Are Handling Online Piracy." Statement before the United States Senate Committee on the Judiciary, Subcommittee on Intellectual Property, Hearing on the Digital Millennium Copyright Act.

Keller, Paul. 2022. "Article 17, the Year in Review (2021 Edition)." *Kluwer Copyright Blog*. http://copyrightblog.kluweriplaw.com/2022/01/24/article-17-the-year-in-review-2021-edition/.

Kjus, Yngvar. 2021. "The Use of Copyright in Digital Times: A Study of How Artists Exercise Their Rights in Norway." *Popular Music and Society* 44: 241–257.

Kjus, Yngvar, and Roy Aulie Jacobsen. 2022. "Will the EU's Directive on Copyright in the Digital Market Change the Power Balance of the Music Industry? Views from Norway." *Nordisk Kulturpolitisk Tidsskrift* 25: 28–42.

Kuczerawy, Aleksandra. 2019. "General Monitoring Obligations: A New Cornerstone of Internet Regulation in the EU?" In *Rethinking IT and IP Law*, edited by Centre for IT and IP Law. Cambridge, UK: Intersentia.

Kuczerawy, Aleksandra. 2020. "From 'Notice and Takedown' to 'Notice and Stay Down': Risks and Safeguards for Freedom of Expression." In *The Oxford Handbook of Online Intermediary Liability*, edited by Giancarlo F. Frosio, 525–543. Oxford: Oxford University Press.

Kulk, Stefan. 2018. "Internet Intermediaries and Copyright Law: Towards a Future-Proof EU Legal Framework." PhD diss., Utrecht University.

Kwall, Roberta R. 2006. "Inspiration and Innovation: The Intrinsic Dimension of the Artistic Soul." *Notre Dame Law Review* 81: 1945–2012.

Landes, William M., and Richard A. Posner. 2003. *The Economic Structure of Intellectual Property Law*. Cambridge, MA: Harvard University Press.

Lange, David. 2002. "Reimagining the Public Domain." *Law and Contemporary Problems* 66: 463–483.

Lessig, Lawrence. 2004. *Free Culture: How Big Media Uses Technology and the Law to Lock Down Culture and Control Creativity*. London: Penguin.

Lester, Toni, and Dessislava Pachamanova. 2017. "The Dilemma of False Positives: Making Content ID Algorithms More Conducive to Fostering Innovative Fair Use in Music Creation." *UCLA Entertainment Law Review* 24: 51–73.

Lunceford, Brett, and Shane Lunceford. 2008. "Meh: The Irrelevance of Copyright in the Public Mind." *Northwestern Journal of Technology and Intellectual Property* 7: 33–49.

Mac Síthigh, Daithí. 2020. "The Road to Responsibilities: New Attitudes Towards Internet Intermediaries." *Information and Communications Technology Law* 29: 1–21.

Metzger, Axel, and Martin Senftleben. 2020. "Selected Aspects of Implementing Article 17 of the Directive on Copyright in the Digital Single Market into National Law." Comment of the European Copyright Society.

Moglen, Eben. 2002. "Anarchism Triumphant: Free Software and the Death of Copyright." In *The Commodification of Information*, edited by Niva Elkin-Koren and Neil Weinstock Netanel, 107–132. The Hague: Kluwer Law International.

Mongnani, Maria Lillà. 2020. "Virtues and Perils of Algorithmic Enforcement and Content Regulation in the EU: A Toolkit for a Balanced Algorithmic Copyright Enforcement." *Case Western Reserve Journal of Law, Technology and the Internet* 11: 1–49.

Montagnani, Maria Lillà, and Alina Trapova. 2019. "New Obligations for Internet Intermediaries in the Digital Single Market—Safe Harbors in Turmoil?" *Journal of Internet Law* 22: 3–11.

Netanel, Neil W. 2007. "Why Has Copyright Expanded? Analysis and Critique." In *New Directions in Copyright Law*, vol. 6, edited by Fiona Macmillan, 3–34. Cheltenham, UK: Edward Elgar.

Okediji, Ruth L. 2009. "The Regulation of Creativity Under the WIPO Internet Treaties." *Fordham Law Review* 77: 2379–2410.

Patry, William. 2009. *Moral Panics and the Copyright Wars*. Oxford: Oxford University Press.

Penney, Jonathon W. 2019. "Privacy and Legal Automation: The DMCA as a Case Study." *Stanford Technology Law Review* 22: 412–486.

Perel, Maayan, and Niva Elkin-Koren. 2016. "Accountability in Algorithmic Copyright Enforcement." *Stanford Technology Law Review* 19: 473–533.

Perel, Maayan, and Niva Elkin-Koren. 2017. "Black Box Tinkering: Beyond Disclosure in Algorithmic Enforcement." *Florida Law Review* 69: 181–221.

Peukert, Alexander, Martin Husovec, Martin Kretschmer, Péter Mezei, and João Pedro Quintais. 2022. "Comment on Copyright and the Digital Services Act Proposal." Comment of the European Copyright Society.

Peukert, Christian. 2019. "The Next Wave of Digital Technological Change and the Cultural Industries." *Journal of Cultural Economics* 43: 189–210.

Quintais, João Pedro. 2020. "The New Copyright in the Digital Single Market Directive: A Critical Look." *European Intellectual Property Review* 42: 28–41.

Quintais, João Pedro, Giancarlo Frosio, Stef van Gompel, P. Bernt Hugenholtz, Martin Husovec, Bernd Justin Jütte, and Martin Senftleben. 2019. "Safeguarding User Freedoms in

Implementing Article 17 of the Copyright in the Digital Single Market Directive." *Journal of Intellectual Property, Information Technology and Electronic Commerce Law* 10: 277–282.

Reda, Julia. 2020. "How Other Countries Are Handling Online Piracy." Statement before the United States Senate Committee on the Judiciary, Subcommittee on Intellectual Property, Hearing on the Digital Millennium Copyright Act.

Rigamonti, Cyrill P. 2006. "Deconstructing Moral Rights." *Harvard International Law Journal* 47: 353–412.

Sag, Matthew. 2018. "Internet Safe Harbors and the Transformation of Copyright Law." *Notre Dame Law Review* 93: 499–564.

Samuelson, Pamela. 2020. "How Other Countries Are Handling Online Piracy." Statement before the United States Senate Committee on the Judiciary, Subcommittee on Intellectual Property, Hearing on the Digital Millennium Copyright Act.

Sawers, Paul. 2018. "YouTube: We've Invested $100 Million in Content ID and Paid over $3 Billion to Rightsholders." VentureBeat. https://venturebeat.com/2018/11/07/youtube-weve-invested-100-million-in-content-id-and-paid-over-3-billion-to-rightsholders/.

Schmitz, Sandra. 2015. *The Struggle in Online Copyright Enforcement: Problems and Prospects*. Baden-Baden: Nomos.

Schwemer, Sebastian Felix. 2020. "Article 17 at the Intersection of EU Copyright Law and Platform Regulation." *Nordic Intellectual Property Law Review* 3: 400–435.

Sell, Susan K. 2003. *Private Power, Public Law: The Globalization of Intellectual Property Rights*. Cambridge: Cambridge University Press.

Senftleben, Martin. 2020. "Institutionalized Algorithmic Enforcement—The Pros and Cons of the EU Approach to UGC Platform Liability." *Florida International University Law Review* 14: 299–328.

Sganga, Caterina. 2018. *Propertizing European Copyright: History, Challenges and Opportunities*. Cheltenham: Edward Elgar.

Shapiro, Ted, and Sunniva Hansson. 2019. "The DSM Copyright Directive: EU Copyright Will Indeed Never Be the Same." *European Intellectual Property Review* 41: 404–414.

Shih Ray Ku, Raymond, Jiayang Sun, and Yiying Fan. 2009. "Does Copyright Law Promote Creativity? An Empirical Analysis of Copyright's Bounty." *Vanderbilt Law Review* 62: 1669–1746.

Simon, David A. 2011. "Culture, Creativity, and Copyright." *Cardozo Arts and Entertainment Law Journal* 29: 279–373.

Spindler, Gerald. 2019. "The Liability System of Art. 17 DSMD and National Implementation." *Journal of Intellectual Property, Information Technology and Electronic Commerce Law* 10: 344–374.

Spindler, Gerald. 2020. "Copyright Law and Internet Intermediaries Liability." In *EU Internet Law in the Digital Era: Regulation and Enforcement*, edited by Tatiana-Eleni Synodinou, Philippe Jougleux, Christiana Markou, and Thalia Prastitou, 3–26. Berlin: Springer.

Spoerri, Thomas. 2019. "On Upload Filters and Other Competitive Advantages for Big Tech Companies Under Article 17 of the Directive on Copyright in the Digital Single Market." *Journal of Intellectual Property, Information Technology and Electronic Commerce Law* 10: 173–186.

Stoner, Robert, and Jéssica Dutra. 2020. *Copyright Industries in the U.S. Economy: The 2020 Report*. Washington, DC: International Intellectual Property Alliance, 2020.

Tóth, Andrea Katalin. 2019. "Algorithmic Copyright Enforcement and AI: Issues and Potential Solutions Through the Lens of Text and Data Mining." *Masaryk University Journal of Law and Technology* 13: 361–387.

Trapova, Alina. 2020. "Reviving Collective Management—Will CMOs Become the True Mediators They Ought to Be in the Digital Single Market?" *European Intellectual Property Review* 42: 272–280.

Travis, Hannibal. 2008. "Opting Out of the Internet in the United States." *Notre Dame Law Review* 84: 331–407.

Travis, Hannibal. 2015. "Free Speech Institutions and Fair Use: A New Agenda for Copyright Reform." *Cardozo Arts and Entertainment Law Journal* 33: 673–737.

US Copyright Office. 2019. *Authors, Attribution, and Integrity: Examining Moral Rights in the United States*. Washington, DC: US Copyright Office.

Vaidhyanathan, Siva. 2003. *Copyrights and Copywrongs: The Rise of Intellectual Property and How It Threatens Creativity*. New York: New York University Press.

Vaidhyanathan, Siva. 2007. "The Googlization of Everything and the Future of Copyright." *UC Davis Law Review* 40: 1207–1231.

van Oranje-Nassau, Constantijn, Jonathan Cave, Martin van der Mandele, Helen Rebecca Schindler, Seo Yeon Hong, Ilian Iliev, and Ingo Vogelsang. 2008. *Responding to Convergence*. Oxford: RAND Corporation.

Waldfogel, Joel. 2017. "How Digitization Has Created a Golden Age of Music, Movies, Books and Television." *Journal of Economic Perspectives* 31: 195–214.

Woodmansee, Martha, and Peter Jaszi. 1994. *The Construction of Authorship: Textual Appropriation in Law and Literature*. Durham, NC: Duke University Press.

Yu, Peter K. 2020. "Can Algorithms Promote Fair Use?" *FIU Law Review* 14: 330–363.

Zimmerman, Diane Leenheer. 2011. "Copyrights as Incentives: Did We Just Imagine That?" *Theoretical Inquiries in Law* 12: 29–58.

Zittrain, Jonathan. 2008. *The Future of the Internet and How to Stop It*. New Haven, CT: Yale University Press.

CHAPTER 13

THE ROLE OF HERITAGE COMMUNITIES IN CULTURAL HERITAGE MANAGEMENT

An International Law Perspective

SIMONA PINTON

Introduction

THIS chapter presents the notion and role of heritage communities (HCs) in the management of cultural heritage (CH) according to new approaches promoted by international legal instruments dealing with CH. It also discusses practices that have been developed to manage CH through participatory and cooperative processes involving multiple stakeholders.[1] The chapter begins by clarifying the notion of CH used here, relying upon Article 2(a) of the Framework Convention on the Value of Cultural Heritage for the Society (the Faro Convention).[2] The Faro Convention's elaboration of the notions of CH, HCs, and European common heritage makes it a highly innovative and far-reaching treaty on culture in the European context (Lixinski 2013; Blake 2015).

The Faro Convention is an international treaty adopted under the aegis of the Council of Europe (CoE), but open to ratification by non-member states and by the European Union.[3] The Convention "emphasizes the important aspects of heritage as they relate to human rights and democracy, [and] promotes a wider understanding of heritage and its relationship to communities and society" (Pejčinović Burić 2020, 4). Thus it encourages inhabitants to engage with CH objects, sites, traditions, and intangible expressions through the meanings and values that these elements represent to them. Indeed, "the need to involve everyone in society in the ongoing process of defining and managing CH" is the vision behind the Convention.[4] The Faro Convention promotes the recognition of CH as a resource useful to address one of the major challenges facing our contemporary societies—namely, the need to ensure the sustainability of future social and economic development in accordance with the UN 2030 Agenda on Sustainable Development Goals. One aspect of this challenge is the delicate issue of the integration of newcomers (migrants, asylum seekers, refugees) and their cultural identities in relation to existing groups and communities and their CH.

The Faro Convention supplements and consolidates the CoE's previous instruments favoring states' cultural goods preservation policies.[5] But aside from the question of whether that generation of agreements was concerned more with the *fabric* of heritage and focused too strongly on conservation for its own sake, the Faro Convention, in line with the Florence Convention,[6] considers CH from the viewpoint of the living people who construct, use, celebrate, or oppose it.[7] Faro addresses the "desire for heritage to become a new instrument serving society and, therefore, balancing the cost of conservation against the value of heritage to everyday public life" (Colomer 2021).

CH and the human right to enjoy and participate in heritage are key aspects of "heritigization processes" (Wolferstan and Fairclough 2013, 43). The "focus on values, rather than constitutive elements of heritage," paves the way to avoiding heritage commodification, because all references to heritage or culture as "concrete entities" are avoided (Lixinski 2013, 79–80).

Specifically, according to Art 2(a), CH is

> a group of resources inherited from the past which people identify, independently of ownership, as a reflection and expression of their constantly evolving values, beliefs, knowledge and traditions. It includes all aspects of the environment resulting from the interaction between people and places through time.

This notion highlights that objects, intangible elements, and places, including all aspects of the environment, are important not just in themselves but also because of their meaning to people. The Faro Convention also includes digital heritage (Art. 14).

The idea of "constantly evolving values," then, indicates living cultures: the main frontier that the Faro Convention urges us to cross is to deal with heritage not by treating it as a limited number of assets to be kept from harm (conservation and restoration) but by considering it as something universal, ubiquitous, for all societies' benefit. Therefore, people create heritage both in the conventional physical sense and in the sense of meaning given to heritage components. CH's significance thus becomes a socially determined process, defined by a group of people with a distinct interest in working for and with an inherited past (Colomer 2021) to be used in the present (Wolferstan and Fairclough 2013) and to be transmitted to younger generations. Thanks to this holistic approach, "ordinary," vernacular, local heritage is retrieved—departing, for example, from the logic of the 1972 UNESCO Convention on the Protection of the World Cultural and Natural Heritage.[8]

The definition of CH in the Faro Convention, however, may appear too wide, dissolving the line between what is heritage and what is not: everything could, in theory, fall under the umbrella of Article 2(a). Faced with such an extensive notion, the safeguarding and management of CH become crucial dimensions to investigate. Which stakeholders are or should be involved in safeguarding and managing CH? How do public authorities and civil society engage to enhance quality of life and respect for the living environment: cultural diversity and social cohesion? How do we develop inclusive and effective governance processes in CH management?

THE NOTION OF (HERITAGE) COMMUNITIES IN THE INTERNATIONAL LEGAL SCENARIO

At the international level, the focus on groups and communities is nowadays part of the debate on cultural diversity and the management of tangible, intangible, and digital heritage. A comprehensive literature exists on the role played by communities in the implementation of international legal instruments' provisions (binding and nonbinding), including on CH (Urbinati 2015, 123–140; Blake 2006; Hausler 2020).

In the realm of international CH instruments, the reference to communities appeared for the first time in the 1996 Operational Guidelines for the Implementation of the 1972 World Heritage Convention, which stated in paragraph 4: "The nominations [for inclusion of cultural properties in the World Heritage List] should be prepared in collaboration with and the full approval of local communities."[9] At the 2000 World Heritage Centre meeting, among the recommendations adopted was the suggestion that there be "emphasis given to the place of local communities in the sustainable heritage management process," including "management systems, language, and other forms of intangible heritage among attributes expressing authenticity." From that date on, the annual Operational Guidelines for the 1972 UNESCO convention have progressively extended references to effective and inclusive participation of local communities, including their spirit, their knowledge, and an understanding of their properties.[10]

In 2007, the states parties to the 1972 UNESCO convention welcomed the proposal by New Zealand to enhance the role of communities in the implementation of the convention by adding a "fifth C"—for "communities"—to the existing strategic objectives.[11] According to that proposal, relevant communities had to be actively involved in the identification, management, and conservation of any site to be added to the World Heritage List. The interests of local/traditional/indigenous people and communities are to be considered and used in a complementary manner, in order not to trump other strategic goals:

> Where community interests are in direct conflict with some of the existing strategic goals, good faith efforts should be made to reconcile the differences in a meaningful and equitable manner.... The identification of communities who have a particular interest is a matter that will require States to develop an explicit methodology.'... Linking communities to heritage protection is a "win-win" scenario.[12]

Along the same lines, in a 2011 report, the UN Independent Expert on Cultural Rights, Farida Shaheed, underlined a shift in emphasis from the preservation and safeguarding of CH for the public at large to the preservation and safeguarding of CH for communities, involving communities in the processes of identification and stewardship (Shaheed 2011, 8). Shaheed recognized differing degrees of access to and enjoyment of CH by social groups. She distinguished between originators or "source communities," who consider themselves the custodians or owners of a specific CH and are keeping CH alive and/or have taken responsibility for it, and individuals and communities—including local communities—who consider a specific CH an integral part of community life but may not be actively involved in its maintenance. She also acknowledged scientists, artists, the general public accessing the CH of others, and the international community acting on behalf of humanity (Shaheed 2011, 16–17).

Interestingly, none of the other instruments mentioned so far details the term "community": it is the Faro Convention that has adopted a specific notion of "heritage community," made explicit in Articles 2 and 12.[13] According to Article 2(b), "a heritage community consists of people who value specific aspects of cultural heritage which they wish, within the framework of public action, to sustain and transmit to future generations." The use of the term "people" indicates that what is at stake is a collective and shared phenomenon (Leniaud 2009, 137), and the notion outlines "the voluntary, public nature of membership . . . as well as the idea that heritage communities exist because their members share common objectives, high among which is the perpetuation of the valued heritage" (Fojut 2009, 20). Moreover, this implies that HCs may reunite people from diverse cultural, religious, ethnic, and linguistic backgrounds over a specific CH they consider to be a common link (Shaheed 2011, 18).

From this essential intertwining of the notions of HC and CH it emerges that "the heritage only grows to the extent that new 'mediators' succeed in adding further heritage categories to a list that is hedged about by criteria selected in a far from diversified or consensual fashion by routine, prejudice and conflicts of power" (Leniaud 2009, 139; see also Greffe 2009, 107). Further, according to a suggestive reading, the innovative notions present in the Faro Convention, and their intersection, promote a "heritigization operation" in which European democracies are able, to this extent, to guarantee cultural rights as part of the fundamental rights of their citizens (Ferracuti 2011, 217–218).

The Faro Convention refers to the notion of HCs in Article 12(b): the parties undertake "[to] take into consideration the value attached by each heritage community to the heritage with which it identifies." The object of the state obligation indicated in Article 12(b) may appear undetermined, although the obligation's existence is not to be doubted: states are required to "undertake," which is a positive commitment, although the convention upholds a state party's "margin of appreciation" as to the ways in which it should respect the role and actions of HCs in relation to CH, as indicated in Article 12. Article 15 complements Article 12 by calling on states parties to develop, "through the CoE, a monitoring function covering legislations, policies and practices concerning CH, consistent with the principles established by this Convention"—a task performed also under the monitoring mechanism referred to in Article 16, which involves the work of the Steering Committee for Culture, Heritage and Landscape (SCCHL).[14]

The apparent indeterminateness of the notion of HC should be interpreted positively and not as a void concept. In other words, in its definition, the notion of an HC values the absence of "predefined societal parameters, national, ethnic, religious, professional or based on class" (Dolff-Bonekämper 2009, 71), as well as the absence of reference to local, regional, national, or global specificities. Communities and individuals constituting HCs can thus move transnationally through Europe (not only in the EU member states); "the same people can belong, simultaneously or in sequence, to several communities," across territories and social groups, thus eventually holding a "plurality of cultural identities" (Zagato and Pinton 2016, 22). Moreover, "individuals may feel an attachment to a heritage in a place where they would like to be, with persons with whom they would like to associate themselves, without this being physically possible. For the concept of heritage community allows for virtual belonging" (Dolff-Bonekämper 2009, 71). Article 4 of the Fribourg Declaration, on cultural communities, reiterates this perspective by affirming that "everyone is free to choose to identify or not to identify with one or several cultural communities, regardless of frontiers, and to modify such a choice"; conversely, "no one shall have a cultural identity imposed or be assimilated into a cultural community against one's will."[15]

Otherwise, compared to the Faro Convention's notion of HC, the definition of "communities, groups and individuals" included in Article 2(1) of the 2003 UNESCO Convention for the Safeguarding of Intangible Cultural Heritage has a more restricted scope. This may be explained by the specific task assigned to it by the 2003 UNESCO convention—namely, "to provide parameters for the identification of social practices to which specific social groups attribute heritage value and, besides this, agree in safeguarding them in the manner established by that legal instrument" (Arantes 2016, 60). The communities and groups of Article 2(1) are "commonly understood as based on membership of an ethnic group, a territory and a shared history" (Colomer 2021; see also Hertz 2015).

> The notion of HCs set in Faro is more inclusive. CH elements are safeguarded not just because they are praised by those who practice them, but also because they are recognized as significant by "outsiders," and "outsiders" are many and varied: they are neighboring communities, agents from governmental entities, experts, academics, visitors, buyers, participants of public performances, and so on.
>
> (Arantes 2016, 61)

In other words, "the Faro perspective suggests that CH is not just "someone's heritage but involves strong symbolic constructs that also interest 'others,' and that touches you and me, not just its bearers or practitioners" (Arantes 2016, 61). The Faro Convention therefore alludes to a broader space of social relationships, in which the development of CH policies would affect, and should engage, all those who consider themselves concerned by that heritage, regardless of any nationality/citizenship link to a country.

As mentioned above, this meaning of HCs may be beneficial to the migration phenomenon and the integration processes it requires. In the processes of community regeneration resulting from constant mobility, multiple identities and narratives emerge that may play an essential role in addressing changing cultural and social challenges. The Faro Convention principles may also contribute to regenerating communities by engaging displaced people in genuine dialogue about CH, contributing ultimately to a more sustained community life and people's well-being (Shearer Demir 2021).[16]

The fundamental trait of HCs with respect to the communities and groups referred to in the 2003 UNESCO Convention thus becomes an elective character that is also self-elective in terms of membership, an attribute that has raised a new challenge in the relationship between civil society and public and private institutions when it comes to safeguarding and managing CH, one that is not without risks. Indeed, the self-elective character of HCs may render them an ambivalent and ambiguous actor (De Marinis 2011).

It is worth reiterating that the approach proposed in this chapter is not to oppose two types of communities or community networks as mutually exclusive, but to evaluate the more elastic and inclusive nature—through space, time, and social and cultural links—of heritage communities and the networks they establish in relation to cultural heritage management.

Does International Law Provide a Role for Heritage Communities in Cultural Heritage Management?

The concept of CH management varies according to the discipline that regulates it, and so a clear definition must be put at the forefront. Although cultural management historically has focused on tangible heritage and dealt with technical conservation issues, such as biological or structural decay, here CH management is meant to encompass all of the practices and competences (skills and knowledge) necessary to safeguard tangible, intangible, and digital heritage, including identification, documentation, research, preservation, protection, promotion, enhancement, and transmission. Moreover, successful CH management must consider various economic, social, and environmental dimensions and a wider range of stakeholders beyond those directly concerned in the heritage sector. This section focuses on a critical analysis of the notion of CH management as it interrelates with the concepts of participation and cooperation of communities with other public and private stakeholders, according to the provisions of CH treaties, in particular the Faro Convention.

As mentioned previously, a role assigned to communities, groups, and in some cases individuals has been acknowledged in relation to the UNESCO conventions of 1972 and 2003. Recently, the 2021 Operational Guidelines for the 1972 convention indicate that states parties should include communities in the preparation and harmonization of Tentative Lists (para. 73); the effective management system (paras. 111–117); the definition of legislation, policies, and strategies affecting World Heritage properties (para. 119); the nomination process (para. 123); the development by member states of educational and capacity-building programs (para. 214bis); and the development of scientific studies and research methodologies, including traditional and indigenous knowledge.[17]

Article 15 of the 2003 convention states: "Within the framework of its safeguarding activities of the intangible cultural heritage, each State Party shall endeavor to ensure the widest possible participation of communities, groups and, where appropriate, individuals that create, maintain and transmit such heritage, and to *involve them actively in its management*" (emphasis added). This provision has been extensively studied by scholars (Hausler 2020; D'amico Soggetti 2020; Jacobs 2020).

In practical terms, state authorities must involve communities, groups, and individuals in processes dealing with the identification and definition of the various elements of the intangible cultural heritage present in the territory and to which the safeguarding measures have to be applied (Art. 11(b) of the 2003 convention); the management of all the safeguarding measures listed in Articles 12, 13, and 14 of the convention to be applied at the domestic level; and the preparation of the periodic reports submitted by states on the legislative, regulatory, and other measures taken for the implementation of the convention (Art. 29).

The Faro Convention promotes an approach to CH management built upon "shared responsibility for cultural heritage and public participation" of several actors (Sec. III, Arts. 11–14). More specifically, according to Article 11, in the management of CH the parties to the convention undertake to

> a) promote an integrated and well-informed approach by public authorities in all sectors and at all levels; b) develop the legal, financial and professional frameworks which make possible joint action by public authorities, experts, owners, investors, businesses, non-governmental organisations and civil society; c) develop innovative ways for public authorities to co-operate with other actors; d) respect and encourage voluntary initiatives which complement the roles of public authorities; e) encourage non-governmental organisations concerned with heritage conservation to act in the public interest.

The Faro Convention then recognizes a role for heritage communities, together with everyone else, to participate in the identification, study, interpretation, protection, conservation, and presentation of the cultural heritage, as well as in "public reflection and debate on the opportunities and challenges which the cultural heritage represents" (Art. 12). According to these provisions, therefore, elected representatives, public institutions, and authorities of the states that ratified the Faro Convention recognize heritage communities as stakeholders in CH management while, in turn, HCs acknowledge their wish to sustain and transmit the CH they value to future generations "within the framework of public action" (Art. 2 (b)).

The convention, however, does not indicate specific measures and policies through which states must ensure community participation in the tasks mentioned in Articles 11 and 12. This is because it is a *framework* convention, which in legal terms means that each state party has a margin of discretion in selecting the policies, measures, and steps it considers most appropriate for achieving the goals of the convention at the domestic level in harmony with its individual political and legal traditions.

Since the adoption of the Faro Convention, the implementation of its provisions by states parties at the international and domestic levels is driven, and coordinated, by means of the Faro Convention Action Plan.[18] The Action Plan, adopted biennially, provides "field based knowledge and expertise for member States to better understand the potentials of the Convention; it helps the Secretariat to highlight and study specific cases in line with the political priorities of the [Council of Europe]; [and it] offers a platform for analysis and recommendations for further steps; and encourages member States to sign and ratify the Convention."[19] In particular, "the operational structure of the Action Plan encourages a dynamic process of action-research-reflection where the concepts on heritage governance, various initiatives for community engagement and cooperation, economic dimension and relationships between heritage and other fields are explored with a synergetic approach" (Faro Convention Action Plan Handbook 2019, 7).

In the 2015–2017 Action Plan, participation was recognized as one of the three main pillars (the other two are narratives and commons) establishing the common frame of reference for understanding and implementing the Faro Convention. The development of participation is also described as one of the convention's main contributions to the social challenges facing many member states in need of "more democracy, more direct citizen participation and better governance based on more effective institutions and on dynamic public-private partnerships" (Wanner 2021, 10). By promoting a type of participation capable of influencing policymaking and rendering it more legitimate and sustainable, the Faro Convention poses civil society as a key component of states' democracy and, in particular, as a crucial actor alongside, and sometimes in the face of, central government, public authorities, and market forces. The type and nature of relations between political authorities, public institutions, private actors, and civil society at large, on one side, and HCs, on the other, are indeed at the core of any system of governance and management.

Since the adoption of the Faro Convention, different experiences have developed in different countries regarding the implementation of the convention's provisions and principles. The Action Plans in many cases drove and also inspired the role of communities and, sometimes, of public authorities more receptive to the convention's approach and framework. Some examples of how HCs act will be provided in the next section.

An interpretation of the type of governance to be established in order to ensure efficient CH management can be found in the statement by the UN Committee on

Economic, Social and Cultural Rights on the "right of everyone to participate in cultural life" (Art. 15, para. 1(a) of the International Convention on Economic, Social and Cultural Rights) (UN Committee 2009). The committee stressed the importance of a core obligation for states that entails at least "the obligation to create and promote an environment within which a person individually, or in association with others, or within a community or group, can participate in the culture of their choice" (UN Committee 2009, 15). Furthermore, the states should enact "appropriate legislation and the establishment of effective mechanisms allowing persons, individually, in association with others, or within a community or group, to *participate effectively* in decision-making processes, to claim protection of their right to take part in cultural life, and to claim and receive compensation if their rights have been violated" (UN Committee 2009, 14, emphasis added).

It is also true that in the last few years the concept of participation, although it is perceived as being inherent in the Faro Convention's logic and meaning, has started to be criticized as counterproductive when initiated by top-down mechanisms and followed up by little feedback from communities on a practical level (Wanner 2021, 13). Terms such as "co-construction," "cooperation," "co-deliberation," and "co-decision" are more meaningful for HCs than the generic "participation," which seems to allocate rights and responsibilities to only one side.

The *Faro Convention Action Plan Handbook 2018–2019* mirrors this shift from participation toward cooperation and co-decision in the definition of priorities, principles, and criteria for the implementation of the convention by all stakeholders. The following definition of "cooperation" is given: "the action of working together [toward the] same goal, beginning from the first steps and gradually constructing together. A special distinction is made here between participation and co-operation, as participating in something denotes lesser influence in decision-making and may exclude certain groups [from] taking [an] active role in the processes" (Faro Convention Action Plan Team 2019, 24).

Since 2018, the focus on heritage governance in terms of both participation and cooperation has been promoted also through the joint CoE–European Commission project The Faro Way: Enhanced Participation in Cultural Heritage.[20] The project encouraged an increased role for civil society in heritage governance by ensuring the commitment of all stakeholders (national authorities in particular) to the Faro Convention principles; showcasing concrete examples of implementing the principles at national, regional, and local levels; and building long-term stakeholders' cooperation to translate the Faro Convention principles into action.

The joint CoE–European Commission project has very much invested in creating a dynamic pan-European network of CH stakeholders, including by means of the Faro Convention Network (FCN), and continues fostering Faro Convention–related actions through the exchange of knowledge and experiences among stakeholders. The FCN is a platform where HCs can come together, exchange their knowledge and experience, and create new synergies and joint initiatives in line with the Faro Convention principles (Faro Convention Action Plan Handbook 2019, 9). The FCN identifies good practices and practitioners, conducts workshops, and supports members' efforts in addressing challenges related to heritage management at the local level, then brings established local good practice to the European governmental level. Among the various topics discussed by the FCN members, the work on dissonant heritage is particularly interesting.[21]

For a HC to become part of the FCN is a self-assessed process; in fact, "interested HCs are encouraged to go through a self-assessment exercise based on the Faro Convention principles and criteria. To conduct the assessment they may rely upon the guidance and support of the CoE secretariat and the other FCN members" (Faro Convention Action Plan Handbook 2019, 9).[22] The FCN is a good example of how knowledge and good practices at the national level may be shared, also inspiring or even convincing national authorities of different states to look into the advantages of getting HCs and other civil society groups fully involved in CH management.

We cannot, however, ignore the fact that some states decide to allow HCs freedom of action and have no interest in cooperative management, often because they are more interested in reducing expenditures on heritage policies. The transfer and sharing of responsibility to HCs should aim at securing local services, but often authorities consider that either as a way of raising revenue (by selling off cultural assets and saving the public costs of maintenance and services) or as a way of extricating state bureaucracies from CH management and leaving administration in the hands of citizens (Colomer 2021). Other administrations simply do not want to share power, knowledge, and heritage decision-making with citizens; the result is that the Faro Convention principles can be implemented only through cosmetic initiatives. The FCN provides aid to HCs in the process of defining and managing CH, especially when the allocation of roles and responsibilities between them and public authorities is critical.

The meaning and value held by HCs may not necessarily coincide with the scientific approach and criteria developed by experts to identify CH. This is particularly salient where the process of defining and identifying CH is centralized in governmental hands. But the Faro Convention promotes HCs' innovative role in a constructive perspective, since "expert, official or orthodox ways of seeing or valuing heritage remain valid but they are now set increasingly against all the other plural ways of seeing and acting" (Wolferstan and Fairclough 2013, 45).

Examples of CH Management at the Domestic Level in Light of the Faro Convention

The centrality of the relationships among public institutions, political representatives, individuals, private entities, experts, and communities, in all their possible forms, represents the main theoretical issue related to the application of the Faro Convention's principles not only at the international and supranational levels but also within the context of domestic legal systems. In this section we will explore how HCs' practices of participation may follow different paths and result in different experiences due to local and national political circumstances (Colomer 2021).

As seen in the previous section, Article 11 of the Faro Convention commits states parties to set in motion a virtuous circle that optimizes the energies, resources, and expertise of different types of actors—institutions, public authorities, elected representatives, civil society (individuals and associationss, businesses, and private entities—in a new perspective on CH governance (Barni 2019). Although a margin of discretion is left to each party on how to implement Article 11's commitments, precisely because of this type of commitment states could make an upstream political choice to take the decision not to ratify the Faro Convention. Ultimately the notions of HCs and of democratic participation/cooperation in the CH management challenge core notions of authority and expertise in the discipline and professional practice of CH. In this frame, among (legal) scholars, one of the debated issues is whether, in order to promote better participatory and cooperative governance mechanisms of HCs in the frame of "public actions," it would be advisable to provide them with a specific legal status, and using this legal status to regulate the HCs' initiatives.

This legal status would help to ensure the protection of traditional knowledge, skills, and identity held by these communities, and to formally regulate the relationship with other public and private actors in CH management (Zagato and Pinton 2016). The issue is truly delicate, placing trust, balance of power, and constructive collaboration at the heart of the cooperative relationship. This process of legal recognition would require the satisfaction of a few preconditions: the readiness of heritage professionals to abandon a top-down model in which they are the ones giving direction to others; civil society stakeholders' interest in engaging in shared management of CH, which would entail all parties having a positive approach to cooperation, a common initial understanding, and professional openness to knowledge of all types; and the acknowledgment that public benefit has to be the primary aim (OMC, Working Group of Member States' Experts 2018).

If we look at the practice developed in the European juridical space, we may distinguish a few legal entities around which heritage communities in charge of CH management have organized themselves. This practice is in line with the fact that the Faro Convention does not indicate a predefined scheme that restricts the structure of a heritage community; all that is required is the intention of the members to act in relation to the CH coming from the past, and their wish to sustain and transmit the CH, in the frame of a public action, to future generations.

The Hôtel du Nord inhabitants' cooperative in Marseille, established in 2011, was set up as a "société coopérative d'intérêt collectif à responsabilité limitée, à capital variable à conseil de surveillance" under the French laws of May 7, 1917, and September 10, 1947, and under Articles 231(1)–231(8) of the French commercial code.[23] Hôtel du Nord is a project made up of a group of small-scale initiatives that create opportunities for local actors to work together to improve the poor living conditions, discrimination, and poverty that affect certain neighborhoods of Marseilles. This goal is achieved through the restoration and enhancement of CH in different neighborhoods of the city, helping to improve the population's living environment. With a view to promoting the hospitality of the city, "heritage walks" are organized by local inhabitants, who welcome guests into their homes to share their daily lives and the very specific heritage of their neighborhood.[24] A recent addition to the work of the Hôtel du Nord is the platform Les Oiseaux de Passage (birds of passage), a travel planning website where French tour operators, cultural facilitators, and local inhabitants jointly promote hospitality and give visitors the chance to discover their local areas and their histories.[25]

In Italy, HCs are more and more adopting the "community cooperative" structure to organize themselves. This form of cooperation is a complex and diversified social institution that works to implement services in local communities by establishing and recognizing a common need in the community and creating relationships with other local stakeholders (citizens, civil society organizations, and sometimes local councils)—surpassing the mutualistic model and paying attention to all the members of the community. Community cooperatives are often characterized by the aim to keep alive and enhance local communities at risk of deterioration, if not extinction (Legacoop 2011, 3–4). The community cooperatives are formally recognized by some regional laws—for instance, the Puglia regional law no. 66,[26] and the law of the Basilicata region on promotion and development of cooperation.[27]

The sharing of responsibilities in CH management may also take the form of a "social contract," as in the example of the village of Viscri, Romania, or of a "strategic plan," as in District 5 in Huelva in Spain.[28] Although each of these initiatives identifies with cooperative principles, they do not have cooperative status or do not use that terminology (Wanner 2021). The first of these, the Whole Village Project, was born as an initiative aimed at preserving the Saxon heritage in the intercultural village of Viscri. The initiative focuses on turning the local heritage into a resource for all community members (Roma, Romanians, Hungarians, and Saxons), enabling them to make the best use of it through tourism, agriculture, and craftsmanship, with the objective of reconciling any potential conflict connected to the challenges of integration.[29]

Cooperative principles and approaches are also often practiced when HCs structure themselves as general nonprofit associations. Faro Venezia, in Italy, for instance, is mainly active in the urban context of Venice. Currently, the city's major problem is related to its depopulation, due to increased mass tourism, which is encouraged by local policies at the municipal level. With the continuous decrease in the number of residents, the city is fast approaching a point of no return, beyond which it will become an empty stage for mass tourism. However, involvement in decision-making processes on these issues has been difficult, as a constructive and open platform for discussions and democratic participation by all stakeholders has been lacking. In this context, several HCs have been created with the aim of preventing tourist exploitation of cultural heritage. Faro Venezia seeks to make Venice more attractive, including to its own residents, through systematic initiatives promoted by a network of local associations (combining research, culture, and art) and implementing different forms of participative democracy to overcome the apparent gap between political leaders, decision-makers, and citizens. To reinforce the attractiveness of the city beyond mass tourism, Faro Venezia's initiatives promote the transformation of heritage sites (such as the Arsenale, the ancient naval production center of the Serenissima) into useful places for all citizens. Faro Venezia also aims to educate local communities about the Faro Convention's principles and approach by collaborating on projects aimed at safeguarding traditional craftsmanship as symbols of intangible cultural heritage, promoting debates on the concepts of active citizenship, and protecting commons. To educate residents and tourists, Faro Venezia organizes heritage walks, often in collaboration with private institutions and other local and regional associations.[30]

In Lithuania, Žemieji Šančiai Bendruomenė is an association situated in a microregion of Kaunas. The association encourages the development of civil society through respect for the CH of its community and active responsibility for self-government. It strengthens community identity by working with people to learn from and experience the places, objects, and stories of Šančiai.[31] Its Cabbage Field Initiative is a contribution to local participation in governance and to the revitalization of an abandoned historical site. The Cabbage Field is a plot of public land that is home to a trio of nineteenth-century vaulted brick structures that were formerly military barracks and have not yet been privatized. Its heritage is of international significance, and the winter cellars that can be found at the site are used to store fermented cabbage, a source of vitamin C—whence the name of the initiative. The Cabbage Field Initiative recognizes and supports the community process of transforming the site into a sustainable public asset. To do this, community art activities are organized on the site to stimulate people's awareness and creative power and to counter excessive urbanization of the area (Council of Europe 2020, 19). In 2020, the Žemieji Šančiai Bendruomenė started a three-year project centered on the notion of genius loci and addressing the public right to participate in decision-making processes concerning environmental matters, combatting aggressive urbanization and enabling residents and other specialists to co-create an architectural and urban plan for the neighborhood. The Žemųjų Šančiai community gives evidence of how community arts became a catalyst for action and how creative approaches may favor both bottom-up and top-down activism. Activities organized around the Nemunas River embankment seek to preserve for future generations its unique architecture, biodiversity, ecosystems, and habitats, as well as facilities dedicated to swimming, fishing, relaxing, and enjoying the riverfront. The action started out as a direct response to plans for a new road along the river but developed into a wider public interest and self-government campaign. The Faro Convention principles have been used to understand how the community seeks to safeguard its unique historic urban landscape and heritage. The initial failure to achieve a constructive dialogue at the municipal level became a driving force for the Žemųjų Šančiai association to press for urban planners to participate *with* rather than exert power *over* communities (Carroll 2021, 19).

Among CH management approaches developed by state authorities, interesting examples come from Finland and the municipality of Fontecchio, Italy. The Faro Convention ratification process adopted by Finland started from a background study carried out in 2014–2015 by the National Board of Antiquities (now the Finnish Heritage Agency) and the Finnish Homeland Association. The purpose of the study was to assess the challenges involved in fostering CH and to create a structured account of citizens' wishes and stakeholders' views about aligning existing cultural practices with the objectives of the Faro Convention.[32] The study acknowledged that both citizen engagement (represented by the Finnish Local Heritage Federation, which includes more than eight hundred member associations around Finland and is an active operator in cultural heritage as well as environmental issues) —and the decentralized heritage administrations were already in alignment with the convention's notions of democratic participation and sharing responsibilities (ICOMOS Finnish National Committee 2020; Salmela 2017; Pinton 2019). The study concluded that the Finnish national heritage legislation met the requirements of the Faro Convention's provisions, and therefore the country did not need further legislative amends in order to proceed with the ratification of the convention, except for further strengthening the democratic model of cooperation. The study acknowledged that embracing the spirit of the Faro Convention goes hand in hand with taking responsibility for driving even further processes of "openness and empowerment in the actions and structures related to cultural heritage administration" (Salmela et al. 2015, 11). These processes include administrative efforts to promote open access to cultural knowledge, promote the co-creation of knowledge, enhance administrative transparency in management decision processes, promote citizens' participation in policymaking processes, open up the role of expert to citizens, and design communication with citizens in plain language to facilitate understanding of technical arguments (Colomer 2021).

In the words of the chief intendant of the Finnish Heritage Agency, in implementing the principles of the Faro Convention the crucial aspect is to

> take a closer look at heritage communities, create dialogue, explore and share existing good practice and create new procedures for cooperation between administration and diverse actors, new innovative and sustainable heritage partnerships. Administration should act more and more as a facilitator, whereas the role of the civil society, with its changing new forms including heritage communities, will grow stronger. Participation and sustainability are among the key words of the implementation.
>
> (Salmela 2017)

In Italy, the municipality of Fontecchio is a pioneer public authority in promoting the creation of and supporting a heritage community that includes public and private stakeholders, both governmental and non\governmental. Fontecchio is a very small village of 350 inhabitants in central Italy. It was damaged by the 2009 earthquake, and the small community had to face the need for both physical and social reconstruction. Local government, together with local associations and facilitators, designed a plan including projects for civic education and citizen participation, care for the landscape, and knowledge and use of CH for economic development, resettlement, and social cohesion, according to Faro Convention principles.

The plan has started to be implemented through a set of initiatives.[33] For instance, Borghi Attivi is a participatory process that since 2011 has involved the population in drawing up guidelines for the aesthetic development of the village, taking into account local construction material and architectonic styles. A set of technical rules for the restoration of private and public buildings was written by citizens, local authorities, and academic experts.

Casa & Bottega is a social housing and urban regeneration project that foresees the development of small apartments to be rented to young families, together with handicraft shops, community gardens where people can cultivate individual plots, and areas of public forest for pasture and wood. A community cooperative manages all services linked to mobility, housing, production, e-commerce, and care of the landscape.[34] Lo Spazio della Memoria is a photographic museum and a multimedia station dedicated to the 2009 earthquake and located inside a medieval tower. Ordine-Caos-Creatività is a collective artwork created by children and families in the new school building. Gardens are at the disposal of citizens, and some mountain paths have been "adopted" by local associations and institutions.

The Fontecchio practice throws light on a model of CH management that is becoming more and more common in other Italian municipalities: a model that encourages shared administration of the commons by different public and private actors through stimulating collective use, management, and ownership of urban assets, services, and infrastructures. This model is called the "pact of collaboration between local administrations and inhabitants," although scholars are still debating the legal nature—private or public—of these pacts (Arena 2016).[35] This chapter will not retrace that investigation. Rather, it is interesting to underline that it does not involve merely conferring on private individuals the responsibility for activities of general interest that the public administration is unable to or does not want to carry out on its own. Rather, the pact wants to establish "a sincere collaboration between 'rulers' and 'ruled,' with the latter motivated by solidarity intentions, a collaboration implemented right from the initial stages concerning the identification of general interests to take care of" (Fidelbo 2018, 8).

CONCLUSIONS

The right to CH as a human right includes the right of individuals and collectivities to know, understand, value, make use of, sustain, and exchange elements of CH and participate in its development, as well as to respect and benefit from the CH of others.[36]

The Faro Convention aims at promoting greater synergy of competencies and actions among all interested public and private actors regarding CH management through the recognition that CH is a crucial resource in several areas: the construction of peaceful and democratic societies, the processes of sustainable development (including economic development), and the promotion of cultural diversity.[37] Cultural heritages—tangible, intangible, and digital—are doomed to die if public authorities, experts, and citizens do not continuously engage in effective and systematic participation, cooperation, and decision-making about which heritage policies to adopt.[38]

Embracing this perspective, this chapter has tried to describe why and how the idea of participatory and cooperative governance—built upon the inclusion of and lively interplay between a diverse range of governmental and nongovernmental shareholders, as promoted by the Faro Convention—is at the heart of sound CH management. Heritage communities have taken seriously the responsibility to safeguard and manage CH, supplementing the policies adopted by their territorial states. HCs' practices have given meaning to the Faro Convention's silence on how, exactly, heritage governance is to be implemented. The variety of practices described in this chapter demonstrates not only that there is no one-size-fits-all process to implement the principles of the convention but also that there is a variety of participatory instruments available and many ways in which they can be implemented. In some countries the legal and political framework regarding CH facilitates participation processes; in others that framework hinders their implementation or even holds back ratification of the Faro Convention. What seems evident, however, is that HCs' mobilization and creative actions have triggered the kind of phenomenon described by some legal doctrine according to which "states' social bases find a way to connect with each other so as to contribute to the creation of transnational legal relationships" beneficial to the societies at large. These relationships shape "fragments of an interindividual organization that crosses borders" (Picchio Forlati 1999, 146).

Accordingly, despite their inconsistencies—and despite the fact that some NGOs and even HCs are in fact under the political control of their respective governments and not able to exercise any kind of control over the government's conduct—these "splinters of transnational interindividual organization" have carved out a significant role in cooperating with, and sometime co-deciding with, intergovernmental bodies in the field of CH policies (Urbinati 2012).

The implementation of the principles of the Faro Convention over the last few years offers further evidence of the positive role played by the CoE Faro intergovernmental institutions (the directorate and the SCCHL) in the attempt to address the reluctance of some European states to ratify the convention and in supporting and disseminating the multiple good practices implemented by HCs with respect to the convention's principles.[39] This has happened sometimes in full harmony with a state's decisions and policies, but more often in a less friendly or even hostile context created by the segment of "heritage experts" still able to influence states' approaches to CH management.[40]

Given the heritage management expertise and the successful dynamics established by many HCs in the European space, one of the priorities of the HCs should be to intensify capacity-building initiatives in tandem with heritage experts in order to understand how much social participation these experts willing are to accept, how much knowledge and power they are willing to give up, and what degree of HC autonomy in CH management they can tolerate. Another priority should be to understand how to draw upon the skills and training of heritage experts to ensure better and more fruitful engagements with HCs that are already following the Faro way (Colomer 2021).

Notes

1. Thus, no analysis is provided in this chapter of the knowledge, skills, and qualities that contribute to and strengthen the quality of CH management professional services. According to *The Competence Framework for Cultural Heritage Management*, the competences of management practitioners include "core competences" (knowledge of heritage principles, ethics and the law), "personal competences" (essential for successful cooperation and facilitation), "managerial competences" (required in order to achieve management goals), and "specialist technical competences." Four levels of professional personnel are covered: skilled workers, middle managers/technical specialists, senior managers, and executives (UNESCO 2021). Competences are only one aspect of successful CH management, alongside financial resources, supporting policies, laws, and regulations.
2. The Council of Europe Framework Convention on the Value of Cultural Heritage for Society (CETS no. 199), signed in Faro on October 27, 2005, entered into force at the international level on June 1, 2011. As of April 20, 2022, twenty-two states had ratified it and six states had signed it.
3. According to Article 19(a), the CoE Committee of Ministers may invite any state that is not a member of the CoE and the EU to accede to the convention by a decision taken by a two-thirds majority of the representatives casting a vote and by the unanimous vote of the representatives of the contracting states entitled to sit on the Committee of Ministers.
4. Faro Convention, Preamble.
5. European Cultural Convention (Paris, December 19, 1954); Convention for the Protection of the Architectural Heritage of Europe (Granada, October 3, 1985); European Convention for the Protection of the Archaeological Heritage (Valletta, January 16, 1992).
6. European Landscape Convention (Florence, October 20, 2000).
7. "Recognizing the need to put people and human values at the centre of an enlarged and cross-disciplinary concept of CH" (Faro Convention, Preamble).
8. Convention Concerning the Protection of the World Cultural and Natural Heritage, adopted by the UNESCO General Conference, November 16, 1972.
9. World Heritage Committee (WHC), WHC-97/2, February 1997, 10. The WHC adopted these operational guidelines beginning in 1977.
10. WHC-05/2, February 2, 2005, 3, 95.
11. The other strategic objectives to promote the implementation of the 1972 convention were defined by the WHC at the 2002 session in Budapest: credibility, conservation, capacity-building, and communication (known as the "4 C's").
12. WHC Committee, WHC-07/31.COM/13B, 6.
13. In the 2007 Fribourg Declaration on Cultural Rights, a "cultural community" is a group of persons who share references that constitute a commo cultural identity that they intend to preserve and develop (Art. 2).
14. See the website for the Steering Committee for Culture, Heritage and Landscape, https://www.coe.int/en/web/cdcpp-committee.
15. Fribourg Declaration on Cultural Rights, May 7, 2007, https://www1.umn.edu/humanrts/instree/Fribourg%20Declaration.pdf.
16. The Faro Principles are: developing democratic participation and social responsibility (Arts. 11, 12, and 13); improving the living environment and quality of life (Art. 8); managing cultural diversity and mutual understanding (Art. 7); and building more cohesive societies (Arts. 8, 9, and 10) (Council of Europe 2021, 8–10).

17. "Knowledge and understanding [of communities] are fundamental to the identification, management, and monitoring of World Heritage properties.... Such studies and research are aimed at demonstrating the contribution that the conservation and management of World Heritage properties, their buffer zones and wider setting make to sustainable development, such as in conflict prevention and resolution, including, where relevant, by drawing on traditional ways of dispute resolution that exist within communities" (para. 215), WHC.21/01, 31 July 2021.
18. "States parties" refers to states that are bound by this convention and among which this convention is in force.
19. See Faro Convention Action Plan, https://www.coe.int/en/web/culture-and-heritage/faro-action-plan.
20. "Enhanced Participation in Cultural Heritage: The Faro Way," https://www.coe.int/en/web/culture-and-heritage/the-faro-way.
21. Ivi for further details.
22. See "Faro Convention Network (FCN)," https://www.coe.int/en/web/culture-and-heritage/faro-community.
23. See Article 1, StatuteMentions légales – Hôtel du Nord (hoteldunord.coop).
24. Hôtel du Nord—Fabrique d'histoires (hoteldunord.coop). Heritage walks constitute an original practice that for HCs also marks a way of self-expression and self-recognition. A heritage walk is conceived and created by those who live and work in a specific territory and who have a particular affinity with that territory and the traditional knowledge and heritages that developed in that place: historical and cultural, in their memory and/or through personal experience. The heritage walk's main objective is to raise awareness among citizens about the value of the CH in the locale which they live and work—namely, about the benefit that derives from living immersed in that heritage because of its historical, cultural and social significance. See "Le Passeggiate Patrimoniali," Faro Venezia, https://farovenezia.org/azioni/le-passeggiate-patrimoniali. The worth of these heritage walks became particularly relevant with the COVID-19 pandemic, which forced us to disengage from places and peoples. Indeed, heritage walks, made by and with HCs, reconnect the community with residents and tourists in a dynamic experience that brings to the forefront traditional knowledge and skills, unknown tangible/intangible heritage, and threats and challenges to the CH.
25. The term "hospitality" defines the act of sharing and reciprocal exchanges between the host and the visitor, where the two parties get to know each other and learn together through their stories and the stories associated with the travel destination. See "Les oiseaux de passage," Les oiseaux de passage.
26. L.R. May 20, 2014, n. 23, "Disciplina delle Cooperative di comunità," in Boll. Uff. Puglia Region n. 66, May 26, 2014.
27. L.R. March 20, 2015, n. 12, "Promozione e sviluppo della cooperazione," in Boll. Uff. Basilicata Region n. 13, March 20, 2015. These cooperatives have a mutualistic purpose, whose object (Article 2) consists in "enhancing the skills of the resident population, cultural traditions and territorial resources," "satisfying the needs of the local community," and "improving the social and economic quality of life through the development of eco-sustainable economic activities aimed at the production of goods and services, the recovery of environmental and monumental goods, the creation of a job offer, and the generation locally of 'social capital.'"

28. See English – Mihai Eminescu Trust and Patrimoni PEU project - Culture and Cultural Heritage (coe.int)
29. See the website of the Mihai Eminescu Trust., http://www.mihaieminescutrust.ro.
30. See the website of Faro Venezia, https://farovenezia.org/.
31. See the website of the Žemieji Šančiai bendruomenė, https://sanciubendruomene.lt/lt/bendruomenes/zsb/. Home - Genius Loci (sanciubendruomene.lt)
32. See Salmela et al. 2015, 8.
33. Il Progetto Casa&Bottega—Comune di Fontecchio, see Brochure 3 (fontecchio.aq.it).
34. A topic that cannot be fully considered in this paper deals with the role and capacity of HCs to create job opportunities, especially for youths.
35. See Article 11, Italian Law, August 7, 1990, n. 241.
36. Remarks by Karima Bennoune, UN Special Rapporteur in the Field of Cultural Rights, Europa Nostra Finland, European Heritage Congress, Turku, May 13, 2017.
37. Article 5: "The Parties undertake to: . . . (d) foster an economic and social climate which supports participation in cultural heritage activities; (e) promote cultural heritage protection as a central factor in the mutually supporting objectives of sustainable development, cultural diversity and contemporary creativity."
38. "The parties recognise that . . . (b) everyone, alone or collectively, has the responsibility to respect the cultural heritage of others as much as their own heritage, and consequently the common heritage of Europe."
39. V. SCCHL, Action Plan 2014–2015 for the Promotion of the FC State of Progress, CDCPP (2015)12, 2015.
40. See the Commons Regulation adopted by the municipality of Padua on December 14, 2021.

REFERENCES

Arantes, Antonio. 2016. "Cultural Heritage Inspires." In Papers Preview, CulturalHeritage-April2016.pdf (unive.it).

Arena, Gregorio. 2016. "Cosa sono e come funzionano i patti per la cura dei beni comuni." Laboratorio per la Sussidiarietà, February 6, 2016. https://www.labsus.org/2016/02/cosa-sono-e-come-funzionano-i-patti-per-la-cura-dei-beni-comuni/.

Barni, Giovanna. 2019. "Convenzione di Faro, Barni: centrale per il principio della partecipazione." Agenzia CULT, March 22, 2019. Convenzione di Faro, Barni: centrale per il principio della partecipazione - AgenziaCult.

Blake, Janet. 2006. *Commentary on the UNESCO 2003 Convention on the Safeguarding of the Intangible Cultural Heritage*. Leicester: Institute of Art & Law.

Blake, Janet. 2015. *International Cultural Heritage Law*. Oxford: Oxford University Press

Carroll, Edmund. 2021. "Genius Loci: Urbanisation and the Imagination of Civil Society." In *People, Places, Stories: Faro Convention Inspired Experiences*, coordinated by the Programa d'Extensió and the Council of Europe, 19–33. Strasbourg: Council of Europe Publishing.

Colomer, Laia. 2021. "Exploring Participatory Heritage Governance After the EU Faro Convention." *Journal of Cultural Heritage Management and Sustainable Development* (ahead of print). doi:10.1108/JCHMSD-03-2021-0041.

Council of Europe. 2021. *The Faro Convention's Role in a Changing Society: Building on a Decade of Advancement*. Strasbourg: Council of Europe Publishing

Council of Europe. 2020. *The Faro Convention: The Way Forward with Heritage*. Strasbourg: Council of Europe Publishing.

Council of Europe. 2019. *Faro Convention Action Plan Handbook 2018-2019*. Strasbourg: Council of Europe Publishing.

D'amico Soggetti, Gabriele. 2020. "Participation of Communities, Groups, and Individuals: Participation and Democracy." In *The 2003 UNESCO Intangible Heritage Convention: A Commentary*, edited by Janet Blake and Lucas Lixinski, 290-305. Oxford: Oxford University Press.

De Marinis, Pablo. 2011. "Derivas de la comunidad: Algunas reflexiones preliminares para una teoría sociológica en (y desde) América Latina." *Revista Eletrônica, Ciências Sociais* 9, no. 1: 92-126.

Dolff-Bonekämper, Gabi. 2009. "The Social and Spacial Frontiers of Heritage—What Is New in the Faro Convention?" In *Heritage and Beyond*, 69-74. Strasbourg: Council of Europe Publishing.

Faro Convention Action Plan Team. 2019. *The Faro Convention Action Plan Handbook 2018-2019*. Strasbourg: Council of Europe Publishing.

Ferracuti, Sandra. 2011. "L'etnografo del patrimonio in Europa: esercizi di teoria, ricerca e cittadinanza." In *Le culture dell'Europa, l'Europa della cultura*, edited by Lauso Zagato and Marilena Vecco, 217-218. Milan: Franco Angeli.

Fidelbo, Eugenio. 2018. "Strumenti di valorizzazione del rapporto tra patrimonio culturale e territorio: il caso dei patti di collaborazione tra amministrazioni locali e cittadini." *Aedon* 3 (online).

Fojut, Noel. 2009. "The Philosophical, Political and Pragmatic Roots of the Convention." In *Heritage and Beyond*, 13-22. Strasbourg: Council of Europe Publishing.

Greffe, Xavier. 2009. "Heritage Conservation as a Driving Force for Development." In *Heritage and Beyond*, 101-112. Strasbourg: Council of Europe Publishing.

Hausler, Kristin. 2020. "The Participation of Non-State Actors in the Implementation of Cultural Heritage Law." In *The Oxford Handbook of International Cultural Heritage Law*, edited by Francesco Francioni and Ana Filipa Vrdoljak. Oxford: Oxford University Press, 760-786.

Hertz, Ellen. 2015. "Bottoms, Genuine and Spurious." In *Between Imagined Communities and Communities of Practice*, edited by Nicolas Adell et al., 25-57. Göttingen: Universitätsverlag Göttingen.

ICOMOS Finnish National Committee. 2020. *Enabling Heritage Involvement: Participatory Models for Cultural Heritage*. Helsinki: Paino, Trinket Oy.

Jacobs, Marc. 2020. "Participation of Communities, Groups, and Individuals: It's Not Just 'the Community.'" In *The 2003 UNESCO Intangible Heritage Convention: A Commentary*, edited by Janet Blake and Lucas Lixinski. Oxford: Oxford University Press, 273-289.

Legacoop. 2011. *Guida alle cooperative di comunità*. Lecce: Officine Cantelmo.

Leniaud, Jean-Marie. 2009. "Heritage, Public Authorities, Societies." In *Heritage and Beyond*, 137-139. Strasbourg: Council of Europe Publishing.

Lixinski, Lucas. 2013. *Intangible Cultural Heritage in International Law*. Oxford: Oxford University Press.

OMC, Working Group of Member States' Experts. 2018. *Report on Participatory Governance in Cultural Heritage*. Luxembourg: Publications Office of the European Union.

Pejčinović Burić, Marija. 2020. "Foreword." In *The Faro Convention: The Way Forward with Heritage*. Strasbourg: Council of Europe.

Picchio Forlati, Laura. 1999. "L'incidenza delle ONG sui rapporti interstatuali." In *Comprendre, l'Europa, la cultura, la pace*, 139–147.

Pinton, Simona. 2019. "La Convenzione di Faro: alcuni di profili internazionali." In *Il valore del patrimonio cultural per la società e comunità patrimoniali. La Convenzione del Consiglio d'Europa tra teoria e prassi*, edited by Luisella Pavan-Woolfe and Simona Pinton, 73–98. Padua: LINEA Edizioni.

Salmela, Ulla. 2017. "Why Finland Signed the Faro Convention and What Is the Added Value." Document on Finnish Heritage Agency's Faro Meeting, Vilnius, November 11, 2017. https://rm.coe.int/finland-ratification-of-the-faro-convention-in-finland-why-how-what-ne/168077fa9f.

Salmela, Ulla, Hannu Matikka, Pauliina Latvala, and Petja Kauppi. 2015. *Kohti Kestävää Kulttuuriperintötyötä: Taustaselvitys Faron yleissopimuksen voimaansaattamiseksi Suomessa*. Vantaa: National Board of Antiquities.

Shaheed, Farida. 2011. "Report of the UN Independent Expert in the Field of Cultural Rights." A/HRC/17/38. United Nations.

Shearer Demir, Hakan. 2021. "Faro Convention and Migration: A Short Study on Heritage, Community Regeneration and the Role of the Faro Convention Principles in Dealing with Displacement." In *The Faro Convention's Role in a Changing Society: Building on a Decade of Advancement*, 66–79. Strasbourg: Council of Europe Publishing.

UN Committee. 2009. "General Comment No. 21: Right of Everyone to Take Part in Cultural Life (Art. 15, Para. 1(a), of the International Covenant on Economic, Social and Cultural Rights)." Doc. E/C.12/GC/21, December 21, 2009.

UNESCO. 2021. *The Competence Framework for Cultural Heritage Management: A Guide to the Essential Skills and Knowledge for Heritage Practitioners*. Paris: UNESCO.

Urbinati, Sabrina. 2012. "Considerazioni su 'comunità, gruppi e, in alcuni casi, individui' nell'applicazione della Convenzione UNESCO per la salvaguardia del patrimonio culturale intangibile." In *Il patrimonio culturale intangibile nelle sue diverse dimensioni*, edited by Tullio Scovazzi et al., 51–73. Milan: Giuffrè.

Urbinati, Sabrina. 2015. "The Community Participation in International Law." In *Between Imagined Communities and Communities of Practice*, edited by Nicolas Adell et al., 123–140. Göttingen: Universitätsverlag Göttingen.

Wanner, Prosper. 2021. "Faro Convention and Participation: Shared Responsibility for Cultural Heritage." In *The Faro Convention's Role in a Changing Society: Building on a Decade of Advancement*, 6–18. Strasbourg: Council of Europe Publishing.

Wolferstan, Sarah, and Graham Fairclough. 2013. "Common European Heritage: Reinventing Identity Through Landscape and Heritage?" In *Heritage Reinvents Europe*, edited by Dirk Callebaut et al., 43–54. Jambes: EAC.

Zagato, Lauso, and Simona Pinton. 2016. "Regime giuridico ad hoc?," in *Antropologia Museale*, n. 37–39: 21–27.

PART IV

LEADERSHIP AND GOVERNANCE IN ARTS AND CULTURAL ORGANIZATIONS

CHAPTER 14

ETHICS IN CULTURAL LEADERSHIP

Relationships of Value

JONATHAN PRICE

Introduction

When the COVID-19 pandemic hit the south Leeds district of Holbeck in March 2020, local theater company Slung Low knew that it was unlikely to be putting on any shows for some time. Instead, it wrote to two hundred local households to put its staff, volunteers, venue, and van at the service of whatever community needs might arise, and ended up running one of the largest food banks in the United Kingdom for fifteen months (Morton 2021; Vinter 2021). Five thousand miles away in Mumbai, theater workers were themselves in need of help as shows closed down and government aid for the mainly freelance backstage crews and front-of-house staff failed to materialize (Sahani 2021). An alliance of senior performing arts figures mobilized to establish a new organization, TheatreDost (*dost* means "friend" in Hindi), to provide emergency support in a variety of forms to the most vulnerable of them, especially the elderly (TheatreDost n.d.). Across the country in Kolkata, Bengali film director and former doctor Kamaleswar Mukherjee put down his camera and picked up his stethoscope for the first time in fourteen years to help marginalized populations in village health camps (Dasgupta 2020). Arundhati Ghosh, executive director of India Foundation for the Arts, recalls him as saying: "In a time of pandemic, what does an artist do? An artist decides not to be an artist, but to be a relief worker."

The individuals and organizations involved in these instances took exceptional actions in exceptional circumstances. They each followed a simple, compelling logic—albeit one that required considerable generosity and determination to enact. They acted not through their expertise in cultural practice but by stepping beyond it. Their actions, therefore, tell us nothing about cultural management. But they are a good starting point for thinking about the place of ethics in cultural leadership.

This chapter will look first at the conceptual relationships between management, leadership, and ethics before looking at the relationship of a cultural organization's vision to its ethical coherence. It introduces a model for mapping the ethical life of cultural organizations across five dimensions, drawing on the public concerns commonly translated into eligibility criteria by cultural funders and authorities in different parts of the world, and proposes principles of sufficiency and consistency according to which their actions can be critiqued. It concludes with observations on the relationship between ethics, leadership, vision, and integrity.

For the purposes of this chapter, the cultural sector is understood in line with the methodology developed by the UK government's Department for Digital, Culture, Media and Sport (2021), according to which it comprises arts, museum activities, music, broadcasting, and heritage, being positioned almost entirely within a larger creative industries sector and overlapping with the tourism and digital sectors.

Leadership, Management, and Ethics

The relationship between leadership and management is the subject of a significant debate in academic and business literature, which veers between viewing the two concepts as identical, mutually exclusive, or interconnected (Edwards et al. 2015). Nahavandi (2012) usefully summarizes the commonly identified distinctions: management's perceived focus on the present and on stability, procedure, structure, and objectivity, as opposed to leadership's greater concern with the future, with creating change and initiating strategy, while being generative of culture, identity, and a connection with followers by appealing to the emotions and to shared values. In this kind of formulation, management is about keeping the vehicle on the road and leadership is concerned with where it is going. However, there is considerable overlap in practice. Effective managers need to be able to inspire and motivate people and to anticipate change, therefore straying into leadership territory, while leaders who create strategy that fails to take into account managerial practicalities are doomed to failure. Nahavandi (2012) ultimately finds sufficient justification for using the terms interchangeably; other theorists, such as Alvesson and Spicer (2011), see management and leadership as intertwined but not identical, identifying elements of managerial work that do not involve leadership. Where these writers agree is in rejecting hard distinctions between leaders and managers, or formulas that tend toward fetishizing or idealizing the leader as some kind of superior being—a tradition traceable to nineteenth-century conceptions of the "great man" who "inhabits a higher sphere of thought" (Emerson [1850] 1901, 3). Nonetheless, it is worth bearing in mind that some of the baggage of this kind of usage still clings to the term "leader."

A trap of the debate is to accept that if management is what managers do, then leadership is simply what leaders do. This imposes a reductive categorical equivalence on the two terms and limits the concept of leadership to a set of tasks and tendencies carried out by a certain class of individuals or within particular roles. Further definitional argument is then limited to a somewhat sterile trading of characteristics between two lists. Leadership can, however, be considered more broadly, following, for example, the thinking of Grint (2005), who identifies some of the ways in which leadership operates through community interactions—the small actions and processes of sense-making undertaken by mutually influential leaders and followers to form hybrid networks in combination with nonhuman forces. Grint's examples of the latter include culture, emotion, and genetics; recent critical leadership scholarship would add race, gender, class, and history (Liu 2021; Knights 2022). Understood in this way, leadership operates both through and beyond formal structures, something that cannot be said nearly as easily for the more rigidly hierarchical construct of management. While the focus of this chapter is primarily on leadership as expressed through the strategic direction and operational management of cultural organizations, this wider understanding of how leadership is constructed is essential to mapping its ethical scope and implications.

Thinking about the place of ethics in this picture introduces another reason to make a distinction between management and leadership. Derived from the thinking of Aristotle, ethics can be defined as "the general theory of right and wrong in choices and actions, and of what is good or bad in dispositions and interpersonal relations and ways of living" (Mackie 1977, 235). According to Singer (1993, 10), "the notion of ethics carries with it the idea of something bigger than the individual." Ethics is concerned with effects that go beyond the immediate interested party: making choices that become desirable because they are known to be right, rather than pursuing actions for the sake of their desirability. It is for this reason, Singer (1993, 10) argues, that "self-interested acts must be shown to be compatible with more broadly based ethical principles if they are to be ethically defensible." Ethics therefore imports a question of responsibility to third parties, an orientation to the exterior, and a concern with consequences.

Mapped onto organizations, any form of direction-finding or decision-making whose priorities exceed the mission-specific interests of the organization is difficult to accommodate within the objective purpose of management—in other words, the service of functional needs internal to the organization. That is not to say that management excludes dealing with questions of ethics or value, because whether an organization is seen to act in a "good" way is directly relevant to the management of external reputation and internal morale, and may need to be balanced against short-term or otherwise limited financial and strategic advantages. So long as justifications can be made strictly in business terms, including through enlightened self-interest, decisions touching on ethical issues can still be considered managerial. Where, however, the consideration is made in the interests of a wider sectoral, social, or moral ideal, then something beyond what can be adequately termed "management" is guiding action. It can further be argued that, where there are competing "goods" (for example, tensions between aesthetic, social, and economic motivations), a form of judgment must be applied to arbitrate between categories that lack a shared index of value. The application of a determining principle in such an instance is at once an ethical choice and an act of leadership.

Ethical decisions that involve considerations not wholly reducible to pure managerial logic represent instances where leadership can be most clearly be disambiguated from management, even if those external considerations are ultimately rejected and the company's self-interest is asserted. To lead is not necessarily to act ethically, but it is to deal with ethicality. Recognizing this also requires recognizing that there are competing moral codes, and that history is littered with dangerous zealots who led in the name of morality (Grint 2005). Leadership has no inherent positive moral charge. It is simply demanded wherever tension arises between logical self-interest and ethical imperatives, and its worth must be judged on the decisions made and on the results. The responsibility is for the outcomes, good or bad, and for the motivations and processes that have led to those outcomes, given that leadership also has to deal with the fact that the consequences of action can rarely be fully foreseen. Acquiring the responsibility is not optional—it goes with the territory. Acting responsibly is another matter.

The picture becomes more fragmented when this association of ethics with leadership is related to the hybridity of leadership. Where does ethical responsibility sit if an organization's actions and direction are not determined by a single leader but by a communal process shaped by history and culture? The difficulty in resolving this is perhaps one reason organizations seen to transgress morally and even legally are rarely held to account effectively in the corporate world (Larkin, Burgess, and Montague 2020). The question can be largely dodged, though organizations may pause to consider the policy issue of how far they consider their responsibilities to stretch, either to follow through on stated ethical commitments or to anticipate and control potential liabilities. Whatever is concluded, other stakeholders may take different views, and given that ethics and leadership are not confined to the managerial boundaries of the organization, their perspectives may not be easily dismissed. The possibility of being held to account does not depend on the company itself actively accepting or recognizing the obligations that may be ascribed to it by others. For these fundamental reasons organizational ethics are complex, contested, and context-specific. They are dependent on value judgments and not reducible to any universally accepted code. Ethical expectations inevitably exceed legal requirements (Mendonca and Kanungo 2007); they are index-linked to ever-evolving societal values.

The potential for ethical complexity and conflict in running organizations becomes apparent if the different categories of ethics common to guiding choice and action in everyday life are considered. Among the main types identified by Larkin, Burgess, and Montague (2020), utilitarian approaches derive from the secular philosophy that advocates achieving the greatest good for the greatest number as the basis for ethical decision-making, judging actions by their consequences (the medical ethic and international law principle of "do no harm" is utilitarian). Deontological approaches, meanwhile, are principled or rule-based, with actions prejudged as right or wrong according to their nature or motivation (religious commandments and other ideologically based behavioral doctrines are deontological). A third category, philosophical egoism, follows socially constructed rules in a self-interested way to achieve approval and avoid punishment.

These are useful primary categories for understanding ethical problems. The moral dilemma encountered by someone who has been brought up to believe it is wrong to lie when faced with a situation where lying would avoid unnecessary harm to a third party finds themselves conflicted between utilitarianism and deontology. The utilitarian impulse asserts that the ends justify the means, but the deontological principle denies this. One value system has to be prioritized over the other, at least temporarily, to resolve the situation. An artist whose determined exercise of freedom of expression breaks taboos and causes offense to a religious community brings about a confrontation between two deontologies. Such instances are far less easily resolved and can escalate.

Philosophical egoism, or "conscientiousness," to use Singer's (1993) term for the same tendency, looks like ethical behavior in that it acts in accordance with the values of society but does not really critically engage with questions of what is or is not right. In philosophical terms, an ethical motivation necessarily involves concern for others (Singer 1993). It is not an ethical choice to take a certain course of action for the sole purpose of avoiding bad PR, for example. Conscientiousness is a usefully conflict-free default position for organizations more concerned with image than belief. Acting conscientiously might involve making apparent sacrifices of self-interest in the short term, but the motivation would still be ultimately self-interested—for example, if based on a calculation that the cultivation of an ethical reputation is of greater long-term value. It may not sound particularly admirable, but in pragmatic terms, this approach at least has the socially desirable effect of causing organizations to consider and mitigate a greater range of their impacts than the single-minded pursuit of narrower business objectives could allow for. Nonetheless, whether consciously or unconsciously adopted, it is a strategy that has limits. If an organization lacks a strong deontological or utilitarian commitment, then there will be a threshold at which its own self-interest will trump its conscientious observance of ethical norms. This is one level at which the gap between what an organization says and what it does can be analyzed.

Locating Ethics in Vision, Mission, and Values

Foster (2018) writes compellingly about the need for arts organizations to pay serious attention to their foundational documents—the articulations of their vision, mission, and values. While most organizations will have these in some form, Foster (2018) identifies a tendency for the statements to be highly generalized and too easily exchangeable between different organizations. In other words, they communicate next to nothing about what is really distinctive or important about the organization they are supposed to represent. Foster (2018) therefore advocates for producing clear and specific documents that identify, differentiate, and connect the organization's vision, mission, core values, artistic intent, and community context. This analysis is important in challenging organizations to describe themselves in terms not only of what they do but also of what they are for. The vision, as Foster (2018) points out, should be a vision of the world as the organization would like it to be—not a vision of what the organization wants to be. Expressed in these terms, the vision should identify clearly and idealistically the form of change the organization exists to produce. The mission then describes the organization's practical purpose, specifying what it does and who it involves. The values are the underpinning principles that the organization commits to applying in the process of carrying out its mission. The vision and the values together constitute the ethical purpose of the organization.

It is enormously easy for an organization's identity to become associated only with the mission—what it is seen to do—rather than the deeper sense of purpose behind the vision. Does this matter? Not always, but in some circumstances it will matter a great deal. Imagine a community arts organization founded in order to bring local people together and celebrate their hometown. Its vision, perhaps, is for the community to be creative, harmonious, and joyful. To achieve this, it stages a summer festival. Over several years, it becomes known for producing the summer festival—that is its primary activity. Therefore, people start to think that the sole purpose of the organization is to produce the festival. What happens, though, if one year it becomes impossible to stage the festival? Does the organization still have a purpose, or any basis for deciding what to do next and how to use its resources? The COVID-19 pandemic asked precisely this question of thousands of cultural sector organizations across the world. This was the situation faced by Slung Low at the beginning of this chapter. The normal mode of delivery—the usual mission of theater-making—was interrupted without warning. In this case, however, the vision of the organization for its community demanded a totally different kind of action to respond to the radically changed circumstances. This allowed the organization to act quickly and decisively at a moment that many would find paralyzing. Similarly, the filmmaker Kamaleswar Mukherjee and the coalition behind TheatreDost acted from an instinctive understanding of duty grounded in values. The mission can change if the vision demands it, which is why a recognition of the community context also needs to be part of an organization's foundational statements, as Foster (2018) insightfully identifies.

In most circumstances, making such extreme changes to activity in order to continue serving the vision is unlikely to be necessary. Nonetheless, losing sight of the difference between vision and mission is to confuse ends and means. This is a danger for cultural organizations, which will often have staff or artists highly focused on specialist areas of work and committed to replicating established processes or patterns of work. Those processes may have served the organization well in the past, and may even have been groundbreaking, but are they still serving the vision? The distinction between vision and mission can become very blurry for those closest to the work, especially if there is strong psychological commitment to it. Part of the role of organizational leadership is to supply perspective and to articulate that difference.

As the vision, mission, and values are foundational to the identity of an organization, they have to be set and owned by whoever has legal and moral responsibility for it, which in most cases (particularly in the nonprofit arts sector) is the board of directors or trustees. If it is accepted that leadership and management are functionally entwined (Alvesson and Spicer 2011; Nahavandi 2012), it is impossibly simplistic to ascribe leadership to the non-executive and management to the executive, but it remains possible to locate the specific corporate responsibility for ethical direction at board level. Allied to the need for clarity in the vision and foundational documents, this emphasizes the centrality of governance to ethical leadership. An organization whose vision is not safeguarded through strong and purposeful governance can hardly expect to maintain a coherent ethical identity in the long term. This should be of concern to any organization whose underpinning relationships depend on clarity of purpose, shared values, and trust.

Ethical Dimensions of Cultural Leadership

Cultural leadership can be very neatly defined as "the act of leading the cultural sector" (British Council 2013), but the simplicity of such a formulation is deceptive. Its origins as a term in policy discourse lie in concerns for the business effectiveness of senior executive managers in large, publicly funded cultural institutions in the United Kingdom in the early 2000s (Hewison 2004). This sense of designating the people and skills needed to run successful cultural organizations remains central, but other interpretations have gained increasing attention: the influence of artists and other cultural workers at all levels of seniority on their own sector; the role of cultural sector leaders in shaping the wider culture of their societies; and the reciprocal influence from other sectors and areas of public life that affect how culture operates and evolves (Leicester 2007; Douglas and Fremantle 2009; British Council 2013; Price 2017). These broader connections are often formalized through non-executive roles, prompting calls for greater attention to their dynamics (Rentschler 2015).

Even where the analytical focus on cultural leadership is restricted to the specialized sense of running cultural organizations, the other definitions are suggestive of the messy connectivity through which the sector's activities are shaped and exert influence. These activities are by their nature bound up with questions of value. Artistic and cultural activities are media through which societies express, reinforce, and challenge their norms and taboos, through which they interpret and reimagine the world. Through culture we celebrate and commemorate, we enjoy ourselves, we make sense of our experiences, and sometimes we criticize or disrupt. Cultural organizations are the vehicles for this precious and sensitive activity, so they need to be trusted by the communities they serve.

Perhaps for this reason, it is sometimes argued that the arts are held to higher standards than other sectors when it comes to ethical questions (Wright 2022). Whether or not this is really true, the perception of ethical inconsistency poses a reputational threat to cultural organizations and individual professionals, with potential knock-on effects for stakeholder relationships. The sheer range of stakeholders an arts or cultural organization needs to serve, sometimes with contradictory interests, is another reason these issues need to be carefully managed (Caust 2018). Yet the majority of cultural organizations lack a clear and coherent policy for managing such tensions (Wright 2018). Having to make policy on the hoof when a crisis hits is fraught with danger, particularly if acting under simultaneous public, media, or political scrutiny, which is frequently the case for cultural organizations due to the profile of their work in the public realm and their funding status.

Further indicators of how the ethical dimensions of cultural leadership can be mapped and categorized are revealed by looking at the concerns that different national policymakers have in common when it comes to justifying and safeguarding their funding interventions in their individual social and political contexts. A comparison of reporting and eligibility criteria across cultural funding programs in the United Kingdom, India, the United States, and Europe reveals strikingly similar sets of requirements running alongside the more obvious concerns for aesthetic quality. India Foundation for the Arts (IFA) focuses on "solidarities, enabling creativity and sustainability" (India Foundation for the Arts n.d.), corresponding closely with the European Commission's priorities of "aesthetics, sustainability and inclusion" (European Commission n.d.), and with Arts Council England's requirements on "equality and diversity," "environmental sustainability," and "artistic and quality assessment" (Arts Council England n.d.). Creative Scotland adds concern with rates of pay and IFA safeguards against "financial delinquency" (Creative Scotland n.d. a), while the National Endowment for the Arts in the US monitors legal requirements on labor rights alongside its requirements on artistic merit, accessibility and nondiscrimination, and observance of environmental policies (National Endowment for the Arts n.d.). There remains the question of whether the cultural work itself is viewed as "good"—or, indeed, morally harmful—according to the different assumptions that public authorities have made in different times and places (Belfiore and Bennett 2007). The criteria around artistic quality and public benefit common to most support programs arguably depend on this tradition. Five areas of ethical concern broadly attributable to the cultural sector can therefore be distilled from these reflections, as illustrated in Figure 14.1: how organizations deal with their staff, artists, volunteers, and other contractors (leading people); who accesses their work or is given a voice at any stage of its development (reach and representation); whether that work is intrinsically harmful or offensive (art and morality); whether the organization is fair, transparent, and trustworthy in its fiscal arrangements (funding and finance); and what level of responsibility it takes ecologically and socially for the implications of its work (environment and impact).

FIGURE 14.1 Ethical dimensions of cultural leadership.

Leading People

Two things consistently agreed on in the literature about the otherwise slippery concept of leadership are that it is necessarily focused on the future and that it works through and with other people as a social process (Grint 2005; Price 2017). Most obviously this happens in formal organizations with the employment of staff, recruitment to boards, hiring of freelancers, and other paid or voluntary roles. How an organization relates to its staff is a fundamental part of its ethical operation and covers multiple individual issues, including pay and working conditions; transparency of recruitment processes; nondiscrimination and equality of opportunity in respect of race, gender, disability, sexual orientation, age, or social class; management style, working culture and expectations; care for health and safety, including mental health; and management of dismissal and layoffs. The specifics of personnel management are rarely addressed in the literature on arts management and cultural leadership, though the role of leadership in setting organizational culture is sometimes emphasized insofar as it sets the tone for how staff are treated (Rentschler 2015).

Arts boards ultimately have responsibility for ensuring that employees and other workers are dealt with fairly, but cultural organizations are by no means immune to labor disputes and allegations of injustice, as cases on the whistleblowing website ArtLeaks regularly testify. The particular characteristics of the cultural workforce nuance the ethical challenge for cultural leaders. These will vary from place to place, but widely prevalent is a heavy reliance on freelance staff, whose working lives are often characterized by precarity (hence the importance of TheatreDost's intervention on behalf of vulnerable theater workers), multiplying the impact if cultural organizations fail to be timely and reliable in their contracting and payments. Such characteristics contribute to problems of structural injustice in the sector, where access to many creative career opportunities becomes limited to the socially privileged (Banks 2017; Brook, O'Brien, and Taylor 2020).

Another problematic feature is the high public profile of some leaders who wield correspondingly high levels of influence and, sometimes, disproportionate power. This reflects a persistent valorization of charismatic leadership within the arts (Nisbett and Walmsley 2016), where organizations often seem to be dazzled by inspirational figureheads and the "aesthetic leadership" represented by their personal styles (Smolović Jones and Jackson 2019, 293). The abuse of power by leaders and managers within companies is often entangled with wider problems of organizational culture (Larkin, Burgess, and Montague 2020). This presents a serious challenge to boards, both ethically and pragmatically. As Gander (2017) points out, creative sector careers are built on reputation, making social capital within the industry a crucial commodity. The potential impact of poor or unjust employment practices on recruitment and retention of staff and artists presents an operational incentive for organizations to manage ethical issues proactively and decisively, although if this is done only for self-interested or "conscientious" reasons (Singer 1993), it has to be questioned how thoroughly or effectively workplace culture issues are likely to be addressed.

Reach and Representation

An ongoing challenge for the cultural sector in many countries, commonly expressed as a policy priority in the funding programs considered above, is to ensure equitable access to the opportunities it represents, both in terms of the people who work within it and the people who access or benefit from its work. While this articulation in policy does not necessarily mean that the challenge is universally embraced across the sector, it is a legitimate ethical concern to inquire who has a voice within cultural institutions, who is visible in the work they represent, whose stories are told, and whose language is used. Within individual organizations, questions to address include whether boards, staff, artists, or artworks are representative of the populations and communities they serve (Azmat and Rentschler 2017).

Principled responses can make a difference. Ghosh describes the importance for India Foundation for the Arts of making its application process available in multiple languages, at significant expense, in order to counteract the privileged status of English-language-users and to ensure accessibility to the program for a broad range of communities. Arts and cultural organizations, with their symbolic power and their ability to articulate inequality and galvanize responses to it, are sometimes presented as part of the solution to social inequality (King's College London 2016). However, in the United Kingdom they are also increasingly called to account for perpetuating barriers to diversity through self-replicating patterns such as access to education and occupational networks, issues that overlap with the problems of leading people discussed above (Banks 2017; Brook, O'Brien, and Taylor 2018, 2020). This is not just a problem for leadership but a problem *of* leadership, particularly where institutions derive prestige, resources, and their worldview from histories of injustice.

The former director of the Queens Museum in New York, Laura Raicovich (2021), articulates the ethical conundrum facing many well-established cultural institutions that view and present themselves as champions of progressive values at the same time as their practices serve to reinforce established narratives and power structures. Raicovich (2021) debunks the concept of neutrality on the basis that people, organizations, and nations taking neutral positions tacitly reinforce the status quo and conceal the ways in which power functions. She calls for a reimagining of cultural space with broad-based public involvement "to actively participate in the change so necessary to create a more equitable world" (Raicovich 2021, 153).

Sharpening the challenge around reach and representation is the question of whether receiving public funding entails its own ethical obligation to the taxpaying public. Making the case, Matarasso and Landry (1999, 19) claim: "Artists, and especially those in receipt of or claiming state funds and support, can no longer claim immunity from public enquiry: they have to be prepared to explain and defend their work in the wider context of democratic policy-making."

Within a democratic system, public funding makes the public as a whole, rather than merely the government (or its agent), into a stakeholder. This does not, however, make it inevitable that a cultural organization will willingly accept or embrace public accountability as an ethical principle. It can be asked whether the ethical responsibility for the use of public funds lies with the funded organizations themselves or with the administrators of the funds, such as arts councils and cultural ministries, whose job it is to ensure that the funded program as a whole delivers the required benefit to the taxpayer. The greater the extent to which the funder imposes conditions and obligations, the closer the subsidized organization is to delivering on a contract or commission, therefore working instrumentally rather than autonomously. Ultimately, the ethical responsibility of any organization relates to its own vision and has to be distinguished from the legal and contractual obligations owed to funders, notwithstanding that these conditions are in turn part of the sector's collective ethical duty to society as a whole. Resolving this is a task for those in positions of leadership within cultural organizations, but the social pressures they will have to take into account are reminders of how cultural leadership can also be understood as a process, operating interactively with other human and nonhuman forces in the way suggested by Grint (2005).

Art and Morality

Another site of potential ethical conflict is the work itself: the issues that arise from within the cultural form, through the nature and legacies of cultural artifacts or productions, as well as their relationships—and the relationships of artists and other cultural figures—to morality and its guardians in any given society. The form of ethical judgment demanded by collisions between culture in its broadest sense and culture in its specialized sense is surely a definitive element of cultural leadership, distinct from the challenges presented in any other field of leadership. It depends simultaneously on the expertise of artists, authors, directors, curators, or choreographers and on the sociocultural context (e.g., secular, religious, conservative, multicultural, patriarchal, postcolonial, urban, or rural). Artists may adopt a strategy of deliberately transgressive taboo-breaking to highlight or protest censorship or hypocrisy (Julius 2002); authorities may co-opt culture to support programs of moral improvement, social control, or nation-building. For whatever purpose and in whichever direction influence is brought to bear, as Caust (2018, 25) notes, "culture plays an important and crucial role in defining a society," while cultural activity must respond to that society in turn.

A typical form of conflict in this dimension is between freedom of creative expression and prevailing social morality. Where it occurs, this is a clash of two deontological positions (positions that the protagonists on either side see as categorically right or wrong from the outset) and as such is not easily resolvable. Cultural leaders can be faced with a conflict between values concurrently held, such as belief in granting autonomy to artists and commitments to working inclusively with local faith communities. This reinforces the need for community context to be actively accounted for within foundational documentation and planning alongside mission, vision, values, and artistic intent (Foster 2018).

Questions of provenance and the ownership of work also need to be addressed. Appropriate management of intellectual property is an important part of cultural administration, with licensing and copyright forming key strands of artistic livelihoods and creators having a fundamental right to be credited for authorship of their work. A further specialized area is the growing field of research and practice in museum decolonization under way in many Western institutions (Giblin, Ramos, and Grout 2019). This is a complex and wide-ranging area of policy and leadership requiring organizations to engage actively with external stakeholders in ethical debates that go beyond purely legal questions of obligation or ownership.

Funding and Finance

Finance is a topic with many aspects demanding sound ethics—probity in accounting, fairness of rates of pay, and avoidance of conflicts of interest, to name a few. As public funding for the arts recedes in many parts of the world and new economic partnerships have to be forged, the ethics of fundraising are becoming increasingly important. For example, regular concerns have emerged in the United Kingdom during the last decade around the motives and suitability of high-profile sponsors from controversial industries such as fossil fuels (Richens 2018). Cultural organizations are increasingly held to account—or drawn into controversy—in terms of the funding partnerships they enter into, which, as Chong (2010) points out, include not only income but also the choices made for investments, a relevant issue for organizations holding significant cash reserves.

There are multiple reasons businesses may want to sponsor arts organizations, ranging from development of staff loyalty to enriching "the quality of life in its operating community" (Chong 2010, 60). For some organizations it is about achieving an increased profile, and for others it is about improving their profile by associating the sponsor with high status and respected activity. Essentially, this becomes a process of exchanging financial capital for social capital—a relationship that can tread a fine line between mutual benefit and exploitation, as alleged in cases of perceived greenwashing of environmentally tainted brands (Miller 2017). Understanding the motivations of a potential sponsor and ensuring that they are consistent with the cultural organization's vision, mission, and values is a crucial task of leadership. Protests against fossil fuel sponsorship, such as those targeted at London's Science Museum in response to its relationship with Shell, which received significant media coverage in the United Kingdom, highlight the reputational dangers for cultural organizations of entering into commercial deals for what appear to be the wrong reasons, or which limit their ability to participate freely in critical debate about the sponsors or their industry (Culture Unstained 2021; Motion 2019; Rawlinson 2021). For its approach to be coherent, a sponsored organization needs to be able to show that the support meets the utilitarian test of doing more good than harm.

It is important to recognize that while suspicion of sponsors' motives has a long history, at least in the United Kingdom (Williams 2007), there are counterarguments to perceptions that corrupting influences or power imbalances are particularly common in the field, as Christine Stanley, an American academic and arts fundraiser, robustly articulates:

> Probably the greatest misconception about what a fundraiser does or what a philanthropist does is that somehow when they give, they are in a position of power within the organization.... Maybe we've watched too many TV shows where there's an evil, rich person in the antagonist role. It is very rare that people who are engaged in philanthropy also want to control things.... [O]ccasionally you get one of those people and you have to weed them out. But, for the most part, there is ... a level of trust, that they have so much respect for the professionals that are doing the work.

Stanley's reference to weeding out highlights the fact that organizations are not obliged to remain tied to problematic sponsors. Indeed, their boards have an obligation to apply their judgment in managing any situation that threatens the central cultural mission. It can also be reasoned that, in some circumstances, public funding might itself become ethically problematic—for instance, if working in settings where being perceived as an instrument of government could be detrimental to an organization's ability to build trust with a particular community. Wright (2018) offers a balanced view in recognizing that while cultural organizations must avoid complicity in unethical activities, what is needed is a specific ethical policy. This can allow coherent management of risk and the emergence of considered, defensible positions driven by trustee leadership, grounded in organizational values, and informed by the experiences of peer organizations. A structured, professional, and principled approach can thereby develop, rather than a series of knee-jerk responses to controversy.

Environment and Impact

The environment has been a growing concern within cultural policy since Arts Council England became the first public funding body globally to introduce a requirement on environmental impact reporting into cultural funding programs (Arts Council England 2021). The European Commission promotes an integration of creative and environmental ideals in its New European Bauhaus initiative, which Creative Europe applicants are now required to address (European Commission n.d.; European Commission 2021), while the United States' National Endowment for the Arts has begun to require certain projects to undergo environmental policy review (National Endowment for the Arts n.d.). Creative Scotland, meanwhile, has commissioned a climate emergency and sustainability plan aimed at identifying the contribution that needs to be made through its own activities and by its target sector (Creative Scotland n.d. b).

The importance of this agenda is rising with the increased recognition of the climate crisis and debate driven by activists such as Creative Carbon Scotland and France's Coalition for Art and Sustainable Development to explore the cultural sector's responsibilities and potential contribution (Van Den Bergh 2016). The challenge to cultural organizations to embrace ecological good practice is ethical in that it means going beyond immediate organizational self-interest to engage with often difficult processes to serve wider interests. The specifics of the challenge vary with the type of work; in England and Scotland respectively, Julie's Bicycle and Creative Carbon Scotland have developed sector support programs to offer structured approaches for events, venues, and touring companies of different scales to address their environmental impact (Julie's Bicycle 2019; Creative Carbon Scotland n.d.).

As well as reassessing their work in relation to sustainability of materials, energy consumption, water usage, travel, and carbon footprint, cultural organizations are well placed to contribute to raising awareness, as for example through the spectacular arts installations that gained international media coverage during the COP26 climate summit in Glasgow (World Architecture Community 2021), drawing on a rich history of environmental art practice (Blanc and Benish 2018). There are unique aspects to both the opportunities and the challenges facing the cultural sector in terms of the environment.

Beneath the big-picture level of saving the planet, this dimension is also about the impact an organization or program of work makes on its immediate physical environment, in the sense of being a good neighbor—dealing with your organization's impact on noise, traffic, litter, and the attractiveness of the locality for the sake of those who share the surrounding space. Other ethical aspects of impact include examination of an organization's supply chain and the standards it demands of others in its business dealings (not exploiting sweatshop labor or giving trade to environmentally irresponsible partners), opening up a disparate set of debates that points up the difficulty of achieving a truly holistic approach to sustainability (Quarshie, Salmi, and Leuschner 2016). Questions that can be asked about the environmental credentials of any cultural organization or project also intersect with the issues around fundraising and sponsorship (Motion 2019; Wright 2021). A primary ethical question for cultural leadership is how far to go and how much responsibility to take across these dimensions (Wright 2022).

Sufficiency and Consistency

Bringing these issues together, there are two fundamental sets of questions that can be asked of a leader, an organization, or a program of work about its ethical approach in each of these dimensions: first, around the consistency between the values espoused and the action taken; second, around the sufficiency of the espoused values themselves (Raelin 1993). Ethical criticisms or objections by stakeholders represent challenges on one of these two levels. Do your commitments go far enough in terms of ambition and your level of commitment? Do they adequately take into account available information, including the concerns and needs of your stakeholders, and the resources that you have at your disposal? If so, are your actions and their effects consistent with the statements, values, and priorities that you have articulated? Does your decision-making match your rhetoric? This model, as presented in Figure 14.2, offers the basis for a scorecard of ethical performance.

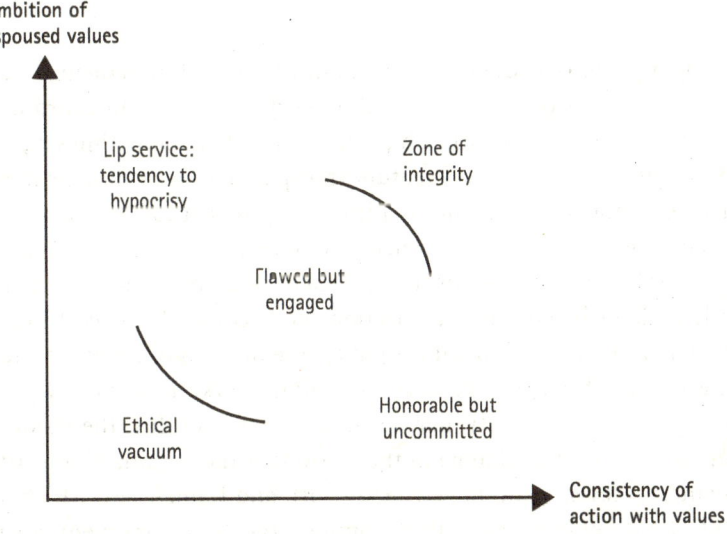

FIGURE 14.2 Locating integrity.

Ethical critique can legitimately attack failings on either axis of the model. An organization that expresses grand ambitions for its contributions to social justice or high standards of financial probity risks looking insincere or hypocritical if its actions fail to follow through. Does the organization have the resources and an operational culture that will allow it to fulfill its promises? It is not good enough to have high ideals that are rarely attained, but at the same time it is pointless to deliver consistently on only the lowest of standards. An individual or organization that makes minimal promises and fails to deliver even on those, meanwhile, could be described as inhabiting an ethical vacuum: it has neither the desire nor capacity to contribute to the well-being of any entity outside of itself. Only setting more exacting standards and matching them with day-to-day behavior can be described meaningfully as a position of integrity, if integrity is understood in its Latin-derived sense of "wholeness" (Bauman 2013).

What remains subjective is where the boundary line of integrity is to be drawn. The dimension of consistency is largely observable, so contradictions can be called out, but what level of ambition is sufficient? This is a question of judgment, and of aligning values, vision, and mission; in short, of leadership. It is a judgment, or set of judgments, that has to be made in relation to public expectations and societal norms (Mendonca and Kanungo 2007). It is therefore a form of judgment that can be challenged by any stakeholder, and not one that lends itself well to being made by a single authoritative leader in isolation. Imagining cultural leadership as a process informed by multiple voices, rather than as a skill set, may be a helpful starting point for organizations seeking to engage meaningfully with their ethical responsibilities. These models can therefore be used for planning as much as for analysis or critique.

Conclusion

Integrity might be an old-fashioned term, but it is a vital ingredient for any organization taking ethics seriously, and few cultural organizations can afford not to if they are ultimately to sustain the relationships they depend on. Sometimes it goes by other names. Beckman (2022, 42) sees "venture transparency" as a fundamental principle of responsible donor management; in a leadership report for Arts Council England, leaders need "commitment to an authentic vision" (King's College London 2018, 5). Foster (2018) provocatively defends the concept of "mission creep," a term usually used pejoratively to describe how an organization can become distracted from its core activities. Foster argues instead that it is right for the mission to change if circumstances have changed; the habitual form and content of the work, though outwardly emblematic of an organization's identity, may cease to be relevant. It is the vision that needs to be held on to—the ideal change in the world that the organization exists to make. At a fundamental level, Slung Low, TheatreDost, and Kamaleswar Mukherjee shared a simple ideal—of being useful to their community—so in a moment of rupture they knew what to do.

Public funders are increasingly tightening their expectations around selected ethical issues, but ultimately the integrity of cultural organizations can only be judged on their own terms, according to their statements and their actions. Critique will inevitably center on questions around the sufficiency and consistency of an organization's ethical approach, though there are no universally applicable standards about what constitutes sufficient ethical commitment in any of the relevant behavioral dimensions. Boards and other decision-makers must meanwhile grapple with competing principles. Are they ticking boxes for funders or are they striving for integrity on their own terms? What are their non-negotiable principles, if any? Do the limits of resources mean that they need to focus on certain ethical commitments above others? The significance of such struggles is heightened within a cultural sector whose work is both reflective and formative of wider social values and debates.

Anyone can share, disagree with, or be concerned about a cultural organization's vision, and any stakeholder has the right to call the organization to account in respect of its integrity as it pursues its mission through its actions. This includes external critics and activists, whether communities contesting the representation of their histories or environmental campaigners challenging cultural institutions on their critical and symbolic role in the public sphere. Their actions may be messy, argumentative, full of frustration, and the cause of frustration in turn, but if cultural leadership has any real meaning, it is to be found in the uneasy relationship between idealism and realism and the choices that have to be made in between. This is the space of ethical decision-making.

Several years ago, Wendy Were, then an executive director at the Australia Council for the Arts, proposed a simple but provocative starting point for arts organizations embarking on evaluation of their work: to ask themselves, "Would people miss us if we went?" (Price 2015). It is difficult to imagine how that question could be answered satisfactorily by any organization whose leadership acts without integrity or fails to exhibit the ethic of care in its dealings with staff, artists, audiences, other stakeholder communities, and the wider environment. To be the organization that people would miss if it were gone means allowing the form of mission creep in which your values, rather than your habits, direct your actions. That will not usually mean downing creative tools and filling a van with medicine and food parcels. But it does involve having real clarity about why your organization exists and what kind of world it wants to create.

REFERENCES

Alvesson, Mats, and André Spicer. 2011. "Theories of Leadership." In *Metaphors We Lead By: Understanding Leadership in the Real World*, edited by Mats Alvesson and André Spicer, 8–30. Abingdon, UK: Routledge.

Arts Council England. n.d. "Requirements of Funded Organisations: Organisational Requirements." https://www.artscouncil.org.uk/npompm-funding-relationships-2018-22/npompm-funding-requirments#section-5.

Arts Council England and Julie's Bicycle. 2021. *Culture, Climate and Environmental Responsibility: Annual Report 2019–20*. Manchester: Arts Council England.

Azmat, Fara, and Ruth Rentschler. 2017. "Gender and Ethnic Diversity on Boards and Corporate Responsibility: The Case of the Arts Sector." *Journal of Business Ethics* 141: 317–336.

Banks, Mark. 2017. *Creative Justice: Cultural Industries, Work and Critique*. London: Rowman and Littlefield.

Bauman, David. 2013. "Leadership and the Three Faces of Integrity." *Leadership Quarterly* 24: 414–426.

Beckman, Gary. 2022. *The New Arts Entrepreneur*. Abingdon: Routledge.

Belfiore, Eleonora, and Oliver Bennett. 2007. "Rethinking the Social Impacts of the Arts." *International Journal of Cultural Policy* 13, no. 2: 135–151.

Blanc, Nathalie, and Barbara Benish. 2018. *Form, Art and the Environment: Engaging in Sustainability*. Abingdon, UK: Routledge.

British Council. 2013. "What Is Cultural Leadership?" https://creativeconomy.britishcouncil.org/media/uploads/files/Cultural_Leadership_2.pdf.

Brook, Orian, Dave O'Brien, and Mark Taylor. 2018. "Panic! Social Class, Taste and Inequalities in the Creative Industries." https://createlondon.org/wp-content/uploads/2018/04/Panic-Social-Class-Taste-and-Inequalities-in-the-Creative-Industries1.pdf.

Brook, Orian, Dave O'Brien, and Mark Taylor. 2020. *Culture Is Bad for You*. Manchester: Manchester University Press.

Caust, Josephine. 2018. *Arts Leadership in Contemporary Contexts*. Abingdon, UK: Routledge.

Chong, Derek. 2010. *Arts Management*. Abingdon, UK: Routledge.

Creative Carbon Scotland. n.d. "Sector Support" https://creativecarbonscotland.com/about/sector-agencies-support/.

Creative Scotland. n.d. a. "Project Monitoring." https://www.creativescotland.com/resources/our-publications/funding-documents/project-monitoring.

Creative Scotland. n.d. b. " A Climate Emergency and Sustainability Plan for Creative Scotland." https://www.creativescotland.com/what-we-do/the-10-year-plan/connecting-themes/environment/a-climate-emergency-and-sustainability-plan-for-creative-scotland.

Culture Unstained. 2021. "Science Museum Faces Backlash over Shell Sponsorship of Climate Exhibition." April 16, 2021. https://cultureunstained.org/2021/04/16/science-museum-faces-backlash-over-shell-sponsorship-of-climate-exhibition/.

Dasgupta, Prijanka. 2020. "Director Goes Back to His Stethoscope After 14 Years." *Times of India*, June 21, 2020. https://timesofindia.indiatimes.com/city/kolkata/director-goes-back-to-his-stethoscope-after-14-years/articleshow/76329879.cms.

Department for Digital, Culture, Media and Sport. 2021. "DCMS Sector Economic Estimates Methodology." Last updated August 26, 2021. https://www.gov.uk/government/publications/dcms-sectors-economic-estimates-methodology/dcms-sector-economic-estimates-methodology.

Douglas, Anne, and Chris Fremantle. 2009. "The Artist as Leader Research Report." https://rgu-repository.worktribe.com/output/247882/the-artist-as-leader-research-report.

Edwards, Gareth, Doris Schedlitzki, Sharon Turnbull, and Roger Gill. 2015. "Exploring Power Assumptions in the Leadership and Management Debate." *Leadership and Organization Development Journal* 36, no. 3: 328–343.

Emerson, Ralph Waldo. [1850] 1901. *Representative Men*. London: J. M. Dent.

European Commission. 2021. "Overview of the Creative Europe Calls for Proposals 2021: Culture Strand." https://culture.ec.europa.eu/news/creative-europe-2021-2027-programme-launch.

European Commission. n.d. "New European Bauhaus." https://europa.eu/new-european-bauhaus/index_en.

Foster, Kenneth. 2018. *Arts Leadership: Creating Sustainable Arts Organizations*. Abingdon, UK: Routledge.

Gander, Jonathan. 2017. *Strategic Analysis: A Creative and Cultural Industries Perspective*. Abingdon, UK: Routledge.

Giblin, John, Imma Ramos, and Nikki Grout. 2019. "Dismantling the Master's House." *Third Text* 33, nos. 4–5: 471–486.

Grint, Keith. 2005. *Leadership: Limits and Possibilities*. Basingstoke, UK: Palgrave Macmillan.

Hewison, Robert. 2004. "The Crisis of Cultural Leadership in Britain." *International Journal of Cultural Policy* 10, no. 2: 157–166.

India Foundation for the Arts. n.d. "Request for Proposals for Arts Platforms." https://indiaifa.org/programmes/arts-practice/request-for-proposals/arts-platforms.html.

Julie's Bicycle. 2019. "Sustainable Events Guides with Manchester City Council." November 5, 2019. https://juliesbicycle.com/resource/sustainable-events-guides-with-manchester-city-council/.

Julius, Anthony. 2002. *Transgressions: The Offences of Art*. London: Thames & Hudson.

King's College London. 2016. "The Civic Role of Arts Organisations: A Literature Review for the Calouste Gulbenkian Foundation." Calouste Gulbenkian Foundation and King's College London.

King's College London. 2018. "Changing Cultures: Transforming Leadership in the Arts, Museums and Libraries." Arts Council England and King's College London.

Knights, David. 2022. "Disrupting Masculinities Within Leadership: Problems of Embodiment, Ethics, Identity and Power." *Leadership* 18, no. 2: 266–276.

Larkin, Roslyn, John Burgess, and Alan Montague. 2020. "Ethical Leadership." In *Organizational Leadership*, edited by John Bratton, 103–122. London: Sage.

Leicester, Graham. 2007. "Rising to the Occasion: Cultural Leadership in Powerful Times." http://culturehive.co.uk/wp-content/uploads/2013/10/23974676-Rising-to-the-Occasion-by-Graham-Leicester-2007_0.pdf.

Liu, Helena. 2021. Redeeming Leadership: An Anti-Racist Feminist Intervention. Bristol: Bristol University Press.

Mackie, John. 1977. *Ethics: Inventing Right and Wrong*. Harmondsworth, UK: Penguin.

Matarasso, Francois, and Charles Landry. 1999. *Balancing Act: 21 Strategic Dilemmas in Cultural Policy*. Strasbourg: Council of Europe.

Mendonca, Manuel, and Rabindra Kanungo. 2007. *Ethical Leadership*. Maidenhead, UK: Open University Press.

Miller, Toby. 2017. Greenwashing Culture. London: Routledge.

Morton, Jeremy. 2021. "'The Best of Us'—the Volunteers at Slung Low's Foodbank." South Leeds Life, February 18, 2021. https://southleedslife.com/the-best-of-us-the-volunteers-at-slung-lows-foodbank/.

Motion, Judy. 2019. "Undoing Art and Oil: An Environmental tale of Sponsorship, Cultural Justice and Climate Change Controversy." *Environmental Politics* 28, no. 4: 727–746.

Nahavandi, Afsaneh. 2012. *The Art and Science of Leadership*. Upper Saddle River, NJ: Pearson.

National Endowment for the Arts. n.d. "Grants for Arts Projects: Award Administration." https://arts.gov/grants/grants-for-arts-projects/award-administration.

Nisbett, Melissa, and Ben Walmsley. 2016. "The Romanticization of Charismatic Leadership in the Arts." *Journal of Arts Management, Law, and Society* 46, no. 1: 2–12.

Price, Jonathan. 2015. "The Art of Valuing." On the Edge Research, March 5, 2015. https://ontheedgeresearch.org/2015/03/04/the-art-of-valuing/.

Price, Jonathan. 2017. "The Construction of Cultural Leadership." *ENCATC Journal of Cultural Management and Policy* 7, no. 1: 5–16.

Quarshie, Anne, Asta Salmi, and Rudolf Leuschner. 2016. "Sustainability and Corporate Social Responsibility in Supply Chains: The State of Research in Supply Chain Management and Business Ethics Journals." *Journal of Purchasing and Supply Management* 22: 82–97.

Raelin, Joseph. 1993. "The Persean Ethic: Consistency of Belief and Action in Managerial Practice." *Human Relations* 46, no. 5: 575–620.

Raicovich, Laura. 2021. *Culture Strike: Art and Museums in an Age of Protest*. London: Verso.

Rawlinson, Kevin. 2021. "Extinction Rebellion Activists Glued to Science Museum Site in Shell Protest." *The Guardian*, August 29, 2021. https://www.theguardian.com/environment/2021/aug/29/extinction-rebellion-protesters-science-museum-shell-sponsorship.

Rentschler, Ruth. 2015. *Arts Governance: People, Passion, Performance*. Abingdon, UK: Routledge.

Richens, Frances. 2018. "Pulse Report: Ethics in Arts Sponsorship." Arts Professional, April 20, 2018. https://www.artsprofessional.co.uk/pulse/survey-report/pulse-report-ethics-arts-sponsorship.

Sahani, Alaka. 2021. "As Covid Downs Curtain on Stage, TheatreDost Helps Mumbai Artistes, Backstage Workers." *Indian Express*, July 17, 2021. https://indianexpress.com/article/cities/mumbai/as-covid-downs-curtain-on-stage-theatredost-helps-mumbai-artistes-backstage-workers-7409744/.

Singer, Peter. 1993. *Practical Ethics*. Cambridge: Cambridge University Press.

Smolović Jones, Owain, and Brad Jackson. 2019. "Seeing Leadership: Becoming Sophisticated Consumers of Leadership." In *Leadership: Contemporary Critical Perspectives* 2, edited by Brigid Carroll, Jackie Ford, and Scott Taylor, 290–309. London: Sage.

TheatreDost. n.d. "About Us." https://theatredost.com/about-us/. Accessed June 2021.

Van Den Bergh, Hannah. 2016. *Art for the Planet's Sake: Arts and Environment*. Brussels: IETM. https://www.ietm.org/system/files/publications/ietm-art-for-the-planets-sake_jan2016.pdf.

Vinter, Robyn. 2021. "'Incredibly Proud': Food Bank Set Up for Pandemic Hands Out Last Package." *The Guardian*, June 26, 2021. https://www.theguardian.com/world/2021/jun/26/incredibly-proud-food-bank-set-up-for-pandemic-hands-out-last-package.

Williams, Raymond. 2007. "Politics and Policies: The Case of the Arts Council." In *Politics of Modernism: Against the New Conformists*, 141–150. London: Verso.

World Architecture Community. 2021. "Es Devlin Creates Conference of the Trees During COP26 Climate Conference." November 10, 2021. https://worldarchitecture.org/architecture-news/empzz/es-devlin-creates-conference-of-the-trees-during-cop26-climate-conference.html.

Wright, Michelle. 2018. "How Bad Is Bad? Are Problems of Ethics in Danger of Making the Arts Unfundable?" Arts Professional, April 25, 2018. https://www.artsprofessional.co.uk/magazine/article/how-bad-bad.

Wright, Michelle. 2021. "Can Corporate Sponsorship be Part of the Environmental Agenda?" Arts Professional, November 10, 2021. https://www.artsprofessional.co.uk/magazine/349/feature/can-corporate-sponsorship-be-part-environmental-agenda.

Wright, Michelle. 2022. "Ethical Trouble at the Top." *Arts Professional*, February 2, 2022. https://www.artsprofessional.co.uk/magazine/351/feature/ethical-trouble-top.

CHAPTER 15

SHARED LEADERSHIP AND THE EVOLUTION OF FESTIVALS

What Can Be Learned?

JOSEPHINE CAUST AND KIM GOODWIN

INTRODUCTION

UNDERSTANDINGS of and the practice of leadership are often a source of conflict within organizations (Grint 2000; Goleman 2000; Yukl 2002). When considering scenarios where specialized knowledge and skills are needed in the leadership of an organization, alternative ways of approaching leadership have developed, where leadership can be shared or distributed among functions (Ansell and Gash 2012). Sharing of the leadership function has been described in several ways: collaborative leadership, co-leadership, shared leadership, plural leadership, distributive leadership, and team leadership (Doos and Wilhelmson 2021). While this phenomenon is most often observed in educational settings, it is also present in other areas in which leaders must have a multiplicity of skills and a wide range of knowledge (Gronn 2002, 2008). Another area in which it appears is the arts, particularly within certain kinds of arts organizations (Reid 2013).

Arts organizations have become more complex in the late twentieth and early twenty-first centuries as they deal with multiple stakeholders such as boards, government funders, sponsors, and philanthropists. This has resulted in changing leadership requirements (Byrnes 2009). It is usually difficult in an age of specialization to find an individual with the capacity to be both a successful artistic leader and a good business manager (Hoyle and Swale 2016; Wester 2016). This has led to the shared/co-leadership model within arts organizations (Reid 2013). However, a shared leadership model requires the participants to have enhanced communication and interpersonal skills (Lash 2012). It has been observed too that contemporary creative models require a collaborative approach rather than a competitive one (Hewison and Holden 2011). Given the links between collaboration and creativity, it is asserted too that artists have enhanced skills in sharing leadership roles (Adler 2006).

Shared or Co-leadership in Arts Organizations

Arts organizations present challenges because of the dual functions of artistic leadership and business management. These functions can be seen as diametrically opposite (Beirne 2012; Cray, Inglis, and Freeman 2007; Hewison and Holden 2002). Unlike mainstream business organizations, leadership of an arts organization is frequently divided between those two functions (Beirne 2012; Lapierre 2001). Within the structure of an arts organization, one or the other of these two roles is perceived as the organizational leader and is given the title of chief executive officer (CEO) or executive director (ED). Traditionally, the title of overall leader was given to the artistic leader, while the administrator/business manager's role was seen as providing support to artists and the artistic program (Pick and Anderton 1996). It has been argued, in fact, that the leadership of arts organizations should always reside with artists (Lapierre 2001). In addition, the model of the artist/impresario as leader, particularly in the case of major arts festivals, continues to be evident, and is often part of the festival's branding (Caust 2004).

In recent times, though, boards of governance or boards of directors, who usually decide on the organizational structure, have often felt more comfortable assigning the overall organizational leadership to the individual responsible for the business side (Caust 2010; Turbide and Laurin 2009). Various factors have an impact on this decision, including managerialism, the increasing complexity of managing arts organizations, and the influence of stakeholders (such as businesspeople) on arts boards (Beirne 2012). In this model, the artistic leader either reports through the CEO/ED to the organizational board or, if reporting directly to the board, is deemed lower in the organizational hierarchy than the CEO. This model can work successfully when the artistic director and CEO/ED understand and support the other's role, but there is also the possibility of conflict between the artistic and business functions, given that the two leadership roles have different priorities (Bilton 2007; Caust 2010; Reynolds, Tonks, and MacNeill 2017). However, "conflict" can also be positively framed within the process of artmaking, given that it is seen as an essential element in creativity (Bilton 2007).

Essentially, an arts organization has a dual mission: it must produce good arts practice, which usually involves some form of risk, to establish and maintain an artistic reputation; yet it must also run as a business, work within its budget, and produce successful financial outcomes (Caust 2010; Douglas and Fremantle 2009). It can be argued these two functions are interdependent, and that because of this duality of function leaders must understand each other's role and expectations and work harmoniously together

(Cray, Inglis, and Freeman 2007; Creese 1997; Bilton 2007). The administrative leader must be sensitive to the needs of, for example, developing an artistic program and supporting artists (Lapierre 2001; Pick and Anderton 1996). Conversely, the artistic leader must understand that there must be sufficient income to deliver the program and that budgets need to be adhered to, otherwise the future of the whole organization is at risk (Douglas and Fremantle 2009; Hewison 2004; Nisbett and Walmsley 2016).

Sometimes, though, when there are two leaders in place, they are given equal status, with both reporting to the board and sharing equal responsibility for the success of the undertaking (Reid 2013). That is, one function is not given delegated power over the other. They are co-leaders of the organization or joint CEOs exercising different responsibilities within it (Reid 2013). There are also models of collaborative leadership that are based on everyone being involved in the process of making and managing work. These might be described as participatory leadership or even collective leadership approaches (Cray, Inglis, and Freeman 2007). Further, it has been observed that some smaller creative groups prefer a model of shared leadership across an organization, seeing it as more effective (Dalbourg and Lofgren 2016).

In a model of shared leadership, though, there are certain challenges from the start. Do the individuals involved share an understanding about the process of collaboration? Does a shared process require specific individual qualities to make it work successfully? What about the time it might take to come to decisions, given the active engagement of several leaders? How will conflict between individuals be managed? While shared or co-leadership models can be a more democratic way of approaching decision-making, they may also present unique organizational challenges.

Methodology

To explore the varied issues around the challenges of shared leadership, this research considers examples of shared or co-leadership in two arts festivals. Case study methodology is used, as it lends itself well to the understanding of complex phenomena and allows a deep engagement with the subject (Yin 2014). The case studies are Rising and Next Wave, two arts festivals located in Melbourne, Australia. These two festivals were chosen as case studies based on convenience sampling. Both Rising and Next Wave are well-established, recognized examples of alternative leadership approaches that have developed over recent years. They are geographically close to the researchers, and their leadership expressed availability and willingness to participate in the research.

In the case of Rising, the leadership model altered in 2019, with the appointment of two artistic directors, Gideon Obarzanek and Hannah Fox. They joined the existing chief executive officer, Kath Mainland, and together they became the three chief executive officers of the organization, all reporting to the board. In the case of Next Wave there is a chief executive officer, Jamie Lewis, who was joined by an artistic directorate of eight individuals in 2021. In both case studies, the pandemic and the ensuing lockdowns affected the artistic undertakings of the organizations. While this is not highlighted dramatically in the chapter, it is referred to from time to time.

To develop a layered picture of each case study, the history of each organization is considered. Then the background of individual key stakeholders is discussed. Following this, the results of interviews with key stakeholders are presented under the headings of leadership, values, governance, and decision-making. In the case of Rising, the researcher conducted an hour-long interview over Zoom with the two artistic directors together; the third member of the triumvirate, the executive director, responded to questions emailed to her by the researcher. In the case of Next Wave, the researcher conducted four hour-long interviews. Three of those interviews were conducted individually with two members of the artistic directorate and the board chair, again using Zoom. One interview was conducted by the researcher in person with the CEO/executive director. In each case the material gathered in the interviews and questionnaires was analyzed by the researchers and coded. The chapter discusses the results of the research, drawing some conclusions about shared models of leadership.

The Case Studies

Rising

Rising is an annual arts festival located in Melbourne, Australia (Rising Festival 2022). In 2019 a triumvirate leadership model was agreed to by the festival's board, and this has continued through 2022. Rising was previously known as the Melbourne Festival of the Arts, and has been in existence for thirty-five years. The Melbourne Festival began as an annual event imported from Spoleto, Italy, with one of the Spoleto festival's original artistic directors, Gian Carlo Menotti, as the inaugural artistic director (Parliament of Victoria 1989). In 1990 the festival changed its name to the Melbourne Festival of Arts. In 2020 it was decided to combine the Melbourne Festival with the White Night Festival, an annual festival that celebrated winter and associated events. The White Night Festival went for a twenty-four-hour period and had been an annual event since 2013 (ToMelbourne n.d.). In this new iteration, the Melbourne Festival was moved from October to May–June, and the combined festivals were renamed Rising (Rising Festival 2022). In both 2020 and 2021 Rising was affected by the pandemic closures and was cancelled at the last minute despite being fully programmed. In 2022, though, Rising was able to go ahead more or less intact.

The executive director of the Melbourne Festival, Kath Mainland, was already in her position and was a member of the panel interviewing candidates for the position of artistic director in 2019. Before taking on the role at the Melbourne Festival in 2016, Mainland had been the CEO of the Edinburgh Fringe for seven years. The appointment of the two co-artistic directors, Gideon Obarzanek and Hannah Fox, at the Melbourne Festival occurred in mid-2019 (Francis 2019). Obarzanek trained as a dancer and worked in Australia and internationally for several years from 1987. In the mid-1990s he established a dance company called Chunky Move in Melbourne, for which he was the CEO and artistic director until 2012. From 2015 to 2017 Obarzanek was an artistic associate at the Melbourne Festival. Fox comes from a visual arts background and prior to working at Rising had been a creative producer at the Mofo and Dark Mofo Festivals in Tasmania, as well as working on festivals and major events in the United Kingdom. Obarzanek and Fox knew each other but had never worked together previously. The idea of a work partnership was suggested by a mutual friend who thought they had complementary skills. Obarzanek approached Fox to see if she was interested in the role of associate artistic director at the Melbourne Festival if he applied for the role of artistic director. Fox responded that she would love to work with Obarzanek but would prefer to be co-artistic director rather than associate artistic director. Obarzanek agreed to this idea, and they then applied for the position of artistic director of the Melbourne Festival as a leadership team. It is important to note that the existing roles of artistic director and executive director of the Melbourne Festival were already designated as *joint* CEO roles. The agreement to there being *three* CEOs (an executive director and two co-artistic directors) clearly sprang out of this existing dual-CEO structure.

Next Wave

Next Wave emerged at the same time as the Melbourne Festival, beginning in 1985 as a biennial multi-arts youth-oriented festival also in Melbourne. The focus of Next Wave has always been on fostering and developing the next generation of artists through career development, presentation opportunity, and multidisciplinary representation (Next Wave n.d. b). Since its inception, Next Wave has concentrated on providing a platform for emerging artists, with it often being their first opportunity to engage in long-term supported development (Gibb 2012). Over the years Next Wave has changed thematically in line with funding, leadership, and artistic priorities; however, an underlying emphasis on early career development and building sustainable arts careers has remained a consistent goal. After a period of self-described reckoning and reflection influenced by staff changes and the COVID-19 shutdowns, in 2021 Next Wave launched an ambitious new leadership model with eight artistic directors, appointed to form an artistic directorate. Next Wave essentially split the artistic director job, in terms of artistic responsibilities and remuneration, into eight distinct roles, one located in each state or territory. The artistic directorate is supported by a CEO/ED, through whom the artistic directorate reports to the board.

Next Wave's CEO/ED is Jamie Lewis, a Singaporean Australian artist-curator, dramaturg, producer, and intercultural facilitator. She had previously worked for Theatre Network Australia and Metro Arts prior to joining Next Wave in late 2020. There was no defined plan to develop an alternate leadership structure before Lewis was appointed to the CEO/ED role. However, she worked closely with members of the board in a concentrated strategic planning process, through which the new structure and shape of the organization emerged over a period of three months. As part of this process, however, several changes in the board membership occurred, because of the recognition that there needed to be an alignment between board members' skills and the new strategic direction of the organization. Amrit Gill, at the time the artistic director and CEO of a similar-sized arts organization, 4A Centre for Contemporary Asian Art in Sydney, joined the board in early 2021 and became chair in 2022 (4A Centre for Contemporary Asian Art n.d.).

As CEO/ED, Lewis undertook a developmental approach in recruiting future members of the artistic directorate. At the end of their two-year tenure, each member of the directorate will then nominate three potential new members for consideration, and the current artistic directorate will collectively curate the makeup of the next iteration. In this way the role of the artistic directorate at Next Wave is not only to curate and build relationships with the producing artists but also to seek out their successors. Two members of the artistic directorate at Next Wave were interviewed for this study. Kirsti Monfries is a Javanese Australian creative producer and curator based in Canberra. Her experience working in experimental art projects across Asia and her passion for working with emerging artists inform her role as a member of Next Wave's artistic directorate (Next Wave n.d. a). The other interviewee, located in Brisbane, was Nathan Stoneham, who comes from a theater/performance background, with experience in cultural and community development as well as social work. Like Monfries, Stoneham's artistic practice has always been embedded with collaborative approaches, and he describes his work as built on a "methodology of friendship."

A final crucial element in the Next Wave model is the shift from being a festival located in one city into a new type of arts organization spread across the country. Thus Next Wave has made a conscious move away from the idea of artistic directors who curate and then transplant works into a central location, culminating in an intense two-week festival. Instead, they are developing an ongoing platform where the members of the artistic directorate facilitate "artists and their arts practices through relationship building and ideas exchange, creative and skill development, and the resources to support the research and presentation of work—across disciplines, art forms and generations" (Next Wave n.d. c).

Interviews and correspondence with the leaders of Rising and Next Wave demonstrate the benefits and challenges that emerge in a more complex approach to leadership. To understand these issues further, the case study data is framed under four themes: leadership, values, governance, and decision-making. By exploring these themes, we identify systems, structures, philosophies, and key skills that may help us understand what makes these multileader approaches work in practice.

LEADERSHIP

An important element for both organizations was the alignment of leadership models with their organizational strategy. In the case of Rising there was a focus on developing new projects with primarily local artists. The new festival also wanted to emphasize large-scale ambitious work that would attract big audiences who may be new to arts practice. Hannah Fox observed, "We're not approaching it as a fusing of the Melbourne International Arts Festival and White Night, but really trying to think about it as an entirely new festival" (Fox quoted in Francis 2019). Kath Mainland, who said she was "super excited" about the possibility of co-leadership and was, as noted, part of the interview panel for the AD recruitment, commented, "I felt having two voices, not one, and those two in particular, would signal a real change for the festival and embrace the change and democratization we were seeking to achieve." Mainland clearly was positive about the co-leadership model and saw the possibility of having two people instead of one in the artistic leadership role as an advantage for the organization. She also saw it in terms of matching the new goals of Rising and its desire to be seen in a different way than its previous iterations. Further, she already had professional respect for the individuals and was excited about the possibilities for all three to work together.

Another unusual aspect of the leadership structure at Rising is the fact that all three people in leadership roles, Mainland, Fox, and Obarzanek, have the same job description with the same delegation of responsibility. In other words, they are all the "boss" and all report directly to the board. In other examples of shared leadership there is usually one person charged with the role of CEO, even though the actions of leadership are shared. In the case of Rising, each person is an organizational leader as well as having specific responsibilities within the triumvirate. They noted that each has areas of specialization; for example, Obarzanek is more responsible for the performing arts and Fox is more responsible for the visual arts. In addition, on the management side, Fox is more experienced in dealing with sponsors, Obarzanek is more knowledgeable about philanthropy, and Mainland focuses more on governance and managing the myriad of stakeholders. All of them have had experience with budgets and complex financial issues. Fox noted that at times they have "leaned" on Mainland because of her long experience in festival governance and dealing with stakeholders—skills that were crucial in dealing with issues arising out of the pandemic, such as last-minute program cancellations.

For Next Wave the change was even more dramatic. The organization moved from a two-week festival based in a single city to a model of ongoing support in multiple locations that includes the development and presentation of work. The board chair, Amrit Gill, noted that while Next Wave has been recognized as a festival, its primary aim has always been on developing emerging artist careers. Now, though, said Gill, the festival has shifted from "shepherding an artist through the creation of one work, to shepherding them through a period of time." This shift was both a response to the external environment, where support for early-career artists had eroded over the previous decade, and a conscious choice to lean into the core purpose of the organization. AD Nathan Stoneham described it this way:

> Next Wave used to reach out across the continent and people. Artists traveled to Melbourne to present their work, but we never had a local person to support its development. There was a sense of transplanting the work from where it was conceived

and made, or where it sometimes belongs. This [new model] lets work be made and shared in the communities and places that they have been designed for.

Next Wave also considers its leadership structure as a triumvirate, but instead of three individuals it has three clusters. These are the eight members of the creatively focused artistic directorate, distributed across the country, with a focus on relationships, curation, and presentation within each locale; the CEO/ED, who leads the administrative and operational part of the organization from the head office in Melbourne; and the board, whose current chair resides in Sydney. While it is possible to see this in hierarchical terms, with the board at the top and the artistic directorate reporting to the CEO/ED (and thus potentially diminishing the directorate's importance), those interviewed were conscious of describing it more in organic terms. The ADs saw CEO/ED Lewis as the central hub that initially connected them together and who formed a conduit to the board, freeing them from the administrative tasks associated with running the organization. Similarly, board chair Gill described her position as "to the side," providing strategic and governance support, with the three clusters of artistic directorate, CEO/ED, and board forming a dispersed creative leadership model.

An important issue, then, is what skills are needed to be successful in these new leadership approaches. Before their appointments to Rising, Fox, Mainland, and Obarzanek had considerable industry experience that was complementary in terms of their knowledge. For example, as the Edinburgh Fringe is an open-access festival, it is likely that the prospect of a democratic approach to programming and organizational structure was something that Mainland was accustomed to and which aligned with her values. As already noted, Fox has a visual arts background, which is different from both Mainland and Obarzanek but important in terms of programming a multi-arts festival. Obarzanek has had a long career in the performing arts, particularly in dance, where collaboration is critical. Further, all of them have had plenty of experience managing money, fundraising, working within tight budgets, and all the other business aspects of managing a major arts festival. All of them talk about having mutual respect for each other's skills and experience, while also noting how important collaboration is in any leadership structure.

For those involved in the more complicated and dispersed Next Wave model, the requisite skills discussed tended to focus largely on interpersonal or soft skills rather than technical background. Monfries and Stoneham both suggested they felt very comfortable working in the collective model, Stoneham because of his background in community development of collective theater and performance works and Monfries because of her extensive experience working in Southeast Asia, where, she said, it is much more common for artists to work collectively. All members of Next Wave interviewed singled out CEO/ED Jamie Lewis's ability to facilitate and manage team processes as being critical for success, while Lewis herself said artists were naturally good at leading in this way because of their ability to hold "critical conversations."

Values

Along with a link between structure and leadership, a second major focus for these organizations is an alignment of personal and organizational values. Members of both organizations reflected on how the structural changes impacted on the role of the leader. Members of both also reflected on the traditional idea of arts organizations centering themselves around a "major personality" who essentially becomes the "branding" of the festival. Instead, Rising wanted the festival to have an image that is not dependent on one charismatic individual but has its own "brand," independent of whoever is leading it. They describe this approach as a "rolling creative leadership model." Fox characterized this approach as demonstrating "a different working model that more closely resembles our creative model of programming itself. We are finding out how best to do our particular parts better over time."

For those associated with Next Wave, the organizational values of justice, friendship, and care are integral to their leadership structure and approach. Gill described the process of developing the new leadership model and organizational strategy as "values-based strategic planning." Monfries suggested that their leadership team has "actually structured an organization around those principles [of justice, friendship, and care]." Similarly, Stoneham, who described the artistic directorate as an "assemblage," noted that for Next Wave,

> the main thing is that it's a shift [away] from having one artistic director who is in control of the main vision, the main program, the programming decision. Instead, it is sharing that role across the continent and allowing more perspectives to inform the decision-making around what the organization is and what the festival becomes.

This value of care can be linked to the focus the Next Wave leaders have on the wellbeing of both arts managers and artists. Monfries suggested it is important that there is a financial acknowledgment of the work the artistic directorate are undertaking, because for many artistic directors in smaller organizations much of the work is unpaid. Both Stoneham and Monfries argued that the triumvirate model removes administrative duties from the job description of artistic directors, particularly given that they are not physically located in the festival's operational center, Melbourne. Stoneham said that they are free to focus on the "rewarding work" of meeting artists, understanding what's happening in their community, and supporting others in developing work. Monfries noted too that the shared workload approach is important in the context of eight people undertaking one role, given that the position of artistic director has a high burnout rate. Thus, in her view, having a distributed leadership model is healthier for all. Monfries added that the traditional notion of the "star-hero" artistic director was dead and that it was time to move toward more of a "shared collaborative community." She believed that a decentralized and distributed structure supported a more collaborative approach, which was "much more contemporary" than the traditional one of a "hero" leader.

Governance

Issues of governance and how the boards responded to the evolution of leadership within these organizations relate in part to the culture of the board itself. In the case of Rising there was some trepidation as to how decision-making by a triumvirate would play out. When discussing how the board felt about the three CEOs, Obarzanek responded:

> I don't think it was easy for them to agree to it. I guess there were previous examples of pairs going off the rails.... There was concern about "decision by committee" and how they would deal with a conflict between the two.

It is apparent in this response that the board members were mindful of how complex the model could become and their potential role in having to both manage a different process and then perhaps sort out any problems or disputes. There is no doubt that if this model did go "off the rails," the board recognized that its role in dealing with the situation would be crucial. Obarzanek added, though, that in agreeing to the shared leadership model, he felt that the organization was "getting a really big deal in terms of breadth of experience and knowledge." Hence he believed that the co-leadership model was a "win-win" for the board as they were getting double the amount of skill, expertise, and arts knowledge from two people than they would from a single artistic director.

For Next Wave, the evolution of the leadership model occurred during a time of board change. The leaders interviewed acknowledged that a few board members felt that the significant changes that occurred at Next Wave, in terms of both artistic direction and leadership, necessitated different governance skill sets, leading to several board members exiting their positions. Gill asserts that the new board members coming on "knew what they were stepping into" and believed strongly in the strategic direction. Next Wave has subsequently established a developmental governance approach, where the board chair has a twelve-month term before moving to the deputy chair role for another twelve-month period. In this way, the board is developing governance skills among its members while ensuring the organization has consistent strategic support with a focus on the skills that are needed. In this way Next Wave is extending its developmental philosophy beyond the operational and artistic leadership of the organization to the governance model as well.

Decision-Making

A final key element to a shared leadership model is the process of decision-making. The advantage of having one leader is that the decision-making process can be quite quick and efficient; decision-making by a group is likely to be much more time-consuming.

Further, the journey of arriving at a shared decision can produce conflict, or one individual can try to push their own agenda onto the others. Finding a way through this, so that everyone can be heard and contribute to a process, is critical. In a group it is also possible that some could side against others, or unofficial hierarchies could emerge.

For Rising, it is a question of how the three individuals interact, and Obarzanek observed that two can overrule one in the decision-making process. Mainland admitted that in the early days of the structure she felt that the artistic leaders had a majority and thus were more likely to be on the same side. However, she thought this has changed over time as the three of them worked together. Mainland described their process as "We talk it out and try to come to a consensus." Obarzanek added, "We discuss almost everything. I think, though it may not be economical, there is a filtering process that pushes ideas and makes the ideas better through that process." Fox suggested that when there is a difference of opinion, the process of discussing it endlessly can end up boring everyone, and as a result they lose interest in the idea they may be pushing. Obarzanek also commented that in relation to artistic ideas, "I think we have a tacit understanding that if one isn't convinced of the other's idea, then we won't go ahead with it." Mainland pointed out, though, that "it's not definitive or frequent that we disagree." They mentioned that there has been one major disagreement, but it was at the board level. One board member was opposed to what they describe as a "high reputational" idea that they, as a leadership team, supported. Given that the organizational leaders were all in agreement, in the end the board supported the idea, despite the opposition of one board member.

For Next Wave, decision-making is more complex, as all choices about participating artists and even the selection of artistic directors are made by the eight-person directorate with support from CEO/ED Lewis. While the eight ADs all bring different skills and experiences to the decision-making table, they also all have skills in critical listening and collaborative process management. Thus, they offer each other mutual respect while listening to everyone's point of view. While the group sometimes splits into smaller working groups to address particular decisions, they do not believe that there are any hierarchies evident in the group. Lewis and Gill also suggested that a clear structure, supported by well-documented and understood human resources policies, provides a framework for decision-making and any conflict management that is needed. Gill asserted:

> When you have a model that is about justice, friendship, and care it is still actually really important to understand how that accountability and care for each other plays out. People need to know what the parameters and expectations are. I think that's been a really, really important bit of work to do, to have a clear process for conflict management.

For those at Next Wave, having a framework built on organizational values, with a clear process and policy from the beginning, has meant that dysfunctional conflict has been avoided. Having so many people involved in decisions, however, can have an impact on the time frames needed to reach an agreement. Nevertheless, the leaders interviewed suggested that the structure and processes in existence make Next Wave both nimbler and more adaptable to external pressures, as they have more expertise to draw on and there is less focus on one individual.

Discussion

This research considers two case studies in which organizations have a shared leadership model. These are Rising, an arts festival that has three leaders, all with equal status within the organizational structure, and Next Wave, an arts organization that has evolved from a traditional festival model and has eight artistic directors and a CEO/ED. Rising's leaders have specific responsibilities. They all share the same job descriptions, are all called CEO, and all report directly to the board of governance. Next Wave's structure of artistic directorate, CEO, and board extends the notion of collaborative or distributed leadership even further, increasing the number of leaders and physically dispersing them across the country. These two cases represent an unusual approach to both leadership and structure, one contrary to that commonly found in the historical literature about leadership, which sees the role of leadership as usually assigned to one individual (Grint 2000; Yukl 2002).

An important aspect of both case studies is the backgrounds of the individuals involved and their commitment to collaboration and shared leadership responsibility. In the case of Rising there is clearly an acknowledged professional respect between the three individuals. This translates to a process in which they can rely on each other during difficult times, as well as hear each other's views. They also embrace a creative process that allows them to explore ideas with each other without feeling that they must defend them forever if it becomes clear that the others don't agree (Bilton 2007; Cray, Inglis, and Freeman 2007). In the case of Next Wave there is a recognition from all the individuals involved that they are committed to the process of collaboration, which involves listening and contributing to a culture centered around the values of justice, friendship, and care. This values-based leadership approach is significant. It changes the conversation from a task-oriented one to one that is more process-focused, with a conscious intent to explore ideas and embrace difference (Dalbourg and Lofgren 2016) while also recognizing the role artistic values play in the leadership and decision-making processes within arts organizations (Hewison 2004; Reynolds, Tonks, and MacNeill 2017).

The approach of both Rising and Next Wave, according to all the leaders interviewed, essentially involves trying to replicate the process of artistic creation, which focuses on taking supported risks, problem-solving, and recognizing and exploring many possible solutions until the right one is found (Adler 2006; Bilton 2007; Douglas and Fremantle 2009; Wester 2016). This may result in a decision-making process that is more time-consuming than, say, if one individual is making the decisions without any real consultation (Nisbett and Walmsley 2016). But in both organizations, there is a conscious rejection of a charismatic or "hero" model of leadership (Nisbett and Walmsley 2016).

The reality is that there are always others contributing to decisions (Ansell and Gash 2012). Thus, creating an organizational model that reflects this process is a significant step and may provide a pathway for others to consider. For it to work, though, requires all leaders to commit equally to both the process and the outcomes (Ansell and Gash 2012; Reynolds, Tonks, and MacNeill 2017). Further, the individuals involved in a shared leadership model must demonstrate a heightened awareness of creating positive relationships, dealing positively with conflict, and enabling open communication (Adler 2006; Lash 2012; Hewison and Holden 2011). The board of the organization must also be committed to the model and recognize its benefits to the organization in the longer term (Bilton 2007; Cray, Inglis, and Freeman 2007). This commitment by the board is evident in both cases discussed here, with the board of Next Wave going even further and changing itself to align with the new leadership approach.

While the impact of COVID-19 has been significant for festivals and the arts sector more broadly during the research period, this is not discussed here at length. But it has had an overhanging influence on both organizations. In the case of Rising it has meant that programming was dramatically affected, with the leaders needing to work closely and collaboratively to manage the outcomes. In the case of Next Wave it has allowed for a deeper discussion about the nature and future of the organization, contributing to significant artistic and organizational changes.

Conclusion

The leadership of arts organizations, and in this case that of arts festivals, is complex. It demands a multitude of skills and knowledge not easily found in one individual. Hence there is a practical rationale for the development of shared leadership models that provide a larger range of skills and knowledge. For a co-leadership model to work successfully, though, requires special qualities from all of those involved.

The co-leaders at Next Wave and Rising have demonstrated that they recognize the challenges implicit in their roles and are committed to working collaboratively for the benefit of both their practices and organizations. Whether these models have broader applicability is not clear, but in both cases cited in this chapter, there is a concerted attempt to align organizational leadership approaches with artistic processes and values. This approach to leadership is an interesting model to consider for future research.

Acknowledgments

The authors would like to thank Rising and its leadership team, Kath Mainland, Hannah Fox, and Gideon Obarzanek, and Next Wave and its leadership representatives, Jamie Lewis, Amrit Gill, Kristi Monfries, and Nathan Stoneham, for agreeing to take part in this research and being so generous with their time, ideas, and reflections about their work.

References

4A Centre for Contemporary Asian Art. n.d. "Amrit Gill." 4A Centre for Contemporary Asian Art, Sydney. https://4a.com.au/creatives/amrit-gill. Accessed September 15, 2022.

Adler, Nancy. 2006. "The Arts and Leadership: Now That We Can Do Anything, What Will We Do?" *Academy of Management and Learning Education* 5, no. 4: 486–499.

Ansell, Chris, and Alison Gash. 2012. "Stewards, Mediators, and Catalysts: Toward a Model of Collaborative Leadership." *The Innovation Journal: The Public Sector Innovation Journal* 17, no. 1: article 7.

Beirne, Martin. 2012. "Creative Tension? Negotiating the Space Between the Arts and Management." *Journal of Arts and Communities* 4, no. 3: 149–160.

Bilton, Chris. 2007. *Management and Creativity: From Creative Industries to Creative Management*. Malden, MA: Blackwell Publishing.

Byrnes, William J. 2009. *Management and the Arts*. Woburn, MA: Focal Press.

Caust, Josephine. 2004. "A Festival in Disarray." *Journal of Arts Management, Law and Society* 34, no. 2: 103–117.

Caust, Josephine. 2010. "Does the Art End When the Management Begins? The Challenges of Making 'Art' for Both Artists and Arts Managers." *Asia Pacific Journal of Arts and Cultural Management* 7, no. 2: 570–584.

Cray, David, Loretta Inglis, and Susan Freeman. 2007. "Managing the Arts: Leadership and Decision Making under Dual Rationalities." *Journal of Arts Management, Law and Society* 36, no. 4: 295–313.

Creese, Elizabeth. 1997. "The Tension Between Artistic Purpose and Management Functions in the Performing Arts." *Aesthetex* 7, no. 1: 57–69.

Dalbourg, Karin, and Mikael Lofgren. 2016. "Cultural Leadership in 3 D." In *The Fika Project: Perspectives on Cultural Leadership*, edited by Karin Dalbourg and Mikael Lofgren, 9–28. Göteborg: Nätverkstan Kultur.

Doos, Marianne, and Lena Wilhelmson. 2021. "Fifty-Five Years of Managerial Shared Leadership Research: A Review of an Empirical Field." *Leadership* 17, no. 6: 715–746.

Douglas, Anne, and Chris Fremantle. 2009. "The Artist as Leader: Research Report." On the Edge Research, Gray's School of Art, and the Robert Gordon University with Cultural Enterprise Office Performing Arts Labs Scottish Leadership Foundation, Aberdeen.

Francis, Hannah. 2019. "Melbourne's Epic New Winter Arts Festival Announces Artistic Directors." *The Age*, July 3, 2019.

Gibb, Susan. 2012. "Next Wave Festival 2012: The Space Between Us Wants to Sing." *Runway* no. 45: 68–71.

Goleman, Daniel. 2000. "Leadership That Gets Results." *Harvard Business Review* 78, no. 2: 78–90.

Grint, Keith. 2000. *The Art of Leadership*. Oxford: Oxford University Press.

Gronn, Peter. 2002. "Distributed Leadership as a Unit of Analysis." *Leadership Quarterly* 13, no. 4: 423–451.

Gronn, Peter. 2008. "The Future of Distributed Leadership." *Journal of Educational Administration* 46: 141–158.

Hewison, Robert. 2004. "The Crisis of Cultural Leadership in Britain." *International Journal of Cultural Policy* 10, no. 2: 157–166.

Hewison, Robert, and John Holden. 2002. "The Task Force Final Report," Clore Leadership Programme, London. https://www.cloreleadership.org/sites/cloreleadership.org/files/task_force_final_report_full.pdf.

Hewison, Robert, and John Holden. 2011. *The Cultural Leadership Handbook: How to Run a Creative Organisation*. Farnham, UK: Gower.

Hoyle, Sue, and Robbie Swale. 2016. "Changing Leaders in Changing Times." *Arts Professional* no. 296. http://www.artsprofessional.co.uk/magazine/296/feature/changing-leaders-changing-time.

Lapierre, Laurent. 2001. "Leadership and Arts Management." *International Journal of Arts Management* 3, no. 3: 4–12.

Lash, Rick. 2012. "The Collaboration Imperative." *Ivey Business Journal: Improving the Practice of Management*, January/February 2012. https://iveybusinessjournal.com/publication/the-collaboration-imperative/.

Next Wave. n.d. a. "Artistic Directorate." Next Wave. Accessed September 15, 2022. https://nextwave.org.au/about/who-we-are/artistic-directorate.

Next Wave. n.d. b. "Next Wave History." Next Wave. Accessed September 7, 2022. https://nextwave.org.au/about/about-next-wave/history.

Next Wave. n.d. c. "Next Wave Vision, Purpose and Values." Next Wave. Accessed September 8, 2022. https://nextwave.org.au/about/about-next-wave/vision-purpose-and-values.

Nisbett, Melissa, and Ben Walmsley. 2016 "The Romanticization of Charismatic Leadership in the Arts." *Journal of Arts Management, Law, and Society* 46: 2–12.

Pick, John, and Malcolm Anderton. 1996. *Arts Administration*. London: Sporn.

Reid, Wendy. 2013. "Dual Executive Leadership in the Arts—Remi Brousseau, Pierre Rousseau and Le Théâtre Denise-Pelletier." In *Arts Leadership—International Case Studies*, edited by Josephine Caust, 96–111. Melbourne: Tilde University Press.

Reynolds, Sarah, Ann Tonks, and Kate MacNeill. 2017. "Collaborative Leadership in the Arts as a Unique Form of Dual Leadership." *Journal of Arts Management, Law and Society* 47, no. 2: 89–104.

Rising Festival. 2022. "Rising: Melbourne." https://rising.melbourne/.

ToMelbourne. n.d. "White Night." ToMelbourne.com.au. Accessed September 15, 2022. https://tomelbourne.com.au/white-night/.

Turbide, Johanne, and Claude Laurin. 2009. "Performance Measurement in the Arts Sector: The Case of the Performing Arts." *International Journal of Arts Management* 11, no. 2: 56–70.

Parliament of Victoria. 1989. *Hansard*, Legislative Council, September 20, 1989. https://www.parliament.vic.gov.au/images/stories/historical_hansard/VicHansardLC_19890920_19890920.pdf.

Wester, Nina. 2016. "I'm a Natural Leader, It's as Simple as That . . ." In *The Fika Project: Narratives by Cultural Change Makers*, edited by Karin Dalborg and Mikael Löfgren, 22–32. Göteborg: Nätverkstan Kultur.

Yin, Robert. 2014. *Case Study Research Design and Methods*. Thousand Oaks, CA: Sage.

Yukl, Gary E. 2002. *Leadership in Organizations*. 5th ed. Upper Saddle River, NJ: Prentice Hall.

CHAPTER 16

THE DEATH OF WHITE SUPREMACY CULTURE IN THE US CREATIVE SECTOR AND IMPLICATIONS FOR ARTS MANAGEMENT

A Critical Race Theory View

QUANICE FLOYD AND ANTONIO C. CUYLER

INTRODUCTION

AMID the COVID-19 pandemic, the summer of 2020 became a pivotal moment for the United States. A Minneapolis police officer put his knee on the neck of George Floyd for over eight minutes, killing him and igniting a global movement for racial justice (Bolden 2020). George Floyd's tragic murder at the hands of a police officer crystallized the cost of racism. A teenager captured his murder on video for the world to watch. Millions grieved worldwide as they finally recognized that these acts of violence were a threat not just to people of the global majority (Black, Indigenous, and People of Color) but to people of conscience everywhere. This brutal act reminded us that the United States still struggles to live up to its founding ideals of equality, freedom, and justice for all.

This devastating event illuminated what Rev. Dr. Martin Luther King Jr. so strongly called "the two Americas." Police are at the center of the destruction of Black bodies at the hands of state-sanctioned actors. These violent images and stories of maimed bodies reinforced for many people of the global majority the daily trauma they go through because they exist in a white-dominated power structure, which seeks to subvert their voice and existence. For older generations of the global majority, it harkened back to a time when law enforcement and government officials could commit acts of violence, mainly with impunity, against people of the global majority, often for exercising political and economic power.

Frustrated with incremental progress, social justice activists organized to support more equitable policies and systems. People of the global majority and their allies flocked to the streets around the United States to protest the inequities that people of the global majority experience daily. Protests disrupted entire industries, similar to how COVID-19 disrupted the nation's comfort, safety, and security. Protests sparked an awakening in every major US city. Despite the gains of the civil rights movement, Black and Brown lives still do not hold the same value as others, and their artistic, economic, educational, and social opportunities for advancement remain limited by current structures and systems. As the United States reckons with the friction between the old and the new, the creative sector also has to consider similar impacts.

As a microcosm of the United States, the creative sector has realized that it is at a crossroads. The sector can no longer accept that millions of dollars in local, state, and federal funding flow to predominantly white-serving organizations while the advancement of organizations by and for people of the global majority is being undermined. In 2017, the Helicon Collaborative published *Not Just Money: Equity Issues in Cultural Philanthropy*, which identified the racial disparities in arts funding. The research found that only 4 percent of foundation arts financing goes to organizations whose main aim is to help communities of the global majority, even though people of this demographic make up 37 percent of the US population. It also said that 25 percent of all arts charities serve communities of color, while only 4 percent of all foundation donations go to these groups.

People of the global majority and their allies demanded that the industry change. From philanthropy to hiring practices to artistic programming, institutions can no longer maintain the status quo. The previous ways of practicing community outreach would not cut it. Those working in the creative sector became acutely aware of the urgency of our times as racial uprisings, COVID-19, and other pressing issues affecting the global majority became more difficult to ignore. This urgency resulted in many cultural institutions publishing statements supporting the Black Lives Matter movement. The ideals of this movement provided a framework for cultural organizations to implement and execute. Some organizations used blanket statements, while others approached writing these statements with intention and action. This issue brought up discussions of how organizations in the creative sector perpetuate white supremacy and have caused harm to people of the global majority. The creative sector must use a critical lens when approaching how they work to help repair the damage that has been done and dismantle the remaining barriers people of the global majority face within the sector.

This chapter examines the arts management field through the lens of critical race theory (CRT). As the field shifts toward a more liberatory, anti-racist culture, there has been little exploration of how CRT and its implications manifest within the field. The tenets of CRT outlined in this chapter are designed to provide guidance to readers on why and how cultural organizations should remain aware of issues of racial inequity, racism, and white supremacy culture within their own institutions.

This chapter will utilize case vignettes to investigate the features of white supremacist culture and critical race theory, explore how CRT contributes to the demise of white supremacy culture in the US creative industry, and discuss the implications for the future of arts management.

Critical Race Theory

Critical race theory is a legal theory that provides a framework for examining how people embed racism and racialized ideologies into government, law, and society. CRT aims to draw attention to how racial biases, prejudices, and stereotypes influence laws, policies, practices, and institutions. The assumption of white superiority has served as the foundation for the dominant ideology and power structures for generations. As early as the 1960s, law and government officials began to concentrate their efforts on eliminating discrimination by implementing civil rights and anti-discrimination legislation. Even though this movement permeated all aspects of the law, the result was a concentration on proving the existence of discrimination. Developed in the late 1970s by Derrick Bell and Kimberlé Crenshaw, CRT has become commonly known but broadly misunderstood due to a conservative backlash against it. CRT primarily sought to dispel the notion that US citizens lived in a colorblind society in which there was no correlation between race and socioeconomic status.

CRT does not imply that white people living in the United States today are necessarily responsible for all racist atrocities throughout history. Instead, white people have a moral obligation to fight the racism of the past and confront racism and racial injustice in the present. It asserts that white people have a distinct advantage over people of the global majority since they live markedly different lives imbued with unearned power and privilege. People of the global majority and white people cannot have non-racialized experiences. CRT can enhance awareness of one's prejudices in the workplace, in one's social connections, and in conversations.

Principles of Critical Race Theory

The principles of CRT offer a framework that those in the creative sector can adopt in order to begin to view the world with a more informed lens regarding the realities of race and racism in US society. Delgado and Stefancic (2017) described the principles of CRT as the following:

> First, racism is ordinary, not aberrational. . . . Second, most would agree that our system of white-over-color ascendancy serves important purposes, both psychic and material, for the dominant group. The first feature, ordinariness, means that

racism is difficult to address or cure because it is not acknowledged. Color-blind, or "formal," conceptions of equality, [are] expressed in rules that insist only on treatment that is the same across the board.... A third theme of critical race theory, the "social construction" thesis, holds that race and races are products of social thought and relations.... Another, somewhat more recent, development concerns differential racialization and its many consequences. At one period, for example, society may have had little use for blacks but much need for Mexican or Japanese agricultural workers.... Closely related to differential racialization—the idea that each race has its own origins and ever-evolving history—is the notion of intersectionality and antiessentialism.... A final element concerns the notion of a unique voice of color. Coexisting in somewhat uneasy tension with antiessentialism, the voice-of-color thesis holds that because of their different histories and experiences with oppression, black, Indigenous, Asian, and Latino/a writers and thinkers may be able to communicate to their white counterparts matters that whites are unlikely to know.
(Delgado and Stefancic 2017, 8–11)

Although these principles were initially created as a framework for law studies and law students, they have integrated themselves into the majority of US society and have implications for the creative sector. If applied to arts management, these principles can provide a lens for arts managers to identify the characteristics of white supremacist culture, making a difference in how we can work toward dismantling white supremacy within the sector.

The Characteristics of white Supremacy Culture

In a recent interview with Shumita Basu (Basu 2021), Jelani Cobb, a historian who was recently appointed dean of the Columbia Journalism School, discussed Bell, one of CRT's founders. Cobb argued that Bell would have predicted today's conservative backlash to honest discussions about race and racial justice. He also described an email in which Bell said that "the election of a Black president would, similar to the *Brown* v. *Board of Education* decision and the 1964 Civil Rights Act, become a moment which promised much, but delivered nothing, except for potentially hastening the premature demise of US democracy." Bell's words were prophetic. The retrenchment and reactionary anti-Obama movement have become so anti-democratic, powerful, and threatening (Basu 2021) that the Electoral College elected the country's first "white" president. While previous white presidents used the passive power of whiteness to propel their political careers, the forty-fifth president explicitly used the ideology of white supremacy to foment his (Coates 2021). But what does this have to do with white supremacy culture?

In 2001, Okun and Jones first published the characteristics of white supremacy culture. As Box 16.1 shows, Okun (2021) identified ten specific behaviors that constitute the

> **Box 16.1 Characteristics of white Supremacy Culture**
>
> 1. Fear
> 2. Perfectionism, one right way, paternalism, and objectivity
> 3. Qualified
> 4. Either/or and the binary
> 5. Progress is bigger/more and quantity over quality
> 6. Worship of the written word
> 7. Individualism and "I'm the only one"
> 8. Defensiveness and denial
> 9. Right to comfort, fear of open conflict, and power hoarding
> 10. Urgency

characteristics of white supremacy culture: fear; perfectionism, "one right way," paternalism, and objectivity; qualified; either/or and the binary; progress is bigger/more and quantity over quality; worship of the written word; individualism and "I'm the only one"; defensiveness and denial; right to comfort, fear of open conflict, and power hoarding; and urgency. Okun (1999) explained that white supremacy targets and violates people of the global majority and their communities with the intent to destroy them directly. It also targets and violates white people with a persistent invitation to collude that will inevitably destroy their humanity. These insights are vital to acknowledging the truth that the social constructions of race, white supremacy culture, whiteness, and the resultant racism harm all humans, including white people. Still, white supremacist culture remains inextricably linked to all the other forms of oppression (Okun 1999). We agree with Okun (2021) that forms of oppression are interconnected, intersecting, and stirred together in a toxic brew that reflects humans' devastation of the air, water, land, and living beings in the name of profit and power. For example, Koch et al. (2019) found that the genocide of people indigenous to Central, North, and South America incited climate change in the 1500s.

When describing fear as a characteristic of white supremacy culture, Okun (2021) argued that "white supremacy culture's number one strategy is to make us afraid." Furthermore, she argued that white supremacy, white supremacy culture, and racism use fear to divide and conquer, always in the service of profit and power for a few at the expense of the many. To address fear, Okun suggested naming it when it arises, whether in a group or individually. She stated, "We must collectively and individually develop skills to meet our fear, sit with our fear, name our fear, and work to avoid letting fear drive our beliefs, actions, and decisions" (Okun 2021, 7). The identification of fear as the first characteristic of white supremacist culture raises a question: is fear the curse of unearned power and privilege? We ask this because across the US creative sector, we have observed people privileged by specific identities fight and resist racial access, diversity, equity, and inclusion (ADEI) out of fear of losing their power and privilege.

Okun (2021) defined perfectionism as the conditioned belief and attitude that humans can exist as perfect based on a standard or set of rules that they did not create but believe will prove their value. Perfectionism is the conditioned belief that humans can determine whether others are showing up as perfect and demand or expect that they do so. One way this occurs is through the belief that there is one right way to do things; presumably, once people are introduced to the right way, they will see the light and adopt it. At the same time, paternalism is the system in which those holding power control decision-making and define standards, perfection, and "one right way." Objectivity is the belief that humans can exist as objective or ' "neutral" beings. As the antidote to these characteristics (perfectionism, "one right way," paternalism, and objectivity), Okun (2021) suggested that individuals and organizations develop a culture of appreciation, take time to make sure that everyone's work and efforts are appreciated, and realize that everybody has a worldview. A globalized view affects the way people understand the world.

When discussing qualifications, Okun (2021) maintained that middle- and owning-class white people who are also formally educated primarily internalize this characteristic. She argued that the culture teaches them that they are qualified and duty-bound to fix the world, save it, and set it straight. She also contends that this characteristic remains closely aligned with the dominant Christian ideology that teaches a Christian duty to convert the "heathen," "impure," and "savage" to "respectable" humans in white people's eyes. This characteristic is particularly violent in its determination to ignore and/or erase the culture, wisdom, genius, and joy of people and communities who need "saving" while seizing their architecture, food, labor, land, music, and other material goods to commodify for profit. She also stressed that while the intention to fix, save, and set straight is often overt, the deviousness of this characteristic is how intensely white middle- and owning-class educated people can internalize the notion and assume their inherent qualifications to "improve" whatever is in front of them that is "broken" without acknowledging or seeing their role in breaking it in the first place (Okun 2021).

The either/or and the binary explore the cultural assumption that humans can and should reduce the complexity of life and the nuances of their relationships with each other and all living things into either/or, yes or no, right or wrong in ways that reinforce toxic power (Okun 2021). As an example, she highlighted positioning or presenting options or issues as either/or—good/bad, right/wrong, with us/against us—and trying to simplify complex things (for example, believing that poverty is simply the result of a lack of education). This is closely linked to perfectionism because binary thinking makes it difficult to learn from mistakes or accommodate conflict. It becomes a strategy used to pit oppressions against each other rather than to recognize how racism and classism intersect and the ways in which both intersect with heterosexism, ageism, and other forms of oppression (Okun 2021).

We see the characteristic of progress as bigger/more and quantity over quality as perpetuating the harmful hustle culture that discourages and undermines self-care.

Okun (2021) describes this characteristic as the cultural assumption that the goal is always to do/get more and do/get bigger. She argued that this leads to an emphasis on what humans can "objectively" measure and how well they are doing at doing/getting more, which is seen as more valuable than the quality of one's relationships to all living beings (Okun 2021). Progress remains narrowly defined as something as superficial as "wealth-building" without considering the emotional and social impacts such pursuits have on humans. Because quantity over quality values counting and producing quantitatively measurable goals, it fosters a discomfort with emotions and feelings and reinforces perfectionism, "one right way," either/or thinking, and urgency thinking (Okun 2021).

Okun (2021) argued that worship of the written word explores the cultural habit of honoring only what is written and, furthermore, only what is written to a narrow standard, even when what is written is full of misinformation and lies. Worship of the written word includes erasure of the wide range of ways humans communicate with each other and all other living things. She clarified that worship of the written word, in her view, is not the same as the ability to write well. For her, worshiping the written word is a white supremacy culture value because it has to do with how white supremacy culture requires documentation of activities, ideas, et cetera to appear in written form, on its terms, in order to preserve power. Examples of how worship of the written word shows up include: if it's not in a memo, it doesn't exist; if it's not grammatically "correct," it has no value; if it's not properly cited according to academic rules that many people don't know or have access to, it's not legitimate. In a context where systemic racism privileges the writing and wisdom of white people, academic standards require "original" work even though humans' knowledge and knowing almost always build on the knowledge and knowing of others, collectively and generationally informed (Okun 2021).

The cultural assumption that individualism is humankind's cultural story and that humans make it on their own (or should), without help, while pulling themselves up by their bootstraps, informs the characteristics of individualism and "I'm the only one." Okun (2021) expressed that US society's cultural attachment to individualism leads to a toxic denial of humans' essential interdependence and the reality that all humans are in this together, like it or not. Three important examples of this characteristic include white people's failure to acknowledge any of the ways dominant identities (able-bodiedness, age, class, education, gender, religion, sexuality) inform belonging to a dominant group that shapes cultural norms and behavior. For people of the global majority, individualism forces the classic double bind in which they are accused of not being "team players," suffering punishment or repercussions for acting as an individual if and when doing so "threatens" the team. Individualism and "I'm the only one" reinforce "one right way" thinking.

Defensiveness and denial reflect the US cultural disease around truth-telling, mainly when speaking truth to power (Okun 2021). White supremacy culture encourages a habit of denying and defending any speaking to or about it. Some examples of defensiveness can be seen in how organizational structures are set up. Much energy is spent trying to prevent abuse and protect power rather than facilitating the capacities of each person or clarifying who has power and how they are expected to use it. People in the organization, particularly those with power, spend a lot of energy trying to make sure that their feelings do not get hurt, forcing others to work around their defensiveness rather than address it head-on. At its worst, they have convinced others to do this work for them. Instead of examining how they might have engaged in racism, white people spend energy defending against charges of racism. And white people targeted by other forms of oppression express resentment because they experience the naming of racism as erasing their experience, which reinforces either/or binary thinking and an oppressive culture where people are afraid to speak their truth. Two critical examples of denial highlighted here include a pattern that often has a white person at a different level of power denying what a person of the global majority or a whole community has said about their experience of racism and claiming the right to define what is and what is not racism.

Right to comfort, fear of open conflict, and power hoarding focus on the cultural assumption that the ones with formal or informal power have a right to comfort, which means they cannot tolerate conflict, particularly open conflict. This assumption supports the tendency to blame the person or group for causing discomfort or conflict rather than address the named issues (Okun 2021). The conservative backlash against protests for racial justice remains an observable phenomenon that supports Okun's assertion. While conservatives have taken many measures to undermine progress on addressing racial justice, including passing legislation to restrict the teaching of CRT in schools and banning books addressing almost any form of oppression (Cheng 2021). One should take note that conservatives have not offered any solutions to the enduring racism in the United States.

Some examples of these characteristics in practice include the belief that those with power have a right to emotional and psychological comfort (another aspect of valuing "logic" over emotion); white people (or those with dominant identities) equating individual acts of unfairness with systemic racism (or other forms of oppression); people in power being scared of expressed conflict and trying to ignore it or run from it; equating the raising of difficult issues with being impolite, rude, or out of line; those in power punishing people either overtly or subtly for speaking out about their truth and/or experience; seeing power as limited, with only so much of it available to go around; and those with power not seeing themselves as hoarding power or as feeling threatened.

Okun (2021) described the final characteristic, urgency, as reflecting the cultural habit of applying a sense of urgency to everyday life in ways that perpetuate power imbalances while disconnecting people from their need to breathe, pause, and reflect. Ironically, this imposed sense of urgency erodes the urgency of tackling racial injustice. A sense of urgency makes it challenging to take time to act inclusively, encourage democratic and/or thoughtful decision-making, think and act long-term, and/or to consider the consequences of the action taken, which frequently results in sacrificing potential allies for quick or apparent results. Examples include sacrificing the interests of people of the global majority and communities to win victories for white people; reinforcing existing power hierarchies that use the sense of urgency to control decision-making in the name of expediency; privileging those who process information quickly (or think they do); and sacrificing and erasing the potential of other modes of knowing and wisdom that require more time (embodied, intuitive, spiritual).

Case Vignettes Across the Creative Sector

In response to the ten characteristics of white supremacist culture, Okun (2021) provided antidotes. However, because white Americans have historically and socially constructed race, structured it, and systematically built it into all aspects of US society, the characteristics of white supremacy culture remain a threat to actualizing racial ADEI for people of the global majority within the creative sector. Now that we have provided a review of CRT and the characteristics of white supremacy culture, we examine how they show up through short case vignettes.

Indianapolis Museum of Art at Newfields

Approximately 22 percent of Indianapolis's population identifies as people of the global majority. However, in January 2021 the Indianapolis Museum of Art at Newfields apologized for a job posting that stated it was seeking a director who would both work to attract a more diverse audience and maintain its "traditional, core, white art audience" (Bahr 2021). The museum's director and chief executive said in an interview "that the decision to use 'white' had been intentional and explained that it had been intended to indicate that the museum would not abandon its existing audience as part of its efforts toward greater diversity, equity, and inclusion" (Bahr 2021). But why did the museum need to signify that its ADEI initiatives would not abandon its existing white audience? Why did the museum not view it equally as essential to convey to people of the global majority that it seeks to build authentic relationships with them, too?

The revised version of the job posting turned out no better, using the phrase "traditional core art audience" (Bahr 2021). The museum compromised its community relevance by disenfranchising Indianapolis residents of the global majority. Malina Simone Jeffers and Alan Bacon, who were guest curators for the museum's show "DRIP: Indy's #BlackLivesMatter Street Mural," decided that they could not remain as guest curators until Newfields included in the exhibition an apology to all artists involved; provided an opportunity for the eighteen visual artists to show their other, personal works with appropriate compensation; and instituted an intentional strategy to display more works from more Black artists in perpetuity. As CRT has encouraged us to see, this incident is not an aberration, as former employees had previously criticized the museum for its "discriminatory" and "toxic" culture (Bahr 2021). Rather, this incident is a primary example of either/or thinking within white supremacy culture. The Indianapolis Museum of Art at Newfields used comfort to ensure that their audiences stayed the same, thus insisting on a right to comfort for those in power.

Heather Mac Donald and the Manhattan Institute

Conservative "cultural critic" Mac Donald (2021) posited that "classical music is under racial attack. Orchestras and opera companies are said to discriminate against black musicians and composers. The canonical repertoire—the product of a centuries-long tradition of musical expression—is allegedly a function of white supremacy." Curiously, she also argued that not one leader in the field had defended Western art music from these charges. We cannot help but wonder whether no leader supported the charge because it is an easily observable fact that classical music has historically, continuously, and proactively excluded most Black Americans. For example, it took the Metropolitan Opera almost 140 years to premiere *Fire Shut Up in My Bones*, its first opera by a Black composer. It makes sense that anti-Black racism is the culprit for such an outcome (Cuyler 2021). Woolfe (2021) documented some of the responses to Black composers' submissions of operas for the Met's consideration. For example, in response to William Grant Still's 1942 submission of the opera *Troubled Island*, the submission ledger commented, "It would be a mere waste of time to go into details about this opera, which is an immature product of two dilettantes."

Another fascinating way some white people in the creative sector express their resistance to racial ADEI is by pivoting to costs, especially given the voluminous grievances Black professionals across the classical music industry expressed after George Floyd's killing in 2020. Mac Donald (2021) argued, "Even in the best of financial circumstances, the racial demands would have been startling in their scope. But at a time when every classical music budget has been blown apart by the coronavirus lockdowns, such ambition requires considerable confidence in one's bargaining power. The bet paid off. Orchestras and opera companies rushed to adopt racial hiring benchmarks and to take on costly new diversity bureaucracy." She made this point because while the Met had to make difficult salary decisions for musicians and staff, it hired its first chief diversity officer (Mac Donald 2021). However, Mac Donald remained remiss by not pointing out that a cultural organization with major contributed and earned income gaps in its budget cannot afford to ignore racial ADEI when it has historically and continuously excluded people of the global majority, especially given the funding system for culture in the United States (Cuyler 2023).

Further demonstrating her protest against racial ADEI and justice in classical music, Mac Donald (2021) used the "token Black" argument to suggest that racism does not exist in classical music. She stated, "Today, black musicians are welcomed with open arms. One musician with a major orchestra marvels at the oppositional stance taken by some of his fellows, such as clarinetist Anthony McGill and his brother, flutist Demarre McGill. 'The business has handed these guys opportunity after opportunity.

To turn around and say: "It's a racist industry!" I want to shake them. They should be ambassadors!'" (Mac Donald 2021).

She also pivoted to a lack of music education as a counterargument, stating, "From 1962 to 1989, the percentage of high schools with orchestras fell from 67 percent to 17 percent, according to *Billboard*. Seventy-seven percent of schools polled in a University of Illinois study dropped piano instruction; 40 percent dropped string instruction. If a child's home is not exposing him to classical music, he is likely not being exposed at all" (Mac Donald 2021). Yet her analysis does not interrogate how US cities fund schools and how those policies and practices impact access to music education for Black students. Nor does she include a discussion of the racial wealth gap (Vox Media Studios 2018), which acknowledges the intersections between class and race and their compounding impacts on the lives of Black people. These omissions of arguments make us question the intellectual honesty of conservative critics such as Mac Donald (2021) and ask whether they are truly prepared to grapple with the realities and enduring impacts of racism on people of the global majority. She also misses the point that a diverse canon constructed on the building blocks of racial ADEI benefits humanity—white people are not the only people who have made meaningful contributions to classical music.

Cases in Dance, Theater, and Arts Journalism

Although space does not permit us to examine cases across all art forms, we see the characteristics of white supremacy culture in dance and theater, too. Although people of the global majority have expressed the harm done by blackface, brownface, and yellowface, some dance companies have struggled to imagine an anti-racist *Nutcracker*, preferring "tradition" over making a more ethical artistic choice. In theater, why does Shakespeare remain the pinnacle of "artistic excellence"? In all art forms, we see the opportunity to imagine a more capacious canon. How might the creative sector decolonize "artistic excellence" so that it is culturally relevant and culturally responsive enough to include all of humankind's contributions to culture?

Arts journalism, too, offers instruction on resistance to ADEI and the characteristics of white supremacy culture in the creative sector. Reynolds (2021) argued that touting all-female composers' programs may do a disservice to the field, limiting audience interest in only old Beethovenian warhorses. He further argued that "the intention is good but placing such works in their own category instead of integrating them into the canon seems slightly misguided. Let's emphasize that these works are wonderful on their own merits instead of emphasizing that they're by composers from historically underrepresented backgrounds" (Reynolds 2021). Meritocracy, in this case, becomes an evaluative mechanism defined by a representative of the dominant gender to evaluate the work of artists of the historically and continuously marginalized gender without any thought to how gender likely informs the creative products that artists create. Why should we not emphasize that composers with historically and continuously marginalized and oppressed identities also contribute to the canon?

These cases highlight how the characteristics of white supremacy culture appear like leitmotifs from a Wagnerian opera throughout the creative sector. White resistance to racial ADEI will rely on these characteristics to maintain white supremacy culture in the creative sector. Indeed, even in racially diverse environments in the creative sector, where people of the global majority achieve a degree of institutional power, whiteness will remain a dominant ingredient of the environment's culture and a determinant of prevailing norms for communication and behavior (Ward 2008). However, people of the global majority and white people can push back against white supremacy culture by adopting anti-racism as a mental model to eradicate racism and heal its enduring impacts on us all. We define anti-racism as abhorring and actively seeking to dismantle and eradicate racist attitudes, behaviors, policies, practices, and the lie of white supremacy in the creative sector (Cuyler 2022).

Implications and Considerations for the US Creative Sector

There are several ramifications to consider when thinking about how white supremacy culture shows up in the US creative sector. The creative sector, which predominantly sits within the nonprofit industrial complex (NPIC), a structure based on capital versus its mission, is a nuanced and complex system warranting racial justice and the dismantling of white supremacy culture. In nonprofits, people redistribute lifesaving resources, share and develop leadership skills, and build radical consciousness and community (Munshi and Willse 2007). When it comes to nonprofits and racial justice work, Rodriguez (2007) states that nonprofit structures are a part of the perpetuation of fears but talks about ways people could work together to abolish systems of white supremacy within the structure:

> The NPIC's well-funded litany of "social justice" agendas, platforms, mission statements, and campaigns offer a veritable smorgasbord of political guarantees that feeds on our cynicism and encourages a misled political faith that stridently bypasses the fundamental relations of dominance that structure our everyday existence in the United States: perhaps it is time that we formulate critical strategies that fully comprehend the NPIC *as the institutionalization of a relation of dominance* and attempt to disrupt and transform the fundamental structures and principals *of a white supremacist US civil society*, as well as the US racist state.
>
> (Rodriguez 2007, 39)

In the years since Rodriguez wrote, white supremacy has still been the law of the land regarding cultural institutions' community engagement, development, marketing, programming, staffing, and so on. According to Gray (2019), Okun and Jones (2001) believed that the standardization of professionalism could serve as a gatekeeping tactic to preserve white supremacy culture:

> The standards of professionalism ... are heavily defined by white supremacy culture—or the systemic, institutionalized centering of whiteness. In the workplace, white supremacy culture explicitly and implicitly privileges whiteness and discriminates against non-Western and non-white professionalism standards related to dress code, speech, work style, and timeliness.
>
> (Gray 2019)

Definitions of professionalism are byproducts of whiteness and white supremacy culture, and they have impactful consequences that often harm people from the global majority. It perpetuates the hierarchy that Western culture and standards are superior to non-Western, non-white culture. This assumption remained evident in the case studies presented earlier in this chapter. Efforts to promote racial justice and combat white normalization and privilege can have far-reaching consequences for organizational development and the sector's progress. This is where we ponder the role of arts management educators in choosing to perpetuate epistemic violence by teaching the nonprofit industrial complex without an interrogation of the ways in which it and its practices harm humans.

In 2018, approximately 82 percent of arts management educators in the United States identified as white. Only 5 percent identified as Black, 3 percent as Asian, and 3 percent as multiracial; none identified as Indigenous (Essig 2018). Unfortunately, more recent data is unavailable because the semi-professional associations that should collect this data annually have not deemed it necessary. However, if 82 percent of arts management educators identify as white, we can hypothesize that at least 77 percent of currently enrolled arts management students identify as white. In addition, arts management alums are primarily identified as female, able-bodied, heterosexual, and millennials (Cuyler, Durrer, and Nisbett 2020). The study aimed to gain a better understanding of how arts alumni valued their degrees but also sought to uncover the demographic profile of arts management graduates internationally.

One argument goes that diversity, equity, and inclusion (DEI) in higher education benefits students. But how? And which students benefit the most from DEI, and at whose expense? Still, most arts management educators (86 percent) teach about diversity issues in their courses, primarily through discussion (91 percent), and almost all (99 percent) expressed that arts management students should receive education on diversity issues in the arts (Cuyler 2017). Furthermore, arts management educators were more likely to report teaching about diversity issues in their courses if they identified as faculty of the global majority, female, or LGBTQ+ (Cuyler 2017). For the 13 percent of educators who expressed that students should receive education on diversity issues but who do not engage in teaching this content themselves, as well as those in the creative sector looking for a way to commit to racial ADEI in the creative sector (or deepen their existing

> **Box 16.2 The Arts Manager's Social Responsibility**
>
> 1. Actively participate in the liberation of the culturally disenfranchised.
> 2. Support and pursue opportunities for decentralized cultural policy.
> 3. Encourage broad-based decision-making and a pluralistic distribution mechanism in financing cultural activities.
> 4. Dedicate a significant period of the workweek to studying the system in order to sharpen understanding of the sociopolitical environment.
> 5. Publicly urge the creation and periodic update of a comprehensive and community cultural assessment.
> 6. Support activism in communities where past exclusionary social patterns have established cultural inequities.
> 7. Maintain an awareness of monopolies in the nonprofit sector while seeking to develop compensatory responses to barriers to public entry.

commitment), we recommend Keller's "The Arts Manager's Social Responsibility" (1989) as a critical start. Ahead of his time, Keller sought to compel arts managers to disrupt the systems of oppression and white supremacy culture within the creative sector. He explained that "we must examine the cultural implications of presiding over institutions whose functions are often restrictive and whose extra-aesthetic and legacies remain undemocratic, exclusionary, and hierarchical in outlook, practice, and community impact" (Keller 1989, 52–53). Keller believed that arts managers have a social responsibility to move the entire sector forward.Box 16.2 highlights seven social responsibilities of arts managers.

Dismantling white supremacy culture in the US creative sector requires examination of all creative practices, including arts management, and imbuing them with anti-capitalism, anti-oppression, anti-racism, and liberation. Though specific to arts managers, Keller's (1989) responsibilities hold implications for all in the creative sector committed to advancing humanity's creative output. With more anti-capitalist, anti-oppressive, anti-racist, and liberatory practices, the creative sector can seismically shift and transform the sector to address creative deficits humanity has long suffered due to all forms of oppression. In closing, we cannot stress enough that the entire US creative sector must understand that the critical lens through which we have viewed the sector and its practices does not only affect people of the global majority; it affects white people as well (Okun 2021). As the Rev. Dr. Martin Luther King Jr. said, "No one is free until we're all free." This is why the creative sector must address racial ADEI now.

References

Bahr, Sarah. 2021. "Indianapolis Museum of Art Apologizes for Insensitive Job Posting." *New York Times*, February 13, 2021. https://www.nytimes.com/2021/02/13/arts/design/indianapolis-museum-job-posting.html.

Basu, Shumita. 2021. "In Conversation: Jelani Cobb on the Backlash to Critical Race Theory." *Apple News Today* (podcast), November 20, 2021. https://apple.news/A0_JyrSS6RlCaRAD AowZGOw.

Bolden, Louis. 2020. "Law Enforcement Officers Have Killed One Black Person per Week This Year, Data Shows." *ClickOrlando*, September 17, 2020. https://www.clickorlando.com/news/local/2020/09/17/law-enforcement-officers-have-killed-1-black-person-per-week-this-year-data-shows/.

Cheng, Yangyan. 2021. "Cancel Culture Isn't the Real Threat to Academic Freedom." *The Atlantic*, November 23, 2021. https://www.theatlantic.com/international/archive/2021/11/china-academic-freedom-cultural-revolution-cancel-culture/620777/?mc_cid=c5984e1 610&mc_eid=4254e9122a.

Coates, Ta-Nehisi. 2021. "Donald Trump Is Out. Are We Ready to Talk About How He Got In? 'The First White President,' Revisited." *The Atlantic*, January 19, 2021. https://www.theatlantic.com/politics/archive/2021/01/ta-nehisi-coates-revisits-trump-first-white-president/617731/

Cuyler, Antonio. 2017. "A Survey of Arts Management Educators' Teaching on Diversity Issues." *Journal of Arts Management, Law, and Society* 47, no. 3: 192–202. https://doi.org/10.1080/10632921.2013.786009.

Cuyler, Antonio. 2021. *Access, Diversity, Equity, and Inclusion in Cultural Organizations: Insights from the Careers of Executive Opera Managers of Color in the US*. London and New York: Routledge.

Cuyler, Antonio. 2022. "Moving Beyond @operaisracist: Exploring Black Activism as a Pathway to Antiracism and Creative Justice in Opera." In *Music as Labour: Inequalities and Activism in the Past and Present*, edited by Dagmar Abfalter and Rosa Reitsamer. London: Routledge, 205

Cuyler, Antonio. 2023. "Access, Diversity, Equity, and Inclusion (ADEI) in Cultural Organizations: Challenges and Opportunities." In *Business Issues in the Arts*, edited by Anthony Rhine and Jay Pension. New York: Routledge, 83–104.

Cuyler, Antonio, Victoria Durrer, and Melissa Nisbett. 2020. "Steadfastly White, Female, Hetero and Abled-Bodied: An International Survey on the Motivations and Experiences of Arts Management Graduates." *International Journal of Arts Management* 22, no. 3: 5–16.

Delgado, Richard, and Stefancic, Jean. 2017. *Critical Race Theory: An Introduction*. New York: New York University Press.

Essig, Linda. 2018. "AAAE Demographic Survey Preliminary Tally." January 25, 2018.

Gray, Aysa. 2019. "The Bias of 'Professionalism' Standards." *Stanford Social Innovation Review*, June 2019. https://ssir.org/articles/entry/the_bias_of_professionalism_standards.

Helicon Collective. 2017. *Not Just Money: Equity Issues in Cultural Philanthropy*. Oakland, CA: Helicon Collective. http://notjustmoney.us/.

Keller, Anthony S. 1989. "The Arts Manager's Social Responsibility." *Journal of Arts Management and Law* 19, no. 2: 44–54.

Koch, Alexander, Chris Brierley, Mark Maslin, and Simon Lewis. 2019. "Earth System Impacts of the European Arrival and Great Dying in the Americas After 1492." *Quaternary Science Reviews* 207, no. 1: 13–36.

Mac Donald, Heather. 2021. "Classical Music's Suicide Pact (Part I)." *City Journal*, Summer 2021. https://www.city-journal.org/classical-music-under-racial-attack-part-1?mc_cid=996 3cfb71a&mc_eid=4254e9122a.

Munshi, Soniya, and Craig Willse. 2007. "Foreword." In *The Revolution Will Not Be Funded: Beyond the Nonprofit Industrial Complex*, edited by Incite. Durham, NC: Duke University Press, xiii–xxii.

Okun, Tema. 1999. "White Supremacy Culture." https://www.whitesupremacyculture.info/characteristics.html.
Okun, Tema. 2021. "White Supremacy Culture—Still Here." May 2021. https://drive.google.com/file/d/1XR_7M_9qa64zZ00_JyFVTAjmjVU-uSz8/view.
Okun, Tema, and Jones, Kenneth. 2001. "The Characteristics of White Supremacy Culture." Dismantling Racism: A Resource Group for Social Change Groups. Western States Center.
Reynolds, Jeremy. 2021. "Is Resonance Works' Emphasis on Diversity the Best Way to Move Classical Music Forward?" *Pittsburgh Post-Gazette*, November 18, 2021. https://www.post-gazette.com/ae/music/2021/11/18/Pittsburgh-Resonance-Works-female-BIPOC-classical-music-programming/stories/202111160103.
Rodriguez, Dylan. 2007. "The Political Logic of the Non-Profit Industrial Complex." In *The Revolution Will Not Be Funded*, edited by Incite, 21–40. Durham, NC: Duke University Press.
Vox Media Studios. 2018. "The Racial Wealth Gap." *Explained* (Netflix series), season 1, episode 3, May 23, 2018. https://www.youtube.com/watch?v=Mqrhn8khGLM.
Ward, Jane. 2008. "White Normativity: The Cultural Dimensions of Whiteness in a Racially Diverse LGBT Organization." *Sociological Perspectives* 51, no 3: 563–586.
Woolfe, Zachary. 2021. "A Black Composer Finally Arrives at the Metropolitan Opera." *New York Times*, September 23, 2021. https://www.nytimes.com/2021/09/23/arts/music/terence-blanchard-met-opera.html.

CHAPTER 17

AN EXPLORATIVE STUDY ON STATE-OWNED MUSEUM PERFORMANCE IN ITALY
The Interplay between the Director's Characteristics and Board Diversity

PAOLA DUBINI AND ALBERTO MONTI

INTRODUCTION

MUSEUMS are organizations whose nature has undergone deep-rooted changes, due to both internal and external forces, particularly over the last three decades (Bertacchini, Dalle Nogare, and Scuderi 2018; Kotler and Kotler 2000; Lindqvist 2012; Rentschler 2004). Museums have evolved from being collection-centered to embracing the so-called audience-centric paradigm (Taheri, Jafari, and O'Gorman 2014). This evolution coincided with a shift away from an established tradition of conservation and research and an image of elitist, top-down, and old-fashioned institutions (Pulh and Mencarelli 2015) and toward a more democratic image, focused on making culture more accessible and diverse, as well as on being more (pro)active toward the community, by joining essential conversations about discrimination and inequality and engaging in efforts to eliminate them (McCall and Gray 2014; see also the new definition of the museum recently proposed by ICOM [n.d.]). Finally, this evolution also paralleled changes happening in cultural policy at the country level, in which traditional models, such as the Continental European or British model, are no longer present in their pure form (Vicente, Camarero, and Garrido 2012). Notwithstanding similarities among countries in their pursuit of cultural objectives, greater variety is now present when it comes to the focus on and level of prioritization attached to goals such as preservation and valorization of cultural heritage or access to and involvement in culture, among others, and the modes of achieving them (e.g., European Commission 2014; Vicente, Camarero, and Garrido 2012).

However, within a shared mixed-methods model, created in response to economic and political events, a wide variety of modes of museum governance across and within countries reflects the diversity of approaches, priorities, and solutions (e.g., Bonet and Donato 2011; Schuster 1998). The process of managerialization and the provision of greater autonomy to the management of museums and art institutions has been mentioned as a promising way for museums to address financial, competitive, and managerial challenges (Zan, Baraldi, and Santagati 2018) as well as to innovate and to cope with external shocks (e.g., ICOM 2020; NEMO 2021). Therefore, determining how new modes of governance affect public museums' ability to perform and pursue different objectives became very important from a policy point of view (e.g., Throsby 2010) and from a more managerial and organizational perspective (e.g., Griffin and Abraham 2000; Turbide 2012).

In this chapter, we address the evolution of the governance of state-owned museums by focusing on the interplay between board members and directors as key interacting players who affect the decision-making process and, therefore, a museum's performance.[1] This choice is in keeping with the definition of governance as "the systems by which organizations are directed, controlled and accountable" (Cornforth 2002, 17). It stresses the role of those in charge of museums in defining policy, providing leadership and management, coordinating and monitoring procedures and resources, and developing a long-term strategy and direction (see Davis and Mort-Putland 2005, 3). Evidence shows that a museum's governance structure and funding might affect strategic decision-making direction and ability to implement their activities (e.g., Oster and Goetzmann 2003; Frey and Meier 2006).

The managerial literature parallels the growing importance of studying the role of the board in affecting organizational effectiveness for both corporations and nonprofit organizations (Cornforth 2001, 2012; Hillman and Dalziel 2003; Jaskyte and Holland 2015; Miller 2002; Miller-Millesen 2003; Minichilli et al. 2009; Turbide 2012). From an analytical point of view, the characteristics of the human capital within the board (Hillman et al. 2008), in particular board diversity (e.g., Tekleab et al. 2016), and their relationship to organizational performance have become the central focus of this stream of research. Notwithstanding this growing body of literature, what is lacking is a shared definition and conceptualization of diversity (Bunderson and Sutcliffe 2002; Harrison and Klein 2007), and the results of the research are often equivocal (Buyl et al. 2011; Yi et al. 2017). This evidence has led scholars to refer to diversity as a double-edged sword (Bunderson and Sutcliffe 2002; Yi et al. 2017), while calling for the development and testing of contingency models able to account for moderators and mediators of such relationships (e.g., Bradshaw 2009; Buyl et al. 2011; Cornforth 2012; Ostrower and Stone 2010; Van Knippenberg, De Dreu, and Homan 2004).

This chapter addresses these calls by examining the interplay between different characteristics of directors and their boards and evaluating the impact of these on the museum's performance (see also Ostrower and Stone 2006). When considering board member attributes, we move away from the more prevalent practice of addressing diversity as demographic characteristics (e.g., Miller and Triana 2009) and instead dig into diversity as it relates to board members' human capital, such as functional diversity and experience (e.g., Tekleab et al. 2016); these latter characteristics have been less explored, especially in the nonprofit literature (e.g., Ostrower and Stone 2006, 2010). We apply the taxonomy created in respect to board composition in the performing arts (Dubini and Monti 2018) to the newly created autonomous state museums in Italy, in order to test the roles of board member diversity and the director's gender and human capital, and the interplay between them, in shaping the organization's performance (e.g., Cornforth 2012; Ostrower and Stone 2010). In particular, we focus our attention on the director's international and curatorial experience with Italian heritage (we indicate the latter with the phrase "curatorial experience") as particularly relevant characteristics that directly impact a museum's performance by way of their interaction with a diverse (as opposed to homogeneous) board.

A reform of the Italian Ministry of Culture (MIC) in 2014 led to legislative innovations intended to give cultural institutions the instruments they need to pursue the new cultural policy (Marzano and Castellini 2018). This reform has paved the way for the establishment of state museums with the specific goal of valorizing their collections, disrupting a tradition and narrative of heritage management built around preservation and the direct involvement of public entities (state, regions, or municipalities). For the study, two elements are worth mentioning: the appointment of a director in charge of the museum's cultural strategy and a board and scientific committee that support the director, and the possibility of managing proceeds from ticket sales directly (for a detailed analysis of the reform, see Forte 2015 and Casini 2014; for an interesting differentiation between governance and management autonomy in the museum context, see Lusiani and Zan 2011). However, ever since the reforms began, there has been a heated debate around the level of independence given to the newly defined organizations, the opportunity to nominate international directors, the effectiveness of boards, and their overall impact on different dimensions of performance (La Repubblica 2015; Sironi 2017).

From a methodological perspective, we use ordinary least-squares regression to test our hypotheses. Our sample consists of the first thirty (out of forty-four) state museums created by law as autonomous organizations between 2014 and 2020. We restricted our selection to those created between 2014 and 2016 to be able to offer robust yet preliminary results, given the limited time in which they have been operating, the magnitude of the institutional change in such bureaucratic organizations (for some of them, the new organizational form took more than a year to be implemented and operational), as well as the need to exclude the impact of the COVID-19 shock on performance.

In line with the literature, our results show that board diversity directly affects an organization's performance. Most importantly, the results help us to understand when diversity matters, given the strategic role of boards of trustees in influencing executives' actions. In particular, we clarify under what conditions the director's gender and human capital matter in terms of an organization's performance. We contribute to the governance literature by explaining when board diversity in interaction with the director helps or hinders the director's ability to exploit their human capital fully (e.g., Khanna, Jones, and Boivie 2014; Westphal and Zajac 2013; Shen, Zhou, and Lau 2016).

The chapter is organized as follows. First, we introduce the context of our study by presenting a brief overview of the reform of Italian state museums. Second, we use a funnel approach to review the literature linking board diversity and performance in for-profit and not-for-profit organizations. The aim is to highlight the potential gaps that we will try to fill by developing our hypotheses related to the impact of the director's characteristics on organizational performance and the interplay of those characteristics with board diversity. Third, we discuss our methodology. Fourth, we present our analytical strategy and the results. Finally, we discuss the results in light of the context and the relevant literature, highlighting our contributions and the limitations of the study.

The Reform of Italian State Museums

Italy has a long-established tradition of heritage preservation; article 9 of its constitution holds the republic responsible for heritage preservation. Such an activity has been traditionally performed by superintendencies, peripheral units throughout the country in charge of both heritage preservation and cultural promotion activities. Starting in 2001, a series of reforms made it possible for a limited number of sites to manage proceeds from tickets directly (Landriani 2012). As a consequence of a series of reforms that began with a ministerial order in late 2014 (DM 23/12/2014), all four hundred Italian state museums have experienced significant institutional change. All state museums have now scientific autonomy and have the authority to manage their collections and to promote their valorization and cultural participation (Forte 2015); their purpose is to enhance knowledge around collections and improve the quality of the visit experience for different audiences (Casini 2016). Forty-four so-called autonomous museums, established between 2015 and 2021, represent a living experiment, as what were once wholly government-owned and -managed organizations now have scientific, financial, administrative, and organizational autonomy and bear responsibility for the specific premises where they operate. They are the contracting authority for concessions and outsourced activities, receive funds from the Ministry of Culture, have direct access to the proceeds of ticket sales, and can solicit private sponsorships. Their governance structure includes a director, a board, a scientific committee, and internal auditors; their responsibility is to set goals and targets; guarantee effectiveness, efficiency, and viability; verify the quality of the scientific offerings; and guarantee the protection and valorization of their collections. The director, who is the president of the board and the scientific committee, sets pricing and ticketing strategies and opening hours, and establishes which activities to outsource through concessions. By law, directors are nominated after an international call. The seniority (in terms of grade and salary) and role of the appointed director depend on the importance of the museum in terms of size, collection, and the number of visitors; of the first thirty museums, ten directors have greater seniority. The ministry nominates each institution's board for terms of five years, with the possibility of that term being renewed once. Board members are not remunerated for their service and cannot have a professional relationship with the museum or participate in initiatives sponsored by the museum. The scientific committee—whose members are nominated by the ministry, the region, and the municipality—has a consulting role in exhibitions organized by the museum and in regulating loans of artifacts belonging to the museum collection. The Ministry of Economy and Finance nominates the president of the internal auditors.

Despite their autonomy, these museums are subject to tight ministry and board control, particularly as far as resource allocation is concerned; furthermore, they have no opportunity to hire and fire, as the Ministry of Culture hires personnel through national calls. At the same time, these museums are not entirely dependent on the ministry because of their autonomy.

The introduction of the reform generated heated internal debate on its appropriateness, resource allocation choices, and boundaries. For this chapter, three critical points of this debate are worth mentioning: the extent of museums' autonomy (the concern was that by following market logic to maximize their attractiveness to tourists, the museums would reduce their educational and public function), the nationality of directors (the concern being that the presence of international directors could undermine the focus on Italian heritage), and the usefulness of boards (here, the concern was that boards would be deemed unnecessary, or a potential).

LITERATURE REVIEW

The managerial literature on the relationship between the board of trustees and organizational effectiveness has grown in importance for both corporations and nonprofit organizations (Cornforth 2001; Hillman and Dalziel 2003; Miller 2002; Miller-Millesen 2003; Turbide 2012; Johnson, Schnatterly, and Hill 2013). From a theoretical perspective, the influence of boards on firm performance has been analyzed primarily through the lens of resource dependence theory, agency theory, and resource-based theory (Boyd 1990; Hillman, Cannella, and Paetzold 2000; Miller 2002; Hillman and Thomas 2011; Jaskyte 2017). According to these perspectives, boards perform three primary activities: "(1) setting organizational direction and strategy, (2) monitoring actions and performance of the executive director, and (3) ensuring that an organization has adequate human and financial resources, representing an organization's interest in society, and advancing the reputation of the organization" (Jaskyte 2017, 454). The empirical literature has concentrated most of its attention on the board's human capital characteristics (Hillman and Thomas 2011), exploring the role of board diversity (e.g., Tekleab et al. 2016) in organizational performance through the lens of the abovementioned activities.

More specifically, most of the published studies analyzing for-profit organizations focus on visible attributes such as gender (e.g., Darmadi 2011; Dunn 2012; Smith, Smith, and Verner 2006), instead of nonvisible ones such as values and professional background (Tekleab et al. 2016). In a similar vein, the literature on nonprofit organizations has only recently paid closer attention to boards' and governance structures' effect on performance (for a review, see Cornforth 2012). In fact, Callen, Klein, and Tinkelman (2010, 105) highlight how "the body of empirical literature dealing with the relation between board governance and non-profit performance is limited and, for the most part, descriptive or exploratory." Similarly, Stone and Ostrower (2007, 420) note that "very few studies ... have asked whether and how board composition affects measures of organizational performance." Much as in the literature on for-profit organizations, empirical studies on board diversity in nonprofits concentrate on visible diversity characteristics, such as gender, or on the size of the board (e.g., Azmat and Rentschler 2017), with few empirical studies looking at deep-level diversity, such as professional background (Bai 2013; Dubini and Monti 2018).

Moreover, these different levels of diversity (e.g., Mannix and Neale 2005) have seldom been applied to both corporate and nonprofit boards (for exceptions, see Brown 2005; Hendry and Kiel 2004; Hillman and Dalziel 2003), which highlights the lack of a shared definition and conceptualization of diversity (Bunderson and Sutcliffe 2002; for a review and conceptualization of diversity, see Harrison and Klein 2007 and Mannix and Neale 2005).

Additionally, the results of studies on the relationship between board diversity and performance are often equivocal (Buyl et al. 2011; Yi et al. 2017), leading scholars to refer to diversity as a double-edged sword (Bunderson and Sutcliffe 2002; Yi et al. 2017). For example, Stone, Hager, and Griffin (2001) assess two hundreds nonprofits operating in Massachuttes that were member of the United Way of Massachusetts Bay and find that both board gender and racial diversity do not affect the percentage of funding received from government or from the United Way association to which the nonprofit belongs. At the same time, board size has a direct negative impact on government funding and a positive effect on the percentage of funds received by the United Way.

By contrast, Callen, Klein, and Tinkelman (2010) find that board size is positively related to direct contributions (i.e., private donations) and the ratio of contributions to administrative expenses. Qualitative research shows that diversity in board composition in terms of gender and ethnicity can positively affect the social performance of not-for profit organizations (e.g., Azmat and Rentschler 2017). Other studies do not consider the direct relationship between board characteristics and organizational performance, but analyze the relationships between board characteristics and activities, correlated with both perceived and objective measures of performance (e.g., Bradshaw, Murray, and Wolpin 1992; Brown 2005; Ostrower and Stone 2010).

The mixed results in assessing the relationship between board characteristics, activities, and performance suggest that the analysis of board composition should adopt an integrated framework (as indicated by Miller-Millesen 2003 and Hillman et al. 2009) to explore how deep-level features (Harrison and Klein 2007) affect different dimensions of organizational performance, in addition to variables such as age, ethnicity, and gender. For example, Bai (2013) finds that the presence (but not the percentage) of government officials on the board is positively related to social performance. Finally, Dubini and Monti (2018) integrate the literature on for-profit organizations and that on nonprofits for board characteristics (Hillman and Dalziel 2003; Turbide 2012). In a longitudinal study of opera houses, they associate the competence profiles of specific board members with different dimensions of performance.

Overall, these studies contribute to our understanding of the relationships between board composition and performance in not-for-profit organizations. Moreover, they highlight the need to develop and test contingency models to explain contradictory findings by looking at potential moderators and mediators of such relationships (e.g., Bradshaw 2009; Cornforth 2012; Ostrower and Stone 2010). Additionally, these ambiguous results parallel the research on board composition and performance in the for-profit sector (for reviews, see Johnson, Schnatterly, and Hill 2013; Rhoades, Rechner, and Sundaramurthy 2000) while amplifying the claims that it is important to study contingencies in such relationships (Boone and Hendriks 2009; Buyl et al. 2011; Van Knippenberg, De Dreu, and Homan 2004).

In this chapter, we build on and extend previous studies by developing a contingency model. In particular, we capitalize on the results of prior research on the governance of cultural organizations (i.e., Dubini and Monti 2018), working on a different subset of organizations—newly created autonomous state museums—treated as a living experiment. However, we advance this work by exploring both the direct impact of the director's characteristics on organizational performance and the interplay of these characteristics with board diversity as that affects performance (Ostrower and Stone 2010). Finally, both surface and deep-level diversity are examined by looking at gender and professional experience for directors and board members. In the following section, we build our contingency model and present our hypothesized relationships.

DIRECTOR'S CHARACTERISTICS AND PERFORMANCE: A CONTINGENCY APPROACH

In one of the early contributions to the analysis of museum governance, Griffin (1991) asked about the role of and relationship between government agencies, museum organization, and the board of trustees in contributing to and improving museum and system performance and effectiveness. Several years later, Rentschler (2004) clarified the importance of studying museums and their specificity while recognizing that "most of the research on governance is conducted in the for-profit arena, with little robust empirical research on non-profit governance" (Rentschler 2004, 30). Rentschler proposes three main reasons for contextualizing research on governance in the nonprofit sector: (1) the inherent differences between for-profit and nonprofit governance, (2) the dynamic and changing nature of the economic and social contracts under which museums operate, and (3) the strict and fiduciary relationships between governance at the organizational level and government in terms of regulation, legislation, and policies.

However, very little work addresses these questions. Oster and Goetzmann (2003) show that governance structure matters in differentiating museums in terms of revenue structure and the ability to attract visitors. Betzler (2015) finds that the presence of donors and business professionals on museum boards is positively related to fundraising in the context of Swiss museums. Finally, Griffin and Abraham (2000) discuss leadership and cohesion as critical factors for a museum's success.

What differentiates the study presented in this chapter from previous studies (e.g., Dubini and Monti 2018) is its analysis of directors' gender and human capital and the interplay of these characteristics with board diversity in influencing the museum's performance, both directly and indirectly. We agree with the literature on for-profit organizations in drawing attention to the potentially unique role that directors play through their interaction with the board or other top members of the management team (Arendt, Priem, and Ndofor 2005; Jaw and Lin 2009; Minichilli et al. 2010). Therefore, we do not treat museum directors as members of the board (in the nonprofit realm, see also Ostrower and Stone 2010).

We expect that directors with significant international experience will be better able to change the status quo than colleagues with expertise developed within the Ministry of Culture and the field of Italian heritage. This argument is backed up by research that shows a direct and positive impact of a CEO's international experience on both the economic performance and internationalization of the organization (e.g., Carpenter, Sanders, and Gregersen 2001; Daily, Certo, and Dalton 2000; Le and Kroll 2017). We therefore state that:

> H1. The international experience of directors positively correlates with museum attendance.

Additionally, we expect that the curatorial experience of the director will affect museum performance. One of the effects of the reform is to allow museums to develop cultural strategies to enhance the value of their collections, therefore internalizing the skills associated with the design and production of exhibits, tasks that generally were outsourced before the reform. Consequently, we expect that:

> H2. The curatorial experience of directors correlates positively with museum attendance.

There is evidence in the literature on for-profit organizations of a link between a CEO's gender and performance (Davis et al. 2010; Khan and Vieito 2013; Smith, Smith, and Verner 2006; Peni 2014; Vieito 2012). However, to the best of our knowledge, no studies address such a relationship in the not-for-profit realm, notwithstanding the greater presence of female managers in top positions in the cultural sector. The majority of existing studies found a positive relationship between the presence of female CEOs or chairs and financial performance (Peni 2014) in very different types of companies and contexts (e.g., Davis et al. 2010; Khan and Vieito 2013; Vieito 2012). However, it should be acknowledged that previous meta-analyses have found no difference in organizational performance between male- and female-led firms (DeRue et al. 2011; Eagly, Karau, and Makhijani 1995). These contradictory findings fostered the need to understand contingencies and mechanisms leading to such potential differences in performance (e.g., Eagly and Carli 2003). Research shows that women in leadership roles—more so than men in leadership roles—express characteristics that relate positively to effectiveness (i.e., Eagly and Carli 2003) and face higher expectations by public opinion due to the difficulties they have had to meet during the selection process over their male counterparts (Dunn 2012; Eagly and Carli 2003). Therefore, we expect that:

H3. Women directors correlate positively with museum attendance.

The Moderating Role of Board Member Diversity

Based on the informational diversity cognitive resource perspective (Tekleab et al. 2016), heterogeneous teams imply the complementarity of individuals' perspectives and capabilities. Consequently, diverse teams result in a higher range of input in discussions and a more thorough analysis of proposed strategic directions and decisions, which in turn lead to above-average performance (Buyl et al. 2011; Jansen et al. 2005; Miller and Triana 2009; Tekleab et al. 2016; Van Knippenberg, De Dreu, and Homan 2004). However, empirical results are controversial (Certo et al. 2006), and the link between diversity, particularly board diversity, and performance is empirically weak (see review in Johnson, Schnatterly, and Hill 2013). According to some authors, one of the reasons is that current studies fail to account for critical moderators (Boone and Hendriks 2009; Buyl et al. 2011). Other studies suggest that research "explore how the benefits and costs of top management team diversity vary depending on the specific attributes on which diversity is being considered" (Nielsen and Nielsen 2013, 378).

Here, we consider as a baseline the positive effect of both gender and background board diversity on performance (e.g., Certo et al. 2006; Dunn 2012; Smith, Smith, and Verner 2006; Tekleab et al. 2016), while exploring how the director's characteristics may affect performance, both directly and through his/her interaction with the board. Previous studies acknowledge the importance of diversity for a board's ability to influence strategic decisions by way of monitoring and advising the CEO. This is documented both in the for-profit sector (e.g., Hillman and Dalziel 2003; Westphal and Zajac 2013) and among non-profit organizations (Brown and Guo 2010). However, few studies draw attention to the interaction between the CEO and the rest of the top management team (e.g., Buyl et al. 2011), or the interactions within the board (e.g., Shen, Zhou, and Lau 2016) as it connects to affecting the relationship between CEO characteristics, board diversity, and performance. We build on these studies and expect that board diversity will positively moderate the international experience of the director due to information processing capability (Le and Kroll 2017). More specifically, we expect a stronger and positive relationship between the director's international experience and the museum performance if compared to cases in which the board is homogeneous. Expanding these arguments, we also expect that board diversity will positively moderate the curatorial experience of the director. Indeed, a diverse board can draw from a wide range of cognitive resources (Miller and Triana 2009) in order to help the director maximize their human capital, characterized by high tacit knowledge in this context (e.g., Crook et al. 2011), in ways that benefit the organization's strategic goals T. Therefore:

> H1a. Board diversity will moderate the relationship between the director's international experience and museum performance. The impact of the director's international experience on attendance is strengthened in the presence of diverse board compared to more homogeneous one.

> H2a. Board diversity will moderate the relationship between the director's curatorial experience and museum performance. The relationship between the director's curatorial experience and museum performance is strengthened in the presence of diverse board compared to more homogeneous one.

Finally, we expect that since several studies suggest women are often better able to manage complexity and decision-making tasks (e.g., Diekman and Eagly 2000; Peni 2014; Schubert 2006), female directors will benefit more than male directors from interacting with a diverse board. Therefore, we expect that:

> H3a. Board diversity will moderate the relationship between the director's gender and performance. Women directors will show better performance in the presence of a diverse board.

Additionally, other important individual characteristics can be considered as potentially interacting with board diversity. It can be argued that the relationship between the director and the board cannot produce performance benefits if diversity triggers interpersonal conflict (Cannella et al. 2008) or leads to slow decision-making (Darmadi 2011). However, social categorization theory (Turner et al. 1987) predicts that team homogeneity lowers the risk of interpersonal conflicts and the danger of subgroup formation while increasing the quality of communication (Harrison et al. 2002; Yi et al. 2017). We extend such reasoning to the relationship between the director and the board, and we expect that foreign directors can trigger in-group/out-group dynamics (Chattopadhyay, Tluchowska, and George 2004; Van Knippenberg, De Dreu, and Homan 2004; Tajfel and Turner 1979) that can reduce the benefit of diversity. Therefore, we expect that:

> H4. Board diversity will moderate the relationship between the director's nationality and museum performance. Italian directors will show better performance in the presence of a diverse board.

One goal of the reform is to allow individual museums to develop cultural strategies consistent with the specificity of their context (Rentschler 2004). Having worked previously within the context of Italian heritage will increase the power and importance of the director's human capital. Additionally, directors with experience in Italian heritage can better interpret and harness board dynamics, given their potentially greater familiarity with the board members' knowledge and experience (Van Knippenberg, De Dreu, and Homan 2004; Tajfel and Turner 1979). In this case, we anticipate that:

> H5. Board diversity will moderate the relationship between the director's experience with Italian heritage and performance. Italian directors will achieve better performance with a homogeneous board.

Methodology

Our sample consists of thirty Italian state museums created by law between December 2014 and January 2016 as part of an ongoing reform process (which has continued into 2023); Table 17.1 shows their characteristics and when they were set up. As superintendencies, the state museums of Pompei and Colosseo in Rome enjoyed some autonomy even before the reform. Museums and sites differ by nature, size, the number of buildings, collections, exhibition areas or sections of archaeological parks responding to the same organization, and characteristics of the collections. We restricted our sample to the autonomous museums created between 2014 and 2016 so as to offer robust yet conservative preliminary results. This sample gives us the possibility to see a potential effect of our hypothesized relationships on a museum's performance given (1) the limited time in which they have been operating, (2) the magnitude of the institutional change in such bureaucratic organizations (for some of them, the new organizational form took more than a year to be realized and become operational), and (3) the desire to exclude the impact of the COVID-19 shock on the organization's performance. Moreover, the fourteen other museums established in 2020 or 2021 have not been in

Table 17.1. Sample Composition

Type of institution	Pre-reform	Setup date				Total
		2014	2016	2019	2021	
Art museums and monuments		16	3	5	2	26
Archeological museums		3	2	2		7
Archaeological sites	2	1	5	1	2	11
Total	2	20	10	8	4	44

Table 17.2. Characteristics of the First 30 Directors

Characteristics of directors	Appointed 2015	Appointed 2017	Situation in 2021
Male	10	6	17
Female	10	4	13
Italian	9	8	25
Non-Italian	7		5
Italian with international experience	4	2	8
Top-tier directors, female	4		3
Top-tier directors, non-Italian	3		4
Total museums	20	10	30

operation long enough to assess the effects on visitors of the interplay between directors and boards.

The directors of these thirty museums were chosen in two batches from an international call; twenty were selected in August 2015 and ten in February 2017. The commissions nominated by the Ministry of Culture to select the directors included international members and partially overlapped. They presented three candidates for each museum, and the minister appointed the eight top-tier directors (who are more senior in grade and salary); the general director for museums decided on the remaining ones. Board members and scientific committees for each museum were nominated by the ministry and chosen from among university professors, experts on the relevant sites or in relevant disciplines, and patrons, and started working at the end of 2016. Table 17.2 shows the characteristics of the directors appointed. The presence of non-Italian directors represents a significant discontinuity in Italian heritage management history; in May 2017, five cases were brought to the administrative court by Italian colleagues who had not been selected. By June 2018, all of them were reintegrated into duty. The presence of female directors is not uncommon in Italian state administration, yet the percentage of female directors in the sample is higher than the average. The last column of Table 17.2 shows the sample's composition today.

Dependent Variable

Given the disruptive nature of the reform and the limited period of the analysis, we assumed that overall visitor attendance would be an adequate proxy to reflect the contributions of board members. We assumed that an increased variety of profiles would increase the museum's reach to a broader set of stakeholders and, therefore, positively impact the total number of visitors. Baia Curioni (2018) compared the change in the number of visitors to state museums with the corresponding change in the number of visitors in the cities where these museums are located and reported better performance of museums over territories in the visitors' attraction, thus confirming our choice of attendance figures as a preliminary proxy for valorization. This approach was used in other studies as well (e.g., Oster and Goetzmann 2003; Noh and Tolbert 2019). Since most of the new museums started operating fully in 2016, we consider each museum's attendance data for the period 2015–2018 as a measure of the impact of the work of the new directors and board members.

Independent Variables

Director's Gender and Human Capital

We used dummy variables to code the director's gender, international experience, job experience within the with Italian heritage, and curatorial experience.

Board Diversity

We applied the five-profile taxonomy developed by Dubini and Monti (2018) to classify board diversity in opera houses to the analysis of 121 curricula vitae of board members for the period in question, to create aggregate indicators of board composition. We began by classifying the number of directors who fell into the categories of "artists," "controllers," "cultural managers," "influential people," and "other specialists" based on the individual's previous experience, education, background, and personal relationships and affiliations (Hillman and Dalziel 2003). Since profiles are not mutually exclusive, we calculated the proportion of profile i as the number of board members having profile i divided by board size. Following Harrison and Klein (2007), we measured board diversity as variety, using the Gini-Simpson Index to account for the diversity in terms of the previously mentioned profile in each board. The index varies from 0 to 1: the greater the index, the greater the diversity of profiles on each board. We also considered the percentage of female board members.

Control Variables

Finally, we included several control variables to account for the museum's and director's characteristics. To account for differences in reputation and attraction capability of different sites, we classified sites in terms of the average number of visitors in the three years before the reform and the level of seniority of the director, which correlates to the importance and visibility of the site or museum (museum status). We also accounted for the director's age and the size of the board, as these can affect the power dynamics in their relationship.

Findings

Descriptive statistics, including means, standard deviations, and minimum and maximum values of the variables, are presented in Table 17.3 along with the intercorrelations

Table 17.3. Means, Standard Deviation, Min, Max, and Pairwise Correlations of the Variables

Variables	Mean	Std. Dev.	Min	Max	Museum Attendance	D_International Experience	D_Internal Career	D_Curatorial Experience	D_Nationality	D_Gender	Board Diversity	D_Age	Museum Status	Board Size
Museum attendance	45850	217707	−964631	347934	1									
D_international experience	0.43	0.50	0	1	−0.2823	1								
D_internal career	0.27	0.45	0	1	0.1218	−0.5273*	1							
D_curatorial experience	0.50	0.51	0	1	−0.2058	0.2018	−0.1508	1						
D_nationality	0.23	0.43	0	1	0.123	0.4718*	−0.3327	0.2364	1					
D_gender	0.57	0.50	0	1	−0.1773	0.086	0.2231	0.2018	−0.3128	1				
Board diversity	0.61	0.12	0.32	0.87	0.4693*	0.0313	−0.2477	0.0788	0.3643*	0.0126	1			
D_age	54	9	38	67	−0.0233	−0.3818*	0.2803	0.1119	−0.097	0.1482	−0.0156	1		
Museum status	0.27	0.45	0	1	0.095	−0.071	−0.0227	0.1508	0.202	0.071	0.2593	0.4897*	1	
Board size	5.07	0.37	4	6	−0.0034	0.025	−0.112	0.1857	0.1171	−0.025	0.4200*	0.0272	0.3079	1
Board_female%	0.47	0.22	0.2	0.8	0.0651	−0.1607	0.2448	−0.1315	−0.4114*	0.5977*	0.0851	0.0337	−0.0874	−0.1206

Notes: D_ = director; number of observations = 30.
* Correlations are significant at 0.05 level.

between constructs. An ordinary least-squares regression procedure is applied to the sample ($N = 30$) to test the formulated hypotheses. Unstandardized and standardized betas, standard errors of the hypothesized relationship, and r-squares of the dependent variable are reported in Tables 17.4, 17.5, 17.6 and 17.7.

Table 17.4 shows the direct effect of the director's international experience and curatorial experience on performance (H1 and H2, respectively). Model 1 shows the impact of the control variables related to both site characteristics and director's characteristics; only board diversity has a positive direct effect on performance. This aligns with our expectations and assumptions and corroborates the need to examine the interaction between board diversity and the director's characteristics for each museum. Model 2 shows the effect of the director's international experience on performance. The results show a nonsignificant direct impact of such variables on performance. We therefore rejected H1. The effect of curatorial experience on performance is tested in Model 3. Again, the findings show a nonsignificant direct effect of having such experience on performance. Thus, we rejected H2. Overall, the full model (Model 4) explains an adjusted cumulative variance of 22 percent compared to the control model's variance of 16 percent.

Table 17.5 shows the results of the interaction between the director's characteristics and board diversity. Model 1 shows that the interaction between board diversity and director's international experience was significant. To interpret and show the effect, we ran the predictive margins routine in Stata (Williams 2012) and present the results in Figure 17.1. As can be seen in the figure, directors with international experience outperform directors with no international experience when the board is highly diverse. We therefore confirmed H1a. Model 2 shows the interaction of board diversity and director's curatorial experience (H2a); Figure 17.2 shows how the relationship between director's curatorial experience and museum performance becomes positive in the presence of board diversity, with the museums run by directors with curatorial experience outperforming museums where the director does not have such experience. Overall, the results confirmed H2a. Finally, the inclusion of the interaction terms in both Model 1 and Model 2 significantly increased the variance explained by these models, moving from 16 percent for the control model to 33 percent and 30 percent, respectively.

To offer a more conservative test for the effect of the director's gender (H3) and its interaction with board diversity (H3a), we included in the model, as a control, both the director's human capital characteristics and the percentage of females on the board. Table 17.6 shows the results of our analysis. Interestingly enough, we did not find a direct effect of gender on performance (Model 1), paralleling previous meta-analyses that found no effect; we therefore rejected H3. However, looking at Model 2, we found significant interaction between gender and board diversity. To better interpret the results, Figure 17.3 shows the marginal effect of being a female or male director contingent upon the degree of diversity of the board. As can be seen, female directors outperform male directors in the presence of a moderately to highly diverse board.

Tables 17.7 and 17.8 show the interaction among director's nationality, experience with Italian heritage, and board diversity, respectively H4 and H5. Model 2, in Table 17.7,

Table 17.4. Regression analysis testing hypotheses H1 and H2

	Model 1				Model 2			
Variables	Coef.	Std. Err.	P>|t|	Beta	Coef.	Std. Err.	P>|t|	Beta
D_international experience					−144853.70	77355.22	0.0740	−0.34
D_curatorial experience								
Board diversity	998063.50	333987.30	0.0060	0.57	986431.80	317864.50	0.0050	0.56
D_gender	−83824.12	74292.92	0.2700	−0.19	−62626.75	71593.58	0.3910	−0.14
D_age	44.69	4962.02	0.9930	0.00	−3958.79	5183.06	0.4530	−0.16
Museum status	19383.58	102150.70	0.8510	0.04	45266.71	98178.74	0.6490	0.09
Board size	−155176.00	115240.20	0.1910	−0.26	−154979.50	109656.20	0.1710	−0.26
Constant	265123.20	630224.80	0.6780		532178.20	616411.30	0.3970	
Number of obs	30.00				30.00			
Prob > F(5, 24)	0.10				0.05			
R-squared	0.31				0.40			
Adj R-squared	**0.16**				**0.24**			

	Model 3				Model 4			
Variables	Coef.	Std. Err.	P>|t|	Beta	Coef.	Std. Err.	P>|t|	Beta
D_international experience	−79342.90	75938.02	0.3070	−0.19	−132216.50	80580.42	0.1150	−0.31
D_curatorial experience	993866.60	333375.40	0.0070	0.57	−50175.39	75414.73	0.5130	−0.12
Board diversity	−68222.54	75639.93	0.3760	−0.16	984792.50	321796.60	0.0060	0.56
D_gender	260.71	4956.88	0.9590	0.01	−54609.80	73471.93	0.4650	−0.13
D_age	25060.26	102100.80	0.8080	0.05	−3472.92	5297.60	0.5190	−0.14
Museum status	−135812.20	116504.20	0.2560	−0.23	46598.49	99410.50	0.6440	0.10
Board size	187166.30	633434.00	0.7700		−142751.20	112520.60	0.2180	−0.24
Constant					459581.10	333486.40	0.4760	
Number of obs	30.00				30.00			
Prob > F(5, 24)	0.11				0.08			
R-squared	0.34				0.41			
Adj R-squared	**0.17**				**0.22**			

Table 17.5. Regression analysis testing hypotheses H1a and H2b

Variables	Model 1				Model 2			
	Coef.	Std. Err.	P>|t|	Beta	Coef.	Std. Err.	P>|t|	Beta
D_international experience	-850982.7	367319.1	0.03	-1.97	-935407.70	377184.70	0.0210	-2.19
D_curatorial experience	278009	469413.8	0.56	0.159	325524.40	421043.40	0.4480	0.19
Board diversity	1152952	587796.8	0.063	1.7009				
D_international experience x board diversity					1426956.00	617905.90	0.0310	2.15
D_curatorial experience x board diversity	-51310.54	67781.07	0.4570	-0.12	-47979.43	69937.36	0.5000	-0.11
D_gender	-4669.645	4902.66	0.3510	-0.19	1122.08	4562.31	0.8080	0.05
D_age	70648.49	93512.84	0.4580	0.15	-20531.49	95716.96	0.8320	-0.04
Museum status	-76509.69	110906.6	0.4970	-0.13	-226436.10	113848.40	0.0590	-0.38
Board size	590735.8	582234.2	0.3210		994008.70	678010.90	0.1570	
Constant	30.00				30.00			
Number of obs	0.02				0.03			
Prob > F(7, 22)	0.49				0.47			
R-squared	**0.33**				**0.30**			
Adj R-squared								

Table 17.6. Regression analysis testing hypotheses H3 and H3a

Variables	Model 1				Model 2			
	Coef.	Std. Err.	P>|t|	Beta	Coef.	Std. Err.	P>|t|	Beta
D_gender	-78711.05	115159.8	0.503	-0.18	-1089947	390092.7	0.012	-2.52
Board diversity	1019406	409716.8	0.022	0.58	-123268.3	555098.1	0.827	-0.07
D_gender × board diversity					1701616	634473.9	0.015	2.51
D_international experience	-97670.4	118987.3	0.422	-0.23	-171678.4	106954.3	0.126	-0.40
D_internal career	98454.06	111668.6	0.389	0.20	37510.34	99604.02	0.711	0.08
D_curatorial experience	-43557.18	84517.68	0.612	-0.10	-20999.36	73878.74	0.779	-0.05
D_nationality	29260.08	135611.1	0.831	0.06	170032.4	128937.3	0.204	0.34
D_age	-3921.179	5603.334	0.493	-0.16	-4880.001	4879.265	0.33	-0.20
Museum status	49339.07	106915.3	0.65	0.10	63397.85	92997.22	0.504	0.13
Board Size	-140158.8	122001.9	0.265	-0.24	-223455.2	110409.5	0.058	-0.37
Board_female%	34303.46	244066.2	0.89	0.03	147450.4	216114.3	0.504	0.15
Constant	395325	683466.9	0.57		1497419	721918.1	0.053	
Number of obs	30				30			
Prob > F(10, 19)	0.22				0.04			
R-squared	0.44				0.60			
Adj R-squared	0.14				0.35			

Table 17.7. Regression analysis testing hypothesis H4

Variables	Model 1				Model 2			
	Coef.	Std. Err.	P>|t|	Beta	Coef.	Std. Err.	P>|t|	Beta
D_nationality	-86220.01	1017786.3	0.406	-0.17	1019422.00	1561069.00	0.521	2.01
Board diversity	1101426	357443.5	0.005	0.6298	1183566.00	379439.80	0.005	0.68
D_nationality × board diversity					-1621673.00	2284680.00	0.485	-2.2
D_gender	-106872.8	79533.37	0.192	-0.247	-124166.30	84015.57	0.1540	-0.29
D_age	-645.5504	5057.553	0.9000	-0.03	-743.39	5114.86	0.8860	-0.03
Museum status	39808.16	105548.2	0.7100	0.08	31365.42	107366.40	0.7730	0.06
Board size	-166172.4	116649	0.1680	-0.28	-185784.50	121121.60	0.1390	-0.31
Constant	323156.3	637657.8	0.6170		392610.90	652033.20	0.5530	
Number of obs	30.00				30.00			
Prob > F(7, 22)	0.18				0.18			
R-squared	0.34				0.34			
Adj R-squared	**0.13**				**0.13**			

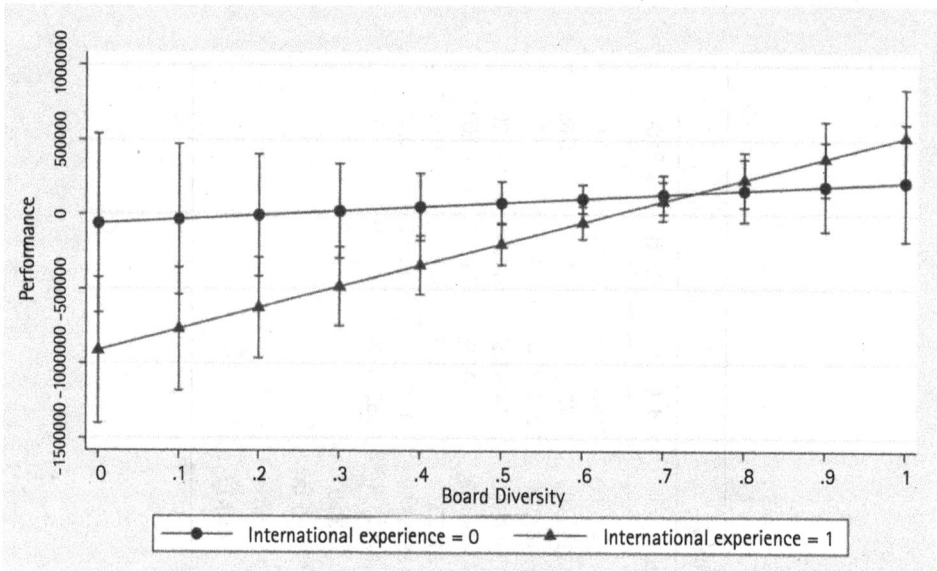

FIGURE 17.1 Marginal effect of interaction between director's international experience and board diversity (H1a).

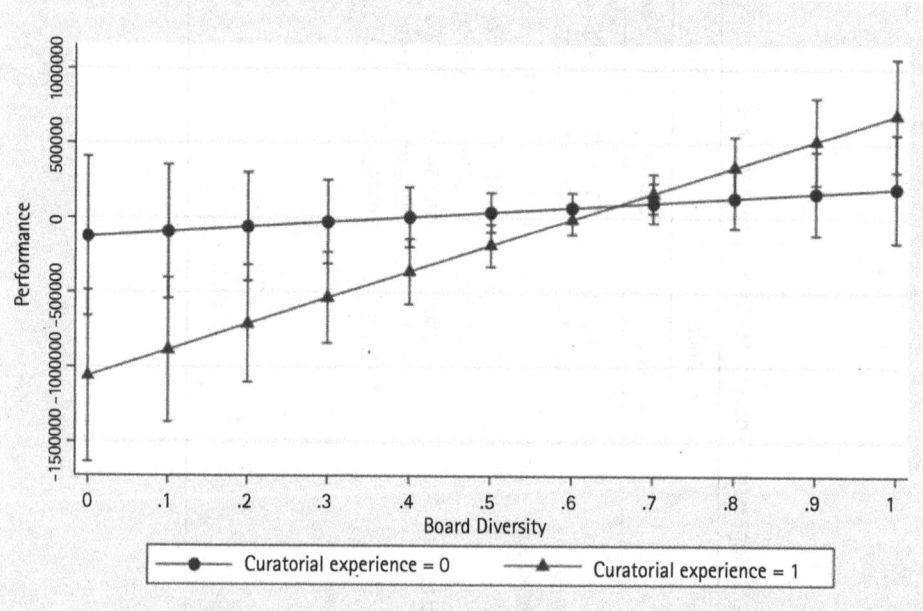

FIGURE 17.2 Marginal effect of interaction between director's curatorial experience and board diversity (H2a)

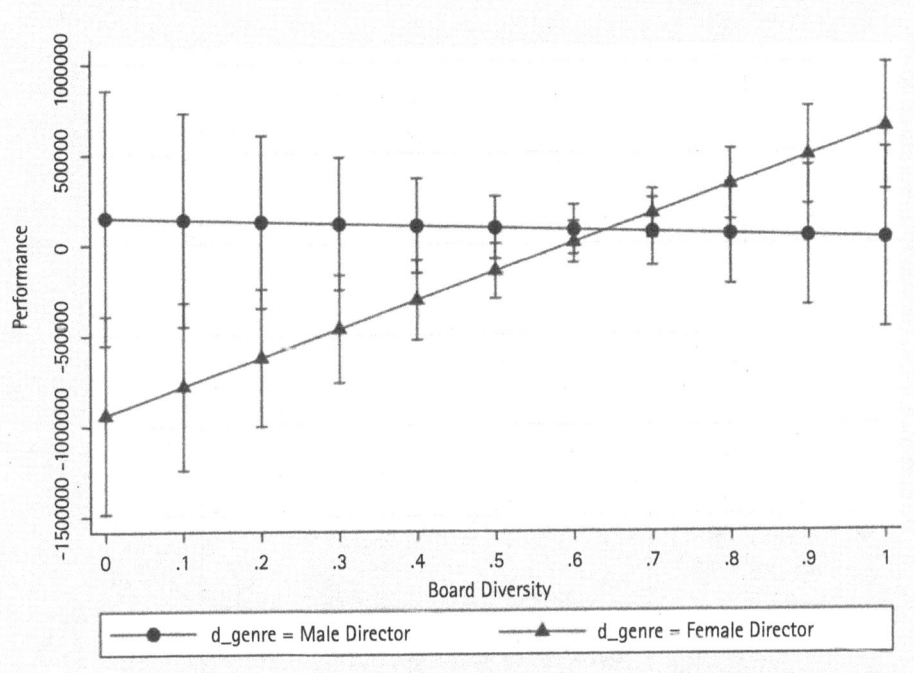

FIGURE 17.3 Marginal effect of interaction between director's gender and board diversity (H3a).

suggests a nonsignificant effect of board diversity on the relationship between director nationality and performance (H4). H4 was therefore not confirmed.

Furthermore, the interaction effect between board diversity and the internal career of the directors in the field of Italian heritage was not validated (Model 2, H5; see Table 17.8). Interestingly enough, before adding the interaction term (i.e., Model 1), we can see both variables' direct and positive effects on museum performance.

Discussion and Implications

The Ministry of Culture's reform is a comprehensive effort to transform how the state manages heritage, and it involves a growing variety of stakeholders. The complexity of the task, the breadth of scope, and the multifaceted array of goals and challenges make it very difficult to assess the effects of the reform so early in the process. The number of ministerial decrees issued between 2014 and 2021 testifies to a dramatic change in the functioning of the peripheral state structures in charge of valorization and preservation. In this chapter, we focused on autonomous state museums in Italy as one key pillar of the reform and sought to relate the contribution of newly mandated governance structures to valorization.

Table 17.8. Regression Analysis Testing Hypothesis H5

Variables	Model 1				Model 2			
	Coef.	Std. Err.	P>|t|	Beta	Coef.	Std. Err.	P>|t|	Beta
D_internal career	165136.30	86534.14	0.0690	0.34				
Board diversity	1127090.00	324126.70	0.0020	0.64				
D_internal career × board diversity					−94477.99	140089.50	0.5070	−0.14
D_gender	−111712.30	72011.84	0.1340	−0.26	−99117.66	75235.37	0.2010	−0.23
D_age	−2640.17	4915.24	0.5960	−0.11	−3694.55	5214.44	0.4860	−0.15
Museum status	42721.69	97722.19	0.6660	0.09	46751.32	99081.67	0.6420	0.10
Board size	−158927.10	109395.20	0.1600	−0.27	−164598.90	111034.20	0.1520	−0.28
Constant	316827.80	59877.60	0.6020		409336.50	621332.00	0.5170	
Number of obs	30.00				30.00			
Prob > F(7, 22)	0.05				0.07			
R-squared	0.40				0.41			
Adj R-squared	0.25				0.23			

The 2014 reform has been disruptive in terms of the role assigned to museums. Contrary to the expectations, this transformation has offered limited opportunities to change people's behavior (through incentives, rotation, or training programs). Thus, the role of directors—and possibly that of the board—becomes very important in determining a new course of action in what have traditionally been very bureaucratic organizations. However, from the beginning there has been a heated debate around the level of independence given to the newly defined organizations, the opportunity to nominate international directors, the effectiveness of boards, and, on the whole, the opportunity to have specific organizations (rather than government agencies) in charge of valorization.

Overall, our findings indicate that individual facets of directors' human capital analyzed in our study do not directly impact museum performance. Additionally, there is no direct effect of director gender on museum performance. One of the possible reasons for these findings is that the time period taken into consideration is too limited; another is that these specific characteristics are not aligned with our dependent variable in terms of impact. Moreover, except for the new directors, virtually all of the museums' employees were the same before and after the reform.

On the other hand, in line with previous studies, results indicate that board diversity does directly affect an organization's performance. Indeed, our results help us understand when diversity matters, given the strategic role of the board in influencing executives' actions and their ability to exploit their human capital fully. More specifically, the director's curatorial experience positively impacts museum attendance in the presence of board diversity, but negatively impacts attendance when the board is homogeneous. This result suggests that trust between director and board on curatorial choices may be built more easily in the presence of complementary competencies, and that heterogeneity of the board may enhance the quality and directions of the choices taken by the directors. A director's nationality does not impact attendance; on the other hand, the director's international experience has a positive impact on attendance in the presence of board diversity. This finding suggests that Italian directors with international experience might play a cultural mediation role in the MIC's complex transformation process and, at the same time, could play a role in public debate by demonstrating the importance of the director's nationality. Finally, the results show that female directors outperform male directors when the board is diverse. This result is interesting because it is the first time this has been documented in the literature on not-for-profit organizations. Additionally, it signals the possibility that women's leadership capability affects organizational performance.

Our findings therefore produce a theoretical contribution to governance literature, suggesting that researchers pay attention to the interplay of competence profiles in building effective governance structures in different types of organizations, particularly in organizations that are starting a structural and cultural transformation with limited resources and several binding conditions, as is the case with MIC. We also contribute to the governance literature by clarifying when board diversity enhances or hinders the director's ability to fully exploit their human capital (e.g., Khanna et al. 2014; Westphal and Zajac 2013; Shen, Zhou, and Lau 2016). Further, we extend the nomological network of the characteristics of the CEO under consideration and their interaction with board characteristics. In particular, the literature on for-profit organizations is limited to the international experience of the CEO and the direct impact of such characteristics on internationalization, with less consideration of the effect on overall firm performance (Daily, Certo, and Dalton 2000; Le and Kroll 2017). And we contribute to the governance literature by showing how different facets of diversity can impact an organization's performance both directly and indirectly (Van Knippenberg et al. 2011).

From a managerial point of view, our findings support paying attention to the selection of board members with complementary profiles when boards are being constituted. In fact, such composition boosts the positive contribution of a director's human capital and the director's ability to become an agent of change, especially for those with an international background or curatorial experience. Our findings suggest that governance structures of museums drive performance. Therefore, policymakers need to push such reform further, explicitly considering the relationships between directors, the MIC, employees, and other governance bodies (boards and scientific committees) and actors (such as private companies operating through concessions) in order to ensure the practical autonomy needed by museums' governance bodies to achieve results related to different stakeholders and objectives (e.g., Bertacchini et al. 2018; Zan, Baraldi, and Santagati 2018). For example, directors' inability to directly manage museum personnel is a crucial difficulty when it comes to ensuring autonomous museums' effective management (Zan et al. 2018). At the same time, MIC's control over directors is hierarchical and de facto only administrative.

Moreover, directors are nominated for four years, with the possibility of being confirmed in the role for one additional four-year term. Individual assessment of directors and communication regarding their turnover or confirmation should be done in a timely manner to foster smoother operation at the museum level. It is, therefore, essential to address the issue of autonomy more comprehensively to allow more effective valorization, while at the same time protecting the institution's public function.

We are fully aware of the limitations of this study, given the magnitude of the change in a highly bureaucratic and conservative environment, the time interval considered, and the limited number of variables taken into consideration. Many processes have been only superficially addressed; therefore, this study is necessarily exploratory. Nevertheless, the setting allows us to consider a specific time frame (one term of museum directors) and compare the extent to which directors' competence base and their interplay with board diversity impact visitor attraction. Our sample size can be considered small, and therefore the results are not as statistically robust as we would like. However, for the reasons specified earlier in the chapter and because of the fact that this sample represents the whole population of autonomous museums in Italy, we are confident about this preliminary finding. An alternative could have been to use a matched sample strategy or, in the future, to consider a longitudinal approach and include all the newly created autonomous museums. Nevertheless, autonomous state museums represent a relevant context in which to study how individual and team competences impact organizational performance. This highlights the importance of following this phenomenon and its implications for policymaking, theory building, and social purposes.

NOTE

1. This work is part of a larger and ongoing project mapping the evolution of the Italian state museums after the 2014 reform. The project aims at exploring the effect of that reform on different outcomes and the relationship between the new governance model giving autonomy to some museums and different aspects of the performance and sustainability of the museums themselves. The data and the main theoretical framework related to board diversity were used for a paper published in the proceedings of the 20th EURAM Conference. We want to thank the participants of the Strategic Interest Group 11_3 on Management and Governance of Culture, Heritage and Tourism for the input that inspired the birth of this work.

REFERENCES

Arendt, Lucy A., Richard L. Priem, and Hermann Achidi Ndofor. 2005. "A CEO-Adviser Model of Strategic Decision Making." *Journal of Management* 31, no. 5: 680–699.

Azmat, Fara, and Ruth Rentschler. 2017. "Gender and Ethnic Diversity on Boardsss and Corporate Responsibility: The Case of the Arts Sector." *Journal of Business Ethics* 141, no. 2: 317–336.

Bai, Ge. 2013. "How Do Board Size and Occupational Background of Directors Influence Social Performance in For-Profit and Non-profit Organizations? Evidence from California Hospitals." *Journal of Business Ethics* 118, no. 1: 171–187.

Baia Curioni, Stefano. 2018. "'I've Seen Fire and I've Seen Rain': Notes on the State Museum Reform in Italy." *Museum Management and Curatorship* 33, no. 6: 555–569.

Bertacchini, Enrico E., Chiara Dalle Nogare, and Raffaele Scuderi. 2018. "Ownership, Organization Structure and Public Service Provision: The Case of Museums." *Journal of Cultural Economics* 42: 619–643.

Betzler, Diana. 2015. "Factors of Board Governance and Fundraising Success: The Composition of Swiss Museum Boards Does Matter." *Journal of Cultural Economy* 8, no. 2: 144–165.

Bonet, Lluís, and Fabio Donato. 2011. "The Financial Crisis and Its Impact on the Current Models of Governance and Management of the Cultural Sector in Europe." *ENCATC Journal of Cultural Management and Policy* 1, no. 1: 4–11.

Boone, Christophe, and Walter Hendriks. 2009. "Top Management Team Diversity and Firm Performance: Moderators of Functional-Background and Locus-of-Control Diversity." *Management Science* 55, no. 2: 165–180.

Boyd, Brian. 1990. "Corporate Linkages and Organizational Environment: A Test of the Resource Dependence Model." *Strategic Management Journal* 11, no. 6: 419–430.

Bradshaw, Pat. 2009. "A Contingency Approach to Nonprofit Organizations." *Nonprofit Management and Leadership* 20, no. 1: 61–81.

Bradshaw, Pat, Vic Murray, and Jacob Wolpin. 1992. "Do Nonprofit Boards Make a Difference? An Exploration of the Relationships Among Board Structure, Process, and Effectiveness." *Nonprofit and Voluntary Sector Quarterly* 21, no. 3: 227–249.

Brown, William A. 2005. "Exploring the Association Between Board and Organizational Performance in Nonprofit Organizations." *Nonprofit Management and Leadership* 15, no. 3: 317–339.

Brown, William A., and Chao Guo. 2010. "Exploring the Key Roles for Nonprofit Boards." *Nonprofit and Voluntary Sector Quarterly* 39, no. 3: 536–546.

Bunderson, J. Stuart, and Kathleen M. Sutcliffe. 2002. "Comparing Alternative Conceptualizations of Functional Diversity in Management Teams: Process and Performance Effects." *Academy of Management Journal* 45, no. 5: 875–893.

Buyl, Tine, Christophe Boone, Walter Hendriks, and Paul Matthyssens. 2011. "Top Management Team Functional Diversity and Firm Performance: The Moderating Role of CEO Characteristics." *Journal of Management Studies* 48, no. 1: 151–177.

Callen, Jeffrey L., April Klein, and Daniel Tinkelman. 2010. "The Contextual Impact of Nonprofit Board Composition and Structure on Organizational Performance: Agency and Resource Dependence Perspectives." *Voluntas: International Journal of Voluntary and Nonprofit Organizations* 21, no. 1: 101–125.

Cannella Jr, Albert A., Jong-Hun Park, and Ho-Uk Lee. 2008. "Top Management Team Functional Background Diversity and Firm Performance: Examining the Roles of Team Member Colocation and Environmental Uncertainty." *Academy of Management Journal* 51, no. 48: 768–784.

Carpenter, Mason A., Wm. Gerard Sanders, and Hal B. Gregersen. 2001. "Bundling Human Capital with Organizational Context: The Impact of International Assignment Experience on Multinational Firm Performance and CEO Pay." *Academy of Management Journal* 44, no. 3: 493–511.

Casini, Lorenzo. 2014. "Il "nuovo" statuto giuridico dei musei italiani." *Aedon* 3.

Casini, Lorenzo. 2016. *Ereditare il futuro: dilemmi sul patrimonio culturale*. Bologna: Il Mulino.

Certo, S. Trevis, Richard H. Lester, Catherine M. Dalton, and Dan R. Dalton. 2006. "Top Management Teams, Strategy and Financial Performance: A Meta-Analytic Examination." *Journal of Management Studies* 43, no. 4: 813–839.

Chattopadhyay, Prithviraj, Malgorzata Tluchowska, and Elizabeth George. 2004. "Identifying the Ingroup: A Closer Look at the Influence of Demographic Dissimilarity on Employee Social Identity." *Academy of Management Review* 29, no. 2: 180–202.

Cornforth, Chris. 2001. "What Makes Boards Effective? An Examination of the Relationships Between Board Inputs, Structures, Processes and Effectiveness in Non-Profit Organisations." *Corporate Governance: An International Review* 9, no. 3: 217–227.

Cornforth, Chris. 2002. "Introduction: the changing context of governance–emerging issues and paradoxes." In *The Governance of Public and Non-Profit Organizations*, edited by C. Cornforth, 13–32. London: Routledge.

Cornforth, Chris. 2012. "Nonprofit Governance Research: Limitations of the Focus on Boards and Suggestions for New Directions." *Nonprofit and Voluntary Sector Quarterly* 41, no. 6: 1116–1135.

Crook, T. Russell, Samuel Y. Todd, James G. Combs, David J. Woehr, and David J. Ketchen Jr. 2011. "Does Human Capital Matter? A Meta-Analysis of the Relationship Between Human Capital and Firm Performance." *Journal of Applied Psychology* 96, no. 3: 443.

Daily, Catherine M., S. Trevis Certo, and Dan R. Dalton. 2000. "International Experience in the Executive Suite: The Path to Prosperity?" *Strategic Management Journal* 21, no. 4: 515–523.

Darmadi, Salim. 2011. "Board Diversity and Firm Performance: The Indonesian Evidence." *Corporate Ownership and Control Journal* 8, nos. 2–4: 450–466.

Davis, Jay, and Laura Mort-Putland. 2005. *Best Practices: Governance.* Victoria, BC: British Columbia Museums Association.

Davis, Peter S., Emin Babakus, Paula Danskin Englis, and Tim Pett. 2010. "The Influence of CEO Gender on Market Orientation and Performance in Small and Medium-Sized Service Businesses." *Journal of Small Business Management* 48, no. 4: 475–496.

Derue, D. Scott, Jennifer D. Nahrgang, Ned E. Wellman, and Stephen E. Humphrey. 2011. "Trait and behavioral theories of leadership: An integration and meta-analytic test of their relative validity." *Personnel Psychology* 64, no. 1: 7–52.

Diekman, Amanda B., and Alice H. Eagly. 2000. "Stereotypes as Dynamic Constructs: Women and Men of the Past, Present, and Future." *Personality and Social Psychology Bulletin* 26, no. 10: 1171–1188.

Dubini, Paola, and Alberto Monti. 2018. "Board Composition and Organizational Performance in the Cultural Sector: The Case of Italian Opera Houses." *International Journal of Arts Management* 20, no. 2: 56–70.

Dunn, Paul. 2012. "Breaking the Boardroom Gender Barrier: The Human Capital of Female Corporate Directors." *Journal of Management and Governance* 16, no. 4: 557–570.

Eagly, Alice H., and Linda L. Carli. 2003. "The Female Leadership Advantage: An Evaluation of the Evidence." *Leadership Quarterly* 14, no. 6: 807–834.

Eagly, Alice H., Steven J. Karau, and Mona G. Makhijani. 1995. "Gender and the Effectiveness of Leaders: A Meta-analysis." *Psychological Bulletin* 117, no. 1: 125.

European Commission. 2014. "Towards an Integrated Approach to Cultural Heritage for Europe." COM 477/2014. https://ec.europa.eu/assets/eac/culture/library/publications/2014-heritage-communication_en.pdf.

Frey, B. S., and S. Meier. 2006. "The Economics of Museums." In *Handbook of the Economics of Art and Culture*, edited by V. Ginsburgh and C. D. Throsby, 99–118. Amsterdam: Elsevier-North Holland.

Forte, Pierpaolo. 2015. "I nuovi musei statali: un primo passo nella giusta direzione." *Aedon* 1: 7–12.

Griffin, Des. 1991. "Museums—Governance, Management and Government: Or, Why Are So Many of the Apples on the Ground So Far from the Tree?" *Museum Management and Curatorship* 10, no. 3: 293–304.

Griffin, Des, and Morris Abraham. 2000. "The Effective Management of Museums: Cohesive Leadership and Visitor-Focused Public Programming." *Museum Management and Curatorship* 18, no. 4: 335–368.

Harrison, David A., and Katherine J. Klein. 2007. "What's the Difference? Diversity Constructs as Separation, Variety, or Disparity in Organizations." *Academy of Management Review* 32, no. 4: 1199–1228.

Harrison, David A., Kenneth H. Price, Joanne H. Gavin, and Anna T. Florey. 2002. "Time, teams, and task performance: Changing effects of surface-and deep-level diversity on group functioning." *Academy of management journal* 45, no. 5: 1029–1045.

Hendry, Kevin, and Geoffrey C. Kiel. 2004. "The Role of the Board in Firm Strategy: Integrating Agency and Organisational Control Perspectives." *Corporate Governance: An International Review* 12, no. 4: 500–520.

Hillman, Amy J., Albert A. Cannella, and Ramona L. Paetzold. 2000. "The Resource Dependence Role of Corporate Directors: Strategic Adaptation of Board Composition in Response to Environmental Change." *Journal of Management Studies* 37, no. 2: 235–256.

Hillman, Amy J., and Thomas Dalziel. 2003. "Boards of Directors and Firm Performance: Integrating Agency and Resource Dependence Perspectives." *Academy of Management Review* 28, no. 3: 383–396.

Hillman, Amy J., Gavin Nicholson, and Christine Shropshire. 2008. "Directors' multiple identities, identification, and board monitoring and resource provision." *Organization Science* 19, no. 3: 441–456.

Hillman, Amy J., Michael C. Withers, and Brian J. Collins. 2009. "Resource Dependence Theory: A Review." *Journal of Management* 35, no. 6: 1404–1427.

ICOM. 2020. "Museums, Museum Professionals and COVID-19." International Council of Museums. https://icom.museum/wp-content/uploads/2020/05/Report-Museums-and-COVID-19.pdf.

ICOM. n.d. "Museum Definition." International Council of Museums. https://icom.museum/en/resources/standards-guidelines/museum-definition/.

Jansen, Justin J. P., Frans A. J. Van den Bosch, and Henk W. Volberda. 2005. "Exploratory Innovation, Exploitative Innovation, and Ambidexterity: The Impact of Environmental and Organizational Antecedents." *Schmalenbach Business Review* 57: 351–363.

Jaskyte, Kristina. 2017. "Board Effectiveness and Innovation in Nonprofit Organizations." *Human Service Organizations: Management, Leadership and Governance* 41, no. 5: 453–463.

Jaskyte, Kristina, and Thomas Holland. 2015. "Nonprofit Boards: Challenges and Opportunities." *Human Service Organizations: Management, Leadership and Governance* 39, no. 3: 163–166.

Jaw, Yi-Long, and Wen-Ting Lin. 2009. "Corporate Elite Characteristics and Firm's Internationalization: CEO-Level and TMT-Level Roles." *International Journal of Human Resource Management* 20, no. 1: 220–233.

Johnson, Scott G., Karen Schnatterly, and Aaron D. Hill. 2013. "Board Composition Beyond Independence: Social Capital, Human Capital, and Demographics." *Journal of Management* 39, no. 1: 232–262.

Khan, Walayet A., and João Paulo Vieito. 2013. "CEO Gender and Firm Performance." *Journal of Economics and Business* 67: 55–66.

Khanna, Poonam, Carla D. Jones, and Steven Boivie. 2014. "Director Human Capital, Information Processing Demands, and Board Effectiveness." *Journal of Management* 40, no. 2: 557–585.

Kotler, Neil, and Philip Kotler. 2000. "Can Museums Be All Things to All People? Missions, Goals, and Marketing's Role." *Museum Management and Curatorship* 18, no. 3: 271–287.

Landriani, Loris. 2012. *Modelli di gestione per le aziende dei beni culturali: l'esperienza delle soprintendenze speciali*. Milan: FrancoAngeli.

Le, Son, and Mark Kroll. 2017. "CEO International Experience: Effects on Strategic Change and Firm Performance." *Journal of International Business Studies* 48, no. 5: 573–595.

Lindqvist, Katja. 2012. "Effects of Public Sector Reforms on the Management of Cultural Organizations in Europe." *International Studies of Management and Organization* 42, no. 2: 9–28.

Lusiani, Maria, and Luca Zan. 2011. "Change and Continuity in Managerialism: 100 Years of Administrative History at the International Museum of Ceramics in Faenza." *Management and Organizational History* 6, no. 1: 59–80.

Mannix, Elizabeth, and Margaret A. Neale. 2005. "What Differences Make a Difference? The Promise and Reality of Diverse Teams in Organizations." *Psychological Science in the Public Interest* 6, no. 2: 31–55.

Marzano, Marianna, and Monia Castellini. 2018. "The Reform of the Italian Ministry of Cultural Heritage: Implications for Governance of the Museum System." *Journal of Arts Management, Law, and Society* 48, no. 3: 206–220.

McCall, Vikki, and Clive Gray. 2014. "Museums and the 'New Museology': Theory, Practice and Organisational Change." *Museum Management and Curatorship* 29, no. 1: 19–35.

Miller, Judith L. 2002. "The Board as a Monitor of Organizational Activity: The Applicability of Agency Theory to Nonprofit Boards." *Nonprofit Management and Leadership* 12, no. 4: 429–450.

Miller, Toyah, and María del Carmen Triana. 2009. "Demographic Diversity in the Boardroom: Mediators of the Board Diversity–Firm Performance Relationship." *Journal of Management Studies* 46, no. 5: 755–786.

Miller-Millesen, Judith L. 2003. "Understanding the Behavior of Nonprofit Boards of Directors: A Theory-Based Approach." *Nonprofit and Voluntary Sector Quarterly* 32, no. 4: 521–547.

Minichilli, Alessandro, Alessandro Zattoni, and Fabio Zona. 2009. "Making Boards Effective: An Empirical Examination of Board Task Performance." *British Journal of Management* 20, no. 1: 55–74.

Minichilli, Alessandro, Guido Corbetta, and Ian C. MacMillan. 2010. "Top management teams in family-controlled companies: 'familiness', 'faultlines', and their impact on financial performance." *Journal of Management Studies* 47, no. 2: 205–222.

NEMO. 2021. "Follow-Up Survey on the Impact of the COVID-19 Pandemic on Museums in Europe—Final Report." Network of Museum Organizations, November 1, 2021. https://www.ne-mo.org/fileadmin/Dateien/public/NEMO_documents/NEMO_COVID19_FollowUpReport_11.1.2021.pdf.

Nielsen, Bo Bernhard, and Sabina Nielsen. 2013. "Top Management Team Nationality Diversity and Firm Performance: A Multilevel Study." *Strategic Management Journal* 34, no. 3: 373–382.

Noh, Shinwon, and Pamela S. Tolbert. 2019. "Organizational Identities of US Art Museums and Audience Reactions." *Poetics* 72: 94–107.

Oster, Sharon, and William N. Goetzmann. 2003. *Does Governance Matter?* Chicago: University of Chicago Press.

Ostrower, Francie, and Melissa M. Stone. 2006. "Governance: Research Trends, Gaps, and Future Prospects." In *The Nonprofit Sector*, 2nd ed., edited by Walter W. Powell and Richard Steinberg, 612–628. New Haven, CT: Yale University Press.

Ostrower, Francie, and Melissa M. Stone. 2010. "Moving Governance Research Forward: A Contingency-Based Framework and Data Application." *Nonprofit and Voluntary Sector Quarterly* 39, no. 5: 901–924.

Peni, Emilia. 2014. "CEO and Chairperson Characteristics and Firm Performance." *Journal of Management and Governance* 18, no. 1: 185–205.

Pulh, Mathilde, and Rémi Mencarelli. 2015. "Web 2.0: Is the Museum Visitor Relationship Being Redefined?" *International Journal of Arts Management* 18, no. 1: 43–51.

Rentschler, Ruth. 2004. "Four by Two Theory of Non profit Museum Governance." *Museological Review* 11: 30–41.

Rhoades, Dawna L., Paula L. Rechner, and Chamu Sundaramurthy. 2000. "Board Composition and Financial Performance: A Meta-analysis of the Influence of Outside Directors." *Journal of Managerial Issues* 12, no. 1: 76–91.

La Repubblica. 2015. "Musei, nominati 20 direttori. Sette sono stranieri." *La Repubblica*, August 18, 2015. repubblica.it/speciali/arte/recensioni/2015/08/18/news/musei_in_arrivo_tanti_direttori_stranieri-121165361/.

Schubert, Renate. 2006. "Analyzing and Managing Risks—On the Importance of Gender Differences in Risk Attitudes." *Managerial Finance* 32, no. 9: 706–715.

Schuster, J. Mark. 1998. "Neither Public Nor Private: The Hybridization of Museums." *Journal of Cultural Economics* 22: 127–150.

Shen, Wei, Qiong Zhou, and Chung-Ming Lau. 2016. "Empirical Research on Corporate Governance in China: A Review and New Directions for the Future." *Management and Organization Review* 12, no. 1: 41–73.

Sironi, Francesca. 2017. "I nuovi musei? Molto marketing, poca sostanza." *La Repubblica*, October 20, 2017. https://espresso.repubblica.it/attualita/2017/10/20/news/i-nuovi-musei-molto-marketing-poca-sostanza-285299495/.

Smith, Nina, Valdemar Smith, and Mette Verner. 2006. "Do Women in Top Management Affect Firm Performance? A Panel Study of 2,500 Danish firms." *International Journal of Productivity and Performance Management* 55, no. 7: 569–593.

Stone, Melissa M., Mark A. Hager, and Jennifer J. Griffin. 2001. "Organizational Characteristics and Funding Environments: A Study of a Population of United Way–Affiliated Nonprofits." *Public Administration Review* 61, no. 3: 276–289.

Stone, Melissa M., and Francie Ostrower. 2007. "Acting in the Public Interest? Another Look at Research on Nonprofit Governance." *Nonprofit and Voluntary Sector Quarterly* 36, no. 3: 416–438.

Taheri, Babak, Aliakbar Jafari, and Kevin O'Gorman. 2014. "Keeping Your Audience: Presenting a Visitor Engagement Scale." *Tourism Management* 42: 321–329.

Tajfel, Henri, and John C. Turner. 1979. "An Integrative Theory of Intergroup Conflict." In *The Social Psychology of Intergroup Relations*, ed. William G. Austin and Stephen Worchel, 33–37. Monterey, CA: Brooks/Cole.

Tekleab, Amanuel G., Ayse Karaca, Narda R. Quigley, and Eric WK Tsang. 2016. "Re-examining the Functional Diversity–Performance Relationship: The Roles of Behavioral Integration, Team Cohesion, and Team Learning." *Journal of Business Research* 69, no. 9: 3500–3507.

Throsby, David. 2010. *The Economics of Cultural Policy*. Cambridge: Cambridge University Press.

Turbide, Johanne. 2012. "Can Good Governance Prevent Financial Crises in Arts Organizations?" *International Journal of Arts Management* 14, no. 2: 4.

Turner, John C., Michael A. Hogg, Penelope J. Oakes, Stephen D. Reicher, and Margaret S. Wetherell. 1987. *Rediscovering the Social Group: A Self-categorization Theory*. Oxford: Blackwell.

Van Knippenberg, Daan, Carsten K. W. De Dreu, and Astrid C. Homan. 2004. "Work Group Diversity and Group Performance: An Integrative Model and Research Agenda." *Journal of Applied Psychology* 89, no. 6: 1008.

Daan Van Knippenberg, Jeremy F. Dawson, Michael A. West, and Astrid C. Homan. 2011." Diversity faultlines, shared objectives, and top management team performance." *Human Relations* 64, no. 3: 307–336.

Vicente, Eva, Carmen Camarero, and María José Garrido. 2012. "Insights into Innovation in European Museums: The Impact of Cultural Policy and Museum Characteristics." *Public Management Review* 14, no. 5: 649–679.

Vieito, Joao Paulo Torre. 2012. "Gender, Top Management Compensation Gap, and Company Performance: Tournament Versus Behavioral Theory." *Corporate Governance: An International Review* 20, no. 1: 46–63.

Westphal, James D., and Edward J. Zajac. 2013. "A Behavioral Theory of Corporate Governance: Explicating the Mechanisms of Socially Situated and Socially Constituted Agency." *Academy of Management Annals* 7, no. 1: 607–661.

Williams, Richard. 2012. "Using the Margins Command to Estimate and Interpret Adjusted Predictions and Marginal Effects." *Stata Journal* 12, no. 2: 308–331.

Yi, Yaqun, Hermann Achidi Ndofor, Xiaoming He, and Zelong Wei. 2017. "Top Management Team Tenure Diversity and Performance: The Moderating Role of Behavioral Integration." *IEEE Transactions on Engineering Management* 65, no. 1: 21–33.

Zan, Luca, Sara Bonini Baraldi, and Maria Elena Santagati. 2018. "Missing HRM: The Original Sin of Museum Reforms in Italy." *Museum Management and Curatorship* 33, no. 6: 530–545.

PART V

MANAGEMENT STRUCTURES AND STRATEGIES FOR ARTS AND CULTURAL ORGANIZATIONS

CHAPTER 18

EVENT CO-CREATION

A Participatory Perspective on Arts and Cultural Management

LEONORE VAN DEN ENDE

Introduction

INCREASINGLY, the evolution of artistic and cultural events like festivals evidences a shift from mere spectatorship to active participation (Chen 2012). In contrast to prior event studies that draw stricter distinctions between organizers and audiences, the latter are more recently perceived as productive agents, too, creatively involved in the making and experience of the event, driven by a desire for more engagement (Caru and Cova 2007). This development of "event co-creation" (Haanpää 2017) increasingly engages participants in artistic and cultural programming with an emphasis on experience, immersion, and play (O'Grady 2015), thereby filling gaps between spectacle and spectator (Robinson 2015, 2). Studying event co-creation necessitates a better grasp of the collective creative activities of multiple stakeholders, not only managers and organizers but also volunteers and attendees (Haanpää 2017).

Situated in the academic debates on arts and cultural management more broadly, and festival and event studies more precisely, this chapter questions whether and how research on event co-creation allows for the development of novel perspectives for arts and cultural management. The field of arts and cultural management, concerned with how cultural organizations, events, and practices are or should be managed, has been dominated by top-down, utilitarian, and reductionist approaches, with little room for bottom-up innovation and critical reflection on practice (Ebewo and Sirayi 2009; DeVereaux 2015; Lang 2015). Similarly, economic, rationalist, and instrumental approaches prevail in the field of festival and event studies, with an evident underrepresentation of interpretive, cultural, and critical perspectives (Frost 2016; Robinson 2015; Getz 2010; Haanpää 2017). The current chapter hopes to address some of these shortcomings by studying event co-creation as an emergent and practice-based process, via the application of ethnographic methods and anthropological theories that emphasize activities of cultural participation and production (Frost 2016; van den Ende 2021b; Jaimangal-Jones 2014; Bourdieu 1993; St John 2008).

To narrow the scope of inquiry, this research focuses on festivals that are organized and produced according to co-creative frameworks in the sense that they promote and facilitate the active participation of multiple actors, such as volunteers and attendees. Theoretically, festivals are understood from a ritual perspective (St John 2008; Turner 1969)—namely, as ritualized events that form temporary, "liminal" spaces intentionally set apart from ordinary, everyday settings and activities (van den Ende 2021b). In the theoretical frame, I explain how this temporary separation from the everyday can stimulate communal creativity and instill the festival with transformative capacity (Abrahams 1987; Turner 1982). Thereafter, in the methods section, I present the ethnographic case study of the festival Tribal Gathering and supplementary data collected via in-depth interviews with various festival organizers concerning the theme of event co-creation. In the findings, I exhibit how festivals are organized and produced to create an immersive and participatory experience and, thereby, to establish a unique event in contrast to a more mainstream festival experience. Analyses indicate that such festivals are constructed as "safe spaces" and "cultural incubators" to stimulate cultural participation and production in a grassroots way. Moreover, rather than this being a purely bottom-up and spontaneous process that emerges in situ, the research shows how event managers and organizers strategically design and program festivals to enable co-creation as a kind of "programmed freedom" (Cova, Dalli, and Zwick 2011), an ironic notion that will be further discussed. Last, the chapter discusses the implications of this research for the development of fresh perspectives for arts and cultural management—theoretically, in terms of a "participatory perspective" for arts and cultural management, and pragmatically, in terms of the organization of liminal, safe spaces that enable cultural participation and (co-)production.

Festival Studies in the Artistic and Cultural Sector

Associated with communal celebration, festivals represent significant artistic and cultural events (Delanty, Giorgi, and Sassatelli 2011) encountered in all human cultures (Falassi 1987). Festivals can be religious, cultural, or political; urban or rural; seasonal or intermittent; artistic or musical (or an amalgamation thereof); focused on a variety of publics, activities, and themes; and found on a scale ranging from local to global. As sites of cultural production and participation, festivals are multifaceted, complex, and dynamic (Frost 2016). While festivals are ancient and historically pervasive, in the last few decades they have flourished in quantity, capacity, variety, and popularity across borders, a development theorized as the "festivalization of culture" (Woodward, Taylor, and Bennett 2014) or the "festivalization of society" (Richards 2007). Due to this development, and to the fact that there is no widely accepted definition of the term "festival," there is quite a deal of variation in terms of how festivals are approached and conceptualized, and research content very much depends on the theoretical perspective utilized (Cudny 2016, chap. 2). Consequently, a broad range of disciplinary perspectives can be found in the relatively young field of festival studies, representing an important subfield within event studies (Getz 2010).

Although the "new" field of festival studies has emerged within event studies in the last decade, the abundant anthropological and sociological research on festivals predates this development (e.g., Turner 1982; Radin 1946; Hartmann 1978; Freed and Freed 1964; Barnett 1949; Duvignaud 1976), focusing on aspects such as culture, ritual, ceremony, celebration, liminality, symbolism, and meaning (Getz 2010, 4). It is odd, then, that a social science perspective is lacking in the current festival studies debate, in which management, tourism, economics, and policymaking have gained a stronger foothold, accompanied by instrumentalist and rationalist approaches (Frost 2016; Anderton 2008). Getz (2012) claims that the difference in perspective, which is apparent not only in festival studies but in event studies more broadly, relates to research focus. While event management and event tourism are more concerned with organizing, policymaking, and marketing from an instrumental and economic perspective, with the aim of mapping out causal relations and impacts, anthropology and sociology emphasize meanings and practices from a critical, cultural, and historical perspective to capture the subjective, lived, and shared experience of events. According to Frost (2016, 570), "anthropology—as critical analytical approach, and as proponent of ethnographic method—is largely absent from the [festival studies] debate" because it is perceived as too "academic" and focused on traditional societies, "with little of value to say to festival organizers and related policy makers."

Frost and others (Robinson 2015; Sherry, Kozinets, and Borghini 2013; Haanpää 2017; Chalcraft and Magaudda 2011) call to reinsert the anthropological perspective and ethnographic methods in festival and event studies, as those tools are means of capturing the social and cultural actors, activities, and contexts of contemporary festivals via in-depth empirical investigation and critical reflection. Similarly, Getz (2010) calls for interdisciplinary theory development, where organization and management studies and anthropology should not shy away from one another but reach out to one another to contribute original insights to festival and event studies. This interdisciplinary connection is precisely what I wish to make in this chapter by combing a focus on festival organization, event co-creation, and anthropological theories and methods to draw out implications for arts and cultural management.

Festival Organization and Event Co-creation

Festivals do not just emerge in situ; rather, they require long-term planning, (de)construction, and stakeholder engagement in pre- and post-festival phases (Wilson et al. 2017). In that sense, festivals are recurrent and complex (inter)organizational productions (Toraldo and Islam 2019), following project-based life cycles, directed by variable agendas, and reliant on an assembly of organizers, producers, attendees, and other stakeholders who co-create the event (St John 2018; Getz 2010; Schüßler and Sydow 2015; Chen 2012). While festivals are themselves temporary events, the organizations, networks, and stakeholders involved have continuity over time (Uriarte et al. 2019; Omidvar, Burke, and Galalae 2020). Moreover, in order to thrive and survive in an increasingly competitive festival market, festivals are never truly temporary but aspire to recur, grow, evolve, and even multiply over time. Encapsulating this paradox of temporality and continuity, festivals can be understood as temporary organizational events embedded in more permanent structures and processes (DeFillippi and Uriarte 2020).

Studying event co-creation can help to gain insight into how festivals are produced and participated in by multiple actors, including organizers and attendees, and such studies have theoretical implications for the field of festival and event studies. According to Haanpää (2017, 17), co-creation remains a relatively uncharted area of research in festival and event studies. Stemming from marketing and consumption research, the concept of co-creation refers mainly to "the production of value that takes place increasingly via the interaction between firm and consumer . . . recognizing that production and consumption are two sides of the same coin" (Cova, Dalli, and Zwick 2011, 232). An important implication is that consumers are not passive recipients of products and/or services but active agents and participants who co-create value through their active engagement in (consumption) experiences (Akaka, Schau, and Vargo 2013; Goolaup and Mossberg 2017). Chen (2012, 571), who draws from ethnographic fieldwork on the co-creative event Burning Man, calls this integration of production and consumption "prosumption," based on a do-it-yourself (DIY) ethos, often encouraged and promoted by organizations in order to decentralize, democratize, build loyalty, innovate, or cut costs. Festivals are especially suitable sites to study co-creation because they provide attendees or consumers with social opportunities to create and share experiences (Goolaup and Mossberg 2017, 41).

While the concept of value co-creation has gained academic cachet, Karababa and Kjeldgaard (2014, 119–120) also point out that it is a notoriously elusive concept because there are multiple understandings of value, based on the fundamental assumptions of diverse theoretical perspectives—for example, economic value, functional value, emotional value, and cultural value. In a similar vein, Ramaswamy (2011, 195) notes that co-creation goes far beyond the conventional products-and-services view of exchange processes, as value is contingent on ongoing human experiences, interactions, and dialogue, which can be facilitated via "engagement platforms." Hence, although this chapter is informed by the debate on value co-creation (particularly the blurring of the boundary between producers and consumers and between organizers and attendees) to depart from the ambiguity of the "value" concept, I understand event co-creation from a practice-based perspective, not merely in terms of the perceived value it may have for diverse actors but also as co-creating the "lived" and shared event itself via cultural participation and production. This approach encapsulates what multiple actors *do* in terms of their co-creative and interactive activities in the making and enactment of events in practice.

Festivals, Liminality, and Creativity

Though festivals involve detailed attention to managerial and organizational aspects such as planning, coordinating, and programming, participation in such events is also emergent, unpredictable, spontaneous, and chaotic, with blurred distinctions between organizers, performers, and attendees (Frost 2016). Studying event co-creation as the integration of production and consumption, and work and leisure, in the organized chaos of festivals requires novel perspectives and empirical inquiry (Toraldo and Islam 2019; Chen 2009).

As stated in the introduction, this chapter aims to investigate event co-creation with an empirical focus on festivals and to highlight the implications for the development of original perspectives for arts and cultural management. I apply a practice-based perspective, informed by anthropological theory, to study the activities through which diverse actors create a festival. Various anthropologists (e.g., Turner 1982; Abrahams 1987; Gilmore 2008; Boissevain 2016; St John 2015) understand festivals as ritualized events—as celebratory and cathartic occasions performed within a temporary, "liminal" space, involving performative activities that construct certain meanings and realities (Schechner 2012; Turner 1982; van den Ende 2021b). As ritualized events, festivals can be perceived as extraordinary and participatory cultural productions, distinguished from more ordinary activities and settings. Here, the concept of "ritualization"—which can be understood as a cultural practice for making distinctions and "making special" (see also Bell 1992)—is useful, as it can show how and why various activities of event (co-)creation produce a contrast between ordinary life and the extraordinary occasion of the event; through this contrast the event establishes its cultural significance and value (van den Ende 2021a). In other words, ritualization encapsulates the ways in which diverse participants create the festival to inscribe it with meaning and intentionally set it apart from quotidian life, having transformative capacity (Turner 1982; Maffesoli 2012). Ritualization can thus be seen as a creative practice through which participants shape events and their experiences (Gordon Lennox 2017).

Fundamental to understanding what ritualization accomplishes is the liminality of festival space (van den Ende 2021b). Ritualization produces a liminal space within which individuals and groups are set apart from mainstream society and the everyday, suspending normal social rules and thus forming a site of playful creativity (Skjoldager-Nielsen and Edelman 2014, 2). Turner (1969) calls this state of temporary suspension from the everyday "anti-structure," which can elicit "communitas" or a sense of togetherness and community through shared experience. Myerhoff (1982, 117) adds that liminal spaces simultaneously question the status quo while providing a source of renewal, innovation, and creativity. Similarly, O'Grady (2017, 3) points out that festival spaces can be consciously constructed to enable cultural expression and participation, setting such playful spaces apart from everyday life. In this way, the liminal spaces of festivals, which are situated in between more stable states and realities, provide occupants with temporary freedom to experiment and explore, from which creativity and novelty emerge, having the potential to enact change or transformation (Kociatkiewicz and Kostera 2015). Various authors (e.g., Robinson 2015; Schmidt 2017; Chen 2009; St John 2017) suggest that event co-creation is associated with the transformative potential of a festival, though this relation is not yet well understood (van den Ende 2021a).

A relevant development in the festival industry is the intentional design of liminal spaces by event producers to create an extraordinary, transitional environment and experience. According to St John (2015, 243), some festival producers engage in intentional ritualization and liminalization to enable participants to enter a transitional space, facilitated through sensorial media, design, and architectonic. Here, festival organizers increasingly utilize a participatory design and multimedia programming, including music, dance, workshops, interactive art, rituals, and ceremonies (Schmidt 2017, 93), to co-produce, together with attendees, an immersive space and an interactive experience that goes beyond a more mainstream presentational, lineup-based festival (Robinson 2015). Evident is the purposeful use of aesthetic design, orchestration, and appropriation, involving aspects such as scenography and choreography that transform conditions and engage the audience in order to elicit particular experiences (van den Ende 2021a). The participatory and immersive activities involved in event co-creation are evidence not only of a current trend in the festival scene but also of an intentional organizational strategy to produce an authentic experience and provide novel cultural value within an increasingly competitive festival market (Johansson and Toraldo 2017; Quinn and Wilks 2017; De Molli, Mengis, and van Marrewijk 2020; St John 2017; van den Ende 2021b).

Methods

A central method utilized in this research is ethnography, which is a qualitative research strategy to describe, interpret, and explain the behavior, meaning, and cultural productions of persons involved in a limited field through direct data collection by researchers who are physically present (Yanow and Schwartz-Shea 2006). The aim is to provide insight into the daily activities and sense-making of the studied population (Bate 1997). This research adopts an interpretive ontology, assuming that knowledge is generated by people who live and work in a particular setting, and that it must be understood through that same point of view (Hatch and Cunliffe 2006).

This research is principally based on an ethnographic case study of a festival called Tribal Gathering, conducted from February 28 to March 16, 2020, right on the brink of the coronavirus pandemic. Curated by the nonprofit organization GeoParadise, primarily to preserve and support indigenous cultures and traditions, Tribal Gathering is an eighteen-day co-creative event that takes place in the Panamanian jungle bordering the Caribbean Sea (GeoParadise 2020). I engaged in participant observation during the festival to gather direct data and to experience and observe the festival space "from the inside." Focusing on themes of festival organization, production, participation, and co-creation, I also carried out twelve in-depth semi-structured interviews as well as multiple conversations with organizers, workers, volunteers, and attendees, selected via snowball sampling during the event. To document findings and (re)analyze the event, I also gathered data in the form of fieldnotes, photographs, and videos.

Because the coronavirus pandemic resulted in the mass cancellation of festivals and other cultural events around the world right after the 2020 Tribal Gathering concluded, my ethnographic participant observation was limited to that particular event, which has consequently become a main focus of the research. To carry on with the research and gather a more diverse dataset, twelve supplementary in-depth interviews were conducted with various professionals in the event industry about their practices of event co-creation, including reflections on other co-creative and participatory events, such as Burning Man events in the United States and other countries and the Boom festival in Portugal. While I did not carry out ethnographic research at these other events, I have attended the Boom festival in Portugal (in 2018 and 2022) and Burning Man regional events in the Netherlands (in 2018, 2019, and 2021) as a participant, thereby gaining firsthand experience to supplement other data. These events have been included in the findings for a more comparative analysis concerning the theme of event co-creation. Supplementary research respondents were purposely chosen because of their engagement with event co-creation and their practices of utilizing festival spaces to facilitate participation and creativity, in line with the focus of this research. Table 18.1 presents a list of interviews.

Festival Organization: The Organized Chaos of Festivals

Co-creative events like Tribal Gathering, Burning Man, and Boom are purposely organized as decentralized, self organizing, and non-sponsored events to facilitate cultural participation and (co-)production. These events fall, to varying degrees, under the category "transformational festival" (e.g., Bottorff 2015; Johner 2015; St John 2020), denoting the idea that the festival can serve as a space for cultural intervention and social change (Wiltshire and Davis 2009, 24). Beyond featuring music, these events often host a wide range of immersive (inter)activities to restore participants' connection to community and environment, guided by principles such as participation, sustainable living, and creative expression (St John 2015, 246).

Tribal Gathering, which serves as the main case study here, is, as noted earlier, an eighteen-day event situated in the jungle, organized by the nonprofit organization

Table 18.1. Research Respondents

Resp.	Role	Gender	Affiliation	Type	Methods
1	Technician	M	Tribal Gathering, Panama	Event	Case study, participant observation, in-depth interviews (2020)
2	Engineer	M			
3	Coordinator	F			
4	Coordinator	F			
5	Photographer	M			
6	Performer	F			
7	Performer	M			
8	Performer	M			
9	Volunteer	M			
10	Attendee/volunteer	M			
11	Attendee/volunteer	M			
12	Attendee	F			
13	Director	M	Burning Man, United States	Event	In-depth interviews (2020–2021)
14	Producer	F		Event	
15	Curator	F	Fusion, Germany	Event	
			Boom, Portugal	Event	
16	Engineer	M	Boom, Portugal	Event	
17	Founder	M	Naam, South Africa	Event	
18	Manager	F	Kamiwaza, France	Event	
			Garbicz, Poland	Event	
19	Founder/manager	F	The Experience Enhancers, Netherlands	Organization	
20	Director/researcher	F	A Greener Festival, United Kingdom	Organization	
21	Founder/director	M	Green Music Initiative, Germany	Organization	
22	Advisor	F	Ministry of Infrastructure and Water, Netherlands	Organization	
23	Programmer	F	Amsterdam Institute for Metropolitan Solutions, Netherlands	Organization	
24	Advisor	M	Performing Arts Fund, Netherlands	Organization	

GeoParadise. There are approximately two thousand participants, half of whom are organizers, workers, performers, and volunteers, and the other half of whom are attendees, though "there's a real blurring between the people who organize stuff and . . . the audience, where people kind of tend to move from one to the other" (respondent 1). The festival is annually (de)constructed, with the aim to "leave no trace" behind in the natural environment. Production of the festival is a cyclical project-based process involving "a high turnover of crew [who would] come do it for a couple of years and then move on and do something else" (respondent 2). Because each event is a unique production, "you never, ever can prepare for any year because every year is different" (respondent 4). As the event is still growing and does not make a profit, according to respondents, the crew members generally don't receive a salary, though their flight ticket, accommodation, and food and drinks are covered.

The event's flexible, multimedia programming, including music, dance, workshops, presentations, exhibitions, rituals, and ceremonies, makes it so that "all [participants] get the chance to involve [themselves] in the creative process" (GeoParadise 2020). An important finding is that Tribal Gathering is "deliberately not coordinated" but it is more "like a set of experiments" (respondent 1). The event organizers and producers build the festival in a more emergent and experimental way, where "people can make their ideas, make their own stuff [and are] like totally self-sufficient" (respondent 2). Evident here is a lack of a clear management style; instead, "you kind of need to take it on and say, OK, I'm going to decide that now because there's no clear instruction" (respondent 3). While respondents, organizers, and attendees alike generally appreciate this flexible organizational structure, it was also described as "chaotic" and "quite frustrating for people if they're used to working in other sites and organizations where things are a bit more organized" (respondent 1).

The concept of maintaining a balance between organization and chaos at festivals, which can be "quite a tricky thing" (respondent 1), relates to prior research on the "creative chaos" of the US Burning Man event, where rapid growth in the 1990s required organizational professionalization to regulate the chaos (Chen 2009). Burning Man has been described as "the biggest community-driven event" (respondent 14), and principles such as participation, communal effort, and self-reliance facilitate its DIY culture. Though there are some seventy thousand participants in its main event in Black Rock City, Nevada, Burning Man is far from being a singular event. Since its commencement in 1986, the main event has proliferated to include eighty-five (and counting) regional events worldwide, indicative of the Burning Man Project's mission to extend its culture into the wider world. "We called it the Burning Man *Project* because it was an ongoing project.... Each year is a different project or manifestation of the social experiment" (respondent 13). Compared to Tribal Gathering, apparent at Burning Man events is a more sophisticated organizational style that evolved over the years as the organization grew to include more participants in multiple events and locales. Whereas in its first decade Burning Man "was a place where you definitely felt a sense of anarchy" and where some members "really valued anarchy over organization" (respondent 13), over time event producers had to adopt a more structured organizational style: "freedom-loving people went to the most removed place from society possible and yet, in order for the experiment to continue, had to adopt tactics of society" (respondent 13). One way in which this is done is by establishing and communicating a distinct ethos and providing clear principles to guide and shape the behavior of its participants, such as "gifting," "communal effort," and "participation" (Burning Man 2022b).

The Boom festival in Portugal, too, has devised principles to shape the culture and practices of its event, including "active participation," "creativity," and "sustainability"

(Boom 2022b). Boom (which typically has about two thousand workers and forty thousand participants) is a biannual "transformational" festival held at a site called Boomland, in the rugged countryside of Idanha-a-Nova municipality. Boom started in 1997 as a psychedelic trance party and evolved into a global celebration of alternative culture. Boom has become a reference point for sustainability in large events, as it uses sustainable energy resources, composts waste, builds with recycled materials, helps to regenerate ecosystems, practices permaculture, and raises environmental awareness. The event also organizes knowledge exchange platforms, lectures, and workshops for learning and stimulating "holistic activism" through its program and venue. Every Boom event has a theme that shapes its program and design; the 2022 theme was "Anthropocene." The organizers describe the theme as a "need to envision new ways of cohabiting harmoniously . . . . [and] conceive innovative ways of doing things," which can be accomplished only by active participants rather than passive observers. (Boom 2022a).

Another aspect that sets Boom apart from a more mainstream festival is its lack of commercial sponsorship—a trait it shares with Tribal Gathering and Burning Man:

> There is no visual pollution like ads. I remember the first time I was blown away; I've never been with so many people in one place without a big sign that says "Heineken," "Telecom," or whatever, "Red Bull." . . . I thought, you need the sponsors, and if you don't have sponsors, you cannot have so many people together. So, there was also this feeling of something very revolutionary and radical, something different now.
>
> (Respondent 15)

Compared to both Tribal Gathering and Boom, Burning Man goes a step further with its principles of "decommodification" and "gifting," which offer an alternative model of exchange to mainstream market capitalism in addition to the absence of corporate sponsors:

> There is no corporate sponsorship. You are entering a "decommodified" space that values who you are, not what you have. You are expected to collaborate, be inclusive, creative, connective and clean up after yourself. Participate actively as a citizen of Black Rock City.
>
> (Burning Man 2022a)

The gift economy and lack of monetary transactions within the festival space are certainly unique to Burning Man events. Yet an engineer at Tribal Gathering (respondent 3) rightly argued that not everyone can afford the time and money needed to attend these festivals, which are "catering for a select middle-class and typically white event-going market" (St John 2017, 11). Participants must cover at least the costs for entrance, travel, and supplies, regardless of whether the event supports monetary transactions within its temporary space or not. Hence, it is important to recognize the human geography and demography of such events, which are found mainly in modern Western societies.

While events like Tribal Gathering, Burning Man, and Boom are distinct in many respects, what they share is their lack of a commercially sponsored setup, their DIY culture, a co-creative framework, and efforts to maintain a balance between more controlled organizational processes and free cultural participation and co-production. Since Tribal Gathering is younger and smaller, the organization is currently more open and chaotic. Hence it will be interesting to observe how the organization develops if Tribal Gathering grows into a larger event, like Burning Man and Boom have done over the last decades, resulting in a need for greater organizational professionalization.

Event Co-creation: Volunteerism and Participation

While festival organizing requires substantial premeditation and coordination, co-creation at events like Tribal Gathering, Burning Man, and Boom is deliberately emergent: "It's a matter of intention . . . the build-up of the festival and who you bring in and how you co-create" (respondent 12). Here the role of the festival organizer is to "ask what is within the visitor and what can you draw out [of them] so that the visitor can contribute to the whole [event]" (respondent 19).

A central aspect characterizing co-created festivals is a large and flexible volunteer base, covering activities such as building, assisting, organizing, administering, cooking, hosting, presenting, and DJing. Some respondents at Tribal Gathering informed me that the purpose of such activities was not to make money—"obviously, the money doesn't matter" (respondent 10)—but rather to meet new people and to add to the experience. Others did mention that for people who have little money volunteering is pragmatic, as they do receive something in exchange for volunteer shifts, whether food and drink, accommodation, a small amount of monetary compensation, or something else: "I saw how brilliant the system is as well, that if you don't have enough money . . . you go there, you sign up, you work five hours, and your dinner and food is sorted" (respondent 3).

Some festival participants start out as a volunteer and work their way up in the organization to becoming a salaried worker. Even then, active participation in the event's co-creation remains a more important motive than financial gain; as one person put it, "I love working in festivals [because] I really like being around very creative people" (respondent 2). Another participant, who has been an attendee, volunteer, and paid worker at the Boom festival, noted:

> The first year I was a volunteer. The second year I got a little bit of money. You don't do this job for money. . . . I was really approaching it like an honor: "Oh my God, I can participate actively to the experience of the Boomers that come from all over the world." It was really very exciting.
>
> (Respondent 15)

There are of course various levels and means of participation in the festival, from attendee to volunteer to worker, depending on what people can afford to do and what it means to them:

> With Burning Man, I was always a volunteer. So, the fifteen years I spent producing all those festivals and all those events, I never got paid ... but some people can afford to give their time and donate their time, and some people can't. Some people need to get paid. There are those people that work the festivals, that work heavy machinery and do rigging and set up stages and sound systems, and they get paid to go from festival to festival. There are people that volunteer, and it's just what you can emotionally, physically, and financially afford, and the importance of it.
>
> (Respondent 14)

Besides a focus on volunteerism, co-creative festivals stimulate the active participation of attendees and other stakeholders: "The attendees, stakeholders, government, and society must directly participate in the festival decisions and moving things in the festival" (respondent 16). Attendees contribute to the festival's spatial production and experience through participatory and immersive programming that emphasizes not only music and dance but also manifold creative (inter)activities. For example, at Burning Man "they do the infrastructure so that you can be the most that you can be and create the most that you can create" (respondent 14). In Burning Man's culture of gifting, everyone is encouraged to be an active participant and contribute to the event's creation, which is seen as a gift: "It's all gifting. It's a gifting academy. Nothing is for bought or sold. There are no transactions" (respondent 14). At both Tribal Gathering and Boom, everyone can sign up to co-create the event, such as via volunteering, making art installations and decorating, giving workshops and presentations, giving performances, or offering therapies.

At Tribal Gathering there was a wide range of creative and cultural (inter)activities, including weaving, knitting, macramé, permaculture, chocolate making, jewelry making, musical instrument making and playing, painting and dyeing with natural materials, yoga, tai chi, reiki, breath work, meditation, sound healing, sweat lodges, sharing circles, tea ceremonies, fire ceremonies, dance ceremonies, cacao ceremonies, and entheogenic medicine ceremonies (see also van den Ende 2021a). During a permaculture workshop I participated in, we learned how to build a wall of the event's "chai shop" from natural materials including earth, clay, and plants. And during an upcycle workshop participants made costumes and art from trash picked up from the beach. In such open and creative spaces, participants gather "with a lot of exchange with the possibility to see what [they] can do" (respondent 7) and come to realize "that a festival can be more than a nice place to dance" (respondent 19). To explain the event's uniqueness and significance, respondents often differentiate between a participatory experience and a more traditional or mainstream hedonistic festival experience: "It's not just music and dance, and there are not just drugs involved. It's just really to connect with yourself, to connect with nature, to do workshops" (respondent 3). Here a main aspect is that co-creative events go beyond the party or music aspect of a festival to produce different kinds of experiences: "Before, some twenty or twenty-five years ago, you had festivals like you have a DJ who shoves music into the crowd and the crowd eats it up. Now there could also be a dialogue and then something *else* happens" (respondent 19).

According to various respondents, co-creation has a deeper meaning in the sense that people can explore their creative potential and tap into their creative selves, which has transformative potential: "Any festival that allows you and gives you permission and encourages you to participate in some way is a transformational festival" (respondent 14). Another respondent who attended Boom even claims that "the main objective of human beings is to co-create and [that] the festival is a very beautiful, pure way to get human beings to use their power of their function in this life" (respondent 16).

LIMINAL FESTIVAL: SAFE SPACES AND CULTURAL INCUBATORS

An essential aspect enabling communal creativity and experimentation to flourish at festivals is the liminal space of the event, which "gives you an open playground to explore the outer boundaries of yourself [and] the freedom to express yourself, however you want" (respondent 14). Respondents often refer to the festival space as a "safe space" where participants feel safe to openly express themselves and experiment with new activities and ideas without experiencing discrimination or judgment. One program curator claimed that "this is really like an art for a festival organizer, [to] create the feeling of trust between the people and the feeling of trust that the space is safe" (respondent 15).

Looking at liminal festival spaces through a lens of ritualization calls attention to the cultural strategy of differentiation, which establishes a contrast between the festival experience and more ordinary or daily experiences. It is this differentiation that instills the festival space with transformative capacity. In such spaces, "people can be free to be themselves separate from the hyper-capitalized [society] that we're experiencing" (respondent 13). Where "there is room for experimentation . . . people can discover what else is possible, beyond what they thought was possible" (respondent 19). And "by experiencing [the festival space], which has been pulling you away from regular society . . . you get into a different state of mind" (respondent 5). An important aspect of liminal spaces is that participants have experiences they usually don't, or can express themselves in ways different from what they do in their ordinary, everyday lives. For this reason, participatory festivals are often experienced as transformational:

> Festivals are the only offering where people are actually paying to undergo a transformation, even if it's only three days, but this is the main reason people attend festivals for. We've been doing so many surveys asking the attendees, why do you attend the festival? And nobody said because of the music. [They said] because we

are meeting new people, we can experience things we usually don't.... I would say this is a rite of passage.

(Respondent 21)

Not only is the demarcated space of festivals fundamental to creating a culturally authentic and transformative experience; equally so is its demarcated time frame. The temporal framework of festivals is perceived as enhancing a transitional environment: "The beauty of a festival is of course that it is temporary, [and] because it's temporary, you can experiment very well. Experiments which you can also carry out in the real world" (respondent 24). An important reference in this quote is a festival's transformative potential *beyond* the festival time-space itself. Specifically, various respondents allude to a festival's potential contribution to society, viewing a festival as a temporary "cultural incubator" (respondent 13) where participants can experiment, innovate, learn, and distill knowledge deemed as valuable to add to society outside the festival, too:

> I believe that our annual gathering and temporary city [Burning Man] has very much functioned as a forum for experimentation, and I often think about what we do as providing a forum to hack society itself in different aspects of society for the better, and the event and temporary city allows our entire community to prototype new technologies, new ways of thinking and even better ways of behaving together in the world.
>
> (Respondent 13)

A participant in Boom explains this transformative potential and contribution to society in terms of establishing a new common perception, which can be accomplished through the temporally and spatially demarcated environment of a co-created festival:

> Festivals are very important to today for the construction of a new society outside. Everybody that has been to a festival like Boom or Burning Man or others around the world. People change. People go outside with new ideas, new insights, new ways of thinking.... When you have this kind of festival people start creating together in a natural way a common sense that is a little bit different from the outside world. So, when you go to this festival [in] these days it's a new common sense. It's a new concept. It's a new way of thinking. And this is the beauty of the festival, is to construct a new paradigm.
>
> (Respondent 16)

Discussion and Conclusion

In this chapter I set out to study event co-creation with an empirical focus on festivals from a theoretical perspective of ritualization, and to explore how this allows for the development of novel perspectives for arts and cultural management. From a perspective of ritualization, a festival can be perceived as the conscious cultural co-production of a

liminal space "removing" participants from ordinary settings of everyday work and life and "transporting" them to an alternative reality and playful arena (van den Ende 2021b; O'Grady 2017) where participation, experimentation, and creativity are stimulated and experienced (Turner 1982). The festival space is thus instilled with transformative potential (Skjoldager-Nielsen and Edelman 2014). This echoes prior research on the ritualization and liminalization of contemporary festivals; St John (2015, 244) addresses "how advanced and complex states of liminality *potentiate* novel cultural forms." Various respondents have alluded to the novelty and creativity inherent in liminal festival spaces, where participants feel liberated to express themselves, and where they gain new ideas, insights, and ways of thinking and behaving through their situated, interactive participation. While this is an event specific and emergent process that transpires in situ, the research findings also indicate that such festivals
tend to be intentionally designed, organized, and programmed to enable and facilitate co-creation and a transitional environment according to participatory ideals.

From a more critical perspective, the co-creative framework of contemporary festivals has been criticized in extant literature, suggesting that consumers play in producing the festival is that of providing "free labor through the expropriation of knowledge, creativity, and communication" (Johansson and Toraldo 2017, 223). For example, Chen (2012), who studies co-created festivals, particularly Burning Man, addresses the tension between democracy and capitalism concerning the benefit attendees gain from partaking in the production of festivals—which she calls "prosumption"—vis-à-vis the exploitation of their knowledge and practices freely given, regardless of the degree of enjoyment of fulfillment experienced. Cova, Dalli, and Zwick (2011) claim this might be a "new form of capitalism" in which the labor of attendees is co-opted by festival organizations to produce festivals, helping to reduce costs and align the festival experience with the desires of visitors. Specifically, they state that "the co-creative model rests on establishing ambiances that program consumer freedom to evolve in ways that permit the harnessing of consumers' newly liberated, productive capabilities" (Cova, Dalli, and Zwick 2011, 233). In the same vein, Schmidt (2017) points out that though certain festivals differentiate themselves from mainstream, capitalist, and consumerist societies, they are nonetheless entangled with and enabled by them. The focus is on the "social differentiation" strategy, through which festival organizations find their niche in the market by highlighting the "atypical quality of the festival experience [and] counterposing it to an underlying idea of what might count as a more traditional festival experience" (Johansson and Toraldo 2017, 229). Framing plays an important role here, as festivals increasingly rely on their "strategic distinction" from other events that "do not offer countercultural authentica in their experiential design" (St John 2017, 11). This "programmed freedom" and framed "otherness" are thus part of a conscious organizational strategy to enable cultural participation and (co-)production, having implications in terms of both the empowerment and exploitation of festival participants. The paradoxical and ambiguous nature of liminal spaces (Turner 1982), particularly festivals (Frost 2016), makes it so that empowerment and exploitation coexist therein, as do freedom and programming. As one respondent said in an interview: "Training in liminality is the training and understanding of how two opposite realities can be present at the same time" (respondent 15).

The findings of this research have implications for the development of novel perspectives for arts and cultural management beyond the context of festival settings and organizations, extending to a broader range of artistic and cultural events and institutes. Arts and cultural management—concerned with the cultivation of the appropriate means and conditions for the production and dissemination of art and culture—is a debated field with ambiguous parameters, riddled with tensions between scholars and practitioners and between the creative practice and economic activity of art and culture (DeVereaux 2018). As the field came to emphasize the marketing, financial aspects, and administration of art and culture stemming from the "management" side, critical scholars have problematized the field for losing sight of the art and culture at its core, and for its indifference to contemporary, postmodern challenges. Instead, they call for more emergent, practice-based perspectives with a focus on cultural participation, decentralization, and co-determination. For example, Brkić (2009, 2–5) criticizes the application of a generic management approach to art and culture as failing to account for the social contextualization and meaning of art and culture or for processes of creativity and innovation integral to the production of art and culture. Rather, he argues, practitioners in the field should be taught and prepared to engage in "new ways of doing things," with an awareness of managerial and economic realities but principally focused on the aesthetic and social side of the field. In a similar vein, Ebewo and Sirayi (2009, 290) state that arts and cultural management tends toward management-centric, utilitarian and reductionist approaches, with little space for bottom-up innovation and critical reflection on its practice. Hence, they call for democratization of the field and propose interdisciplinary approaches concerned with the promotion of creativity and renewal, such as the need for cultural organizations to provide "the right atmosphere for people to exhibit their cultural expression." Similarly, Lang (2015, 31) proposes the emancipation of cultural management, so that culture can be actively shaped and co-produced beyond an instrumental and economic focus. One way to do this is by establishing temporary "in-between spaces" that provide open and safe settings for participatory culture to thrive, in turn allowing for the renegotiation of an extant status quo to enable social change. And Ramaswamy (2011, 195) highlights the need for "engagement platforms" to enable co-creation beyond conventional exchange processes via human interaction and dialogue.

Fittingly, this research on co-creative festivals as liminal spaces and significant artistic and cultural events helps to provide insight into how these in-between spaces, open atmospheres, and engagement platforms instill and reinforce cultural participation and co-production. The contribution of this chapter is thus a participatory perspective for arts and cultural management via which various cultural events and spaces, such as but not limited to festivals, can be intentionally designed, organized, and managed as cultural incubators to amplify communal creativity as a practice-based and relational process. This, in turn, allows for bottom-up change and innovation by exploring and devising alternative ways of doing, thinking, and being in the world that significantly depart from, challenge, or transform the status quo. While the tension between the symbolic expression and economic activity of arts and cultural management will remain here (as it does for festival organization), a main implication of this research is a critical rethinking of organization and management practices to explore alternatives to predominantly economic and management-centric approaches—preferably via the application of critical, interpretive perspectives and anthropological theories and methods, and an empirical focus on participatory activities such as co-creating, innovating, volunteering, and gifting, as the findings of this research have shown. In sum, both the practice and the academic discipline of arts and cultural management should disengage from traditional, generic management ideals and become more concerned with how to create safe, liminal spaces for free artistic expression and cultural co-production, essential for establishing a new common perception and facilitating a paradigmatic shift toward a socially sustainable future in which art and culture can and should play prominent, constructive roles.

References

Abrahams, Roger D. 1987. "An American Vocabulary of Celebrations." In *Time out of Time: Essays on the Festival*, edited by Alessandro Falassi, 173–183. Albuquerque: University of New Mexico Press.

Akaka, Melissa Archpru, Hope Jensen Schau, and Stephen L Vargo. 2013. "The Co-creation of Value-in-Cultural-Context." In *Consumer Culture Theory*, edited by Russell W. Belk, Linda Price, and Lisa Peñaloza, 265–284. Research in Consumer Behavior, vol. 15. Bingley, UK: Emerald.

Anderton, Chris. 2008. "Commercializing the Carnivalesque: The V Festival and Image/Risk Management." *Event Management* 12, no. 1: 39–51.

Barnett, James H. 1949. "The Easter Festival—a Study in Cultural Change." *American Sociological Review* 14, no. 1: 62–70.

Bate, Paul. 1997. "Whatever Happened to Organizational Anthropology? A Review of the Field of Organizational Ethnography and Anthropological Studies." *Human Relations* 50, no. 9: 1147–1171.

Bell, C. 1992. *Ritual Theory, Ritual Practice*. Oxford: Oxford University Press.

Boissevain, Jeremy. 2016. "The Dynamic Festival: Ritual, Regulation and Play in Changing Times." *Ethnos* 81, no. 4: 617–630.

Boom. 2022a. "2022 Theme." Boom Festival Organization. Accessed 26 April 2022. https://boomfestival.org/boom2022/vision/2022-theme/.

Boom. 2022b. "Our Principles." Boom Festival Organization. Accessed 26 April 2022. https://boomfestival.org/boom2022/vision/our-principles/.

Bottorff, David Lane. 2015. "Emerging Influence of Transmodernism and Transpersonal Psychology Reflected in Rising Popularity of Transformational Festivals." *Journal of Spirituality in Mental Health* 17, no. 1: 50–74.

Bourdieu, Pierre. 1993. *The Field of Cultural Production*. Edited by R. Johnson. Cambridge: Polity Press.

Brkić, Aleksandar. 2009. "Teaching Arts Management: Where Did We Lose the Core Ideas?" *Journal of Arts Management, Law, and Society* 38, no. 4: 270–280.

Burning Man. 2022a. "First-Timer's Guide." Accessed August 24, 2022. https://burningman.org/event/preparation/black-rock-city-guide/first-timers-guide.

Burning Man. 2022b. "The 10 Principles of Burning Man." Burning Man Project. Accessed April 26, 2022. https://burningman.org/about/10-principles/.

Caru, Antonella, and Bernard Cova, eds. 2007. *Consuming Experience*. New York: Routledge.

Chalcraft, Jasper, and Paolo Magaudda. 2011. "Space Is the Place." In *Festivals and the Cultural Public Sphere*, edited by Gerard Delanty, Liana Giorgi, and Monica Sassatelli, 173–189. London: Routledge.

Chen, Katherine K. 2009. *Enabling Creative Chaos: The Organization Behind the Burning Man Event*. Chicago: University of Chicago Press.

Chen, Katherine K. 2012. "Artistic Prosumption: Cocreative Destruction at Burning Man." *American Behavioral Scientist* 56, no. 4: 570–595.

Cova, Bernard, Daniele Dalli, and Detlev Zwick. 2011. "Critical Perspectives on Consumers' Role as 'Producers': Broadening the Debate on Value Co-creation in Marketing Processes." *Marketing Theory* 11, no. 3: 231–241.

Cudny, Waldemar. 2016. *Festivalisation of Urban Spaces: Factors, Processes and Effects*. Cham, Switzerland: Springer.

De Molli, Federica, Jeanne Mengis, and Alfons van Marrewijk. 2020. "The Aestheticization of Hybrid Space: The Atmosphere of the Locarno Film Festival." *Organization Studies* 41, no. 11: 1491–1512.

DeFillippi, Robert, and Yesim Tonga Uriarte. 2020. "The Belonging Paradox and Identities in Festivals." In *Tensions and Paradoxes in Temporary Organizing*, edited by Timo Braun and Joseph Lampel, 17–36. Research in the Sociology of Organizations, vol. 67. Bingley, UK: Emerald.

Delanty, Gerard, Liana Giorgi, and Monica Sassatelli. 2011. *Festivals and the Cultural Public Sphere*. London: Routledge.

DeVereaux, Constance. 2015. "Cultural Management and the Discourse of Practice." In *Forschen im Kulturmanagement*, edited by Sigrid Bekmeier-Feuerhahn et al., 155–168. Bielefeld, Germany: Transcript Verlag.

DeVereaux, Constance. 2018. *Arts and Cultural Management: Sense and Sensibilities in the State of the Field*. New York: Routledge.

Duvignaud, Jean. 1976. "Festivals: A Sociological Approach." *Cultures* 3, no. 1: 14–25.

Ebewo, Patrick, and Mzo Sirayi. 2009. "The Concept of Arts/Cultural Management: A Critical Reflection." *Journal of Arts Management, Law, and Society* 38, no. 4: 281–295.

Falassi, Alessandro, ed. 1987. *Time out of Time: Essays on the Festival*. Albuquerque: University of New Mexico Press.

Freed, Ruth S., and Stanley A. Freed. 1964. "Calendars, Ceremonies, and Festivals in a North Indian Village: Necessary Calendric Information for Fieldwork." *Southwestern Journal of Anthropology* 20, no. 1: 67–90.

Frost, Nicola. 2016. "Anthropology and Festivals: Festival Ecologies." *Ethnos* 81, no. 4: 569–583.

GeoParadise. 2020. "Tribal Gathering." Accessed April 2020. https://www.tribalgathering.com.

Getz, Donald. 2010. "The Nature and Scope of Festival Studies." *International Journal of Event Management Research* 5, no. 1: 1–47.

Getz, Donald. 2012. "Event Studies: Discourses and Future Directions." *Event Management* 16, no. 2: 171–187.

Gilmore, Lee. 2008. "Of Ordeals and Operas: Reflexive Ritualizing at the Burning Man Festival." In *Victor Turner and Contemporary Cultural Performance*, edited by Graham St John, 211–226. New York: Berghahn Books.

Goolaup, Sandhiya, and Lena Mossberg. 2017. "Exploring Consumers' Value Co-creation in a Festival Context Using a Socio-cultural Lens." In *The Value of Events*, edited by Erik Lundberg, John Armbrecht, Tommy D. Andersson, and Donald Getz, 39-57. New York: Routledge.

Gordon-Lennox, Jeltje, ed. 2017. *Emerging Ritual in Secular Societies: A Transdisciplinary Conversation*. London: Jessica Kingsley.

Haanpää, Minni. 2017. "Event Co-creation as Choreography: Autoethnographic Study on Event Volunteer Knowing." PhD thesis, University of Lapland.

Hartmann, Roswith. 1978. *The Art of the Festival, as Exemplified by the Fiesta of the Patroness of Otuzco, La Virgen de la Puerta*. Publications in Anthropology, no. 6. Lawrence: Department of Anthropology, University of Kansas.

Hatch, Mary Jo, and Ann L. Cunliffe. 2006. *Organization Theory: Modern, Symbolic, and Postmodern Perspectives*. 2nd ed. Oxford: Oxford University Press.

Jaimangal-Jones, Dewi. 2014. "Utilising Ethnography and Participant Observation in Festival and Event Research." *International Journal of Event and Festival Management* 5, no. 1: 39-55.

Johansson, Marjana, and Maria Laura Toraldo. 2017. "'From Mosh Pit to Posh Pit': Festival Imagery in the Context of the Boutique Festival." *Culture and Organization* 23, no. 3: 220-237.

Johner, Andrew. 2015. "Transformational Festivals: A New Religious Movement?" In *Exploring Psychedelic Trance and Electronic Dance Music in Modern Culture*, edited by Emilia Simão, Armando Malheiro da Silva, and Sérgio Tenreiro de Magalhães, 58-86. Hershey, PA: Information Science Reference.

Karababa, Emingül, and Dannie Kjeldgaard. 2014. "Value in Marketing: Toward Sociocultural Perspectives." *Marketing Theory* 14, no. 1: 119-127.

Kociatkiewicz, Jerzy, and Monika Kostera. 2015. "Into the Labyrinth: Tales of Organizational Nomadism." *Organization Studies* 36, no. 1: 55-71.

Lang, Siglinde. 2015. "Between 'What Is' and 'What Might Be': Towards a Participatory Understanding of Arts and Cultural Management." *Media Transformations* 11: 30-49.

Maffesoli, Michel. 2012. "Tribal Aesthetic." In *Consumer Tribes*, edited by Bernard Cova, Robert Kozinets, and Avi Shankar, 43-50. London: Routledge.

Myerhoff, Barbara. 1982. "Rites of Passage: Process and Paradox." In *Celebration: Studies in Festivity and Ritual*, edited by Victor Turner, 109-135. Washington, DC: Smithsonian Institution Press.

O'Grady, Alice. 2015. "Alternative Playworlds: Psytrance Festivals, Deep Play and Creative Zones of Transcendence." In *The Pop Festival: History, Music, Media, Culture*, edited by George McKay, 149-164. New York: Bloomsbury.

O'Grady, Alice. 2017. "Dancing Outdoors: DIY Ethics and Democratized Practices of Well-Being on the UK Alternative Festival Circuit." In *Weekend Societies: Electronic Dance Music Festivals and Event-Cultures*, edited by Graham St John, 137-158. New York: Bloomsbury.

Omidvar, Omid, Gary Thomas Burke, and Cristina Galalae. 2020. "The Cyclic Organization of Festivals as Temporary Events: The Critical Role of Spatial Practices." *Academy of Management Proceedings* 2020, no. 1: 21769.

Quinn, Bernadette, and Linda Wilks. 2017. "Festival Heterotopias: Spatial and Temporal Transformations in Two Small-Scale Settlements." *Journal of Rural Studies* 53: 35-44.

Radin, Paul. 1946. "Japanese Ceremonies and Festivals in California." *Southwestern Journal of Anthropology* 2, no. 2: 152-179.

Ramaswamy, Venkat. 2011. "It's About Human Experiences ... and Beyond, to Co-creation." *Industrial Marketing Management* 40, no. 2: 195-196.

Richards, Greg. 2007. "The Festivalization of Society or the Socialization of Festivals? The Case of Catalunya." In *Cultural Tourism: Global and Local Perspectives*, edited by Greg Richards, 257–280. Binghamton, NY: Haworth.

Robinson, Roxy. 2015. *Music Festivals and the Politics of Participation*. London: Routledge.

Schechner, Richard. 2012. *Performance Studies: An Introduction*. 2nd ed. New York: Routledge.

Schmidt, Bryan. 2017. "Boutiquing at the Raindance Campout: Relational Aesthetics as Festival Technology." In *Weekend Societies: Electronic Dance Music Festivals and Event-Cultures*, edited by Graham St John, 93–114. London: Bloomsbury.

Schüßler, Elke, and Jörg Sydow. 2015. "Organizing Events for Configuring and Maintaining Creative Fields." In *The Oxford Handbook of Creative Industries*, edited by Candace Jones, Mark Lorenzen, and Jonathan Sapsed, 284–300. Oxford: Oxford University Press.

Sherry, John F., Jr., Robert V. Kozinets, and Stefania Borghini. 2013. "Agents in Paradise: Experiential Co-creation Through Emplacement, Ritualization, and Community." In *Consuming Experience*, edited by Antonella Caru and Bernard Cova, 31–47. New York: Routledge.

Skjoldager-Nielsen, Kim, and Joshua Edelman. 2014. "Liminality." *Ecumenica* 7, nos. 1–2: 33–40.

St John, Graham, ed. 2008. *Victor Turner and Contemporary Cultural Performance*. New York: Berghahn Books.

St John, Graham. 2015. "Liminal Being: Electronic Dance Music Cultures, Ritualization and the Case of Psytrance." In *The Sage Handbook of Popular Music*, edited by Andy Bennett and Steve Waksman, 243–260. London: Sage.

St John, Graham. 2017. "Introduction: Dance Music Festivals and Event-Cultures." In *Weekend Societies: Electronic Dance Music Festivals and Event-Cultures*, edited by Graham St John, 1–21. London: Bloomsbury.

St John, Graham. 2018. "Civilised Tribalism: Burning Man, Event-Tribes and Maker Culture." *Cultural Sociology* 12, no. 1: 3–21.

St John, Graham. 2020. "Ephemeropolis: Burning Man, Transformation and Heterotopia." *Journal of Festive Studies* 1, no. 2: 289–322.

Toraldo, Maria Laura, and Gazi Islam. 2019. "Festival and Organization Studies." *Organization Studies* 40, no. 3: 309–322.

Turner, Victor. 1969. *The Ritual Process: Structure and Anti-structure*. London: Routledge.

Turner, Victor, ed. 1982. *Celebration: Studies in Festivity and Ritual*. Washington, DC: Smithsonian Institution Press.

Uriarte, Yesim Tonga, Robert DeFillippi, Massimo Riccaboni, and Maria Luisa Catoni. 2019. "Projects, Institutional Logics and Institutional Work Practices: The Case of the Lucca Comics and Games Festival." *International Journal of Project Management* 37, no. 2: 318–330.

van den Ende, Leonore. 2021a. "Festival Co-creation and Transformation: The Case of Tribal Gathering in Panama." In *Festival Cultures: Mapping New Fields in the Arts and Social Sciences*, edited by Maria Nita and Jeremy Kidwell, 195–226. London: Palgrave Macmillan.

van den Ende, Leonore. 2021b. "The Spatial Production of Festivals: Ritualization, Liminality and Performativity." In *The Metamorphosis of Cultural and Creative Organizations: Exploring Change from a Spatial Perspective*, edited by Federica De Molli and Marilena Vecco, 93–108. Abingdon, UK: Routledge.

Wilson, Juliette, Norin Arshed, Eleanor Shaw, and Tobias Pret. 2017. "Expanding the Domain of Festival Research: A Review and Research Agenda." *International Journal of Management Reviews* 19, no. 2: 195–213.

Wiltshire, Kyer, and Erik Davis. 2009. *Tribal Revival: West Coast Festival Culture*. San Francisco: Lovevolution Press.

Woodward, Ian, Jodie Taylor, and Andy Bennett, eds. 2014. *The Festivalization of Culture*. Burlington, VT: Ashgate.

Yanow, Dvora, and Peregrine Schwartz-Shea, eds. 2006. *Interpretation and Method: Empirical Research Methods and the Interpretive Turn*. Armonk, NY: M. E. Sharpe.

CHAPTER 19

KNOWLEDGE MANAGEMENT IN ARTS AND CULTURAL ORGANIZATIONS

A Conceptual Framework for Organizational Performance

NEVILLE VAKHARIA

Introduction

Arts and cultural organizations are becoming increasingly reliant on the need to strategically use data, information, and organizational knowledge to advance their goals and missions (Dalle Nogare and Murzyn-Kupisz 2021; Gerrard, Sykora, and Jackson 2017; Mason 2015; Vakharia and Janardhan 2017). Efforts to increase organizational effectiveness, improve organizational performance, and increase innovation require a deeper understanding of organizational knowledge management. However, there has been only limited study of how organizational knowledge management can be applied to arts and cultural organizations. This is in part due to the fact that knowledge management has multiple broad and debated definitions (Blair 2002; Faucher, Everett, and Lawson 2008; Gourlay and Nurse 2005; Wallace 2007). Further, the study of knowledge management draws from multiple bodies of literature and fields of study, including information science, organizational behavior, and strategic management (Bellarby and Orange 2006; Desouza and Paquette 2011; McInerney 2002), which complicates its applicability to arts and cultural organizations.

To fully understand the role of knowledge management in arts and cultural organizations, it could be more effective to assess the factors that enable knowledge management and the organizational practices that result. Understanding these factors could provide a better understanding of how arts and cultural organizations can be effective in managing knowledge. The concepts of knowledge management enablers and a knowledge management orientation provide the necessary approach and serve as the basis for the proposed conceptual framework. Understanding how these two constructs are related and their impact on organizational performance opens a new and relevant body of research in the study of arts and cultural organizations. This chapter presents a new conceptual framework to assess how arts and cultural organizations create, manage, and share organizational knowledge and its relationship to organizational performance. Specifically, extant literature is used to develop a conceptual framework that suggests a series of relationships between enabling factors and practices of knowledge management and organizational performance in the arts and cultural context.

Organizational Knowledge and Knowledge Management

The process of institutionalizing knowledge manifests itself through the theory of organizational knowledge creation (Nonaka 1994). Nonaka, von Krogh, and Voelpel (2006, 1179) define organizational knowledge creation as "the process of making available and amplifying knowledge created by individuals as well as crystallizing and connecting it with an organization's knowledge systems." This seminal theory views knowledge as being first created by individuals within an organization, with the organization serving as a platform through which knowledge is amplified and systematized (Nonaka 1994).

Knowledge within individuals creates organizational knowledge through the conversion of tacit knowledge to explicit knowledge, from individuals to groups and then to the entire organization (Nonaka 1991). Tacit knowledge refers to those things that are difficult to communicate or formalize (Polanyi 1962), including mental models, "know-how," and skills that cannot be readily articulated verbally (Nonaka 1994). Tacit knowledge is rooted in ideals, values, emotions, and intuition (Polanyi 1962; Nonaka, Toyama, and Konno 2000). Explicit knowledge refers to knowledge that is readily systematic, formalized, and codified (Nonaka and Takeuchi 1995). Explicit knowledge can be easily transmitted, processed, and stored (Nonaka, Toyama, and Konno 2000). The theory of organizational knowledge creation identifies tacit and explicit knowledge as complementary. It is the interactions between tacit and explicit knowledge that create organizational knowledge. This theory of organizational knowledge creation differs from the traditional Western epistemological view of knowledge as explicit only, which has broadened the study of how organizational knowledge is created, managed, and shared in organizations.

"Knowledge management" is a term that is broadly used, broadly debated, and defined in a bewildering plethora of ways (Blair 2002; Faucher, Everett, and Lawson 2008; Gourlay and Nurse 2005; Wallace 2007). In fact, some state that knowledge is not even something that can be managed (Desouza and Paquette 2011). It is simultaneously viewed as a theory, a construct, a practice, a field of study, and more (Alavi and Leidner 2001; Dalkir and Leibowitz 2011; McInerney 2002; Wallace 2007). It is also a relatively new term on which multiple streams of study are simultaneously occurring, each with their own areas of focus. As a result, there is no singular definition of or construct for knowledge management that can be uniformly applied to arts and cultural organization. Rather, knowledge management can be studied through its antecedents and through elements of its practice. The concepts of knowledge management enablers and a knowledge management orientation serve as a means to create a framework to understand organizational knowledge and its management.

Knowledge Management Enablers

In order for organizations to effectively manage organizational knowledge, the conditions that enable it must exist. The concept of knowledge management enablers provides the ability to understand both the human and technical conditions that support knowledge management. Just as Nonaka's (1994) definition of organizational knowledge refers to its ability to enable effective action, understanding these enablers and their effects on knowledge management practices is necessary to identify how organizations leverage their human and technical resources to allow for effective action or practices to take place.

Knowledge management enablers can be described as the influencing factors that foster knowledge consistently within an organization (Ichijo, von Krogh, and Nonaka 1998) and initiate knowledge creation and sharing (Stonehouse and Pemberton 1999). These enablers are considered the most prominent factors that facilitate knowledge activities in an organization (Palacios-Marqués and Simón 2006). Knowledge management enablers have been identified and studied from multiple perspectives. Early research on knowledge management enablers identified broad categories of both human and technical dimensions of these influencing factors. While common elements of knowledge management enablers exist, and there is a shared belief that these enablers are indispensable, some variation is present.

Early studies of knowledge management enablers identified five enabling factors that overcome impediments to knowledge development: (1) mindset of firm members, (2) communication in the firm, (3) the firm's structure, (4) relationship among firm members, and (5) human resource management (Shah and Kant 2018; Leonard-Barton 1995). The mindset of firm members refers to shared values of the importance of knowledge within the organization. Communication relates to the ability of an individual with knowledge to share and codify the knowledge for others. The structure of an organization relates to the rigidity or openness of the roles and functions within the organization. The relationship among firm members is related to communications among members but is more focused on members' willingness to share their individual tacit knowledge in a deliberative and trustful manner. Human resource management relates to how an organization recognizes, cultivates, values, and rewards individuals who share their knowledge and experience (Ichijo, von Krogh, and Nonaka 1998). In this definition, knowledge management enablers are clearly focused on the individual and organizational factors that relate to people.

A more commonly accepted view of knowledge management enablers combines elements of the factors listed above but also includes a technological component. According to Leonard-Barton (1995), "knowledge building activities" comprise the physical systems, skills, managerial systems, and values that enable knowledge management practices to occur. Operationalizing Leonard's framework, Lee and Choi (2003), among others, identified four dimensions of knowledge management enablers: (1) organizational culture of collaboration and trust, (2) organizational structure that is decentralized and nonhierarchical, (3) worker skills that are T-shaped (workers have deep knowledge in their own areas but also broad knowledge of what others do), and (4) information technology that is used well and supported (see also Appleyard 1996; Bennett and Gabriel 1999; Kogut and Zander 1992). These four dimensions of knowledge management enablers have been studied in multiple industries and organization types, including marketing firms, semiconductor manufacturers, and pharmaceutical companies throughout the world (Bennett and Gabriel 1999; Bierly and Chakrabarti 1996; Gupta and Govindarajan 2000). These studies identified important relationships between knowledge management enablers and various aspects of organizational performance, identifying both direct relationships and the presence of mediating variables.

Organizational culture relates to the shared basic assumptions, values, and beliefs that characterize a setting (Serrat 2017) and has been shown to be one of the most important factors for successful knowledge management (Chase 1997; Davenport, De Long, and Beers 1998; Demarest 1997; Gold, Malhotra, and Segars 2001). Organizational culture, in turn, defines the value an organization places on knowledge and determines the types of knowledge that are most essential for success (De Long 1997). An organizational culture that fosters the creation and sharing of organizational knowledge is one that is built on collaboration, trust, and learning (Lee and Choi 2003).

Organizational structure relates to the amount of centralization and formalization of roles within the organization. Centralization relates to how much decision-making is relegated to the top levels of the organization (Caruana, Morris, and Vella 1998), while formalization relates to the extent that rules and policies define roles, authority, and procedures (Jaworski and Kohli 1993). Organizational structure has been widely studied through centralization and formalization, showing that structure has significant effects on organizational outcomes, including the effectiveness of knowledge management efforts (Eppler and Sukowski 2000; Jarvenpa and Staples 2000; Lubit 2001).

Worker skills are defined as the extent to which workers have T-shaped skills (Hamdi et al. 2016; Madhavan and Grover 1998). Workers with T-shaped skills have the ability to combine theoretical and practical knowledge while also being able to collaborate synergistically with those in other work units or departments (Madhavan and Grover 1998).

Finally, information technology in the context of knowledge management enablers relates to technology infrastructure and its capabilities. As an enabler, information technology serves to connect people with reusable codified knowledge and supports the creation of new knowledge (Lee and Choi 2003). Information technology in this context also includes organizational support for it, as any effective technology for knowledge management requires an organizational focus on its use and support (Stonehouse and Pemberton 1999).

The four dimensions of knowledge management enablers have served as the basis for many empirical studies, and while many studies adapted their own versions of the enabling factors, core to their descriptions are the human aspects of culture, structure, and people along with some prevailing role of information technology (Yeh, Lai, and Ho 2006). Empirical studies of knowledge management enablers typically view them as an antecedent to some aspect of an organizational outcome (see Ho 2009; Migdadi 2009; Wong and Aspinwall 2005; Yasir and Majid 2017). Shah and Kant's (2018) meta-analysis of knowledge management enablers identified 1,050 research investigations, demonstrating the maturity of this construct as well as the continued interest in its study.

In the arts and cultural sector, knowledge management enablers as a construct of study have not yet emerged in the relevant literature. However, some elements of knowledge management enablers have begun to appear in several studies, primarily focused on museums. In a case study of a US art museum, Jung (2016) studied how a museum's management structure influenced its organizational culture, finding that an unstable organizational structure negatively impacted its culture and claiming that an emphasis on organizational learning could improve its organizational performance. With regard to information technology as a knowledge management enabler, Peacock (2008) describes how museums can better adapt to new technologies through an organizational change approach that includes a museum's staff skills and structure. In a study of collaborative exhibitions, Moussori (2012) identified how a shared knowledge management system combined with a community of practice and situated learning (Lave and Wenger 1991) played a key role in enhancing professional development and on-the-job training of museum staff. In a study of technology projects in five US museums, Mason (2015) identified interdisciplinary collaboration as a key success factor. The study was grounded in Nonaka and Takeuchi's (1995) knowledge creation model as a means to understand the conversion and sharing of knowledge. Finally, Marty's (1999) assessment of a university museum in the United States demonstrated the important relationship between a museum's social structure and its information systems, identifying cooperative problem-solving and collaborative help-giving (Rouncefield et al. 1994; Twidale, Nichols, and Paice 1997) as critical success factors in the use and implementation of new technologies.

While these museum-focused studies have helped uncover the importance of certain concepts related to knowledge management enablers, they do not collectively assess or reference all four elements of Lee and Choi's (2003) categorization of knowledge management enablers, nor do they use the methods necessary to do so. Applying these four elements of the knowledge management enablers construct, as shown in Table 19.1, to

Table 19.1. Knowledge Management Enabler Dimensions and Components

Knowledge management enabler dimensions (Lee and Choi 2003)	Dimension components
Organizational culture	• Collaboration • Trust • Learning
Organizational structure	• Centralization • Formalization
Staff skills	• T-shaped skills • Sharing skills with others
Technology use and support	• Technology for communications • Effective technology systems • Technology support

arts and cultural organizations would provide a more comprehensive understanding of how organizational knowledge is created and shared. This could be accomplished by adapting the construct scales to the arts and cultural organizational context and assessing them in a broad sample of organizations. Using construct validity methods, a valid scale of knowledge management enablers could be developed that quantifies the level of knowledge management enablers within an organization.

By adapting the four elements of knowledge management enablers and assessing them broadly in a large sample of arts and cultural organizations, a more comprehensive understanding of their role could be achieved. For example, some knowledge management enablers may be more prominent than others, or some may support knowledge management practices more than others. Undertaking a rigorous study of knowledge management enablers in arts and cultural organizations could also provide the benefit of bringing the sector into the broader study of knowledge management enablers, helping to understand similarities to and differences from other industries and sectors, and opening up new research areas for scholars from multiple disciplines.

While knowledge management enablers address how an organization creates the environment in which knowledge management practices and behaviors can take place, it is important to understand if these practices and behaviors are occurring, and if so, to what extent. The study of a knowledge management orientation serves as the basis from which this understanding can occur.

Knowledge Management Orientation

The underlying philosophy within an organization that dictates its internal and external activities and practices is known as its strategic orientation (Day 1990; Kohli and Jaworski 1990; Kotler 2000). An organization's strategic orientation can predict its behaviors (Hakala 2011) and provide a higher-order view of the practices that help it achieve its goals (Narver and Slater 1990). Commonly studied strategic orientations include a customer orientation (Appiah-Adu and Singh 1998; Brady and Cronin 2001; Deshpandé, Farley, and Webster 1993), a competitor orientation (Armstrong and Collopy 1996; Cooper 1984; Kaliappen and Hilman 2013), a technology orientation (Al-Henzab, Tarhini, and Obeidat 2018; Chen et al. 2014; Workman 1993), and an innovation orientation (Ayuso et al. 2011; Siguaw, Simpson, and Enz 2006; Talke, Salomo, and Kock 2011). These studies typically investigate strategic orientations as antecedents or mediators toward an organizational outcome such as operational performance, financial performance, or employee satisfaction.

A knowledge management orientation builds on the constructs of the strategic orientations of the firm. An organization with a knowledge management orientation is one that uses knowledge management behaviors and practices to achieve its goals (Darroch 2003; Darroch and McNaughton 2003; Darroch 2005). Both Darroch (2003, 2005) and Wang, Ahmed, and Rafiq (2008) have empirically developed, tested, and validated knowledge management orientation, though each with a differing approach. These definitions and instruments for assessing knowledge management orientation serve as the basis for the study of this construct.

Darroch (2003) identified knowledge management practices and behaviors through interviews and a statistically validated survey instrument. Building on Bennett and Gabriel's (1999) definition of knowledge management, Darroch creates her own definition as "the process that creates or locates knowledge and manages the dissemination and use of knowledge within and between organizations" (Darroch 2003, 41). From this definition, she identifies three distinct components of knowledge management practices: (1) knowledge acquisition, (2) knowledge dissemination, and (3) responsiveness to knowledge.

Knowledge acquisition refers to practices of finding, creating, or discovering knowledge that relates to any aspect of the organization's function. Darroch further describes how this knowledge acquisition can typically arise from the use of data and information that become institutionalized into organizational knowledge. Knowledge dissemination relates to the practices that allow for knowledge to be shared from individuals to groups to the entire organization. Darroch uses Nonaka's (1994) SECI model in her framing of knowledge dissemination. Responsiveness to knowledge refers to how an organization responds to and uses the knowledge it has, but it also relates to the timeliness and quality of such a response (Darroch 2003). Knowledge usage is only an effective practice if an organization achieves some benefit from its use. Darroch's three categories of knowledge management practices and behaviors were empirically tested using these categories in a cohort of organizations with fifty or more employees. The results of this study identified a finalized set of scale items in each of the three categories that could be validated statistically and used for further study.

With validated results, Darroch's (2005) subsequent study of knowledge management practices and behaviors used the term "knowledge management orientation," positioning it as a new strategic orientation. This study found significant associations between a knowledge management orientation and organizational innovation as well as a range of performance measures.

Despite Darroch's originating use of the term "knowledge management orientation," Wang, Ahmed, and Rafiq (2008) claim to introduce the term in their study, defining it as "the degree to which a firm demonstrates behaviors of organized and systematic knowledge management (KM) implementation" (219). They develop their theoretical framework from four foundational theories: information processing theory (Huber 1991; Simon 1978), organizational learning theory (Fiol and Lyles 1985; Sinkula, Baker, and Noordewier 1997), the knowledge-based view of the firm (Grant 1996), and organizational knowledge creation (Nonaka and Takeuchi 1995).

Like Darroch, Wang, Ahmed, and Rafiq view a knowledge management orientation as a second-order latent construct with observable indicators but identify four factors that it comprises. Their four factors of knowledge management orientation are (1) organizational memory, (2) knowledge sharing, (3) knowledge absorption, and (4) knowledge receptivity.

Both Darroch's (2003, 2005) and Wang, Ahmed, and Rafiq's (2008) models of knowledge management orientation have become the basis for the study of this construct, primarily as an antecedent to some aspect of organizational performance. These subsequent studies of knowledge management orientation have demonstrated that consideration must be given to the type of organization studied, the industry, the geographic location, and other factors. As a result, it is necessary that any scales of knowledge management orientation be adapted to the unit of study.

As with knowledge management enablers, there is currently no study of the construct of knowledge management orientation in arts and cultural organizations within the relevant literatures. However, some studies of the behaviors and practices of arts and cultural organizations as related to knowledge management provide insight into how a knowledge management orientation for these organizations could be developed, though most studies were focused specifically on museums. Hemmings et al. (1997) identified the situated character of information and knowledge in museums, describing how technology must be embedded or situated within the local practices of the museum employees. Their ethnographic study of two British museums focused on the curatorial and collections aspects of museum work but was among the first to analyze the practices of how workers interacted with the museum's database systems. The authors describe how the use of a database system must take into account the multiple ways in which museum workers interact with it and conclude that the success of its use depends on understanding organizational practices that affect its use.

In her commentary in *Museum Management and Curatorship*, Nancy Fuller (2005) describes how museums must improve their on-the-job training, mentorship, and professional development to stimulate the expansion of knowledge. These elements can all be related to aspects of a knowledge management orientation. From a more empirical perspective, Thepthepa and Mitsufuji (2016) investigated the concept of knowledge processes in two science museums in Thailand. They define knowledge processes as processes that enhance the use of knowledge by employees. These processes are knowledge acquisition, knowledge dissemination, and knowledge utilization. Despite naming two of the three elements of Darroch's (2003, 2005) knowledge management orientation, there is no reference to her work, nor is it placed within the broader empirical work in this area. In a study of performing arts organizations in the United States, Vakharia et al. (2018) studied specific knowledge-related practices, finding an association between certain practices and organizational performance. However, these knowledge-related practices were not based on the components of a knowledge management orientation.

The study of the established construct of a knowledge management orientation, as shown in Table 19.2, could be adapted to arts and cultural organizations to broaden how practices and behaviors are studied and bring them into the substantive study of strategic orientations. A valid scale of a knowledge management orientation could be developed for arts and cultural organizations that could be used with the scale for knowledge management enablers, as described above.

By adapting the three elements of a knowledge management orientation to arts and cultural organizations' behaviors and practices, deeper insights into the behaviors that favor effective knowledge management practices can be objectively examined. Combining the study of a knowledge management orientation with knowledge management enablers in arts and cultural organizations could provide a comprehensive view of how knowledge is created, managed, and shared. It also provides the added benefits of bringing these organizations into the broader study of these constructs and the potential to engage a broader diversity of scholars.

Assessing knowledge management enablers as an antecedent to a knowledge management orientation could provide insights into how an organization creates an environment in which knowledge management practices occur. Assessing the relationship between these two constructs could identify which enabling factors are most associated with which practices, and which have the strongest effects. Finally, empirically testing these two constructs in relation to an organization's performance could create an

Table 19.2. Knowledge Management Orientation Scale and Dimension Components

Knowledge management orientation element dimensions (Darroch 2003, 2005)	Dimension components
Knowledge acquisition	• Market/customer knowledge • Staff training and development
Knowledge dissemination	• Formalized meetings and communications • Mentoring and coaching • Documented policies and procedures
Knowledge receptivity	• Adapting to technology changes • Responsiveness to customer needs • Quality improvements

understanding of the value of these two constructs in helping improve organizational effectiveness and performance.

Organizational Performance

Organizational performance is one of the most important constructs in the study of organizations, often described as the ultimate evaluative dependent variable and the ultimate goal of modern industrial activity (Richard et al. 2009). Despite its prominence in many streams of research studies, how organizational performance is assessed and measured varies tremendously. This is primarily due to the fact that organizational performance can be measured both objectively and subjectively, both directly and indirectly (Richard et al. 2009).

Much of the organizational science and strategic management literature on organizational performance uses financial and accounting measures of organizational performance such as sales, profitability, market share, shareholder return, and other objective measures (March and Sutton 1997; Jung and Takeuchi 2010). A growing movement toward broadening this view of performance emerged with Kaplan and Norton's (1992, 1996) concept of a Balanced Scorecard. The Balanced Scorecard framework includes financial and accounting measures of performance but adds three additional dimensions—a customer dimension, an internal business process dimension, and a learning and growth dimension—to provide a broader, holistic view of organizational performance. The Balanced Scorecard is widely used and adapted (Ahn 2001; Chavan 2009; Niven 2002).

The customer dimension focuses on measures of how customers view the organization and its performance from the customer's perspective. The internal business process dimension focuses on measures of organizational processes that help achieve goals, including information technology use, employee skills, and quality improvement efforts. The learning and growth dimension relates to measures of organizational learning, innovation, and product/service improvements. Adding these dimensions to existing financial performance measures creates a broader view of understanding organizational performance. A key challenge of using these approaches to organizational performance is the fact that the measures are typically tailored to a specific organization, making broader, sector-wide research studies significantly challenging (Neely and Bourne 2000; Schneiderman 1999). As a result, the narrower financial and accounting measures of organizational performance remain common in most studies of multiple organizations or of a particular industry sector.

Objective measures of organizational performance have been studied in conjunction with both knowledge management enablers and a knowledge management orientation using singular financial and accounting measures in order to assess comparable data among organizations. Lee and Choi's (2003) seminal empirical study of knowledge management enablers used just five comparative measures of organizational performance related to profitability, market share, and growth as subjectively assessed by survey respondents. Their study found a positive association between knowledge management enablers and organizational performance. Despite the subjectivity of the performance measures, this approach to assessing organizational performance is not unusual with large samples of organizations (Avlonitis and Gounaris 1999; Deshpandé, Farley, and Webster 1993; Jaworski and Kohli 1993). With regard to knowledge management orientation, Darroch's (2005) empirical study also collected subjective organizational performance measures from respondents, finding a positive association between a knowledge management orientation and organizational performance. However, only a limited number of these associations were related to respondents' subjective views of their own internal performance measures. Respondents were more likely to identify strong organizational performance in their own organization compared to other organizations, possibly due to a halo effect. Ultimately, Darroch finds mixed results when looking comprehensively at a knowledge management orientation and both internal and external assessments of organizational performance.

In the nonprofit and cultural sectors, organizational performance is a growing area of study, receiving increasing attention from scholars and researchers, though one that remains more complex than in other organizations. This is due to the fact that these organizations have multiple stakeholders and a public benefit mission requiring different performance assessment approaches (Carnochan et al. 2014; Forbes 1998). Various models have been developed that expand performance beyond financial and accounting measures. Moore's (1995) theory of public value has been conceptualized into a public value scorecard, though little has been empirically studied using this concept (Meynhardt et al. 2017). Sowa, Selden, and Sandfort's (2004) multidimensional, integrated model of nonprofit organizational effectiveness (MIMNOE) views organizational performance along two dimensions—management effectiveness and program effectiveness—though it, too, remains primarily conceptual. Within the performing arts sector, Pandey, Kim, and Pandey (2017) analyzed organizational performance through instrumental and expressive measures, combining financial and nonfinancial measures to demonstrate a broader view of organizational performance.

However, Kaplan and Norton's (1996) Balanced Scorecard remains the most frequently adapted and studied tool for a broad assessment of organizational performance in the nonprofit sector, and its approach is most relevant to cultural institutions. In fact, Kaplan (2001) created a version of the Balanced Scorecard for nonprofit organizations, applying it to specific nonprofit organizations individually to demonstrate its use. Within the nonprofit cultural sector, it has been adapted to assess broader dimensions of organizational performance, including the performing arts (Weinstein and Bukovinsky 2009; Turbide and Laurin 2009) and museums (Basso, Casarin, and Funari 2018; Camarero and Garrido 2009; Haldma and Lääts 2012).

Despite the complexity of assessing organizational performance beyond purely financial measures, a broader view of performance that also includes customer/stakeholder perspectives, internal processes, and learning and growth provides deeper

Table 19.3. Organizational Performance for Arts and Cultural Organizations Aligned with Balanced Scorecard Dimensions

Organizational performance adapted for arts and cultural organizations (Likert items: "Our organization is:")	Balanced scorecard performance dimension (Kaplan and Norton 1996)
Managed and led effectively	Internal business process dimension
Effectively serving a diverse community	Customer dimension
Governed effectively	Internal business process dimension
Financially stable	Financial dimension
Innovative	Learning and growth dimension
A valued community asset	Customer dimension
Operating efficiently	Internal business process dimension
Continually learning as an organization	Learning and growth dimension
Providing engaging visitor experiences	Customer dimension
Supported by a broad base of individual and institutional donors	Financial dimension

insights into a holistic view of performance. Additionally, this view of organizational performance can be studied through the lens of knowledge management enablers and a knowledge management orientation as factors that impact performance.

From this broader view of organizational performance, and using the Balanced Scorecard model, the following elements are proposed for an organizational performance metric scale tailored to arts and cultural organizations, as shown in Table 19.3. These performance elements can be used as a scale that could be tested and validated with the proposed scales of knowledge management enablers and a knowledge management orientation.

Conceptual Framework

With proposed scales for knowledge management enablers, a knowledge management orientation, and organizational performance, a conceptual framework can be proposed that demonstrates the relationships between each of these three constructs. This framework adapts Hackerman and Morris's (1975) input-process-output model. In this widely adapted model, inputs are individual, group, or environmental factors that take in information; process refers to group interactions and practices serving as a mediating force; and output refers to some form of performance outcome. In the proposed conceptual framework, knowledge management enablers serve as inputs, while a knowledge management orientation serves as a process, with organizational

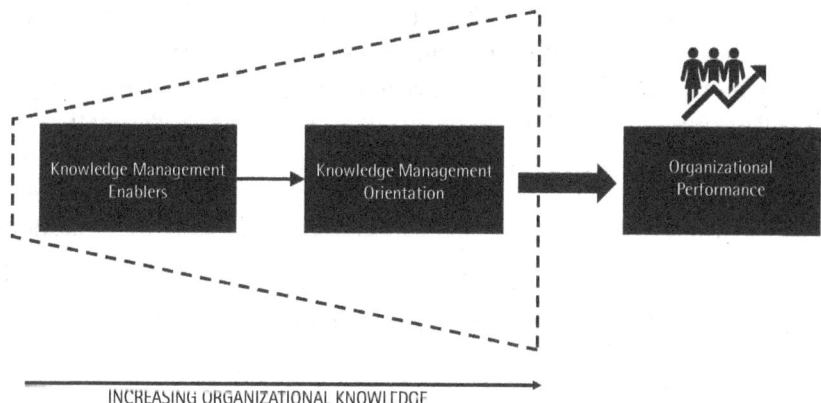

FIGURE 19.1 Conceptual framework of knowledge management enablers, knowledge management orientation, and organizational performance.

performance as an output. The conceptual model showing the constructs and relationships is shown in Figure 19.1.

Adapting Lee and Choi's (2003) framework of knowledge management enablers with Darroch's (2003, 2005) framework on knowledge management orientation and adapting the Balanced Scorecard for organizational performance, this new conceptual framework defines knowledge management enablers as an antecedent to a knowledge management orientation, with both constructs increasing organizational knowledge and linking to organizational performance. This framework offers the following propositions for future empirical study:

P1. An increased presence of the four dimensions of knowledge management enablers are associated with an increased presence of the three dimensions of knowledge management orientation.

P2. An increased presence of the four dimensions of knowledge management enablers is associated with higher levels of the four dimensions of the Balanced Scorecard's measures of organizational performance.

P3. An increased presence of the three dimensions of knowledge management orientation is associated with higher levels of the four dimensions of the Balanced Scorecard's measures of organizational performance.

P4. Knowledge management orientation mediates the relationship between knowledge management enablers and organizational performance.

These propositions are based on and build on extant relationships from the literature and related empirical studies on knowledge management enablers, knowledge management orientation, and organizational performance. More importantly, the propositions and new framework would be tailored to the arts and cultural sector, providing insights and analyses specific to the sector. However, the use of extant constructs and prior frameworks could also allow for broader comparisons to other sectors.

These propositions can be empirically tested by creating a cross-sectional survey that is based on validated scales of each construct assessed using Likert-type items. Because the survey items would be adapted to the specific environment and terminologies of arts and cultural organizations, findings would be highly relevant to leaders of these organizations. By surveying a large enough sample of arts and cultural organizations to allow for the potential of statistically significant results, the conceptual framework could serve as the basis for a new body of research in the study of arts and cultural organizations.

Conclusion

In a knowledge-driven society, organizations that can effectively enable and manage the creation of organizational knowledge will be more effective in adapting to a rapidly changing knowledge society. While knowledge management remains a nebulous subject of study, understanding the conditions that enable knowledge management practices provides a concrete and measurable means to understand how organizational knowledge is created. Similarly, understanding a knowledge management orientation provides insight into the behaviors and practices an organization undertakes to leverage organizational knowledge. Linking these two constructs to organizational performance in a conceptual framework could help assess how knowledge management enablers and a knowledge management orientation link to performance.

Building on extant literature and empirical studies of knowledge management enablers, a knowledge management orientation, and organizational performance, a novel conceptual framework has been proposed that describes how enabling forces could affect practices and behaviors that in turn ultimately affect performance. This new framework provides the arts and cultural sector with a much needed, holistic understanding of how organizational practices that foster the effective creation, management, and sharing of organizational knowledge can improve organizational performance, delivering new insights for practitioners and researchers. Practitioners, especially senior leaders of arts and cultural organizations, would gain a clearer understanding of their role in fostering an environment in which their organizational culture, structure, staff skills, and technical systems are focused on knowledge acquisition, dissemination, and responsiveness. Researchers studying the arts and cultural sector can now seek to operationalize and test this conceptual framework, opening up new streams of research inquiry while also bringing arts and cultural research into the broader study of knowledge management.

References

Ahn, Heinz. 2001. "Applying the Balanced Scorecard Concept: An Experience Report." *Long Range Planning* 34, no. 4: 441–461.

Alavi, Maryam, and Dorothy E. Leidner. 2001. "Review: Knowledge Management and Knowledge Management Systems: Conceptual Foundations and Research Issues." *MIS Quarterly* 25, no. 1: 107–136.

Al-Henzab, Jawaher, Ali Tarhini, and Bader Yousef Obeidat. 2018. "The Associations Among Market Orientation, Technology Orientation, Entrepreneurial Orientation and Organizational Performance." *Benchmarking: An International Journal* 25, no. 8: 3117–3142.

Appiah-Adu, Kwaku, and Satyendra Singh. 1998. "Customer Orientation and Performance: A Study of SMEs." *Management Decision* 36, no. 6: 385–394. https://doi.org/10.1108/0025174981 0223592.

Appleyard, Melissa M. 1996. "How Does Knowledge Flow? Interfirm Patterns in the Semiconductor Industry." *Strategic Management Journal* 17, no. S2: 137–154.

Armstrong, J. Scott, and Fred Collopy. 1996. "Competitor Orientation: Effects of Objectives and Information on Managerial Decisions and Profitability." *Journal of Marketing Research* 33, no. 2: 188–199. https://doi.org/10.2307/3152146.

Avlonitis, George J., and Spiros P. Gounaris. 1999. "Marketing Orientation and Its Determinants: An Empirical Analysis." *European Journal of Marketing* 33, nos. 11–12: 1003–1037.

Ayuso, Silvia, Miguel Ángel Rodríguez, Roberto García-Castro, and Miguel Ángel Ariño. 2011. "Does Stakeholder Engagement Promote Sustainable Innovation Orientation?" *Industrial Management and Data Systems* 111, no. 9: 1399–1417. https://doi.org/10.1108/02635571111182764.

Basso, Antonella, Francesco Casarin, and Stefania Funari. 2018. "How Well Is the Museum Performing? A Joint Use of DEA and BSC to Measure the Performance of Museums." *Omega* 81: 67–84. https://doi.org/10.1016/j.omega.2017.09.010.

Bellarby, Lizzie and Orange, Graham. 2006. Knowledge sharing through communities of practice in the voluntary sector. In *Encyclopedia of communities of practice in information and knowledge management*, edited by Elayne Coakes and Steve Clarke, pp. 301–306. Hershey, PA: IGI Global. https://10.4018/978-1-59140-556-6.ch051.

Bennett, Roger, and Helen Gabriel. 1999. "Organisational Factors and Knowledge Management Within Large Marketing Departments: An Empirical Study." *Journal of Knowledge Management* 3, no. 3: 212–225. http://dx.doi.org.ezproxy2.library.drexel.edu/10.1108/13673279910288707.

Bierly, Paul, and Alok Chakrabarti. 1996. "Generic Knowledge Strategies in the U.S. Pharmaceutical Industry." *Strategic Management Journal* 17: 123–135.

Blair, David C. 2002. "Knowledge Management: Hype, Hope, or Help?" *Journal of the American Society for Information Science and Technology* 53, no. 12: 1019–1028. https://doi.org/10.1002/asi.10113.

Brady, Michael K., and J. J. Cronin. 2001. "Customer Orientation: Effects on Customer Service Perceptions and Outcome Behaviors." *Journal of Service Research* 3, no. 3: 241–251.

Camarero, Carmen, and María-José Garrido. 2009. "Improving Museums' Performance Through Custodial, Sales, and Customer Orientations." *Nonprofit and Voluntary Sector Quarterly* 38, no. 5: 846–868. https://doi.org/10.1177/0899764008319230.

Carnochan, Sarah, Mark Samples, Michael Myers, and Michael J. Austin. 2014. "Performance Measurement Challenges in Nonprofit Human Service Organizations." *Nonprofit and Voluntary Sector Quarterly* 43, no. 6: 1014–1032.

Caruana, Albert, Michael H. Morris, and Anthony J. Vella. 1998. "The Effect of Centralization and Formalization on Entrepreneurship in Export Firms." *Journal of Small Business Management* 36, no. 1: 16–29.

Chase, Rory L. 1997. "The Knowledge-Based Organization: An International Survey." *Journal of Knowledge Management* 1, no. 1: 38–49. https://doi.org/10.1108/EUM0000000004578.

Chavan, Meena. 2009. "The Balanced Scorecard: A New Challenge." *Journal of Management Development* 28, no. 5: 393–406.

Chen, Yang, Guiyao Tang, Jiafei Jin, Qinghong Xie, and Ji Li. 2014. "CEOs' Transformational Leadership and Product Innovation Performance: The Roles of Corporate Entrepreneurship and Technology Orientation." *Journal of Product Innovation Management* 31, no. 51: 2–17.

Cooper, Robert G. 1984. "How New Product Strategies Impact on Performance." *Journal of Product Innovation Management* 1, no. 1: 5–18.

Dalle Nogare, Chiara, and Monika Murzyn-Kupisz. 2021. "Do Museums Foster Innovation Through Engagement with the Cultural and Creative Industries?" *Journal of Cultural Economics* 45, no. 4: 671–704. https://doi.org/10.1007/s10824-021-09418-3.

Dalkir, Kimiz, and Jay Liebowitz. 2011. *Knowledge Management in Theory and Practice*. Cambridge, MA: MIT Press.

Darroch, Jenny. 2003. "Developing a Measure of Knowledge Management Behaviors and Practices." *Journal of Knowledge Management* 7, no. 5: 41–54. http://dx.doi.org.ezproxy2.library.drexel.edu/10.1108/13673270310505377.

Darroch, Jenny. 2005. "Knowledge Management, Innovation and Firm Performance." *Journal of Knowledge Management* 9, no. 3: 101–115. http://dx.doi.org.ezproxy2.library.drexel.edu/10.1108/13673270510602809.

Darroch, Jenny, and Rod McNaughton. 2003. "Beyond Market Orientation: Knowledge Management and the Innovativeness of New Zealand Firms." *European Journal of Marketing* 37, nos. 3–4: 572–593. https://doi.org/10.1108/03090560310459096.

Davenport, T.H., David W. De Long, and Michael C. Beers. 1998. "Successful Knowledge Management Projects." *Sloan Management Review* 39, no. 2: 43–57.

Day, George S. 1990. *Market Driven Strategy: Processes for Creating Value*. New York: Free Press.

De Long, David. 1997. "Building the Knowledge-Based Organization: How Culture Drives Knowledge Behaviors." Working paper, Centers for Business Innovation.

Demarest, Marc. 1997. "Understanding Knowledge Management." *Long Range Planning* 30, no. 3: 374–384. https://doi.org/10.1016/S0024-6301(97)90250-8.

Deshpandé, Rohit, John U. Farley, and Frederick E. Webster. 1993. "Corporate Culture, Customer Orientation, and Innovativeness in Japanese Firms: A Quadrad Analysis." *Journal of Marketing* 57, no. 1: 23–37. https://doi.org/10.2307/1252055.

Desouza, K. C., and Scott Paquette. 2011. *Knowledge Management: An Introduction*. New York: Neal-Schuman.

Eppler, Martin J., and Oliver Sukowski. 2000. "Managing Team Knowledge: Core Processes, Tools and Enabling Factors." *European Management Journal* 18, no. 3: 334–341. https://doi.org/10.1016/S0263-2373(00)00015-3.

Faucher, Jean-Baptiste P. L., André M. Everett, and Rob Lawson. 2008. "Reconstituting Knowledge Management." *Journal of Knowledge Management* 12, no. 3: 3–16. https://doi.org/10.1108/13673270810875822.

Fiol, C. Marlene, and Marjorie A. Lyles. 1985. "Organizational Learning." *Academy of Management Review* 10, no. 4: 803–813. https://doi.org/10.5465/AMR.1985.4279103.

Forbes, Daniel P. 1998. "Measuring the Unmeasurable: Empirical Studies of Nonprofit Organization Effectiveness from 1977 to 1997." *Nonprofit and Voluntary Sector Quarterly* 27, no. 2: 183–202. https://doi.org/10.1177/0899764098272005.

Fuller, Nancy J. 2005. "Recognizing and Responding to the Knowledge Needs of Museums." *Museum Management and Curatorship* 20, no. 3: 272–276. https://doi.org/10.1080/09647770500902003.

Gerrard, David, Martin Sykora, and Thomas Jackson. 2017. "Social Media Analytics in Museums: Extracting Expressions of Inspiration." *Museum Management and Curatorship* 32, no. 3: 232–250. https://doi.org/10.1080/09647775.2017.1302815.

Gold, Andrew H., Arvind Malhotra, and Albert H. Segars. 2001. "Knowledge Management: An Organizational Capabilities Perspective." *Journal of Management Information Systems* 18, no. 1: 185–214.

Gourlay, Stephen, and Andrew Nurse. 2005. "Flaws in the 'Engine' of Knowledge Creation." In *Challenges and Issues in Knowledge Management*, edited by Anthony F. Buono, Flemming Poulfelt, and Handelshøjskolen i København, 293–251. Greenwich, CT: Information Age.

Grant, Robert M. 1996. "Toward a Knowledge-Based Theory of the Firm." *Strategic Management Journal* 17: 109–122.

Gupta, Anil K., and Vijay Govindarajan. 2000. "Knowledge Flows Within Multinational Corporations." *Strategic Management Journal* 21, no. 4: 473–496.

Hackman, J. Richard, and Charles G. Morris. 1975. "Group Tasks, Group Interaction Process, and Group Performance Effectiveness: A Review and Proposed Integration." In *Advances in Experimental Social Psychology*, edited by Leonard Berkowitz, 8:45–99. New York: Academic Press. https://doi.org/10.1016/S0065-2601(08)60248-8.

Hakala, Henri. 2011. "Strategic Orientations in Management Literature: Three Approaches to Understanding the Interaction Between Market, Technology, Entrepreneurial and Learning Orientations." *International Journal of Management Reviews* 13, no. 2: 199–217. https://doi.org/10.1111/j.1468-2370.2010.00292.x.

Haldma, Toomas, and Kertu Lääts. 2012. "The Balanced Scorecard as a Performance Management Tool for Museums." In *Best Practices in Management Accounting*, edited by Greg N. Gregoriou and Nigel Finch, 232–252. London: Palgrave Macmillan. https://doi.org/10.1057/9780230361553_16.

Hamdi, Shabnam, Abu Daud Silong, Zoharah Binti Omar, and Roziah Mohd Rasdi. 2016. "Impact of T-Shaped Skill and Top Management Support on Innovation Speed: The Moderating Role of Technology Uncertainty." *Cogent Business and Management* 3, no. 1: 1153768. https://doi.org/10.1080/23311975.2016.1153768.

Hemmings, Terry, Dave Randall, Dave Francis, Liz Marr, Colin Divall, and Gaby Porter. 1997. "Situated Knowledge and the Virtual Science and Industry Museum: Problems in the Social-Technical Interface." *Archives and Museum Informatics* 11, no. 2: 147–164.

Ho, Chin-Tsang. 2009. "The Relationship Between Knowledge Management Enablers and Performance." *Industrial Management and Data Systems* 109, no. 1: 98–117. https://doi.org/10.1108/02635570910926618.

Huber, George P. 1991. "Organizational Learning: The Contributing Processes and the Literatures." *Organization Science* 2, no. 1: 88–115.

Ichijo, Kazuo, Georg von Krogh, and Ikujiro Nonaka. 1998. "Knowledge Enablers." *Knowing in Firms: Understanding, Managing and Measuring Knowledge*. Thousand Oaks, CA: SAGE.

Jarvenpaa, S. L., and D. S. Staples. 2000. "The Use of Collaborative Electronic Media for Information Sharing: An Exploratory Study of Determinants." *Journal of Strategic Information Systems* 9, no. 2: 129–154. https://doi.org/10.1016/S0963-8687(00)00042-1.

Jaworski, Bernard J., and Ajay K. Kohli. 1993. "Market Orientation: Antecedents and Consequences." *Journal of Marketing* 57, no. 3: 53–70. https://doi.org/10.2307/1251854.

Jung, Yuha. 2016. "Micro Examination of Museum Workplace Culture: How Institutional Changes Influence the Culture of a Real-World Art Museum." *Museum Management and Curatorship* 31, no. 2: 159–177. https://doi.org/10.1080/09647775.2015.1117393.

Jung, Yuhee, and Norihiko Takeuchi. 2010. "Performance Implications for the Relationships Among Top Management Leadership, Organizational Culture, and Appraisal Practice: Testing Two Theory-Based Models of Organizational Learning Theory in Japan." *International Journal of Human Resource Management* 21, no. 11: 1931–1950. https://doi.org/10.1080/09585192.2010.505093.

Kaliappen, Narentheren, and Haim Hilman Abdullah. 2013. "Enhancing Organizational Performance Through Strategic Alignment of Cost Leadership Strategy and Competitor Orientation." *Middle-East Journal of Scientific Research* 18, no. 10: 1411–1416.

Kaplan, Robert S. 2001. "Strategic Performance Measurement and Management in Nonprofit Organizations." *Nonprofit Management and Leadership* 11, no. 3: 353–370. https://doi.org/10.1002/nml.11308.

Kaplan, Robert S., and David P. Norton. 1992. "The Balanced Scorecard—Measures That Drive Performance." *Harvard Business Review* 70, no. 1: 71–79.

Kaplan, Robert S., and David P. Norton. 1996. "Linking the Balanced Scorecard to Strategy." *California Management Review* 39, no. 1: 53–79.

Kogut, Bruce, and Udo Zander. 1992. "Knowledge of the Firm, Combinative Capabilities, and the Replication of Technology." *Organization Science* 3, no. 3: 383–397.

Kohli, Ajay K., and Bernard J. Jaworski. 1990. "Market Orientation: The Construct, Research Propositions, and Managerial Implications." *Journal of Marketing* 54, no. 2: 1–18. https://doi.org/10.2307/1251866.

Kotler, Philip. 2000. *Marketing Management: The Millennium Edition*. Upper Saddle River, NJ: Prentice Hall.

Lave, Jean, and Etienne Wenger. 1991. *Situated Learning: Legitimate Peripheral Participation*. Cambridge: Cambridge University Press.

Lee, Heeseok, and Byounggu Choi. 2003. "Knowledge Management Enablers, Processes, and Organizational Performance: An Integrative View and Empirical Examination." *Journal of Management Information Systems* 20, no. 1: 179–228. https://doi.org/10.1080/07421222.2003.11045756.

Leonard-Barton, Dorothy. 1995. *Wellsprings of Knowledge*. Boston: Harvard Business School Press.

Lubit, Roy. 2001. "Tacit Knowledge and Knowledge Management: The Keys to Sustainable Competitive Advantage." *Organizational Dynamics* 29, no. 3: 164. https://doi.org/10.1016/S0090-2616(01)00026-2.

Madhavan, Ravindranath, and Rajiv Grover. 1998. "From Embedded Knowledge to Embodied Knowledge: New Product Development as Knowledge Management." *Journal of Marketing* 62, no. 4: 1–12. https://doi.org/10.2307/1252283.

March, James G., and Robert I. Sutton. 1997. "Crossroads—Organizational Performance as a Dependent Variable." *Organization Science* 8, no. 6: 698–706. https://doi.org/10.1287/orsc.8.6.698.

Marty, Paul F. 1999. "Museum Informatics and Collaborative Technologies: The Emerging Socio-Technological Dimension of Information Science in Museum Environments." *Journal of the American Society for Information Science* 50, no. 12: 1083–1091. https://doi.org/10.1002/(SICI)1097-4571(1999)50:12<1083::AID-ASI7>3.0.CO;2-B.

Mason, Marco. 2015. "Prototyping Practices Supporting Interdisciplinary Collaboration in Digital Media Design for Museums." *Museum Management and Curatorship* 30, no. 5: 394–426. https://doi.org/10.1080/09647775.2015.1086667.

McInerney, Claire. 2002. "Hot Topics: Knowledge Management—A Practice Still Defining Itself." *Bulletin of the American Society for Information Science and Technology* 28, no. 3: 14–15. https://doi.org/10.1002/bult.235.

Meynhardt, Timo, Steven A. Brieger, Pepe Strathoff, Stefan Anderer, Anne Bäro, Carolin Hermann, Jana Kollat, Paul Neumann, Steffen Bartholomes, and Peter Gomez. 2017. "Public Value Performance: What Does It Mean to Create Value in the Public Sector?" In *Public Sector Management in a Globalized World*, edited by René Andeßner, Dorothea Greiling, and Rick Vogel, pp. 135–160. Wiesbaden: Springer Fachmedien. https://doi.org/10.1007/978-3-658-16112-5_8.

Migdadi, Mahmoud. 2009. "Knowledge Management Enablers and Outcomes in the Small and Medium Sized Enterprises." *Industrial Management and Data Systems* 109, no. 6: 840–858. https://doi.org/10.1108/02635570910968072.

Moore, Mark H. 1995. *Creating Public Value: Strategic Management in Government*. Cambridge, MA: Harvard University Press.

Moussouri, Theano. 2012. "Knowledge Management for Collaborative Exhibition Development." *Museum Management and Curatorship* 27, no. 3: 253–272. https://doi.org/10.1080/09647775.2012.701996.

Narver, John C., and Stanley F. Slater. 1990. "The Effect of a Market Orientation on Business Profitability." *Journal of Marketing* 54, no. 4: 20–35. https://doi.org/10.2307/1251757.

Neely, Andy, and Mike Bourne. 2000. "Why Measurement Initiatives Fail." *Measuring Business Excellence* 4, no. 4: 3–7.

Niven, Paul R. 2002. *Balanced Scorecard Step-by-Step: Maximizing Performance and Maintaining Results*. New York: John Wiley & Sons.

Nonaka, Ikujiro. 1991. "The Knowledge-Creating Company." *Harvard Business Review* 69, no. 6: 96.

Nonaka, Ikujiro. 1994. "A Dynamic Theory of Organizational Knowledge Creation." *Organization Science* 5, no. 1: 14–37.

Nonaka, Ikujiro, and Hirotaka Takeuchi. 1995. *The Knowledge-Creating Company: How Japanese Companies Create the Dynamics of Innovation*. New York: Oxford University Press.

Nonaka, Ikujiro, Georg von Krogh, and Sven Voelpel. 2006. "Organizational Knowledge Creation Theory: Evolutionary Paths and Future Advances." *Organization Studies* 27, no. 8: 1179–1208. https://doi.org/10.1177/0170840606066312.

Nonaka, Ikujiro, Ryoko Toyama, and Noboru Konno. 2000. "SECI, Ba and leadership: a unified model of dynamic knowledge creation." *Long Range Planning* 33, no. 1: 5–34. https://doi.org/10.1016/S0024-6301(99)00115-6

Palacios Marqués, Daniel, and Fernando José Garrigós Simón. 2006. "The Effect of Knowledge Management Practices on Firm Performance." *Journal of Knowledge Management* 10, no. 3: 143–156. https://doi.org/10.1108/13673270610670911.

Pandey, Sheela, Mirae Kim, Sanjay K. Pandey. 2017. "Do mission statements matter for nonprofit performance? Insights from a study of US performing arts organizations." *Nonprofit Management and Leadership* 27, no. 3: 389–410. https://doi.org/10.1002/nml.21257

Polanyi, Michael. 1962. "Tacit knowing: Its bearing on some problems of philosophy." *Reviews of Modern Physics* 34, no. 4: 601–616.

Peacock, Darren. 2008. "Making Ways for Change: Museums, Disruptive Technologies and Organisational Change." *Museum Management and Curatorship* 23, no. 4: 333–351. https://doi.org/10.1080/09647770802517324.

Richard, Pierre J., Timothy M. Devinney, George S. Yip, and Gerry Johnson. 2009. "Measuring Organizational Performance: Towards Methodological Best Practice." *Journal of Management* 35, no. 3: 718–804.

Rouncefield, Mark, John A. Hughes, Tom Rodden, and Stephen Viller. 1994. "Working with 'Constant Interruption': CSCW and the Small Office." In *Proceedings of the 1994 ACM Conference on Computer Supported Cooperative Work*, pp. 275–286. New York: ACM.

Schneiderman, Arthur M. 1999. "Why Balanced Scorecards Fail." *Journal of Strategic Performance Measurement* 2, no. 11: 6–11.

Serrat, Olivier. 2017. "A Primer on Organizational Culture." In *Knowledge Solutions*, edited by Olivier Serrat, pp. 355–358. Singapore: Springer.

Shah, H.G. and Ravi Kant. 2018. "Knowledge Management Enablers: Metadata Analysis for KM Implementation." *Journal of Information & Knowledge Management* 17, no. 4: 1850036-1–1850036-29. https://doi.org/10.1142/S0219649218500363

Siguaw, Judy A., Penny M. Simpson, and Cathy A. Enz. 2006. "Conceptualizing Innovation Orientation: A Framework for Study and Integration of Innovation Research." *Journal of Product Innovation Management* 23, no. 6: 556–574. https://doi.org/10.1111/j.1540-5885.2006.00224.x.

Simon, Herbert A. 1978. "Information-Processing Theory of Human Problem Solving." In *Handbook of Learning and Cognitive Processes*, edited by William K. Estes, 5, pp. 271–295. Hillsdale, NJ: Lawrence Erlbaum.

Sinkula, James M., William E. Baker, and Thomas Noordewier. 1997. "A Framework for Market-Based Organizational Learning: Linking Values, Knowledge, and Behavior." *Journal of the Academy of Marketing Science* 25, no. 4: 305–318.

Sowa, Jessica E., Sally Coleman Selden, and Jodi R. Sandfort. 2004. "No Longer Unmeasurable? A Multidimensional Integrated Model of Nonprofit Organizational Effectiveness." *Nonprofit and Voluntary Sector Quarterly* 33, no. 4: 711–728. https://doi.org/10.1177/0899764004269146.

Stonehouse, George H., and Jonathan D. Pemberton. 1999. "Learning and Knowledge Management in the Intelligent Organisation." *Participation and Empowerment: An International Journal* 7, no. 5: 131–144. https://doi.org/10.1108/14634449910287846.

Talke, Katrin, Søren Salomo, and Alexander Kock. 2011. "Top Management Team Diversity and Strategic Innovation Orientation: The Relationship and Consequences for Innovativeness and Performance." *Journal of Product Innovation Management* 28, no. 6: 819–832. https://doi.org/10.1111/j.1540-5885.2011.00851.x.

Thepthepa, Nopparat, and Toshioa Mitsufuji. 2016. "Knowledge Process and Learning Organization Development in Science Museums." *Procedia Computer Science* 99: 157–170. https://doi.org/10.1016/j.procs.2016.09.108.

Turbide, Johanne, and Claude Laurin. 2009. "Performance Measurement in the Arts Sector: The Case of the Performing Arts." *International Journal of Arts Management* 11, no. 2: 56–70.

Twidale, Michael B., David M. Nichols, and Chris D. Paice. 1997. "Browsing Is a Collaborative Process." *Information Processing and Management* 33, no. 6: 761–783. https://doi.org/10.1016/S0306-4573(97)00040-X.

Vakharia, Neville K., and Divya Janardhan. 2017. "Knowledge-Centric Arts Organizations: Connecting Practice to Performance." *International Journal of Arts Management* 19, no. 2: 14–31.

Vakharia, Neville, Marilena Vecco, Andrej Srakar, and Divya Janardhan. 2018. "Knowledge Centricity and Organizational Performance: An Empirical Study of the Performing Arts." *Journal of Knowledge Management* 22, no. 5: 1124–1152.

Wallace, Danny P. 2007. *Knowledge Management: Historical and Cross-Disciplinary Themes*. Westport, CT: Libraries Unlimited.

Wang, Catherine L., Pervaiz K. Ahmed, and Mohammed Rafiq. 2008. "Knowledge Management Orientation: Construct Development and Empirical Validation." *European Journal of Information Systems* 17, no. 3: 219–235. http://dx.doi.org.ezproxy2.library.drexel.edu/10.1057/ejis.2008.12.

Weinstein, Larry, and David Bukovinsky. 2009. "Use of the Balanced Scorecard and Performance Metrics to Achieve Operational and Strategic Alignment in Arts and Culture Not-for-Profits." *International Journal of Arts Management* 11, no. 2: 42–55.

Wong, Kuan, and Elaine Aspinwall. 2005. "An Empirical Study of the Important Factors for Knowledge-management Adoption in the SME Sector." *Journal of Knowledge Management* 9, no. 3: 64–82. https://doi.org/10.1108/13673270510602773.

Workman, John P., Jr. 1993. "Marketing's Limited Role in New Product Development in One Computer Systems Firm." *Journal of Marketing Research* 30, no. 4: 405.

Yasir, Muhammad, and Abdul Majid. 2017. "Impact of Knowledge Management Enablers on Knowledge Sharing: Is Trust a Missing Link in SMEs of Emerging Economies?" *World Journal of Entrepreneurship, Management and Sustainable Development* 13, no. 1: 16–33. https://doi.org/10.1108/WJEMSD-02-2016-0010.

Yeh, Ying-Jung, Sun-Quae Lai, and Chin-Tsang Ho. 2006. "Knowledge Management Enablers: A Case Study." *Industrial Management and Data Systems* 106, no. 6: 793–810. https://doi.org/10.1108/02635570610671489.

CHAPTER 20

PROJECT MANAGEMENT FOR CULTURAL EVENTS

Toward a Systemic Approach

LUCIO ARGANO

INTRODUCTION

EXTRAORDINARY events date back a long time—one might think of the Olympics, which first took place in 776 BCE. Today, events characterize many dimensions of our social, economic, and political life (Ferrari 2018). An event can be defined as "an occurrence at a given place and time; a special set of circumstances; a noteworthy occurrence" (Getz 2007, 18).

Events play a major role in terms of aggregation, communication, and marketing. They contribute to promoting locations, building up the reputation of local areas, and attracting tourists (Dwyer and Wickens 2013; Long and Robinson 2004; Watt 1998; Betteridege 1997; Walo, Bull, and Breen 1996; Hall 1992).[1] Events also have a transformational function, in that they generate new economies and relations, which in turn lead to increased competitiveness as well as social and urban regeneration (Smith 2012) — for example, the designation of European Capitals of Culture (Evans 2001; Landry and Bianchini 1995). In this respect, Richards and Palmer (2010) use the expression "eventful cities" to refer to cities animated by events as a form of urban revitalization.

As early as the 1990s, event management studies were characterized by an interdisciplinary approach (Ferrari 2018; Raj, Walters, and Rashid 2017; Dowson and Bassett 2015; Claveau 2015; Page and Connell 2012; Allen et al. 2011; Bowdin et al. 2011; Berridge 2007; Getz 2007; Van Der Wagen and Carlos 2005; Baron, Bovis, and Sauvageot 2004; Goldblatt 1990). In order to contribute to this research strand, this chapter discusses events in different artistic and cultural fields (see Table 20.1). Specifically, emphasis will be placed upon creative and narrational events taking place in a well-defined spatial and temporal dimension and featuring symbolic, artistic, and sensorial codes.

Table 20.1. Types of Cultural Events

Cultural field	Types of events
Art and heritage	Exhibitions, installations, vernissage, public art, performances
Intangible cultural heritage	Popular festivals, celebrations, inaugurations, carnival, pyrotechnics events, historical reinterpretations, religious events and processions
Performing arts	Special shows, festivals, reviews, retrospectives, major concerts
Cinema, video, radio, and audiovisual	Festivals, special screening, previews, installations, retrospectives, presentations
Television and radio	Special broadcasts, awards, media and brand events
Humanities and scientific disciplines	Festivals, conferences, congresses, meetings, readings, talks

Cultural events celebrate the culture of a given area or a social group (Bladen et al. 2012). They help to showcase new artistic languages and talent, giving rise to cognitive, emotional, aesthetic, and ethical experiences at both individual and collective levels (Getz 2007). Cultural events bring together historical, cultural, and artistic themes, as well as social, patriotic, and ceremonial ones (Sonder 2004). As an important component of cultural policies, cultural events are collective occasions that promote social cohesion and inclusion (Picard and Robinson 2006; Quinn 2005). Festivals are the most widespread cultural events, and scholars have investigated different types of them (Cudny 2014, 2016; Yeoman et al. 2004; Formica 1998), particularly those associated with cultural tourism (Lashua, Spracklen, and Long 2014; Quinn 2010; Richards 2007; McKercher and du Cros 2002) and local marketing (Paiola and Grandinetti 2009; Mehmetoglu and Ellingsen 2005; Mayfield and Crompton 1995).[2]

This chapter puts forward the argument that although cultural events are meticulously planned, they are actually complex phenomena to which project management practices cannot be applied fully. A systemic approach is therefore suggested, along with a review of traditional planning strategies.

Cultural Events as Complex Systems and Plans: A Review

Cultural events present some features of projects—that is, they are limited in time, they are unique in terms of planning and final outcome, and they are characterized by the variability of related tasks and possible risks and resources allocated (Pielichaty et al. 2017; Bladen et al. 2012; O'Toole and Mikolaitis 2002). Also, they include correlated tasks, temporarily allocated resources, coordinated actions, and assigned objectives (Kerzner 1989; Graham 1985; Archibald 1976).

Project management applies specific methodologies and standards (notably ISO 21500, Guidance on Project Management) to projects carried out in a number of industries: technology, infrastructure, scientific research, software development, international cooperation, and new products and services.

Many scholars have linked event management to project management (Van Der Wagen and White 2015; APMA 2012; Cserhàti and Szabo 2014; Allen et al. 2011; Bowdin et al. 2011; O'Toole and Mikolaitis 2002; O'Toole 2000), highlighting the commonalities of terminology, stakeholder accountability, the major role of planning, and knowledge transfer. Furthermore, it has been argued that the tools employed in project management can be also used in event management; examples include the work breakdown structure (WBS), task analysis, the resource breakdown structure (RBS), the Gantt chart, network analysis, activity on node, critical path analysis, and the PERT chart.

With a view toward investigating the similarities and differences between cultural events and projects, it is useful to examine the special character of cultural events using the lens of complexity theory. Edgar Morin (1990) states that complexity is characterized by a quantity of interactions and interferences between a large number of entities. Complexity also includes uncertainties, indeterminacies, and random phenomena, and thus entails a mixture of order and disorder. Complexity is linked to system, which Morin (1977) defines as an organized global unity of interrelationships between elements, actions, or individuals. Complexity itself is characterized by instability, unpredictability, turbulence, ambiguity, absence of linearity, and variance (variety, intensity, and variability of elements). Cultural events are complex systems—sets of symbolic and behavioral elements, both tangible and intangible (Morin 1977), that are embedded in conceptual, creative, and organizational processes that generate mutual dependence and conditioning (Miller 1965).

Two events may have the same or a similar structure, but one may feature a lower degree of complexity because it is based on defined rules and so is arranged using traditional models and formats (e.g., a film festival). Depending on the structure, cultural events might have interrelated subsystems with consistent levels within the same organizational units. For example, a festival may occur simultaneously in different places in the same city. Conceived as a system, a cultural event consists of many components, both complementary to and integral to one another.

The realization of cultural events might be affected by unexpected circumstances. There are a number of variables that can cause instability and jeopardize an initial plan. Continuous effort is therefore needed to harmonize the different parts of the system and set a clear development strategy.

In this sense, cultural events are fraught with unforeseeable factors, as their environmental, creative, financial, and operational dynamics feature a high degree of uncertainty (for example, acquisition of rights, artists, and works; authorizations; space use; deadlines; and technical and safety issues).

The organization of cultural events is marked by novel situations and behaviors that can be either predictable or unpredictable (Battram 1999). Farsightedness gives way to variations and plan changes. Events depend on the pace of the system and its interior linkages (which are sometimes covert), and these are mutually influenced, generating both actions and reactions.

In the context of cultural events, space and time are closely intertwined and at times binding, for they condition the layout, process, and final outcome (Dowson and Bassett 2015). Events can take place in areas already designated to accommodate cultural activities (exhibition venues, concert halls, theaters) or in public or private spaces utilized for other civil or social purposes (streets, squares, gardens, stadiums, or factories). In the first case the event may need to adapt to the venue, while in the second case, significant albeit temporary changes are made that may impact routine life (e.g., residents, shops, mobility) until the space is restored to its usual function. If events are held in different areas of the same urban district, or if they are traveling shows, the scope of the system might widen.

Timing includes both the duration of the event and the time needed to create and organize the event. Cultural events might be brief or longer-lasting; they might be scheduled or be held more spontaneously; they might occur regularly, occasionally, or on a one-time basis. This way of organizing time constitutes both a paradox and a hindrance, in that the need to comply with deadlines leading up to the event forces planners to prioritize calendar time (Boutinet 1990) over the time needed for creativity, generating a conflict between planning and designing. Like project management, cultural event management rests on sequential steps. However, adjustments in a step generate intermediate outcomes and further developments (Cerezuela 2004).

Finally, cultural events are cognitive systems and communication systems. They produce, disseminate, and mediate thoughts, awareness, and knowledge, which are conveyed through specific language (for example, signs, messages, and meanings), terminology, and register (for example, in the form of narration, epic, divulgation, description, exploration), creating their own identity.

Cultural Events: Degrees of Complexity

Observing the numerous festivals that take place in cities—for example, large art exhibitions, public art initiatives (such as "The Floating Piers" on Iseo Lake in 2016 by the artist Christo or the temporary participatory monumental constructions by Olivier Grossetête), we can see that cultural events feature four degrees of complexity, as illustrated in Figure 20.1.

The first degree of complexity has to do with the fact that cultural events are open systems where regular interaction and relations take place in a given context, providing and collecting information that affects creation and planning. Here, the context includes the external environment, the organization in charge of the event, and the area in which competitors operate (e.g., the sectoral and local levels). The variations in setting produce

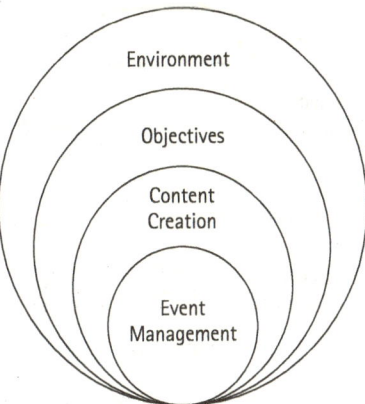

FIGURE 20.1 Degrees of complexity in cultural events.

ambiguous, ever-changing, and sometimes harsh conditions, which necessitate a continuous search for links, adjustments, and balances, limiting the scope for change. As they contribute to social construction, cultural events are exposed to opportunities, challenges, and changes from both the internal and external contexts in which they take place, both conditioning those contexts and being conditioned by them. Cultural events are also adaptive because the adjustment processes of their components have an impact on the system, and this system reacts to external and internal stimuli, collecting information on a regular basis (Holland 1992).

The way the environment affects cultural events is evident at the macro level (i.e., society, culture, economics, politics and evolution of technology), at the meso level (i.e., funds and partnerships), and at the micro level (i.e., resources, staff and organization), particularly considering the tension between tradition and innovation (Bladen et al. 2012). Although the scope of the system is defined by the project—for example, its content, the geography, the field—there is a certain permeability, so the system and the surrounding context overlap. This process is even more evident in events held in public spaces and in those that involve the audience in the creation, design, and planning stages. Beginning in 2007, the Kilowatt Festival (held in Sansepolcro, Tuscany, Italy), an important event dedicated to contemporary performing arts, developed a format called "The Visionaries": a group of citizens is involved in programming nine performances, while the other part of the schedule is determined by the artistic directors of the festival. This initiative turned out to be very successful and has become a European best practice (the Be SpectACTive project).

This degree of complexity has to do with the heterogeneous relations established with different groups of stakeholders, who have different interests, different cultural backgrounds, and different levels of influence and power. Stakeholders express a polygon of relational and fiduciary forces that operate in multiple directions. Many of them are project actors, sometimes principal ones. Each stakeholder has its own world, and the possible project of the cultural event lies in the interaction or overlap between the

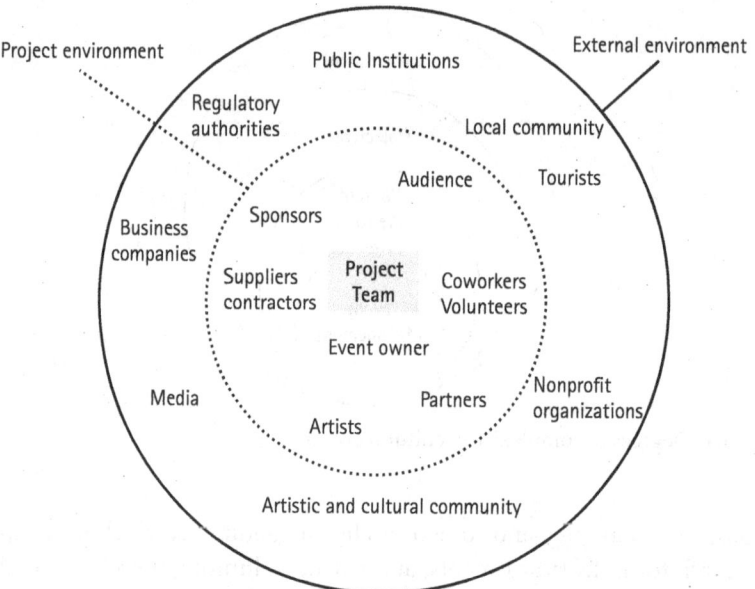

FIGURE 20.2 Stakeholders of cultural events.

lived worlds. A multistakeholder environment may threaten to erode the event's space of independence, leading to continuous realignment and negotiation. The number and variety of stakeholders in cultural events can be seen in Figure 20.2.

The degree of complexity also depends on the audience's behavior, cultural habits, and practices, and the larger consumer base (from which that audience is drawn) and its sociocultural background. Other factors might include the effectiveness of services or offers in relevant sectors (e.g., the opportunity to preview a movie in film festivals). It is worth noticing that contextual factors might have a role independent of the event itself—for example, the weather conditions in the event of open-air shows, or applicable legislation.

The second degree of complexity arises from the different objectives the event intends to pursue, even those contained in its subsystem. These can be cultural objectives (related to artists' intentions) but may also be strategic objectives and purposes set out by organizers (Bladen et al. 2012) (such as increasing participation in a festival or widening a network of artists). Normally, the main objectives of a cultural event are artistic, economic, and competitive, and they can conflict or change priorities. Stakeholders can also lay out objectives (such as maximizing the sponsor's visibility or extending the local tourist season). Cultural events must also pursue project-related goals (those concerning budget, timing, quality of performances and services, safety, media coverage and communication, sales, participation, and satisfaction). Harmonizing these different objectives can be complicated, especially considering that the outcome cannot be predicted or assessed beforehand, as the audience is the ultimate judge.

The third degree of complexity involves project content. In the implementation phase there are many intangibles, along with a degree of originality, exclusivity, and unpredictability related to artistic creation (which is unforeseeable by definition), and these can drive the innovation of processes and products.

In this respect, cultural events include dynamics that lead to invention and remodulation (such as of shapes, themes, and layouts). The space for creative and conceptual elaboration is peculiar in three ways: in terms of situations, authors and players involved, and feedback provided (Boutinet 1990). Events also make use of interdisciplinary content and offerings: languages, practices, references, and messages combine. Many theaters and dance festivals feature performing arts that involve hybrid language and shapes, moving away from predefined and recognizable genres. Cultural festivals (e.g., festivals of philosophy, literature, economy, and creativity) are a further example of the transformative nature of cultural events. Any content-related amendment necessarily presupposes a change to the project (Thiry-Cherques 2006).

The elaboration of concepts for content and programming produces instability and variability with regard to initial assumptions, priorities, and circumstances, as well as issues concerning resource evaluation. All these require continuous adjustments. Planning cultural events involves seeking discontinuity, which is imaginative, cognitive, and operational in nature (Boutinet 1990). This is so because creativity in cultural events pursues "the adjacent possible" (Kauffman 2000), introducing novelties and giving rise to generative and selection phenomena.

With the COVID-19 pandemic, many cultural events have been transformed into digital activities, changing the format, the mode of use (exclusively online, or as a mix of online and on-site), and often the structure of the content. The speed of the digital transition increased the complexity of cultural events, due to the impact of new technologies and media, the characteristics of digital times and languages, and the redefinition of the concept of aggregation and collective experience. This is not to mention both the impact on the project team of a cultural event (both its numbers and its professionalism) and the arising and integration of new organizational processes.

The last degree of complexity is linked to the management of cultural events (i.e., resources, risks, constraints). Events require heterogeneous and interdependent resources other than human, material, and financial ones—for example, information, relations, signs, and value. The relevance of the human factor can be seen in the variety of expertise needed (featuring different specializations) but also in the number of unskilled jobs generated (often filled by volunteers). Cultural events bring together authors, artists, technicians, managers, and laborers, combining different cultural, professional, and organizational aspects as well as distinct perceptions and practices. Even suppliers have a relevant role. Cultural events are "multi-minded" systems (Gharajedaghi 1999); this can manifest both formally and informally, giving rise to different lexicons and new planning mindsets.

Event management might adapt to others planning times and requirements. This way, events can be placed in the system of the entity organizing them, which in turn can contain complex subsystems (as, for example, temporary exhibitions promoted by a museum). Yet a division might arise between top artists and managers, which poses a leadership issue during the project, leading to negotiations and divergences (such as about the use of resources), and so project managers frequently might perform a double role (artistic and managerial functions).

The content and realization of the event affect the allocation of material resources, which combine old-fashioned practices and new technologies. Financial resources are also relevant, because economic feasibility might depend on variable costs and other revenue sources, which in turn rest on the quality of the event and fundraising skills. It might be the case that the actual costs wind up being higher than the estimates, even though control mechanisms were put in place. More likely than not, cultural events have to deal with limited funding and must search for further resources. This aspect brings to mind the complexity concerning objectives and context, as this may bring forward the need to review event-related goals and implementation aspects. Organizational complexity arises because cultural events face many risks, whether internal (little expertise, difficulties with supplies, contractual issues, unforeseen costs, cancellations, technical problems) or external (adverse weather conditions, security, audience flows and behavior, poor ticket sales).

Besides the three elements traditionally limiting project management—costs, timing, and scope—event management must deal with further hurdles (such as legal, physical, or ethical issues that arise from sectoral practices and space use), which can become part of the project itself and affect the event. Quality constitutes a constraint in project management (Archibald 1976); this constraint is even more pronounced in cultural events, as quality is the result of organizational, artistic, and communication skills (Argano 2012).

Finally, cultural events that collaborate with local, national, and international networks (for example, in the co-production and distribution of works) bring in other aspects of management complexity in terms of decisions, rules, agreements, resources to be committed, and rights to be shared between heterogeneous subjects that have different levels of influence and power.

The Rationale of Project Management and Cultural Events

The rigid application of traditional project management rules and standards—which require full control over activities—might prove ineffective in the complex scenarios that characterize cultural events. Project management involves planning actions in advance, dividing them into detailed tasks, and defining deliverables with specific requirements. Traditional WBS has a divisive and analytical character, as it is used to organize single elements in a hierarchical fashion, without acknowledging existing links and relations.

The success of a project depends on consistency with the initial plan, so variables are regarded as issues or interference to be dealt with during the recovery phase of the initial plan. The relevance attached to planning—which, in project management, limits design and claims to provide future projections—presupposes the predictability of actions and makes them final when implemented. This approach neither considers possible evolutions nor the intangibles that inhere in cultural events. The need to proceed smoothly when organizing cultural events is evident when looking at their life cycle (see Figure 20.3), which features a number of phases both independent and interconnected. While some processes end in the span of one phase (e.g., the setting up of exhibitions), others overlap, influencing different processes and the project as a whole. This aspect can be seen when examining the link between creation and implementation, where project feasibility is evaluated. Ideating a cultural event rests on a set of assumptions, needs, hypotheses, and themes (Argano 2012) and calls for continuing investigation in order to come up with a meta-project summarizing the event concept, its related strategy, and the main characteristics (location, timing, guests, etc.).

The event concept is the result of individual acts that look to balance critical and spontaneous elements, making the project an open platform with options and revelations; consequently, there are many moments in which organizational, communicative, and artistic aspects are scrutinized. During the implementation phase—in which major revisions take place—the structure of the event will be finalized, including schedule, offerings, and positioning. The development stage of the event can be seen in its entirety only upon completion. Shone and Perry (2010) have pointed out one possible limitation when applying project management to event management: the absence of a clear definition of the event in its initial phase (though cultural events feature an ongoing creative process), which does not allow one to identify which tasks need be planned. Furthermore, overly formalized plans, procedures, and documents might affect plan management and cause inertia and excessive red tape, with potential consequences for certain aspects (e.g., the involvement of volunteers) (Bowdin et al. 2011).

During cultural events, aspects such as the engagement, wishes, and needs of the audience come into play (Pielichaty et al. 2017), producing new and unexpected dynamics. Because of this, soft skills and relationship management skills can be seen as criteria essential to success (Cserhàti and Szabo 2014). Interacting with an audience made up mostly of stakeholders requires some compromises (O'Toole 2000), which in turn might cause changes that impact planning. While the linear approach adopted in project management speeds up decision-making, the operational dimension of cultural events requires flexibility in choices due to ever-changing scenarios.

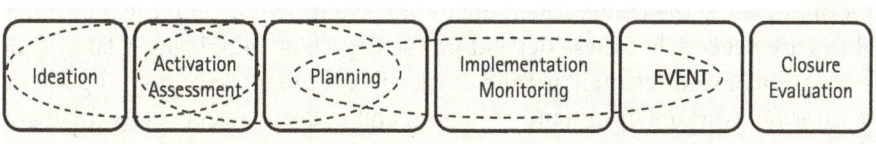

FIGURE 20.3 Cultural event life cycle.

Traditional project management places emphasis on process groups, regardless of the outcome (Silvers et al. 2006); however, when planning cultural events, the outcome is a major driver. *A Guide to the Project Management Body of Knowledge*, or *PMBOK Guide*, released by the Project Management Institute, has identified ten areas of knowledge and management (integration, scope, schedule, cost, quality, resources, communications, risk, procurement, stakeholders) through which processes and deliverables are identified and evaluated against conformity principles (O'Toole 2000). However, these principles are difficult to establish in cultural events. The *International Event Management Book of Knowledge Framework*, or *EMBOK* (Silvers et al. 2006, 52), presents a set of areas in need of supervision and reconnection for all events. The EMBOK framework, which considers all types of events in all fields, proposes the following domains and classes of knowledge:

1. *Administration:* financial, human resources, information, procurement, stakeholders, systems, time
2. *Design:* catering, content, entertainment environment, production, program, theme
3. *Marketing:* marketing plan, materials, merchandise, promotion, public relations, sales, sponsorship
4. *Operations:* attendees, communication, infrastructure, logistics, participants, site, technical resources
5. *Risk:* emergency, health and safety, insurance, legal and ethics, decision analysis, security

When it comes to cultural events, these areas might fit rigid standards and models only to a limited extent, as this adaptation risks altering the nature of the event itself.

It is therefore advisable to move from a linear style of organization to a holistic one, so as to promote the innovative character of cultural events and to adapt planning on a case-by-case basis.

Cultural Events: A Systemic Approach

Cultural event management can benefit from a more holistic approach, one that accounts for interconnections rather than single components. In order to facilitate a systemic approach to the management of cultural events, clarity and organizational capabilities are needed, but these depend on the degree of complexity. Clarity calls for the adoption of some elementary and quick rules in order to promote alignment, a more informal work environment, cohesion, and collective support in the team, as well as greater individual contributions and their integration. According to the model advanced by De Toni, Comello, and Ioan (2011), the organizational capabilities that favor a systemic approach are interconnection, abundance, sharing, and reconfiguration. The interconnection of those involved in the project (people and the organization) is based on networking, cooperation, and a focus on stakeholders and the audience.

Networking works if based on a model open to horizontal relations. Cooperation takes place both within the event and outside it, establishing synergies and alliances (even if temporary ones) through genuine collaborations. This allows one to overturn habitual practices by cooperating with other players who might contribute to the event. The management of relations in a less compartmentalized way is especially important when attempting to strike a balance between different groups of stakeholders, whose behaviors might change as events develop. It might be useful to draw a map of stakeholders, identifying for each of them not only their interests but also their expectations, features, languages, conflict-ridden situations, ways of interacting with them, and ways of managing information flows concerning project developments. The abundance of information, interaction, knowledge, skills, and approaches (Bergami 2009) is a fundamental aspect of the cultural event. They represent fundamental resources people can refer to when attempting to move beyond mere tasks and functions (Nonaka and Takeuchi 1995).

Sharing originates from disseminating values and focusing on the event as a catalyst for the engagement of stakeholders, the team, and the audience. Sharing also has an effect on the management of the event and the definition of outcomes, which of course may be reviewed and changed. Sharing helps one to think about future prospects, to deal with possible constraints, and to understand options, raising awareness of one's room to maneuver in order to come up with an overall strategy. By way of example, it might be sensible to draw up a project manifesto laying out the event's mission, goals, and values.

Sharing also promotes self-organization and fruitful dialogue, especially between the team and stakeholders, enhancing participation, bottom-up support, and the exchange of information in difficult situations. Furthermore, sharing has been reported to increase interactions and rational and affective trust (Peters 1992). Finally, sharing might serve as a sense-maker, enabling those involved in the cultural event to interpret situations through direct experience (Plowman et al. 2007).

The capability of reconfiguration is tied in with the innovative nature of the event, its process, and the final layout. Reconfiguration is also a response to emerging needs, content, and change, and so it implies operational and strategic flexibility when developing the project. Reconfiguration is closely linked with event feasibility—namely, the plausibility and relevance of the project, as well as its consistency with the needs and objectives initially identified. This task calls for a wider perspective that takes other factors into consideration, such as content-related needs, especially mandatory ones (artists, guests, works, rights); the actions to be performed; the skills required; possible constraints, necessary resources, and in-house facilities; and costs and revenues.

A more systemic feasibility analysis can benefit from tools that consider all aspects of a given task. An example of this approach is a SWOT analysis (strength, weaknesses, opportunities, and threats) (Pielichaty et al. 2017), which highlights the interrelations among these forces, their relevance, and priorities. Furthermore, a systemic examination should be performed to identify objective risks (by means of what-if scenario analyses) in order to understand the probability of occurrence, the degree of tolerance, and the actions to be taken in terms of risk elimination, risk acceptance, risk mitigation, alternatives, and risk transfer. This state of affairs enables one to draw a distinction between the notion of risk generally and operational issues that need short-term solutions. An overview of the project helps to identify possible shortcomings that should be dealt with from the very beginning by reviewing choices and processes. Many projects are unsuccessful because the early warning signs of possible problems are neglected rather than being managed promptly.

Another relevant aspect is the integration of processes, resources, and activities. While this is based on established operational procedures, it should be adjusted regularly because of the uniqueness of the event and because few actions can be standardized. Integration takes place within the event, though sometimes a need for harmonization of different projects or aspects will emerge. Reconfiguring means interpreting reality, forming a mental picture, increasing leverage, and understanding the overall context within which the event takes place. Examining the surrounding environment in terms of situations (Bowdin et al. 2011) might give us only a static picture. For this reason, the analysis should consider the dynamics between all the players as the event develops, looking for possible links.

Planning mechanisms can also be reviewed, especially when stakeholders must be involved in decision-making or when responsibilities must be extended to others, provided that new rules are laid out in a project charter. This might happen when collaboration involves public institutions or when partnerships are established concerning services, financial resources, sales, cultural aspects, or co-production.

Systemic Approach versus Project Management Tools

The systemic approach employs traditional project management tools in a more adaptive and flexible way. This chapter's author shares the views of Paradiso and Ruffa (2009), who argue that in ever-changing projects such as cultural events, a shift should take place from routine project planning to project building. The latter approach can bring together those activities necessary to arrange the event with possible adjustments and changes resulting from organizational and creative processes and stakeholders' expectations. This way, the project is simply overseen rather than strictly controlled. Furthermore, while traditional project management follows a linear path featuring an orderly series of activities, in cultural events the reverse takes place, because the start of the event is the key point. Drawing on Goldratt's (1997) critical chain project management, or CCPM, it is therefore more sensible to proceed backward for time management purposes (O'Toole 2000). Thanks to this approach, the project enjoys more development paths and outcomes. As most aspects of an event require precise planning (such as artistic production, setting up, accommodations, logistics, marketing, sales, fundraising, and communication), a Gantt chart can be used. But this tool should be seen as a road map and frequently reviewed according to the development of the project, taking account of the links between different aspects, parallel actions, and overall consistency, using milestones not as hard-and-fast principles but as elements that might be subject to change.

Specific plans must also have systemic character. For instance, well-attended cultural events require emergency planning in order to deal with unforeseeable events (Berlonghi 1995). Here a systemic approach involves considering the actions to be taken but also predicting participants' behavior, identifying access points (for both people and emergency vehicles), estimating the number of security staff needed, outlining the issues to tackle, and identifying people to be involved in the team.

In Italy, the Rome Film Fest has adopted a systematic map for the programming of film screenings, working on both a "typical day" and a dynamic schedule that can easily accommodate changes in the program (such as changes in the duration of the films, operational and technical needs, and requests from directors). The planning for Rome Film Fest is inspired by agile project management (Bowdin et al. 2011; Argano 2012), which is an incremental approach that prioritizes people over tools, utilizes short development iterations (known as sprints), promotes cooperation with stakeholders, regularly redefines priorities, and deals with changes by using small plans rather than attempting to strictly adhere to guidelines laid down in advance.

The systemic map should also include the WBS, although that focuses on the scope of the project and is unable to identify all the work that needs to be performed. The WBS helps to define the main tasks, moving from a top-down structure to mental and conceptual maps. The WBS should provide an overall picture of the event, which includes the links between actions while ensuring the adaptability and flexibility of its components. Reconfiguring means being fast, enabling the project to develop, and encouraging an entrepreneurial drive among team members. One project management tool that can be used is the responsibility assignment matrix (RAM), which gives priority to ever-changing tasks over roles. Using the RAM, each task can be linked to one or more members of the project team by establishing who is responsible, who must approve, who must be informed, and who must provide support. For the purposes of clarity, the project can also be supplemented with guidelines, checklists, flexible policies, and information flows made available through knowledge repositories, avoiding prescriptive procedures that might hamper operational activities.

From a systemic perspective, monitoring and control—which are important when assessing the project and its progress—can be reviewed in terms of project-driving (Paradiso and Ruffa 2009), which considers in a more dynamic way some key aspects illustrated in the systemic map (e.g., timing, costs, and tasks). Normally, project management places much emphasis on performance evaluation, especially when there are deviations in cost, time, or quality. An evaluation is done by means of earned value management, which takes account of planning, costs, and scope to assess performance based on real values or quantitative criteria (e.g., return on investment, ROI, or return on equity, ROE). The recourse to key performance indicators (KPIs) in cultural events ensures the fulfillment of the main strategic and operative objectives, as well as assessment of the impact of event on local areas and on the community as a whole (from social, cultural, economic, political, and reputational points of view). This aspect further reasserts the effectiveness of the systemic approach in terms of dealing with context and stakeholders (Getz 2018; Colombo 2015; Baker and Draper 2013; Fredline, Jago, and Deery 2003; Ritchie 1984). Finally, for cultural events that involve the construction of the project through participatory processes with citizens and other stakeholders, the Event Canvas methodology (conceived by Roel Frissen, Ruud Janssen, and Dennis Luijer and made available through the Event Design Collective) can be an excellent tool; it uses a collaborative and evolutionary approach to design the artistic, cultural, and experiential path (Frissen, Janssen, and Luijer 2016).

Conclusion

Understood as complex systems, cultural events are a halfway point between order and disorder. In Langton's words, they are on the "edge of chaos" (Langton 1990). In this creative space (Merry 1995), strategic and organizational opportunities arise, the old and the new clash, and every step is risky. Managing a cultural event more dynamically is possible if one is willing to deal with project-related issues and their contradictions in a flexible way. To this end, it is necessary to make the tools and aspects of project management more consistent with the ever-changing nature of cultural events, in which the project is considered as a component of a system.

In this respect, cultural events are likely to present new challenges to management. For example, the increasing attention paid to environmental sustainability (Schäfer 2020; Meegan 2017; Pernechy and Lük 2013; Getz 2009) affects organization, practices, equipment, choice of suppliers, and content. In the future, impact evaluation of a cultural event should give greater attention to environmental and social sustainability criteria (for example, by applying the UNESCO Culture|2030 Indicators, which concern environment and resilience, prosperity and livelihood, knowledge and skills, and inclusion and participation). Another aspect that needs to be stressed is the ability of cultural events to generate managerial skills through the "try and learn" principle. Here, cognitive skills (for example, reading the context, or the ability to formulate displays and scenarios), strategic skills (such as defining an overall strategy for the event with a systematic vision), relational skills, assistance skills, and service skills become increasingly important as the ability to engage in complex thinking increases. Knowledge is developed through a passage of memory and storytelling of team members in relation to events organized in the past. Nevertheless, as in so many fields, this can only be done when we learn from past errors and failures and move on from established assumptions; this is the key to widening our knowledge and applying it to future cultural events.

Notes

1. Getz (2008) and Getz and Page (2016) describe the close link between event studies and tourism.
2. Getz (2010) examined more than 400 academic papers dealing with the nature and the scope of research on festivals.

References

Allen, Johnny, William O'Toole, Robert Harris, and Ian McDonnell. 2011. *Festival and Special Event Management*, 5th ed. Brisbane: Wiley & Sons Australia.

APMA. 2012. *Event Project Management Body of Knowledge*. Colorado Springs, CO: American Project Management Association.

Archibald, Russel D. 1976. *Managing High Technologies Programs and Projects*. New York: Wiley & Sons.

Argano, Lucio. 2012. *Manuale di progettazione della cultura. Filosofia progettuale, design e project management in campo culturale e artistico*. Milan: Franco Angeli.

Baker, Kristi L., and Jason Draper. 2013. "Importance-Performance Analysis of the Attributes of a Cultural Festival." *Journal of Convention and Event Tourism* 14, no. 2: 104–123. https://doi.org/10.1080/15470148.2013.783772.

Baron, Eric, Rémy Bovis, and Pierre Sauvageot. 2004. *Organiser un événement artistique sur l'espace public. Quelle liberté, quelles contraintes*. Paris: Irma Editions.

Battram, Arthur. 1999. *Navigating Complexity: The Essential Guide to Complexity Theory in Business and Management*. London: Industrial Society.

Bergami, Bruna. 2009. "Il valore della ridondanza." In *Il project management emergente. Il progetto come sistema complesso*, edited by Francesco Varanini and Walter Ginevri, 275–292. Milan: Guerini e Associati.

Berlonghi, Alexander E. 1995. "Understanding and Planning for Different Spectator Crowds." *Safety Science* 18, no. 4: 239–247. https://doi.org/10.1016/0925-7535(94)00033-Y.

Berridge, Graham. 2007. *Events Design and Experience*. Abingdon, UK: Routledge.

Betteridege, Debbie. 1997. *Event Management in Leisure and Tourism*. London: Hodder & Stoughton.

Bladen, C., J. Kennel, E. Abson, and N. Wilde. 2012. *Events Management: An Introduction*. Abingdon, UK: Routledge.

Boutinet, Jaen-Pierre. 1990. *Anthropologie du projet*. Paris: Presses Universitaires de France.

Bowdin, G., I. McDonnell, J. Allen, and W. O'Toole. 2011. *Events Management*, 3rd ed. Oxford: Butterworth-Heinemann.

Claveau, Philippe. 2015. *Management de projets événementiels*. Grenoble: Presses Universitaires de Grenoble.

Cerezuela, David R. 2004. *Diseño y evaluaciòn de proyectos culturales*. Barcelona: Ariel.

Colombo, Alba. 2015. "How to Evaluate Cultural Impacts of Events? A Model and Methodology Proposal." *Scandinavian Journal of Hospitality and Tourism* 16, no. 4: 500–511. doi:10.1080/15022250.2015.1114900.

Cserhàti, Gabriella, and Lajos Szabò. 2014. "The Relationship Between Success Criteria and Success Factors in Organisational Event Projects." *International Journal of Project Management* 32, no. 4: 613–624. doi:10.1016/j.ijproman.2013.08.008.

Cudny, Waldemar. 2014. "The Phenomenon of Festivals: Their Origins, Evolution, and Classifications." *Anthropos* 2, no. 109: 640–656. doi:10.5771/0257-9774-2014-2-640.

Cudny, Waldemar. 2016. *Festivalisation of Urban Spaces: Factors, Processes and Effects*. Berlin: Springer.

De Toni, Alberto F., Luca Comello, and Lorenzo Ioan. 2011. *Auto-organizzazioni. Il mistero dell'emergenza nei sistemi fisici, biologici e sociali*. Venice: Marsilio.

Dowson, Ruth, and David Bassett. 2015. *Event Planning and Management: Principles, Planning and Practice*. PR in Practice. London: Kogan Page.

Dwyer, Larry, and Eugenia Wickens. 2013. *Event Tourism and Cultural Tourism: Issues and Debates*. Abingdon, UK: Routledge.

Evans G. 2001. *Cultural Planning: An Urban Renaissance?* Abingdon, UK: Routledge.

Ferrari, Sonia. 2018. *Event marketing: i grandi eventi e gli eventi speciali come strumenti di marketing*. Padua: Cedam.

Formica, Sandro. 1998. "The Development of Festivals and Special Events Studies." *Festival Management and Event Tourism* 5, no. 3: 131–137.

Fredline, Liz, Leo Jago, and Margaret Deery. 2003. "The Development of a Generic Scale to Measure the Social Impact of Events." *Event Management* 8, no. 1: 23–37. doi:10.3727/152599503108751676.

Frissen, Roel, Ruud Janssen, and Dennis Luijer. 2016. *Event Design Handbook*. Amsterdam: Bis.

Getz, Donald. 2008. "Event Tourism: Definition, Evolution, and Research." *Tourism Management* 29: 403–428. https://doi.org/10.1016/j.tourman.2007.07.017.

Getz, Donald. 2009. "Policy for Sustainable and Responsible Festivals and Events: Institutionalization of a New Paradigm." *Journal of Policy Research in Tourism, Leisure and Events* 1, no. 1: 61–78. https://doi.org/10.1080/19407960802703524.

Getz, Donald. 2010. "The Nature and Scope of Festival Studies." *International Journal of Event Management Research* 5, no. 1: 1–47. https://www.ijemr.org/wp-content/uploads/2014/10/Getz.pdf.

Getz, Donald. 2018. *Event Evaluation: Theory and Methods for Event Management and Tourism*. Oxford: Goodfellow.

Getz, Donald. 2007. *Event Studies: Theory, Research and Policy for Planned Events*. Oxford: Butterworth-Heinemann.

Getz, Donald, and Stephen J. Page. 2016. "Progress and Prospects for Event Tourism Research." *Tourism Management* 52: 593–631. https://doi.org/10.1016/j.tourman.2015.03.007.

Gharajedaghi, Jamshid. 1999. *Systems Thinking: Managing Chaos and Complexity*. Boston: Butterworth-Heinemann.

Goldblatt, Joe J. 1990. *Special Events: The Art and Science of Celebration*. New York: Van Nostrand Reinhold.

Goldratt, Eliyahu M. 1997. *Critical Chain*. Great Barrington, MA: North River Press.

Graham, Robert J. 1985. *Project Management: Combining Technical and Behavioral Approaches for Effective Implementation*. Melbourne: Van Nostrand Reinhold.

Hall, Colin M. 1992. *Hallmark Tourist Events: Impacts, Management, and Planning*. London: Belhaven.

Holland, John H. 1992. *Adaptation in Natural and Artificial Systems: An Introductory Analysis with Applications to Biology, Control and Artificial Intelligence*. Cambridge, MA: MIT Press.

Kauffman, Stuart A. 2000. *Investigations*. Oxford: Oxford University Press.

Kerzner, Harold. 1989. *Project Management: A System Approach to Planning, Scheduling, and Controlling*. Melbourne: Van Nostrand Reinhold.

Landry, Charles, and Franco Bianchini. 1995. *The Creative City*. London: Demos.
Langton, Chris G. 1990. "Computation at the Edge of Chaos: Phase Transitions and Emergent Computation." *Physica D: Nonlinear Phenomena* 42, nos. 1–3: 12–37. https://doi.org/10.1016/0167-2789(90)90064-V.
Lashua, Brett, Karl Spracklen, and Phil Long. 2014. "Introduction to the Special Issue: Music and Tourism." *Tourist Studies* 14, no. 1: 3–9. https://doi.org/10.1177/1468797613511682.
Long, Philip, and Mike Robinson. 2004. *Festivals and Tourism: Marketing, Management and Evaluation*. Sunderland, UK: Business Education Publishers.
Mayfield, Teri L., and John L. Crompton. 1995. "The Status of the Marketing Concept Among Festival Organizers." *Journal of Travel Research* 33, no. 4: 14–22. https://doi.org/10.1177/004728759503300403.
McKercher, Bob, and Hilary du Cros. 2002. *Cultural Tourism*. New York: Haworth.
Meegan, Jones. 2017. *Sustainable Event Management: A Practical Guide*. Abingdon, UK: Routledge.
Mehmetoglu, Mehmet, and Kristen A. Ellingsen. 2005. "Do Small-Scale Festivals Adopt 'Market Orientation' as a Management Philosophy?" *Event Management* 9, no. 3: 119–132. https://doi.org/10.3727/152599505774791176.
Merry, Uri. 1995. *Copying with Uncertainty*. Westport, CT: Praeger.
Miller, James G. 1965. "Living Systems: Basic Concepts." *Behavioral Science* 10, no. 3: 193–237. doi:10.1002/bs.3830100302.
Morin, Edgar. 1977. *La méthode I. La nature de la nature*. Paris: Le Seuil.
Morin, Edgar. 1990. *Introduction à la pensée complexe*. Paris: ESF.
Nonaka, Ikujiro, and Hiro Takeuchi. 1995, *Knowledge Creating Company: How Japanese Companies Create the Dynamics of Innovation*. Oxford: Oxford University Press.
O'Toole, William. 2000. "Towards the Integration of Event Management Best Practice by the Project Management Process." In John Allen, Robert Harris, Leo K. Jago, and A. J. Veal, eds., *Events Beyond 2000: Setting the Agenda: Proceedings of Conference on Event Evaluation, Research and Education*, 86–92. Sidney: Australian Centre for Event Management.
O'Toole, William, and Phyllis Mikolaitis. 2002. *Corporate Event Project Management*. New York: John Wiley & Sons.
Page, Stephen J., and Joanne Connell, eds. 2012. *The Routledge Handbook of Events*. Abingdon, UK: Routledge.
Paiola, Marco, and Roberto Grandinetti. 2009. *Città in festival. Nuove esperienze di marketing territoriale*. Milan: FrancoAngeli.
Paradiso, Livio, and Michela Ruffa. 2009. *Il progetto oltre la WBS*. In *Il project management emergente. Il progetto come sistema complesso*, edited by Francesco Varanini and Walter Ginevri, 147–182. Milan: Guerini e Associati.
Pernecky, Tomas, and Michael Lük, eds. 2013, *Events, Society and Sustainability: Critical and Contemporary Approaches*. Abingdon, UK: Routledge.
Peters, Tom. 1992. *Liberation Management: Necessary Disorganization for Nanosecond Nineties*. London: Macmillan.
Picard, David, and Mike Robinson, eds. 2006. *Festivals, Tourism and Social Change: Remaking Worlds*. Clevedon, UK: Channel View.
Pielichaty, Hanya, Georgiana Els, Ian Reed, and Vanessa Mawer. 2017, *Events Project Management*. Abingdon, UK: Routledge.
Plowman, Donde Ashmos, Stephanie Solansky, Tammy E. Beck, Lakami Baker, Mukyta Kulkarni, and Deandra Villarreal Travis. 2007. "The Role of Leadership in Emergent,

Self-Organization." *Leadership Quaterly* 18, no. 4: 341–356. https://doi.org/10.1016/j.leaqua.2007.04.004.

Quinn, Bernadette. 2005. "Arts Festival and the City." *Urban Studies* 42, nos. 5–6: 927–943. https://journals.sagepub.com/doi/10.1080/00420980500107250.

Quinn, Bernadette. 2010. "Arts Festivals, Urban Tourism and Cultural Policy." *Journal of Policy Research in Tourism, Leisure and Events* 2, no. 3: 264–279. https://doi.org/10.1080/19407963.2010.512207.

Raj, Razaq, Paul Walters, and Tahir Rashid. 2017. *Events Management: Principles and Practice*. London: Sage.

Richards, Greg, ed. 2007. *Cultural Tourism: Global and Local Perspectives*. New York: Haworth.

Richards, Greg, and Robert Palmer. 2010. *Eventful Cities: Cultural Management and Urban Revitalisation*. Oxford: Butterworth Heinemann.

Ritchie, Brent J. 1984. "Assessing the Impact of Hallmark Events: Conceptual and Research Issues." *Journal of Travel Research* 22, no. 1: 2–11. https://doi.org/10.1177/004728758402300101.

Schäfer, Paul. 2020. *Sustainable Event Management. The Socio-Economic Challenges of Hosting an Eco-Friendly Music Festival*. Munich: GRIN Verlag.

Shone, Anton, and Bryn Perry. 2010. *Successful Event Management*, 3rd ed. London: Cengage Learning.

Silvers, Julia R., Glenn Bowdin, William O'Toole, and Kathleen B. Nelson. 2006. "Towards an International Event Management Body of Knowledge (EMBOK)." *Event Management* 9, no. 4: 185–198. doi:10.3727/152599506776771571.

Smith, Andrew. 2012. *Events and Urban Regeneration: The Strategic Use of Events to Revitalise Cities*. Abingdon, UK: Routledge.

Sonder, Mark. 2004. *Event Entertainment and Production*. Hoboken, NJ: John Wiley and Sons.

Thiry-Cherques, Hermano R. 2006. *Techniques de modélisation de projets culturels*. Paris: L'Harmattan.

Van Der Wagen, Lynn, and Brenda R. Carlos. 2005. *Event Management: For Tourism, Cultural, Business and Sporting Events*. Hoboken, NJ: Pearson Prentice Hall.

Van Der Wagen, Lynn, and Lauren White. 2015. *Human Resource Management for the Event Industry*, 2nd ed. Abingdon, UK: Routledge.

Walo, Maree, Adrian Bull, and Helen Breen. 1996. *Festival Management and Event Tourism*. London: Cameron Mackintosh.

Watt, David. 1998. *Event Management in Leisure and Tourism*. Harlow, UK: Addison Wesley Longman.

Yeoman, Ian, Martin Robertson, Jane Ali-Knight, Siobhan Drummond, and Una McMahon-Beattie. 2004. *Festival and Events Management: An International Arts and Culture Perspective*. Oxford: Butterworth Heinemann.

CHAPTER 21

A NEW FUTURE FOR CULTURAL UNION WORKERS?

RACHEL SHANE AND JOSII AUSTIN

Introduction

Picket line checklist: Skimpy bathing suit, *check*. Five-inch stilettos, *check*. Club music playlist, *check*. Fabulous wig, *check*. Stage name, *check*. Slip-and-slide, *check*.

In lieu of Scabby the Rat[1]—a mainstay spectacle of labor demonstrations—the dancers at the North Hollywood Star Garden Topless Dive Bar hosted costumed supporters, a surprise musical act, and a slip-and-slide (McClear 2022). The glitz and glam of the dancers' ongoing picket in August 2022 not only tethered them to thousands of workers across the United States, who in increasing numbers are demanding equity, inclusivity, and safer working conditions on the job (Taylor 2022), but also showcased an important and ongoing progression in the labor movement. As this chapter explores, Star Garden is representative of a broader union effort that is shifting organizing to workers. This evolution has the potential to redefine the role and purpose of cultural unions in the United States.

Cultural unions represent actors, artists, singers, dancers, musicians, stagehands, stage managers, technical performing arts and film employees, choreographers, directors—anyone involved in the creation of arts and cultural products. Most cultural unions formed around the turn of the twentieth century. Since formation, little has changed within these unions in terms of structure, membership, or member incentives. However, into the twenty-first century, substantive changes are burgeoning that have the potential to shift cultural employment significantly.

Notably, to the surprise of some, the Star Garden Dancers organized with Actors' Equity Association (Equity or AEA), the century-old labor union traditionally representing stage actors and stage managers working within the United States. This widened the understanding of the union's jurisdiction, expanded its scope of membership, and repurposed union goals and values. The union election at Star Garden, which was contested by the employer with a hearing scheduled for May 2023 with the National Labor Relations Board (NLRB), is just one contemporary example of how the cultural labor sector is adjusting and transforming between long periods of equilibrium.

Equity has a storied history of progressive and inclusive ideals. The union has battled politically and socially for decades, having stood up for racial integration in theaters, launching Broadway Cares/Equity Fights AIDS during the AIDS crisis, and, in one of its more recent endeavors, initiating Open Access, which radically shifted union membership eligibility (Actors' Equity Association 2021b). Yet research into the union's history, current footing in the labor movement, and collective power suggests that sociopolitical and cultural clashes are what drive the membership to force union-wide introspection and change. Would Equity have welcomed the adult dancers so willingly ten years ago? Five? Would Open Access have been considered a viable union entry point three years ago? We are not so sure.

In this chapter, we look at what is causing the contemporary shift in workplace and membership policies impacting theatrical actors. We center our research around Equity, as it is the active community and governing body that dictates working conditions for what is considered the American professional theater. Through a theoretical framework that positions collective action, social identity, and punctuated equilibrium theories, we layer and match real-time events to significant disruptions in the union's equilibrium, which often resulted in public member engagement as well as an organizational shift in behaviors and values. For instance, we draw from the devastating impact of the COVID-19 pandemic, the increased awareness of Black Lives Matter, and trending shifts in unionism to connect theory and demonstrative actions taken by Equity in response to its members.

What follows in this chapter is an analysis of historical and contemporary circumstances that have impacted the union and thus rippled across the theatrical industry in the United States. After outlining the historical context of AEA, we focus on recent Equity activities—its response to the pandemic, the introduction of Open Access, and the union's recent organizing efforts on tour and at Star Garden—to highlight both theoretical and practical implications of the union and, subsequently, the industry's transformation. While periods of equilibrium ebb and flow and lasting outcomes remain unclear, such examples undergird ways in which union members (the actors) and the union itself can better harness periods of disruption to ultimately transform itself and reach a new state of equilibrium.

METHODOLOGY

We carried out a qualitative study, using historical inquiry, document analysis, and semistructured interviews (2022) with three Equity leaders from the executive and senior staff.

Historical inquiry allows us to investigate the past through the process of asking questions, analyzing past events, and considering the broader context of the events.

This undertaking allows for an examination of evidence that finds patterns and analyzes participants' perspectives with the goal of connecting the past and present.

In our effort to understand the current political and social context of the union and its initiatives, previous research and reporting contributed to our assessment of internal and external structures, values, and actions. In addition to limited previous scholarly research on the union, we relied heavily on reports and press materials released by the union throughout its history as well as press coverage. These documents are useful to understand the union's perspective, values, and stance on issues over time.

In order to present a contrast to the union's perspective when appropriate, we utilized media such as reported articles, industry blogs, and social media. Numerous union members have voiced agitation and support through articles and social media platforms. These opinions provide critical insight into the internal culture of the union—from how members view themselves within the broader ecosystem of Equity to how members value Equity in their workplaces.

Lastly, this research utilized field interviews with three leaders of Actors' Equity Association in 2022. The focus of these interviews was on the leaders' perspectives on the role of the union in a pandemic/early post-pandemic context. Three types of questions were asked: descriptive, structural, and contrast. In particular, we asked questions about how events in the union's recent history impacted policies, structures, and operations. These questions are intended to showcase how Actors' Equity is evolving from a professional organization to a more traditional labor union.

Theoretical Framework

This study investigates the transformations of a creative sector union through the theoretical lenses of collective action, social identity, and punctuated equilibrium. Each of the theories offers a different perspective for understanding Actors' Equity Association as an institution, its organizing behavior, and the actions of members, as well as the mobilization movements that reshaped the unionization in the twentieth century and again a hundred years later.

Collective action theory provides insights into the behavior of the organization. Social identity theory examines how individuals perceive their own value through membership affiliation. Punctuated equilibrium theory explains abrupt change within typically static organizations. After discussing each of the specific theories, we outline the framework of this study and how the three theories will be utilized together for this inquiry.

Collective Action Theory

Contemporary origins of collective action theory are credited to the work of economist Mancur Olson. In his 1965 book *The Logic of Collective Action*, Olson questioned how and why individuals would collaborate as a group, given that an individual's self-interest does not always coincide with the group interest. Olson argued that participation and cooperation would depend on numerous factors, including the size of the group; the type of benefits received for participation; reputation, trust, and reciprocity within the group; and the group's ability to limit "free riders" (members of the group who do not contribute to the collective good).

His theory about group interests was centered on the concept of collective goods. Olson (1965) defined a collective good as one that could not be withheld from any other member if it was provided to one member of the group. Thus if a good was available to one union member, it would be available to all union members.

Additionally, he suggested that a collective good cannot be withheld from nonparticipating group members. This dynamic creates "free riders"—people who join the group and collect the benefits but do not contribute to the group. Significantly, Olson (1965) argued that free riding is the behavior of a *rational* individual.

Because collective action is irrational, Olson theorizes that in order for a group to be successful it must be coercive, provide incentives for its members, and be small in terms of member numbers. Coercion can refer to the recruitment of members, or it could mean the mechanism by which collective goods are obtained. Olson says that the group must have some mechanism or authority for coercing people to join and securing collective goods. Additionally, Olson argued that collective action must be accompanied by an excludable incentive that could reward participants and/or punish nonparticipants. Lastly, he offered that to lessen the free-rider problem, group membership should be kept small.

In a chapter on the specifics of labor unions and collective action, Olson (1965) states that labor unions are created to demand collective goods. Collective goods for a labor union have been historically defined as higher wages, shorter hours, and better working conditions. In the labor union, coercion may take the form of compulsory membership for those who want to work in a specific field. Thus, the largest incentive to join the union is to obtain work.

While Olson's work was focused on identifying benefits as primarily material—for instance, wages and insurance benefits—Clark and Wilson (1961) and Wilson (1973) identified three different types of incentives: material, solidary, and purposive. Solidary incentives stem from social ties and include honor, prestige, and respect (with nonparticipation leading to shame, contempt, and exclusion). Purposive incentives are the satisfactions one obtains by involvement in the group.

Bowman, Ippolito, and Donaldson (1969) found purposive incentives to be the most important incentive to political activism and material incentives the least important. However, their study also suggested that, over time, purposive incentives wane, because purposive (and material) goals prove more difficult to achieve. Subsequently, the solidary incentives become the most important.

Finally, the most logical argument that runs counter to Olson's theories is that despite the irrationality of joining groups, people do it. Political scientists have asked how, if Olson is correct, large-membership groups (e.g., environmental groups) can grow rapidly despite the lack of incentives. Salisbury and Conklin (1998, 268) approach this contradiction from the standpoint of the need for expression for a specific cause: "At the core of expressive political action is the idea that political success is not a necessary condition... making the effort is its own reward."

The concept of collective action theory can be utilized to examine the behavior of cultural unions, specifically Actors' Equity Association.

Social Identity Theory

If "making the effort is its own reward," as Salisbury and Conklin asserted, it would seem reasonable to consider why individuals behave as they do when within a group. While Olson and collective action theory examines group behavior through an economist's perspective, Henri Tajfel considered the behavior of individuals in group environments from a psychological perspective. Social identity theory posits that a person's sense of self is based on their group membership (Tajfel 1974). Tajfel proposed that a person's sense of self-esteem and pride are linked to the groups that people belong to. Tajfel and Turner (1979) suggest that within the process of social identity, there are three consecutive mental processes that are used to create a social identity and evaluate others: social categorization, social identification, and social comparison.

The first stage is social categorization, where people categorize people, including themselves, in order to understand a social environment. Social categories can include race, religion, societal roles, jobs, and so on. These categories provide people with a mechanism for understanding and contextualizing the roles for themselves and others. People define appropriate behavior by reference to the norms of the groups they belong to, and individuals can belong to multiple groups.

In the second stage, social identification, people begin to adopt the identity of the groups that they belong to and conform to the norms of the group. Self-esteem begins to be tied to group membership. Lastly, once people have categorized themselves, they will compare their group with others. The comparative process can lead to competition and hostility (McLeod 2019). Identity theory hypothesizes that identities are made salient and prominent through commitments to networks and relationships (Davis, Love, and Fares 2019).

Social identity theory combined with a collective-action understanding of solidary incentives can help explain why actors would join Actors' Equity even without the benefit of material incentives.

Punctuated Equilibrium Theory

Policy models are traditionally utilized to explain either stability or change. Punctuated equilibrium theory (True, Jones, and Baumgartner 1999) seeks to explain why policies that are in stasis for long periods of time are interrupted by significant change.

The model of punctuated equilibrium is embedded within the context of pluralism, which exists in the American political system. Within pluralist systems, power and decision-making are dispersed among various concerned participants, which may be government, industry, or civic groups. These groups are considered subsystems. If the participants in these subsystems are benefiting, there is considerable interest in maintaining the status quo. "Existing policies can be reinforced or questioned. Reinforcement creates great obstacles to anything but modest change, but the questioning of policies at the most fundamental levels creates opportunities for dramatic reversals of policy outcomes" (True, Jones, and Baumgartner 1999, 98). Thus, the natural state is equilibrium. During equilibrium, policy changes are marginal and small.

Such equilibrium can be disrupted by conflict expansion (Cobb and Elder 1983). Conflict expansion occurs when an increasing number of people mobilize around an issue. As the number of participants increases, the risk that the associated subsystem will collapse also grows (Masse Jolicoeur 2018).

Baumgartner and Jones contend that the policy's image—that is, how the policy is framed in the media and public—influences the development of conflict expansion. A policy's image can be positive or negative. The more positive the public feels about a policy, the more likely the policy retains equilibrium. The more negative the policy image, the more probable it is that a period of significant change will occur (Baumgartner and Jones 1991).

A subsystem's role is typically to reinforce its preferred policy image and negate facts that would disrupt equilibrium. Yet the accumulation of unaddressed or unresolved negative facts can put the policy at risk of a period of significant change.

"The institutional locations where authoritative decisions are made concerning a given issue" are called policy venues (Baumgartner and Jones 1991, 32). Each policy venue has an inherent decision-making bias because of the values, concerns, and participants specific to that venue.

According to the punctuated equilibrium model, the interactions between policy venues and policy images explain the creation, maintenance, alterations, and destruction of political subsystems. When policy images are positive, subsystems and venues thrive. Yet subsystems may be dismantled and venues replaced when policy images are negative. The policy image and venue are so intertwined that as long as the venue retains a monopoly and the image is positive, the policy is unlikely to experience change, promoting stasis or policy equilibrium. Should the policy image shift, new information is more inclined to be received sympathetically, which can lead to policy change.

The punctuated equilibrium model is key to examining Actors' Equity policy modifications in terms of membership structure and union identity.

An Examination of Actors' Equity Association

The formative years of performing arts unions (late 1800s–early 1900s) followed the traditional path of trade unionism in many respects. Mobilization of workers originated from the desire to improve working conditions and pay. The following sections trace the key maneuvers of Actors' Equity Association from union formation to the second decade of the twenty-first century.

Union Formation

The late 1800s and early 1900s were the formative years for unionization within the performing arts in the United States. The industrial revolution crossed the Atlantic Ocean and farms were gradually replaced with factories. Soon monopolies, also known as trusts, flourished as a few people gained control over entire industries. Business trusts became commonplace—US commerce was dominated by those who owned Standard Oil, US Steel, and American Tobacco. Following this employment trend, more and more laborers no longer cultivated fields; they worked with machinery.

Similarly, while theater had always been an aspect of the American culture, the twentieth century brought formalization and institutionalization to the practice. Theater took shape as an industry—one that generated profit, employed workers, and contributed to the economy. By the turn of the twentieth century, theatrical producers had created something that had never existed in the United States before: "a centralized, national theater system" (Berheim 1932, 1).

As theater transformed into an industry, theater artists began organizing in an effort to represent their needs and interests. Following the trends of trade unionism, mobilization originated from the artists' desire to improve working conditions and pay within their respective fields. Yet the adaptation of a traditional union structure was complicated for artists. Actors, musicians, and stagehands worked in separate groups to represent each group's interests in the industry. Complicating the adaptation of unionism, actors and musicians did not conventionally see themselves as unionists. Often artists held a dual role both as an artist and as the manager of a group of artists, in the actor-manager or musician-manager model. This duality made it difficult for most performing artists to align with industrial workers initially.

The first theatrical workers to unionize were stagehands, as the National Alliance of Theatrical Employes in 1893.[2] Stagehands may have had an easier time viewing themselves as members of the rank and file, as their role was considered more industrial and technical. Musicians followed in 1896 and organized as the American Federation of Musicians.

Actors' Equity Association (Equity) was formed as an entity representing actors in 1913. Equity attempted to negotiate with theatrical producers unsuccessfully for three years. The inability to negotiate with producers led Equity to call a membership vote in order to determine whether it should affiliate with the American Federation of Labor (AFL) in 1916.

Francis Wilson, Equity president in 1916, expressed his frustration with attempts at negotiation without unionization: "I am perfectly convinced that it is absolutely impossible for us to believe that we can effect an equitable contract between actor and manager unless we adopt just such methods as have been adopted by the musicians' union, by the mechanics' union, and by the unions of the other trades and other professions." By a vote of 718 to 13, the members of Actors' Equity Association authorized its alliance with the American Federation of Labor "at the discretion of the council" (Gemmill 1926, 41). However, due to issues joining AFL, it would be another three years before Actors' Equity officially joined the unionized labor movement.

Meanwhile, the producers were banding together to form a united front in their own group, to be known as the Producing Managers' Association (PMA). The PMA agreed to union-breaking tactics, including attacking union leaders, offering advantageous contracts to actors to keep them from joining Equity, and organizing a rival company union that the producers ultimately controlled. Subsequently, the PMA refused to negotiate with Equity.

Actors' Equity leadership knew that they would have to demonstrate their power to the producers to force them to negotiate. Thus, Equity leaders instructed ten Equity members to walk out of rehearsals of the Broadway musical *Chu Chin Chow*. However, only four members responded to the strike call and walked out. The remaining six members resigned from Equity and continued rehearsing.

The incident raised significant questions about the support Equity actually had within its own ranks. However, within one week, Equity leaders were able to get members to agree to refuse work from any member of the PMA until the managers had recognized the association as the representative for actors. On the evening of August 7, 1919, approximately 100 actors refused to perform, closing the majority of Broadway's theaters. The first strike by Actors' Equity had begun. The union hoped that a strike would earn them recognition from the producers as the negotiating organization for the actors, a standardized contract with minimum rates of pay, rehearsal pay, and coverage of clothing and shoe expenses.

When it came to its membership, Equity leaders faced several challenges. First, many actors were not convinced that the best maneuver was to align themselves with organized labor. The leadership had never managed to convince all its members or potential members that art and labor were compatible. Second, some actors felt they had moral and legal obligations to uphold the contracts they were operating under with the managers, and so they did not feel they could respond to the call for a strike. Third, many actors, and specifically those who were not well known, such as chorus members, had to face the predicament of choosing between Equity and their own ambitions. With many of the stars out on strike, the situation posed a potential opportunity for these actors to propel themselves into leading roles, even if that meant they were "scabs" (strikebreakers). Ultimately, however, Equity was effective at convincing the majority of the value of the cause, and the newly formed union prevailed.

The strike lasted thirty days, forced the closure of thirty-seven plays, and prevented the opening of sixteen others in eight cities. The strike had significant monetary costs for both managers and actors. It is estimated that the strike cost the managers $3 million, and it cost Equity approximately $5,000 per day, which resulted in an accumulated debt of over $120,000.

The strike also resulted in the largest membership gain for Equity in its history. When the strike began, Equity had approximately 2,700 members. By the time it was over, the membership had swelled to over 14,000. While many Equity members were dissatisfied with the final agreement that was reached with the producers, the strike had successfully established the power and influence of Actors' Equity Association in the theatrical industry—so much so that it would be more than forty years before another strike occurred.

In these early days, Actors' Equity had to use the most vigorous form of collective action—the strike. The union was still small and had little political power within the industry prior to the strike. However, union leadership competently utilized the strike to its advantage.

In order to gain a victory against the producers, the union began an open membership drive, admitting virtually anyone. This action enabled the union to bring into its ranks any performer who the producers might attempt to use as strikebreakers. Notably, chorus workers were imperative to Equity's success during the strike. Equity needed support from all theatrical workers in order to win against the producers. Historically, Actors' Equity had refused to allow membership to chorus members (or vaudeville performers). During the strike, however, Actors' Equity offered to share its name with chorus members and created an auxiliary organization known as Chorus Equity Association (CEA). While CEA was organized as a separate union, Equity kept control of the CEA by requiring that two-thirds of its board be members of Actors' Equity. The hierarchy established by Equity was visible throughout the strike: "The contrast between the French-heeled slippers of the leading ladies and the unfashionable boots of their less-successful sisters brought home to the spectators lining the sidewalks the economic gulf which divided those at the top of the acting profession from those at the bottom" (Holmes 1994, 139).

This example of the relationship between the actors and chorus members highlights the strong social identity of actors from the beginning of unionization:

> [Equity's] founders, members of a relatively affluent theatrical elite, had aimed to raise the social status of the American actor by challenging the autocratic powers of the managerial moguls and, at the same time, by imposing their own class-specific vision of what it meant to be an actor upon their fellow performers. Initially, at least, they had articulated their occupational aspirations in the rather nebulous language of professionalism. But the obduracy of the managerial establishment had compelled them to adopt a more aggressive organizational strategy and, ultimately, much like other groups of white-collar workers for whom the professional model proved problematic—teachers, social workers, and nurses, for instance—they had affiliated with the organized labor movement. However, the uneasy compromise between professional pretension and trade-union practice generated powerful tensions within the Equity as its leaders struggled to reconcile the needs of their constituents with their own desire for greater occupational prestige.
>
> (Holmes 1994, 185)

While Actors' Equity did eventually join the growing union movement in the United States, it would be a century before it modified its original principle: "This is not a trades union but a professional association which aims to assume such magnitude as to make membership in the association tantamount with membership in the profession" (McArthur 2000, 1). This founding philosophy proved to be aligned with both the social identity of actors and the purposive (cause or issue-based) incentives provided by Equity to its membership.

In its founding ideals, Actors' Equity was representative of the larger cultural union development that occurred at the turn of the twentieth century. Cultural union creation allowed actors, artists, and musicians to be recognized as workers within an industry. Yet, despite joining the labor movement, these members did not want to be thought of as "unionists." For that reason they actively dismissed requests to participate in broader union activities, including strikes and boycotts of employers on behalf of other unions.

A Century of Status Quo

Since its formation and the early tumultuous years of finding its footing as a labor union, Actors' Equity has enjoyed a relatively steady hundred-year period in which significant internal conflicts were rare. Rather, the mid-twentieth century proved to be a period of progressive evolution for the union. As the nation matured and faced increasingly complex and interconnected problems, the union led the way in fighting for its members and, more broadly, the theater industry.

For example, Equity has long championed inclusion in the union, onstage, and out in the house. Throughout the 1940s, the union took steps to force producers to integrate their theaters (Simonson 2013). Paul Robeson, the first Black man to portray Othello on Broadway in 1943, experienced constant discrimination. While on a subsequent tour, he was forbidden to stay at the same hotels or dine at the same restaurants as his white costars (Actors' Equity Association n.d. a). In response, Equity created the Hotel Accommodations Committee with the intent of locating inclusive and safe accommodations for traveling Black actors (Simonson 2013).

Later that decade, in 1947, Equity sent a message to producers nationally: no more segregation in live theater. Using Washington, DC's National Theatre as the example, the union wrote, "We state now to the National Theatre . . . and to a public which is looking to us to do what is just and humanitarian, that unless the situation at the National Theatre is remedied within twelve months from June 1, 1947, we will be forced to forbid our members to play there," (Actors' Equity Association n.d. a). While three theaters in the District of Columbia reversed their segregation policies, the National Theatre transformed into a movie house rather than reverse its segregation policy.

Politically, Equity consistently leaned liberal. Heading into the 1950s and the Cold War, the union released the following statement: "Participants in the Communist Conspiracy should be exposed as enemies of the nation" ("Equity Declared Reds Are Menace" 1951). The union's statement was in reaction to the US House Committee on Un-American

Activities, which had begun targeting actors for allegedly being communists. The union had previously condemned slanderous blacklisting in Hollywood and on Broadway in the late 1940s, going so far as to create a rule that an Equity member may not defame another member (Actors' Equity Association n.d. a).

The 1960s started with what the *New York Post* called "the Cold War on Broadway" (Actors' Equity Association n.d. b). In the largest work stoppage since its inaugural strike in 1919, Equity members from twenty-two Broadway companies were locked out on June 2, 1960—one day after the company of *The Tenth Man* did not take the stage because of an Equity rules violation. A program insert for the show read, "The actors you miss tonight are at a meeting called by their union, Actors' Equity Association, to discuss the refusal of the producers to bargain fairly on: 1. Salary increases; 2. Expanded welfare benefits; 3. A pension plan; 4. Working conditions . . . The managers have threatened closing of all theaters as a substitute for fair and reasonable collective bargaining" (Stevens-Garmon 2013). With pensions a particular sticking point in these negotiations with the Broadway League, the New York City mayor's office stepped in with a plan to support actor pensions and keep Broadway running.

In 1964, Equity struck again, this time for twenty-seven hours. Arguing over minimum salaries, rehearsal pay, a day off each week during the rehearsal period, an antidiscrimination clause ("Negotiators Reach Tentative Pact in Theater Strike" 1964), the union and the Broadway League (then the League of New York Theaters) had reached a deadlock. Yet again the New York City mayor's office stepped in to resolve the dispute between the actors and the producers, reaching a deal at 3 a.m. in the mayor's official residence, Gracie Mansion.

Equity would again call a strike in 1968. The three-day affair was another fight against the Broadway League, which saw the closure of nineteen Broadway shows and nine touring productions (Shepard 1968). The main issues included wage increases, issues of jurisdictional control, benefits for those performing on tour, and working conditions.

A little over a year later, in November 1970, Equity members working Off-Broadway went on strike to advocate for better wages and benefits. Angus Duncan, the executive secretary of the union, noted that Off-Broadway had become a bona fide big business, yet actors and stage managers still worked for "peanuts" (Calta 1970a). The thirty-one-day strike ended in December with help from the New York State Mediation Board (Calta 1970b) when both parties agreed to a binding arbitration that adjusted wages to a sliding scale.

By the late 1980s, the union had grown to represent nearly 40,000 members (Actors' Equity Association, n.d. c) across the United States. While the majority of its members' work was based in New York City, the union's council eventually turned its eyes to Los Angeles, and implemented new rules for members working in spaces with less than 100 seats (Shirley 1989). In response, Equity members filed a lawsuit against the union. The case was settled out of court, and the settlement stipulated that should the union revise those rules in any way, it must bring the issue back to the members, who could vote on the proposed changes via referendum (Shirley 1989). The settlement agreement, known as the 99-Seat Theater Agreement, allowed Equity members to work outside of

California's minimum wage laws (Robb 2015). As a result, some Equity actors worked for $7 to $9 a performance, and in many instances the actors used their own funds toward costumes and resources for building sets, along with "volunteering" during rehearsals (Gelt 2015).

While most of the twentieth century saw stability within Actors' Equity, during the 1950s and 1960s the union worked to expand its influence through traditional collective action behavior—strikes and expansion of the union's influence. In addition to focusing on increasing theatrical employment opportunities for its membership, Actors' Equity was also concerned with preventing its own membership from working without a union contract, and so it took hundreds of actions against its own members who took nonunion work. This coercive action stemmed from the union's recognition that it needed to both control employment and protect its only valuable good from theatrical managers.

A New Century

The turn of the twenty-first century did not bring good news for labor unions in the United States. Union density—the percentage of the total number of employees in a given industry or country who are union members—continued the downward trend that had begun in the 1960s, with union density in the US workforce and in the US public sector dropping a full percentage point in five years (even though local government has the highest density of union members, with 41.9 percent—attributable to the highly unionized professions of teachers, police officers, and firefighters) and density in the private sector falling even more, by 1.2 percent (Bureau of Labor Statistics 2001).

Since 2003, union membership has remained below 16 million; not since 1952 had union membership in the United States been so low. The continued decline in union membership was attributed to several factors. There was a decline in the once highly unionized manufacturing industries. In 1961, 51 percent of production employees were unionized; however, in 2005, only 13 percent held union cards. Contributing to this decline is the movement of manufacturing plants from generally pro-union states such as Michigan, Pennsylvania, and New York to right-to-work states in the South,[3] where union membership has remained low (Mosca and Pressman 1995). Additionally, "during the 1980s, much of the decrease in unionization stemmed from the disproportionate growth of nonunion employment... management's opposition to representation elections, the downsizing of manufacturing operations with high union representation, the replacement of striking workers, and the subcontracting of previously unionized work all contributed to the declining unionization" (Mosca and Pressman 1995, 160). According to a Gallup poll, only 60 percent of Americans approved of labor unions in 2001. This continued the downward trend of support for unions, which had reached its high of 75 percent in 1953.

In addition to declining numbers, organized labor faced internal fractures. In 2005, the AFL-CIO marked its fiftieth anniversary, but instead of celebrating, the federation was desperately attempting to retain its membership.⁴ Its efforts were unsuccessful. In July, the two largest unions in the AFL-CIO, the International Brotherhood of Teamsters and the Service Employees International Union (SEIU), announced their departure from the federation. Shortly thereafter, a third union, the United Food and Commercial Workers, announced that it too was leaving. The exodus of these unions resulted in a loss of nearly one-third of the AFL-CIO's membership.

The unions left the AFL-CIO because of a mounting disagreement over how to retain union strength and build membership. The president of the SEIU stated, "Our world has changed, our economy has changed, employers have changed; but the AFL-CIO is not willing to make fundamental changes as well" (Associated Press 2005). The three unions joined several others in forming a new group called the Change to Win Coalition, which claimed it would provide new alternatives for securing the role of unions in the twenty-first century. In the wake of the coalition's establishment, two more unions announced that they would leave the AFL-CIO. In February 2006, two of the largest construction trade unions—with a combined 1.1 million members—joined several other construction unions in the creation of the National Construction Alliance.

The current difficulties of labor have prompted Bennett and Kaufman (2002) to ask a poignant question about the future of labor unions: Have labor unions been victims of their own political success? It certainly raises the question of whether workers actually need unions any longer to protect them in the workplace. Since the creation of the modern union in the United States, unions have steadfastly labored to ensure the protection of employees. This protection has taken the form of internal negotiations and political advocacy. Yet "the more success unions achieve in the legislative and regulatory arenas, the less future workers will have to gain, relative to their colleagues from the past, from joining a union" (Bennett and Kaufman TKTK, 245).

Lichtenstein (2013) agreed that the nation's workforce has largely turned its back on unions in favor of governmental protection. However, he contends that there are problems with an absolute substitution of governmental regulation for unions. The first problem that arises is enforcement. Lichtenstein argues that the current regulatory and legal system is incapable of enforcing the inner workings of the millions of US businesses. He also argues that employee rights suffer when regulatory mechanisms are removed from the control of those who are directly involved and are handed over to the National Labor Relations Board or the court system.

There are few who would argue that organized labor is not in trouble. In May 2006, *Forbes* magazine, in an article entitled "Jobs That Will Disappear," predicted that the twenty-first century would not need union organizers or union leaders: "The labor movement has not come to terms with the knowledge economy at all" (Forbes 2006). The question that remains is: What can be, or should be, done to save labor unions? Certainly, there are millions of unionists who strongly support the resurrection of union ideals. However, even union leaders disagree on how to revitalize organized labor.

While the first twenty years of the twenty-first century saw considerable union decline, the COVID-19 pandemic triggered a drastic shift in support for unions. By August 2022, the number of Americans who supported unions reached a record high not seen since 1965, with 71 percent of Americans approving of labor unions—a significant rise since the start of the pandemic (McCarthy 2022). It was argued that the low employment rate during the pandemic shifted the balance of power between employees and employers, creating an environment ripe for union development at several high-profile companies including Amazon and Starbucks. This shift of power was also seen within the membership at Actors' Equity Association.

Change Is Brewing

Equity's long period of equilibrium abruptly came to an end in 2020. In March of that year, the COVID-19 pandemic shuttered live performances across the nation. Actors (along with freelance and company artists in the United States) were among the most severely impacted professions, with 63 percent experiencing unemployment and 95 percent losing income from creative work because of the pandemic (Cohen 2022). When the industry went dark, the union had to quickly rethink how to support its suddenly unemployed membership.

Equity's first task was to understand the scope of the pandemic and how it would impact union members and the industry. The union hired several public health consultants to guide the union's policies and terms (Huston 2022). Equity would go on to release several iterations of return-to-work guidelines, making sure that any and every process was cleared by the union. However, a year into the pandemic, Equity members grew tired of waiting for the union to implement return-to-work protocols. A *New York Times* article noted that "nearly 2,000 members of Actors' Equity have signed a petition that asks the simple question, 'When are we going to talk about the details of getting back to work?'" A union representative said that he and his Equity colleagues felt unheard, left out of discussions, and further behind other industries in getting back to work (Paulson 2021). When the article appeared, the union had approved safety plans from only twenty-two theaters across the nation, and many producers felt that the union was obstructing progress.

Frustrations over Equity's transparency and inclusion of member voices roiled the union in the spring of 2021. In April the union was scheduled to host its first national convention. However, the convention coincided with the public release of harassment allegations against theatrical producer Scott Rudin. Rudin was accused of "acts of intimidation" and humiliation against employees going back decades (Marks 2021). Just days before the convention, hundreds of theater workers marched down Broadway to protest Equity's failure to list Rudin's shows on the Do Not Work list (Tran 2021).[5] Equity contended that the list was only for nonunion productions. Furthermore, some Equity members reportedly felt that the union was "ineffective in protecting its membership from racism, sexism, and unsafe work environments" (Tran 2021). Some members began the campaign #NoNewsNoDues and stopped paying their monthly union dues in protest. The organizers of the protest had six demands for the union: one was to pressure the Broadway League to remove Rudin, another was "visibility on how the national council votes for policies," and a third involved "efforts to improve diversity with the council" (The Race Against Race 2021).

The convention ended abruptly after delegates—predominately members of color—walked out of the convention. Afterward, union members took to social media and other outlets to protest what they saw as "white supremacy culture" within the union's structures (Peterson 2021). In a response to the entire membership, president Kate Shindle wrote, "Although I am deeply saddened and sorry for any pain that was caused at the convention, this experience has presented a true opportunity to identify and interrupt this harmful pattern of behavior" (Kumar 2021). The convention ultimately adopted forty-one resolutions put forth by members, many of which sought to reprioritize inclusion and equity internally and externally (Actors' Equity Association 2021a).

Notably, these incidents made visible the brewing animosity between Equity leadership and some of its membership. While there had been other times in the union's history when there was public outcry from its members against union policies (such as the protest that resulted in the 99-Seat Theater Agreement), these incidents would mark the beginning of a period of significant change within the union.

OPEN ACCESS

Perhaps in response to member outcry, during the summer of 2021 Equity announced a major shift in its membership policy based on a core question: "How do we diversify our union if marginalized people do not have access to join?" (Bellinger 2021). The resulting initiative, Open Access, radically shifted how individuals could join the union. Traditionally, union membership had been gained either by getting hired on a union contract or by working a specified amount of weeks as an Equity membership candidate. With this sudden shift in policy, actors and stage managers were invited to join if they could prove (via a pay stub, W-2 form, etc.) that they have worked "professionally" in the United States (Actors' Equity Association 2021b). While Open Access was planned to be in effect only through May 1, 2023, the union has pledged to develop a "permanent gateway to membership that addresses racial inequities in accessing membership in the union" (Actors' Equity Association 2021b).

Importantly, the messaging around Open Access directly reframed how the union positioned itself within the theatrical sector, seemingly claiming a newfound power. Kate Shindle, president of Actors' Equity Association, said in a statement, "The old system had a significant flaw: It made employers the gatekeepers of Equity membership, with almost no other pathways to joining. . . . The union has inadvertently contributed to the systemic exclusion of BIPOC artists and others with marginalized identities by maintaining a system in which being hired to work those contracts was a prerequisite of membership" (American Theatre Editors 2021).

Still, the reform and sharpened focus on racial equity in the industry and within the union led many members to publicly question the motives of the union and to reflect on the working value of Equity membership:

> "I've dreamed about joining Equity since I was 12, but I have no intention of joining through this new program, nor do I know of anyone else who is planning to join," says theater artist Madeline Wall, a 2020 University of Minnesota graduate.
>
> "All of my Equity weeks were acquired pre-pandemic," she continues, "and the last year has made developing relationships with Equity theaters near-impossible. I could join—and pay thousands of dollars to do so—but it could be years before I am cast by Equity companies, and during those years, I would be shut out from any non-Equity opportunities."
>
> "If you join Equity too soon and are still finding your feet as an actor," [an actor wrote], "you may limit the work opportunities you have due to the plethora of Equity actors that will be vying for the same jobs."
>
> (Gabler 2021)

YouTube blogger Kent James Collins inquired how the union intended to support a sudden influx of new members, mentioning the need for increased audition slots, more contracts, and member education. He also addressed ongoing criticisms that the union was using open access as a "cash grab" (Half Hour Call 2021). During the height of the pandemic in the 2020–2021 season, nearly 70 percent of Equity members made less than $10,000 (Stamp 2021), and some members believed that Open Access was an attempt to help the union recuperate from the associated drop in dues coming in to fund the organization's operational capacities.

Equity president Kate Shindle went on the record to rebuff such claims (American Theatre Editors 2021). Rather, as union leaders told us in a 2022 interview, the Open Access program and any future policy designed to address restrictive racial barriers to union membership are about redistributing the power within the theatrical industry. Such moves are tethered to the notion of collectively reenvisioning Equity members— the professional actor and stage manager—as workers first.

This long-standing tension between the roles of artist and worker continues to underlie many implicit narratives regarding those who have an Equity card and those who do not. While the union does not engage in that rhetoric, the sudden shift in ideology is palpable throughout the membership and across the entertainment industry. As the union's leadership told us, "A union isn't for art. A union is so that you can go do your art and not have to worry whether or not your check will clear."

The Open Access initiative was only the second time in the history of Equity that membership was broadly extended to anyone who desired it (the first time being in 1919). This policy change will change Equity primary incentive for membership— legitimacy as an actor. Legitimacy—or professional status—is tied directed to the social identity of actors.

Equity's Card Campaign

"Sugar, Butter, Union" (Actors' Equity Association 2022b). This was Equity's social media slogan in front of its efforts to organize a nonunion, national tour of *Waitress: The Musical* during spring 2022. In the United States, all theaters—including national Broadway tours—operate with one of two employment agreements, union or nonunion. Historically, Equity has kept a list of producers operating nonunion productions. This list, the Do Not Work list, indicates to its membership that they are forbidden from working on these productions because they do not recognize the union contract. While Equity has prohibited its members from working for producers on the Do Not Work list, that was largely its only action taken against nonunion producers.

Nonunion productions are typically produced by companies that only operate nonunion shows. However, *Waitress* was an exception. According to the union's Action Network petition, two *Waitress* tours went out on the road: one union and one nonunion. Performers in the latter tour, according to Equity, earned a third of the pay with far fewer workplace protections than performers in the unionized tour (Actors' Equity Association 2022b). The same company was producing both touring shows. So for the first time in twenty years, Equity attempted to unionize a national tour (Levin 2022).

Equity made contact with the actors and stage managers on the non-Equity tour and began a card campaign, which empowers workers to sign a union authorization card instead of immediately committing to an election. The goal of this type of organizing campaign is to prove to employers that a majority of their workers want union representation ("Card Check: Learn the Basics" 2013). Typically, this effort urges employers to voluntarily recognize the union. However, the producers of the non-Equity tour declined to recognize the union.

Next, Equity tried a different tactic. Withdrawing their petition for union representation, the union instead filed a grievance with the National Labor Relations Board[6] alleging that the producers were "double-breasting" by running both tours (Paulson 2022). The union asserted that the non-Equity tour violated its right to be the "exclusive bargaining representative of performers and stage managers" (Huston and Kilkenny 2022). The union posited that because the producers were already signatories to union agreements--including as part of the Broadway League—Equity agreements applied to "any and all corporations, co-partnerships, enterprises and/or groups which said signers or each of them directs, controls, or is interested in" (Huston and Kilkenny 2022). While, as of 2022, the grievance was still ongoing at the NLRB and as the tour has since closed, Equity hoped to garner retroactive pay and benefits for those workers and force any upcoming iterations of the nonunion tour to instead go on a union contract.

According to Equity's organizing director, Stef Frey, whom we interviewed in 2022, the card campaign was a reflection of Equity's changing "organizing philosophy," in which increased member engagement and focus on worker power paved the way for organizing effort—successful or not. For instance, union leadership cites a shared and reinvigorated labor landscape in America, one in which organizing efforts at workplaces at large companies inspired union and nonunion members alike.

A Culture of Yes: Star Garden

On August 17, 2022, Equity issued a press release with the following headline: "Actors' Equity Association to Unionize Strippers at the Star Garden" (Actors' Equity Association 2022c). Quickly picked up by media outlets, the story garnered national attention. If successful, the effort would make Star Garden the only unionized strip club in the United States (Fuster 2022). Absent from the public conversation, however, was the fact that strippers were organizing with a theatrical stage union.

Just as the union saw Open Access as an important opportunity to reshape members' positions of power within the industry, this opportunity presented a chance to rethink the union's own position in the live performance sector. One member of Equity's leadership noted to us that several entertainment unions have been among the last to catch up to exploring their jurisdictional reach and how they might cover a different type of worker—such as strippers, or real estate actors (those who use their acting skills in real-life role playing activities), or medical performers.

For the union, and with unanimous support from Equity's National Council,[7] this foray into live performance (rather than just live theater) means an ongoing transformation of internal values and processes. This includes not just internal decision-making structures but also external organizing practices. Leadership noted that Equity had always employed a top-down approach to organizing, depending on the employer to grant voluntary recognition.

That culture was no longer working for the union. Instead, new executive leadership hired in 2022 at the union's highest levels embraced what they called a "culture of yes," or fostering a member-driven, bottom-up approach that has increased member communication and engagement in the union's processes. Leadership cited contract negotiations at the Second City comedy club in Chicago, where they developed a member-led contract action team to support the bargaining committee. In addition, members were brought in as observers who were encouraged to provide feedback and learn about the negotiation process.

The leadership said in our interview with them that member priorities have shifted too. The Star Garden dancers, for instance, came to Equity with issues regarding unsafe stages, being filmed without consent, illegal payments, and unfair pay. Quality-of-life issues such as work-life balance and mental health have become key bargaining matters at the negotiating table as Equity looks to break down harmful practices (such as the demanding hours of what's commonly called "tech week"—the week leading up to opening night which incorporates all the technical elements of a production such as set, lighting, sound, costumes, and props). During this week, it has been union standard to work 10 hours out of 12 hours.

At the end of 2022, Equity was just beginning the bargaining process for its next sit-down production agreement with the Broadway League. Leadership has sensed a collective shift in how members see themselves and how they talk about themselves. One leader said this is now "workers seeing themselves *as workers* deserving of basic dignity."

The Star Garden campaign has been a crucial example of this paradigm shift. The dancers remain locked out of their workplace by their employers, having been locked out shortly after announcing their organizing drive in 2021. The dancers' Instagram account depicts picket lines with signs that state "Everyone Deserves Safety" and "Strippers' Safety over Bosses' Profits," (Stripper Action Updates 2022). Most recently, the dancers voted to be represented by a union, "but the final result was delayed when the employer challenged all but one of the mail ballots" (Actors' Equity Association 2022d). At the time of writing (late 2022), the dancers were still on strike while the union awaited an NLRB ruling on the challenged votes.

In a statement, union president Kate Shindle said, "This effort reflects Equity's revitalized commitment to collaborating with live performers seeking to organize their workplaces, and our core belief that every worker who wants a union deserves a union. We anticipate the cooperation of the City of Los Angeles and look forward to bargaining a fair contract very soon" (Actors' Equity Association 2022a). The statement ends by encapsulating this new organizing mindset and giving nonunion workers a call to action, urging them to know their worth: "Equity encourages all workers in live performance who feel they would benefit from a union contract to contact the union's organizing department."

Throughout its history, Actors' Equity has regularly utilized collective action as a means of establishing, expanding, and maintaining control of theatrical employment. Its founding principle and primary collective good remained stable for a century—to make membership in the union tantamount to membership within the profession.

Despite the union's high level of unemployment and lack of collective goods, "professionalism" correlated so significantly to its members' social identity that the union enjoyed 100 years of equilibrium. It was not until the global pandemic that the union made significant changes to its membership structure and collective action activity.

The period of significant change resulted in the union altering its policies on membership access, which subsequently changed the collective goods and incentives offered to members and potential members. The union's repositioning has resulted in beseeching its members to shift their social identity from "actor" to "unionist." It remains to be seen if Equity members will embrace this new proposition. As one of the union's leaders explained, "[Equity] is no longer a professional affiliation.... It is no longer a token of professionalism.... We are a motherfucking labor union."

Conclusion

Actors' Equity and the broader theatrical landscape in America are evolving. As a response to the COVID-19 pandemic and ensuing calls for social justice across the United

States, this paradigmatic shift embeds inclusion as an ideological tenet of collective action. The long-standing normative institutionalization of hierarchal leadership and related structures in cultural unions is being examined as contributing mechanisms that discourage organizational participation and hinder equitable progress and inclusion. Since the start of the pandemic in the United States, this shared cultural reflection has engendered introspection that has empowered systematic change for many institutions.

As a leading cultural and labor organization, Equity is a critical example that, theoretically and practically, demonstrates such change. The union is not only assessing pathways of engagement and membership but also actively redefining the notion of the theater professional and subsequently reworking ideals of membership eligibility. Recent organizing drives, changes to membership policy, and a public push centering worker power have shifted the dynamics that guide Equity's internal culture and external engagement within the labor movement. Seemingly, the union has evolved from its founding philosophies through grassroots and member-led initiatives triggered by a global crisis.

As Equity and its members reconsider the value and meaning of organized labor, the changes in its organizational structure and the connected social identity of actors will impact the theater sector, the cultural labor movement, and the role of cultural workers in the field.

Notes

1. Scabby the Rat is a giant inflatable rodent whose presence indicates an active labor dispute.
2. The National Alliance of Theatrical Stage Employees (later the international alliance) had until 2001 used the older spelling of the word, "employe." In 2001, delegates voted to update the spelling to the contemporary "employee."
3. A right-to-work state is a state that has enacted legislation that guarantees that no individual can be forced as a condition of employment to join or pay dues or fees to a labor union. Whereas a pro-union state can require union membership for employment within certain industries.
4. The American Federation of Labor and Congress of Industrial Organizations (AFL-CIO) is the largest federation of unions in the United States. It is made up of fifty-six national and international unions representing more than twelve million active and retired workers. The performing arts unions, including Actors' Equity Association, the American Federation of Musicians, and IATSE, are all members of the AFL-CIO.
5. Equity's Do Not Work list identifies productions that its membership cannot work on because the productions do not recognize the union contract.
6. The National Labor Relations Board is an independent agency of the US federal government with the responsibility of enforcing US labor laws in relationship to collective bargaining and unfair labor practices.
7. National Council is Equity's decision-making body regarding policy, finance and appeals. It also has the authority to adopt rules supplementing the constitution and by-laws. The council consists of eight officers and seventy-five councilors.

References

Actors' Equity Association. 2021a. "Actors' Equity Association Concludes First-Ever Convention." Press release. April 28, 2021. https://www.actorsequity.org/news/PR/FirstConventionConclulsion/.

Actors' Equity Association. 2021b. "Open Access." https://actorsequity.org/join/openaccess/.

Actors' Equity Association. 2022a. "Actors' Equity Association Reaches New Heights by Organizing Lecturers at the Griffith Observatory Planetarium." Press release, September 19, 2022. https://actorsequity.org/news/PR/GriffithObservatory91922/.

Actors' Equity Association. 2022b. "Show Your Support for the Touring Company of Waitress Unionizing!" Action Network petition. https://actionnetwork.org/petitions/sugar-butter-union/?clear_id=true.

Actors' Equity Association. 2022c. "Actors' Equity Association to Unionize Strippers at Star Garden." Press release, August 17, 2022. https://actorsequity.org/news/PR/StarGarden/.

Actors' Equity Association. 2022d. "LA Strippers Unionizing with Actors' Equity Association a Step Closer to the Bargaining Table After NLRB Vote Count Today." Press release, November 2022. https://actorsequity.org/news/PR/SGCount/.

Actors' Equity Association. n.d. a. "AEA Timeline | 1940's." Equity Timeline 100 Years. https://www.actorsequity.org/timeline/timeline_1940.html.

Actors' Equity Association. n.d. b. "AEA Timeline | 1960s." Equity Timeline 100 Years. https://www.actorsequity.org/timeline/timeline_1960.html.

Actors' Equity Association. n.d. c. "AEA Timeline | 1980s." Equity Timeline 100 Years. https://www.actorsequity.org/timeline/timeline_1980.html.

American Theatre Editors. 2021. "Actors' Equity Announces 'Open Access' to Membership." *American Theatre*, July 21, 2021. https://www.americantheatre.org/2021/07/21/actors-equity-announces-open-access-to-membership/.

Associated Press. 2005. "Teamsters split with AFL-CIO." *The Denver Post*. July 25, 2005. https://www.denverpost.com/2005/07/25/teamsters-split-with-afl-cio/.

Baumgartner, Frank R., and Bryan D. Jones. 1991. "Agenda Dynamics and Policy Subsystems." *Journal of Politics* 53, no. 4: 1044–1074.

Bellinger, Bear. 2021. "Open Access." Press release, Actors' Equity Association. https://actorsequity.org/resources/diversity/diversityblog/OpenAccess/.

Bennett, James. T., and Bruce E. Kaufman. 2002. *The Future of Private Sector Unionization*. New York: Routledge.

Bernheim, Alfred L. 1932. *The Business of the Theatre: An Economic History of the American Theatre, 1750–1932*. New York: Benjamin Blom.

Bowman, Lewis, Dennis Ippolito, and William Donaldson. 1969. "Incentives for the Maintenance of Grassroots Political Activism." *Midwest Journal of Political Science* 13, no. 1: 126–139.

Bureau of Labor Statistics. 2001. "Union Members in 2000." Press release, January 18, 2001. https://www.bls.gov/news.release/history/union2_01182001.txt.

Calta, Luisa. 1970a. "Off Broadway Actors Go on Strike." *New York Times*, November 17, 1970. https://www.nytimes.com/1970/11/17/archives/off-broadway-actors-go-on-strike.html.

Calta, Luisa. 1970b. "Accord Reached in Off-Broadway Strike." *New York Times*, December 17, 1970. https://www.nytimes.com/1970/12/17/archives/accord-reached-in-off-broadway-strike.html.

"Card Check: Learn the Basics." 2013. US Chamber of Commerce, December 19, 2013. https://www.uschamber.com/employment-law/unions/card-check-learn-the-basics.

Clark, Peter Bentley, and James F. Wilson. 1961. "Incentive Systems: A Theory of Organizations." *Administrative Science Quarterly* 6: 129–166.

Cobb, Roger W., and Charles D. Elder. 1983. *Participation in American Politics: The Dynamics of Agenda-Building*. 2nd ed. Baltimore: Johns Hopkins University Press.

Cohen, Randy. 2022. "COVID-19's Pandemic's Impact on The Arts: Research." Americans for the Arts, National Arts Administration and Policy Publications Database, May 12, 2022. https://www.americansforthearts.org/node/103614.

Davis, Jenny, Tony Love, and Phoenicia Fares. 2019. "Collective Social Identity: Synthesizing Identity Theory and Social Identity Theory Using Digital Data." *Social Psychology Quarterly* 82, no. 3: 254–273. https://doi.org/10.1177/0190272519851025.

"Equity Declared Reds Are Menace." 1951. *New York Times*, April 20, 1951. https://www.nytimes.com/1951/04/20/archives/equity-declares-reds-are-menace-actors-union-takes-stand-on.html.

Forbes. 2006. "Jobs that will disappear." *Forbes*, May 18, 2006.

Fuster, Jeremy. 2022. "North Hollywood Strippers Move to Unionize with Actors' Equity in Historic Labor Vote." The Wrap, August 17, 2022. https://www.thewrap.com/star-garden-strippers-union-actors-equity/.

Gabler, Jay. 2021. "Open Access Invites More Actors to Join the Union, but There's a Catch." Racket, November 16, 2021. https://racketmn.com/open-access-invites-more-actors-to-join-the-union-but-theres-a-catch/.

Gelt, Jessica. 2015. "Actors' Equity and L.A.'s 99-Seat Theaters: A Brief History." *Los Angeles Times*, May 15, 2015. https://www.latimes.com/entertainment/arts/theater/la-ca-cm-the-road-theater-sidebar-20150517-story.html.

Gemmill, Paul Fleming. 1926. *Collective Bargaining by Actors: A Study of Trade-Unionism Among Performers of the English-Speaking Legitimate Stage in America*. Washington, DC: US GPO.

Half Hour Call. 2021. "Are Millennials Killing the Equity Card Industry?? | Actors' Equity Association Open Access." YouTube, posted July 26, 2021. https://www.youtube.com/watch?v=FO_zDlTyG4I.

Holmes, Sean. 1994. "Weavers of Dreams, Unite! Constructing an Occupational Identity in the Actors' Equity Association, 1913–1934." Ph.D. dissertation, New York University.

Huston, Caitlin. 2022. "Actors' Equity Appoints New Team of COVID-19 Safety Consultants." Broadway News, February 7, 2022. https://broadwaynews.com/2022/02/07/actors-equity-appoints-new-team-of-covid-19-safety-consultants/.

Huston, Caitlin, and Katie Kilkenny. 2022. "Actors' Equity Expands 'Waitress' Unionizing Fight to Entire Broadway Touring Industry (Exclusive)." *Hollywood Reporter*, May 5, 2022. https://www.hollywoodreporter.com/business/business-news/actors-equity-waitress-unionizing-fight-to-entire-broadway-touring-industry-exclusive-1235141202/.

Kumar, Naveen. 2021. "Broadway Is Back, and May Finally Confront Its Racism." *Daily Beast*, May 29, 2021. https://www.thedailybeast.com/broadway-is-back-and-may-finally-confront-its-racism.

Levin, Annie. 2022. "Non-Equity 'Waitress' Musical Tour Files for Union Recognition." *Observer*, April 26, 2022. https://observer.com/2022/04/non-equity-waitress-musical-tour-files-for-union-recognition/.

Lichtenstein, Nelson. 2013. *State of the Unions: A Century of American Labor*. Princeton, NJ: Princeton University Press.

Marks, Peter. 2021. "Broadway Producer Scott Rudin Steps Aside amid Accusations of Abusive Behavior Going Back Decades, Apologizes for Pain He Caused." *Washington Post*, April 17, 2021.

Masse Jolicoeur, M. 2018. "An Introduction to Punctuated Equilibrium: A Model for Understanding Stability and Dramatic Change in Public Policies." National Collaborating Centre for Healthy Public Policy, Montreal. https://www.ncchpp.ca/docs/2018_ProcessPP_Intro_PunctuatedEquilibrium_EN.pdf.

McArthur, Benjamin. 2000. *Actors and American Culture, 1850–1920*. Iowa City: University of Iowa Press, 2000.

McCarthy, Justin. 2022. "U.S. Approval of Labor Unions at Highest Point Since 1965." Gallup, August 30, 2022. https://news.gallup.com/poll/398303/approval-labor-unions-highest-point-1965.aspx.

McClear, Sheila. 2022. "The Striking Strippers of North Hollywood Could be Joining Actors' Equity." *Los Angeles Magazine*, August 17, 2022. https://www.lamag.com/citythinkblog/the-striking-strippers-of-north-hollywood-could-be-joining-actors-equity/.

McLeod, S. A. 2019. "Social Identity Theory." Simply Psychology, October 24, 2019. www.simplypsychology.org/social-identity-theory.html.

Mosca, Joseph B., and Steven Pressman. 1995. "Unions in the 21st Century." *Public Personnel Management* 24, no. 2: 159–166. https://doi.org/10.1177/009102609502400205.

"Negotiators Reach Tentative Pact in Theater Strike." 1964. *New York Times*, June 8, 1964. https://www.nytimes.com/1964/06/08/archives/negotiators-reach-tentative-pact-in-theater-strike.html.

Olson, Mancur. 1965. *The Logic of Collective Action: Public Goods and the Theory of Groups*. Cambridge, MA: Harvard University Press.

Paulson, Michael. 2021. "Theater Actors Step Up Push for Union to Allow Them to Work." *New York Times*, March 19, 2021. https://www.nytimes.com/2021/03/19/theater/actors-equity-frustration-petition.html.

Paulson, Michael. 2022. "Equity Drops 'Waitress' Unionization Effort and Files Grievance." *New York Times*, May 6, 2022. https://www.nytimes.com/2022/05/05/theater/waitress-equity.html.

Peterson, Christopher. 2021. "Actors' Equity Convention Ends with Walkout by BIPOC Delegates After Failure to Address 'White Supremacy Culture.'" *OnStage Blog*, April 29, 2021. https://www.onstageblog.com/editorials/2021/4/29/actors-equity-convention-end-with-walkout-by-bipoc-delegates-after-failure-to-address-white-supremacy-culture.

The Race Against Race (@50milerunforjusticeprotest). 2021. "March on Broadway—Full List of Demands." Instagram, April 22, 2023. https://www.instagram.com/p/CN-Op9BDyLt/?hl=en.

Robb, David. 2015. "Lawsuit Filed to Stop Actors Equity from Forcing Small Theatres to Pay Minimum Wage." Deadline, October 18, 2015. https://deadline.com/2015/10/actors-equity-la-99-seat-waiver-los-angeles-1201587087/.

Salisbury, Robert H., and Lauretta Conklin. 1998. "Instrumental Versus Expressive Group Politics: The National Endowment for the Arts." In *Interest Group Politics*, edited by Allan J. Cigler and Burdett A. Loomis, chap. 13. Washington, DC: CQ Press.

Shepard, Richard F. 1968. "Strike by Actors Closes 19 Shows Along Broadway." *New York Times*, June 18, 1968. https://www.nytimes.com/1968/06/18/archives/strike-by-actors-closes-19-shows-along-broadway-equity-orders.html.

Shirley, Don. 1989. "Out-of-Court Settlement Puts an End to Waiver Wars . . . for Now." *Los Angeles Times*, April 24, 1989. https://www.latimes.com/archives/la-xpm-1989-04-24-ca-1738-story.html.

Simonson, Robert. 2013. "Equity at 100: How Actors' Equity Pushed for Racial Equality." *Playbill*, February 13, 2013. https://playbill.com/article/equity-at-100-how-actors-equity-pushed-for-racial-equality-com-202475.

Stamp, Joey. 2021. "2020–2021 Theatrical Report." Actors' Equity Association. https://www.actorsequity.org/aboutequity/annualstudy/2020-2021-annual-study.

Stripper Action Updates (@stripperstrikenoho). 2022. "The group on the picket line tonight..." Instagram post, September 25, 2022. https://www.instagram.com/p/Ci7WLP3ufDe/?hl=en.

Stevens-Garmon, Morgen. 2013. "100 Years of the Actors' Equity Association." *MCNY Blog: New York Stories*, May 21, 2013. https://blog.mcny.org/2013/05/21/100-years-of-the-actors-equity-association/.

Tajfel, Henri. 1974. "Social Identity and Intergroup Behaviour." *Social Science Information* 13, no. 2: 65–93.

Tajfel, Henri, and John Turner. 1979. "An Integrative Theory of Intergroup Conflict." In *Organizational Identity: A Reader*, edited by Mary Jo Hatch and Majken Schultz, 56–65. New York: Oxford University Press.

Taylor, Erin. 2022. "Inside LA's Star Garden Strike: Strippers are Organizing Whether You Like It or Not." *Observer*, August 25, 2022. https://observer.com/2022/08/inside-las-star-garden-strike-strippers-are-organizing-whether-you-like-it-or-not/.

Tran, Diep. 2021. "Why Some Members of Actors' Equity Association Aren't Paying Their Dues." *Backstage*, April 24, 2021. https://www.backstage.com/magazine/article/actors-equity-association-protest-dues-73140/.

True, James L., Bryan D. Jones, and Frank R. Baumgartner. 1999. "Punctuated-Equilibrium Theory Explaining Stability and Change in Public Policymaking." In *Theories of the Policy Process*, edited by Paul Sabatier, 155–123. Boulder, CO: Westview Press.

Wilson, James Q. 1973. *Political Organizations*. New York: Basic Books.

PART VI

MARKETING FOR ARTS AND CULTURAL ORGANIZATIONS

PART VI

MARKETING FOR ARTS AND CULTURAL ORGANIZATIONS

CHAPTER 22

GAMES AND MUSEUMS

A Novel Approach to Attracting and Retaining Audiences

MARTA PIZZETTI AND GIULIA MINIERO

Introduction

THE cultural sector was one of those most affected by the COVID-19 pandemic (ILO 2020): cultural institutions were forced to stay closed for several months during and after the generalized lockdowns that paralyzed the world. Even before the pandemic, cultural institutions faced the challenge of developing tools to maintain a relationship with visitors when they cannot visit the institution; the spread of COVID-19 has further exacerbated this challenge.

Relational marketing offers various tools to build and maintain customer loyalty through a deep understanding of customers' needs, customization of the experience, and continuous interaction with the customer. Digitalization is at the heart of relational marketing, because new technologies foster customer involvement and thereby reduce uncertainty and distance between consumers and aesthetic objects. Today, an increasing number of art institutions have taken up the challenge of digitalization to rejuvenate their image and to better align with audience expectations. The use of digital technologies is especially expected by younger generations, who may value digitization efforts made by cultural institutions that otherwise are seen as boring and old-fashioned (Hughes and Moscardo 2019; Passebois Ducros and Euzeby 2021).

Initially, digital technology has been used to facilitate interactions with the customer base using email campaigns, the institution's website, and social media (Courchesne, Ravanas, and Pulido 2019). Social media channels and podcasts have proliferated: the Uffizi Museum joined TikTok, and the Leonardo da Vinci Science and Technology Museum in Milan produced a podcast series on Leonardo's works. Other digital tools offer new interactions that can enrich the customer experience before, during, or after the visit, such as augmented reality apps for immersive tours and multimedia access to collections (Camarero, Garrido, and San José 2016). For example, the British Museum has developed a 360-degree virtual tour of its exhibitions. Gamification—the incorporation of game elements in activities (Robson et al. 2015)—is another digital tool that cultural institutions can use to build and maintain a relationship with customers (De Angeli 2018). Gamification influences contemporary life in many ways, as expectations of interactivity and reward have become embedded within everyday activities. Indeed, gamification has already been successfully applied in other contexts, such as education, and it is an effective tool for engaging customers by fostering intrinsic and extrinsic motivation (Hamari and Koivisto 2015; Mitchell, Schuster, and Drennan 2017). Nowadays, games are an important component of individuals' lives: we play games everywhere and engage in such activities for extended periods. The industry is constantly growing; it had a 2021 value of $178.3 billion and is expected to increase by 50 percent over the next four years, reaching a value of $268.8 billion in 2025 (Juniper Research 2021). Despite its multiple successful applications, gamification remains underused in cultural institutions. This is because of a general skepticism within such institutions about gamification, which, it is feared, could transform the cultural experience into an amusement park (i.e., Disneyfication) and even alienate part of the audience (Balloffet, Courvoisier, and Lagier 2014).

Current literature has mainly focused on using digital tools during the visit—that is, when the consumer is physically close to the cultural institution (e.g., Errichiello et al. 2017). Conversely, less is known about the benefits offered by such technologies when the cultural institution and the consumer are not close—that is, when the consumer does not or cannot visit the cultural institution.

Expanding our understanding of how consumers respond to digital experiences when they are at home or do not have access to the institution, like during the COVID-19 pandemic, would provide timely suggestions to cultural institution marketers who strive to find effective ways to maintain their institution's relevance in consumers' minds and to establish and develop a relationship with consumers. Increased competition (Colbert and Dantas 2019), the inherent constraints on institutions' availability (Preece and Wiggins Johnson 2011), and the need to attract new segments of consumers (Miniero and Holst 2020) force cultural institutions such as museums to offer a more customized and interactive experience outside the museum walls. In addition, audiences nowadays expect easy access to arts and culture for minimal cost, and more institutions are embracing the idea of open access to collection items (Australia Council for the Arts 2021).

The aim of the present chapter is twofold. First, it sheds light on consumers' responses to the digital experience offered by museums. Specifically, it focuses on gamification, a recent and promising tool for cultural institutions, and compares it to other popular digital tools—namely, virtual tours of and podcasts about collections. Such an analysis is relevant for the strategic implementation of digital experiences that are effective in retaining and/or attracting the target audience. Second, it examines whether digital experiences can be risky for cultural institutions because they might reduce the perceived authenticity of the offer. More specifically, we aim to contribute to the current debate on the risks of gamification for cultural institutions by empirically examining the perceived authenticity of the digital experience. With these objectives in mind, the present chapter aims to provide answers to the following research questions:

> RQ1: How do consumers respond to gamification as a strategy to offer digital museum experiences compared to other popular digital tools (i.e., virtual tours and podcasts)?
>
> RQ2: Does gamification reduce the perceived authenticity of cultural institutions?

The chapter develops as follows. First we review the current literature on gamification and its application in the cultural industry. Then we describe how cultural institutions can use gamification and other digital experiences to manage relationships with their target audience effectively. Based on this literature review, we derive working hypotheses. Second, we describe the experimental design conducted to test hypotheses on the effect of gamification on perceived authenticity, novelty, intention to use the digital experience, and attitude toward the cultural institution, compared to the effects of virtual tours and podcasts. The chapter ends with a discussion of theoretical contributions, a recommendation for practitioners, and suggestions for future research avenues.

Theoretical Background and Hypothesis Development: Gamification in the Arts and Culture

Initially, gamification entered the museum world as video games displayed (or even playable) in museum collections. Beginning in 2012, the Museum of Modern Art (MOMA) in New York has included video games in its permanent collection, considering them as artworks (Goodlander and Mansfield 2013; Izzo 2017) or as a form of modern life and culture (Muriel and Crawford 2018). More recently, cultural institutions have started to employ gamification as a communication tool in the effort to engage and educate their audience (De Angeli 2018). Gamification may offer customers new, engaging, and attractive experiences. For example, the British Museum launched a game called Young Explorer, to help visitors between the ages of nine and fourteen approach history. In Spain, the Thyssen-Bornemisza Museum implemented the Nubla Project, intended to help visitors experience the collection differently and in a more engaged manner through gaming.

Research suggests that the gaming experience at museums elicits positive feelings and increases the time spent visiting the cultural institution while fostering a positive attitude toward exploring the museum environment (Xhembulla et al. 2014). Gamification appears to be a successful tool for engaging audiences, especially children (Xhembulla et al. 2014), while facilitating the learning experience. Providing playful and fun experiences helps individuals stay focused and increases their level of attention (Hunter and Werbach 2012). For instance, children aged six through nine interacting with a mobile game at the British Museum showed an unexpected learning outcome in terms of kinesthetic skills: they could improve their coordination by scanning tags to activate them as they progressed in the game (Mannion 2012).

Games can be much more than an educational tool, and cultural institutions have the potential to use gamification to strengthen the emotional attachment between them and their audience through social interactions. At the Asian Civilizations Museum in Singapore, a mobile game developed to convey cultural content on Chinese terracotta warriors effectively fostered purposeful social interaction between parents and children (Thian 2012) and peer-to-peer interaction (Waycott, Jones, and Scanlon 2005). This effect is highly desirable for museums: beyond learning, a noteworthy outcome of the experience at a museum is the creation and reinforcement of a positive attitude toward exploration of the institution, and younger generations of visitors value peer interactions in cultural contexts (Xhembulla et al. 2014; Hughes and Moscardo 2019).

Games are especially attractive for younger visitors, who are generally not very prone to dedicate their leisure time to cultural experiences (NEA 2015). Gamification turns what young consumers see as a not-fun activity into an engaging experience, during which they can feel empowered to customize their experience with the cultural environment through interaction and active participation. Choosing and interacting with different game settings, collecting points or badges, and appearing on the leaderboard are all typical in-game mechanisms that might help visitors to increase their engagement with the game (Hunter and Werbach 2012). For example, the Tate Museum invested in the game Race Against Time, a free mobile game in which gamers accumulate tokens that enable them to progress further in the game. This might augment the likelihood that visitors keep interacting with the game when the experience at the museum is over. If the game is engaging and fun and provides them with cultural value, most likely they will keep playing even outside the institutional environment (Schaller 2011).

Gamification as a Customer Relationship Management Tool

Many tools based on gamification have been implemented to enrich the visitor experience. However, gaming elements could also be strategically used to foster audience development, engagement, and participation in a time frame different from the one in which the visit takes place (Viola 2015). In Italy, for example, the National Archeological Museum in Naples created a game, Father and Son, to create and maintain a relationship with its audience outside of the museum (Solima 2018).

Gamification can be strategically used to keep a cultural institution present in customers' minds and to maintain, reinforce, and even create relationships with actual and potential visitors (Preece and Wiggins Johnson 2011). However, so far, gamification has been less frequently employed than other, more traditional tools of customer relationship management (e.g., email campaigns, customer profiling, and dynamic pricing; Courchesne et al. 2019) or other new digital technologies, such as websites and social media profiles (Garrido and Camarero 2014). These digital tools have the primary function of increasing transactions by making access to the institution easier and faster (e.g., buying online tickets) (Courchesne et al. 2019) and informing customers about events, collections, and activities (Palumbo 2021). Museums have also developed podcasts about their collections. For example, Art Fund (UK's national charity for art) has developed a series of podcasts featuring famous actors in collaboration with museums and art galleries across the UK, such as the Art Gallery & Museum of Glasgow. Podcasts are particularly suited to attract those visitors who look for a wide variety of cultural offerings (Gürel and Nielsen 2019) because they increase visitors' ability to select, access, and retrieve information (Calcagno and Biscaro 2012).

More recently, museums have started to leverage the emotions new technologies may generate by implementing virtual tours, in some cases also involving virtual reality (Atzeni, Del Chiappa, and Pung 2022). Virtual tours are enjoyable and allow consumers to experience artifacts and emotionally connect to them even before seeing them physically (Alelis, Bobrowicz, and Ang 2015).

Studies on the use of digital technologies by museums suggest that not all technologies contribute similarly to the customer's experience (Sundar et al. 2015). Virtual tours of and podcasts about art collections are among the most common forms of digital content that museums offer, whether as a tryout of the collection or as a way to expand the lifetime of a temporary exhibition (Hume and Mills 2011). These digital tools use storytelling in the service of traditional didactic and learning outcomes: they leverage the cognitive experience to promote familiarity (Roederer, Revat, and Pallud 2020) and create bonds with the artworks (Di Blasio and Di Blasio 1983), which may promote the success of educational objectives. Indeed, a study demonstrated that consumers actively look for podcasts when searching for information and might become irritated if the podcast does not provide the information needed (Florenthal et al. 2012). Building on this, virtual tours and podcasts might be seen as convergent with the traditional representation of museums: they use a language aligned with the traditional educational aim of cultural institutions but may limit a consumer's scope for personal interpretation. Moreover, the experience is guided by the institution, with limited possibilities for personalization and co-creation by the consumer, who has to follow the pattern suggested by the "expert" (Calcagno and Biscaro 2012; Srinivasan et al. 2009).

Gamification helps consumers express their preferences and customize their experience, increasing their sense of ownership of the experience (Hammady, Ma, and Temple 2016). Moreover, gamification involves interactive storytelling, in which the customer has an active role and is engaged both cognitively and emotionally (Kidd 2011). Such characteristics diverge from the way many consumers perceive museums: as places for contemplation, rich with information to learn but not interactive and fun (Hughes and Moscardo 2019). Conversely, offering a gamified experience diverges from the traditional museum offering. Therefore, gamification may be perceived as unexpected, incongruent with the traditional museum experience, and more novel than virtual tours or podcasts. We therefore posit:

> H1: Gamification is perceived as significantly more novel than other popular digital experiences, namely virtual tours and podcasts of artworks.

It is paramount for cultural institutions to offer experiences perceived as novel in order to remain salient for target customers. Novelty has been found to boost salience, attention, and interest; it facilitates the creation of memories (Bechkoff 2019) and increases enjoyment (Yim, Chu, and Sauer 2017). In the marketing domain, novelty is a driver of competitive advantage by differentiation (Bloch 1995). Perceived novelty induces a positive psychological response: it instills in consumers the belief that their experience will be more enjoyable, leading to more positive attitudes (Yim, Chu, and Sauer 2017) and facilitating subsequent behaviors (Bloch 1995; Hetet, Ackermann, and Mathieu 2016). We therefore hypothesize:

> H2: Perceived novelty mediates the relationship between digital experiences and attitudes toward the museum.

Downsides of Digitalization in Cultural Industries

Despite the potential benefits of digital tools, many professionals in the cultural industry are still reluctant to use them or cautious about relying on them because of the fear of losing the museum's character and authenticity (Balloffet, Courvoisier, and Lagier 2014; Passebois Ducros and Euzéby 2021). The concern is rooted in the traditional mission of cultural institutions, which is primarily education. The fear is that heavily leveraging digital tools might dilute the identity and the institutional role of cultural institutions.

Authenticity is vital for cultural institutions because it is considered an essential element of distinctiveness (Thyne and Hede 2016), a factor involved in choosing to visit a place (Correia Loureiro 2019; Atzeni, Del Chiappa, and Pung 2022), and a driver of loyalty toward the cultural institution (Forgas-Coll et al. 2017). For these reasons, it is crucial to adopt digital tools that foster authenticity instead of jeopardizing it, but to date limited research has been conducted on the differential effect of digital tools on perceived authenticity. Studies suggest that when a virtual tour experience is perceived as authentic, it elicits positive emotional response, attachment, and behavioral intentions (Atzeni, Del Chiappa, and Pung 2022). However, to elicit authenticity, virtual tours must be high-resolution 360-degree experiences in which the consumer has complete control of the path to follow (Spielmann and Orth 2021). Conversely, in the context of cultural institutions, virtual tours often present a non-immersive experience (Atzeni, Del Chiappa, and Pung 2022), with static images that decrease perceived authenticity (Spielmann and Orth 2021).

Podcasts also may positively affect perceived authenticity, but such a perception is mainly driven by the viewer's familiarity with the podcast host or the host's ability to communicate the message in their own words (Brinson and Lemon 2022). In the context of podcasts about museum artworks, the host is likely to read a script that informs the audience about the artwork's history or characteristics. The use of formal and informative language, although aligned with traditional forms of communication by cultural institutions, may impede the development of a relationship between the audience and the podcast host (Brinson and Lemon 2022), negatively influencing perceived authenticity.

Gamification might be more effective in fostering visitors' perception of authenticity because it elicits transportation (absorption in a story) and imagination (Green and Brock 2000), which are drivers of perceived authenticity (Hede and Thyne 2010; Derbaix and Gombault 2016). Indeed, transportation is more likely if the content presents events that are known, familiar, and culturally close to the user (Bilandzic and Busselle 2008; Larsen and László 1990). Specifically, research has indicated that realism in a portrayal can be leveraged to drive transportation (Beverland, Lindgreen, and Vink 2008; Brown, Kozinets, and Sherry 2003; Gilmore and Pine 2007). We argue that gamification increases the perceived authenticity of the museum, thanks to an increase in transportation, which in turn affects the consumer's intention to experience the digital content. Studies in tourism, a sector that has already implemented digital tools to attract consumers, suggest that authenticity positively influences future behaviors (Atzeni, Del Chiappa, and Pung 2022). More formally, we specify:

H3: Gamification is perceived as significantly more authentic than other digital experiences—namely, virtual tours and podcasts.

H4: Perceived authenticity mediates the relationship between digital experiences and intention to use the digital tool.

The Study

The present study aims at providing timely answers regarding the benefits and risks gamification delivers to cultural institutions by investigating how gamification affects consumers' responses compared to the popular digital experiences of virtual tours of museums and podcasts about artworks. The digital experiences under investigation in this study have been mostly examined as tools to enhance the experience at the time of

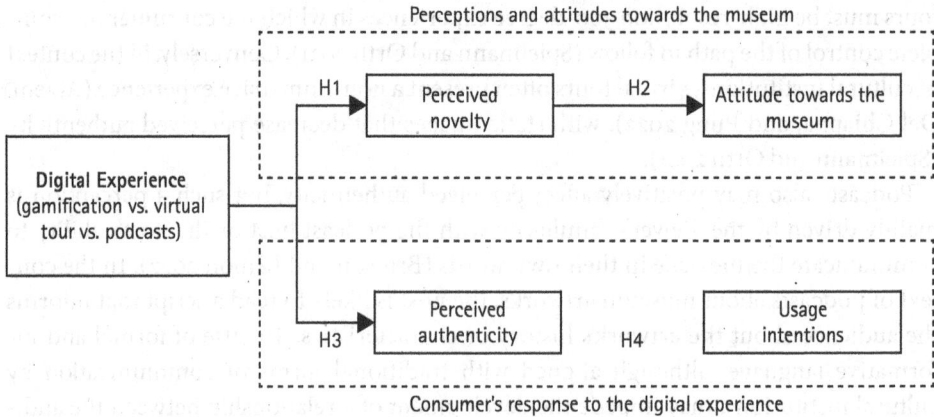

FIGURE 22.1 Graphical representation of tested hypotheses.

the visit, while less is known about their effectiveness in maintaining the relationship with a customer (Sundar et al. 2015) when the customer is not close to the museum.

To empirically test and compare the effect of the three forms of digital experience on consumer response, an experimental design was deemed suitable because it permits the testing of cause-and-effect relationships by controlling for extraneous and intervening variables. Experimental designs are widely used in the consumer behavior and marketing field and have been successfully applied to the cultural sector (e.g., Miniero, Rurale, and Addis 2014; Xhembulla et al. 2014).

In the present study, we investigate two classes of dependent variables. The first deals with the effects of the digital experience on consumers' perceptions of and attitudes toward museums. The second relates to consumers' response to the digital experience. Analyzing these two classes of variables allows us to measure the effects of digital experiences on the overall perceptions of the museum and to provide a fine-grained understanding of how consumers react to digital experiences in terms of the perceived authenticity of what is being offered as well as in terms of usage intention. For the two classes of variables, we expected a differential effect of the three types of digital experiences, as hypothesized above. Figure 22.1 graphically illustrates the variables and hypotheses tested.

Procedures

This study adopted a scenario-based experimental design. A total of 121 participants (M_{age} = 33.17; 47.9 percent female) took part in a single-factor (digital experience: gamification vs. virtual tour vs. podcasts) between-subject experimental design. Participants were recruited from the UK-resident panel of Prolific Academic, a crowdsourcing platform that connects researchers with potential study participants. Such crowdsourced samples have proven reliable and suitable for investigating certain variables, including perceptions and attitudes (Goodman and Paolacci 2017). Participants were provided an online link to access the related questionnaire through Prolific Academic, and received a small reward for completing it. Participants were asked to read a short text on a digital experience offered by a museum and answer questions related to the dependent variables under investigation (perceived novelty, attitude toward the museum, perceived authenticity of the museum, and digital experience usage intention).

Participants were randomly assigned to the three experimental conditions. The scenarios described a fictitious digital experience offered by a fictitious museum (though the scenarios drew inspiration from museums' actual offers). This choice was made in order to avoid recall bias. The scenario on gamification described an interactive game to be played at home that allows the player to discover the museum's collection of artworks. Specifically, the game asks players to put themselves in the shoes of the son of an archeologist, who has to discover his father's life by learning about the museum collection and interacting with other players.[1] In the virtual tour condition, the user can discover the museum collection by choosing between different itineraries. The podcast condition describes a collection of videos on the museum's most important artworks, narrated by museum researchers.

After presenting the scenario, we measured the dependent variables: perceived novelty (two items from Wiebe et al. 2014; Cronbach's α = .923), attitude toward the museums (five items from Spears and Singh 2004; Cronbach's α = .908), perceived authenticity of the offer (three items from Newman and Dhar 2014; Cronbach's α = .721), and digital experience usage intention (three items from Badrinarayanan et al. 2012; Cronbach's α = .931).

As a control variable, we measured involvement with art (six items from Chang and Gibson 2011; Cronbach's α = .954) because it influences perceptions of museum experience (Forgas-Coll et al. 2017). We found that participants differ between conditions ($F = 3.106, p = .05$), and we included involvement with arts as a covariate in our analysis. All scales were measured on a seven-point Likert scale. The questionnaire also included demographic questions that were administered at the end.

To measure the effectiveness of our manipulation, we included a manipulation check, which consisted of a multiple-choice question. Specifically, we asked participants to indicate what the fictitious museum's new offer was: an online game, a virtual tour, or a selection of podcasts. Participants who indicated the wrong option were excluded from further analysis. The final sample was 89 participants ($n_{gamification} = 31$; $n_{virtual\_tour} = 38$; $n_{podcasts} = 20$).

Findings

Analyses of covariance (ANCOVA) were performed on each dependent variable, with involvement with art as covariate. Table 22.1 reports the mean and standard deviations for each experimental condition and each dependent variable.

Table 22.1. Mean (and Standard Deviation) of Experimental Conditions for Each Dependent Variable

	Gamification	Virtual tour	Podcasts
Perceived novelty	5.68 (1.08)	4.86 (1.70)	4.95 (1.23)
Attitudes toward the museum	6.10 (.63)	5.64 (1.12)	5.70 (1.10)
Perceived authenticity	5.76 (.76)	5.26 (.87)	5.45 (.70)
Usage intention	5.28 (1.56)	4.32 (1.71)	4.87 (1.75)

Effects of the Digital Experience on Overall Perceptions of the Museum

Perceived novelty. The ANCOVA revealed a significant difference between conditions ($F = 4.786$, $p < .01$) and that involvement with arts is significantly related to perceived novelty ($F = 10.718$, $p < .01$). Planned contrasts tests show that gamification is perceived as significantly more novel compared to the virtual tour and the podcasts ($M_{gamification} = 5.68$ (1.08) vs. $M_{virtual\_tour} = 4.86$ (1.70) vs. $M_{podcasts} = 4.95$ (1.23); $t = 2.427$, $p < .05$). Specifically, it is perceived as significantly more novel compared to the virtual tour ($t = 2.411$, $p < .05$) and slightly significantly more novel compared to podcasts ($t = 1.800$, $p = .075$). No other significant differences were found.

Attitude toward the museum. When we controlled for involvement with arts ($F = 14.188$, $p < .001$), we found a significant difference between conditions ($M_{gamification} = 6.10$ (.63) vs. $M_{virtual\_tour} = 5.64$ (1.12) vs. $M_{podcasts} = 5.70$ (1.10); $F = 3.620$, $p < .05$). Further analysis revealed that participants have a slightly significantly more positive attitude toward the museum when it offers gamification compared to a virtual tour ($t = 1.928$, $p = .057$). Attitude does not differ between the gamification and podcast conditions, nor between virtual tours and podcasts. A bootstrapping analysis with 5,000 resamples based on PROCESS procedures (Hayes 2022) supported the idea that there is an indirect effect between digital experience, perceived novelty, and attitude toward the museum ($b = -.2138$; .0963; $-.4192 <$ CI 95% $< -.0425$).

Consumer Responses to the Digital Experience

Perceived authenticity. We found significant differences between conditions ($F = 3.737$, $p < .05$) when involvement with arts was kept constant ($F = 4.024$, $p < .05$). Planned contrasts tests revealed that gamification offers the most authentic experience compared to the other two conditions ($M_{gamification} = 5.76$ (.76) vs. $M_{virtual\_tour} = 5.26$ (.87) vs. $M_{podcasts} = 5.45$ (.70), $t = 2.628$, $p < .05$). More specifically, it is perceived as significantly more authentic than the virtual tour ($t = 2.599$, $p < .05$) and slightly significantly more authentic than podcasts ($t = 1.959$, $p = .053$). Virtual tours and podcasts do not differ ($t = -.244$, $p = .81$).

Digital experience usage intention. The ANCOVA revealed that usage intention significantly varies between conditions ($M_{gamification} = 5.28$ (1.56) vs. $M_{virtual\_tour} = 4.32$ (1.71) vs. $M_{podcasts} = 4.87$ (1.75); $F = 3.372$, $p < .05$) when involvement with arts was kept constant ($F = 7.624$, $p < .01$). Further analysis revealed that participants are significantly more eager to try the gamification compared to the virtual tour ($t = 2.389$, $p < .05$). No other significant differences were found.

We tested the mediated relationship (testing H4) involving digital experience, perceived authenticity, and usage intention following the PROCESS procedure with 5,000 resamplings (Hayes 2022, model 4). Bootstrap output revealed a significant indirect effect of perceived authenticity on usage intention ($b = -.1835$; .0958; $-.3956 < $ CI 95% $< -.0272$).

Discussion

The experiment's findings support our intuition that gamification can be a viable tool for museums to maintain a relationship with customers when they are not on-site. Our fine-grained results show that gamification, compared to the other popular strategies of virtual tours and podcasts, is the most appreciated digital experience (greater perceived authenticity and higher usage intention) and has the most positive effect on the overall perception of the museum (higher novelty and more positive attitudes). Gamification, indeed, is found to have the highest scores for both classes of variables under investigation, and its scores are always significantly higher than the scores for virtual tours.

We found that gamification can be effective in renovating the image of the museum. Indeed, the museum offer is perceived as more novel when it involves gamification compared to virtual tours or podcasts (H1 is supported). We also found that perceived novelty is important for attitudes toward the museum, which are more positive when gamification is employed—something that is explained by perceived novelty (in line with H2). Specifically, consumers are more willing to experience the gamification tool, though not significantly more than the podcasts about artworks. Moreover, gamification is perceived as the most authentic digital experience compared to both the virtual tour and the podcasts (supporting H3). In line with our expectations, we found that perceived authenticity explains usage intentions (confirming H4).

Our data also reveal that podcasts about artworks can be suitable for marketers aiming to improve their relationship with customers. Podcasts are considered the second-best option by our participants. As the dependent variable means illustrate (see Table 22.1), podcasts have the second-highest score for each dependent variable, and those scores are not significantly lower than the scores for gamification regarding usage intentions and attitudes toward the museum. These results can be explained by podcasts' ability to increase transparency of and social connection with the cultural institution, characteristics that consumers look for. Indeed, podcasts about artworks provide access to the backstage of the museum and its secrets, which may be valued as evidence of the museum's willingness to be transparent and authentic with its customers (Pulh, Mencarelli, and Chaney 2019). Moreover, podcasts often feature museum employees narrating the artwork's story. Giving a face to the museum instead of interacting with a faceless organization may create social intimacy and relational connection—museums are incarnated by their employees (Pulh, Mencarelli, and Chaney 2019; Fournier 1998).

Conclusions and Implications for Management

Cultural institutions can employ a wide array of digital tools that offer the opportunity to build, maintain, and reinforce the relationship with actual or potential customers (De Molli and Vecco 2021). However, the use of new technologies is not free of risks, and different tools may affect the audience differently, depending on audience characteristics or features of the digital tool. The present study contributes to the current debate on the use of new digital strategies for managing the relationship with customers by focusing on the opportunities offered by gamification.

First, our findings emphasize the need for cultural institutions to embrace the opportunities offered by digital tools. Despite the differences, the three digital tools examined here (gamification, virtual tours, and podcasts) generated positive responses from participants, with high scores for each dependent variable (means above 4). In this context, gamification emerges as the most effective digital tool among those examined. It triggers the most positive responses toward the digital experience (in terms of authenticity and usage intention) and the cultural institution (in terms of perceived novelty and attitudes toward the museum). The consumer may perceive gamification as a conscious effort made by cultural institutions to fit into modern lifestyles, in which games and new technologies are pervasive. Gamification may therefore be a strategy that allows museums to modernize their image—an element particularly relevant for young consumers and digital natives. Recent findings suggest that young adults perceive museums not as linked to them but rather as a place for schools, families, or an elite of consumers (Hughes and Moscardo 2019). Young adults demand more interactive experiences, and gamification may be the right tool to attract this difficult-to-target segment. Thanks to gaming, visitors may also become learners: not only do they interact with the devices in specifically situated physical and social contexts, but these interactions generate new contexts and places that may ultimately affect the learning process. As a consequence, the evaluation of gamification experiences with museums should also consider the extent to which such applications can foster the development of new learning processes (Addis 2005).

Our second contribution is the finding that the risk most commonly associated with gamification in recent literature—that is, the Disneyfication of cultural institutions (Balloffet, Courvoisier, and Lagier 2014)—is not as great as has been portrayed. Our findings shed a more positive light on how digital experience generally, and gamification specifically, affects consumers' perceptions. Digital experiences do not jeopardize the authenticity of the museum experience; conversely, gamification seems to be the most viable tool for cultural institutions to maintain a relationship with visitors without compromising the perceived authenticity of the institutions.

From a managerial perspective, gamification appears to be an effective tool for stimulating future visits, especially for eliciting distant interactions with the institutions and creating positive attitudes toward them. Gamification can help build and maintain a relationship with target visitors who are looking for a more modern way of getting in touch with cultural institutions. The importance of this has been demonstrated by the COVID-19 pandemic and the consequent economic downturn, which considerably reduced visitors' physical presence in these institutions.

It is also essential to acknowledge that because gamification is so widespread across industries, it is more accessible to cultural institutions as well. Today's technology is way more affordable than in the past, and developers and educators have acquired significant expertise with it; therefore, such initiatives can be implemented more frequently and with more success.

Moreover, given the wide use of gamification in the educational context (Hamari and Koivisto 2015; Mitchell, Schuster, and Drennan 2017), managers in the cultural sector should closely collaborate with policymakers and other public institutions, such as schools, to develop a coordinated use of gamification for fostering culture and young people's interest in the arts.

On the other hand, we acknowledge that other digital tools, such as podcasts about artworks, may be less technologically complex and therefore might allow the institution to rely more on existing internal capabilities. As our study showed, podcasts are particularly welcomed by consumers, despite being rated lower than gamification. Such a result suggests that marketing managers in cultural institutions should carefully consider the use of digital tools and make choices based on the goals they aim to achieve. For instance, when informing (rather than the perception of novelty) is central, podcasts can be effective ways to maintain a close relationship with the audience.

Limitations and Future Research

Future research may extend the present findings by investigating the effect of gamification on specific segments of consumers. The present study involved a homogeneous sample with limited information on their characteristics (e.g., we did not ask questions about their family composition). Literature on gamification suggests that consumers vary in terms of what they look for when they play a game (Robson et al. 2015) as well as their motivations to visit museums (Gürel and Nielsen 2019). It is therefore important to understand the individual characteristics of the cultural institution's target customers in order to propose experiences they will find enjoyable.

Moreover, gamification has been shown to improve families' experience during museum visits (de La Ville, Badulescu, and Delestage 2021). Gamification might be further leveraged to encourage families to interact with the museum even before the visit. Attracting children is of primary importance for cultural institutions because early experiences constitute the basis for a taste for cultural consumption that endures into the future (Borrione, Friel, and Segre 2021).

A second limitation of our study is the use of a scenario-based experiment. Although it allows controlling for extraneous variables, a field experiment would permit us to collect information about more nuances of the experience, such as emotions, attention, and behavior. Another interesting avenue of research would be measuring the long-term effects of exposure to gamification. We measured variables immediately after the scenario; it would be interesting to understand how long the effects might last.

A third limitation relates to the difference in popularity of the digital experience analyzed. While we argue that gamification is perceived as more novel than virtual tours and podcasts because of its intrinsic divergence from traditional museum language, another reason for this may be that consumers are less familiar with game-based experiences with museums. Studies suggest that the standard tools of Web 2.0, such as podcasts or social media channels, are so widely diffused that they do not surprise consumers anymore or produce greater involvement (Pulh and Mencarelli 2015). More research is therefore needed to capture whether the effervescence of gamification may decrease when this tool becomes more routinely used.

Future areas of development in this domain might involve adding connectivity elements so that some elements of the gaming experience could be shared through social media platforms and translated to the everyday life of the learners. This could enhance visitors' experience by adding the social dimension that is intrinsically embedded in almost every digital experience. Finally, creating a game that offers the user a higher degree of control could represent another possible work direction, making the application even more responsive to visitors' choices and resulting in a more personalized experience. This would reinforce the sense of connection and attachment that visitors might experience with the cultural institution.

Note

1. This scenario was developed by the authors based on the game Father and Son created by Museo Mann in Naples.

References

Addis, Michela. 2005. "New Technologies and Cultural Consumption—Edutainment Is Born!" *European Journal of Marketing* 39, nos. 7–8: 729–736. https://dx.doi.org/10.2139/ssrn.319503.

Alelis, Genevieve, Ania Bobrowicz, and Chee Siang Ang. 2015. "Comparison of Engagement and Emotional Responses of Older and Younger Adults Interacting with 3D Cultural Heritage Artefacts on Personal Devices." *Behaviour and Information Technology* 34, no. 11: 1064–1078. http://dx.doi.org/10.1080/0144929X.2015.1056548.

Atzeni, Marcello, Giacomo Del Chiappa, and Jessica Mei Pung. 2022. "Enhancing Visit Intention in Heritage Tourism: The Role of Object-Based and Existential Authenticity in Non-immersive Virtual Reality Heritage Experiences." *International Journal of Tourism Research* 24: 240–255.

Australia Council for the Arts. 2021. "In Real Life: Mapping Digital Cultural Engagement in the First Decades of the 21st Century." July 17, 2021. https://australiacouncil.gov.au/advocacy-and-research/in-real-life/.

Badrinarayanan, Vishag, Enrique P. Becerra, Chung-Hyun Kim, and Sreedhar Madhavaram. 2012. "Transference and Congruence Effects on Purchase Intentions in Online Stores of Multi-Channel Retailers: Initial Evidence from the US and South Korea." *Journal of the Academy of Marketing Science* 40, no. 4: 539–557.

Balloffet, Pierre, François H. Courvoisier, and Joëlle Lagier. 2014. "From Museum to Amusement Park: The Opportunities and Risks of Edutainment." *International Journal of Arts Management* 16, no. 2: 4–16.

Bechkoff, Jennifer. 2019. "Gamification Using a Choose-Your-Own-Adventure Type Platform to Augment Learning and Facilitate Student Engagement in Marketing Education." *Journal for Advancement of Marketing Education* 27, no. 1: 13–30.

Beverland, Michael B., Adam Lindgreen, and Michiel W. Vink. 2008. "Projecting Authenticity Through Advertising." *Journal of Advertising* 37, no. 1: 5–15. https://doi.org/10.2753/JOA0 091-3367370101.

Bilandzic, Helena, and Rick W. Busselle. 2008. "Transportation and Transportability in the Cultivation of Genre-Consistent Attitudes and Estimates." *Journal of Communication* 58, no. 3: 508–529. https://doi.org/10.1111/j.1460-2466.2008.00397.x.

Bloch, Peter H. 1995. "Seeking the Ideal Form: Product Design and Consumer Response." *Journal of Marketing* 59, no. 3: 16–29.

Borrione, Paola, Martha Friel, and Giovanna Segre. 2021. "'Kids, Today We're Going to the Museum!' Discriminating Factors in Museum Visiting for Families with Children in Italy." *International Journal of Arts Management* 23, no. 3: 21–31.

Brinson, Nancy H., and Laura L. Lemon. 2022. "Investigating the Effects of Host Trust, Credibility, and Authenticity in Podcast Advertising." *Journal of Marketing Communications* (online). https://doi.org/10.1080/13527266.2022.2054017.

Brown, Stephen, Robert V. Kozinets, and John Sherry. 2003. "Sell Me the Old, Old Story: Retromarketing Management and the Art of Brand Revival." *Journal of Customer Behaviour* 2, no. 2: 133–147.

Calcagno, Monica, and Claudio Biscaro. 2012. "Designing the Interactions in the Museum: Learning from Palazzo Strozzi." *International Studies of Management and Organization* 42, no. 2: 43–56.

Camarero, Carmen, María José Garrido, and Rebeca San José. 2016. "Efficiency of Web Communication Strategies: The Case of Art Museums." *International Journal of Arts Management* 18, no. 2: 42–62.

Chang, Seohee, and Heather J. Gibson. 2011. "Physically Active Leisure and Tourism Connection: Leisure Involvement and Choice of Tourism Activities Among Paddlers." *Leisure Sciences* 33, no. 2: 162–181.

Colbert, François, and Danilo D. Dantas. 2019. "Customer Relationship in Arts Marketing: A Review of Key Dimensions in Delivery by Artistic and Cultural Organizations." *International Journal of Arts Management* 21, no. 2: 4–14.

Courchesne, André, Philippe Ravanas, and Christian Pulido. 2019. "Using Technology to Optimize Customer Relationship Management: The Case of Cirque du Soleil." *International Journal of Arts Management* 21, no. 2: 83–93.

Correia Loureiro, Sandra Maria. 2019. "Exploring the Role of Atmospheric Cues and Authentic Pride on Perceived Authenticity Assessment of Museum Visitors." *International Journal of Tourism Research* 21: 413–426.

De Angeli, Daniela. 2018. "GameTale: Facilitating the Design of Gameful Museum Experiences." *Economia della cultura* 28, no. 3: 311–320.

De La Ville, Valérie-Inés, Cristina Badulescu, and Charles-Alexandre Delestage. 2021. "Welcoming Families to the Museum: Reconsidering Forms of Cultural Mediation for Parent/Child Autonomous Visits." *International Journal of Arts Management* 23, no. 3: 32–45.

De Molli Federica, and Marilena Vecco. 2021. *The Metamorphosis of Cultural and Creative Organizations: Exploring Change from a Spatial Perspective*. Routledge Research in the Creative and Cultural Industries. New York: Routledge.

Derbaix, Maud, and Anne Gombault. 2016. "Selling the Invisible to Create an Authentic Experience: Imagination at Work at Cézanne's Studio." *Journal of Marketing Management* 32, nos. 15–16: 1458–1477.

Di Blasio, Margaret, and Raymond Di Blasio. 1983. "Constructing a Cultural Context Through Museum Storytelling." *Roundtable Reports* 8, no. 3: 7–9.

Errichiello, Luisa, Roberto Micera, Marcello Atzeni, and Giacomo Del Chiappa. 2017. "Exploring the Implications of Wearable Virtual Reality Technology for Museum Visitors' Experience: A Cluster Analysis." *International Journal of Tourism Research* 21: 590–605.

Florenthal, Bela, Priscilla A. Arling, Deborah Skinner, Kathryn W. King, and Patrick Rondeau. 2012. "Enhancing the Traditional IMC Recruitment Plan to Gauge the Impact of Vodcast Usage on Students' Attitudes and Behavioral Intentions." *International Journal of Integrated Marketing Communications* 4, no. 1: 61–77.

Forgas-Coll, Santiago, Ramon Palau-Saumell, Jorge Matute, and Salomé Tárrega. 2017. "How Do Service Quality, Experiences and Enduring Involvement Influence Tourists' Behavior? An Empirical Study in the Picasso and Miró Museums in Barcelona." *International Journal of Tourism Research* 19: 246–256.

Fournier, Susan. 1998. "Consumers and Their Brands: Developing Relationship Theory in Consumer Research." *Journal of Consumer Research* 24, no. 4: 343–373.

Garrido, Maria José, and Carmen Camarero. 2014. "Learning and Relationship Orientation: An Empirical Examination in European Museums." *International Journal of Nonprofit and Voluntary Sector Marketing* 19: 92–109. https://doi.org/10.1002/nvsm.1490.

Gilmore, James H., and B. Joseph Pine. 2007. *Authenticity: What Consumers Really Want*. Boston, MA: Harvard Business School Press.

Goodlander, Georgina, and Michael Mansfield. 2013. "Press Start: Video Games in an Art Museum." *Journal of Interactive Humanities* 1, no. 1: 4.

Goodman, Joseph K., and Gabriele Paolacci. 2017. "Crowdsourcing Consumer Research." *Journal of Consumer Research* 44: 196–210.

Green, Melanie C., and Timothy C. Brock. 2000. "The Role of Transportation in the Persuasiveness of Public Narratives." *Journal of Personality and Social Psychology* 79, no. 5: 701–721. https://doi.org/10.1037//0022-3514.79.5.701.

Gürel, Eda, and Axel Nielsen. 2019. "Art Museum Visitor Segments: Evidence from Italy on Omnivores and Highbrow Univores." *International Journal of Arts Management* 21, no. 2: 55–69.

Hamari, Juho, and Jonna Koivisto. 2015. "Why Do People Use Gamification Services?" *International Journal of Information Management* 35, no. 4: 419–431. https://doi.org/10.1016/j.ijinfomgt.2015.04.006.

Hammady, Ramy, Minhua Ma, and Nicholas Temple. 2016. "Augmented Reality and Gamification in Heritage Museums." Proceedings of the 2nd International Joint Conference on Serious Games. *Lecture Notes in Computer Science* 9894: 181–187.

Hayes, Andrew F. 2022. *Introduction to Mediation, Moderation, and Conditional Process Analysis*. 3rd ed. New York: Guilford Press.

Hetet, Blandine, Claire-Lise Ackermann, and Jean-Pierre Mathieu. 2016. "La nouveauté perçue: Fondements conceptuels et proposition d'une echelle de mesure." *Revue française du marketing* 256, no. 2/4: 61–79.

Hede, Anne-Marie, and Thyne Maree. 2010. "A Journey to the Authentic: Museum Visitors and Their Negotiation of the Authentic." *Journal of Marketing Management* 26, nos. 7–8: 686–705.

Hughes, Karen, and Gianna Moscardo. 2019. "For Me or Not for Me? Exploring Young Adults' Museum Representations." *Leisure Sciences* 41, no. 6: 516–534. https://doi.org/10.1080/01490400.2018.1550455.

Hume, Margee, and Michael Mills. 2011. "Building the Sustainable iMuseum: Is the Virtual Museum Leaving Our Museums Virtually Empty?" *International Journal of Nonprofit and Voluntary Sector Marketing* 16: 275–289. https://doi.org/10.1002/nvsm.425.

Hunter, Dan, and Kevin Werbach. 2012. *For the Win*. Philadelphia: Wharton Digital Press.

ILO. 2020. "COVID-19 and the Media and Culture Sector." International Labour Organization. July 10, 2020. https://www.ilo.org/sector/Resources/publications/WCMS_750548/lang--en/index.htm.

Izzo, Filomena. 2017. "Museum Customer Experience and Virtual Reality: H. Bosch Exhibition Case Study." *Modern Economy* 8, no, 4: 531–536.

Juniper Research. 2021. "Video Games 2020–2023 Market Summary." Accessed December 9, 2021. https://www.juniperresearch.com/infographics/video-games-statistics.

Kidd, Jenny. 2011. "Enacting Engagement Online: Framing Social Media Use for the Museum." *Information Technology and People* 24, no. 1: 64–77.

Larsen, Steen F., and János László. 1990. "Cultural-Historical Knowledge and Personal Experience in Appreciation of Literature." *European Journal of Social Psychology* 20, no. 5: 425–440.

Mannion, Shelley. 2012. "Beyond Cool: Making Mobile Augmented Reality Work for Museum Education." Paper presented at the conference Museums and the Web

Miniero, Giulia, and Christian Holst. 2020. "Corporate Communication and the Arts: The Mistake of Not Engaging." In *Managing the Cultural Business: Avoiding Mistakes, Finding Success*, edited by Michela Addis and Andrea Rurale, 311–346. London: Routledge.

Miniero, Giulia, Andrea Rurale, and Michela Addis. 2014. "Effects of Arousal, Dominance, and their Interaction on Pleasure in a Cultural Environment." *Psychology and Marketing* 31, no. 8: 628–634.

Mitchell, Robert, Lisa Schuster, and Judy Drennan. 2017. "Understanding How Gamification Influences Behaviours in Social Marketing." *Australasian Marketing Journal* 25, no. 1: 12–19.

Muriel, Daniel, and Garry Crawford. 2018. *Video Games as Culture: Considering the Role and Importance of Video Games in Contemporary Society.* Abingdon, UK: Routledge.

NEA. 2015. "How a Nation Engages with Art. Highlights from the 2012 Survey of Public Participation in the Arts." National Endowment for the Arts, Washington, DC. https://www.arts.gov/sites/default/files/highlights-from-2012-sppa-revised-oct-2015.pdf.

Newman, George E., and Ravi Dhar. 2014. "Authenticity Is Contagious: Brand Essence and the Original Source of Production." *Journal of Marketing Research* 51, no. 3: 371–386.

Palumbo, Rocco. 2021. "Enhancing Museums' Attractiveness Through Digitalization: An Investigation of Italian Medium and Large-Sized Museums and Cultural Institutions." *International Journal of Tourism Research* 24, no. 2: 1–14. https://doi.org/10.1002/jtr.2494.

Passebois Ducros, Juliette, and Florence Euzéby. 2021. "Investigating Consumer Experience in Hybrid Museums: A Nethnographic Study." *Qualitative Market Research: An International Journal* 24, no. 2: 180–199. https://doi.org/10.1108/QMR-07-2018-0077.

Preece, Stephen B., and Jennifer Wiggins Johnson. 2011. "Web Strategies and the Performing Arts: A Solution to Difficult Brands." *International Journal of Arts Management* 14, no. 1: 19–31.

Pulh, Mathilde, and Mencarelli Rémy. 2015. "Web 2.0: Is the Museum-Visitor Relationship Being Redefined?" *International Journal of Arts Management* 18, no. 1: 43–51.

Pulh, Mathilde, Mencarelli Rémy, and Damien Chaney. 2019. "The Consequences of the Heritage Experience in Brand Museums on the Consumer-Brand Relationship." *European Journal of Marketing* 53, no. 10: 2193–2212.

Robson, Karen, Kirk Plangger, Jan H. Kietzmann, Ian McCarthy, and Leyland Pitt. 2015. "Is It All a Game? Understanding the Principles of Gamification." *Business Horizons* 58, no. 4: 411–420.

Roederer, Claire, Robert Revat, and Jessie Pallud. 2020. "Does Digital Mediation Really Change the Museum Experience? Museomix in the Lyon-Fourvière Archaeological Museum." *International Journal of Arts Management* 22, no. 3: 108–123.

Schaller, David T. 2011. "The Meaning Makes It Fun: Game-Based Learning for Museums." *Journal of Museum Education* 36, no.3: 261–268.

Spielmann, Nathalie, and Ulrich R. Orth. 2021. "Can Advertisers Overcome Consumer Qualms with Virtual Reality? Increasing Operational Transparency Through Self-Guided 360-Degree Tours." *Journal of Advertising Research* 61, no. 4: 147–163. https://doi.org/10.2501/JAR-2020-015.

Solima, Ludovico. 2018. "Il gaming per i musei. L'esperienza del Mann." *Economia della cultura* 28, no. 3: 275–290.

Spears, Nancy, and Surendra N. Singh. 2004. "Measuring Attitude Toward the Brand and Purchase Intentions." *Journal of Current Issues and Research in Advertising* 26, no. 2: 53–66.

Srinivasan, Ramesh, Robin Boast, Jonathan Furner, and Katherine M. Becvar. 2009. "Digital Museums and Diverse Cultural Knowledges: Moving Past the Traditional Catalog." *The Information Society* 25: 265–278.

Sundar, S. Shyam, Eun Go, Hyang-Sook Kim, and Bo Zhang. 2015. "Communicating Art, Virtually! Psychological Effects of Technological Affordances in a Virtual Museum." *International Journal of Human-Computer Interaction* 31: 385–401.

Thian, Cherry. 2012. "Augmented Reality—What Reality Can We Learn from It." Paper presented at the conference Museums and the Web.

Thyne, Maree, and Anne-Marie Hede. 2016. "Approaches to Managing Co-production for the Co-creation of Value in a Museum Setting: When Authenticity Matters." *Journal of Marketing Management* 32, no. 15–16: 1478–1493. http://dx.doi.org/10.1080/0267257X.2016.1198824.

Viola, Fabio. 2015. "Videogiochi nelle strategie museali." GamEifications, October 13, 2015. http://www.gameifications.com/case-study/videogiochi-nelle-strategie-museali/.

Waycott, Jenny, Ann Jones, and Eileen Scanlon. 2005. "PDAs as Lifelong Learning Tools: An Activity Theory Based Analysis." *Learning, Media and Technology* 30, no. 2: 107–130.

Wiebe, Eric N., Allison Lamb, Megan Hardy, and David Sharek. 2014. "Measuring Engagement in Video Game-Based Environments: Investigation of the User Engagement Scale." *Computers in Human Behavior* 32: 123–132.

Xhembulla, Jetmir, Irene Rubino, Claudia Barberis, and Giovanni Malnati. "Intrigue at the Museum: Facilitating Engagement and Learning Through a Location-Based Mobile Game." In *Proceedings of the 10th International Conference on Mobile Learning 2014*, 41–48. Graz: Graz University of Technology.

Yim, Mark Yi-Cheon, Shu-Chuam Chu, and Paul L. Sauer. 2017. "Is Augmented Reality Technology an Effective Tool for E-commerce? An Interactivity and Vividness Perspective." *Journal of Interactive Marketing* 39: 89–103.

CHAPTER 23

THE RELATIONSHIP BETWEEN MARKETING AND FUNDRAISING FOR ARTS AND CULTURAL ORGANIZATIONS

HYUNJUNG LEE, KYOUNGNAM HA, AND YOUNGSEON KIM

INTRODUCTION

A nonprofit organization practicing marketing places supporters right at the center of everything the organization does (Sargeant 2009). Marketing-oriented organizations provide offerings that meet their supporters' needs and wants to acquire and retain support for their organizations. While the marketing concept applies across contexts (Wymer, Gross, and Helmig 2016), arts and cultural organizations (ACOs) have adopted marketing concepts and tactics to increase fundraising effectiveness. Fundraising activity brings donations, which are a major revenue source for ACOs; therefore, increasing the efficacy of fundraising activities has been a priority in ACO operations. As a result, much research has reported various marketing practices that ACOs have implemented to attract more support and resources and the role of marketing in organizational performance, including fundraising (Boorsma and Chiaravalloti 2010).

This chapter aims to outline the relationship between marketing and fundraising by reviewing relevant scholarly research on this topic. We start with an overview of marketing practices in ACOs. We then discuss the role of marketing in fundraising activities. Finally, we conclude with a discussion of the relationship between marketing and fundraising in ACOs in terms of carrying out their missions and creating goodwill for the public, and we mention future directions for research.

Marketing in ACOs

Marketing is defined as "the activity, set of institutions, and processes for creating, communicating, delivering, and exchanging offerings that have value for customers, clients, partners, and society at large" (American Marketing Association 2017). In the definition, creating offerings refers to the development of a product or service to satisfy consumers' needs and wants. Communicating is promoting the product or service and reaching out to customers through various marketing communication tools such as advertising, public relations (PR), direct marketing, personal selling, sponsorship, events, sales promotions, and social media communications. Delivering the product or service leads to a distribution channel strategy of making the product available at the right place and at the right time for customers convenience. Exchanging offerings is related to the pricing of the product or service. This definition demonstrates that marketing is a multifaceted and dynamic process that can facilitate the exchange of values between an organization and its target customers. By deconstructing each component in the definition of marketing, we can see that some of the marketing components may be less applicable to fundraising activities than others. For example, the pricing of the product and service component may not be readily applicable to fundraising.

ACOs have adopted marketing to improve overall financial performance, even though marketing concepts were not well accepted by the ACO community initially due to their origin in the for-profit sector (Arnold and Tapp 2003; Boorsma and Chiaravalloti 2010; Lee, Ha, and Kim 2018). More than four decades ago Kotler (1979, 44) stated, "Within another decade, marketing will be a major and accepted function within the nonprofit sector." As he predicted, more nonprofit ACOs have adopted marketing as a part of their operations.

As more ACOs have begun to use marketing concepts, misunderstandings about the application of marketing concepts in the ACO context have grown. While Colbert (2009, 14) defined marketing as "the art of putting oneself in the consumer's shoes," many ACOs would consider marketing as "selling" and thus "immoral" (Sargeant 2009, 35 and 44, respectively). Misunderstandings about and the devaluation of marketing in the nonprofit community resulted in slow adoption of marketing and the use of ineffective marketing practices. Even though there has come to be increased acceptance of marketing among ACOs over time, many managers are still confused about the marketing concept and where marketing can be applied in ACOs (Cuadrado, Gil, and Molla 2000). For example, ACOs tend to mainly utilize promotional tactics such as PR even though the scope of marketing is broader than promotion (Cuadrado, Gil, and Molla 2000; McDonald and Harrison 2002). PR is a marketing communication tool that belongs to promotion, one element of the marketing mix. It does not represent marketing entirely and is not in an independent realm outside marketing. However, considering that fundraising is one of the major operations in ACOs, it is understandable that ACOs have relied on PR to promote their public image to the relevant communities and stakeholders, publicize fundraising events, and encourage people to become supporters by purchasing a single ticket, a membership, or a subscription. PR tools such as publicity and press releases are effective and efficient ways of reaching out to a larger audience to raise awareness and do not cause much concern about the credibility of information sources (McDonald and Harrison 2002). These functional or task-specific executions of promotion show that ACOs do not approach marketing holistically as a strategy to increase support from their various stakeholders. Rather, ACOs have often adopted marketing in a piecemeal fashion, focusing on marketing's promotional function.

This narrow scope of marketing executions in ACOs coincides with a lack of scholarly research about marketing and fundraising practices in ACOs. Wymer (2021, 1) stated that the nonprofit marketing literature is "discordant and fragmented." Researchers have pointed out that the lack of scholarly research about marketing in ACOs may have contributed to the piecemeal approach to marketing taken by ACOs and their late adoption of the marketing concept (Betzler and Gmür 2016; Jung 2015). Thus, some researchers have recommended that ACOs view marketing as an underlying management process or philosophy (Narver and Slater 1990; Sargeant 2009) and embrace marketing as a way to help identify, anticipate, and satisfy supporters' needs and wants, and eventually to achieve sustainability (Liao, Foreman, and Sargeant 2001; Sargeant, Foreman, and Liao 2002).

Marketing in Fundraising

Market Orientation and Fundraising

Fundraising is an essential everyday operation for an ACO, which in order to achieve its social mission needs to increase its organizational capability through contributions and grant income (Byrnes 2014). The organization's fundraising capabilities can significantly impact its effective functioning and ultimately its survival (Kim, Gupta, and Lee 2021). Weinstein and Barden (2017, 3) defined successful fundraising as "the right person asking the right prospect for the right amount for the right project at the right time in the right way." They particularly highlighted the six *rights* as critical success factors in any fundraising, as more than 80 percent of a nonprofit's total revenue typically results from less than 20 percent of its donors (a variation of Pareto's 80/20 rule); in some mature fundraising programs, 90 percent of total revenue comes from 10 percent of donors. Even though these findings are not specific to ACO fundraising, they bring attention to matters of prospective donors and how to approach them to maximize an ACO's fundraising performance. As the perception of fundraising has evolved from a money-raising practice to a more systematic, sustainable, and strategic initiative for ACO sustainability, much attention has been devoted to how to effectively develop fundraising

(Jung 2015). Marketing is one of the ways to create a systematic, sustainable, and strategic fundraising practice. Čačija (2013) claimed that fundraising serves as feedback for a nonprofit organization's strategic marketing movement.

Market orientation explains how to implement marketing concepts in an organization. Two commonly used perspectives for assessing market orientation are *cultural* and *behavioral*. Narver and Slater's (1990) cultural perspective suggests that an organization that practices marketing has three cultural orientations: (1) customer orientation, (2) competitor orientation, and (3) interfunctional coordination. Kohli and Jaworski's (1990) behavioral perspective suggests that an organization implementing a marketing concept presents three behaviors: (1) intelligence generation, (2) intelligence dissemination, and (3) responsiveness. Studies show a positive relationship between market orientation and organizational performance (Hult, Ketchen, and Slater 2005; Shoham, Rose, and Kropp 2005). Market orientation is a long-term-focused marketing strategy that helps an organization gain a competitive advantage. Because of the strategy's centrality in business success and growth, many studies about marketing in the for-profit sector have investigated the effect of market orientation on the for-profit organization's performance. However, only a relatively small number of studies have examined the impact of market orientation on the ACO's performance. Gainer and Padanyi (2002, 2005) showed a positive relationship between market orientation and organizational performance: ACOs that implemented market-driven activities in their operation were more likely to develop a market-oriented culture, which led not only to growth in resources and customer satisfaction but also to an improved reputation among peers. The researchers emphasize the importance of being attentive to and coping with market forces, as this can increase revenue without sacrificing the organization's artistic reputation and integrity. This finding aligns with Kohli and Jaworski's (1990) and Narver and Slater's (1990) work viewing market orientation from behavioral and cultural perspectives. Frey and Meier (2006) discovered that museums with market-oriented management earned higher revenue by catering to visitor interests than museums without such an approach. Voss and Voss (2000), however, reported that market orientation in nonprofit professional theaters is negatively associated with earned revenue, total revenue, and net revenue.

Although market orientation has a substantial, tangible application for ACOs, it is still challenging to fully implement market orientation in ACOs without adjustments, because market orientation was originally developed for large business organizations with customers and competitors and was structured into the functional business area (Wymer, Boenigk, and Möhlmann 2015). Thus, Liao, Foreman, and Sargeant (2001) proposed societal orientation as an alternative to market orientation for nonprofit organizations, to distinguish nonprofit organizations' mission pursuit and operational environment from for-profit organizations' profit-seeking and market environment. Furthermore, as nonprofits have adopted marketing concepts through market orientation, the nonprofit sector has created the term *donor-centricity*, which is more applicable to nonprofits (Bennett 1998; Institute for Sustainable Philanthropy 2021).

Relationship Marketing and Fundraising

A major recent trend in marketing is a shift away from transactional marketing and toward relationship marketing (Andreasen and Kotler 2007). The basic idea of relationship marketing is to treat different customers differently and achieve organizational sustainability and long-term stability by building a strong relationship with loyal customers. A large body of research on nonprofits has paid attention to this transition in marketing focus and has strived to suggest ways to build a steady relationship with donors and patrons (Fillis 2011; Rentschler et al. 2002). Kotler (1980, xv) observed that many ACOs have adopted relationship marketing as their strategy: "marketing becomes the critical mechanism for building enduring and satisfying relationships between the arts organization and its target audience."

The core strategies of relationship marketing have three primary parts: acquisition, retention, and growth (Rentschler et al. 2002). Research on relationship marketing emphasizes retention, which involves cultivating a strong relationship between an organization and its supporters (Rentschler and Radbourne 2008; Lee and Lee 2017), because acquiring new donors is more costly than keeping loyal donors (Jung 2015; Kim, Gupta, and Lee 2021). Sargeant (2013) found that recruiting a donor costs nonprofits two to three times as much as their first donation. Considering that it typically takes twelve to eighteen months before a new donor becomes profitable and about half of new donors are lost after their first donation, it is not surprising that many nonprofits suffer from the instability of individual giving (Gaffny 1996; Khodakarami, Petersen, and Venkatesan 2015; Sargeant and Woodliffe 2007). Therefore, retaining and growing existing donors has become a desired strategy for nonprofit organizations (Sargeant and Jay 2004). Similarly, Byrnes (2014) and Čačija (2013) noticed that long-term relationships with donors and well-organized marketing strategies are the keys to successful fundraising.

ACOs that apply relationship marketing to keep and grow the value of donors through an in-depth understanding of those donors enhance their fundraising performance. Rentschler et al. (2002) proposed a loyalty ladder that demonstrates how a prospect for an ACO becomes a single-ticket buyer, repeat buyer, subscriber or member or donor, and long-term advocate. Scherhag and Boenigk (2013) supported the application of relationship marketing to ACOs by reporting a positive effect of relationship marketing on fundraising performance for ACOs in Germany. They showed that ACOs that treated donors differently according to their donation amount achieved more positive fundraising results than those that treated all donors equally. Jung (2015) emphasized the importance of building relationships with the local community to develop inclusive fundraising strategies for a museum. Kotler, Kotler, and Kotler (2016) highlight the role of relationship marketing as a proactive form of fundraising, which requires segmentation of the donor market, evaluation of the potential of each segment, and allocation of resources to the segments based on their respective potential for donation. Kim, Gupta, and Lee (2021) also suggest that nonprofit organizations should make additional efforts to identify prospective loyal donors and develop a marketing plan to appeal to them.

As nonprofits have adopted marketing concepts through practicing relationship marketing, the nonprofit sector has also developed the term *relationship fundraising* (Burnett 2002). In relationship fundraising, fundraisers recognize each donor as unique in their donation history, motivation for donation, and expectations for the organization they support. A relationship fundraising strategy is a long-term-oriented strategy that focuses on donor acquisition and donor retention. Nonprofit organizations should implement such a strategy even though the return on investment for relationship fundraising is not immediate, as the potential future revenue from the relationship fundraising strategy far outweighs the investment (Sargeant 2001). In addition, cultivating donor relationships in nonprofits can increase donation revenue (Sargeant 2009).

Despite the need for long-term relationships and corresponding marketing strategies for successful fundraising, academic research about the determinants of switching behavior (e.g., switching from being a one-time donor to being a regular donor) and lapse behavior, which may give practitioners insight into how to retain the existing donors, has been lacking (Burnett 2002).

An ACO's marketing concept adoption can be observed through the market orientation and relationship marketing practices in its fundraising operations. To implement market orientation and relationship marketing in fundraising, ACOs need to develop strategic marketing planning to help them build a competitive advantage in the fundraising market.

Developing Strategic Marketing Planning for Fundraising

Market orientation and relationship fundraising are two vital strategic directions ACOs have adopted to improve their operations, especially their fundraising. Well-developed marketing strategic planning plays a crucial role in executing a successful fundraising campaign (Maple 2013). The first step in implementing both market orientation and relationship fundraising is to identify the needs and wants of various groups of potential and current donors and patrons so that ACOs can serve them with customized messages, offerings, and benefits (Andreasen and Kotler 2007; Kotler, Kotler, and Kotler 2016).

Understanding ACO Supporters

Understanding ACO supporters is the first step to developing a marketing strategy for effective fundraising. Bennett (1998) reported that in the United Kingdom, small and medium-sized nonprofit organizations that understood supporters' characteristics and motivations for donation improved their fundraising performance. Tajtáková and

Arias-Aranda (2008) suggest that marketing strategies should be based on consumers' motivations, interests, attendance, barriers, and expectations. The organization's knowledge of donor demographic and psychographic profiles, including motivations, guides the development of customized messages for different potential and current donors. Personalized communication is the outcome of a market-oriented strategy and the most effective way to build relationships between organizations and donors. Streed (2020) suggests that arts consumers may present substantial differences in profile, expectations, and behavior due to the heterogeneous nature of performing arts.

A large body of research in the nonprofit literature has identified ACO supporters' characteristics and motivations (Ateca-Amestoy and Gorostiaga 2022; Bekkers and Wiepking 2011; Neumayr and Handy 2019). Colbert (2003) reported heterogeneity among arts patrons. For example, consumers of high art tend to have a higher education level than the general population: 85 to 90 percent of contemporary art institutions' patrons hold a university degree, and 65 percent of the audience of symphony orchestras and theaters have a university degree. Donors for ACOs are typically white (Jung 2015), older, more educated (Pompe, Tamburri, and Munn 2020), and wealthy (Kottasz 2004). They tend to live in an affluent area, occupy managerial or professional roles (Carpenter, Connolly, and Myers 2008; Mohan and Bulloch 2012), and hold high social status (Wiepking 2007). Kottasz (2004) suggests that high-income young male professionals can be a new target donor group for ACOs, having observed that young wealthy men in London are more likely to donate to arts organizations than to other types of charities.

While the motivation for contributions differs by socioeconomic status (Radley and Kennedy 1992), multiple motivations for supporting ACOs have been identified, including self-interest (Sargeant and Shang 2010), altruism (Sargeant and Shang 2010; Wiepking 2007), awareness of need (Wiepking 2007), solicitation (Bekkers and Wiepking 2007; Wiepking and Maas 2009), psychological benefits (Wiepking 2007; Bekkers and Wiepking 2011), norms of social responsibility (Barnes 2011), social status (Kolhede and Gomez-Arias 2016), tax incentives (Bertacchini, Santagata, and Signorello 2011), individual experiences and desire for impact (Breeze 2013), and sense of connection (Payton and Moody 2008). In addition, recent research confirms that art consumption experiences (e.g., visiting theaters and viewing visual arts) and active participation are positively correlated with donations (Ateca-Amestoy and Gorostiaga 2022; Bourgeon-Renault et al. 2006; Conway and Leighton 2012; Petkus 2004). This finding emphasizes the experiential aspect of ACO offerings. Offering a superior experience to its audience can create a positive attitude toward the ACO and result in donation behavior. ACOs that are perceived as providing high-quality programs and services tend to receive more donations (Krawczyk, Wooddell, and Dias 2017).

The research found that different donor groups preferred different fundraising approaches and techniques. Thus, developing distinct fundraising strategies helps ACOs appeal effectively to diverse donor segments with specific demographic and psychographic profiles (Petkus 2004; Schlegelmilch and Tynan 1989a, b). Fundraising, especially museum fundraising, has concentrated on the needs and interests of donors in traditional demographic profiles (white, affluent, and educated), but clinging only to this demographic may not improve fundraising outcomes considering the changing trends in the US population (Bell 2012; Jung 2015; Smithsonian Institution 2001). Individual charitable giving rates among low- and middle-income donors in the United States are declining due to recent tax policy changes and organizations' greater reliance on high-income donors. A recent study from the European Union confirms the demographic profile of arts patrons as older and with higher education levels (Ateca-Amestoy and Gorostiaga 2022; Rooney et al. 2020; Urban Institute 2021). Therefore, embracing diversity and inclusion efforts is necessary to increase the chances of successful fundraising and expand the base of patrons for future growth (Pettey and Wagner 2007; Faculty of the Lilly Family School of Philanthropy 2020). In this vein, segmenting donor groups and executing relevant fundraising marketing programs for each segment are recommended more than ever.

Segmentation, Targeting, and Positioning

When an ACO understands its potential or current supporters, the organization can develop a marketing strategy through the STP approach: segmentation, targeting, and positioning. Market segmentation can be applied to fundraising by grouping heterogeneous supporters into segments that share common properties in terms of demographic, geographic, behavioral, and psychographic characteristics. After segmentation, an ACO can choose appropriate target donor groups and develop a positioning strategy to communicate why the target market donor groups should support the organization. An ACO's understanding of its donors, grouping them into segments (segmentation), selecting particular groups to focus on (targeting), and executing positioning strategy (positioning) to appeal to the chosen target donors will impact their fundraising outcomes positively (Colbert and Ravanas 2019). The STP approach implies a donor priority strategy that treats donors differently according to their contribution and offers personalized services, yielding greater fundraising performance (Scherhag and Boenigk 2013). In terms of positioning, both academics and professionals have emphasized building a favorable, unique, and strong brand (Aaker 1992; Wymer, Gross, and Helmig 2016). Positioning strategy influences how an ACO is perceived and understood by its target public audience. Building a positive brand image in the minds of the target donors will play a crucial role in improving fundraising performance (Wymer, Boenigk, and Möhlmann 2015; Wymer, Gross, and Helmig 2016).

Branding

The American Marketing Association defines *brand* as "a name, term, design, symbol or any other feature that identifies one seller's goods or service as distinct from those of other sellers" (American Marketing Association n.d.). This definition simply refers to brand elements intended to identify a brand and differentiate it from its competitors.

However, a brand represents something bigger than the combination of brand elements, and it is this that ultimately gives the customer a reason to choose it over its competitor. Therefore, brand strength comes less from the functional performance of products than from intangibles such as brand awareness, brand meaning built in the customer's mind, the customer's emotional connection to the brand, brand image, and company reputation (Keller and Swaminathan 2020). These intangible assets constitute brand equity, defined as "the marketing effects or outcomes that accrue to a product with its brand name compared with those that would accrue if the same product did not have the brand name" (Ailawadi, Lehmann, and Neslin 2003, 1). In particular, what resides in the customer's mind regarding a brand—for example, their feelings, thoughts, or understanding— matters to building a strong brand. Therefore, a customer-based brand equity approach emphasizes looking at brand equity from the consumer's perspective, orienting from the customer's mindset (Keller and Lehmann 2003). It provides the customer with a reason to buy the brand instead of its competitors and to be loyal to the brand.

Brand equity serves as an organization's competitive advantage, something that a competitor may not easily take over or imitate. Therefore, building a strong brand and maintaining it over time are crucial to an organization's long-term sustainability. Holt and Cameron (2010) developed a cultural brand strategy that guides organizations to build a strong brand with innovative ideologies. This strategy emphasizes cultural innovation—creating an innovative cultural expression that resonates with the target market's ideological needs through myth and cultural code to build an iconic brand (Holt 2012). Schroeder (2009) also emphasized the cultural aspect of brand and identified brand culture as the third dimension of brand research, in conjunction with the more traditional research areas of brand identity and brand image. Art marketing researchers have suggested that arts marketing theory should take into account cultural and social issues as well as economic factors, and have reported that arts and cultural branding works best when it includes context such as social, political, and cultural components (Baumgarth and O'Reilly 2014; O'Reilly 2005).

As the competition to attract and retain support among ACOs grows, the role of the brand becomes more significant for fundraising (Colbert 2009; Scott 2000). Research shows that the branding principle applies to organizations in the nonprofit sector due to its essential role in fundraising (Wymer, Boenigk, and Möhlmann 2015). According to Sargeant and Woodliffe (2007), a well-known nonprofit organization with a clear mission identity tends to receive a greater amount of donations. Higher levels of brand recognition and understanding by the public are positively associated with superior fundraising performance (Sargeant and Woodliffe 2007). Furthermore, studies in the nonprofit sector show that brand familiarity leads to a favorable attitude toward the organization, resulting in a greater amount of donations and support (Lee and Lee 2017). Brand familiarity is also found to have a positive impact on earned revenue. For example, Urrutiaguer (2014) reported that the local audience's paid attendance for arts performances tended to be low when the performances were launched by an emerging but less well-known performing arts company. Positive brand attitude and attachment to the brand are likely to increase visitors' behavioral loyalty (reflected in volunteering and an enhanced likelihood of donating) in addition to their impact on financial performance (Baumgarth 2014). Being well-known, building a favorable image among the target groups of current and prospective supporters, and offering supporters good-quality artistic programs and services that are differentiated from those offered by peer organizations are the prerequisites for an ACO to be a strong brand (Wymer, Gross, and Helmig 2016). Best (2012) recognizes brand reputation and unique programs and services as potential sources for an ACO's competitive advantage. Streed (2020) claimed that performing arts managers should develop distinctive marketing strategies to embrace heterogeneous customers and expand their customer base.

In sum, a strong brand provides reasons for potential supporters to consider supporting a particular ACO over another and for current supporters to continue to support it. ACOs with strong brand equity (high awareness, relevance, perceived quality, and knowledge) have improved fundraising outcomes. From the brand management perspective, revitalizing the brand and staying relevant in supporters' minds are critical. Courchesne, Ravanas, and Pulido (2017) highlight that an ACO needs to develop a brand repositioning strategy that it can implement when its current brand becomes irrelevant to supporters and loses its appeal. An ACO can improve a weakened brand image and increase its earned and donation income by offering a new product or service (e.g., doing social good) or launching a new communication channel (e.g., a social media platform or a web-based blog).

Designing a Marketing Mix: The 4 P's

Having a strong brand helps ACOs become more effective in their fundraising. The strategic approaches to building strong brand equity have evolved from market orientation to service orientation to experiential orientation (Colbert and Dantas 2019). The marketing mix (product, price, place, promotion—the 4 P's) involves marketing activities that help an organization build a competitive advantage, such as strong brand equity. Designing marketing mix programs is a vital part of brand-building strategies. Even though the traditional marketing 4 P's may not directly relate to ACO fundraising, they can still provide some useful insights.

Product

For ACOs, a broad product definition may include "tangible goods, a service, an experience, a cause, or an idea. Product is associated with any result of the creative act—for example, a performance, a festival event, exhibition, a painting, a CD or music download, a book, a film, or a television program" (Colbert and Ravanas 2019, 24). Both market orientation and relationship marketing strategy emphasize the importance of product offerings in developing a marketing strategy. Quality of the artistic product and communication about the artistic work are vital to developing a competitive advantage in the saturated arts market (Colbert 2003). However, the literature finds evaluating artistic and cultural product quality to be challenging. When customers evaluate the quality of ACO offerings, they consider artistic product quality, which is subjective, and their art consumption experience. Thus, Davis and Swanson (2009) introduce five service attributes—employees, showtime, facility access, ancillary quality, and visual aesthetics—that cultural event attendees use to evaluate the service quality of performing arts products. This perspective suggests the need for co-production or co-creation of art products, emphasizing the active roles consumers play in creating value from their arts experiences (Boorsma 2006). Stavraki, Plakoyiannaki, and Clarke (2018) provide theoretical insight into the consumption of art experiences and examine the interpretive responses to an aesthetic experience.

As ACOs implement market orientation, the market's influence on the artistic product development process becomes a question: how much should the market influence creativity in art production? ACOs' products or programs influence demand among a target segment (Courchesne, Ravanas, and Pulido 2017; Urrutiaguer 2014). Voss and Voss (2000) reported that professional theaters that present innovative artistic products receive less revenue than theaters that offer less innovative products. ACOs suffer from an artistic deficit due to their preference for commercial, risk-free, popular works over more creative pieces (Heilbrun and Gray 1993). However, some researchers found that market-oriented ACOs understand customers' cultural consumption patterns and preferences and increase innovativeness in their programs (Burton, Louviere, Young. 2009; Camarero, Garrido, and Vicente 2011). While ACOs continuously make a trade-off between the objectives of increasing audience and innovating the art form through programs, innovative products that require higher marketing costs to educate the audience and that are associated with uncertainty in ticket sales are considered to be high-risk products (Bakhshi and Throsby 2010; DeLong and Vijayaraghavan 2012; Frumkin and Andre-Clak 2000; McDonald 2007). Research suggests that the arts and culture industry must constantly balance artistic aspirations with commercial realities to achieve ongoing success (e.g., Dempster 2006; Holbrook and Zirlin 1985). Entrepreneurial marketing, a combination of entrepreneurship and marketing, is proposed as a new paradigm to balance artistic innovation and market needs in ACOs (Fillis and Telford 2020; Parkman, Holloway, and Sebastiao 2012; Rentschler and Geursen 2004). Entrepreneurial marketing emphasizes innovation and creativity in product/programing development and marketing execution (Fillis and Rentschler 2005). It has been adopted in the arts and cultural sector and garnered remarkable success by enhancing the user experience through creative artistic innovation (Fillis, Lehman, and Miles 2017).

Price

Price is the value of goods and services. There are several factors involved in determining price: customer perception, cost, product type, competitors' products, and external factors. According to Hill, O'Sullivan, and O'Sullivan (2017, 159), some individuals who join an "arts organization's Friends scheme" may actively support the organization and its work, which becomes a solid foundation for fundraising, and higher price encourages them to pay more in return for greater engagement with the organization.

This phenomenon leads to two questions: how should an ACO estimate the value of its products, and what determines the price of the product? A theory of price strategy for nonprofit organizations is still in its embryonic stage. Thus, most studies regarding price in nonprofits rely on specific cases. For example, Birnberg, Choi, and Presslee (2021) conducted a field study and found that pay-what-you-want may not be the best pricing strategy for a performing arts theater. Estelami, Estelami, and Lichtmann (2019) examine locational variables (e.g., the location of a seat) as a factor that determines ticket prices. Labaronne and Slembeck (2015) show that dynamic pricing strategies such as auctions can help performing arts organizations adapt to temporal demand fluctuation.

Place

Place is defined as the ensemble of activities that make the product or service available to consumers. The place strategy that determines how and where to distribute products must be based on consumers' points of view and convenience (Colbert and Ravanas 2019). Thus a multichannel strategy to promote and deliver cultural and artistic products, services, and fundraising has become the industry norm. As digital technology evolves, ACOs have embraced digital channels as a way of delivering their artistic products and services. For example, Behzadi (2013) reported that the website of the Metropolitan Opera serves as a distribution channel because it provides online box office functions and opera streaming services.

Gallagher and Sowa (2014) pay attention to the way social media are used to manage the engagement of donors, members, and volunteers in ACOs. Many studies have examined the effectiveness of fundraising using these channels. For example, Bhati and McDonnell (2020) reported that a nonprofit's Facebook network size, activity, and audience engagement are positively related to fundraising success, measured by the number of donors and amount of donations. Lee and Shon (2021) also found a close connection between the number of followers on social media platforms and both donation revenue and the number of volunteers: the number of Facebook followers is positively associated with individual donations and the number of full-time-equivalent volunteers, while the number of Twitter followers has a positive impact on donations but not on the number of full-time equivalent volunteers.

Promotion

Promotion is responsible for communicating marketing offers to the target market. Organizations use promotional tactics to deliver messages conveying the positioning of an organization and its offerings to the target audience. ACOs recognize the strategic role of promotion to reach out to their supporters, maintain relationships with their publics, and enhance their reputation (Hooper-Greenhill 2000). While traditional promotional tools such as advertising, public relations, sales promotion, personal selling, direct marketing, and sponsorship have proven to be effective, nontraditional communication channels such as social media platforms are increasingly utilized to promote performing arts products (Hausmann 2012). Hausmann and Poellmann (2013) reported that ACOs adopt social media marketing techniques to strategically manage communication, innovation, and reputation. Several studies claim that web-based communication tools such as social media, blogs, mobile apps, podcasting, and streaming services enable ACOs to co-create brands with supporters and to provide more personalized services to their supporters through two-way interactive communication; this increases the target audience's knowledge about the ACOs and their satisfaction with the organization's programs and services (Bertacchini and Morando 2013; Capriotti and Kuklinski 2012; Sigala 2005; Teather and Wilhelm 1999). Camarero, Garrido, and San Jose (2016) investigated the determinants of museum success as measured by website traffic and showed that content- and interaction-oriented online communication strategies generate high website traffic. Other studies explore the use of online communication strategies by cultural organizations (Padilla-Meléndez and del Águila-Obra 2013) and the motivation for visiting online museums (Goldman and Schaller 2004) and suggest metrics to evaluate online communication performance in ACOs (Cunliffe, Kritou, and Tudhope 2001; Padilla-Meléndez and del Águila-Obra 2013).

The Relationship between Marketing and Fundraising

The central purpose of the marketing concept is to positively influence an organization's performance. As more ACOs have adopted marketing concepts from the for-profit sector to increase revenues and improve financial sustainability, the number of studies that examine the effect of marketing on a nonprofit's performance has increased. However, few studies have explicitly examined the relationship between marketing and fundraising. Most studies looked at a nonprofit's marketing activity and the financial outcomes, mainly using the amount of support acquired (e.g., as measured by ticket sales, donations, and grants). There seem to be mixed relationships between marketing and financial viability for ACOs: while a majority of research found a positive relationship between marketing activity and financial health in nonprofits, some studies found a negative association between them (e.g., Eikenberry and Kluver 2004; Kirchner, Markowski, and Ford 2007).

The Smithsonian Institution reviewed marketing activities in art museums and found that the higher the marketing expenditure, the higher the general admission sales to the public (Smithsonian Institution 2001). This finding demonstrates that increases in art museums' marketing activity produced increases in earned revenue. Arnold and Tapp (2003) also found that direct marketing efforts increase earned income (e.g., ticket sales) and donations in ACOs. Grizzle (2015) reported that marketing and advertising expenses for fundraising increase donation revenue in ACOs. Lee, Ha, and Kim (2018) further investigated the relationship and noted that an ACO's marketing expense is more strongly associated with earned income than with donation revenue. Lee (2021) reported that the art sector spends more on marketing than other nonprofit sectors do and found a positive relationship between marketing expenditures and earned revenue and donations. When the two relationships are compared, the relationship between marketing and earned income is seen to be stronger than that between marketing and donations.

Marketing activities also increase the amount of money ACOs can raise from businesses. Thomas, Pervan, and Nuttall (2009) show that market-oriented ACOs can attract more business sponsorships without sacrificing their artistic and social goals. Lee, Kim, and Ranucci (2021) extended the finding by examining the relationship through longitudinal data and reported a positive association between marketing emphasis in an ACO's operations and the acquisition of corporate support.

Our literature review confirms that ACOs have adopted marketing concepts to improve their performance. These have included market orientation and relationship marketing strategies, which share the tenet that an organization's marketing strategy starts from understanding the supporter's unmet needs and wants in order to satisfy them with the organization's offerings. In return, these satisfied supporters will provide more resources to organizations, allowing them to better meet their social goals.

Going Forward: Future Research

This chapter reviewed scholarly works to discuss how marketing is related to fundraising in ACOs. The adoption of marketing concepts in ACO fundraising and marketing strategies plays a vital role in successful fundraising. For successful fundraising, organizations must build a strong brand and cultivate relationships with donors, because a strong brand lures new supporters and solid donor relationships keep current supporters donating. Marketing was adopted initially as just a promotional tactic, but more ACOs have come to embrace marketing as a whole strategy for their organizational health. Although ACOs have adopted various marketing strategies and tactics, in this chapter we mainly focused on the two most-researched topics in marketing and fundraising: market orientation and relationship marketing. As nonprofits adopted and practiced more marketing strategies, they realized that some adjustments were necessary to successfully apply marketing strategies rooted in the for-profit sector to nonprofit organizations. Among the nonprofit-specific marketing strategies they have developed are donor-centricity and relationship fundraising. Considering that fundraising is an everyday operation essential to ACOs' sustainability, examining whether marketing strategy has helped ACOs improve fundraising performance is a necessary and meaningful pursuit for research. However, there seems to be a lack of research investigating the effects of marketing strategies on fundraising performance. Therefore, we conclude this chapter with suggestions for future studies in the relevant areas.

First, more empirical research should be conducted to shed light on the relationship between marketing and fundraising. The tasks for research include identifying the scope of marketing activities in ACOs' fundraising/development function. There are many overlaps between marketing and fundraising. For example, when an ACO sends direct mail to a longtime donor for a capital campaign, that can be considered both a marketing activity to build a long-term relationship with the current donor and a part of fundraising activity to acquire necessary funds. However, there are no widely accepted rules for identifying marketing activity in ACO operations or for parsing out marketing from development.

Another topic for future research is developing valid and reliable measures of marketing and fundraising outcomes (Wymer 2021). Developing nonprofit fundraising outcome measures is challenging because the outcomes often depend on behavioral and attitudinal changes among target donors (Shah and George 2021). Boorsma and Chiaravalloti (2010) claimed that financial outcome and audience numbers are not sufficient to measure marketing contributions to arts organizations; instead, they suggest using mission-based measurements to assess marketing effects in ACOs. Even in the for-profit sector, measuring marketing effectiveness is a challenging task. However, developing a valid and reliable measurement for relevant constructs is the first step in measuring marketing effectiveness. Without proper measures, it is not possible to precisely assess the effect of marketing on fundraising. Researchers have utilized different subjective and objective constructs and measures to evaluate marketing and fundraising success in ACOs. For example, Arnold and Tapp (2003) measured an organization's marketing effort through the annual expenditures allocated to marketing activities. Lee, Ha, and Kim (2018) and Lee, Kim, and Ranucci (2021) used marketing for programs, marketing for fundraising, and marketing emphasis to measure ACO's marketing activity level and annual marketing expenditure data from a secondary database. Thomas, Pervan, and Nuttall (2009) assessed marketing through market orientation, measured by asking market orientation questions during individual interviews.

Building a long-term relationship with loyal donors and developing corresponding marketing strategies are critical factors in successful fundraising from a relationship marketing perspective. However, academic research on donors' switching and lapse behaviors is scant even though the research findings from such studies have many practical implications for professionals (Burk 2003; Burnett 2002). Furthermore, the emphasis remains firmly on donor acquisition rather than donor retention or growth (Sargeant and Hudson 2008). Thus, factors that influence donor churn should be investigated in the future. While a large body of research in relationship marketing emphasizes the importance of keeping loyal supporters, Kim, Gupta, and Lee (2021) insist that long-lapsed members are still worth pursuing for renewal, though they are less productive for repeat giving. This suggestion leads to the need for donor valuation based on loyalty.

Developing a reputable brand, finding the right supporters, and personalized communication with potential and current supporters are well-established marketing strategy recommendations that ACOs should implement to acquire and retain supporters. However, how successfully these marketing concepts are implemented varies among ACOs. Moreover, despite the rapidly growing use of digital channels in creating brand image, building relationships, and communicating with current and potential supporters, little research deals with this topic in ACOs. Therefore, future research should explore the development of web-based marketing strategies for ACOs and assess their effects on ACOs' fundraising.

References

Aaker, David A. 1992. "The Value of Brand Equity." *Journal of Business Strategy* 13, no. 4: 27–32. https://doi.org/10.1108/eb039503.

Ailawadi, Kusum L., Donald R. Lehmann, and Scott A. Neslin. 2003. "Revenue Premium as an Outcome Measure of Brand Equity." *Journal of Marketing* 67, no. 4: 1–17. https://doi.org/10.1509/jmkg.67.4.1.18688.

American Marketing Association. 2017. "What Is Marketing? The Definition of Marketing." https://www.ama.org/the-definition-of-marketing-what-is-marketing/.

American Marketing Association. n.d. "Branding." Accessed December 10, 2021. https://www.ama.org/topics/branding/.

Andreasen, Alan R., and Philip Kotler. 2007. *Strategic Marketing for Non-Profit Organizations*. 7th ed. Upper Saddle River, NJ: Prentice-Hall.

Arnold, Mark J., and Shelley R. Tapp. 2003. "Direct Marketing in Non-profit Services: Investigating the Case of the Arts Industry." *Journal of Services Marketing* 17, no. 2: 141–160. https://doi.org/10.1108/08876040310467916.

Ateca-Amestoy, Victoria, and Arantza Gorostiaga. 2022. "Donating Money and Time to Cultural Heritage: Evidence from the European Union." *Journal of Cultural Economics* 46, no. 1: 101–133. https://doi.org/10.1007/s10824-021-09409-4.

Bakhshi, Hasan, and David Throsby. 2010. "Culture of Innovation." Research report. NESTA, London. http://www.nesta.org.uk/publications/culture-innovation.

Baumgarth, Carsten. 2014. "'This Theatre Is a Part of Me': Contrasting Brand Attitude and Brand Attachment as Drivers of Audience Behaviour." *Arts Marketing: An International Journal* 4, nos. 1–2: 87–100. https://doi.org/10.1108/AM-01-2014-0007.

Barnes, Martha L. 2011. "'Music to Our Ears': Understanding Why Canadians Donate to Arts and Cultural Organizations." *International Journal of Nonprofit and Voluntary Sector Marketing* 16, no. 1: 115–126. https://doi.org/10.1002/nvsm.405.

Baumgarth, Carsten, and Daragh O'Reilly. 2014. "Brands in the Arts and Culture Sector." *Arts Marketing: An International Journal* 4, no. 1/2: 2–9. doi: 10.1108/AM-08-2014-0028.

Behzadi, Houman. 2013. "Met Opera on Demand." *Music Reference Services Quarterly* 16, no. 3: 178–180. https://doi.org/10.1080/10588167.2013.811380.

Bekkers, René, and Pamala Wiepking. 2007. "Generosity and Philanthropy: A Literature Review." Available at SSRN: http://ssrn.com/abstract=1015507.

Bekkers, René, and Pamala Wiepking. 2011. "A Literature Review of Empirical Studies of Philanthropy: Eight Mechanisms That Drive Charitable Giving." *Nonprofit and Voluntary Sector Quarterly* 40, no. 5: 924–973. https://doi.org/10.1177/0899764010380927.

Bell, Ford. 2012. "How Are Museums Supported Financially in the US?" https://static.america.gov/uploads/sites/8/2016/03/You-Asked-Series_How-Are-Museums-Supported-Financially-in-the-US_English_Lo-Res_508.pdf.

Bennett, Roger. 1998. "Market Orientation Among Small to Medium Sized UK Charitable Organisations: Implications for Fund-Raising Performance." *Journal of Nonprofit and Public Sector Marketing* 6, no. 1: 31–45. https://doi.org/10.1300/J054v06n01_03.

Bertacchini, Enrico, and Federico Morando. 2013. "The Future of Museums in the Digital Age: New Models for Access to and Use of Digital Collections." *International Journal of Arts Management* 15, no. 2: 60–72.

Bertacchini, Enrico, Walter Santagata, and Giovanni Signorello. 2011. "Individual Giving to Support Cultural Heritage." *International Journal of Arts Management* 13, no. 3: 41–55. https://papers.ssrn.com/abstract=1844292.

Best, Roger. 2012. *Market-Based Management*. 6th ed. Boston: Pearson.

Betzler, Diana, and Markus Gmür. 2016. "Does Fundraising Professionalization Pay? The Impact of Organizational Fundraising Capability on a Charity's Net Revenue from Private Donations." *Nonprofit Management and Leadership* 27, no. 1: 27–42. https://doi.org/10.1002/nml.21212.

Bhati, Abhishek, and Diarmuid McDonnell. 2020. "Success in an Online Giving Day: The Role of Social Media in Fundraising." *Nonprofit and Voluntary Sector Quarterly* 49, no. 1: 74–92. https://doi.org/10.1177/0899764019868849.

Birnberg, Jacob, Jongwoon (Willie) Choi, and Adam Presslee. 2021. "Giving Customers Decision Rights: A Field Study of Pay-What-You-Want Pricing at a Performing Arts Theater." *Accounting Perspectives* 20, no. 2: 201–225. https://doi.org/10.1111/1911-3838.12251.

Boorsma, Miranda. 2006. "A Strategic Logic for Arts Marketing." *International Journal of Cultural Policy* 12, no. 1: 73–92. https://doi.org/10.1080/10286630600613333.

Boorsma, Miranda, and Francesco Chiaravalloti. 2010. "Arts Marketing Performance: An Artistic-Mission-Led Approach to Evaluation." *Journal of Arts Management, Law, and Society* 40, no. 4: 297–317. https://doi.org/10.1080/10632921.2010.525067.

Bourgeon-Renault, Dominique, Caroline Urbain, Christine Petr, Marine Le Gall-Ely, and Anne Gombault. 2006. "An Experiential Approach to the Consumption Value of Arts and Culture: The Case of Museums and Monuments." *International Journal of Arts Management* 9, no. 1: 35–47.

Breeze, Beth. 2013. "How Donors Choose Charities: The Role of Personal Taste and Experiences in Giving Decisions." *Voluntary Sector Review* 4, no. 2: 165–183. https://doi.org/10.1332/204080513X667792.

Burnett, Ken. 2002. *Relationship Fundraising: A Donor-Based Approach to the Business of Raising Money*. San Francisco: Jossey-Bass.

Burk, Penelope. 2003. *Donor-Centered Fundraising*. Chicago: Cygnus Applied Research.

Burton, Christine, Jordan Louviere, and Louise Young. 2009. "Retaining the Visitor, Enhancing the Experience: Identifying Attributes of Choice in Repeat Museum Visitation." *International Journal of Nonprofit and Voluntary Sector Marketing* 14, no. 1: 21–34. https://doi.org/10.1002/nvsm.351.

Byrnes, William. 2014. *Management and the Arts*. 5th ed. New York: Routledge. https://doi.org/10.4324/9781315755380.

Capriotti, Paul, and Hugo P. Kuklinski. 2012. "Assessing Dialogic Communication Through the Internet in Spanish Museums." *Public Relations Review* 38, no. 4: 619–626.

Čačija, Ljiljana. 2013. "Fundraising in the Context of Nonprofit Strategic Marketing: Toward a Conceptual Model." *Management: Journal of Contemporary Management Issues* 18, no. 1: 59–78.

Camarero, Carmen, M. José Garrido, and Rebeca San José. 2016. "Efficiency of Web Communication Strategies: The Case of Art Museums." *International Journal of Arts Management* 18, no. 2: 42–62.

Camarero, Carmen, M. Jose Garrido, and Eva Vicente. 2011. "How Cultural Organizations' Size and Funding Influence Innovation and Performance: The Case of Museums." *Journal of Cultural Economics* 35, no. 4: 247–266.

Carpenter, Jeffrey, Cristina Connolly, and Caitlin Knowles Myers. 2008. "Altruistic Behavior in a Representative Dictator Experiment." *Experimental Economics* 11, no. 3: 282–298. doi: 10.1007/s10683-007-9193-x.

Colbert, François. 2003. "Entrepreneurship and Leadership in Marketing the Arts." *International Journal of Arts Management* 6, no. 1: 30–39.

Colbert, François. 2009. "Beyond Branding: Contemporary Marketing Challenges for Arts Organizations." *International Journal of Arts Management* 12, no. 1: 14–20.

Colbert, François, and Danilo C. Dantas. 2019. "Customer Relationships in Arts Marketing: A Review of Key Dimensions in Delivery by Artistic and Cultural Organizations." *International Journal of Arts Management* 21, no. 2: 4–14.

Colbert, François, and Philippe Ravanas. 2019. *Marketing Culture and the Arts*. 5th ed. Montreal: HEC Montreal.

Conway, Tony, and Debra Leighton. 2012. "'Staging the Past, Enacting the Present': Experiential Marketing in the Performing Arts and Heritage Sectors." *Arts Marketing: An International Journal* 2, no. 1: 35–51. https://doi.org/10.1108/20442081211233007.

Courchesne, André, Philippe Ravanas, and Cristian Pulido. 2017. "Doing Well by Doing Good: Les Grands Ballets Canadiens de Montréal Offers Dance Therapy as a Strategic Initiative." *International Journal of Arts Management* 20, no. 1: 78–83.

Cuadrado, Manuel, Irene Gil, and Alejandro Molla. 2000. "Empirical Evidence of Marketing Practices in the Nonprofit Sector: The Case of Performing Arts." *Journal of Nonprofit and Public Sector Marketing* 8, no. 3: 15–24.

Cunliffe, Daniel, Efmorphia Kritou, and Douglas Tudhope. 2001. "Usability Evaluation for Museum Web Sites." *Museum Management and Curatorship* 19, no. 3: 229–252.

Davis, J. Charlene, and Scott R. Swanson. 2009. "The Importance of Being Earnest or Committed: Attribute Importance and Consumer Evaluations of the Live Arts Experience." *Journal of Nonprofit and Public Sector Marketing* 21, no. 1: 56–79. https://doi.org/10.1080/10495140802111968.

DeLong, Thomas J., and Vineeta Vijayaraghavan. 2012. "Should You Listen to the Customer?" *Harvard Business Review* 90, no. 9 (online). http://www.hbs.edu/faculty/Pages/item.aspx?num=42930.

Dempster, Anna M. 2006. "Risky Business: The Art of Managing Creative Ventures." In *Cultural Industries: The British Experience in International Perspective*, edited by Christine Eisenberg, Rita Gerlach, and Christian Handke (online). Berlin: Humboldt University. https://edoc.hu-berlin.de/handle/18452/1851.

Eikenberry, Angela M., and Jodie Drapal Kluver. 2004. "The Marketization of the Nonprofit Sector: Civil Society at Risk?" *Public Administration Review* 64, no. 2: 132–140.

Estelami, Hooman, Nicole N. Estelami, and John Lichtmann. 2019. "Determinants of Prices for the Performing Arts." *Journal of Promotion Management* 25, no. 6: 890–906. https://doi.org/10.1080/10496491.2018.1536622.

Faculty of the Lilly Family School of Philanthropy. 2020. "Inclusive Philanthropy." *Stanford Social Innovation Review* 18, no. 4: 38–43. https://doi.org/10.48558/GTA9-WJ43.

Fillis, Ian, Kim Lehman, and Morgan P. Miles. 2017. "The Museum of Old and New Art: Leveraging Entrepreneurial Marketing to Create a Unique Arts and Vacation Venture." *Journal of Vacation Marketing* 23, no. 1: 85–96. https://doi.org/10.1177/1356766716634153.

Fillis, Ian, and Ruth Rentschler. 2005. "Using Creativity to Achieve an Entrepreneurial Future for Arts Marketing." *International Journal of Nonprofit and Voluntary Sector Marketing* 10, no. 4: 275–287. https://doi.org/10.1002/nvsm.26.

Fillis, Ian, and Ruth Rentschler. 2011. "The Evolution and Development of Arts Marketing Research." *Arts Marketing: An International Journal* 1, no. 1: 11–25. https://doi.org/10.1108/20442081111129842.

Fillis, Ian, and Nick Telford. 2020. *Handbook of Entrepreneurship and Marketing*. Cheltenham, UK: Edward Elgar.

Frey, Bruno S., and Stephan Meier. 2006. "The Economics of Museums." In *Handbook of the Economics of Art and Culture*, edited by Victor A. Ginsburg and David Throsby, 1:1017–1047. Elsevier. https://doi.org/10.1016/S1574-0676(06)01029-5.

Frumkin, Peter, and Alice Andre-Clark. 2000. "When Missions, Markets, and Politics Collide: Values and Strategy in the Nonprofit Human Services." *Nonprofit and Voluntary Sector Quarterly* 29, no. 1 (suppl.): 141–163. https://doi.org/10.1177/0899764000291S007.

Holbrook, Morris B., and Robert B. Zirlin. 1985. "Artistic Creation, Artworks, and Aesthetic Appreciation: Some Philosophical Contributions to Nonprofit Marketing." *Advances in Nonprofit Marketing* 1, no. 1: 1–54.

Holt, Douglas. 2012. "Cultural Brand Strategy." In *Handbook of Marketing Strategy*, edited by Venkatesh Shankar and Gregory S. Carpenter, 306–317. Cheltenham, UK: Edward Elgar.

Holt, Douglas, and Douglas Cameron. 2010. *Cultural Strategy: Using Innovative Ideologies to Build Breakthrough Brands*. Oxford: Oxford University Press.

Hult, G., Tomas M., David J. Ketchen Jr., and Stanley F. Slater. 2005. "Market Orientation and Performance: An Integration of Disparate Approaches." *Strategic Management Journal* 26, no. 12: 1173–1181. https://doi.org/10.1002/smj.494.

Gaffny, Thomas. 1996. "Advanced Techniques of Donor Recognition." *International Journal of Nonprofit and Voluntary Sector Marketing* 1, no. 1: 41–49. https://doi.org/10.1002/nvsm.6090010107.

Gainer, Brenda, and Paulette Padanyi. 2002. "Applying the Marketing Concept to Cultural Organisations: An Empirical Study of the Relationship between Market Orientation and Performance." *International Journal of Nonprofit and Voluntary Sector Marketing* 7, no. 2: 182–193. https://doi.org/10.1002/nvsm.178.

Gainer, Brenda, and Paulette Padanyi. 2005. "The Relationship Between Market-Oriented Activities and Market-Oriented Culture: Implications for the Development of Market Orientation in Nonprofit Service Organizations." *Journal of Business Research* 58, no. 6: 854–862. https://doi.org/10.1016/j.jbusres.2003.10.005.

Gallagher, Kathleen, and Jessica Sowa. 2014. "Leveraging Social Media to Engage and Retain: Art/Culture Organization Donors, Members, and Volunteers." In *The Routledge Companion to Arts Marketing*, edited by Daragh O'Reilly, Ruth Rentschler, and Theresa Kirchner, 170–179. New York: Routledge.

Goldman, Kate Haley, and David T. Schaller. 2004. "Exploring Motivational Factors and Visitor Satisfaction in On-Line Museum Visits." Paper presented at the International Conference for Culture and Heritage Archive. https://www.eduweb.com/motivational_factors.pdf.

Grizzle, Cleopatra. 2015. "Efficiency, Stability and the Decision to Give to Nonprofit Arts and Cultural Organizations in the United States." *International Journal of Nonprofit and Voluntary Sector Marketing* 27, no. 1: 67–97.

Hausmann, Andrea. 2012. "Creating 'Buzz': Opportunities and Limitations of Social Media for Arts Institutions and Their Viral Marketing." *International Journal of Nonprofit and Voluntary Sector Marketing* 17, no. 3: 173–182. https://doi.org/10.1002/nvsm.1420.

Hausmann, Andrea, and Lorenz Poellmann. 2013. "Using Social Media for Arts Marketing: Theoretical Analysis and Empirical Insights for Performing Arts Organizations."

International Review on Public and Nonprofit Marketing 10, no. 2: 143–161. https://doi.org/10.1007/s12208-013-0094-8.

Heilbrun, James, and Charles M. Gray. 1993. *The Economics of Arts and Culture: An American Perspective*. New York: Cambridge University Press.

Hill, Liz, Carolin O'Sullivan, and Terry O'Sullivan. 2017. *Creative Arts Marketing*. 3rd ed. Amsterdam: Taylor & Francis.

Hooper-Greenhill, Eilean. 2000. "Changing Values in the Art Museum: Rethinking Communication and Learning." *International Journal of Heritage Studies* 6, no. 1: 9–31. https://doi.org/10.1080/135272500363715.

Institute for Sustainable Philanthropy. 2021. "Donor Centricity: Where Did It Come From and Why Does It Matter?" April 1, 2021. https://www.philanthropy-institute.org.uk/blog/donor-centricity-where-did-it-come-from-and-why-does-it-matter.

Jung, Yuha. 2015. "Diversity Matters: Theoretical Understanding of and Suggestions for the Current Fundraising Practices of Nonprofit Art Museums." *Journal of Arts Management, Law and Society* 45, no. 4: 255–268. https://doi.org/10.1080/10632921.2015.1103672.

Keller, Kevin Lane, and Donald R. Lehmann. 2003. "How Do Brands Create Value?" *Marketing Management* 12, no. 3: 26–31.

Keller, Kevin Lane, and Vanitha Swaminathan. 2020. *Strategic Brand Management: Building, Measuring, and Managing Brand Equity*. 5th ed. Hoboken, NJ: Pearson.

Khodakarami, Farnoosh, J. Andrew Petersen, and Rajkumar Venkatesan. 2015. "Developing Donor Relationships: The Role of the Breadth of Giving." *Journal of Marketing* 79, no. 4: 77–93. https://doi.org/10.1509/jm.14.0351.

Kim, Sungjin, Sachin Gupta, and Clarence Lee. 2021. "Managing Members, Donors, and Member-Donors for Effective Nonprofit Fundraising." *Journal of Marketing* 85, no. 3: 220–239. https://doi.org/10.1177/0022242921994587.

Kirchner, Theresa A., Edward P. Markowski, and John B. Ford. 2007. "Relationships Among Levels of Government Support, Marketing Activities, and Financial Health of Nonprofit Performing Arts Organizations." *International Journal of Nonprofit and Voluntary Sector Marketing* 12, no. 2: 95–116.

Kohli, Ajay K., and Bernard J. Jaworski. 1990. "Market Orientation: The Construct, Research Propositions, and Managerial Implications." *Journal of Marketing* 54, no. 2: 1–18. https://doi.org/10.2307/1251866.

Kolhede, Eric John, and J. Tomas Gomez-Arias. 2016. "Segmentation of Infrequent Performing Arts Consumers." *Arts and the Market* 6, no. 1: 88–110. https://doi.org/10.1108/AAM-04-2014-0015.

Kotler, Neil, Philip Kotler, and Wendy Kotler. 2016. *Museum Marketing and Strategy: Designing Missions, Building Audiences, Generating Revenue and Resources*. Hoboken, NJ: John Wiley & Sons.

Kotler, Philip. 1979. "Strategies for Introducing Marketing into Nonprofit Organizations." *Journal of Marketing* 43, no. 1: 37–44. https://doi.org/10.1177/002224297904300104.

Kotler, Philip. 1980. "Foreword." In *Marketing the Arts*, edited by Michael Mokwa, William Dawson, and Arthur Prieve, xii–xv. New York: Praeger.

Kottasz, Rita. 2004. "Differences in the Donor Behavior Characteristics of Young Affluent Males and Females: Empirical Evidence from Britain." *Voluntas: International Journal of Voluntary and Nonprofit Organizations* 15, no. 2: 181–203. https://doi.org/10.1023/B:VOLU.0000033180.43496.09.

Krawczyk, Kelly, Michelle Wooddell, and Ashley Dias. 2017. "Charitable Giving in Arts and Culture Nonprofits: The Impact of Organizational Characteristics." *Nonprofit and Voluntary Sector Quarterly* 46, no. 4: 817–836. https://doi.org/10.1177/0899764017692038.

Labaronne, Leticia, and Tilman Slembeck. 2015. "Dynamic Pricing in Subsidized Performing Arts." *International Journal of Nonprofit and Voluntary Sector Marketing* 20, no. 2: 122–136.

Lee, Hyunjung, Kyoungnam Catherine Ha, and Youngseon Kim. 2018. "Marketing Expense and Financial Performance in Arts and Cultural Organizations." *International Journal of Nonprofit and Voluntary Sector Marketing* 23, no. 3: e1588. https://doi.org/10.1002/nvsm.1588.

Lee, Hyunjung, Youngseon Kim, and Rebecca Ranucci. 2021. "Stability and Compatibility in the Receptivity of US Arts and Culture Organizations to Corporate Support." *International Journal of Arts Management* 23, no. 2: 43–55.

Lee, Woo Jin, and Lee Soo Hee. 2017. "Marketing from the Art World: A Critical Review of American Research in Arts Marketing." *Journal of Arts Management, Law, and Society* 47, no. 1: 17–33. https://doi.org/10.1080/10632921.2016.1274698.

Lee, Young-Joo. 2021. "Nonprofit Marketing Expenses: Who Spends More than Others?" *Journal of Nonprofit and Public Sector Marketing* 33, no. 3: 385–402. https://doi.org/10.1080/10495142.2019.1707743.

Lee, Young-Joo, and Jongmin Shon. 2021. "Nonprofits' Online Social Capital and Charitable Support." *Journal of Nonprofit & Public Sector Marketing* 0, no. 0 (October 15, 2021): 1–18. https://doi.org/10.1080/10495142.2021.1982112.

Liao, Mei-Na, Susan Foreman, and Adrian Sargeant. 2001. "Market Versus Societal Orientation in the Nonprofit Context." *International Journal of Nonprofit and Voluntary Sector Marketing* 6, no. 3: 254–268. https://doi.org/10.1002/nvsm.151.

Maple, Peter. 2013. *Marketing Strategy for Effective Fundraising*. London: Directory of Social Change.

McDonald, Heath, and Paul Harrison. 2002. "The Marketing and Public Relations Practices of Australian Performing Arts Presenters." *International Journal of Nonprofit and Voluntary Sector Marketing* 7, no. 2: 105–117. https://doi.org/10.1002/nvsm.172.

McDonald, Robert E. 2007. "An Investigation of Innovation in Nonprofit Organizations: The Role of Organizational Mission." *Nonprofit and Voluntary Sector Quarterly* 36, no. 2: 256–281. https://doi.org/10.1177/0899764006295996.

Mohan, J., and L. Bulloch. 2012. "The Idea of a 'Civic Core': What Are the Overlaps between Charitable Giving, Volunteering, and Civic Participation in England and Wales." Working Paper 73. Third Sector Research Centre Working Paper. https://www.birmingham.ac.uk/documents/college-social-sciences/social-policy/tsrc/working-papers/working-paper-73.pdf

Narver, John C., and Stanley F. Slater. 1990. "The Effect of a Market Orientation on Business Profitability." *Journal of Marketing* 54, no. 4: 20–35. https://doi.org/10.2307/1251757.

Neumayr, Michaela, and Femida Handy. 2019. "Charitable Giving: What Influences Donors' Choice Among Different Causes?" *Voluntas: International Journal of Voluntary and Nonprofit Organizations* 30, no. 4: 783–799. https://doi.org/10.1007/s11266-017-9843-3.

O'Reilly, Daragh. 2005. "Cultural Brands/Branding Cultures." *Journal of Marketing Management* 21, no. 5–6: 573–588. doi: 10.1362/0267257054307336

Padilla-Meléndez, Antonio, and Ana Rosa del Águila-Obra. 2013. "Web and Social Media Usage by Museums: Online Value Creation." *International Journal of Information Management* 33, no. 5: 892–898. https://doi.org/10.1016/j.ijinfomgt.2013.07.004.

Parkman, Ian D., Samuel S. Holloway, and Helder Sebastiao. 2012. "Creative Industries: Aligning Entrepreneurial Orientation and Innovation Capacity." *Journal of Research in Marketing and Entrepreneurship* 14, no. 1: 95–114. https://doi.org/10.1108/14715201211246823.

Payton, Robert L., and Michael P. Moody. 2008. *Understanding Philanthropy: Its Meaning and Mission*. Bloomington: Indiana University Press.

Petkus, Ed, Jr. 2004. "Enhancing the Application of Experiential Marketing in the Arts." *International Journal of Nonprofit and Voluntary Sector Marketing* 9, no. 1: 49–56. https://doi.org/10.1002/nvsm.232.

Pettey, Janice Gow, and Lilya Wagner. 2007. "Introduction: Union Gives Strength—Diversity and Fundraising." *International Journal of Educational Advancement* 7, no. 3: 171–175. https://doi.org/10.1057/palgrave.ijea.2150059.

Pompe, Jeffrey, Lawrence Tamburri, and Johnathan Munn. 2020. "Marketing Strategies for Performing Arts Audiences: Characteristics of Ticket Purchasers." *Journal of Nonprofit and Public Sector Marketing* 32, no. 5: 453–464. https://doi.org/10.1080/10495142.2019.1589631.

Radley, Alan, and Marie Kennedy. 1992. "Reflections upon Charitable Giving: A Comparison of Individuals from Business, 'Manual' and Professional Backgrounds." *Journal of Community and Applied Social Psychology* 2, no. 2: 113–129. https://doi.org/10.1002/casp.2450020208.

Rentschler, Ruth, and Gus Geursen. 2004. "Entrepreneurship, Marketing and Leadership in Non-Profit Performing Arts Organisations." *Journal of Research in Marketing and Entrepreneurship* 6, no. 1: 44–51. https://doi.org/10.1108/14715200480001354.

Rentschler, Ruth, and Jennifer Radbourne. 2008. "Relationship Marketing in the Arts: The New Evoked Authenticity." In *The Routledge Companion to Nonprofit Marketing*, edited by Adrian Sargeant and Walter Wymer, 241–252. London: Routledge.

Rentschler, Ruth, Jennifer Radbourne, Rodney Carr, and John Rickard. 2002. "Relationship Marketing, Audience Retention and Performing Arts Organisation Viability." *International Journal of Nonprofit and Voluntary Sector Marketing* 7, no. 2: 118–130. https://doi.org/10.1002/nvsm.173

Rooney, Patrick, Sasha Zarins, Jon Bergdoll, and Una Osili. 2020. "The Impact of Five Different Tax Policy Changes on Household Giving in the United States." *Nonprofit Policy Forum* 11, no. 4: 20200040. https://doi.org/10.1515/npf-2020-0040.

Sargeant, Adrian. 2001. "Relationship Fundraising: How to Keep Donors Loyal." *Nonprofit Management and Leadership* 12, no. 2: 177–192. https://doi.org/10.1002/nml.12204.

Sargeant, Adrian. 2009. *Marketing Management for Nonprofit Organizations*. 3rd ed. Oxford: Oxford University Press.

Sargeant, Adrian. 2013. "Donor Retention: What Do We Know and What Can We Do About It?" *Nonprofit Quarterly*, summer 2013, 12–23.

Sargeant, Adrian, Susan Foreman, and Mei-Na Liao. 2002. "Operationalizing the Marketing Concept in the Nonprofit Sector." *Journal of Nonprofit and Public Sector Marketing* 10, no. 2: 41–65. https://doi.org/10.1300/J054v10n02_03.

Sargeant, Adrian, and Jane Hudson. 2008. "Donor Retention: An Exploratory Study of Door-to-Door Recruits." *International Journal of Nonprofit and Voluntary Sector Marketing* 13, no. 1: 89–101. https://doi.org/10.1002/nvsm.301.

Sargeant, Adrian, and Elaine Jay. 2004. *Fundraising Management: Analysis, Planning and Practice*. London: Routledge.

Sargeant, Adrian, and Jen Shang. 2010. *Fundraising Principles and Practice*, vol. 17. Hoboken, NJ: John Wiley & Sons.

Sargeant, Adrian, and Lucy Woodliffe. 2007. "Gift Giving: An Interdisciplinary Review." *International Journal of Nonprofit and Voluntary Sector Marketing* 12, no. 4: 275–307. https://doi.org/10.1002/nvsm.308.

Scherhag, Christian, and Silke Boenigk. 2013. "Different or Equal Treatment? Donor Priority Strategy and Fundraising Performance Assessed by a Propensity Score Matching Study: Different or Equal Treatment?" *Nonprofit Management and Leadership* 23, no. 4: 443–472. https://doi.org/10.1002/nml.21074.

Schlegelmilch, B. B., and A. C. Tynan. 1989a. "Market Segment-Oriented Fund-Raising Strategies: An Empirical Analysis." *Marketing Intelligence and Planning* 7, nos. 11–12: 16–24. https://doi.org/10.1108/EUM0000000001065.

Schlegelmilch, B. B., and A. C. Tynan. 1989b. "The Scope for Market Segmentation Within the Charity Market: An Empirical Analysis." *Managerial and Decision Economics* 10, no. 2: 127 134.

Schroeder, Jonathan E. 2009. "The Cultural Codes of Branding." *Marketing Theory* 9, no. 1: 123–126. https://doi.org/10.1177/1470593108100067.

Scott, Carol. 2000. "Branding: Positioning Museums in the 21st Century." *International Journal of Arts Management* 2, no. 3: 35–39.

Shah, Denish, and Morris George. 2021. "Linking Marketing to Nonprofit Performance." *Journal of Public Policy and Marketing* 40, no. 4: 571–583. https://doi.org/10.1177/0743915620978538.

Shoham, Aviv, Gregory M. Rose, and Fredric Kropp. 2005. "Market Orientation and Performance: A Meta-analysis." *Marketing Intelligence and Planning* 23, no. 5: 435–454. https://doi.org/10.1108/02634500510612627.

Sigala, Marianna. 2005. "A Learning Assessment of Online Interpretation Practices: From Museum Supply Chains to Experience Ecologies." In *Information and Communication Technologies in Tourism 2005*, edited by Andrew J. Frew, 67–78. Vienna: Springer. https://doi.org/10.1007/3-211-27283-6_7.

Smithsonian Institution. 2001. "Art Museums and the Public." Smithsonian Institution, Washington, DC. https://www.si.edu/Content/opanda/docs/Rpts2001/01.10.ArtPublic.Final.pdf.

Stavraki, Georgia, Emmanuella Plakoyiannaki, and Jackie Clarke. 2018. "The Appropriation Cycle: Novice and Expert Consumers." *European Journal of Marketing* 52, nos. 9–10: 1886–1908. https://doi.org/10.1108/EJM-08-2017-0527.

Streed, Odile. 2020. "Revisiting Segmentation for the Performing Arts: Strategic Implications." *Journal of Marketing Trends* 6, no. 1: 36–47.

Tajtáková, Mária, and Daniel Arias-Aranda. 2008. "Targeting University Students in Audience Development Strategies for Opera and Ballet." *Service Industries Journal* 28, no. 2: 179–191. https://doi.org/10.1080/02642060701842191.

Teather, Lynn, and Kelly Wilhelm. 1999. "Web Musing: Evaluating Museums on the Web from Learning Theory to Methodology." In *Museums and the Web 1999: Selected Papers*, edited by Jennifer Trant and David Bearman, 131–143. Archives and Museum Informatics.

Thomas, Sarah R., Simon J. Pervan, and Peter J. Nuttall. 2009. "Marketing Orientation and Arts Organizations: The Case for Business Sponsorship." *Marketing Intelligence and Planning* 27, no. 6: 736–752.

Urban Institute. 2021. "Nonprofit Trends and Impacts 2021." Research report. Urban Institute, Washington, DC.

Urrutiaguer, Daniel. 2014. "Programming Strategies and Demand in the Performing Arts: The Case of the Forum in Le Blanc-Mesnil, France." *International Journal of Arts Management* 17, no. 1: 31–42.

Voss, Glenn B., and Zannie Giraud Voss. 2000. "Strategic Orientation and Firm Performance in an Artistic Environment." *Journal of Marketing* 64, no. 1: 67–83.

Weinstein, Stanley, and Pamela Barden. 2017. *The Complete Guide to Fundraising Management*. Hoboken, NJ: John Wiley & Sons.

Wiepking, Pamala. 2007. "The Philanthropic Poor: In Search of Explanations for the Relative Generosity of Lower Income Households." *Voluntas: International Journal of Voluntary and Nonprofit Organizations* 18, no. 4: 339–358. https://doi.org/10.1007/s11266-007-9049-1.

Wiepking, Pamala, and Ineke Maas. 2009. "Resources That Make You Generous: Effects of Social and Human Resources on Charitable Giving." *Social Forces* 87, no. 4: 1973–1995. https://doi.org/10.1353/sof.0.0191.

Wymer, Walter. 2021. "Nonprofit Marketing Research: Developing Ideas for New Studies." *SN Business and Economics* 1, no. 7: 90. https://doi.org/10.1007/s43546-021-00095-0.

Wymer, Walter, Silke Boenigk, and Mareike Möhlmann. 2015. "The Conceptualization of Nonprofit Marketing Orientation: A Critical Reflection and Contributions Toward Closing the Practice-Theory Gap." *Journal of Nonprofit and Public Sector Marketing* 27, no. 2: 117–134. https://doi.org/10.1080/10495142.2014.965078.

Wymer, Walter, Hellen P. Gross, and Bernd Helmig. 2016. "Nonprofit Brand Strength: What Is It? How Is It Measured? What Are Its Outcomes?" *Voluntas: International Journal of Voluntary and Nonprofit Organizations* 27, no. 3: 1448–1471. https://doi.org/10.1007/s11266-015-9641-8.

CHAPTER 24

CREATION AND CONSUMPTION EXPERIENCE OF CULTURAL VALUE IN CONTEMPORARY ART

IAN FILLIS, BORAM LEE, AND IAN FRASER

Introduction

WE inform understanding of the cultural value surrounding contemporary art by focusing on stakeholder interactions relating to an annual high-profile contemporary art exhibition. The chapter is structured as follows. We assess the meaning of contemporary art before evaluating its connection with cultural value. We then utilize marketing and consumption theory to enhance understanding. Insight is provided through our qualitative cultural value research on an annual contemporary art exhibition. Finally, we discuss our findings and make a number of suggestions for future research.

We respond to broader criticisms that research on the impact of the arts tends to have conceptual and methodological weaknesses (McCarthy et al. 2001) by progressing theory grounded in a robust conceptual framework. We build on Jafari, Taheri, and vom Lehn (2013) by moving beyond affective, recreational, and cognitive experiences to account for the social context of exhibition attendance. For some consumers, aesthetic and everyday consumption experiences are intertwined as they embrace the arts within their lives (Venkatesh and Meamber 2008).

The notion of "customer" does not fit clearly with visual art consumption. Instead, both art for art's sake and art for business's sake philosophies impact (Fillis 2006). Joy and Sherry (2003, 155) evaluate the relationship between art market and artwork by considering the actions of each stakeholder:

> The relationship between art and market can be rendered visible only by closely examining the actions of contemporary artists, art critics, and writers, and the efforts

of gallery and auction house merchandisers. A market orientation is just one way of evaluating the activities of the art world. Art and market are not reducible to each other.... While the market operates on a narrative that valorizes the latest trend in image-making... it is neither the only or the most important arbitrator of value for the viewer.

This raises both philosophical and practical value issues with respect to producing what a potential buyer might want (customer orientation) versus producing from within and then stimulating demand for the artwork (self or intrinsic creation). Our research involves consumers as gallery visitors and buyers, artists, the art institution, gallerists, and investors. All of these create and receive value in both the short and long terms, and may even only recognize value well after any encounter with the art as they reflect on the experience. Gummerus's (2013) positioning of value as experience outcomes fits well here.

What Is Contemporary Art?

Some critics view art as no more than an industrial product, while others see it as possessing an aesthetic culturally defined sign (Mick 1986; Barrere and Santagata 1999). Venkatesh and Meamber (2008) interpret engagement with art as simultaneous production and consumption. Art consists of artifacts, images, or performances that contain rich, complex, direct, and symbolic meanings. Contemporary art can be shocking, modernizing, and retro-sensationalist (Smith 2009). It can also be postcolonial in being influenced not by any art movement but, rather, by diversity, identity, and critique. Contemporary art as counterculture (Roszak 1995; Desmond, McDonagh, and O'Donohoe 2000) can be seen in small-scale artist-run initiatives, taking control away from the art institution in shaping value.

Plattner (1998, 482) considers the market for contemporary art,

> where producers do not make work primarily for sale, where buyers often have no idea of the value of what they buy, and where middlemen routinely claim reimbursement for sales of things they have never seen to buyers they have never dealt with.

It has also been described as a Veblen good (Veblen 1973), with high price approximating to high elite value. Joy and Sherry (2004, 307) think of contemporary, avant-garde art as being capable of "bursting the frame" by "continuously critiquing and pushing the boundaries in the creation of art."

According to Bourdieu (1993, 36), believing in the value of an artwork constitutes part of its full reality, although other factors also shape its perceived value:

> There is... every reason to suppose that the constitution of the aesthetic gaze... capable of considering the work of art in and for itself... is linked to the institution of the

work of art as an object of contemplation, with the creation of private and . . . public galleries and museums, and the parallel development of a corps of professionals appointed to conserve the work of art, both materially and symbolically.

A work of art, he asserts, can only receive value from a position of collective belief. Many artists create value through producing work reflecting their inner motivation (intrinsic value) and not through adherence to market principles (Holbrook and Zirlin 1985).

Communicating the value associated with art concerns the expression of feelings and ideas about it. When we are attracted to an artwork, we experience mental and sensual, aesthetic arousal (Venkatesh and Meamber 2008). Value is created from the written, verbal, and visual narratives surrounding the art. Experience is an additional source of value in being memorable, personal, and founded on sensations (Pine and Gilmore 2011), moving between passive and active participation in involving consumption through absorption and immersion, signaling the co-creation of value (Prahalad and Ramswamy 2004; Vargo and Lusch 2014). This results in the construction of new value and meanings associated with the art (Minkiewicz, Evans, and Bridson 2014).

Defining Cultural Value

Crossick and Kaszynska (2014, 124) view cultural value in terms of "the effects that culture has on those who experience it and the difference it makes to individuals and society."

Geursen and Rentschler (2003) evaluate both its aesthetic context (relating to quality of life and the social and psychological values of cultural capital) and its neoclassical economic interpretation (measuring its economic output and monetary value to the economy). O'Brien (2015) reveals that a "true understanding of the value of culture is impossible without the disciplines and fields that are currently peripheral to both government social science and, more broadly, higher education in the UK." Art as a cultural object (Duhaime, Joy, and Ross 1995) contains a range of both stable and subjective values expressed through our interpretations of meaning as we interact with the object (or the experience). When an art object is located in a museum or gallery, this gives it an aura of value. When we enter a gallery space, we do not enter blind but, rather, come in with presuppositions about what we might find there and how we might react in terms of

> the knowledge, the expectations, the mental schema, and the values that individuals bring to their experience of art . . . When a cultural object brings to the fore some of these assumptions held by individuals, a cultural interaction or positive encounter is said to have occurred.
>
> (Duhaime, Joy, and Ross 1995, 356)

Fillis (2006, 2010) critiques the tensions between artistic and market orientation in visual art, noting the limitations of long-held marketing assumptions in assisting artists to advance their artistic standing. The distinction between producer/consumer relationships in the arts and those elsewhere is clarified by Lehman and Wickham (2014, 665):

> Unlike the dyadic relationship that exists between manufacturer and final consumer in the traditional marketing sense, the arts marketing context comprises a complex set of collaborative interrelationships between art producers, their audience, and key intermediaries.

The arts and related cultural phenomena represent activities that have value and benefits for government, organizations, and consumers. Instrumental benefits pertain to social, economic, or policy outcomes (Belfiore 2002). Intrinsic benefits are less obvious, but the ability of arts and cultural experiences to transform people is of central interest to cultural policy and practice (Radbourne, Glow, and Johanson 2010). Cultural production concerns "the process by which cultural products (including goods, artifacts, visual and experiential objects, services and art forms) are created, transformed and diffused in the constitution of consumer culture" (Venkatesh and Meamber 2006, 12, in Lash and Urry 1994/2002).

Art and cultural value is expressed through involvement (Slater and Armstrong 2010). However, collectors of art and museum and gallery visitors express different desires based on their perception of value (Chen 2009). Belk's (1982, 1995) work on collecting behavior further informs understanding of contemporary art's appeal; he describes collecting as an obsessive and addictive behavior rather than an everyday consumer behavior relating to lower-value goods and services.

Art products are difficult to value due to the individual experiences of stakeholders (Johnson 2014). Throsby's (2001) six forms of value (aesthetic, spiritual, social, historical, symbolic, and authentic), however, help to provide a framework for understanding the elements of cultural value. Preece (2014) investigates value as a social, co-created phenomenon in the visual arts market, where both art and artists have socially constructed meaning and context. She identifies a lack of transparency, making the identification of value associations challenging.

Our understanding of how consumers make decisions concerning their evaluations of art is limited (Moulard et al. 2014). Although technical characteristics are important (Marshall and Forrest 2011), the impact of visual aesthetics and visual consumption is also part of the value surrounding contemporary art (Schroeder 2002, 2006). The perceived authenticity of artists and their work also shapes artists' brand value (Beverland, Lindgreen, and Vink 2008) and consumers' experiences (Beverland and Farrelly 2010). The authenticity of the artist can affect the valuation of the art as well as consumers' behavioral intentions (Fine 2003). The art market is reliant on brand image, identity, and value, signaling the need for deeper investigation (Schroeder 2002).

Improving Understanding of Contemporary Art as Cultural Value

Cultural value, marketing value, and consumption value are inextricably linked, even though there is little extant research that examines this intersection (O'Reilly 2005; Larsen, Lawson and Todd 2013). Value emerges from what people do via "the social pursuit of those meaningful distinctions typically through the exchange of resources between actors" (Arnould 2014, 13). Levy's symbolic value (Levy 1959) and Peñaloza and Venkatesh's sign value (Peñaloza and Venkatesh 2006) help us to understand consumption activity and the economy, since any market can be viewed as a social/cultural constructed system of created meanings.

Overlapping partly with Throsby (2001), Karababa and Keldgaard (2014) consider how value is produced and consumed within a cultural paradigm involving, for example, co-creation of value, aesthetic value, and identity. Co-creation concerns "the processes by which both consumers and producers collaborate, or otherwise participate, in creating value" (Pongsakornrungsilp and Schroeder 2011). An additional contributor is experiential consumption, where higher-level hedonic activities are categorized and prioritized by individuals as they seek to manage their decision-making (Shah and Alter 2014). Value is also located in the arousal and pleasure experienced in cultural environments where consumers can escape from daily routines (Miniero, Rurale, and Addis 2014). The atmosphere or ambience of the cultural space also contributes to the experience's perceived value (Goulding 2000). Consumer value of an arts and cultural experience can be viewed holistically, "as it incorporates all the stimuli, emotions, ambience and environment that shape an artistic performance [or] exhibition" (Miniero, Rurale, and Addis 2014, 629). Experiential value is central to many activities relating to visual art, as some consumers become heavily engaged with the artist and the artwork while, for others, this is less important (Holbrook and Hirschman 1982).

Co-production or co-creation of value can also be understood from a network perspective; for example, artists, peers, galleries, dealers, and consumers interact directly and indirectly to create value. This value is co-produced within networks involving the interaction of social and economic stakeholders (Jyrama 2002). Rodner and Thomson (2013) help us to appreciate the contributions of the various actors in the art market network, including the artists, art schools, galleries, critics, auction houses, museums, and collectors, in what they term the "art machine."

Factors influencing how we value visual art include trust, experience, image, talent, standards, taste, reputation of the artist (and experts referred to for confirmation of value), and cultural knowledge generally.

Qualitative Insight into Creation and Consumption Experience of Cultural Value in Contemporary Art

The research site was an annual contemporary art exhibition in a prominent art institution in a major UK city. We focused on the relationships between interested stakeholders and their perceptions of this value. Twenty-six interviews were carried out: fifteen with a selection of the artists, four with institution staff, two with the exhibition selection panel, and five with major prize-givers. All interviews were semi-structured and recorded digitally. Exhibiting artists (current and past) were asked, for example, about their participation in the exhibition, their longer-term ambitions, the value associated with their work, marketplace engagement, the impact of their work, and their relationship with the institution. The transcribed interviews were coded for analysis using Nvivo. We used thematic analysis (Boyatzis 1998) to assess the role of the exhibition as a launching platform for career development and engagement by the artists with the institution. We used pseudonyms or institutional functions to ensure anonymity.

The interviews assessed how each stakeholder constructed and understood the marketing and consumption aspects of cultural value, as visualized in Figure 24.1. This tripartite conceptual framework shows how value is created and consumed through the platform (the annual exhibition) as the initial value creation point, and the three major value recipients and creators (the exhibitor, the organizer, and the public) within the value creation channels. This value is also shared over time with other communities and stakeholders. The institution is the organizer, the public are the visitors to the exhibition, and the artists are those currently or previously exhibiting at the exhibition. Co-creation and other marketing and consumption activities occur between the different stakeholders. Direct value is illustrated through the solid lines in Figure 24.1, with indirect value visualized as dotted lines.

Creation of Value

An exhibiting artist revealed challenges in identifying the different values involved in both producing the work and communicating its value:

> Value is a really hard thing for me as an artist. I know the value that's the lower part of value, the main dimension of value, would be the actual chance to get to make it and to have the space to show it in because I can't show that in my living room at home. . . . [I]t's just getting the idea out and doing it and the value of speaking to people and getting these images back. Maybe having it on my CV.

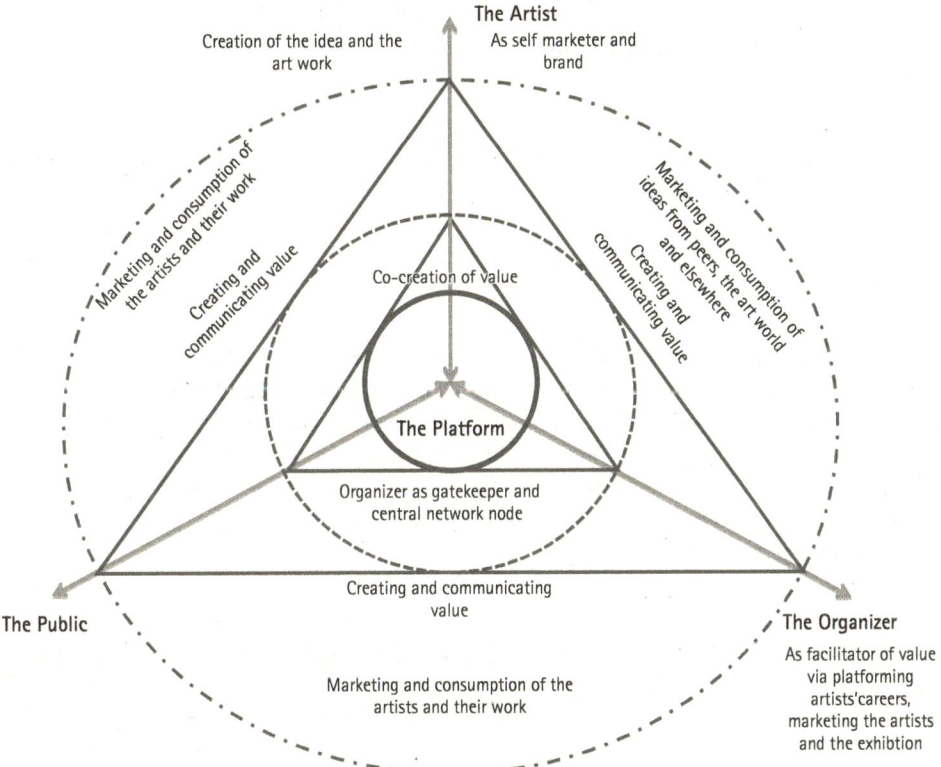

FIGURE 24.1 Cultural value of contemporary art: Creation and consumption.

Making the work is where most value lies for another artist. The value to the artist may have more to do with their own value as a brand rather than with the artwork's value (Schroeder 2009), even though this may be problematic for some:

> I don't like that really that the artist holds the value rather than their artwork, but I think [that's] an honest perspective and the direction they've taken. . . . I don't like that an artist . . . could hold . . . the value and I think it's nice that an artwork can just go off and do something and have its own value.

Another artist explains value priorities as an artist, even if the artwork doesn't sell:

> Selling is a weird one because it's like people can obviously appreciate things really much and then they don't want to buy it. It could just be because it's absolutely massive or whatever and they don't want to buy it for that reason but they might really appreciate it. So the value for me is I don't really generally care about selling the work. I know that sounds odd, but I've never sold anything and it's never really bothered me and I'm happy to spend money making new stuff. It's more, I suppose, the feedback and knowing people enjoy it. For me the value is probably more to do with the actual feedback and knowing people enjoy it.

Artists talked about the value of the institution in helping secure publicity, as well as in launching their careers and acting as a catalyst in developing intrinsic and extrinsic value. The exhibition is

> of great value to the graduate artists and to the contemporary art world and culture that there is that profile, that focuses on emerging talent.
> (Assistant director of major printmakers)

Reaching new audiences was also enabled beyond peers and other close stakeholders:

> I think it would get more exposure from people who aren't necessarily that interested in art to start with because I was thinking even people's mums and dads, uncles and aunties and people are coming to see this and they're all possibly not art-minded and all have different views and that can add value because you can make somebody interested in art and also it can be beneficial to you ... because they could know somebody or you could be the first piece of work that they ever invest in. . . . It hits a really wide audience.

CREATION OF INTRINSIC VALUE AND SOCIAL VALUE

One of the buyers at the exhibition, the director of a program called Art in Healthcare, talked about the ability of purchased contemporary art to "quite easily and cost-effectively and quickly transform the healing space to create something... more familiar, less threatening" via the intrinsic values relating to the work. Art in Healthcare is a charity with a vision of "art for every healthcare setting in Scotland" and a mission to use visual art to improve health and well-being. Co-creation occurs here, following purchase of selected artworks:

> We... have an outreach program where we hire artists to take a couple of works from our collection and just go to a local care home or the children's hospital or a hospice and put on a two-hour art workshop and get the people involved so that it's another way to engage with the collector itself and to learn about the artists and to learn about the artwork and the processes and then ... it inspires them to create their own work in response to that piece.
> (Art in Healthcare director)

An artist who had exhibited at a previous year's exhibition and was selected for a major retrospective of the country's work reflected on the value created, indicating its longitudinal worth:

> The value isn't monetary, I don't think, because it's an emotional, more spiritual connection that you have with a piece that can't be quantified and it's so personal to everyone who looks at it.

Co-creation of value was identified through interaction between the various stakeholders, as well as with the artwork and the exhibition setting (Prahalad and Ramswamy 2004; Vargo and Lusch 2014). The assistant director of a major printmaker, which offers a scholarship prize, revealed the importance of co-creating:

> That's the richness of just not knowing how it's going to look, reacting to it . . . you haven't entirely created it, it's come from your relationship with this material, with this process.

The program coordinator of the art institution also reveals how co-creation of value occurs:

> So it's really kind of making it a value to the artist while making it accessible to visitors who don't have the same understanding perhaps, but saying, "Look, this is what's coming out of art school and this is good, this is exciting." . . . [I]t's valuable for people coming in to have just insight or understanding because maybe people who don't look at art at all will find some work very inaccessible and just a sort of slight introduction or a way of how to understand or look at it makes such a difference, and I think that creates value, interpretation.

Utilizing Public Reaction to the Exhibition to Inform Understanding of Contemporary Art

Several visitors viewed the quality of the work and its perceived derivative nature negatively. Underpinning this was the notion that the idea behind the work was being promoted over technical skill and artistry. In fact, our data confirms a conflict between consumers about their perceptions of what constitutes art more generally, from specific notions of it "hanging on a wall" to wider, looser interpretations involving the value of the idea behind it (Danto 2013). An older lawyer explained his expectations and subsequent experiences of the current exhibition:

> My expectations were of more representative art and what I saw wasn't the kind of stuff I would hang and therefore it didn't get me excited, enthused. There was no way I would go to that exhibition and to the people that I know would I say "You've got to go to that," but that's because I've a very narrow set of tastes.

A regular visitor who collected art raised concerns about the quality of some work but thought that this year's exhibition was better than those from previous years, stimulating him to buy an artwork:

> This year was very interesting in the sense that I thought that the quality was overall much higher than I've seen and because of that . . . there was one of the pieces that

I bought, so . . . that was encouraging. It was nice to see something where you go, "Right, I can see there's some real quality going on here," some real craftsmanship, for want of a better word, and I think previously I was left to think the single thing that I felt has been most lacking. . . . [I]t's almost like there's no . . . craft gone into the work so . . . in the four years that they've been studying they haven't learnt how to apply paint in any kind of meaningful way, they haven't learnt how to even display their works . . . in a way that suggests they've even cared about what they're presenting.

For this individual, the technical skill behind the production of the artwork impressed him the most and this then shaped its value (Marshall and Forrest 2011).

For a retired engineer, an unplanned visit resulted in positive impressions of the exhibition, although this person was disinclined to purchase:

It was a very wet day and I was passing . . . so I went in. . . . I really was expecting to see . . . what is in the market. . . . I was overwhelmed by the sheer scale and for me it became far too much after a while and the rain had stopped. I didn't get to see it all but I was impressed by what I saw. I wouldn't say I would have bought very much if I'd had the money.

He considers the role of the market (Fillis 2006) and how people define art. Not all art can be innovative and that realistic expectations relating to the need to sell the work at a lower price can also occur.

Authenticity concerns are also raised, which have an impact on the art's perceived value (Beverland, Lindgreen, and Vink 2008; Beverland and Farrelly 2010):

I think that . . . artists have to live and . . . there are market forces and presumably artists want to sell their work generally. . . . So . . . there is definitely a place for . . . art which is not completely cutting-edge but it's better than buying a reproduction in the shop down the road. So, I think we have to be very careful here about how we define what art is all about. . . . I don't think art has to be cutting-edge because artists have to make a living and not everybody wants . . . some weird thing on their walls.

In stating this, however, he also recalls the work of a performance artist at the exhibition. Even though it was not to his taste, he had clearly thought about and engaged with the performance:

What I remembered about that was thinking . . . that guy has a lot of guts to sit there all day doing that. That's what I remember about it and thinking, "I couldn't do that" and "What's it all about?" . . . but I admired . . . his character and guts for doing it but . . . this is not recommending you fill that place with people like that.

Discussion and Conclusion

Value is communicated to and from each of the parties (exhibition, artists, institution, and public). The artist initially generates value through the creation of the idea underpinning the artwork and then enhances this as it becomes a "product." Consumption of peers' ideas also informs artists' creation of value. The findings indicate elements of sacred or special value being experienced, although lower levels may also be experienced (Belk, Wallendorf, and Sherry 1989). Figure 24.1 shows the constitution of a network of cultural value creation and dissemination. The institution, as organizer, is the gatekeeper and central node of the network. The institution also acts as a facilitator of value by acting as a platform for artists to develop their careers and for marketing the artist and the exhibition itself.

Our visual representation of value creation uncovers collaborative value creation. In understanding how this value is individually or co-created, we acknowledge the personal values of the artist and visualize these on an intrinsic-extrinsic value continuum. These values have implications for market creation, market-following behavior, and engagement with the public as consumers. In addition, we consider the personal value and the cultural value of individual artists' work, alongside that of the exhibition and the venue, as well as wider societal impacts. The exhibition enabled the social construction of cultural value, including its marketing, experiential components, and other consumption components. Validation of the artist occurs through art-making, marketing, and consumption processes relating to cultural value creation and dissemination. Cultural value is created through marketing and consumption discourses relating to the exhibition, the artists, the venue, and stakeholder interactions during and after the visit.

Our work has heightened insight into value creation and consumption from a cocreation perspective, moving beyond the perspective of artist as producer. Value is socially and culturally constructed in direct and indirect ways as part of both everyday and special or sublime consumption practices. Creativity results in cultural value with input from artists, institution, exhibition, venue, the public, and other stakeholders. Our data indicates high levels of engagement and therefore high cultural value, despite some traditionalists expressing lower levels of satisfaction. How we actually value art depends on the interrelationships between market and nonmarket measures. Value has several dimensions: economic, aesthetic, spiritual, social, historical, and symbolic (Throsby 2001; Levy, Venkatesh, and Peñaloza 2014). Value can also lie in the spectacular (Debord 1977; Peñaloza 1998). Hedonic, symbolic, intrinsic, extrinsic, and instrumental aspects of art consumption combine to shape the cultural value of an exhibition. Symbolic value can refer to the acquisition of cultural and symbolic capital (Bourdieu 1983). Other relevant forms of value relate to authenticity, visual consumption (Schroeder 2002), experiential consumption, and the artist's brand. Authenticity, perceived and actual, has an impact on cultural value (e.g., whether an audience believes the exhibited art to be original or derivative). However, it doesn't seem to matter to some consumers if the art is technically inauthentic, so long as it has meaning and value to them (Fillis 2014). We create value through our co-created consumption and production activities. The art consumer can be seen as a producer of both consumption and cultural value. Value is created through our discourses and practices relating to art—for example, in the meanings, interactions, and artifacts of art. Value is produced and consumed in a cultural paradigm of exchange and perceived value. We can visualize a circle of value involving culture, marketing, and consumption where meanings are made (O'Reilly 2005). Our research has demonstrated that art consumption moves beyond Arnould's (2014) functional exchange and uses value to involve cultural knowledge and competency.

When we visit an art exhibition or other arts and cultural site, we exhibit collective belief in the value of artworks through social shaping. The "art for art's sake" versus "art for business's sake" continuum also impacts our interpretations of art's cultural value and its marketing and consumption dimensions. Artists create as expressions of their vision, emotions, and aesthetic ideal, irrespective of whether they are intent on creating a market or following demand for their work. Our findings demonstrate a philosophical clash from a consumer perspective when some voice support for contemporary art that pushes the boundaries of perception while others prefer more traditional ways of conveying art knowledge through "nice" painting and sculpture. The former acts as a counterculture to the latter. So value moves between commercial (extrinsic, profane) and production (intrinsic, sacred) positions. We can visualize a value competency spectrum, dependent on each stakeholder's cultural capital and the sign value from each aesthetic sign perceived by them. Cultural value will vary depending on the availability of the art (unique art versus mass appeal), but Benjamin's (1970) mechanical reproduction thesis tells us that mass appeal also drives cultural value (Fillis 2014).

Our research demonstrates the co-creation of cultural value in practice. Our findings confirm that both cultural value and cultural experience are co-created through stakeholder value and the development of social value around the exhibition. This results in the formation of networks of cultural value development via the exhibition's marketing and consumption processes. Our results demonstrate both the role of the institution and a moving away from it in communicating, sharing, and consuming cultural value. It is important to note the dynamic nature of cultural value and its associated marketing and consumption values.

Limitations of our study include the focus on one particular arts and cultural site, although it can be argued that this site is representative of similar sites elsewhere. The data assessed here is part of a much larger cultural value project involving both quantitative and qualitative research, including a visitor survey, with findings reported elsewhere. It should be possible to replicate our study in other geographical locations in the United Kingdom, Europe, and elsewhere.

Although the site for our investigation was an art institution, there are lessons for the creative and cultural industries more broadly. The principal contributions of this research have been the ability to investigate the nonfinancial, intrinsic factors involved in the marketing and consumption of cultural value, factors that to date have been underresearched. We need to think more about how we value art qualitatively by investigating dimensions such as trust, experience, standards, taste, and artist reputation.

Acknowledgment

The research utilized in this chapter was funded by the Arts and Humanities Research Council (AHRC) Cultural Value Project, grant number AH/L014750/1.

References

Arnould, Eric J. 2014. "Rudiments of a Value Praxeology." *Marketing Theory* 14, no. 1: 129–133. doi.org/10.1177/1470593113500384.

Barrère, Christian, and Walter Santagata. 1999. "Defining Art: From the Brancusi Trial to the Economics of Artistic Semiotic Goods." *International Journal of Arts Management* 1, no. 2: 28–38.

Belfiore, Eleonora. 2002. "Art as a Means of Alleviating Social Exclusion: Does It Really Work? A Critique of Instrumental Cultural Policies and Social Impact Studies in the UK." *International Journal of Cultural Policy* 8, no. 1: 91–106. doi.org/10.1080/102866302900324658.

Belk, Russell W. 1982. "Acquiring, Possessing, and Collecting: Fundamental Processes in Consumer Behavior." In *Marketing Theory: Philosophy of Science Perspectives*, edited by Ronald F. Bush and Shelby D. Hunt, 185–190. Chicago: American Marketing Association.

Belk, Russell W. 1995. "Collecting as Luxury Consumption: Some Effects on Individuals and Households." *Journal of Economic Psychology* 16, no. 1: 477–490. doi.org/10.1016/B978-0-12-374522-4.00004-4.

Belk, Russell W., Melanie Wallendorf, and John F. Sherry Jr. 1989. "The Sacred and the Profane in Consumer Behavior: Theodicy on the Odyssey." *Journal of Consumer Research* 16, no. 1: 1–38. doi.org/10.1086/209191.

Benjamin, Walter. 1970. "The Work of Art in the Age of Mechanical Reproduction." In *Illuminations: Essays and Reflections*, translated by H. Zohn, 219–253. London: Jonathan Cape.

Beverland, Michael B., and Francis J. Farrelly. 2010. "The Quest for Authenticity in Consumption: Consumers' Purposive Choice of Authentic Cues to Shape Experienced Outcomes." *Journal of Consumer Research* 36, no. 5: 838–856. doi.org/10.1086/615047.

Beverland, Michael B., Adam Lindgreen, and Michiel W. Vink. 2008. "Projecting Authenticity Through Advertising: Consumer Judgments of Advertisers' Claims." *Journal of Advertising* 37, no. 1: 5–15. doi.org/10.2753/JOA0091-3367370101.

Bourdieu, Pierre. 1983. "The Forms of Capital." In *The Handbook of Theory and Research for the Sociology of Education*, edited by John G. Richardson, 241–258. New York: Greenwood.

Bourdieu, Pierre. 1993. *The Field of Cultural Production: Essays on Art and Literature*. Edited by Randal Johnson. New York: Columbia University Press.

Boyatzis, Richard E. 1998. *Transforming Qualitative Information: Thematic Analysis and Code Development*. Thousand Oaks, CA: SAGE.

Chen, Yu. 2009. "Possession and Access: Consumer Desires and Value Perceptions Regarding Contemporary Art Collection and Exhibit Visits." *Journal of Consumer Research* 35, no. 6: 925–940. doi.org/10.1086/593699.

Crossick, Geoffrey, and Patrycja Kaszynska. 2014. "Under Construction: Towards a Framework for Cultural Value." *Cultural Trends* 23, no. 2: 120–131. doi.org/10.1080/09548963.2014.897453

Danto, Arthur C. 2013. *What Art Is*. New Haven, CT: Yale University Press.

Debord, Guy. 1977. *Society of the Spectacle*, rev. ed. Detroit: Black & Red.

Desmond, John, Pierre McDonagh, and Stephanie O'Donohoe. 2000. "Counter-Culture and Consumer Society." *Consumption, Markets and Culture* 4, no. 3: 241–279. doi.org/10.1080/10253866.2000.9670358.

Duhaime, Carole, Annamma Joy, and Chris Ross. 1995. "Learning to 'See': A Folk Phenomenology of the Consumption of Contemporary Canadian Art." In *Contemporary Marketing and Consumer Behavior: An Anthropological Source Book*, edited by John F. Sherry Jr., 351–398. Thousand Oaks, CA: SAGE.

Fillis, Ian. 2006. "Art for Art's Sake or Art for Business Sake: An Exploration of Artistic Product Orientation." *Marketing Review* 6, no. 1: 29–40. doi.org/10.1362/146934706776861573.

Fillis, Ian. 2010. "The Tension Between Artistic and Market Orientation in Visual Art." In *Marketing the Arts: A Fresh Approach*, edited by Daragh O'Reilly and Finola Kerrigan, 51–59. London: Routledge.

Fillis, Ian. 2014. "The Impact of Aesthetics on the Celtic Craft Market." *Consumption, Markets and Culture* 17, no. 3: 274–294. doi.org/10.1080/10253866.2013.763603.

Fine, Gary Alan. 2003. "Crafting Authenticity: The Validation of Identity in Self-Taught Art." *Theory and Society* 32, no. 2: 153–180. doi.org/10.1023/A:1023943503531.

Geursen, Gus, and Ruth Rentschler. 2003. "Unraveling Cultural Value." *Journal of Arts Management, Law, and Society* 33, no. 3: 196–210.

Goulding, Christina. 2000. "The Museum Environment and the Visitor Experience." *European Journal of Marketing* 34, nos. 3–4: 261–278. doi.org/10.1108/03090560010311849.

Gummerus, Johanna. 2013. "Value Creation Processes and Value Outcomes in Marketing Theory: Strangers or Siblings?" *Marketing Theory* 13, no. 1: 19–46. doi.org/10.1177/1470593112467267.

Holbrook, Morris B., and Elizabeth C. Hirschman. 1982. "The Experiential Aspects of Consumption: Consumer Fantasies, Feelings, and Fun." *Journal of Consumer Research* 9, no. 2: 132–140. doi.org/10.1086/208906.

Holbrook, Morris B., and Robert B. Zirlin. 1985. "Artistic Creation, Artworks, and Aesthetic Appreciation: Some Philosophical Contributions to Nonprofit Marketing." *Advances in Nonprofit Marketing* 1, no. 1: 1–54.

Jafari, Aliakbar, Babak Taheri, and Dirk vom Lehn. 2013. "Cultural Consumption, Interactive Sociality, and the Museum." *Journal of Marketing Management* 29, nos. 15–16: 1729–1752. doi.org/10.1080/0267257X.2013.811095.

Johnson, Jennifer Wiggins. 2014. "Audience Valuation and Pricing the Performing Arts." In *The Routledge Companion to Arts Marketing*, edited by Daragh O'Reilly, Ruth Rentschler, and Theresa A. Kirchner, 109–118. New York: Routledge.

Joy, Annamma, and John F. Sherry Jr. 2003. "Speaking of Art as Embodied Imagination: A Multisensory Approach to Understanding Aesthetic Experience." *Journal of Consumer Research* 30, no. 2: 259–282. doi.org/10.1086/376802.

Joy, Annamma, and John F. Sherry Jr. 2004. "Framing Considerations in the PRC: Creating Value in the Contemporary Chinese Art Market." *Consumption, Markets and Culture* 7, no. 4: 307–348. doi.org/10.1080/1025386042000316306.

Jyrämä, Annukka. 2002. "Contemporary Art Markets—Structure and Actors: A Study of Art Galleries in Finland, Sweden, France and Great Britain." *International Journal of Arts Management* 4, no. 2: 50–65.

Karababa, Eminegül, and Dannie Kjeldgaard. 2014. "Value in Marketing: Toward Sociocultural Perspectives." *Marketing Theory* 14, no. 1: 119–127. doi.org/10.1177/1470593113500385.

Larsen, Gretchen, Rob Lawson, and Sarah Todd. 2013. "The Symbolic Consumption of Music." In *New Horizons in Arts, Heritage, Nonprofit and Social Marketing*, edited by Roger Bennett, Finola Kerrigan, and Daragh O'Reilly, 89–104. Abingdon, UK: Routledge.

Lash, S. and Urry, J. (1994/2002) *Economies of Sign and Space*. London: Sage.

Levy, Sydney J. 1959. "Symbols for Sale." *Harvard Business Review*, March–April, 117–124.

Lehman, Kim, and Mark Wickham. 2014. "Marketing Orientation and Activities in the Arts-Marketing Context: Introducing a Visual Artists' Marketing Trajectory Model." *Journal of Marketing Management* 30, nos. 7–8: 664–696.

Marshall, Kimball P., and P. J. Forrest. 2011. "A Framework for Identifying Factors That Influence Fine Art Valuations from Artist to Consumers." *Marketing Management Journal* 21, no. 1: 111–123.

McCarthy, Kevin F., Elizabeth H. Ondaatje, Laura Zakaras, and Arthur Brooks. 2001. *Gifts of the Muse: Reframing the Debate About the Benefits of the Arts*. Santa Monica, CA: RAND Corporation.

Mick, David Glen. 1986. "Consumer Research and Semiotics: Exploring the Morphology of Signs, Symbols, and Significance." *Journal of Consumer Research* 13, no. 2: 196–213.

Miniero, Giulia, Andrea Rurale, and Michela Addis. 2014. "Effects of Arousal, Dominance, and Their Interaction on Pleasure in a Cultural Environment." *Psychology and Marketing* 31, no. 8: 628–634.

Minkiewicz, Joanna, Jody Evans, and Kerrie Bridson. 2014. "How Do Consumers Co-create Their Experiences? An Exploration in the Heritage Sector." *Journal of Marketing Management* 30, nos. 1–2: 30–59.

Moulard, Julie Guidry, Dan Hamilton Rice, Carolyn Popp Garrity, and Stephanie M. Mangus. 2014. "Artist Authenticity: How Artists' Passion and Commitment Shape Consumers' Perceptions and Behavioral Intentions Across Genders." *Psychology and Marketing* 31, no. 8: 576–590.

O'Brien, Dave. 2015. "Cultural Value, Measurement and Policy Making." *Arts and Humanities in Higher Education* 14, no. 1: 79–94.

O'Reilly, Daragh. 2005. "Cultural Brands/Branding Cultures." *Journal of Marketing Management* 21, nos. 5–6: 573–588.

Peñaloza, Lisa. 1998. "Just Doing It: A Visual Ethnographic Study of Spectacular Consumption Behavior at Nike Town." *Consumption, Markets and Culture* 2, no. 4: 337–400.

Peñaloza, Lisa, and Alladi Venkatesh. 2006. "Further Evolving the New Dominant Logic of Marketing: From Services to the Social Construction of Markets." *Marketing Theory* 6, no. 3: 299–316.

Pine, B. Joseph, and James H. Gilmore. 2011. *The Experience Economy*, updated ed. Boston: Harvard Business School Press.

Plattner, Stuart. 1998. "A Most Ingenious Paradox: The Market for Contemporary Fine Art." *American Anthropologist* 100, no. 2: 482–493.

Pongsakornrungsilp, Siwarit, and Jonathan E. Schroeder. 2011. "Understanding Value Co-creation in a Co-consuming Brand Community." *Marketing Theory* 11, no. 3: 303–324.

Prahalad, Coimbatore K., and Venkat Ramaswamy. 2004. "Co-creation Experiences: The Next Practice in Value Creation." *Journal of Interactive Marketing* 18, no. 3: 5–14.

Preece, Chloe. 2014. "The Fluidity of Value as a Social Phenomenon in the Visual Arts Market." In *The Routledge Companion to Arts Marketing*, edited by Daragh O'Reilly, Ruth Rentschler, and Theresa A. Kirchner, 344–352. New York: Routledge.

Radbourne, Jennifer, Hilary Glow, and Katya Johanson. 2010. "Measuring the Intrinsic Benefits of Arts Attendance." *Cultural Trends* 19, no. 4: 307–324.

Rodner, Victoria L., and Elaine Thomson. 2013. "The Art Machine: Dynamics of a Value Generating Mechanism for Contemporary Art." *Arts Marketing: An International Journal* 3, no. 1: 58–72.

Roszak, Theodore. 1995. *The Making of a Counter Culture: Reflections on the Technocratic Society and Its Youthful Opposition.* Berkeley: University of California Press.

Schroeder, Jonathan E. 2002. *Visual Consumption.* London: Routledge.

Schroeder, Jonathan E. 2006. "Introduction to the Special Issue on Aesthetics, Images and Vision." *Marketing Theory* 6, no. 1: 5–10.

Schroeder, Jonathan E. 2009. "The Cultural Codes of Branding." *Marketing Theory* 9, no. 1: 123–126.

Shah, Anuj K., and Adam L. Alter. 2014. "Consuming Experiential Categories." *Journal of Consumer Research* 41, no. 4: 965–977.

Slater, Alix, and Kate Armstrong. 2010. "Involvement, Tate, and Me." *Journal of Marketing Management* 26, nos. 7–8: 727–748.

Smith, Terry. 2009. *What Is Contemporary Art?* Chicago: University of Chicago Press.

Throsby, David. 2001. *Economics and Culture.* Cambridge: Cambridge University Press.

Vargo, Stephen L., and Robert F. Lusch. 2014. "Evolving to a New Dominant Logic for Marketing." In *The Service-Dominant Logic of Marketing: Dialog, Debate, and Directions*, edited by Robert F. Lusch and Stephen L. Vargo, 21–46. New York: Routledge.

Veblen, Thorstein. 1973. *The Theory of the Leisure Class.* Boston: Houghton Mifflin.

Venkatesh, Alladi, and Laurie A. Meamber. 2006. "Arts and Aesthetics: Marketing and Cultural Production." *Marketing Theory* 6, no. 1: 11–39.

Venkatesh, Alladi, and Laurie A. Meamber. 2008. "The Aesthetics of Consumption and the Consumer as an Aesthetic Subject." *Consumption, Markets and Culture* 11, no. 1: 45–70.

Venkatesh, Alladi, and Lisa Peñaloza. 2014. "The Value of Value in CCT." *Marketing Theory* 14, no. 1: 135–138.

CHAPTER 25

SERVICESCAPE CONCEPT IN THE CULTURAL AND CREATIVE SECTORS

CHRISTIAN JULMI

INTRODUCTION

THE atmospheric design of the environment not only is a key activity in retail but is also becoming increasingly commonplace in the cultural and creative sectors. This activity seeks to influence the affective experience of those present and to encourage them to behave or feel in a certain way. In this context, the concept of servicescape refers to the spatial setting in which a service process takes place. It includes physical, social, and psychological aspects of the service setting and is perceived holistically by those present (Bitner 1992; Tombs and McColl-Kennedy 2003). Research suggests that customer satisfaction with an organization's servicescape also increases satisfaction with the complete service encounter (Hutton and Richardson 1995; Ezeh and Harris 2007). Through the holistic perception of the servicescape, the concept of servicescape is closely related to or even synonymous with the concept of atmosphere, referred to as atmospherics—a term credited to Kotler (1973)—or store atmosphere (Mari and Poggesi 2013; Hoffman and Turley 2002). The servicescape may thus be defined as "the atmospherics of service" (Nilsson and Ballantyne 2014, 374).

Although there is overlap between servicescapes in retail, on the one hand, and in cultural and creative sectors, on the other, there are also important differences. For example, while the design of a store atmosphere is intended to encourage customers to buy a specific product, art and culture provide experiences that are consumed for their own sake (Miniero, Rurale, and Addis 2014). Accordingly, the design of the servicescape is more about influencing factors such as visitor satisfaction, loyalty, or recommendation intention. Therefore, the study of the servicescape in the cultural and creative sectors should be regarded as a separate research area. Against this background, the aim of this chapter is to give an overview of the theoretical underpinnings and empirical findings from the literature on the servicescape concept in the cultural and creative sectors.

The structure of the chapter follows Schultze and Stabell's (2004) distinction between dualism and duality. Whereas dualism implies either/or thinking and constructs the world in terms of mutually exclusive opposites, duality rests upon both/and thinking, denying dichotomies such as subjective/objective or person/environment (Julmi 2017c). The distinction between dualism and duality is especially useful for systemizing conceptions of such a holistic and vague phenomenon as servicescape, which can be phenomenologically described as being somewhere in between object (or artifact) and subject (or perceiver) (Böhme 1993). Dualistic approaches to servicescape have their roots in environmental psychology and assume that the stimuli of an environment incite the cognitive and emotional state of an individual and subsequently evoke a certain behavior. To study this influence, the environment is usually operationalized into single stimuli whose effects are studied more or less in isolation. In contrast, nondualistic approaches to servicescape take a phenomenological lens and try to study servicescapes more holistically. Such approaches conceptualize servicescapes as something irreducible that lies in between or goes beyond subject and object.

Dualistic Approaches to Servicescape

For dualistic approaches to servicescape, this section summarizes the basic assumptions, considered servicescape dimensions, and empirical findings in the cultural and creative sectors.

Theoretical Underpinnings

Dualistic servicescape research generally follows the stimulus-organism-response (S-O-R) paradigm, which assumes that an external stimulus (S) affects an internal state within an organism (O) leading to a specific behavioral response (R) (Spangenberg, Crowley, and Henderson 1996; Woodworth and Marquis [1908] 1947). Bitner's (1992, 59) generally accepted conceptualization of servicescapes reflects this paradigm. She states that "a variety of objective environmental factors are perceived both by customers and employees and that both groups may respond cognitively, emotionally and physiologically to the environment. Those internal responses to the environment influence in turn the behavior of individual customers and employees in the servicescape." Within this paradigm, servicescape research is most commonly grounded in environmental psychology—namely, in the pleasure-arousal-dominance (P-A-D) emotional state model from Mehrabian and Russell (1974), also known as the M-R model—which was initially adapted to the context of store atmospheres by Donovan and Rossiter (1982). According to this view, the servicescape "evokes emotions, these emotions help determine value, and this value motivates customers to patronize a given choice repeatedly" (Babin and Attaway 2000, 93).

More specifically, the P-A-D model operationalizes the stimuli of an environment into single variables (e.g., color, temperature, light, acoustic, smell, taste) that influence the perceiver's emotional state. The induced emotional state is operationalized into the three independent variables pleasure, arousal, and dominance. Pleasure refers to the extent someone feels good, happy, and/or joyful; arousal relates to the degree someone feels active, stimulated, and/or excited; dominance denotes the extent someone feels in control, influential, and/or important (Ellen and Zhang 2014). Finally, the emotional state leads to a behavioral response. Mehrabian and Russell distinguish between approach- and avoidance-related behavior. Approach behaviors are reflected in a desire to enter or stay in a particular place, whereas avoidance behaviors imply a desire to leave or avoid that place.

Following this model, the independence of the emotional state dimensions of pleasure and arousal could be empirically confirmed to a large extent (Russell 1979, 1980; Donovan and Rossiter 1982; Watson and Tellegen 1985). Russell (1980) develops from this independence the so-called circumplex model of affective states, which uses self-assessments to span the field of affect (or emotional response) across the two dimensions of pleasure (pleasure/displeasure) and arousal (arousal/sleepiness). The four resulting quadrants of the model each represent a specific type of affective response: distress (arousal/displeasure), excitement (arousal/pleasure), relaxation (sleepiness/pleasure), and depression (sleepiness/displeasure). Russell's circumplex model of affective states is the leading model conceptualizing affect in the services literature (Wirtz, Mattila, and Tan 2000).

As Russell and Pratt (1980) show with their circumplex model of affective qualities of the environment, a person's affective state also directly affects how the environment is perceived. The affective quality of an environment is defined as the emotion-provoking quality that people verbally attribute to an environment. The authors show that the description of affective environmental qualities can also be mapped over the two dimensions pleasant/unpleasant and arousing/sleepy. Here, however, it is not the person who is, for example, in a festive or hectic mood, but the environment itself that is perceived as a festive or hectic environment. Figure 25.1 shows the two models at a glance. The left-hand model of Russell represents the structure of affective states (e.g., feeling relaxed, feeling depressed); the right-hand model of Russell and Pratt shows affective qualities attributed to environments (e.g., relaxing places, gloomy places).

Whether dominance is also an independent dimension has not yet been conclusively determined. In some studies, dominance was found to be independent (Russell and Mehrabian 1977; Yalch and Spangenberg 2000; Yani-de-Soriano and Foxall 2006), whereas other studies could not confirm an independence (Russell 1979; Donovan and Rossiter 1982; Donovan et al. 1994). Despite this ambivalence of the dominance dimension, the P-A-D model is often used in the study of the servicescape (Mari and Poggesi 2013). For the cultural and creative sectors, researchers typically assume that

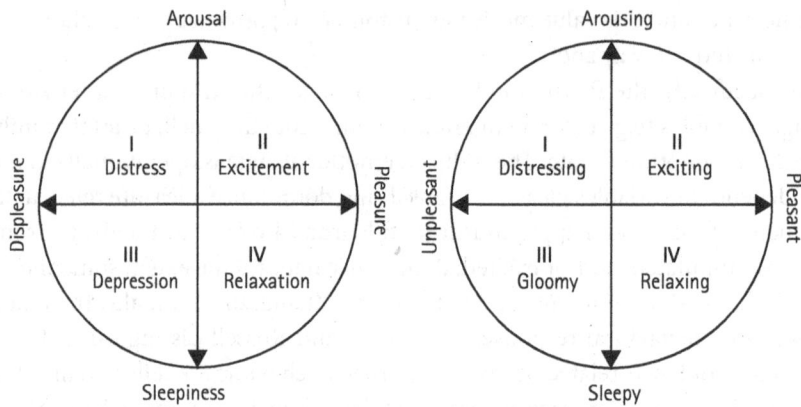

FIGURE 25.1 The circumplex models of affect and affective qualities.

consumption of arts and culture is hedonic and therefore, by definition, pleasure-oriented (Miniero, Rurale, and Addis 2014).

Servicescape Dimensions

Customers and employees face a multiplicity of impressions in the servicescape. In order to capture this multiplicity analytically and to theorize servicescapes in a more systematic manner, researchers have proposed various servicescape models. In his pioneering work, Kotler (1973) broke down the atmospheric quality of an environment into the main sensory channels of sight, sound, scent, and touch. According to Kotler, the main visual dimensions are color, brightness, size, and shapes, the main aural dimensions are volume and pitch, the main olfactory dimensions are scent and freshness, and the main tactile dimensions are softness, smoothness, and temperature. With his concept of atmospherics, Kotler analyzed the influence of exterior architecture, interior design, and window dressing on store sales volume.

Following these ideas, Bitner (1992) developed her seminal servicescape model to typologize the physical surroundings of the service environment and their effects on customers and employees in a more comprehensive manner. She distinguishes between three dimensions of the physical surroundings: (1) ambient conditions, (2) spatial layout and functionality, and (3) signs, symbols, and artifacts. Ambient conditions affect the five senses and thus correspond to Kotler's atmospheric qualities. They encompass background characteristics such as temperature, lighting, noise, music, and scent. Ambient conditions are usually below the level of our complete awareness and may even be totally imperceptible in the case of gases, chemicals, or infrasound. Spatial layout and functionality refer to the arrangement, size, and shape of objects (spatial layout) and their ability to facilitate performance and the accomplishment of goals (functionality). The main elements of this dimension are architectural layout, equipment, and furnishings. Signs, symbols, and artifacts reflect the objects' explicit or implicit signals that communicate about the place to its users. For example, signs on the exterior or interior can be used as labels (e.g., the name of a company), for directional purposes (e.g., an entrance or exit sign), or to communicate rules of behavior (e.g., a No Smoking sign). Similarly, personal artifacts and style of decor (e.g., artworks, presence of certificates, floor coverings, or photographs) communicate symbolic meaning.

Whereas Bitner's (1992) servicescape model focuses on dimensions of the physical environment, scholars have subsequently expanded her model by adding dimensions of the social environment. For example, Bitner (2000) emphasized that the employees and customers themselves shape and influence the environment and are an important part of the perceived servicescape. For the customer component, Brocato, Voorhees, and Baker (2012) empirically identified three subdimensions: similarity (i.e., the extent to which customers perceive other customers as being similar to themselves), physical appearance (i.e., the physical characteristics and overall look of other customers), and suitable behavior (i.e., the extent to which customers perceive other customers as behaving appropriately given the consumption context).

In their social-servicescape model, Tombs and McColl-Kennedy (2003) conceptualized the social density and the displayed emotions of other consumers as key elements of the perceived social environment that have an impact on the perceivers' affective states and their responses. Rosenbaum and Montoya (2007) added place identity—defined as the congruency between a perceiver's self-identity and a place—to the social environment of the servicescape, arguing that a congruent place identity is more likely to encourage an approach behavior. Rosenbaum (2005) complemented Bitner's (1992) perceived physical servicescape with a perceived symbolic servicescape, defined "as signs, symbols, objects and artifacts contained within a consumption setting that possess a common interpretation among consumers belonging to a specific ethnic group" (257). In contrast to the signs and symbols of the physical environment, the signs and symbols of the symbolic servicescape are meant to be interpreted by a specific ethnic group only.

In order to synthesize the disparate servicescape approaches in the literature, Rosenbaum and Massiah (2011) proposed their expanded servicescape model. In addition to Bitner's consideration of physical stimuli, the authors include the environment's social, socially symbolic, and natural stimuli. Social conditions are employees, customers, social density, and displayed emotions of others. The socially symbolic setting consists of "signs, symbols, and artifacts that are laden with socio-collective meanings to influence approach behaviors among groups of customers with a unique ethnic, sub-cultural, or marginalized societal status" (Rosenbaum and Massiah 2011, 478). Lastly, natural stimuli refer to elements of the servicescape that are restorative to human well-being. The authors distinguish between three restorative stimuli: being away, fascination, and compatibility. Being away refers to stimuli that evoke feelings of breaking free to a different place or world. Fascination is reflected in stimuli that capture

Table 25.1. Environmental Dimensions of the Servicescape

Environment	Definition	Elements	Sources
Physical environment			
Ambient conditions	Background characteristics of the environment that affect the five senses and are below the level of our complete awareness	Air quality, noise, music, odor, color schemes, lighting, cleanliness	Kotler 1973; Bitner 1992; Rosenbaum and Montoya 2007; Rosenbaum and Massiah 2011
Spatial layout and functionality	Arrangement, size, and shape of objects (spatial layout) and their ability to facilitate performance and the accomplishment of goals (functionality)	Architectural layout, equipment, furnishings	Bitner 1992; Rosenbaum and Montoya 2007; Rosenbaum and Massiah 2011
Signs, symbols, and artifacts	Object's explicit or implicit signals that communicate about the place to its users	Signage, personal artifacts, style of decor	Bitner 1992; Rosenbaum and Montoya 2007; Rosenbaum and Massiah 2011
Social environment			
Social conditions	Customer and employee elements that are encapsulated in a consumption setting	Social density, privacy, displayed emotions, place identity, similarity, physical appearance, suitable behavior	Tombs and McColl-Kennedy 2003; Rosenbaum and Montoya 2007; Rosenbaum and Massiah 2011; Brocato, Voorhees, and Baker 2012
Socially symbolic setting	Signs, symbols, and artifacts that are laden with socio-collective meanings	Ethnic signs/symbols, Ethnic objects/artifacts	Rosenbaum 2005; Rosenbaum and Massiah 2011
Natural environment	Natural stimuli in customer-environmental behaviors	Being away, fascination, compatibility	Rosenbaum and Massiah 2011

a person's attention. Compatibility evokes feelings of belonging among those present (see also Ong and Yap 2017).

Table 25.1 synthesizes the discussed environmental dimensions of the servicescape.

It should not go unmentioned that scholars also proposed alternative distinctions and/or extensions of the servicescape. For instance, Baker (1987) distinguishes between ambient factors, design factors, and social factors. Further operationalizations can be found in Turley and Milliman (2000); Vilnai-Yavetz, Rafaeli, and Schneider-Yaacov (2005); Grayson and McNeill (2009); Berman and Evans ([1979] 2017); Line, Hanks, and Kim (2018); Line and Hanks (2019); Pizam and Tasci (2019); and Siguaw, Mai, and Wagner (2019).

Empirical Findings from the Literature

There is now a large body of empirical research on the servicescape concept. Most empirical studies examine commercial consumption settings such as hospitality (e.g., restaurants, cafés, bars, wineries), tourism (e.g., hotels, casinos, airports, theme parks), and retail (e.g., stores, shopping malls) (Cortes-Navas and Rojas-Berrio 2018; Pizam and Tasci 2019). However, since "there is no ideal servicescape composition for all industries" (Ezeh and Harris 2007, 63), findings from these areas cannot simply be transferred to the cultural and creative sectors. There have been several empirical studies in this area to date, the most important of which will be summarized below.

With regard to museums, Goulding (2000) has already pointed out the importance of the service encounter experience in museums. She noticed that "the museum product is delivered in a physical environment or site which encompasses the land or building area, shape, lighting, means of orientating the visitor, queues, waiting, crowding, and methods of stimulating interest and engagement" (Goulding 2000, 261). Empirical research suggests that the servicescape in museums does indeed play an important role for visitors. Kottasz (2006) quantitatively explored the experience of visitors to a selection of London museums. She found that the interior (lighting, special effects) and decoration elements (signage accompanying the exhibition displays) had significant effects on the pleasure, arousal, and dominance felt by visitors. Moreover, novelty (an environment that is different and new), complexity (visual richness, ornamentation, the rate at which information is presented), coherence (order, clarity, and unity) and mystery (that which is secret and inexplicable) not only had a significant effect on visitors' affective states but also partially determined the intention to revisit the museum. Bonn et al. (2007) investigated the effect of the servicescape on visitors to four Florida cultural attractions using multiple regression analyses. The authors found that elements such as lighting, color, and signage, combined with design factors such as spaciousness and traffic flow, were much more important than elements such as facility attractiveness, tour guide availability, music, and merchandise quality. According to the authors, this stands in contrast to findings from the retailing sector, where social factors have proven to have a huge impact on the customer's behavior. In their qualitative study, Ardley et al. (2012) explored visitor perceptions of the Magna Carta exhibition in Lincoln Castle, in the United Kingdom. The authors found that the visitors problematized especially three characteristics of the servicescape. First, they complained about the inferior quality of lighting, which made them go through the exhibition much too quickly without being able to engage with the documents. Second, they felt the size of the exhibition was too small for such important documents. Third, they criticized the lack of exhibition signage, which made it difficult for them to navigate to and through the exhibition. From these results, the authors derived measures to improve the investigated servicescape. Recently, Conti et al. (2020) examined the influence of the servicescape of three Italian national art museums on the positive word of mouth of visitors. They define the term museumscape as "the physical space and the general atmosphere experienced by museum visitors during their whole museum visiting experience" (Conti et al. 2020, 4) and

Table 25.2. Summary of Museum Servicescape Variables

Environment	Elements
Physical environment	
Ambient conditions	Color schemes, lighting, flooring, materials selection, sounds, aromas, temperature, special effects, novelty, complexity, coherence, mystery
Spatial layout and functionality	Architectural style, setting of museum, spaciousness, size of the exhibition, positioning of entrance, visitor comfort, visitor flow, audio guides, allocation of space to exhibitions, programs, areas, catering, retail, spatial arrangement of exhibitions, grouping of exhibits, location of ticketing, individual exhibits and displays, individual exhibits and images, display case layouts
Signs, symbols, and artifacts	Exterior decoration and signage, signage accompanying the exhibition displays, interpretative signage and object labels, interactive instruction labels
Social environment	
Social conditions	Appearance of floor staff, availability and perception of floor staff, helpfulness, courtesy and knowledge of floor staff, crowding, interactions with other visitors

Source: Adapted from Forrest 2013.

identified six attributes as particularly relevant for the museum context: (1) ambient conditions, (2) staff behavior (in terms of helpfulness, courtesy, and knowledge), (3) collateral services and facilities (such as audio guides, guides, bars, and restaurants), (4) art gallery quality (in terms of the museum's collection and the architecture), (5) exhibition space aesthetics, and (6) signs and signage. Their quantitative study revealed significant effects of exhibition space, art gallery quality, and staff behavior on visitors' positive word of mouth. In contrast, the remaining three components were not significantly related with visitors' positive word of mouth. Summarizing these museum-related studies and taking into account the museum servicescape variables compiled by Forrest (2013), a number of relevant museum servicescape elements emerge, as shown in Table 25.2. These indicate a neglect of the socially symbolic setting and the natural environment (for their relevance, see Gilmore and Magee 2018).

Another area where the servicescape is being examined is festivals. In this context, Lee et al. (2008, 57) introduced the festivalscape as "the general atmosphere experienced by festival patrons." Several studies use structural equation modeling to investigate consequences of different festivalscape characteristics. In their study of the International Andong Mask Dance Festival, in South Korea, Lee et al. (2008) identified seven dimensions determining the festivalscape: convenience, staff, information, program content, facilities, souvenirs, and food quality. The authors found festival program content to be the most important driver of emotions and patron satisfaction, followed by food quality and facilities. Yoon, Lee, and Lee (2010) conducted a study at the Punggi Ginseng Festival in South Korea. Results showed that the four festivalscape dimensions of program, souvenirs, food, and facilities influence festival value, which in turn contributes to visitors' festival satisfaction and loyalty, whereas the festivalscape dimension of informational service did not prove to have a significant effect. Also in South Korea is the Boryeong Mud Festival, whose festivalscape Lee, Lee, and Choi (2011) have examined. The authors investigated the impact of five dimensions of the festivalscape: festival program, informational services, festival products (souvenirs and food), convenient facilities, and natural environment. Results showed that festival program, convenient facilities, and natural environment influence emotional value (e.g., the festival was perceived as pleasurable), whereas festival program and convenient facilities also influence functional value (e.g., the festival was perceived as affordable). In this way, these dimensions indirectly contributed to festival satisfaction and behavioral intentions. Grappi and Montanari (2011) examined the case of the Festival della Filosofia (Festival of Philosophy) in Italy, focusing on the following dimensions of the festivalscape: program content, staff behavior, locations and atmosphere, information and facilities, hotel and restaurant offerings, and souvenir availability. Apart from the facility dimension, all dimensions showed significant effects on at least one of the three variables of positive emotion, negative emotion, and hedonic value. Overall, the research model showed that the festivalscape has indirect effects on attendees' intention to patronize the festival again. In terms of the food and wine event Friuli Doc in Italy, Mason and Paggiaro (2012) conceptualized the festivalscape as one variable encompassing aspects of fun, comfort, and food. Their study revealed significant direct effects of the festivalscape on satisfaction, which in turn significantly influenced behavioral intention. Choe et al. (2018) explored festivalscape factors at an international wine-and-dine festival in Macau, China. They found that the festivalscape had an overall significant positive effect on perceived value for money, overall satisfaction, and intention to revisit. In an additional exploratory factor analysis, they identified five distinct festivalscape dimensions: quality of the festival venue, cost and wine, festival entertainment and program, logistics, and helpfulness of service staff. For three local and small Italian culinary festivals, Vesci and Botti (2019) found food and beverage quality, staff service, and information to be predictors of attendee attitude toward local festivals and their revisiting intentions. Overall, it is apparent that—despite similar methodological approaches—these studies of festivalscape operationalize the environment quite differently. Nevertheless, it is consistently shown that the festivalscape not only influences the affective state of visitors but also indirectly influence their approach or avoidance behavior.

Researchers have also looked at the servicescape of operas and theaters. In their study on opera-goers at the Palau de les Arts Reina Sofía in Valencia, Spain, Tubillejas-Andrés, Cervera-Taulet, and Calderon Garcia (2021) found that the artscape—defined as "servicescape applications in performing arts" (156)—has a direct impact on loyalty in performing arts attendees. They further showed that the physical dimensions (exterior and interior elements) and the social dimensions (employees' characteristics, attendees' characteristics, employee and attendee interactions, and attendees' interactions) of the artscape have to be considered together. Tubillejas-Andrés, Cervera-Taulet, and

Calderón García (2020) showed with the same sample that the positive (negative) emotional experience of a servicescape was positively (negatively) associated with attendees' behavior in terms of perceived utilitarian and hedonic value, satisfaction, and loyalty.

Regarding theaters, Jobst and Boerner (2015) surprisingly found in their study on theater-goers in twelve German-speaking theaters that the perceived servicescape is of only minor relevance for customer satisfaction (as compared with primary services such as artistic quality). Of the six dimensions considered, only (1) seating and view and (2) other customers' behavior showed significant but weak effects. In contrast, no effects could be detected for (3) ambiance and interior decor, (4) navigation, (5) employees, and (6) catering, cloakroom, and sanitary facilities. However, further research is needed in this context to assess and compare these outcomes in operas and theaters.

Nondualistic Approaches to Servicescape

For nondualistic approaches to servicescape, this section summarizes the basic assumptions, considered servicescape dimensions, and empirical findings in the cultural and creative sectors.

Theoretical Underpinnings

Dualistic research on servicescape assumes that dimensions and/or elements of the environment can be isolated and general patterns can be explored (Bitner 1992). However, regarding the concept of atmosphere, the dichotomous distinction between external stimuli and internal states raises serious problems. As a holistic quality, the atmosphere cannot be cut off either from its perceiver as an external quality (the same environment may evoke different feelings) nor from the environment as an internal quality (the atmosphere is perceived as belonging to a certain environment) (Bille 2015; Julmi 2015, 2017b). As a consequence, different dualistic researchers come to different conclusions regarding whether the atmosphere is an external or internal feature. Whereas some researchers locate the atmosphere within the external environment (Grossbart et al. 1990; Rayburn and Voss 2013; Tombs and McColl-Kennedy 2003; Turley and Milliman 2000; Yani-de-Soriano and Foxall 2006), others treat the atmosphere as a psychological variable (Berman and Evans [1979] 2017; Buckley 1987; Ghosh 1990; Foxall, Goldsmith, and Brown [1994] 1998) and argue that atmospheres "[do not] refer to the objective physical and social factors . . . but to the subjective feelings these factors engender in consumers" (Foxall, Goldsmith, and Brown [1994] 1998, 201). It is therefore not surprising that in dualistic studies on servicescape, atmosphere remains an undertheorized concept and an overused metaphor (Julmi 2017c). Symptomatically, Kotler et al. (2009,

679) begin their section "Service Atmosphere" by remarking that "atmosphere is a major marketing element" but then do not use the term again in the rest of the chapter.

In contrast, the central assumption of nondualistic approaches to servicescape is that the servicescape does not exist independently from the perceiver and is co-constructed by those present. From this view, the holistic atmosphere becomes the central aspect of the servicescape, because "this in-between, by means of which environmental qualities and states are related, is atmosphere" (Böhme 1993, 114). Atmospheres "exceed that from which they emanate"; they "are quasi-autonomous" (Anderson 2009, 80), "quasi-things" (Griffero 2017), or "half-things/entities" (Schmitz 2019, 99). They manifest themselves as in-betweens that bridge subject and object, as a glue that sticks both sides together.

In general, studies such as those of Böhme (2016) and Griffero (2014) have made the concept of atmosphere acceptable in recent years and contributed to its international dissemination in research. These studies originated in the so-called new phenomenology of Hermann Schmitz (Julmi 2017c; Pfister 2019), who is becoming "increasingly familiar to the Anglophone world" (Philippopoulos-Mihalopoulos 2015, 123). Schmitz developed his theory of atmospheres as early as the 1960s (Schmitz 1969) and defines atmosphere as "the unbounded occupation of a surfaceless space in the region of what is experienced as present" (Schmitz 2019, 94). Taking up the thoughts of Schmitz (cf. Kazig 2016), Böhme (1993) defines atmosphere as the sphere of what is experienced as corporeally present in relation to the environment. Similar to Böhme, Anderson (2009, 79) emphasizes the elusiveness and ephemerality of atmospheres: "Atmospheres are perpetually forming and deforming, appearing and disappearing, as bodies enter into relation with one another. They are never finished, static or at rest." This dynamic and temporal character of atmospheres is considered highly relevant in marketing (Hill, Canniford, and Eckhardt 2021; Steadman et al. 2021).

According to nondualistic approaches to servicescape, the stimuli of the environment cannot be cut off from the perceivers' affective states. Hence, the qualities that are of primary relevance are those that serve as a bridge between subject and object on an affective level. Following Schmitz, the affective interplay between person and environment is based on so-called bridging qualities (Schmitz 2019; Schmitz, Müllan, and Slaby 2011). Bridging qualities are present in the surroundings on existing shapes, but at the same time they belong to the perceiver's affective experience. With Schmitz, two kinds of bridging qualities can be distinguished: kinesthetic and synesthetic qualities (cf. Julmi 2016). Bridging qualities correspond to what Böhme calls ecstasies: "things articulate their presence through qualities—conceived as ecstasies" (Böhme 1993, 122).

Kinesthetic qualities are suggestions or omens of motions, which can emanate from executed motions as well as from latent ones. Examples of kinesthetic qualities are a glare, a pointed finger that stabs the person pointed at like a dagger, an eye-stinging smell, the branches of a weeping willow, the rhythm of a piece of music, and the affordance of a doorknob (Gibson 1977).

Another example is the dynamic design of a sports car: even if the car is not moving, its shape corporeally suggests a dynamic motion and therefore is perceived as dynamic (Haverkamp 2013). Kinesthetic qualities are organized through the shape of gestalts.

An artifact like a huge Christmas tree being located immediately behind a small entrance, for example, suggests a motion from the bottom up, which manifests itself in a corresponding movement of one's head (Großheim, Kluck, and Nörenberg 2015). Likewise, the kinesthetic quality of fast music as a suggestion of motion makes people not only move but also drink faster (McElrea and Standing 1992). In their study, Bonnin and Goudey (2012) explicitly stressed the importance of kinesthetic (or kinetic) qualities regarding the perception of store environments. The authors define kinesthetic quality as "the appreciation of the store with regard to the movements and gestures that can be performed during the shopping trip." It is the "configuration of the store, its layout and more broadly its design" that "channel the movements and gestures of shoppers and probably influence the kinetic quality of the store" (Bonnin and Goudey 2012, 637). Another example of a kinesthetic quality is crowdedness, which may emanate from other customers or the physical layout of a store (Ballantine, Parsons, and Comesky 2015).

Synesthetic qualities are qualities that go beyond the allocation to individual genres of perception, such as colors, temperatures, noise, and light. A color is perceived not only as red or brown but also as bright (light) or warm (temperature). Sounds are perceived as heavy, dense, or hard (mass), but also as dark (light), cold (temperature), or fast (velocity). In general, synesthetic characters stand out due to plus qualities such as bright, warm, fast, and loud and minus qualities such as dark, cold, calm, and quiet (and a neutral zone between them). The relevance of synesthetic qualities in the context of atmospheres within marketing research has been highlighted by several researchers (Sharma and Stafford 2000; Joy and Sherry 2003; Biehl-Missal and Saren 2012; Biehl-Missal 2013; Haverkamp 2013). For example, Biehl-Missal and Saren (2012, 173) state: "Because of its synesthetic character, which is informed by different senses, we are able to describe material's warmth or coolness in an atmospheric sense." In terms of store atmospheres, Spence et al. (2014, 481) acknowledge that an "area of growing research interest pertains to the synesthetic (and surprising) correspondences that exist between the senses."

Servicescape Dimensions

Different types of servicescapes can be differentiated analogously to the circumplex models introduced above. In his circumplex model of affective atmospheres, Julmi (2022) differentiates atmospheres on the basis of two dimensions: (1) inviting/repellent atmospheres and (2) narrowing/widening atmospheres. Inviting atmospheres have a pull effect and invite the person present to stay or enter; repellent atmospheres, on the other hand, have a push effect and induce the feeling of wanting to leave an environment or not be there. Narrowing atmospheres have a concentric tendency from the spatial environment to one's own felt presence and emphasize the absolute location of spatially felt "here"; widening atmospheres, in contrast, have an eccentric tendency, directed from one's own sensed presence into the spatial environment, so that one feels detached

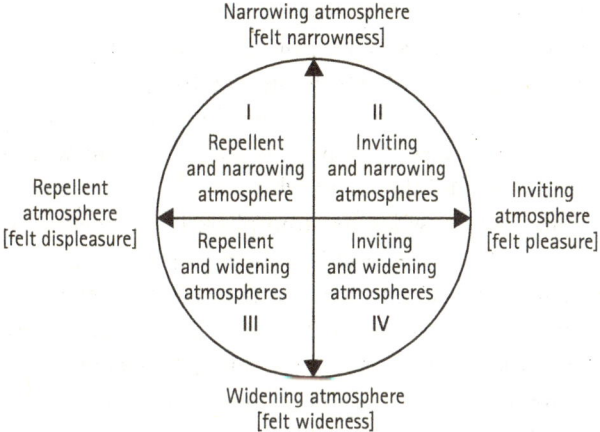

FIGURE 25.2 The circumplex model of affective atmospheres.

Source: Reprinted with permission from Julmi 2017a.

in the wideness from the spatially felt "here." These two dimensions lead to the development of four ideal types of atmospheres relevant to the servicescape: repellent and narrowing atmospheres, inviting and narrowing atmospheres, repellent and widening atmospheres, and inviting and widening atmospheres (see Figure 25.2).

The repellent-narrowing atmosphere has a narrowing effect with concentric character and generates repulsive pressure with connotations of displeasure. Atmospheres that can be assigned to this ideal type are usually associated with an unpleasant tension, which the affected person usually feels at the mercy of. Owing to its concentric character, the environment has a controlling and dominant effect, which is perceived as threatening, oppressive, or intrusive. Often there is no possibility of retreat, which gives the narrowness an additional intensity (e.g., when someone feels trapped in a tightly packed crowd).

The inviting-narrowing atmosphere is characterized by its perceived pleasant activating and stimulating effect. This effect can be based on the presence of others and manifest itself in a pleasant closeness and intimacy between them. The stimulating effect of others is an invitation to seek contact with others and to engage with relish with the possibility of the environment. This possibility does not necessarily presuppose the presence of other people and can also be revealed in the joyful expectation of a visit or a call.

The repellent-widening atmosphere is reflected in its uncomfortable, eccentric character, which points to the wideness of space. The spatial experience is associated with a noticeable and unpleasant expansion. The structuring narrow element is missing, which is why those affected corporeally lose themselves in the wideness of space. This is reflected in the atmosphere of boredom: although there is no danger, we feel uncomfortable in the spatial wideness. Examples of repellent-widening atmospheres are desolate, lost, yearning, dreary, strange, monotonous, Kafkaesque, and bizarre atmospheres.

Inviting-widening atmospheres have an attracting, eccentric character. Their focus is less on closeness and intimacy and more on relaxation and privacy. They invite those present to linger, to spread out, and to recharge their batteries without being affected by disturbances. The affected person feels a balanced relaxation, in which no suggestion for any side is forced with determination. They are in harmony with themselves or are invited atmospherically to find their center by collecting themselves and relaxing. An apt description of an inviting-widening atmosphere is provided by an actor in an article by De Molli (2020, 9), "who reported that being surrounded by unknown, yet calm, people who were behaving in an informal way (e.g. a festival attendee taking a nap in a public park), in a general atmosphere of calm and relaxation, in a fresh and open-air setting, prompted him to behave likewise (e.g. deciding, for example, to take off his shoes and relax in the same space)." Further examples of inviting-widening atmospheres are serene, tolerant, and devotional atmospheres.

Basically, it can be assumed that the servicescape is designed to create inviting atmospheres and avoid repellent atmospheres. For museum/art gallery visits and their desired properties, the distinction between inviting-widening and inviting-narrowing atmospheres corresponds with the two forms of museum and art gallery experience space characteristics contrasted by McIntyre (2009). On the one hand, the experience stands as a "contemplative bath," which can be associated with an inviting and widening atmosphere. In such an atmosphere, those present come to rest, in order to breathe the aura of aesthetic artifacts in a devotional way and to take them in receptively (Rauh 2018). On the other hand, the experience stands as an "entertaining show" that can be described as being affected by an inviting and narrowing atmosphere.

Even though no deterministic assignment is possible, the four ideal types of atmospheres each correspond to certain kinesthetic and synesthetic qualities. Table 25.3 gives an overview of these assignments.

Empirical Findings from the Literature

Since nondualistic approaches to servicescape do not strictly separate the environment from its perceiver, elements of the environment cannot be conceptualized as independent variables. Accordingly, the servicescape is difficult to study using quantitative research methods. Instead, this area is dominated by phenomenological analyses and qualitative studies. Since there are many rich descriptions of atmospheres in cultural sites in the literature, only a selection of a few works on exhibitions and/or tours will be considered below to give a rough impression of the study of atmospheres in the cultural and creative sectors from a nondualistic perspective. There are also, for example, several works on atmospheres in and of urban nightlife (e.g., Oznobikhina 2021; Biehl and Vom Lehn 2022), festivals (e.g., De Molli, Mengis, and van Marrewijk 2020; Alves et al. 2021), and Christmas markets/grottos (e.g., Julmi 2016; Hancock 2020).

For the hall of the *Mona Lisa*, Rauh (2018) demonstrates that the repellent-narrowing atmosphere of the hall prevents visitors from adequately engaging with the artwork: "the

Table 25.3. Ideal Types of Atmospheres and Corresponding Bridging Qualities

Ideal type	Kinesthetic qualities	Synesthetic qualities
Repellent-narrowing atmosphere	Hard, angular, piercing, drilling, pricking, sharp, reinforcing, stressful, intrusive, depressing, oppressive, heavy	Dark, gloomy, black, red, garish, sharp, annoyingly loud, oppressively silent, short-tempered
Inviting-narrowing atmosphere	Open, playful, frisky, sparkish, uplifting, exhilarated, stimulating, excitatory, animate, engaging, charming, elated, light	Radiant, shiny, bright, warm, fresh, cheerful, blazing, sanguine, pastel-colored, well-tempered
Repellent-widening atmosphere	Inert, restless, denying, prohibitive, unbearable, isolating, inaccessible, standoffish, aloof, perfunctory, sketchy, messy	Murky, pale, cool, gray, shabby, dull, characterless, vapid, bizarre, stifling, monotonous, miserable, ill-tempered
Inviting-widening atmospheres	Round, damp, relieving, completive, liberating, remote, sedative, compensative, acquiescent, relieving, cozy	Calm, smooth, lucid, balanced, soft, blue, green, respectful, amicable, thoughtful, value-free, limpid, even-tempered

Source: Adapted from Julmi 2015; Wolf 2018.

hectic atmosphere within the hall of the Mona Lisa does not allow for a contemplative perception of the painting" (Rauh 2018, 48). Here the author suggests that the atmosphere would have to be suitably inviting and widening to allow for a contemplative bath, "to soak up the atmosphere in isolation" (Goulding 2000, 263).

Madsen's (2018) analysis of the blue and octagon-shaped Dome Gallery at Faaborg Museum, Denmark, reveals its inviting and widening atmosphere. The pompous room has been designed predominantly in blue, which synesthetically gives the room the character of calm and as a kinesthetic quality also has something receding, which contributes to the widening effect of the surroundings. The peaceful place invites visitors to linger and soon forget the hustle and bustle of the streets.

Stenslund (2018) investigated the atmosphere of an exhibition entitled "Biography" by the Scandinavian artist duo Elmgreen & Dragset at the National Gallery of Denmark. One section of the show consisted of a long labyrinthine corridor bringing several of the artists' pieces together (e.g., porcelain washbowls, seats of a waiting room, several doors). Although unintentional, the installation has created a hospital atmosphere for many visitors.

Interestingly, several of them have attached this impression to a specific smell, although the smell was not altered curatorially and the artists had not given the corridor any anchoring to a hospital. The perceived smells were described quite differently (e.g., sterility, stuffiness, bad breath, filth, cleanliness, clinic, doctor, rubber, alcohol, cucumber, disinfectants, and death), but all of these were associated with the same atmosphere, as if one were directly taken to a hospital. Moreover, the descriptions of the atmospheres were strongly enriched with synesthetic and kinesthetic qualities: "the unpleasant smell of claustrophobia and powerlessness," "the clean smell of death," "the bright light causing a dark mood," experiencing "silence, sterility, sadness and coldness," "a nasty smell . . . like being punched in the stomach" (Stenslund 2018, 168).

Vaujany et al. (2019) described how tour guides use kinesthetic and synesthetic qualities during tours of collaborative spaces to convey particular atmospheres. The tour guides intertwined their narratives with intentionally designed quasi objects such as light, smell, colors, and textures to contrast the open, colored, casual, and personal (i.e., inviting-narrowing) atmosphere of the collaborative spaces with the closed, gray, serious, and impersonal (i.e., repellent-widening) atmosphere of more traditional work environments.

Finally, the idea that cultural sites such as museums should have an inviting atmosphere is also viewed critically. Biehl-Missal and Vom Lehn (2015, 242) acknowledge that "many art and history museums emphasize the controversial potential of their artifacts and the generally challenging potential of art, which allows for unexpected and unpleasant experiences." They illustrate their critical marketing approach with a variety of empirical examples. For instance, they describe how the installation "Shalechet" (Fallen Leaves) by Menashe Kadishman "filled one of the voids at the Jewish Museum in Berlin with countless small 'screaming' faces made of iron which, via synaesthetic perception, produce a doubly mute situation because of the absence of sound mimetically connotated by open mouths; this produces a solely material echo of the past laments that is as cold and metallic as the iron is for us" (Biehl-Missal and Vom Lehn 2015, 248).

Julmi (2022) similarly analyzed the atmosphere of the monument to the murdered Jews of Europe in Berlin in terms of the circumplex model of atmospheres. Drawing on the study from Steinberg (2014), he described how the architecture triggers feelings among visitors—on the one hand, feelings such as fear, threat, nausea, constriction, and oppression (as repellent and narrowing atmospheres), but on the other hand feelings of loneliness and abandonment (as repellent and widening atmospheres). The steles in particular had an oppressive effect on many visitors as kinesthetic qualities, whereby this effect was enhanced by synesthetic qualities such as heaviness, cold, darkness, and silence. Through their affective concern with the atmosphere of the monument, visitors can thus acquire a vague impression of the hopeless situation of the Jews under the regime of Adolf Hitler and the National Socialists.

Conclusion

The aim of this chapter was to summarize for both dualistic and nondualistic approaches to servicescape the basic assumptions, considered servicescape dimensions, and empirical findings in the cultural and creative sectors. For these approaches, an increasing interest in research can be observed, both in general and in relation to the cultural and creative sectors. As the practical relevance of the servicescape will continue to increase and the existing studies do not yet provide a comprehensive picture of how the servicescape is perceived and co-created by those present, there is still a great need for future research to conduct further studies. On the one hand, this applies to conducting empirical studies in areas of the cultural and creative sectors that have been neglected so far. In the cultural sector, for example, a more in-depth study of artscape in the performing arts would be desirable. In the creative sector, there is an overall lack of empirical evidence on the design and impact of servicescapes (e.g., with regard to co-working spaces). In addition, researchers should pay more attention to servicescapes in virtual spaces, which have been gaining importance, and not only since the COVID-19 pandemic (Amitrano, Russo Spena, and Bifulco 2021). On the other hand, servicescape research in the cultural and creative sectors is highly fragmented. In order to establish this field as a research area of its own, a theoretical and empirical synthesis of the existing literature is needed as well as theoretical approaches that go beyond a mere operationalization of the servicescape.

The overview of servicescape research in the cultural and creative sectors provided here also has practical implications for the design of the servicescape. In general, the findings from the literature gathered here are useful clues for managers as to which elements of the servicescape are particularly suited in which context to elicit a specific effect among those present. It should be noted, however, that the practical relevance of dualistic and nondualistic approaches must be distinguished. Dualistic approaches provide instrumental knowledge about which stimuli can be used to manipulate which experiences and behaviors. In contrast, nondualistic approaches create conceptual knowledge about how atmospheres are (co-)created in a particular setting and how they are perceived holistically. Both refer to two different kinds of knowledge. Whereas instrumental knowledge usually requires "no understanding of the larger context within which that knowledge was developed," conceptual knowledge broadens our understanding and requires "an—at least rudimentary—understanding of the theoretical context in which that knowledge is embedded" (Nicolai and Seidl 2010, 1276). Thus, although dualistic and nondualistic approaches are scientifically incommensurable in that each provides "an alternative view of what constitutes the scientist's relevant universe" (Astley 1985, 498), they are complementary in terms of their practical relevance.

References

Alves, Susana, Maria Di Gabriele, Saverio Carillo, Massimiliano Masullo, and Luigi Maffei. 2021. "Exploring the Soundscape and the Atmosphere of the Gigli Di Nola Cultural Festival in Italy." *Emotion, Space and Society* 41: 100848. https://doi.org/10.1016/j.emospa.2021.100848.

Amitrano, Cristina Caterina, Tiziana Russo Spena, and Francesco Bifulco. 2021. "Augmented Servicescape: Integrating Physical and Digital Reality." In *Digital Transformation in the Cultural Heritage Sector*, edited by Tiziana Russo Spena and Francesco Bifulco, 181–197. Cham: Springer International. https://doi.org/10.1007/978-3-030-63376-9_9.

Anderson, Ben. 2009. "Affective Atmosphere." *Emotion, Space and Society* 2: 77–81. https://doi.org/10.1016/j.emospa.2009.08.005.

Ardley, Barry, Nick Taylor, Emily McLintock, Frankii Martin, and Gavin Leonard. 2012. "Marketing a Memory of the World: Magna Carta and the Experiential Servicescape." *Marketing Intelligence and Planning* 30, no. 6: 653–665. https://doi.org/10.1108/0263450121 1262618.

Astley, W. Graham. 1985. "Administrative Science as Socially Constructed Truth." *Administrative Science Quarterly* 30, no. 4: 497–513. https://doi.org/10.2307/2392694.

Babin, Barry J., and Jill S. Attaway. 2000. "Atmospheric Affect as a Tool for Creating Value and Gaining Share of Customer." *Journal of Business Research* 49, no. 2: 91–99. https://doi.org/10.1016/S0148-2963(99)00011-9.

Baker, Julie. 1987. "The Role of the Environment in Marketing Services: The Consumer Perspective." In *The Services Challenge: Integrating for Competitive Advantage*, edited by John A. Czepiel, Carole Congram, and James Shanahan, 79–89. Chicago: American Marketing Association.

Ballantine, Paul W., Andrew G. Parsons, and Katrina Comesky. 2015. "A Conceptual Model of the Holistic Effects of Atmospheric Cues in Fashion Retailing." *International Journal of Retail and Distribution Management* 43, no. 6: 503–517. https://doi.org/10.1108/IJRDM-02-2014-0015.

Berman, Barry, and Joel R. Evans. (1979) 2017. *Retail Management. A Strategic Approach*. 13th ed. Boston: Pearson.

Biehl, Brigitte, and Dirk Vom Lehn. 2022. "Atmospheres as Dynamic Configurations: The Case of a Museum and a Techno Club." In *The Metamorphosis of Cultural and Creative Organizations: Exploring Change from a Spatial Perspective*, edited by Federica De Molli and Marilena Vecco, 27–39. New York: Routledge. https://doi.org/10.4324/9781003134671-4.

Biehl-Missal, Brigitte. 2013. "The Atmosphere of the Image: An Aesthetic Concept for Visual Analysis." *Consumption Markets and Culture* 16, no. 4: 356–367. https://doi.org/10.1080/10253866.2012.668369.

Biehl-Missal, Brigitte, and Michael Saren. 2012. "Atmospheres of Seduction: A Critique of Aesthetic Marketing Practices." *Journal of Macromarketing* 32, no. 2: 168–180. https://doi.org/10.1177/0276146711433650.

Biehl-Missal, Brigitte, and Dirk Vom Lehn. 2015. "Aesthetics and Atmosphere in Museums: A Critical Marketing Perspective." In *Museum Media*, edited by Michelle Henning, 235–258. Chichester, UK: Wiley-Blackwell. https://doi.org/10.1002/9781118829059.wbihms311.

Bille, Mikkel. 2015. "Hazy Worlds: Atmospheric Ontologies in Denmark." *Anthropological Theory* 15, no. 3: 257–274. https://doi.org/10.1177/1463499614564889.

Bitner, Mary J. 1992. "Servicescapes: The Impact of Physical Surroundings on Customers and Employees." *Journal of Marketing* 56, no. 2: 57–71. https://doi.org/10.1177/002224299205600205.

Bitner, Mary J. 2000. "The Servicescape." In *Handbook of Services Marketing and Management*, edited by Teresa A. Swartz and Dawn Iacobucci, 37–50. Thousand Oaks, CA: Sage.

Böhme, Gernot. 1993. "Atmosphere as the Fundamental Concept of New Aesthetics." *Thesis Eleven* 36, no. 1: 113–126. https://doi.org/10.1177/072551369303600107.

Böhme, Gernot. 2016. *The Aesthetics of Atmospheres*. Milton, UK: Taylor & Francis. https://doi.org/10.4324/9781315538181.

Bonn, Mark A., Sacha M. Joseph-Mathews, Mo Dai, Steve Hayes, and Jenny Cave. 2007. "Heritage/Cultural Attraction Atmospherics: Creating the Right Environment for the Heritage/Cultural Visitor." *Journal of Travel Research* 45, no. 3: 345–354. https://doi.org/10.1177/0047287506295947.

Bonnin, Gaël, and Alain Goudey. 2012. "The Kinetic Quality of Store Design: An Exploration of Its Influence on Shopping Experience." *Journal of Retailing and Consumer Services* 19, no. 6: 637–643. https://doi.org/10.1016/j.jretconser.2012.08.006.

Brocato, E. Deanne, Clay M. Voorhees, and Julie Baker. 2012. "Understanding the Influence of Cues from Other Customers in the Service Experience: A Scale Development and Validation." *Journal of Retailing* 88, no. 3: 384–398. https://doi.org/10.1016/j.jretai.2012.01.006.

Buckley, Patrick G. 1987. "The Internal Atmosphere of a Retail Store." *Advances in Consumer Research* 14, no. 1: 568.

Choe, Jaeyeon, Xinyi Qian, Michael O' Regan, and Matthew H. T. Yap. 2018. "Macau Wine Festivalscape: Attendees' Satisfaction and Behavioural Intentions." *Hospitality and Society* 8, no. 3: 273–295. https://doi.org/10.1386/hosp.8.3.273_7.

Conti, Emanuela, Massimiliano Vesci, Paola Castellani, and Chiara Rossato. 2020. "The Role of the Museumscape on Positive Word of Mouth: Examining Italian Museums." *TQM Journal* (online, July 7, 2020). https://doi.org/10.1108/TQM-12-2019-0306.

Cortes-Navas, Sandra Liliana, and Sandra Rojas-Berrio. 2018. "Servicescape Concept Evolution: Systematic Review of Literature 1995–2017." *Espacios* 39, no. 13: 30.

De Molli, Federica. 2020. "Participatory Interpretation: A Way to Overcome Analytical Challenges in Organizational Aesthetic Research." *Culture and Organization* 41, no. 3: 1–14. https://doi.org/10.1080/14759551.2020.1806839.

De Molli, Federica, Jeanne Mengis, and Alfons van Marrewijk. 2020. "The Aestheticization of Hybrid Space: The Atmosphere of the Locarno Film Festival." *Organization Studies* 41, no. 11: 1491–1512. https://doi.org/10.1177/0170840619867348.

Donovan, Robert J., and John R. Rossiter. 1982. "Store Atmosphere: An Environmental Psychology Approach." *Journal of Retailing* 58, no. 1: 34–57.

Donovan, Robert J., John R. Rossiter, Gilian Marcoolyn, and Andrew Nesdale. 1994. "Store Atmosphere and Purchasing Behavior." *Journal of Retailing* 70, no. 3: 283–294. https://doi.org/10.1016/0022-4359(94)90037-X.

Ellen, Tristan, and Ran Zhang. 2014. "Measuring the Effect of Company Restaurant Servicescape on Patrons' Emotional States and Behavioral Intentions." *Journal of Foodservice Business Research* 17, no. 2: 85–102. https://doi.org/10.1080/15378020.2014.902642.

Ezeh, Chris, and Lloyd C. Harris. 2007. "Servicescape Research: A Review and a Research Agenda." *Marketing Review* 7, no. 1: 60–78. https://doi.org/10.1362/146934707X180677.

Forrest, Regan. 2013. "Museum Atmospherics: The Role of the Exhibition Environment in the Visitor Experience." *Visitor Studies* 16, no. 2: 201–216. https://doi.org/10.1080/10645578.2013.827023.

Foxall, Gordon R., Ronald E. Goldsmith, and Stephen Brown. (1994) 1998. *Consumer Psychology for Marketing*. 2nd ed. London: Thomson.

Ghosh, Avijit. 1990. *Retail Management*. Chicago: Dryden Press.

Gibson, James J. 1977. "The Theory of Affordances." In *Perceiving, Acting, and Knowing: Toward an Ecological Psychology*, edited by Robert Shaw and John Bransford, 67–82. Hillsdale, NJ: Erlbaum.

Gilmore, Audrey, and Roxana Magee. 2018. "Re-Thinking Places: From Dark Heritage Sites to Socially Symbolic Scapes." In *Cultural Heritage*, edited by Adriana Campelo, Laura Reynolds, Adam Lindgreen, and Michael Beverland, 221–234. London: Routledge.

Goulding, Christina. 2000. "The Museum Environment and the Visitor Experience." *European Journal of Marketing* 34, nos. 3–4: 261–278. https://doi.org/10.1108/03090560010311849.

Grappi, Silvia, and Fabrizio Montanari. 2011. "The Role of Social Identification and Hedonism in Affecting Tourist Re-Patronizing Behaviours: The Case of an Italian Festival." *Tourism Management* 32, no. 5: 1128–1140. https://doi.org/10.1016/j.tourman.2010.10.001.

Grayson, Rollo A. S., and Lisa S. McNeill. 2009. "Using Atmospheric Elements in Service Retailing: Understanding the Bar Environment." *Journal of Services Marketing* 23, no. 7: 517–527.

Griffero, Tonino. 2014. *Atmospheres: Aesthetics of Emotional Space*. Farnham, UK: Ashgate.

Griffero, Tonino. 2017. *Quasi-Things: The Paradigm of Atmospheres*. Albany: SUNY Press.

Grossbart, Sanford, Ronald Hampton, B. Rammohan, and Richard S. Lapidus. 1990. "Environmental Dispositions and Customer Response to Store Atmospherics." *Journal of Business Research* 21, no. 3: 225–241. https://doi.org/10.1016/0148-2963(90)90030-H.

Grossheim, Michael, Steffen Kluck, and Henning Nörenberg. 2015. *Kollektive Lebensgefühle. Zur Phänomenologie Von Gemeinschaften*. Rostock: Universität Rostock, Institut für Philosophie.

Hancock, Philip. 2020. "Organisational Magic and the Making of Christmas: On Glamour, Grottos and Enchantment." *Organization* 27, no. 6: 797–816. https://doi.org/10.1177/1350508419867205.

Haverkamp, Michael. 2013. *Synesthetic Design: Handbook for a Multi-Sensory Approach*. Basel: Birkhäuser.

Hill, Tim, Robin Canniford, and Giana M. Eckhardt. 2021. "The Roar of the Crowd: How Interaction Ritual Chains Create Social Atmospheres." *Journal of Marketing* 86, no. 3: 002224292110233. https://doi.org/10.1177/00222429211023355.

Hoffman, K. Douglas, and L. W. Turley. 2002. "Atmospherics, Service Encounters and Consumer Decision Making: An Integrative Perspective." *Journal of Marketing Theory and Practice* 10, no. 3: 33–47.

Hutton, James D., and Lynne D. Richardson. 1995. "Healthscapes: The Role of the Facility and Physical Environment on Consumer Attitudes, Satisfaction, Quality Assessments, and Behaviors." *Health Care Management Review* 20, no. 2: 48–61. https://doi.org/10.1097/00004010-199502020-00008.

Jobst, Johanna, and Sabine Boerner. 2015. "The Impact of Primary Service and Servicescape on Customer Satisfaction in a Leisure Service Setting: An Empirical Investigation Among Theatregoers." *International Journal of Nonprofit and Voluntary Sector Marketing* 20, no. 3: 238–255. https://doi.org/10.1002/nvsm.1522.

Joy, Annamma, and John F. Sherry, JR. 2003. "Speaking of Art as Embodied Imagination: A Multisensory Approach to Understanding Aesthetic Experience." *Journal of Consumer Research* 30, no. 2: 259–282. https://doi.org/10.1086/376802.

Julmi, Christian. 2015. *Atmosphären in Organisationen: Wie Gefühle das Zusammenleben in Organisationen beherrschen*. Bochum, Freiburg: Projektverlag.

Julmi, Christian. 2016. "Conquering New Frontiers in Research on Store Atmospheres: Kinetic and Synesthetic Qualities." *Ambiances: International Journal of Sensory Environment, Architecture and Urban Space* 2. https://doi.org/10.4000/ambiances.723.

Julmi, Christian. 2017a. "Ein Circumplex-Modell der Atmosphären." *Sociologia Internationalis* 55, no. 2: 191–211.

Julmi, Christian. 2017b. *Situations and Atmospheres in Organizations: A (New) Phenomenology of Being-in-the-Organization*. Milan: Mimesis International.

Julmi, Christian. 2017c. "The Concept of Atmosphere in Management and Organization Studies." *Organizational Aesthetics* 6, no. 1: 4–30.

Julmi, Christian. 2022. "Atmosphere in Cultural Organisations: A Circumplex Model of Affective Atmospheres." In *The Metamorphosis of Cultural and Creative Organizations: Exploring Change from a Spatial Perspective*, edited by Federica De Molli and Marilena Vecco, 13–26. New York: Routledge. https://doi.org/10.4324/9781003134671-3.

Kazig, Rainer. 2016. "Presentation of Hermann Schmitz' Paper, 'Atmospheric Spaces.'" *Ambiances: International Journal of Sensory Environment, Architecture and Urban Space* 2. https://doi.org/10.4000/ambiances.709.

Kotler, Philip. 1973. "Atmospherics as a Marketing Tool." *Journal of Retailing* 49, no. 4: 48–64.

Kotler, Philip, Kevin L. Keller, Mairead Brady, Malcolm Goodman, and Torben Hansen. 2009. *Marketing Management*. Harlow, UK: Pearson.

Kottasz, Rita. 2006. "Understanding the Influences of Atmospheric Cues on the Emotional Responses and Behaviours of Museum Visitors." *Journal of Nonprofit and Public Sector Marketing* 16, nos. 1–2: 95–121. https://doi.org/10.1300/J054v16n01_06.

Lee, Jin-Soo, Choong-Ki Lee, and Youngjoon Choi. 2011. "Examining the Role of Emotional and Functional Values in Festival Evaluation." *Journal of Travel Research* 50, no. 6: 685–696. https://doi.org/10.1177/0047287510385465.

Lee, Yong-Ki, Choong-Ki Lee, Seung-Kon Lee, and Barry J. Babin. 2008. "Festivalscapes and Patrons' Emotions, Satisfaction, and Loyalty." *Journal of Business Research* 61, no. 1: 56–64. https://doi.org/10.1016/j.jbusres.2006.05.009.

Line, Nathaniel D., and Lydia Hanks. 2019. "The Social Servicescape: A Multidimensional Operationalization." *Journal of Hospitality and Tourism Research* 43, no. 2: 167–187. https://doi.org/10.1177/1096348018767948.

Line, Nathaniel D., Lydia Hanks, and Woo Gon Kim. 2018. "An Expanded Servicescape Framework as the Driver of Place Attachment and Word of Mouth." *Journal of Hospitality and Tourism Research* 42, no. 3: 476–499. https://doi.org/10.1177/1096348015597035.

Madsen, Tina Anette. 2018. "Walking and Sensing at Faaborg Museum: Atmosphere and Walk-Along Interviews at the Museum." *Nordisk Museologi* 24, no. 2: 124–141. https://doi.org/10.5617/nm.6351.

Mari, Michela, and Sara Poggesi. 2013. "Servicescape Cues and Customer Behavior: A Systematic Literature Review and Research Agenda." *Service Industries Journal* 33, no. 2: 171–199. https://doi.org/10.1080/02642069.2011.613934.

Mason, Michela C., and Adriano Paggiaro. 2012. "Investigating the Role of Festivalscape in Culinary Tourism: The Case of Food and Wine Events." *Tourism Management* 33, no. 6: 1329–1336. https://doi.org/10.1016/j.tourman.2011.12.016.

McElrea, Heather, and Lionel Standing. 1992. "Fast Music Causes Fast Drinking." *Perceptual and Motor Skills* 75, no. 2: 362. doi:10.2466/PMS.75.5.362-362.

McIntyre, Charles. 2009. "Museum and Art Gallery Experience Space Characteristics: An Entertaining Show or a Contemplative Bathe?" *International Journal of Tourism Research* 11, no. 2: 155–170. https://doi.org/10.1002/jtr.717.

Mehrabian, Albert, and James A. Russell. 1974. *An Approach to Environmental Psychology*. Cambridge, MA: MIT Press.

Miniero, Giulia, Andrea Rurale, and Michela Addis. 2014. "Effects of Arousal, Dominance, and Their Interaction on Pleasure in a Cultural Environment." *Psychology and Marketing* 31, no. 8: 628–634. https://doi.org/10.1002/mar.20723.

Nicolai, Alexander T., and David Seidl. 2010. "That's Relevant! Different Forms of Practical Relevance in Management Science." *Organizational Studies* 31, nos. 9–10: 1257–1285. https://doi.org/10.1177/0170840610374401.

Nilsson, Elin, and David Ballantyne. 2014. "Reexamining the Place of Servicescape in Marketing: A Service-Dominant Logic Perspective." *Journal of Services Marketing* 28, no. 5: 374–379. https://doi.org/10.1108/JSM-01-2013-0004.

Ong, Derek Lai Teik, and Wei Xin Yap. 2017. "The Impact of Fitness Center Servicescape on Individual Behavior: The Mediating Role of Emotional Response." *Journal of Global Sport Management* 2, no. 2: 128–142. https://doi.org/10.1080/24704067.2017.1314177.

Oznobikhina, Irina Igorevna. 2021. "What Urban Nightlife Feels Like: Atmospheric Narratives and Public Spaces." In *Transforming Urban Nightlife and Development of Smart Public Places*, edited by Hisham Abusaada, Abeer Elshater, and Dennis Rodwell, 40–53. Hershey, PA: IGI Global. https://doi.org/10.4018/978-1-7998-7004-3.ch004.

Pfister, Dieter. 2019. "The Concept of Atmosphere from a Multidisciplinary Perspective." In *Atmospheric Turn in Culture and Tourism: Place, Design and Process Impacts on Customer Behaviour, Marketing and Branding*, edited by Michael Volgger and Dieter Pfister, 31–43. Bingley, UK: Emerald. https://doi.org/10.1108/S1871-317320190000016007.

Philippopoulos-Mihalopoulos, Andreas. 2015. *Spatial Justice: Body, Lawscape, Atmosphere*. Abingdon, UK: Routledge.

Pizam, Abraham, and Asli D. A. Tasci. 2019. "Experienscape: Expanding the Concept of Servicescape with a Multi-Stakeholder and Multi-Disciplinary Approach." *International Journal of Hospitality Management* 76:25–37. https://doi.org/10.1016/j.ijhm.2018.06.010.

Rauh, Andreas. 2018. *Concerning Astonishing Atmospheres: Aisthesis, Aura, and Atmospheric Portfolio*. Milan: Mimesis International.

Rayburn, Steven W., and Kevin E. Voss. 2013. "A Model of Consumer's Retail Atmosphere Perceptions." *Journal of Retailing and Consumer Services* 20, no. 4: 400–407. https://doi.org/10.1016/j.jretconser.2013.01.012.

Rosenbaum, Mark S. 2005. "The Symbolic Servicescape: Your Kind Is Welcomed Here." *Journal of Consumer Behavior* 4, no. 4: 257–267. https://doi.org/10.1002/cb.9.

Rosenbaum, Mark S., and Carolyn Massiah. 2011. "An Expanded Servicescape Perspective." *Journal of Service Management* 22, no. 4: 471–490. https://doi.org/10.1108/09564231111155088.

Rosenbaum, Mark S., and Detra Y. Montoya. 2007. "Am I Welcome Here? Exploring How Ethnic Consumers Assess Their Place Identity." *Journal of Business Research* 60, no. 3: 206–214. https://doi.org/10.1016/j.jbusres.2006.09.026.

Russell, James A. 1979. "Affective Space Is Bipolar." *Journal of Personality and Social Psychology* 37, no. 3: 345–356.

Russell, James A. 1980. "A Circumplex Model of Affect." *Journal of Personality and Social Psychology* 39, no. 6: 1161–1178.

Russell, James A., and Albert Mehrabian. 1977. "Evidence for a Three Factor Theory of Emotions." *Journal of Research in Personality* 11, no. 3: 273–294.

Russell, James A., and Geraldine Pratt. 1980. "A Description of the Affective Quality Attributed to Environments." *Journal of Personality and Social Psychology* 38, no. 2: 311–322.

Schmitz, Hermann. 1969. *System Der Philosophie, Bd. III: Der Raum, 2. Teil: Der Gefühlsraum*. Bonn: Bouvier Verlag.

Schmitz, Hermann. 2019. *New Phenomenology: A Brief Introduction*. Milan: Mimesis International.

Schmitz, Hermann, Rudolf O. Müllan, and Jan Slaby. 2011. "Emotions Outside the Box: The New Phenomenology of Feeling and Corporeality." *Phenomenology and the Cognitive Sciences* 10, no. 2: 241–259. https://doi.org/10.1007/s11097-011-9195-1.

Schultze, Ulrike, and Charles Stabell. 2004. "Knowing What You Don't Know? Discourses and Contradictions in Knowledge Management Research." *Journal of Management Studies* 4, no. 4: 549–573. https://doi.org/10.1111/j.1467-6486.2004.00444.x.

Sharma, Arun, and Thomas F. Stafford. 2000. "The Effect of Retail Atmospherics on Customers' Perceptions of Salespeople and Customer Persuasion: An Empirical Investigation." *Journal of Business Research* 49, no. 2: 183–191.

Siguaw, Judy A., Enping Mai, and Judy A. Wagner. 2019. "Expanding Servicescape Dimensions with Safety: An Exploratory Study." *Services Marketing Quarterly* 40, no. 2: 123–140. https://doi.org/10.1080/15332969.2019.1592860.

Spangenberg, Eric R., Ayn E. Crowley, and Pamela W. Henderson. 1996. "Improving the Store Environment: Do Olfactory Cues Affect Evaluations and Behaviors?" *Journal of Marketing* 60, no. 2: 67–80.

Spence, Charles, Nancy M. Puccinelli, Dhruv Grewal, and Anne L. Roggeveen. 2014. "Store Atmospherics: A Multisensory Perspective." *Psychology and Marketing* 31, no. 7: 472–488.

Steadman, Chloe, Gareth Roberts, Dominic Medway, Steve Millington, and Louise Platt. 2021. "(Re)Thinking Place Atmospheres in Marketing Theory." *Marketing Theory* 21, no. 1: 135–154. https://doi.org/10.1177/1470593120920344.

Steinberg, Katharina. 2014. *Das Denkmal für die ermordeten Juden Europas und seine Wirkung auf die Besucher*. Berlin: Humboldt Universität zu Berlin.

Stenslund, Anette. 2018. "The Harsh Smell of Scentless Art: On the Synaesthetic Gesture of Hospital Atmosphere." In *Exploring Atmospheres Ethnographically*, edited by Sara A. Schroer and Susanne B. Schmitt, 153–171. London: Routledge. https://doi.org/10.4324/9781315581613-11

Tombs, Alastair, and Janet R. McColl-Kennedy. 2003. "Social-Servicescape Conceptual Model." *Marketing Theory* 3, no. 4: 447–475. https://doi.org/10.1177/1470593103040785.

Tubillejas-Andrés, Berta, Amparo Cervera-Taulet, and Haydee Calderón García. 2020. "How Emotional Response Mediates Servicescape Impact on Post Consumption Outcomes: An Application to Opera Events." *Tourism Management Perspectives* 34:100660. https://doi.org/10.1016/j.tmp.2020.100660.

Tubillejas-Andrés, Berta, Amparo Cervera-Taulet, and Haydee Calderon Garcia. 2021. "Assessing Formative Artscape to Predict Opera Attendees' Loyalty." *European Business Review* 33: 154–179. https://doi.org/10.1108/EBR-10-2019-0273.

Turley, L. W., and Ronald E. Milliman. 2000. "Atmospheric Effects on Shopping Behavior: A Review of the Experimental Evidence." *Journal of Business Research* 49, no. 2: 193–211. https://doi.org/10.1016/S0148-2963(99)00010-7.

Vaujany, François-Xavier de, Aurore Dandoy, Albane Grandazzi, and Stéphanie Faure. 2019. "Experiencing a New Place as an Atmosphere: A Focus on Tours of Collaborative Spaces." *Scandinavian Journal of Management* 35, no. 2: 101030. https://doi.org/10.1016/j.scaman.2018.08.001.

Vesci, Massimiliano, and Antonio Botti. 2019. "Festival Quality, Theory of Planned Behavior and Revisiting Intention: Evidence from Local and Small Italian Culinary Festivals." *Journal of Hospitality and Tourism Research* 38:5–15. https://doi.org/10.1016/j.jhtm.2018.10.003.

Vilnai-Yavetz, Iris, Anat Rafaeli, and Caryn Schneider-Yaacov. 2005. "Instrumentality, Aesthetics and Symbolism of Office Design." *Environment and Behavior* 37, no. 4: 533–551. https://doi.org/10.1177/0013916504270695.

Watson, David, and Auke Tellegen. 1985. "Toward a Consensual Structure of Mood." *Psychological Bulletin* 98, no. 2: 219–235.

Wirtz, Jochen, Anna S. Mattila, and Rachel L. P. Tan. 2000. "The Moderating Role of Target-Arousal on the Impact of Affect on Satisfaction: An Examination in the Context of Service Experiences." *Journal of Retailing* 76, no. 3: 347–365. https://doi.org/10.1016/S0022-4359(00)00031-2.

Wolf, Barbara. 2018. "Atmosphären als sozialisierende Einflussgröße." In *Stimmungen und Atmosphären: Zur Affektivität des Sozialen*, edited by Larissa Pfaller and Basil Wiesse, 169–196. Wiesbaden: Springer. https://doi.org/10.1007/978-3-658-18439-1_8.

Woodworth, Robert S., and Donald G. Marquis. (1908) 1947. *Psychology*. 5th ed. New York: Henry Holt.

Yalch, Richard F., and Eric R. Spangenberg. 2000. "The Effects of Music in a Retail Setting on Real and Perceived Shopping Times." *Journal of Business Research* 49, no. 2: 139–147. https://doi.org/10.1016/S0148-2963(99)00003-X.

Yani-de-Soriano, M. Mirella, and Gordon R. Foxall. 2006. "The Emotional Power of Place: The Fall and Rise of Dominance in Retail Research." *Journal of Retailing and Consumer Services* 13, no. 6: 403–419. https://doi.org/10.1016/j.jretconser.2006.02.007.

Yoon, Yoo-Shik, Jin-Soo Lee, and Choong-Ki Lee. 2010. "Measuring Festival Quality and Value Affecting Visitors' Satisfaction and Loyalty Using a Structural Approach." *International Journal of Hospitality Management* 29, no. 2: 335–342. https://doi.org/10.1016/j.ijhm.2009.10.002.

PART VII
FINANCING AND FUNDRAISING FOR ARTS AND CULTURAL ORGANIZATIONS

PART VII

CHAPTER 26

AN INTERNATIONAL PERSPECTIVE ON ARTS AND CULTURAL FUNDING

Private, Public, and Hybrid Models

YI LIN AND HUIHUI LUO

INTRODUCTION

RESEARCH on the funding structures of arts and cultural organizations is normally explored in two different aspects: in terms of cultural policies, at the macro level, and in terms of financial data, at the micro level.

At the macro level, different funding structures reflect different market environments, which in turn result from different cultural policies. Milton C. Cummings and Richard S. Katz (1987, 18) proposed three types of arts and cultural policies that accord with the historical origins of the European governance system. The first type is the direct intervention model, represented by France and Austria, in which artists and arts organizations are directly overseen and subsided by the government's cultural department. The second type is the artistic autonomy and depoliticization model, represented by the United Kingdom and the Netherlands. In this model an arts fund is governed and managed by an arts council, and the government can only decide how much money to give, not to whom. The role of the government is to ensure that artists or arts organizations receive sufficient funds to build their capabilities, rather than ultimately develop a dependence on state funding. The third type is a hybrid of the other two, with Italy and Germany as the representatives. In this model there are both ministries of culture and art-related funds and associations.

Another art policy model in the Western world is the US model of assistance and guidance. The US government's support for art has two facets: direct support from the National Endowment for the Arts and other public funding at the state and local levels, and indirect support through tax incentives. In Asia, Japan follows the American model, while China draws from European models. This chapter takes an international perspective and will mainly compare and contrast the Chinese example with the US example.

Given the various art and cultural policy models just described, it is no surprise that the funding structure for art and cultural organizations varies around the world. At the micro level, from the perspective of accounting and finance, funding structure is the proportion of funds received through each funding channel, such as government funding, self-derived income, and private sector funding (including individual donors, corporation sponsorship, and private foundations) (Harsell 2013). Given the differences in cultural policies between countries, the relative size of each funding source for arts organizations accordingly differs. For example, while organizations in the United States rely more on funding from the private sector, organizations in Britain and other European countries normally rely heavily on government funds (Kim and Van Ryzin 2013; Mahieu 2017; Alexander 2018; Luccasen and Thomas 2020; Poling 2021). However, no matter how arts organizations get funding, governments, corporations, and the general public are the three main sources.

This chapter argues that funding structure should not be regarded simply as the proportion of funds provided by each funding source, nor should the formation of capital structure be simply attributed to market environmental factors such as external cultural policies. The essence of the funding structure is actually an indicator of the interrelationship of the influential driving forces behind arts and cultural organizations. From March and Simon's research (1993) on different motivations of organizations to Moeran and Pederson's research (2011) on value negotiation, there has been a great deal of discussion in academia about how to understand organizations' justifications of their behavior in an environment of multiple and possibly contradictory logics.

The aim of this chapter is to identify a model for the financing mechanism that could provide insight into these kinds of interrelationships, and which may inspire arts managers to realize the self-directed financing ability of arts and cultural organizations. After a brief overview of how government, corporations, and the general public serve as the three main external funding sources, this chapter raises the question of what makes each willing to fund the arts. By exploring Boltanski and Thévenot's (2006) theory of the six "orders of worth" or "worlds" of justification that are drawn upon by social actors during disputes, we provide a critical elaboration of these six worlds and define five forces—academic force, market force, innovation force, reputation force, and institutionalization force—in order to examine the above questions. Exploring why different funders support arts organizations is actually about the driving forces behind the funders' behavior—in other words, the funders' values and their "value order worlds" (to use Boltanski and Thévenot's terminology). Only when funders feel that it is beneficial to fund arts and cultural organizations according to their own value order world will they actually fund them. Therefore, it is necessary not only to understand funding structure from the perspective of economics and accounting but also to examine the tensions behind the forces driving funders.

The chapter then outlines how a financing mechanism is constructed by linking the driving system, the operation system, and the external environment, and it describes the collisions, interactions, and coordination that occur within the system as a whole. It concludes with a reflection on how arts organizations could change in order to achieve sustainable, self-directed funding, and then suggests some potential areas for future research.

Three Main External Funding Sponsors for Arts and Cultural Organizations

As we mentioned above, government, corporations, and the general public are the three main funding sources for arts and cultural organizations, since the money, whether as public funding, corporate sponsorship, foundation support, individual giving, or consumption behavior, comes from one of those three sources.

Government

There is an ongoing debate about whether the government should fund the arts. Brooks (2001) found that variables like political opinions, gender, income, previous donations to the arts, and geographic location all influence public attitudes toward government funding of the arts. For example, in the United States, Democrats typically support government funding for the arts, while Republicans oppose it (Brooks 2003). However, no matter whether people take an elitist perspective that the arts should be funded for their artistic and aesthetic value or a populist perspective that arts should be funded as long as they benefit the public, the arts seem to have every right to be subsidized and funded by the government (Bell 1992).

With the rise of the market economy, art has become a part of the cultural industry, which not only makes profits from commercial operations but also drives regional economies as tourist destinations (Jolliffe and Cave 2012; Franklin 2018), and government support for the arts is seen as a way to stimulate the cultural industry. Such support is also seen as a way to improve the popularity of art, enhance people's sense of responsibility, improve the creativity and diversity of arts, ensure equality and accessibility, and help people feel more integrated with the local community (Martell 2004; Harsell 2013).

However, the stability of public funding is uncertain due to its close relationship with laws, policies, and regulations (Martell 2004; Harvie 2015). For example, in the United Kingdom, arts funding was reduced after the 2010 general election. The government not only reduced the number of recipients but also reduced the total amount of funding. Some local governments have cut funding for the arts entirely. This forced many arts organizations to close, or come very close to closing (Harvie 2015). With the disappearance of these arts organizations, there would also be harm to artistic innovation and employment (Harvie 2015). Another concern with government funding is the independence of the arts. Edward Banfield once argued that it is political forces rather than economic forces that interfere with artistic freedom (Banfield 1984).

Corporations

Corporations that fund the arts usually have specific purposes for doing so. For example, they may expect to improve their own image and reputation through sponsorship or donation (Preece 2015). Arts organizations are increasingly coming under pressure from corporate donations, which no longer are just charitable acts but also become investments, as in the concept of "venture philanthropy" (Harrow, Palmer, and Bogdanova 2006; Grossman, Appleby, and Reimers 2013; Merchant 2015; Esparza 2019; Avci 2021). Cobb (2002) explained that a foundation who adopts "philanthropic venture capital" aims at funding nonprofit organizations under the condition of avoiding budget increases and capital loses. One possible way of conducting venture philanthropy is for a foundation to lend funds or lease assets to other nonprofit organizations or socially responsible for-profit enterprises, and then those organizations refund the proceeds and principal to the foundation (Cobb 2002). Instead of providing sustaining funding to nonprofit organizations, venture philanthropists tend to help those organizations grow larger, which may bring them new opportunities to access long-term funding streams (Grossman, Appleby, and Reimers 2013). Venture philanthropy is gradually gaining popularity around the world, appearing in North America in the 1990s, spreading into Europe in the 2000s, and getting a foothold in Asia in the 2010s (Merchant 2015).

However, the abuse of private funding can cause serious problems. For example, it may lead to a situation in which financial elites decide the objects of funding and product creation, or it may cause a situation of inequality in which large arts organizations benefit more, since private funders may tend to choose conservative and relatively safe institutions (Harvie 2015). In the United Kingdom, for example, the competitive need for private charitable donations in the theater industry has aggravated elitism, urbanism, and the imbalances of industrial structure (Harvie 2015).

The Public in General

Individual donations, crowdfunding, ticket sales, and product consumption are the main ways in which the general public normally gives its financial support to arts and cultural organizations. Individual donations can reflect the degree of social support for the arts. People's arts-related donation behavior could be affected by personal factors like gender, individuals' intrinsic motivations, interest in arts and culture, social responsibility, household income, personal taste, and sense of honor (Barnes 2011; Ki and Oh 2018), or by extrinsic factors such as the quality of arts activities, tax incentive policies, tax mechanisms, monetary and social rewards, ecological context, organizational identity, and social network ties (Vesterlund 2006; Ressler, Paxton, and Velasco 2020; Abínzano, López-Arceiz, and Zabaleta 2022).

The literature has examined the relationships between different funding sources (Payne 1998, 2001; Kim and Van Ryzin 2013), laying a foundation for further study of funding structure and its mechanisms. In this literature, researchers seemed to hold two assumptions, consciously or unconsciously: that a single funding source's effect on organizational performance is observable and measurable, and that the relationship between public funding and private funding is in a great state of tension, with conflicting values.

However, this chapter takes the perspective of system theory and argues that an organization's success depends on the overall funding structure of the organization, which means that the observable and measurable result of an organization is actually a result of the joint action of different funding sources. In the overall funding structure, different funding sources may have a range of relationships with each other, not only conflicting but also coordinating and facilitating. This will be discussed in later sections.

Funding Structure of Arts and Cultural Organizations

In terms of economic and accounting concepts, the funding structure is simply the proportion of each funding source to the total income that appears on the balance heet. Take the organizations in Figure 26.1 as examples.

As Figure 26.1 shows, organizations' funding structures can vary. There are purely government-funded arts organizations, such as arts organizations at the national and provincial levels in most European countries and China. There are also purely privately funded arts organizations, such as the Getty Museum and the Pola Museum of Art. Most museums adopt a hybrid funding structure, obtaining income from government, corporations, and the public.

However, a funding structure is not just simple proportions of funding sources; more importantly, it is a final result or a certain state that is formed by different conflicting or coordinating logics of value assessment that are behind or represented by different funding sources. Research has been done to explore different funders' judgment and evaluation criteria regarding funding decisions. For example, Preece (2015) interviewed fifty-two newly formed arts organizations and found that while governmental, the funding, and foundations value arts organizations' mission, vision, and institutionalization, corporations pay more attention to organizational structure and management capability.

From the perspective of practical sociology, Boltanski and Thévenot (2006) put forward a theory of six "worlds of value order" in their book *On Justification: Economies*

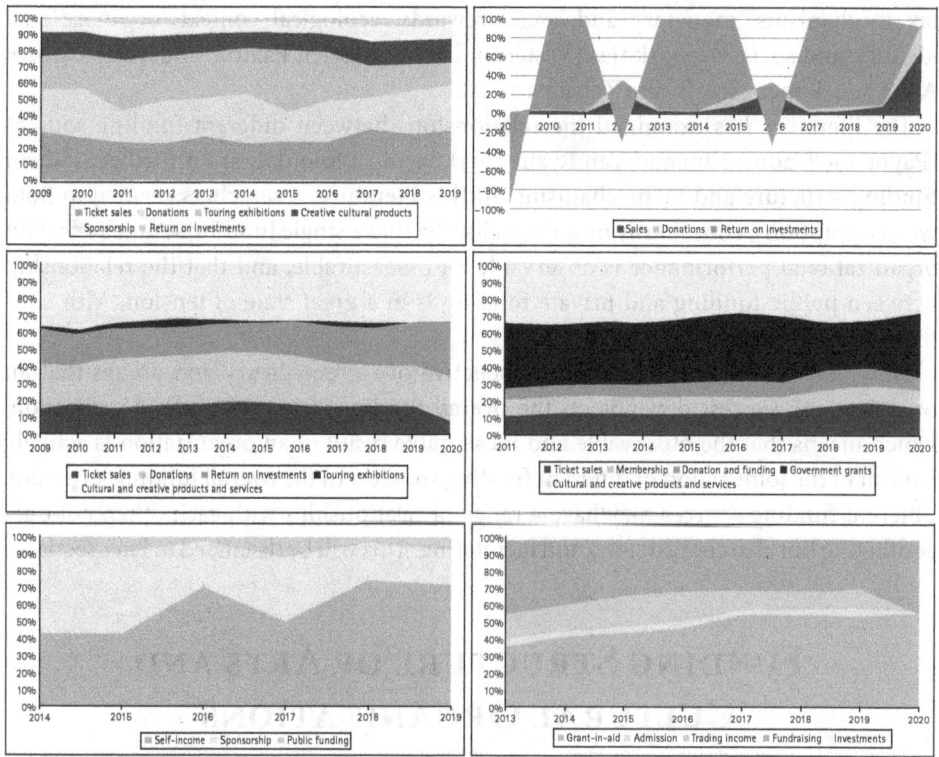

FIGURE 26.1 Various types of funding for arts and cultural organizations.
Source: Annual reports of the Guggenheim Museum, the Museum of Modern Art, the Metropolitan Museum of Art, the Getty Museum, the Today Art Museum, and the British Museum.

of Worth. They believe that people's differences in real life may be conflicts between the values in these different worlds. The values in each of these six worlds are different, and so are the value evaluation criteria (see Table 26.1).

A critical elaboration of Boltanski and Thévenot's (2006) theory of the six "orders of worth" or "worlds of value order" allows us to identify, define, and categorize the value assessment criteria behind an arts organization's overall funding structure and allows us to isolate the reasons for or against the idea of giving financial support to arts organizations common to each of the three types of funder (government, corporations, and the public). The six orders of worlds can be juxtaposed with five forces, including the academic force, market force, innovation force, force of credibility (reputation force), and institutionalization force, to create a new model detailing the driving forces behind attracting financial capital for the arts and culture from government, corporations, and the public.

When it comes to the field of arts and culture, the world of industry might not be seen as an independent world, as it overlaps with all five other value order worlds. For example, a dance group or a play production company collaborates with or sells products to a theater company. The production efficiency and quality of the production are directly linked to market sales, public reputation, and peer evaluation. Therefore,

Table 26.1. The Value and Criteria for Evaluating Value in the Six Worlds

Six common value order worlds	Value	Value evaluation
Market world	Competition, interest, consumers' choices	Price
Civic world	Equality, social benefits, social participation	Voting, laws, rights
Domestic world	Responsibility, convention, collective credit	Responsibilities
Inspired world	Inspiration, creativity	Rarity, uniqueness
World of fame	Public opinion	Public relations, public recognition
Industrial world	Production efficiency, planning process	Functionality

Table 26.2. The Linkage between Five Driving Forces and Five Common Value Order Worlds

Five common value order worlds	Value	Value evaluation	Five driving forces behind funding sources
Market world	Competition, interest, consumers' choices	Price	Market force: the power of market capability
Civic world	Equality, social benefits, social participation	Voting, laws, rights	Academic force: the power of academic ability
Domestic world	Responsibility, convention, collective credit	Responsibilities	Institutionalization force: the power of institutionalization
Inspired world	Inspiration, creativity	Rarity, uniqueness	Innovation force: the power of creativity
World of fame	Public opinion	Public relations, public recognition	Reputation force: the power of credibility

the exploration of the common value order world behind the funders does not include the world of industry. The five driving powers behind funding sources could be listed as in Table 26.2.

In this perspective, exploring the reasons different sponsors fund arts organizations is actually a research question that involves exploring the funders' values and their value order world. Only when funders feel that it is valuable to fund arts and cultural

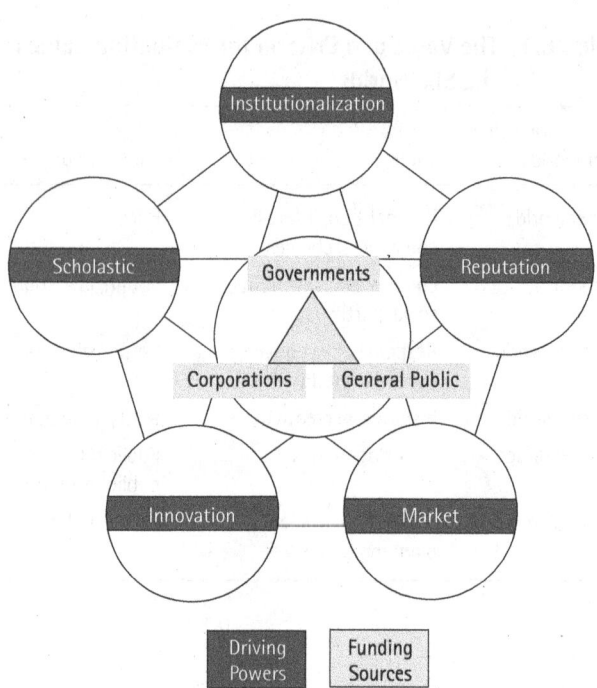

FIGURE 26.2 The model of funding structure.

organizations in their own value order world will they actually fund them. Therefore, it is necessary to understand funding structure not only from the perspective of economics and accounting but also in terms of the tensions behind the forces driving funders. The whole funding structure of arts organization could be presented as in Figure 26.2.

Reputation Force (The Power of Credibility)

Corresponding to the world of fame, where the highest value is prestige or honor given by others and public opinion becomes the highest standard of evaluation, the reputation force, which could also be called the power of credibility, refers to the quality of being trusted; it is constructed by public perceptions.

Trust and reputation are often not clearly separated. Trust is the core component in the relationship between organizations and their stakeholders and between organizations and the public. The higher the trust in an organization or its information, the more credible the communications from that organization are considered to be. Scholars generally believe that credibility is a multidimensional perceptual structure. As Jackob (2008) pointed out, public reliability is a perceived state—that is, the result of the attribution process. In this process, the information receiver forms a judgment regarding its source, so as to evaluate information's credibility. Bigné, Chumpitaz, and Curás (2010) regard credibility as trustworthiness and expertise; similarly, Fombrun (1996) regards credibility as trustworthiness and expertise and found that the audience's perception of organizational credibility can enhance their perception of the brand as well as their consumption intention. Mahieu (2017) found that representativeness and international renown change the nature of public support for visual art creation. These researchers laid a foundation for understanding how the reputation force, which is closely related to public perception of credibility, could influence support for public funding of arts organizations at both the individual and national levels.

Much research has shown that public donations and government funding are closely related to the credibility and trust of arts organizations (Roberson 2015; Cascino, Correia, and Tamayo 2019; Luccasen and Thomas 2020). For example, an art museum's credibility depends not just on its collections, exhibitions, and education programs but also the credibility of the museum's funding sources. Funding sources can impact museum exhibition formats and contents (Alexander 1996), and museums may plan exhibitions that fit a funder's preferences (Bradburne 2010). Whether funds can be used as the donor intends is the most important thing for donors. Research on credibility or trust-building in other fields (Chan 2007; Moore 2018; Yan, Wang, and Wu 2020) suggests that openness and transparency regarding donated funds could be one of the standards used to measure an arts organization's credibility.

Innovation Force (The Power of Creativity)

The innovation force uses the same value evaluation criteria as the inspired world, which thinks highly of creativity. This need not be limited to artistic creativity; it may include, among other things, programming, product development, and approaches to fundraising. Exhibitions and educational programs are the core competitive strength for museums to differentiate themselves; therefore, unique museum features or innovative community or family projects can give them an advantage when competing for limited funds in the market. The development of cultural and creative products is a common embodiment of creativity in museums. The British Museum, the Forbidden City in China, and the Museum of Modern Art in New York all perform well in this field. The construction of an online sales platform also helped arts organizations reach a wider range of consumer groups. Private art galleries in Suzhou and Shanghai have innovated their marketing methods and adopted a ticket linkage to help each other attract visitors.

The emergence of arts crowdfunding has become an innovative fundraising method in the arts field and established a new operational mode of solidarity, collaboration, and sharing. Crowdfunding refers to organizations receiving funds from a relatively large number of individuals. It is a collective effort of consumers, with each providing a relatively small amount of money to support projects or organizations (Fehrer and Nenonen 2020). In a broader sense, the concept of crowdfunding also involves *crowd creation*, which gives consumers the opportunity to choose which products to put on the market and the ability to change the creative orientation of a project (Chaney 2019). A crowdfunding event could be a crowd pre-sale, crowd donations, crowd equity, or crowd lending activities (Crosetto and Regner 2018). There are five different forms of crowdfunding: royalty-based, equity-based, donation-based, lending-based, and reward-based (Belleflamme and Lambert 2016). Apart from being an alternative source of funding, crowdfunding could also be seen as an innovative way to search for approval for a project and manage community (Chaney 2019).

There are other examples of arts institutions searching for the public's help in innovative ways. For example, UCCA Center for Contemporary Art adopted charity sales as a fundraising innovation. The amount raised through seat pledges and a public auction at a gala dinner was enough to support the annual operating expenses. The exquisite foreign-language books and artist co-branded products in the museum store also bring a lot of income to the museum. The Metropolitan Museum of Art in the United States has also made innovations in fundraising methods. In 2015, Thomas Campbell, the museum's director, took the unprecedented step of issuing $250 million of taxable bonds (Goldstein 2017; Cohan 2017) to help the museum renovate and maintain its infrastructure. Although the move was not successful in the long run and the museum's financial deficit increased significantly due to mistakes in operational decision-making, ultimately causing Campbell to lose his position, this creative financing idea was worth considering.

Scholastic Force (The Power of Scholastic Ability)

The academic force corresponds to the civic world, where the highest value is social benefit and social participation. In this sense, the scholastic force could be explained as the educational incentive that was created by organizations themselves for social benefits. The power of academic ability is the foundation of art organizations, and it is also an important standard for public donations and government funding. The presentation of academic power is reflected in the construction of curation teams and academic boards, the production of core products, and the output of academic achievements.

Taking art museums as an example, scholastic strength is reflected in the level of curation and scholarly achievements. The touring exhibition is an important source of income for art museums such as the Museum of Modern Art and the Guggenheim Museum. Exhibitions for which the planning relies on scholastic strength not only show the world the ability of curation and research but also bring in income from the intellectual property created along with the exhibition. However, exhibitions may be on loan, as many are in Chinese art museums; sometimes items are on loan, and sometimes the whole exhibition is on loan, as a so-called canned exhibition. In most cases of loaned exhibitions, art museums are treated as exhibition venues; the museums must make high payments for the loaned items or exhibitions, and they then cannot highlight any of their own academic ability. When a canned exhibition is of poor quality, whether in terms of the curation or the display, audiences may absorb little knowledge, and the poor reputation of the exhibition may lead to a reduction in audience attendance.

Market Force (The Power of Market Capability)

Corresponding to the market world, the market force also highly values competition, interest, and consumers' choice. To be specific, the power of market capability contains the driving force of market economy and market communication. Many corporations and individuals invest in or sponsor organizations in the arts and cultural field in order to realize their own economic interests; this is especially the case with corporate sponsorship. The market economy can also become the standard by which the value of government support, such as whether it drives local employment and economic development.

Another manifestation of market power is the force of communication, which includes two functions: communicating information and guiding consumption (Lin 2017). The communication power can be explained in two ways: one is that the organization tries to convey some information to visitors, collectors, and the public through their cultural and artistic products; the other is that relevant media exposure and activities, as communication channels, affect the public's awareness and stimulate their interest in consumption and having an experience.

Institutionalization Force (The Power of Institutionalization)

The domestic world values responsibility, convention, and collective credit, and it prioritizes group order and hierarchy; the institutionalization force assesses value similarly. The power of institutionalization is mainly reflected in an organization's internal policies and management system. In American museums, for example, the prosperity and development of the field are largely due to adequate financial support, which is made possible in great part by the US policy system. There is no specific governmental cultural agency in the United States to supervise, govern, and fund art museums; rather, support for arts and organizations is mainly a product of government policies and systems, especially the provisions of the Internal Revenue Service (IRS), including tax exemption policies, such as sections 501(c)(3), 4940(d)(2), and 4942(J)(3) of the tax code.

The power of institutionalization can to some extent be seen in an organization's internal management system, in particular the structure of the management team and their working process. For example, a museum with a clear management structure, a team of fundraising specialists or public affairs professionals, and standardized curation and operations processes would have a greater chance to gain government and/or foundation financial support (Preece 2015).

Financing Mechanisms for Arts and Cultural Organizations

The word "mechanism" has three meanings, according to the *Collins English Dictionary*: (1) "In a machine or piece of equipment, a mechanism is a part, often consisting of a set of smaller parts, which performs a particular function"; (2) "A mechanism is a special way of getting something done within a particular system"; and (3) "A mechanism is a part of your behavior that is automatic and that helps you to survive or to cope with a difficult situation." The financing mechanism could be explained as a special way of getting funds, consisting of different parts, to help organizations cope with financial needs.

Financing mechanisms in the area of education were a subject of academic interest in the late 1990s. Education, especially higher education, is a public good that needs diversified financial support. Arts and culture are also public goods (Jung 2018), and the social environment for art organizations is quite similar to the situation educational institutions were facing two decades ago; therefore, a review of previous research on school financing mechanisms could provide some valuable insights.

During the 1990s, many countries faced significant changes in their economies, forcing reform in their systems for financing higher education. More new funders needed to be attracted, and multiple funding channels needed to be developed; at the same time, existing participants in the funding system needed encouragement to invest more (Carnoy 2000). Lin (2006) combined soft system methodology with the methodology of open complex giant systems and higher education system thinking to set up a conceptual model to address the relationship between higher education institutions and donations to institutions of higher education by enterprises, social groups, and individual citizens, and linked these to the external environment of policy and market in order to construct a system perspective on educational financing mechanisms.

System thinking has also recently been brought into the arts and cultural field. Jung (2017) explored the application of system thinking to understanding arts and educational organizations as open, complex systems interconnected with external environments. Jung and Love (2017) further discussed the theory and practice of system thinking in museums. Jung and Vakharia (2019) brought the insights of open systems theory into the field of arts and cultural organization management, suggesting that this might enhance organizations' performance in both financial and nonfinancial areas; they also pointed out that arts and cultural organizations should be seen as open and networked structures that are part of and affected by external environments. These research tracks suggest that the funding mechanisms of arts organizations could be studied from the perspective of system thinking as open complex systems that are closely linked to external environments.

The PEST model, which represents four aspects of environments (political, economic, social, and technological), is a powerful and widely used tool for analyzing external environments (Aguilar 1967; Sammut-Bonnici and Galea 2015) that could offer a better understanding of factors influencing organizational development (Matović 2020). It could also be used with arts and cultural organizations, examining the political, economic, social, and technological aspects of their complex financing systems.

The political environment could influence the direction and mode of government funding, which in turn could have an impact on the content and staff composition of arts organizations' production. The technological environment could influence ways of curating exhibitions or fundraising channels. The economic environment could refer not only to the economic status of the society but also to ecological changes that might have economic impacts, such as the COVID-19 pandemic. These in turn might affect the structure of arts and cultural organizations, the content they produce, and their ability to raise funds. The social environment also has a profound impact on the financing of arts and cultural organizations. Comparing China and the United States, the differences between the countries' cultures of donation and patterns of cultural consumption behavior are the main reason for the different funding structures of arts and cultural organizations in the two countries.

Besides the external environment, research has shown a mutually influencing relationship between the internal environment of an arts organization and its funders. Alexander (1996), drawing on organizational theory, found that different funders' tastes were translated into different exhibition formats and content. Stockenstrand and Ander (2014) compared the stability, business strategy, and management of Swedish orchestras and British orchestras and suggested that funding sources might influence how organizations perceive the importance of communication and knowledge management. Preece (2015) found that funders make funding decisions based on the quality of an organization's products and services, mission and vision, organizational structure, and management capability. Hence, there is theoretical and empirical evidence that organizational outcomes are shaped not just by internal management but also by funding sources.

Drawing together all the themes discussed so far, we can see that the financing mechanism of arts and cultural organizations consists of three subsystems, including the driving power system, the operational system, and the external environment (see Figure 26.3). The driving power system is the funding structure that was mentioned previously, which includes three funding sources and five driving powers (see Figure 26.2). The operational system refers to the process in which an arts organization uses its personnel, management structure, and projects to connect to government, corporations, and the public in order to obtain external financial support under the allocation of the five driven powers. The external environment refers to the dynamically changing environment of technological, political, social, and economic factors.

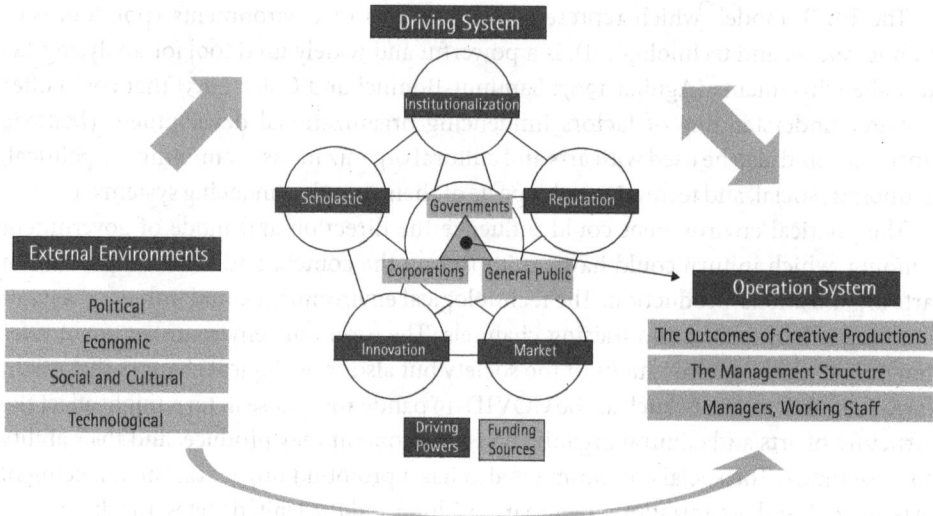

FIGURE 26.3 The financing mechanisms of arts organizations.

Intertwining Relationships within the Financing Mechanism

As the financing mechanism of arts and cultural organizations is an open complex system that involves so many participants and influencers, there is inevitably some interplay among funders, driving forces, and environmental changes.

Positive and Negative Relationships between Funders

Within a funding system, there are positive and negative correlations between different funding sources. As an example, the funds provided to US arts organizations by the National Endowment for the Arts (NEA) account for only 1 percent of those organizations' total funding, but its strategy is to use those allocations to encourage organizations to actively seek diversified incomes. The NEA's supportive attitude drives active investment by states, local governments, foundations, corporations, and individuals. The public is more willing to donate to arts organizations if the projects seeking funding have received grants from or been recommended by the government.

But research conducted by Kim and Van Ryzin (2013) showed that government funding can have a "crowding-out" effect on private donations. That is, individuals might reduce or eliminate the amount they donate to arts and cultural organizations that receiving government funding, regardless of what percentage of total income that government funding provides.

Another example of these correlations is provided by Today Art Museum (TAM) in Beijing. It opened in 2002, funded by a real estate company. TAM focused on discovering and promoting young artists and emerging artists and was recognized by the art community for its exhibition quality. Many of the artists who exhibited at TAM later became famous, and TAM gained status and a strong reputation. However, in recent years real estate has become less profitable and the company reduced its funding to the museum, so TAM has had to become financially independent. TAM tried to maintain its previous peak by relying on corporate sponsorship and venue fees. However, considering the lack of supportive tax policies, limited returns from sponsorship returns, a reduction of quality in exhibitions that leased space at TAM, and many other factors, TAM sought other strategies. One was to import more blockbuster exhibitions sponsored by corporations, such as Mi, Van Cleef & Arpels, and Paul Smith. The admission fees for these exhibitions are much higher than the normal fees. But, under the pressure of having to change its funding structure, TAM also saw its academic reputation decrease to some degree.

TAM has continued to identify new sources of funding. For example, frequent visitors could be cultivated and become potential individual sponsors through a membership plan. Drawing on Hirschman's (1983) three-market segmentation theories (artists, art peers, and the public) and Lin and Colbert's research (2018) showing that people with an educational or professional arts background are more active in art consumption and find it easier to establish emotional contact with art-related activities and objects, TAM could also attempt to transfer existing participants to the next level of giving by actively encouraging the patrons to develop more ties to the arts, which would increase their likelihood of donating.

The Coordination Effect between the Driving Forces

There could be coordination effects between different driving forces. For example, the institutionalization force may facilitate the reputation force. In the United States, an organization recognized by the IRS with 501(c)(3) tax exemption status is considered more formal and credible in the eyes of the public and other entities. At the Metropolitan Museum of Art, only forty more or less elective trustees have the right to vote; the five-year tenure system and annual election of one-fifth of the board ensure that the organization is not affected by the will of any single group, which guarantees credibility and public trust. Under the requirements of the institutionalization force, credibility could also have a positive effect on government funding. For example, in Suzhou, the government organizes a centralized review of private art organizations applying for subsidies or awards from June to August every year. In addition to reviewing the written application materials these organizations provide, the government also refers to the documents issued by the Municipal Art Museum Association and third-party evaluators' assessments of the organizations' operations. The results of these evaluations are publicized after being examined and approved by the municipality's department of culture and its financial department. Private art galleries that fail to pass the annual inspection, fail to complete a statistical survey, or fail to pass a random inspection twice a year will not be eligible to submit an application for an award application in that year. Private art organizations that provide false application materials or otherwise violate laws, regulations, or rules are penalized by not being able to participate for five years.

The Conflict Effect Inside the System

The conflict effect also plays a part in funding systems. In 1983, the UK's Arts Council received criticism from the public for its £50,000 sponsorship of a controversial visual art piece by David Mach—a representation of a submarine constructed of waste tires. In another example from 1989, NEA-funded artist Robert Mapplethorpe exhibited works related to homosexuality in a retrospective titled "The Perfect Moment." The organizer of the exhibition was the Institute of Contemporary Arts in Philadelphia, which had received a $30,000 NEA grant and had plans for the exhibition to visit Chicago, Washington, DC, and other cities. The exhibition angered conservative senator Jesse Helms and led the Senate to vote to prevent the NEA from supporting "obscene or vulgar" works. Not only was the credibility of the organization mounting the exhibition challenged, but also the government that provided funding was questioned. These incidents highlight the struggle between artistic freedom and control and reveal the conflicts between the public, government, and the professional aesthetic standards of the art world. They also suggest some of the types of conflicts that arts organizations might face when they search for funds, since it is impossible to make every stakeholder happy.

Another example of conflict would be the Tate Modern's controversial sponsorship relationship with the oil company BP. In 2016, BP announced that it was ending its twenty-seven-year sponsorship of the Tate, largely because of public protest. Art collectives and some members of the general public believed that oil companies giving sponsorship to arts organization was a way to legitimize their devastation of the environment and their reckless business practices, and that receiving funds from oil companies represents a serious stain on the United Kingdom's cultural patrimony (Tate à Tate n.d.). Besides oil companies, other corporate sponsors have also been criticized, including investment banks, tobacco companies, and wines and spirits companies. They are believed to be participating in arts philanthropy in order to keep the policy environment favorable to the industry, not just simply to promote sales (Smith 2008; Chong 2018). In such cases, it is difficult for arts organizations not to lose credibility when they accept donations from questionable funding sources. At the same time, the arts organizations had an urgent need for funds, showing the conflicts that can exist between the market force and credibility.

Dynamic Changes in the External Environment of Fundraising

The COVID-19 pandemic was a shock to the arts and cultural field, creating challenges but also offering opportunities. This is an example of how a change in environment can lead to the adjustment of funding structures and the operation of financing mechanisms.

During COVID-19, the arts and cultural industry faced not only the same challenges as other industries but also a long and unstable road to recovery. Due to the lockdowns, many art venues had to close down or to restrict the number of visitors per day and/or per show. Since the 2008 financial crisis, arts organizations had been relying more on revenue from ticket and product sales to deal with the impact of the reduction of public funds, commercial sponsorship, and charitable donations. However, this kind of funding structure made arts and cultural organizations more vulnerable to the pandemic's impact and in many cases has threatened the viability of the organizations.

Arts and cultural organizations sought to adjust their mode of operations and seek new ways of funding during and after the pandemic. These organizations were able to leverage information technology to spread culture and art during the outbreak of the pandemic in a way that had not been possible ten years earlier. According to a survey of 19,398 cultural and art institutions conducted between March 2020 and February 2021, 72 percent have adjusted their operations mode, and of these 73 percent chose to increase online content in order to compete for public attention and support (Americans for the Arts 2021). This example shows how the external environment influences the operational system of organizations and the forces of market and innovation, demonstrating the dynamic and self-adjusting nature of fundraising mechanisms.

Conclusion

This chapter has illuminated funding structures and financing mechanisms in order to help arts and cultural organizations move toward achieving sustainable and stable financing. Arts managers may use this understanding in their decision-making, and researchers may investigate this mechanism further—for example, focusing on questions such as how to target appropriate funders, how to establish a hierarchy of donors by educating and cultivating them, and how to use driving forces in the funding structure to face risk and challenges.

References

Abínzano, Isabel, Francisco J. López-Arceiz, and Idoia Zabaleta. 2022. "Can Tax Regulations Moderate Revenue Diversification and Reduce Financial Distress in Nonprofit Organizations?" *Annals of Public and Cooperative Economics* (online). https://doi.org/10.1111/apce.12370.

Aguilar, Francis J. 1967. *Scanning the Business Environment.* New York: Macmillan.

Alexander, Victoria. D. 1996. "Pictures at an Exhibition: Conflicting Pressures in Museums and the Display of Art." *American Journal of Sociology* 101, no. 4: 797–839.

Alexander, Victoria D. 2018. "Heteronomy in the Arts Field: State Funding and British Arts Organizations." *British Journal of Sociology* 69: 23–43.

Americans for the Arts. 2021. "The Impact of COVID-19 on the Arts and Cultural Sector of the United States." https://www.americansforthearts.org/by-topic/disaster-preparedness/the-economic-impact-of-coronavirus-on-the-arts-and-culture-sector.

Avci, Sureyya Burcu. 2021. "The New Venture Philanthropy." In *Innovations in Social Finance*, edited by Thomas Walker, Jane McGaughey, Sherif Goubran, and Nadra Wagdy, 483–503. Cham: Springer.

Banfield, Edward. 1984. *The Democratic Muse: Visual Arts and the Public Interest.* New York: Basic Books.

Barnes, Martha L. 2011. "Music to Our Ears: Understanding Why Canadians Donate to Arts and Cultural Organizations." *International Journal of Nonprofit and Voluntary Sector Marketing* 16: 115–126.

Bell, Jeffery. 1992. *Populism and Elitism: Politics in the Age of Equality.* Washington, DC: Regnery.

Belleflamme, Paul and Thomas Lambert. 2016. "An Industrial Organization Framework to Understand the Strategies of Crowdfunding Platforms." In *International Perspectives on Crowdfunding*, ed. J. Méric, I. Maque, and J. Brabet, 1–19. Bingley: Emerald. https://doi.org/10.1108/978-1-78560-315-020151001.

Bigné Alcañiz, Enrique, Ruben Chumpitaz Cáceres, and Rafael Curás Pérez. 2010. "Alliances Between Brands and Social Causes: The Influence of Company Credibility on Social Responsibility Image." *Journal of Business Ethics* 96, no. 2: 169–186. http://www.jstor.org/stable/40863730.

Boltanski, Luc, and Laurent Thévenot. 2006. *On Justification: Economies of Worth.* Princeton, NJ: Princeton University Press.

Bradburne, James M. 2010. "Wagging the Dog: Managing Museum Priorities in a Different Economy." *Journal of Museum Education* 35, no. 2: 141–152.

Brooks, Arthur C. 2001. "Who Opposes Government Arts Funding?" *Public Choice* 108, nos. 3–4: 355–367. http://www.jstor.org/stable/30026370.

Brooks, Arthur C. 2003. "Public Opinion and the Role of Government Arts Funding in Spain." *Journal of Comparative Policy Analysis: Research and Practice* 5, no. 1: 29–38, doi:10.1080/13876980308412690.

Carnoy, Martin. 2000. "School Choice? Or is it Privatization?" *Educational Researcher* 29, no.7: 15–20. https://doi.org/10.3102/0013189X029007015

Cascino, Stefano, Maria Correia, and Ane Tamayo. 2019. "Does Consumer Protection Enhance Disclosure Credibility in Reward Crowdfunding?" *Journal of Accounting Research* 57: 1247–1302.

Chan, Kenneth S. 2007. "Trade, Social Values, and the Generalized Trust." *Southern Economic Journal* 73, no. 3: 733–753. http://www.jstor.org/stable/20111921.

Chaney, Damien. 2019. "A Principal-Agent Perspective on Consumer Co-Production: Crowdfunding and the Redefinition of Consumer Power." *Technological Forecasting and Social Change* 141: 74–84.

Chong, Derrick. 2018. "The Ethics of Museum Sponsorship and Arts Activism." SAGE Business Cases. https://dx.doi.org/10.4135/9781526439963.

Cobb, Nina Kressner. 2002. "The New Philanthropy: Its Impact on Funding Arts and Culture." *Journal of Arts Management, Law, and Society* 32, no. 2: 125–143. doi:10.1080/10632920209596969.

Cohan, William D. 2017. "Inside a Met Director's Shocking Exit and the Billion Dollar Battle for the Museum's Future." *Vanity Fair*, March 19, 2017. https://www.vanityfair.com/news/2017/03/thomas-campbell-met-director-exit.

Crosetto, Paolo, and Tobias Regner. 2018. "It's Never Too Late: Funding Dynamics and Self Pledges in Reward-Based Crowdfunding." *Research Policy* 47, no. 8: 1463–1477. https://doi.org/10.1016/j.respol.2018.04.020.

Cummings, Milton C., and Richard S. Katz. 1987. *The Patron State*. New York: Oxford University Press.

Esparza, Erin. 2019. "Nonprofit and Foundation Sponsored Research: Developing New Models of Collaboration for Research and Development." *Academic Entrepreneurship for Medical and Health Scientists* 1, no. 2: article 7.

Fehrer, Julia, and Suvi Nenonen. 2020. "Crowdfunding Networks: Structure, Dynamics and Critical Capabilities." *Industrial Marketing Management* 88: 449–464. https://doi.org/10.1016/j.indmarman.2019.02.012.

Franklin, Adrian. 2018. "Art Tourism: A New Field for Tourist Studies. " *Tourist Studies* 18, no. 4: 399–416. https://doi.org/10.1177/1468797618815025.

Fombrun, Charles J. 1996. *Reputation: Realizing Value from the Corporate Image*. Boston, MA: Harvard Business School Press.

Goldstein, Andrew. 2017. "Mutiny at the Met? Thomas Campbell on the Price of Modernization at America's Greatest Museum." Artnet, September 6, 2017. https://camd.org.au/mutiny-at-the-met-thomas-campbell/.

Grossman, Allen, Sarah Appleby, and Caitlin Reimers. 2013. "Venture Philanthropy: Its Evolution and Its Future." Harvard Business School Background Note N9-313-111.

Harrow, Jenny, Paul Palmer, and Mariana Bogdanova. 2006. "Business Giving, the Tsunami and Corporates as Rock Stars: Some Implications for Arts Funding?" *Cultural Trends* 15, no. 4: 299–323. doi:10.1080/09548960600922640.

Harsell, Dana Michael. 2013. "My Taxes Paid for That?! Or Why the Past Is Prologue for Public Arts Funding." *PS: Political Science and Politics* 46, no. 1: 74–80. doi:10.1017/s1049096512001266.

Harvie, Jen. 2015. "Funding, Philanthropy, Structural Inequality and Decline in England's Theatre Ecology." *Cultural Trends* 24, no. 1: 56–61. doi:10.1080/09548963.2014.1000586.

Hirschman, Elizabeth C. 1983. "Aesthetics, Ideologies and the Limits of the Marketing Concept." *Journal of Marketing* 47, no. 3: 45. doi:10.2307/1251196.

Jackob, Nikolaus. 2008. "Credibility Effects." In *International Encyclopedia of Communication*, edited by W. Donsbach, 1044–1047. Malden, MA: Blackwell.

Jolliffe, Lee, and Jenny Cave. 2012. "Arts Tourism." In *Tourism: The Key Concepts*, edited by P. Robinson, 13–15. London: Routledge.

Jung, Yuha. 2017. "Systems Thinking in Organizations: Applying It to Study Arts and Educational Settings." *Journal of Art for Life* 9: 1–17.

Jung, Yuha. 2018. "Economic Discussion of Conflict between Public Education Policies and Common Good Arts in the United States." *The Journal of Arts Management, Law, and Society* 48: 98–107.

Jung, Yuha, and Ann Rowson Love. 2017. *Systems Thinking in Museums: Theory and Practice*. Lanham, MD: Rowman & Littlefield.

Jung, Yuha, and Neville Vakharia. 2019. "Open Systems Theory for Arts and Cultural Organizations: Linking Structure and Performance." *Journal of Arts Management, Law and Society* 49, no. 4: 257–273.

Ki, Eyun-Jung, and Jeyoung Oh. 2018. "Determinants of Donation Amount in Nonprofit Membership Associations." *International Journal of Nonprofit and Voluntary Sector Marketing* 23, no. 3: article e1609.

Kim, Mirae, and Gregg G. Van Ryzin. 2013. "Impact of Government Funding on Donations to Arts Organizations." *Nonprofit and Voluntary Sector Quarterly* 43, no. 5: 910–925. doi:10.1177/0899764013487800.

Lin, Yi. 2017. "Promotion or Communication: This Is a Question." Paper presented at the International Conference on Arts and Cultural Management, Beijing, China, June 28, 2017.

Lin, Yi. 2006. *An Innovative Methodology for Analysing Policy and Finance for Higher Education in China*. Beijing: Central Radio and TV University Press.

Luccasen, R. Andrew, and M. Kathleen Thomas. 2020. "Voluntary Taxation and the Arts." *Journal of Cultural Economics* 44, no. 4: 589–604.

Mahieu, Sandrine. 2017. "The Impact of Public Funding on Contemporary Visual Arts." *Political Quarterly* 88: 622–630. https://doi.org/10.1111/1467-923X.12396.

March, James, and Herbert Simon. 1993. *Organizations*. 2nd ed. Cambridge, MA: Blackwell.

Martell, Christine R. 2004. "Dedicated Funding for Arts, Culture, and Science." *Public Finance and Management* 4, no. 1: 50–74.

Matović, Ivana Marinović. 2020. "PESTEL Analysis of External Environment as a Success Factor of Startup Business." in the ConSciens Conference Proceedings, September 28-29, 2020, pages 96–102.

Merchant, Joshua D. 2015. "From Altruism to Investment: Venture Philanthropy and Its Impact on Shared Governance at Liberal Arts Colleges." PhD diss., Western Michigan University.

Moeran, Brian, and Jesper Strandgaard Pederson. 2011. *Negotiating Values in the Creative Industries: Fairs, Festivals, and Competitive Events*. New York: Cambridge University Press.

Moore, Sarah. 2018. "Towards a Sociology of Institutional Transparency: Openness, Deception and the Problem of Public Trust." *Sociology* 52, no. 2: 416–430. https://www.jstor.org/stable/26558712.

Payne, A. Abigail. 1998. "Does the Government Crowd-Out Private Donations? New Evidence from a Sample of Non-Profit Firms." *Journal of Public Economics* 69: 323–345.

Payne, A. Abigail. 2001. "Measuring the Effect of Federal Research Funding on Private Donations at Research Universities: Is Federal Research Funding More than a Substitute for Private Donations?" *International Tax and Public Finance* 8: 731–751.

Poling, Jessica. 2021. "Art in the Time of Frugality: Scarcity, Cooperation, and Change in American Art Museums." *Sociological Forum* 36: 226–247. https://doi.org/10.1111/socf.12670.

Preece, Stephen B. 2015. "Acquiring Start-Up Funding for New Arts Organizations." *Nonprofit Management and Leadership* 25, no. 4: 463–474. doi:10.1002/nml.21131.

Ressler, Robert W., Pamela Paxton, and Kristopher Velasco. 2020. "Donations in Social Context." *Nonprofit Management and Leadership* 31: 693–715.

Roberson, Belinda Gail. 2015. "Examining the Relationship Between Trust, Credibility, Satisfaction, and Loyalty Among Online Donors." PhD diss., Walden University. https://scholarworks.waldenu.edu/dissertations/1862/.

Sammut-Bonnici, Tanya, and Galea, David. 2015. "PEST Analysis" In *Wiley Encyclopedia of Management*, edited by C.L. Cooper, J. McGee and T. Sammut-Bonnici. https://doi.org/10.1002/9781118785317.weom120103

Smith, Elizabeth A. 2008. "Tobacco Industry Sponsorship of Arts Organizations." Paper presented at the 136th APHA Annual Meeting and Exposition.

Stockenstrand, Anna-Karin, and Owe Ander. 2014. "Arts Funding and Its Effects on Strategy, Management and Learning." *International Journal of Arts Management* 17, no. 4: 43–53.

Tate à Tate. n.d. "Introduction to Oil Sponsorship of the Arts." https://tateatate.org/sponsorship.html, accessed December 30, 2022.

Vesterlund, Lise. 2006. "Why Do People Give?" In *The Nonprofit Sector*, 2nd ed., edited by R. Steinberg and W. Powell, 568–587. New Haven, CT: Yale University Press.

Yan, Bo, XiaoHu Wang, and Jiannan Wu. 2020. "Fiscal Transparency Online and Public Trust: An Exploratory Study on Baimiao Township Government." *China Review* 20, no. 3: 99–126. https://www.jstor.org/stable/26928113.

CHAPTER 27

CONTEMPORARY FINDINGS ON INDIVIDUAL DONATIONS AND FUNDRAISING STRATEGIES

JENNIFER WIGGINS

THE Great Recession, from December 2007 to June 2009, had a significant impact on the ability of nonprofit arts organizations to raise funds. In the United States, the arts sector experienced a decrease in assets of more than 20 percent, with a 9 percent decrease in revenues in 2009 alone (McCambridge and Dietz 2020). This was primarily driven by a drop in investment value, accompanied by smaller decreases in contributions as donors and corporate sponsors rethought their budgets and government funding was redirected toward pressing economic needs (McCambridge and Dietz 2020). In Europe, arts organizations that had historically relied on public funding found themselves struggling to shift toward private contributions in response to cuts in government support and a drop in corporate sponsorships (Krebs, Rieunier, and Urien 2015). In recognition of these struggles, academic research on charitable donations experienced a surge, both in mainstream journals and in journals dedicated to the nonprofit and arts industries.

Accompanying this growing interest was an increase in the availability of data on fundraising effectiveness. The Cultural Data Project, now DataArts, was founded in 2004 with the goal of amassing a large dataset of financial information on the nonprofit arts industry in the United States (DataArts n.d.). Crowdfunding websites such as Kickstarter and KIVA made basic financial data on their campaigns publicly available. Combined with existing resources like Guidestar, now Candid, which digitizes US IRS 990 forms for nonprofit organizations, researchers had access to better and more complete data that enabled more nuanced analyses of fundraising practices and successes (Candid n.d.). Collectively, this has led to a wealth of new knowledge about individual donations and effective fundraising strategies. The goal of this chapter is to conduct a review of the literature on individual donations published after the start of the Great Recession, combining systematic and narrative methods, with a focus on identifying best practices for arts organizations.

METHOD AND ANALYSIS

A search of the Business Source Complete database was conducted for the keyword "donation" with the results limited to publications between 2008 and 2021. Additional keyword searches were planned, but as the initial search resulted in more than seven thousand hits, and it is unlikely that a publication on charitable donations would not include the word "donation," further searches were deemed moot. Removing duplicates and limiting the results to high quality international journals in English (see Appendix) revealed 506 articles and conference proceedings across the fields of consumer research, marketing strategy, nonprofit management, business ethics, accounting, advertising, and arts management. The sample was further refined based on the abstracts to focus on individual donation behavior, excluding research on corporate philanthropy, corporate social responsibility, cause-related marketing, and the development of professional fundraising as a field, and to focus on those findings that are most relevant to the arts industries, for example, excluding research on blood and organ donation or children in poverty, resulting in a final sample of 208 publications. This literature was reviewed with a goal to let the underlying themes in the literature emerge naturally to provide a comprehensive overview of our current understanding of individual charitable donation behavior.

The analysis revealed five primary research streams co-occurring in the literature, which reflect differences in the theoretical and methodological approaches taken by various research fields. The first stream seeks to identify antecedents and drivers that can explain and predict individual donation behavior. Spanning consumer research, marketing strategy, nonprofit management, and arts management, this research primarily relies on experimental and survey methodologies to test the impact of individual and situational factors on likelihood to donate. The second stream considers social influences, including social information, public recognition, and the influence of donors' social networks. This research has been influenced by prior work in economics (Johnson and Grimm 2012) and has now been incorporated into consumer research as well as nonprofit and arts management. This research has primarily relied on experimental methods, but more recently it has incorporated network analysis using secondary data.

While researchers looking from a psychological or sociological perspective have examined the individual's donation decision and the influence of other donors in the social network, an economic perspective suggests that there are also structural dynamics that can have an influence on the individual's donation behavior. Access to financial data enabled a revived interest in the crosswise dynamics between different sources of revenue in the nonprofit management and marketing strategy fields. Researchers in this area have primarily used secondary datasets and econometric analyses to examine the interplay among different sources of funding and the impact of alternative funding sources on the overall amount of individual donations within an organization or industry. Research from an accounting perspective has taken a different approach to understanding the individual donor's response to funding structure, examining the impact of an organization's financial transparency and accountability on individual donation decisions. This stream similarly relies on secondary data and econometric analysis, with some use of experimental methodology. Finally, research continued to probe perhaps the longest-running research question in this area: how to optimize the effectiveness of fundraising appeals. This stream spans consumer research, marketing strategy, and advertising, and primarily uses experimental methods to test the effectiveness of various aspects of fundraising requests and messages. Table 27.1 provides an overview of the distribution of these five streams across the publication years 2008–2021. This chapter reviews each of these streams in turn, followed by implications for future research on individual donations to the arts.

Antecedents and Drivers of Individual Donation Behavior

Much historical research has focused on understanding the intrinsic or altruistic motives for donation (Johnson and Grimm 2012). Intrinsically motivated donors may be driven by empathy for the beneficiaries (Ein-Gar and Levontin 2013; Verhaert and Van den Poel 2011a), regret over not donating in the past (Bennett 2009b), or an internalized norm of social responsibility (Barnes 2011). Donors may be driven by a personal connection to the cause (Lin-Healy and Small 2012), a desire to support their local community (Kim, Gibson, and Ko 2011), or the wish to leave an impact on the future for posterity (Krebs, Rieunier and Urien 2015). Donation behavior also seems to be a way to assuage guilt over unrelated behaviors. Consumers who have engaged in indulgent consumption or made an immoral choice are more likely to donate immediately afterward (Chatterjee, Mishra, and Mishra 2010; Gneezy, Imas, and Madarász 2014), as are consumers who have been exposed to appeals linking a suggested donation amount to the price of a hedonic product, such as a pint of gourmet ice cream (Savary, Goldsmith, and Dhar 2015).

Researchers have also examined donors' responses to extrinsic incentives and rewards. Donor acquisition increases when fundraising appeals include low-value monetary gifts (such as stamps or a coin); however, average donation amounts and return on investment decrease (Yin, Li, and Singh 2020). Reframing gifts as charitable purchases and not rewards for donations can mitigate this effect (Savary, Li, and Newman 2020). Adding a "bonus trigger incentive" that adds a predetermined dollar amount to gifts

Table 27.1. Distribution of Research Streams by Publication Year

	2008	2009	2010	2011	2012	2013	2014	2015	2016	2017	2018	2019	2020	2021	Total	Percent
Antecedents and drivers	0	2	2	7	4	4	6	7	1	0	1	3	4	2	43	21%
Social influences	1	1	0	0	0	1	1	1	2	3	3	3	9	5	31	15%
Crosswise dynamics	0	0	0	0	2	1	1	1	3	2	2	1	5	3	25	12%
Transparency and accountability	0	3	0	1	1	4	1	2	3	6	6	3	5	4	34	16%
Fundraising appeals	2	5	2	4	5	7	4	4	6	6	6	6	9	7	75	36%
Total	3	11	4	13	12	17	14	15	15	17	18	16	32	21	208	100%

also increases donor acquisition and willingness to donate, but only when the incentive is large enough to be impactful (Helms-McCarty, Diette, and Holloway 2016). Donors continue to be responsive to benefits offered for different donation amounts (Boenigk and Scherhag 2014; Scherhag and Boenigk 2013). However, emphasizing these benefits increases donors' attributions of their donations to the benefits received, making them more likely to lapse if benefits are removed (Johnson and Ellis 2011). Similarly, incentivizing supporters to persuade others to donate leads to persuasion tactics that are perceived as less sincere, reducing their effectiveness (Barasch, Berman and Small 2014). Interestingly, while extrinsic motivations have often been viewed as less desirable, intrinsically motivated donors do not donate more to the arts than their extrinsically motivated counterparts (Johnson and Ellis 2011). Donors evaluate rewards only after considering the needs of the beneficiaries, and are willing to help in the absence of a reward if that need is great (Abbate and Ruggieri 2011).

Researchers have also examined the processes that donors use to decide whether to donate, to whom, and how much. The choice to donate tends to be determined by factors internal to the individual, but donation amount is more influenced by external factors like perceived need of the beneficiaries, effectiveness of the organization, or the overall economic environment (Fajardo and Townsend 2012; Osili, Ackerman, and Li 2019). Donors to only one organization tend to select one to which they feel a personal connection; however, the choice of a second recipient organization is also influenced by self-image fit and reputation, seeing others donate, and receiving promotional materials (Bennett 2012; Bennett and Ali-Choudhury 2009). Donors prefer to distribute their donations among multiple organizations rather than concentrating on one, and donate more money overall when they choose the recipient organizations before the total amount to be donated (Okutur and Berman 2020; Sharps and Schroeder 2019).

Attention has also been paid to the relationships that are cultivated between nonprofit organizations and potential donors. Donation intention is increased by positive past experiences with the organization as a customer, member, or audience member (Beldad, Snip, and van Hoof 2014; Kim, Gupta, and Lee 2021; Moon and Azizi 2013; Swanson and Davis 2012). These effects can be enhanced when the donor identifies strongly with the organization (Boenigk and Helmig 2013; Fang, Fombelle, and Bolton 2021) and when they have donated to a broad variety of projects within the organization (Khodakarami, Petersen, and Vekatesan 2015). However, strong identification with other members of the organization increases member retention but decreases donations (Fang, Fombelle, and Bolton 2021). Relationships with arts organizations have also been divided into exchange relationships, which assume equitable outcomes, and communal relationships, which do not. Arts consumers' perceptions of whether they have an exchange or communal relationship with the organization does not always match how they are segmented by the organization, making prediction of donation behavior based on purchase behavior challenging (Johnson, Peck, and Schweidel 2014). Consumers can even perceive both exchange and communal relationships with arts organizations simultaneously, and both can motivate them to donate even in the absence of rewards (Johnson and Grimm 2010).

Donation behavior has also been found to exhibit cross-cultural differences. Cultures with high individualism and low uncertainty avoidance demonstrate higher propensities to engage in prosocial behavior (Luria, Cnaan, and Boehm 2015). High power distance has been linked to lower perceptions of individual responsibility to help, and therefore lower donation behavior (Luria, Cnaan, and Boehm 2015; Winterich and Zhang 2014). Responses to donation appeals have also been shown to vary across cultures. Donors from tight cultures with more formal norms are more likely to respond to donation requests, while donors from loose cultures with less formal norms are more likely to donate in the presence of others (Siemens et al. 2020). Self-benefit appeals are more effective in individualistic cultures, while other-benefit appeals are more effective in collectivistic cultures (Ye et al. 2015), and donors with an independent self-construal are more likely to donate to charities with high rates of support, while donors with an interdependent self-construal are more likely to donate to charities with low rates of support (Allen, Eilert, and Peloza 2018).

The presence of this stream in contemporary research suggests that this topic is still of interest to understanding individual donation behavior. However, its focus on the motivations and responses of individual donors suggests a limited view of the donation decision as residing only in the donor's mind. Researchers have also begun to take a broader, more complex view of donation behavior, examining social, structural, and economic influences on individual donations.

Social Influences on Individual Donation Behavior

While past research on antecedents of donation behavior largely focused on intrinsic and extrinsic motivations, there has been increasing interest in the impact of social or reputational motivations (Johnson and Grimm 2012). Information about others' donation behavior positively affects donor acquisition and likelihood to donate (Shang and Sargeant 2016; Shang, Reed, and Croson 2008; Verhaert and Van den Poel 2011a); however, the impact on amount donated been mixed (Croson, Handy, and Shang 2009; Minguez and Sese 2021). Social information influences donation decisions by communicating social norms, increasing awareness of need, and acting as a quality signal for the organization (van Teunenbroek, Bekkers, and Beersma 2020). However, it can also communicate that the donor's contribution will have less impact and negatively affect the donor's identity membership esteem (Shang and Sargeant 2016; van Teunenbroek, Bekkers, and Beersma 2020).

The impact of social information is sensitive to the identity of the donors being used as examples. The positive effect is stronger when the sample donor is similar to the prospective donor (James 2019; Shang, Reed, and Croson 2008; Tian and Konrath 2021), especially when the prospective donor is more collectivist or other-focused (Shang, Reed, and Croson 2008). However, the effect has a limit—a sample donor who is too similar to the prospective donor can decrease likelihood to donate by making the prospective donor feel less unique (Tian and Konrath 2021). Prospective donors are also more willing to donate when the example donors come from lower-class backgrounds (Cha, Yi, and Lee 2020). When other donors are perceived to be wealthier, prospective donors "pass the buck" and donate less (Berman et al. 2020).

Current research on public recognition as a donation reward is primarily focused on explaining a history of mixed results. For example, public recognition is an effective reward in arts crowdfunding when there are no material rewards offered, but in the presence of material rewards it becomes ineffective (Boeuf, Darveau, and Legoux 2014). Public recognition increases donation intentions and amounts donated for donors with an independent, but not interdependent, self-construal (Simpson, White, and Laran 2018) and for donors with a high, but not low, need for social approval (Denis, Pecheux, and Warlop 2020). Public recognition increases donations to out-groups but not to in-groups, because in-group donations are expected and therefore the social benefits of recognition are diminished (Han, Lee, and Winterich 2020). And public recognition decreases donation likelihood when it is perceived to create ambiguity in the attributions that will be made about the donor's motivation (Savary and Goldsmith 2020). This concern about attributed motivation leads donors to show an aversion to being required to publicize their own donations, despite receiving reputational benefits (Wang and Tong 2015).

Researchers have also noted donors' tendency to communicate to others about their own donation behavior. Donors choose to share charity brands and donor recognitions on social networking sites for a variety of reasons, including self-enhancement, impression management, high involvement with the cause, advocacy for the nonprofit, or conformity to site norms (Chell, Russell-Bennett, and Mortimer 2020; Wallace, Buil, and de Chernatony 2017). Promoting one's own prosocial behavior can communicate good deeds, but it can also signal selfish motivations, especially if the behavior is already known by others (Berman et al. 2013). Interestingly, communications about donations of time receive greater social benefits and admiration than donations of money because they are more costly to the donor, even though they are perceived to be less effective (Johnson and Park 2021).

Researchers have also examined more general social network effects on donation behavior. Individuals are more likely to become donors, donate more frequently, and donate higher amounts when they have stronger social networks (Reddick and Ponomariov 2012; Unger, Papastamatelou, and Arpagaus 2021), are more involved in their civic community (Wu et al. 2018), and have more ties with organizations and associations in their community (Hossain and Lamb 2017). Individuals also donate more when their primary social network ties are also donors (Herzog and Yang 2018). Peer-to-peer fundraising solicitations, which rely on social ties, have been found to be more effective when the fundraiser emphasizes information about themselves and their investment in the fundraising campaign than when they emphasize information about the efficacy of their charity (Chapman, Masser, and Louis 2019).

Finally, researchers have examined the practice of giving charitable donations as gifts. Recipients of donations as gifts are less likely to donate time or money to the organization in the future because they lack agency in the decision to donate and ownership of the donation (Ok, Habib, and Aquino 2020). This is mitigated if the recipient is allowed to select how the funds are allocated among various charities, as this restores the missing sense of agency and ownership (Mulder and Joireman 2016), or if the gift was requested, as on a gift registry (Ok, Habib, and Aquino 2020). However, gift registries that ask for donations receive less money than those that ask for cash because gift-givers anchor the amount on a typical donation rather than a typical gift (Samper, Chan, and Hamilton 2017).

These findings suggest that the social dynamics among donors can have a significant impact on their decision to donate and their choices of organization and donation amount, which is not accounted for in the literature on individual antecedents and motivations. Donation decisions are made not in isolation but rather in the context of a network of social influences that can override or alter individual inclinations.

Crosswise Dynamics among Funding Sources

Research on the interplay between sources of funding has long focused on the interplay between public versus private funding, finding evidence of both crowding-out effects, in which government funds substitute for private donations, and crowding-in effects, in which government funds signal that the organization is worth supporting and private donations increase (Alexiou, Wiggins, and Preece 2020). Recent research suggests possible explanations for these conflicting findings, including the age of the organization (Lu 2016), the size of the organization (Hughes, Luksetich, and Rooney 2014), the specific nonprofit sector (Lu 2016), and whether the study methodology is experimental or non-experimental (de Wit and Bekkers 2017). The effect of government funding also varies by level of government. Support from more central levels of government increases private donations but decreases funding from more local levels of government, and support from multiple levels of government decreases private donations (de Wit and Bekkers 2017; Schatteman and Bingle 2017). Finally, recent research finds that the crowding-out effect of government support does not apply to volunteers. The presence of volunteers from national service programs has a positive effect on volunteer and individual donation rates (Messamore, Paxton, and Velasco 2021).

Largely using data from the Cultural Data Project, researchers have also identified potential crowding out of donations by earned revenue from program activities and ticket sales. There appears to be a trade-off between donations and audience size, with organizations that attract larger audiences and more visitors to their websites receiving fewer contributions from foundations (Charles and Kim 2016), and organizations that gain more than 50 percent of their revenue from donations having lower attendance figures (Kim 2017). Charles and Kim (2016) suggest that organizations with larger audiences project an image of success that makes them appear less in need. The effects of revenue, however, may be more complex. Krawczyk, Wooddell, and Dias (2017) find that earned revenue is positively related to donations, but the effect sizes are so small as to be managerially useless. However, Lee, Ha, and Kim (2018) find that marketing expenses used for programming, not fundraising, have a positive influence on donation revenue. This is consistent with the idea that arts organizations can be segmented into those that focus on engaging with audiences and those that focus on engaging with donors (Besana 2012), but it suggests that efforts to engage with one group may spill over onto the other group, further complicating the dynamics between purchases and donations.

Several researchers have examined the impact of commercialization or social enterprise activities, again to mixed results. The initial introduction of a profit-generating social enterprise decreases individual donations, with the effect partially mitigated when the social enterprise is consistent with the organization's mission and competently operated (Smith, Cronley, and Barr 2012). However, ongoing engagement with a profit-generating social enterprise increases donations when the profits of the enterprise are not distributed to owners or equity investors (Faulk et al. 2020). Consistent with these mixed results, a meta-analysis of nonprofit commercialization found 110 positive effects on donation income, 30 null effects, and 155 negative effects, with an overall small but significant crowding-out effect (Hung 2020a). In contrast to Smith, Cronley, and Barr's (2012) findings, Hung (2020a) finds that the negative effect of commercialization on donation income is greater when the commercial income is mission-related than when it is unrelated, and that the crowding-out effect is stronger in sectors where organizations rely primarily on donation revenue.

Researchers have also examined the impact of corporate sponsorship, and again the results have been mixed. Sponsorship reduces willingness to donate if donors perceive their individual contributions to matter less in light of the corporate funding (Bennett, Kim, and Loken 2013). The effect can be mitigated or reversed by the donor's identification with the sponsor, the size of the corporate donation, and the donor's attitude toward the nonprofit organization (Bennett, Kim, and Loken 2013; Kwak and Kwon 2016). Sponsorship crowds in individual donations if it increases the visibility of the nonprofit organization and signals willingness to work hard, increasing perceptions of donation impact (Goh, Pappu, and Chien 2021).

Researchers have also found crosswise dynamics among other sources of contributed income. Mio and Fasan (2015) find that museums that focus on attracting monetary donations have more independent boards and higher individual donation rates, while museums that focus on in-kind contributions have smaller boards and higher volunteer rates. Hung (2020b) examines the interplay between volunteerism and donation and finds that volunteers are only willing to donate money to the organization if they are satisfied with their volunteer experience. And Alexiou, Wiggins, and Preece (2020) find that the impact of crowdfunding campaigns on other funding depends on organization age. Young organizations are legitimated by a successful campaign, but funds raised in the campaign substitute for other donations, while established organizations see an increase in funding from other sources regardless of campaign success.

Finally, researchers have studied the competitive dynamics among organizations within a geographic area and found a positive effect on donations. Increased nonprofit density increases awareness of the nonprofit sector and its actions, leading to increased confidence in nonprofit performance among donors (McDougle and Lam 2014). Successful capital campaigns by arts organizations also have a positive effect on the fundraising success of both other arts organizations (Woronkowicz and Nicholson-Crotty 2017) and non-arts organizations (Woronkowicz 2018) in the geographic area, perhaps because they increase awareness of the need for services. Interestingly, these same successful campaigns can decrease the size of a local nonprofit ecology because capital campaigns capture the core donor segment, leaving only peripheral sources of support for the rest of the sector (Woronkowicz 2018).

Competitive dynamics are sensitive to perceptions of equity. Equal distribution of revenue among organizations in the same geographic context increases overall donations (Ressler, Paxton, and Velasco 2021). When distribution of revenue is unequal, fundraising success has been linked to emphasizing connections to the local geographic community (Ressler, Paxton, and Velasco 2021) and to emphasizing relative need, as individuals who are choosing among a group of charities are more likely to donate to the charity with the least prior support (Bradley, Lawrence, and Ferguson 2019). Data from China suggests that government funding can also exhibit a crowding-in effect among a network of linked organizations; when one organization experiences an increase in government funding, neighbor organizations in the network experience a corresponding increase in individual donations as donors redistribute funds to even out the resources among the group (Ma 2020).

This research suggests that individual donation decisions are influenced not only by their own social networks but also by the organization's network of funding sources and neighboring or competing organizations. Individual donors are aware of the overall structure of nonprofit funding sources and the dynamics of funding, and appear to adjust their donation behavior in response to changes in the donation behavior of nonindividual entities as well as other individual donors.

Transparency and Accountability

Prospective donors are sensitive to information about an organization's effectiveness in fulfilling its mission (Bertacchini, Santagata, and Signorello 2011; Cryder, Loewenstein, and Scheines 2013; Katz 2018). Providing tangible details about organizational effectiveness increases donations by increasing perceptions of donation impact (Cryder, Loewenstein, and Scheines 2013) and trust in the organization (Alhidari et al. 2018; Cheng and Wu 2021; Evers and Gesthuizen 2011; Wymer, Becker, and Boenigk 2021) and can be more effective than tax rebates and incentives in soliciting donations

(Bertacchini, Santagata, and Signorello 2011). This transparency can be achieved by disclosing financial information to potential donors, for example, providing web access to IRS 990 forms (Blouin, Lee, and Erickson 2018) or presenting detailed disclosures in annual financial reports (Rossi, Leardini, and Landi 2020). Donors particularly value indicators that provide information about medium-term outcomes over indicators of immediate output or long-term impact (Bodem-Schrötgens and Becker 2020).

Organizations can increase perceptions of effectiveness by promoting signals of external validation. For example, indicating that the organization meets the standards of the Better Business Bureau increases donations (Chen 2009; Sloan 2009), although the information primarily affects donation amount rather than donation likelihood (Agyemang et al. 2019). Stronger forms of voluntary nonprofit accountability, such as external certifications, have also been linked to higher donation amounts (Becker 2018). Web assurance seals, while uncommon and primarily used by large, less efficient organizations, also increase donor support (Canada and Harris 2020). Interestingly, mere evaluation by a third party may be enough to signal that the organization values transparency and accountability. Among US nonprofit organizations, receiving a rating from a large charity rating organization increased donations even if the rating was negative, although a positive rating was more beneficial (Harris and Neely 2016).

Prospective donors are also sensitive to information about the organization's efficiency in using donated revenue. Indications of financial efficiency increase donations through strengthening donor confidence (Li, McDowell, and Hu 2012) and affect choice of organization by changing perceptions of the most and least efficient organizations in the group (van der Heijden 2013). Studies using Cultural Data Project data have found that fundraising efficiency is positively associated with both individual and foundation donations (Charles and Kim 2016; Grizzle 2015; Krawczyk, Wooddell, and Dias 2017). The role of administrative efficiency is less clear, with findings of both significant and non-significant effects on donations (Grizzle 2015; Krawczyk, Wooddell, and Dias 2017). Prospective donors are not affected by the amount of debt an organization holds (Charles 2018; Grizzle 2015), but they are sensitive to donated revenue being used to service interest on outstanding debt (Charles 2018). In general, arts organizations are seen as most efficient at creating art, followed by fundraising, and least efficient in creating social impact (Del Barrio-Tellado, Prieto, and Murray 2020).

Researchers have identified strategies that can mitigate the negative effect of inefficiency, including allowing donors to restrict how their donation can be used (Li, McDowell, and Hu 2012), informing donors that someone else has already covered overhead costs (Charles, Sloan, and Schubert 2020), and using money from "tainted" sources, like corporate support from a tobacco company, to cover administrative expenses (Bluvstein et al. 2019). Donors who are committed to the cause are more focused on outcomes than organizational intentions, and therefore more willing to accept overhead being covered from donated revenue (Newman et al. 2019). The impact of administrative inefficiency has also been found to be lower in the arts sector than in other nonprofit sectors (Jacobs and Marudas 2009) and to dissipate when expenses are described as building long-term organizational capacity and not as "overhead" (Qu and

Daniel 2021). There may also be a lower limit to "overhead aversion." In a review of more than 95,000 IRS 990 forms, Ressler, Paxton, and Velasco (2021) found that organizations with less than 15 percent overhead received lower donations than their higher-overhead counterparts.

Recent findings suggest that concerns about financial inefficiency may be exaggerated. Donors are influenced by a variety of information disclosed by the organization, and they often base their decisions on nonfinancial information such as goals, outcomes, programs, and mission (Harris, Petrovits, and Yetman 2015; McDowell, Li, and Smith 2013). Financial information seems to have its strongest effect on knowledgeable, sophisticated donors who donate larger amounts (Balsam and Harris 2014; Bourassa and Stang 2016). Less sophisticated donors do not judge the quality of financial information and are more likely to respond to media reports than to information disclosed on an IRS 990 form (Balsam and Harris 2014; Yetman and Yetman 2013). Finally, even when information is provided that an organization is less effective than its peers, donations are still likely when the cause is subjectively preferred (Berman et al. 2018).

This stream suggests that individual donation decisions are influenced by perceptions of the organization's funding and administrative structure as a whole. Prospective donors consider the organization's effectiveness in fulfilling its mission and efficiency in using donated funds as part of the decision to contribute to the organization's efforts. This research suggests that the organization may be influencing donation decisions indirectly, through their management and administrative decisions and their financial disclosures. While social and crosswise influences may be beyond the organization's control, these dimensions represent potential areas of organizational influence. However, this requires organizations to recognize that fundraising is a more global function within the organization than previously considered.

OPTIMIZING FUNDRAISING APPEALS

Perhaps the largest stream of research on donations continues to focus on optimizing the effectiveness of fundraising appeals. Researchers have tested a variety of appeal messages, finding success with appeals that emphasize emotional engagement, a service orientation, a unique voice, a strong tradition (Sargeant, Ford, and Hudson 2008), personal nostalgia (Ford and Merchant 2010), credibility (Goering et al. 2011), and awe (Guan et al. 2019). Several studies have compared an altruistic or other-focused appeal with an egoistic or self-focused appeal and found that altruistic appeals are more effective for donations of time versus money (Kim 2014), when donations are public versus private (White and Peloza 2009; Wu, Gao, and Mattila 2017), and for in-group versus out-group beneficiaries (Park and Lee 2015), with egoistic appeals exhibiting the opposite effects. Appeals that focus on the donor increase donation likelihood, while appeals that emphasize the organization increase the amount donated, with mixed appeals decreasing both likelihood to donate and amount donated (Fajardo, Townsend, and Bolander 2018). Messages that emphasize the organization's successes are more effective in individualist cultures, while emphasizing donor contribution and group effort is more effective in collectivist cultures (Laufer et al. 2010). Celebrity endorsements can increase donations and reduce fundraising expenses (Harris and Ruth 2015), especially if the celebrity is unexpected and therefore attracts attention (Panic, Hudders, and Cauberghe 2016). Finally, inducing potential donors to imagine how their funds would be used to help beneficiaries can overcome the tendency to help in-groups more than out-groups (Gaesser, Shimura, and Cikara 2020) and to value in-kind donations over cash (Zhou and Gonçalves 2020).

Considerable research has focused on the framing of messages. Loss/negative/prevention-framed messages increase donations more than their gain/positive/promotion-framed counterparts (Bullard and Penner 2017; Cao 2016; Erlandsson, Nilsson, and Västfjäll 2018; Lee, Fraser, and Fillis 2017); however, a recent meta-analysis suggests that the overall effect may be null (Xu and Huang 2020). Promotion-framed messages increase donations more when a campaign has had a publicly known unsuccessful start (Le, Supphellen, and Bagozzi 2021). Framing the message from the perspective of the beneficiary, as opposed to the perspective of the donor, increases donations and improves the effectiveness of vivid information (Hung and Wyer 2009, 2011). However, activating donor identity increases donations for in-group beneficiaries and for frequent donors (Kessler and Milkman 2018; Kwan and Wyer 2016). Mentioning or showing money primes a self-sufficient mindset, which reduces donation behavior, but this can be mitigated by efforts such as using opaque rather than transparent collection boxes (Ekici and Shiri 2018). Finally, framing donations as an infrequent or exceptional expense increases donations and decreases donors' likelihood to consider their budgets in the donation decision (Sussman, Sharma, and Alter 2015).

One rich substream of message framing has examined the role of construal level in the processing of appeals. Messages that use concrete language or identify specific beneficiaries or donation targets are more effective for current fundraising campaigns, as opposed to campaigns in the future (Ein-Gar and Levontin 2012), when the request is for monetary donations, as opposed to donations of time (MacDonnell and White 2012; Song and Kim 2020), when the psychological distance between the donor and the beneficiaries is low (Ein-Gar and Levontin 2013), when the donor feels closer to the brand (Connors et al. 2021), and when the message includes specific information about how the donation would be used (Gu and Chen 2021). Concrete framing also increases the personal happiness of the donor (Rudd, Aaker, and Norton 2013). Donations are also more likely when there is low geographic or psychological distance between the donor and the beneficiaries (Paniculangara and He 2012; Touré-Tillery and Fishbach 2017); however, this can be overcome when donors have a strong global identity and perceive themselves to be world citizens (Wang, Kirmani, and Li 2021).

A second substream has examined the "identified victim effect," the tendency of donors to give more to a specifically identified beneficiary than to multiple beneficiaries. This effect can be overcome when the beneficiaries are viewed as entitative or forming a cohesive group, as long as the group is viewed as sharing positive traits (Smith, Faro, and

Burson 2013). However, this is more effective for donations of time than money (Liu, He, and Wang 2019). The negative effect of multiple beneficiaries can also be overcome by encouraging the donor to take the perspective of a single beneficiary prior to making the donation decision (Jang 2020), asking the donor how much they would donate to help one person before asking for the donation to help the group (Hsee et al. 2013), or increasing the donor's perceived self-efficacy and therefore the perceived efficacy of their donation (Sharma and Morwitz 2016). Donors are also more likely to opt out of donating when they must choose between two similar beneficiaries, unless there is an option to treat them fairly (Ein-Gar, Levontin, and Kogut 2021).

Researchers have also examined the use of numerical information in appeals and the resulting anchoring effects. One common anchor is the use of a donation scale, which generally increases donation amounts and net margins but exhibits asymmetrical effects. A lower leftmost anchor increases donation likelihood but decreases donation amounts, while a steeper increase in the amounts on the scale increases donation amounts (De Bruyn and Prokopec 2013; De Bruyn and Prokopec 2017). A similar effect has been found for setting a donation amount as a default, with lower defaults increasing the donation rate, but higher defaults increasing donation amounts (Goswami and Urminsky 2016). Suggesting a personalized donation amount can be effective in increasing donation rates, but the effects of specific suggestions depend on whether the campaign goal is new donor acquisition, donor retention, or lapsed donor reactivation (Verhaert and Ven den Poel 2011b). Setting a donation goal (for example, on a tote board or "thermometer") increases donation amounts, while messages that legitimate paltry contributions increase the donation rate (Jensen, King, and Carcioppolo 2013). Finally, incorporating a "none" option into the donation scale and shifting the message from "will you give" to "how much will you give" increases donation rates (Moon and VanEpps 2019).

Researchers have also identified effective persuasion tactics to incorporate into appeal messages, including offering to match donations either unconditionally or conditioned on reaching a certain response rate (Anik, Norton, and Ariely 2014; Charness and Holder 2019), allowing donors to earmark their donations for specific purposes (Fuchs, de Jong, and Schreier 2020; Kessler, Milkman, and Zhang 2019), framing donations as a dollar amount per day as opposed to the total donation amount (Atlas and Bartels 2018), including information about how past donations were used (Shehu et al. 2017), and allowing donors to use small donations to indicate an unrelated preference (vote for cats versus dogs, vanilla versus chocolate ice cream) that provides them with an opportunity for self-expression (Rifkin, Du, and Berger 2021).

Beyond message content, researchers have examined the aesthetic aspects of fundraising appeals. Using warm colors induces feelings of warmth and increases volunteerism, while cool colors induce perceptions of competence and increase monetary donations (Mehta et al. 2011). Congruity with the message can change this, however, with a negative message paired with warm colors, or a positive message paired with cool colors, increasing attention, emotional responses, and donations (Choi et al. 2020). Empathy for beneficiaries, and subsequent donations, can be induced through incorporating rough (versus smooth) haptic elements when the beneficiaries are perceived to be less fortunate (Wang, Zhu, and Handy 2016), or through displaying the appeal on a concave (versus convex) surface, priming a need to belong (Zhang and Wang 2019). Caution should be used with aesthetics, however, as Townsend (2017) finds that only aesthetic design elements that do not have cost implications increase donations, while those that are perceived as costly to the organization decrease donations.

Finally, researchers have examined the impact of fundraising media. Direct mailings from the same organization have been found to increase donor irritation and to cannibalize donations; however, competitive direct mailings increase the total amount donated to the group of charities (van Diepen, Donkers, and Franses 2009a, 2009b). Direct mailings are primarily effective in increasing donation incidence for active donors and are somewhat effective in reviving lapsed donors; however, lapsed donors who received multiple direct mailings prior to lapse have a lower chance of revival (Feng 2014; Schweidel and Knox 2013). Viewing fundraising appeals in virtual reality increases donations of time and money through the mechanisms of increased social presence, empathy, and responsibility (Yoo and Drumwright 2018; Kandaurova and Lee 2019). Attention has also been given to the impact of online engagement on donations, since organizations now obtain a significant portion of their donations from online giving (Bennett 2008). Organization websites that create an emotional response are more effective in eliciting small impulsive donations (Bennett 2009a), and organizations with stronger online social networks, greater social media engagement of their followers, and the ability to mobilize their online support networks receive more donations (Bhati and McDonnell 2020; Lee 2021; Lucas 2017; Saxton and Wang 2014).

The prevalence of this research stream suggests that the field perceives there to still be much to learn about how best to solicit donations from individuals. As individual donation behavior has become more complex and organizations have faced increasing competition for donated funds, there persists a goal to identify a more refined or creative approach to donation appeals to trigger the conversion from prospect to donor.

Future Research on Individual Donations to the Arts

Collectively, these five research streams suggest that while there exists an understanding of what motivates donors and a plethora of persuasive options in designing an effective fundraising appeal, the interaction between a nonprofit arts organization and its prospective donors should not be as simple as receiving a communication from a development department. Donors are influenced by a wide variety of information and interactions with the organization, from their experience as an audience member to their engagement with the organization on social media to the organization's financial disclosures. Their decisions to donate are influenced by the behavior of other donors to the organization, their own social networks, and even example donors described in the organization's fundraising appeals. They may base their donation on a long-standing relationship with the organization developed over time, or they may be choosing how to allocate their donation budget across a group of organizations that they wish to support. The decision to donate is far more complex than a response to a particular fundraising request.

The interplay among sources of revenue also suggests that organizations need to view their fundraising efforts as part of a multifaceted interaction with their donor community and ecological environment. Donors look to non-individual funders or ticket buyers to signal an organization's effectiveness and the worthiness of its cause, but they can also interpret institutional support or large audiences as evidence that individual donations are not needed. The actions of competitor organizations can affect fundraising success, from siphoning off core donors in a capital campaign to overwhelming potential donors with direct mailings. Decisions made in one aspect of fundraising strategy can have a significant impact not only on the organization's overall funding model but also on the fundraising success of its geographic and industry neighbors.

Future research should shift away from the approach of testing the response of an individual donor with a specific motivation or characteristic to a specific type of persuasive appeal, and instead consider fundraising as a global phenomenon that involves all aspects of the organization's interactions with the prospective donor and the fundraising environment. Donors do not view the organization as a series of silos that interact with them separately, and they do not necessarily view themselves as being part of a unique segment, separate from audience members, volunteers, or institutional supporters. Their interaction with the organization is a holistic one, incorporating various aspects of who they perceive the organization to be, who they perceive themselves to be, and how they interface with all aspects of the organization.

The financial repercussions of the Great Recession spurred a great deal of valuable inquiry into the complexity of donation behavior, and the increased availability of data has enabled researchers to examine donation behavior in context, including within the individual's and the organization's social networks. This contextual approach to understanding donation behavior is likely to yield valuable insights for both researchers and arts organizations in the years to come.

References

Abbate, Costanza Scaffidi, and Stefano Ruggieri. 2011. "The Fairness Principle, Reward, and Altruistic Behavior." *Journal of Applied Social Psychology* 41, no. 5: 1110–1120.

Agyemang, Isaac, Darlene D. Bay, Gail L. Cook, and Parunchana Pacharn. 2019. "Individual Donor Support for Nonprofits: The Roles of Financial and Emotional Information." *Behavioral Research in Accounting* 31, no. 1: 41–54.

Alexiou, Kostas, Jennifer Wiggins, and Stephen B. Preece. 2020. "Crowdfunding Acts as a Funding Substitute and a Legitimating Signal for Nonprofit Performing Arts Organizations." *Nonprofit and Voluntary Sector Quarterly* 49, no. 4: 827–848.

Alhidari, Ibrahim S., Tania M. Veludo-de-Oliveira, Shumaila Y. Yousafzai, and Mirella Yani-de-Soriano. 2018. "Modeling the Effect of Multidimensional Trust on Individual Monetary Donations to Charitable Organizations." *Nonprofit and Voluntary Sector Quarterly* 47, no. 3: 623–644.

Allen, Alexis M., Meike Eilert, and John Peloza. 2018. "How Deviations from Performance Norms Impact Charitable Donations." *Journal of Marketing Research* 55, no. 2: 277–290.

Anik, Lalin, Michael I. Norton, and Dan Ariely. 2014. "Contingent Match Incentives Increase Donations." *Journal of Marketing Research* 51, no. 6: 790–801.

Atlas, Stephen A., and Daniel M. Bartels. 2018. "Periodic Pricing and Perceived Contract Benefits." *Journal of Consumer Research* 45, no. 2: 350–364.

Balsam, Steven, and Erica E. Harris. 2014. "The Impact of CEO Compensation on Nonprofit Donations." *Accounting Review* 89, no. 2: 425–450.

Barasch, Alixandra, Jonathan Berman, and Deborah Small. 2014. "When Payment Undermines the Pitch: On the Persuasiveness of Pure Motives in Fund-Raising." *Psychological Science* 27, no. 10: 1388–1397.

Barnes, Martha L. 2011. "'Music to Our Ears': Understanding Why Canadians Donate to Arts and Cultural Organizations." *International Journal of Nonprofit and Voluntary Sector Marketing* 16, no. 1: 115–126.

Becker, Annika. 2018. "An Experimental Study of Voluntary Nonprofit Accountability and Effects on Public Trust, Reputation, Perceived Quality, and Donation Behavior." *Nonprofit and Voluntary Sector Quarterly* 47, no. 3: 562–582.

Beldad, Ardion, Babiche Snip, and Joris van Hoof. 2014. "Generosity the Second Time Around: Determinants of Individuals' Repeat Donation Intention." *Nonprofit and Voluntary Sector Quarterly* 43, no. 1: 144–163.

Bennett, Christine M., Hakkyun Kim, and Barbara Loken. 2013. "Corporate Sponsorships May Hurt Nonprofits: Understanding Their Effects on Charitable Giving." *Journal of Consumer Psychology* 23, no. 3: 288–300.

Bennett, Roger. 2008. "Research into Charity Advertising Needs a New Direction." *International Journal of Advertising* 27, no. 1: 161–164.

Bennett, Roger. 2009a. "Impulsive Donation Decisions During Online Browsing of Charity Websites." *Journal of Consumer Behavior* 8: 116–134.

Bennett, Roger. 2009b. "Regret and Satisfaction as Determinants of Lapsed Donor Recommencement Decisions." *Journal of Nonprofit & Public Sector Marketing* 21, no. 4: 347–366.

Bennett, Roger. 2012. "What Else Should I Support? An Empirical Study of Multiple Cause Donation Behavior." *Journal of Nonprofit & Public Sector Marketing* 24, no. 1: 1–25.

Bennett, Roger, and Rehnuma Ali-Choudhury. 2009. "Second-Gift Behaviour of First-Time Donors to Charity: An Empirical Study." *International Journal of Nonprofit and Voluntary Sector Marketing* 14, no. 3: 161–180.

Berman, Jonathan Z., Amit Bhattacharjee, Deborah A. Small, and Gal Zauberman. 2020. "Passing the Buck to the Wealth*ier*: Reference-Dependent Standards of Generosity." *Organizational Behavior and Human Decision Processes* 157: 46–56.

Berman, Jonathan Z., Alixandra Barasch, Emma E. Levine, and Deborah Small. 2018. "Impediments to Effective Altruism: The Role of Subjective Preferences in Charitable Giving." *Psychological Science* 29, no. 5: 834–844.

Berman, Jonathan Z., Emma E. Levine, Alixandra Barasch, and Deborah A. Small. 2013. "The Braggart's Dilemma: On the Social Rewards and Penalties of Advertising Prosocial Behavior." *Advances in Consumer Research* 41: 74–75.

Bertacchini, Enrico, Walter Santagata, and Giovanni Signorello. 2011. "Individual Giving to Support Cultural Heritage." *International Journal of Arts Management* 13, no. 3: 41–55.

Besana, Angela. 2012. "Alternative Resources: Revenue Diversification in the Not-for-Profit USA Symphony Orchestra." *Journal of Arts Management, Law, and Society* 42, no. 2: 79–89.

Bhati, Abhishek, and Diarmuid McDonnell. 2020. "Success in an Online Giving Day: The Role of Social Media in Fundraising." *Nonprofit and Voluntary Sector Quarterly* 49, no. 1: 74–92.

Blouin, Marie C., Roderick L. Lee, and G. Scott Erickson. 2018. "The Impact of Online Financial Disclosure and Donations in Nonprofits." *Journal of Nonprofit & Public Sector Marketing* 30, no. 3: 251–266.

Bluvstein, Shirly, Dafna Goor, Vicki Morwitz, and Alixandra Barasch. 2019. "Dirty Motivation: Using Donations to Mitigate Overhead Aversion." *Advances in Consumer Research* 47: 363–366.

Bodem-Schrötgens, Jutta, and Annika Becker. 2020. "Do You Like What You See? How Nonprofit Campaigns with Output, Outcome, and Impact Effectiveness Indicators Influence Charitable Behavior." *Nonprofit and Voluntary Sector Quarterly* 49, no. 2: 316–335.

Boenigk, Silke, and Bernd Helmig. 2013. "Why Do Donors Donate? Examining the Effects of Organizational Identification and Identity Salience on the Relationships Among Satisfaction, Loyalty, and Donation Behavior." *Journal of Service Research* 16, no. 4: 533–548.

Boenigk, Silke, and Christian Scherhag. 2014. "Effects of Donor Priority Strategy on Relationship Fundraising Outcomes." *Nonprofit Management & Leadership* 24, no. 3: 307–336.

Boeuf, Benjamin, Jessica Darveau, and Renaud Legoux. 2014. "Financing Creativity: Crowdfunding as a New Approach for Theatre Projects." *International Journal of Arts Management* 16, no. 3: 33–48.

Bourassa, Maureen A., and Abbey C. Stang. 2016. "Knowledge Is Power: Why Public Knowledge Matters to Charities." *International Journal of Nonprofit and Voluntary Sector Marketing* 21, no. 1: 13–30.

Bradley, Alex, Claire Lawrence, and Eamonn Ferguson. 2019. "When the Relatively Poor Prosper: The Underdog Effect on Charitable Donations." *Nonprofit and Voluntary Sector Quarterly* 48, no. 1: 108–127.

Bullard, Olya, and Sara Penner. 2017. "A Regulatory-Focused Perspective on Philanthropy: Promotion Focus Motivated Giving to Prevention-Framed Causes." *Journal of Business Research* 79, no. 3: 173–180.

Canada, Joseph, and Erica E. Harris. 2020. "The Role of Web Assurance Seals in Nonprofit Giving." *Journal of Information Systems* 34, no. 2: 131–148.

Candid. n.d. https://candid.org/about/our-story. Accessed December 2, 2021.

Cao, Xiaoxia. 2016. "Framing Charitable Appeals: The Effect of Message Framing and Perceived Susceptibility to the Negative Consequences of Inaction on Donation Intention." *International Journal of Nonprofit and Voluntary Sector Marketing* 21: 3–12.

Cha, Moon-Kyug, Youjae Yi, and Jaehoon Lee. 2020. "When People Low in Social Class Become a Persuasive Source of Communication: Social Class of Other Donors and Charitable Donations." *Journal of Business Research* 112: 45–55.

Chapman, Cassandra M., Barbara M. Masser, and Winnifred R. Louis. 2019. "The Champion Effect in Peer-to-Peer Giving: Successful Campaigns Highlight Fundraisers More than Causes." *Nonprofit and Voluntary Sector Quarterly* 48, no. 3: 572–592.

Charles, Cleopatra. 2018. "Nonprofit Arts Organizations: Debt Ratio Does Not Influence Donations—Interest Expense Ratio Does." *American Review of Public Administration* 48, no. 7: 659–667.

Charles, Cleopatra, and Mirae Kim. 2016. "Do Donors Care About Results? An Analysis of Nonprofit Arts and Cultural Organizations." *Public Performance & Management Review* 39, no. 4: 864–884.

Charles, Cleopatra, Margaret F. Sloan, and Peter Schubert. 2020. "If Someone Else Pays for Overhead, Do Donors Still Care?" *American Review of Public Administration* 50, nos. 4–5: 415–427.

Charness, Gary, and Patrick Holder. 2019. "Charity in the Laboratory: Matching, Competition, and Group Identity." *Management Science* 65, no. 3: 1398–1407.

Chatterjee, Promothesh, Arul Mishra, and Himanshu Mishra. 2010. "The Reparation Effect: Indulgent Consumption Increases Donation Behavior." *Advances in Consumer Research* 37: 527–528.

Chell, Kathleen, Rebekah Russell-Bennett, and Gary Mortimer. 2020. "Exploring Psychological Determinants of Sharing Donor Recognition on Social Networking Sites." *International Journal of Nonprofit and Voluntary Sector Marketing* 25:e1666. https://doi.org/10.1002/nvsm.1666.

Chen, Greg. 2009. "Does Meeting Standards Affect Charitable Giving? An Empirical Study of New York Metropolitan Area Charities." *Nonprofit Management & Leadership* 19, no. 3: 349–365.

Cheng, Yuan, and Zhongsheng Wu. 2021. "The Contingent Value of Political Connections on Donations to Chinese Foundations: Exploring the Moderating Role of Transparency." *Administration & Society* 53, no. 1: 36–63.

Choi, Jungsil (David), Yexin Jessica Li, Priyamvadha Rangan, Bingqing (Miranda) Yin, and Surendra N. Singh. 2020. "Opposites Attract: Impact of Background Color on Effectiveness of Emotional Charity Appeals." *International Journal of Research in Marketing* 37, no. 3: 644–660.

Connors, Scott, Mansur Khamitov, Matthew Thomson, and Andrew Perkins. 2021. "They're Just Not That into You: How to Leverage Existing Consumer-Brand Relationships Through Social Psychological Distance." *Journal of Marketing* 85, no. 5: 92–108. doi:10.1177/0022242920984492.

Croson, Rachel, Femida Handy, and Jen Shang. 2009. "Keeping Up with the Joneses: The Relationship of Perceived Descriptive Social Norms, Social Information, and Charitable Giving." *Nonprofit Management & Leadership* 19, no. 4: 467–489.

Cryder, Cynthia E., George Loewenstein, and Richard Scheines. 2013. "The Donor Is in the Details." *Organizational Behavior and Human Decision Processes* 120, no. 1: 15–23.

DataArts. n.d. "Our History." https://culturaldata.org/about/history/. Accessed December 2, 2021.

De Bruyn, Arnaud, and Sonja Prokopec. 2013. "Opening a Donor's Wallet: The Influence of Appeal Scales on Likelihood and Magnitude of Donation." *Journal of Consumer Psychology* 23, no. 4: 496–502.

De Bruyn, Arnaud, and Sonja Prokopec. 2017. "Assimilation-Contrast Theory in Action: Operationalization and Managerial Impact in a Fundraising Context." *International Journal of Research in Marketing* 34, no. 2: 367–381.

de Wit, Arjen, and René Bekkers. 2017. "Government Support and Charitable Donations: A Meta-Analysis of the Crowding-Out Hypothesis." *Journal of Public Administration Research and Theory* 27, no. 2: 301–319.

Del Barrio-Tellado, María José, Luis César Herrero Prieto, and Clare Murray. 2020. "Audience Success or Art for Art's Sake? Efficiency Evaluation of Dance Companies in the United States." *Nonprofit Management & Leadership* 31: 129–152.

Denis, Etienne, Claude Pecheux, and Luk Warlop. 2020. "When Public Recognition Inhibits Prosocial Behavior: The Case of Charitable Giving." *Nonprofit and Voluntary Sector Quarterly* 49, no. 5: 951–968.

Ein-Gar, Danit, and Liat Levontin. 2012. "How Does Construal Level Influence Donations to Individuals and Organizations." *Advances in Consumer Research* 38: 657–658.

Ein-Gar, Danit, and Liat Levontin. 2013. "Giving from a Distance: Putting the Charitable Organization at the Center of the Donation Appeal." *Journal of Consumer Psychology* 23, no. 2: 197–211.

Ein-Gar, Danit, Liat Levontin, and Tehila Kogut. 2021. "The Adverse Effect of Choice in Donation Decisions." *Journal of Consumer Psychology* 31, no. 3: 579–586. doi:10.1002/jcpy.1230.

Ekici, Ahmet, and Aminreza Shiri. 2018. "The Message in the Box: How Exposure to Money Affects Charitable Giving." *Marketing Letters* 30, no. 1: 137–149.

Erlandsson, Arvid, Artur Nilsson, and Daniel Västfjäll. 2018. "Attitudes and Donation Behavior When Reading Positive and Negative Charity Appeals." *Journal of Nonprofit & Public Sector Marketing* 30, no. 4: 444–474.

Evers, Anouk, and Maurice Gesthuizen. 2011. "The Impact of Generalized and Institutional Trust on Donating to Activist, Leisure, and Interest Organizations: Individual and Contextual Effects." *International Journal of Nonprofit and Voluntary Sector Marketing* 16, no. 4: 381–392.

Fajardo, Tatiana M., and Claudia Townsend. 2012. "Splitting the Decision: Increasing Donations by Recognizing the Differential Impact of Internal and External Considerations." *Advances in Consumer Research* 40: 252–253.

Fajardo, Tatiana M., Claudia Townsend, and Willy Bolander. 2018. "Toward an Optimal Donation Solicitation: Evidence from the Field of the Differential Influence of Donor-Related and Organization-Related Information on Donation Choice and Amount." *Journal of Marketing* 82, no. 2: 142–152.

Fang, Di, Paul W. Fombelle, and Ruth N. Bolton. 2021. "Member Retention and Donations in Nonprofit Service Organizations: The Balance Between Peer and Organizational Identification." *Journal of Service Research* 24, no. 2: 187–205.

Faulk, Lewis, Sheela Pandey, Sanjay K. Pandey, and Kristen Scott Kennedy. 2020. "Donors' Responses to Profit Incentives in the Social Sector: The Entrepreneurial Orientation Reward and the Profit Penalty." *Journal of Policy Analysis and Management* 39, no. 1: 218–242.

Feng, Shanfei. 2014. "Getting Lapsed Donors Back: An Empirical Investigation of Relationship Management in the Post-Termination Stage." *Journal of Nonprofit & Public Sector Marketing* 26, no. 2: 127–141.

Ford, John B., and Altaf Merchant. 2010. "Nostalgia Drives Donations: The Power of Charitable Appeals Based on Emotions and Intentions." *Journal of Advertising Research* 50, no. 4: 450–459.

Fuchs, Christoph, Matrijn G. de Jong, and Martin Schreier. 2020. "Earmarking Donations to Charity: Cross-Cultural Evidence on Its Appeal to Donors Across 25 Countries." *Management Science* 66, no. 10: 4820–4842.

Gaesser, Brendan, Yuki Shimura, and Mina Cikara. 2020. "Episodic Simulation Reduces Intergroup Bias in Prosocial Intentions and Behavior." *Journal of Personality and Social Psychology: Interpersonal Relations and Group Processes* 118, no. 4: 683–705.

Gneezy, Uri, Alex Imas, and Kristóf Madarász. 2014. "Conscience Accounting: Emotion Dynamics and Social Behavior." *Management Science* 60, no. 11: 2645–2658.

Goering, Elizabeth, Ulla M. Connor, Ed Nagelhout, and Richard Steinberg. 2011. "Persuasion in Fundraising Letters: An Interdisciplinary Study." *Nonprofit and Voluntary Sector Quarterly* 40, no. 2: 228–246.

Goh, Iris K. L., Ravi Pappu, and P. Monica Chien. 2021. "Investigating the Impact of Perceived Nonprofit Sponsorship Engagement on Prosocial Behavior." *Journal of Business Research* 126: 113–125.

Goswami, Indranil, and Oleg Urminsky. 2016. "When Should the Ask Be a Nudge? The Effect of Default Amounts on Charitable Donations." *Journal of Marketing Research* 53, no. 5: 829–846.

Grizzle, Cleopatra. 2015. "Efficiency, Stability, and the Decision to Give to Nonprofit Arts and Cultural Organizations in the United States." *International Journal of Nonprofit and Voluntary Sector Marketing* 20, no. 3: 226–237.

Gu, Yu, and Rong Chen. 2021. "How Does Money Phrasing Influence Intention to Donate: The Role of Construal Level and Fit." *Psychology & Marketing* 38, no. 11: 1911–1927. doi:10.1002/mar.21551.

Guan, Fang, Jun Chen, Outong Chen, Lihong Liu, and Yuzhu Zha. 2019. "Awe and Prosocial Tendency." *Current Psychology* 38, no. 4: 1033–1041.

Han, Eunjoo, Saerom Lee, and Karen Page Winterich. 2020. "How Public Recognition Promotes Donations to Out-Groups." *Advances in Consumer Research* 48: 385–388.

Harris, Erica E., and Daniel G. Neely. 2016. "Multiple Information Signals in the Market for Charitable Donations." *Contemporary Accounting Research* 33, no. 3: 989–1012.

Harris, Erica, Christine M. Petrovits, and Michelle H. Yetman. 2015. "The Effect of Nonprofit Governance on Donations: Evidence from the Revised Form 990." *Accounting Review* 90, no. 2: 579–610.

Harris, Erica E., and Julie A. Ruth. 2015. "Analysis of the Value of Celebrity Affiliation to Nonprofit Contributions." *Nonprofit and Voluntary Sector Quarterly* 44, no. 5: 945–967.

Helms-McCarty, Sara E., Timothy M. Diette, and Betsy Bugg Holloway. 2016. "Acquiring New Donors: A Field Experiment Using Bonus Trigger Incentives." *Nonprofit and Voluntary Sector Quarterly* 45, no. 2: 261–274.

Herzog, Patricia Snell, and Song Yang. 2018. "Social Networks and Charitable Giving: Trusting, Doing, Asking, and Alter Primacy." *Nonprofit and Voluntary Sector Quarterly* 47, no. 2: 376–394.

Hossain, Belayet, and Laura Lamb. 2017. "Associational Capital and Adult Charitable Giving: A Canadian Examination." *Nonprofit and Voluntary Sector Quarterly* 46, no. 5: 963–983.

Hsee, Christopher K., Jiao Zhang, Zoe Y. Lu, and Fei Xu. 2013. "Unit Asking: A Method to Boost Donations and Beyond." *Psychological Science* 24, no. 9: 1801–1808.

Hughes, Patricia, William Luksetich, and Patrick Rooney. 2014. "Crowding-Out and Fundraising Efforts: The Impact of Government Grants on Symphony Orchestras." *Nonprofit Management & Leadership* 24, no. 4: 445–464.

Hung, ChiaKo. 2020a. "Commercialization and Nonprofit Donations: A Meta-Analytic Assessment and Extension." *Nonprofit Management and Leadership* 31: 287–309.

Hung, ChiaKo. 2020b. "Converting Volunteers to Donors: Fundraising Strategies for Professional Associations." *International Journal of Nonprofit and Voluntary Sector Marketing* 26, no. 3: e1697. https://doi.org/10.1002/nvsm.1697.

Hung, Iris W., and Robert S. Wyer Jr. 2009. "Differences in Perspective and the Influence of Charitable Appeals: When Imagining Oneself as the Victim Is Not Beneficial." *Journal of Marketing Research* 46, no. 3: 421–434.

Hung, Iris W., and Robert S. Wyer Jr. 2011. "When Imagining Oneself as the Victim is Not Always Beneficial: The Impact of Differences in Perspectives on Effectiveness of Charitable Advertisements." *European Advances in Consumer Research* 9: 514.

Jacobs, Fred A., and Nicholas P. Marudas. 2009. "The Combined Effect of Donation Price and Administrative Inefficiency on Donations to US Nonprofit Organizations." *Financial Accountability & Management* 25, no. 1: 33–53.

James, Russell N., III. 2019. "Using Donor Images in Marketing Complex Charitable Financial Planning Planning Instruments: An Experimental Test with Charitable Gift Annuities." *Journal of Personal Finance* 18, no. 1: 65–73.

Jang, Hyunkyu. 2020. "Increasing Donations for Multiple Victims." *Advances in Consumer Research* 48: 430–431.

Jensen, Jakob D., Andy J. King, and Nick Carcioppolo. 2013. "Driving Toward a Goal and the Goal-Gradient Hypothesis: The Impact of Goal Proximity on Compliance Rate, Donation Size, and Fatigue." *Journal of Applied Social Psychology* 43, no. 9: 1881–1895.

Johnson, Jennifer Wiggins, and Bret Ellis. 2011. "The Influence of Messages and Benefits on Donors' Attributed Motivations: Findings of a Study with 14 American Performing Arts Presenters." *International Journal of Arts Management* 13, no. 2: 4–15.

Johnson, Jennifer Wiggins, and Pamela E. Grimm. 2010. "Communal and Exchange Relationship Perceptions as Separate Constructs and Their Role in Motivations to Donate." *Journal of Consumer Psychology* 20, no. 3: 282–294.

Johnson, Jennifer Wiggins, and Pamela E. Grimm. 2012. "Motivations to Donate: New Perspectives from Psychology, Economics, and Marketing." In *Handbook on Psychology of Motivation: New Research*, edited by Jason N. Franco and Alexander E. Svensgaard, 35–60. Hauppauge, NY: Nova Science.

Johnson, Jennifer Wiggins, Joann Peck, and David A. Schweidel. 2014. "Can Purchase Behavior Predict Relationship Perceptions and Willingness to Donate?" *Psychology & Marketing* 31, no. 8: 647–659.

Johnson, Samuel G. B., and Seo Young Park. 2021. "Moral Signaling Through Donations of Money and Time." *Organizational Behavior and Human Decision Processes* 165: 183–196.

Kandaurova, Maria, and Seung Hwan (Mark) Lee. 2019. "The Effects of Virtual Reality (VR) on Charitable Giving: The Role of Empathy, Guilt, Responsibility, and Social Exclusion." *Journal of Business Research* 100: 571–580.

Katz, Hagai. 2018. "The Impact of Familiarity and Perceived Trustworthiness and Influence on Donations to Nonprofits: An Unaided Recall Study." *Journal of Nonprofit & Public Sector Marketing* 30, no. 2: 187–199.

Kessler, Judd B., and Katherine L. Milkman. 2018. "Identity in Charitable Giving." *Management Science* 64, no. 2: 845–859.

Kessler, Judd B., Katherine L. Milkman, and C. Yiwei Zhang. 2019. "Getting the Rich and Powerful to Give." *Management Science* 65, no. 9: 4049–4062.

Khodakarami, Farnoosh, J. Andrew Petersen, and Rajkumar Venkatesan. 2015. "Developing Donor Relationships: The Role of the Breadth of Giving." *Journal of Marketing* 79, no. 4: 77–93.

Kim, May, Heather Gibson, and Young Jae Ko. 2011. "Understanding Donors to University Performing Arts Programs: Who Are They and Why Do They Contribute?" *Managing Leisure* 16, no. 1: 17–35.

Kim, Mirae. 2017. "The Relationship of Nonprofits' Financial Health to Program Outcomes: Empirical Evidence from Nonprofit Arts Organizations." *Nonprofit and Voluntary Sector Quarterly* 46, no. 3: 525–548.

Kim, Namin. 2014. "Advertising Strategies for Charities: Promoting Consumers' Donation of Time Versus Money." *International Journal of Advertising* 33, no. 4: 707–724.

Kim, Sungjin, Sachin Gupta, and Clarence Lee. 2021. "Managing Members, Donors, and Member-Donors for Effective Nonprofit Fundraising." *Journal of Marketing* 85, no. 3: 220–239.

Krawczyk, Kelly, Michelle Wooddell, and Ashley Dias. 2017. "Charitable Giving in Arts and Culture Nonprofits: The Impact of Organizational Characteristics." *Nonprofit and Voluntary Sector Quarterly* 46, no. 4: 817–836.

Krebs, Anne, Sophie Rieunier, and Bertrand Urien. 2015. "Generativity: Its Role, Dimensions, and Impact on Cultural Organizations in France." *International Journal of Arts Management* 17, no. 3: 28–45.

Kwak, Dae Hee, and Youngbum Kwon. 2016. "Can an Organization's Philanthropic Donations Encourage Consumers to Give? The Roles of Gratitude and Boundary Conditions." *Journal of Consumer Behavior* 15: 348–358.

Kwan, Candice M. C., and Robert S. Wyer. 2016: "The Effects of Self-Identity Activation and Emotions on Donation Decisions." *Advances in Consumer Research* 44: 526–527.

Laufer, Daniel, David H. Silvera, J. Brad McBride, and Susan M. B. Schertzer. 2010. "Communicating Charity Successes Across Cultures: Highlighting Individual or Collective Achievement?" *European Journal of Marketing* 44, nos. 9–10: 1322–1333.

Le, Nhat Quang, Magne Supphellen, and Richard P. Bagozzi. 2021. "Effects of Negative Social Information on the Willingness to Support Charities: The Moderating Role of Regulatory Focus." *Marketing Letters* 32, no. 1: 111–122.

Lee, Boram, Ian Fraser, and Ian Fillis. 2017. "Nudging Art Lovers to Donate." *Nonprofit and Voluntary Sector Quarterly* 46, no. 4: 837–858.

Lee, Hyunjung, Kyoungnam Catherine Ha, and Youngseon Kim. 2018. "Marketing Expense and Financial Performance in Arts and Cultural Organizations." *International Journal of Nonprofit and Voluntary Sector Marketing* 23:e1588. https://doi.org/10.1002/nvsm.1588.

Lee, Young-Joo. 2021. "Liked on Facebook, Liked for Real? Nonprofits' Online Popularity and Financial Performance." *Nonprofit Management & Leadership* 31, no. 3: 609–621.

Li, Wei, Evelyn McDowell, and Michael Hu. 2012. "Effects of Financial Efficiency and Choice to Restrict Contributions on Individual Donations." *Accounting Horizons* 26, no. 1: 111–123.

Lin-Healy, Fern, and Deborah A. Small. 2012. "Cheapened Altruism: Discounting Personally Affected Prosocial Actors." *Organizational Behavior and Human Decision Processes* 117, no. 2: 269–274.

Liu, Fan, Xin He, and Ze Wang. 2019. "The Differential Impact of Group Entitativity on Donation of Time Versus Money." *Advances in Consumer Research* 47: 750–751.

Lu, Jiahuan. 2016. "The Philanthropic Consequence of Government Grants to Nonprofit Organizations: A Meta-Analysis." *Nonprofit Management & Leadership* 26, no. 4: 381–400.

Lucas, Evie. 2017. "Reinventing the Rattling Tin: How UK Charities Use Facebook in Fundraising." *International Journal of Nonprofit and Voluntary Sector Marketing* 22: e1576. https://doi.org/10.1002/nvsm.1576.

Luria, Gil, Ram A. Cnaan, and Amnon Boehm. 2015. "National Culture and Prosocial Behaviors: Results from 66 Countries." *Nonprofit and Voluntary Sector Quarterly* 44, no. 5: 1041–1065.

Ma, Ji. 2020. "Funding Nonprofits in a Networked Society: Toward a Network Framework of Government Support." *Nonprofit Management & Leadership* 31: 233–257.

MacDonnell, Rhiannon, and Katherine White. 2012. "How Construals of Money Versus Time Impact Consumer Charitable Giving." *Journal of Consumer Research* 42, no. 4: 551–563.

McCambridge, Ruth, and Nathan Dietz. 2020. "Nonprofits in Recession: Winners and Losers." *Nonprofit Quarterly* 27, no. 1. https://nonprofitquarterly.org/the-great-recession-nonprofit-winners-and-losers/.

McDougle, Lindsey, and Marcus Lam. 2014. "Individual- and Community-Level Determinants of Public Attitudes Toward Nonprofit Organizations." *Nonprofit and Voluntary Sector Quarterly* 43, no. 4: 672–692.

McDowell, Evelyn A., Wei Li, and Pamela C. Smith. 2013. "An Experimental Examination of US Individual Donors' Information Needs and Use." *Financial Accountability & Management* 29, no. 3: 327–347.

Mehta, Ravi, Boyoun (Grace) Chae, Rui (Juliet) Zhu, and Dilip Soman. 2011. "Warm or Cool Colors? Exploring the Effects of Color on Donation Behavior." *Advances in Consumer Research* 39: 190–191.

Messamore, Andrew, Pamela Paxton, and Kristopher Velasco. 2021. "Can Government Intervention Increase Volunteers and Donations? Analyzing the Influence of VISTA with a Matched Design." *Administration & Society* 53, no. 10: 1547–1579. doi:10.1177/00953997211009885.

Minguez, Ana, and Francisco Javier Sese. 2021. "Social Norms and Recognition in Social Fundraising Campaigns: The Moderating Role of Self-Construal." *International Journal of Nonprofit and Voluntary Sector Marketing* 27, no. 1: e1706. https://doi.org/10.1002/nvsm.1706.

Mio, Chiara and Marco Fasan. 2015. "The Impact of Independent Directors on Organizational Effectiveness in Monetary and In-Kind Stakeholder Dialogue Museums." *Journal of Arts Management, Law, and Society* 45, no. 3: 178–192.

Moon, Alice, and Eric VanEpps. 2019. "Beyond Whether to Give: Using Continuous Requests to Increase Donation Rates." *Advances in Consumer Research* 47: 775.

Moon, Sangkil, and Kathryn Azizi. 2013. "Finding Donors by Relationship Fundraising." *Journal of Interactive Marketing* 27, no. 2: 112–129.

Mulder, Mark R., and Jeff Joireman. 2016. "Encouraging Charitable Donations via Charity Gift Cards: A Self-Determination Theoretical Account." *Journal of Nonprofit & Public Sector Marketing* 28, no. 3: 234–251.

Newman, George E., Adam Shniderman, Daylian M. Cain, and Kyle Sevel. 2019: "Do the Ends Justify the Means? The Relative Focus on Overhead Versus Outcomes in Charitable Fundraising." *Nonprofit and Voluntary Sector Quarterly* 48, no. 1: 71–90.

Ok, Ekin, Rishad Habib, and Karl Aquino. 2020. "Don't Take My Warm Glow: Unasked Prosocial Gifts Reduce Subsequent Donations." *Advances in Consumer Research* 48: 101–103.

Okutur, Nazli Gurdamar, and Jonathan Zev Berman. 2020. "Doing More Good: On the Process of Constructing Donation Portfolios." *Advances in Consumer Research* 48: 568–569.

Osili, Una O., Jacqueline Ackerman, and Yannan Li. 2019. "Economic Effects on Million Dollar Giving." *Nonprofit and Voluntary Sector Quarterly* 48, no. 2: 417–439.

Panic, Katarina, Liselot Hudders, and Veroline Cauberghe. 2016. "Fundraising in an Interactive Online Environment." *Nonprofit and Voluntary Sector Quarterly* 45, no. 2: 333–350.

Paniculangara, Joseph, and Xin He. 2012. "Empathy, Donation, and the Moderating Role of Psychological Distance." *Advances in Consumer Research* 40: 251–252.

Park, Kiwan, and Seojin Stacey Lee. 2015. "The Role of Beneficiaries' Group Identity in Determining Successful Appeal Strategies for Charitable Giving." *Psychology & Marketing* 32, no. 12: 1117–1132.

Qu, Heng, and Jamie Levine Daniel. 2021. "Is 'Overhead' a Tainted Word? A Survey Experiment Exploring Framing Effects of Nonprofit Overhead on Donor Decision." *Nonprofit and Voluntary Sector Quarterly* 50, no. 2: 397–419.

Reddick, Christopher G., and Branco Ponomariov. 2012. "The Effect of Individuals' Organization Affiliation on Their Internet Donations." *Nonprofit and Voluntary Sector Quarterly* 42, no. 6: 1197–1223.

Ressler, Robert W., Pamela Paxton, and Kristopher Velasco. 2021. "Donations in Social Context." *Nonprofit Management & Leadership* 31, no. 4: 693–715.

Rifkin, Jacqueline R., Katherine M. Du, and Jonah Berger. 2021. "Penny for Your Preferences: Leveraging Self-Expression to Encourage Small Prosocial Gifts." *Journal of Marketing* 85, no. 3: 204–219.

Rossi, Gina, Chiara Leardini, and Stefano Landi. 2020. "The More You Know, the More You Give: Influence of Online Disclosure on European Community Foundations' Donations." *Nonprofit Management & Leadership* 31: 81–101.

Rudd, Melanie, Jennifer Aaker, and Michael I. Norton. 2013. "Leave Them Smiling: How Concretely Framing a Prosocial Goal Creates More Happiness." *Advances in Consumer Research* 41: 73–74.

Samper, Adriana, Cindy Chan, and Ryan Hamilton. 2017. "Giving to Versus on Behalf of: Charitable Gift Requests Lead to Less Generous Giving." *Advances in Consumer Research* 45: 271–272.

Sargeant, Adrian, John B. Ford, and Jane Hudson. 2008. "Charity Brand Personality: The Relationship with Giving Behavior." *Nonprofit and Voluntary Sector Quarterly* 37, no. 3: 468–491.

Savary, Jennifer, and Kelly Goldsmith. 2020. "Unobserved Altruism: How Self-Signaling Motivations and Social Benefits Shape Willingness to Donate." *Journal of Experimental Psychology: Applied* 26, no. 3: 538–550.

Savary, Jennifer, Kelly Goldsmith, and Ravi Dhar. 2015. "Giving Against the Odds: When Tempting Alternatives Increase Willingness to Donate." *Journal of Marketing Research* 52, no. 1: 27–38.

Savary, Jennifer, Charis X. Li, and George E. Newman. 2020. "Exalted Purchases or Tainted Donations? Self-Signaling and the Evaluation of Charitable Incentives." *Journal of Consumer Psychology* 30, no. 4: 671–679. doi:10.1002/jcpy.1157.

Saxton, Gregory, and Lili Wang. 2014. "The Social Network Effect: The Determinants of Giving Through Social Media." *Nonprofit and Voluntary Sector Quarterly* 43, no. 5: 850–868.

Schatteman, Alicia M., and Ben Bingle. 2017. "Government Funding of Arts Organizations: Impact and Implications." *Journal of Arts Management, Law, and Society* 47, no. 1: 34–46.

Scherhag, Christian, and Silke Boenigk. 2013. "Different or Equal Treatment? Donor Priority Strategy and Fundraising Performance Assessed by a Propensity Score Matching Study." *Nonprofit Management & Leadership* 23, no. 4: 443–472.

Schweidel, David A., and George Knox. 2013. "Incorporating Direct Marketing Activity into Latent Attrition Models." *Marketing Science* 32, no. 3: 471–487.

Shang, Jen, Americus Reed II, and Rachel Croson. 2008. "Identity Congruency Effects on Donations." *Journal of Marketing Research* 45, no. 3: 351–361.

Shang, Jen, and Adrian Sargeant. 2016. "Social Norms and Fundraising: The Trade-Off Between Enhanced Donations and Donor Identity Esteem." *Journal of Nonprofit & Public Sector Marketing* 28, no. 4: 351–363.

Sharma, Eesha, and Vicki G. Morwitz. 2016. "Saving the Masses: The Impact of Perceived Efficacy on Charitable Giving to Single vs. Multiple Beneficiaries." *Organizational Behavior and Human Decision Processes* 135: 45–54.

Sharps, Daron L., and Juliana Schroeder. 2019. "The Preference for Distributed Helping." *Journal of Personality and Social Psychology: Interpersonal Relations and Group Processes* 117, no. 5: 954–977.

Shehu, Edlira, Michael Clement, Karen P. Winterich, and Ann-Christin Langmaack. 2017. "'You Saved a Life': How Past Donation Use Increases Donor Reactivation via Impact and Warm Glow." *Advances in Consumer Research* 45: 272–273.

Siemens, Jennifer Christie, Mary Anne Raymond, Yunsik Choi, and Jayoung Choi. 2020. "The Influence of Message Appeal, Social Norms and Donation Social Context on Charitable Giving: Investigating the Role of Cultural Tightness-Looseness." *Journal of Marketing Theory and Practice* 28, no. 2: 187–195.

Simpson, Bonnie, Katherine White, and Juliano Laran. 2018. "When Public Recognition for Charitable Giving Backfires: The Role of Independent Self-Construal." *Journal of Consumer Research* 44, no. 6: 1257–1273.

Sloan, Margaret F. 2009. "The Effects of Nonprofit Accountability Ratings on Donor Behavior." *Nonprofit and Voluntary Sector Quarterly* 38, no. 2: 220–236.

Smith, Brett R., Maria L. Cronley, and Terri F. Barr. 2012. "Funding Implications of Social Enterprise: The Role of Mission Consistency, Entrepreneurial Competence, and Attitude Toward Social Enterprise on Donor Behavior." *Journal of Public Policy & Marketing* 31, no. 1: 142–157.

Smith, Robert W., David Faro, and Katherine A. Burson. 2013. "More for the Many: The Influence of Entativity on Charitable Giving." *Journal of Consumer Research* 39, no. 5: 961–976.

Song, Doori, and Dong Hoo Kim. 2020. "'I'll Donate Money Today and Time Tomorrow': The Moderating Role of Attitude Toward Nonprofit Organizations on Donation Intention." *International Journal of Nonprofit and Voluntary Sector Marketing* 25: e1659. https://doi.org/10.1002/nvsm.1659.

Sussman, Abigail B., Eesha Sharma, and Adam L. Alter. 2015. "Framing Charitable Donations as Exceptional Expenses Increases Giving." *Journal of Experimental Psychology: Applied* 21, no. 2: 130–139.

Swanson, Scott R., and J. Charlene Davis. 2012. "Delight and Outrage in the Performing Arts: A Critical Incident Analysis." *Journal of Marketing Theory and Practice* 20, no. 3: 263–278.

Tian, Yuan, and Sara Konrath. 2021. "Can Too Much Similarity Between Donors Crowd Out Charitable Donations? An Experimental Investigation of the Role of Similarity in Social Influence on Giving Behavior." *Current Psychology* 40, no. 1: 1546–1558.

Touré-Tillery, Maferima, and Ayelet Fishbach. 2017. "Too Far to Help: The Effect of Perceived Distance on the Expected Impact and Likelihood of Charitable Action." *Journal of Personality and Social Psychology* 112, no. 6: 860–876.

Townsend, Claudia. 2017. "The Price of Beauty: Differential Effects of Design Elements with and Without Cost Implications in Nonprofit Donor Solicitations." *Journal of Consumer Research* 44, no. 4: 794–815.

Unger, Alexander, Julie Papastamatelou, and Jürg Arpagaus. 2021. "Do Social Networks Increase Donation Frequency? The Swiss Context." *Current Psychology* (online). https://doi.org/10.1007/s12144-020-01335-6.

van der Heijden, Hans. 2013. "Charities in Competition: Effects of Accounting Information on Donating Adjustments." *Behavioral Research in Accounting* 25, no. 1: 1–13.

van Diepen, Merel, Bas Donkers, and Philip Hans Franses. 2009a. "Does Irritation Induced by Charitable Direct Mailings Reduce Donations?" *International Journal of Research in Marketing* 26, no. 3: 180–188.

van Diepen, Merel, Bas Donkers, and Philip Hans Franses. 2009b. "Dynamic and Competitive Effects of Direct Mailings: A Charitable Giving Application." *Journal of Marketing Research* 46, no. 1: 120–133.

van Teunenbroek, Claire, René Bekkers, and Bianca Beersma. 2020. "Look to Others Before You Leap: A Systematic Literature Review of Social Information Effects on Donation Amounts." *Nonprofit and Voluntary Sector Quarterly* 49, no. 1: 53–73.

Verhaert, Griet A., and Dirk Van den Poel. 2011a. "Empathy as Added Value in Predicting Donation Behavior." *Journal of Business Research* 64, no. 12: 1288–1295.

Verhaert, Griet A., and Dirk Van den Poel. 2011b. "Improving Campaign Success Rate by Tailoring Donation Requests Along the Donor Lifecycle." *Journal of Interactive Marketing* 25, no. 1: 51–63.

Wallace, Elaine, Isabel Buil, and Leslie de Chernatony. 2017. "When Does 'Liking' a Charity Lead to Donation Behavior." *European Journal of Marketing* 51, nos. 11–12: 2002–2029.

Wang, Chen, Rui (Juliet) Zhu, and Todd C. Handy. 2016. "Experiencing Haptic Roughness Promotes Empathy." *Journal of Consumer Psychology* 26, no. 3: 350–362.

Wang, Xia, and Luqiong Tong. 2015. "Hide the Light or Let It Shine? Examining the Factors Influencing the Effect of Publicizing Donations on Donors' Happiness." *International Journal of Research in Marketing* 32, no. 4: 418–424.

Wang, Yajin, Amna Kirmani, and Xiaolin Li. 2021. "Not Too Far to Help: Residential Mobility, Global Identity, and Donations to Distant Beneficiaries." *Journal of Consumer Research* 47, no. 6: 878–889.

White, Katherine, and John Peloza. 2009. "Self-Benefit Versus Other-Benefit Marketing Appeals: Their Effectiveness in Generating Charitable Support." *Journal of Marketing* 73, no. 4: 109–124.

Winterich, Karen Page, and Yinlong Zhang. 2014. "Accepting Inequality Deters Responsibility: How Power Distance Decreases Charitable Behavior." *Journal of Consumer Research* 41, no. 2: 274–293.

Woronkowicz, Joanna. 2018. "The Effects of Capital Campaigns on Local Nonprofit Ecologies." *Nonprofit and Voluntary Sector Quarterly* 47, no. 3: 645–656.

Woronkowicz, Joanna, and Jill Nicholson-Crotty. 2017. "The Effects of Capital Campaigns on Other Nonprofits' Fundraising." *Nonprofit Management & Leadership* 27, no. 3: 371–387.

Wu, Laurie, Yixing (Lisa) Gao, and Anna S. Mattila. 2017. "The Impact of Fellow Consumers' Presence, Appeal Type, and Action Observability on Consumers' Donation Behaviors." *Cornell Hospitality Quarterly* 58, no. 2: 203–213.

Wu, Zhongsheng, Rong Zhao, Xiulan Zhang, and Fengqin Liu. 2018. "The Impact of Social Capital on Volunteering and Giving: Evidence from Urban China." *Nonprofit and Voluntary Sector Quarterly* 47, no. 6: 1201–1222.

Wymer, Walter, Annika Becker, and Silke Boenigk. 2021. "The Antecedents of Charity Trust and Its Influence on Charity Supportive Behavior." *International Journal of Nonprofit and Voluntary Sector Marketing* 26: e1690. https://doi.org/10.1002/nvsm.1690.

Xu, Jie, and Guanxiong Huang. 2020. "The Relative Effectiveness of Gain-Framed and Loss-Framed Messages in Charity Advertising: Meta-Analytic Evidence and Implications."

International Journal of Nonprofit and Voluntary Sector Marketing 25: e1675. https://doi.org/10.1002/nvsm.1675.

Ye, Nan, Lefa Tang, Ying Yu, and Yingyuan Wang. 2015. "'What's In It for Me?': The Effect of Donation Outcomes on Donation Behavior." *Journal of Business Research* 68, no. 3: 480–486.

Yetman, Michelle H., and Robert J. Yetman. 2013. "Do Donors Discount Low-Quality Accounting Information?" *Accounting Review* 88, no. 3: 1041–1067.

Yin, Bingqing (Miranda), Yexin Jessica Li, and Surendra Singh. 2020. "Coins Are Cold and Cards Are Caring: The Effect of Pregiving Incentives on Charity Perceptions, Relationship Norms, and Donation Behavior." *Journal of Marketing* 84, no. 6: 57–73.

Yoo, Seung-Chul, and Minette Drumwright. 2018. "Nonprofit Fundraising with Virtual Reality." *Nonprofit Management & Leadership* 29: 11–27.

Zhang, Yuli, and Chen Wang. 2019. "Shape Up the Behavior: A Concave Display Board Promotes Charitable Donations." *Advances in Consumer Research* 47: 940–941.

Zhou, Xiaozhou (Zoe), and Dilney Gonçalves. 2020. "Donating Cash or Donating Objects? How Donation Type Determines Donation Likelihood." *Advances in Consumer Research* 48: 814–815.

APPENDIX

Journals Included in Initial Search Criteria

Academy of Management Journal
Academy of Management Review
Accounting Horizons
The Accounting Review
Administration & Society
Administrative Science Quarterly
Administrative Sciences
Advances in Consumer Research
American Behavioral Scientist
American Political Science Review
American Review of Public Administration
American Sociological Review
Artivate: A Journal of Entrepreneurship in the Arts
Asian Pacific Advances in Consumer Research
Basic and Applied Social Psychology
Behavioral Research in Accounting
British Journal of Psychology
Business & Society
Business Ethics Quarterly
Business Ethics: A European Review
California Management Review
Cognition and Emotion
Contemporary Accounting Research
Cornell Hospitality Quarterly

Corporate Reputation Review
Creative Industries Journal
Current Psychology
Entrepreneurship Research Journal
European Advances in Consumer Research
European Journal of Marketing
European Management Journal
European Management Review
Family Business Review
Financial Accountability & Management
Information & Management
International Journal of Advertising
International Journal of Arts Management
International Journal of Human-Computer Interaction
International Journal of Information Management
International Journal of Nonprofit and Voluntary Sector Marketing
International Journal of Psychology
International Journal of Research in Marketing
Journal of Advertising
Journal of Advertising Research
Journal of Applied Social Psychology
Journal of Arts Management, Law, and Society
Journal of Business Ethics
Journal of Business Research
Journal of Consumer Behaviour
Journal of Consumer Psychology
Journal of Consumer Research
Journal of Electronic Commerce Research
Journal of Experimental Psychology: Applied
Journal of Hospitality Marketing & Management
Journal of Information Systems
Journal of Interactive Marketing
Journal of International Management
Journal of Management Studies
Journal of Marketing
Journal of Marketing Management
Journal of Marketing Research
Journal of Marketing Theory and Practice
Journal of Nonprofit & Public Sector Marketing
Journal of Organizational Behavior
Journal of Personal Finance
Journal of Personality and Social Psychology
Journal of Personality and Social Psychology: Attitudes and Social Cognition
Journal of Personality and Social Psychology: Interpersonal Relations and Group Processes
Journal of Policy Analysis and Management
Journal of Product & Brand Management
Journal of Public Administration Research and Theory

Journal of Public Policy & Marketing
Journal of Public Relations Research
Journal of Service Research
Journal of Services Marketing
Journal of the Academy of Marketing Science
Journal of the Association for Consumer Research
Journal of the Association for Information Systems
Latin American Advances in Consumer Research
Management Science
Managing Leisure
Marketing Letters
Marketing Science
Nonprofit and Voluntary Sector Quarterly
Nonprofit Management & Leadership
Organizational Behavior and Human Decision Processes
Psychological Science
Psychology & Marketing
Public Performance & Management Review
Research Policy
The Service Industries Journal
Small Business Economics
Strategic Management Journal

CHAPTER 28

TAX INCENTIVES FOR ARTS AND CULTURAL ORGANIZATIONS

SIGRID HEMELS

Introduction

"But in this world, nothing can be said to be certain but death and taxes!" American founding father Benjamin Franklin wrote this in a letter to Jean-Baptiste Le Roy on November 13, 1789 (Franklin 1817, 266), but it is still true. Tax is a relevant and unavoidable factor in social and business life, including the arts. Countries do not only use tax as a means to fund government expenditures. Many governments use tax legislation as a cultural policy instrument. This includes tax benefits for arts organizations and their benefactors. Such benefits are commonly known as *tax incentives*.

This chapter analyzes what a tax incentive is, what its positive and negative sides are, and how it is used to support the arts and cultural organizations. Several important incentives for the sector are discussed: tax incentives for giving, the possibility of paying tax with art, value added tax exemptions, exemptions of customs duties, and reduced value added tax rates for art.[1] This includes an analysis of these incentives in cross-border situations, such as cross-border fundraising and importing works of art. One word of warning: this chapter is not a social sciences paper, nor a US-style legal paper. It adheres to the continental European legal tradition of doctrinal research, taking an internal view on tax legislation (for the differences between legal scholarship in the United States and the European continent, refer to Schön 2016) and might therefore differ from what the reader is used to.

It is important that cultural organizations and researchers in the field of the arts know about tax incentives because of their significant impact on funding strategy and financial situations. Similarly, tax legislators and judges should acknowledge arts research. This chapter aims to add to mutual understanding and to exchanges of ideas between arts researchers and lawyers. It intends to inspire scholars in the field of arts and cultural management to include tax in their work, and to provide them with tools for this venture.

Concept

The primary function of taxation is to fund government expenditures. In addition, tax legislation may be used to promote policy goals. Given the incentivizing aim tax legislation has in those cases, these benefits are called tax incentives.[2] The Organisation for Economic Co-operation and Development (OECD 2010, 12) defined tax incentives as "provisions of tax law, regulation or practices that reduce or postpone revenue for a comparatively narrow population of taxpayers relative to a benchmark tax."

Tax incentives can take various forms. For example, cultural organizations that are listed as a charity are often exempt from taxes such as corporate income tax, gift tax, or inheritance tax. Another example is gift deduction, when one gives to a listed museum. Tax incentives can also take the form of a reduced rate—for example, a reduced value added tax (VAT) rate for entrance tickets for theater performances.

The aim of these tax incentives is—or should be—meeting a specific cultural policy object.[3] One example is enabling arts and cultural organizations to obtain additional funding or to increase consumption of cultural goods and services. Whether such a policy goal is achieved depends on various factors, including price elasticity. A good is price-elastic if, all else being equal, the quantity consumed of a good increases if its price decreases. For price-elastic goods, a price-reducing government policy can have the desired effect. For example, if giving is price-elastic, making giving cheaper through a gift deduction increases giving. However, if a good is price-inelastic, a change in price will not significantly change demand. In some cases, this might be a desired policy effect. For example, if the demand for opera tickets is price-inelastic, a reduction in VAT rate might not lead to a reduction in the ticket price. Instead, the company selling the tickets may keep the tax benefit. This might be a desired effect (for example, if a government wants opera companies selling tickets to have more funding) or an undesired one (for example, if tickets are sold by commercial companies who use the rate decrease to increase their profits). Unfortunately, many governments base a tax incentive on a "gut feeling" that a decrease in price will increase demand without properly surveying price elasticity aspects and the question of who will actually benefit. This leads to failed tax incentives.

Tax incentives may be perceived as free lunches, but they are not. A tax incentive reduces the tax income of a government, thus requiring either a cutback of direct spending or tax increases. Just like direct subsidies, tax incentives are a cost for the government, hence the alternative term "tax expenditures." Government agencies sometimes prefer a tax incentive over a direct subsidy, as these do not reduce their budget, but only reduce the income of the ministry of finance. For a ministry of culture, a tax incentive might seem more attractive than a more effective direct subsidy that reduces its budget. For the government as a whole, it is not desirable when a less effective tax incentive is introduced just because the ministry of culture does not want a more effective direct subsidy reducing its budget.

Pros and Cons of Tax Incentives

Many tax experts are not in favor of tax incentives. Some of their arguments apply to direct subsidies as well, but others are more specific to tax incentives. The OECD (2010) identified several theoretical and practical allegations against tax incentives. First are considerations of fairness. Lobby groups can have a strong political influence when pleading for tax incentives. The benefit of such an incentive is big for the small group that benefits, and the costs are borne by a large group of anonymous taxpayers. Second, there may be issues with the efficiency and effectiveness of tax incentives; it is difficult to evaluate existing tax incentives, and there are weaknesses in reporting in the budget. Third, tax incentives can increase the complexity of the tax system. Fourth, it is difficult to estimate the costs of tax incentives. Fifth, tax incentives tend to evade systematic and critical review. As a result, they can grow over time and avoid reform, reduction, or repeal.

The OECD (2010) also identified conditions under which tax incentives are most likely to be successful policy tools to achieve their objectives. These include administrative economies of scale and scope, as tax incentives might lead to lower administrative costs than direct subsidies. In addition, where detailed verification is not necessary and there is a limited probability of abuse or fraud, a tax benefit can be cost-effective, especially as information from third sources is available that can be used to check the claim of the taxpayer. Furthermore, in the case of a wide range of taxpayer choice, the distinctions among different activities that qualify for governmental support may not be considered important. In such cases a simpler reporting and verification process through the tax system might be more efficient than a direct subsidy.

Tax incentives are not necessarily a better or worse policy instrument but must be considered relative to alternative policy tools such as spending programs, regulation, and information campaigns. Policy objects and fiscal policy considerations should determine the best instrument. In addition, tax incentives must be democratically controlled, accounted for, and evaluated in the same way as direct subsidies. As this is currently not always the case, tax incentives are, in that respect, inferior to direct subsidies.

TAX INCENTIVES FOR GIVING TO THE ARTS AND CULTURAL ORGANIZATIONS

Private gifts can have several functions for cultural institutions. First of all, these broaden the institution's financial base by providing an additional source of income. Second, private gifts strengthen the financial base, as this source of funding may be less sensitive to political and economic changes. Third, private gifts can be used to strengthen the social base of cultural institutions, as private gifts provide an opportunity to create and foster a bond with the public.

Many governments support private donations to the arts and cultural organizations by tax incentives (OECD 2020). In addition, many governments exempt cultural organizations from paying gift and inheritance tax on donations they receive. This is the case both for countries that do not have large direct spending programs for the arts, such as the United States, and for countries that give substantial funding to cultural organizations, such as in Europe. Tax incentives for giving are designed in various ways. Examples are an income deduction, such as in the United States, Germany, the Netherlands, and Japan; a tax credit (a deduction of tax payable), such as in Canada and France; and a tax refund to cultural organizations, such as the gift aid scheme in the United Kingdom.

Some countries apply the tax incentive both to cash gifts and to objects, while other countries restrict it to cash gifts. The reason for the latter is often that it is difficult to value works of art. The donor benefits from a valuation that is as high as possible, as this will significantly reduce her tax assessment. The donor might be a wealthy individual or an artist donating her own work. If museums are involved in such valuations, they must ensure that they are not too obliging. They must make sure that valuations are reasonable. Otherwise, they might end up in the press as accomplices of tax fraud by overstating the value of a gift in kind.

Often, cultural organizations must meet formal and factual requirements, including having a charity registration, before the organization and its donors can apply tax incentives. Examples are the 501(c)(3) status in the United States for nonprofit organizations (named after the section of the US Internal Revenue Code in which it is included) or the inclusion in the charity register in the UK.

Cross-Border Charitable Giving: Problems and Solutions

Historically, countries restricted the application of tax incentives for giving to only resident cultural organizations. This is still the norm outside the European Union—for example, in Japan, the United States, and Australia. The idea behind this restriction is usually that countries want tax incentives to be beneficial to their own country (Bater 2004; Heidebauer et al. 2013; Buijze 2020).

This principle is often not applied consistently (TGE and EFC 2014). Resident charities are usually allowed to fund activities abroad. This has led to charities raising funds for foreign cultural organizations. For example, the American Friends of the Louvre is a US-resident charity with 501(c)(3) status.[4] US donors do not get a tax benefit if they donate directly to the French museum. By using this intermediary, they can get a gift deduction.

Other cultural organizations have not established a charity in the United States themselves but make use of, for example, the King Baudouin Foundation United States

(KBFUS).[5] KBFUS has the US 501(c)(3) status and enables US donors to obtain a tax benefit on their donations to cultural organizations in Europe and Africa, among other organizations. With an American Friends Fund at KBFUS, European and African nonprofits can receive tax-deductible gifts from US donors without having to set up and maintain their own US charity. At the time of writing, KBFUS had 199 projects in the "Arts, Culture and Historical Preservation" category.[6] To name just a few examples showing the wide range of projects: the Arcangelo Recording Fund, Giving for Giotto, Abbaye de Sept Fons, African Burns Creative Projects, American Friends of Museo Egizio (just one of many museums in the list), the Bayerische Staatsoper, the English National Ballet, the Nordic Symphony, and the Synagogue Borculo Foundation.

Similar initiatives are KBF Canada (enabling Canadian donors to donate internationally with a tax benefit),[7] Give2Asia (for US donors who want to support charities in twenty-three countries across the Asia-Pacific region and receive a tax benefit),[8] and Give2Asia Foundation Ltd. (for international giving with a tax benefit for Hong Kong donors).[9]

The European Court of Justice (ECJ) made it clear in several judgments between 2006 and 2015 that EU member states may not restrict their tax incentives for giving to resident cultural organizations (Hemels 2020a). However, as member states may still impose other requirements, including the requirement to register, there is still not a single market for philanthropy (Korzeniewska and Surmatz 2021). For that reason, even EU donors and cultural organizations make use of intermediary organizations, such as Transnational Giving Europe (TGE). TGE enables secure and tax-effective cross-border giving for charitable organizations and their donors in twenty-one European countries. TGE mentions museums as a specific example of organizations benefiting from this network, but other examples include the Gustav Mahler Jugendorchester (Austria), the Stichting International Theater Amsterdam (Netherlands), the Pro Patrimonio Foundation (Romania), the Gstaad Menuhin Festival (Switzerland), and the Glyndebourne Opera House (United Kingdom).[10]

Sometimes cultural organizations establish a joint charity in a country with significant fundraising potential. An example is the Dutch Masters Foundation.[11] This is a London-based registered charity founded in 2011 to support three Dutch cultural organizations: the Nederlands Dans Theater, the Royal Concertgebouw Orchestra, and the Royal Picture Gallery Mauritshuis.

Knowledge and Communication Are Key

Knowledge of tax incentives for giving is crucial for arts organizations. A donor will not give just because she can obtain a tax incentive. A donation will always cost money. But if it is correctly communicated that a tax incentive may be obtained, this might induce the donor to give more. Information on tax incentives is preferably included on the website of cultural organizations, as it is the first point of access for many donors. The information should be clear and easy to find. For small cultural organizations, information on national tax incentives will probably suffice. For large cultural organizations with an international audience, it may be beneficial to include options for cross-border donations. In order to avoid legal liabilities, it is important not to make any promises about benefits and to emphasize that the website is not meant to, nor can be understood to, provide tax advice and that for the tax effects in a specific situation a potential donor should seek the advice of a tax specialist. Knowledge about tax incentives is relevant not only for the fundraising team of a cultural organization. At least some basic knowledge is expected from everyone in the organization who is in contact with (potential) donors, including employees in the management and curatorial departments.

Paying Taxes with Important Works of Art or Cultural Heritage

Substantial amounts of cultural heritage are in private hands. Several countries implemented a tax incentive to induce owners of important works of art, archives, and other cultural objects to transfer ownership to the state in exchange for a reduced tax liability. This may include various taxes, most dominantly inheritance tax.

In Ireland, for example, cultural heritage can be used to obtain a tax credit from income tax, corporation tax, capital gains tax, gift tax, or inheritance tax liabilities. In Italy, an even wider range of taxes can be paid by the transfer of cultural heritage. Through this tax incentive, the National Library of Ireland managed to acquire a six-page James Joyce manuscript in spring 2006 after failing to buy it in 2004 (Murphy 2012). The Allied Irish Bank bought the manuscript for €1.17 million at auction to donate it to the National Library and credit the value against its corporation tax liabilities. Through the incentive, the manuscript is now available to the public and researchers.

Most countries limit the incentive to inheritance tax. They see it as a risk that at the death of the owner of important works of art, the heirs may want to sell the works, possibly to a foreign seller, if only to pay the inheritance tax on the whole estate. Cultural organizations might not be able to obtain sufficient funds in time to purchase these important works of art when they become available. This tax incentive, through which tax is paid by transferring the ownership of cultural heritage to the state, has the advantage that the budget is already there, which enables acting quickly.

The United Kingdom introduced the "acceptance in lieu" scheme in 1910 for historic buildings. In 1956, it was expanded to moveable property without a link to historic buildings. France introduced the incentive in 1968 under the name *dation en paiement*. Other countries with such incentives include Belgium, the Netherlands, and Spain.

The European Commission (1985) suggested a European framework to settle inheritance tax through the transfer of important works of art. The Economic and Social Committee of the European Communities (1985) unanimously supported this initiative. However, it was withdrawn (European Commission 1991), apparently because ministers of finance of the EU member states objected to it and argued that it was not within the competence of ministers for cultural affairs, as it had to do with taxation.

Common Features

The incentive differs between countries. A common feature is that it does not apply to all cultural heritage. It has to be of significant cultural or historical value. For example, the United Kingdom requires the item to be preeminent for its national, scientific, historic, or artistic interest, and in France it must have high artistic or historic value. In most countries moveable cultural heritage such as art, manuscripts, archives, archeological objects, and historic documents may qualify. In some countries, such as the United Kingdom and Italy, certain immovable property such as buildings and land is also acceptable. Ireland has set a minimum value threshold of €75,000. Most countries have special committees that advise on the acceptance (or rejection) of the cultural objects.

Usually, the state becomes the owner of the object, which can subsequently be given on loan to a museum, library, or archive. This is the case in France, the United Kingdom, and the Netherlands. In Ireland the state donates the objects to a specific museum, archive, or library. The Dutch incentive does not oblige the state to put the cultural heritage on public display, but it was customary to give it on loan to a museum or archive. However, the Dutch television program *Zembla* (2019) reported that the heirs of former Queen Juliana obtained a discount of €8.8 million through this incentive in 2004, without the most important work obtained, Willem van de Velde's pen painting *Vloot op de rede*, being on public display. This painting, valued at €2.5 million, was located in the office of King Willem-Alexander in the Dam Square Palace in Amsterdam. This office is not open to the public even though the Dutch Advisory Committee insisted that the painting should be accepted only if it would be placed in a museum. After questions from Parliament, Prime Minister Mark Rutte (2020) stated that even though it is customary to place the objects in a museum, this is not an obligation. This example shows the importance of requiring public access in the legislation. Especially in situations involving royals or other powerful persons, this requirement precludes public funds being used without the public benefiting from it.

Publicity on the Incentive Differs

The way information on objects obtained through the incentive is provided varies widely. In the Netherlands, nothing is systematically communicated. It depends on individual museums. For example, in 2009, the Rijksmuseum in Amsterdam organized a special exhibition of sixteen drawings it obtained through the tax incentive. The amount of money involved is almost never made public in the Netherlands. When a citizen requested documents on the application of this incentive, the State Secretary of Finance (2019) partly granted it. It seems that not much has been documented on this tax incentive, as only thirteen documents were found for the years 2012–2019. These included the annual reviews for the years 2011–2018 of the Advisory Commission. The information was very limited, as the artist, the value of the object, and the museum to which it was given on loan were not made public, the reason given being the obligation of secrecy in tax matters. The information is limited to descriptions such as "a painting," "a sculpture," "part of an archive," and "a collection." The lack of information means that neither the Dutch Parliament nor Dutch taxpayers can check how the money is spent. The Dutch incentive, therefore, does not meet the transparency and accountability requirements one would expect.

In Italy, the incentive seems to be rather unknown and is used sporadically even though it has existed since 1982. According to Traballi (2019) and Bisogno (2020), this is due to the lack of interest shown in its disclosure by the state, as well as to inconsistencies in the legislation and the cumbersome procedure. Traballi (2019) suggested that the state has little interest in acquiring works of art and prefers cash payments of taxes. Ireland is much more open than the Netherlands and Italy. It publishes a list with a description and the value of each object and the name of the receiving organization.[12]

The United Kingdom has the best practice on how to account for this tax incentive. Every year, Arts Council England publishes on its website an illustrated report with descriptions of the objects, the value of the tax incentive, and the receiving organization.[13] Where the Netherlands is very secretive, the UK government and museums give substantial publicity to the incentive and its successes. The tax incentive has been important in acquiring major works now available to the public. For example, in the fiscal year 2019–2020 were acquired, among others, a Manet painting, a Gauguin manuscript, a Chagall gouache, Rembrandt etchings, five antique pianos, and a Churchill letter (Arts Council England 2020). These items were distributed to a range of cultural organizations all over the United Kingdom, including museums, archives, and the Royal Academy of Music.

For museums, archives, and other cultural organizations that may obtain (if only on loan from the state) valuable cultural heritage through this incentive, it is important to be aware of it and its requirements. This will enable cultural organizations to introduce it in their conversations with owners of such objects. They can also fulfill a role in increasing public awareness by giving publicity to the works acquired through this incentive. This is even more the case in countries such as the Netherlands and Italy, where the state does not communicate about the acquired works. In times of tight acquisition budgets, this incentive provides an interesting option, but as long as it is unknown to the public and cultural organizations, it remains a sleeping beauty.

Value Added Tax: Ambiguous Incentives

Many countries apply taxes on consumption. Well known is the harmonized VAT in the EU. EU member states must base their national VAT legislation on the EU VAT

Directive (EU Council 2006). VAT is collected from entrepreneurs who are taxable persons for VAT purposes (a taxable person can be a natural person, a legal person, or something else such as a partnership). As entrepreneurs are obliged to include the VAT in the price of the goods or services they sell, the tax is, in fact, paid by consumers. This makes VAT an indirect tax, as the taxable person (the entrepreneur) is not the person who is supposed to bear the tax. Furthermore, insofar as taxable persons (entrepreneurs) use goods and services (inputs) for taxed transactions, they are entitled to deduct the VAT on supplies obtained from another taxable person (Article 168 of the VAT Directive). This results in a tax that is levied from entrepreneurs but in fact is a tax burden for consumers and other end users who are not able to get a refund, as they are not taxable persons for VAT. This consumption tax has been copied in many countries around the world. A similar tax is charged in Australia, India, Canada, New Zealand, Singapore, and Hong Kong under the name "goods and services tax." The US sales tax is a different kind of consumption tax, as it is only collected by the retailer when the final sale in the supply chain is reached. VAT is collected by all sellers in each stage of the supply chain, but with a refund of tax for entrepreneurs. Hence the name "value added tax"; in each stage of the chain only the value added during that stage is taxed. As VAT is the most dominant consumption tax in the world, and as many countries have copied the EU VAT system, this chapter will focus on the EU VAT Directive to show the impact of consumption taxes on the arts and cultural organizations.

Being a Taxable Person for VAT May Be Beneficial

It may be counterintuitive, but unlike with most taxes, such as corporate income tax, it may be beneficial for cultural organizations to be a VAT taxable person. Cultural organizations that are taxable for VAT may be able to recover VAT they paid on their inputs. This is especially important if such input VAT is high, as is the case, for example, for museums and theaters that incur high costs for maintenance and renovation of their buildings.

In order to be a taxable person, a cultural organization has to carry out an economic activity (Article 9 of the VAT Directive). For the VAT concept of "economic activity," it is not relevant that activities are not for profit. It includes various activities of cultural organizations such as ticket sales, selling goods in museum shops, and activities in return for sponsorship. If a cultural organization only provides services free of charge, it is not a taxable person. The same applies if a cultural organization only receives voluntary donations and public grants.

The fact that if a cultural organization only provides services free of charge it is not a taxable person caused a problem when, in 1998, the UK government restored free public access to the principal collections on display in museums and galleries. Having lost their economic activity, these museums and galleries could no longer recover (part of) the VAT they paid on their inputs. Insofar as they charged entry fees for special exhibitions or sold products in their shops, they were still taxable persons, but they could only deduct the input VAT related to those activities. To compensate for this disadvantage of free access, in 2001 the United Kingdom introduced a special VAT refund scheme for museums and galleries (HM Revenue and Customs 2001) that met strict requirements (VAT Notice 998 [HM Revenue and Customs 2017]; Article 33A of the VAT Act 1994), allowing them to reclaim VAT incurred in relation to free admission. The scheme does not form part of the general VAT system, but certain rules in UK VAT legislation apply to it. It is, strictly speaking, not a tax incentive but a direct grant.

This UK example shows that policy decisions that are meant to have a positive effect (free admission to museums) can have a counteractive VAT effect (increase in costs because of losing the right to a VAT refund). Policymakers must take such effects into account. If policymakers seem to be unaware of these effects, cultural organizations should make them aware. When implementing such policies, policymakers may consider redressing the negative effects by direct grants, as was the case in the United Kingdom. As the grants are compensated for by higher VAT income because cultural organizations can no longer request a refund, the effect is neutral both for the state and for cultural organizations. The European Commission (2011, 10) called on member states to alleviate the VAT burden for nonprofit organizations by introducing such targeted compensation mechanisms outside the VAT system.

VAT Exemptions May Not Always Be Beneficial

The VAT Directive includes various exemptions. In contrast with other taxes, being exempt from VAT is often not beneficial. The reason for this is that insofar as a taxable person uses goods and services for exempt transactions, the input VAT is not deductible. This might be detrimental when input VAT is high. This is relevant for cultural organizations and cultural policymakers, as EU member states are allowed to exempt the supply of certain cultural services and the supply of goods closely linked thereto (Article 132(1)(n) of the VAT Directive). EU member states are relatively free—within the restrictions of the directive and general EU law—to decide whether or not to apply such exemption and if so, what its scope will be. Not all cultural services that meet the requirements of the directive must be exempt (for more elaborate discussions and references to case law, see Hemels 2023).

Cultural organizations must be aware that being exempt might be a financial drawback. For example, in the Netherlands, museums were exempt from VAT until 1996. Upon the wish of the museum sector, the exemption was abolished to enable museums to get a refund on their input VAT.

Reduced VAT Rates for Admission to Cultural Organizations

EU member states must apply a regular VAT rate of at least 15 percent (Article 98 of the VAT Directive). They are allowed to apply a reduced VAT rate of, in principle, at least

5 percent on certain goods and services included in Annex III of the VAT Directive. This includes admission to shows, theaters, circuses, fairs, concerts, museums, cinemas, exhibitions, and similar cultural events and facilities. A reduced rate does not restrict the possibility of deducting input VAT irrespective of whether that input VAT was based on the regular rate or a reduced rate. For cultural organizations with a high input VAT, a reduced rate is therefore more attractive than an exemption. For that reason, Dutch museums preferred a reduced VAT rate applied on their entry tickets as of 1996 to an exemption. The reduced rate is a tax incentive that is beneficial to cultural organizations, as it reduces the price of their entrance tickets.

Some member states may apply rates below 5 percent. They already had such rates before January 1, 1991, and have been "temporarily" allowed to keep them. France, for example, applies a rate of 2.1 percent to specific tickets for certain theatrical performances and circus performances.[14] The theatrical performances of drama, opera, music, or choreography must be of newly created works or of classic works in a new staging. The circus performances must feature exclusively original creations designed and produced by the company and using the regular services of a group of musicians. The rate only applies to the first 140 performances. This incentive keeps the refund of input VAT intact but reduces the tax burden on such performances.

Exemption from Customs Duties

If certain requirements are met, works of art can be imported into the EU and into many other countries free of customs duties—for example, by certain museums and for exhibitions. This exemption is a true tax incentive (as is the reduced VAT rate), as it makes it possible for museums to import works of art for temporary exhibitions without the additional costs of customs duties.

The tax incentive makes museums vulnerable to artists or major donors who want the museum to import works of art that are, in fact, destined not for the museum but for themselves. This happened to the Stedelijk Museum in Amsterdam. Five works by Dutch artist Karel Appel, coming from the United States, had been sitting for years in customs at Amsterdam's Schiphol airport. If the artist had taken these out of customs, he would have had to pay import duty. As they were taken out as loans to the Stedelijk Museum, no import duty was due. However, instead of being delivered directly to the museum, the works ended up in Appel's Amsterdam residence and were only handed over to the museum when the museum found out that the works were not in the collection. When this came out, the museum director was dismissed. Later the public prosecutor acquitted him of all charges, as it turned out that he was not aware that the works had not been transferred to the museum. A scandal like this can do serious harm to both the museum and its management. It is important that museum employees who might have to deal with such requests from artists do not give in, instead making sure that the works end up in the museum in order to remain within the law and not harm the reputation of the museum.

Reduced VAT Rates for Works of Art

Not only cultural organizations but also the arts, more specifically artists and their heirs, can benefit from reduced VAT rates. EU member states have the option to apply a reduced VAT rate to the importation of works of art. In that case, the reduced rate may also be applied to the supply of works of art by the artist or his heirs (Article 103 and Annex IX of the VAT Directive). Member states may also allow art dealers to apply the margin scheme to works of art, meaning that instead of applying the VAT rate on the sales price, the VAT rate is applied on the art dealer's margin (the difference between the purchase price and selling price).

These tax incentives apply only to art that meets the tax definition of "work of art." For customs duties, this definition is included in Chapter 97 of the so-called Combined Nomenclature (CN), which is based on the internationally used Harmonized System run by the World Customs Organization. The works of art included in this chapter are:

9701 Paintings, drawings, and pastels, executed entirely by hand
9702 Original engravings, prints, and lithographs
9703 Original sculptures and statuary, in any material

Since 1995, Article 311(2) of the VAT Directive defines "works of art" as the objects listed in Directive Annex IX, Part A:

1. Pictures, collages, paintings, and drawings executed entirely by hand by the artist (CN code 9701)
2. Original engravings, prints, and lithographs (impressions produced in limited numbers) executed entirely by hand by the artist, irrespective of the process or of the material employed, but not including any mechanical or photomechanical process (CN code 9702)
3. Original sculptures and statuary, in any material, provided that they are executed entirely by the artist, including sculpture casts the production of which is limited to eight copies and supervised by the artist or the artist's successors in title (CN code 9703)
4. Tapestries and wall textiles made by hand from original designs provided by artists, provided that there are not more than eight copies of each
5. Individual pieces of ceramics executed entirely by the artist and signed by the artist
6. Enamels on copper, executed entirely by hand, limited to eight numbered copies bearing the signature of the artist or the studio
7. Photographs taken by the artist and printed by the artist or under the artist's supervision, signed and numbered and limited to thirty copies, all sizes and mounts included

Art that does not fall into one of these categories is not eligible for the VAT benefits. The ECJ had to interpret the definitions of "works of art" on several occasions, both for customs duties and for VAT. The case law concerns works by various famous artists. For example, regarding a work by Claes Oldenburg (*Model, Motor Section, Giant Soft Fan*), the German customs authorities questioned whether this was a sculpture, as in their view only objects having a sculptural form made by traditional techniques could be classified as such. The ECJ disagreed and ruled that all three-dimensional artistic productions, irrespective of the techniques and materials used, may be sculptures.[15]

Similarly, the German customs found that a work by László Moholy-Nagy entitled *Konstruktion in Emaille I (Telefonbild)* was not a painting. However, the ECJ decided that paintings are all pictorial works executed entirely by hand on a support of any kind of material and that for that reason the steel plate with a fused coating of enamel glaze colors was a painting.[16] Apparently nobody had told the ECJ why the work was called *Telefonbild* (telephone picture). In 1922, Moholy-Nagy ordered by telephone five paintings in porcelain enamel from a sign factory. He had the factory's color chart before him and he sketched his paintings on graph paper. At the other end of the telephone, the factory supervisor had the same kind of paper. He took down the dictated shapes in the correct position. Moholy-Nagy (1947, 79) acknowledged that these pictures do not have the quality of the "individual touch" (and are not, in the words of the ECJ, "executed entirely by hand"). However, he was of the opinion that mathematically harmonious shapes, executed precisely, are filled with emotional quality, and that they represent the perfect balance between feeling and intellect. The effect of the judge's mistake was that this work could, in line with how it is viewed by art historians, be classified as art for customs duty purposes.

On the other hand, in 1989 the ECJ observed that thirty-six photographs by Robert Mapplethorpe could not be brought in under any of the CN codes of Chapter 97. The court ruled that although the photographer may, by the choice of subject and techniques used, confer some artistic merit to the work, the original is always the result of a technical process consisting in fixing the image of objects on a sensitive surface by the action of light. For that reason the court was of the opinion that the original could not be considered to be wholly executed by hand and held that art photographs could not be classified as art under the CN codes.[17] Currently this is not a problem, as photographs can be imported duty free in the EU under CN heading 4911.

Point 7 of Annex IX to the VAT Directive does include a specific reference to photographs. However, the ECJ stretched this definition to any photograph that meets the objective requirements included in that point, including non-artistic photographs such as wedding photos.[18]

In contrast the European Commission (2010, L214/3) explicitly denied a work of video art by Bill Viola and a work of light art by Dan Flavin the art status for VAT purposes. Viola's work is described as a video sound installation consisting of ten DVD players, ten projectors, ten loudspeakers, and twenty DVDs "containing recorded works of 'modern art' in the form of images accompanied by sound." The work of Dan Flavin was described as "A so-called 'light installation' consisting of six circular fluorescent lighting tubes and six lighting fittings of plastics." The European Commission decided that both works could not be classified as sculptures, notwithstanding the fact that in 2008 the London VAT and Duties Tribunal classified these works, which were identified by Valentin (2011) as *Hall of Whispers* by Bill Viola and *Six Alternating Cool White/Warm White Fluorescent Lights Vertical and Centered* (1973) by Dan Flavin, as sculptures. Before coming to this judgment, the UK judges heard various expert witnesses, including a museum director, a curator, and an art critic, to give evidence on the character of the works (Adam 2010) and went to the Tate Modern Museum to view a similar Flavin work (paragraph 16 of the judgment). The London VAT and Duties Tribunal regarded it as "absurd to classify any of these works as components ignoring the fact that the components together make a work of art" (paragraph 49 of the judgment).

These kinds of qualification problems are not new, nor are they unique to the EU. In 1928, the US Customs Court had to decide on whether or not various works by Constantin Brancusi, including the famous *Bird in Space*, were works of art. This court also heard various expert witnesses. In recognizing the "so-called new school of art," the court acknowledged an art movement "whose exponents attempt to portray abstract ideas rather than to imitate natural objects."[19] As a result, *Bird in Space* was categorized as art and could be imported tax-free. Tischler (2012, 1688) points out that the court relied on the principle of "objective acceptance," which subordinates conflicting subjective responses of the court to expert testimonials and recognizes shifting trends within the art world. This also seems to have been the approach of the UK Tribunal in 2008, which even mentioned the Brancusi case in paragraph 30 of its judgment.

It is worrying that the ECJ does not take the same approach of objective acceptance. The ECJ did not hear expert witnesses in any of the cases discussed. This resulted in a divergence between what is regarded as art in the art world and the definition of art for VAT and customs duties purposes. As a consequence, VAT and customs duties incentives favor traditional forms of art over contemporary art forms.

Conclusion

Tax incentives for arts and cultural organizations have implications for the finances of cultural organizations and their fundraising strategy. They provide for additional possibilities to increase collections and have an impact on their costs.

On the other hand, tax incentives can be a threat for cultural organizations. This may be the case if major donors or artists try to use cultural organizations to import art tax free or to obtain higher tax deductions by inflating the value of donations in kind. Such schemes are tax fraud, and not only illegal but also detrimental to the reputation of cultural organizations.

Conversely, tax legislators and judges should be aware of the negative effect resulting from tax incentives being based on a rather conservative definition of art. This excludes various forms of contemporary art and forms a hindrance—in any case not an incentive—for the development of new art forms. Such disparities between the fields of tax and arts make it even more important that the two fields communicate and learn from each other, not only in daily life but also in academia.

Notes

1. Readers who need a wider-ranging and more in-depth discussion than is possible within the confines of this book chapter should see Hemels and Goto 2017.
2. One of the alternative terms is "tax expenditure." For a more elaborate discussion, see Hemels and Goto 2017), chap. 4.
3. Tax incentives can also be a reflection of pure lobbying power.
4. American Friends of the Louvre, https://aflouvre.org/about/.
5. King Baudouin Foundation United States, https://kbfus.org/.
6. King Baudouin Foundation United States, "Find Giving Opportunities," https://kbfus.net workforgood.com/projects?utf8=%E2%9C%93&cat=545&search_string=.
7. KBF Canada, https://www.kbfcanada.ca/en/.
8. Give2Asia, https://give2asia.org/.
9. Give2Asia (Hong Kong), https://give2asia.org/hongkong/.
10. Transnational Giving Europe, https://www.transnationalgiving.eu/.
11. Dutch Masters Foundation, http://www.dutchmasters.org.uk/.
12. Department of Tourism, Culture, Arts, Gaeltacht, Sport and Media, Government of Ireland, "Tax Relief for Heritage Donations," June 10, 2020, https://www.gov.ie/en/publication/d5404-tax-relief-for-heritage-donations/.
13. Arts Council England, "Acceptance in Lieu," https://www.artscouncil.org.uk/tax-incentives/acceptance-lieu.
14. Article 281 quater, Code général des impôts, https://www.legifrance.gouv.fr/codes/section_lc/LEGITEXT000006069577/LEGISCTA000006191656/#LEGISCTA000006191656.
15. ECJ, May 15, 1985, Case 155/84, *Reinhard Onnasch v. Hauptzollamt Berlin—Packhof*, https://eur-lex.europa.eu/legal-content/en/TXT/?uri=CELEX:61984CJ0155.
16. ECJ, November 8, 1990, Case C-231/89, *Krystyna Gmurzynska-Bscher, Galerie Gmurzynska v. Oberfinanzdirektion Köln*, https://eur-lex.europa.eu/legal-content/en/TXT/?uri=CELEX:61989CJ0231.
17. ECJ, December 13, 1989, Case C-1/89, *Ingrid Raab v. Hauptzollamt Berlin-Packhof*, https://eur-lex.europa.eu/legal-content/HR/TXT/?uri=CELEX:61989CJ0001.
18. ECJ, September 5, 2019, Case C-145/18, *Regards Photographiques SARL v. Ministre de l'Action et des Comptes publics*, https://eur-lex.europa.eu/legal-content/en/TXT/?uri=CELEX:62018CJ0145. For an extensive discussion of this case and its implications, see Hemels 2020b.
19. *Brancusi v. United States*, US Customs Court, November 26, 1928, T. D. 43063, 54 Treas. Dec. 428, p. 3, https://www.robertocaso.it/wp-content/uploads/2020/04/54_Treas._Dec._428_1928_Cust._Ct_Brancusi-v-US.pdf.

References

Adam, G. 2010. "Flavin and Viola Light Works Ruled 'Not Art.'" *The Art Newspaper* no. 219: 59.
Arts Council England. 2020. "Cultural Gifts Scheme & Acceptance in Lieu Report 2020." https://www.artscouncil.org.uk/sites/default/files/download-file/CGS_AIL_Website_Download_201920_FINAL_23%20DEC_0.pdf.
Bater, Paul. 2004. "Introduction: International Tax Issues Relating to Non-Profit Organisations and Their Supporters." In *The Tax Treatment of NGOs*, edited by Paul Bater, Frits W. Hondius, and Penina Kessler Lieber, 1–29. The Hague: Kluwer Law International.

Bisogno, M. 2020. "L'adempimento tributario Mediante cessione di opere d'arte: Spunti per un'analisi comparata." *Rivista Trimestrale di Diritto Tributario* no. 1: 7–27.

Buijze, Renate. 2020. *Tackling the International Tax Barriers to Cross-Border Charitable Giving*. Amsterdam: IBFD.

Economic and Social Committee. 1985. "Bulletin 11/1983, Item 14." http://aei.pitt.edu/50776/1/B0191.pdf.

European Commission. 1985. "Draft Resolution of the Council and of the Ministers Responsible for Cultural Affairs Meeting Within the Council Concerning the Adoption of Tax Measures in the Cultural Sector, Com/85/194 Final." https://ec.europa.eu/commission/presscorner/detail/en/P_85_33.

European Commission. 1991. "91/C 186/03." *Official Journal of the European Communities*, July 18, 1991, 12. https://eur-lex.europa.eu/legal-content/lv/TXT/?uri=OJ:C:1991:186:TOC.

European Commission. 2010. "Commission Regulation (EU) No 731/2010 of 11 August 2010." https://eur-lex.europa.eu/legal-content/EN/TXT/?uri=CELEX%3A32010R0731.

European Commission. 2011. "Communication from the Commission to the European Parliament, the Council and the European Economic and Social Committee. On the future of VAT Towards a Simpler, More Robust and Efficient VAT System Tailored to the Single Market, 6 December 2011, COM(2011/851)." https://eur-lex.europa.eu/legal-content/EN/ALL/?uri=celex%3A52011DC0851.

EU Council. 2006. "Council Directive 2006/112/EC of 28 November 2006 on the Common System of Value Added Tax as Later Amended." https://eur-lex.europa.eu/legal-content/EN/ALL/?uri=CELEX:32006L0112.

Franklin, Benjamin. 1817. "To Mr. Le Roy, of Paris. On the Affairs of France. Philadelphia, Nov. 13, 1789." In *The Private Correspondence of Benjamin Franklin*, 1:265–266. London: Henry Colburn. https://books.google.se/books?id=6Pyx4bCPwEYC&pg=PR7&source=gbs_selected_pages&cad=2#v=onepage&q&f=false.

Heidebauer, S., S. J. C. Hemels, B. W. Muehlman, M. Stewart, O. Thoemmes, and T. Tukic. 2013. "Cross Border Charitable Giving and Its Tax Limitations." *Bulletin for International Taxation* 67, no. 11: 611–625.

Hemels, Sigrid. 2020a. "Charitable Organisations." In *Research Handbook on European Union Taxation Law*, edited by C. H. J. I. Panayi, W. Haslehner, and E. Traversa, 248–268. Cheltenham, UK: Edgar Elgar.

Hemels, Sigrid. 2020b. "Say Cheese! Photographs and the Definition of Works of Art for VAT Purposes." *FIRE Journal* 2020, no. 1: 1–18. https://www.djoef-forlag.dk/publications/fire/files/2020/2020-1/Artikel_1_1.pdf.

Hemels, Sigrid. 2023. "Charities and VAT." In Marta Papis (ed.) *Ben Terra's European Tax Law: Value Added Tax and Beyond*. Amsterdam: IBFD.

Hemels, Sigrid, and Kazuko Goto. 2017. *Tax Incentives for the Creative Industries*. Singapore: Springer.

HM Revenue and Customs. 2017. VAT Notice 998. "VAT Refund Scheme for Museums and Galleries." https://www.gov.uk/guidance/vat-refund-scheme-for-museums-and-galleries-notice-998.

HM Revenue and Customs. 2001. "VAT (Refund of Tax to Museums and Galleries) Order 2001 (SI 2001/2879)." https://www.gov.uk/guidance/vat-refund-scheme-for-museums-and-galleries-notice-998#annex.

Korzeniewska, Anna, and Hanna Surmatz. 2021. "A Single Market for Philanthropy in the EU." https://www.philanthropyadvocacy.eu/news/a-single-market-for-philanthropy-in-the-eu/.

London VAT and Duties Tribunal. 2008. Haunch of Venison Partners Limited v. HM Revenue and Customs, C 00266, 11 December 2008. https://www.casemine.com/judgement/uk/5a8ff78e60d03e7f57eaf152.

Moholy-Nagy, László. 1947. "Abstract of an Artist" (1944). In *The New Vision and Abstract of an Artist*. New York: Wittenborn, Schultz.

Murphy, S. J. 2012. "Irish Historical Mysteries: The Trade in Joyce Manuscripts." http://homepage.eircom.net/~seanjmurphy/irhismys/joyce.htm.

OECD. 2010. "Tax Expenditures in OECD Countries." http://www.oecd.org/gov/budgeting/taxexpendituresinoecdcountries-oecdpublication.htm.

OECD. 2020. "Taxation and Philanthropy." https://www.oecd-ilibrary.org/taxation/taxation-and-philanthropy_df434a77-en.

Rutte, Mark. 2020. "Letter of 24 January 2020, Reference 4112217." https://www.rijksoverheid.nl/documenten/kamerstukken/2020/01/24/beantwoording-kamervragen-over-kunstverkoop-oranjes-en-een-historische-kunstverkoop-door-koninklijk-huis.

Schön, Wolfgang. 2016. "Tax Law Scholarship in Germany and the United States." Working Paper No. 2016-7. Max Planck Institute for Tax Law and Public Finance. https://ssrn.com/abstract=2775191 or http://dx.doi.org/10.2139/ssrn.2775191.

State Secretary of Finance. 2019. "Letter of 12 July 2019, Nr. 2019-0000089981." https://open.overheid.nl/Details/ronl-4df60583-a136-4181-8187-4325c0d305eb/1.

TGE and EFC. 2014. "Taxation of Cross-Border Philanthropy in Europe After Persche and Stauffer: From Landlock to Free Movement?" Transnational Giving Europe and European Foundation Centre. https://efc.issuelab.org/resources/18545/18545.pdf.

Tischler, Rachel J. 2012. "'The Power to Tax Involves the Power to Destroy': How Avant-Garde Art Outstrips the Imagination of Regulators, and Why a Judicial Rubric Can Save It." *Brooklyn Law Review* 77, no. 4: 1665–1705. https://brooklynworks.brooklaw.edu/blr/vol77/iss4/8/.

Traballi, Alberto. 2019. "Pagare le imposte mediante cessione di opere d'arte, un'opportunità poco conosciuta." https://www.traballitaxadvisor.com/pagare-imposte-con-opere-d-arte/.

Valentin, P. 2011. "UK: The European Commission Says It's Not Art." Mondaq. https://www.mondaq.com/uk/music-and-the-arts/135086/the-european-commission-says-its-not-art.

Zembla. 2019. "Duurste kunstwerk uit erfenis van prinses Juliana weggehouden van publiek." BNNVARA, December 18, 2019. https://www.bnnvara.nl/zembla/artikelen/duurste-kunstwerk-uit-erfenis-van-prinses-juliana-weggehouden-van-publiek.

CHAPTER 29

NON-FUNGIBLE TOKENS AND NONPROFIT MANAGEMENT

Participation, Revenue Generation, and Strategic Planning

HEATHER R. NOLIN AND AMY C. WHITAKER

THE COVID-19 pandemic has highlighted the necessity of financial stability for arts and cultural institutions. According to the American Alliance of Museums' National Survey of COVID-19 Impact on United States Museums, conducted in June 2020, the vast majority (87 percent) of the 521 museum respondents reported that they had only twelve months or less of financial operating reserves remaining. A majority (56 percent) of respondents reported that if the pandemic closures had extended another six months and they were unable to secure additional funding—whether from governments, foundations, individual donors, museumgoers, shop visitors, or other means—they were going to have to close (AAM 2020). Fully 70 percent reported a loss of revenue of 70 percent since the start of the COVID-19 pandemic, highlighting that museums require ample and sustained funding to stay in operation.

At the same time that cultural institutions have faced these tough financial challenges, the non-fungible token (NFT) has entered the public consciousness as a new form of art, a rapidly evolving technology, and a sometimes profitable market phenomenon (cf. Nadini et al. 2021).[1] From 2019 to 2021, the NFT marketplace grew from $4.6 million to $11.1 billion (McAndrew 2022, 14). In 2021, the artist Mike Winkelmann (known professionally as Beeple) sold an NFT at Christie's for $69.346 million, and the State Hermitage Museum in St. Petersburg, Russia, sold NFTs based on five of its most prized and recognizable works for a total of $440,000 (Kishkovsky 2021). Given the positive financial outcomes of these activities against a backdrop of financial distress, it stands to reason that museums and other cultural organizations may be tempted to engage with NFTs either as artworks or as means of revenue generation. The financial, artistic, and cultural differences between the Beeple and Hermitage NFT projects highlight the critical question of NFT strategy in cultural institutions: if NFTs are to achieve their maximum financial potential for the institution, do they need to function as unique works of art? Furthermore, if they function not as art but as something like postcards or souvenirs, how can institutions cultivate a reciprocal sense of connection with their audiences?

In this chapter, we present five case studies that explore some possible answers to these questions as well as various applications of NFTs to core nonprofit missions and activities of individual museums and the larger field. Mission-related goals of individual museums include collections development, policies, and care; audience engagement; and scholarly contribution. The mission-related goals of the museum field extend to the stewardship and preservation of objects and the prioritization of collective field-level interest over situations in which an institution has a self-interest—for instance, ensuring that objects are kept in publicly accessible collections or that institutions are not deaccessioning objects for financial gain.

The five use cases for NFTs in museums are drawn from real-world examples or fully developed hypotheticals. These cases include revenue generation from general and more specialized audiences, deaccessioning, restitution of cultural heritage, and audience relationship-building and fundraising via NFTs of a cultural institution itself. While we focus on art museums, other collecting institutions, such as libraries and archives, and those that typically do not collect, such as heritage sites, *Kunsthallen*, and performing arts organizations, may find these observations and strategic planning tools valuable. We hope to show our readers that this new technology can function within the museum ecosystem as much more than a novel type of artwork or a new means of fundraising. NFTs can encapsulate institutional creativity in uncovering new ways of thinking, solving problems, and engaging audiences.

For any of these strategies or use-cases, there is no one answer or knowable outcome as much as there is a process of engagement with fundamentally open-ended questions of strategy, mission, and financial planning. To be sure, the future of NFTs changes daily. Even as we write, news breaks about the volatility of the value of NFTs, about museums selling traditional artworks to fund the purchase of NFTs, and about the rapid evolution of financial structures around cryptocurrencies.[2] For any individual, whether a legendary curator, tech pioneer, or someone new to NFTs, reconciling NFT futures and museum practices calls anyone's bluff on believing only in their own opinion and that they know everything about this new digital form. Therefore, we invite the reader to keep an open mind and think creatively and financially about the support required to run twenty-first-century cultural organizations and the realities and possibilities of NFTs as a new, messy, evolving technology.

Are NFTs Art?

Are NFTs art, something else, or both? At least for a time, Wikipedia editors declined even to classify NFTs as art (Artnet News 2022), leaving record sales by the artists Beeple and Pak off lists of the most expensive artworks by living artists. As recently as October 2022, writers have suggested that NFTs are a Ponzi scheme—not artworks with aesthetic value but tokens to be offloaded for profit (Escalante-de Mattei 2022; Levine 2022). Especially given this controversy, questions of connoisseurship and the artist's intent must be part of the discussion at any institution considering a strategic plan that will include NFTs.

NFTs present new variations on problems of connoisseurship, authenticity, and ownership that have long characterized a "work of art," however defined. Consider, for example, the difference between an NFT and works of art created for devotional rather than aesthetic or financial purposes. The sculpted portrait of the first Venetian Patriarch and later saint, Lorenzo Giustiniani (1381–1456), once attributed to Jacopo Bellini (probably 1396–1470/1471), is considered powerful and valuable to its audience because the artist carved Giustiniani's image directly from the priest's likeness. Thus the sanctity of the priest is transferred to the object itself, and the marble becomes imbued with the magical power of its subject.[3] Indeed, Venetians, including the Doge (Venetian head of state) in 1477, prayed to this likeness, which originally crowned Giustiniani's tomb in the basilica of San Pietro di Castello, to ask him to end several severe outbreaks of the plague that ravaged the city in the fifteenth, sixteenth, and seventeenth centuries.[4] What would it mean to make an NFT of such an object?

In addition to considering to what degree the power of the subject is imbued in a work of art, one must also consider to what extent the "hand" of the artist is discernable and how and to what degree their "hand" needs to be present in order for the work of art to be regarded as an autograph work. Consider the case of *Salvator Mundi* (ca. 1500), an artwork attributed to Leonardo da Vinci (1452–1519) when it sold at Christie's in November 2017 for $450.3 million. The work was heavily restored by master conservator Dianne Modestini (Reyburn 2022). Even if Leonardo were the painter of the original, at what point would the artwork no longer be by his hand? Or there is the example of the *Ecce Homo* (Jesus Christ's face) frescoed in 1930 on the wall of a church in Borja, Spain, by Elías García Martínez (1858–1934). In 2012, in an attempt to preserve the work, an untrained but enthusiastic restorer rendered the image unrecognizable. Even though the work became a tourist attraction, specifically because the face of Jesus came to resemble a "blurry potato," that notoriety does not cancel out the question of whether the overly restored fresco may still be considered a work by Martínez (Kussin 2016).

While authenticity—of the artwork, its subject, and its artist—is what traditionally defines physical works of art, even for editioned works that exist in multiple copies, what sets NFTs apart is the question of ownership. The Beeple work exists in infinite high-resolution copies as a JPEG file, but because it is registered to the blockchain only one collector owns the $69.346 million NFT. These examples encapsulate, even for more recent work, the dilemma of bridging from a traditional work of art to its digital copy and, by extension, the tension between art's artistic and financial natures.

A Creative Approach to Strategic Planning: Mapping the Financial and Philosophical

Strategic planning is a framework for approaching institutional questions and ways of thinking about the organization's future. With its focus on mission, values, goals, and long-view time horizons, the greatest benefit of the process—often more important than the final plan—is getting people to think together and to work differently, including realigning shared assumptions about what that future might hold.

Any initiative involving NFTs at a museum is also an exercise in strategic planning, and much can be learned from NFT-related strategic planning in museums. This far-flung and rapidly evolving topic—spoken about in grandiose terms or discussed as a utopian future within the hermetically sealed microcosm of pandemic Zoom calls from basement offices lined with apocalyptic quantities of paper towels—challenges exactly this gap between the realities of institutions historically designed to care for and store tangible objects and a digital future of ever-changing bounds of art and finance. Because NFTs acutely invite institutions to balance their mission-driven priorities and financial requirements, we introduce here a Venn-diagramming method of strategic planning. As a shorthand, we call this mapping tool and process the Nolin-Whitaker Method (NWM).

Even without injecting NFTs into the equation, many museums and other arts and cultural institutions may fall flat in strategic planning processes. This could be because they rely on general, inflexible templates often used for planning in hospitals, universities, or for-profit organizations; they fail to implement the plan because of lack of leadership or cultural buy-in and engagement; or they return to methods of thinking and working that they had before the planning process.[5] While we do not profess to offer a panacea for these shortfalls, we argue that the difficulty of grappling with the sheer newness of NFTs can offer the counterintuitive gift of leaving these templated methods behind and inviting cultural institutions to think about their artistic and economic lives in new ways. The Venn-diagramming tools, presented here for use with NFTs, also provide tools to overcome obstacles that can stymie successful strategic planning more generally.

The Nolin-Whitaker Method (NWM) is a visual mapping tool and conceptual framework to guide strategic planning processes. Organizations may use this approach to visualize and articulate ways to balance often-competing impulses and goals: emotional versus intellectual, aspirational versus realistic, and right-brained versus left-brained ways of thinking about the future. The essence of this dual approach is the creation of multiple Venn-diagram overlaps that offer perspective on how museums can engage meaningfully and purposefully in areas of both mission-driven values and financial necessity.

NFTs are unique in their peculiar tripartite nature as art, as governance and investment structures, and as potential revenue sources. As we will show, this level of complexity presents additional—and unusual—challenges for the future of cultural institutions trying to balance an aspirational vision with the realities of executing and sustaining that vision in the longer term. The Venn-diagramming method lends itself to understanding and expressing ideas visually, which can have particular resonance for staff working in organizations such as museums that, being dedicated to the visual arts, often require staff to have strong visual acuity and thinking skills.

Strategic planning in museums is itself artistic in the sense that it is a generative organizational process that requires creative thinking about how to balance care and interpretation of collections that are held in the public trust with the need to leverage those collections in some ethical way for financial gain to cover that same care and interpretation. Rather than reducing the process to a single outcome, strategic planning is an act of gathering (Parker 2018), an open-ended exercise in convening people to discuss values and to decide what they will or will not do and how they will do it together. It is also a rare moment within an institution to address, navigate, and reconcile what we term an organization's "financial" and "philosophical" needs and priorities (see Figure 29.1), which are by turns competing and overlapping.

In our model, we use "financial" to mean engaging with art markets and with the more fundamental operational aspects of running a museum, including the structural necessity or institutional algebra of covering costs and finding economic sustainability for the short and long term.[6] These questions of the philosophical and the financial—that is, the relationship of art and money—map onto sociological theories of the uneasy intersections of art and commerce—that is, the debate between warring worldviews of Hostile Worlds and Nothing But (Velthuis 2005). In Hostile Worlds, art and commerce

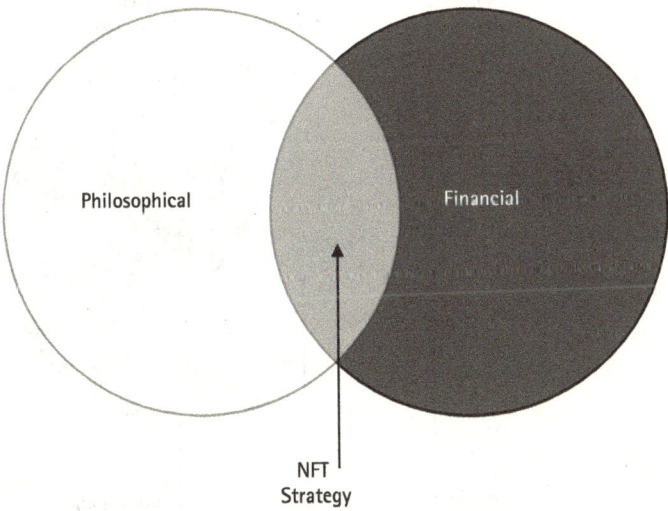

FIGURE 29.1 The financial and the philosophical.

must be kept apart because markets taint art. In Nothing But, markets can metabolize all forms of value—cultural, social, artistic—into price (Grampp 1989). The arts rely on "circuits of commerce" (Velthuis 2005; Zelizer 2000) in which those things that are most difficult to price, like art, exist in constellation with the need of art institutions, like museums, to sustain themselves financially. The Nolin-Whitaker Method offers one possible way to harmonize the two warring points of view.

As part of the strategic planning process, we encourage the reader to develop and customize the diagrams we present to reflect their own institutional values and priorities and those from the field and society that they want to incorporate into their planning processes. While we focus here on balancing specific aspects of the philosophical and the financial in NFT strategies, and specifically consider novel approaches to restitution or to audience engagement, the diagrams could be formulated to reflect an institution's desire to engage in other work, including philanthropy, open-source sharing of collections, or development of more representative and diverse audiences and staff.

Figure 29.2 shows an expanded version of this philosophical and financial overlap. In the philosophical realm, we highlight key areas that NFT strategy especially activates: *scholarship*, which includes the creation, collection, and dissemination of knowledge about NFTs as art and within the context of longer histories of art, both digital and analog; *connoisseurship*, which dovetails with scholarship but focuses on ascertaining and then stewarding the value of art; *audience engagement*, which includes inviting new audiences into museums; and *artistic practice*, which includes the museum's stewardship not only of objects but also of ongoing creative practice, including in the form of commissioning new artworks as NFTs. In the financial, we highlight three especially active areas: *investment management*, which refers primarily to the organization's

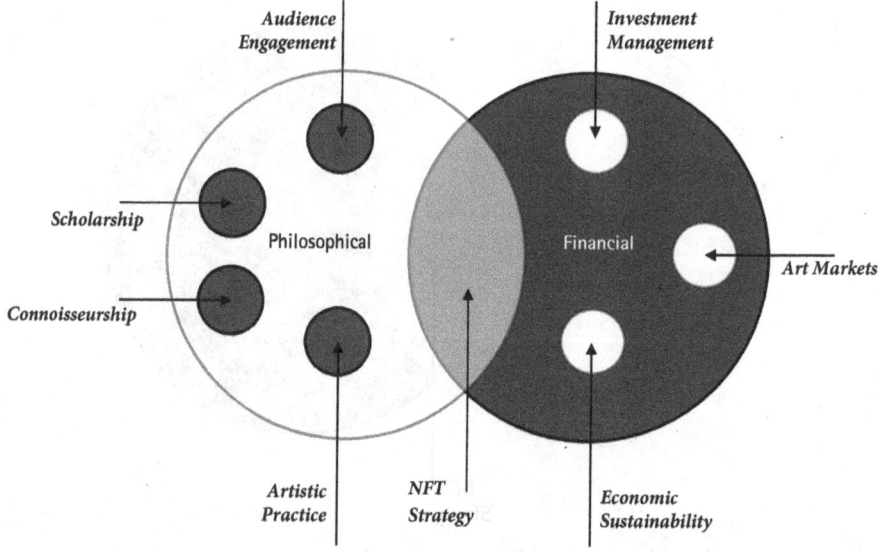

FIGURE 29.2 Breakdown of the financial and philosophical.

endowment but also includes other assets that would be listed on a balance sheet, such as gift shop inventory, facilities, and grants; *art markets*, which mirror connoisseurship in the art historical sense by appraising market value and which include sales platforms for art such as auction houses and commercial galleries as well as online platforms for NFT sales; and *economic sustainability*, which refers to an institution's ability to support itself day in, day out. In the cases we study here, we see some strategies that earn revenue for direct operating expenses and others that contribute to endowments, creating longer-term revenue support through investment gains.

The real-world and hypothetical case studies that we workshop in this chapter show that the remit of a cultural institution is varied and complex and requires many forms of expertise and specialization. There can be a lack of consensus about what an organization is trying to achieve by discussing NFTs. As we have seen in some of the cases below, NFT strategy has received more scrutiny from boards of trustees, at the same time that the boards generally would not oversee such operating decisions.[7] In addition, NFTs are new and typically not well understood by stakeholders without a technical background in computer programming. Therefore, they add even more complexity to team discussion and decision-making. What work-culture divides need to be crossed for teams to come together on NFT strategies? What financial and philosophical approaches can be melded to always keep art at the center—including finding the money to do so? Teams must be open to learning together the intricacies of collecting, preserving, and displaying this art form born in the computer age. As we hope to show in the case studies, for NFTs to be truly meaningful and impactful for the organization, the teams must also be open to new ways of implementing their strategies.

Case Studies

We now turn to cases of revenue generation and then expand to hypotheticals that extend to deaccessioning and institutional decision-making.

NFT as Revenue Generator

With the outsized market returns of NFTs, it is understandable that nonprofit institutions might create NFTs from their existing collections or otherwise use NFTs to make money. Some of these efforts seem conspicuously and primarily about revenue. At the same time, others have succeeded in generating revenue while also engaging in mission-critical activities such as conservation and acquisitions.

Case Study I: *NFTs of Collection Objects for Conservation—MFA Boston*

In June 2022, the Museum of Fine Arts Boston announced that the institution was partnering with LaCollection, a for-profit company that has cultivated relationships with other encyclopedic museums, to create NFTs of a group of Impressionist pastels owned by the MFA Boston for buyers to "collect" (LaCollection n.d.).[8] Inspired by the 2018–2019 exhibition "French Pastels: Treasures from the Vault," the sale rolled out in two phases. In total, LaCollection offered for sale on its website roughly two thousand NFTs of twenty-four different pastels at €299 ($316) each (MFA Boston 2022a). The sale, split across two NFT issuances spaced several months apart, was designed, according to the museum, to benefit the needed conservation of two of their Degas paintings.[9] In August 2022, the first group of eleven NFTs was also displayed in a digital exhibition at Claude Monet's gardens in Giverny, France; the exhibition was free to anyone who purchased admission to the gardens.[10]

In the announcement of the first NFT sale, the MFA Boston spokesperson, chief operating officer Eric Woods, expressed the NFT strategy in terms of audience outreach, saying: "There are myriad virtual outreach modalities that have really come to the fore" (Yerebakan 2022). When the authors subsequently interviewed Debra LaKind, senior director of intellectual property and business development at the MFA Boston, about the strategy, she stated that it was a way to expand the institution's reach and engage with new audiences, and she framed the project as a "test" or experiment to see how NFTs benefit both the museum's marketing strategy and collections care priorities. These statements highlight that the museum's strategy was intentionally experimental in nature—prototyping different ways to make NFTs work within the overall strategies of an organization. The licensing team led the project with conservation and curatorial taking part in the decision-making. The reader might consider how the complexion of the project could have changed had a different department led the effort. The MFA Boston case highlights the ways in which exploratory NFT strategies serve as a lens over a specific intersection of the financial and the philosophical, giving the institution new information for future experiments. Figure 29.3 shows the philosophical and financial strategy areas that are activated in this case.

The MFA Boston's efforts to raise funds for conservation are poignant in that collecting organizations routinely have more works in need of conservation than time, funds, and staff to treat them. An extreme example is the municipality of Florence, Italy. In the early morning of November 5, 1966, the Arno River overran its banks, flooding the city and inundating its streets and buildings with water and mud. More than four thousand works of art and four million books and manuscripts were severely damaged. One work symbolizes the tragedy: the fourteen-foot-high *Crucifix* by Cimabue (ca. 1240–before 1302). The artist painted it in egg tempera with gold leaf on wood sometime before 1288 for the Franciscan friars of Santa Croce. For nearly seven hundred years the cross hung unmolested in various parts of the church. Once the floodwaters receded in the afternoon of November 5, 1966, the object, which had been submerged in water for hours, was caked in mud. Ultimately, almost 60 percent of the paint and gold leaf lifted off the wood and floated away. It took more than fifteen years to stabilize and restore the work. Stories like these make a clear case for the need for funds to conserve works of cultural patrimony.

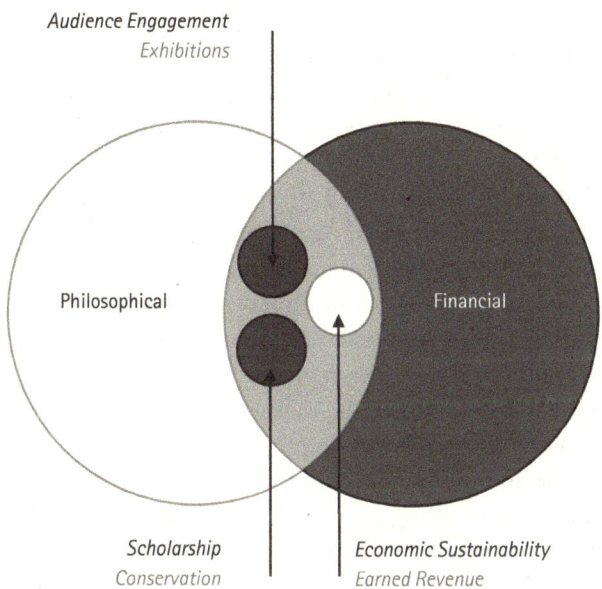

FIGURE 29.3 Case study I: MFA Boston.

Arguably, the 1966 flood example evokes an emotional resonance far greater than the MFA Boston case because of the epic scale and suddenness of the devastation and because it touches upon a larger collective urge to preserve our humanity alongside our cultural patrimony. In considering the MFA Boston's NFT strategy, even given the clear need for restoration of significant works of art, one may consider the difference in feeling between the two cases—or, put another way, how the "philosophical" side of the Venn diagram is weighted in each instance. What could the MFA Boston learn from the comparison? Consider also that perhaps the MFA Boston was uncomfortable navigating the crossover of money and art, whether the institution was fearful of NFTs as a new technology or was hopeful that NFTs would be an easy source of revenue.[11] In either case, how would a museum make decisions about partnering with a for-profit entity such as LaCollection, and how would any cultural organization decide which works to conserve or, more broadly, what part of the museum's mission to tie to the revenue raised? The reader can consider whether the "philosophical" parts of this project could have been more authentic and robust and less shellacked onto what appears to have been primarily an economic motivation.

Case Study II: *NFTs of Collections Objects for Revenue Generation—British Museum*

The Boston MFA case shares a revenue-forward approach with the NFT projects of the British Museum.[12] In fact, this approach even more strongly characterizes the British Museum NFT, also managed by the company LaCollection, because for the British Museum the revenue was not explicitly tied to a mission-centric purpose such as conservation. Concurrent with its Katsushika Hokusai (1760–1849) exhibition ("Hokusai: The Great Picture Book of Everything," September 2021–January 2022), the British Museum minted an NFT of the artist's work, which sold for $20,000 and then dropped to an estimated price of $5,000; Bendor Grosvenor (2022) noted, "You can still buy an actual Hokusai print for less." Like the marketing for the MFA Boston sale, this strategy feels engineered, down to LaCollection's offsetting the carbon footprint of minting the NFT by planting trees. Again, the museum's communication strategy used the language of audience engagement, focusing in this case on the surprising fact that museum website usage had, LaCollection claimed, fallen during the pandemic.[13] Figure 29.4 shows the rather singular focus on revenue generation despite the concurrent timing with the museum's exhibition program.

The reader can consider whether there are ways the British Museum could have engineered the strategy differently. As simple as the question seems, what might have been some of the museum's underlying motivations to make an NFT? Was it out of hopefulness for a successful fundraising plan, an experiment with a trending technology, or a gambit to reach new audiences? If the purpose was to generate revenue, would there be ways to generate that revenue that more successfully married those economics to the museum's mission?

These efforts by the MFA Boston and British Museum encapsulate a pattern of NFT strategy that other cultural institutions have followed with varying degrees of philosophical and financial success: Take a work of art from the institution's collection, turn it into a salable object, then attach the sale to a mission-centric purpose such as conservation and to positive initiatives such as exhibitions or carbon offsets. It is perhaps not surprising that museums most often choose this approach when deciding to dip their toes into the NFT waters, as it most closely resembles how they have traditionally monetized their collections and justified doing so. As an example, the Metropolitan Museum's

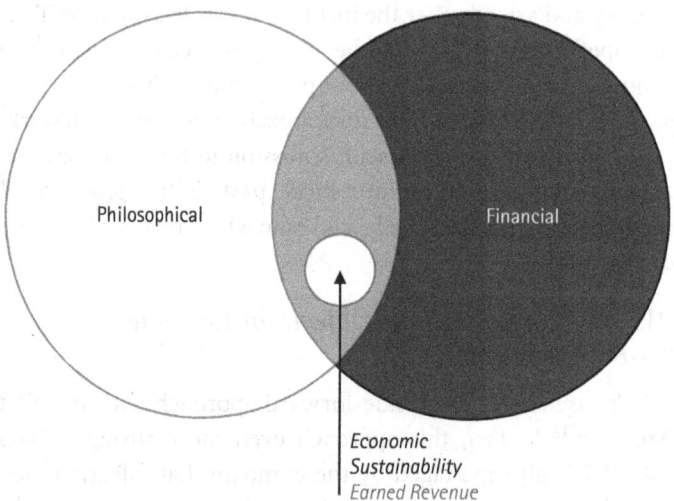

FIGURE 29.4 Case study II: The British Museum.

store describes the mugs, jewelry, scarves, and other goods that it sells to the public as "revenue-generating reproductions of works in [the Met's] collection," and states that "every purchase supports The Met's collection, study, conservation, and presentation of 5,000 years of art" (Metropolitan Museum of Art n.d.). Does the focus on revenue reduce an NFT of the masterpiece to a collectible rather than an artwork? And does that focus minimize the engagement of the work philosophically and the institution's more nuanced responsibilities toward connoisseurship?[14] Like a postcard that one brings home to remember highlights of a museum visit, an NFT can create visitor engagement outside the walls of a museum. Given that US-based museums that are structured as 501(c)3 nonprofit organizations are tax exempt, museums have an added incentive to make their gift shop wares related to their mission in order to avoid paying unrelated business income tax (UBIT).[15] Thus, sales and engagement mirror the complex overlaps of the philosophical and financial realms, for digital as well as analog goods.

Case Study III: *NFT as New Artwork—Museum of Modern Art*

Other museum revenue strategies have expanded to encompass many points of philosophical as well as financial engagement. In 2021, the Museum of Modern Art in New York engaged with NFTs differently by commissioning well-known digital artist Refik Anadol (b. 1985) to create NFTs not from singular works of art but from the archive of digital records of artworks in the collection and from the collection's metadata (Anadol et al. 2021).[16] The NFTs were exhibited and sold through Feral File, an NFT curatorial platform that the artist Casey Reas (b. 1972) started with the company Bitmark.[17] With the support of Glenn Lowry, the museum's director, a team comprised of Paola Antonelli, the senior curator of architecture and design and director of R&D; Michelle Kuo, the Marlene Hess Curator of Painting and Sculpture; and Jan Postma, the chief financial officer, offered support to Anadol's studio and Feral File with the first exhibition and NFT auction derived from this data.[18] In describing the project, Antonelli said that MoMA did not intend to collect any of the works that the artist minted for this project; in fact, it would appear to be a conflict of interest to do so. Instead, the sale raised enough funding to support collections care and to endow a position for a new "web3" associate.[19]

This case raises interesting questions and potential models for working groups and strategic planning around NFTs. First, the NFTs complement the collection and are not weak copies of a single object. Rather than taking Vincent van Gogh's *Starry Night* or another well-known MoMA work and selling the equivalent of a baseball card NFT of it, they imagined artists making new work tied to MoMA via records of all of the museum's collection. Second, the engagement of selling and collecting is noteworthy and recalls our discussion of art and money. The works were sold to support museum programs but were not collected by the museum. Selling and collecting were held apart. Similarly to NFT sales such as those of the MFA Boston, the work raised funds that are tied to a need such as conservation. However, in this case, the funds went not only to collections care but also to fund the larger ability of the museum to support NFT exploration going forward through an endowed position or investment in infrastructure such as NFT display screens. The financial engagement rises from supporting the ongoing costs of the museum to the institution's investment management via the endowment of funds to support ongoing operating expenses.

Antonelli described her work in design and how this project was different. Design typically is a less scrutinized area; in this case, everything changed because, as Antonelli said, "it is art and not design." She continued, "There is more scrutiny but also more excitement.... [T]here is more pressure, but also more participation, which is good" (author interview, August 24, 2022).

Antonelli said the project also brought in audiences "that had never been interested in MoMA, or maybe did not even know what MoMA was." Because the NFT was paired with a membership to the museum, the project introduced these new audiences to the more traditional core of MoMA's collections and other exhibitions and programs.

Figure 29.5 shows this nexus of philosophical and financial activity. By our estimates, based on publicly available data from Feral File, the project grossed $2,026,200 in the primary market, with MoMA receiving $337,700 of that in the primary market and $469,897 total as of January 10, 2023, with an additional $132,197 in revenue to MoMA from secondary-market royalties, with 3 percent of the works having been resold.[20] Philosophically, the work supports artistic practice by commissioning new work and generating $1.6 million in estimated revenue for the artist. Consider the contrast of this strategy to that of making an NFT that represents an existing object in the museum's collection. By taking the MoMA collection metadata as the subject of the work, the

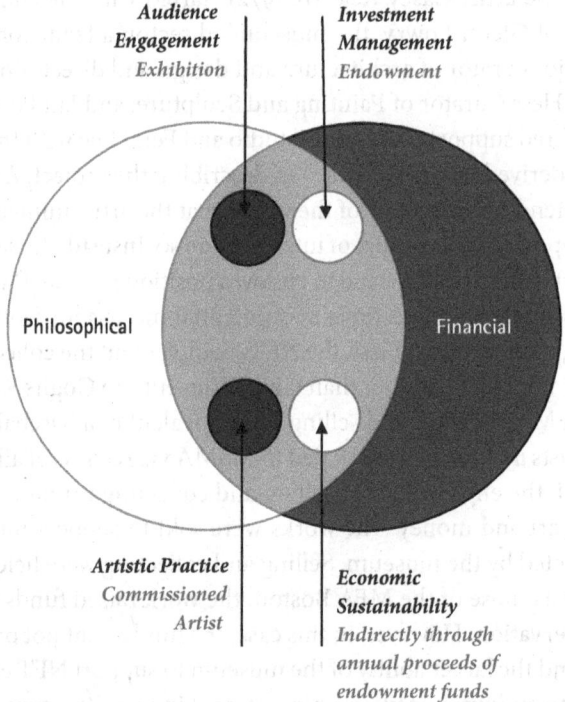

FIGURE 29.5 Case study III: The Museum of Modern Art.

commission uniquely relates to the museum. In addition, the work supports audience engagement and exhibition through its successful initial sale (and museum membership given to the collectors) and through a physical exhibition of the work, *Refik Anadol: Unsupervised*, that was mounted in November 2022.[21] Financially, the project differs from the MFA Boston and British Museum cases in that it raised funds to put into an endowment rather than spendable income for specific projects. The endowment indirectly supports annual operating expenses, in this case the staff position and collections care. Thus, ongoing expenses are supported but in a more holistic and long-term way, including the generative revenue of selling works for which the museum receives a 5 percent royalty in any future secondary-market sales.

This case may seem unique to a well-resourced modern and contemporary art museum. Yet the reader may want to consider whether even more groundbreaking strategies are possible at long-established institutions such as the Morgan Library or the Opera del Duomo di Firenze, or at museums on academic campuses such as the Williams College Museum of Art, where robust metadata of collections exists but apart from a mandate to focus solely on contemporary artistic practice. There does not need to be like-for-like thinking in which digital sales fund digital strategy. Accordingly, how might an organization capture some of this creative strategizing and learn, subtly or structurally, from the MoMA case? For example, what staff (a new manuscripts curator, conservator, or academic outreach manager) or projects (a new facility, enhanced community programming, or publications) might these organizations choose to prioritize over new digital team members or technology projects to benefit from money generated by NFT endeavors like that at MoMA and from the teaching and subsequent knowledge gained as a result of the process? Moreover, given academic museums' explicit mission to engage faculty and students in interdisciplinary research, what kinds of cross-disciplinary projects could also emerge from enacting an NFT strategy similar to that of MoMA?

NFT as an Asset

Most museum NFT collaborations have been concerned with revenue from the issuance of NFTs, yet more insights can be gleaned from more speculative and hypothetical cases, which we present here. First, we consider what it would mean for a museum to sell NFTs that transfer partial financial ownership of works in the collection, and the applications of this strategy to deaccessioning and restitution. Then in the following section, we consider a hypothetical in which an institution issues NFTs to grant decision-making or governance rights to the NFT owners.

The MFA Boston and British Museum sales did not confer public ownership of the artwork in the museums' collections. Museums rarely sell art from their collection precisely because of the tensions inherent in the overlap of the financial and the philosophical. Typically, when a museum deaccessions—that is, sells—a work of art, the museum is bound, via the rules of professional bodies such as the Association of Art Museum Directors (AAMD), the American Alliance of Museums (AAM), or the International Council of Museums (ICOM), to use the proceeds of the sale only for the acquisition of new works. According to AAMD, a museum may use the practice to "refine and enhance the quality, use, and character of [its] holdings" and "proceeds from a deaccessioned work are used *only* [emphasis original to the source] to acquire other works of art" (AAMD 2011). The practice garnered particular scrutiny in 2020 after the AAMD shifted its policy in response to the dire financial consequences of COVID-19 on museums to allow them to use sales proceeds from deaccessioned art for more broadly defined operating expenses and other purposes beyond acquiring new work (Gold and Jandl 2020). This change opened up the possibility not only of selling artworks in museum collections but also of selling fractions of them. In September 2022, after significant backlash from the field, which most publicly resulted in the Baltimore Museum of Art halting its sale of three works from its collection (Jackson 2020), the AAMD clarified its policy to exclude salaries and other operating expenses not directly tied to collections and their care (Kamp 2022). In this section, however, we imagine using an NFT as an asset in which the financial nature of the artwork is fractionalized and sold, in order to explore deaccessioning and restitution.

Using blockchain, and by extension NFTs, has been proposed as a new avenue of restitution. This is because of blockchain's structural nature as a record-keeping system, which allows for tracking of information such as provenance—that is, the history of ownership of the object. If traditional works of art and antiquities are linked to the blockchain as NFTs, we can have a publicly accessible record of the ownership and exhibition of these objects. Blockchain could be used to "split the rights stack" of these works so that ownership could be returned to source countries. Those countries in return could decide to allow any institution to continue to exhibit and care for the work (Whitaker et al. 2021). In Sarr and Savoy's (2018) report on works of African art and culture held in European museums—a report commissioned by French president Emmanuel Macron—the authors found that tens of thousands of significant objects were held in European museums, and over 90 percent of African cultural artifacts were located outside the African continent. If these African cultural objects were registered to the blockchain as NFTs then the smart contracts that govern NFTs could be used to codify agreements so that the terms, once agreed, can be executed automatically without one party having administrative authority.[22] For instance, the institution could send payments to a source country, to whom ownership of a work previously in the institution's collection has been returned, in exchange for ongoing rights to exhibit or publish the work. In the case of portfolios of objects, a portion could return to the source country, a portion could be gifted or sold to the museum housing them, and a portion could be sold into the market with proceeds shared with the source country. A wide array of negotiated outcomes are possible.

This financialization of a work of art is markedly different from the revenue-generation NFTs in the MFA Boston and British Museum cases. For instance, consider the difference between, hypothetically, the MoMA selling an NFT of Vincent van Gogh's *Starry Night* and selling it as an asset token of the work that confers a percentage of ownership—whether 0.01 percent or 10 percent—to the holder of the token. Putting aside the heated deaccessioning debate that would ensue, there would be the difficulty of pricing the work, since art prices are typically set through sale at auction or private gallery. This case brings together the art and money sides of a museum in ways that are usually firewalled—the pricelessness of the work of art. Typically, museums' art and money sides are held separate: the pricelessness of the work of art and the necessity of funding, including the implicit and explicit expectations of financial contributions from generous donors. The fractional selling of art would be a form of fracking the financial structure of the museum, creating micro-financialization across a collection.

Case Study IV: *Deaccessioning and Restitution NFTs—Hypothetical*

Imagine that a museum received a donation of objects, including antiquities, from a now-deceased donor in the middle of the twentieth century. Years later, as the curator reviews that collection, they discover that most works need more detailed provenance information. The museum then undertakes research and learns that some of the works were illegally removed from the source country and sold via a gray market for antiquities. The museum, which is obligated by the field to collect in an ethical and legal way, wishes to amend the situation and contacts the source country to offer to return the objects. Many different outcomes are possible. First, suppose the source country claims the works outright, and the museum returns them. In addition to the revised digital record of the work that will live in perpetuity in the museum's collection database, the museum may choose to also register NFTs of the works on a blockchain as a digital record of the objects' tenure in the museum before return. Second, suppose the source country appreciates the recognition but does not wish to accept the formal return of the objects. In this case, the blockchain can be used to register the transfer of ownership back to the source country without the need to physically return the objects.

In addition, many other, more kaleidoscopic solutions are possible here. For instance, the museum might keep physical possession (or ownership, outright or partially) and return cash flows to the source country for a period of time or indefinitely. The source country could delimit this relationship temporally and allow the museum to keep the objects on display for a fixed term before returning them. The museum may be paying for conservation, as in the case of the Byzantine frescoes at the Menil Collection (Whitaker et al. 2021). Or the museum could send cash flows for this finite period. An NFT and its related smart (self-executing) contract (see note 1) could automate these payments and provide a public record. In addition, the museums could designate the use of funds as they saw fit, whether as spendable income for immediate projects or as endowment contributions for longer-term initiatives.[23]

This strategy dovetails with two other areas of strategic planning. The first is standardizing how institutions gather provenance information about works of art. This kind of information-gathering protocol is well-established practice at collecting institutions that acquire contemporary artworks with complex installation and conservation needs associated with their long-term preservation. For example, an artist questionnaire typically accompanies the acquisition of time-based media and other works incorporating media that may become outdated, such as Betamax video tapes or cathode-ray tube televisions, or media that may decay or degrade, such as apples or petroleum jelly.[24] Museums could develop similar standards for provenance information gathering about antiquities in both existing and newly acquired collections. Academic museums may especially consider undertaking this provenance research, given their parallel focus on teaching and research. Second, questions of provenance and restitution naturally expand the philosophical side of strategy planning from the values of just *the institution* to the overall values of *the field* (see Figure 29.6). The stewardship of the work of art becomes more important than the institution's decisions to be the specific steward, and the process of revisiting these works with care shifts the association of these objects from black-market thievery to a more positive frame of careful stewardship and transparent communications.

Figure 29.6 shows this more complex dynamic in which there are the philosophical values of the institution but also of the field. These sometimes overlap and sometimes conflict, for instance, if the institution wishes to keep an object, but there is a higher interest in restitution. In this case, the institution is enacting the higher values of the field by returning the objects to the source countries. Sometimes the institution's desire to maintain possession of an object can be in tension with others who champion restitution.

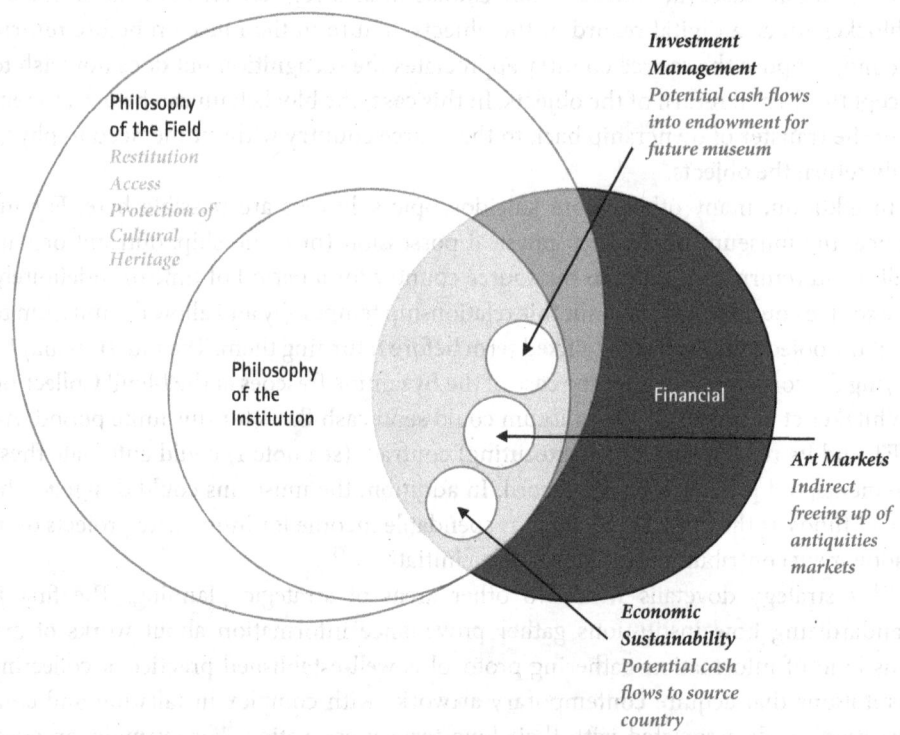

FIGURE 29.6 Deaccessioning and restitution NFTs: Hypothetical.

While possession and restitution can be in tension as zero-sum, this line of thinking—and the related applications of blockchain and NFTs—opens new approaches to seemingly intractable restitution problems. More broadly, this approach is a model for collaborative and shared solutions that merge artistic, financial, and societal values, even with the trade-offs of placing trust in technological infrastructure and navigating cultural resistance to new technology within the field. In this case, NFTs create a public and automated contract or governance arrangement between the institutions, source countries, and other parties.

NFTs as the Institution

In 2021, when the Hermitage Museum issued the NFTs mentioned earlier in this chapter, the offerings were signed by the Hermitage director, Mikhail Piotrovsky, as if he were the artist of the institution. As Piotrovsky said, the sale was "an important stage in the development of the relationship between person and money, person and thing" (Kishkovsky 2021). The sale was also important in developing relationships among an institution, its audiences, and its fellow institutions. How might institutions structure their relationships with stakeholders using blockchain registration and NFTs, and what are the arguments in favor of implementing such a structure?

Consider the case of two organizations thousands of miles apart that house some of the most important art, artifacts, and archives related to the American West. Among the vast holdings of the Beinecke Rare Book and Manuscript Library at Yale University is the Yale Collection of Western Americana, a group of sixty-five thousand printed objects, four thousand manuscripts, tens of thousands of photographs, and hundreds of works on paper and paintings. Another institution two time zones away, the Denver Museum of Art, is home to the Petrie Institute of Western American Art, which oversees and promotes the study of the museum's collection of two hundred years of Western sculpture, paintings, and works on paper. What would it mean for these institutions to employ NFTs as a frame for collaboration, or to assemble teams from these two organizations to work on shared projects? How might they design a strategic planning process if the purpose was reputation-building, resource-sharing for scholars, or pedagogy and student learning? Recalling the relationship of blockchain and provenance, this potential collaboration involves library science, archival practice, registrars, and the managerial representatives of both institutions.

Case Study V: *NFTs as Administrator—Hypothetical*

An institutional token can give the holder the right to participate in an organization's decision-making and thus opens them up to this larger sphere of overall governance. In the case of the Beinecke Library and Petrie Institute, the partner institutions would make decisions about joint acquisitions or programming. However, consider a more speculative and potentially dangerous case in which expertise-reliant organizations issue institutional tokens to the public to allow them to vote on whatever topic the organization wants feedback on. In the case of museums, it could be which works should come out of storage or which exhibitions they want to see in the galleries.

While other forms of technology—for instance, Qualtrics or SurveyMonkey questionnaires—already allow museums to survey their audiences, in this case a token could give their audience actual decision-making control. One could imagine extreme versions of these hypotheticals that remove all reliance on subject matter expertise and, in the process, potentially topple the institution's authority. What if an NFT allowed the public to decide on museum exhibitions or hours, like stockholders in a corporation?

Figure 29.7 shows this larger sphere of governance. Whereas Figure 29.6 shows the values of the field as larger than the values of the organization, Figure 29.7 shows this governance or decision-making as a larger context around the institution's financial management. For instance, the audience is engaged with art by participating in decisions around what works are on view. But the audience is also engaged via participation in managerial decision-making. Museums could decide whether participation is free or if audience members pay to participate, in which case the sale of these institutional or decision-making NFTs would raise revenue or also create an endowment for the museum, depending on how the NFT is conceived. Museums can choose to use smart contracts to automate these decisions, closing the gap between audience participation and decisions taken. The reader could imagine the risks, future states, and uncharted legal frontiers that may unfold with NFTs that are not symbolic—as in the souvenir or baseball card of a masterpiece—but that are structural—as in a financial share or decision-making right.

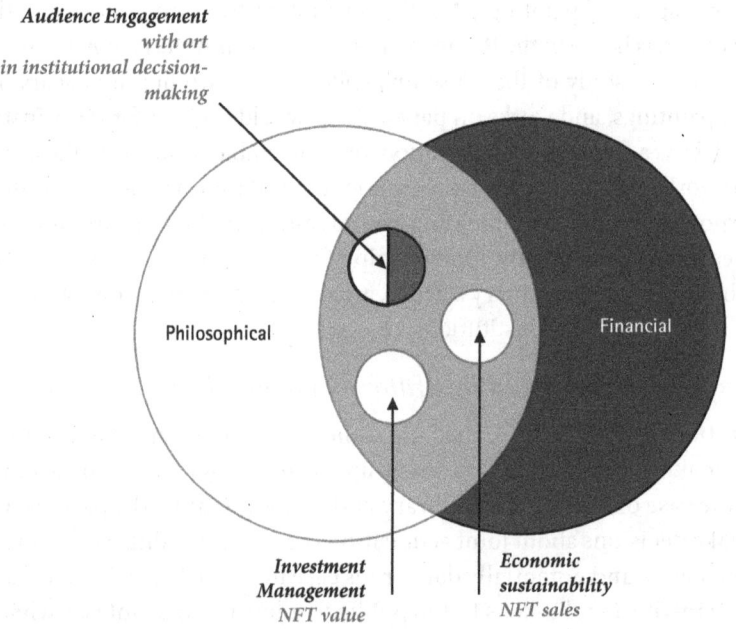

FIGURE 29.7 NFTs as administrator: Hypothetical.

Managerial Implications

NFTs provide an interesting litmus test for cultural organizations managing their artistic programming and financial needs. In the cases we have seen, "revenue for revenue's sake" might work for the bottom line but may fall short on philosophical grounds. The appearance of squeezing money from a lauded artwork may come at a reputational cost. Instead, complementary approaches to the museum's collection have been promising—commissioning works by new artists based on collections, for instance. In addition, the speculative futures of NFTs are aligned with important values in the field, whether the restitution and stewardship of cultural heritage or the more fundamental aspects of a museum's balancing of its focus on scholarship and its relationship to its public.

These findings likely apply to other cultural institutions such as theaters, libraries, and archives. Theaters may find revenue-based NFTs more successful because they can be paired with season tickets, and audiences have expectations of more ephemeral performance. An NFT associated with a symphony or play has a different character than one associated with a painting because the former is performed in many different venues by many different artists and takes its own shape each time. Libraries and archives may find affinities with institutional NFTs and collaboration with museums and other cultural institutions. And museums wishing to explore NFTs around restitution can benefit from strategic planning collectives across institutions.

With frontier technology such as NFTs, navigating institutional strategy becomes something of an art project itself. Thus, museum leaders and managers of cultural institutions become collaborative artists, experimenting and building future systems. In this way, strategic planning is a creative and open-ended practice. One can learn from the "bright spot" examples of successful strategy and try to avoid those initiatives that have been read as disingenuous, but ultimately NFTs as a kind of trial-and-error approach that could risk failing in public—an especially scary prospect in the current climate of cancel culture or for those hesitant to make what they perceive to be the right decision for the long term that may appear to be the wrong one in the short term. These factors make strategic planning even more important as a process for engaging with both staff within the institution and the collective public. NFT strategy also uniquely engages the role of trustees, including those with a fiduciary duty and those who are advisors.[25]

The Nolin-Whitaker Method of Venn-diagram mapping represents this creative and synthesizing process of strategic planning as bringing together groups of people with overlapping—and not overlapping—interests, knowledge, and priorities. The method also brings to the surface the necessity of simultaneously thinking about mission and finances—the why and the how. Revenue-focused approaches may fall flat, whether out of sheer chance or a lack of artistic energy. Thus, this model offers an ongoing set of tools for managing many priorities and designing a holistic strategy that simultaneously serves an institution's philosophical and financial values. The various NFT strategies and the convening of stakeholders also raise new questions about forms of expertise needed on the staff and boards of organizations, whether in art, technology, or finance, and the strength of leadership, management, and vision needed in the heads of nonprofits, especially collecting institutions.

Conclusions

NFT strategy may allow organizations to focus on the larger societal pulls and challenges of the time, including navigating complex ethical and societal gray areas while envisioning how museums can become more than just repositories of objects. Instead, we imagine resilient organizations constantly engaged with making meaning and creating a purpose for themselves and their collections by interrupting internal stagnation and resistance and engaging in larger questions of the intersections of creative, economic, and civic life.

While many avenues of research and practice will continue to unfold, perhaps the biggest lesson of NFTs is remembering not only the art but also the artists and the museums' audiences. The most successful projects have invited engagement with collections by creating new work, not just technological copies of objects already in the collection.

Strategic planning is really a catchphrase for thinking about the future of the organization. And when confronted with thinking about that future—whether that be short term or long term, staffing or mission—oftentimes the strategic planning process assumes that everybody in the organization is in lockstep, that everybody agrees on what will happen and where the organization needs to go. NFTs—specifically this intersection of art and money—force the organization to discuss these aspects of their existence. In bringing the financial and philosophical together, NFTs hold up a mirror to the culture of an organization and its values. It is difficult to think of another example where that would be so clear and force such a reckoning of the organization.

An organization, of course, can decide not to engage with NFTs—not to collect them, not to issue them, or to engage with them only in certain ways—but even to arrive at this answer requires some investigation into the most fundamental questions philosophically and financially that the organization wrestles with. It is, therefore, useful to arm ourselves with conceptual frameworks around art and money that form a reckoning with technology, audience, and collections.

If the last five years have taught us anything, it is how big cultural shifts can happen with little warning and that the organizations that thrive because of these shifts are the ones with creative minds, solid disaster recovery plans, and usually solid financial reserves. These elements will undoubtedly continue to merge as society continues to navigate social, political, and financial upheaval, pandemics, and anything else that is waiting to come our way in the future. NFT strategy is emblematic of this process of developing the flexibility and resilience needed to deal with the unknown, and the clarity and coalition-building to confront whatever events the future may bring. Navigating these intersections and constellations of the philosophical and the financial is a process of curiosity, collaboration, creative resourcefulness, and shared process.

Acknowledgments

We gratefully acknowledge the generous conversations, advising, and resource-sharing of Paola Antonelli, Erin Benay, Christina Ferando, Pamela Franks, Lara Hughes, Debra LaKind, Anne Moore, Sean Moss-Pultz, Michael Nguyen, Margriet Schavemaker, the editors, and others who have contributed to our thinking.

Notes

1. An NFT is a unique digital identifier that is registered to a blockchain, creating digital provenance records and digital scarcity (one unique identifier for many interchangeable copies of a digital file). An NFT includes a smart contract that governs actions associated with the token, such as paying an artist a resale royalty when ownership of a work is transferred. Blockchains are decentralized databases that record transactions or other pieces of information (ledgers) that exist in many interconnected digital copies. The purpose of interconnecting copies is to enable anyone to—in theory—trust the information without needing to trust a single person or entity, such as a museum, university registrar, bank, et cetera, to maintain and authenticate the record (Whitaker and Abrams 2023). Through their registry to a blockchain, NFTs share with museums an interest in provenance, that is, in records of ownership. For further background reading on NFTs, see Levine 2022 (general cryptocurrency primer), Jung 2022 (NFTs and museums), Antonelli et al. 2022 ("The Third Web" as subject of the MoMA R&D Salon), and and Whitaker 2022 (NFTs, the art market, and the larger arts ecosystem). The term "smart contract" refers to a piece of computer programming that can automatically execute a transaction—for instance, to automatically pay an artist a resale royalty when an artwork is sold. The smart contract and the digital identifier or "token" come together to allow an NFT to create new models of ownership, provenance, and digital record-keeping. A group of smart contracts may be put together to create a decentralized autonomous organization (DAO). A DAO can be thought of as a cooperative governance structure that codifies a group's decision-making agreements into an automated organizational structure.
2. Regarding volatility of NFTs, the *New York Times* recently reported that in 2021 the trading volume in NFTs fell 97 percent (Small 2022). From 2021 to the fall of 2022, the average price of an art NFT fell from $3,200 to $1,200 (NonFungible 2022a, 2022b). Regarding selling traditional artworks, the Museum of Modern Art had stored the art collection of William S. Paley, the founder of CBS, from Paley's death in 1990 until fall 2022. The eighty-one works under MoMA's care were sold at auction at Sotheby's, with a portion of the proceeds going to fund the museum's digital initiatives (Jhala 2022). The museum received a reported $47 million from the sale (Villa and Cassady 2022). Regarding cryptocurrency, the rapidly evolving financialization and potential for Ponzi schemes of some cryptocurrency structures has led to episodes of apparent fraud. In November 2022, around the time of this writing, FTX Trading Limited, a crypto exchange with 100,000 creditors and assets estimated at between $10 and $50 billion, filed for bankruptcy (Yaffe-Bellany 2022).

3. This idea of imbuing the artwork with the power of its subject is akin to the belief in the act of transubstantiation of the Eucharistic elements into the body and blood of Christ during Roman Catholic mass.
4. The sculpted likeness of Giustiniani is still in the Venetian church of San Pietro di Castello. It was removed from his burial chapel and placed in the Lando family chapel off the left aisle around 1571. Giustiniani's remains were transferred to a lavish silver and marble sarcophagus above the high chapel of San Pietro, which now celebrates the life of the saint in its lateral and apse frescoes, where he continues to be venerated for his healing powers.
5. These observations stem from Nolin's work running a strategic planning consultancy for museums and partnering with institutions whose teams are seeking more creative approaches after standard templates have failed as tools for the specific needs of arts organizations.
6. Financial concerns vary substantially depending on a museum's business model and the size, diversification, and management of its endowment (cf. Yermack 2017), as well as on market performance and public and private funding, among many other important factors in museum management (cf. Jung and Love 2017). Philosophical concerns vary widely, too: across collecting and noncollecting institutions, each organization makes decisions based upon its unique mission, values, history, and other attributes. But generally speaking, the sturdier the sources of accessible and unrestricted funding for any institution, the more creative and artistic risk an institution may take.
7. Following principles of nonprofit governance, the board of trustees would typically not be involved in NFT strategy unless it overlapped with the organization's fiduciary responsibilities, in which case at least the board's finance committee, if not the full board, would be involved in the decision-making process.
8. The pastels had recently been shown in the exhibition "French Pastels: Treasures from the Vault" (June 30, 2018–January 6, 2019) but had not previously been displayed publicly for many years. The MFA Boston pastels are by artists including Edgar Degas (1834–1917), Edouard Manet (1832–1883), Claude Monet (1840–1926), and Camille Pissarro (1830–1903). The pastel medium becomes unstable when exposed to substantial light over long periods of time, and thus works in this medium are less frequently exhibited. Also, the MFA Boston's collection consists of over half a million works (MFA Boston 2022b), only a fraction of which can be displayed to the public at any one time.
9. The authors interviewed Debra LaKind, senior director of intellectual property and business development at the MFA Boston, on January 18, 2023, after the completion of the first NFT sale and the announcement but not completion of the second sale. The two Degas paintings that benefitted from the NFT sales are *Edmondo and Thérèse Morbilli*, about 1865, oil on canvas, 116.5 × 88.3 cm (45 7/8 × 34 3/4 in.), Gift of Robert Treat Paine, 2nd, 31.33 and *Degas's Father Listening to Lorenzo Pagans Playing the Guitar*, about 1869–72, oil on canvas, 81.6 × 65.1 cm (32 1/8 × 25 5/8 in.), Bequest of John T. Spaulding, 48.533.
10. In a related marketing strategy, the NFTs went on sale on July 14, Bastille Day.
11. When asked how much revenue the MFA Boston earned from the sale of NFTs from their collection, LaKind replied, "We don't share financial information."
12. The authors contacted the British Museum seeking more information about the museum's 2021 issue of NFTs of Hokusai and their more recent issue of NFTs of Piranesi prints from the museum's collection. We specifically asked about their underlying motivations for making the NFTs, the percentage of total NFTs that were sold, and the total revenue the sales generated. Craig Bendle, manager of product licensing and wholesale merchandise

at the British Museum, replied that he was "unable to agree to an interview on this topic, as [they] are under strategic review for this area, as well as potentially for commercial reasons."

13. Some museums, including Tate, found unique website visitors to go up yearly from 2019 to 2020 (Tate Gallery 2020).
14. Perhaps the role of museums and for-profit institutions such as LaCollection and the Italian company Cinello explains, at least in part, the Italian government's decision (Batycka 2022) to halt NFT sales by Italian museums This suspension of Italian museum NFT sales in July 2022 followed the 2021 sale by the Uffizi Gallery of an NFT of Michelangelo's *Doni Tondo* for €240,000. Cinello, which managed the sale, split proceeds with the Uffizi 50-50—after subtracting costs of production, which, including taxes, NFT costs, physical framing, a platform commission, and a 20 percent operating fee, totaled €100,000. Thus, the museum only made half of €140,000, or €70,000. In collaboration with London-based dealer Unit, the NFT was issued in an edition of nine (priced from €100,000 to €250,000), creating other revenue but still with the hefty share to Cinello (Batycka 2022).
15. According to the IRS website, UBIT is "income from a trade or business, regularly carried on, that is not substantially related to the charitable, educational, or other purpose that is the basis of the organization's exemption" (IRS 2022). An example that might compel a museum to pay UBIT on profits is the selling of food or coffee in its museum café or receiving revenue from a parking garage that it owns.
16. Metadata are the descriptors that give information about other data—essentially data of data. Metadata of an image of a work of art typically includes the artist's information, the title and medium of the work of art, copyright notices, keywords, and a description of the work. In 2015, MoMA posted all its metadata on Github, a platform for sharing computer code.
17. Both Reas and the co-author Whitaker are advisors to Bitmark. Whitaker was not involved in the MoMA project.
18. Casey Reas, the founder of Feral File, the curatorial platform with which MoMA partnered, is also a professor at the University of California, Los Angeles, and the co-inventor of a visually driven computer programming language called Processing. Anadol, described by Antonelli as a protegé of Reas, created a work called *Unsupervised*. Anadol trained an algorithm to create new artworks from metadata associated with real works of art in the collection. The MoMA project is part of Anadol's larger series *Machine Hallucinations*, "an ongoing project exploring data aesthetics based on collective visual memories" (Feral File 2021). The Feral File show consisted of three single-edition algorithmic works, which sold in the $300,000 to $500,000 range; nine prints, titled *MoMA Dreams A* through *H*, which were issued in editions of 100 for each print; and one "global AI [artificial intelligence] data painting" in a twenty-second video format (MP4), which was sold in an edition of 5,000, with a price of approximately $500 (Feral File 2021).
19. "Web3" is the term for the new, more participatory internet that some proponents of NFTs and blockchain imagine, moving from the "web2" platforms of large technology companies to distributed ownership of data using blockchain.
20. This estimate is based on the following: Three works were editions of one and sold for, respectively, $510,000, $306,000, and $310,000. A further nine works were editions of 100 and sold for $1,000 each (or $1,002 in the case of the "A" edition). An additional work, *Data Universe*, sold in an edition of 5,000 at a primary-market price of $100. The total revenue

of all of these sales was $2,026,200. In the primary market, one-sixth of the total revenue went to MoMA, one-sixth to Feral File, and the remaining four-sixths (two-thirds) to the artist's studio. In the secondary market, 80 percent went to the collector, 10 percent to the artist, and 5 percent each to MoMA and to Feral File. In the secondary market, via the platform OpenSea, the total sales volume up to January 10, 2023, was 1,977 ETH or $2,643,941 (computed at an ETH-USD exchange rate of $1,337,35). The project to date has generated $1,615,194 for the artist and $469,897 for the Museum of Modern Art (and the same for Feral File). Data are available in Feral File 2023.

21. In November 2022, the Museum of Modern Art opened a physical exhibition of Anadol's project on a 24-by-24-foot LED screen in the museum's atrium. Through Bitmark, the company that hosts Feral File, gave away NFT "gifts"—not artworks—to visitors who scanned a QR code on the wall of the museum. The Anadol exhibition was originally scheduled to be on view from November 19, 2022, until March 5, 2023 (MoMA 2022) as was extended to an "ongoing" exhibition at the time of press.

22. A smart contract is a piece of computer programming that can automatically execute a transaction—for instance, to automatically pay an artist a resale royalty when an artwork is sold. The smart contract and the digital identifier or "token" come together to allow an NFT to create new models of ownership, provenance, and digital record-keeping. Decentralized autonomous organizations, or DAOs, are a collection of associated smart contracts that can, together, function as an organization or set of automated decision-making. DAOs can be thought of as cooperative governance structures, or ways for people to agree on decision-making processes as a collective and then to execute those decisions automatically.

23. While such NFT use cases are still speculative, recent creative institutional arrangements outside of blockchain and NFTs are noteworthy cases about which we can ask whether these new technologies could be helpful. For example, in 2022, the Metropolitan Museum of Art in New York, the Museum of Cycladic Art in Athens, Greece, the Greek state, and a new Delaware-based nonprofit organization, the Hellenic Ancient Culture Institute, entered into a novel arrangement around 161 works of ancient Cycladic art held in the collection of Leonard N. Stern (Moynihan 2022). By the agreement, formal ownership of the works was returned to Greece, by way of a donation of the artworks by Stern to the Hellenic Ancient Culture Institute. In turn, a group of fifteen of the sculptures went on view at the Museum of Cycladic Art in Athens in November 2022, and then those works, along with others from the Stern collection, are to go on view at the Metropolitan Museum in January 2024 and to stay on view for at least ten years. While blockchain may not be needed for such an arrangement, at the same time a public ledger could be useful in the transparency of the agreement. In the future, institutions entering into restitution arrangements might wish to automate cash flows using smart contracts or to sell related NFTs.

24. In 1993, the Yale University Art Gallery was gifted one of five versions of *Unit Bolus*, a work Matthew Barney (b. 1967) created in 1990–1991. The work consists of a stainless-steel rack, cast petroleum jelly 8-pound dumbbell, and electric freezing device. Anne Morgan, the gallery's collections registrar, with whom we spoke for this chapter, said that the museum has on file interviews with the artist and his studio assistants that capture the artist's intentions for the material future of his work. The gallery has a mold for replacing the dumbbell, because it damages easily, and protocols for tracking the original and copies.

25. NFTs can be meaningfully explored concerning financial support, commissioning and collecting artworks, caring for collections, and codifying relationships with communities

and other institutions. In the existing research on blockchain and museums (cf. Liddell 2021), the nature of blockchain as a registry of information dovetails with what Liddell calls "guardianship" of museum objects. At the same time, as Susan Taylor, director of the New Orleans Museum of Art, has said, "The museum field is looking at its mandate and approach in new ways. We are evolving from an object-centric institution to a people-centric institution" (Haimerl 2021). These priorities of museums—caring for objects and supporting their staff members and audiences—require budgetary support, regardless of how laudable the aims.

REFERENCES

AAM. 2020. "National Survey of COVID-19 Impact on United States Museums." American Alliance of Museums, Washington, DC. https://www.aam-us.org/wp-content/uploads/2020/07/2020_National-Survey-of-COVID19-Impact-on-US-Museums.pdf.

Anadol, Refik, Casey Reas, Michelle Kuo, and Paola Antonelli. 2021. "Modern Dream: How Refik Anadol Is Using Machine Learning and NFTs to Interpret MoMA's Collection." *MoMA Magazine*, November 15, 2021.https://www.moma.org/magazine/articles/658.

Antonelli, Paola, Helena Klevorn, Bruce Afua, Kyle Chayka, Stephanie Dinkins, Michelle Kuo, Rafaël Rozendaal, Mindy Seu, Scott Wang, Tricia Brett, Amy Whitaker, and Alex Zhang. 2022. "MoMA R&D Salon 40: Web3The Third Web," October 24, 2022. http://momarnd.moma.org/salons/salon-40-the-third-web/http://momarnd.moma.org/salons/.

Artnet News. 2022. "Wikipedia Editors Have Voted Not to Classify NFTs as Art, Sparking Outrage in the Crypto Community." *Artnet News*, January 13, 2022. https://news.artnet.com/market/wikipedia-editors-nft-art-classification-2060018.

AAMD. 2011. "Art Museums and the Practice of Deaccessioning." Association of Art Museum Directors, New York. https://aamd.org/sites/default/files/document/PositionPaperDeaccessioning%2011.07.pdf.

Batycka, Dorian. 2022. "Italy Instructs Museums to Halt Contracts with NFT Companies, Citing 'Unregulated' Terms That Could Affect the Country's Cultural Heritage." *Artnet News*, July 11, 2022. https://news.artnet.com/market/cinello-nft-michaelangelo-2145003.

Escalante-De Mattei, Shanti. 2022. "Bloomberg's Massive Crypto Article Derides NFTs as Nothing More than a Ponzi Scheme." *Artnews*, October 25, 2022. https://www.artnews.com/art-news/news/bloomberg-crypto-nfts-matt-levine-1234644343/.

Feral File. 2021. "Deep Modern." Exhibition note for Refik Anadol, *Unsupervised*, November 2021. https://feralfile.com/exhibitions/unsupervised-sla.

Feral File. 2023. Auction results for Refik Anadol, *Unsupervised—Machine Hallucinations—MoMA*, January 2023. https://feralfile.com/highest-bid-auction/d281d2e7-7209-46a3 973b b9061bd9f442.

Gold, Mark S., and Stefanie S. Jandl. 2020. "Why the Association of Art Museum Directors's Move on Deaccessioning Matters So Much." *The Art Newspaper*, May 18, 2020. https://www.theartnewspaper.com/2020/05/18/why-the-association-of-art-museum-directorss-move-on-deaccessioning-matters-so-much.

Grampp, William D. 1989. *Pricing the Priceless: Art, Artists, and Economics*. New York: Basic Books.

Grosvenor, Bendor. 2022. "British Museum Presses on Minting NFTs Despite Crypto Crash—When Will UK Museums Stop Seeing Artworks as Assets?" *The Art Newspaper*, June

22, 2022. https://www.theartnewspaper.com/2022/06/22/british-museum-presses-on-minting-nfts-despite-crypto-crashwhen-will-uk-museums-stop-seeing-images-of-artworks-as-assets.

Haimerl, Amy. 2021. "What Keeps U.S. Museums Running—and How Might the Pandemic Change That?" *ARTnews*, March 3, 2021. https://www.artnews.com/art-news/news/united-states-art-museum-financing-123458493.

IRS. 2022. "Unrelated Business Income Tax." Internal Revenue Service, Washington, DC, August 22, 2022. https://www.irs.gov/charities-non-profits/unrelated-business-income-tax.

Jackson, Christine. 2020. "The BMA Deaccessioning Scandal, Explained." *Baltimore Magazine*, October 22, 2020. https://www.baltimoremagazine.com/section/uncategorized/the-bma-deaccessioning-scandal-explained/.

Jhala, Kabir. 2022. "Sotheby's to Sell $70m of Art Stored at MoMA to Benefit New York Museum's Digital Initiatives." *The Art Newspaper*, September 14, 2022. https://www.theartnewspaper.com/2022/09/14/sothebys-70m-william-paley-collection-museum-modern-art

Jung, Yuha. 2022. "Current Use Cases, Benefits and Challenges of NFTs in the Museum Sector: Toward Common Pool Model of NFT Sharing for Educational Purposes." *Museum Management and Curatorship*, published online October 10, 2022. https://doi.org/10.1080/09647775.2022.2132995.

Jung, Yuha, and Anne Rowson Love. 2017. *Systems Thinking in Museums: Theory and Practice* New York: Rowman & Littlefield, 2017.

Kamp, Justin. 2022. "Following Controversial Sales, US Museums Association Revises Its Deaccessioning Policy." *The Art Newspaper*, September 30, 2022. https://www.theartnewspaper.com/2022/09/30/new-museum-deaccessioning-rule-association-of-art-museum-directors.

Kishkovsky, Sophia. 2021. "Hermitage Museum Mints Leonardo, Monet, Van Gogh, NFTs to Raise Funds." *The Art Newspaper*, July 27, 2021. https://www.theartnewspaper.com/2021/07/27/hermitage-museum-mints-leonardo-monet-van-gogh-nfts-to-raise-funds.

Kussin, Justin. 2016. "Infamous Botched Jesus Painting Now a Major Tourist Attraction." *New York Post*, March 12, 2016. https://nypost.com/2016/03/12/infamous-botched-jesus-painting-now-a-major-tourist-attraction/.

LaCollection. n.d. Website. LaCollection.io, accessed August 28, 2022.

Levine, Matt. 2022. "The Crypto Story." *Bloomberg Businessweek*, October 31, 2022. https://www.bloomberg.com/features/2022-the-crypto-story/?leadSource=uverify%20wall#trust-money-community.

Liddell, Frances. 2021. "Building Shared Guardianship Through Blockchain Technology and Digital Museum Objects." *Museum and Society* 19, no. 2: 220–236.

Metropolitan Museum of Art. n.d. "About the Met Store." https://store.metmuseum.org/about-us, accessed December 7, 2022.

McAndrew, Clare. 2022. *The Art Market 2022*. Basel: Art Basel and UBS, 2022. https://artbasel.com/about/initiatives/the-art-market.

MFA Boston. 2022a. "MFA Boston and LaCollection.io Offer NFT Collection of Rarely Seen 19th-Century French Impressionist Pastels." Museum of Fine Arts, Boston, June 23, 2022. https://www.mfa.org/press-release/mfa-boston-and-lacollectionio-offer-nft-collection.

MFA Boston. 2022b. "MFA Boston Adds 35 Martin Barooshian Works to Its Collection." Museum of Fine Arts, Boston, February 28, 2022. https://www.mfa.org/press-release/martin-barooshian-acquisition.

MoMA. 2022. "Refik Anadol: Unsupervised." Press release, Museum of Modern Art, New York. http://press.moma.org/exhibition/refik-anadol-unsupervised/.

Moynihan, Colin. 2022. "Leonard Stern's Cycladic Art Will Be Shown at the Met but Owned by Greece." *New York Times*, October 11, 2022. https://www.nytimes.com/2022/10/11/arts/design/stern-cycladic-antiquities-met-museum-greece.html.

Nadini, Matthieu, Laura Alessandretti, Flavio Di Giacinto, Mauro Martino, Luca Maria Aiello, and Andrea Baronchelli. 2021. "Mapping the NFT Revolution: Market Trends, Trade Networks, and Visual Features." *Nature: Scientific Reports*, article no. 20902. https://www.nature.com/articles/s41598-021-00053-8.

NonFungible. 2022a. "Quarterly NFT Market Report: Q3 2022." NonFungible Corporation. https://nonfungible.com/reports/2022/en/q3-quarterly-nft-market-report.

NonFungible. 2022b. "Yearly NFT Market Report 2021: How NFTs Affect the World" (free edition). NonFungible Corporation. https://nonfungible.com/reports/2021/en/yearly-nft-market-report.

Parker, Priya. 2018. *The Art of Gathering*. New York: Riverhead.

Reyburn, Scott. 2022. "Five Years Since the $450m Salvator Mundi Sale: A First-Hand Account of the Non-Sensical Auction." *The Art Newspaper*, November 15, 2022. https://www.theartnewspaper.com/2022/11/15/five-years-since-the-450m-salvator-mundi-sale-a-first-hand-account-of-the-nonsensical-auction.

Sarr, Felwine, and Bénédicte Savoy. 2018. "The Restitution of African Cultural Heritage: Toward a New Relational Ethics." Translated by Drue S. Burk. https://www.about-africa.de/images/sonstiges/2018/sarr_savoy_en.pdf.

Small, Zachary. 2022. "Even as NFTs Plummet, Digital Artists Find Museums Are Calling." *New York Times*, October 31, 2022. https://www.nytimes.com/2022/10/31/arts/design/nfts-moma-refik-anadol-digital.html.

Tate Gallery. 2020. "The Board of Trustees of the Tate Gallery: Annual Accounts 2019–2020." Tate Gallery, London. https://www.tate.org.uk/documents/1668/tate_gallery_annual_accounts_2019-20_web_accessible.pdf.

Velthuis, Olav. 2005. *Talking Prices: Symbolic Meanings of Prices on the Market for Contemporary Art*. Princeton, NJ: Princeton University Press.

Villa, Angelica, and Daniel Cassady. 2022. "Record-Breaking Mondrian Painting Carries Sotheby's Tepid Modern Art Sales to $391.2M." *ArtNews*, November 14, 2022. https://www.artnews.com/art-news/news/mondrian-sothebys-auction-record-william-paley-david-solinger-1234646724/.

Whitaker, Amy. 2022. "Exhibit 2: NFTs and the Art Market." In Clare McAndrew, *The Art Market 2022*, 49–55. Basel: UBS and Art Basel. (Republished as "The Artistic Value of an NFT." https://www.artbasel.com/stories/art-market-report-amy-whitaker?lang=en.)

Whitaker, Amy, and Nora Burnett Abrams. 2023. *The Story of NFTs: Artists, Technology, and Democracy*. New York: Rizzoli and MCA Denver.

Whitaker, Amy, Anne Bracegirdle, Susan de Menil, Michelle Ann Gitlitz, and Lena Santos. 2021. "Art, Antiquities, and Blockchain: New Approaches to the Restitution of Cultural Heritage." *International Journal of Cultural Policy* 27, no. 3: 312–329. https://doi.org/10.1080/10286632.2020.1765163.

Yaffe-Bellany, David. 2022. "Embattled Crypto Exchange FTX Files for Bankruptcy." *New York Times*, November 11, 2022. https://www.nytimes.com/2022/11/11/business/ftx-bankruptcy.html.

Yermack. David. 2017. "Donor Governance and Financial Management in Prominent US Art Museums." *Journal of Cultural Economics* 41: 215–235.

Yerebakan, Osman Can. 2022. "Museum of Fine Arts, Boston Selling NFTs of Rarely-Exhibited French Impressionist Pastels to Raise Funds for Conservation." *The Art Newspaper*, June 28, 2022. https://www.theartnewspaper.com/2022/06/28/mfa-boston-nfts-conservation-french-impressionist-pastels-degas.

Zelizer, Viviana. 2000. "How and Why Do We Care About Circuits?" *Accounts Newsletter of the Economic Sociology Section of the American Sociological Association* 1 (2000): 3–5.

PART VIII

AUDIENCE DEVELOPMENT
Participation, Engagement, and Evaluation

CHAPTER 30

IMPROVING ACCESSIBILITY AND INCLUSION IN THE PERFORMING ARTS FOR PEOPLE WITH DISABILITIES

Moving Beyond a "Checking-the-Boxes" Approach

ALLISON AMIDEI AND ELENA SV FLYS

Introduction

At this pivotal moment in the movement for social justice and inclusion, there exists a contradiction in the performing arts field. Article 27 of the United Nations Universal Declaration of Human Rights states that "everyone has the right freely to participate in the cultural life of the community, to enjoy the arts and to share in scientific advancement and its benefits" (United Nations 1948). While performing arts organizations aim to be inclusive and welcoming, there still exist many obstacles for people with disabilities to participate. According to the World Health Organization, 15 percent of the world's population has a disability (World Health Organization 2021). Moreover, the United Nations notes that aging populations are increasing, and since those same populations have a higher risk of disability, there will likely be further increases in the disabled population of the world (United Nations n.d.). However, as the "world's largest minority," disabled people are one of the most marginalized groups in our society according to metrics such as poverty, education, health, housing, and a lack of available services (Goodman, Morris, and Boston 2019, 21). It is also a group that any one of us can join at any time in our lives. Despite the significant size of this demographic, people with disabilities experience disproportionate barriers to participation in the performing arts. For example, they are the least represented on stage and screen, with 95 percent of roles going to able-bodied actors (Woodburn and Kopić 2016, 1). Moreover, Leahy and

Ferri (2022) point out that adults with disabilities had a lower rate of engagement with the arts than other adults and a lower rate of being an artist or cultural producer. In addition to this, there are many performing arts sites that do not offer access services for their content. In order to address this contradiction, the performing arts sector needs to engage in a major change. The first step is to move beyond a "checking-the-boxes" approach for providing access and inclusion for the disabled community based solely on what is legally required. To illustrate some of the possible changes to enact, we will examine the challenges and benefits of incorporating accessibility in performing arts organizations and offer the perspective of performing arts practitioners with disabilities from the United States and Spain. These perspectives will come from conducting qualitative surveys of performing artists with expertise in accessibility and inclusion. By considering access barriers, funding concerns, employment and representation issues, and attitudinal challenges common to the accessibility implementation process, performing arts managers can improve access inclusion for people with disabilities in the performing arts.

Only by making structural and systematic changes in performing arts practices can full access and inclusion of the disabled community be achieved. Thus, in addition to theoretical perspectives from disability studies scholars and sector reports, this chapter uses interviews with arts practitioners from the disability community in the United States and Spain to discuss accessibility. While this research study focused on the performing arts, the recommendations and results could potentially be applied across the rest of the arts disciplines. Through an analysis of access implementation and a study of the artistic, technical, organizational, and attitudinal issues that arise, this chapter can show potential areas for improvement that arts leaders can consider in order to achieve a more inclusive environment for the disabled community.

Literature Review: Highlighting the Contradiction

Despite the ideal of the Universal Declaration of Human Rights, in reality participation is not possible for all due to a lack of access services provided within the arts sector and a lack of knowledge about accessibility and disability among arts sector leaders (Lamarre, Rice, and Besse 2021, 186).

Access Barriers: A Call to Disrupt Ableism

The November 2021 "Time to Act" report (Floch and Portolés 2021) surveyed European cultural operators from forty-two countries about disability access and inclusion. While 57 percent of the organizations had worked to improve physical access, only 16 percent of European arts sector leaders reported having a good knowledge of the work of artists with disabilities and only 17 percent mentioned dedicated programming to engage with artists with disabilities (Floch and Portolés 2021). Furthermore, 33 percent of arts venues and festivals stated that they do not consider audiences with disabilities on a regular basis when determining things like programming or marketing (Floch and Portolés 2021). The 24 percent of venues that did actively engage with audiences with disabilities did not have a specific strategy for doing so (Floch and Portolés 2021). Given this data, it appears that creators and audiences with disabilities are being left on the margins.

As reinforced by the "Time to Act" report, approaches to accessibility in the cultural sector often focus on structural modifications to architecture rather than centering an arts-going experiencing and the myriad of more complex barriers to inclusion (as stated by several authors such as Barton-Farcas 2018; Kleege 2018; SV Flys 2018). Disability rights experts advocate for thinking more creatively about access and decentering nondisabled persons. For example, Kelly and Orsini (2021, 293) point out that if access is only considered in terms of necessary "adjustments" rather than in making a patron with disabilities feel welcome, then the messaging is that the venue is only interested in the "non-disabled art consumer." Lamarre, Rice, and Besse (2021, 188) parallel this: "We must interrogate access beyond making changes in spaces, policies, and procedures to meet legislative requirements. We might additionally consider how we can creatively reimagine the role of disability and of mind-body differences in enlivening public spaces." Mashburn and Papalia (2019) call for arts leaders to "disrupt ableism" and be "guided by those at the margins" (para. 20), while the World Health Organization (2011, 169) calls for organizations to build a "culture of accessibility."

Funding

Funding is an important consideration for performing arts administrators looking to improve access within their organizations. There are potential grants and other opportunities that could be accessed for organizations supporting and serving people with disabilities. Some foundations and grant-making organizations, such as South Arts in Atlanta, list access as a core value and require that grantees provide access services for their constituents. The Oregon Arts Commission provides funds to offset expenditures for specific access-related expenses. The Michigan Council for Cultural Affairs is another organization that requires access as part of their funding program. Similarly, Spain has grants from Fundación Once, Fundación Universia, and Fundación Caixa, among others, that provide funds related to access and inclusion.

Although money should not be the reason behind access and inclusion, it is worth stating that there is a significant audience group left behind when art organizations are not accessible. Data from the Australian National Arts Participation Survey of 2016 demonstrates that people with disabilities are more likely to donate money to the arts (21 percent compared to 9 percent donated by people without disabilities) (Australia Council for the Arts 2017). As noted in the introduction, since 15 percent of the population has a disability and this percentage is increasing, it could be said that as the population with disabilities increases, the number of potential arts patrons who will require access services to engage with the arts also increases.

However, the impact of the global pandemic poses a real growth threat for audiences with disabilities. In the UK Disability Arts Alliance 2021 Survey, "82 percent of respondents expressed concern about continued provision of access for disabled audiences through reopening," and the study's author stresses that "the cultural sector needs to offer reassurance that access remains a top priority" (Gentry 2021, 2). The report also cited "continued access provision for disabled people in general" and "failure to meet individual personal access needs" as some of the top concerns as the culture sector reopens (Gentry 2021, 4). Gentry (2021) further argues that the survey results suggested that disabled respondents have little faith in the arts sector's prioritization of access services.

Employment: Representation in the Performing Arts

Just as accessibility improvements focused only on structural modifications to architecture are limiting, a focus on inclusion for audiences with disabilities while failing to increase the representation of people with disabilities performing onstage is also limiting. Addressing this point, Sandals (2016, n.p.) quotes Eliza Chandler, the artistic director of the nonprofit Tangled Art + Disability, saying that people with disabilities "aren't just audiences, they are artists and creators too." This is seen in the arguable dominance of standardized aesthetic bodies on the stage and screen (Ojeda and SV Flys 2015; Hermans 2016). To break these exclusive practices, one could argue that audience members, directors, and producers need to be challenged in order to deconstruct and embrace an aesthetic of difference. Hermans (2016, 161) speaks to the harm caused by omitting disabled bodies: "By opposing the disabled to the abled (the abnormal versus the normal), the disabled body is reduced to a thing to be looked at, even stared at. Under the gaze of the social other, the disabled body is constructed and filled with preexisting expectations and by stereotypical thinking." In the film sector, sixty-two actors have been nominated for an Oscar for playing a disabled character.[1] Twenty-eight of those nominated for portraying a disabled character have won, but of those winners, only three have actually had a disability (Troy Katsur in 2022, Marlee Matlin in 1987, and Harold Russell in 1947; see Lopez 2023).

This lack of interpreters with disabilities portraying their own disability has also been pointed out by scholars such as Sandahl (2019) and Corbella and Sánchez-Guijo (2010). Therefore, the data shows a potential contradiction in the sector, where stories with disabled characters and the act of "playing disability" are seen as award-worthy, but actors with the lived/embodied experience of disability are rarely given the chance to play any role at all, not even the roles in which a disability is integral to the performance. Barton-Farcas (2018, 4) argues that organizations fear that the work from artists with disabilities "won't be good enough," which will require them to "ask the audience to applaud substandard work out of pity." Ironically, Barton-Farcas (2018) indicates that, based on her experience, this type of fear usually comes specifically from those who also do not make efforts to be inclusive.

Attitudinal Changes: Addressing a Culture of Exclusion in the Performing Arts

Holmes (2018, 24) points out that incorporating access can be a real struggle for an organization that lacks the "full picture of how the existing culture perpetuates exclusion." Considering that 15 percent of the world's population experiences some form of disability, we could argue that this lack of awareness around the need for accessibility teeters on the edge of negligence and fuels a cycle of exclusion and discrimination. As an example, Darren Walker, president of the Ford Foundation, admitted in a 2016 statement that the foundation had completely failed to address the disabled community (Walker 2016). This resonates further with the earlier data presented in the "Time to Act" report, in which most of the managers admitted having poor to very poor knowledge of disability art and artists. As Holmes (2018) notes, those in senior leadership roles are key to making inclusion central in an organization's culture; therefore, this lack of knowledge can potentially harm the inclusiveness of the performing arts sector.

Considering this knowledge gap around disability, Durrer and Miles (2009, 229) argue for arts administrators to consider their role as that of a "cultural intermediary" tasked with breaking down the barriers to inclusion. Similarly, Michael Achtman of Graeae Theatre promotes the concept of "creative enablers" (2014, 36). These are individuals trained to assist and facilitate disabled artists to allow more artistic autonomy (Gold 2021, 221). For some disabled artists, these creative enablers might take the form of a scribe for notes or someone to help with lines, while others seek out an enabler to establish more of an artistic partnership (Gold 2021, 222). Similarly, arts administrators could train to become a creative enabler facilitating inclusion within their organization. Authors such as Silverman et al. (2012), Kelly and Orsini (2021), Lamarre, Rice, and Besse (2021), and Garland-Thompson (2017) point out the relevance of orientation and training to best create accommodations to improve accessibility. They suggest engaging access occupational therapists, advisors, and people with disabilities to create and sustain accessible practices. Moving beyond training, Walker (2016) suggests that arts leaders also be open to receiving negative feedback from the disabled community as a means to become more accountable, see missed opportunities, and be open to change.

Research Study Methodology

Thus far we have included different perspectives and literature reviews giving an overview of the state of access and inclusion in the arts. Following the disability rights rallying cry "Nothing About Us, Without Us" (Charlton 2000), we now provide feedback on access and inclusion directly from experts and arts practitioners from the disability community. Our goal is to compare what we have found in the literature with the experience of professionals in the field.

One of the goals of this chapter is to raise awareness about the current situation. In order to do so and to better understand the state of accessibility in the performing arts field, we conducted qualitative surveys targeting performing artists, managers, and leaders with expertise in accessibility and asked for recommendations to improve inclusion for people with disabilities. Our objective is to compare what was stated in the literature review with our respondents' opinions. Invitations to participate were sent to performing arts organizations with missions focused on disability as well as shared through performing arts disability affinity groups on social media. Respondents were screened for those who self-identified as having a disability (59.3 percent of respondents), those who had prior experience working with individuals with disabilities, or those who had prior experience working at organizations with missions centering disability and inclusion. Interviews were conducted within the researchers' home countries, the United States and Spain.[2] We had thirty completed interviews (twenty-one from the United States and nine from Spain) during a six-month period in 2021. The interviews included a series of prepared questions about demographic data and the interviewee's professional performing arts experiences. In order to have a range of accessible options, respondents could complete the interview questions online or choose to have a recorded Zoom interview. Recorded interviews were then transcribed. Due to the requirements of institutional review boards and ethical committees in both countries, interviewees' personal information was removed from the data and participants were coded by letter and number to maintain anonymity. Besides the ethical requirements, maintaining anonymity was important for our participants to feel comfortable sharing their personal experiences without risk of potential backlash. We initially analyzed the responses using a verbatim coding method to find common words and phrases from the data.[3] We then considered how these common themes in the data related to the work of performing arts managers, who would be responsible for accessibility implementation within their organizations. This resulted in the data responses being coded into the following categories addressed in the literature review: access barriers, funding, employment, and attitudinal changes. Funding and employment (human resources) are two of the main areas covered within the arts administration sector (as stated in textbooks and by scholars and associations),[4] and access barriers and attitudinal changes are categories highlighted by experts in the field of accessibility and inclusion in the cultural sector (e.g., Gallego-Noche et al.

Table 30.1. Interview Respondent Demographics

Person 1	US	Performing arts manager
Person 2	US	Arts administrator, director
Person 3	US	Drama therapist, director, educator
Person 4	US	Arts administrator
Person 5	US	Performer, choreographer, educator
Person 6	US	Student, educator
Person 7	US	Performer, teaching artist
Person 8	US	Theater artist and designer
Person 9	US	Poet, artist
Person 10	US	Theater artistic director
Person 11	Spain	Director, performer
Person 12	Spain	Special educator, arts administrator
Person 13	Spain	Director, educator
Person 14	Spain	Artist, actor
Person 15	Spain	Artist, dramaturge
Person 16	Spain	Actress, dancer
Person 17	Spain	Director
Person 18	Spain	Actress
Person 19	Spain	Artist
Person 20	US	Access and inclusive programs manager
Person 21	US	Accessibility specialist
Person 22	US	Performer, arts manager
Person 23	US	Performer
Person 24	US	Educator, performing arts manager
Person 25	US	Educator, performer
Person 26	US	Performing arts manager, performer
Person 27	US	Performer, playwright
Person 28	US	Performing arts manager, technician
Person 29	US	Designer, educator
Person 30	US	Designer, educator

2021, referencing attitudinal barriers as nonrecognition; Shevlin, Kenny, and McNeela 2004). For reference, we present a table with participants, their job in the arts, and the country they reside in (see Table 30.1).

Access Barriers

The World Health Organization and World Bank *World Report on Disability* (WHO 2011) describes access barriers as being physical, social, and attitudinal. The report recommends that initial efforts to improve access should begin with the removal of physical barriers; however, the social and attitudinal barriers must also be addressed because the areas are interconnected. By raising the access standards in all three areas, organizations can build a "culture of accessibility" for people with disabilities (WHO 2011, 169). This sentiment is echoed in our study responses. One of the participants, a performing arts manager and theater technician from the United States, said that organizations that consider accessibility often provide more thoughtful experiences: "It is much more welcoming at every level. So, generally, the ones that have lots of accessibility considerations, they thought about a lot of things to make the experience pleasurable for folks and entertaining and valuable for everyone that walks in the door" (Person 28). Similarly, Person 10 said, "The focus on audience access made for a deeper artistic experience for both the company of performers and the audience members whether or not they had a disability."

The responses also illuminated how the culture of accessibility can be broken down when these three areas (physical, social, and attitudinal) are not addressed. Among the data, there were frequent references to the inaccessibility of performing-arts-related spaces. Person 4 suggested that organizations should conduct "an assessment of their venue to ensure that it is physically accessible." According to the participant, even when a space is technically accessible, it is often not a pleasant or even logical user experience. Person 26 wanted not only an "eye for access, but the eye for the nuance of access. It is not just 'Can you get people in the door?'" and also noted, "I think there are ways to think about access from the ground up so that it's not feeling like an add-on." For example, this person mentioned how accessible audience seating only on the perimeter is a "check-the-box" access failure: "What if you had the modular ability to always be adding wheelchair seats wherever somebody wants to sit, where any seat in the entire venue could be accessible to somebody in a wheelchair?" (Person 26).

Respondents also spoke of the content, quality, and frequency of access services. Just as access for physical spaces should be incorporated in initial building plans, organizations should avoid "tacking on" accessibility at the end of the process or only when a patron requests an accommodation. "They need to listen to disabled people and build it in from the very start; not try to fit it on top of something that was created with no consideration for inclusion" (Person 1). Respondents talked about the need for effective communication. For example, Person 14 mentioned offering sign language or captions in every performance. This participant also spoke to the relevance of having many of these accommodations for actors who have a disability, such as light warning signals backstage so that deaf actors would know when to enter a scene. In addition, several respondents wanted access services to be available regularly and not relegated to only one or two performance dates. Person 22, for example, requested "video and printed social stories of every venue; large-print programs; accessible signage with pictures and words; gender-neutral restrooms; captioning and ASL translation at least 1x/week rather than 1x/run; relaxed performances of shows for adults, not just shows for children" as options. In other words, most performances could follow universal design principles, which establish how everything should be created with everyone in mind from conception and not just adapted to comply with the law.

Funding

Funding was also important to our interviewees when considering accessibility implementation. Person 1 suggested that grantors require that a portion of larger grants be used for access-related expenses like sign language interpreters and audio descriptions for performances. Person 13 denounced organizational complaints that accessibility is difficult and expensive to provide: "All this is a convenient attitude" and "a regrettably palliative bet in the face of a lack of rigor" and "the professional need that it entails." Person 1 emphasized the importance of properly budgeting for access and expressed a desire for the funding to be tied to inclusive practices. It was further noted that organizations "should stop making work that isn't accessible. And if they don't stop, they should stop taking public funds to make inaccessible work, at least" (Person 1). By contrast, Person 22 acknowledged that offering affordable, quality programming is a challenge. Notably, there are potential grants and targeted funding opportunities for organizations genuinely dedicated to inclusive, equitable practices for people with disabilities.[5] However, respondents (nine out of the thirty interviewed) spoke of uneven support for accessibility in funding models. Similarly, Person 4 wanted "to see more funding allocated to accessible programs, even if through grants."

Despite the challenges, achieving *inclusion for real* means it is important to realize that access services cannot be treated as optional, nor cut as a cost-saving measure in austere times. Moreover, accessibility should be fundamentally integral to the programming of all arts organizations and budgeted as such. "For people in management and/or production training, I think it is essential to understand that inclusion can never be an end, but a means. We cannot continue generating inclusive spaces or inclusive projects, because inclusion must be an intrinsic condition and not an addition" (Person 12). Moreover, respondents also suggested that training in accessibility would be necessary for organizations not currently incorporating access into their work (seven respondents in total). This is reinforced by authors such as Silverman et al. (2012), Lamarre, Rice, and Besse (2021), and Garland-Thompson (2017), who have all pointed out the importance of training around access implementation by engaging accessibility advisors and hiring people with disabilities as consultants. Person 20, an access and inclusive programs manager in the United States, said, "As a result of requiring that all staff across the institution attend disability awareness training presented in partnership with community members with disabilities, we have noticed an increase in thinking about accessibility on the front end across the institution and increased requests to learn more about accessibility." They added, "Accessibility and inclusion is the work of everyone in the organization, not just a select few individuals" supporting the organization-wide training

(Person 20). These comments could also be related to attitudinal barriers, which, as will be discussed later, could be reduced through training.

Employment

Overwhelmingly, nearly all respondents wanted to see organizations regularly employ more people with disabilities and build relationships with disabled communities. "Actively seek out artists with disabilities to be a part of your administration and stages. . . . Hire experts in disability on your staff" (Person 2). But real inclusion seems to be more than just having one person from a historically marginalized community as a token to demonstrate the diversity of an organization. One participant defined tokenism as being "the practice of making only an effort to be inclusive with members of minority groups to give the appearance of equal rights" (Person 19). As an example, Person 15 shared the experience of being valued only as a "marketing object" and not for their talents as an artist. "People who have disabilities should not be treated like 'team mascots' but as equal artistic collaborators who have lots of *great* ideas" (Person 3, emphasis in original). Since disability is not a monolith, a multitude of voices should be involved in a participatory process to best establish truly inclusive practices. Holmes (2018, 80) argues that "unchecked assumptions about any group of people, especially when treated as a monolithic group, might misdirect us towards ineffective, even offensive, solutions." Thus, representation is critical for decision-making and forging an organization's path. Similarly, Person 10 noted, "All presently marginalized groups, POC, Indigenous, LGBTQ, low-income folks need to be represented on the management and organizational levels. Disability is often left off this list. It needs to be part of a social justice approach to the arts." Person 28 echoes this: "Why are no people of X community or whatever community here?" and "Racial recognition has changed the way I've considered the spaces I've been. . . . With disability, just looking around the room: who's here and who's not here? And, do I really want to come back here?"

Several respondents noted that the lack of equitable pay for people with disabilities was an obstacle to participation in the performing arts. Hadley (2019, 349) indicated that while arts jobs are always financially perilous, the situation for disabled artists is made worse by cuts to the arts sector coinciding with cuts to financial and disability support systems that enable their ability to be in the workforce. Person 17 shared frustration with providing expertise about disability to organizations and then not being compensated or even credited for that work. Person 28 agreed: "We should pay people for their time and their knowledge."

Respondents also pointed out that lack of time flexibility among organizations presents a challenge. Therefore, it may be important that as access and inclusion expand, organizations and managers consider time flexibility, or as Jones, Changfoot, and Johnston call it, "crip time" (2021, 313).[6] As an example, building flexibility into a rehearsal schedule would allow more time to make accommodations for disabled performers or technicians, thus providing more space for them to do their work. Consider that a typical rehearsal break, per Actors' Equity rules, is ten minutes. But would ten minutes be enough time for a performer in a wheelchair to navigate to an accessible bathroom and back? "Theater is a huge time commitment that needs you to function at a high level in many roles. . . . Even if it means a longer process, slow down and spread work more equitably" (Person 8). Moreover, rethinking long workdays has intersectional benefits that would increase equity for many involved in the performing arts. Flexibility in rehearsal could help performers who are caregivers, are parents, or have second jobs. For example, many theater artists are questioning the effectiveness of a standard "10 out of 12" technical rehearsal, requiring artists and crew to work for ten or more hours.[7] Person 30, a theater designer in the United States, makes the connection between financial hardship, pay inequality, and poor treatment still experienced by many creatives:

> We have for many years created a philosophy of self-harm when it comes to abusive labor practices and the amount of hours. And so we have built this entire system on top of martyrdom and very real exhaustion and financial poverty at the expense of many. And so those who are able to financially be in theater usually means that they're able to be financially anywhere they want to be. And so theater is a choice for them and the rest of us are trying to survive. And we've been forced to fight over scraps all these years and we've been fighting each other when we really should have been fighting the structure that was putting us in a system of fighting over scraps.

Just by implementing a more "humane" rehearsal schedule, an organization would put inclusion into practice. Relatedly, the pandemic has shown the potential of remote work and flexible hours. Therefore, why not consider possibilities like these that will positively impact people with diverse requirements and needs?

Person 2 questioned, "Why wouldn't you actively choose to engage neurodiverse brains, physically challenged bodies, and nonverbal communicators (just to name a few) in the creation of new work and/or provide a fresh take on an existing piece of work?" A shift in perception (Person 27) and perspective (Person 29) were also noted outcomes of more inclusive artistic practices and programming:

> You never know what somebody else brings to the table in terms of ways of doing things. It's more innovative or just interesting aesthetically, figuring out ways to do things faster or better. I just see it as the human capital thing that we need to include everybody because everybody has all these gifts that they can contribute to the whole situation. (Person 29)

Aichner (2021) makes a strong economic argument, noting that people with disabilities are highly motivated to work, promote a positive work environment, and are better able to identify creative solutions. Person 26 agrees: "The disability community is just ripe with so many different approaches simply because the work has to happen in a different way." Further, a workplace that is inclusive of people with disabilities will strengthen the diversity of the organization as well as broaden internal perspectives (Kuligowski 2020). Person 26 explains:

> What we've seen is if you can open yourself to being inclusive of those individuals in those communities, it naturally pushes people out of their box and makes people more creative if they embrace it and if they go with it and say yes. I think it's mostly just tapping into these creative assets and you have these amazing artists that too often are not included in spaces. They're gonna bring something different to the work.

Similarly, lighting designer Annie Weigand, who is Deaf, gives an example of the way her disability brings a different perspective:

> I am very visual based, very reliant on my eyes; they're clearly my strongest tool. With this unique toolset, I'm able to bring a different perspective on things to the table. For instance, maybe there's a part in a show that's conveyed through sound only, and I always question whether a sound component can be supported visually. I would offer that perspective to the director. Changes might be made to make something more visual, as opposed to only audio. (Maag and Weigand 2021, 7)

Attitudinal Changes: Avoiding the "Check-the-Box" Mentality

Respondents cited a "check-the-box" mentality as a concern. There was frustration that inclusion is sometimes publicly pushed as an important organizational value even as the experience of actually working with the company is far from inclusive. "I work for a program now that absolutely puts [accessibility] all on the surface and doesn't allow this to be in the fabric of the program.... It does not actually fundamentally change the culture and fix the issue" (Person 24). "Culture is democratic, communal, not elitist, and a part of our daily life in many ways. The entire population must be proactive in its cultural contribution to society" (Person 11).

Relying on legislation to regulate access and inclusion within organizations often "causes changes to be slow and arduous" (Person 17). Person 28 lamented that "the bare minimum is what a lot of [organizations] hit" and asked for a "higher standard of what the baseline is." In the United States, the Americans with Disabilities Act (ADA) was passed in 1990. Spanish democracy only began in 1975, with some of the first national disability decrees not established until 2007. Since these disability rights laws are fairly recent, changes made in response to these laws are still catching up. Echoing this, Person 17 had mixed feedback about the current state of arts access and inclusion in Spain:

> Honestly, I don't think a good job is being done. In fact, I think that this work has not even begun seriously.... It is true that we are a young country, where democracy is forty years old, and this undoubtedly means that, in some aspects, there are things that have not even been tried. The good thing, without a doubt, is that everything remains to be done.

To make a real and lasting impact, respondents desired more widely disseminated resources and a higher standard for what constitutes access and inclusion. Person 28 echoes this sentiment:

> There hasn't necessarily been an established baseline of what organizations should do. And with all things considered, there's the ADA and people are not even meeting that. But rarely beyond the ADA. They're trying to do their best. A lot of them are well-intended but everything changes every minute. So I hope that soon there will be some more available resources that would provide an understanding of what a baseline is for even general accessibility.

Similarly, while anything that adds more access moves us closer to meaningful inclusion, the dominant culture often prioritizes access improvements that do not disrupt established systems while continuing to keep disabled people on the margins (Lobel and Thom 2019, 250).

In response to sentiments such as these, the arts should move beyond this deficit-based approach to access and inclusion: "This sector offers exciting opportunities to explore how accessibility can become more than an exercise of ticking boxes in response to legislation by fully and artistically engaging with the idea of access" (Lamarre, Rice, and Besse 2021, 186). By engaging in inclusive practices that move beyond the legal minimum requirements, organizations that proactively integrate access into programming and organizational structures can create "a message of social commitment" (Person 12).

When asked how to convince managers to improve access, Person 11, an arts administrator and a disabled person, stated that "administrations must provide these accessible and inclusive spaces, promote and favor them, to generate a more egalitarian, non-exclusive society," highlighting the need for administrators to become a leading force. Person 3 spoke of the fundamental shifts in attitude needed in order to fully adopt inclusive practices:

> Arts managers need to understand that people who have disabilities are people first and therefore part of the general public and deserve access to the arts. They need to learn how to make access available and to keep up with the latest technology that makes the arts accessible. . . . They also need to be willing to listen to artists, audience members, and arts participants who have disabilities when they have ideas of what would make their programming more accessible. Most importantly, the attitudes of all who work for the organization need to be welcoming, willing to learn more about how to make their classes, performances, exhibits, etc., accessible and welcoming.

Some respondents shared stronger opinions about arts leaders: "If they don't want to include access and inclusion, they are terrible people. There are laws against excluding disabled people but clearly that isn't enough for them" (Person 1). Considering the disconnect between leadership and moral/legal access obligations, Person 3 stated, "I think that those who are disconnected think of people who need accommodations as burdens who are creating expenses for the organization that are too costly and may bankrupt the organization. They are thinking of artists and audience members with disabilities as 'other' and not as equal humans."

Some respondents experienced a total failure of organizations to address any accessibility needs. Person 28 noted that some have a "narrow frame of focus" on what accessibility really means. As an example, they shared their experiences around accessible audience seating for wheelchairs being relegated to undesirable locations in the theater or only made available as an afterthought: "I've seen some really unfortunate language around like, 'Well, we'll remove chairs if we have to . . . if we must.'" Person 29 expressed frustration about organizations not taking feedback about inequitable practices: "When I've said something, because I always say something, I feel like I get blowback: 'Well, that's not in our repertory.' I feel like I'm doing an advocacy-education thing in the moment, but with someone who has already made decisions about how things are going to be. I'm not talking to somebody who is open-minded about it." Person 6 said some organizations focused on providing access for individuals with sensory and physical disabilities while failing to expand offerings for those with cognitive disabilities, and notes that what work is being done for neurodiverse audiences is overwhelmingly focused on children and young adults, leaving out adults entirely.

Echoing Gold's study (2021) concerning the lack of representation of neurodivergent artists, Person 3, a drama therapist and educator, shared that a real change in attitude most strongly comes through having a connection to people with disabilities:

> But I think they will only really "get it" [when] they have an immersive, creative experience with people who have disabilities so they can see that they have the same feelings, dreams, and creativity as anyone else. I think changes in attitude, acceptance, and value come only through experiences with others, not with disembodied information.

In this sense, many respondents noted the importance of seeking out regular feedback from participants and artists with disabilities on improving access services (Persons 1, 2, 3, 10, and 30):

> Everyone has some disability at some point in their life, whether it's temporary or long-term. The disability I have in my hands was something I got as an adult, I didn't start off with it. . . . How do you get people to be not only more inclusive in their actions, but in their philosophy and their thought process in the way they actually approach things? A lot of people can be more inclusive. (Person 30)

Still other respondents called for more humane treatment overall and consideration when working with the disabled community. One participant said, "Above all, patience" (Person 19), referring to the need for people to understand diverse needs (e.g., needing more time, less content, etc.). For example, many asked for more time in art-making processes (Person 25). Others emphasized art as a human right: "Access and inclusion [help] people who have been marginalized to become independent and confident, to feel respected, accepted, and valued as equal human beings in the community" (Person 3). There also were calls for an attitudinal shift for critics considering works of art created by persons with disabilities (e.g., discounting work as therapeutic rather than artistic).

What Does "Accessibility for Real" Look Like?

Based on our responses, artistic inclusion and accessibility for real will only be fully realized when people with disabilities are participating in the performing arts at every level within a performing arts organization and not just when it directly relates to disability (Persons 11, 12, 14, and 18). For some this means removing the "inclusive" label so that access and inclusion become fully normalized (Persons 11 and 12). The goal would be for organizations to have a dedicated accessibility coordinator/designer on staff. Person 6 states, "I would like to see more companies including an access designer from the outset of a project rather than shoehorning in access at the very end of the process." Echoing the need for training and creative enablers (Achtman 2014), Person 13 emphasized the importance of a design plan, trained personnel, and "a guarantee of permanent dissemination and realization" in order to fully integrate accessibility. This would not only benefit the organization and patrons but also improve the connection between access services and programming.

However, respondents noted that already successful inclusive performing arts organizations such as Graeae Theatre in the United Kingdom, Phamaly Theatre in the United States, and Palmyra Teatro and the Apropa Culture program in Spain can serve as models of inclusion for real in the arts. These organizations implement access and inclusion not only from the beginning of their processes but also as an integral part of their organizational existence. In addition, all of them hire people with disabilities. For example, everyone working for Phamaly Theatre has a disability. Moreover, these companies are considered professional companies and not amateur. They show how inclusive work should be considered professional and not just tagged as a therapeutic or social service venture based on a paternalistic, condescending approach. Rather, let us redefine what meaningful inclusion entails by "learning, inviting, copying, and adapting the mechanisms of these companies that have been in business for years ... We don't have to 'invent' anything" (Person 17). This way, access services and inclusive practices can move beyond being just a tool and become a means to further explore art and content (Person 16).

Conclusion

We have presented different perspectives from research reports, disability studies theories, and feedback on access and inclusion directly from performing arts practitioners from the disability community, thereby highlighting some of the obstacles to access and inclusion in the performing arts. Further, we shared suggestions to improve accessibility implementation and considered the important role current and future performing arts administrators have in disrupting exclusive systems. First and foremost, we would like to remind performing arts administrators of the benefits of hiring people with disabilities as staff, consultants, and artists who bring dynamic creativity in addition to the lived/embodied knowledge of disability into an organization. Moreover, leaders can responsibly use funding to create meaningful approaches to inclusion for artists and audiences with disability and not just "check the box" to fulfill legal requirements. We argued that arts administrators could become creative enablers who embrace inclusion and facilitate the ability for everyone to participate in performing arts autonomously. By acknowledging both the individual and institutional privilege contributing to injustice, arts administrators can serve as cultural intermediaries to address knowledge gaps and ignorance in order to make space for true inclusion. Given the limitations of legislation in guaranteeing inclusion and access, transformative change is needed to ensure that real inclusion is not only about fully accessible physical spaces but also about content and participation in performing arts being accessible to everyone.

Authors' Note

We have no conflicts of interest to disclose.

Notes

1. Many professionals from the performing arts sector, such as actors or costume designers, will work in parallel in the film sector. That is why this chapter considers it important to have both fields represented.
2. Both researchers have worked in the United States, and Elena SV Flys now works in Spain. The goal was to see if there were major differences between the countries.
3. Realizing that there were no major differences between respondents in the United States and Spain.
4. E.g., textbooks such as Rosewall 2021, Korza, Brown, and Dreeszen 2007, and Byrnes 2014, and undergraduate/graduate curriculum standards of the Association of Arts Administration Educators.
5. The Oregon Arts Commission provides funds to offset expenditures for specific access-related expenses. The Michigan Council for Cultural Affairs is another organization that requires access as part of its funding program. Similarly, Spain has grants from Fundación Once, Fundación Universia, and Fundación Caixa, among others, that provide funds related to access and inclusion.
6. "A concept arising from disabled experience that addresses the ways that disabled/chronically ill and neurodivergent people experience time (and space) differently than ablebodyminded folk." Critical Disability Studies Collective n.d.
7. See the website of No More 10 Out of 12s, https://nomore10outof12s.com/.

References

Achtman, Michael. 2014. "How Creative Is the Creative Enabler?" *Alt.theatre: Cultural Diversity and the Stage* 11, no. 3: 36.
Aichner, Thomas. 2021. "The Economic Argument for Hiring People with Disabilities." *Humanities and Social Sciences Communications* 8, no. 1: 1–4.
Australia Council for the Arts. 2017. *Connecting Australians: Results of the National Arts Participation Survey*. Surry Hills, NSW: Australia Council for the Arts. https://australiacouncil.gov.au/advocacy-and-research/connecting-australians/.

Barton-Farcas, Stephanie. 2018. *Disability and Theatre: A Practical Manual for Inclusion in the Arts*. New York: Routledge.

Byrnes, William. 2014. *Management and the Arts*. 5th ed. New York: Routledge.

Charlton, James I. 2000. *Nothing About Us Without Us: Disability Oppression and Empowerment*. Berkeley: University of California Press.

Corbella, Marta, and Fernando Sánchez-Guijo. 2010. "La representación de las personas con discapacidad visual en el cine." *Revista de Medicina y Cine* 6, no. 2: 69–77.

Critical Disability Studies Collective. n.d. "Terminology." University of Minnesota. https://cdsc.umn.edu/cds/terms#:~:text=Crip%20time%3A%20A%20concept%20arising,differently%20than%20able%2Dbodyminded%20folk.

Durrer, Victoria, and Steven Miles. 2009. "New Perspectives on the Role of Cultural Intermediaries in Social Inclusion in the UK." *Consumption Markets and Culture* 12 no. 3: 225–241.

Floch, Yohann, and Jordi Baltà Portolés. 2021. "Time to Act: How Lack of Knowledge in the Cultural Sector Creates Barriers for Disabled Artists and Audiences." British Council. https://www.disabilityartsinternational.org/wp-content/uploads/2021/04/Time-to-Act-embargoed-report.pdf.

SV Flys, Elena. 2018. "ADA and Communication: Accessibility in Theatre." *Culturework* 22, no. 1 (online). https://scholarsbank.uoregon.edu/xmlui/bitstream/handle/1794/23403/n01SVFlys.pdf?seque nce=2&isAllow.

Gallego-Noche, Beatriz, Cristina Goenechea, Inmaculada Antolínez-Domínguez, and Concepción Valero-Franco. 2021. "Towards Inclusion in Spanish Higher Education: Understanding the Relationship Between Identification and Discrimination." *Cogitatio* 9, no. 3: 81–93. https://doi.org/10.17645/si.v9i3.4065.

Garland-Thompson, Rosemarie. 2017. *Extraordinary Bodies: Figuring Physical Disability in American Culture and Literature*. New York: Columbia University Press.

Gentry, Alistair. 2021. "We Shall Not Be Removed: 2021 Summary Report." UK Disability Arts Alliance. https://usercontent.one/wp/www.weshallnotberemoved.com/wp-content/uploads/2021/05/STANDARD-PRINT-UK-Disability-Arts-Alliance-2021-Survey-Report-1.pdf.

Gold, Becky. 2021. "Neurodivergency and Interdependent Creation: Breaking into Canadian Disability Arts." *Studies in Social Justice* 15, no. 2: 209–229.

Goodman, Nanette, Michael Morris, and Kelvin Boston. 2019. "Financial Inequality: Disability, Race and Poverty in America." National Disability Institute, Washington, DC. https://www.nationaldisabilityinstitute.org/wp-content/uploads/2019/02/disability-race-poverty-in-america.pdf.

Hadley, Bree. 2019. "Disability Arts in an Age of Austerity." In *Routledge Handbook of Disability Arts, Culture, and Media*, edited by Bree Hadley and Donna McDonald, 347–361. London: Routledge.

Hermans, Carolien. 2016. "Differences in Itself: Redefining Disability Through Dance." *Social Inclusion* 4, no. 4: 160–167.

Holmes, Kat. 2018. *Mismatch: How Inclusion Shapes Design*. Cambridge, MA: MIT Press.

Jones, Chelsea, Nadine Changfoot, and Kirsty Johnston. 2021. "Representing Disability, D/Deaf, and Mad Artists and Art in Journalism: Identifying Ableist Fault Lines and Promising Crip Practices of Representation." *Studies in Social Justice* 15, no. 2: 307–333.

Kelly, Christine, and Michael Orsini. 2021. "Beyond Measure? Disability Art, Affect and Reimagining Visitor Experience." *Studies in Social Justice* 15, no. 2: 288–306.

Kleege, Georgina. 2018. *More than Meets the Eye: What Blindness Brings to Art*. New York: Oxford University Press.

Korza, Pam, Maren Brown, and Craig Dreeszen. 2007. *Fundamentals of Arts Management*. Amherst: Arts Extension Service, University of Massachusetts.

Kuligowski, Kiely. 2020. "How Hiring People with Disabilities Helps Business." Business.com, December 30, 2020. https://www.business.com/articles/hire-disabled-people/.

LaMarre, Andrea, Carla Rice, and Kayla Besse. 2021. "Letting Bodies Be Bodies: Exploring Relaxed Performance in the Canadian Performance Landscape." *Studies in Social Justice* 15, no. 2: 184–208.

Leahy, Ann, and Delia Ferri. 2022. "Barriers and Facilitators to Cultural Participation by People with Disabilities: A Narrative Literature Review." *Scandinavian Journal of Disability Research* 24, no. 1: 68–81. http://doi.org/10.16993/sjdr.863.

Lobel, Brian, and Jess Thom. 2019. "On the Fringe of the Fringe." In *Routledge Handbook of Disability Arts, Culture, and Media*, edited by Bree Hadley and Donna McDonald, 243–250. London: Routledge.

Lopez, Kristen. 2023. "Disabled Audiences Knew 'Coda' Wouldn't Change Things—Even after Its Best Picture Win." *IndieWire*. January 12, 2023. https://www.indiewire.com/2023/01/coda-oscar-win-representation-one-year-1234796049/.

Maag, Michael, and Annie Wiegand. 2021. "Illuminating the Careers of Disabled Lighting Designers." HowlRound Theatre Commons, February 25, 2021. https://howlround.com/illuminating-careers-disabled-lighting-designers.

Mashburn, Whitney, and Carmen Papalia. 2019. "Meaningful Inclusion." *C Magazine*, Winter. https://cmagazine.com/issues/140/meaningful-inclusion.

Ojeda, D., and E. SV Flys. 2015. "La creación espectacular con personas con discapacidad y la accesibilidad universal del arte y la cultura escénica." *Acotaciones* 35: 1–28.

Rosewall, Ellen. 2021. *Arts Management: Uniting Arts and Audience in the 21st Century*. 2nd ed. Oxford: Oxford University Press.

Sandahl, Carrie. 2019. "It's All the Same Movie: Making Code of the Freaks." *Journal of Cinema and Media Studies* 58, no. 4: 145–150.

Sandals, Leah. 2016. "8 Things Everyone Needs to Know About Art and Disability." *Canadian Art*, March 3, 2016. https://canadianart.ca/features/7-things-everyone-needs-to-know-about-art-disability/.

Shevlin, Michael, Mairin Kenny, and Eileen McNeela. 2004. "Participation in Higher Education for Students with Disabilities: An Irish Perspective." *Disability and Society* 19, no. 1: 15–30. https://doi.org/10.1080/0968759032000155604.

Silverman, Fern, Bradford Bartley, Ellen Cohn, Ingrid Kanics, and Lynn Walsh. 2012. "Occupational Therapy Partnerships with Museums: Creating Inclusive Environments that Promote Participation and Belonging." *International Journal of the Inclusive Museum* 4, no. 4: 15–31.

United Nations. n.d. "Ageing and Disability." Department of Economic and Social Affairs. https://www.un.org/development/desa/disabilities/disability-and-ageing.html.

United Nations. 1948. "Universal Declaration of Human Rights." https://www.un.org/en/about-us/universal-declaration-of-human-rights.

Walker, Darren. 2016. "Ignorance Is the Enemy Within: On the Power of Our Privilege, and the Privilege of Our Power." Ford Foundation. September 12, 2016. https://www.fordfoundation.org/just-matters/just-matters/posts/ignorance-is-the-enemy-within-on-the-power-of-our-privilege-and-the-privilege-of-our-power/.

WHO. 2011. *World Report on Disability*. Geneva: World Health Organization and World Bank. https://www.who.int/publications/i/item/9789241564182.

WHO. 2021. "Disability and Health Fact Sheet." World Health Organization. https://www.who.int/en/news-room/fact-sheets/detail/disability-and-health.

Woodburn, Danny and Kristina Kopic. 2016. "On Employment of Actors with Disabilities in Television." The Ruderman White Paper. Ruderman Family Foundation, July n.d. https://issuu.com/rudermanfoundation/docs/tv_white_paper_final.final

CHAPTER 31

PERFORMANCE EVALUATION IN THE ARTS

A Multidisciplinary Review and a New Pragmatic Research Agenda

FRANCESCO CHIARAVALLOTI

INTRODUCTION

IN a context of growing government control of public expenditures, publicly funded arts organizations are asked to account for the value they create for their stakeholders (Belfiore 2004; Caust 2003; Gstraunthaler and Piber 2007; Meyrick 2016; Meyrick et al. 2019; Oakes, Townley, and Cooper 1998; Ter Bogt and Tillema 2016 Townley 2002; Zan 2000; Zan ET al. 2000). Consistent with both its arts advocacy mission (see Pick and Anderton 1996; Bendixen 2000) and its largely applied nature (see Evrard and Colbert 2000), arts management research has promptly reacted to this practical need of arts organizations by suggesting models and techniques of performance evaluation that have mainly been imported from the business sector, or at least inspired by those used there. In business management, "evaluation occurs when feedback about the system's current level of performance is compared to the planned level so that any discrepancies can be identified and corrective action prescribed" (Atkinson, Kaplan, and Young 2004, 283). One well-known example concerns the models based on Kaplan and Norton's (1992) Balanced Scorecard (see Weinstein and Bukovinsky 2009; Boorsma and Chiaravalloti 2010; Zorloni 2012). In most cases, models and techniques of performance evaluation in the arts have been suggested without a prior in-depth empirical investigation of the variety of meanings attributed to performance, and of the variety of evaluative practices already in use in the specific contexts in which individual arts organizations operate (Chiaravalloti and Piber 2011). A contextual understanding of the values created by arts organizations and a thorough understanding of the practice of evaluation in arts organizations are preconditions for the development and implementation of performance evaluation systems that are useful both for the organizations and for their stakeholders (Chiaravalloti 2016). A task for research is to fill this gap in understanding.

Two disciplines that have recently paid increasing attention to performance evaluation in the arts promise to contribute substantially to filling this gap in understanding: critical accounting studies and valuation studies. Accounting is the discipline in which the topic of performance evaluation has its roots (Kaplan 1984), and it is thus by definition a relevant contributor to research on performance evaluation. In particular, critical accounting studies expressly focuses on understanding the impact of accounting systems on the individual, organizational, and sociopolitical levels, rather than on developing accounting techniques and procedures (Hopwood 1983; Roberts and Scapens 1985; Chiaravalloti 2014). Valuation studies aim at "a better understanding of valuation and evaluative processes and practices" (Lamont 2012, 203) in order to find appropriate answers to some of the main social problems faced by contemporary societies, such as growing inequality in income and in cultural and political representation (Lamont 2012). As the literature review presented in this chapter shows, critical accounting studies on the practice of evaluation in the arts contribute to a better understanding of the friction between economic and artistic logics that emerges from the implementation of the currently dominant procedures of evaluation, which are inspired by new public-management-oriented reforms. In particular, it highlights the limits of accounting in representing the alternative logics and systems of evaluation applied by arts organizations in order to compensate for the inadequacy of those imposed by regulatory bodies. Valuation studies on the arts improve our understanding of performance in arts organizations by stimulating the adoption of a broader concept of value that is not limited to the dominant economic one. This is particularly important considering that, despite the instrumental turn in the cultural political debate on the values of art in Europe since the 1980s (Belfiore 2004; Vestheim 1994; Vuyk 2010), the creation of artistic value is still considered paramount among the objectives of publicly funded arts organizations (Chong 2000). In addition, by valorizing other logics of evaluation, such as the aesthetic logic versus the scientific logic, valuation studies on the arts highlight forms of judgment that provide alternatives to the currently dominant calculative technologies of evaluation.

Despite their substantive relevance for the study of performance evaluation in the arts, these two disciplines have thus far largely remained outside the arts management debate on performance evaluation. The objective of this contribution is to bring their insights into the arts management debate on performance evaluation. In particular, by looking at differences and similarities between research motivations, topics, and methods in the different disciplines, an agenda for further research on performance evaluation in the arts will be set—one that, in line with a new pragmatic agenda (Wicks and Freeman 1998; Chiaravalloti and Piber 2011), is able to create knowledge that is useful to individual arts organizations and their stakeholders.

A multidisciplinary literature review forms the central section of this chapter and is mainly meant to introduce the contributions from critical accounting studies and valuation studies, which have remained lateral to arts management research on performance evaluation so far. The results of this review inform the new pragmatic research agenda on performance evaluation in the arts that is presented and discussed in the following section. Finally, the conclusion places this contribution within the broader endeavor of establishing arts management as a distinct and legitimate academic discipline, with its own theoretical and methodological frameworks (Chiaravalloti and Piber 2011).

Performance Evaluation in the Arts: A Multidisciplinary Literature Review

This section introduces two main streams of recent academic discussions on performance evaluation in the arts: critical accounting studies and valuation studies. The topic of performance evaluation in the arts has only recently gained momentum in critical accounting studies (e.g., Mariani and Zan 2011; Nørreklit 2011; Sundström 2011; Bialecki, O'Leary, and Smith 2016; Coslor 2016; Crepaz, Huber, and Scheytt 2016; Donovan and O'Brien 2016; Ellwood and Greenwood 2016) and in sociologically informed valuation studies (e.g., Lamont 2012; Chong 2013, 2015; Haywood et al. 2014; Brewer 2015; Farías 2015; Hutter 2015; Hutter and Stark 2015; Pinch 2015). By contrast, performance evaluation has been debated for some time in arts management literature (e.g., Gstraunthaler and Piber 2007; Turbide and Laurin 2009; Boorsma and Chiaravalloti 2010; Chiaravalloti and Piber 2011; Zorloni 2012; Badia and Donato 2013; Chiaravalloti 2014; Hadida 2015; Williams-Burnett and Skinner 2017; Agostino 2018). After a concise overview of the current state of arts management research on performance evaluation, we turn to the new insights coming from critical accounting studies and valuation studies, then summarize the similarities and differences between research motivations, topics, and methods in the three disciplines.

The State of Arts Management Research on Performance Evaluation in the Arts

Arts management research deals with the organizational structures, processes, practices, and actors of the cultural sector and how they are influenced by cultural, social, economic, and political developments (Evrard and Colbert 2000). In a context of growing government control of publicly funded arts organizations based on quantitative indicators of performance (Zan et al. 2000; Belfiore 2004; Lindqvist 2012; Meyrick 2016; Meyrick et al. 2019), arts management, consistent with its arts-advocacy mission (e.g., Pick and Anderton 1996 and Bendixen 2000), has been the academic discipline that has paid most attention to performance evaluation in the arts so far (e.g., Gstraunthaler and Piber 2007; Turbide and Laurin 2009; Boorsma and Chiaravalloti 2010; Chiaravalloti and Piber 2011; Zorloni 2012; Badia and Donato 2013; Chiaravalloti 2014; Hadida 2015; Williams-Burnett and Skinner 2017; Agostino 2018). Consistent with its largely applied nature (e.g., Evrard and Colbert 2000), arts management research has suggested a plethora of "how-to" models and techniques for the evaluation—and, in many cases, for the *measurement*—of performance in arts organizations (Gilhespy 1999, 2001; Soren 2000; Boerner and Renz 2008; Weinstein and Bukovinsky 2009; Radbourne et al. 2009; Boorsma and Chiaravalloti 2010; Zorloni 2012; Badia and Donato 2013).[1] By contrast, there is a lack of in-depth empirical investigation of the different meanings attributed to performance by the different evaluators (organizational actors and stakeholders; see Chiaravalloti and Piber 2011) and of the different evaluative practices already in use in arts organizations. Research on the practice of evaluation in arts organizations is mainly limited to inventories of performance measurement and management procedures and indicators, as well as how their implementation is perceived by the organizational actors involved in evaluation procedures (Gstraunthaler and Piber 2007, 2012; Turbide and Laurin 2009; Velli and Sirakoulis 2018; Alcouffe et al. 2019). Among this literature, which unanimously highlights the difficulty of grasping the complex range of values created by arts organizations through performance measurement systems, only Gstraunthaler and Piber (2012) research those forms of "artistic evaluation" (Chiaravalloti and Piber 2011, 258) that are actually used by museum managers and that could consequently inspire alternative systems of evaluation.

Drawing on the same field work as their 2007 work, in their 2012 article Gstraunthaler and Piber report that museum managers evaluate the "aesthetic and cultural quality" of their organization's work using a specific "aesthetic-expressive" logic that is based on their own expert frames of reference and cannot "be fully explained" without difficulty (Gstraunthaler and Piber 2012, 38). This kind of evaluation happens outside organizational procedures; it is embedded in "everyday communication processes," such as those occurring in the workday routine of museum employees, for instance during coffee and lunch breaks (Gstraunthaler and Piber 2012, 38). Gstraunthaler and Piber suggest making this expert knowledge explicit and these informal practices of evaluation "institutionalized," in order to embed artistic language in evaluation procedures (2012, 39). The use of narrative forms of evaluation, such as comments by artists, curators, and other professionals, in communicating organizational performance to external stakeholders is considered necessary by museum managers for the purpose of complementing numerical information that would otherwise be "meaningless" (Gstraunthaler and Piber 2012, 39).

Gstraunthaler and Piber's important beginning, focusing on the process of understanding the various meanings attached to performance by managers and employees of arts organizations, and on practices of evaluation other than merely procedural ones, has not found a substantial continuation in arts management research. Rather, the most recent discussion on performance evaluation again reflects the largely applied and often uncritical nature of arts management research. The focus continues to be on suggesting new solutions for what Zan calls the "informative premise" of accountability (Zan 2006, 6–7)—the need for information that is capable of representing the values that arts organizations are accountable for to their various stakeholders.

Meyrick et al. (2019) have recently discussed the potential of narratives to communicate artistic values—a potential that, as mentioned earlier, had already emerged from Gstraunthaler and Piber's field work in museums (2012). Meyrick et al. stress the ability of narrative to contextualize information to support understanding and, in particular, to grasp "long-term evaluative concepts such as heritage value, intergenerational value, and legacy value" (2019, 379). Considering the importance of narrative in accountability processes in general, they find that "intuitively, narrative presents an appropriate communication tool for what cultural organizations actually do" (Meyrick et al. 2019, 379). However, despite their suggestion of general directions for the use of narratives in cultural reporting, they recognize that the real challenge still consists in finding a language that is able to express the values emerging from experiences with the arts (Meyrick et al. 2019). Unlike Gstraunthaler and Piber (2012), who suggest facing this challenge by eliciting that language from the arts practitioners, Meyrick suggests a priori what such a language should look like (2016), falling again in the "how-to" trap that has largely characterized arts management research on performance evaluation to date. Belfiore and Bennett (2007) had already warned about the disjunction between the academic language of artistic values and the language required in order to describe experiences *of* and *with* art as they actually happen. Instead, ethnography-inspired immersive research techniques for the investigation of those experiences can both contribute to an understanding of the values of art and provide a firsthand language to communicate about them—the language that is used by arts practitioners, audiences, and other users, and that is patiently elicited from them by researchers (Chiaravalloti 2020).

For instance, Foreman-Wernet and Dervin (2017) show how an in-depth investigation of audiences' experiences with the arts provides rich information and narratives on the meanings and values of art, which can be used to inform cultural policy. However, thus far there is a lack of similar in-depth investigation of how other internal organizational actors (e.g., arts managers) value the artistic work of their organizations. Together with audiences, critics, peers, government representatives or agencies, and the arts field in general, managers of arts organizations are fundamental actors of evaluation (Chiaravalloti and Piber 2011). As they are the experts in their field, the investigation of their subjective experiences of evaluation promises new, rich information on the values of art and especially on the nature of the artistic logic that is assumed to guide artistic evaluations (Gstraunthaler and Piber 2012). In order to collect this kind of information, which may inspire an alternative artistic language to communicate artistic values, arts management research on performance evaluation should temporarily put aside its characteristically applied nature and instead patiently pursue an understanding-driven approach through "an intensive immersion in the field and the use of in-depth, mainly qualitative research techniques" (Chiaravalloti 2020, 136; see also Walmsley 2018).

As we will see, critical accounting studies and valuation studies share the use of immersive research approaches and an understanding-driven approach. Their studies of the practice of evaluation in the arts thus promise to further our understanding of the various meanings of performance and of the different evaluative practices in arts organizations. This is a precondition for developing and implementing performance evaluation systems that are useful both to the organizations and to their stakeholders (Chiaravalloti 2016).

The Contribution of Critical Accounting Studies to Our Understanding of Performance Evaluation in the Arts

The idea that closely investigating actors of evaluation will deliver new insights into evaluative practices that are alternative or at least complementary to the dominant calculative ones was a chief finding of the first accounting article devoted to the arts and cultural sector (Mautz 1988). Mautz recommended observing how managers in not-for-profit arts organizations evaluate performance, what kind of information they use, and how they form their judgments, in order to discover new forms of performance evaluation that go beyond the largely inadequate but dominant accounting-related ones.

Accounting is the discipline in which the topic of performance evaluation is rooted (Kaplan 1984) and is thus a relevant contributor to research on performance evaluation, regardless of the specific disciplinary angle from which the topic is studied. In particular, "critical accounting studies ... share sociology's concern with the problem of social order, the practical enactment of organizational and societal control and accountability, the exercise of power both through and by accounting, and accounting's role in producing organizational and cultural identity" (Alvesson et al. 2011, 473–474).

In general, accounting research developed a substantial critical stream as early as the 1980s, following the publication of Hopwood's (1983) seminal article "On Trying to Study Accounting in the Contexts in Which It Operates." However, with respect to the arts sector, such issues as processes of acceptance of, or resistance to, mandatory accounting procedures and standards and how these processes are influenced by different logics were treated in accounting literature for the first time at the turn of the century (Christiansen and Skærbæk 1997; Zan 1998, 2002; Hooper, Kearins, and Green 2005). In particular, the topic of performance evaluation entered the critical accounting debate only years later, with contributions by Mariani and Zan (2011), Nørreklit (2011), and Sundström (2011). These three contributions focus on the performing arts sector and show the importance of the evaluator's individual subjectivity and of professional logics in making sense of performance; more generally, they address the importance of the very practice of evaluation.[2]

Critical accounting research's interest in the arts has gained momentum since then. Between 2012 and 2017 three authoritative accounting journals devoted special issues to the relation between accounting and artistic and cultural practices. The special issue of the *Accounting, Auditing and Accountability Journal* on "Accounting and Popular Culture," published in 2012, and the special issue of *Management Accounting Research* on "Managing Popular Culture," published in 2017, focus on a broad meaning of culture as "the regular rituals that pervade the everyday" (Jeacle 2012, 580) and include not only mass culture, such as television, pop music, and blockbuster movies, but also sports (Jeacle 2017).[3] By contrast, more traditional arts organizations and artistic objects—the main domain of arts management research so far—are the chief focus of the special issue of *Critical Perspectives on Accounting* devoted to the relations between "accounting, culture and the state" and published in 2016 (Jeacle and Miller 2016); four contributions to this special issue deal with evaluative practices.

However, out of these four contributions only the article by Oakes and Oakes (2016) highlights both the possibilities offered by alternative, non-numerical forms of performance information and the necessity to go beyond economic values while accounting for the complex range of values created by arts organizations. The other contributions, unlike what we will see with valuation studies on the arts in the next section, do not fully embrace the emancipatory potential of a critical approach in giving artistic values and logics a central role in research on evaluative practices. In fact, Donovan and O'Brien (2016) focus on governments' calculative practices of valuing culture, in which economic value largely dominates. Even their suggested approach to the inclusion of non-economic aspects in the valuation of culture ultimately flows, for the sake of data commensurability, into a numerical operationalization of non-economic information. The authors mention narrative techniques that promise to contribute to a more holistic approach to valuation that is respectful of the nature of art and thus acceptable within the cultural sector. However, no detail is given on these techniques. Crepaz, Huber, and Scheytt (2016, 47) also observe "artistic modes of valuation" applied to balance the weight of accounting practices in cultural political decision-making in their case study of RUHR.2010, the campaign that earned the Ruhr region recognition as a European Capital of Culture in 2010. However, these modes are neither specified nor investigated further. Their main focus is on "accounting as a valuation producing machine attaching value to an entity," a value that is mainly economic (Crepaz, Huber, and Scheytt 2016, 39). Finally, Ellwood and Green (2016) deal with the capitalization of museums' collection items in the financial statements of museums' annual reports. Their focus is on how capitalization as the attribution of economic value to cultural objects also affects the perceived cultural value of those objects. Their case studies show that this can happen and even lead to undesirable loss of cultural value—for instance, in small organizations and communities, when a small economic value attributed to an object leads to its disposal.

It is thus mainly Oakes and Oakes (2016) who offer new insights into evaluative practices that are alternative or at least complementary to the dominant calculative ones. In their study of the impact of austerity on English arts organizations striving to help widen arts engagement in England, they show that the managers of the investigated organizations find numerical indicators inadequate for capturing the created artistic values. Consequently, the managers try to supplement quantitative information with qualitative information of a narrative and visual nature. However, despite their committed efforts to find a way to account for artistic values, the interviewed managers seem aware that "the essence of the arts is always out of reach" (2016, 50). On the one hand, these findings confirm that the scientific logic from which the "dream of measuring the world" (Chiaravalloti and Piber 2011, 263) originates is inadequate for artistic evaluations; on the other hand, they also show that the nature of the alternative "artistic" logic that seems to naturally inform artistic evaluations is still far from being fully grasped. On a more applied level, in a previous article based on the same field work, Oakes and Oakes (2015) had already shown how accounting is unable to provide managers of arts organizations with a thorough and reflective tool for artistic evaluations. However, they had also pointed to a possibility for accounting to develop itself in new directions, "towards a broader notion of quantitative and qualitative accountability" (Oakes and Oakes 2015, 756)—a possibility that they seem to give up in their later article.

Mautz's (1988) invitation to observe how managers of not-for-profit arts organizations actually evaluate performance, in order to discover innovative solutions to the problem of accounting for the performance of these organizations, is thus yet to be fully embraced (Chiaravalloti 2014). This can only be partially explained by the understanding-driven approach of critical accounting research. In fact, there seem to be inherent limits to accounting in its ability to look beyond accounting techniques and procedures. The understanding-driven endeavor of critical accounting research has focused on existing procedures, their perception, and their limitations, but it has not focused on alternative or at least complementary evaluative practices applied by arts organizations in order to offset the inadequacy of those imposed by regulatory bodies. The limits of accounting also relate to its inability to renew itself from within the discipline. Apart from Donovan and O'Brien's (2016) suggestion of a mixed-methods approach to cultural political evaluation that would incorporate qualitative and quantitative indicators (the development of which should be, in their opinion, a main concern of academics), critical accounting has not come up with suggestions for alternative evaluative practices. Incremental, endogenous accounting innovation seems unable to provide arts organizations with information and procedures that are able to mirror the nature of artistic logics, values, and (e)valuations. More radical, exogenous innovation coming from outside accounting is required, in line with Miller's theorization of accounting as a discipline and a practice that evolves mainly "at its margins" (Miller 1998, 605); this is a challenge and, at the same time, an opportunity for the "artistic" side of arts management research.

The Contribution of Valuation Studies to Our Understanding of Performance Evaluation in the Arts

The sociopolitical concern of critical accounting studies, as described at the beginning of the previous section, is shared by sociologically informed valuation studies (Lamont 2012). This gives critical accounting research an important role to play in that "good amalgamating arena" of disciplines from which advances in valuation studies are expected (Helgesson and Muniesa 2013, 3). Valuation studies, also known as the sociology of valuation and evaluation, is a transdisciplinary, emerging field dealing with "any social practice where the value or values of something are established, assessed, negotiated, provoked, maintained, constructed and/or contested" (Doganova et al. 2014,

87). The broad relevance of this emerging field of research for contemporary societies was clearly illustrated somewhat earlier by Lamont (2012) in her review of Western (North American and European) literature on the sociology of valuation and evaluation. In order to find adequate answers to some of the main social problems faced by contemporary societies, such as growing inequality in income and in cultural and political representation, research should focus on how dynamics of conflict and coexistence between different systems of values and (e)valuation emerge and shape exclusive versus inclusive models of social organization (Lamont 2012). The precondition for this kind of research is, according to Lamont, "a better understanding of valuation and evaluative processes and practices" (Lamont 2012, 203), as they have become focal issues within the current political context:

> Questions of performance and its evaluation have gained greater social and scholarly prominence in recent years. With neoliberalism and the spread of market fundamentalism, governments have turned to new public management tools to ensure greater efficacy, with the result that quantitative measures of performance and benchmarking are diffusing rapidly and are having important structuring effects on a range of institutions and domains of human activity.
>
> (Lamont 2012, 202)

In this political context, values "that are not based on market performance tend to lose their relevance" (Lamont 2012, 210), and individuals who do not meet the neoliberal standards of social and economic success are not considered valuable and are excluded from society economically, culturally, and politically.

This also applies to organizations, especially to those organizations that create values that have a nature different from those in business and which are thus difficult to quantify. The limits of numerical forms of evaluation and the consequent necessity to rely on "forms of human judgments" clearly emerge from Lamont's review (Lamont 2012, 204). The arts offer a rich case for research on those "forms of human judgments," because of the special role of subjectivity and the assumed relativism of taste in artistic evaluation (Chong 2013). As Chong states in her study of critics' quality judgment of new fiction books, "subjectivity operates as an epistemic virtue in artistic evaluation" (Chong 2013, 265) and emerges "as a mode of knowledge making rather than as a mere impediment to objective evaluation" (Chong 2013, 266); "emotions, personal preference, and taste are fundamental ways of relating to artistic objects" and assume the same role in "the epistemic logic of aesthetics" that objectivity and rationality have in "the scientific world" (Chong 2013, 276). Considering that critics' individual perception of quality is influenced by the norms and practices of the literary field (Chong 2013)—in line with Zuckerman's conception of evaluation practices as "products of social interaction" (Zuckerman 2012, 224)—Chong's immersion in the knowledge-making subjectivity of critics by means of in-depth interviews about how they evaluate new books contributes to our understanding of both the individual judgment of each critic and how this emerges in mutual interaction with other critics' judgments and with the norms and practices of the literary field.

The special role of subjectivity and the assumed relativism of taste in artistic evaluation are not the only factors that make the arts an academically relevant case for research on (e)valuation. Researching evaluative practices in the arts also stimulates the adoption of a broader concept of value—one that goes beyond economic values—and more creativity in developing new methodologies for valuation studies, above all with respect to the study of non-economic values (Haywood et al. 2014). Both elements contribute to the academic and political relevance of valuation studies by pushing the focus of this emerging field of research beyond the calculative practices of evaluation and toward those "social practices through which transcendental, moral and plural values, judgments and justifications are enacted" (Haywood et al. 2014, 75).

The choice to focus research on certain kinds of evaluative practices is indeed associated with the choice of the sector in which to study those practices. This becomes evident with the almost contemporaneous publication, in 2015, of two edited books by the same publisher (Oxford University Press): *Making Things Valuable* (Kornberger et al. 2015) and *Moments of Valuation* (Berthoin Antal, Hutter, and Stark 2015). The first collection of articles focuses on those calculative practices by which objects are made valuable—mainly in an economic sense—such as "rankings, ratings, reviews, standards, classifications, and categorizations" (Kornberger et al. 2015, 1). It investigates those practices mainly in business organizations. The second collection focuses on a broader spectrum of evaluative practices than on calculative practices only. It includes experiments, meetings, and longer periods of time in which evaluation standards emerge and/or change—what Hutter and Stark define as "moments of valuation" (Hutter and Stark 2015, 2). Specifically, it focuses on those "moments of valuation" through which something is eventually recognized as innovative and thus "positioned as valuable in communities, organizations, and markets"—not necessarily in an economic sense. This collection gives the arts and, more generally, aesthetic objects a central role in the investigation of evaluative practices: synthesized sound (Pinch 2015), wine (Hennion 2015), creative products (Hutter 2015), paintings (Brewer 2015; Kharchenkova and Velthuis 2015), books (Chong 2015), architectural design (Farías 2015), and artistic interventions in organizations (Berthoin Antal 2015). In particular, the contributions on evaluative practices in the arts confirm that, in artistic evaluations, the aesthetic logic prevails over the scientific logic (Brewer 2015); that the emotional, cognitive, and cultural subjectivity of the evaluators is central (Brewer 2015; Chong 2015; Kharchenkova and Velthuis 2015); and that this develops and deploys in interplay with other actors and technologies of evaluation (Brewer 2015; Pinch 2015). Finally, Chong (2015) insists on the importance of investigating the evaluators' subjective experiences in order to gain a thorough understanding of evaluative practices, in line with valuation studies' preference for the use of immersive approaches in research aimed at the understanding of alternative forms of value and valuations (Otto and Dalsgaard 2016).

Comparative Summary

This multidisciplinary review shows that, despite their slightly different motivations for research on evaluative practices in the arts, arts management research, critical accounting studies, and valuation studies largely converge on what the relevant topics and methods for further research are.

With regard to the slightly different motivations, arts management studies are interested in research on evaluative practices in the arts mainly from an applied perspective (Chiaravalloti and Piber 2011). As an interdisciplinary arena unified by an interest in the practice of arts organizations and of the cultural sector in general (Rentschler and Shilbury 2008), they promptly reacted to publicly funded arts organizations' urgent need to adopt performance evaluation systems in order to comply with governments' growing accountability requirements. However, the urgency to provide arts organizations with performance evaluation models and techniques has largely prevailed over the necessity to understand the meaning of performance and its evaluation in the specific contexts in which individual organizations operate (Chiaravalloti and Piber 2011). The latter is a precondition for the development of performance evaluation systems that mirror the reality of artistic work and are thus useful both for the organizations and for their stakeholders (Chiaravalloti 2016). In addition, a deep understanding of the meaning of performance and its evaluation, centered on the values emerging from experiences with the art, promises to contribute to an evidence base of the value that arts organizations contribute to society, and to inform the development of a new artistic language of accountability (Gstraunthaler and Piber 2012; Meyrick et al. 2019) supporting a content-based dialogue about those values (Foreman-Wernet and Dervin 2017).

Critical accounting studies is interested in research on evaluative practices in the arts because publicly funded arts organizations offer a quintessential case for the investigation of the consequences of the invasive spread of accounting into the management practices of the public sector (Zan 2006). Many arts organizations are directly a branch of the public sector or are substantially dependent on public funding (Zan 2006). Being artistic-mission-driven organizations (Boorsma and Chiaravalloti 2010), they constitute a subsector of the wider public sector that possibly creates the values that are most difficult to operationalize—let alone quantify—for communities (Zan 1998; Boorsma and Chiaravalloti 2010). Consequently, they offer the ultimate case for the investigation of potential conflicts between the economic logic propagated by new public-management-oriented reforms, mainly through the use of quantitative measures of performance inspired by accounting (Hood 1991), and the professional logics that have traditionally characterized the different subsectors of the public sector (Zan et al. 2000). Consistent with its intention to articulate its criticism of the intrusion of accounting in many domains of public life, critical accounting research on evaluative practices in publicly funded arts organizations has focused on highlighting moments of friction between those logics in different organizational processes (Oakes and Oakes 2015, 2016) rather than on understanding the specific nature of "artistic" logics and their role in artistic evaluation. Thus, Mautz's (1988) invitation to draw on that understanding and to apply it to the development of innovative solutions to the problem that arts organizations face when they have to account for the value they create for the communities in which they operate has largely been neglected by critical accounting studies (Chiaravalloti 2014).

Valuation studies are interested in research on evaluative practices in the arts for three main reasons. First, research on evaluative practices in the arts highlights "forms of human judgment" (Lamont 2012, 204) that are alternative or at least complementary to the currently dominant calculative technologies of evaluation. Second, this research valorizes other logics of evaluation, such as the aesthetic logic, versus the scientific one (Chong 2013). Third, it stimulates the adoption of a broader meaning of value in society, not limited to the dominant economic one (Haywood et al. 2014). By doing this, research on evaluative practices in the arts helps to rehabilitate the role in society of individuals, organizations, and communities that do not match the neoliberal standards of social economic success and fight to remain included economically, culturally, and politically.

With regards to topics and methods for further research on evaluative practices in the arts, all three literatures reviewed here converge on the importance of the evaluators' subjectivity (Mariani and Zan 2011; Nørreklit 2011; Sundström 2011; Gstraunthaler and Piber 2012; Chong 2013; Brewer 2015; Chong 2015; Kharchenkova and Velthuis 2015) and of a not yet further specified aesthetic logic in forming judgments on artistic performance (Mariani and Zan 2011; Nørreklit 2011; Sundström 2011; Gstraunthaler and Piber 2012; Chong 2013; Brewer 2015). While for an understanding of evaluative practices in general case studies are the most-used research approach (e.g. Gstraunthaler and Piber 2012; Crepaz, Huber, and Scheytt 2016), in-depth interviews with the different actors involved in evaluation—for example, artists, managers, audiences, and administrators— appear to be the most promising technique for gaining insights into evaluators' subjective experiences (e.g., Chong 2015; Oakes and Oakes 2015, 2016; Foreman-Wernet and Dervin 2017). This is also the case because this form of immersive qualitative research provides narrative accounts of the values of art that can immediately inform a new, artistic language to account for the complex range of values that arts organizations contribute to society (Foreman-Wernet and Dervin 2017).

PERFORMANCE EVALUATION IN THE ARTS: A NEW PRAGMATIC RESEARCH AGENDA

A thorough understanding of the actual practice of evaluation in individual organizations and subsectors of the arts sector is a precondition for developing evaluation procedures that reflect the organizational and institutional reality in which these organizations operate (Chiaravalloti 2016). This includes the understanding of the different meanings of performance and forms of evaluation in the specific contexts in which individual organizations operate. Arts management research has made a beginning with this endeavor (Gstraunthaler and Piber 2007, 2012); critical accounting studies and valuation studies can further it, by offering insights that are peculiar to their disciplinary motivation for research on evaluative practices in the arts. With their focus on processes of acceptance of, or resistance to, the application of mandatory performance evaluation systems, critical accounting studies can substantially improve our understanding of what new performance evaluation systems for arts organizations should *not* look like. This refers not only to the technical aspects of the systems but also to the organizational process of adoption and implementation of those systems. With their focus on non-calculative forms of evaluation and on non-economic logics and values, valuation studies offer an alternative way to look at performance and its evaluation in arts organizations. In particular, their in-depth investigation of the subjectivity of the different actors involved in evaluation can both improve our understanding of artistic logics and provide inspiration for alternative artistic systems of evaluation—that is, systems that mirror the logic, content, and language of evaluation of the investigated actors. Performance evaluation systems that mirror the reality of artistic work promise to be more useful for arts organizations and their stakeholders, evaluating the actual work of the organization, than the managerial ones inspired by the business sector and imposed by new public-management-oriented reforms.

Recognizing the necessity to fill the understanding gap in arts management research on performance evaluation does not mean neglecting the arts-advocacy mission and the largely applied nature of the discipline. In line with Wicks and Freeman's new pragmatic approach to organization studies (1998), a deep and thorough understanding of the practice of evaluation is not an endeavor to be pursued for its own sake. The purpose is to develop and implement new systems of evaluation that would be useful for those involved in arts organizations and for their wider communities:

> Pragmatism allows researchers to . . . develop research that is focused on serving human purposes—i.e., both morally rich and useful to organizations and the communities in which they operate. . . . Researchers doing this type of work would see organization studies as a vehicle to help people lead better lives. It would be characterized by a focus on the practical relevance of research as well as a desire to search for novel and innovative approaches ("experimentation") that may help serve human purposes.
>
> (Wicks and Freeman 1998, 123–124)

A new pragmatic approach to the study of performance evaluation in the arts thus means that a deep understanding of the practice of evaluation is only a first step, though a necessary one, toward the formulation of contextually useful solutions for the different kinds of organizations within the arts sector (see also Scapens 2006). However, as we have seen, the completion of this first step is still far from being reached. In fact, the process of understanding the practice of evaluation in arts organizations is just beginning. Much more research is required in order to answer fundamental understanding-driven questions: What does performance mean according to the different actors of evaluation in arts organizations and the communities in which they operate? What are the forms of human judgments (Chong 2013) adopted by actors of evaluation in the arts? What is an artistic logic? What and whom is the evaluation for? Immersive research techniques inspired by ethnography (Chiaravalloti 2020; Walmsley 2018) should be applied to answer these questions with respect to the different subsectors of the arts (e.g., orchestras, theaters, museums, media, popular music, film).

Within a new pragmatic research agenda that is respectful of the arts-advocacy mission and the largely applied nature of arts management research, the next step would be to use the gathered knowledge to develop and implement new and better—or, in other words, useful—performance evaluation systems. While the reviewed literature recognizes the existence and use of alternative, artistic information regarding performance—information that is able to represent the values for which arts organizations have to account to their different stakeholders, or what Zan (2006) defines as the informative premise of accountability—it does not suggest how such alternative information could be translated into a usable form (e.g., a language) in order to be integrated into existing performance evaluation systems or shape new ones.

Considering that the pressure for accountability to external stakeholders is unlikely to diminish in the near future, arts organizations will need to find effective ways to explain their value to external stakeholders. Consequently, a key challenge will be to translate that alternative, artistic information about performance into a form that can be used to communicate to both internal and external stakeholders of the organization. As seen in the review, quantitative indicators of performance do not fit within the aesthetic epistemology of artistic evaluations; by contrast, a richer and deeper artistic language of evaluation capable of supporting a content-oriented dialogue between the organizations and their external environment probably would.

For this scope, an important role is left to the humanistic side of arts management research (Sicca 1997). It is unlikely that accounting and organization studies, and perhaps even valuation studies, will provide a language that is capable of explaining the substantive aspects and criteria used for artistic evaluation. This should be a concern of the humanities. If the arts world justifiably refuses to conceive of its value only in the economic terms provided by the mainstream language of business and neoliberalism, then it should be a task for arts-related disciplines to offer arts organizations a richer and deeper language to support a content-oriented dialogue about their organizational performance with the external environment. The new pragmatic approach offers the right epistemological framework for bringing together social sciences and humanities knowledge, despite their different research traditions and methodologies. Wicks and Freeman (1998, 137–138) call for "theoretical integration: . . . a detailed rationale for researchers to reject the separate but (un)equal view of normative and empirical research . . . and to work systematically for, at a minimum, various forms of symbiosis." With respect to the search for a new, artistic language of evaluation, systematic reviews of the academic literature in specific artistic disciplines offer a useful method for exploiting existing normative knowledge. In-depth interviews with all those directly involved in the processes of programming, production, and reception of the arts—artists, managers, audiences—offer the possibility of eliciting new, empirical knowledge about the unwritten and tacit ways these actors of evaluation make sense of artistic performance.

When the potential offered by systematic literature reviews and in-depth interviews for the identification of a new, artistic language of evaluation has been exploited, in line with Wicks and Freeman's call for "experimentation" (1998, 124), participatory action research could be used to test the contextual usefulness of this newly developed artistic language for individual arts organizations and their communities. That is, does the new artistic language help the organizations to effectively account for the value they create for the communities in which they operate?

Conclusion

While this multidisciplinary review contributes to closing the current understanding gap in arts management research on performance evaluation (which forms the first step in the suggested new pragmatic agenda for research on performance evaluation in the arts), there is a more general consideration that deserves attention, especially among those researchers who are interested in establishing arts management as a distinct discipline (Evrard and Colbert 2000). The new pragmatic agenda for research on performance evaluation offers an important road map for the development of arts management as a distinct and legitimate academic discipline. Researching performance evaluation in the arts, not just as the application of a predefined set of more or less sophisticated managerial and political procedures but as the exploration of an unelicited set of practices that are naturally embedded in the artistic work of arts organizations, makes clear how these organizations actually work. Artistic processes are a neglected research topic in arts management research, as the focus has mainly been on the import and application of management techniques from business in an attempt to improve the supporting processes of arts organizations. If it only maintains this focus, arts management cannot become a distinct discipline, and will remain an application of existing management knowledge. Understanding what management means in the arts and cultural sector and whether there is a special way of managing arts and cultural organizations—and thus focusing on what management means in respect of artistic processes—should produce management knowledge that can emerge only from the arts and cultural sector with its specific characteristics (e.g., Zan 2006, 2012). Consequently, this arts management knowledge might also add to management studies in general, and even to other disciplines (e.g., cultural economics, sociology of arts, cultural studies, cultural policy studies), thereby legitimating the ambition of arts management to become a distinct academic discipline (Evrard and Colbert 2000). A new pragmatic research agenda supports this endeavor. First, it shifts the focus of arts management research away from the application of standardized managerial models and techniques and toward the understanding of actual practices of management in individual arts organizations. Second, it promotes a respectful integration of the specific artistic knowledge involved in managing arts organizations, both the practical knowledge of the arts practitioners and the academic knowledge of the scholars in the respective artistic disciplines. Third, it tests the validity of the created knowledge in terms of its usefulness for creating better arts organizations and better communities. Ultimately, a new pragmatic research agenda will help to establish arts management as a distinct discipline by supporting a shift in focus from the managerial to the artistic in managing arts organizations.

Notes

1. For a detailed overview and analysis of different performance evaluation models for arts organizations, see Chiaravalloti and Piber 2011.
2. For a thorough, systematic literature review of accounting literature on the arts and cultural sector until 2014, see Chiaravalloti 2014.
3. In doing so, they reflect not only the broader notion of popular culture and the cultural policy shift toward everyday creativity but also the critical approach to the very definition of culture that characterizes cultural studies.

References

Agostino, Deborah. 2018. "Can Twitter Add to Performance Evaluation in the Area of Performing Arts? Reflections from La Scala Opera House." *Journal of Arts Management, Law, and Society* 48, no. 5: 321–338.

Alcouffe, Simon, Pascale Amans, Isabelle Assassi, and Fabienne Oriot. 2019. "French Budget Act (LOLF) Indicators as Seen Through the Lens of the National Drama Centres: A Case Study." *International Journal of Arts Management* 21, no. 3: 57–72.

Alvesson, Mats, Todd Bridgman, Hugh Willmott, Mahmoud Ezzamel, and Keith Robson. 2011. "Accounting." In *The Oxford Handbook of Critical Management Studies*, edited by Mats Alvesson, Todd Bridgman, and Hugh Willmott, 473–498. New York: Oxford University Press. www.oxfordhandbooks.com/view/10.1093/oxfordhb/9780199595686.001.0001/oxfordhb-9780199595686-e-023.

Atkinson, Anthony A., Robert S. Kaplan, and S. Mark Young. 2004. *Management Accounting*, 4th ed. Upper Saddle River, NJ: Pearson Prentice Hall.

Bialecki, Michael, Susan O'Leary, and David Smith. 2016. "Judgement Devices and the Evaluation of Singularities: The Use of Performance Ratings and Narrative Information to Guide Film Viewer Choice." *Management Accounting Research* 35: 56–65.

Badia, Francesco, and Fabio Donato. 2013. "Performance Measurement at World Heritage Sites: Per Aspera ad Astra." *International Journal of Arts Management* 16, no. 1: 20–34.

Belfiore, Eleonora. 2004. "Auditing Culture." *International Journal of Cultural Policy* 10, no. 2: 183–202.

Belfiore, Eleonora, and Oliver Bennett. 2007. "Determinants of Impact: Towards a better Understanding of Encounters with the Arts." *Cultural Trends* 16, no. 3: 225–275.

Bendixen, Peter. 2000. "Management Skills and Roles: Concepts of Modern Arts Management." *International Journal of Arts Management* 2, no. 3: 4–13.

Berthoin Antal, Ariane. 2015. "Sources of Newness in Organizations: Sand, Oil, Energy, and Artists." In *Moments of Valuation: Exploring Sites of Dissonance*, edited by Ariane Berthoin Antal, Michael Hutter, and David Stark, 290–311. Oxford: Oxford University Press.

Berthoin Antal, Ariane, Michael Hutter, and David Stark, eds. 2015. *Moments of Valuation: Exploring Sites of Dissonance*. Oxford: Oxford University Press.

Boerner, Sabine, and Sabine Renz, S. 2008. "Performance Measurement in Opera Companies: Comparing the Subjective Quality Judgments of Experts and Non-Experts." *International Journal of Arts Management* 10, no. 3: 21–37.

Boorsma, Miranda A., and Francesco Chiaravalloti. 2010. "Arts Marketing Performance: An Artistic-Mission-Led Approach to Evaluation." *Journal of Arts Management, Law, and Society* 40, no. 4: 297–317.

Brewer, John. 2015. "Evaluating Valuation: Connoisseurship, Technology, and Art Attribution in an American Court of Law." In *Moments of Valuation: Exploring Sites of Dissonance*, edited by Ariane Berthoin Antal, Michael Hutter, and David Stark, 89–107. Oxford: Oxford University Press.

Caust, Jo. 2003. "Putting the 'Art' Back into Arts Policy Making: How Arts Policy Has Been 'Captured' by the Economists and the Marketers." *International Journal of Cultural Policy* 9, no. 1: 51–63.

Chiaravalloti, Francesco. 2014. "Performance Evaluation in the Arts and Cultural Sector: A Story of Accounting at Its Margins." *Journal of Arts Management, Law, and Society* 44, no. 2: 61–89.

Chiaravalloti, Francesco. 2016. "Performance Evaluation in the Arts: From the Margins of Accounting to the Core of Accountability." PhD diss., University of Groningen, SOM Research School.

Chiaravalloti, Francesco. 2020. "Stop Measuring, Start Understanding! An Arts Policy and Management Researcher's Autobiographic Account of the Urgency of an Ethnographic Turn in Research on the Values of Art." *Art and the Public Sphere* 9, nos. 1–2: 131–143.

Chiaravalloti, Francesco, and Martin Piber. 2011. "Ethical Implications of Methodological Settings in Arts Management Research: The Case of Performance Evaluation." *Journal of Arts Management, Law, and Society* 41, no. 4: 240–266.

Chong, Derrick. 2000. "Why Critical Writers on the Arts and Management Matter." *Culture and Organization* 6, no. 2: 225–241.

Chong, Philippa K. 2013. "Legitimate Judgment in Art, the Scientific World Reversed? Maintaining Critical Distance in Evaluation." *Social Studies of Science* 43, no. 2: 265–281.

Chong, Philippa K. 2015. "Playing Nice, Being Mean, and the Space in Between: Book Critics and the Difficulties of Writing Bad Reviews." In *Moments of Valuation: Exploring Sites of Dissonance*, edited by Ariane Berthoin Antal, Michael Hutter, and David Stark, 133–146. Oxford: Oxford University Press.

Christiansen, John K., and Peter Skærbæk. 1997. "Implementing Budgetary Control in the Performing Arts: Games in the Organizational Theatre." *Management Accounting Research* 8, no. 4: 405–438.

Coslor, Erica. 2016. "Transparency in an Opaque Market: Evaluative Frictions Between 'Thick' Valuation and 'Thin' Price Data in the Art Market." *Accounting, Organizations and Society* 50: 13–26.

Crepaz, Lukas, Christian Huber, and Tobias Scheytt. 2016. "Governing Arts Through Valuation: The Role of the State as Network Actor in the European Capital of Culture 2010." *Critical Perspectives on Accounting* 37: 35–50.

Doganova, Liliana, Martin Giraudeau, Claes-Fredrik Helgesson, Hans Kjellberg, Francis Lee, Alexandre Mallard, Andrea Mennicken, Fabian Muniesa, Ebba Sjögren, and Teun Zuiderent-Jerak. 2014. "Valuation Studies and the Critique of Valuation." *Valuation Studies* 2, no. 2: 87–96.

Donovan, Claire, and Dave O'Brien. 2016. "Governing Culture: Legislators, Interpreters and Accountants." *Critical Perspectives on Accounting* 37: 24–34.

Ellwood, Sheila, and Margaret Greenwood. 2016. "Accounting for Heritage Assets: Does Measuring Economic Value 'Kill the Cat'?" *Critical Perspectives on Accounting* 38: 1–13.

Evrard, Yves, and François Colbert. 2000. "Arts Management: A New Discipline Entering the Millennium?" *International Journal of Arts Management* 2, no. 2: 4–13.

Farías, Ignacio. 2015. "Epistemic Dissonance: Reconfiguring Valuation in Architectural Practice." In *Moments of Valuation: Exploring Sites of Dissonance*, edited by Ariane Berthoin Antal, Michael Hutter, and David Stark, 271–289. Oxford: Oxford University Press.

Foreman-Wernet, Lois, and Brenda Dervin. 2017. "Hidden Depths and Everyday Secrets: How Audience Sense-Making Can Inform Arts Policy and Practice." *Journal of Arts Management, Law, and Society* 47, no. 1: 47–63.

Gilhespy, Ian. 1999. "Measuring the Performance of Cultural Organizations: A Model." *International Journal of Arts Management* 2, no. 1: 38–52.

Gilhespy, Ian. 2001. "The Evaluation of Social Objectives in Cultural Organizations." *International Journal of Arts Management* 4, no. 1: 48–57.

Gstraunthaler, Thomas, and Martin Piber. 2007. "Performance Measurement and Accounting: Museums in Austria." *Museum Management and Curatorship* 22, no. 4: 361–375.

Gstraunthaler, Thomas, and Martin Piber. 2012. "The Performance of Museums and Other Cultural Institutions: Numbers or Genuine Judgments?" *International Studies of Management and Organization* 42, no. 2: 29–42.

Hadida, Allègre. 2015. "Performance in the Creative Industries." In *The Oxford Handbook of Creative Industries*, edited by Candace Jones, Mark Lorenzen, and Jonathan Sapsed, 219–247. Oxford: Oxford University Press.

Haywood, Gordon, Johan Nilsson, Michael Franklin, Paul Gilbert, Linus Krafve Johansson, Lisa Lindén, Mark MacGillivray, and Robert Meckin. 2014. "Valuation Studies: A Collaborative Valuation in Practice." *Valuation Studies* 2, no. 1: 71–85.

Helgesson, Claes-Fredrik, and Fabian Muniesa. 2013. "For What It's Worth: An Introduction to Valuation Studies." *Valuation Studies* 1, no. 1: 1–10.

Hennion, Antoine. 2015. "Paying Attention: What Is Tasting Wine About?" In *Moments of Valuation: Exploring Sites of Dissonance*, edited by Ariane Berthoin Antal, Michael Hutter, and David Stark, 37–56. Oxford: Oxford University Press.

Hood, Christopher. 1991. "A Public Management for All Seasons?" *Public Administration* 69, no. 1: 3–19.

Hooper, Keith, Kate Kearins, and Ruth Green. 2005. "Knowing 'the Price of Everything and the Value of Nothing': Accounting for Heritage Assets." *Accounting, Auditing and Accountability Journal* 18, no. 3: 410–433.

Hopwood, Anthony G. 1983. "On Trying to Study Accounting in the Contexts in Which It Operates." *Accounting, Organizations and Society* 8, nos. 2–3: 287–305.

Hutter, Michael. 2015. "Dissonant Translations: Artistic Sources of Innovation in Creative Industries." In *Moments of Valuation: Exploring Sites of Dissonance*, edited by Ariane Berthoin Antal, Michael Hutter, and David Stark, 57–88. Oxford: Oxford University Press.

Hutter, Michael, and David Stark. 2015. "Pragmatist Perspectives on Valuation: An Introduction." In *Moments of Valuation: Exploring Sites of Dissonance*, edited by Ariane Berthoin Antal, Michael Hutter, and David Stark, 1–12. Oxford: Oxford University Press.

Jeacle, Ingrid. 2012. "Accounting and Popular Culture: Framing a Research Agenda." *Accounting, Auditing and Accountability Journal* 25, no. 4: 580–601.

Jeacle, Ingrid. 2017. "Managing Popular Culture." *Management Accounting Research* 35: 1–4.

Jeacle, Ingrid, and Peter Miller. 2016. "Accounting, Culture, and the State." *Critical Perspectives on Accounting* 37: 1–4.

Kaplan, Robert S. 1984. "The Evolution of Management Accounting." *Accounting Review* 59, no. 3: 390–418.

Kaplan, Robert S., and David P. Norton. 1992. "The Balanced Scorecard—Measures That Drive Performance." *Harvard Business Review*, January–February, 71–79.

Kharchenkova, Svetlana, and Olav Velthuis. 2015. "An Evaluative Biography of Cynical Realism and Political Pop." In *Moments of Valuation: Exploring Sites of Dissonance*, edited by Ariane Berthoin Antal, Michael Hutter, and David Stark, 108–130. Oxford: Oxford University Press.

Kornberger, Martin, Justesen, Lise, Koed Madsen, Anders, and Jan Mouritsen. 2015. *Making Things Valuable*. Oxford: Oxford University Press.

Lamont, Michèle. 2012. "Toward a Comparative Sociology of Valuation and Evaluation." *Annual Review of Sociology* 38: 201–221.

Lindqvist, Katja. 2012. "Effects of Public Sector Reforms on the Management of Cultural Organizations in Europe." *International Studies of Management and Organization* 42, no. 2: 9–28.

Mariani, Marcello M., and Luca Zan. 2011. "The Economy of Music Programs and Organizations: A Micro Analysis and Typology." *European Accounting Review* 20, no. 1: 113–148.

Mautz, R. K. 1988. "Monuments, Mistakes, and Opportunities." *Accounting Horizons* 2, no. 2: 123–128.

Meyrick, Julian. 2016. "Telling the Story of Culture's Value: Ideal-Type Analysis and Integrated Reporting." *Journal of Arts Management, Law, and Society* 46, no. 4: 141–152.

Meyrick, Julian, Tully Barnett, Heather Robinson, and Matt Russell. 2019. "What's the Story? 'Credible' Narrative in the Evaluation of Arts and Culture." *Journal of Arts Management, Law, and Society* 49, no. 6: 375–388.

Miller, Peter. 1998. "The Margins of Accounting." *European Accounting Review* 7, no. 4: 605–621.

Nørreklit, Hanne. 2011. "The Art of Managing Individuality." *Qualitative Research in Accounting and Management* 8, no. 3: 265–291.

Oakes, Helen, and Steve Oakes. 2015. "An Analysis of Business Phenomena and Austerity Narratives in the Arts Sector from a New Materialist Perspective." *Accounting and Business Research* 45, nos. 6–7: 738–764.

Oakes, Helen, and Steve Oakes. 2016. "Accounting Colonisation and Austerity in Arts Organisations." *Critical Perspectives on Accounting* 38: 34–53.

Oakes, Leslie S., Barbara Townley, and David J. Cooper. 1998. "Business Planning as Pedagogy: Language and Control in a Changing Institutional Field." *Administrative Science Quarterly* 43, no. 2: 257–292.

Otto, Ton, and Steffen Dalsgaard. 2016. "Guest Editorial: Alternative Valuations." *Valuation Studies* 4, no. 1: 1–9.

Pick, John, and Malcolm Anderton. 1996. *Arts Administration*, 2nd ed. London: Spon Press.

Pinch, Trevor. 2015. "Moments in the Valuation of Sound: The Early History of Synthesizers." In *Moments of Valuation: Exploring Sites of Dissonance*, edited by Ariane Berthoin Antal, Michael Hutter, and David Stark, 15–36. Oxford: Oxford University Press.

Radbourne, Jennifer, Johanson, Katya, Glow, Hilary, and Tabitha White. 2009. "The Audience Experience: Measuring Quality in the Performing Arts." *International Journal of Arts Management* 11, no. 3: 16–29.

Rentschler, Ruth, and Brad Shilbury. 2008. "Academic Assessment of Arts Management Journals: A Multidimensional Rating Survey." *International Journal of Arts Management* 10, no. 3: 60–71.

Roberts, John, and Robert Scapens. 1985. "Accounting Systems and Systems of Accountability: Understanding Accounting Practices in Their Organizational Context." *Accounting, Organizations and Society* 10, no. 4: 443–456.

Scapens, Robert W. 2006. "Understanding Management Accounting Practices: A Personal Journey." *British Accounting Review* 38, no. 1: 1–30.

Sicca, Luigi Maria. 1997. "The Management of Opera Houses: The Italian Experience of the Enti Autonomi." *The International Journal of Cultural Policy* 4, no. 1: 201–224.

Soren, Barbara J. 2000. "The Learning Cultural Organization of the Millennium: Performance Measures and Audience Response." *International Journal of Arts Management* 2, no. 2: 40–49.

Sundström, Andreas. 2011. "Framing Numbers 'at a Distance': Intangible Performance Reporting in a Theater." *Journal of Human Resource Costing and Accounting* 15, no. 4: 260–278.

Ter Bogt, Henk, and Sandra Tillema. 2016. "Accounting for Trust and Control: Public Sector Partnerships in the Arts." *Critical Perspectives on Accounting* 37: 5–23.

Townley, Barbara. 2002. "The Role of Competing Rationalities in Institutional Change." *Academy of Management Journal* 45, no. 1: 163–179.

Turbide, Johanne, and Claude Laurin. 2009. "Performance Measurement in the Arts Sector: The Case of the Performing Arts." *International Journal of Arts Management* 11, no. 2: 56–70.

Velli, Vasiliki, and Kleanthis Sirakoulis. 2018. "Performance Measurement in Non-Profit Theatre Organizations: The Case of Greek Municipal and Regional Theatres." *International Journal of Arts Management* 21, no. 1: 49–60

Vestheim, Geir. 1994. "Instrumental Cultural Policy in Scandinavian Countries: A Critical Historical Perspective." *International Journal of Cultural Policy* 1, no. 1: 57–71.

Vuyk, Kees. 2010. "The Arts as an Instrument? Notes on the Controversy Surrounding the Value of Art." *International Journal of Cultural Policy* 16, no. 2: 173–183.

Walmsley, Ben. 2018. "Deep Hanging Out in the Arts: An Anthropological Approach to Capturing Cultural Value." *International Journal of Cultural Policy* 24, no. 2: 272–291.

Weinstein, Larry B., and David Bukovinsky. 2009. "Use of the Balanced Scorecard and Performance Metrics to Achieve Operational and Strategic Alignment in Arts and Culture Not-for-Profits." *International Journal of Arts Management* 11, no. 2: 42–55.

Wicks, Andrew C., and R. Edward Freeman. 1998. "Organization Studies and the New Pragmatism: Positivism, Anti-Positivism, and the Search for Ethics." *Organization Science* 9, no. 2: 123–140.

Williams-Burnett, Nicola Jayne, and Heather Skinner. 2017. "Critical Reflections on Performing Arts Impact Evaluations." *Arts and the Market* 7, no. 1: 32–50.

Zan, Luca. 1998. "Piano, with Harmony: Analyzing the Imola Academy from a Management Study Perspective." *Financial Accountability and Management* 14, no. 3: 215–231.

Zan, Luca. 2000. "Managerialisation Processes and Performance in Arts Organisations: The Archeological Museum of Bologna." *Scandinavian Journal of Management* 16, no. 4: 431–454.

Zan, Luca. 2002. "Renewing Pompeii, Year Zero: Promises and Expectations from New Approaches to Museum Management and Accountability." *Critical Perspectives on Accounting* 13, no. 1: 89–137.

Zan, Luca. 2006. *Managerial Rhetoric and Arts Organizations*. Basingstoke, UK: Palgrave Macmillan.

Zan, Luca. 2012. "Research on Arts Organizations and the Lazy Community of Management Studies." *International Studies of Management and Organization* 42, no. 2: 3–8.

Zan, Luca, Anthony Blackstock, G. Cerutti, and Claudio Mayer. 2000. "Accounting for Art." *Scandinavian Journal of Management* 16, no. 3: 335–347.

Zorloni, Alessia. 2012. "Designing a Strategic Framework to Assess Museum Activities." *International Journal of Arts Management* 14, no. 2: 31–47.

Zuckerman, Ezra W. 2012. "Construction, Concentration, and (Dis)Constinuities in Social Valuations." *Annual Review of Sociology* 38: 223–245.

CHAPTER 32

EVALUATING CULTURAL VALUE

The Quintessential Wicked Problem

BEN WALMSLEY

Introduction

Cultural value is a notoriously elusive concept. It is also a notoriously political construct. These two characteristics combined make it what I have previously termed a "wicked problem" for scholars and practitioners alike (Walmsley 2019, 91). Rittel and Webber (1973) were the first scholars to fully formalize a theory of wicked problems, defining them as problems that lack a definitive formulation, are unique, lack an enumerable set of potential solutions and evade testable solutions, exist as symptoms of other problems, and have no "stopping rule." In the course of this chapter, I will argue that all of these characterizations apply to questions of cultural value and that this presents a number of significant but nonetheless fascinating and resolvable challenges for cultural evaluation.

As both an academic field and as an area of cultural policy and practice, cultural value is a particularly interdisciplinary endeavor, and alongside the hotly contested notions of cultural versus economic and social value, this is one of the main sources of its inherent tensions. However, the contested and interdisciplinarity nature of cultural value also presents a range of opportunities to arts managers and to the field of arts management more broadly; when co-created in a spirit of honesty, curiosity, and empathy, cultural evaluation can offer valuable insights into the immediate and cumulative impacts that engaging with the arts and culture can have on people's lives and into the broader social and economic benefits of cultural activity. This is why it remains a live and hotly debated issue for artists, producers, managers, and policymakers all over the world.

This chapter begins by synthesizing the core tensions that underlie discussions about cultural value. It then explores the meaning and etymology of evaluation. Following an in-depth application of the different qualities of a wicked problem onto cultural value and evaluation, the chapter reviews the policy and methodological tensions that have consistently plagued attempts to value and evaluate cultural participation and engagement. It illustrates these attempts through a series of examples and case studies drawn from England and Canada—two countries with starkly contrasting policy approaches to understanding and evaluating cultural value. Finally, the chapter offers a critical appraisal of competing and complementary approaches to cultural evaluation and makes the case for a creative, people-centered, mixed-methods, and multidimensional approach that places audiences and participants at the heart of evaluation and addresses the needs and interests of arts and cultural managers, producers, marketers, scholars, funders, and policymakers alike.

Cultural Value

Debates about cultural value are beset with a number of tensions and abstractions that appear to have effected a damaging epistemological stasis. Philosophical debates about cultural value have been hampered by the dualistic separation between economics and aesthetics exacerbated by the rise of utilitarianism (Taylor 2015). Policy debates are often obstructed by the false dichotomization of intrinsic and instrumental value (Belfiore and Bennett 2008) and reduced by the cynical prioritization of quantitative data over qualitative insights. In the global North, the instrumental quantification of culture has arisen from decades of neoliberal attempts to co-opt economic logic into the public policy case for arts and culture (Taylor 2015). Although debates about cultural value are certainly not new, they have recently been hijacked by vain attempts of politicians, civil servants, policymakers, and academics to measure cultural value for the purposes of calculating return on public investment to inform future funding decisions.

Despite the political pressure to measure cultural value, myriad academic studies have challenged the premise of trying to quantify cultural value (e.g., Matarasso 1996; Walmsley 2012; Vuyk 2010; Walmsley and Meyrick 2022). Leading cultural economists such as Throsby (2006) and Klamer (2017) also concede that certain expressions of cultural value transcend valuation, as they are rooted in shared social experiences; as Nye (2009, 11) contends, culture is the manifestation of "values and practices that create meaning for a society." A broad conclusion of the growing number of critical qualitative studies on this topic is that attempts to quantify the effects of the arts at the level of social impact (e.g., through Subjective Wellbeing or Social Return on Investment methods) are flawed and deeply problematic, essentially because they are neither sophisticated nor reflexive enough to account for the immeasurable realms of emotion and spirituality (Holden 2012) nor for the vital notions of context and praxis (Oliver and Walmsley 2011). The benefits of a reflexive approach to exploring cultural value are also championed by Scott (2010, 2), who warns that when public funding decisions rely on measurable results rather than complex outcomes, cultural policy becomes stuck in "the bind of instrumentality."

Mindful of the fact that none of the recent attempts to capture cultural value "commanded widespread confidence," the United Kingdom's Arts and Humanities Research Council (AHRC) put out a call in 2013 to fund a series of ambitious new research projects to advance discussions on cultural value and develop the range of methods deployed to evaluate it (Arts and Humanities Research Council 2013). In foregrounding the subjective and intersubjective experiences of cultural audiences and participants, the Cultural Value Project represented an open challenge to the Green and Magenta Book approaches that had been championed and/or adopted in recent UK studies on cultural value (e.g., O'Brien 2010; EPPI Centre 2010).[1]

The diverse and comprehensive responses that this call produced constituted a rich, polyvocal, and critical account of the impacts of arts and culture on individuals and communities. Despite highlighting the significant and growing body of evidence to support the positive impacts of arts and culture on society, the authors of the summative report ultimately called for more mixed-methods and longitudinal studies of value and impact to support or challenge existing claims of cultural value and for the establishment of a new center dedicated to this endeavor (Crossick and Kaszynska 2016). One of the key roles of this new center would be to advance thinking and practices related to cultural evaluation.

Defining Evaluation

At first sight, evaluation appears to be an accessible, if not self-explanatory, concept. It is not only an everyday term, meaning "to judge the value or condition of (someone or something) in a careful and thoughtful way" (as the Merriam-Webster dictionary defines it); it is also deployed widely in the arts and cultural sector to refer to activities that reflect back on a project or program, consulting with key stakeholders, analyzing key data, and ultimately making judgments about an activity's relative success. So far, so good. But there is an acknowledged crisis in evaluation (Walmsley and Meyrick 2022), and in particular with regard to its relationship with cultural value (Holden 2006). This crisis has several underlying causes. First, there is confusion among cultural practitioners, and sometimes a deliberate blurring, regarding processes of monitoring, reporting, advocacy, and evaluation. Although these processes should absolutely be complementary and conjoined, they should also be discrete and independent. Second, there is a widespread reticence across the cultural sector to acknowledge failure, driven by a fear of alienating or upsetting funders. This creates "a cultural policy landscape that is not conducive to honesty or critical reflection" (Jancovich and Stevenson 2021) and ultimately affects a sector-wide knowledge management problem (Brown 2017), where seemingly negative findings are not shared, lessons are not learned, and wheels are constantly reinvented. Third, there is currently a disproportionate amount of evaluation in the cultural sector, which means that practitioners generally lack the time or resources to undertake it properly and funders lack the time or resources to engage with it properly. Fourth, there are significant skills gaps across the sector that lead to methods being poorly or inappropriately applied, ethical standards being compromised, and analyses often being deeply flawed. This in turn produces a problem of legitimacy, whereby evaluation is often not taken seriously: "The arts and cultural sector struggles to provide arguments about the overall quality of its work in a way that both has credibility with funders and other stakeholders, and has the support of the arts sector" (Bunting and Knell 2014, 4). Finally, there are structural issues at the policy level, including the false prioritization of econometric methods (Scott 2010; Galloway et al. 2005), the prevalence of vested interests, and inevitable imbalances of power. Combined, these factors create a dysfunctional evaluation culture where valid learning often goes unheeded, where the voices of audiences and participants are seldom heard, and where the potential to develop a meaningful knowledge and evidence base is generally missed.

The etymology of the term "evaluation" is significant, but it is often forgotten or disregarded entirely in discussions and applications of the practice. According to the Online Etymology Dictionary, the term derives from the Latin verb *valere*, which means to "be strong, be well; be of value, be worth." Matarasso (1996, 3) accordingly reminds us that value lies at the heart of evaluation, and defines evaluation as a value-based "process of calculating worth." The essential challenge with evaluation is implicit within this definition, and as Matarasso (1996, 3) points out, difficulties arise from the "essentially relative nature of worth." Similarly, Vecco (2018) asserts that values attributed to cultural heritage are contingent and dependent on their social, historical, political, and cultural context. Returning to the word's Latin roots, the other potential definition of "evaluation"—"to be strong or well"—is often overlooked. This is a damaging oversight, as this alternative understanding offers an important insight into the overarching purpose of evaluation, which is to become better or stronger by fostering better practice. This connection is suggested by Robinson (2010, 13), who discusses resilience in terms of an organization's capacity for "learning and adaptation" and ultimately its capacity to adapt and change.

Following this review of the literature, we might therefore define evaluation as *an honest and open process of reflective learning and analysis that engages with key data and stakeholders to calculate worth, promote resilience, and drive positive change*. Prima facie, this would seem to offer a comprehensive definition that captures the core processes and intended outcomes of rigorous evaluation. However, it still leaves us with the contested issue of "worth," an issue that infuses any discussion about cultural value.

A Wicked Problem

Even when stakeholders accept a common definition of evaluation, attempts to evaluate culture are beset with a number of further research, policy, and management-related challenges. Drawing on Rittel and Webber (1973), I earlier defined a wicked problem as one that lacks a definitive formulation, is unique, lacks an enumerable set of potential solutions and evades testable solutions, exists as a symptom of other problems, and/or has no "stopping rule." Let's now take these characteristics in order to illuminate the complex and contested nature of evaluation even further.

The first issue to explore is the extent to which *cultural value lacks a definitive formulation*. We have already seen the definitional tensions and ambiguities that plague the evaluation of cultural value, and these highlight the complexities involved in accurately formulating the nature of the problem at hand. But over and above the problems of how to evaluate cultural value there are of course more fundamental questions of what the term "culture" means. What do we mean by "culture"? Whose culture? Do we mean everyday cultural activities like drinking tea (Williams 1958) or Culture with a capital C—so-called high culture, such as opera and ballet? Should we take an "omnivorous" approach to cultural engagement (Peterson and Simkus 1992)? How might we reflect timely questions of cultural democracy and diversity in our understanding of cultural value?

Then we have the definitional problem of "value," which is certainly no less complex. As Matarasso observes in relation to evaluation: "The important, and essentially political, question about evaluation is which value system is used to provide benchmarks against which work will be measured—in other words, who defines value" (1996, 2). As we saw earlier, value can only ever be relative, and value systems are inherently subjective and political: Who decides what is valuable or worthy and what isn't? What kind of value is at play—social, cultural, educational, economic . . . ? On which bases or criteria are judgments about worth and value made? Some of these questions might be answered by an organization's mission. In the context of arts and cultural evaluation, this would generally entail placing the artistic mission at the center (Boorsma and Chiaravalloti 2010) and so prioritizing cultural or artistic value. Other answers might be found in a cultural project or program's core strategic objectives, which might target local economic growth and regeneration, for example. However, although this approach could offer a neat strategic management solution by basing key performance indicators (KPIs) for evaluation on the underlying strategic purpose of an activity, it does not circumnavigate the inherently political nature of evaluation and the tensions that often spring up between cultural funders, producers, artists, audiences, and policymakers. In other words, there remain "fundamental tensions and contradictions inherent in the strategic convergence of the social, the cultural . . . and the economic" (Stevenson, Rowe, and McKay 2010, 249). In short, even if we could define "culture" and "value" objectively and as independent terms, which of course we never really could (or even should), as a composite entity or concept cultural value resists systematic analyses and ultimately evades any exhaustive formulation.

Second is the question of whether *cultural value is an essentially unique "problem."* Rittel and Webber (1973, 165) describe a unique problem as one whose "particulars" override its "commonalities with other problems already dealt with." In this sense we might ask ourselves whether questions related to cultural value are replicable in other contexts and whether they can be formulated into a family of related concepts. While we might productively align cultural value with other complex areas of public policy such as poverty or environmentalism, cultural value's roots and conditions undoubtedly present a sufficient number of "additional distinguishing properties of overriding importance" (Rittel and Webber 1973, 164) to classify it as a wicked problem. Examples here include cultural value's epistemological grounding in philosophy, arts, and aesthetics, and its specific application to the idiosyncratic cultural and creative industries.

Third, we should determine whether *cultural value lacks an enumerable (or an exhaustively describable) set of potential solutions and evades testable solutions*. Rittel and Webber (1973, 164) fortuitously answer the first question for us:

> Chess has a finite set of rules, accounting for all situations that can occur. In mathematics, the tool chest of operations is also explicit; so, too, although less rigorously, in chemistry. But not so in the world of social policy.

Connected as it is to questions of cultural democracy and policy, cultural value is a heterogenous and amorphous construct, comprising infinite questions that have preoccupied philosophers since at least the days of Plato. So to that extent it again emerges as a wicked problem. But does it evade testable solutions? Attempted solutions to wicked problems "generate waves of consequences over an extended—virtually an unbounded—period of time" and "may yield utterly undesirable repercussions which outweigh the intended advantages" (Rittel and Webber 1973, 163). The fact that artists, arts managers, academics, philosophers, funders, and policymakers have been arguing about cultural value for decades, if not centuries, suggests that testable solutions will always prove elusive. We must conclude, therefore, that cultural value does indeed evade testable solutions and once again presents as a wicked problem.

Fourth, we need to reflect on the extent to which *questions of cultural value exist as symptoms of other problems*. If we consider cultural value as a contested area of policy, then we can appreciate how it might be symptomatic of higher-level problems such as public engagement, participation, co-creation, poverty, education, and health. In epistemological terms, it is similarly a subdiscipline of higher-level questions related to philosophy, ethics, sociology, and aesthetics. So even if we could "solve" the "problem" of cultural value, its higher-level problems would remain unsolved, and attempts to cure the symptom would ultimately prove futile.

Finally, if we want to understand the extent to which it might be described as a wicked problem, we must investigate the hypothesis that *cultural value has no "stopping rule."* In other words, following Rittel and Webber (1973), the question here is whether attempts to "solve the problem" of cultural value can ever be deemed to be complete. According to the "no stopping rule" definition, we would once again have to conclude that cultural value is indeed a wicked problem because there are no ends to the "causal chains" that connect its constituent parts and any "additional investment of effort" would not necessarily "increase the chances of finding a better solution" (Rittel and Webber 1973, 162).

In other words, the problem characterizing cultural value is certainly not that it has not been sufficiently debated, investigated, and researched.

In summary, cultural value represents a wicked problem on all counts and attempts to evaluate it are beset with a number of intractable challenges. Rittel and Webber's thesis on the nature of social policy problems encapsulates the implications of these challenges.

> The search for scientific bases for confronting problems of social policy is bound to fail, because of the nature of these problems. They are "wicked" problems, whereas science has developed to deal with "tame" problems. Policy problems cannot be definitively described. Moreover, in a pluralistic society there is nothing like the undisputable public good; there is no objective definition of equity; policies that respond to social problems cannot be meaningfully correct or false; and it makes no sense to talk about 'optimal solutions' to social problems unless severe qualifications are imposed first. Even worse, there are no 'solutions' in the sense of definitive and objective answers. (1973, 155)

The nature of cultural value evaluation, as exposed brutally here (albeit in the broader context of social policy) by Rittel and Webber, means that attempts to provide objective, scientific, or calculable "solutions" to it can only ever be both reductive and disingenuous. This does not imply, of course, that we should abandon cultural value evaluation altogether; rather, we must embrace its plurality and messiness in order to really get under the skin of the fundamental issues at stake. In order to assess the feasibility of applying this challenge in practice, in the following sections we will explore contrasting approaches to developing frameworks to evaluate cultural value.

Evaluation Frameworks

It is widely acknowledged that current methods for evaluating the impact of the arts and culture are based on "a fragmented and incomplete understanding of the cognitive, psychological and socio-cultural dynamics that govern the aesthetic experience" (Belfiore and Bennett 2007, 225). It is worth pausing at this point in the chapter to dissect the various rationales for this "incomplete understanding" and assess the respective outcomes of different methodological approaches to developing new evaluation frameworks. English cultural policy offers a revelatory case study (Yin 2009) of the limited, instrumental approach.

Although often praised for their sophisticated approach to arts marketing, audience research, and cultural evaluation, English institutions have actually been the biggest proponent of quantitative methodologies over the past two decades—probably largely a result of their early adoption of the new public management principles advocated by the New Labour government post-1997 (O'Brien 2013). Two recent examples of reductionist cultural evaluation frameworks are Arts Council England's (2021a) Impact and Insight Toolkit and the Department for Culture, Media and Sport (DCMS)'s Valuing Culture and Heritage Capital framework (Sagger, Philips, and Haque 2021). The Impact and Insight Toolkit is a metrics-based framework that combines self-assessment with assessments from peers and audiences based on a series of artistic criteria: concept, presentation, distinctiveness, challenge, captivation, enthusiasm, local impact, relevance, rigor, originality, risk, and excellence. The toolkit is mandatory for larger regularly funded organizations because according to the arts council, the framework helps to ensure that arts and cultural organizations "are using consistent metrics to collect their data, making it easier to measure and demonstrate the value of the whole arts and culture sector" (Arts Council England 2021a).

Although the framework has been championed by a small number of consultants and arts funders, it has equally been subjected to fierce criticism and rejected by the Canada Council for the Arts as well as the Australian state funding body Creative Victoria. The main critique leveled at the framework is that it offers a time-consuming and reductive proxy for artistic value that is open to political abuse: "Metrics-based approaches to understanding the value of culture imply homogeneity of artistic purpose, invite political manipulation and demand time, money and attention from cultural organisations without proven benefit" (Phiddian et al. 2017, 174). The framework was developed over time from significant empirical research with both arts organizations and audiences, and although it offers a relatively complex and multidimensional evaluation system that triangulates the perspectives of three core stakeholder groups, the framework has also been criticized for its "unemotional and cognitive bias" (Walmsley 2019, 103).

DCMS recently took a very different approach to evaluating cultural value based on the econometric methods (notably the Social Cost Benefit Analysis principles) advocated in the Treasury's Green Book. The Valuing Culture and Heritage Capital framework reflects DCMS's ambition "to develop a formal approach to value culture and heritage assets [and] to create publicly available statistics and guidance that will allow for improved articulation of the value of the culture and heritage sectors in decision making" (Sagger, Philips, and Haque 2021, 2). Significantly, the framework acknowledges the limitations of economic and quantitative methods in providing a complete understanding of cultural value:

> Economic methodology should be used alongside other information, both quantitative and qualitative, to create a robust evidence base for decision making. Therefore, while economic methodologies will take centre stage, a cross-disciplinary approach is needed, for example linking economic valuation methodologies to heritage science.
>
> (Sagger, Philips, and Haque 2021, 2)

While the recognition of the need for a mixed-methods and cross-disciplinary approach represents a welcome addition to the UK government's traditional approaches to evaluating public spending, in the "wicked" context of culture, which, as we have seen, is characterized by competing and contested notions and systems of value, DCMS's insistence on prioritizing economic methodologies appears at best arbitrary and at worst ideological. As Throsby (2020, 169) argues, cultural capital must also encapsulate assets that "embody, store or give rise to cultural value" over and above any economic value they may possess. It is also worth noting that this initial framework only focuses on *tangible* cultural assets, relegating the more complex evaluation of intangible assets, intellectual property, and soft power to a subsequent study.

The DCMS framework acknowledges that in order to estimate the value of a culture and heritage asset to an individual, "we must look beyond market prices" (Sagger, Philips, and Haque 2021, 15). It cites three reasons for this: first, admission to cultural venues is often free or subsidized; second, culture is often "consumable without entry"; and third, "people attribute value to culture and heritage without directly consuming it themselves (non-use value)" (Sagger, Philips, and Haque 2021, 15). In lieu of market price, the framework advocates assessing the value of a cultural asset according to the following criteria: asset life, usage, service quality, the length of the policy or intervention, and discount rate.[2] What the framework fails to recognize is the growing body of evidence demonstrating that audiences (beneficiaries) do not perceive culture in monetary or economic terms and that market price is therefore one of the least apposite means of evaluating cultural value. Moreover, the assessment criteria are uniquely instrumental, failing to capture the breadth and diversity of cultural value on any intrinsic terms or to account for the fact that many cultural and heritage assets actually *appreciate* (rather than depreciate) over time.

These two contrasting attempts to construct a national evaluation framework for culture reflect attempts to solve the problem of cultural value from two very different perspectives (audience-based versus asset-based) and methodologies (survey-based versus econometric). Although both of the frameworks have certainly advanced knowledge of cultural value in very different ways and opened up a generally constructive critical debate about cultural value and evaluation, it is clear that neither approach has managed to produce an overarching measurement of the value of culture to society, nor even garner a critical mass of support from key stakeholders, including arts and cultural organizations themselves. As Rittel and Webber (1973, 157) note, "attempts to build systems of social indicators . . . are in effect surrogates for statements of desired conditions. As we all now know, it has turned out to be terribly difficult, if not impossible, to make either of these systems operational."

A Multidimensional Approach

Reflecting the limitations of the two frameworks explored above, Piber and Chiaravalloti (2011, 242) argue that most approaches to evaluation "fail to make sense of the contextual complexity of artistic activities, overestimating the general validity of methods and underestimating the richness and diversity of the contexts in which they might be applied." This view is supported by Jancovich and Stevenson (2021), who distinguish between two often competing types of evaluation: evaluation for accountability and evaluation for improvement. The former, they argue, encourages a positivist monitoring of KPIs to support evidence-based policymaking, while the latter encourages complexity and learning throughout the process, based on an interpretative philosophy that "any knowledge (or evidence) is both constructed and contingent" (Jancovich and Stevenson 2021, 968).

In relation to this latter mode, Matarasso proposes that arts evaluation needs to adopt "sensitive, creative, people-centred approaches" that focus on outcomes rather than outputs (1996, 13). This people-centered approach reflects the general direction of travel in public (including cultural) policy toward participatory and co-creative practices. Within the English context explored above, it also reflects Arts Council England's "Let's Create" strategy, which represents a significant policy turn toward amateur culture and everyday creativity: "By 2030, we want England to be a country in which the creativity of each of us is valued and given the chance to flourish" (Arts Council England 2021b, 15).

There is growing consensus among cultural policymakers, funders, and evaluators that mixed-methods, multidimensional models offer the most rigorous, sensitive, and apposite means of evaluating cultural value and impact. As we have seen, England offers a particularly fruitful context for exploring how cultural evaluation is applied in practice, essentially because it has highly instrumentalized and deeply embedded mechanisms of policy evaluation. Canada offers the perfect antidote to the English model, as Canadian cultural policymakers have resisted the instrumental approach and opted for a deeply intrinsic model. In order to illustrate these divergent approaches, the following section presents three short case studies of cultural evaluation frameworks that take a people-centered, mixed-methods, and multidimensional approach. Following Yin (2009), they therefore represent contrasting case studies to the two examples presented above. However, they also act as revelatory case studies (Yin 2009), neatly illustrating the contrasting cultural policy contexts of the two countries in scope.

Case Study 1: Impacts 08

A good example of a mixed-methods, creative, and people-centered approach is the Impacts 08 evaluation of Liverpool's year as European Capital of Culture. The evaluation comprised over thirty qualitative and quantitative research projects and incorporated a range of longitudinal evaluation methodologies, including stakeholder analysis, economic impact analysis, media impact analysis, business impact analysis, demographic analysis, and social anthropology. The evaluation was based on a highly complex multidimensional framework designed to develop an enhanced evidence base for the multiple impacts of culture, including the lived experiences of residents. It aimed to explore processes as well as outcomes of different cultural impact activities and to contextualize impact data by assessing surrounding narratives (Garcia, Melville, and Cox 2010).

The evaluation analyzed the impact of the year of culture on aspects of access and inclusion, images and perceptions of Liverpool, governance and delivery, cultural vibrancy, social capital, physical infrastructure, the local economy, and tourism (Garcia, Melville, and Cox 2010). In order to address these diverse objectives and stakeholders, the evaluation methods deployed by the research team included depth interviews, focus groups and community workshops, participant observation, cognitive mapping, surveys, questionnaires, and economic impact assessment. The framework incorporated analysis of longitudinal impact and has left the legacy of a replicable research framework, which can be (and indeed has been) used to explore the impacts of future culture-led regeneration.[3] The framework offers a starkly contrasting model to the limited quantitative approaches and methods proposed by Arts Council England and DCMS. By taking a radically mixed-methods and cross-disciplinary approach, the Impacts 08 framework addressed both the accountability and reflective learning aspects of cultural evaluation identified by Jancovich and Stevenson (2021). It also incorporated the sensitive, creative, and people-centered approaches advocated by Matarasso and embraced the contextual complexity highlighted by Piber and Chiaravalloti.

Case Study 2: Canada Council for the Arts

In 2017, Canada Council for the Arts commissioned the US arts consultancy firm WolfBrown to develop a bespoke qualitative impact framework that would reflect "the complexity of the Canadian arts ecology" and enable it "to better articulate the many ways in which Canadians' lives are enhanced by the arts" (Canada Council for the Arts 2019). The research team behind the framework explained their methodology and rationale as follows: "Our focus on intrinsic impacts and qualitative methods will complement the well-established quantitative measures of economic impact, health benefits, and other so-called 'instrumental' impacts... [and] tell a richly textured and rigorously researched story about how its [Canada Council's] investments... benefit the breadth and diversity of the Canadian public" (Brown, Carnwath, and Dueser 2019, 4). This focus on the breadth, diversity, and complexity afforded by a bespoke and deeply qualitative approach marks a stark contrast to the English models explored in the previous section, which prioritized the quantitative evaluation of tangible cultural value.

The Canada Council's focus on the cultural ecology incorporates both the "upstream" and "downstream" impacts of arts funding. The framework thus explores the impact of public investment on direct beneficiaries (such as artists and arts organizations) and indirect beneficiaries (such as audiences, cultural participants, and wider communities). It attempts to afford a meaningful voice to these key stakeholder groups and to reflect value in their own terms rather than via proxy measures such as contingent valuation or subjective wellbeing and encompasses tangible as well as intangible culture. This culminates in the evaluation of a rich range of cultural and social outcomes, ranging from changes to artistic practice to the relationship between creative engagement and social cohesion or community development. As the framework is implemented across Canada's arts sector over the coming years, the council is planning to fund a number of research projects to explore how the organizations it funds can articulate the broader impacts they have on their communities.

Case Study 3: Centre for Cultural Value

A recent UK-wide cultural sector survey on evaluation undertaken by the Centre for Cultural Value highlighted the mismatched priorities in evaluation practice between the cultural sector and its funders as well as the significant skills gaps in evaluation practice, in particular with regard to analysis and mixed-methods practice (McDowell 2020). When asked to define evaluation, most respondents connected the activity to processes of assessing success, evidencing impact, deepening understanding, and enhancing practice (McDowell 2020, 12ff.) and 73 percent of respondents believed that "explaining activity and impact to funders" was an "extremely important" priority when determining their evaluation aims (19). Overall, the survey revealed a deep sense of insecurity across the UK cultural sector about the purpose and process of evaluation alongside an inability to equate it with reflective learning.

In response to this baseline research, in 2021 the Centre for Cultural Value collaborated with an expert working group of forty-six academics, funders, cultural leaders, and consultants to co-create a new set of principles to guide cultural evaluation. After a series of interactive discussions and workshops, the group cohered around four key principles: that evaluation should *be beneficial, robust, people-centered, and connected* (Centre for Cultural Value 2021). As illustrated in Table 32.1, a set of twelve subprinciples lies beneath these core values to offer the nuance required of cultural evaluation.

Table 32.1. Cultural Evaluation Principles

Beneficial	Robust
Committed to learning and/or change	Rigorous
Ethical	Open-minded
Applicable	Proportionate
People-centred	Connected
Empathetic	Transparent
Many-voiced	Aware
Socially engaged	Shared

Source: Centre for Cultural Value (2021, 5)

Collectively, these interconnected principles represent a new way of thinking about evaluation that places audiences and participants at its heart. While fully cognizant of the need for rigorous assessment of strategic objectives, as set by cultural funders and by artists and organizations themselves, the principles privilege meaningful learning, reflection, and positive change over empty justification and advocacy. Like the Impact 08 model, the principles respond to Matarasso's appeal for a sensitive, creative, and values-based approach to evaluation, and to Piber and Chiaravalloti's call to make sense of the contextual complexity of arts and cultural activity. They encompass both intrinsic and instrumental impacts and aim to move beyond the false dichotomy between these two approaches by synthesizing different types of data and by deliberately blurring the boundaries between what have traditionally been presented as discrete benefits. Like the Canada Council framework, the principles prioritize social over economic impact, but the model is much more open and loosely structured, based on a set of ethical and methodological principles designed to be adaptable to the evolving and unique contexts of artists, cultural programs, and organizations.

Conclusion

We have seen in this chapter that the task of evaluating cultural activity is beset by a range of seemingly intractable challenges, ranging from agreeing on a common definition, methodology, and approach to understanding the nature of the problem to be solved in the first place. As Rittel and Webber conclude:

> One of the most intractable problems is that of defining problems (of knowing what distinguishes an observed condition from a desired condition) and of locating problems (finding where in the complex causal networks the trouble really lies). In turn, and equally intractable, is the problem of identifying the actions that might effectively narrow the gap between what-is and what-ought-to-be. (1973, 159)

While we can relatively easily establish broad consensus on a definition of cultural evaluation—based on accepted notions and principles of reflective learning, data analysis, stakeholder engagement, calculating worth, and promoting positive change—a definition of cultural value ultimately proves elusive. This is essentially because cultural value is a quintessentially wicked problem—particularly, it seems, in the context of English cultural policy—that lacks a definitive formulation, is unique, exists as a symptom of other problems, lacks an enumerable set of potential solutions and evades testable solutions, and has no stopping rule.

Consensus on questions of cultural value presupposes the existence of an agreed value system, but the politics inherent to cultural value highlight the contested nature of "worth" and the intractable tensions between social, cultural, and economic value. This is evident in the contrasting approaches to developing frameworks to evaluate cultural value that we have reviewed in the chapter. Ultimately, we must concur with Rittel and Webber that in a pluralistic society there is no indisputable public good, nor any objective definition of equity. We might even go further and contend that in a diverse and pluralistic society there is no objective definition of value. As Rittel and Webber conclude themselves, it therefore becomes "morally objectionable . . . to tame a wicked problem prematurely, or to refuse to recognize the inherent wickedness of social problems" (1973, 161).

Despite the contested nature of cultural value, we have seen in this chapter how philosophical, epistemological, and methodological approaches to cultural evaluation are evolving. Frameworks and principles such as those advanced by the Canada Council for the Arts and the Centre for Cultural Value advocate multidimensional, people-centered models of cultural evaluation that combine intrinsic and instrumental benefits, encompass diversity and polyvocalism, and embrace complexity. Such models aim to capture the processes as well as the diverse and contested outcomes of arts and cultural engagement; they prioritize reflective learning, acknowledge constructive failure, and generate meaningful narratives rather than simply measuring outputs and outcomes and reducing them to quantitative data. This evolution represents a quiet revolution in cultural and wider public policy, a rejection of new public management and its obsession with preordained targets and measurable social outcomes and a return to the "policy ambiguity" (Gray 2015) advocated back in 1973 by Rittel and Webber, who assert in their final analysis that "there are no value-free, true-false answers to any of the wicked problems governments must deal with" (169). We have perhaps, then, come full circle.

Notes

1. The Green Book is produced for the UK Government by HM Treasury to provide guidance for public sector bodies on how to appraise proposals before committing funds to a policy, program, or project. The Magenta Book provides complementary guidance on the evaluation of ensuing policies, programs, and projects.
2. Discounting is an accounting method used to compare costs and benefits occurring over different periods of time to convert costs and benefits into present values while accounting for depreciation.
3. Evaluation of the impacts of Liverpool 2008 was revisited by the research project Impacts 18, funded by the UK's Arts and Humanities Research Council.

References

Arts and Humanities Research Council. 2013. "Cultural Value Project." Arts and Humanities Research Council. http://www.ahrc.ac.uk/Funded-Research/Funded-themes-and-programmes/Cultural-Value-Project/Pages/default.aspx.
Arts Council England. 2021a. "Impact and Insight Toolkit." https://www.artscouncil.org.uk/advice-and-guidance-library/impact-and-insight-toolkit.

Arts Council England. 2021b. *Let's Create: Strategy 2020–2030*. Manchester: Arts Council England.

Belfiore, Eleonora, and Oliver Bennett. 2007. "Determinants of Impact: Towards a Better Understanding of Encounters with the Arts." *Cultural Trends* 16, no. 3: 225–275. https://doi.org/10.1080/09548960701479417

Belfiore, Eleonora, and Oliver Bennett. 2008. *The Social Impact of the Arts: An Intellectual History*. Basingstoke, UK: Palgrave Macmillan.

Boorsma, Miranda, and Francesco Chiaravalloti. 2010. "Arts Marketing Performance: An Artistic-Mission-Led Approach to Evaluation." *The Journal of Arts Management, Law and Society* 40, no. 4: 297–317. https://doi.org/10.1080/10632921.2010.525067.

Brown, Alan. 2017. "Audience Research Gone Wild: Keynote Address at the Second Symposium of the International Network for Audience Research in the Performing Arts (Inarpa)." *Participations* 14, no. 2: 53–62.

Brown, Alan, John Carnwath, and James Doeser. 2019. "Canada Council for the Arts: Qualitative Impact Framework." WolfBrown, San Francisco.

Bunting, Catherine, and John Knell. 2014. "Measuring Quality in the Cultural Sector: The Manchester Metrics Pilot: Findings and Lessons Learned." Arts Council England, London.

Canada Council for the Arts. 2019. "Qualitative Impact Framework." Canada Council for the Arts. https://canadacouncil.ca/research/research-library/2019/12/qualitative-impact-framework.

Centre for Cultural Value. 2021. "Evaluation Principles." Centre for Cultural Value, Leeds.

Crossick, G., and P. Kaszynska. 2016. "Understanding the Value of Arts and Culture. The Ahrc Cultural Value Project." Arts and Humanities Research Council, Swindon.

EPPI Centre. 2010. "Understanding the Drivers, Impact and Value of Engagement in Culture and Sport: An Overarching Summary of the Research." Arts Council England, DCMS, English Heritage, Museums Libraries Archives Council, Sport England London.

Galloway, Susan, Christine Hamilton, Adrienne Scullion, and David Bell. 2005. "Quality of Life and Well-Being: Measuring the Benefits of Culture and Sport: Literature Review and Thinkpiece. Scottish Executive Social Research, Edinburgh.

Garcia, Beatriz, Ruth Melville, and Tamsin Cox. 2010. "Creating an Impact: Liverpool's Experience as European Capital of Culture." University of Liverpool and Liverpool John Moores University.

Gray, Clive. 2015. "Ambiguity and Cultural Policy." *Nordic Journal of Cultural Policy* 1, no. 18: 66–80.

Holden, John. 2006. *Cultural Value and the Crisis of Legitimacy: Why Culture Needs a Democratic Mandate*. London: Demos.

Holden, John. 2012. "New Year, New Approach to Wellbeing?" *Guardian Professional*, January 5, 2012. http://www.guardian.co.uk/culture-professionals-network/culture-professionals-blog/2012/jan/03/arts-heritage-wellbeing-cultural-policy.

Jancovich, Leila, and David Stevenson. 2021. "Failure Seems to Be the Hardest Word to Say." *International Journal of Cultural Policy* 27, no. 7: 967–981. https://doi.org/10.1080/10286632.2021.1879798.

Klamer, Arjo. 2017. *Doing the Right Thing: A Value Based Economy*. London: Ubiquity Press.

Matarasso, François. 1996. "Defining Values: Evaluating Arts Programmes." Working paper. Comedia, Stroud.

McDowell, Emma. 2020. "The Role of Evaluation and Research in Arts, Cultural and Heritage Organisations: Sector Survey Key Findings August 2020." Centre for Cultural Value, Leeds.

Nye, Joseph S., Jr. 2009. *Soft Power: The Means to Success in World Politics*. New York: Public Affairs.

O'Brien, Dave. 2010. "Measuring the Value of Culture: A Report to the Department for Culture Media and Sport." Department for Digital, Culture, Media and Sport, London.

O'Brien, Dave. 2013. *Cultural Policy: Management, Value and Modernity in the Creative Industries*. London: Routledge.

Oliver, James, and Ben Walmsley. 2011. "Assessing the Value of the Arts." In *Key Issues in the Arts and Entertainment Industry*, edited by Ben Walmsley, 83–101. Oxford: Goodfellow.

Peterson, Richard A., and Albert Simkus. 1992. "How Musical Tastes Mark Occupational Status Groups." In *Cultivating Differences: Symbolic Boundaries and the Making of Inequality*, edited by Michèle Lamont and Marcel Fournier, 152–186. Chicago: University of Chicago Press.

Phiddian, Robert, Julian Meyrick, Tully Barnett, and Richard Maltby. 2017. "Counting Culture to Death: An Australian Perspective on Culture Counts and Quality Metrics." *Cultural Trends* 26, no. 2: 174–180.

Piber, Martin, and Francesco Chiaravalloti. 2011. "Ethical Implications of Methodological Settings in Arts Management Research: The Case of Performance Evaluation." *The Journal of Arts Management, Law, and Society* 41: 240–266. https://doi.org/10.1080/10632921.2011.628210.

Rittel, Horst W. J., and Melvin M. Webber. 1973. "Dilemmas in a General Theory of Planning." *Policy Sciences* 4: 155–169.

Robinson, Mark. 2010. "Making Adaptive Resilience Real." Arts Council England, London.

Sagger, Harman, Jack Philips, and Mohammed Haque. 2021. "Valuing Culture and Heritage Capital: A Framework Towards Informing Decision Making." Department for Culture, Media and Sport, London.

Scott, Carol A. 2010. "Searching for the 'Public' in Public Value: Arts and Cultural Heritage in Australia." *Cultural Trends* 19, no. 4: 273–289. https://doi.org/10.1080/09548963.2010.515003.

Stevenson, Deborah, David Rowe, and Kieryn McKay. 2010. "Convergence in British Cultural Policy: The Social, the Cultural, and the Economic." *The Journal of Arts Management, Law and Society* 40: 248–265. https://doi.org/10.1080/10632921.2010.500926.

Taylor, Calvin. 2015. "Cultural Value: A Perspective from Cultural Economy." Arts and Humanities Research Council, Swindon.

Throsby, David. 2006. "The Value of Cultural Heritage: What Can Economics Tell Us?" Paper presented at the Capturing the Public Value of Heritage Conference, January 25–26, 2006, London.

Throsby, David. 2020. "Cultural Capital." In *Handbook of Cultural Economics*, edited by Ruth Towse, 168–173. Cheltenham, UK: Edward Elgar.

Vecco, Marilena. 2018. "Value and Values of Cultural Heritage." In *Cultural Heritage*, edited by Adriana Campelo, Laura Reynolds, Adam Lindgreen, and Michael Beverland, 23–38. London: Routledge.

Vuyk, Kees. 2010. "The Arts as an Instrument? Notes on the Controversy Surrounding the Value of Art." *International Journal of Cultural Policy* 16, no. 2: 173–183. https://doi.org/10.1080/10286630903029641.

Walmsley, Ben. 2012. "Towards a Balanced Scorecard: A Critical Analysis of the Culture and Sport Evidence (Case) Programme." *Cultural Trends* 21, no. 4: 325–334.

Walmsley, Ben. 2019. *Audience Engagement in the Performing Arts: A Critical Analysis*. London: Palgrave Macmillan.

Walmsley, Ben, and Julian Meyrick. 2022. "Critical Perspectives on Valuing Culture: Tensions and Disconnections Between Research, Policy and Practice." In *Routledge Companion to Audiences and the Performing Arts*, edited by Matthew Reason, Lynne Conner, Katya Johanson, and Ben Walmsley, 229–240. London: Routledge.

Williams, Raymond. 1958. *Culture and Society*. London: Chatto and Windus.

Yin, R. K. 2009. *Case Study Research: Design and Methods*. 4th ed. London: Sage.

CHAPTER 33

MEASURING CUSTOMER MULTISENSORY EXPERIENCE IN LIVE MUSIC

MANUEL CUADRADO-GARCÍA,
JUAN D. MONTORO-PONS, AND
CLAUDIA E. GOYES-YEPEZ

Introduction

LIVE music had been notably evolving for a decade, until the arrival of the COVID-19 pandemic, as a result of several changes in the music industry. Specifically, in the case of Spain, a wide and varied offering of live events, including music festivals, has consolidated itself. This showed that live music, as an industry with a high volume of business, not only was generating knock-on effects in other sectors, such as hospitality and tourism (Cuadrado-García, Miquel-Romero, and Montoro-Pons 2019) but also was attracting large audiences. Although the number of concerts and spectators has been fluctuating during the last decade (Table 33.1), revenues have been going up (SGAE 2021), and Spaniards' interest in live music concerts remains high: on a scale of 1 to 10, 70.4 percent of the population rate their interest at a 7 or above, 39.5 percent have attended a live concert, and 87.2 percent listen to music (with that being the most frequent cultural activity) (Ministerio de Cultura y Deportes 2019). The main motives for attending live shows are joy, experiences, and emotions (Cuadrado-García and Montoro-Pons 2021), proving that individuals are increasingly seeking experiences and immersion when attending these types of events. In this regard, some festivals and music promotors are gradually introducing new efforts to make the attendee experience multisensory, which enables them to reach new audiences, including those with visual or auditory impairments.

Table 33.1. Music Concerts, Attendees, and Revenue in Spain 2011–2020

	2011	2012	2013	2014	2015	2016	2017	2018	2019	2020
Concerts	121,722	116,446	103,208	94,549	90,212	88,259	87,924	89,440	91,106	45,306
Attendees (millions)	28,544	27,659	24,940	24,827	24,791	25,360	26,801	27,750	28,273	5,938
Revenue (millions of euros)	208,931	212,155	202,148	229,798	254,673	297,619	330,372	358,191	382,495	102,331

Source: SGAE 2021.

An experience is a personal event with an important emotional meaning. It is produced by a person's interaction with the stimuli consumed (Hoolbrok and Hirschman 1982)—that is, both the service (core product) and goods (peripheral products). The aim, according to Pine and Gilmore (1998), is to create a memorable event. This has led to studying people's experiences, as well as their motivations and cognitive processes (Malter et al. 2020), in order to improve both the marketing strategy of companies and consumer welfare. Within the marketing discipline, experience has been discussed from different approaches, such as the consumer experience, experiential marketing, and the brand experience.

The concept of consumer experience—initially introduced by Hirschman and Holbrook (1982) in relation to hedonic products, that is, those associated with pleasure, excitement, and satisfaction—contemplated multisensory, fantasy, and emotional aspects. This, together with the increasing personalization of products and the development of relationship marketing (Addis and Holbrook 2001), has emphasized the importance of considering customers as interlocutors and involving them in the production process, which entails greater applicability of the experiential perspective. In this sense, subjectivity becomes important, but also important is considering each experience as extraordinary (Carù and Cova 2003), as well as the notion that immersion in a consumer experience is not an immediate phenomenon but rather something more progressive (Carù and Cova 2006).

Schmitt's (1999) experiential marketing perspective contemplates experiences through a model that designs, manages, and integrates five relevant dimensions: sensory (sense); affective (feel); physical, behavioral, and lifestyle (act); cognitive-creative (think); and social identity (relate). Specifically, the *sensory* dimension refers to creating sensory experiences through sight, hearing, smell, taste, and touch. The *affective* dimension contemplates the consumer's internal feelings and emotions with the aim of creating experiences; that is, it emphasizes the hedonic and pleasure-seeking aspects of moods, emotions, or other affective responses. The *physical, behavioral, and lifesyle* dimension refers to a wide spectrum of activities related to lifestyle. The *cognitive-creative* dimension appeals to the intellect in order to create cognitive and problem-solving experiences to engage consumers creatively. And the *social identity* dimension contains aspects of the previous dimensions and expands beyond the individual and their personal and private feelings, relating a person to society.

From the above, it can be inferred that experience together with perception and satisfaction are key factors in the live music context. The central aim of this study is to analyze the consumer experience from the perspective of multisensory perception. To do so, this chapter begins by describing multisensory perception and consumer experience and their relationship, proposing a theoretical model. Next, the empirical research conducted to test the model is described, both the objectives and the methodology. This chapter continues with the description of the main results and ends with a section discussing the conclusions.

Multisensory Perception

Perception, the awareness of sensory information and sensation that occurs when a stimulus affects the receptor cells of an organ (Krishna 2012), has been widely analyzed in literature, both from a reductionist approach, considering just one or two senses, and a holistic approach, integrating the five senses (Fenko, Schifferstein, and Hekkert 2010; Krishna 2012; Haase and Wiedmann 2018; Haase, Wiedmann, and Labenz 2018; Wiedmann et al. 2018). The holistic approach refers to multisensory perception, which considers the joint analysis of the visual, auditory, olfactory, gustatory and tactile dimensions. This implies a total and global integration of perception with the senses.

In addition, according to Haase, Wiedmann, and Labenz (2018), multisensory perception refers to the evaluation of an object by the consumer, which determines the degree of attractiveness of that object to the five human senses. A high evaluation represents a positive sensory perception, while a low evaluation indicates a negative sensory perception. In this context, Haase and Wiedmann (2018) construct and validate a multisensory perception scale considering the previous five dimensions, noting that they can have different levels of importance depending on the product. In other words, there is a dominant sensory dimension, according to Fenko, Schifferstein, and Hekkert (2010), that depends on the period of use and the type of product. When buying a physical product, vision is initially the most important dimension; after one month of use, touch becomes dominant; and after one year, vision, touch, and hearing become equally important. In addition, Helmefalk and Hultén (2017) consider that visual, acoustic, olfactory, gustatory, and tactile dimensions have positive effects on shopper emotions and purchasing behavior in a retail environment. Similarly, the common theory of two systems of cognitive psychology (Neys 2006; Sloman 2002; Stanovich and West 2002) suggests that consumers evaluate the results of cognitive information processing through the subconscious (implicit system) and consciousness (explicit system). In this regard, live music could be perceived by consumers through their five senses if those senses are activated in the performance. Otherwise, only sight and hearing would be involved.

Sensory perception was measured by Haase and Wiedmann (2018), who constructed and validated a scale composed of twenty adjectives (four per sense), resulting in a reliable and consistent measurement tool for the five sensory dimensions. This scale was validated by Haase, Wiedmann, and Labenz (2018) and Wiedmann et al. (2018). The former show that the brand experience plays an important role as a mediator between sensory perception and consumer responses. The latter confirm the significative and positive relationship between multisensory marketing and the brand experience. In addition, Iglesias, Markovic, and Rialp (2019) determine that multisensory perception is positively related to consumer experience: the higher the multisensory perception, the better the experience perceived by the consumer.

CUSTOMER EXPERIENCE

Experience has become increasingly relevant as customers seek pleasurable and multisensory experiences (Schmitt 1999). According to Brakus, Schmitt, and Zarantonello (2009), *experience* refers to consumers' internal subjective responses (sensations, feelings, and cognitions) and behavioral responses provoked by the stimulus of the product—responses that are essential to make customers happy (Schmitt, Brakus, and Zarantonello 2014). Specifically, Pine and Gilmore (1998) state that an experience occurs when a company intentionally uses services as a central element and goods as accessories to attract individual customers in a way that creates a memorable event. This entails considering experience as a multidimensional construct that can be multisensory. The more senses that are developed in an experience, the more effective and memorable it can be. Experiential marketing is based on strategic experiential dimensions: sensory (sense), affective (feel), cognitive-creative (think), physical, behavioral, and lifestyle (act), and social identity (relate), as determined by Schmitt (1999). Gentile, Spiller, and Noci (2007) add a pragmatic component.

The literature has studied experience in relation to brands (Khan and Rahman 2015), events (Zarantonello and Schmitt 2013), and consumers (Holbrook and Hirschman 1982). Numerous empirical studies have been carried out in different industries (food and beverages, automobile, electronics, footwear, clothing, tourism and hospitality, financial services, telecommunications, retail, media, and entertainment). Consumers look for brands that offer attractive and engaging experiences to which they can relate and which they can incorporate into their lifestyles; they expect something different that dazzles their senses, touches their hearts, and stimulates their minds (Schmitt 1999).

But how has experience been measured? Some authors have considered customer experience as consisting of four dimensions: sensory, affective, cognitive, and behavioral (Brakus, Schmitt, and Zarantonello 2009; Tsai, Chang, and Ho 2015; Xie, Poon, and Zhang 2017). For example, Brakus, Schmitt, and Zarantonello (2009) constructed a scale of experience that originally considered five dimensions (sensory, affective, behavioral, intellectual, and relational), but these authors were able to confirm the existence of just four of them, eliminating the relational dimension. Several authors then took this four-dimensional scale as a reference and validated it in different product and service environments. For instance, Iglesias, Singh, and Batista-Foguet (2011) empirically show that affective commitment completely mediates the relationship between brand experience and brand loyalty. Zarantonello and Schmitt (2013) confirm that attendance at events has an impact on the brand experience. Lin (2015) reveals that brand experience has a positive impact on brand equity and satisfaction. Moreira, Fortes, and Santiago (2017) show that the use of multisensory stimulation has positive effects on customers' brand experiences, brand equity, and purchase intentions. And Xie, Poon, and Zhang

(2017) reveal that brand quality has a mediating effect between the brand experience and aspects of customer behavior toward other customers and toward the organization; in addition, they point out that the strongest impact is in the behavioral dimension, followed by the affective one. Finally, Wiedmann et al. (2018) conducted an empirical study in a service industry (luxury hotels) and showed that multisensory marketing notably influences the brand experience, the value perceived by the customer, and the construction of brand strength. These findings provided interesting clues for designing experiential marketing.

Other researchers consider five dimensions of experience, adding the relational dimension (based on the experiential marketing model in Schmitt 1999). Nysveen, Pedersen, and Skard (2013) point out that experience dimensions had not been empirically studied as individual variables in prior research. Their research shows the individual effects of each dimension of brand experience, contributing to a deeper understanding of the complexity of the experience construct. Cleff, Walter, and Xie. (2018) demonstrate a positive effect of online brand experience on brand loyalty. They highlight that the affective and behavioral brand experiences have a high impact on brand loyalty. Hultén (2011) determines that the sensory dimension is intended to characterize the identity of a brand in relation to each of the five senses, and also notes that a multisensory brand experience offers behavioral, emotional, cognitive, sensory, or symbolic value at a more internal level. In this regard, a smell, sound, sight, taste, or touch can reinforce a positive feeling, which generates value for individuals and, in particular, creates a brand image. Cleff, Lin, and Walter (2014) find that experiences create sensory stimulation through the senses of sight, hearing, smell, taste, and touch and play a central role in creating brand equity.

Some studies have focused on the sensory experience. Iglesias, Markovic, and Rialp (2019) confirm that multisensory perception is positively related to consumer experience. That is, the higher the multisensory perception, the better the experience perceived by the consumer. The existing research in this context also analyzes the effects of the experience on other variables, mainly satisfaction (Brakus, Schmitt, and Zarantonello 2009; Iglesias, Markovic, and Rialp 2019) and loyalty (Brakus, Schmitt, and Zarantonello 2009; Iglesias, Singh, and Batista-Foguet 2011; Mukerjee 2018). Nysveen, Pedersen, and Skard (2013) demonstrate that the five dimensions of experience are important predictors of customer satisfaction and loyalty.

With the aim of measuring multisensory perception and consumer experience, we will adapt the five-dimensional construct to the music context. Live music is consumed in groups and so should be analyzed considering the five experiential dimensions (including the social dimension of the relations among attendees). We propose the following two hypotheses:

H1: Multisensory perception has a positive effect on customer experience

H2: Customer experience has a positive effect on satisfaction

From these two hypotheses, a theoretical model is proposed (Figure 33.1).

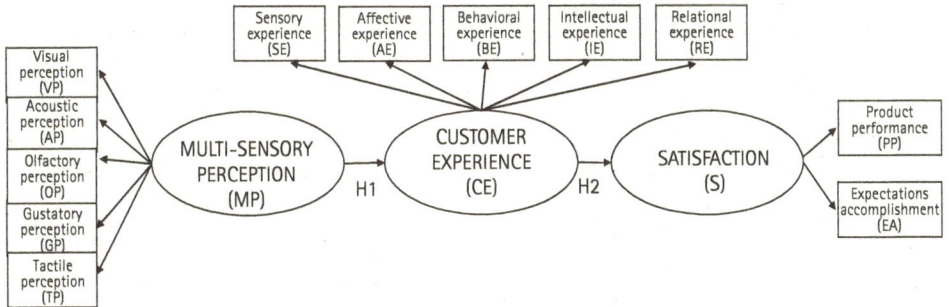

FIGURE 33.1 Theoretical model and hypotheses.

Empirical Research: Objectives and Methodology

Empirical research was undertaken to test the theoretical model and hypotheses. The central aim of this research was to analyze the consumer experience in the context of live music from a multisensory approach. The specific objectives were the following:

- Analyze the multisensory perception and experience among subsamples (gender, level of education, family situation, and disability).
- Validate the five dimensions of the multisensory perception scale: visual, acoustic, olfactory, gustatory, and tactile.
- Validate the five dimensions of the consumer experience scale: sensory, affective, behavioral, intellectual, and relational.
- Analyze the effects of visual, auditory, olfactory, taste and tactile perception in multisensory perception.
- Analyze the effects of sensory, affective, behavioral, intellectual, and relational experience on the consumer experience.
- Study the relationship among multisensory perception, consumer experience, and satisfaction.

To collect the data, we conducted a self-administered survey through a structured questionnaire handed out to the attendees of a multisensory concert, expressly produced for the occasion, as explained next. The design of the questionnaire was based on an analysis of the literature, a review by three academic experts in consumer behavior and experiential marketing, and a pre-test carried out with a group of ten individuals. The final questionnaire was divided into three parts: (1) habits of attendance at music shows (type, frequency, sources of information, and motives for attendance), (2) scales (multisensory perception, customer experience, and satisfaction), and (3) sociodemographic variables (age, gender, level of education, occupation, and disability).

The main variables were measured through multi-item (Table 33.2) and five-point Likert scales (1 = strongly disagree to 5 = strongly agree).

Table 33.2. Scales of Measurement

Variable/Dimensions	Items	Source
Multisensory perception		Adapted from Haase and Wiedmann 2018
Visual perception	1. What I saw was unique 2. What I saw was attractive 3. What I saw was impressive 4. What I saw seemed nice to me	
Acoustic perception	5. The sound was nice 6. The music sounded good 7. The voices were melodic 8. The sound was of good quality	
Olfactory perception	9. The room smelled good 10. The smell was pleasant 11. I liked the scent of the environment 12. I perceived a good scent	
Gustatory perception	13. What I ate tasted good 14. What I ate was nice 15. What I ate had a special flavor 16. What I ate was delicious	
Tactile perception	17. I was comfortable with the physical contact from the artists 18. I found the physical contact from the artists pleasant 19. The physical contact generated well-being 20. I liked the physical contact on my body	
Customer experience		Adapted from Schmitt 1999 and Brakus, Schmitt, and Zarantonello 2009
Sensory experience	1. It made a strong impression on my senses 2. It was interesting for my senses 3. It was attractive to my senses	
Affective experience	4. It generated feelings in me 5. It generated strong emotions in me 6. It was very emotional	
Behavioral experience	7. It allowed me to let myself be carried away by my senses 8. It made me to do things 9. It led me to want to see it again	
Intellectual experience	10. It made me think 11. I was curious 12. It can help me solve problems	
Relational experience	13. It made me feel accompanied 14. It made me feel part of a community 15. It made me feel part of a family	
Satisfaction		Adapted from Oliver 1980
	1. It made me feel satisfied 2. It met my expectations	

A descriptive statistical analysis was undertaken to determine the differences among subsamples. Then, to confirm the model, the SmartPLS3 software (Ringle, Wende, and Becker 2015) was used through a structural equation model (SEM) based on the variance through partial least squares (PLS-SEM). First the reflective measurement model was solved, then the path of coefficients in the structural model was calculated, and finally the global analysis was done.

The Multisensory Musical Concert

The empirical research was carried out among attendees to a multisensory concert expressly produced for the occasion. The event, for which a low admission fee was charged, was performed for people both with and without aural and/or visual impairment. Some were relatives and friends of the university students responsible for organizing the event. Others came because of the promotion of the concert among local organizations for disabled people. The concert was called Concierto Sentido—a pun in Spanish, because not only does *concierto* mean "concert" and *sentido* mean "sense" (in other words, a concert for the senses) but *con cierto*, "with a certain," used before *sentido*, "sense," means "meaningful"—so it is not only a concert for the senses but also evocative.

The concert was a song recital performed by Las Reinas Magas (The Wise Women), composed of eight women: four instrumentalists (harp, accordion, guitar and clarinet) and four voices. The performance consisted of a series of versions of well-known songs but in a multisensory way: the voices and music (acoustic), the sight of the performers (visual), the scents of the aromatic plants distributed at the entrance and the essential oils that emanated from different spots in the venue (olfactory), the flavors of seasonal fruits and vegetables (gustatory), and the vibration of the voices as the singers placed their hands on people's heads or shoulders (tactile). The concert was performed twice in the Matilde Salvador Auditorium at the Arts Center La Nau (Universitat de València, Spain) in November 2019, with a total of 196 attendees.

Fieldwork was performed by students at the University of Valencia. They handed the questionnaires out to all the spectators once the concert was over, helping those with disabilities. In the case of those visually impaired, fieldworkers asked them every single question orally, subsequently registering their answers. Questions and answers were transformed into variables and data producing a dataset.

Participants' Profiles

The sociodemographic profile of attendees to the multisensory concert is presented in Table 33.3. The mean age of participants, who range from fourteen to seventy-nine years old, was 35.53 years. Regarding gender, 34.4 percent were men and 65.6 percent

Table 33.3. Sociodemographic Profile of the Sample

Variables		N	%
Age	14–31	107	54.6
	32–49	37	18.9
	> 50	52	26.5
Gender	Men	68	34.4
	Women	128	65.6
Level of education	No education	2	1.0
	Primary-secondary	14	7.1
	High school	75	38.3
	University	105	53.6
Family status	No partner/no children	85	43.4
	No partner/children	10	5.1
	Partner/no children	55	28.1
	Partner/children	45	23.0
Occupational status	Student	99	50.5
	Employed	48	24.5
	Self-employed	11	5.6
	Unemployed	10	5.1
	Retired	20	10.2
	Housework	7	3.6
Disability	Yes	58	29.58
	No	138	70.41

were women. In addition, 50.8 percent of those attending the concert were students, and 53.6 percent had studied at the university level. Those without a partner and children accounted for 43.4 percent, and those with Spanish nationality for 87.7 percent. Finally, the population with disabilities was 29.58 percent of the total number of interviewees. This last figure refers not only to those who came because they had heard about the concert through an organization for disabled persons but also to those with some form of visual impairment (e.g., wearing glasses).

Results

As stated previously, a descriptive analysis was first undertaken in relation to the main variables considered: multisensory perception and customer experience. Then, in order to confirm the model (namely, the relationship among these two variables plus satisfaction), a structural equation model was created, and its results described.

Multisensory Perception and Experience: Values and Differences

In relation to multisensory perception, all the items in the scale got scores higher than 4, meaning the perception was very positive (Table 33.4). Specifically, the four most highly valued items were the ones linked to the acoustic sense: "The music sounded good" (4.71), "The sound was pleasant" (4.65), "The voices were melodic" (4.64), and "The sound was of good quality" (4.57). On the other hand, a couple of items linked to taste got the lowest scores, although they were above the midpoint of the scale: "What I ate had a special flavor" (3.56) and "What I ate was delicious" (3.62).

Statistical tests were conducted to identify differences among sociodemographic groups. The variables "gender" and "level of education" only showed statistically significant differences in the item "What I ate was delicious," with women and those with less education giving it a higher assessment. "What I saw was impressive" scored higher among those with lower education levels. Surprisingly, those with children (whether partnered or not) and those having a disability gave higher assessments to the four items of the tactile dimension: "I was comfortable with the physical contact from the artists," "I found the physical contact from the artists pleasant," "The physical contact generated well-being," and "I liked the physical contact on my body."

Regarding the experience by attendees (Table 33.4), all the items of the scale were above the midpoint of the scale but lower than 4 except "It was interesting for my senses" (4.03), "It was attractive for my senses" (4.00)—with those two items linked to the sensory dimension—and "I was curious" (4.02), which scored greater than 4.

The experience was also different by group. Women gave higher values to different items than men did, especially those connected to the cognitive experience. However, those with a lower level of education seemed to have a better experience, as almost all the items were scored higher. Similarly, those with children gave higher values to almost all the items in the scale than those without children did, except "I was curious" and "It made me think." Finally, impaired people assessed the behavioral, intellectual, and relational dimensions of the experience much higher than those not having any disability.

The Relationship among Multisensory Perception, Experience, and Satisfaction

To test the model and the hypotheses, the measurement model was first evaluated with the corresponding criteria: Cronbach's alpha (CA), composite reliability (CR), convergent validity (AVE), discriminant validity, and cross loads. As shown in Tables 33.5 and 33.6, all of these criteria confirmed that the measurement was satisfactory.

Once we had verified that the measurement model was satisfactory, we moved on to the structural model. According to Hair, Ringle, and Sarstedt (2017), it should be

Table 33.4. Multisensory Perception and Experience

Variable/Dimensions		Min.	Max.	Mean	St. dev.
Multisensory perception					
Visual perception	1. What I saw was unique	1	5	4.40	0.894
	2. What I saw was attractive	1	5	4.30	0.848
	3. What I saw was impressive	1	5	4.16	0.900
	4. What I saw seemed nice to me	1	5	4.53	0.699
Acoustic perception	5. The sound was nice	2	5	4.65	0.628
	6. The music sounded good	1	5	4.71	0.636
	7. The voices were melodic	1	5	4.64	0.669
	8. The sound was of good quality	1	5	4.57	0.736
Olfactory perception	9. The room smelled good	1	5	4.27	0.848
	10. The smell was pleasant	1	5	4.31	0.805
	11. I liked the scent of the environment	1	5	4.13	0.926
	12. I perceived a good scent	1	5	4.14	0.906
Gustatory perception	13. What I ate tasted good	1	5	4.26	0.900
	14. What I ate was nice	1	5	4.31	0.848
	15. What I ate had a special flavor	1	5	3.56	1.141
	16. What I ate was delicious	1	5	3.62	1.068
Tactile perception	17. I was comfortable with the physical contact from the artists	1	4	4.02	1.201
	18. I found the physical contact from the artists pleasant	1	5	4.01	1.211
	19. The physical contact generated well-being	1	5	4.00	1.218
	20. I liked the physical contact on my body	1	5	3.91	1.244
Customer experience					
Sensory experience	1. It made a strong impression on my senses	1	5	3.81	0.881
	2. It was interesting for my senses	1	5	4.03	0.896
	3. It was attractive to my senses	1	5	4.00	0.923
Affective experience	4. It generated feelings in me	1	5	3.99	0.966
	5. It generated strong emotions in me	1	5	3.61	1.083
	6. It was very emotional	1	5	3.81	1.009
Behavioral experience	7. It allowed me to let myself be carried away by my senses	1	5	3.73	1.006
	8. It made me to do things	1	5	3.36	1.226
	9. It led me to want to see it again	1	5	3.66	1.144
Intellectual experience	10. It made me think	1	5	3.77	1.026
	11. I was curious	1	5	4.02	0.870
	12. It can help me solve problems	1	5	2.99	1.225
Relational experience	13. It made me feel accompanied	1	5	3.74	1.061
	14. It made me feel part of a community	1	5	3.46	1.139
	15. It made me feel part of a family	1	5	3.13	1.169

Table 33.5. Reliability and Convergent Validity of the Measurement Instrument

Factor	Indicator	Load	t Value	CA (0.7)	CR (0.8)	AVE (0.5)
Multisensory perception	VP	0.815***	29.054	0.919	0.929	0.522
	AP	0.785***	23.851			
	OP	0.625***	9.525			
	GP	0.623***	11.134			
	TP	0.741***	13.543			
Customer experience	SE	0.886***	50.634	0.954	0.959	0.942
	AE	0.917***	81.555			
	CE	0.908***	76.326			
	IE	0.863***	38.338			
	RE	0.820***	26.214			
Satisfaction	PP	0.917***	19.498	0.791	0.905	0.827
	EA	0.902***	35.501			

CA = Cronbach's alpha; CR = composite reliability; AVE = average extracted variance; VP = visual perception; AP = acoustic perception; OP = olfactory perception; GP = gustatory perception; TP = tactile perception; SE = sensory experience; AE = affective experience; CE = cognitive experience; IE = intellectual experience; RE = relational experience; PP = product performance; EA = expectations accomplishment
*** $p < 0.01$

Table 33.6. Discriminant Validity

	MP	CE	S
Multisensory perception (MP)	0.722	0.731	0.767
Customer experience (CE)	0.701	0.97	0.944
Satisfaction (S)	0.67	0.823	0.91

MP = multi-sensory perception; CE = customer experience; S = satisfaction

evaluated based on the following criteria: (1) size and significance of path coefficients, (2) coefficients of determination R2, (3) predictive relevance Q2, (4) effect size f2, and (5) effect size q2. As shown in Table 33.7, bootstrapping was used, indicating that the path coefficient between the multisensory perception construct (MP) and the consumer experience construct (CE) is 0.701, which confirms hypothesis H1. Similarly, the relationship between the consumer experience construct (CE) and the satisfaction construct (S) demonstrated a path coefficient of 0.823, confirming hypothesis H2.

The effect of the dimensions in their respective constructs was also calculated, although for the sake of clarity tables are not provided.

Table 33.7. Structural Model Measurements

Hypotheses	Path coefficient	t Value (bootstrap)	Confidence level 2.5%	97.5%	Dependent construct R2	Predictive relevance Q2
H1: MP–CE	0.701**	19.498	0.621	0.770	0.491	0.298
H2: CE–S	0.823**	35.501	0.778	0.866	0.677	0.554

** $p < 0.01$

Based on the results obtained and the analysis of previous studies in the literature, several relevant contributions to this field of research can be highlighted. To begin with, this study has validated the scale of the five dimensions of multisensory perception (visual, acoustic, olfactory, gustatory, and tactile) proposed by Haase and Wiedmann (2018) and endorsed by Haase, Wiedmann, and Labenz (2018) and Wiedmann et al. (2018). In addition, the five-dimensional consumer experience scale (sensory, affective, behavioral, intellectual, and relational) by Brakus, Schmitt, and Zarantonello (2009) was also validated, as ratified by Nysveen, Pedersen, and Skard (2013) and Cleff, Walter, and Xie (2018).

Furthermore, the effects of visual, auditory, olfactory, gustatory, and tactile perception on multisensory perception were analyzed, as well as the effects of sensory, affective, behavioral, intellectual, and relational experience as measures of the explanatory and predictive power of the structural model. It was found that visual, acoustic, and tactile perception have a large effect on multisensory perception, or high explanatory power, while olfactory and gustatory perception have a medium effect. The affective and behavioral experiences have a large effect on the consumer experience, while the sensory, intellectual, and relational experiences have a medium effect on the consumer experience. Consumer experience has a large explanatory effect on satisfaction, and multisensory perception has a medium explanatory effect on consumer experience. With regard to the effects as a measure of predictive power, it was found that tactile perception has a large effect on multisensory perception, auditory and visual perception a medium effect, and olfactory perception a small effect. Affective experience has a large predictive effect on consumer experience, sensory experience a medium effect, and relational and behavioral experience a small effect. Taste perception and intellectual experiences have a negative effect on endogenous constructs.

Finally, the structural equation model analysis empirically tested the direct relationship between multisensory perception, consumer experience, and satisfaction in the context of live music. The findings are consistent with existing research, highlighting the positive relationship between these variables. Specifically, the results indicate that multisensory perception is a strong predictor of the consumer experience (Hultén 2011; Brakus, Schmitt, and Zarantonello 2009; Haase, Wiedmann, and Labenz 2018; Haase and Wiedmann 2018; Iglesias, Markovic, and Rialp 2019;

Wiedmann et al. 2018). Likewise, consumer experience shows a strong and highly significant effect on satisfaction (Brakus, Schmitt, and Zarantonello 2009; De Oliveira et al. 2018; Ha and Perks 2005; Haase, Wiedmann, and Labenz 2018; Lin 2015; Nysveen, Pedersen, and Skard 2013). In detail, visual, auditory, and tactile perceptions are the most important dimensions (they have the highest loads), followed by olfactory and taste perceptions, which also play a significant role but are less important in multisensory perception. These findings are consistent with the results of research by Haase, Wiedmann, and Labenz (2018) and Krishna (2012), in which visual perception has one of the greatest weights in the construct of multisensory perception. Similarly, affective and behavioral experiences are the most important dimensions in the consumer experience (they have the highest loads), followed by the sensory, intellectual, and relational dimensions. These findings are in line with the study proposed by Xie, Poon, and Zhang (2017).

Conclusions

The main contribution of this study is to provide empirical evidence regarding the causal relationships involving multisensory perception, consumer experience, and satisfaction. Results support the two research hypotheses described in the conceptual model, indicating a causal chain of direct effects between the three latent dimensions. The five dimensions of the multisensory perception scale were validated (visual, acoustic, olfactory, gustatory, and tactile), as were the five dimensions of the consumer experience scale (sensory, affective, behavioral, intellectual, and relational).

This chapter provides valuable information on the importance of multisensory perception in creating unique consumer experiences. The main focus of marketing practice is still on visual stimuli. However, this study provides empirical evidence of the importance of an integrated approach in addressing all the senses. In the case of live music, the potential lies especially in the visual, acoustic, and tactile senses, which generate significant affective and cognitive experiences and, therefore, satisfaction in the consumer. At an applied level, sensory stimuli could be established through the five senses, thus giving rise to a positive multisensory perception and, therefore, to greater success in the market. Other practitioners could also benefit from the research model by adapting it to other contexts. The results have implications as well for music organizations and those creating and performing music. Knowing that multisensory perception—namely, activating more than the traditional two senses (visual and acoustic)—can lead to a greater customer experience and satisfaction within the context of live music could lead to different decisions being made. In this regard, implementation of experiential marketing, as the use of different peripheral sensory attributes and tools, could produce more intense and satisfactory experiences for attendees. This could enlarge audiences, as such experiences target impaired people, who tend to have difficulty finding enjoyment at these types of events and so attend them less often. And consumers who are more satisfied, because of having experienced and enjoyed a different, more intense, and multisensory experience—both people with disabilities and those without disabilities—are likely to become more loyal and eager to act as ambassadors, spreading their enthusiasm among other potential attendees.

Finally, this study has some limitations that offer possible starting points for future research. The model was tested on a limited and relatively homogeneous sample. Therefore, new research should use more heterogeneous and representative samples of the population. Additionally, the data presented here are related to the specificity of the live music context, and findings could be different for other areas. Therefore, future research could analyze these relationships in different areas within the cultural sector. On the other hand, data analysis has focused on causal relationships through structural equation models. To gain a better understanding of the effects of sensory marketing activities, one could examine the moderating effects of sociodemographic aspects (such as gender, age, and people with or without functional diversity).

References

Addis, Michela, and Morris B. Holbrook. 2001. "On the Conceptual Link Between Mass Customisation and Experiential Consumption: An Explosion of Subjectivity." *Journal of Consumer Behaviour* 1, no. 1: 50–66. https://doi.org/10.1002/cb.53.

Brakus, J. Josko, Bernd H. Schmitt, and Lia Zarantonello. 2009. "Brand Experience: What Is It? How Is It Measured? Does It Affect Loyalty?" *Journal of Marketing* 73, no. 3: 52. https://doi.org/http://dx.doi.org/10.1509/jmkg.73.3.52.

Carù, Antonella, and Bernard Cova. 2003. "Revisiting Consumption Experience: A More Humble but Complete View of the Concept." *Marketing Theory* 3, no. 2: 267–286. https://doi.org/10.1177/14705931030032004.

Carù, Antonella, and Bernard Cova. 2006. "How to Facilitate Immersion in a Consumption Experience: Appropriation Operations and Service Elements." *Journal of Consumer Behaviour* 5, no. 1: 4–14. https://doi.org/10.1002/cb.30.

Cleff, Thomas, I. Chun Lin, and Nadine Walter. 2014. "Can You Feel It? The Effect of Brand Experience on Brand Equity." *IUP Journal of Brand Management* 11, no. 2: 7–27.

Cleff, Thomas, Nadine Walter, and Jing Xie. 2018. "The Effect of Online Brand Experience on Brand Loyalty: A Web of Emotions." *IUP Journal of Brand Management* 15, no. 1: 7–24.

Cuadrado-García, Manuel, María-José Miquel-Romero, and Juan D. Montoro-Pons. 2019. "Género, motivaciones y frenos en el consumo de música en directo." *Cuadernos Económicos del ICE* 98: 105–124. https://roderic.uv.es/handle/10550/74765.

Cuadrado-García, Manuel, and Juan D. Montoro-Pons. 2021. "LGB's Arts Affinity: An Empirical Study of Theater Audiences Based on Motivations." *Journal of Homosexuality* 69, no. 8: 1322–1341. https://doi.org/10.1080/00918369.2021.1912557.

de Oliveira, Fernando, Wagner Junior, Claudio Hoffmann, and Diego Costa. 2018. "The Brand Experience Extended Model: A Meta-analysis." *Journal of Brand Management* 25, no. 6: 519–535. https://doi.org/http://dx.doi.org/10.1057/s41262-018-0104-6.

Fenko, Anna, Hendrik N. J. Schifferstein, and Paul Hekkert. 2010. "Shifts in Sensory Dominance Between Various Stages of User–Product Interactions." *Applied Ergonomics* 41, no. 1: 34–40. https://doi.org/https://doi.org/10.1016/j.apergo.2009.03.007.

Gentile, Chiara, Nicola Spiller, and Giuliano Noci. 2007. "How to Sustain the Customer Experience: An Overview of Experience Components That Co-create Value with the Customer." *European Management Journal* 25, no. 5: 395–410. https://doi.org/10.1016/j.emj.2007.08.005.

Ha, Hong-Youl, and Helen Perks. 2005. "Effects of Consumer Perceptions of Brand Experience on the Web: Brand Familiarity, Satisfaction and Brand Trust." *Journal of Consumer Behaviour* 4, no. 6: 438–452. https://doi.org/10.1002/cb.29.

Haase, Janina, Klaus-Peter Wiedmann, and Franziska Labenz. 2018. "Effects of Consumer Sensory Perception on Brand Performance." *Journal of Consumer Marketing* 35, no. 6: 565–576. https://doi.org/doi:10.1108/JCM-10-2017-2404.

Haase, Janina, and Klaus-Peter Wiedmann. 2018. "The Sensory Perception Item Set (SPI): An Exploratory Effort to Develop a Holistic Scale for Sensory Marketing." *Psychology and Marketing* 35, no. 10: 727–739. https://doi.org/http://dx.doi.org/10.1002/mar.21130.

Hair, Joseph F., Christian M. Ringle, and Marko Sarstedt. 2017. "Partial Least Squares Structural Equation Modeling." In *Handbook of Market Research*, edited by C. Homburg, M. Klarmann, and A. Vomberg, 1–40 (Cham: Springer). https://doi.org/10.1007/978-3-319-05542-8_15-1.

Helmefalk, Miralem, and Bertil Hultén. 2017. "Multi-Sensory Congruent Cues in Designing Retail Store Atmosphere: Effects on Shoppers' Emotions and Purchase Behavior." *Journal of Retailing and Consumer Services* 38: 1–11. https://doi.org/https://doi.org/10.1016/j.jretconser.2017.04.007.

Hirschman, Elizabeth C., and Morris B. Holbrook. 1982. "Hedonic Consumption: Emerging Concepts, Methods and Propositions." *Journal of Marketing* 46, no. 3: 92–101. https://doi.org/10.2307/1251707.

Holbrook, Morris B., and Elizabeth Hirschman. 1982. "The Experiential Aspects of Consumption: Consumer Fantasies, Feelings, and Fun." *Journal of Consumer Research* 9, no. 2: 132–140. https://doi.org/10.1086/208906.

Hultén, Bertil. 2011. "Sensory Marketing: The Multi-sensory Brand-Experience Concept." *European Business Review* 23, no. 3: 256–273. https://doi.org/http://dx.doi.org/10.1108/09555341111130245.

Iglesias, Oriol, Stefan Markovic, and Josep Rialp. 2019. "How Does Sensory Brand Experience Influence Brand Equity? Considering the Roles of Customer Satisfaction, Customer Affective Commitment, and Employee Empathy." *Journal of Business Research* 96: 343–354. https://doi.org/https://doi.org/10.1016/j.jbusres.2018.05.043.

Iglesias, Oriol, Jatinder J. Singh, and Joan M. Batista-Foguet. 2011. "The Role of Brand Experience and Affective Commitment in Determining Brand Loyalty." *Journal of Brand Management* 18, no. 8: 570–582. https://doi.org/http://dx.doi.org/10.1057/bm.2010.58.

Khan, Imran, and Zillur Rahman. 2015. "A Review and Future Directions of Brand Experience Research." *International Strategic Management Review* 3, no. 1: 1–14. https://doi.org/https://doi.org/10.1016/j.ism.2015.09.003.

Krishna, Aradhna. 2012. "An Integrative Review of Sensory Marketing: Engaging the Senses to Affect Perception, Judgment and Behavior." *Journal of Consumer Psychology* 22, no. 3: 332–351. https://doi.org/10.1016/j.jcps.2011.08.003.

Lin, Yi Hsin. 2015. "Innovative Brand Experience's Influence on Brand Equity and Brand Satisfaction." *Journal of Business Research* 68, no. 11: 2254–2259. https://doi.org/https://doi.org/10.1016/j.jbusres.2015.06.007.

Malter, Maayan S., Morris B. Holbrook, Barbara E. Kahn, Jeffrey R. Parker, and Donald R. Lehmann. 2020. "The Past, Present, and Future of Consumer Research." *Marketing Letters* 31, nos. 2–3: 137–149. https://doi.org/10.1007/s11002-020-09526-8.

Moreira, António C., Nuno Fortes, and Ramiro Santiago. 2017. "Influence of Sensory Stimuli on Brand Experience, Brand Equity and Purchase Intention." *Journal of Business Economics and Management* 18, no. 1: 68–83. https://doi.org/10.3846/16111699.2016.1252793.

Ministerio de Cultura y Deportes. 2019. "Encuesta de hábitos y prácticas culturales en España 2018–19." División de Estadística y Estudios, Secretaría General Técnica. https://www.culturaydeporte.gob.es/dam/jcr:1712f192-d59b-427d-bbe0-db0f3e9f716b/encuesta-de-habitos-y-practicas-culturales-2018-2019.pdf.

Mukerjee, Kaushik. 2018. "The Impact of Brand Experience, Service Quality and Perceived Value on Word of Mouth of Retail Bank Customers: Investigating the Mediating Effect of Loyalty." *Journal of Financial Services Marketing* 23, no. 1: 12–24. https://doi.org/http://dx.doi.org/10.1057/s41264-018-0039-8.

Neys, Wiem D. 2006. "Dual Processing in Reasoning: Two Systems but One Reasoner." *Psychological Science* 17: 428–433.

Nysveen, Herbjorn, Per E. Pedersen, and Siv Skard. 2013. "Brand Experiences in Service Organizations: Exploring the Individual Effects of Brand Experience Dimensions." *Journal of Brand Management* 20, no. 5: 404–423. https://doi.org/http://dx.doi.org/10.1057/bm.2012.31.

Oliver, Richard L. 1980. "A Cognitive Model of the Antecedents and Consequences of Satisfaction Decisions." *Journal of Marketing Research* 17, no. 4: 460. https://doi.org/10.2307/3150499.

Pine, B. Joseph, and James H. Gilmore. 1998. "Welcome to the Experience Economy." *Harvard Business Review* 76, no. 4: 97–105.

Ringle, Christian. M., Sven Wende, and Jan-Michael Becker. 2015. *SmartPLS 3*. 3rd ed. Bönningstedt: SmartPLS. http://www.smartpls.com.

Schmitt, Bernd H. 1999. "Experiential Marketing." *Journal of Marketing Management* 15, nos. 1–3: 53–67. https://doi.org/10.1362/026725799784870496.

Schmitt, Bernd H., Josko Brakus, and Lia Zarantonello. 2014. "The Current State and Future of Brand Experience." *Journal of Brand Management* 21, no. 9: 727–733. https://doi.org/http://dx.doi.org/10.1057/bm.2014.34.

SGAE. 2021. "Anuario SGAE de las artes escénicas, musicales y audiovisuales 2021." Fundación SGAE. http://www.anuariossgae.com/anuario2021/frames.html.

Sloman, Steven A. 2002. "Two Systems of Reasoning." In *Heuristics and Biases: The Psychology of Intuitive Judgment*, edited by D. Griffin, D. Kahneman, and T. Gilovich, 379–396. Cambridge: Cambridge University Press. https://doi.org/DOI:10.1017/CBO9780511808098.024.

Stanovich, Keith E., and Richard F. West. 2002. "Individual Differences in Reasoning: Implications for the Rationality Debate?" In *Heuristics and Biases: The Psychology of Intuitive Judgment*, edited by D. Griffin, D. Kahneman, and T. Gilovich, 421–440. Cambridge: Cambridge University Press. https://doi.org/DOI: 10.1017/CBO9780511808098.026.

Tsai, Yi-Ching, Chang, Hui-Chen, and Kung-Chun Ho. 2015. "A Study of the Relationship Among Brand Experiences, Self-Concept Congruence, Customer Satisfaction, and Brand Preference." *Contemporary Management Research* 11, no. 2: 97–115. https://doi.org/10.7903/cmr.12970.

Wiedmann, Klaus-Peter, Franziska Labenz, Janina Haase, and Nadine Hennigs. 2018. "The Power of Experiential Marketing: Exploring the Causal Relationships Among Multisensory Marketing, Brand Experience, Customer Perceived Value and Brand

Strength." *Journal of Brand Management* 25, no. 2: 101–118. https://doi.org/http://dx.doi.org/10.1057/s41262-017-0061-5.

Xie, Lishan, Patrick Poon, and Wenxuan Zhang. 2017. "Brand Experience and Customer Citizenship Behavior: The Role of Brand Relationship Quality." *Journal of Consumer Marketing* 34, no. 3: 268–280. https://doi.org/10.1108/JCM-02-2016-1726.

Zarantonello, Lia, and Bernd H. Schmitt. 2013. "The Impact of Event Marketing on Brand Equity." *International Journal of Advertising* 32, no. 2: 255–280. https://doi.org/10.2501/IJA-32-2-255-280.

PART IX

ENTREPRENEURSHIP AND INTRAPRENEURSHIP IN ARTS AND CULTURAL ORGANIZATIONS

CHAPTER 34

ENTREPRENEURSHIP IN CULTURE

Concepts, Perspectives, Success Factors

ELMAR D. KONRAD AND MARILENA VECCO

Introduction

Private cultural enterprises are measured not only by the quality of their artistic offerings and social impact but also by their economic success. Particularly in view of tight public budgets and the increasing number of start-ups and project initiatives in the cultural sector, interaction of and a synthesis between artistic output and economic efficiency are desirable. Entrepreneurship and culture and not mutually incompatible. This was reinforced all the more by the COVID-19 pandemic from 2020 onward (Harper 2020; Betzler et al. 2021; Khlystova, Kalyuzhnovac, and Beltiski 2022).

In this context, private cultural enterprises are understood as comprising both for-profit and nonprofit organizations. These differ from purely publicly financed cultural institutions in Europe, especially in Germany. Founders and managers of such private cultural enterprises therefore increasingly refer to, and apply, entrepreneurial measures of success to assess their status. In this chapter, the influence of entrepreneurial behavior on success in the private cultural sector is analyzed by using tools of entrepreneurship research (Gehman and Soublière 2017; Klamer 2011). The focus on private cultural enterprises is justified by the increasing importance that such kinds of enterprises are currently assuming in supporting and developing initiatives in the cultural sphere in local, regional respectively rural and urban contexts (Konrad and Höllen 2021; Vecco and Srakar 2020).

By relying on cultural management and entrepreneurship, we extend the entrepreneurial excellence model (EEM; Gemünden, Salomo, and Müller 2005) to the cultural sector, in what we call the cultural entrepreneurship excellence model (CEEM). The present study shows that the presence of entrepreneurial competences and entrepreneurial behavior by the founders and managers of private cultural enterprises are indeed fundamental to success in the cultural sector.

The chapter is structured as follows. The next section reviews the main concepts of cultural management and entrepreneurship relevant to the EEM. The following section introduces the CEEM and presents various hypotheses developed on the basis of the existing literature. Next, the chapter presents an empirical verification of the hypotheses previously developed. The final section provides the conclusions and discusses some implications and limitations of our research.

Conceptual Basics

Aspects of Cultural Management

For a considerable time, management and entrepreneurship research has been intensively focused on the question of what distinguishes successful from unsuccessful business start-ups (Keane and Chen 2019; Spiegel et al. 2016; Konrad 2013). The academic knowledge gained from study of the management of commercial enterprises was partly transferred to the cultural sector, which led to a wealth of specialist literature on subareas of cultural management with a more practical orientation, such as sponsorship, patronage, nonprofit marketing, event marketing, and festivalization. Disciplines such as marketing and financial management had wide application in the arts and cultural sectors. Research on the formation of a cultural management theory has so far been only rudimentary. According to Bendixen (1996), a good theory of cultural management should examine the gap between the traditional profit-oriented and entrepreneurial economy and the traditional cameralistically managed public cultural sector committed to an idealistic concept of culture; it should also treat the social and historical background and, above all, the economic energies that drive events. The insights provided by such a theory should then be passed on to cultural practitioners. Moreover, cultural management is not merely the application of management to culture in the same way that cultural entrepreneurship is not just the application of entrepreneurship to culture; it should also identify and valorize the specificities of culture (Colbert 2003; Evard and Colbert 2000).

In terms of business management, existing cultural management theoretical approaches focus almost exclusively on publicly owned cultural enterprises, even though by far the largest part of the turnover generated is in the private cultural sector. The content-related objectives of privately run cultural institutions are usually different from those of public institutions (Birnkraut 2019), which means that the resulting program decisions have different contours. These privately run organizations, as well as their founders and leaders, need functioning tools of organizational management and marketing suited to them, rather than those more appropriate for public institutions, which are often embedded in a bureaucratic structure. Theories and constructs of cultural management should include tools that can effectively and efficiently address communication, technological, organizational, social, legal, and economic tasks and challenges. Despite various scholars' attempts, no significant studies or results are yet available for the development of a general, robust, cultural management theory.

Aspects of Entrepreneurship

Economic theories often have widely differing views of the role of the entrepreneur and entrepreneurship; this is particularly the case for cultural entrepreneurship (Gartner et al. 1994). To overcome this potential fragmentation of the discipline, Vecco (2020) proposed a model to connect cultural entrepreneurship to entreprencurship more broadly conceived. The underlying principle was to focus on entrepreneurship as a behavior, a mindset, a process, and skills that can be applied in different contexts and environments, with different goals and values. Despite the diversity of approaches, common ground can be found in the definition provided by Bygrave and Hofer (1991, 12), who define an entrepreneur as someone "who perceives an opportunity and creates an organization to pursue it." In addition to simply recognizing opportunities, creating opportunities is an important impetus for entrepreneurs (Suddaby, Bruton, and Si 2015). This approach is applicable to the creation of both for-profit and nonprofit cultural enterprises. It also applies to arts entrepreneurship, in the sense of the realization of an artistic or creative project; art entrepreneurs, like other entrepreneurs, need to build networks, tap resources, and develop strategies. We believe this definition is applicable to almost all cultural entrepreneurs, who see possibilities—opportunities as well as market niches—for concrete cultural work and create a suitable organization, such as an association, with which to realize these opportunities (Kirzner 1997). However, the focus in the remainder of this chapter will be more on the creation and buildup of cultural enterprises comparable to emerging organizations (Katz and Gartner 1988).

The organizational elements in entrepreneurship models can essentially be summarized under the terms *strategy*, *culture* (in the sense of organizational culture), *structure*, and *networks*. For the start-up and establishment phases of enterprises, strategy was found to be a success-promoting influence, particularly when it features a balance of proactive and reactive principles of action. With regard to the (organizational) culture of start-ups, entrepreneurship research favors an open organizational culture that emphasizes growth, risk-taking, and flexibility (Wasserman 2012; Gregoire, Shepherd, and Schurer Lambert 2010). The intensity and quality of the interconnectedness of different tasks and functions are assumed to have a positive influence on the growth and survival of a company.

The literature on entrepreneurship research contains numerous proposals for measuring the success of (young) companies (Vecco and Srakar 2018, 2020). A distinction is frequently made between subjective and objective measures of success. When measuring subjective success, the issue at hand is the achievement of the company's goals (for example, planned sales growth, customer loyalty, or expected cost advantages over competitors). By contrast, objective measures of success are economic variables such as turnover, profit, profitability, employment figures, and growth. The present study takes into account both these objective measures as well as other operationalized measures of success, such as the degree of establishment inside the creative sector or cultural network and level of awareness among the population and in the media.

Entrepreneurial Excellence Model (EEM)

In this section, the core framework of the entrepreneurial excellence model (EEM) is outlined and developed on the basis of the existing literature (Viedma Marti & do Rosário Cabrita 2012; Grichnik, Baierl, and Faschingbauer 2016). Since the cultural and creative sector can be regarded as highly innovative (O'Connor 2000), our development of the model incorporates research findings on entrepreneurial behavior as a significant success factor in another innovative industry, technology-oriented start-ups (Gemünden and Konrad 2000). In a second step, the EEM is expanded to include specific prerequisites for cultural entrepreneurs (Gemünden, Salomo, and Müller 2005). These prerequisites, derived from innovation and entrepreneurship research (Gemünden and Konrad 2000), include competences (particularly social competences), experience (especially cultural sector knowledge), methodological competences (especially management skills), and motivation (in particular, the need for achievement). These elements will be incorporated into the hypotheses we will develop and test.

In the standard framework, processes and structures are understood as frames within which leading individuals in the cultural sector recognize an opportunity to establish a business, create an organization, or shape an existing business or organization (Figure 34.1). Such organizations are not necessarily traditional profit-oriented companies. Many of them are private companies, but their nonprofit legal status excludes profit as an objective. Seen in this light, other criteria of success, such as image and reputation, may be relevant. However, these criteria are also relevant for profit-oriented cultural enterprises. The leaders of these organizations act as cultural entrepreneurs.

Core Model of Cultural Entrepreneurship Excellence

Personal behavior and a specific entrepreneurial attitude are important variables influencing the success of a company. As Slevin and Covin (1995) demonstrate, a pronounced entrepreneurial attitude—comprising initiative and proactivity, market orientation, and a growth-oriented mindset—prevails among successful entrepreneurs (Wales et al. 2021; Mendy 2021; Jiang et al. 2018; Lurtz and Kreutzer 2017). An enterprise-oriented leadership style and risk-taking behavior that emerges from critical thinking and calculation of risk (McMullen and Shepherd 2006) are also key factors in success.

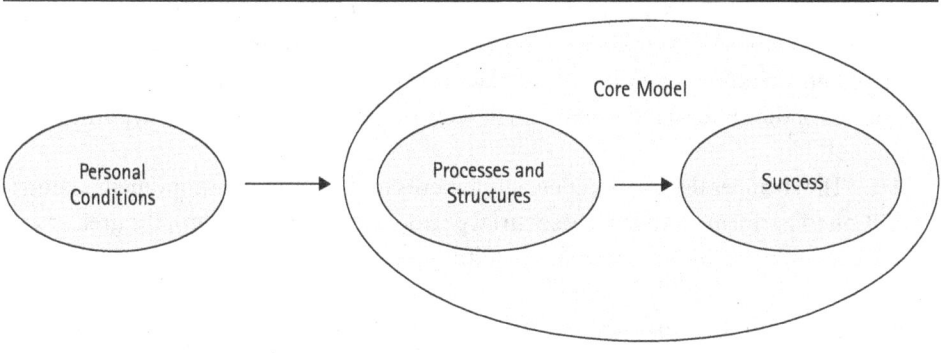

FIGURE 34.1 Standard framework of cultural entrepreneurship excellence.
Source: Created by the authors based on Konrad 2010, 100–101.

Private cultural enterprises, whether for-profit or nonprofit, are usually very small organizations. The leaders are often also the founders and owners of the organization. In such small structures, the transition from entrepreneurial decisions to management activities is fluid, and oftentimes the two can hardly be separated. In cultural enterprises, a major factor in direct economic success is the personal strategic actions of the cultural entrepreneur. For example, cultural entrepreneurs act and make decisions faster and more innovatively than managers in the publicly funded cultural sector (Höllen, Lengfeld, and Konrad 2020). Another direct pathway from a cultural entrepreneur's entrepreneurial performance to corporate success is associated with how management tasks are carried out (Konrad 2010). Cultural entrepreneurs are confronted with a variety of different tasks and duties within their business, which may be sporadic or permanent, procedural or behavioral, and entrepreneurs must be flexible, effective, and efficient. These characteristics also rely on the cultural entrepreneur's access to and efficient utilization of resources.

A central factor in the cultural entrepreneurship excellence model (CEEM) is the entrepreneurial performance of the cultural entrepreneur or the leader of a private cultural organization. This performance consists of several entrepreneurial elements: (1) relationship management, (2) design and management of networks, (3) functional-operational tasks, and (4) procedures for entrepreneurial-strategic decision-making (Konrad 2013; Santos, Marques, and Ferreira 2020).[1]

Network-specific and relationship-specific activities and actions, particularly those directed toward identifying and solving problems, are outstanding contributors to operational success. By appropriately initiating and maintaining personal relationships with opinion leaders and decision-makers in the cultural field, a cultural entrepreneur can obtain important information that permits the entrepreneur to handle problems and tasks more quickly and effectively. In addition, building a network of relationships with potent partners can help the entrepreneur overcome serious barriers by tapping into necessary resources and gaining support. Intensive exercise of relationship-specific functions in the cultural sector, which can be seen as strategic cooperation and interaction within a network of actors, increases the efficiency of resource exploitation.

These considerations regarding the relationship of entrepreneurial performance to the success of the cultural enterprise can be summarized in the following hypothesis:

> H1: The stronger the entrepreneurial elements in the cultural entrepreneur's contribution to performance (entrepreneurial performance contribution), the greater and more sustainable the success of their cultural enterprise.

In addition to the process construct of entrepreneurial performance, which is shaped by the behavior and activities of the entrepreneur, structure-related constructs, such as the quality of the relationship portfolio and the characteristics of the internal organizational culture, have an influence on success. These structure-related factors are also directly influenced by the cultural entrepreneur. In the CCEM, therefore, a relationship portfolio includes contacts and connections with organizations and third parties that have resources relevant to cultural entrepreneurs, such as financial resources, information, power, and further contacts (Konrad and Vecco 2020). A cultural entrepreneur in possession of a comprehensive, balanced relationship portfolio can efficiently seek out, bring together, and influence important actors across organizational boundaries in ways that benefit the entrepreneur's projects and activities (Vecco and Konrad 2018; Hausmann and Heinze 2016; Walter 1999). Good personal relationships help a cultural entrepreneur to move in the desired direction and to gain support (Konrad 2013). The quality of a relationship portfolio is essentially based on the type and cultivation of the resources of the respective partners, as well as the character of the personal relationships with these actors.[2] Operating in a web of social relationships, these actors can control resources relevant to themselves and to their direct and indirect network partners. This means that they may have access to important resources themselves, are able to open up those resources to others, or may block others from accessing those resources. Such resources—including public funding, financial sponsorships, and audience growth through media reports, recommendations by influencers and statements by public opinion leaders—have a direct effect not only on a cultural enterprise's economic success but also on its level of awareness and degree of establishment. For this reason, the second hypothesis regarding success can be formulated as follows:

> H2: As the quality of the cultural entrepreneur's relationship portfolio increases, so does the success of their enterprise.

In addition to these structural influences, the characteristics and performance of the cultural enterprise as a whole must of course also be taken into account. One yardstick for this is the typology of the enterprise's organizational culture, with an entrepreneurial, innovative, and market-oriented organizational culture tending to promote success.

Privately owned cultural enterprises are typically small to very small organizations (Thorsby 2008), and so management—that is, the cultural entrepreneur—has an outsized influence on organizational culture, both directly and indirectly (Konrad 2013; Kuratko et al. 1993). Because most tasks within the enterprise must be carried out by a small group of people, fostering entrepreneurial thinking leads to more effective performance of those tasks and the ability to recognize market potential in the cultural sector.[3] Entrepreneurial thinking, whether across levels or within a group of equals, is more likely if employees have decision-making powers and are willing to take risks.

Such an orientation toward innovation, recognizing and taking advantage of market opportunities, entrepreneurship, and risk-taking, coupled with the will to perform and succeed (assessed in terms of measurable goals), increases the social skills of staff by fostering an environment in which information is shared constantly, spontaneously, intentionally, and comprehensively. Further development and goal achievement are central elements of an entrepreneurial, market-oriented organizational culture.[4] Therefore:

> H3: The more entrepreneurial and market-oriented the organizational culture (entrepreneurial corporate culture), the greater the success of the cultural enterprise.

In order to have a balanced, well-developed relationship portfolio that can assist in the achievement of these strategic considerations, it is important for the cultural entrepreneur to initiate and cultivate personal relationships and to engage in network-shaping activities. Walter's (1999) and Konrad's (2013) findings on relationship promoters highlight the influence of these activities on the relationship portfolio. The process-oriented approaches of the various promoter models allow us to recognize the effect of entrepreneurial performance contribution on the quality of the relationship portfolio.

Beyond purely relationship- and network-specific activities, organizational and functional duties and tasks also have an influence on the quality of the relationship portfolio. Thus:

> H4: The stronger the entrepreneurial elements in the cultural entrepreneur's contribution (entrepreneurial performance contribution), the better the quality of their relationship portfolio.

As already mentioned, private cultural enterprises are usually very small and thus very strongly shaped by the cultural entrepreneurs themselves. Whether the enterprise involves creating a new business, making a new entry into an existing market, or moving into a new market, it can be assumed that the cultural entrepreneur's performance contribution has a direct influence on organizational culture—the strategic content and form of the entrepreneur's actions help to anchor the entrepreneurial, market-oriented organizational culture in the employees, and thus promote dynamic-entrepreneurial as well as competitive and performance-oriented behavior. The entrepreneur's performance contribution also helps to set the innovation and

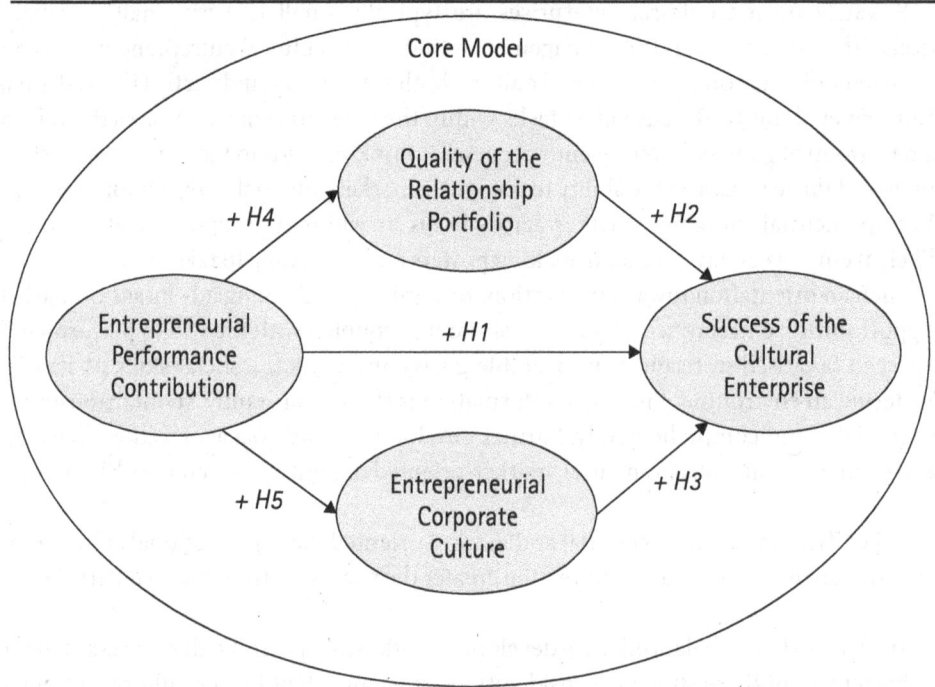

FIGURE 34.2 Standard hypotheses on cultural entrepreneurship excellence (core model).
Source: Created by the authors based on Konrad 2010, 125.

risk levels of market orientation strategies. Thus, the final impact hypothesis can be formulated as follows:

H5: As the entrepreneurial contribution of the cultural entrepreneur increases (entrepreneurial performance contribution), so does the entrepreneurial-market-oriented organizational culture of their cultural enterprise (entrepreneurial corporate culture).

Figure 34.2 summarizes the cultural entrepreneurship excellence model, including the core hypotheses and effects on success. The construct of the entrepreneurial performance contribution is seen as a process-oriented variable, and the constructs of the relationship portfolio and the organizational culture are structure-oriented variables.

Extended Cultural Entrepreneurship Excellence Model

The core model presented previously is expanded in the following sections to include four explanatory variables: social competence, cultural knowledge, business knowledge, and entrepreneurial motivation. It can be assumed for all variables that they positively influence the entrepreneurial activities of the individual in question (Gemünden and Konrad 2000). Motivations are relatively stable drivers of human behavior. And the establishment of good personal relationships with partners relevant to cultural enterprises depends on social skills such as communication, sociability, empathy, coordination, and flexibility, which help cultural entrepreneurs to deal appropriately and effectively with partners (Konrad 2017; Goleman 2000; Walter 1999).[5]

Social Competence

Since it can be very difficult to fully grasp the complexity of a situation, possible courses of action, related consequences, and their probabilities, cultural entrepreneurs frequently resort to standardized rules of conduct and everyday knowledge in order to reduce complexity. But entrepreneurs must therefore be very attentive to their environment; keeping an ear open to the ideas and wishes of their partners in the cultural sector is of major importance, allowing them to react quickly and effectively to any emerging changes. Various elements of social competence (Timmons and Spinelli 2004), such as empathy, sociability, and the ability to coordinate, are crucial prerequisites for shaping the relationship portfolio as well as for acting within the personal network. Within the organization, the presence of strong social competences is also vital, so that when it comes to functional tasks and duties the concerns of staff, partners, and clients can be identified and responded to positively. The above connections are summarized in the following hypothesis:

> H6: The more pronounced the social competences of the cultural entrepreneur, the more positive the effect on the entrepreneurial performance contribution of the cultural entrepreneur.

Cultural Knowledge

Cultural knowledge can be regarded as a part of human capital. Thus, cultural knowledge can be interpreted as a manifestation of industry-specific experience and professional competences or knowledge.[6] Industry-related experience is particularly relevant to start-ups, as it helps with information procurement and strategic planning. This specific knowledge, whether acquired theoretically or through practical experience, reduces the barriers to accessing a market and increases the probability that a newly founded company will survive. Knowledge of the cultural sphere allows the cultural entrepreneur to orient themselves within the cultural sphere and identify important individuals, both of which have a direct, positive effect on their relationship-specific performance contribution.

Similarly, people who have a high level of knowledge of culture and the general cultural scene, as well as professional competence in cultural practice, are attractive partners for other actors in the cultural sector and thus more likely to be sought out. This makes it easier to initiate and maintain relationships with important people in the cultural sector, which then has a direct, positive impact on the subconstructs of maintaining and shaping personal relationships and networks. Furthermore, cultural knowledge creates a certain security in strategic decision-making processes, and thus favors proactive and risky actions—in other words, cultural knowledge promotes an orientation toward entrepreneurial action.

From the previous arguments, the influence of cultural knowledge can thus be summarized in the following hypothesis:

> H7: The higher the cultural knowledge (expertise) of the cultural entrepreneur, the more positive the effect on their entrepreneurial performance contribution.

Business Knowledge

The presence of organizational skills and competences in leadership-oriented tasks must be considered as prerequisites for effective and efficient network management; by helping the enterprise avoid mistakes and execute tasks more efficiently and effectively, they have a direct effect on the cultural entrepreneur's network-specific performance contributions. Knowledge of marketing policy, experience in public relations, and knowledge of relevant legal and financial aspects facilitate the recognition of problems, and thus facilitate problem-solving (Konrad and Höllen 2021). We can assume that someone who has a high level of professional competences and experience, as well as realistic ideas of personal and entrepreneurial goals, can afford to concentrate on the essential strategic planning and market concepts, and thereby also optimize the activities and performance of the enterprise. And the personal objectives of entrepreneurs are strongly related to the knowledge of how to achieve their goals. For example, the personal goal of presenting an innovative product within the cultural sector gives rise to a strategy for developing and facilitating a good cultural program. Taken together, all these elements of business knowledge offer the entrepreneur a sound base from which to make strategic decisions, and so favor proactive and risky actions. In other words, business knowledge, like cultural knowledge, promotes the orientation of entrepreneurial action.[7]

In summary, these arguments regarding the interdependencies of business knowledge and the entrepreneur's contribution of entrepreneurial performance lead to the following hypothesis:

> H8: The greater the cultural entrepreneur's business knowledge and management know-how, the more positive the effect will be of their entrepreneurial performance contribution.

Motivation

In entrepreneurship research, the explanatory construct of motivation is not necessarily sufficient to establish a direct link to the success of an enterprise. Rather, the concept of motivation is a way to account for why someone does something, and possibly to account for how intensively, persistently, or frequently they do it. Motivation therefore serves as a partial explanatory construct for activities and modes of action. In the literature, two motives in particular have emerged to explain entrepreneurial behavior, action patterns, and performance contributions: performance motivation and feasibility thinking.

An essential prerequisite to entrepreneurial action is the will to perform. This achievement motivation is based on the work of McClelland (1966) and has been empirically tested by several scholars (among others, Smith and Karaman 2019). It can be described as striving for efficient performance. Highly motivated people prefer goals that are high but achievable, and they avoid ones that are unrealistically high. Thus, the achievement of realistically high goals is largely dependent on commitment, risk awareness, and a sense of one's own efficiency (process-oriented activity variables); it is less dependent on external circumstances. Money is not a motivation for action, but rather a measure of one's own performance in terms of performance contribution. Furthermore, the desire for autonomy, self-realization, and self-sufficiency—in other words, the desire to take responsibility for oneself—is a vital motive in the decision to become self-employed or to act entrepreneurially. Since the construct of the cultural entrepreneur's entrepreneurial contribution is composed of entrepreneurial activities, tasks, and orientation of actions, we can establish a direct, positive impact of these entrepreneurial motives. We can now expect that classical entrepreneurial motives such as achievement motivation, striving for autonomy or self-realization, willingness to take risks and striving for power are also important prerequisites for the specific activities of a cultural entrepreneur. Making decisions and acting under uncertain conditions and under the pressure of a highly competitive environment require a certain willingness to take risks (Antoncic et al. 2018).

In conclusion, these arguments regarding the interdependencies of entrepreneurial motivation and the cultural entrepreneur's entrepreneurial performance contribution can be presented in the following final hypothesis:[8]

H9: The more pronounced the entrepreneurial motivation of the cultural entrepreneur, the more positive the effect it has on their entrepreneurial performance contribution.

The overall hypotheses of the extended model are once again graphically presented in Figure 34.3.

Empirical Verification

In order to empirically confirm the CEEM, we draw on a large-scale study of cultural entrepreneurship from Germany. This study began in the early 2000s and was completed in 2009 with wave-like follow-up and control surveys (Konrad 2010). Since the focus was on private cultural enterprises nationwide, both nonprofit and for-profit, this study can be considered representative of the European cultural sector. For the present chapter, we will mainly refer to the first wave of the survey.

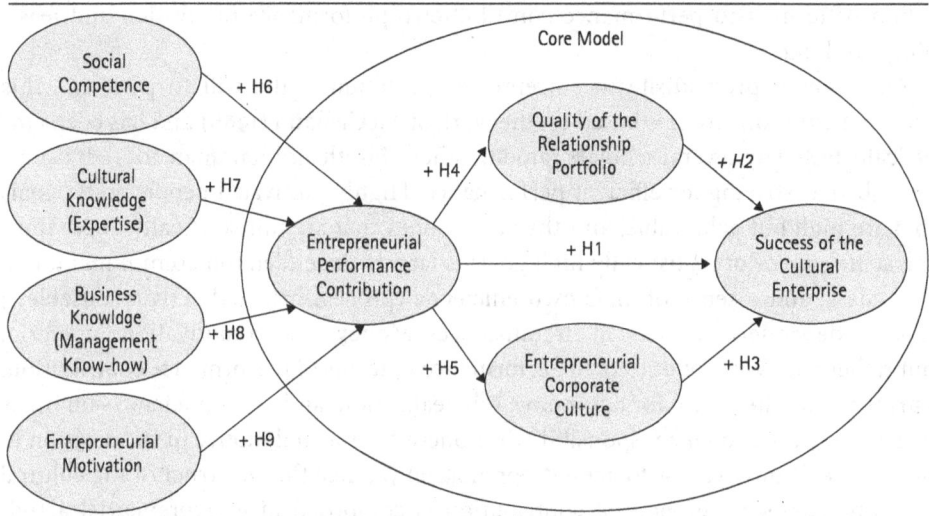

FIGURE 34.3 All hypotheses for the CEEM (extended model).

Source: Created by the authors based on Konrad 2010, 132.

Data Collection and Sample

To gain a better understanding of cultural entrepreneurship excellence and the personality of the cultural entrepreneur, a qualitative preliminary study was conducted. Intensive interviews in the form of guided discussions were conducted with nine managers and directors of selected German cultural enterprises, as well as with four senior editors of regional cultural magazines, in seven different cities in Germany during the first six months of 2000. In one important result of this preliminary investigation, we found that the characteristics of the relevant determinants of success varied considerably between the cultural enterprises. We also were able to determine that the managers of such private cultural enterprises were suitable key informants.

A total of 167 successful face-to-face interviews were conducted on-site at private cultural enterprises throughout Germany, using a highly standardized interview guide. Three companies from France were also included in the sample. About 80 percent of the companies in the sample were located in urban areas; the rest were in rural areas. Of the 167 cultural enterprises, 76 had a profit-oriented legal form and 91 of them had a nonprofit-oriented legal form. Of all the respondents, 52.7 percent described themselves as founders and another 34.7 percent as sole directors from the beginning of the venture. The remainder of the respondents work on a management team or were chairpersons of a cultural association. The vast majority of the organizations in the sample had eight to ten employees. The mean age of the cultural enterprises was ten years; about 25 percent had been founded around three years prior to the time of the survey. It is also interesting to note that about 80 percent of the respondents were male.

In addition to the main investigation with the founders and managers of the cultural enterprises, brief interview guidelines were developed for external experts, so as to be able to include an independent assessment of the success of the cultural enterprises. In addition to purely economic success data such as profitability and sales growth, factors such as image, degree of establishment, and name recognition were also taken into account. To ensure a valid assessment, the enterprises would be evaluated in terms of these success measures by external respondents, not by the cultural enterprises themselves. Senior representatives of local cultural administrations and authoritative media representatives from feature pages and cultural departments were selected by telephone to serve as external experts on the degree of establishment of the cultural institutions. The respondents assessed the success of the cultural enterprises on a seven-point Likert scale. A total of eighty-one representatives from the cultural administrations and eighty-six media representatives were successfully interviewed in the period 2000–2001. Thus, it was possible to assess the success of each cultural enterprise especially in terms of its degree of establishment by consulting at least one external expert representative.[9]

Testing the Hypotheses

We find it logical to adopt an external validation of the degree of establishment as a separate measure of success, since such an evaluation cannot be verified by objective, concrete facts; a self-assessment by the cultural entrepreneur themselves might well be distorted by wishful thinking or a lack of objective distance. The external media representatives or representatives of cultural administrations were interviewed by telephone after the main investigation had been completed. The economic measures of success were not taken into account here, as the preliminary study had established that the external experts usually had no insight in this regard.

A series of multiple regression analyses were conducted to test the CEEM. The regression findings confirmed all the identified relationships. The entrepreneurial performance contribution has a highly significant effect on the success of the cultural enterprise ($.287; p < .001$), the quality of the relationship portfolio ($.641; p <. 001$), and the entrepreneurial, market-oriented organizational culture ($.683; p < .001$). Overall, 37.4 percent of the variance in the cultural entrepreneur's success, 40.8 percent of the variance in the quality of the cultural entrepreneur's personal relationship portfolio, and 46.3 percent of the variance in the entrepreneurial market-oriented organizational culture are explained. Figure 34.4 summarizes the regression coefficients and the corrected coefficients of determination of all the final and intermediate constructs of the cultural entrepreneurship model. In this study, the self-assessment of success by the cultural entrepreneur can be considered representative, as shown by the relatively high agreement between self-assessment of the degree of establishment and the external assessments.

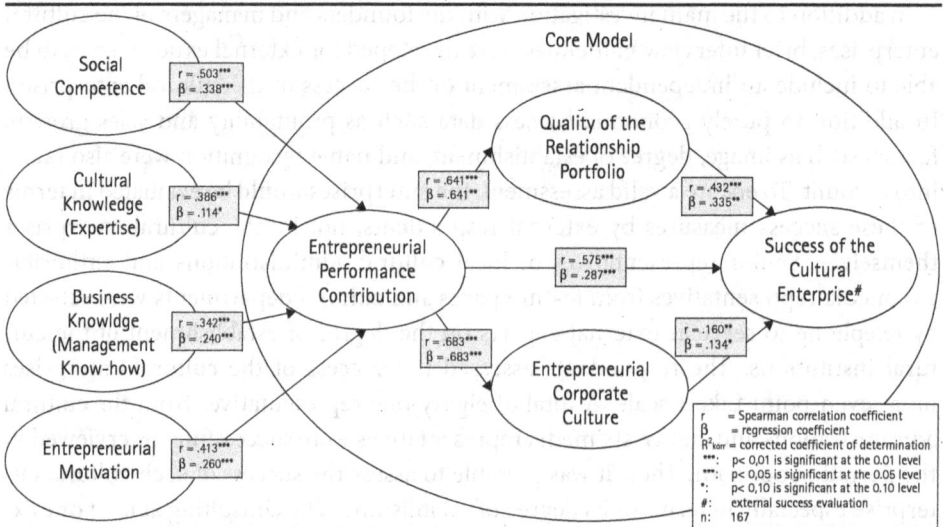

FIGURE 34.4 Results for the CEEM (extended model).

Source: Created by the authors based on Konrad 2010, 163.

Concluding Remarks

Summary of Findings

The main goal of this chapter was to show how entrepreneurship can explain and even promote the success of private cultural enterprises. Private cultural enterprises are usually very small organizations, which means that the entrepreneurial and strategic activities of their leaders and managers, who are usually also the founders and owners, have a direct impact. With the development of the cultural entrepreneurship excellence model, these effects on success can be put on a theoretical level and empirically tested. This chapter aims to contribute to the further development of a cultural management theory by establishing the significance of entrepreneurship within private cultural enterprises, using the instruments of entrepreneurship research.

In brief, the conclusion to be drawn is that entrepreneurial action and behavior, by founders and owners as well as managers and directors of cultural enterprises, represent important prerequisites for economic success. In addition to the purely economic effects, this type of entrepreneurship has a strong influence on these companies' degree of establishment and level of awareness. More specifically, we note the following findings.

Leaders and founders of cultural enterprises operate in a network of relationships. Successful cultural entrepreneurs seek out and maintain these relationships, thus forming a personal portfolio of relationships. The relationships of individual actors to each other within this portfolio can influence further relationships of other actors. But they are also influenced by the cultural entrepreneurs themselves through system-oriented and relationship-specific actions and activities. This network-specific behavior represents an important part of the entrepreneurial performance contribution. On the one hand, determinants of successful cultural entrepreneurs coming from outside can be compensated for by appropriate entrepreneurial measures and networking if these influences have a negative impact on the results of the cultural enterprise. On the other hand, these can also be promoted and used and thus strengthened if they have positive effects. These network- and relationship-oriented activities within the entrepreneurial performance contribution offer important advantages to cultural entrepreneurs.

The quality of the cultural entrepreneur's relationship portfolio has a very positive influence on success. Because cultural enterprises are usually small, the personality of the cultural entrepreneur is the linchpin of the relationship network. Moreover, the indirect influence of the cultural entrepreneur's performance contribution to success is enhanced by his or her network- and relationship-specific actions and activities. Therefore, cultural entrepreneurs should build and maintain strong relationships with relevant people in the cultural sector.

Because most private cultural enterprises are small, the cultural entrepreneur's performance contribution has a strong influence on the form and reach of the organizational culture. One can certainly speak meaningfully of the organizational culture as an extended arm of the cultural entrepreneur within their company. Entrepreneurial decisions and the way they are implemented in terms of strategy, personnel matters, programming, and management are very important elements of the performance contribution. An organizational culture oriented toward entrepreneurship, innovation, and marketing has a strong positive effect on the success of the cultural enterprise. Because of this indirect effect, the cultural entrepreneur's entrepreneurial contribution to the organization's success has an even higher value.

In the private cultural sector in particular, it is evident that the motives, knowledge, and experience of cultural entrepreneurs have a strong influence on their activities and entrepreneurial decisions, as is the case with innovation-oriented start-ups in other industries. These factors have the same or similar effects in both for-profit and nonprofit private cultural enterprises.

Implications and Limitations

Of course, the CEEM presented in this chapter also has some weaknesses. It can be assumed that the model represents a very basic and also quite comprehensive framework that explains and allows us to measure the success of cultural enterprises in relation to the characteristics and behavior of cultural entrepreneurs. However, the difficulty is how one determines what "success" means in the cultural sector. Particularly in the case of private nonprofit cultural organizations, classic economic measures of success such as profit and growth are rarely applicable. Image, reputation, level of awareness, and degree of establishment are usually much more important measures of success, but evaluating them is difficult. Evaluation by external experts and those familiar with an organization's local or regional cultural scene should help circumvent this dilemma. However, this can also be viewed critically, since in the end, despite standardized Likert-scale-based questions, they are subjective assessments. A comprehensive, generally valid measurement of success in the cultural sector is and remains a challenge.

Finally, another limitation is that the model has a very Central European, especially German, perspective. It would be interesting to see whether the model could also be applied to an Anglo-American or Asian context and lead to similar results.

In principle, however, we are convinced that the CEEM can map basic impacts quite well and can also be expanded or varied to study other areas of the cultural and creative sector. For example, many artists and creative professionals are self-employed—that is, artistic entrepreneurs (Vakharia 2016). For them, many factors of successful artistic and professional work are the same or similar to those of private cultural enterprises. Another field would be publicly funded cultural institutions. So far, entrepreneurship research has not dealt with this issue in detail. Sometimes the research refers to certain branches, like theaters or museums, or uses entrepreneurship aspects as an approach to or underpinning for marketing concepts or innovation drivers in such cultural institutions (Fillis and Lehman 2021). However, cultural management research and research on the arts is increasingly beginning to deal with entrepreneurial aspects in these sectors (Callander and Cummings 2021). Therefore, it would be worth considering whether the CEEM could be varied to apply to this context, specifically management personnel such as museum, theater, and opera directors.

Furthermore, the cultural entrepreneurship excellence model can provide a good basis for funding guidelines, assessment of personal success, strategic planning decisions, teaching, and educational programs relevant to the cultural sector, and even for the further development of a new approach to cultural management. The development of such a new approach to cultural management should make it clear that without artists and cultural workers operating as cultural entrepreneurs, there is no need for the profession of arts manager. After all, first come the cultural entrepreneurs, who build something creative or artistic; then come the arts managers, who operationally and strategically manage what has already been created (Konrad 2006).

The present findings can help founders of cultural organizations and aspiring cultural entrepreneurs to do business successfully. Likewise, public authorities can provide recommendations for effective support and advice for promising entrepreneurial activities. If satisfactory answers can be found to the question of what factors promote success in the cultural sector, public funds can be used in a much more targeted way to promote start-ups and cultural entrepreneurial activities. Similarly, specific tools can be created or adapted to promote, advise, and develop economically and culturally interesting cultural businesses. This will improve their position in their locale and allow them to hold their own in the market. Diverse and attractive cultural offerings sustainably improve an area's quality of life.

Notes

1. The entrepreneurial performance contribution consists of four subconstructs. The subconstruct "relationship management activities" consists of five items as factor loadings. "Design and management of networks" also consists of five items, as does "functional-operational tasks." The fourth subconstruct, "procedures for entrepreneurial-strategic decision-making," is based on three items. A lower limit of .50 was set as a minimum requirement for the factor loadings of an indicator. High factor loadings of the individual indicators as well as a high variance of all indicators explained by the extracted factor form a measure of the internal consistency of the item group. A minimum value of 50 percent was set as the lower limit for the variance explained by the factor for the present investigation. All further analyses of this study are based on the extracted factor values. For a detailed description of all items, see Konrad 2010, 148–150.
2. The construct quality of the relationship portfolio was determined based on the quality of relationships (assessed on a seven-point Likert scale) with the following groups: (1) representatives and decision-makers in cultural policy, (2) representatives of the media, (3) people in business, (4) important people in cultural life, and (5) other opinion leaders. For a detailed description of all items, see Konrad 2010, 151–152.
3. In the present case, the focus is primarily how the cultural entrepreneurs influence the acting team in terms of organizational structure and culture. In very small cultural enterprises, team-based work is always present. A dedicated examination of teamwork quality and teamwork performance was not undertaken.
4. The construct of organizational culture is based on Cameron and Freeman's (1991) characterization of the four types of organizational culture. According to Minzberg (1991), the adhocracy culture and the market culture in particular are crucial for an entrepreneurial and market-oriented organizational culture. Therefore, two factors with four items each were included in the assessment. For a description of all items, see Konrad 2010, 154.
5. The social competence construct consists of three factors: empathy (five items), sociability (five items), and coordination skills (six items). For a description of all items, see Konrad 2010, 151.
6. The cultural knowledge construct consists of knowledge and experience in the cultural sector, knowledge regarding cultural policy and administration, and knowledge of media and public relations in the cultural sector. For a description of all items, see Konrad 2010, 151–152.
7. The business knowledge (or management know-how) construct consists of items that measure knowledge and understanding of financing issues, legal issues, accounting, marketing, human resources, and business skills. For a description of all items, see Konrad 2010, 152.
8. The entrepreneurial motivation construct takes as its basis the six motive bundles described by McClelland (1965, 1966). For a description of all items, see Konrad 2010, 152–153.
9. The external performance measurement construct—assessed once from the perspective of representatives of cultural policy and once from the perspective of media representatives—consists of seven items. For a description of all items, see Konrad 2010, 158.

References

Antoncic, Jjasna, Bostjian Antoncic, Matjaz Gantar, Robert D. Hisrich, Lawrence J. Marks, Alexandre A. Bachkirov, Zhaoyang Li, Pierre Polzin, Jose L. Borges, Antonio Coelho, and

Marja-Liisa Kakkonen. 2018. "Risk-Taking Propensity and Entrepreneurship: The Role of Power Distance." *Journal of Enterprising Culture* 26: 1–26.

Bendixen, Peter. 1996. "Kultur management theories." In *Kulturmanagement in Europa*, edited by M. Fischer, H. Rauhe, and J. W. Wiesand, 50–61. Bonn: ARCult Media.

Betzler, Diana, Ellen Loots, Marek Prokůpek, Lenia Marques, and Petja Grafenauer. 2021. "COVID-19 and the Arts and Cultural Sectors: Investigating Countries' Contextual Factors and Early Policy Measures." *International Journal of Cultural Policy* 27, no. 6: 796–814.

Birnkraut, Gesa. 2019. "Empfehlungen an Kulturinstitutionen und Kulturpolitik." In *Evaluation im Kulturbetrieb. Kunst- und Kulturmanagement*, 109–113. Wiesbaden: Springer.

Bygrave, William D., and Charles W. Hofer. 1991. "Theorizing About Entrepreneurship." *Entrepreneurship Theory and Practice* 16, no. 4: 13–22.

Callander, Adrienne, and Michael E. Cummings. 2021. "Liminal Spaces: A Review of the Art in Entrepreneurship and the Entrepreneurship in Art." *Small Business Economics* 57: 739–754.

Cameron, Kim S., and Sarah Freeman. 1991. "Cultural Congruence, Strength and Type: Relationships to Effectiveness." In *Research in Organizational Change and Development*, vol. 5, edited by Richard W. Woodman and William A. Pasmore, 23–58. Greenwich, CT: JAI Press.

Colbert, François. 2003. "Entrepreneurship and Leadership in Marketing the Arts." *International Journal of Arts Management* 6, no. 1: 30–39.

Evard, Yves, and François Colbert. 2000. "Arts Management: A New Discipline Entering the Millennium?" *International Journal of Arts Management* 2, no. 2: 4–13.

Fillis, Ian, and Kim Lehman. 2021. "Art Collecting as Consumption and Entrepreneurial Marketing as Strategy." *Arts and Market* 11, no. 3: 171–185.

Gartner, William B., Kelly G. Shaver, Elizabeth Gatewood, and Jerome A. Katz. 1994. "Finding the Entrepreneur in Entrepreneurship." *Entrepreneurship Theory and Practice* 18, no. 3: 5–9.

Gehman, Joel, and Jean-François Soublière. 2017. "Cultural Entrepreneurship: From Making Culture to Cultural Making." *Innovation: Organization and Management* 19: 61–73.

Gemünden, H. G., and E. D. Konrad. 2000. "Unternehmerisches Verhalten als bedeutender Erfolgsfaktor von technologieorientierten Unternehmensgründungen." *Die Unternehmung. Schweizerische Zeitschrift für betriebswirtschaftliche Forschung und Praxis* 54, no. 4: 247–272.

Gemünden, Hans G., Søren Salomo, and Thilo Müller. 2005. *Entrepreneurial Excellence*. Wiesbaden: Springer.

Goleman, Daniel. 2000. "Emotional Intelligence: Issues in Paradigm Building." In *The Emotionally Intelligent Workplace: How to Select for, Measure, and Improve Emotional Intelligence in Individuals, Groups, and Organizations*, edited by Daniel Goleman and Cary Cherniss, 1–13. San Francisco: Jossey-Bass.

Gregoire, Denis A., Dean A. Shepherd, and Lisa Schurer Lambert. 2010. "Measuring Opportunity-Recognition Beliefs: Illustrating and Validating an Experimental Approach." *Organizational Research Methods* 13, no. 1: 114–145.

Grichnik, Dietmar, Ronny Baierl, and Michael Faschingbauer. 2016. "Effectuation: Control the Future with the Entrepreneurial Method." In *Design Thinking for Innovation*, edited by W. Brenner and F. Uebernickel, 115–129. Cham: Springer.

Harper, Graeme. 2020. "Creative Industries Beyond COVID-19." *Creative Industries Journal* 13, no. 2: 93–94.

Hausmann, Andrea, and Anne Heinze. 2016. "Entrepreneurship in the Cultural and Creative Industries: Insights from an Emergent Field." *Artivate: A Journal of Entrepreneurship in the Arts* 5: 7–22.

Höllen, Max, Christian Lengfeld, and Elmar D. Konrad. 2020. "Business Success for Creative and Cultural Entrepreneurs: Influences of Individual- and Firm-Related Factors on Revenue and Satisfaction." *International Journal for Arts Management* 22, no. 2: 52–65.

Jiang, Xu, Heng Liu, Carl F. Fey, and Feifel Jiang. 2018. "Entrepreneurial Orientation, Network Resource Acquisition, and Firm Performance: A Network Approach." *Journal of Business Research* 87: 46–57.

Katz, Jerome A., and William Gartner. 1988. "Properties of Emerging Organizations." *Academy of Management Review* 13, no. 3: 429–441.

Keane, Michael, and Ying Chen. 2019. "Entrepreneurial Solutionism, Characteristic Cultural Industries and the Chinese Dream." *International Journal of Cultural Policy* 25, no. 6: 743–755.

Khlystova, Olena, Yelena Kalyuzhnovac, and Maksim Belitski. 2022. "The Impact of the COVID-19 Pandemic on the Creative Industries: A Literature Review and Future Research Agenda." *Journal of Business Research* 139: 1192–1210.

Kirzner, Israel M. 1997. *How Markets Work: Disequilibrium, Entrepreneurship and Discovery*. London: Institute of Economic Affairs.

Klamer, Arjo. 2011. "Cultural Entrepreneurship." *Review of Austrian Economics* 24, no. 2: 141–156.

Konrad, Elmar D. 2006. "Erst kommt der Kultur-Unternehmer dann der Kultur-Manager – Betrachtung am Beispiel privater Kulturveranstaltungsbetriebe." In *Unternehmertum und Führungsverhalten im Kulturbereich*, edited by Elmar D. Konrad, 22–50. Münster: Waxmann.

Konrad, Elmar D. 2010. *Kulturmanagement und Unternehmertum*. Stuttgart: Kohlhammer.

Konrad, Elmar D. 2013. "Cultural Entrepreneurship: The Impact of Social Networking on Success." *Creativity and Innovation Management* 39: 307–319.

Konrad, Elmar D. 2017. "How Affects Cultural Entrepreneurship the Financing Structures in Creative Industries: A Survey About Start-ups and Young Growing Firms in Germany." In *Entrepreneurship Issues in Creative Industries—Corporate and Spatial Perspectives*, edited by Elisa Innerhofer, Harald Pechlaner, and Elena Borin, 25–44. Wiesbaden: Springer.

Konrad, Elmar D., and Max Höllen. 2021. "The Regional Context in Entrepreneurial Finance of Cultural Business: Urban Versus Rural Space for Creative and Cultural Entrepreneurship." In *The Metamorphosis of Cultural and Creative Organizations: Exploring Change from a Spatial Perspective*, edited by Federica De Molli and Marilena Vecco, 155–176. London: Routledge.

Konrad, Elmar D., and Marilena Vecco. 2020. "Anatomy of Cultural and Creative Entrepreneurship: Past, Present and Future." *International Journal of Entrepreneurship and Small Business* 40, no. 2: 147–153.

Kuratko, Donald F., Jeffrey S. Hornsby, Douglas W. Naffziger, and Ray V. Montagno. 1993. "Implementing Entrepreneurial Thinking in Established Organizations." *S.A.M. Advanced Management Journal* 58, no. 1: 28–33.

Lurtz, Kathrin, and Karin Kreutzer. 2017. "Entrepreneurial Orientation and Social Venture Creation in Nonprofit Organizations: The Pivotal Role of Social Risk Taking and Collaboration." *Nonprofit and Voluntary Sector Quarterly* 46, no. 1: 92–115.

McClelland, David C. 1965. "Achievement and Entrepreneurship: A Longitudinal Study." *Journal of Personality and Social Psychology* 1, no. 4: 389–392.

McClelland, David C. 1966. "Does Education Accelerate Economic Growth?" *Economic Development and Cultural Change* 14, no. 3: 257–278.

McMullen, Jeffrey S., and Dean A. Shepherd. 2006. "Entrepreneurial Action and the Role of Uncertainty in the Theory of Entrepreneur." *Academy of Management Review* 31, no. 1: 132–152.

Mendy, John. 2021. "Performance Management Problem of Four Small and Medium-Sized Enterprises (SMEs): Towards a Performance Resolution." *Journal of Small Business and Enterprise Development* 28, no. 5: 1–13.

Mintzberg, Henry. 1991. *The Effective Organization: Forces and Formes. Sloan Management Review* 32, no. 2: 54–67.

O'Connor, Justin. 2000. "The Definition of the 'Cultural Industries.'" *European Journal of Arts Education* 2, no. 3: 15–27.

Santos, Gina, Carla S. Marques, and João J. M. Ferreira. 2020. "Passion and Perseverance as Two New Dimensions of an Individual Entrepreneurial Orientation Scale." *Journal of Business Research* 112, no. 3: 190–199.

Slevin, Dennis P., and Jeffrey G. Covin. 1995. "Entrepreneurship as Firm Behavior: A Research Model." *Advances in Entrepreneurship, Firm Emergence and Growth* 2, no. 18: 175–224.

Smith, Robert L., and Mehmet A. Karaman. 2019. "Development and Validation of the Contextual Achievement Motivation Measure." *International Journal of Psychology and Educational Studies* 6, no. 3: 16–26.

Spiegel, Olav, Puja Abbassi, Matthäus P. Zylka, Daniel Schlagwein, Kai Fischbach, and Detlef Schoder. 2016. "Business Model Development, Founders' Social Capital and the Success of Early Stage Internet Start-ups: A Mixed-Method Study." *Information Systems Journal* 26, no. 5: 421–449.

Suddaby, Roy, Garry D. Bruton, and Steven X. Si. 2015. "Entrepreneurship Through a Qualitative Lens: Insights on the Construction and/or Discovery of Entrepreneurial Opportunity." *Journal of Business Venturing* 30, no. 1: 1–10.

Thorsby, David. 2008. "Modelling the cultural industries." *International Journal of Cultural Policy* 14, no. 3: 217–232.

Timmons, Jeffrey A., and Stepen Spinelli. 2004. *New Venture Creation: Entrepreneurship for the 21st Century*, 6th ed. New York: McGraw-Hill/Irwin.

Vakharia, Neville. 2016. "Perspectives on Arts Entrepreneurship: Knowledge Centricity and the Artist Entrepreneur." *Artivate: A Journal of Entrepreneurship in the Arts* 5, no. 2: 3–6.

Vecco, Marilena. 2020. "Artpreneurs' Lessons to Traditional Entrepreneurs." *International Journal of Entrepreneurship and Small Business* 40, no. 2: 154–170.

Vecco, Marilena, and Elmar D. Konrad. 2018. *The Power of Partnership: Necessity or Luxury in the Cultural and Creative Sectors?* Dortmund: European Center for Creative Economy.

Vecco, Marilena, and Andrej Srakar. 2018. "Nascent Cultural and Creative Entrepreneurship: Between Entrepreneurial Economics and Institutional Entrepreneurship." In *Nascent Entrepreneurship and Successful New Venture Creation*, edited by Marilena Vecco and Andrej Srakar, 175–202. Hershey, PA: IGI Global.

Vecco, Marilena, and Andrej Srakar. 2020. "Direct, Indirect and Cross-Lagged: The Effects of Cultural Policy on Nascent Cultural Entrepreneurship." *International Journal of Arts Management* 22, no. 2: 67–82.

Viedma Marti, José M., and Maria do Rosário Cabrita. 2012. *Entrepreneurial Excellence in the Knowledge Economy: Intellectual Capital Benchmarking Systems*. Wiesbaden: Springer.

Wales, William J., Sascha Kraus, Matthias Filser, and Christoph Stoekmann. 2021. "The Status Quo of Research on Entrepreneurial Orientation: Conversational Landmarks and Theoretical Scaffolding." *Journal of Business Research* 128: 564–577.

Walter, Achim. 1999. "Relationship Promoters: Driving Forces for Successful Customer Relationships." *Industrial Marketing Management* 28, no. 5: 537–551.

Wasserman, Noam. 2012. *The Founder's Dilemmas: Anticipating and Avoiding the Pitfalls That Can Sink a Startup*. Princeton, NJ: Princeton University Press.

CHAPTER 35

ENGAGED DISSENT

Entrepreneurship and Critique in the Institutional Practice of Three Contemporary Artists

ADRIENNE CALLANDER

Introduction

DEFINED broadly, institutions are socially constructed environments that shape individual and collective action and belief (Thornton, Ocasio, and Lounsbury 2012; Besharov and Smith 2014). Deviation from institutional rules and norms exacts a toll on individuals and organizations, most notably a reduction in legitimacy and in access to the resources that legitimacy can engender (DiMaggio and Powell 1983; Lawrence, Suddaby, and Leca 2009; Suddaby, Bitektine, and Haack 2017). A degree of leeway to interrogate and dissent from normative pressures is a defining feature of both entrepreneurship and art (Callander and Cummings 2021) and their respective subfields, institutional entrepreneurship and institutional critique. Institutional entrepreneurship, concerned with the emergence, alteration, and erosion of institutions (DiMaggio 1988), permits its practitioners a de facto degree of divergence from the status quo as they actively seek a structural transformation (Misangyi, Weaver, and Elms 2008; Hjorth 2011; McMullen, Brownell, and Adams 2021). Similarly, in art, in the practice of institutional critique, artists are "critically distanced from the status quo both politically and aesthetically" (Piper 1992, 5). They resist a dominant practice in order to speak truth to power or to opt out of artistic restriction (Adorno 1945; Piper 1992; Schaefer 2002; Faris 2004; Dodd 2014; Heffernan 2015). Remarkably, however, while both fields offer strategies and tactics for navigating the peril of subversion, their synergistic relationship in this regard is underexplored in the art, entrepreneurship, and arts entrepreneurship literatures (Bureau and Zander 2014). This chapter addresses that gap by examining how key theories and methods of entrepreneurship and art operated and interacted with one another in the institutional practice of visual artists Nan Goldin, Theaster Gates, and Yayoi Kusama.

These artists, recognized internationally for their artistic accomplishment and for their institutional impact within and beyond art, challenged the status quo. At the same time, they remained deeply invested in the structural shapes and outcomes of the institutions they challenged. Goldin founded an organization to expose and transform art museums inured to the opioid plague that fueled their funding. Gates formed a Chicago-based network of nonprofits to support and promote Black art and enterprise effaced by the art establishment. Kusama synthesized commercial and artistic practices to both provoke and command an art market that would have otherwise marginalized her. While their strategy varied according to their goals and contexts, all three borrowed from entrepreneurship and art as they acted to both subvert an established practice and introduce a new one. They differed from those who merely reinforce institutional norms or those who reject them in that they answered authority not with conformity or simple protest but with an alternative: a form of refusal that remained engaged.

The multiple-case study that follows examines the specific ways that Goldin, Gates, and Kusama acted to transform norms in the social environments within which they and their work operated. Case analysis narrows its focus to each artist's exercise of emancipatory, public, or effectual models of entrepreneurship within aesthetic frameworks informed by art practices ranging from punk to performance to social practice to Pop Art, in tandem with a lived experience of marginalization. As backdrop to the cases, this chapter bridges institutional entrepreneurship and institutional critique to establish a transdisciplinary theoretical baseline for agency: the capacity to make "critical interventions that set the course of institutional development" (DiMaggio and Powell 1991, 9). In the process, it discerns the potential for entrepreneurship studies to bolster and renew institutional practice in art.

Methodology

The transdisciplinary focus of this chapter warranted bridging the literatures of institutional entrepreneurship and institutional critique to establish a theoretical baseline (Eisenhardt and Graebner 2007) for agency. Against this backdrop, descriptive in- and cross-case analysis (Miles and Huberman 1994) of the institutional practice of three international visual artists was conducted. Given the complex relational processes that institutional change entails (Garud and Karnøe 2001; Hardy and Maguire 2008; Seo and Creed 2002), the "real-world context" (Eisenhardt and Graebner 2007, 25) of artists' institutional practice, and the theory-driven nature of this study (Lee and Sabylinski 1999), the multiple-case study was selected for its potential to support the discovery of unexpected and divergent phenomena that characterizes theory building (King, Felin, and Whetten 2009). The nested nature of individual experience and action within organization- and system-level interactions supports individual-level analysis of the tension between agency and institutional structure (Battilana 2006; Lawrence, Suddaby, and Leca 2011).

Merging the selection criteria of Csikszentmihalyi (1996) and Bureau and Zander's (2014) conditions for subversive power in art and in entrepreneurship, the selection of case subjects relied on three main criteria: first, selected artists needed to be recognized in their field and beyond for artistic achievement; second, selected artists needed to be recognized in their field and beyond for institutional impact; and third, the subjects' reflections on their own artistic and institutional practice needed to be accessible. All three artists studied here—Nan Goldin, Theaster Gates, and Yayoi Kusama—have been internationally profiled in academic and popular journals and/or filmed documentaries about their artistic and institutional impact, and each has spoken publicly and/or written extensively on the intersection of art and institutional work in their respective practices. Variation in case study subjects' age, gender, sexual orientation, race, and national identity enhanced the scope of the study, while restriction to the visual arts productively limited analysis and discussion of the findings.

Three models of entrepreneurship—*emancipation* (Rindova, Barry, and Ketchen 2009), emphasizing change creation over wealth creation; *public entrepreneurship* (Hjorth and Bjerke 2006; Hjorth 2013), increasing social exchange between people in public spaces; and *effectuation* (Sarasvathy 2001), privileging creative over causal approaches to venturing—were observed across all three cases. To productively limit the scope of analysis, a single entrepreneurship model was isolated and analyzed within each case. While each case was analyzed through the lens of a single entrepreneurship model, the full range of each artist's art practice was examined, in tandem with their respective lived experiences, to support comparison of the aesthetic frameworks they employed in their respective approaches to institutional practice.

Bridging Institutional Entrepreneurship and Institutional Critique

The philosopher Theodor Adorno writes that art "was, and is, a force of protest of the humane against the pressure of domineering institutions" (Adorno 1945, 237). Lawrence, Suddaby, and Leca (2011) offer a conceptualization of institutional work as a more quotidian process that captures "the efforts of individuals and collective actors to cope with, keep up with, shore up, tear down, tinker with, transform, or create anew the institutional structures within which they live, work, and play" (53). Thus, the intersection of art and entrepreneurship in the realm of institutional practice might call for a balance between heroic resistance to the forces of structuration and a continuous relinquishing of the sense of arrival, stability, or finality as one structure gives way to another. In that same vein, what follows is not an exhaustive review of institutional entrepreneurship and institutional critique scholarship that culminates in a definitive stance but a carving out of key theories of agency and an examination of the contours of their operation in successive waves of institutional critique practice.

Interrogating the position that organizations passively accept institutional pressures and norms (Suddaby 2010) and the parallel position that organizations are "unaffected by the particular interests of politically conceived actors" (DiMaggio 1988, 4), the institutional entrepreneurship literature emerged as scholars began to analyze institutional change and the exercise of individual and collective agency. Agency, defined in the entrepreneurship literature as the capacity to disrupt, alter, or maintain institutional structures (DiMaggio 1988; Beckert 1999; Battilana and D'Aunno 2009) and in the art literature as transformative, constitutive, or institutive power (Sedgwick 2003; Ahmed 2004; Peltomäki 2007), sparks a constructivist concern: how do institutional actors "enact change within a context that theoretically determines their values and behaviors" (McMullen, Brownell, and Adams 2021, 1208)? How do they escape—in order to reshape—the social structures that seek to bind them? Alternately, how do they penetrate—in order to reshape—the social structures that seek to exclude them? In entrepreneurship and in art, practitioners who dissent from established norms, "in some cases out of necessity, but in others as a strategy for horizontal resistance to vertical consolidation of both economic power and cultural pluralities" (Callander and Cummings 2021, 749), enact a legitimating condition of the field (Butler 2009) that sanctions resistance to the pressure to conform. Adrian Piper, an artist associated with institutional critique, situates this critical distance in the margin, where artists "see the mainstream clearly because they've been excluded from it while having to navigate through it" (Piper 1992, 5). The entrepreneurship literature cautions against overromanticization of resource-poor margins (Dodd, Prett, and Shaw 2016) but nonetheless urges consideration of the political, artistic, or economic periphery as a staging ground for meaningful challenges to institutional norms (Dodd 2014). Greenwood and Suddaby (2006) note, "New ideas occur at the margins of a field because it is there that organizations are less embedded, less privileged, and more exposed to institutional contradictions" (30). In condoning dissent and activation of the margin, institutional entrepreneurship and institutional critique grant sufficient latitude—or degrees of agency—for the development of "attitudes, dispositions, or strategies that immunize individuals to the action-adverse conditions" (McMullen, Brownell, and Adams 2021, 1214) of institutional environments.

Not all challenges to institutional norms prove impactful. Transformation of institutional structures is possible to the extent that those who would defend a system's norms believe the challenge to the status quo will benefit the institution and its actors (Goddard 2020; Wijnberg and Gemser 2000; McMullen, Brownell, and Adams 2021). Cultures morph as new perspectives are introduced and eventually accepted by established systems, but not all are eager to cross the *value boundary* (Groys 2014) between sanctioned and unsanctioned ideas to engage in cultural revision (Sturken 1997). The mobilization of allies in support of institutional change extends beyond those already invested in a course of action to those who might still need convincing (Battilana, Leca, and Boxenbaum 2009). Bureau and Zander (2014) capture this tension: "If subversive attitudes and activities are needed to launch and develop new ideas and projects, whether in art or entrepreneurship, resistance is found on the other side of the coin" (125). Thus, negotiation between the familiar and the unfamiliar and the ability to strategically "engage others in collective action" (Fligstein 2001 105) are fundamental to institutional change (DiMaggio 1988; Alvarez et al. 2005; Henfridsson and Yoo 2014; Zhao et al. 2018).

The *paradox of embedded agency* (Seo and Creed 2002; Greenwood and Suddaby 2006; Battilana 2006; Mutch 2007; Garudy, Hardy, and Maguire 2007; Battilana and D'Aunno 2009) frames agency as an inter-actor (Hardy and Maguire 2008) process of negotiation in which change agents navigate familiar systems to reshape the larger social structures to which they belong. It acknowledges that individuals and organizations remain implicated in the institutional spaces they seek to change. Thus, institutional entrepreneurs must calibrate their own marginality in order to act with and within a structure even as they leverage resources to counter and change it. Institutional critique contends with this paradox. It recognizes the making of art as inseparable from the institutional spaces within which it is "produced, presented, and circulated" (MTL Collective 2018, 194). At the same time, it articulates a distance between agent and structure, between artist and the administration of art.

Operating as both "critical method and artistic practice" (Sheikh 2009, 29), first-wave institutional critique arose in the late 1960s and early 1970s in artworks, performative interventions, publications, and "(art-)political activism" (Sheikh 2009, 29) that took an antagonistic stance toward art museums and "white box" gallery spaces perceived as practicing cultural confinement (Smithson 1972) in what art critic Lucy Lippard refers to as "the sacrosanct ivory walls and heroic, patriarchal mythologies with which the 1960s opened" (Lippard 1973, vii). This antagonism toward art world gatekeepers did not constitute support for wholesale detachment from the art world. Rather, it called for a new kind of artwork, one that resisted hegemonic cultural determinism (Raunig 2009). Artists critiqued and evaded institutional intermediaries and controls by eschewing traditional modes of production and exhibition that could be captured, cataloged, or otherwise enclosed by the curatorial class (Lippard 1973; Alberro 2012). However, subversions could elicit institutional penalty. Hans Haacke's *Shapolsky et al. Manhattan Real Estate Holdings, a Real-Time Social System, as of May 1, 1971* (1971)—a series of photographs coupled with data pulled from public records—exposed, as artwork, a New York City slumlord's decades-long fraud. Deemed "incompatible with the functions of a prestigious art institution" (Deutsche 1996, 159), Haacke's 1971 solo exhibition at the Guggenheim Museum of Art—which would have debuted *Shapolsky et al.*—was canceled before it opened (Hileman 2010).

By the late 1980s and early 1990s, a "second wave" of institutional critique moved from frontal antagonism and separation from institutional spaces to a deeper acceptance of the artist as problematic participant in systems of cultural confinement. Artists Andrea Fraser and Fred Wilson, both of whom created works in which they performed as art the duties of a museum guide or guard, interrogated and attempted to negotiate the condition of their own institutionalization (Fraser 2005; Holms 2009). Fraser dismissed the idea that there could be any distance between artist and institution: "It's not a question of being against the institution: We are the institution. It's a question of what kind of institution we are" (Fraser 2005, 105). As artists expanded the framework for institutional critique to include a critique of the role of the artist (Sheikh 2009), emergent strategies included integration of non-art practices and communal and collaborative approaches to the production of art (Bishop 2004). The artist, an extension of the institution, performed a refusal of art world norms by crossing into non-art realms. The exercise of agency in this new landscape entailed deemphasis of the role of the artist—now complicit in the structures being critiqued—in favor of a more community-oriented approach not only to art viewing but also to art making. Rirkrit Tiravanija, an artist associated with Relational Aesthetics (Bourriaud 1998; Dezeuze 2006)—socially oriented artwork that is "openended, interactive, and resistant to closure" (Bishop 2004, 52)—turned 303 Gallery in New York City into a kitchen that served visitors free Thai curry. This performative installation, *Untitled (Free)* (1992), did not disavow the art world so much as intervene in its operations by disrupting the concepts of "gallery," "art," and "audience." Artists' *transfiguration of the commonplace* (Danto 1981; Bourriaud 1998; Dezeuze 2006) elevated familiar acts like cooking and eating to the status of art while handing activation and completion of the artwork to the audience. In such ways, institutional critique came to operate inside institutional spaces, where it was accepted as an art practice.

By the late 1990s and early 2000s, institutional critique sought new modes for escape from and resistance to institutional pressures. One tactic was to transfer the strategy of communal and collaborative art making and the elevated status of everyday actions and materials to the emerging context of global art fairs and biennials. For Documenta 11, Cildo Meireles's *Disappearing Element/Disappeared Element (Imminent Past)* (2002) entailed street vendors selling flavorless water popsicles throughout the festival host city of Kassel, Germany. The words "Disappeared Element" became legible on the sticks as festival goers—consumers of the popsicles, the festival, contemporary art, and its critique—licked and dissolved (and transformed) the work (Brett 2008; Castellano 2018). Engaging "the relationship between art prestige, economics and ecology," Castellano writes, "[*Disappearing Element/Disappeared Element*] denounces the volatility of a globalised and biennial-driven art world" (Castellano 2018, 60) while, nonetheless, participating in it. The rise in popularity of international art fairs and biennials initially stemmed, in part, from the impulse to dissolve museums' national—and nationalistic—identities (Kastner 2009; Castellano 2018). But this tactic would inevitably be criticized for its complicity in global systems of disparity and exclusion (Brett 2008; Castellano 2018). The perennial dilemma was renewed: how to calibrate embeddedness in order to work within institutional structures without sacrificing agency.

Inherently political, institutional entrepreneurship is a discursive and collective (Seo and Creed 2002; Hardy and Maguire 2008) process that aims to "dislodge existing practices ... introduce new ones, and then ensure that these become widely adopted and taken for granted by other actors in the field" (Hardy and Maguire 2008, 204). By this definition, institutional entrepreneurs seek to stabilize the structural changes they instigate and, ultimately, to institutionalize new norms. However, the relational nature of institutional entrepreneurship continuously invites new actors to institute new forms and practices in social structures that then morph in response, only to elicit new refusals and trajectory shifts (Henfridsson and Yoo 2014) in an ongoing process that staves off institutional ossification or authoritarian pressure. Citing Foucault's 1978 lecture "What Is Critique?," Raunig (2009) frames institutional critique as "a permanent process of instituting" (4). The instituent practice "does not oppose the institution, but it does flee from institutionalization" (Raunig and Ray 2009, xvii). As institutional critique evolves new modes of art making and new formats for delivery to evade capture by art world structures that seek to catalog and enclose its outputs, its practitioners remain vigilant to the peril of embedding "only into the surface of the institution without materially altering the institution or its organization in any deeper sense" (Steyerl 2009, 17). To avoid having institutional critique become subject to the very rules and pressures it seeks to resist, Raunig (2009) calls for it to "link up with other forms of critique both within and outside the art field" (3). This strategy opens the door for institutional critique to closely consider entrepreneurship and its tactics for navigating the peril of subversion in acts of dissension from and transformation of established systems. What follows is a multiple-case study of the "linking up" of art with entrepreneurship in the institutional practice of three visual artists as they acted to transform the status quo.

Case Analysis

The following cases examine the ways that visual artists Nan Goldin, Theaster Gates, and Yayoi Kusama navigated the dynamic tension between agency and the isomorphic pressure to conform that is central to structuration (Greenwood and Suddaby 2006; Garudy, Hardy, and Maguire 2007; Lawrence, Suddaby, and Leca 2011). In their efforts to effect institutional change, all three artists relied on their extensive knowledge of art world operations and their connections in and beyond art as they leaned into their respective art practices and the lived experience that informed those practices to uniquely craft an approach to instigating change. Overlaps between cases highlight performance art, sector spanning, and marginalization as factors in all three artists' instigation of institutional change, while the exercise of emancipatory, public, or effectual principles of entrepreneurship demonstrates the synergistic potential for impact that entrepreneurship offers institutional practice in art.

Nan Goldin

A fierce empathy is discernible in Nan Goldin's activism and artwork; in both, the body is a battleground. Described as a "punk-sex" photographer and a documentary realist (Qualls 1995, 26), Goldin photographed, and photographed from within, a social fringe where she and her close circle of friends—her chosen family (Als 2016)—celebrated (and mourned) one another, together. Goldin's influential early collection of photographs, *The Ballad of Sexual Dependency* (1979–86), looks intimately at addiction, domestic violence, sexual vulnerability, and the toll of AIDS on her close-knit community on Manhattan's Lower East Side. *The Ballad of Sexual Dependency*, exhibited as a slide show of images projected on the wall with the whir of the projector's lamp and the clatter of the carousel advancing each slide in the background, ported easily between punk clubs on New York City's Lower East Side (Ruddy 2009). Exemplifying the mid-1970s to mid-1980s punk and post-punk era's "powerful insertion of the queer body into contemporary art," *Ballad* expressed Goldin's subcultural community's rejection of "binaries and their reach into the politics of race, gender, sexuality, class and the segregation of urban space" (Hart 2008). As a participant-observer (Edmonston 1983; Yi 2013; Cook 2015), Goldin captured "the random gestures and colors of the universe of sex and dreams, longing and breakups" (Als 2016). Of the work and its "emotional swells of existence" (LaForce 2018), Goldin explains, "It's not about a style or a look or a setup. It's about emotional obsession and empathy" (O'Brien 2011). Qualls (1995) argues that in documenting her own experience of domestic abuse Goldin transitioned from participant-observer (Edmonston 1983; Yi 2013; Cook 2015) to photographic performer, "defining herself not just as a journalist-chronicler of the scene in which she was involved but also as a performer . . . not an actor analyzing another's text, but one using their own lives as the canvas" (Qualls 1995, 31).

Decades later, with her formation of the organization Prescription Addiction Intervention Now (P.A.I.N.), Goldin's artistic impulse to make visible the vulnerable, including herself, took an entrepreneurial turn. Goldin formed P.A.I.N. to challenge museum funding practices, specifically museums' ties to the Sackler family, major museum patrons implicated in the US opioid epidemic (Jobey 2019; di Liscia 2020; Viveros-Fauné 2021). In "Nan Goldin Gets Your P.A.I.N.," Viveros-Fauné (2021) describes the scope of Goldin's impact:

> The activist group she founded . . . has drawn a bead on the numbered Swiss bank accounts of pharmaceutical giant Purdue Pharma, along with those of its owners, the billionaire Sackler family, unrepentant profiteers of the Oxycontin scourge. The "most evil family in America"—according to Tennessee Congressman Jim Cooper—is currently mired in bankruptcy court, thanks in no small part to Goldin.

Artist-led calls for change tend to be radical in nature, provocative in their affect, and impactful (Serafini 2018; Jobey 2019; di Liscia 2021). In her organized resistance to museum funding strategies that relied on the Sackler family's philanthropy, Goldin activated principles of *emancipatory entrepreneurship* (Rindova, Barry, and Ketchen 2009). The emancipation model, emphasizing change creation over wealth creation, destabilizes the narrow view that entrepreneurship is merely a free-market weapon for dismantling social safety nets (Bonin-Rodriguez 2012). In emancipatory entrepreneuring, the act of *making declarations* works in tandem with the principles of *seeking autonomy* and *authoring* to create new norms. *Seeking autonomy* describes the dual action of not only breaking free of an authority but also breaking up an operational status quo to enable others to join in the shaping of new institutional forms and practices. *Authoring* describes an alliance between the entrepreneur and "high-status actors who increase legitimacy and survival chances" (Rindova, Barry, and Ketchen 2009, 480) while sharing in the mission to enact meaningful change. Practicing an "aesthetics of tactical embarrassment" (Sholette 2003), Goldin *made declarations* by participating in on-site protests in which members of P.A.I.N. performed "die-ins" in museum lobbies and on front steps, scattering pill bottles and lying prone as if dead (Jobey 2019). In an open letter in *Artforum* Goldin declared: "I've started a group ... to hold [the Sacklers] accountable. To get their ear, we will target their philanthropy. They have washed their blood money through the halls of museums and universities around the world" (Goldin 2018). Goldin *authored* with political leaders seeking to hold the Sacklers accountable by testifying before the US Congress about the impact of her own addiction to Oxycontin. And she *sought autonomy* for herself and others via her organization's campaign to change major arts institutions' funding methods.

A participant-observer in her photographic work (Edmonston 1983; Yi 2013; Cook 2015), with deep knowledge of art world operations and firsthand experience of opioid addiction, Goldin formed an organization to expose an abuse, build support for its address, and pressure arts administrators, as financial agents (Férnandez-Blanco and Prieto-Rodriguez 2020), to calculate their own risks and uncertainties (McMullen and Shepherd 2006) in their decision to perpetuate or end a moral hazard. She did this while maintaining a sense of allegiance to the very system she critiqued. Walking through the Metropolitan Museum of Art soon after the removal of the Sackler family name from its walls, Goldin noted that museums collect "the spoils of civilization" and then added, "But I still love them" (Schulman 2022).

Theaster Gates

In 2007, Theaster Gates—a sculptor, ceramicist, musician, and installation artist whose social practice entails performance, community organizing, and "large-scale urban intervention" (Austen 2013)—delivered a performance at Chicago's Hyde Park Art Center that resonates today throughout his multivalent practice (McGraw 2012; Mannes-Abbott 2013). *Plate Convergence* (2007), curated by Gates, presented the work of Japanese master potter Shoji Yamaguchi. Gates described how Yamaguchi had "fled Hiroshima, married a black civil rights activist, and instituted a ritual called Plate Convergences" that gathered people together to discuss "race, political difference and inequity" (Wei 2011). The exhibition consisted of long ceramic plates; a video of the plates in use at a series of community dinners; wall vinyl that provided a timeline for the "Yamaguchi Institute"; and a recreation of one of the community dinners for those in attendance. In reality, Yamaguchi was a fiction. The works in the exhibition, the dinner, the institute, and Yamaguchi himself were all Gates's creations. Gates explained that he invented Yamaguchi as an alter ego to help him navigate the marginalization he experienced as a Black artist (Austen 2013). Through Yamaguchi, Gates performed tropes of tradition, gathering, craft, and exoticism to reject the curatorial exclusion that he himself experienced while, at the same time, transforming perceptions of what—and whom—curatorial practice could entail (Reinhardt 2015).

With *Plate Convergence*, Gates performed a blueprint for the intersection of community engagement and artistic practice and "the ethical impact of the discursive interactions and the social work they perform" (Reinhardt 2015). He would unfold this blueprint across the city of Chicago over the next fifteen years. Gates's drive to preserve, protect, and promote Black culture and enterprise, and by extension his own practice, led to *Dorchester Projects* (2009), "an artwork open to the public" (Adams 2015), which gathered people together to share meals and exchange with one another, engage with and support Black culture, and strengthen the economic health of the project's predominantly Black neighborhood on Chicago's South Side without gentrifying it. Gates established the Rebuild Foundation—"a platform for art, cultural development, and neighborhood transformation" (Gates n.d.)—to support his community-building efforts. By 2022, Rebuild Foundation's network had expanded to include Black Cinema House, Stony Island Arts Bank, Dorchester Industries, Black Artists Retreat, and Dorchester Art + Housing Collaborative. McGraw (2012) writes, "Under Gates's framework, cultural institutions are part of the problem—they adhere to systemic inequities—and one must either remake them from within or invent new forms" (McGraw 2012, 91). With Rebuild Foundation, Gates did not depart the art world; rather, he created a parallel system, one from which he influenced the art establishment and the philanthropic and political elite, in and beyond Chicago. In an interview with *Art in America*, Gates explained, "I realized that if I had the courage to make work outside the institution, then institutions might actually be interested in the work" (Wei 2011).

Gates's community-building ethos enacted principles of *public entrepreneurship*, a model of entrepreneurship that aims to increase opportunities for exchange between people in public spaces (Hjorth and Bjerke 2006). Pushing back against the characterization of social problems—such as precarity induced by marginalization—as "economic problems in need of 'better management'" (Hjorth and Bjerke 2006, 119), public entrepreneurship counters the prevalent reduction of social concerns to merely a "form of the economic" (103) with a conceptualization of entrepreneurship as a "sociality-creating force" (109). *Sociality*, a collective form of engagement, emphasizes belonging and positions the entrepreneur as a citizen-actor "relationally defined by an ethics of responsibility for the creation and re-creation of the public" (Hjorth 2013, 44). Beyes (2015) notes that public entrepreneurship, concerned with social transformation, resonates in contemporary art's attention to "socio-political effects" (445). In "The Artist Corporation and the Collective" (2014), Gates writes, "Collectivity, collections, collectives, those things for me have everything to do with our willingness to understand the economies between political space and people" (Gates 2014, 78). Thus, Gates bridged art making and the making of a public sphere.

Gates, not averse to making a profit, exercised a hybrid form of public entrepreneurship in which he leveraged public and private resources to bolster a social practice (McGraw 2012; Adams 2015; Reinhardt 2015) that in turn supported Black art, artists, and community. Speaking with Chicago mayor Rahm Emanuel in 2019, Gates spoke of the potential for artists who know how a city works to advance equity (Emanuel 2019). Despite his degree in urban development, Gates eschewed the title of developer: "What I am is really just an expanded individual, a complicated individual that both wants for himself and wants for the world" (Gates 2014, 78).

Yayoi Kusama

Nonagenarian visual artist and fashion icon Yayoi Kusama, the "world's top-selling living female artist" (Allen 2020), first demonstrated her capacity for cross-boundary disruption (Burgelman and Grove 2007) sixty years ago by embracing the commercial transaction as an artistic gesture. Kusama's early practice, influenced by "happenings" and Pop Art, offers insight into her later address of the art world's systems of selection and control of distribution. Happenings, which emerged in the late 1950s as improvisational precursors to performance art, were inherently cross-disciplinary, drawing on theater, visual art, music, and poetry. At the same time, they were ephemeral and time-based and thus resisted commodification. Happenings also broke the traditional artist-audience divide. For Kusama's *Anatomic Explosions* (1968–69), a series of happenings staged throughout Manhattan, "participants stripped naked and donned an assortment of masks while Kusama painted polka dots on their bodies" (Kennell 2019, 202). The polka dot, Kusama's obsessive motif adorning her sculptures and installations, became a hallmark of her collaboration with the Louis Vuitton fashion brand, but Kusama attributes her use of polka dots to hallucinations she first experienced as a child. In her own writings, Kusama describes the depersonalization she experienced as a result of her neurodivergence: "I don't consider myself an artist; I am pursuing art in order to correct the disability which began in my childhood" (Pollock 2006, 133).

Kusama's early practice also drew on Pop Art's embrace of consumer culture to undermine perceptions that the art object was precious or unique. Of her guerrilla performance *Narcissus Garden*, performed outside the 1966 Venice Biennale, she says, "What was most important... was my action of selling the mirror balls on the site, as if I were selling hot dogs or ice cream cones" (Artspace 2017). "Lampooning the art market" (Selvin 2020), Kusama used "performance art as her business model" (Allen 2020) as she implemented the aesthetics of advertising and the mechanics of retail as tools of provocation that challenged the role of art's institutional intermediaries. In her fusion of Pop Art and happenings, Kusama blurred the line between fine art and consumer culture and diminished the boundary between artist and audience. With *Narcissus Garden*, the business transaction became an artistic medium (Callander 2019). Kusama challenged cultural confinement (Smithson 1972) by eliminating the fine art "middleman" and centered the artist in both creative and commercial components of cultural production. At the same time, Kusama aggressively pursued inclusion by leading galleries, collectors, and critics. Kusama worked to expand the institutional environment to make room for her avant-garde experiments within central art world structures, entry to which Kusama, an Asian woman in a male-dominated Eurocentric selection system, was frequently denied.

In her challenge to institutional norms, Kusama practiced the improvisational model of *effectual entrepreneurship*. *Effectuation* seeks to "control an unpredictable future rather than predict an uncertain one" (Sarasvathy 2001, 259) through principles of *affordable loss*, *exploitation of contingencies*, *strategic alliance*, and *control of an unpredictable future*. In effectual entrepreneuring, the entrepreneur leverages available resources, welcomes unexpected events, and prioritizes networking over competitive analysis. These principles were evident in Kusama's embrace of experimentation, flexibility, and collaboration not only within established art circles but also across sectors. Kusama's involvement with fashion is popularly chronicled as beginning in 2006 when Louis Vuitton artistic director Marc Jacobs visited her in her Tokyo studio, but she first experimented with fashion in her 1960s New York City boutique, where she staged shows featuring clothing with erotic cutouts. When her fashion experiments attracted mainstream commercial attention, Kusama negotiated her way into a central channel of commercial distribution by collaborating with the company she suspected of stealing her designs (Artspace 2017).

Of her provocations, Kusama says, "I wanted to overturn the conventions" (Artspace 2017). An "eminently pragmatic upstart" and a "networking warrior" (Swanson 2012) who "long had viral ambitions" (Allen 2020), Kusama balanced her capacity for upending norms with a keen awareness of market operations to establish *optimal distinctiveness* (Alvarez et al. 2005; Zhao et al. 2018), wherein inclusion (allowing the artist to obtain resources) and differentiation (allowing the artist to attain recognition) are achieved via the breaking of conventions and the maintaining of control over the "coupling of art and business" (Alvarez et al. 2005, 864). Kusama challenged art world brokers and assumed their role herself to bridge the divide between art and its commercialization.

Kusama's involvement with fashion is popularly chronicled as beginning in 2006 when Louis Vuitton artistic director Marc Jacobs visited her in her Tokyo studio, but she first experimented with fashion in her 1960s New York City boutique, where she staged shows featuring clothing with erotic cutouts. When her fashion experiments attracted mainstream commercial attention, Kusama negotiated her way into a central channel of commercial distribution by collaborating with the company she suspected of stealing her designs (Artspace 2017).

Concluding Discussion

The main motivation of this study was to examine the synergistic relationship between entrepreneurship and art in the institutional practice of Nan Goldin, Theaster Gates, and Yayoi Kusama, artists recognized internationally for their artistic accomplishment and institutional impact in and beyond art. All three artists exercised degrees of agency to effectively manage a highly relational process (Fligstein 2001; Garud and Karnøe 2001; Hardy and Maguire 2008) that required, at once, a degree of immunization against the pressure to conform, knowledge of the systems to be impacted, and a facility in negotiating the social networks that would oppose or support their structural interventions (McMullen, Brownell, and Adams 2021). As they defined the terms of their relationship to the social structures they navigated, in ways exemplary or adversarial (Finkelpearl 2013), Goldin, Gates, and Kusama activated principles of emancipatory, public, and effectual entrepreneurship in their pursuit of institutional interventions and the fomenting of structural change. In all three cases, the artists confronted the administration of art: Goldin challenged museum funding practices, Gates rejected curatorial exclusion, and Kusama questioned the role of brokers.

As they activated a degree of immunity against isomorphic pressures, tapped their knowledge of the system(s) they hoped to influence, and built alliances across a range of competing interests and investments, Goldin, Gates, and Kusama exercised, and extended, *temporal agency* (Mead 1932; Emirbayer and Mische 1998; Battilanan and D'Aunno 2009; Garud, Kumaraswamy, and Karnøe 2010), a process of social engagement informed by the past, oriented toward the future, and sensitive to present contingencies (Emirbayer and Mische 1998). For artists, present actions and future projections are informed by pasts spent developing aesthetic frameworks that are, in turn, informed by their practice of art—in both its material and philosophical considerations—and the lived experience that informs that practice. This aesthetic dimension of temporal agency, derived from the "interplay of our sensory and evaluative capacities" (Creed, Taylor, and Hudson 2020, 416), posits that in the attempt to "contextualize past habits and future projects within the contingencies of the moment" (Emirbayer and Mische 1998, 963), artists as institutional entrepreneurs implement a distinct interpretive framework. Goldin's emancipatory challenge (Rindova, Barry, and Ketchen 2009) to art museums' embrace of predatory philanthropy referenced the punk, performative, and documentary aspects of a photography practice that responded to and captured Goldin's experience of queerness, addiction, and subcultural solidarity. Gates's public entrepreneuring (Hjorth and Bjerke 2006) in response to the exclusion of Black culture and enterprise mirrored a social practice that propelled Gates's harnessing of craft, commerce, and community building to counter the effects of racist marginalization. Kusama's early effectual command (Sarasvathy 2001) of the crossover between art and its commercialization as she navigated the sexism and xenophobia that contributed to her socioeconomic exclusion reflected the influence of an improvisational practice characterized by street-level performance and Pop Art's "vernacular of consumer culture" (Callander 2019, 64). It is beyond the scope of this study to fully consider the implications of the extension of temporal agency via the aesthetic frameworks of artists who engage institutional practice, but the role of performance art, cross-sector activity, and social marginalization are factors worth exploring in any future examination of the impact of artistic practice on the mechanics of agency, a core concern for institutional entrepreneurship studies.

Mindful that institutional critique seeks its own continuous renewal, this study narrows its focus to the potential impact institutional entrepreneurship studies offers institutional practice in art. The subject of this study has been artists who mitigated risk and uncertainty (McMullen and Shepherd 2006) as they deployed degrees of iteration, projection, and practical evaluation (Battilana and D'Aunno 2009; Kier and McMullen 2018) in the instigation of trajectory shifts (Henfridsson and Yoo 2014) that transformed institutional norms. Each practiced an engaged form of dissent to challenge the art world, a system in which they remained deeply invested. Callander and Cummings (2021) note that an emphasis on "renewal" characterizes the dominant conceptualization of entrepreneurship in the arts management literature, "which seeks not the formation of ventures so much as the reorganization or redirection of established entities" (747). The framing of entrepreneurship as an *intrapreneurial* pursuit (Antoncic and Hisrich 2003), wherein administrators merely seek "to maintain or grow the financial health of an organization as it encounters changing market demands and shifting policy environments" (Callander and Cummings 2021, 747), limits the full potential of entrepreneurship in the administration of the arts. Possibly, a more porous membrane exists between the arts and their administration—one in which there is not only a synergy between artist and administrator but even a symbiosis or a changing of the guard, or no guard at all. Not every artist makes for an administrator, but the administrator who can dial up creative, social, and practical imaginativeness (Kier and McMullen 2018) might view management as a medium for the shaping and reshaping of the structures within which art operates, thus blurring the line between entrepreneurship and management in the administration of art.

References

Adams, Tim. 2015. "Chicago Artist Theaster Gates: 'I'm Hoping Swiss Bankers Will Bail Out My Flooded South Side Bank in the Name of Art.'" *The Guardian*, May 3, 2015. https://www.theguardian.com/artanddesign/2015/may/03/theaster-gates-artist-chicago-dorchester-projects.

Adorno, Theodor W. 1945. "Theses upon Art and Religion Today." *Kenyon Review* 7, no. 4: 677–682.

Ahmed, Sara. 2004. "Affective Economies." *Social Text* 22, no. 2: 17–39.

Alberro, Alexander. 2012. "Michael Asher." *Art in America*, December 19, 2012. https://www.artnews.com/art-in-america/features/michael-asher-62960/.

Allen, Greg. 2020. "The Kusama Industrial Complex: How Yayoi Kusama Came to Captivate the World, Fueling Museums and the Market." *ArtNews*, July 21, 2020. https://www.artnews.com/art-news/artists/yayoi-kusama-museum-favorite-art-market-rise-1202694918/.

Als, Hilton. 2016. "Nan Goldin's 'The Ballad of Sexual Dependency.'" *New Yorker*, July 4, 2016. https://www.newyorker.com/magazine/2016/07/04/nan-goldins-the-ballad-of-sexual-dependency.

Alvarez, José Luis, Carmelo Mazza, Jesper Strandgaarde Pedersen, and Sylvia Svejenova. 2005. "Shielding Idiosyncrasy from Isomorphic Pressures: Towards Optimal Distinctiveness in European Filmmaking." *Organization* 12, no. 6: 863–888. https://journals.sagepub.com/doi/10.1177/1350508405057474.

Antoncic, Bostjan, and Robert D. Hisrich. 2003. "Clarifying the Intrapreneurship Concept." *Journal of Small Business and Enterprise Development* 10, no. 1: 7–24.

Artspace. 2017. "'It Feels Good to Be an Outsider': Yayoi Kusama on Avoiding Labels, Organizing Orgies, and Battling Hardships." *Artspace*, May 8, 2017. https://www.artspace.com/magazine/interviews_features/book_report/it-feels-good-to-be-an-outsider-yayoi-kusama-on-avoiding-labels-organizing-orgies-and-battling-54768.

Austen, Ben. 2013. "Chicago's Opportunity Artist." *New York Times Magazine*, December 20, 2013. https://www.nytimes.com/2013/12/22/magazine/chicagos-opportunity-artist.html.

Battilana, Julie. 2006. "Agency and Institutions: The Enabling Role of Individuals' Social Positions." *Organization* 13, no. 5: 653–676.

Battilana, Julie, and Thomas D'Aunno. 2009. "Institutional Work and the Paradox of Embedded Agency." In *Institutional Work*, edited by Thomas B. Lawrence, Roy Suddaby, and Bernard Leca, 29–58. Cambridge: Cambridge University Press.

Battilana, Julie, Bernard Leca, and Eva Boxenbaum. 2009. "How Actors Change Institutions: Towards a Theory of Institutional Entrepreneurship." *Academy of Management Annals* 3, no. 1: 65–107.

Beckert, Jens. 1999. "Agency, Entrepreneurs, and Institutional Change: The Role of Strategic Choice and Institutionalized Practices." *Organization Studies* 20, no. 5: 777–799.

Besharov, Marya L., and Wendy K. Smith. 2014. "Multiple Institutional Logics in Organizations: Explaining Their Varied Nature and Implications." *Academy of Management Review* 39, no. 3: 364–381.

Beyes, Timon. 2015. "Fictions of the Possible: Art, the City, and Public Entrepreneurship." *Journal of Management Inquiry* 24, no. 4: 445-449.

Bishop, Claire. 2004. "Antagonism and Relational Aesthetics." *October* 110: 51–79.

Bonin-Rodriguez, Paul. 2012. "What's in a Name? Typifying Artist Entrepreneurship in Community Based Training." *Artivate: A Journal of Entrepreneurship in the Arts* 1, no. 1: 9–24.

Bourriaud, Nicolas. 1998. *Relational Aesthetics*. Dijon, France: Les Presses du Réel, 1998.

Brett, Guy. 2008. "Corners and Crossroads." *Frieze* 117 (September 9, 2008). https://www.frieze.com/article/corners-and-crossroads.

Bureau, Sylvain, and Ivo Zander. 2014. "Entrepreneurship as an Art of Subversion." *Scandinavian Journal of Management* 30, no. 1: 124–133.

Burgelman, Robert A., and Andrew S. Grove. 2007. "Cross-Boundary Disruptors: Powerful Interindustry Entrepreneurial Change Agents." *Strategic Entrepreneurship Journal* 1, nos. 3-4: 315–327. https://doi.org/10.1002/sej.27.

Butler, Judith. 2009. "Critique, Dissent, Disciplinarity." *Critical Inquiry* 35: 773–797.

Callander, Adrienne. 2019. "Artmaking as Entrepreneurship: Effectuation and Emancipation in Artwork Formation." *Artivate: A Journal of Entrepreneurship in the Arts* 8, no. 2: 61–77.

Callander, Adrienne, and Michael Cummings. 2021. "Liminal Spaces: The Art in Entrepreneurship and the Entrepreneurship in Art." *Small Business Economics* 57, no. 2: 739–754.

Castellano, Carlos Garrido. 2018. "The Institution of Institutionalism: Difference, Universalism and the Legacies of Institutional Critique." *Culture, Theory and Critique* 59, no. 1: 59–73.

Cook, Chuck. 2015. "The Photographer as Participant Observer: Ed Wheeler and the Gulf Oil Rigs, 1981–1985." *Southern Quarterly* 52, no. 4: 104–121.

Creed, W. E. Douglas, Steven S. Taylor, and Bryant Ashley Hudson. 2020. "Institutional Aesthetics: Embodied Ways of Encountering, Evaluating, and Enacting Institutions." *Organization Studies* 41, no. 3: 415–435.

Csikszentmihalyi, Mihaly. 1996. *Creativity: Flow and the Psychology of Discovery and Invention*. New York: HarperCollins.

Danto, Arthur C. *The Transfiguration of the Commonplace: A Philosophy of Art*. Cambridge, MA: Harvard University Press, 1981.

Deutsche, Rosalyn. 1996. "Property Values: Hans Haacke, Real Estate, and the Museum." In *Evictions: Art and Spatial Politics*, 159–192. Cambridge, MA: MIT Press.

Dezeuze, Anna. 2006. "Everyday Life, 'Relational Aesthetics' and the 'Transfiguration of the Commonplace.'" *Journal of Visual Art Practice* 5, no. 3: 143–152.

di Liscia, Valentina. 2020. "Nan Goldin Testifies at Landmark Hearing on Purdue Pharma's Role in Opioid Crisis." Hyperallergic, December 21, 2020. https://hyperallergic.com/609594/nan-goldin-testifies-at-landmark-hearing-on-purdue-pharmas-role-in-opioid-crisis/.

di Liscia, Valentina. 2021. "Citing Job Insecurity, Whitney Museum Workers Are Unionizing." Hyperallergic, May 18, 2021. https://hyperallergic.com/646835/whitney-museum-workers-are-unionizing/.

DiMaggio, Paul J. 1988. "Interest and Agency in Institutional Theory." In *Institutional Patterns and Organizations: Culture and Environment*, edited by Lynne G. Zucker, 3–21. Cambridge, MA: Ballinger.

DiMaggio, Paul J., and Walter W. Powell. 1983. "The Iron Cage Revisited: Institutional Isomorphism and Collective Rationality in Organizational Fields." *American Sociological Review* 48, no. 2: 147–160.

DiMaggio, Paul J., and Walter Powell. 1991. "Introduction." In *The New Institutionalism in Organizational Analysis*, edited by Walter P. Powell and Paul J. DiMaggio, 1–40. Chicago: University of Chicago Press.

Dodd, Sarah. 2014. "Roots Radical—Place, Power and Practice in Punk Entrepreneurship." *Entrepreneurship and Regional Development* 26, no. 1: 165–205. http://doi.org/10.1080/08985626.2013.877986.

Dodd, Sarah, Tobias Pret, and Eleanor Shaw. 2016. "Advancing Understanding of Entrepreneurial Embeddedness: Forms of Capital, Social Contexts and Time." In *A Research Agenda for Entrepreneurship and Context*, edited by Friederike Welter and William B. Gartner, 120–134. Cheltenham, UK: Edward Elgar.

Edmonston, Paul. 1983. "Participant Observation and Visual Documentation as Modes of Inquiry in the Visual Arts." *Visual Arts Research* 9, no. 1: 78–87.

Eisenhardt, Kathleen M., and Melissa E. Graebner. 2007. "Theory Building from Cases: Opportunities and Challenges." *Academy of Management Journal* 50, no. 1: 25–32.

Emanuel, Rahm, host. 2019. "Ep. 93: Theaster Gates's Community Canvas." *Chicago Stories with Mayor Rahm Emanuel*. Chicago Mayor's Office, April 30, 2019. Video. https://www.youtube.com/watch?v=CoVdzD6eKYg.

Emirbayer, Mustafa, and Ann Mische. 1998. "What Is Agency?" *American Journal of Sociology* 103, no. 4: 962–1023.

Faris, Marc. 2004. "'That Chicago Sound': Playing with (Local) Identity in Underground Rock." *Popular Music and Society* 27, no. 4: 429–454.

Fernández-Blanco, Víctor, and Juan Prieto-Rodríguez. 2020. "Museums." In *Handbook of Cultural Economics*, edited by Ruth Towse and Trilce Navarrete Hernández, 349–357. Cheltenham, UK: Edward Elgar.

Finkelpearl, Tom. 2013. *What We Made: Conversations on Art and Social Cooperation*. Durham, NC: Duke University Press.

Fligstein, Neil. 2001. "Social Skill and the Theory of Fields." *Sociological Theory* 19, no. 2: 105–125.

Fraser, Andrea. 2005. "From the Critique of Institutions to an Institution of Critique." *Artforum*, September: 278–283.

Garud, Raghu, Cynthia Hardy, and Steve Maguire. 2007. "Institutional Entrepreneurship as Embedded Agency: An Introduction to the Special Issue." *Organization Studies* 28, no. 7: 957–969.

Garud, Raghu, and Peter Karnøe. 2001. "Path Creation as a Process of Mindful Deviation." In *Path Dependence and Creation*, edited by Raghu Garu and Peter Karnøe, 1–40. Mahwah, NJ: Lawrence Erlbaum.

Garud, Raghu, Arun Kumaraswamy, and Peter Karnøe. 2010. "Path Dependence or Path Creation?" *Journal of Management Studies* 47, no. 4: 760–774. https://onlinelibrary.wiley.com/doi/10.1111/j.1467-6486.2009.00914.x.

Gates, Theaster. 2014. "The Artist Corporation and the Collective." *Nka: Journal of Contemporary African Art* 34: 74–79.

Gates, Theaster. n.d. "Rebuild Foundation." Theaster Gates (website). https://www.theastergates.com/project-items/rebuild-foundation.

Goddard, Stacie E. 2020. "Revolution from the Inside: Institutions, Legitimation Strategies, and Rhetorical Pathways of Institutional Change." *Global Policy* 11, no. 3: 83–92.

Goldin, Nan. 2018. "Nan Goldin." *Artforum*, January 2018. https://www.artforum.com/features/nan-goldin-2-237147/.

Greenwood, Royston, and Roy Suddaby. 2006. "Institutional Entrepreneurship in Mature Fields: The Big Five Accounting Firms." *Academy of Management Journal* 49, no. 1: 27–48.

Groys, Boris. 2014. *On the New*. Translated by G. M. Goshgarian. New York: Verso Books.

Hardy, Cynthia, and Steve Maguire. 2008. "Institutional Entrepreneurship." In *The Sage Handbook of Organizational Institutionalism*, edited by Royston Greenwood, Christine Oliver, Thomas B. Lawrence, and Renate E. Meyer, 198–217. London: Sage.

Hart, Stephanie. 2008. "Ways of See(th)ing: A Record of Visual Punk Practice." *Postmodern Culture* 18, no. 2. https://muse.jhu.edu/article/245448.

Heffernan, Nick. 2015. "No Parents, No Church, No Authorities in Our Films: Exploitation Movies, the Youth Audience, and Roger Corman's Counterculture Trilogy." *Journal of Film and Video* 67, no. 2: 3–20.

Henfridsson, Ola, and Youngjin Yoo. 2014. "The Liminality of Trajectory Shifts in Institutional Entrepreneurship." *Organization Science* 25, no. 3: 932–950. https://www.tandfonline.com/doi/abs/10.1080/08985626.2012.746883.

Hileman, Kristen. 2010. "Romantic Realist: An Interview with Hans Haacke." *American Art* 24, no. 2: 75–93.

Hjorth, Daniel. 2011. "On Provocation, Education and Entrepreneurship." *Entrepreneurship and Regional Development* 23, nos. 1–2: 49–63.

Hjorth, Daniel. 2013. "Public Entrepreneurship: Desiring Social Change, Creating Sociality." *Entrepreneurship and Regional Development*, 25, nos. 1–2: 34–51. https://doi.org/10.1080/08985626.2012.746883.

Hjorth, Daniel, and Bjorn Bjerke. 2006. "Public Entrepreneurship: Moving from Social/Consumer to Public/Citizen." In *Entrepreneurship as Social Change: A Third Movements in Entrepreneurship Book*, edited by Chris Steyaert and Daniel Hjorth, 97–120. Cheltenham, UK: Edward Elgar.

Holms, Brian. 2009. "Extradisciplinary Investigations: Towards a New Critique of Institutions." In *Art and Contemporary Critical Practice: Reinventing Institutional Critique*, edited by Gerald Raunig and Gene Ray, 53–61. London: Mayfly Books.

Jobey, Liz. 2019. "Nan Goldin on Art, Addiction and Her Battle with the Sacklers over Opioids." *Financial Times*, November 8, 2019. https://www.ft.com/content/d6500c16-002a-11ea-b7bc-f3fa4e77dd47.

Kastner, Jens. 2009. "Artistic Internationalism and Institutional Critique." In *Art and Contemporary Critical Practice: Reinventing Institutional Critique*, edited by Gerald Raunig and Gene Ray, 43–51. London: Mayfly Books.

Kennell, Amanda. 2019. "Yayoi Kusama, the Modern Alice." *Journal of Adaptation in Film and Performance* 12, no. 3: 195–210.

Kier, Alexander S., and Jeffery S. McMullen. 2018. "Entrepreneurial Imaginativeness in New Venture Ideation." *Academy of Management Journal* 61, no. 6: 2265–2295.

King, Brayden G., Teppo Felin, and David A. Whetten. 2009. "Comparative Organizational Analysis: An Introduction." In *Studying Differences Between Organizations: Comparative Approaches to Organizational Research*, edited by Brayden G. King, Teppo Felin, and David A. Whetten, 3–19. Vol. 26 of Research in the Sociology of Organizations. Bingley, UK: Emerald. https://www.emerald.com/insight/content/doi/10.1108/S0733-558X(2009)0000026002/full/html.

La Force, Thessaly. 2018. "Nan Goldin Survived an Overdose to Fight the Opioid Epidemic." *New York Times Style Magazine*. June 11, 2018. https://www.nytimes.com/2018/06/11/t-magazine/a-heroin-chic-photographers-new-project-tackling-the-opioid-epidemic.html.

Lawrence, Thomas B., Bernard Leca, and Roy Suddaby. 2009. "Introduction: Theorizing and Studying Institutional Work." In *Institutional Work: Actors and Agency in Institutional Studies of Organizations*, edited by Thomas B. Lawrence, Roy Suddaby, and Bernard Leca, 1–27. Cambridge, UK: Cambridge University Press.

Lawrence, Thomas, Roy Suddaby, and Bernard Leca. 2011. "Institutional Work: Refocusing Institutional Studies of Organization." *Journal of Management Inquiry* 20, no. 1: 52–58.

Lee, T. L., Mitchell, and C. J. Sablynski. 1999. "Qualitative Research in Organizational and Vocational Psychology: 1979–1999." *Journal of Vocational Behavior* 55: 161–187.

Lippard, Lucy. 1973. *Six Years: The Dematerialization of the Art Object*. New York: Praeger.

Mannes-Abbott, Guy. 2013. "Theaster Gates: 'My Labor Is My Protest.'" *Third Text* 27, no. 6: 811–814.

McGraw, Hesse. 2012. "Theaster Gates: Radical Reform with Everyday Tools." *Afterall: A Journal of Art, Context and Enquiry* 30: 86–99.

McMullen, Jeffery S., and Dean A. Shepherd. 2006. "Entrepreneurial Action and the Role of Uncertainty in the Theory of the Entrepreneur." *Academy of Management Review* 31, no. 1: 132–152.

McMullen, Jeffery, Katrina Brownell, and Joel Adams. 2021. "What Makes an Entrepreneurship Study Entrepreneurial? Toward a Unified Theory of Entrepreneurial Agency." *Entrepreneurship Theory and Practice* 45, no. 5: 1197–1238.

Mead, George Herbert. 1932. *The Philosophy of the Present*. Chicago: University of Chicago Press.

Miles, Matthew B., and A. Michael Huberman. 1994. *Qualitative Data Analysis: An Expanded Sourcebook*. Newbury Park, CA: Sage.

Misangyi, Vilmos F., Gary R. Weaver, and Heather Elms. 2008. "Ending Corruption: The Interplay Among Institutional Logics, Resources, and Institutional Entrepreneurs." *Academy of Management Review* 33, no. 3: 750–770.

MTL Collective. 2018. "From Institutional Critique to Institutional Liberation? A Decolonial Perspective on the Crises of Contemporary Art." *October* 165: 192–227.
Mutch, Alistair. 2007. "Reflexivity and the Institutional Entrepreneur: A Historical Exploration." *Organization Studies* 28, no. 7: 1123–1140.
O'Brien, Glenn. 2011. "Nan Goldin: In the Frame." *Harper's Bazaar*. October 19, 2011. https://www.harpersbazaar.com/culture/features/a822/nan-goldin-in-the-frame-1111/.
Peltomäki, Kirsi. 2007. "Affect and Spectatorial Agency: Viewing Institutional Critique in the 1970s." *Art Journal* 66, no. 4: 36–51.
Piper, Adrian. 1992. "The Joy of Marginality." In "The Nineties: Moving Forward, Reaching Back: A Multicultural Odyssey," edited by Susan Sherman, special issue, *Ikon* 12–13: 3–8.
Pollock, Griselda, ed. 2006. *Psychoanalysis and the Image: Transdisciplinary Perspectives*. Malden, MA: Blackwell.
Qualls, Larry. 1995. "Performance/Photography." *Performing Arts Journal* 17, no. 1: 26–34.
Raunig, Gerald. 2009. "Instituent Practices: Fleeing, Instituting, Transforming." In *Art and Contemporary Critical Practice: Reinventing Institutional Critique*, edited by Gerald Raunig and Gene Ray, 3–12. London: Mayfly Books.
Raunig, Gerald, and Gene Ray, eds. 2009. *Art and Contemporary Critical Practice: Reinventing Institutional Critique*. London: Mayfly Books.
Reinhardt, Kathleen. 2015. "Theaster Gates's Dorchester Projects in Chicago." *Journal of Urban History* 41, no. 2: 193–206.
Rindova, Violina, Daved Barry, and David Ketchen. 2009. "Entrepreneuring as Emancipation." *Academy of Management Review* 34, no. 3: 477–491.
Ruddy, Sarah. 2009. "'A Radiant Eye Yearns from Me': Figuring Documentary in the Photography of Nan Goldin." *Feminist Studies* 35, no. 2: 347–380.
Sarasvathy, Saras D. 2001. "Causation and Effectuation: Toward a Theoretical Shift from Economic Inevitability to Entrepreneurial Contingency." *Academy of Management Review* 26, no. 2: 243–263.
Schaefer, Eric. 2002. "Gauging a Revolution: 16 mm Film and the Rise of the Pornographic Feature." *Cinema Journal* 41, no. 3: 3–26.
Schulman, Michael. 2022. "Nan Visits the De-Sacklered Met." *New Yorker*, November 21, 2022. https://www.newyorker.com/magazine/2022/11/21/nan-goldin-visits-the-de-sacklered-met.
Sedgwick, Eve Kosofsky. 2003. *Touching Feeling: Affect, Pedagogy, Performativity*. Durham, NC: Duke University Press.
Selvin, Claire. 2020. "Yayoi Kusama's Storied 'Narcissus Garden' Installation Goes on View in Arkansas." *ArtNews*, April 12, 2020. https://www.artnews.com/art-news/news/yayoi-kusamas-narcissus-garden-the-momentary-arkansas-1202696665/.
Seo, Myeong-Gu, and W. E. Douglas Creed. 2002. "Institutional Contradictions, Praxis, and Institutional Change: A Dialectical Perspective." *Academy of Management Review* 27, no. 2: 222–247.
Serafini, Paula. 2018. *Performance Action: The Politics of Art Activism*. London: Routledge.
Sheikh, Simon. 2009. "Notes on Institutional Critique." In *Art and Contemporary Critical Practice: Reinventing Institutional Critique*, edited by Gerald Raunig and Gene Ray, 29–32. London: Mayfly Books.
Sholette, Gregory G. 2003. "Dark Matter, Las Agencias, and the Aesthetics of Tactical Embarrassment." *Journal of Aesthetics and Protest* 1, no. 2. https://www.joaap.org/1/yomango/.

Smithson, Robert. 1972. "Cultural Confinement." *Artforum*, October. https://www.artforum.com/features/cultural-confinement-2-215283/.

Steyerl, Hito. 2009. "The Institution of Critique." In *Art and Contemporary Critical Practice: Reinventing Institutional Critique*, edited by Gerald Raunig and Gene Ray, 13–20. London: Mayfly Books.

Sturken, Marita. 1997. *Tangled Memories: The Vietnam War, the AIDS Epidemic, and the Politics of Remembering*. Berkeley: University of California Press.

Suddaby, Roy. 2010. "Challenges for Institutional Theory." *Journal of Management Inquiry* 19, no. 1: 14–20.

Suddaby, Roy, Alex Bitektine, and Patrick Haack. 2017. "Legitimacy." *Academy of Management Annals* 11, no. 1: 451–478.

Swanson, Carl. 2012. "The Art of the Flame-Out." *New York Magazine*, July 6, 2012. https://nymag.com/arts/art/features/yayoi-kusama-2012-7/.

Thornton, Patricia H., William Ocasio, and Michael Lounsbury. 2012. *The Institutional Logics Perspective: A New Approach to Culture, Structure and Process*. Oxford: Oxford University Press.

Viveros-Fauné, Christian. 2021. "Nan Goldin Gets Your P.A.I.N." *Village Voice*, April 21, 2021. https://www.villagevoice.com/2021/04/21/nan-goldin-gets-your-p-a-i-n.

Wei, Lilly. 2011. "In the Studio: Theaster Gates." *Art in America* 99: 120–126.

Wijnberg, Nachoem, and Gerda Gemser. 2000. "Adding Value to Innovation: Impressionism and the Transformation of the Selection System in Visual Arts." *Organization Science* 11, no. 3: 323–329.

Yi, Hyewon. 2013. "Photographer as Participant Observer: Larry Clark, Nan Goldin, Richard Billingham, and Nobuyoshi Araki." PhD diss., City University of New York.

Zhao, Eric Y., Masakazu Ishihara, P. Devereaux Jennings, and Michael Lounsbury. 2018. "Optimal Distinctiveness in the Console Video Game Industry: An Exemplar-Based Model of Proto-Category Evolution." *Organization Science* 29, no. 4: 588–611. https://pubsonline.informs.org/doi/10.1287/orsc.2017.1194.

CHAPTER 36

ASSESSING THE BUSINESS MODEL OF CREATIVE AND CULTURAL ORGANIZATIONS PARTICIPATING IN THE EUROPEAN CAPITAL OF CULTURE PROGRAM

GIOVANNI SCHIUMA, DANIELA CARLUCCI,
FRANCESCO SANTARSIERO, AND
ROSARIA LAGRUTTA

Introduction

EUROPEAN Capital of Culture (ECoC) is one of the European Union's most highly praised initiatives. The initiative's aim is to bring fresh life to the city chosen as ECoC and boost its cultural, social, and economic development. The city nominated ECoC has a full year to celebrate arts and the great cultural diversity that characterizes European countries. It designs and develops a cultural program with a solid European dimension that involves citizens living in the city and its surroundings and those from elsewhere. Broad citizen participation in the ECoC program is a key factor in the success of an ECoC year. Citizens should be actively engaged throughout the entire process, from the bidding phase through the implementation and ending with evaluating the mega-event's legacy. Creative and cultural organizations are crucial in engaging citizens, creating opportunities for a wide range of people to proactively and actively participate in the development of cultural projects and events included in the program. Boosting and widening access to culture, they act as a powerful engine of the ECoC initiative.

In recent years there has been an interesting debate regarding the role that ECoCs play in the development and growth of creative and cultural organizations operating in designated capital cities, their region, and beyond (e.g., Campbell 2011; Garcia et al. 2009 b; Garcia, Melville, and Cox 2010; Langen and Garcia 2009). Palmer (2004) stated that most ECoC cities consider the expansion of creative industries to be one of their economic priorities. The United Kingdom's Department for Culture, Media and Sport (2008) claimed that the increased level of activity within creative industries associated with ECoC status can assist in the revitalization of the city.

Examining the long-term impacts of the ECoC program over the past thirty years and exploring successful strategies and best practices, Garcia and Cox (2013, 113) pointed out that the "impacts upon the host city's existing cultural system and plans for cultural activity are the most prolific areas of reported beneficial impact from ECoCs. Benefits include projects that continue beyond the hosting year, increased collaboration and networking between cultural providers, and increased capacity and ambition within the sector." However, the same scholars also highlighted that "even with sustained and tangible plans, there is unlikely to be a strong legacy of creative industries' development resulting from the recent ECoC programs" (143). Campbell (2011) argued that there is no strong evidence of linkage between cultural initiatives in the ECoC setting and creative industry development.

So while the ECoC designation of a city has a broader impact on the city's profile and potentially increases the credibility of its creative and cultural offerings, there are different experiences regarding the impact on creative and cultural organizations directly involved in the project (Campbell 2011; Garcia et al. 2009 a), and additional research on ECoC's impact on creative and cultural industries would be of benefit.

This chapter attempts to contribute to the debate on the effects of ECoC events on creative and cultural organizations participating in the ECoC program. The focus is on the impacts on such organizations' business models. The study used an exploratory research and qualitative approach, focusing on the ECOC program of Matera, Italy, that is one of the two cities named ECOC in 2019. Extensive documentary research was done, along with in-depth interviews conducted with creative practitioners actively engaged in the Matera ECOC program. Interviews were conducted a few months before and shortly after the 2019 ECoC program was complete. They involved project and cultural managers of five local creative and cultural organizations that implemented large cultural projects as part of the program. The research attempted to capture and analyze the effects of the Matera 2019 experience on how the investigated creative and cultural organizations create, distribute, and capture value. Particular attention was paid to changes of their business model. These effects were explored and analyzed through the lenses of the Business Model Prism (Schiuma and Lerro 2017), a multidimensional framework describing the structure and logic of the business model of a creative and cultural organization. Specifically, we asked: *Has developing big projects included in the ECoC program produced some changes in how the examined organizations translate resources into projects and results and create value? What kind of changes occurred?*

The remainder of the chapter is organized as follows. First the chapter provides a view of the evaluation of ECoC impacts. Then it addresses some critical issues regarding the business modeling of creative and cultural organizations and describes the Business Model Prism. After that, the chapter illustrates the research method and the findings of the case studies analysis. Finally, concluding remarks and suggestions for future research work are presented.

Evaluating the Impacts of ECoC

The European Capital of Culture program was born in 1985, thanks to Greek minister of culture Melina Mercouri. Her idea was to designate a city as an ECoC to celebrate arts and culture throughout the year and highlight the richness of the great cultural diversity that characterizes the European countries. According to the European Union (2015), the ECoC program has grown yearly, becoming the most significant European cultural event. It impacts the cultural sphere of each city designated as an ECoC and has social, educational, urban planning, and economic impacts on the surrounding region.

The mega-event acts as a catalyst that fosters a changed perception of the European image and serves as an engine of development. ECoC, initially seen as a celebratory event, is nowadays considered a transformational process for the hosting city, part of a long-term culture-based development strategy designed to improve the hosting city's international profile, enhance its residents' pride and self-confidence, and produce sustainable socioeconomic impacts (Burksiene, Dvorak, and Burbulyte-Tsiskarishvili 2018; European Union 2015; Fox and Rampton 2016; Garcia 1990; Rampton et al. 2011). The cities chosen as ECoCs have an excellent opportunity to reinvent themselves, starting from their cultural resources and investing in new growth paths. Each city exploits this advantage by designing its cultural program to take advantage of its features and strengths. Over the years the cities have assessed the impacts of such events in heterogeneous ways (Ebejer, Xuereb, and Avellino 2021).

Most of the evaluation studies were final reports written by the staff members of the organization responsible for ECoC implementation or studies commissioned by independent bodies or developed by research centers (e.g., Liu 2019b; Palmer and Richard 2004; Steiner, Frey, and Hotz 2015; Van der Steen and Richards 2021). Several ECoCs (e.g., Luxembourg in 2007, Liverpool in 2008, Essen in 2010, and Mons in 2015) developed indicators and methodologies to assess the event's impacts across different areas, including culture, the economy, image, the environment, and policies. Recently, the European Commission introduced new assessment requirements for ECoCs post-2019. From 2020 to 2033, each city will be responsible for evaluating the results of its year as ECoC.

Great attention has been paid to macro effects of the ECoC designation. Some scholars (e.g., Ebejer, Xuereb, and Avellino 2021; Liu 2019 a; Nobili 2005; Richard and Wilson 2004; Turşie and Perrin 2020) analyzed the impacts of the mega-event in terms of image branding and repositioning as well as in terms of the social and sustainability effects. Srakar and Vecco (2017) and Gomes and Librero-Cano (2018) applied, respectively, an econometric model and a difference-in-differences approach to measuring the effects of cultural events on GDP, the employment growth, and other economic dimensions. Several scholars investigated ECoC impacts in terms of tourism and economic growth, image and perceptions, social goals, sustainability, and urban and political facets (e.g., Garcia et al. 2008; Garcia et al. 2009 b, 2010; Garcia and Cox 2013; Hughes 2003; Myerscough 1994; Palmer and Richard 2004; Richards and Wilson 2004; Richards, Hitters, and Fernandes 2002).

The studied impacts have both common and unique traits. This is understandable given the differences in the sixty cities that received the ECoC designation between 1985 and 2019. Investigating success strategies and long-term effects of ECoCs in three decades, Garcia and Cox (2013) and Garcia (2019) examined the published material produced by ECoC host cities. They reviewed the evidence of impacts and long-term effects from cultural, economic, social, and policy viewpoints. The scholars highlighted that after three decades, the ECoC is a crucial platform for city positioning and a catalyst for economic and cultural regeneration (Balsas 2004). They have identified some areas of positive impact for which evidence is relatively robust: cultural and image impacts, economic impacts, and social impacts.

Cultural and image impacts. ECoC produced substantial effects on a city's cultural vibrancy by reinforcing formal and informal networks, creating opportunities for new collaborations and new work, and nurturing the capacity and ambition of the cultural sector. Hosting ECoC also produced an image renaissance for low-profile (or negative-profile) cities by attracting considerable media attention and improving local, national and international perceptions.

Economic impacts. ECoC produced a substantial immediate to medium-term effect on tourism development. Regarding long-term effects, scholars have concluded that cities undergoing major repositioning during or post-ECoC can sustain growth in tourism visits and expenditures in the long term. However, cities' assertions of positive economic impacts have been overinflated or are lacking in robust evidence, particularly in terms of job creation.

Social impacts. Hosting ECoC improved local perceptions of the city. Many recent ECoCs claim that 50 to 90 percent of their local population feel that their city is a "better place" after hosting the mega-event. Hosting ECoC fostered local pride and a can-do attitude and produced an increase in the volume and diversity of cultural audiences during the ECoC year. Some cities declared that over half of their local population engaged with their ECoC program.

About other areas of impact, from physical to policy and political effects, it is harder to prove the added value of the ECoC program, due to the complexity of methodologies required for capturing such effects.

The literature review on the impacts of ECoC shows that in most cases, studies provided a macro-scale analysis of the cultural, social, and economic impacts of ECoC. This is reasonable, as the ECoC title is perceived as an essential part of a local development strategy pursuing mainly socioeconomic growth. However, it is equally important to understand the micro-level effects that such an event produces on citizens and organizations experiencing ECoC and directly involved in its implementation. In this regard, Fišer and Kožuh (2019) and Steen and Richards (2021), focusing respectively on Maribor ECoC 2012 and La Valletta ECoC 2018, analyzed the impact on feelings of community reputation and pride. Garcia et al. (2009 a) and the investigated the impacts of Liverpool ECoC on residents, artists, and creative and cultural organizations. Stipanović, Rudan, and Zubović (2019) analyzed the role of cultural and creative industries in creating innovative urban tourism, considering them as critical stakeholders in transforming Rijeka from an industrial city into a city with a strong cultural identity. Boyko (2007) examined the impact of the ECoC program on place meanings for the local community in the city of Bruges, focusing mainly on the event's social, physical, and psychological effects on the resident population.

Understanding the impacts of an ECoC on its key actors such as citizens and creative and cultural organizations is crucial. The effects and lasting legacy of an ECoC depend indeed on solid, continuous, and participation by citizens in the cultural life of the city. They depend as well on capacity building in cultural and creative organizations to increase their sustainability and competitiveness. We next explore how developing an ECoC program can lead such organizations to modify the ways they combine their assets and activities to create and deliver social, economic, and cultural value for individuals, groups, and society as a whole.

Grasping the Business Model in Creative and Cultural Organizations: The Business Model Prism

The Business Model in Creative and Cultural Organizations

Given their intrinsic orientation toward value creation in terms of social impacts rather than profits, creative and cultural organizations are reluctant to consider themselves as organizations doing some form of business. Undoubtedly, there are differences between the main concerns and scopes of a creative and cultural organization and those of a for-profit business, even though both have to achieve financial viability. However, business modeling remains fundamental for creative and cultural organizations that aim to remain competitive and deliver sustainable value over time (Laasch 2018; Schiuma and Lerro 2017).

The literature on business models in the arts and cultural sector is still fragmented and embryonic. This is probably due to the heterogeneity of the creative and cultural sector, which includes several types of organizations with specific missions, aims, and orientations toward the market.

Focusing on museums, Falk and Sheppard (2006) highlight the importance of a radical new business model for these organizations to survive the transition into the knowledge age. The scholars offer insights for planning a business model to preserve museums' financial viability and artistic integrity. Referring again to museums, Decker-Lange, Singer, and Schrander (2019) illustrate how stakeholders' fluctuating emphasis on economic, cultural, and political logics influences the content, structure, and governance of the activities constituting the business models of research museums. For visual arts organizations, Royce (2011, 32) highlights the necessary traits of a robust business model, including "financial viability, sound managerial systems and human resource practices, good leadership and clear governance, a sound knowledge of present and future audiences, participants and customers, strong networks and good relationships with stakeholders, customers and suppliers." Rodríguez (2016) argues that there is a need to eradicate false distinctions between business and the arts and cultural sector, and provides some ideas from management studies that may lead arts managers to adopt more strategic approaches for their organizations. Li (2020) focuses on business model innovation in creative industries, and argues that such innovations are primarily digital.

Despite the heterogeneity of studies, it is clear that business modeling is a valuable means for creative and cultural organizations to articulate their values and objectives and connect them to their customers, suppliers, and partners through proper exploitation of organizational assets and processes.

By modeling their business, creative and cultural organizations can describe how they create, deliver, and capture value (Osterwalder and Pigneur 2010) and update their strategy to consider socioeconomic challenges and trends.

The Business Model Prism

Business modeling is increasingly acknowledged as essential to creative and cultural organization success. It allows such organizations to understand better how they create, deliver, and capture value. This is particularly relevant since today creative and cultural organizations are challenged to achieve financial viability without compromising their mission and not-for-profit values, to spur social innovation, and to serve as a catalyst for change for organizations operating in other traditional sectors (Schiuma and Lerro 2017). The methods and tools for describing and managing tailor-made business models in the creative and cultural sectors are still being studied (Dümcke 2015; Li 2020; Munoz-Seca 2011; Schiuma and Lerro 2017).

Recently, Schiuma and Lerro (2017) proposed a multidimensional framework, the Business Model Prism (BMP), as a way to map the structure and logic of creative and cultural organizations' business models. Built on the findings of a comprehensive review of the literature concerning business models in the creative and cultural sector, the BMP describes the business model of a creative and cultural organization through seven facets, shown in Figure 36.1. The upper facet refers to social and cultural value and impact; the lower facet refers to funding and financial resilience. The other five

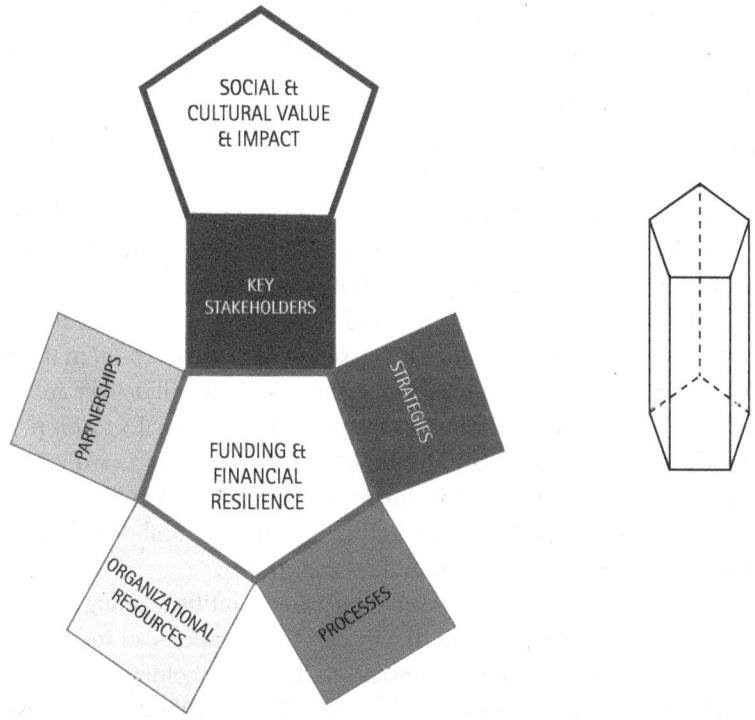

FIGURE 36.1 The Business Model Prism.
Source: Schiuma and Lerro 2017, 8, Creative Commons Attribution 4.0 International License.

facets describe the remaining critical dimensions of a business model: stakeholders, strategies, processes, organizational resources, and partnerships. The seven facets are interrelated and provide an organization with lenses through which to think about the critical questions it wants to address when seeking to manage its activities. Each facet is described by specific questions that allow us to fully understand a creative and cultural organization's internal working mechanisms and value creation dynamics:

> *Social and Cultural Value and Impact.* Why do we exist? What impact do we want to have? Which values do we wish to propose and offer? What are our mission and vision?
> *Stakeholders.* Who are our key stakeholders? What are their wants, needs, expectations, and dreams?
> *Strategies.* What are we doing to satisfy our stakeholders and deliver value for them? What are the leading products and services we offer? What is our legal structure? What is our current organizational structure?
> *Processes.* What are our existing processes? How do we manage our projects and programs? What are the characteristics of our productions? How do we generate and sustain demand? How do we carry out research and development?
> *Organizational Resources.* What resources do we need in order to implement, exploit, and enhance our processes?

Partnerships. What partnerships do we need to build and enhance in order to implement our strategy, communicate our social and cultural values, and guarantee our impact?

Funding and Financial Resilience. What are our current costs and incomes? What is our financial status?

According to Schiuma and Lerro (2017, 9), these "key questions define the main issues to be addressed and managed to support the development of the fundamental theoretical pillars distinguishing the business model of an arts/culture organization." The basic assumption of the BMP is that a creative and cultural organization must have a clear picture of its value creation dynamics to be sustainable and successful in the long term. It must define what social and cultural value and impact it will deliver and for whom; consequently, it has to define its mission, vision, and strategies. To accomplish this, an organization has to identify its key stakeholders. Schiuma and Lerro (2017) identify the following critical categories of stakeholders for creative and cultural organizations: users, artists, members, staff, volunteers, other arts and cultural organizations, public administration and institutions, communities, and society.

Once the most influential key stakeholders are identified, along with their primary wants, needs, expectations, and dreams, an organization can focus on designing its strategy. The organization must translate its key stakeholders' requirements into pragmatic objectives and outputs to be delivered. The identification of these strategic objectives can be complemented with an analysis of the products and services the organization is delivering or developing. In addition, the strategy should encompass the organization's legal structure and its organizational chart.

Next, the organization must undertake an analysis of the processes needed to achieve the targeted strategic objectives: creating and offering value, reaching audiences and users, supporting audience development, managing stakeholder relationships, generating revenues, and controlling costs. The analysis of such processes must be complemented with an understanding of the organizational resources available and needed for their implementation. Organizational resources include people, practices, technologies, and infrastructures.

Then the partners playing a pivotal role in successful strategy implementation must be identified. Creative and cultural organizations can create partnerships to optimize operations and better allocate resources; reduce risk and uncertainty; acquire specific resources, knowledge, and licenses; or explore new opportunities and potential markets. Four main types of partnerships have been identified: partnerships with other arts and cultural organizations, partnerships with businesses, partnerships with communities and nongovernmental organizations, and partnerships with public authorities.

Finally, the business model requires an understanding of the organization's economic and financial sustainability, specifically in terms of funding and financial resilience.

BMP is a multidimensional framework that encourages managers to think through the links between the strategy, resources, and activities that underpin value creation.

Discerning the Effects of ECoC on Creative and Cultural Organizations' Business Models Through the Lens of the Business Model Prism

Methods

This research used a case study approach to investigate the effects of ECoC on the business model of the creative and cultural organizations leading the ECoC projects. The case study method was applied since it is the most appropriate one for probing beneath the surface of a situation and producing a rich context for deep understanding of the investigated phenomenon. It enriches the empirical base, especially when quantitative or statistical data are difficult to extract (Robinson and Shumar 2014).

Extensive documentary research and a series of semistructured research interviews were carried out with creative practitioners actively involved in implementing the ECoC program in Matera in 2019. The interviews were conducted from September 2019 to early March 2020, before the outbreak of the COVID-19 pandemic. They involved project and cultural managers of five creative and cultural organizations that implemented big cultural projects in the Matera 2019 program. The Matera Basilicata 2019 Foundation suggested the organizations, with the idea of ensuring, through the proposed sample, a sort of representativeness of all organizations involved in the program (in terms of organizational configuration, site of operation, and sector). Therefore, the analyzed organizations have different organizational configurations (one social cooperative, one theater company, and three cultural associations), come from different territories (two from Matera, two from Potenza, and one from Pisticci), and operate in various creative-cultural sectors (two in theater, one in visual arts and education, one in audiovisual, and one in the integration of migrants and disabled individuals). Together with other creative and cultural organizations, these organizations developed a remarkable part of the Matera 2019 cultural program. From a total of eighty-one applicants that responded to a public call in 2017, twenty-seven local creative and cultural organizations were selected and named project leaders (PLs).

The development of these projects proceeded in two phases. In the first phase, the selected PLs attended a capacity-building program (the Build Up project) that focused on several themes: the European dimension, the artistic facet, management, production of outputs for the audience, and production sustainability. During the Build Up project, the PLs had the chance to collaborate, share experiences, and plan an in-depth executive project. Next, in 2018, the PLs had the opportunity to meet the public and evaluate their projects' technical and economic feasibility through so-called crash tests. This allowed them to refine and calibrate their projects' objectives and activities. Overall, then, the PLs embarked on a two-year journey that included capacity-building activities, project co-creation paths, tests, and finally the accomplishment of cultural productions that involved local communities and large interested audiences. During this journey, the PLs got involved in an experimental process of artistic and cultural production and social innovation, working for and with citizens and collaborating with other local, national and international institutions and organizations.

Through a series of meetings and semistructured interviews, the scholars probed different facets of interviewees' experiences of Matera 2019, capturing their perceptions about the changes in their business model against their participation in the mega event. All the interviews were—with the consent of the PLs—recorded and transcribed. This provided a reliable information base that accurately reflected the interviewees' thoughts. Each interview had an average duration of four hours. Manual coding was used for analyzing data. The interview guide was designed in such a way as to allow analysis of changes in business model as described in the BMP. The BMP was chosen as a lens to investigate the effects of Matera 2019 on organizations' business models since it allows for a deep analysis from multiple angles. The interviews helped produce reasonably accurate data concerning the interviewees' perceptions of the changes in their business model a few months after the conclusion of their projects and Matera 2019.

Findings

The projects developed by the investigated organizations were original productions in which citizens became actors and co-authors themselves. Citizens had the opportunity to play an active role in the project development and choose their engagement level. This was intended to accomplish one of the main aims of Matera ECoC 2019: stimulating social innovation in the community. Table 36.1 shows a summary of the projects developed by the five PLs.

Designing and managing a big project for Matera 2019 forced the studied organizations to reflect on their value proposition and strategic objectives as well as on the use of organizational resources, the development of activities and relationships, and the management of financial resources.

In the following, the main findings from the joint analysis of the five case studies are described through the seven dimensions of the BMP.

Social and Cultural Value and Impact

The Matera 2019 experience corroborated the social and cultural value proposition of each PL. All the interviewed managers emphasized that developing a big project for Matera 2019 confirmed their aim to use art in multiple ways: as a social activator; as a tool for connecting people; as a means of dialogue with reality, the city, and its inhabitants; as a way of promoting the cultural regeneration of communities; as a way of

Table 36.1. Projects Developed by the Examined Project Leaders

Organization	Project
A	A traveling theater recalling an abandoned ship that traveled through five peripheral communities by narrating stories extrapolated from the experiences of people living in the peripheral areas. The project aimed to communicate the identity of the peripheral region of Basilicata all over Europe and ignite social activation and innovation.
B	Approximately 300 Matera inhabitants co-created an emotional map with the project leader, illustrating their most beloved places. The project aimed to promote a different way to live in the city and unveil the soul of the places through the soul of the person who generously shared their story. The map has been presented as a multisensory installation piece and in several other ways.
C	The project leader shared and gave voice to immigrants' talent through workshops and events. The project aimed to stimulate inclusion and social integration through work and art.
D	A traveling museum that exhibits fragments, traces, and small items collected during a journey in Mediterranean areas. Retracing the stories contained within the recovered objects offered an opportunity for reflection on the relationships among the people, places, and cultures within which these things were born, exchanged, handled, and experienced. The project leader wanted to provide a space for reflection on places and people's identity.
E	A film highlighting some big issues of the peripheral European areas, involving the community in the content production and the cinematographic work. The project aimed to promote a cinematographic language, stimulate audience development, and give voice to territories and local realities.

increasing and strengthening the identity of the places where people live; and as a means of giving life to peripheral areas.

Strategies

Analyzing the effects of Matera 2019 revealed a common tendency of the PLs to define new strategic objectives or to remodel existing ones to capitalize on their ECoC experience. The specificity of each project experience led each PL to formulate some specific objectives. However, it is possible to identify some macro strategic objectives common to all the interviewees. These macro objectives can be grouped into three main areas. The first area concerns openness to collaborations at the national/international level. The analyzed organizations aim to establish and strengthen their collaboration at the national/international level and to participate in international (European) networks. The second area has to do with capitalizing on the project: (1) scaling up and capitalizing on the methodological framework underlying the project carried out for Matera 2019,

(2) ensuring continuity of the project carried out for Matera 2019 at regional, national, and international levels, and (3) expanding and further improving the project carried out for Matera 2019 by involving old and new audiences. Finally, the third area concerns the financial dimension. All the organizations declared the objective of achieving financial sustainability in the medium and long terms. This sustainability has to be increasingly independent of public funds.

Processes

The joint analysis of the case studies highlighted some improvements common to the interviewed PLs regarding project management, communication, and marketing activities. Designing and managing significant projects for Matera 2019 allowed organizations to improve the management of complex projects (with particular reference to cost and time management dimensions), to increase their commitment to achieving the projects' objectives (paying particular attention to efficiency and time management), and to improve the selection and planning of projects as well as the simultaneous administration of parallel processes and activities. Regarding communication and marketing activities, from the interviews it emerged that all the PLs experienced an improvement in planning and management of advertising/promotion/marketing activities as well as of communication activities, primarily through more comprehensive and effective exploitation of social media.

Organizational Resources

PLs increased their tangible assets by producing physical project outputs (e.g., artistic works, film productions, books, games) and developing specific technological equipment and improved communication sites and channels (e.g., apps, technologies for augmented reality, advanced equipment for filming).

Further impacts on organizational resources concerned improvements in intangible resources, such as organizational reputation and image. Moreover, managing big cultural projects characterized by a certain level of complexity and budget size, forced the PLs to improve their managerial, communication, accounting, and digital competencies.

The Build Up project was an essential step in developing organizational resources. The PLs perceived it as a practice that, appropriately revised, can represent a legacy for the next ECoCs. However, the PLs had different opinions of its efficacy. Generally, the Build Up helped organizations develop, to some extent, skills related to communication, event planning, and digital content management. Furthermore, the Build Up acted as a turbo boost for developing the PLs' projects. However, the PLs claimed that they had improved their skills mainly autonomously, according to a "learning by doing" logic.

Partnerships

For all the PLs, carrying out a big project for Matera 2019 allowed them to expand their network, getting in touch with others operating in the creative and cultural sector and with public and private organizations operating in other sectors at local, national, and international levels. However, with some exceptions, the impact on partnership development was limited. Specifically, there was an increase in contacts with artists and other organizations. However, at the time of the interviews, the expansion of the network did not mean the growth of stable partnerships. Moreover, the forms of cooperation mainly involved the PLs and an artist or an organization in a narrow collaboration. However, these relationships and embryonic partnerships have great value for the PLs and represent a seed to nurture through new projects.

Stakeholders

Matera 2019's effect on the stakeholder dimension of the business model was, to a certain extent, different for each PL. All the PLs expanded their stakeholder networks. In particular, the PLs improved their relationships with their stakeholders and enhanced their reputation and image at local and national levels. At the local level, the changes included strengthening and expanding relationships with public organizations (e.g., schools and universities) and private organizations (e.g., companies involved in the project's implementation) as well as with local communities and with public bodies (even though some PLs described the relations with local public bodies as a factor hindering agile project development). On the other side, the PLs noticed a marginal improvement in the relationships among organizations operating in the creative and cultural sector at the local level and a limited strengthening of the networking among the PLs involved in the Matera 2019 program. According to most of the interviewed PLs, this had to do with two factors: the absence of clear programmatic lines aimed at driving all the PLs toward a shared vision, mission, and network activity, and structural characteristics of the local creative and cultural sector (e.g., management style, a low propensity to share information). At the national level, participating in ECoC allowed the PLs to establish or consolidate relationships with well-known associations and organizations operating in the creative and cultural sector and with public schools. Finally, the PLs have started to create and reinforce relationships with artists and organizations to develop specific or European projects at the international level.

Funding and Financial Resilience

Funding and financial resilience represent a tricky facet of the business model of creative and cultural organizations. Developing a big project for Matera 2019 generated exposure to debt situations, albeit temporary (PLs had to advance one part of the capital required by the project). This produced a certain level of apprehension, amplified by the fact that the financial reporting mechanisms and rules were changed several times during the project. The changes in the reporting system made some PLs uneasy. Indeed, most of the examined organizations did not have employees adequately skilled in managing economic/financial matters and able to respond promptly to changes in reporting requirements.

The interviews highlighted some critical concerns regarding the financial and economic dimension after the ECoC year. The PLs were worried about the absence of public policies and programs to guarantee the continuation and enhancement of the implemented projects after 2019 and the existence of proper financial resources for capitalizing on artistic and cultural outputs and tangible and intangible organizational heritage built through Matera 2019 projects. Beyond these concerns, the ECoC experience ignited new intentions and actions. From the interviews, it emerged that PLs were working to rely less and less on public funds in favor of seeking private funds (e.g., sponsors) and identifying new ways of financially exploiting the outputs from projects developed for Matera 2019.

Conclusions

Evaluating the impacts of an ECoC is still a challenging task. Assessing such a big event against its set goals and the program's objectives through several perspectives—cultural, social, economic, and environmental—is difficult (Gomez and Librero-Cano 2018; Langen and Garcia 2009). This is in part because of the lack of shared and well-founded methods for getting evidence of short- and long-term effects after the event has been hosted.

The evaluation has to encompass both a macro-scale analysis of the cultural, social, and economic impacts of ECoC and an understanding of the effects that such an event produces at the micro level—that is, on citizens and organizations experiencing ECoC directly involved in its implementation.

Most of the studies done to date adopt a macro scale to investigate the impact of ECoC. This is understandable, as hosting this mega-event is seen as an opportunity for urban regeneration and a catalyst for social, cultural, and economic development. But micro-scale lenses enrich the understanding of the impacts generated by this peculiar event on its participants. They shed more light on participants' experiences of ECoC and can highlight issues regarding the context-specific effects of the event. This research adopted micro-scale lenses to explore the experiences of some creative and cultural organizations during Matera's year as ECoC in 2019. Specifically, it looked at how participation in the event impacted their business model. To the best of our knowledge, this area of exploration is still insufficiently investigated. We propose using the BMP framework to comprehensively analyze the effects of ECoC on the business model of creative and cultural organizations actively involved in the program.

Several clear findings emerged from this research that may have particular relevance to cultural policymakers in the hosting city and region. These results suggest key subjects for building an environment that nurtures future creative and cultural practices.

The joint analysis of the case studies revealed that each PL had strengthened its value proposition, defined new strategic objectives to be pursued in the near future, enriched its wealth of tangible and intangible assets, partially modified its processes, woven new partnerships (albeit in a very limited way), and strengthened its relationships with stakeholders. The project implementation generated an exposure of the PLs to debt situations, although temporary. This produced a certain level of apprehension among the organizations, amplified by the fact that the reporting mechanisms and rules changed several times during the project. On the other hand, the ECoC experience reinforced the PLs' desire to acquire greater financial resilience by relying less on public funding and developing projects/activities that contribute to achieving greater economic sustainability.

Overall, Matera 2019 was a transformational event for the analyzed PLs. It pushed them to rethink and improve their business model and, in line with the "Open Future" slogan of Matera 2019, to project themselves into the future. Developing big cultural projects provided them with new strengths to leverage for future growth from an entrepreneurial point of view.

The study contributes to the broader research puzzle on evaluating ECoC impacts by offering a fresh perspective on the effects of this event. It is crucial to understand the influence of the ECoC on the value creation dynamics of the creative and cultural organizations that serve as a major pillar of the mega-event. The success and lasting legacy of an ECoC depend on the capacity of local creative and cultural organizations to remain competitive and continue to create and deliver value beyond the hosting year.

Further development of the study could include increasing the number of creative and cultural organizations examined as well as investigating and differentiating the impacts in various creative and cultural sectors. Moreover, it would be interesting to monitor the impacts over time. This would allow an assessment of the medium and long-term legacy of the ECoC program.

The main limitation of the study concerns the generalizability of the results. The researchers had the opportunity to examine only a sample of the PLs involved in realizing the Matera 2019 program. Moreover, the findings reflect the managers' perception of the impacts on the business model at the time of the interviews. A longitudinal study would further enrich the knowledge of the effects generated over time.

References

Balsas, Carlos J. L. 2004. "City Center Regeneration in the Context of the 2001 European Capital of Culture in Porto, Portugal." *Local Economy* 19, no. 4: 396–410.

Boyko, Christopher T. 2007. "Are You Being Served? The Impacts of a Tourist Hallmark Event on the Place Meanings of Residents." *Event Management* 11, no. 4: 161–177.

Burksiene, Valentina, Jaroslav Dvorak, and Gabriele Burbulyte-Tsiskarishvili. 2018. "Sustainability and Sustainability Marketing in Competing for the Title of European Capital of Culture." *Organizacija* 51, no. 1: 66–78. doi:10.2478/orga-2018-0005.

Campbell, Peter. 2011. "Creative Industries in a European Capital of Culture." *International Journal of Cultural Policy* 17, no. 5: 510–522. doi:10.1080/10286632.2010.543461.

Department for Culture, Media and Sport. 2008. *Creative Britain: New Talents for the New Economy*. London: DCMS.

Decker-Lange, Carolin, Marie-Noëlle Singer, and Florian Schrander. 2019. "Balancing Evolving Logics: Business Model Change in the Leibniz Research Museums." *Science and Public Policy* 46, no. 3: 430–440.

Dümcke, Cornelia. 2015. "New business models in the Cultural and Creative Sectors (CCSs). European Expert Network on Culture (EENC)." https://static1.squarespace.com/static/59f7358a9f8dce60489b6448/t/5b0dfe6b88251b536ef13e7f/1527643756357/2015_Cornelia+Du%CC%88mcke_EENC_Ad+hoc+question_New+Business+Models+in+the+CCSs+June+2015.pdf

Ebejer, John, Karsten Xuereb, and Marie Avellino. 2021. "A Critical Debate of the Cultural and Social Effects of Valletta 2018 European Capital of Culture." *Journal of Tourism and Cultural Change* 19, no. 1: 97–112. doi:10.1080/14766825.2020.1849240.

European Union. 2015. *European Capital of Culture, 30 Years*. Luxembourg: Publications Office of the European Union.

Falk, John H., and Beverly K. Sheppard. 2006. *Thriving in the Knowledge Age: New Business Models for Museums and Other Cultural Institutions*. Lanham, MD: Altamira Press.

Fišer, Suzana Žilič, and Ines Kožuh. 2019. "The Impact of Cultural Events on Community Reputation and Pride in Maribor, the European Capital of Culture 2012." *Social Indicators Research* 142, no. 3: 1055–1073. doi:10.1007/s11205-018-1958-4.

Fox, Tim, and James Rampton. 2016. *Ex-Post Evaluation of the 2015 European Capitals of Culture, Final Report: A Study Prepared for the European Commission by Ecorys and the Centre for Strategy and Evaluation Services (CSES)*. Luxembourg: Publications Office of the European Union.

Garcia, Beatriz. 1990. "Deconstructing the city of culture: The long-term cultural legacies of Glasgow." *Urban studies* 42, 5–6: 841–868.

Garcia, Beatriz. 2019. "European Capitals of Culture: Success Strategies and Long-Term Effects (1985–2019)." https://www.europarl.europa.eu/cmsdata/192028/GARCIA_ECoC-30years-original.pdf.

Garcia, Beatriz, and Tasmin Cox. 2013. *European Capitals of Culture: Success Strategies and Long Term Effects*. Luxembourg: EUR-OP.

Garcia, Beatriz, Ruth Melville, and Tasmin Cox. 2008. "Impacts 08—The Liverpool Model." Understanding the Effect of Cultural Regeneration in the Lead to Liverpool." http://iccliverpool.ac.uk/wp-content/uploads/2013/04/Impacts082008BURAMagazine-FINAL.pdf

Garcia, Beatriz, Ruth Melville, and Tasmin Cox. 2010. "Creating an Impact: Liverpool's Experience as European Capital of Culture." https://www.liverpool.ac.uk/media/livacuk/impacts08/pdf/pdf/Creating_an_Impact_-_web.pdf

García, Beatriz, Ruth Melville, Tasmin Cox, and Kate Rodenhurst. 2010. "Neighborhood Impacts: A Longitudinal Research Study into the Impact of the Liverpool European Capital of Culture on Local Residents." https://www.liverpool.ac.uk/media/livacuk/impacts08/pdf/pdf/Neighbourhood_Impacts.pdf

Garcia, Beatriz, Ruth Melville, Tasmin Cox, and Kate Rodenhurst. 2009a. "Liverpool's Arts Sector—Sustainability and Experience: How Artists and Arts Organisations Engaged with the Liverpool European Capital of Culture." https://www.liverpool.ac.uk/media/livacuk/impacts08/publications/liverpools-arts-sector.pdf

Gomes, Pedro, and Alejandro Librero-Cano. 2018. "Evaluating Three Decades of the European Capital of Culture Programme: A Difference-in-Differences Approach." *Journal of Cultural Economics* 42, no. 1: 57–73. doi:10.1007/s10824-016-9281-x.

Hughes, Howard L. 2003. "European Capital of Culture and Its Significance for Tourism and Culture: The Case of Krakow 2000." *International Journal of Arts Management* 5, no. 3: 12–23.

Langen, Floris, and Beatriz Garcia. 2009. *Measuring the Impacts of Large Scale Cultural Events: A Literature Review*. Liverpool: Impacts 08.

Laasch, Oliver. 2018. "Beyond the Purely Commercial Business Model: Organisational Value Logics and the Heterogeneity of Sustainable Business Models." *Long Range Planning* 51, no. 1: 158–183. doi:10.1016/j.lrp.2017.09.002.

Li, Feng. 2020. "The digital transformation of business models in the creative industries: A holistic framework and emerging trends." *Technovation* 92–93, 102012. doi:https://doi.org/10.1016/j.technovation.2017.12.004

Liu, Yi- De. 2019 a. "Event and Sustainable Culture-Led Regeneration: Lessons from the 2008 European Capital of Culture, Liverpool." *Sustainability* 11, no. 7: 1869. doi:10.3390/su11071869.

Liu, Yi- De. 2019 b. "The Cultural Legacy of a Major Event: A Case Study of the 2008 European Capital of Culture, Liverpool." *Urban Science* 3, no. 3: 79. doi:10.3390/urbansci3030079.

Garcia, Beatriz, Ruth Melville, and Tasmin Cox. 2009b. "Liverpool's Creative Industries: Understanding the Impact of Liverpool European Capital of Culture 2008 on the City Region's Creative Industries." https://www.liverpool.ac.uk/media/livacuk/impacts08/publications/liverpools-creative-industries.pdf

Muñoz-Seca, Beatriz. 2011. "A business model for cultural services: Joint design and production of a customer experience." https://media.iese.edu/research/pdfs/DI-0941-E.pdf

Myerscough, John. 1994. *European Cities of Culture and Cultural Months*. Glasgow: Network of Cultural Cities of Europe.

Nobili, Valentina. 2005. "The Role of European Capital of Culture Events Within Genoa's and Liverpool's Branding and Positioning Efforts." *Place Branding* 1, no. 3: 316–328. doi:10.1057/palgrave.pb.5990031.

Osterwalder, Alexander, and Yves Pigneur. 2010. *Business Model Generation: A Handbook for Visionaries, Game Changers and Challengers*. Hoboken, NJ: John Wiley & Sons.

Palmer, R. 2004. "European Cities and Capitals of Culture: Study Prepared for the European Commission Part I." Palmer-Rae Associates, Brussels.

Palmer, Robert, and Greg Richard. 2004. "European Cities and Capitals of Culture: Part I and II." Palmer-Rae Associates, Brussels.

Rampton, James, Nick McAteer, Neringa Mozuraityte, Márta Levai, and Selek Akçeli. 2011. "Ex-Post Evaluation of 2010 European Capitals of Culture: Final Report for the European Commission Directorate General for Education and Culture." Ecorys UK Ltd., Birmingham.

Richards, Greg, and Julie Wilson. 2004. "The Impact of Cultural Events on City Image: Rotterdam, Cultural Capital of Europe 2001." *Urban Studies* 41, no. 10: 1931–1951. doi:10.1080/0042098042000256323.

Richards, Greg, Erik Hitters, and Carlos Fernandes. 2002. *Rotterdam and Porto, Cultural Capitals 2001: Visitor Research*. Arnhem: Atlas.

Robinson, Sarah, and Wesley Shumar. 2014. "Ethnographic Evaluation of Entrepreneurship Education in Higher Education: A Methodological Conceptualisation." *International Journal of Management Education* 12, no. 3: 422–432. doi:10.1016/j.ijme.2014.06.001.

Rodriguez, José. 2016. "To Sell or not to Sell? An Introduction to Business Model (Innovation) for Arts and Culture Organisations."https://www.ietm.org/system/files/publications/ietm_business-models_2016.pdf

Royce, Susan J. 2011. "Business Models in the Visual Arts: An Investigation of Organisational Business Models for the Turning Point Network and Arts Council England." Arts Council England, Manchester.

Schiuma, Giovanni, and Antonio Lerro. 2017. "The Business Model Prism: Managing and Innovating Business Models of Arts and Cultural Organisations." *Journal of Open Innovation: Technology, Market, and Complexity* 3, no. 3: 13. doi:10.1186/s40852-017-0066-z.

Srakar, Andrej, and Marilena Vecco. 2017. "Ex-Ante Versus Ex-Post: Comparison of the Effects of the European Capital of Culture Maribor 2012 on Tourism and Employment." *Journal of Cultural Economics* 41, no. 2: 197–214. doi:10.1007/s10824-017-9294-0.

Steiner, Lasse, Bruno Frey, and Simone Hotz. 2015. "European Capitals of Culture and Life Satisfaction." *Urban Studies* 52, no. 2: 374–394. doi:10.1177/0042098014524609.

Stipanović, Christian, Elena Rudan, and Vedran Zubović. 2019. "Cultural and Creative Industries in Urban Tourism Innovation—The Example of the City of Rijeka." *Tourism in South East Europe* 5: 655–666.

Turşie, Corina, and Thomas Perrin. 2020. "Assessing the social and cultural impacts of the European Capital of Culture programme in cross-border regions. A research agenda." *Eastern Journal of European Studies* 11, special issue: 77–98.

Van Der Steen, Tessa, and Greg Richards. 2021. "Factors Affecting Resident Support for a Hallmark Cultural Event: The 2018 European Capital of Culture in Valletta, Malta." *Journal of Policy Research in Tourism, Leisure and Events* 13, no. 1: 107–123. doi:10.1080/19407963.2019.1696352.

CHAPTER 37

CULTURAL FIRMS' PERFORMANCE FROM A REGIONAL DEVELOPMENT PERSPECTIVE

Evidence from Europe

ANDREJ SRAKAR AND MARILENA VECCO

Introduction

ENTREPRENEURSHIP is commonly seen as an important driver of economic development, employment, and growth. This belief is grounded on an extensive body of literature that addresses both the determinants and outcomes of entrepreneurship at different levels of analysis (Wennekers and Thurik 1999). It is recognized that entrepreneurship is a complex phenomenon that is driven by individuals but embedded in a wider economic and societal context; the wider regional context regulates the quality and outcomes of this process (Acs, Autio, and Szerb 2014).

While there is no generally accepted definition of entrepreneurship that covers all levels of analysis, there is broad agreement that entrepreneurial behaviors and actions comprise multiple dimensions, such as opportunity recognition, risk-taking, resource mobilization, innovation, and the creation of new organizations (Autio 2005, 2007; Praag and Versloot 2007). The range of different activities and outcomes associated with entrepreneurship suggests that a multidimensional definition of entrepreneurship is probably more suited to understanding the economic and societal benefits generated by entrepreneurs (Gartner 1985; Cooper and Dunkelberg 1986; Acs, Audretsch, and Evans 1994; Blanchflower, Oswald, and Stutzer 2001; Carree et al. 2002; Reynolds et al. 2005; Acs, Arenius, and Minniti 2005; Grilo and Thurik 2005; Bosma et al. 2009). In recent years, cultural and/or creative entrepreneurship has been presented as a specific research and practice field (e.g., Lindqvist 2011; Meisiek and Haefliger 2011). The definition of cultural entrepreneurship adopted within this article draws on the insight, first introduced by DiMaggio (1982), that actively maintaining a network of contacts, seeking ways to stimulate the interest of curators and critics, engaging in self-marketing activities such as branding, and proactively seeking to increase sales as opposed to waiting for the tide constitutes a form of entrepreneurship (Klamer 2011).[1] Scherdin and Zander (2011, 3) define cultural entrepreneurship as "the discovery and pursuit of new art ideas, using a multitude of artistic expressions and organizational forms as vehicles by which to express and convey these ideas to the public." The presence of micro-enterprises in the art sector gives an extended meaning to entrepreneurship, related to the parallelism between arts organizations and small and medium enterprises (SMEs) (Moureau and Sagot-Duvaroux 2010; Fillis and Rentschler 2005; Fillis 2000, 2004). The main difference between an entrepreneur and a cultural entrepreneur is the difference in the roles of profit and the creation of wealth: profit is not the main drive behind a cultural entrepreneur's activity. Despite embracing one definition of and approach to cultural entrepreneurship, we strongly think that there is a clear need to more deeply investigate how and why cultural and creative entrepreneurship is assumed to be different from other varieties of entrepreneurship (Vecco 2020). Entrepreneurship is considered one of the most crucial factors in economic progress. The establishment of new firms and enterprises may play a significant role in regional economies because of the knowledge and novelties that they bring to the market. Several studies proved that entrepreneurship has a positive effect on economic growth in developed countries (Acs and Audretsch 1988; Acs and Varga 2005; van Stel, Carree, and Thurik 2005; Acs and Szerb 2007).

It is commonly recognized that although individuals' motivations drive the entrepreneurial process, the environment regulates the quality and outcomes of this process (Shane, Locke, and Christopher 2003). In this chapter, the focus is on the regional dimension of entrepreneurship in the cultural sector in Europe. An important issue to guide the development of the hypotheses of this study is the influence of entrepreneurial development on organizational performance at the European regional level. Our contribution to literature is twofold. First, as the topic of empirical research in cultural entrepreneurship is still underresearched, we decided to measure and evaluate the performance of cultural firms by using some objective and direct metrics. Second, we provide evidence of the role played by cultural firms in regional development in 2013, showing the relevance of the regional level.

The chapter is structured as follows. The following section introduces the literature review and the hypotheses developed for the present study. The next section describes our database and the methodological approach adopted. The third section outlines the results, tested for robustness, while the last section discusses the hypotheses with the support of the results and concludes by providing some policy implications of the study.

Literature Review

As Audretsch and Thurik (2001) stated, changes in economic theories about entrepreneurship have been supported by the shift in the broader economic environment. Specifically, they identified fourteen trade-offs concerning the differences between the "managed economy" and the "entrepreneurial economy." If the blueprints of the "managed economy" were capital, labor, the concentration of big and dominant enterprises, mass production, and economies of scale, the entrepreneurial economy has been characterized by small and medium firms adopting a strategy of diversification and flexibility. In this context, the role of local policies, as well as that of the local and regional space, became more significant than in the managed economy (Audretsch and Thurik 2001; Audretsch 2009).

For a more complete understanding of how entrepreneurship contributes to economic and societal development, it is important to recognize the contextually embedded quality of entrepreneurial actions and behaviors in national-, regional-, and city-level contexts (Szerb et al. 2013). In this analysis, the focus is on the regional dimension. This is a useful level of analysis for three reasons (Szerb et al. 2013). First, most entrepreneurial businesses operate locally or regionally and are therefore subject to local or regional contextual influences. Second, particularly in larger countries, there could be significant variations in industry structure and economic base across regions. Third, as a practical issue, the EU systematically collects harmonized data across EU regions.

Our focus on regions also resonates with a substantial body of literature on the intersection of regional economic development and entrepreneurship (Baumgartner, Pütz, and Seidl 2013; Trettin and Welter 2011; Acs and Szerb 2009, 2010, 2011; Acs, Autio, and Szerb 2014), which started to emerge as central areas of inquiry in the early 1990s (Sternberg 2009). In this study, the Regional Entrepreneurship and Development Index (REDI) as developed in the European Commission report of Szerb et al. (2013) is used. The REDI is assumed to capture the quality of entrepreneurial ecosystems in European regions, specifically its systemic nature in the context of entrepreneurship. Moreover, it seeks to capture the ability of the regional entrepreneurial ecosystem to support economic regional development (Szerb, Vörös, et al. 2017).

The main idea of the REDI is that system performance at the regional level is co-produced by its constituent elements. This assumes that the fourteen pillars are interrelated and act as complements to one another. The combination of pillar components shows whether the entrepreneurial ecosystem of a region functions well or not. The REDI incorporates three sub-indices, fourteen pillars, twenty-eight variables (divided into fourteen that are institutional and fourteen that are individual), forty-four indicators, and sixty sub-indicators (Table 37.1). The structure of the index, created by the Global Entrepreneurship Development Institute, is based on the Global Entrepreneurship and Development Index (GEDI). The GEDI relies on a composite index that measures productive entrepreneurship in a multidimensional way.

Table 37.1. The Structure of the Regional Entrepreneurship and Development Index

Regional Entrepreneurship Index

Sub-indexes	Pillars	Variables (Ind./Inst.)	Entrepreneurship attributes
Attitudes Sub-Index	Opportunity perception	Opportunity recognition Market agglomeration	Market and regulation
	Start-up skills	Skill perception Quality of education	Human capital/education
	Risk acceptance	Risk perception Business risk	Cultural, regulation
	Networking	Know entrepreneur Social capital	Networks
	Cultural support	Career status Open society	Cultural
Abilities Sub-Index	Opportunity start-up	Opportunity motivation Business environment	Regulation
	Technology adoption	Technology level Absorptive capacity	Knowledge creation/dissemination
	Human capital	Educational level Education and training	Human capital/education
	Competition	Competitors Business strategy	Infrastructure
Aspiration Sub-Index	Product innovation	New product Technology transfer	Knowledge creation/dissemination
	Process innovation	New technology Technology development	Knowledge creation/dissemination
	High growth	Gazelle clustering	Infrastructure and finance
	Globalization	Export Connectivity	Market
	Financing	Informal investment Financial institutions	Finance

An important question to guide the development of the hypotheses of this study is the influence of entrepreneurial development on organizational performance. Studies in entrepreneurial orientation (individual aspects of the REDI) began in the early 1980s, and researchers continually found that it has a significant effect on firm performance (Covin and Slevin 1991; Zahra and Covin 1995; Dess, Lumpkin, and Covin 1997; Lumpkin and Dess 1996). Kreiser and colleagues found a positive relationship between high innovativeness and proactiveness and organizational performance in terms of sales level, sales growth, and gross profit (Kreiser, Marino, and Weaver 2002; see also Lumpkin and Dess 2001). Awang et al. (2009) found that different entrepreneurial orientation dimensions (autonomy, innovativeness, proactiveness, and risk-taking) contribute independently to explaining organizational performance. Slater and Narver (2000), Pulendran, Speed, and Widing (2000), and Tay and Morgan (2002) identified significant, positive links between market orientation and organizational performance, and Subramanian and Nilakanta (1996) and Tidd, Bessant, and Pavitt (2001) found a relationship between innovativeness and better organizational performance. Van Praag and Versloot (2007) demonstrate the value of entrepreneurship in terms of employment generation and dynamics, innovation, productivity and growth, and individuals' utility. The impacts of entrepreneurship can also include knowledge spillovers and "creative destruction" (Autio 2005, 2007). The existing literature has argued that many of the characteristics of the entrepreneurial process are locally inherent (see Müller 2016 for an exhaustive literature review). For example, regional specificities related to firms' accessibility to financing and innovation needs or the proximity to scientific and technological infrastructures are among the most important characteristics that shape regional entrepreneurial and innovative climates (Audretsch and Feldman 1996; Boschma and Lambooy 1999; Feldman 2001; Andersson, Quigley, and Wilhelmsson 2005).

Previous research showed that regional conditions may influence firm start-up rates and that the local social and economic milieu is fundamental in fostering entrepreneurship (Garofoli 1994), whereas entrepreneurship also had a positive impact on regional development in terms of growth and job creation (Dejardin and Fritsch 2011). This suggests that regional structural conditions influence entrepreneurial activities, and that, in turn, entrepreneurial activities influence regional structures in terms of development. The literature shows a positive effect of different dimensions of entrepreneurial orientation on organizational performance on the national and regional levels. To the best of our knowledge, no such study has been done before focusing solely on cultural firms. Related to cultural firms, we would expect to find significant heterogeneity, as we include in the analysis both "core" arts organizations and cultural and creative industries (Throsby 2001; Hesmondhalgh 2002; Miller 2009; Mato 2009). Furthermore, significant differences in terms of observing individual and institutional REDI indicators might be expected. Some of the differences are in the measurement, as individual indicators are unidimensional measures while institutional indicators are mainly composite. Moreover, individual indicators do not take into account the different environmental factors, efficiency, and quality of an institutional setup, which can have a major influence on the quality of entreprencurship and on the economic and societal impact eventually realized through entrepreneurial action (Szerb et al. 2013).

As the topic of empirical research in cultural entrepreneurship is still underresearched, we decided to measure and evaluate the performance of cultural firms by using some objective and direct metrics. According to Song, Di Benedetto, and Nason (2007), measures like turnover, profit, productivity, size, age, social capital, and so on can be used to define the performance and growth of firms. The performance assessment used within this study is based on management-driven indicators: capital, level of debt, size in terms of employees, and stability of operating revenues. Based on the previous literature review, we expect that regional entrepreneurial development as a value-enhancing instrument would have an ambiguous but likely positive effect on the size of the firm (in terms of employment) and a negative effect on the instability of revenues. Although the evidence is mixed, a firm's mode of financing may have some effects as well. For example, Modigliani and Miller (1958) examine the effect of capital structure on firm value and propose that firms should employ as much debt as possible given the limits of their finances (Modigliani and Miller 1963). Recent studies also showed a shift in focus, from the trade-off theory to the pecking order theory (Quan 2002; Mazur 2007); the latter suggests that firms have a particular preference order for capital used to finance their businesses (Myers and Majluf 1984). Owing to the information asymmetries between a firm and potential investors, a firm will prefer retained earnings to debt, short-term debt over long-term debt, and debt over equity (Chen and Chen 2011).

Following this literature, we assume some positive effects and benefits of debt financing and therefore expect to find positive effects of regional entrepreneurial development on the level of debt and negative on the level of capital. Considering the abovementioned firm measures, the two following hypotheses (with subhypotheses) have been developed:

H1: The Regional Entrepreneurship and Development Index has a significant effect on the performance of cultural firms.
H1a: A higher REDI is correlated with lower instability of revenues for cultural firms.
H1b: A higher REDI is correlated with a higher number of employees in cultural firms.
H1c: A higher REDI is correlated with a higher level of debt financing for cultural firms.
H1d: A higher REDI is correlated with a lower level of capital financing for cultural firms.
H2: The relationship between REDI and the performance of cultural firms is moderated by the sector of the cultural firm and by the dimension (individual/institutional) of the index.

Data and Method

This analysis is developed using Amadeus, which is a database of comparable financial information for public and private firms covering forty-three countries. It presents comprehensive information on Europe's largest 500,000 public and private firms by total assets. In our analysis, we use thirteen selected European countries: the United Kingdom, Sweden, Slovenia, Slovakia, Poland, Lithuania, Latvia, Italy, Hungary, Germany, France, Estonia, and the Czech Republic.[2] To discern the firms working in the cultural and creative sector, we use a detailed NACE II classification.[3] We organized the firms under three main categories (following the original classification in Söndermann 2010): the market-oriented class comprises commercial, for-profit activities; the mixed class covers firms that are both market-oriented and non-market-oriented (activities that are nonprofit, publicly financed, or funded by private donations), and the third class encompasses "firms that carry out related or partly cultural activities" (Table 37.2).

Because the REDI is of a cross-sectional nature (only one time value is calculated for each unit and variable), the data we used is for the most recent year of this index, 2013, and collects a sample of 41,119 firms from the thirteen European countries mentioned previously. In total, 1,623 firms—representing 3.95 percent of the total firms—were cultural firms. These firms represent our final sample in the analysis. Some basic descriptive characteristics of the dataset are presented below (Table 37.3).

The main independent variable of interest is the Regional Entrepreneurship and Development Index, which serves as proxy for the development of entrepreneurship in a region. The REDI (Szerb et al. 2013) introduces a new approach to measuring entrepreneurship in EU regions. As noted earlier, the REDI consists of three sub-indices (measuring entrepreneurial attitudes, abilities, and aspirations), fourteen pillars, and twenty-eight variables, and while the individual variables are mainly unidimensional, the institutional indicators are mostly composites. The index-building logic differs from other widely applied indices in three respects. First, it combines individual-level variables with institutional variables to capture contextual influences. Second, it equates the fourteen pillar values by equalizing their marginal effects. Third, it allows index pillars to "co-produce" system performance. These features set the REDI apart from simple summative indices that assume full substitutability between system components, making it uniquely suited to profiling regional systems of entrepreneurship in EU regions (Szerb et al. 2013).

As an econometric tool, we used generalized linear mixed models (GLMMs). In general, mixed-effect models are generalizations of linear models, including additional random-effect terms, and are often appropriate for representing clustered dependent data—arising, for example, when data are collected hierarchically, when observations are taken on related individuals, or when data are gathered over time on the same individuals (see Galwey 2014. GLMMs allow for non-normal distribution of the error term in the mixed effects regression. In our case we have (non-negative) continuous dependent variables with a positive skew in distribution; hence we use gamma regression with an inverse Gaussian link function. In generalized linear models (linear regression models that allow an arbitrary distribution for the standard error), a link function maps a nonlinear relationship to a linear one, which means you can fit a linear model to the data. More specifically, it connects the predictors in a model with the expected value of the dependent variable in a linear way. An inverse Gaussian link function uses normal distribution for the error term but with inverse values (instead of x it uses $1/x$) for dependent variables and/or predictors. For each variable, we estimate two different models: first, the reduced model without interaction variables; and second, the full model, including all the relevant interactions. In this way we are also able to verify hypothesis H2.

Table 37.2. Classification of the Activities in the Three Classes

Market-oriented class	Mixed-orientation class	Related or partly cultural activities class
47.61 Retail sale of books in specialized stores	60.10 Radio broadcasting	18.11 Printers of daily newspapers
47.62 Retail sale of newspapers and stationery in specialized stores	60.20 Television programming and broadcasting activities	18.12 Other printers
47.63 Retail sale of music and video recordings in specialized stores	85.52 Cultural education	18.20 Reproduction of recorded media
58.11 Book publishing	90.01 Performing arts	32.20 Manufacture of musical instruments
58.13 Publishing of newspapers	90.03 Artistic creation	47.78 Other retail sale of new goods in specialized stores
58.14 Publishing of journals and periodicals	91.01 Library and archives activities	47.79 Retail sale of secondhand goods
58.21 Publishing of computer games	91.02 Museums activities	47.89 Retail sale via stalls and markets of other goods
59.11 Motion picture, video, and television program production activities	91.03 Operation of historical sites and buildings and similar visitor attractions	47.91 Retail sale via mail order houses or via Internet
59.12 Motion picture, video, and TV program postproduction activities		
59.13 Motion picture, video, and television program distribution activities		
59.14 Motion picture projection activities		
59.20 Sound recording and music publishing activities		
63.91 News agency activities		
71.11 Architectural activities		
73.11 Advertising agencies		
74.10 Specialized design activities		
74.20 Photographic activities		
74.30 Translation and interpretation activities		
77.22 Renting of videotapes and disks		
90.02 Support activities for performing arts		
90.04 Operation of arts facilities		

Source: Elaboration based on classification in Söndermann 2010.

Table 37.3. Descriptive Statistics of the Main Variables in the Studied Sample of Cultural and Creative Firms

Sector	%	N	
Market-oriented firms	68.02	1,104	
Mixed-orientation firms	13.37	217	
Related or partly cultural activities' firms	18.61	302	
Total		1,623	
Dependent variables	Average	Median	N
Operating revenues (in Euros)	219,563.00	71,081.00	1,281
Number of employees	12.93	5.02	1,173
Capital financing	191,506.91	2,403.00	1,090
Level of debt	181,056.09	11,102.00	1,054

Source: Authors' calculations.

The reduced model reads as follows:

$$y_i \sim f(y; \mu_i, \phi)$$

$$g(\mu_i) = \eta_i$$

$$\eta_i = \beta' x_i$$

$$\left(\frac{1}{\mu_i}\right) = \eta_i = depvar_{ij} = \alpha + \beta_1 REDI + \beta_2 X_{2ij} + \beta_3 Z_{3ij} + b_{i1} country_{1ij} + b_{i2} region_{2ij} + \varepsilon_{ij}$$

x_i is a vector of values of the predictor variables, β is a vector of regression coefficients, and $f(y; \mu_i, \phi) = \frac{1}{\Gamma(\phi)\mu^\phi} y^{\phi-1} e^{-\frac{y}{\mu}}$ is a gamma distribution with $\Gamma(\cdot)$ the gamma function; $depvar$ is the dependent variable: stability of operating revenues (measured as the variance of the operating revenues of past three years); employment (in number of employees); firm's capital (in logarithms); and firm's level of debt (in logarithms) for firm i in group j; REDI is the value of the Regional Entrepreneurship and Development Index; X is a vector of additional variables, encompassing (logarithm of) GDP per capita, sector variables and their interactions with REDI variables; Z is a vector of control variables, encompassing, among others, balance sheet items, profit and loss account items, current, monthly and annual market capitalisation figures and ownership variables; country and region are the random effect regressors; ε_{it} is the random error component.

Results

The main results of this chapter are presented in the following tables. Table 37.4 shows the results of generalized linear mixed modeling of the influence of the independent variable of REDI and other main independent variables on the performance measures of the firms. First, we can observe that the main relevant variable is a country-level one: GDP per capita (which we model on level 1 and not as part of random effects). Here, a higher value is related to lower instability of revenues, higher number of employees, lower capital, and debt financing. For the level of capital, we also find a relationship with REDI: the mixed-orientation firms have in general a higher level of capital than firms carrying out related or partly cultural activities (the reference group). However, the ones located in regions with a higher level of regional entrepreneurial development tend to have an additional and strongly statistically significant negative relationship with the level of capital financing. Based on the financial theory previously mentioned (Modigliani and Miller 1958, 1963), we would assume that, at least to a certain extent, debt financing is preferred over capital financing.[4] Therefore, this can be interpreted as a sign of a firm's sound financial policy related to higher regional entrepreneurial development; that is, in regions with a higher regional entrepreneurial development, the entrepreneurs and firms follow what the finance literature acknowledges to be good practices (debt financing is preferred over capital). Furthermore, firms located in regions with a higher REDI have higher instability of firm revenues and a higher level of debt financing. None of those results is moderated by the effects of the cultural sector, which means that all cultural firms regardless of their specific cultural sector have equal results in this aspect.

Table 37.5 displays the results obtained by including the individual and institutional dimensions of the REDI. Again, one of the main predictors is the level of GDP per capita, which is related to the performance measures in broadly the same manner as in Table 37.4. Noticeably, there is a difference between the two dimensions of the REDI index in terms of instability of revenues. Firms in countries with a higher institutional and lower individual REDI have higher instability of revenues, which broadens the results of Table 37.4. The mixed-orientation firms with a better institutional REDI have a slightly higher number of employees than the firms that carry out related or partly cultural activities. In previous work, the authors attributed the higher number of employees found in cultural firms to the firms' inefficiency (see Vecco and Srakar 2018a). In this manner, the findings can be explained as the mixed firms exploiting the institutional environment for enhancing their employment, but with some expected drawbacks in terms of efficiency of production. Additionally, the results show that the mixed-orientation firms tend to have higher capital on average. Finally, there is a strong (positive) relationship of the REDI to debt financing, with firms with higher individual and institutional REDI having higher levels of debt financing.

Table 37.4. Results of Gamma Regression, Total REDI

	Instability of revenues			Employment			Employment			Capital			Capital			Firm debt			Firm debt		
	Coef. [z]	Sig.	Coef. [z]	Sig.	Coef. [z]	Sig.	Coef. [z]	Sig.	Coef. [z]	Sig.	Coef. [z]	Sig.	Coef. [z]	Sig.	Coef. [z]	Sig.	Coef. [z]	Sig.	Coef. [z]	Sig.	Coef. [z]	Sig.
Market-oriented	-0.23 [-1.58]		0.35 [0.50]		0.01 [0.23]		0.01 [0.04]		-0.04 [-0.25]		0.40 [0.64]		-0.17 [-1.80]	*	-0.51 [-1.32]	
Mixed-orientation	0.82 [2.20]	**	2.06 [0.88]		0.20 [1.61]		0.40 [0.82]		-0.29 [-0.85]		3.03 [2.33]	***	-0.39 [-1.86]	*	-0.28 [-0.35]	
Log GDP pc	-7.13 [-5.11]	***	-7.05 [-5.08]	***	0.46 [1.47]		0.46 [1.47]	*	-3.68 [-2.69]	***	-3.69 [-2.69]	***	-1.96 [-1.84]	*	-1.98 [-1.85]	*
REDI	0.03 [3.20]	***	0.03 [3.32]	***	0.00 [1.59]		0.00 [1.49]		0.01 [1.36]		0.02 [1.67]	*	0.03 [4.55]	***	0.02 [3.99]	***
Market × REDI			-0.01 [-0.85]				0.00 [0.01]				-0.01 [-0.74]				0.01 [0.91]	
Mixed × REDI			-0.02 [-0.54]				0.00 [-0.42]				-0.05 [-2.64]	***			0.00 [-0.13]	
Nr. Obs.	1623		1623		1623		1623		1623		1623		1623		1623	
Wald chi2	92.96	***	94.46	***	72.05	***	72.28	***	130.94	***	138.4	***	118.37	***	119.22	***
Log likelih.	-1186.50		-1186.03		-2352.28		-2352.19		-4170.40		-4166.87		-3243.48		-3243.03	
Var Country	0.1051		0.1008		0.0253		0.0254		1.1737		1.1887		0.8772		0.8802	
Var Region	0.1196		0.0000		0.0055		0.0053		0.4805		0.4740		0.0465		0.0484	
Var Residual	2.6159		2.6123		1.0372		1.0372		7.3275		7.2988		2.8668		2.8639	
LR vs. lin.reg.	8.24	**	7.67		13.57	***	13.40	**	171.30	***	163.9	***	214.42	***	214.88	***

Notes: In all models, all controls are included. Statistical significance:
*** 1%; ** 5%; * 10%. In brackets are the z statistics.

Source: Authors' calculations.

Table 37.5. Results of Gamma Regression, Individual and Institutional REDI

	Instability of revenues		Employment		Capital		Firm debt	
	Coef. [z]	Sig.	Coef. [z]	Sig.	Coef. [z]	Sig.	Coef. [z]	Sig.
Market oriented	0.22 [0.32]		0.01 [0.25]		0.28 [0.95]		-0.03 [-0.23]		0.68 [0.89]		-0.16 [-1.76]		-0.67 [-1.38]	*
Mixed oriented	4.66 [0.73]		0.20 [1.59]		1.29 [1.80]	*	-0.29 [-0.85]		4.41 [2.37]	**	-0.39 [-1.84]	*	-0.26 [-0.22]	
Log GDP pc	-11.12 [-7.01]	***	0.73 [1.56]		0.68 [1.47]		-3.06 [-1.79]	*	-3.13 [-1.82]	*	-0.88 [-0.63]		-0.84 [-0.59]	
REDI Indiv	-0.04 [-2.11]	**	0.01 [1.47]		0.02 [1.87]	*	0.04 [0.92]		0.05 [1.09]		0.07 [2.06]	**	0.07 [1.98]	**
REDI Inst	0.05 [3.82]	***	0.00 [1.24]		0.00 [1.44]		0.01 [0.92]		0.02 [1.28]		0.02 [2.46]	**	0.02 [2.03]	**
Market × REDIInd	-0.04 [-1.81]	*	-0.01 [-1.40]				-0.02 [-0.86]				0.01 [0.78]			
Market × REDIInst	0.01 [0.13]		-0.04 [-0.56]				-0.01 [-0.89]				0.01 [1.08]			
Mixed × REDIInd	0.00 [0.17]		0.00 [-1.78]	*			-0.11 [-1.82]	*			0.00 [-0.07]			
Mixed × REDIInst	-0.07 [-0.54]		0.00 [-1.25]				-0.06 [-2.80]	***			0.00 [-0.12]			

Nr. Obs.	1623		1E23		1623		1623		1623		1623		1623		1623	
Wald chi2	135.86	***	140.35	***	73.61	***	78.91	***	131.53	***	140.42	***	119.80	***	120.96	***
Log likelih.	−1182.62		−1180.78		−2351.60		−2349.13		−4170.22		−4166.03		−3242.59		−3241.96	
Var Country	0.0000		0.0000		0.0304		0.0290		1.1455		1.1599		0.9870		1.0061	
Var Region	0.0000		0.0000		0.0047		0.0057		0.4785		0.4702		0.0428		0.0435	
Var Residual	2.6082		2.5928		1.0363		1.0325		7.3277		7.2941		2.8643		2.8613	
LR vs. lin.reg.	8.41	*	10.03	***	14.93	***	14.54	***	152.96	***	146.99	***	207.93	***	207.56	***

Notes: In all models, all controls are included. Statistical significance:
*** 1%; ** 5%; * 10%. In brackets are the z statistics.

Discussion and Conclusion

In this section, the findings are presented and discussed according to our hypotheses stated above.

H1a: A higher REDI is correlated with lower instability of revenues of the cultural firms.

We have found strong evidence to reject subhypothesis H1a. Higher levels of entrepreneurship are related to higher instability of firm revenues. We explain this finding in light of cultural firm characteristics—they have lower revenues and are substantially younger than firms in the economy in general. As stated by Katherine Lucas McKay, "Lower instability of firm revenues is often the consequence of their low savings. Remarkably low savings levels create financial uncertainty and instability at both the business and household levels. Businesses with no savings tend to be younger, have lower revenues, and have lower total household incomes" (Lucas McKay 2014).

H1b: A higher REDI is correlated with higher number of employees in cultural firms.

Likewise, no evidence for H1b has been identified. As previously noted, GDP per capita was a stronger predictor than REDI for this performance measure. We interpreted this in light of previous findings (see, e.g., Vecco and Srakar 2018a; 2018b). A higher number of employees is not always associated with good firm performance, and in the future, additional mediating and moderating relationships could provide more explanation of this finding and whether it is related to a relationship we did not control for in our model.

H1c: A higher REDI is correlated with a higher level of debt financing.
H1d: A higher REDI is correlated with a lower level of capital financing for cultural firms.

We found positive evidence for H1c, H1d, and H2, specifically for the level of capital (the mixed-orientation firms have in general a higher level of capital than the firms that carry out related or partly cultural activities firms with partly cultural activities, while the ones with a higher level of regional entrepreneurial development tend to have an additional and strongly significant lower level of capital than those firms) and debt financing (countries with a higher level of entrepreneurship have higher levels of debt financing, a finding that holds for both individual and institutional REDI). Findings can be explained by referring to previous literature in finance, specifically the capital structure irrelevance principle (the so-called Modigliani-Miller theorems; for more, see Modigliani and Miller 1958, 1963).

H2: The relationship between REDI and the performance of cultural firms is moderated by the sector of the cultural firm and by the dimension (individual/institutional) of the index.

We have found that none of the results is moderated by the effects of the cultural sector, which means that all cultural firms regardless of their specific cultural sector have equal results in this aspect. But we have found evidence of moderating relationships of the dimensions of the REDI index, as related to instability of revenues, capital, and debt financing. Firms in countries with a higher institutional and lower individual REDI have higher instability of revenues. The mixed-orientation firms with a better institutional REDI index have a slightly higher number of employees than firms with partly cultural activities As noted previously, earlier work by the authors linked a higher number of employees of cultural firms with inefficiency, and so the findings can be explained as the mixed firms (which include public sources of funds in their financing) exploiting the institutional environment for enhancing their employment, but with some expected drawbacks in efficiency of production. Additionally, as said earlier, the results show that mixed-orientation firms tend to have higher capital on average, and there is a strong (positive) relationship of the REDI to debt financing, with firms in both countries with higher individual and institutional REDI having higher levels of debt financing.

To strengthen these results, we performed a sensitivity analysis, which we do not present here in detail due to limited space. First, we performed the basic correlations and linear (OLS) regressions using the same variables as in Tables 37.3 and 37.4. Findings were in line with the above. It would be interesting to implement the analysis also on the full set of the EU countries to get better insights into this observation in the future. Additionally, we performed the analysis using different combinations of independent variables, a superior hierarchical level of the entrepreneurial regime (following, e.g., Dilli and Elert 2016), and a more common welfare regime typology (following Esping-Andersen 1990). Not many different results were found. More research is needed to clarify entrepreneurial regime classifications (Vecco and Srakar 2018a; 2018b; Srakar and Vecco 2021).

Some limitations of the present study can be identified in the composition of the REDI, as the component collection is rather ad hoc (Szerb, Lafuente, et al. 2017). Some important attributes of entrepreneurial ecosystems may be added to the REDI sub-indicators, in particular in terms of number of variables used and their time dimension. If the market, the regulatory environment, human capital and education, knowledge creation and dissemination, and the financial and infrastructure dimensions are comprehensively captured, specific indicators for supporting services and leadership would be included. Other limitations refer to the sample selected, for, as we have mentioned, the study uses thirteen of the twenty-eight European countries in the year 2013 without taking into account how the economic and political regimes of the different countries could affect the regional growth and performance of the firms under examination.

Some policy recommendations are relevant here. Through this analysis, we were unable to confirm that the regional dimension is very strongly related to the performance of cultural firms. Nevertheless, the relationship to the type of financing has been confirmed. To stimulate cultural entrepreneurship at the European level, policymakers should focus on the regional dimension more in terms of the modes of firm financing. This may imply the identification of better measures of performance success; in our study we have included only the broadest ones. Firm success can be measured by many criteria, and measures should be chosen based on the policy objective (by referring, for example, to the renowned Du Pont scheme of performance indicators; see, e.g., Bodie, Kane, and Marcus 2004).

On the firm level, cultural firms should choose the location of their activities based on both the development of the local business environment (the entrepreneurial dimension) and the general welfare of the location (the gross domestic product dimension). We were not able to find sufficient evidence to claim that the regional entrepreneurship development dimension is sufficiently important to merit firms' singular attention; rather, it has to be combined with other factors important for selecting the location of activity. Firms could also exploit policy factors related to stimulating the development of entrepreneurship based on the regional structure, in particular as related to measures to stimulate different forms of firm financing (by, for example, choosing the location of their activity based on those factors, applying for government funds as appropriate, and cooperating with governmental authorities on the appropriate level).

Future research can focus on localized entrepreneurship: how entrepreneurs are embedded in and interact with their immediate spatial context and use existing resources. This will allow a better understanding of why some places are more entrepreneurial than others, and why certain types of entrepreneurship prevail in specific regions. Furthermore, future research could explore the genesis and dynamics of the diversity of regional entrepreneurship. Adopting a micro approach, we may see that although the entrepreneurial activity may statistically be lower in some regions, a specific entrepreneurial activity linked and embodied in that specific region can emerge by utilizing and valorizing place-specific resources (Korsgaard and Anderson 2011). To be effective, policies have to abandon the best-practice approach of replicating what other regions or countries do, in order to develop their own context-specific, tailor-made program (Huggins and Williams 2011). The specificities of the capabilities and structures of spatial contexts and entrepreneurial culture have to be taken into account (North and Smallbone 2006; Venkataraman 2004) to develop effective policies to foster local entrepreneurial intentions, attitudes, and activity (Bosma and Schutjens 2011).

Notes

1. Throughout the article we use "cultural entrepreneurship" to refer both to firms in the cultural sector and to firms in the creative sector.
2. The choice of the countries was guided by data availability and geographic representation of the European countries.
3. NACE II is the revised Nomenclature of Economic Activities (NACE), used for the European statistical classification of economic activities.
4. Related to the topic, we could also mention the works of DeAngelo and Masulis (1980); Taggart (1985); Ashton (1989); Adedeji (1998); Klapper, Saria-Allende, and Sulla (2002); Graham (2003); and Frank and Goyal (2005).

References

Acs, Zoltán J., Pia Arenius, and Maria Minniti. 2005. *Global Entrepreneurship Monitor: 2004 Executive Report.* London: London Business School and Babson College.

Acs, Zoltán J., and David B. Audretsch. 1988. "Innovation in Large and Small Firms: An Empirical Analysis." *American Economic Review* 784: 678–690.

Acs, Zoltán J., David B. Audretsch, and David S. Evans. 1994. "Why Does the Self-Employment Rate Vary Across Countries and over Time?" CERP Working Paper no. 871, Center for Economic Policy Research.

Acs, Zoltán J., Erkko Autio, and László Szerb. 2014. "National Systems of Entrepreneurship: Measurement Issues and Policy Implications." *Research Policy* 43, no. 3: 476–494. http://dx.doi.org/10.1016/j.respol.2013.08.016.

Acs, Zoltán J., and László Szerb. 2007. "Entrepreneurship, economic growth, and public policy." *Small Business Economics* 28: 109–122.

Ács, Zoltán J., and László Szerb. 2009. "The Global Entrepreneurship Index (GEINDEX)." *Foundations and Trends in Entrepreneurship* 5, no. 5: 341–435.

Ács, Zoltán J., and László Szerb. 2010. *The Global Entrepreneurship and Development Index 2011.* Cheltenham: Edward Elgar.

Ács, Zoltán J., and László Szerb. 2011. *The Global Entrepreneurship and Development Index 2012.* Cheltenham: Edward Elgar.

Acs, Zoltán J., and Attila Varga. 2005. "Entrepreneurship, Agglomeration, and Technological Change." *Small Business Economics* 24: 323–334.

Adedeji, Abimbola. 1998. "Does the Pecking Order Hypothesis Explain the Dividend Payout Ratios of Firms in the UK?" *Journal of Business Finance and Accounting* 25: 1127–1157.

Andersson, Roland, John M. Quigley, and Mats Wilhelmsson. 2005. "Agglomeration and the Spatial Distribution of Creativity." *Papers in Regional Science* 84, no. 3: 445–464.

Ashton, David J. 1989. "The Cost of Capital and the Imputation Tax System." *Journal of Business Finance and Accounting* 16, no. 1: 75–88.

Audretsch, David B. 2009. "The Entrepreneurial Society." *Journal of Technology Transfer* 34: 245–254.

Audretsch, David B., and Maryann P. Feldman. 1996. "R&D Spillovers and the Geography of Innovation and Production." *American Economic Review* 86, no. 3: 630–640.

Audretsch, David B., and Roy Thurik. 2001. "What's New About the New Economy? Sources of Growth in the Managed and Entrepreneurial Economies." *Industrial and Corporate Change* 10, no. 1: 267–315.

Autio, Erkko. 2005. *Global Entrepreneurship Monitor: 2005 Report on High-Expectation Entrepreneurship.* London: London Business School and Babson College.

Autio, Erkko. 2007. *Global Entrepreneurship Monitor: 2007 Global Report on High Growth Entrepreneurship.* Wellesley, MA: Babson College and London Business School.

Awang, Amran, Shaiful Annuar Khalid, Ab Aziz Yusof, Kamsol Mohamed Kassim, Mohammad Ismail, Rozihana Shekh Zain, and Abdul Rashid Sintha Madar. 2009. "Entrepreneurial Orientation and Performance Relations of Malaysian Bumiputera SMEs: The Impact of Some Perceived Environmental Factors." *International Journal of Business and Management* 4, no. 9: 84–96.

Baumgartner, Daniel, Marco Pütz, and Irmi Seidl. 2013. "What Kind of Entrepreneurship Drives Regional Development in European Non-core Regions? A Literature Review on

Empirical Entrepreneurship Research." *European Planning Studies* 21, no. 8: 1095–1127. doi:10.1080/09654313.2012.722937.

Blanchflower, David G., Andrew Oswald, and Alois Stutzer. 2001. "Latent Entrepreneurship Across Nations." *European Economic Review* 45, nos. 4–6: 680–691.

Bodie, Zane, Alex Kane, and Alan J. Marcus. 2004. *Essentials of Investments*. 5th ed. New York: McGraw-Hill Irwin.

Boschma, Ron A., and Jen Lambooy. 1999. "Evolutionary Economics and Economic Geography." *Journal of Evolutionary Economics* 9, no. 4: 411–429.

Bosma, Niels, Zoltán J. Acs, Erkko Autio, Alicia Coduras, and Jonathan Levie. 2009. *GEM Executive Report 2008*. Babson College, Universidad del Desarrollo, and Global Entrepreneurship Research Consortium.

Bosma, Niels, and Veronique Schutjens. 2011. "Understanding Regional Variation in Entrepreneurial Activity and Entrepreneurial Attitude in Europe." *Annals of Regional Science* 47, no. 3: 711–742. doi:10.1007/s00168-010-0375-7.

Carree, Martin, André van Stel, Roy Thurik, and Sander Wennekers. 2002. "Economic Development and Business Ownership: An Analysis Using Data of 23 OECD Countries in the Period 1976–1996." *Small Business Economics* 19, no. 3: 271–290.

Chen, Li-Ju, and Shun-Yu Chen. 2011. "How the Pecking-Order Theory Explains Capital Structure." *Journal of International Management Studies* 6, no. 3: 92–100.

Cooper, Arnold C., and Williams C. Dunkelberg. 1986. "Entrepreneurship and Paths to Business Ownership." *Strategic Management Journal* 7, no. 1: 53–68.

Covin, Jeffrey G., and Dennis P. Slevin. 1991. "A Conceptual Model of Entrepreneurship as Firm Behavior." *Entrepreneurship Theory and Practice* 16, no. 1: 7–25.

DeAngelo, Harry, and Donald R. Masulis. 1980. "Optimal Capital Structure Under Corporate and Personal Taxation." *Journal of Financial Economics* 8: 3–29.

Dejardin, Marcus. 2011. "Linking Net Entry to Regional Economic Growth." *Small Business Economics* 36, no. 4: 443–460. doi:10.1007/s11187-009-9255-x.

Dess, Gregory G., G. Thomas Lumpkin, and Jeffrey G. Covin. 1997. "Entrepreneurial Strategy Making and Firm Performance: Tests of Contingency and Configurational Models." *Strategic Management Journal* 18: 677–695.

Dilli, Selin, and Niklas Elert. 2016. "The Diversity of Entrepreneurial Regimes in Europe." Paper presented at the 14th Interdisciplinary European Conference on Entrepreneurship Research, Chur, Switzerland.

DiMaggio, Paul. 1982. "Cultural Capital and School Success: The Impact of Status Culture Participation on the Grades of U.S. High School Students." *American Sociological Review* 47: 189–201.

Esping-Andersen, Gøsta. 1990. *The Three Worlds of Welfare Capitalism*. Princeton, NJ: Princeton University Press.

Feldman, Maryann P. 2001. "The Entrepreneurial Event Revisited: Firm Formation in a Regional Context." *Industrial and Corporate Change* 10, no. 4: 861–891.

Fillis, Ian. 2000. "Being Creative at the Marketing/Entrepreneurship Interface: Lessons from the Art." *Journal of Research in Marketing and Entrepreneurship* 2: 125–137.

Fillis, Ian. 2004. "The Entrepreneurial Artist as Marketer: Drawing from the Smaller-Firm Literature." *International Journal of Arts Management* 7: 9–21.

Fillis, Ian, and Ruth Rentschler. 2005. "Using Creativity to Achieve an Entrepreneurial Future for Arts Marketing." *International Journal of Nonprofit and Voluntary Sector Marketing* 10, no. 4: 275–287.

Frank, Murray Z., and Vidhan K. Goyal. 2005. "Trade-off and Pecking Order Theories of Debt." In *Handbook of Corporate Finance: Empirical Corporate Finance*, edited by E. Eckbo, chap. 7. Handbooks in Finance Series. Amsterdam: Elsevier/North Holland.

Galwey, Nicholas W. 2014. *Introduction to Mixed Modeling Beyond Regression and Analysis of Variance*. Hoboken, NJ: John Wiley & Sons.

Garofoli, Gioacchino. 1994. "New Firm Formation and Regional Development: The Italian Case." *Regional Studies* 28, no. 4: 381–393. doi:10.1080/00343409412331348346.

Gartner, Williams B. 1985. "A Conceptual Framework for Describing the Phenomenon of New Venture Creation." *Academy of Management Review* 10, no. 4: 696–706.

Graham, John R. 2003. "Taxes and Corporate Finance: A Review." *Review of Financial Studies* 16, no. 4: 1075–1129.

Grilo, Isabel, and Roy Thurik. 2005. "Latent and Actual Entrepreneurship in Europe and the US: Some Recent Developments." *International Entrepreneurship and Management Journal* 1, no. 4: 441–459.

Hesmondhalgh, David. 2002. *The Cultural Industries*. London: Sage.

Huggins, Robert, and Nick Williams. 2011. "Entrepreneurship and Regional Competitiveness: The Role and Progression of Policy." *Entrepreneurship and Regional Development* 23, nos. 9–10: 907–932. doi:10.1080/08985626.2011.577818.

Klamer, Arjo. 2011. "Cultural Entrepreneurship." *Austrian Economics* 24, no. 2: 141–156.

Klapper, Leora, Virginia Saria-Allende, and Victor Sulla. 2002. "Small- and Medium-Size Enterprise Financing in Eastern Europe." World Bank Policy Research Working Paper 2933.

Korsgaard, Steffen, and Alistair R. Anderson. 2011. "Enacting Entrepreneurship as Social Value Creation." *International Small Business Journal* 29, no. 2: 135–151. doi:10.1177/0266242610391936,

Kreiser, Patrick M., Louis D. Marino, and K. Mark Weaver. 2002. "Assessing the Psychometric Properties of the Entrepreneurial Scale: A Multi-Country Analysis." *Entrepreneurship Theory and Practice* 26: 71–92.

Lindqvist, Katja. 2011. "Artists Entrepreneurs." In *Art Entrepreneurship*, edited by Michael Sherdin and Ivo Zander, 10–22. Cheltenham, UK: Edward Elgar.

Lucas McKay, Katherine. 2014. "Achieving Financial Security Through Entrepreneurship. Policies to Support Financially Vulnerable Microbusiness Owners." CFED, Washington, DC.

Lumpkin, G. Tom, and Gregory G. Dess. 1996. "Clarifying the Entrepreneurial Construct and Linking It to Performance." *Academy of Management Review* 21: 135–172.

Lumpkin, G. Tom, and Gregory G. Dess. 2001. "Linking Two Dimensions of Entrepreneurial Orientation to Firm Performance: The Moderating Role of Environment and Industry Life Cycle." *Journal of Business Venturing* 16: 429–451.

Mato, Daniel. 2009. "All Industries Are Cultural." *Cultural Studies* 23, no. 1: 70–87.

Mazur, Kinga. 2007. "The Determinants of Capital Structure Choice: Evidence from Polish Companies." *International Atlantic Economic Society* 13: 495–514.

Meisiek, Stefan, and Stefan Haefliger. 2011. "Inventing the Unexpected: Entrepreneurship and the Arts." In *Art Entrepreneurship*, edited by Michael Sherdin and Ivo Zander, 78–97. Cheltenham, UK: Edward Elgar.

Miller, Toby. 2009. "From Creative to Cultural Industries." *Cultural Studies* 23, no. 1: 88–99.

Modigliani, Franco, and Marcus H. Miller. 1958. "The Cost of Capital, Corporation Finance and the Theory of Investment." *American Economic Review* 48, no. 3: 261–297.

Modigliani, Franco, and Merton H. Miller. 1963. "Corporate Income Taxes and the Cost of Capital: A Correction." *American Economic Review* 53: 433–443.

Moureau, Nathalie, and Dominique Sagot-Douvaroux. 2010. *Le marché de l'art contemporain*. Paris: La Découverte.

Müller, Sabine. 2016. "A Progress Review of Entrepreneurship and Regional Development: What Are the Remaining Gaps?" *European Planning Studies* 24, no. 6: 1133–1158.

Myers, Stewart C., and Nicholas Majluf. 1984. "Corporate Financing and Investment Decisions When Firms Have Information That Investors Do Not Have." *Journal of Financial Economics* 13: 187–221.

North, David, and David Smallbone. 2006. "Developing Entrepreneurship and Enterprise in Europe's Peripheral Rural Areas: Some Issues Facing Policy-Makers." *European Planning Studies* 14, no. 1: 41–60. doi.10.1080/09654310500339125.

Pulendran, Sue, Richard Speed, and Robert E. Widing II. 2000. "The Antecedents and Consequences of Market Orientation in Australia." *Australian Journal of Management* 25, no. 2: 119–143.

Quan, Vuong Due Hoang. 2002. "A Rational Justification of the Pecking Order Hypothesis to the Choice of Sources of Financing." *Management Research News* 25: 74–90.

Reynolds, Paul, Niels Bosma, Erkko Autio, Steve Hunt, Natalie De Bono, Isabel Servais, and Nancy Chin. 2005. "Global Entrepreneurship Monitor: Data Collection Design and Implementation 1998–2003." *Small Business Economics* 24, no. 3: 205–231.

Scherdin, Mikael, and Ivo Zander (Edited). 2011. Art Entrepreneurship. Cheltenham, UK: Edward Elgar.

Shane, Scott, Edwin A. Locke, and John Christopher. 2003. "Entrepreneurial Motivation." *Human Resource Management Review* 13, no. 2: 257–279.

Slater, Stanley F., and John C. Narver. 2000. "The Positive Effect of a Market Orientation on Business Profitability: A Balanced Replication." *Journal of Business Research* 48, no. 1: 69–73.

Söndermann, Michael. 2010. "Definition of Cultural Industries Within the TF3 Framework." In European Commission, *European Competitiveness Report 2010: An integrated Industrial Policy for the Globalisation Era. Putting Competitiveness and Sustainability at Front Stage*. Brussels: European Commission.

Song, Michael C., Anthony Di Benedetto, and Robert W. Nason. 2007. "Capabilities and Financial Performance: The Moderating Effect of Strategic Type." *Journal of the Academy of Marketing Science* 35: 18–34.

Srakar, Andrej, and Marilena Vecco. 2021. "Classification of Entrepreneurial Regimes: A Symbolic Polygonal Clustering Approach." In *Data Analysis and Rationality in a Complex World*, edited by T. Chadjipadelis, 261–271. Studies in Classification, Data Analysis, and Knowledge Organization. Cham, Switzerland: Springer.

Sternberg, Rolf. 2009. "Regional Dimensions of Entrepreneurship." *Foundations and Trends in Entrepreneurship* 5, no. 4: 211–340. doi:10.1561/0300000024.

Subramanian, Ashok, and Sreevatsalan Nilakanta. 1996. "Organizational Innovativeness: Exploring the Relationship Between Organizational Determinants of Innovation, Types of Innovations, and Measures of Organizational Performance." *Omega* 24, no. 6: 631–647.

Szerb, László, Zoltán J. Acs, Erkko Autio, Raquel Ortega-Argilés, and Eva Komlósi. 2013. *REDI: The Regional Entrepreneurship and Development Index—Measuring Regional Entrepreneurship. Final Report*. Brussels: European Commission.

Szerb, László, Esteban Lafuente, Krisztina Horvath, Balázs Páger, Mark Sanders, and Erik Stam. 2017. "Cross-Sectional Analysis of REDI and Regional Growth Performance Measures." EU Project FIRES.

Szerb, László, Aidis Ruta, and Zoltán J. Acs. 2013. *A Comparative Analysis of Hungary's Entrepreneurial Performance in the 2006–2010 Time Period Based in the GEM and the GEDI Methodologies*. Pécs: PTE-KTK.

Szerb, László, Zoltan Vörös, Eva Komlósi, Zoltán J. Acs, Balázs Pager, and Raquel Ortega-Argilés. 2017. "The New Regional Entrepreneurship and Development Index: Structure, Data and Description of Methodology." Unpublished manuscript.

Taggart, Robert A., Jr. 1985. "Effects of Regulation on Utility Financing: Theory and Evidence." *Journal of Industrial Economics* 33, no. 3: 257–267.

Tay, Linda, and Neil A. Morgan. 2002. "Antecedents and Consequences of Market Orientation in Chartered Surveying Firms." *Construction Management and Economics* 20, no. 4: 331–341.

Throsby, David. 2001. *Economics and Culture*. Cambridge, UK: Cambridge University Press.

Tidd, Joe, John Bessant, and Keith Pavitt. 2001. *Integrating Technological, Market and Organisational Change*. Chichester, UK: John Wiley and Sons.

Trettin, Lutz, and Frielerike Welter. 2011. "Challenges for Spatially Oriented Entrepreneurship Research." *Entrepreneurship and Regional Development* 23, nos. 7–8: 1–28. doi:10.1080/08985621003792988.

Van Praag, C. Miriam, and Peter H. Versloot. 2007. "What Is the Value of Entrepreneurship: A Review of Recent Research." *Small Business Economics* 29, no. 4: 351–382.

van Stel, André, Martin Carree, and Roy Thurik. 2005. "The Effect of Entrepreneurial Activity on National Economic Growth." *Small Business Economics* 24: 311–321.

Vecco, Marilena, and Andrej Srakar. 2018a. "Nascent Cultural and Creative Entrepreneurship: Between Entrepreneurial Economics and Institutional Entrepreneurship." In *Nascent Entrepreneurship and Successful New Venture Creation*, edited by A. C. Moreira, J. G. Dantas, and F. M. Valente, 175–202. Hershey, PA: IGI Global.

Vecco, Marilena, and Andrej Srakar. 2018b. "Modelling Cultural Entrepreneurial Regimes in Central and Eastern Europe: A Symbolic Data Analysis Approach." In *Creative Industries and Entrepreneurship: Paradigms in Transition from a Global Perspective*, edited by L. Lazzeretti and M. Vecco, 156–176. Cheltenham, UK: Edward Elgar.

Vecco, Marilena. 2020. "Artpreneurs' lessons to traditional business." *Home International Journal of Entrepreneurship and Small Business* 40, no. 2: 154–170.

Venkataraman, S. Shankar. 2004. "Regional Transformation Through Technological Entrepreneurship." *Journal of Business Venturing* 19, no. 1: 153–167. doi:10.1016/j.jbusvent.2003.04.001.

Wennekers, Sander, and Roy Thurik. 1999. "Linking Entrepreneurship and Economic Growth." *Small Business Economics* 13, no. 1: 27–56.

Zahra, Shaker A., and Jeffrey G. Covin. 1995. "Contextual Influences on the Corporate Entrepreneurship-Performance Relationship: A Longitudinal Analysis." *Journal of Business Venturing* 10: 43–58.

PART X
FUTURE DIRECTIONS FOR ARTS AND CULTURAL MANAGEMENT

PART X

CHAPTER 38

THE GLOBALIZED AND CHANGING LANDSCAPE OF THE ARTS

The Era of Post-Pandemic and Civil Unrest

PIER LUIGI SACCO

INTRODUCTION: THE POST-PANDEMIC ERA AS A POINT OF NO RETURN FOR CULTURAL AND CREATIVE SECTORS

THE global COVID-19 pandemic has had an enormous impact on all spheres of human activity at the economic, social, and environmental levels (Rahman et al. 2021), and likely also at the sociocultural level, although a clear understanding of such changes will only become possible in a medium- to long-term perspective (Sacco and De Domenico 2021). In this general context of large-scale system disruption, the cultural and creative sectors have been struck with particular intensity (OECD 2020). At the root of this problem are the high levels of fragmentation and the extreme incidence of very small and micro firms (Gundolf, Jaouen, and Gast 2018) and individual freelance professionals (Mould, Vorley, and Liu 2014) across such sectors (Comunian and England 2020). Due to this extreme heterogeneity, policymakers often lack a deep understanding of the complex functioning of cultural production systems (Pratt 2009), and consequently of the specific needs and characteristics of cultural and creative activities and jobs (Markusen 2006). The actual levels of welfare protection and economic support provided by different countries have therefore depended upon the specific structure of local creative economies, the relative importance of market-mediated sustainability strategies compared to government-funded ones, and the actual characteristics of relief packages

(Betzler et al. 2021). Moreover, sectoral statistics are often incomplete and flawed by serious definitional and methodological issues (Foord 2008), making it difficult to acquire an accurate and reliable picture of the status quo.

However, the overall impact of the pandemic on cultural and creative sectors has not been entirely negative. Some important positive effects are also emerging, partly as a result of an imposed service innovation effect, which emerged in several different sectors as a response to the pandemic shock (Heihonen and Strandvik 2021). More specifically, those sectors whose value creation relies, or can be quickly redesigned to rely, on digital platforms and remote access have responded well and even thrived, whereas those whose value creation depends on access in the physical space have struggled (Jeannotte 2021). Such tendencies are not likely to exert only temporary effects but will also characterize future trends in the medium to long run, so each sector's specific capacity to integrate digital elements and to monetize remote access will play an important role in their future evolution (Khlystova, Kalyuzhnova, and Belitski 2022). The future evolution of cultural and creative sectors will therefore be characterized by an increasing complementarity between physical and digital dimensions of production and access.

As already remarked, this tendency is clearly being amplified by the pandemic crisis, but it was already ongoing before the pandemic shock, so the latter compounds with other, important drivers that push in the same direction. There is reason to believe that the current transitional phase is not temporary but marks a point of no return with respect to the pre-pandemic status quo, so the pandemic can be retrospectively interpreted as the triggering shock that moved the system across the threshold of change toward which it was already heading. Putting such drivers into focus and understanding the general picture that results from their complex interaction is therefore key to figuring out the future post-pandemic scenarios of cultural and creative production at the global scale. This is the purpose of the present chapter. There are at least four different drivers that need to be considered in this regard: the shifting global geography of cultural production and access; the advent of participatory, decentralized content creation; the consolidation and evolution of digital content mega-platforms; and the tension between democratic and authoritarian forces in the shaping of global cultural conversations. We will briefly explore them one by one in the following sections.

The Shifting Global Geography of Cultural Production and Access

Between the end of World War II and the early 2000s, the global geography of cultural production and access was firmly controlled, both economically and symbolically, by Western countries, and in particular by the United States and Europe (O'Connor 2020). As a result of a peculiar constellation of sociopolitical and cultural conditions (Wilson

2000; Bowditch 2001), Europe has been, historically, the cradle of the patronage regime of cultural production in its full-fledged form (Bullard 2002). Patronage, in turn, has been essential for the development of the notion of highbrow culture and of cultural institutions such as the museum, the theater, and the library in their modern form (Fischer-Lichte 1997; Battles 2003; Abt 2006). The global diffusion of such institutions has been crucially enabled by European colonial empires, as part of a political strategy aimed at establishing the Western models of socioeconomic organization as the benchmark of human civilization (Bowden 2019) and, consequently, at imposing European values, social norms and lifestyles as an ideal model to be imitated, and to some extent customized, by non-European societies, with culture as a key symbolic marker of this process of assimilation (Bernal 1994).

The advent of the cultural industry at the transition between the nineteenth and twentieth centuries has further consolidated Western supremacy (Jenkins 2003). There has been, however, a significant shift of the key momentum from Europe to the United States. Somewhat ironically, Europe had developed both the social conditions and the technology for the cultural industry revolution (Sassoon 2006), but the new production regime was basically challenging the vested interests related to the incumbent patronage regime, and primarily those of the cultural gatekeepers who administered it (Shrum 1996).

The idea of a mass cultural production where the standards of success and legitimization were determined by box office response rather than by critical appreciation was shaking the patronage regime at its foundations. In particular, it was overturning the principle that the experts know better than anyone else what kind of culture should be accessed—and produced with public money (Bourdieu 1996). For this reason, Europe essentially handed over the innovation leadership in the cultural industry to the United States (Trumpbour 2002). The emerging North American global power was ideally qualified not only to embrace and develop the new production regime but also to make it a quintessential element of its own cultural identity.

The new cultural regime allowed the United States to build an idiosyncratic national culture that was not derivative of the European one but rather was built upon dialectically opposite principles (Huyssen 1986). At the same time, it was also reshaping the very notion of patronage in new, different forms (Mulcahy 2003). Moreover, being a cauldron of different ethnicities and mostly European cultures, the new cultural industry allowed the United States to construct a new shared imagery that could at the same time represent, and offer convenient cultural niches to, all of them at the same time (Powell 2000), shaping a national cultural identity that avoided the consolidation of an archipelago of culturally parochial, ethnoculturally centered subcultures. Furthermore, the cultural industry provided the United States with an ideal solution to the issue of creating a national culture in a geographically vast and dispersed country where technologically reproducible content could circulate much more quickly than nonreproducible content and live performances. A further advantage was that of ensuring that even relatively remote centers lacking major museums or theaters could nevertheless gain timely access to new cultural content (Tapia 1997).

In addition, the "spectacle culture" of the emerging cultural industry, tapping into preexisting visual tropes, transformed the American landscape itself into a new cultural landmark, strongly identified with American cultural identity (Tenneriello 2013). Finally, the emerging American business culture could be seamlessly applied to the nascent cultural industry, providing it with sophisticated business models. This helped the American cultural industry to quickly grow to become the undisputed global content leader (Gomery 2005).

From a European perspective rooted in the patronage system, a business-driven logic of cultural production was highly controversial; in a sense, the basic rationale of patronage is exactly that of enabling cultural producers to create without having to accommodate the compromises of market demand and to maintain their creative independence and integrity (Bowditch 2001). Rather than challenging the United States on the new ground, Europe therefore did not fully compete for it, only to regain interest in cultural and creative industry and entrepreneurship as an economic growth driver from the early 1980s onward (Lee et al. 2014). This does not mean, of course, that Europe didn't develop its own cultural industry—it rather means that the European cultural industry has traditionally been, unlike its American counterpart, very sensitive to the standards and criteria of the highbrow culture typical of the patronage regime (de Valck 2016). In European cinema, music, or literature, with the partial exception of the United Kingdom, which has built a cultural industry that has a closer exchange with the American one for clear linguistic and sociocultural reasons, critical acclaim counts as much as box office returns, and sometimes more. Excessive market success may be accordingly regarded by peers as suspicious, in that it signals an excessive concession to the demands and expectations of an unsophisticated mass demand (Bauman 2008). Even today, when cultural industries are in a mature stage of development, these dialectical tensions are still very strong in the European Union, which maintains a distinctive positioning with respect to the American cultural industry. Rather than directly challenging its leadership in global mass content markets except for specific, somewhat isolated attempts, European cultural industries are consolidating their occupation of content niches that are mostly amenable to well-educated, culturally cosmopolitan global audiences (Lewis and Canning 2020).

This combination of factors provides an explanation of why Europe, despite its social and technological leadership at the turn of the century, handed over to the United States the global leadership in the industrial production of cultural and creative content—a crucial turn that is at the root of American soft power in the second half of the twentieth century (Nolan 2015).

Although the "Western" cultural sphere is much less compact than one would think, and despite the clear gulf between the European and the American production systems, up until very recently the conventional wisdom has been that the West basically ruled the global cultural ecosystem—Europe primarily in its highbrow dimension, the United States primarily in the mass culture dimension. Which, in practical terms, given the relative size and economic impact of highbrow and mass culture, amounted to recognizing the United States as the global cultural leader and Europe as its learned appendix (with a correspondingly intermediate positioning for other Western countries, mostly from the British Commonwealth, such as Canada and Australia).

This is not to say that non-Western cultures have been generally deemed irrelevant. In his global survey of cultural and creative ecosystems, Martel (2011) documented how new cultural production hubs had been blossoming practically everywhere, and in some cases, such as India's Bollywood and Nigeria's Nollywood, not to speak of the pan-Arabic content empire built by the Rotana Group, they were quickly becoming major economic powerhouses. However, Martel concluded that all such new hubs, however impressive in their scale and speed of development, were eminently local in scope and would hardly be able to compete with the United States for global leadership. A particularly telling example is the brief coverage, and somewhat condescending comments, that Martel devotes to one such instance of a local emerging cultural powerhouse, South Korea. This is a clear example of how the "conventional wisdom" approach to global content ecosystems has considered non-Western cultural production as local phenomena that could only be appealing to culturally homogeneous neighbors and whose role in Western cultural palimpsests could be that of (orientalist?) curiosities (Gaupp 2020), with the United States as the sole cultural superpower that could successfully reach a truly global audience. The only partial exception at the end of the 2010s could be considered to be Japan, with the global explosion of the manga and anime culture—once again, however, a niche phenomenon, although very successful with the younger generations, and not a truly alternative cultural industry paradigm in the global context (Kawashima 2018).

However, the case of South Korea is precisely the example that shows how narrow that view was. Today, South Korea is rapidly ascending to the status of a global cultural and creative powerhouse (Lee and Nornes 2015), with big American studios such as Disney and key digital platforms such as Netflix opening their Korean studios and production lines—as business partners rather than as "cultural colonizers" (Jin 2021; Ju 2022), though Korea has long been sensitive to the cultural dominance exerted by the US cultural industry (Jin 2007). A more recent, partial analogue to Martel's book, Pecqueur's (2020) *Atlas de la culture*, draws a very different global picture only ten years after. One witnesses a steep transition from the essentially unipolar vision of Martel to an essentially multipolar vision in which the Far East, and increasingly the global South, move toward the center of the scene, being limited more by the current availability of financial resources (with notable exceptions such as China—where, however, the main limitation comes from political constraints to free expression) than from the appeal and vibrancy of their creative production. The creative contents from the emerging hubs look particularly "fresh" and attractive if compared to the increasingly repetitive and predictable products of the mainstream cultural industry, which unsurprisingly systematically "borrows" new ideas and languages from what it considers the cultural fringe, repackaging them in its traditional formats and narratives (Bustamante 2004).

What is particularly telling is that in the 2010s, when Martel was conducting his global survey, South Korea was already a booming cultural powerhouse, and the Hallyu (the "Korean Wave") was clearly the coolest new trend in Asian culture. However, that trend was dismissed as local, like the others examined in Martel's book, because there was no reason to expect that audiences outside of Asia would find that kind of content of any interest, no more than they did for Bollywood movies. In an irony of history—which is, however, not difficult to rationalize—the West has been in fact the last geocultural area to be taken over by the latest waves of the Hallyu, with the Muslim world widely embracing Korean content when in Europe it was still a niche trend (Elaskary 2018). The Muslim world offered to Korean content a vast new audience that resonated with many aspects of its value systems and was especially interested in exploring content other than mere local remixing of the Western mainstream (Kaptan and Tutucu 2022).

Although at face value Korean content could be easily mistaken as essentially complying with the Western values of individualistic consumption, as a matter of fact it develops a critical attitude toward the West and positions itself as a counterhegemonic cultural force (Kim 2021). Now, however, Hallyu is getting very popular across Western audiences as well, and has become a real global sensation, to the point of having K-pop bands such as BTS topping Billboard charts and co-featuring big Western bands like Coldplay, and Korean movies winning the Oscar for Best Film (and not just Best Foreign Film), as in the case of *Parasite* (Kim 2022).

It is likely that, despite its exceptional speed and scale of success, South Korea will be not an isolated example of a non-Western country making it to the global mainstream but rather a pioneer of a new phase in which geographically and culturally diverse voices take center stage. This is mainly, and somewhat inevitably, due to the increasing role of digital channels of content dissemination, and this trend is likely to be further accelerated in the post-pandemic scenario, where digital access has become, even more than before, the "new normal" (or at least a substantial part of it).

We must therefore be prepared for a new global scenario of cultural and creative production in which Western culture is no longer the default choice of most audiences, and where Western notions of cultural relevance (Rad, Martingano, and Ginges 2018) and creativity (Sundararajan and Raina 2015) are no longer necessarily naturalized. The West is demographically declining, whereas the global South is rising, and even though financial resources, and thus production capacity, are still mostly concentrated in the West, global audiences are increasingly non-Western. There is therefore a clear competitive push toward broadening the spectrum of content away from Western-centrism (Sommer and Sacco 2019). Despite the fact that for the moment most of the platforms offering them are Western and could consequently appropriate culturally diverse content as a mere form of product diversification, the projected growth rates of emerging economies from Asia, and in the future also Africa, suggest that the entrance of big, non-Western digital content platforms in the global arena is only a matter of time (Miller 2012). The pandemic crisis contributed to a substantial extent to new habits of digitally mediated access to content in market segments that were previously mostly focused on physical access, and this has created new opportunities of exposure for culturally and geographically peripheral voices (Vlassis 2021). This will likely accelerate the consolidation of a multipolar structure of the global arena of cultural content.

The Advent of Participatory, Decentralized Content Creation

One of the most important innovations related to the digital revolution is the possibility of new forms of increasingly participatory and decentralized content creation (Jenkins, Ito, and boyd 2015). While this possibility is clearly enabled by digital technology, it would be misleading to think that such a social trend is the *product* of digital technologies. A social demand for increased social agency in creative content production and dissemination has emerged and has been steadily building up from the countercultural revolutions of the late 1950s and 1960s onward, and with the consequent flourishing of subcultures (Jenks 2005). The typical small-group dynamic that is characteristic of the core members of a new subculture makes it inevitable that all involved subjects share a possibility of, and an aspiration to, contributing to the definition of the subculture's aesthetics, language, and semantics (Fine 2012). Therefore, in the subcultural context the usual partition between "producers" and "audience" blurs, and as the subculture expands its social reach through gradual processes of co-optation and affiliation, this horizontal logic of content creation persists, only to vanish when the scale of diffusion turns it into a commodified mass phenomenon (Schiele and Venkatesh 2016). But the crucial contribution of the digital revolution has been exactly preserving this possibility of decentralized contribution even at large scale (Lin and de Kloet 2019)—an option that would be impossible through nondigital tools of content creation and access.

The proliferation of digital content "bubbles" enabled by the digital revolution is therefore an evolution of the pre-digital logic of self-identity building through subcultural creation and participation (Chen 2016), with the important difference that the intrinsically fluid character of digital interaction makes such bubbles more volatile than traditional, pre-digital subcultural movements, while at the same time allowing multiple, parallel affiliations to different bubbles, favoring the development of potentially "multiple digital personalities" (Jain et al. 2021).

However, the promise of a massively decentralized active digital participation is still unfulfilled to a large extent. Preliminary analyses show that having the possibility to engage in content creation does not necessarily amount to exploiting such opportunity. Online communities are still mostly populated by total or partial "lurkers" who absorb content produced by others, with a very basic personal contribution or reaction in the form of likes, resharing, minimal comments, and so on.

Most of the content created and shared online is still produced by a relatively small group of digital influencers who are able to shape and orientate global conversations (Sacco et al. 2021). Of course, the actual social dynamics may be extremely complex and difficult to predict without a sophisticated toolbox of nonlinear modeling and simulation tools, so the importance of the choices of relatively non-active users in the access and dissemination of content should not be overlooked. However, it is undeniable that the potentially disruptive agenda-setting capacity of massively decentralized digital participation has been only minimally exploited so far, and this is the result of our still limited capability to use digital tools to their full capacity, even at the current state of technological advancement (Bosello and van den Haak 2022). Moreover, while there is a tendency to think that we have gained a solid proficiency with digital tools and platforms, we still largely ignore the long-term effects of digital participation both at the micro scale of human cognition, affect, and motivation (Firth et al. 2019) and at the macro scale of the social dynamics of attitudinal and behavioral change (Chayko 2008).

The most important critical factors in this context are therefore digital capability building and empowerment. In a digitally powered knowledge society, even basic digital literacy is not enough to acquire real citizenship. It is, moreover, necessary to develop the capacity to become part of an increasingly diverse number of conversations and processes of collective deliberation as new, emerging forms of social governance (Mäkinen 2006). Human development has been made possible by the social orientation of our brains (Muthukrishna and Heinrich 2016), which supports the crucial processes of cumulative culture. Being kept out of such social conversations means being excluded from key resources and opportunities to improve one's sense of meaning in life, well-being, education, access to social and economic processes, and political representation.

The pandemic crisis has clearly exposed some critical points in this regard. The first is the still dramatic inequality of opportunity of digital connectivity: from remote schooling to access to all kinds of knowledge and social resources from home during lockdowns, the social divide between those who have regular and safe access to high-quality, high-speed digital connectivity and those who don't has never been so evident in its social consequences (Katz, Jordan, and Ognyanova 2021). Consequently, there is now a growing conviction that fair digital access should be added to the list of basic human rights (Von Braun, Zamagni, and Sánchez-Sorondo 2020). The second is that, even in the presence of digital access of good quality, differences in digital capabilities have further widened the gap between those who were able to access crucial resources to cope with the psychosocial effects of the pandemic (for instance, access to quality content to manage emotional overload and mood instability in a situation of constant stress and alert) and those who didn't (Henry, Kayser, and Egermann 2021). Epidemiologists have clearly warned us that the current global pandemic, even when it is (hopefully) definitely over, is likely not the last, and that similar crises will have to be faced in the future, in addition to the likely crises related to the consequences of climate change. Therefore, digital access and literacy should be seen as a critical precondition to a suitably updated notion of welfare, and as an important factor to improve the resilience of our socio-sanitary systems in response to major structural crises.

Once again, we witness major differences at the global scale in terms of quality of digital access and of development of basic digital capabilities, and especially so between the global North and South. However, it is also interesting to stress that it is especially in socioeconomically deprived areas, such as in most of Africa, that new forms of frugal technological innovation are quickly emerging, developing ingenious solutions to important social challenges but also testing radically new approaches to the building of inclusive content platforms (Madichie and Hinson 2022).

In the future, however, we can expect an increase in decentralized forms of creativity, where individual authorship will be gradually complemented by collective authorship (Bantinaki 2016); the more this is the case, the more digital capability-building and empowerment goals will be reached at all territorial scales. We already have interesting signs of this new trend in traditional, vertical cultural production arenas: for instance, the 2021 Turner Prize shortlisted artists were all art collectives, and the curators of Documenta 15 are an Indonesian artist collective, ruangrupa, who invited mostly artist collectives—a clear sign that there is a fundamental shift in perspective as to the relevance of collective artistic agency in the new sociocultural context (Zarobell 2022). The passage from the institutionalized artistic sphere to the domain of massively decentralized cultural production is neither easy nor obvious, but the trend is set, and it is likely a long-term one.

The Consolidation and Evolution of Digital Content Mega-Platforms

The digital mega-platforms play a central role in the new global ecosystem of cultural and creative content, and it could be natural to think of them as the frontier of innovation in the field. However, this intuition suffers from a lack of historical perspective. In the past, the countries that have been leading the technological innovation behind the emergence of a new regime have not been the ones that became the innovation leaders in content production, as was the case for the emergence of the cultural and creative industries. This could happen again, and the real content innovation could rather be driven by the latecomers, not the incumbents. Let us see why.

Somewhat ironically, the rapid escalation of the new non-Western cultural superpowers such as South Korea reflects, *mutatis mutandis*, the same deep logic that brought the US takeover of the global cultural industry. The United States benefited from Europe's unwillingness to tap into the world of opportunity they crucially contributed to create with the industrial revolution and with technological innovations in content reproduction such as cinema, photography, and the radio, to cite a few obvious examples. Europe clearly made use of such technologies and developed a mass culture, but without bringing it to its most innovative and transformational consequences, preferring to preserve its leadership in the preexisting patronage regime, which evolved into the public patronage of twentieth-century public cultural policy (Sacco, Ferilli, and Tavano Blessi 2018). Likewise, the United States has been the major force behind the development of the digital content economy. However, one of the key features of digital content is its fluid character, which fits poorly into the straitjacket of the intellectual property system that has been created for, and tailored around, pre-digital media. As a consequence, to preserve the profitability of its cultural industry, the United States has severely limited the development of post-copyright business models and has tried to remodel as much as possible the developmental strategy of the new digital content platforms in terms of the well-established models of twentieth-century cultural industry (Fuchs 2011).

Because of this, the business model of virtually all of the digital mega-platforms is based on the extractive exploitation of digital participation. The more people use the platform and provide content, the greater the value of the eyeballs, customer profiling, social trend analysis, and so on that can be monetized on the respective markets (Barns 2019). What is actually shared on the platform makes no difference insofar as it generates traffic (Myllylahti 2018). However, it was inevitable that some restriction on content had to be introduced in view of the concerning implications of the proliferation of fake, deceiving, and manipulative content of all sorts (Wingfield, Isaac, and Benner 2016)—but once again, only as a way of maximizing traffic flows under viability constraints. This means that, essentially, the mega-platforms of today are not interested in becoming enablers of collective action but rather function as all-purpose containers for individual ego-casting—in a nutshell, the extension of the familiar principle of pre-digital media such as television, where the real restriction that is now lifted is that everybody can have their own bundle of "channels" to broadcast their daily life, travels, creations, thought, and just about anything else, and interact (i.e., create traffic) with those of others (Leask, Fyall, and Barron 2014). But any real attempt at using the platform in a massively coordinated, socially transformational way would be immediately seen as a threat, as a potential hijacking of the control over the platform itself. Any kind of transformational collective coordination may only happen at the scale and under the forms decided by the platform designers and administrators.

This is perfectly consequential, but on the other hand it is more of a digital upscaling of the logic of the cultural and creative industries production regime than a real deployment of the potential of digital platforms, where what makes the difference with respect to the past is exactly the power of societal transformation that emerges from decentralized production and dissemination of content. An immediate corollary of this logic is the questioning of intellectual property as the basic principle of governance of content production and dissemination (Menell 2015)—that is, the very foundation of the value chain of traditional cultural and creative industries. The current mega-platforms have no interest in dismantling intellectual property even when they do not sell the streaming of copyrighted material, insofar as they can provide their users with alternative material that is explicitly engineered to circulate as shareable items (such as memes and user-generated content).

This focus on preserving the status quo as much as possible in terms of the logic of value creation is what prevents the United States from being the innovation leader for the next regime, and what is empowering new players such as South Korea to occupy the space that is left available by the United States' defense of its incumbent advantage in the old regime. In the case of South Korea, as its emergence as a global content leader has largely coincided with the digital revolution, business models and the organizational logic of the respective content ecosystems have evolved accordingly. There are in particular two features among many that make a difference with respect to the currently prevailing models. The first is the development of what we could call post-copyright business models. The Korean cultural industry is obviously profiting from the monetization of intellectual property, but strategically one of the main drivers of the global popularity of Korean content is the fact that they are freely available (or almost so) online (Hassim, Jayasainan, and Khalid 2019). K-dramas are freely accessible and downloadable hours after their broadcast on Korean TV, professionally subtitled in English and often in other languages. Other forms of content are directly designed for value creation on digital platforms, rather than to deploy digital platforms as a distributional channel, as happens in the readaptation of pre-digital business models (Jin 2018). K-pop bands are not simply selling music. They are part of an experience industry that responds to the logic and criteria of digital fandom (Parc and Kawashima 2018), which offers plenty of opportunities for monetization without the need to enforce intellectual property: live and online concerts, merchandising (fans would not be interested in counterfeited merchandise, they want the original), product placement, et cetera. Likewise for online gaming and so on.

Being freely distributed online, Korean content has a wide global circulation that facilitates the creation of large national and regional fan bases, paving the way to otherwise implausible business opportunities such as selling of broadcast rights and increased value of product placement for artists, TV series, and so forth. Without this free online circulation, Korean content would have never scaled globally. Moreover, the high levels of digital literacy in Korean society allow a strong interaction between cultural producers and fans. For instance, in the case of K-dramas, thanks to the adoption of the live shoot system, which allows a partial overlap between the shooting and broadcasting phases, it becomes possible to take into account direct feedback from viewers in fine-tuning the storyline, the construction and evolution of characters, the emotional valence of the story, and so on, leading to a real process of content co-creation that has had a profound impact on the evolution of the topics, tropes, style, and aesthetics of Korean TV series (Lucchi Basili and Sacco 2020). The combination of these two elements (post-copyright business model and content co-creation with users) is a clear example of the innovation frontier on which the American cultural industry is not just lagging behind but not even trying, with the result that North American audiences are now being increasingly attracted by natively digital, non-Western content ecosystems such as the Korean one (Jin 2016).

However, somewhat paradoxically, now that the American cultural industry has recognized Korea as a cultural powerhouse that deserves direct investment, it is trying to push Korean content production models back on the familiar track (Ju 2020). For instance, K-dramas produced by Netflix are entirely shot before broadcasting, and their free availability online is being progressively restricted. If Korea adapts to the new rules, despite the possible short-term advantages, it also possibly gives up some of the key elements that make Korean content globally attractive in the first place, so that, in the long term, abandoning the most innovative features of the current model could backfire. Had Korea adopted the mainstream model from the beginning, a partnership with Netflix or Disney would have likely produced a temporary burst of global coolness but little more than that, with the mega-platform moving on to appropriate and maximize value from another source of "local cool," extending the extractive logic to the content sourcing sphere. Now that Korea has already gained global traction, it could probably maintain it even if folding back to more traditional productive models, at least in the medium term. However, whether or not Korea will persist in the development of its own model rather than complying with the mainstream one, it is highly likely that the next emerging cultural powerhouses will follow the original Korean model rather than the current mainstream one, as this would be much more effective in the global positioning of the country as a source of fresh, interesting content rather than as a local thematic entry in the catalog of the mega-platforms.

In the full-fledged version of the new, massively decentralized cultural production regime driven by content co-creation, it can be expected that the innovation leaders will be different from the incumbent ones, and there is reason to expect that they could come from the Far East and from the global South. Once again, the acceleration of online access to content sparked by the global pandemic is already promoting the development of digital content industries in several countries from these regions, and such trends could start becoming globally visible in the next few years.

Another important driver of change in this regard is the increasingly hybrid digital-physical environments that are being developed in the post-pandemic scenario (Sui and Shaw 2022). Despite the big ongoing investments in the mainstreaming of the metaverse as the new enabling platform for cultural ecosystems, the role of physical spaces and places remains crucial, as many experiences (such as those involving smell, taste, or touch, for instance) cannot be fully enjoyed in a purely digital context (Harley et al. 2018). For this reason, it is likely that the hybridization of digital and physical reality will become another important driver for the consolidation of a multipolar geography of cultural production in which the attractiveness/meaningfulness of physical locations is strategically complementary to digital platformization and identity.

Democratic versus Authoritarian Approaches to Global Cultural Conversations

A last, crucial element of the future scenario is the dialectical tension between democratic and authoritarian regimes in the shaping of global cultural conversations. Countries like China are natural candidates to emerge as future cultural powerhouses, and China's focus on soft power clearly points in this direction (Shambaugh 2015). However, it is still controversial whether countries that substantially constrain freedom of expression can produce appealing content outside of their closer geographical sphere of sociopolitical influence. So far, China is essentially producing content for its internal market, which, however big and quickly growing (Shan 2014), does not make it much different from the equally large but regional Indian content ecosystem.

As the incumbent mega-platforms are facing a dilemma in terms of maintaining and consolidating their control of the digital space, there is a parallel dilemma in terms of making content accessible online in a free or restricted way for political-ideological reasons. China clearly has the potential to build a giant content ecosystem at the national scale (Chang 2009), but its cultural and ideological homogeneity would fatally impoverish content innovation, which essentially thrives upon diversity, not homogeneity. Therefore, maintaining authoritarian control over content production could imply the impossibility of scaling up as a global cultural powerhouse, apart from the possibility of delivering content to other authoritarian governments that restrict choice according to a similar logic. And this would imply, in turn, giving up one of the most powerful, if not *the* most powerful, drivers of soft power. This is of course a problem for all authoritarian governments, and even more so for smaller countries that cannot rely upon an internal market as large as the Chinese one. For some emerging cultural powerhouses such as Turkey that are at a crossroads between authoritarianism and democracy, this choice may be especially crucial in terms of their future opportunities in the global creative arena (Cevik 2019).

On the other hand, given the emerging configuration of the new, multipolar world order in which there is an increasingly clearer contraposition between a democratic bloc and an authoritarian bloc, one cannot take for granted that democracy can be taken as the implicit benchmark of global governance systems. If the conflict further escalates, we could even witness a strong weaponization of culture as an ideological tool of persuasion and mobilization, in which political goals take over economic ones, let alone creative and expressive ones. And therefore, in spite of all the promise of future scenarios of massive, horizontal co-creation of cultural content, we could also land in a dystopian scenario in which culture is recruited by propaganda in a context of global conflict, as has happened for significant portions of the past century.

Conclusions

We are living in a very turbulent and uncertain historical moment, in which many possible future scenarios could materialize. Global pandemics, climate change, and a return of a possible cold war logic in international relations are rapidly and strongly reshaping our societies and economies, and are changing perceptions, expectations, and behaviors in many domains. Culture makes no exception, and it is possibly among the most affected. There is a possible scenario characterized by a multipolar arena of cultural powerhouses, by massively decentralized processes of cultural co-creation, by next-generation digital platforms whose business models and organizational principles are designed around the native characteristics of digital content creation processes rather than upon adaptations of pre-digital cultural industry models, and by a democratic and inclusive global governance that favors cultural dialogue and hybridization guaranteed by free cultural expression and respect of basic human rights. This is to some extent the promise behind emerging Web3 models (Voshmgir 2020), although a full understanding and assessment of these dynamics is not possible yet.

But we could also face a future scenario in which the development of new, emergent cultural powerhouses is thwarted by neocolonial forms of political and military conquest and control by a small number of superpowers, where cultural participation is organized by extractive digital platforms to favor commodification and monetization of experiences and collective action is practically impeded, and where authoritarian political models embrace an essentially anti-democratic policy of suppression of free cultural expression and appreciation of critical thinking and diversity.

There is much at stake. And, possibly now more than ever, culture might make a difference. From the viewpoint of the shifting geography of cultural production, we may expect that multipolarism may favor the emergence of a less centralized and more inclusive global cultural ecosystem (Collective Eye 2022). From the point of view of participatory, decentralized content creation, we may expect that moving beyond content creation informed by intellectual property and by the enforcement of individual authorship will favor the development of radically innovative forms of collective intelligence that could improve human capacities to address societal challenges more creatively and effectively (Jones 2016). From the viewpoint of the evolution of digital mega-platforms, we may expect that the possible emergence of nonextractive, decentralized platforms where users become more aware of the costs and social implications of profiling and digital exploitation will favor more democratic digital governance systems and more inclusive ownership (Cammaerts and Mansell 2020). And finally, from the point of view of democratic versus authoritarian forces, we may expect that a more democratic, inclusive, active, and purposeful digital participation may favor the transition toward democratic peace as the overarching governance principle of human societies (Richmond 2020).

Such engrossing, constructive perspectives are, however, far from given or simple to attain. The future is still very open and uncertain. But the fact that cultural production, in and of itself, is a very important angle from which to analyze and interpret such trends and the underlying key issues testifies to the increasing relevance that this once neglected dimension is assuming in the current policy agendas. And this is a first, important milestone in its own right.

References

Abt, Jeffrey. 2006. "The Origins of the Public Museum." In *A Companion to Museum Studies*, edited by Sharon Macdonald, 115–134. Oxford: Blackwell.

Bantinaki, Katerina. 2016. "Commissioning the (Art) Work: From Singular Authorship to Collective Creatorship." *Journal of Aesthetic Education* 50, no. 1: 16–33. https://doi.org/10.5406/jaesteduc.50.1.0016.

Barns, Sarah. 2019. "Negotiating the Platform Pivot: From Participatory Digital Ecosystems to Infrastructures of Everyday Life." *Geography Compass* 13, no. 9: e12464. https://doi.org/10.1111/gec3.12464.

Battles, Matthew. 2003. *Library: An Unquiet History*. New York: W. W. Norton.
Bauman, Shyon. 2008. *Hollywood Highbrow: From Entertainment to Art*. Princeton, NJ: Princeton University Press.
Bernal, Martin. 1994. "The Image of Ancient Greece as a Tool for Colonialism and European Hegemony." In *Social Construction of the Past: Representation as Power*, edited by George C. Bond and Angela Gilliam, 119–128. Abingdon, UK: Routledge.
Betzler, Diana, Ellen Loots, Marek Prokupek, Lénia Marques, and Petja Grafenauer. 2021. "COVID-19 and the Arts and Cultural Sectors: Investigating Countries' Contextual Factors and Early Policy Measures." *International Journal of Cultural Policy* 27, no. 6: 796–814. https://doi.org/10.1080/10286632.2020.1842383.
Bosello, Greta, and Marcel van den Haak. 2022. "#Arttothepeople? An Exploration of Instagram's Unfulfilled Potential for Democratizing Museums." *Museum Management and Curatorship*, advance online publication. https://doi.org/10.1080/09647775.2021.2023905.
Bourdieu, Pierre. 1996. *The Rules of Art: Genesis and Structure of the Literary Field*. Stanford, CA: Stanford University Press.
Bowden, Brett. 2019. "In the Name of Civilization: War, Conquest, and Colonialism." *Pléyade* 23: 73–100. http://dx.doi.org/10.4067/S0719-36962019000100073.
Bowditch, Phebe L. 2001. *Horace and the Gift Economy of Patronage*. Berkeley: University of California Press.
Bullard, Melissa M. 2002. "Heroes and Their Workshops: Medici Patronage and the Problem of Shared Agency." In *The Italian Renaissance*, edited by Paula Findlen, 299–316. Oxford: Blackwell.
Bustamante, Enrique. 2004. "Cultural Industries in the Digital Age: Some Provisional Conclusions." *Media, Culture and Society* 26, no. 6: 803–820. https://doi.org/10.1177/0163443704047027.
Cammaerts, Bart, and Robin Mansell. 2020. "Digital Platform Policy and Regulation: Toward a Radical Democratic Turn." *International Journal of Communication* 14: 11182.
Cevik, Senem B. 2019. "Turkey in Global Entertainment: From the Harem to the Battlefield." In *World Entertainment Media: Global, Regional and Local Perspectives*, edited by Paolo Sigismondi, 116–123. Abingdon, UK: Routledge.
Chang, Shaun. 2009. "Great Expectations: China's Cultural Industry and Case Study of a Government-Sponsored Creative Cluster." *Creative Industries Journal* 1, no. 3: 263–273.
Chayko, Mary. 2008. *Portable Communities: The Social Dynamics of Online and Mobile Connectedness*. Albany: SUNY Press.
Chen, Chih-Ping. 2016. "Forming Digital Self and Parasocial Relationships on YouTube." *Journal of Consumer Culture* 16, no. 1: 232–254. https://doi.org/10.1177/1469540514521081.
Collective Eye. 2022. *The Collective Eye in Conversation with ruangrupa: Thoughts on Collective Practice*. Berlin: Distanz Verlag.
Comunian, Roberta, and Lauren England. 2020. "Creative and Cultural Work Without Filters: COVID-19 and Exposed Precarity in the Creative Economy." *Cultural Trends* 29, no. 2: 112–128. https://doi.org/10.1080/09548963.2020.1770577.
de Valck, Marijke. 2016. "Fostering Art, Adding Value, Cultivating Taste: Film Festivals as Sites of Cultural Legitimization." In *Film Festivals: History, Theory, Method, Practice*, edited by Marijke de Valck, Brendan Kredell, and Skadi Loist, 100–116. Abingdon, UK: Routledge.
Elaskary, Mohamed. 2018. "The Korean Wave in the Middle East: Past and Present." *Journal of Open Innovation: Technology, Market and Complexity* 4, no. 4: 51. https://doi.org/10.3390/joitmc4040051.

Fine, Gary A. 2012. *Tiny Publics: Idiocultures and the Power of the Local*. New York: Russell Sage Foundation.

Firth, Joseph, et al. 2019. "The 'Online Brain': How the Internet May Be Changing Our Cognition." *World Psychiatry* 18, no. 2: 119–129. https://doi.org/10.1002/wps.20617.

Fischer-Lichte, Erika. 1997. *The Show and the Gaze of Theatre: A European Perspective*. Iowa City: University of Iowa Press.

Foord, Jo. 2008. "Strategies for Creative Industries: An International Review." *Creative Industries Journal* 1, no. 2: 91–113.

Fuchs, Christian. 2011. "The Contemporary World Wide Web: Social Medium or New Space of Accumulation?" In *The Political Economies of Media: The Transformation of the Global Media Industries*, edited by Dwayne Winseck and Dal Yong Jin, 201–220. London: Bloomsbury Academic.

Gaupp, Lisa. 2020. "The 'West' Versus 'the Rest'? Festival Curators as Gatekeepers for Sociocultural Diversity." In *Managing Culture: Reflecting on Exchange in Global Times*, edited by Victoria Durrer and Raphaela Henze, 127–153. Cham, Switzerland: Palgrave Macmillan. https://doi.org/10.1007/978-3-030-24646-4_6.

Gomery, Douglas. 2005. *The Hollywood Studio System: A History*. London: BFI Publishing.

Gundolf, Katherine, Annabelle Jaouen, and Johanna Gast. 2018. "Motives for Strategic Alliances in Cultural and Creative Industries." *Creativity and Innovation Management* 27, no. 2: 148–160. https://doi.org/10.1111/caim.12255.

Harley, Daniel, Alexander Verni, Mackenzie Willis, Ashley Ng, Lucas Bozzo, and Ali Mazalek. 2018. "Senory VR: Smelling, Touching and Eating Virtual Reality." In *Proceedings of the Twelfth International Conference on Tangible, Embedded, and Embodied Interaction (TEI '18)*, 386–397. New York: ACM.

Hassim, Nurzihan, Sheila Y. Jayasainan, and Nur L. Khalid. 2019. "Exploring Viewer Experiences with *Sageuk* K-Dramas from a Parasocial Relations Perspective." *SEARCH Journal of Media and Communication Research* 11, no. 1: 77–94. https://expert.taylors.edu.my/file/rems/publication/100975_6486_1.pdf.

Heihonen, Kristina, and Tore Strandvik. 2021. "Reframing Service Innovation: COVID-19 as a Catalyst for Imposed Service Innovation." *Journal of Service Management* 32, no. 1: 101–112.

Henry, Noah, Diana Kayser, and Hauke Egermann. 2021. "Music in Mood Regulation and Coping Orientation in Response to COVID-19 Lockdown Measures Within the United Kingdom." *Frontiers in Psychology* 12: 647879. http://doi.org/10.3389/fpsyg.2021.647879.

Huyssen, Andreas. 1986. *After the Great Divide: Modernism, Mass Culture, Postmodernism*. Bloomington: Indiana University Press.

Jain, Varsha, Russell W. Belk, Anupama Ambika, and Manisha Pathak-Shelat. 2021. "Narratives Selves in the Digital World: An Empirical Investigation." *Journal of Consumer Behavior* 20, no. 2: 368–380. https://doi.org/10.1002/cb.1869.

Jeannotte, M. Sharon. 2021. "When the Gigs Are Gone: Valuing Arts, Culture and Media in the COVID-19 Pandemic." *Social Sciences and Humanities Open* 3, no. 1: 100097. https://doi.org/10.1016/j.ssaho.2020.100097.

Jenkins, Barbara. 2003. "Creating Global Hegemony: Culture and the Market." In *Rethinking Global Political Economy: Emerging Issues, Unfolding Odysseys*, edited by Mary Ann Tetreault, Robert A. Denemark, Kenneth P. Thomas, and Kurt Burch, 65–85. Abingdon, UK: Routledge.

Jenkins, Henry, Mizuko Ito, and danah boyd. 2015. *Participatory Culture in a Networked Era: A Conversation on Youth, Learning, Commerce and Politics*. Cambridge: Polity Press.

Jenks, Chris. 2005. *Subculture: The Fragmentation of the Social*. London: Sage.

Jin, Dal Yong. 2007. "Reinterpretation of Cultural Imperialism: Emerging Domestic Market vs. Continuing US Dominance." *Media, Culture and Society* 29, no. 5: 753–771. https://doi.org/10.1177/0163443707080535.

Jin, Dal Yong. 2016. *New Korean Wave: Transnational Cultural Power in the Age of Social Media*. Urbana: University of Illinois Press.

Jin, Dal Yong. 2018. "An Analysis of the Korean Wave as Transnational Popular Culture: North American Youth Engage Through Social Media as TV Becomes Obsolete." *International Journal of Communication* 12: 404–422.

Jin, Dal Yong. 2021. "Cultural Production in Transnational Culture: An Analysis of Cultural Creators in the Korean Wave." *International Journal of Communication* 15: 1810–1835.

Jones, Garett. 2016. "Hive Mind: How Your Nation's IQ Matters So Much More than Your Own." Stanford, CA: Stanford University Press.

Ju, Hyejung. 2020. *Transnational Korean Television: Cultural Storytelling and Digital Audiences*. Lanham, MD: Lexington Books.

Ju, Hyejung. 2022. "K-Dramas Meet Netflix: New Models of Collaboration with the Digital West." In *The Soft Power of the Korean Wave: Parasite, BTS and Drama*, edited by Youna Kim, 171–183. Abingdon, UK: Routledge.

Kaptan, Yesim, and Murat Tutucu. 2022. "The Rise of K-Dramas in the Middle East: Cultural Proximity and Soft Power." In *The Soft Power of the Korean Wave: Parasite, BTS and Drama*, edited by Youna Kim, 196–207. Abingdon: Routledge.

Katz, Vikki S., Amy B. Jordan, and Katherine Ognyanova. 2021. "Digital Inequality, Faculty Communication, and Remote Learning Experiences During the COVID-19 Pandemic: A Survey of US Undergraduates." *PLoS ONE* 16, no. 2: e0246641. https://doi.org/10.1371/journal.pone.0246641.

Kawashima, Nobuko. 2018. "'Cool Japan' and Creative Industries: An Evaluation of Economic Policies for Popular Culture Industries in Japan." In *Asian Cultural Flows: Creative Economy*, edited by Nobuko Kawashima and Hye-Kyung Lee, 19–36. Singapore: Springer https://doi.org/10.1007/978-981-10-0147-5_2.

Khlystova, Olena, Yelena Kalyuzhnova, and Maksim Belitski. 2022. "The Impact of the COVID-19 Pandemic on the Creative Industries: A Literature Review and Future Research Agenda." *Journal of Business Research* 139: 1192–1210. https://doi.org/10.1016/j.jbusres.2021.09.062.

Kim, Ju Oak. 2021. "BTS as Method: A Counter-Hegemonic Culture in the Network Society." *Media, Culture and Society* 43, no. 6: 1061–1077. https://doi.org/10.1177/0163443720986029.

Kim, Youna, ed. 2022. *The Soft Power of the Korean Wave: Parasite, BTS and Drama*. Abingdon, UK: Routledge.

Leask, Anna, Alan Fyall, and Paul Barron. 2014. "Generation Y: An Agenda for Future Visitor Attraction Research." *International Journal of Tourism Research* 16, no. 5: 462–471 https://doi.org/10.1002/jtr.1940.

Lee, David, David Hesmondhalgh, Kate Oatley, and Melissa Nisbett. 2014. "Regional Creative Industries Policy-making Under New Labour." *Cultural Trends* 23, no. 4: 217–223. https://doi.org/10.1080/09548963.2014.912044.

Lee, Sangjoon, and Abé Mark Nornes. 2015. *Hallyu 2.0: The Korean Wave in the Age of Social Media*. Ann Arbor: University of Michigan Press.

Lewis, Ingrid, and Laura Canning. 2020. "Introduction: The Identity of European Cinema." In *European Cinema in the Twenty-First Century*, edited by Ingrid Lewis and Laura Canning, 1–11. Cham, Switzerland: Palgrave Macmillan. https://doi.org/10.1007/978-3-030-33436-9_1.

Lin, Jian, and Jeroen de Kloet. 2019. "Platformization of the Unlikely Creative Class: *Kuaishou* and Chinese Digital Cultural Production." *Social Media + Society* 5, no. 4: online. https://doi.org/10.1177/2056305119883430.

Lucchi Basili, Lorenza, and Pier Luigi Sacco. 2020. "*Jealousy Incarnate*: Quiet Ego, Competitive Desire, and the Fictional Intelligence of Long-Term Mating in a Romantic K-Drama." *Behavioral Sciences* 10, no. 9: 134. https://doi.org/10.3390/bs10090134.

Madichie, Nnamdi O., and Robert E. Hinson. 2022. *The Creative Industries and International Business Development in Africa*. Bingley, UK: Emerald.

Mäkinen, Maarit. 2006. "Digital Empowerment as a Process for Enhancing Citizens' Participation." *E-Leaning and Digital Media* 3, no. 3: 381–395. https://doi.org/10.2304/elea.2006.3.3.381.

Markusen, Ann. 2006. "Urban Development and the Politics of a Creative Class: Evidence from a Study of Artists." *Environment and Planning A: Economy and Space* 38, no. 10: 1921–1940. https://doi.org/10.1068/a38179.

Martel, Frédéric. 2011. *Mainstream. Enquête sur la guerre globale de la culture et des médias*. Paris: Flammarion.

Menell, Peter S. 2015. "Adapting Copyright for the Mashup Generation." *University of Pennsylvania Law Review* 441: 164.

Miller, Jade. 2012. "Global Nollywood: The Nigerian Movie Industry and Alternative Global Networks in Production and Distribution." *Global Media and Communication* 8, no. 2: 117–133. https://doi.org/10.1177/1742766512444340.

Mould, Oli, Tim Vorley, and Kai Liu. 2014. "Invisible Creativity? Highlighting the Hidden Impact of Freelancing in London's Creative Industries." *European Planning Studies* 22, no. 12: 1436–1255. https://doi.org/10.1080/09654313.2013.790587.

Mulcahy, Kevin V. 2003. "Entrepreneurship or Cultural Darwinism? Privatization and American Cultural Patronage." *Journal of Arts Management, Law and Society* 33, no. 3: 165–184. https://doi.org/10.1080/10632920309597344.

Muthukrishna, Michael, and Joseph Heinrich. 2016. "Innovation in the Collective Brain." *Philosophical Transactions of the Royal Society B* 371: 20150192. https://doi.org/10.1098/rstb.2015.0192.

Myllylahti, Merja. 2018. "An Attention Economy Trap? An Empirical Investigation into Four News Companies' Facebook Traffic and Social Media Revenue." *Journal of Media Business Studies* 15, no. 4: 237–253. https://doi.org/10.1080/16522354.2018.1527521.

Nolan, Mary. 2015. "Negotiating American Modernity in Twentieth-Century Europe." In *The Making of European Consumption*, edited by Per Lundin and Thomas Kaiserfeld, 17–44. London: Palgrave Macmillan. https://doi.org/10.1057/9781137374042_2.

O'Connor, Justin. 2020. "The Creative Imaginary: Cultural and Creative Industries and the Future of Modernity." In *Handbook on the Geographies of Creativity*, edited by Angeline de Dios and Lily Kong, 15–36. Cheltenham, UK: Elgar. https://doi.org/10.4337/9781785361647.00009.

OECD. 2020. "Culture Shock: COVID-19 and the Cultural and Creative Sectors." Organisation for Economic Co-operation and Development, Paris. https://www.oecd.org/coronavirus/policy-responses/culture-shock-covid-19-and-the-cultural-and-creative-sectors-08da9e0e/.

Parc, Jimmyn, and Nobuko Kawashima. 2018. "Wrestling with or Embracing Digitalization in the Music Industry: The Contrasting Business Strategies of J-Pop and K-Pop." *Kritika Kultura* 30: 23–048.

Pecqueur, Antoine. 2020. *Atlas de la culture. Du soft power au hard power: comment la culture prend le pouvoir*. Paris: Autrement.

Powell, Timothy B. 2000. *Ruthless Democracy: A Multicultural Interpretation of American Renaissance*. Princeton, NJ: Princeton University Press.

Pratt, Andy. 2009. "Policy Transfer and the Field of Cultural and Creative Industries: What Can Be Learned from Europe?" In *Creative Economies, Creative Cities*, edited by Lily Kong and Justin O'Connor, 9–23. Dordrecht: Springer. https://doi.org/10.1007/978-1-4020-9949-6_2.

Rad, Mostafa S., Alison J. Martingano, and Jeremy Ginges. 2018. "Toward a Psychology of *Homo sapiens*: Making Psychological Science More Representative of the Human Population." *Proceedings of the National Academy of Sciences* 115, no. 45: 11401–11405. https://doi.org/10.1073/pnas.1721165115.

Rahman, M. D. Mofijur, et al. 2021. "Impact of COVID-19 on the Social, Economic, Environmental and Energy Domains: Lessons Learnt from a Global Pandemic." *Sustainable Production and Consumption* 26: 343–359. https://doi.org/10.1016/j.spc.2020.10.016.

Richmond, Oliver P. 2020. "Peace in Analog/Digital International Relations." *Global Change, Peace and Security* 32, no. 3: 317–336.

Sacco, Pier Luigi, and Manlio De Domenico. 2021. "Public Health Challenges and Opportunities After COVID-19." *Bulletin of the World Health Organization* 99, no. 7: 529–535. https://dx.doi.org/10.2471/BLT.20.267757.

Sacco, Pier Luigi, Guido Ferilli, and Giorgio Tavano Blessi. 2018. "From Culture 1.0 to Culture 3.0: Three Socio-Technical Regimes of Social and Economic Value Creation Through Culture, and Their Impact on European Cohesion Policies." *Sustainability* 10, no. 11: 3923. https://doi.org/10.3390/su10113923.

Sacco, Pier Luigi, Riccardo Gallotti, Federico Pilati, Nicola Castaldo, and Manlio De Domenico. 2021. "Emergence of Knowledge Communities and Information Centralization During the COVID-19 Pandemic." *Social Science and Medicine* 285: 114215. https://doi.org/10.1016/j.socscimed.2021.114215.

Sassoon, Donald. 2006. *The Culture of the Europeans: From 1800 to the Present*. London: Harper Collins.

Schiele, Kristen, and Alladi Venkatesh. 2016. "Regaining Control Through Reclamation: How Consumption Subcultures Preserve Meaning and Group Identity After Commodification." *Consumption, Markets and Culture* 19, no. 5: 427–450. https://doi.org/10.1080/10253866.2015.1135797.

Shambaugh, David. 2015. "China's Soft Power Push: The Search for Respect." *Foreign Affairs* 94, no. 4: 99–107.

Shan, Shi-lian. 2014. "Chinese Cultural Policy and the Cultural Industries." *City, Culture and Society* 5, no. 3: 115–121. https://doi.org/10.1016/j.ccs.2014.07.004.

Shrum, Wesley M., Jr. 1996. *Fringe and Fortune: The Role of Critics in High and Popular Art*. Princeton, NJ: Princeton University Press.

Sommer, Doris, and Pier Luigi Sacco. 2019. "Optimism of the Will: Antonio Gramsci Takes in Max Weber." *Sustainability* 11, no. 3: 688. https://doi.org/10.3390/su11030688.

Sui, Daniel, and Shih-Lung Shaw. 2022. "New Human Dynamics in the Emerging Metaverse: Towards a Quantum Phygital Approach by Integrating Space and Place." *Leibniz International Proceedings in Informatics* 240: 11.1–11.13.

Sundararajan, Louise, and Maharaj K. Raina. 2015. "Revolutionary Creativity, East and West: A Critique from Indigenous Psychology." *Journal of Theoretical and Philosophical Psychology* 35, no. 1: 3–19. https://doi.org/10.1037/a0037506.

Tapia, John E. 1997. *Circuit Chautauqua: From Rural Education to Popular Entertainment in Early Twentieth Century America*. Jefferson, NC: McFarland.

Tenneriello, Susan. 2013. *Spectacle Culture and American Identity, 1815–1840*. New York: Palgrave Macmillan.

Trumpbour, John. 2002. *Selling Hollywood to the World: US and European Struggles for Mastery of the Global Film Industry, 1920–1950*. Cambridge: Cambridge University Press.

Vlassis, Antonios. 2021. "Global Online Platforms, COVID-19, and Culture: The Global Pandemic, an Accelerator Towards Which Direction?" *Media, Culture and Society* 43, no. 5: 957–969. https://doi.org/10.1177/0163443721994537.

Von Braun, Joachim, Stefano Zamagni, and Marcelo Sánchez-Sorondo. 2020. "The Moment to See the Poor." *Science* 368: 214. https://doi.org/10.1126/science.abc2255.

Voshmgir, Shermin. 2020. *Token Economy: How the Web3 Reinvents the Internet*. 2nd ed. Luxembourg: Amazon Media.

Wilson, Peter. 2000. *The Athenian Institution of the Khoregia: The Chorus, the City and the Stage*. Cambridge: Cambridge University Press.

Wingfield, Nick, Mike Isaac, and Katie Benner. 2016. "Google and Facebook Take Aim at Fake News Sites." *New York Times*, November 14, 2016. https://www.nytimes.com/2016/11/15/technology/google-will-ban-websites-that-host-fake-news-from-using-its-ad-service.html.

Zarobell, John. 2022. "Global Art Collectives and Exhibition Making." *Arts* 11, no. 2: 38. https://doi.org/10.3390/arts11020038.

CHAPTER 39

ALIGNING ARTS RESEARCH WITH PRACTITIONER NEEDS

Beyond Generalizations

SUNIL IYENGAR

Overview

AMONG policymakers and philanthropic funders in the United States, it is a commonplace that COVID-19 heightened public awareness about social, racial, and economic disparities that existed long before the pandemic. "Disparities," in this context, signifies differential access to health and educational services, as well as diverse outcomes for population subgroups. In the United States, growing recognition of these factors coincided with a nation's public reckoning over traumas from racially or ethnically motivated violence and related injustices.

For many arts organizations and their funders, there has been a parallel process of awakening. At different stages during the pandemic, and with varying levels of intensity, the field has rallied to three imperatives: (1) reengaging artists, audiences, and learners through a combination of in-person and digital experiences, (2) embracing practices that more fully reflect the values of diversity, equity, inclusion, and accessibility (DEIA), and (3) reorienting the arts as an opportunity for community healing and transformation.

These themes are not mutually exclusive, and not all arts managers will view them in the same terms or give them equal weight. As this chapter will show, however, each theme has roots in arts management research and cultural policy discourses going back at least a decade. By the same token, each theme not only suggests new research topics for arts management and cultural policy but also shifts the burden of any prospective research agenda from studies gathering empirical insights about *why* the arts matter—findings that can be used for case-making and advocacy purposes—to studies that can guide evidence-based practice for greater societal impacts.

This subtle shift of emphasis is displayed in the National Endowment for the Arts (NEA) research agenda for 2022–2026. A relatively small agency of the US government, the NEA nonetheless remains the nation's flagship entity for supporting arts and cultural research. To that extent, the agency's five-year research agenda can be seen as broadly representative of US cultural researchers' current patterns of engagement with the themes given above. As the NEA's research agenda suggests, the study topics that correspond with these themes increasingly will require more qualitative approaches, including community participatory research methods (NEA 2021b). Along with such studies, steady curation of key statistical indicators in the arts—again, supported by NEA research—will help US arts managers better anticipate and address trends affecting their sector.

Before tracing the development of the three themes listed above, and showing how they track with needs of the sector and with ongoing programs at the NEA, it will be helpful in each case to review a brief history of relevant research investments by the United States' premier arts agency.

Reengaging Artists, Audiences, and Learners

The NEA launched a research function in 1975, a decade after the agency's own establishment. Initial research reports included descriptive statistics about US artists, arts institutions, and arts participation.

Early in its career, the entity that would come to be known as the NEA's Office of Research and Analysis initiated the mining of US Census Bureau datasets for many of these analyses—a pattern that persists today. A landmark research initiative for the office has been the cultivation of a data partnership with the Census Bureau, resulting in a periodic, nationally representative survey of arts participation. Since 1982, the NEA has conducted seven waves of the Survey of Public Participation in the Arts (SPPA) as supplements to questionnaires fielded by the Census Bureau.

More recently, the NEA has introduced a short-form version of the SPPA, the Arts Basic Survey (ABS). The ABS, too, is conducted in partnership with the Census Bureau. Complementing these data collections is a NEA-designed module of the General Social Survey (GSS), administered by NORC at the University of Chicago. Past survey questions on this module have focused on motivations and barriers affecting public participation in the arts. Throughout the evolution of these instruments, there has been a tension between the desire to preserve question items so that responses can be compared across survey years and the need to accommodate new items that account for demographic, cultural, and technological shifts affecting arts participation.

In June 2014, the NEA and the United Kingdom's Arts and Humanities Research Council hosted a joint research symposium at the Gallup headquarters in Washington,

DC. At the event, researchers, policymakers, and arts practitioners interrogated the strengths and weaknesses of common methods, cultural data sources, and variables used to report statistics about who participates in the arts, how so, and how often (NEA 2014). Roughly a year later, NORC and the James Irvine Foundation issued "The Cultural Lives of Californians," a report that challenged a conventional narrative of declining participation in the arts, as measured by attendance at art museums or performing arts events.

The NORC/Irvine survey used a "larger aperture" than afforded by the NEA's own surveys. The California survey began, for instance, with "an open-ended question about respondents' own description of their creative, cultural, and artistic activities." Also, in inquiring about participation habits, the survey placed less emphasis on specific arts genres than did past versions of the SPPA, and it offered examples from a range of cultural activities in an effort to elicit more "inclusive" responses (Novak Leonard et al. 2015, 8, 11).

The Gallup event and the NORC/Irvine report reinforced the NEA's commitment to ensuring that its own surveys about arts participation capture the full array of arts and cultural experiences in the United States. This commitment took the form of substantial revisions to the 2012 and 2017 SPPA instruments. Since the 2012 SPPA report, moreover, the NEA has used a different slate of metrics for reporting on arts participation.

These metrics consider the total universe of participants not only in terms of arts attendance but also by their reported levels of engagement with art making, arts learning, and digital consumption of the arts. In previous decades, for example, the national discourse around arts participation—with reference to the NEA statistics—focused on declining attendance rates for various art forms. The NEA's 2008 SPPA report noted that 35 percent of adults had visited an art museum or gallery or attended one of six types of "benchmark" arts activities in the preceding year (NEA 2009). This share of adults contrasted with the 39 percent who had attended such activities four years earlier.

By contrast, the 2017 SPPA report found that 54 percent of the US adult population had attended any number of "artistic, creative, or cultural activities," not limited to the previous benchmark items (NEA 2019). Also reported were the 74 percent who used media to consume artistic or arts-related content; the 57 percent who read novels or short stories, poetry, plays, or books in general; the 54 percent who created or performed art; the 17 percent who learned an art form informally; and the 9.5 percent who took formal classes or lessons in the arts.

For a national public funder of the arts, the single most important reason for tracking arts participation trends is to understand how best to enable people from all demographic, geographic, and socioeconomic backgrounds to take part in these life-affirming experiences. In particular, the SPPA data can and does reveal large subgroups for whom arts participation—even when broader measures are applied—does not register as highly as it does with other, often more socioeconomically privileged subgroups. These equity-related considerations will resurface in the next section of this chapter.

For now, let us assume access to a far more dynamic and capacious framework than is often used in representing arts participation as a human activity. When, in early 2020, the sector ground to a halt because of the COVID-19 pandemic, managers were pressed to reach into their communities and identify other ways of engaging them with arts offerings. The most common of these strategies has been virtual engagement—whether with live or archived content—but the general effect of this disruption to arts administration was to accelerate learning about audience development models "beyond attendance."

The phrase comes from the title of a NEA research report dating nearly ten years prior to the pandemic. The report, subtitled "A Multi-Modal Understanding of Arts Participation," examined how different routes of arts participation—for example, attendance, creation and performance, and digital media consumption—correspond with one another, and it urged arts organizations to address this plurality in their own programming (NEA 2011).

Other pre-pandemic reports from the NEA also had compared audiences for visual and performing arts events with those consuming the arts through digital media and with participants in "informal" arts activities. More than a decade ago, the NEA published a two-volume study of outdoor arts festivals, noting that young adults, in particular, "crave a new level of interactivity, they value personal creation and performance as part of the overall arts experience, and they appear to prefer those activities in informal settings" (NEA 2010, 7).

Now, in the wake of the pandemic, it is worth asking whether such demands and opportunities still motivate arts participation in the United States. Two NEA research reports in 2020 anticipated this question for arts managers in a post-COVID-19 environment. Although each report relied on 2016–2017 survey data, the findings still can guide organizations seeking to reengage with in-person and virtual audiences or learners.

One report noted that the desire to socialize with family and friends remained a top driver for adults' participation in most types of arts activities (NEA 2020b). For Generation Z adults (those born after 1997), "an inability to find someone to go with" was the most commonly reported barrier to arts attendance. Members of racial or ethnic minority groups, meanwhile, were significantly more likely than most whites to identify "celebrating their cultural heritage" as a reason for arts participation (NEA 2020b).

The other research report, titled "Paths to Participation: Understanding How Art Forms and Activities Intersect" (NEA 2020a), highlighted correlations among various modes of arts participation. It found that adults who used media to consume visual art or music, dance, or theater performances were at least five times as likely as other adults to attend in-person arts events. (In arriving at this ratio, the researchers accounted for differences in the race, ethnicity, gender, age, and educational background of participants.)

Researchers also learned that adults who did theater activities (e.g., attended theater live or virtually, or did acting) were four times as likely as other adults to participate in visual art activities (e.g., attending an exhibit or creating artwork). Further, adults who participated in literary arts activities (e.g., read or listened to books or literature or went to book clubs) were two to three times as likely as other adults to do one of the following activities: attend an arts event, create or perform art, take arts-related classes or lessons, or use media to consume art.

The mutually reinforcing relationships of these different forms of arts participation can give hope to organizations seeking to rebuild audiences after the pandemic. But the data also tells arts managers that values such as socialization and pride in one's cultural heritage are, and likely will remain, integral to different demographic subgroups, depending on the art form or activity type.

Beyond awaiting results from periodic surveys such as the SPPA, the ABS, and the GSS, managers can benefit from hypothesis-driven studies about processes and practices that improve the quality of arts organizations' engagement with audiences and learners. The NEA's research agenda for 2022–2026 will incentivize such studies, along with the development of evidence-based guides and tools, not only for arts audience engagement but also for the purpose of better understanding the rapidly evolving "arts ecology" in the United States—as represented also by artists, arts and cultural workers, arts organizations, and venues (NEA 2021b, 10).

In the NEA's new research agenda, the precise wording for this topic area is:

> How is the U.S. arts ecosystem (e.g., arts organizations and venues, artists and arts workers, and participants and learners) **adapting and responding** to social, economic, and technological changes and challenges to the sector, including trends accelerated by the COVID-19 pandemic? What are promising practices and/or replicable strategies for responding to such forces, for different segments of the arts ecosystem?
>
> (NEA 2021b, 1)

Regarding research topics specific to artists, arts audiences, arts learners, and arts organizations, the document lists sample questions for each category. The agency's primary engine for driving this work will be two research funding programs: Research Grants in the Arts and NEA Research Labs. Concurrently, the NEA will establish a National Arts Statistics and Evidence Reporting Center (NASERC) to complement its National Archive of Data on Arts and Culture (NADAC).

NASERC will work with a diverse pool of arts practitioners, funders, and policymakers to identify key indicators that can be created through national statistics, including some of the data sources already mentioned. The indicators will guide a periodic schedule of reporting so that the sector can anticipate the release of these data points and more clearly perceive their relevance to questions and challenges it is facing. Alongside these indicators will be a series of evidence-based reports (including field scans) on topics deemed useful to the broader arts field.

The need for a user-friendly statistical framework for the routine measurement of variables pertaining to the US arts ecology was revealed in the first few months after COVID-19 struck the United States. In that tumultuous period, analysts, arts funders, and journalists struggled to obtain real-time facts and figures about how the sector was being affected.

Surveys or analyses by organizations such as LaPlaca Cohen and Slover Linett (2020), WolfBrown (2020), SMU DataArts and TRG Arts (SMU/TRG 2020), and Americans for the Arts (n.d.) all contributed snapshots of this impact. The NEA also fielded surveys of national arts service organizations and conducted interviews with arts leaders and researchers-consultants to learn about trends in reopening (NEA 2021a). In addition, the agency supported a "COVID-19 sector benchmark dashboard" that TRG Arts developed as a tool for performing arts managers (SMU/TRG n.d.). The scramble for data suggested that a statistical clearinghouse for arts practitioners—if not quite a rapid surveillance reporting center—would be a welcome new resource.

Ultimately, the NEA collaborated with the Federal Emergency Management Agency (FEMA) and Argonne National Laboratory to produce a white paper about the impacts of COVID-19 on the arts sector (Guibert and Hyde 2021). In blogs and presentations, NEA researchers also reported data from the US Census Bureau's Small Business Pulse Survey and the Current Population Survey, and from the Bureau of Economic Analysis, to describe factors such as artist unemployment rates, revenue losses to arts businesses, and consumer spending on the arts (Iyengar 2020). Ideally, NASERC will help arts managers better to understand how such different data sources relate to each other, and which statistics will be useful under which circumstances.

Statistics about artists and their conditions have not been discussed in this chapter—but ongoing curation of these data, too, will be critical to NASERC. Curation of US data about "arts learners," however, is complicated by a variety of state educational systems, policies, and data reporting requirements.

In 2020, in partnership with the Education Commission of the States, the NEA unveiled the State Data Infrastructure Project for Arts Education: a suite of resources to help organizations request, extract, and report state data about arts education access and enrollment levels in public elementary, middle, and high schools (ECS n.d.). Thus, in scenarios when it is not feasible routinely to report arts data at the national level, it remains possible for the NEA to develop guidance and tool kits for communities, arts practitioners, and local policymakers to help themselves.

Embracing Practices That More Fully Reflect the Values of DEIA

In 2011, the National Committee for Responsive Philanthropy published the report "Fusing Arts, Culture and Social Change: High Impact Strategies for Philanthropy." Authored by Holly Sidford, the president of Helicon Collaborative, the critique prompted greater reflection among funders about the degree to which arts grantmaking practices account for "the country's [United States] evolving cultural landscape and . . . changing demographics" (Sidford 2011, 1). Subsequent research reports and articles have improved the state of evidence on this topic, not only for arts funders but also for arts managers and cultural policymakers.

At the NEA, a comprehensive approach for promoting equity, and DEIA practices in general, has been directed by the highest levels of government. As one of his first presidential actions, Joe Biden announced the executive order "Advancing Racial Equity and Support for Underserved Communities Throughout the Federal Government" (White House 2021).

For the NEA, the call has spurred reexamination of the agency's administrative data fields and forms for collecting information from prospective grant applicants and from grantees. This assessment is still under way, but it will be guided and strengthened by the NEA's new strategic plan, which carries a "cross-cutting objective": "The NEA will model diversity, equity, inclusion, and accessibility in the arts through all of its activities and operations" (NEA 2022c, 3). Accordingly, the agency has designed metrics for monitoring its performance on this objective.

Changes to these administrative data fields and forms may permit better tracking of the racial/ethnic characteristics of those benefiting from NEA grants, even as such data will improve the agency's capacity to reach organizations working with historically underserved groups. Yet one already can make a few generalizations about racial/ethnic equity and the arts in the United States, based on nationally representative data on arts participation and the arts and cultural workforce. Here are some relevant findings:

- Based on the NEA's Survey of Public Participation in the Arts, African American, Hispanic, and Asian adults repeatedly show lower rates of arts attendance compared with non-Hispanic whites. Yet differences in venue type (e.g., formal versus informal) and art form or genre (e.g., culturally specific forms of arts participation, such as Latin/Spanish/salsa music events) can narrow these differences considerably (NEA 2019).
- The 2017 SPPA data revealed that African Americans and Hispanics were less likely than whites to report the availability of arts and cultural activities in their neighborhoods, opportunities to take part, and access to information about those opportunities (NEA 2019).
- As a whole, artists in the United States are less diverse than the workforce in general. For the period covering 2015–2019, American Community Survey data show that 38 percent of US workers were nonwhite or Hispanic, while among artists the share was just under 27 percent. However, the finding does not apply evenly to artist occupations. For example, 44 percent of dancers and choreographers and 36 percent of announcers were nonwhite or Hispanic (NEA 2022a).

All these observations stem from self-reported data, but they are consistent with larger structural inequities that have shown up elsewhere in the social impact sector. As with education and public health, for example, it is necessary to understand the distinctive needs of communities that are targeted through public policy and grant opportunities in the arts, so that funders can avoid making unwarranted assumptions about which programs and interventions to support.

One recent attempt by the NEA to arrive at a better understanding of culturally specific needs is demonstrated by a partnership with the Native Arts and Cultures Foundation. In 2021, the organizations published "Native Arts and Culture: Resilience, Reclamation, and Relevance," a report summarizing proceedings from a historic gathering at the NEA. Participants included members from more than forty tribal nations, Native artists and students, government agency representatives, nonprofit professionals, and funders (Native Arts and Cultures Foundation 2021).

Subsequently, in May 2021, the NEA joined the Association of Tribal Archives, Libraries, and Museums to host a Native Artists Summit, titled "Sustaining and Advancing Indigenous Cultures." Most recently, the NEA has announced a tribal consultation policy (NEA 2021c), responding to President Biden's "Memorandum on Tribal Consultation and Strengthening Nation-to-Nations Relationships."

Apart from using surveys and administrative data—and the power of convening—to identify and address inequities in the US arts ecosystem, the NEA has begun to contribute to a body of evidence about (1) how the arts themselves can be used to address racial/ethnic biases in the public sphere and (2) positive outcomes resulting from successful integration of race/ethnicity-specific factors in art making or arts education.

Following are examples of NEA-funded grant projects that have supported this research.

- At George Mason University in Fairfax, Virginia, researchers are examining the longitudinal effects of marching band participation on university students from different racial/ethnic backgrounds. The study will assess student outcomes across three types of institutions: an institution representing historically black colleges and universities (HBCUs), a university with a racially/ethnically diverse student body, and a university with mostly white students. Outcomes to be measured include self-efficacy, stress, "belongingness," and attitudes about diversity. Researchers also will use social network analyses to track development of cross-race friendships arising from marching band participation.
- The ability of school-based dance/movement therapy to foster empathy and prevent school violence and ethnic bullying is the focus of a study at Drexel University in Philadelphia, Pennsylvania. Analyses will include measures of group synchrony, empathy, quality of peer relationships, and frequency of verbal and/or physical aggression from middle school students with diverse racial and ethnic backgrounds, tracked before, during, and after intervention.
- Researchers at Governors State University in University Park, Illinois, are conducting a mixed-methods study of the importance of arts participation in cultivating a sense of belonging and positive academic outcomes among university students of color. Students will be recruited from two public universities, the first composed primarily of African American students and the second a Hispanic-serving institution.
- In another mixed-methods study, Boston Chinatown Neighborhood Center will explore how collaborative art making by artists and local residents can improve community social cohesion. The study will investigate the Pao Arts Center's

Residence Lab (in Boston, Massachusetts), a program uniting Asian and Pacific Islander artists with Boston Chinatown residents so they can use storytelling and the co-creation of artwork to shape the future of Chinatown and expand its cultural footprint. Researchers will rely mainly on ethnographic and qualitative research methods.
- At the University of Texas at El Paso, a qualitative research study is examining how community arts programs align with the cultural learning practices of Latinx youth. The study will determine how the motivations, aspirations, and cultural backgrounds of children, family, and educators can interact to produce a responsive learning environment for Latinx students in these community arts programs. Regarding the Latinx arts field in general, the National Association of Latino Arts and Culture (NALAC), with a research grant from the NEA, is analyzing the size and scope of charitable support for Latinx arts and culture in specific geographic regions.
- Based on a series of experimental studies, researchers at Los Angeles, California-based Occidental College find that in a museum and lab setting, cultural biases about American Indians were "stubbornly resistant to change and, in some cases, appeared more frequently for participants encouraged to adopt others' perspectives" (Sherman, Cupo, and Mithlo 2020). The studies, which analyzed perceptual, cognitive, emotional, and physiological responses to American Indian photographs from the 1860s to the 1930s, led the researchers to conclude in a working paper that "interventions in cultural intolerance—both standard educational approaches in the museum . . . as well as psychological approaches—cannot be uniformly applied, but must be unique to each cultural group impacted." The researchers have since published their findings.

Within the US arts sector, the push to achieve equitable outcomes for different racial/ethnic subgroups will require not exclusively academic research approaches but also community-based participatory research practices. The individual voices and the collective agency of community members who participate in such studies must be honored and respected if these studies are to yield meaningful insights for arts practitioners and policymakers.

Shared definitions, goals, and outcome measures are fundamental to the process. At the same time, more research resources are necessary for a greater understanding of how effective interventions can be scaled and replicated in communities of different types. Again, the NEA's Research Grants in the Arts and its Research Labs program will be the primary vehicles for supporting such studies. The agency's 2022–2026 research agenda includes the following topic area:

> What is the state of **diversity, equity, inclusion, and accessibility in the arts**? What progress has been made in achieving these outcomes for arts administration, employment, learning, and participation? What are some promising practices and/or replicable strategies in these domains, and what are appropriate markers of success?
>
> (NEA 2021b, 1)

In describing the research topic, the agenda lists a series of sample questions for potential grant applicants. Those questions are:

- How have arts organizations diagnosed and addressed inequities in their practices and policies, and how can progress toward becoming a fully equitable organization be measured?
- How do decision-making processes change when an arts organization commits to an equity framework?
- What is the relationship between commitment to an equity agenda and the financial stability of an arts organization?
- What are the costs and opportunities associated with adopting, or failing to adopt, strategies in support of diversity, equity, inclusion, and accessibility in the arts?
- How have artists and arts organizations created greater public awareness about inequities within the communities they serve?
- To what extent, and under what conditions, have technological innovations improved access to the arts across diverse communities? (NEA 2021b, 6)

Much of the foregoing section has emphasized racial and ethnic dimensions of DEIA. Nevertheless, as demonstrated by the agency's research agenda questions, the pursuit of equity—through research and practice—extends to a range of demographic, geographic, and socioeconomic parameters. In April 2022, the NEA published an equity action plan in response to the President's executive order on addressing racial equity and supporting underserved communities (NEA 2022b). The plan describes the NEA's own efforts to improve data collection and reporting that will advance these goals.

Reorienting the Arts as an Opportunity for Community Healing and Transformation

For several years, the NEA has encouraged and funded experimental and quasi-experimental studies that aim to establish causal relationships between the arts and positive outcomes in health and education. Arts interventions that seek to improve individual health and well-being may be considered as falling into two types: creative arts therapies (delivered by certified therapists in art, music, dance, or drama, for example) or arts-in-health programs, in which the arts consumption or art making is not guided by a certified therapist.

Through the Creative Forces: NEA Military Healing Arts Network, the agency works with the US Departments of Defense and Veterans Affairs to place creative arts therapists at the core of patient-centered care at clinical sites throughout the country, including telehealth services. The initiative also increases access to community arts activities to promote health, well-being, and quality of life for military and veteran populations exposed to trauma, as well as for their families and caregivers. The Creative Forces clinical research team published twenty-three studies in peer-reviewed journals between 2016 and October 2021. Other studies are in progress, including four feasibility studies that will lay the groundwork for randomized controlled trials on the efficacy of creative arts therapy interventions for military and/or veteran populations (NEA n.d.).

In addition to clinical research associated with the Creative Forces initiative, the agency supports experimental and quasi-experimental studies about the arts and health through research grants and the NEA Research Labs program. Here the focus is not limited to creative arts therapies but includes the study of arts interventions or variables that contribute to social or emotional well-being or to physical health outcomes. Many NEA research-grant-funded projects have supported such studies over the last several years, as have NEA Research Labs around the country.

Beginning in 2019, moreover, the NEA has joined the National Institutes of Health (NIH) in supporting biomedical and behavioral research grants investigating the relationship of music to health and wellness (NIH 2019). This partnership stems from an initiative called Sound Health, a partnership between the John F. Kennedy Center for the Performing Arts and NIH, in association with the NEA. In early 2021, the NEA and the University of California, San Francisco, opened the Sound Health Network, an online hub that includes a clearinghouse of research articles, a directory, a webinar series, and other resources to strengthen research and practice collaborations in music, health, and healing.

So far, all the research projects referenced in this section have focused on understanding the arts' health benefits for individuals. Yet COVID-19 exposed the importance of community-led strategies to improve public health conditions. Even before the pandemic, the organization Art Place America and the University of Florida's Center for Arts in Medicine had produced a white paper, "Creating Healthy Communities: Arts + Public Health in America," designed to help advance this cross-sectoral collaboration (Sonke et al. 2019).

Similarly, the NEA and the Robert Wood Johnson Foundation, along with several other funders, supported the development of a research report to encourage place-based arts strategies that can foster social cohesion as a conduit to greater public health equity. The report, titled "WE-Making: How Arts and Culture Unite People to Work Toward Community Well-Being," is accompanied by a conceptual framework, a theory of change, case studies, a literature review, and recommendations for future research and practice (PolicyLink, n.d.).

All of these projects began well before COVID-19, and yet during the pandemic they yielded immediate tools for funders and policymakers seeking to embed the arts in public health interventions. In the wake of these activities, the Centers for Disease Control and Prevention (CDC) issued evidence-based guidelines to help professionals in public health and health communications partner successfully on vaccine campaigns with local artists, culture-bearers, and arts organizations.

Then, in August 2021, NEA and CDC officials participated in a public webinar titled "Trusted Messengers and Trusted Spaces: Engaging Arts and Culture for COVID-19 Vaccine Confidence in Your Community" (Center for Arts in Medicine 2021). During this event, the CDC Foundation announced a funding opportunity to support community efforts using the arts to build vaccine confidence. Then, in October 2021, the NEA signed a memorandum of understanding with the CDC and the CDC Foundation to design and implement a grant program, which resulted ultimately in awards to thirty arts and cultural organizations nationwide (CDC Foundation 2022).

The University of Florida's Center for Arts in Medicine had been involved in early efforts with the CDC and the CDC Foundation to promote public awareness of the arts' potential in boosting vaccine confidence. The center also runs EpiArts Lab, a NEA Research Lab co-funded by Bloomberg Philanthropies to mine longitudinal datasets for a better understanding of the relationships between the arts and healthy outcomes in the general public. Another recent example of the NEA's investment in research on the arts and public health is production of a report about arts strategies for addressing the opioid crisis (NEA 2020c).

By and large, however, the NEA's portfolio of research awards and publications focused on health benefits from the arts has looked at individual-level rather than community-level outcomes. Regarding NEA research grant awards, this tendency may be partly a function of the program's application guidelines, which over the years have prioritized experimental and quasi-experimental study designs; these are often more conducive to clinical, classroom, or psychology lab settings than population cohorts within a community.

Creative placemaking, as exemplified by the NEA's Our Town initiative, offers another avenue for arts managers to take in engaging with public health practitioners. Our Town grant projects integrate arts, culture, and design activities into efforts that strengthen communities by advancing local, economic, physical, and/or social outcomes. Through a program evaluation that led to the development of a theory of change and logic model for the initiative, the NEA identified sustainable "systems changes" as distal outcomes of the program.

Within this framework, longer-term public health goals certainly are viable for an Our Town grant applicant. (A 2019 article co-authored by CDC and NEA staff described the role of such projects in "creating healthy communities" [Cornett et al. 2019].) But these outcomes may be coextensive with other physical, economic, or social changes at the community level. Indeed, as part of the NEA's new strategic plan, the agency seeks not only to fuse the arts with public health practice but, more broadly, to "embed the arts in system-wide initiatives that strengthen or heal communities" (NEA 2022c, 2).

Accordingly, the NEA's 2022–2026 research agenda includes the following priority research area:

In what ways do the arts contribute to the healing and revitalization of communities? What factors mediate these contributions, and for the benefit of which populations?

What are common elements of such programs or practices, and what are appropriate measures of success?

Again, the agency's Research Grants in the Arts and NEA Research Labs programs will be used to incentivize studies in this topic area. Sample research questions in this area include:

- How can the arts and artists help to heal social or ideological divides within a community, and to improve relations among different subgroups?
- How can the arts and artists improve attachment to communities, social capital, civic engagement, and other drivers of social cohesion?
- How do the arts and artists mobilize communities for collective action—e.g., to address inequities or to support trauma recovery, emergency preparedness, or public health response efforts?
- How can the arts and artists contribute to trust in public institutions or in the democratic process?
- How do the arts and artists contribute to the development of leadership skills in youth and the emergence of new community leaders?
- How have artists contributed successfully to community healing and transformation, and what are common characteristics of those who have done so? (NEA 2021b, 6)

Many of these questions, as with the ones listed under the DEIA research topic area, do not lend themselves neatly to experimental or quasi-experimental study designs. This is because the interrogative word is often, if not always, "how." Rather than seek to measure the strength or direction of the relationship of the arts to positive individual or societal outcomes, the foregoing research questions are largely about mechanisms of action. Here is an elevated role for qualitative research in hypothesis building, for community engagement in the research process, and for the production of evidence-based guides that can help accomplish the outcomes of interest. These research investments should yield knowledge that arts practitioners can use in designing, refining, and evaluating their programs or activities.

Before leaving this section, it should be understood that all three central topics guiding the NEA's research agenda are conducive not only to the formulation of novel questions and approaches but also to the production of insights that arts managers and cultural policymakers can bring to their future work.

In drafting this research agenda, the NEA deliberately heeded voices representing different sets of practices, theoretical perspectives, and lived experiences either within the arts sector or adjacent to it. Most of these inputs concerned the US arts and cultural ecosystem. Although academic literature was consulted on occasion, the agenda was created primarily by engaging with its prospective users and beneficiaries—a constituency that transcends the individual disciplines or conceptual models that occupy arts and cultural research as a field.

To foster this engagement, the NEA commissioned a planning study. This included a portfolio review of the NEA research awards programs, a scan of arts-related research projects supported by other US federal agencies, and focus group meetings and interviews with experts nationwide.

The title of the resulting report, "Yes, 'Art Works'—Now What?," signals a shift in emphasis that had been urged by many focus group participants. They had articulated the need for an agenda that, in the report's words, would go "beyond supporting research that is used primarily in 'case-making' about the arts' value as a public good." Rather, according to the report, the NEA should favor "more research that will help decision-makers and arts practitioners understand various dynamics at work within communities, arts organizations, artists' careers, and specific arts disciplines and fields" (NEA 2022d, 12).

Addressing findings from the planning study, a draft research agenda was posted to the NEA website for public comment. It also was distributed widely to arts and cultural researchers and practitioners. The final agenda avoids prescriptive overtones. Instead, it allows multiple points of entry for prospective researchers, arts practitioners, and NEA partners seeking to respond to sector-wide challenges through knowledge production.

As a menu, the agenda offers just enough specificity (through sample research questions) to elicit concrete proposals from future applicants to the NEA's research awards program, but it also provides a sufficiently flexible basis for welcoming the unexpected. This approach contrasts to the one used by the NEA's prior research agenda, which had itemized questions, study designs, and products and publications that the agency would pursue over a five-year period.

Ultimately, the new agenda serves multiple purposes. To NEA research grant applicants, it broadcasts priorities that may be used in designing studies and research programs around arts and cultural management and policy. But even for other entities—arts organizations, funders, and educators, in the United States or abroad—the agenda charts a path forward for shared discourse about evidentiary needs for today's arts and cultural practitioners as a collective enterprise. The agenda makes explicit some of the most pressing societal issues facing the sector today, and converts them into research topics and questions of interest not just to the NEA but arguably to arts and cultural practitioners in the United States and abroad. Post-pandemic engagement with artists, students, and art-goers through in-person or virtual opportunities; the arts' integration with community healing and trauma recovery strategies; and the monitoring of DEIA concerns as they affect arts practice—all of these themes currently motivate policymakers and funders in contemplating or effecting programmatic reforms. At the same time, the community-based participatory approaches that are encouraged by the NEA's research agenda are consonant with contemporary efforts among researchers—of all disciplinary backgrounds—to include more diverse voices and perspectives in policy-relevant studies.

A Postscript: To Enhance and Not Abandon Studies of Value and Impact

Apart from incentivizing research in the three topic areas outlined above, the NEA will continue to support research about the value and impact of the arts, especially in relationship to three key domains: health and well-being, cognition and learning, and economic growth and innovation.

Among specific sample questions for each domain, however, the NEA's research agenda encourages grant applicants to propose studies that ask "for whom" and "under which circumstances" any positive impacts are to be realized. By renewing support of experimental and quasi-experimental studies about the arts' effects on individuals and society, the agency will extend the line of progress achieved by NEA grant-funded researchers who, over the last decade, have investigated causal claims about the arts. Yet those studies will be complemented by many more research projects that seek to understand how optimal outcomes may be achieved, with the goal of replicating and expanding those benefits for more people and communities.

This realignment of the NEA research agenda is based on the realization that generalized statements about "value and impact"—even if supportable by causal inferences about the arts—will ring hollow unless clear conditions and pathways are adumbrated for arts practitioners pursuing those outcomes. Randomized, controlled studies still serve an indispensable function in the arts and cultural research arena. It is just that—in the United States and elsewhere—arts research administrators must balance these efforts with the recruitment of policymakers, practitioners, and prospective beneficiaries who can take part in qualitative, collaborative research aiming to describe, in richly layered detail, the mechanisms of action governing effective program design and delivery. For its part, the NEA's research grant program will encourage a blend of quantitative and qualitative methodologies while cultivating tool kits and evidence-based guides that can help arts managers and others in using data and metrics to improve services for artists, audiences, and learners, to heal communities through the arts, and to ensure equitable access to arts opportunities and their attendant benefits.

References

Americans for the Arts. n.d. "The Economic Impact of Coronavirus on the Arts and Culture Sector." Americans for the Arts, Washington, DC. https://www.americansforthearts.org/by-topic/disaster-preparedness/the-economic-impact-of-coronavirus-on-the-arts-and-culture-sector.

CDC Foundation. 2022. "CDC Foundation Supports Arts and Cultural Organizations to Build Confidence in COVID-19 and Seasonal Influenza Vaccines." CDC Foundation, Atlanta, GA. https://www.cdcfoundation.org/pr/2022/arts-and-cultural-organizations-build-vaccine-confidence.

Center for Arts in Medicine. 2021. "Trusted Messengers and Trusted Spaces: Engaging Arts and Culture for Vaccine Confidence in Your Community." Center for Arts in Medicine, University of Florida, August 24. https://www.vaccinate.arts.ufl.edu/.

Cornett, Kelly, Bray-Simons, Katherine, Devlin, Heather M., Iyengar, Sunil, Shaffer, Patricia Moore, and Fulton, Janet E. 2019. "Creating Activity-Friendly Communities: Exploring the Intersection of Public Health and the Arts." *Journal of Physical Activity and Health*, Human Kinetics Journals, Champaign, IL., USA, Vol. 16, Issue 11, 937-939. https://journals.humankinetics.com/view/journals/jpah/16/11/article-p937.xml.

ECS. n.d. "State Data Infrastructure Project for Arts Education." Education Commission of the States, Denver, CO. https://www.ecs.org/initiatives-projects/state-data-infrastructure-project-for-arts-education/.

Guibert, Greg, and Iain Hyde. 2021. "Analysis: COVID-19's Impact on Arts and Culture." Argonne National Laboratory, Washington, DC. https://www.arts.gov/sites/default/files/COVID-Outlook-Week-of-1.4.2021.pdf.

Iyengar, Sunil. 2020. "Taking Note: COVID-19 Arts Watch—Federal Data Update." National Endowment for the Arts, Washington, DC. https://www.arts.gov/stories/blog/2020/taking-note-covid-19-arts-watch-federal-data-update.

LaPlaca Cohen and Slover Linett. 2020. "Culture + Community in a Time of Crisis: A Special Edition of Culture Track: Key Findings from Wave 1." LaPlaca Cohen and Slover Linett Audience Research, New York. https://s28475.pcdn.co/wp-content/uploads/2020/09/CCTC-Key-Findings-from-Wave-1_9.29.pdf.

Native Arts and Cultures Foundation. 2021. "Native Arts and Culture: Resilience, Reclamation, and Relevance." Native Arts and Cultures Foundation, in partnership with the National Endowment for the Arts and the National Endowment for the Humanities. https://www.nativeartsandcultures.org/wp-content/uploads/2021/02/Native-Arts-Culture-Conference-Full-Report_FINAL.pdf.

NEA. 2009. "2008 Survey of Public Participation in the Arts." National Endowment for the Arts, Washington, DC. https://www.arts.gov/sites/default/files/2008-SPPA.pdf.

NEA. 2010. *Live from Your Neighborhood: A National Study of Outdoor Arts Festivals: Volume One, Summary Report*. Research Report #51. Washington, DC: National Endowment for the Arts. https://www.arts.gov/sites/default/files/Festivals-Report.pdf.

NEA. 2011. "Beyond Attendance: A Multi-Modal Understanding of Arts Participation." National Endowment for the Arts, Washington, DC. https://www.arts.gov/sites/default/files/2008-SPPA-BeyondAttendance.pdf.

NEA. 2014. *Measuring Cultural Engagement: A Quest for New Terms, Tools, and Techniques*. Washington, DC: National Endowment for the Arts. https://www.arts.gov/impact/research/publications/measuring-cultural-engagement-quest-new-terms-tools-and-techniques.

NEA. 2019. "U.S. Patterns of Arts Participation: A Full Report of the 2017 Survey of Public Participation in the Arts." National Endowment for the Arts, Washington, DC. https://www.arts.gov/sites/default/files/US_Patterns_of_Arts_ParticipationRevised.pdf.

NEA. 2020a. "Paths to Participation: Understanding How Art Forms and Activities Intersect." National Endowment for the Arts, Washington, DC. https://www.arts.gov/sites/default/

files/Paths-to-Participation-Understanding-How-Art-Forms-and-Activities-Intersect-1-2021.pdf.

NEA. 2020b. "Why We Engage: Attending, Creating, and Performing Art." National Endowment for the Arts, Washington, DC. https://www.arts.gov/sites/default/files/Why-We-Engage-0920_0.pdf.

NEA. 2020c. "Arts Strategies for Addressing the Opioid Crisis: Examining the Evidence." National Endowment for the Arts, Washington, DC. https://www.arts.gov/impact/research/publications/arts-strategies-addressing-opioid-crisis-examining-evidence.

NEA. 2021a. "The Art of Reopening: A Guide to Current Practices Among Arts Organizations During COVID-19." National Endowment for the Arts, Washington, DC. https://www.arts.gov/sites/default/files/The%20Art-of-Reopening.pdf.

NEA. 2021b. "National Endowment for the Arts Research Agenda—FY 2022 to FY 2026." National Endowment for the Arts, Washington, DC. https://www.arts.gov/sites/default/files/NEA-research-agenda-12.21.pdf.

NEA. 2021c. "Tribal Consultation Policy." National Endowment for the Arts, Washington, DC. https://www.arts.gov/sites/default/files/Tribal%20Consultation%20Policy%20NEA%202021%20Final.pdf.

NEA. 2022a. "Artists in the Workforce: Selected Demographic Characteristics Prior to COVID-19." National Endowment for the Arts, Washington, DC. https://www.arts.gov/sites/default/files/Artists-in-the-Workforce-Selected-Demographic-Characteristics-Prior-to-COVID%E2%80%9019.pdf.

NEA. 2022b. "Equity Action Plan of the National Endowment for the Arts." National Endowment for the Arts, Washington, DC. https://www.arts.gov/sites/default/files/EquityActionPlan_041422.pdf.

NEA. 2022c. "Strategic Plan, FY 2022–2026." National Endowment for the Arts, Washington, DC. https://www.arts.gov/sites/default/files/2022-2026-Strategic-Plan-Feb2022.pdf.

NEA. 2022d. "Yes, 'Art Works'—Now What? Preparing the NEA's FY 2022–2026 Research Agenda." National Endowment for the Arts, Washington, DC. https://www.arts.gov/sites/default/files/Yes-Art-Works-Now-What.pdf.

NEA. n.d. Creative Forces National Resource Center. National Endowment for the Arts, Washington, DC. https://www.creativeforcesnrc.arts.gov/our-impact/clinical-research-findings.

NIH. 2019. "NIH Awards $20 million over Five Years to Bring Together Music Therapy and Neuroscience." News release. National Institutes of Health, Bethesda, MD. https://www.nih.gov/news-events/news-releases/nih-awards-20-million-over-five-years-bring-together-music-therapy-neuroscience.

Novak-Leonard, Jennifer, Michael Reynolds, Ned English, and Norman Bradburn. 2015. "The Cultural Lives of Californians: Insights from the California Survey of Arts and Cultural Participation." NORC at the University of Chicago and the James Irvine Foundation. https://www.irvine.org/wp-content/uploads/Cultural_Lives_of_Californians_Report.pdf.

PolicyLink. n.d. "Social Cohesion and Well-Being." Arts, Culture, and Community Development. PolicyLink, Oakland, CA. https://communitydevelopment.art/issues/social-cohesion.

Sherman, Aleksandra, Cupo, Lani, and Mithlo, Nancy Marie. 2020. "Perspective-Taking Increases Emotionality and Empathy but Does Not Reduce Harmful Biases Against American Indians: Converging Evidence from the Museum and Lab." *PLOS One*, February 24, 2020. https://journals.plos.org/plosone/article?id=10.1371/journal.pone.0228784.

Sidford, Holly. 2011. *Fusing Arts, Culture and Social Change: High Impact Strategies for Philanthropy*. Washington, DC: National Center for Responsive Philanthropy. https://bjn9t2lhlni2dhd5hvym7llj-wpengine.netdna-ssl.com/wp-content/uploads/2016/11/Fusing_Arts_Culture_and_Social_Change-1.pdf.

SMU/TRG. 2020. "Arts and Cultural Organizations: In It For the Long Haul." https://culturaldata.org/pages/long-haul/.

SMU/TRG. n.d. "COVID-19 Sector Benchmark Dashboard." SMU DataArts and TRG Arts, Dallas, TX. Accessed November 8, 2021. https://culturaldata.org/covid-19-sector-benchmark-dashboard/about-the-project/.

Sonke, J., T. Golden, S. Francois, J. Hand, A. Chandra, L. Clemmons, D. Fakunle, M. R. Jackson, S. Magsamen, V. Rubin, K. Sams, and S. Springs. 2019. "Creating Healthy Communities: Arts + Public Health in America." University of Florida Center for Arts in Medicine/ArtPlace America. https://arts.ufl.edu/sites/creating-healthy-communities/resources/white-paper/.

White House. 2021. "Executive Order on Advancing Racial Equity and Support for Underserved Communities Through the Federal Government." https://www.whitehouse.gov/briefing-room/presidential-actions/2021/01/20/executive-order-advancing-racial-equity-and-support-for-underserved-communities-through-the-federal-government/.

WolfBrown. 2020. "WolfBrown Announces the COVID-19 Audience Outlook Monitor." WolfBrown, Detroit, MI. https://www.wolfbrown.com/post/wolfbrown-announces-the-covid-19-audience-outlook-monitor.

Index

For the benefit of digital users, indexed terms that span two pages (e.g., 52–53) may, on occasion, appear on only one of those pages.

Tables, figures, and boxes are indicated by *t*, *f*, and *b* following the page number

303 Gallery (New York), 727–28
4A Centre for Contemporary Asian Art, 287–88
99-Seat Theater Agreement, 421–22

A

ableism, 624–25
Abraham, Morris 322
Abzug, Rikki, 65–66
academic force, 532–33
academic research
    on the arts, 806–7, 808, 809–10, 813–19
    structure of, 23–24
Académie des sciences morales et politiques (France), 23
accessibility, 624–25, 627, 628–29, 634–38
accountability, 644
accounting, 546, 642, 646–48, 654–55, 676n.2
Accounting, Auditing and Accountability Journal, 646–47
Achtman, Michael, 627
acoustics, 694
activism
    art and, 727, 730–31
    arts management and, 300, 311–12
    environmental, 251
    festivals and, 357–58
    for racial justice, 300
actors
    COVID-19 and, 424
    disabilities and, 626–27, 630–31, 632–33
    unionization of, 411–12, 417, 426–28, 429
Actors' Equity Association, 411–13, 415, 416, 417–22, 423–30, 633
Administrative Sciences Association of Canada (ASAC), 26
Adorno, Theodor W., 67, 725–26
advertising, 358
aesthetics
    fundraising and, 558–59
    institutions and, 725
    logic of, 642, 650
AFL-CIO, 422–23, 430n.4, *See also* American Federation of Labor (AFL)
Africa
    ACOs in, 578–79
    art in, 606
    arts research in, 67–68
    economy of, 790
    technology in, 792
African Americans, 302
    art and, 724, 731–32, 735
    in the arts, 307–9
    in arts management, 311
    arts participation of, 811, 812
    cultural diplomacy and, 190
    music education and, 309
    in politics, 302
agency, 726, 727, 735, 791
agency theory, 84–85, 91–92, 319
Agreement on Trade-Related Aspects of Intellectual Property Rights (TRIPS), 222, 223–25
Ahearne, Jeremy, 173
Ahmed, Pervaiz K., 377, 378
Aichner, Thomas, 633–34
AIDS crisis, 412, 729–30
Alasuutari, Pertti, 167–68

Alexander, Victoria D., 535
Alexiou, Kostas, 553–54
algorithmization, 184, 189–94, 197, 198
algorithms, 226–30
　influence of, 192–93, 196
Allied Irish Bank, 580
Alvesson, Mats, 264
Amadeus (database), 766–67
Amazon, 423–24
Amazon Prime, 50
American Alliance of Museums (AAM), 593, 605–6
American Federation of Labor (AFL), 417–18, 605–6. *See also* AFL-CIO
American Federation of Musicians, 417
American Friends of the Louvre, 578
American Marketing Association, 458, 464–65
Americans for the Arts, 44, 204, 809–10
American Sign Language, 631
Americans with Disabilities Act (ADA), 634, 635
American Tobacco, 417
American West, 609
Amsterdam, 581–82, 585
Anadol, Refik, 603
Anatomic Explosions (Kusama), 733
Ander, Owe, 535
Anderson, Ben, 507
Andreasen, A., 123–24
Angelini, Francesco, 120
Anglophone world, 507
animals, 104
Anthropocene, 357–58
anthropology, 63
　cultural policy and, 173
　event studies and, 349–50, 351, 353, 364–65
anti-racism, 310, 312
Antiracism, Diversity, Equity, and Inclusion (ADEI), 303–4, 307, 308–10, 311–12. *See also* Diversity, Equity, Inclusion and Antiracism (DEIA)
anti-structure, 353–54
antitrust law, 125
Antonelli, Paola, 603, 604, 613
Appel, Karel, 585
Apple, 49
Apropa Culture program, 637

Arabic language, 789
Arantes, Antonio, 243
archaeology, 325–26
architecture, 626
Ardley, Barry, 503–4
Argonne National Laboratory, 810
Arias-Aranda, Daniel, 462–63
Aristotle, 103, 265
Arnold, Mark J., 469–70, 471
Arno River, 600
Arnould, Eric J., 491–92
Arostegui, Juan Arturo Rubio, 170–71
Arsenale (Venice), 250–51
art
　authenticity of, 595
　commerce and, 597–98
　contemporary, 481, 482–83, 484, 485–86, 489–90
　devotional, 595
　entrepreneurship and, 724–29
　festivals and, 396
　importation of, 585
　institutional critique and, 723–24, 725–29, 735–36
　legal definition of, 588
　market for, 482, 484
　NFTs and, 593–95, 612
　as product, 482, 491
　taxes on, 586–88
　value of, 481–83, 484, 485–86, 487f, 488–89, 491–92
　values of, 642, 645, 647
Artforum, 730–31
Art Fund (UK), 441
art galleries, 727–28
　atmosphere of, 510
Art Gallery & Museum of Glasgow, 441
artificial Intelligence, 183–85, 192–94, 198
Art in America, 732
Art in Healthcare (charity), 488
"Artist Corporation and the Collective, The" (Gates), 732
artistic directors, 79, 84, 284, 286–87, 291, 294
artists
　disabilities and, 632
　as entrepreneurs, 718
　ethics and, 267, 273

funding of, 523
institutional critique and, 723–24, 734–36
leadership and, 284–85
NFTs and, 595
perceptions of, 67
views of value, 486–88
Artivate (journal), 153–54, 153*t*
Art Place America, 815
arts
  access to, 438
  activism and, 251
  authenticity and, 83
  benefits of, 131–33, 814–18, 819
  community turn in, 205, 209–11, 218
  copyright and, 221–22
  cultural diplomacy and, 185
  cultural planning and, 208
  DEIA and, 813
  disabilities and, 623–24, 626–27, 628, 635, 636, 637–38
  economics and, 132–33, 664, 670–71
  economic sector, 44, 48
  evaluation of, 642, 643–55, 669–71, 672
  government support of, 206
  Great Recession and, 545
  impacts of, 481, 665, 814–19
  literary, 808
  market for, 128–31
  morality and, 273–74
  participation in, 122–23, 806–7, 808–9, 812
  politics and, 525–26
  popular culture and, 129
  pricing in, 133–35
  as products, 466–67
  research on, 806–7, 808, 809–10, 813–19
  subjectivity and, 649–50
  taxes and, **575–76**
  theories of, 148*t*
  value of, 819
  values and, 527–28
  Visual, 286–87, 808
  women and, 217
arts administration. *See also* arts and cultural management
  name, 6
"Arts Administration: A Field of Dreams?", 6
arts and cultural management
  activism and, 312, 312*b*, 805
  applications of, 15
  approaches to, 12, 349–50, 353, 362–63, 364–65
  in Canada, 25–28
  copyright and, 230–31
  COVID-19 and, 807–8
  critical race theory and, 300, 302
  cultural diplomacy and, 183
  cultural heritage and, 244
  debates in, 349–50, 364
  definition of, 59, 60–61
  digitalization and, 198
  disability access and, 635, 637–38
  disciplines and, 24, 32
  economics and, 119–20, 135
  entrepreneurship and, 704, 735–36
  evaluation of, 17
  as field, 24, 25, 32, 38–39
  field of, 3–5, 6, 7, 10–11, 12, 19, 143, 154–57
  funding and, 16, 31–36, 33*t*, 539
  gamification and, 449
  geography of, 5–6, 9–11, 10*f*, 19
  habitus of, 144
  history of, 5–6, 64*t*, 66–68, 69, 69*t*
  interdisciplinarity of, 141–42, 147, 152, 154–57
  journals and, 145–46, 152–54, 153*t*
  journals of, 6, 60–61, 62*f*
  legitimacy of, 60, 61–62, 65–66, 67–68, 69*t*
  mapping theories of, 144–45, 146, 148*t*, 153*t*, 156*f*
  methods in, 59–60, 62–69, 70–71
  open systems theory in, 101–3, 106, 108–10, 114, 534
  paradigms of, 63–64
  performance evaluation and, 641–46, 651, 654–55
  policy and, 13
  pricing in, 133–34
  publications on, 28–31, 29*t*, 546
  race and, 300, 311–12
  research and, 819
  research chairs in, 36–37
  servicescapes and, 513
  taxes and, 575–76
  theories of, 12, 70, 141–42, 147–52, 704–5
  training in, 216

arts and cultural organizations (ACOs), 12, 13–15, 17, 18
  audiences and, 94, 809
  in Australia, 288
  boards of, 79–80, 84–86, 93–94
  branding of, 464–66
  business models of, 744, 747–50, 751–52
  credibility of, 530–31, 532–33, 538
  cultural planning and, 203, 204, 207, 210, 211, 216–17
  DEIA and, 814
  digitalization and, 437–39, 441, 442–43, 448, 468, 471–72
  diversity and, 110–14
  donors to, 549, 554–55, 559–60
  ecosystem of, 42
  entrepreneurship and, 761–62, 766, 770, 774–75
  environment and, 276–77
  environment of, 101–2, 110–11
  ethics and, 264, 267–77, 278, 279
  evaluation of, 641–42, 643–44, 645–46, 651–54
  evolution of, 50, 51*t*
  festivals and, 351
  funding of, 274–76, 523–27, 529*t*, 531–32, 536–37, 593, 599–610
  funding mechanisms for, 534–35, 536, 536*f*
  funding structure of, 527–33, 530*f*, 539
  fundraising of, 458–60, 462–64, 467–68, 469–72, 554
  gamification and, 439, 442, 443–44, 448, 449
  governance of, 79–82, 84, 91–92
  institutions and, 533
  knowledge and, 371–73, 376, 378–79
  leadership of, 283–85, 295
  marketing and, 457, 458–59, 461, 464, 466–67, 469–72
  markets and, 533
  motives of, 524
  NFTs and, 599, 608*f*, 611–13
  open systems theory and, 109, 112–13
  perceptions of, 555
  performance of, 381–82, 382*t*, 384
  pricing and, 134–35
  promotion of, 468–69
  race and, 300
  regional variation of, 770
  resource acquisition by, 90–91
  status of, 94
  strategic planning and, 596–99
  supporters of, 462–64, 471–72
  tax incentives and, 575–76, 577–80, 582–84, 588
  values of, 647–48
Arts and Health (journal), 153, 153*t*
Arts and Humanities Research Council (AHRC), 492–93, 665, 676n.3, 806–7
Arts Basic Survey (ABS), 806, 809
Arts Center La Nau, 689
Arts Council of Greater New Haven, 205
Arts councils, 523
Arts Council (UK), 270, 278, 538, 582, 669–70, 672, 673
arts education
  data on, 810
arts-in-health programs, 814
arts journalism, 309
arts managers
  roles of, 110
"Arts Manager's Social Responsibility, The" (Keller), 311–12
arts sector. *See also* creative sector; cultural sector
  inequality in, 813
Asia
  arts research in, 67–68, 70–71
  cultural policy in, 523–24
  economy of, 790
  philanthropy in, 526
Asian Americans
  in arts management, 311
  arts participation of, 811
Asian Civilizations Museum, 440
Association canadienne-française pour l'avancement des sciences (ACFAS), 27
Association for Cultural Economics International, 122
Association francophone pour le savoir, 27
Association internationale de management de l'art et de la culture (AIMAC), 27–28
Association of Art Museum Directors (AAMD), 605–6
Association of Arts Administration Educators (AAAE), 25–26

Association of Tribal Archives, Libraries, and Museums, 812
Ateca-Amestoy, Victoria, 122–23, 127, 131
Athens, 616n.23
athletics
 reputation in, 89
Atlanta, Georgia, 625
Atlantic Ocean, 417
Atlas de la culture (Pecqueur), 789
atmospheres, 512
 study of, 508, 513
 types of, 508–10, 509*f*, 511*t*
atmospherics, 497–98, 500, 506–7
attendance
 at Italian museums, 326–27, 328*t*, 337, 338–39
 museum directors and, 322, 323
audience-centric paradigm, 315–16
audiences
 ACOs and, 94, 809
 participation of, 349–50, 397, 791
Audretsch, David B., 124–25, 763
Australia
 arts and cultural management in, 5–6, 19, 25
 cultural evaluation in, 670
 cultural planning in, 206, 208
 cultural policy in, 43, 67
 cultural production in, 788–89
 disability access in, 625–26
 festivals in, 286–88
 publications in, 29, 29*t*
 tax incentives in, 578
Australia Council for the Arts, 279
Australian Centre for the Moving Image, 195–96
Austria, 523
 Copyright in, 229–30
Austrian economics, 121–22, 124–25
authenticity
 of ACOs, 80–81, 82, 84, 88, 89, 90–91, 92–94
 of art, 490
 of copies, 186–87
 expressive, 83
 of museums, 442–43, 446–47, 449
 NFTs and, 595
 nominal, 83
 types of, 83
authoritarianism, 786, 789, 796–97, 798
avant-garde, 733–34

B
Bacon, Alan, 307–8
Baeker, Greg, 203
Bai, Ge, 320–21
Baker, Julie, 501, 502
Bakhshi, Hasan, 125–26
Balanced Scorecard, 380, 381, 382, 382*t*, 641–42
Baldin, Andrea, 133–34
Ballad of Sexual Dependency, The (Goldin), 729–30
Baltimore Museum of Art, 605–6
Banefield, Edward, 525–26
Bannerman, Sarah, 37
Barden, Pamela, 459–60
Barney, Matthew, 616n.24
Barton-Farcas, Stephanie, 626–27
Basilicata (region), 751, 753*t*
Baskerville, Richard L., 49
Bastille Day, 614n.10
Basu, Shumita, 302
Batista-Foguet, Joan M., 685–86
Baumgartner, Frank R., 416
Baumol, William J., 124–25, 151
Becker, Gary, 128–29
Beckman, Gary, 278
Beeple (artist), 593–95
behavioral economics, 122–24
Behzadi, Houman, 468
Beijing, 537
Beinecke Rare Book and Manuscript Library, 609–10
Belfiore, Eleonora, 645
Belgium, 31, 580
Belk, Russell W., 123–24, 484
Bell, Derrick, 301
Bellini, Jacopo, 595
Benay, Erin, 613
Bendixen, Peter, 704
Bendle, Craig, 614–15n.12
Benjamin, Walter, 186–87, 492
Bennett, James T., 423
Bennett, Oliver, 645
Bennett, Roger, 377, 462–63
Berlin, 512
Berne Convention for the Protection of Literary and Artistic Works (1886), 223–25
Bérubé, Julie, 6–7

Besse, Kayla, 625, 635
Best, Roger, 465–66
Betamax video, 607–8
Better Business Bureau, 555
Betzler, Diana, 170–71, 322
Beyes, Timon, 732
Bhati, Abhishek, 468
Bianchini, 208, 216
Bickerton, Craig, 131
Biden, Joe, 811, 812
Biehl-Missal, Brigitte, 508, 512
big data, 195, 196
Bigné Alcañiz, Enrique, 530–31
Billboard, 309, 790
binary thinking, 303*b*, 304
biodiversity, 251
"Biography" (Elmgreen & Dragset), 511–12
biology, 103, 108
Bird in Space (Brancusi), 588
Birnberg, Jacob, 467–68
Bisogno, M., 582
Bitmark, 603
Bitner, Mary J., 498–99, 500–2
Black Americans
    art and, 724, 731–32, 735
    in the arts, 307–9
    in arts management, 311
    arts participation of, 811, 812
    cultural diplomacy and, 190
    music education and, 309
    in politics, 302
blacklisting, 420–21
Black Lives Matter movement, 152, 300
    unions and, 412
Black Rock City, Nevada, 357
blockchain, 16, 595, 606, 609, 613n.1
    research and, 68
boards of directors, 80, 316
    of ACOs, 284
    composition of, 79–80, 84–86, 93
    decision-making by, 86–88, 93–94
    diversity of, 323–25, 327, 329–35, 334*f*, 335*f*, 337, 338–39
    ethics and, 269, 279
    NFTs and, 599, 614n.7
    shared leadership and, 290, 292
    study of, 316–17, 319–21, 327, 328*t*, 338

Boenigk, Silke, 461
Boerner, Sabine, 506
Böhme, Gernot, 507
Boix, Rafael, 44
Bollywood, 789–90
Boltanski, Luc, 524, 527–28
Bonnin, Gaël, 507–8
Bonn, Mark A., 503–4
books, 807
    digitalization of, 122
Boom festival, 355, 356*t*, 357–58, 359, 360, 361, 362
Boorsma, Miranda, 471
Borja, Spain, 595
Borowiecki, Karol J., 130
Borrup, Tom, 204, 209, 210, 211, 214, 216, 217
Borwick, Doug, 112–13
Boryeong Mud Festival, 504–5
Boston, 65–66, 88, 112, 812–13
Boston Chinatown Neighborhood Center, 812–13
Boston Symphony Orchestra, 88, 111–12
Botti, Antonio, 504–5
Boudreaux, Kevin J., 49–50
Boulding, Kenneth E., 104
Bourdesian theory, 69
Bourdieu, Pierre, 129, 142, 143–44, 146–51, 155, 156, 482–83
Bowen, William, 151
Bowman, Lewis 414
Boyko, Christopher T., 746–47
BP (oil company), 538
Brakus, J. Josko, 685–86
Brancusi, Constantin, 588
branding, 464–66, 471–72
    of charities, 551
    experiences and, 684, 685, 686
Brazil, 187, 190–91
bridging qualities, 507, 510–11
Brisbane, Australia, 288
British Commonwealth, 788–89
British Council, 185, 190–91
British Museum, 437–38, 439–40, 531
    NFTS and, 601–3, 602*f*, 604–7, 614–15n.12
Brittany, 126
Brkić, Aleksandar, 364
Broadway, 418, 420–21, 427
Broadway League, 421, 424–25, 427, 429

Brocato, E. Deanne, 501
Brooks, Arthur C., 525
Brown v. Board of Education, 302
Bruges, Belgium, 746–47
BTS (band), 790
Budapest, 187, 255n.11
Buddhism, 103–4
bullfights, 129
Bureau of Economic Analysis, 810
Bureau, Sylvain, 725, 726–27
Burgess, John, 266
Burke, Andrew E., 124–25
Burning Man (festival), 352, 355, 356t, 360, 362
    economics of, 358–59, 363–64
    history of, 357
Burns, Tom, 107–8
business
    ACOs and, 79–80
    art and, 481–82, 492, 597–98
    arts and cultural management and, 59
    cultural production and, 787, 788
    cultural sector and, 747–48
    economics and, 121–22
    knowledge of, 710–11, 712
    open systems theory in, 106
business management
    of ACOs, 283–84
Business Model Prism, 744–45, 747–50, 749f, 751–52, 756
business models, 744, 748–50, 751–52, 755, 756
business-to-consumer logic, 50
Business Week rankings, 94
Bustamante, Mauricio, 181n.8
Bygrave, William D., 705
Byrnes, William, 461
Byzantine frescoes, 607

C

Cabane, Charlotte, 133
Cabbage Field Initiative, 251
Čačija, Ljiljana, 459–60, 461
Calderón García, Haydee, 505–6
California, 46, 421–22, 806–7
Callander, Adrienne, 723–24, 735–36
Callen, Jeffrey L., 319–20
Camarero, Carmen, 468–69
Cameron, Douglas, 465

Cameron, Kim S., 719n.4
Cameron, Samuel, 120–21
Campbell, Peter, 744
Campbell, Thomas, 532
Canada
    arts and cultural management in, 6–7, 25–28, 36–37, 38–39
    copyright in, 221–22
    cultural planning in, 203, 206
    cultural production in, 788–89
    cultural value in, 663–64, 670, 673
    funding in, 31–36, 33t, 34t
    publications in, 28–31, 29t
    tax incentives in, 578
Canada Council for the Arts, 32, 670, 673–74, 675, 676
Canada Research Chairs (CRC), 37, 38–39
Canadian Association of Arts Administration Educators (CAAAE), 25–26
Canadian Communication Association (CCA), 26
Canadian Political Science Association (CPSA), 26
Canberra, Australia, 288
capitalism
    alternatives to, 358
    culture and, 122
    democracy and, 363–64
    festivals and, 358, 361, 363–64
Capone, Francesco, 44
carbon footprint, 601–2
Caribbean Sea, 354–55
Carmelle and Rémi Marcoux Research Chair on Arts Management, 36
Castellani, Massimiliano, 120
Castellano, Carlos Garrido 728
Castiglione, Concetta, 127
Caust, Josephine, 121, 273–74
CBS, 613n.2
CDs
    streaming and, 126
Cellini, Roberto, 127–28
censorship, 789
Centers for Disease Control and Prevention (CDC), 815–16
Central Europe, 718
Centre for Cultural Value, 674–75, 676

Cerf, Vint, 231n.6
Cervera-Taulet, Amparo, 505–6
Chaire Fernand-Dumont sur la culture, 36–37
Charles, Cleopatra, 552–53
Chandler, Eliza, 626
Change to Win Coalition, 423
Changfoot, Nadine, 632–33
charities
  tax exemptions for, 576
chatbots, 191–92
Chen, Katherine K., 352, 363–64
Cherbo, Joni, 181n.10
chess, 668
Chiaravalloti, Francesco, 471, 643–44, 645–46, 647–48, 652–53, 671–72, 673, 675
Chicago, 88, 428, 538, 724, 731–32, 733
Chicago Symphony Orchestra, 88, 134–35
Chicago, University of, 806
Chief Executive Officers (CEOs), 79, 284, 285–88, 289, 290, 294
  experience of, 322, 337–38
  gender of, 322–23
children
  gamification and, 439–40
China
  ACOs in, 535
  arts research in, 67–68
  authoritarianism in, 789, 796–97
  cultural policy of, 523–24, 527
  cultural production in, 789, 796
  fundraising in, 554
  museums in, 531, 532–33
Choe, Jaeyeon, 504–5
Choi, Byounggu, 374, 375–76, 380–81, 383
Choi, Jongwoon, 467–68
Choi, Youngjoon, 504–5
Chong, Derek, 274–75
choreography, 811
Chorus Equity Association (CEA), 419
Christianity, 304
Christie's, 593–94
Christmas markets, 510
Christmas trees, 507–8
Christo (artist), 396
Chu Chin Chow (musical), 418
Chumpitaz Cáceres, Ruben, 530–31
Chunky Move (dance company), 286–87

Cimabue, 600
circuses, 129
Cirque du Soleil, 53
cities
  ACOs in, 109
  art and, 733
  cultural events and, 393, 396
  ECoC and, 743–44, 746
City Beautiful movement, 205
city planning, 205, 209–10
City University (London), 5–6
civic improvement groups
  cultural planning and, 205
Civil Rights Act, 302
civil rights movement, 300
Clarke, Jackie, 466–67
Clark, Peter Bentley, 414
class
  art and, 88
  art donors and, 463–64
  festivals and, 358
  theatre and, 419
classical music, 308
Cleff, Thomas, 686
Cleveland, Ohio, 65–66, 88
climate change, 49, 276, 302–3, 792, 797–98
Coalition for Art and Sustainable Development (France), 276
Coate, Bronwyn, 122
Cobb, Jelani, 302
Cobb, Nina Kressner, 526
co-creation
  of events, 349–50, 351–53, 355–61, 362, 363–64
  of value, 485, 488
coercion
  collective action and, 414, 422
Colbert, François, 6, 36, 141, 458–59, 463, 537
Cold War, 180n.1, 190, 420–21
  artists and, 164
collaborative governance, 171f
collective, 732
collective action, 413–15, 419, 429
collective goods, 414
collectivism
  donations and, 550–51, 556–57
Collins, Kent James, 426

colonialism, 786–87
  culture and, 215
color
  fundraising and, 558–59
  servicescapes and, 511–12
Colosseo (Museum), 325–26
Columbia Journalism School, 302
Comello, Luca, 402–3
commerce
  as art, 733–34
  art and, 597–98
commodification, 798
commodities
  culture as, 128–29
communication
  diplomacy and, 190, 198
  ECoC and, 754
  markets and, 533
  theories of, 148t
communism, 420–21
Communitas, 353–54
communities
  festivals and, 357
  online, 791
  organizations and, 110–14
Community arts movement, 205
community engagement, 112–13
community turn (arts), 205, 209–11, 218
competition, 124–28, 132
  gamification and, 442
  for legitimacy, 108
  in performing arts, 92
  of social groups, 415
complexity, 47–53, 394–96
computers, 223
Comunian, Roberta, 45, 46
concerts
  attendees of, 681, 682t, 689–90, 690t
  digital music and, 126
  multisensory, 681, 687–89
Concierto Sentido, 689
conferences, 27
  in Canada, 26
conflict, 306
conflict effect, 538
conformity, 415
  artists and, 724, 726

Conklin, Lauretta, 414–15
connoisseurship, 598–99
conscientiousness, 267
conservation
  of art, 600, 601–2
  of culture, 52, 240
  museums and, 315–16
conservatism, 538
  CRT and, 301, 306
  racism and, 306, 309
consumer demand theory, 123
consumer experience, 685–86, 687–90, 694–96
consumerism, 363–64
consumers
  of art, 481–82, 484, 491–92
consumer theory, 128–29
content creation, 791–93
ContentID, 223–25, 227–29
Conti, Emanuela, 503–4
cooperation
  cultural events and, 402–3
Cooper, Jim, 730
COP26 summit, 276
copyright, 223–27, 230–31, 231n.1
  creativity and, 221–23
  criticism of, 222–23, 231n.5
  enforcement of, 225–30
  in the EU, 225–27
  value and, 43–44
Corbella, Marta, 626–27
Corporation for Public Broadcasting, 174
corporations
  art funding and, 524, 525, 526, 538
  boards of, 79–80, 88
  ethics and, 266
  funding from, 81–82, 553, 555–56
Council of Europe (CoE), 164–65, 166, 239–40, 255n.3
counterculture, 363–64, 482
Courchesne, André, 466
Court of Justice of the European Union (CJEU), 229–30
Cova, Bernard, 363–64
COVID-19, 300, 751
  ACOs and, 263, 268
  arts and, 170–71, 174, 807–8, 809–10, 815

corporations (*cont.*)
  arts leadership and, 14, 18
  awareness of disparities and, 805
  cultural diplomacy, 184
  cultural economics and, 126
  cultural enterprises and, 703
  cultural events and, 399
  cultural sector and, 437, 785–86, 796
  digitalization and, 186, 196–97, 438, 449
  festivals and, 285–86, 287, 295, 354–55
  funding and, 539, 593, 605–6
  impacts of, 535, 785–86, 792
  music and, 681
  open systems theory and, 101
  servicescapes and, 512–13
  unions and, 412, 413, 423–24, 429–30
  in the USA, 299
Covin, Jeffrey G., 706
Cowen, Tyler, 120–21, 122
Cox, Tasmin, 744, 746
Cray, David, 87, 93–94
creative arts therapies, 814
Creative Carbon Scotland, 276
creative commons, 120
creative ecology, 46, 47
Creative Forces: NEA Military Healing Arts Network, 814–15
creative industries, 43, 44, 49, 67
  funding for, 32, 33–34, 34t
"Creative Nation: Commonwealth Cultural Policy" (report), 43
Creative Scotland, 270
creative sector. *See also* cultural sector
  activism and, 311–12
  complexity of, 47–53
  COVID-19 and, 785–86
  critical race theory and, 301, 302, 303–4, 307–10
  digital revolution and, 49–50
  evolution of, 51t, 52
  inequality in, 813
  mapping of, 50–53
  race and, 300, 310, 312
  servicescape and, 497–98, 499–500, 506, 512–13
  taxonomy of, 42–47, 53–54
Creative Victoria, 670

creativity
  commercialism and, 467
  cultural value and, 491
  decentralization of, 793, 797–98
  everyday, 656n.3
  government and, 81–82
  law and, 221–22
credibility
  fundraising and, 556–57
  power of, 530–31
Crenshaw, Kimberlé, 301
Crepaz, Lukas, 647
critical accounting studies, 642–43, 646–49, 651–53
critical chain project management (CCPM), 404–5
Critical Disability Studies Collective, 638n.6
Critical Perspectives on Accounting (journal), 646–47
critical race theory (CRT), 300, 301–2, 307–8
  censorship of, 306
critical systems theory, 113
critical theory, 148t, 152, 154
critical viewpoint, 65
critics, 81–82, 83–84, 87–88
Cronley, Maria L., 553
Crossick, Geoffrey, 483
crowd creation, 531–32
crowdfunding, 531–32, 545–46, 551, 553–54
  history of, 16
Crucifix (Cimabue), 600
cryptocurrency, 594, 613n.2
  research and, 68
Csikszentmihalyi, Mihaly, 725
Cuccia, Tiziana, 127–28
culinary festivals, 504–5
cultural bureaucracy, 166–67, 169f, 170f, 171f
cultural capital, 670–71
  arts management and, 143
Cultural Data Project, 545–46, 552–53
cultural democracy, 24, 39n.1, 667
cultural development
  policy and, 164, 170–71
Cultural Development (Girard), 166
cultural diplomacy, 13, 183, 189
  definition, 183
  technology and, 183–89, 193–98

cultural diversity
  policy and, 170–71
cultural economics, 48, 119–21, 135
  behavioral economics and, 122–24
  competition and, 124–28
  criticism of, 119, 121–22, 135
  influence of, 121
  pricing and, 133–35
  values and, 120, 121–22
cultural enterprises, 703–4
  success of, 703, 706, 714–15, 716–17
cultural entrepreneurship, 703–4, 705, 706–11, 712, 713, 714–15, 761–62, 765–66
  regional variation in, 770
cultural entrepreneurship excellence model (CEEM), 703–4, 706–15, 707f, 710f, 716f, 716–18
cultural events, 401f, 402–6. See also festivals
  complexity of, 394–400, 397f, 406
  evolution of, 349
  history of, 393
  impact of, 393, 394, 406, 745–46
  location of, 396–97
  study of, 393, 394
  sustainability and, 406
  types of, 394t
cultural heritage, 48–49, 243–44. See also heritage communities
  communities and, 241
  definition, 240–41
  management of, 239, 240–41, 244–54, 255n.1
  preservation of, 52, 240, 242
  right to, 240, 253
  tax incentives for, 580
cultural incubators, 350, 361–62
cultural industry, 67
  art and, 525
cultural leadership, 263–64, 269–77
"Cultural Lives of Californians, The" (report), 806–7
cultural management, 3. See also arts and cultural management
cultural perspective (marketing), 460
cultural planning, 13, 203, 206–9, 211–13, 214–17
  community turn and, 209–11, 218
  culture and, 214–15, 218
  expectations of, 212f, 213f
  history of, 204, 205–6
  inequities in, 214, 218
  training in, 216
  in the USA, 204, 206–7, 210, 216
  women and, 217
Cultural Planning at 40 (Borrup), 210
cultural policy, 13, 27, 164, 172f, 173–74, 523, 656n.3
  copyright and, 230–31
  cultural events and, 394
  ECoC and, 757
  economics and, 119
  entrepreneurship and, 775–76
  environment and, 276–77
  evaluation and, 645, 648
  French model of, 164–71
  history of, 315–16
  in Italy, 325–26, 335–37
  mapping and, 163, 171–73, 174, 178, 179–80
  taxes and, 575, 576
  types of, 523–24
  in the USA, 173–79, 175f, 176f, 177f
  value and, 663–64, 665–66
Cultural Policy: A Preliminary Study (Girard), 165–66
cultural production, 484, 786–90, 798
  theories of, 148t
cultural sector, 119–20, 123, 125, 272–73. See also creative sector
  business models in, 747–50, 755
  complexity of, 47–50
  COVID-19 and, 437, 449, 785–86, 796
  cultural planning and, 209–10, 212, 214, 216–17, 218
  definition of, 264
  digitalization and, 49–50, 442–43
  entrepreneurship in, 703–4, 761–62, 770, 775
  environment and, 270
  in Europe, 762
  evaluation and, 652–55
  evolution of, 51t, 52
  gamification and, 439–40, 449
  knowledge from, 655–56
  knowledge management in, 375
  leadership in, 269

cultural sector (*cont.*)
  mapping of, 50–53
  performance in, 381–82
  servicescape and, 497–98, 499–500, 506, 512–13
  taxonomy of, 42–47, 53–54
  in the UK, 674–75
cultural spaces, 485
cultural studies, 656n.3
Cultural Trends (journal), 29, 135–36n.1
cultural unions, 411, 415, 420, 429–30. *See also* unions
cultural value, 120, 482, 492, 663–65, 667–72, 675–76. *See also* value
  definition of, 483–84, 665–66
  understanding of, 481, 484, 485
Cultural Value Project, 665
culture
  brands and, 465
  definition of, 214–15, 656n.3, 667
  democratization of, 24, 39n.1
  entrepreneurship and, 703–4
  impact of, 665
  festivals and, 350–51
  as need, 163
  right to, 163
  rituals and, 646–47
  value of, 663–66, 667–72, 675–76
  values and, 527–28
  views of, 215
Culture Chatbot Generic Services project, 191
culture ministries, 167–68
Culture Wars (USA), 179
Cummings, Michael, 723–24, 735–36
Cummings, Milton C., 523
Cunningham, Stuart, 43
Curás Pérez, Rafael, 530–31
Curioni, Baia, 326–27
Cuseum, 186–87
customer experience, 685–90, 687f, 688t, 691–95, 692t
customer satisfaction, 506
customs law, 585
Cuyler, Antonio C., 6
cybernetics, 107
Czech Republic, 766–67

D
Dakar, Senegal, 167–68
Dalí Museum, 192–93
Dalí, Salvador, 192–93
Dalli, Daniele, 363–64
dance, 286–87, 290, 811
Darroch, Jenny, 377–79, 380–81, 383
data
  cultural planning and, 209–10, 214
  quantitative, 664
DataArts, 545–46
datafication, 184, 193–97, 198
Da Vinci, Leonardo, 437–38, 595
Davis, Gerald F., 104–5
Davis, J. Charlene, 123–24, 466–67
deaf community, 630–31, 634
De Bernard, Manfredi, 46
decentralized autonomous organization (DAO), 613n.1
decision-making
  boards and, 86–89, 93–94
  shared leadership and, 292–94
Decker-Lange, Carolin, 748
decommodification, 358
de Coquet, Mary Rozsa, 90, 92, 109–10
"deep hanging out" approach, 63
Defense Department (USA), 814–15
Degas, Edgar, 596, 614nn.8–8
Degas's Father Listening to Lorenzo Pagans Playing the Guitar (Degas), 614n.9
Dejean, Sylvain, 126
De la Vega, Pablo, 126–27
Delaware, 616n.23
Delgado, Richard, 301–2
democracy, 786, 796–98
  arts funding and, 273
  capitalism and, 363–64
Democratic Party (USA), 525
democratization
  of culture, 24, 39n.1, 171–73
demography
  of festivals, 358
De Molli, Federica, 510
Denmark, 511
Denver Museum of Art, 609
deontology, 266, 274
Department of Canadian Heritage, 35–36

Department of Commerce (USA), 173–74
Department of Culture, Media and Sports (DCMS) (UK), 43, 264, 669–71, 673, 744
Department of the Interior (USA), 173–76
Department of Veterans Affairs (USA), 814–15
Dervin, Brenda, 645
De Toni, Alberto F., 402–3
Devereaux, Constance, 6
Devotional art, 595
Dewey, John, 148t
Dias, Ashley, 552–53
Di Benedetto, Anthony, 765–66
digital engagement, 15
digital home entertainment, 125
digitalization, 122, 126–27, 185–89, 437–41, 444–45, 448
  cultural sector and, 786, 791–96
Digital Millennium Copyright Act (DMCA), 223–25
digital museum diplomacy, 185–87
digital revolution
  cultural sector and 49
Digital Services Act (EU), 230–31
Digital Single Market Strategy (EU), 225
digitization, 222–25, 227–29
Dimaggio, Paul J., 108, 111–12, 147–51, 724, 726, 761–62
Directive on Copyright in the Digital Single Market (CDSM), 225–26, 229–31
disabilities, people with
  accessibility for, 624–25, 627, 628–29, 634–36, 637–38
  concerts for, 689–90
  participation in arts, 623–24, 626–27, 628–29, 632–34, 636, 637–38
Disappearing Element/Disappeared Element (Imminent Past) (Meireles), 728
disciplinary model, 23–24
disciplines, 4, 6–7, 23–24
  definition of, 11–12
disinformation, 193
Disney, 789, 795–96
Disneyfication, 437–38, 449
diversity
  ACOs and, 110–14
  art and, 482
  of artists, 811
  in arts education, 309, 311–12
  attitudes to, 812
  of authors, 8–9
  board-director interaction and, 334f, 335f
  of boards, 316–17, 318, 319–20, 323–25, 327, 329–35, 337, 338–39
  cultural heritage and, 252, 253–54
  cultural planning and, 204, 207–8, 210, 214, 218
  cultural production and, 796, 798
  cultural value and, 667
  ethics and, 271
  of museum directors, 326t
  museums and, 307
  of roles on boards, 84–86, 93
  in the UK, 272–73
  of unions, 425
diversity, equity, and inclusion (DEI), 311–12
  open systems theory and, 102–3, 110–14
diversity, equity, inclusion, and accessibility (DEIA), 805, 810–14, 817, 818
Documenta 15, 793
Dome Gallery (Faaborg Museum), 511
Donaldson, William, 414
donations
  individual, 545–46, 547–50
  influences on, 550–59
  study of, 545–50, 548t, 559–60
donor-centricity, 460
donors
  involvement of, 16
Donovan, Claire, 647, 648
Donovan, Robert J., 498–99
Dorchester Projects (Gates), 732
Dorn, Charles M., 6–7
Dorries, Nadine, 194–95
Dowling, Robyn, 208
Downward, Paul, 131
Dreeszen, Craig, 204, 211
  community turn in the arts and, 210, 213
  on cultural planning, 205, 206–7, 208, 209, 210, 211–12
Drexel University, 812
dualism, 498–500, 506–7, 512–13
duality, 498
Dubini, Paola, 85–86, 93, 320–21, 322, 327
Duhaime, Carole, 483

Dumont, Fernand, 36–37
Duncan, Angus, 421
Durrer, Victoria, 627
Dutch Advisory Committee, 581–82
Dutch Masters Foundation, 579
Dutch Parliament, 581
dynamic pricing, 134, 135

E
earthquakes, 251–52
eastern philosophy, 103–4, 114
Ebewo, Patrick, 364
Ecce Homo, 595
ecology, 535, 560
    art and, 728
    of arts, 673–74, 809
    of culture, 45–46, 47
econometrics, 120–21, 665–66, 671, 767
economic activity (legal definition), 583
Economic and Social Committee of the
    European Communities, 580–81
economics
    antitrust law and, 125
    arts and cultural management and, 5, 12,
        17–18, 119–20, 135
    complexity in, 47
    of cultural enterprises, 703
    cultural policy and, 664–65, 670–71
    cultural sector and, 41, 43–44, 50, 785–86
    ECoC and, 745–46, 756
    entrepreneurship and, 761–62, 763
    event studies and, 349–50, 364–65
    heterodox, 121–22
    theories from, 148*t*, 151, 152–53, 155
    values and, 647, 648–49, 652
Economics and Culture (Throsby), 131
economic value, 120
ecosystems
    of arts, 809, 812, 817
    cultural, 788–89
    of cultural industries, 42, 45, 46, 51*t*, 52,
        53–42
    entrepreneurial, 763
    preservation of, 251
    social, 106
Edelstein, Leonard, 59–60
Edinburgh Fringe (festival), 286–87, 290

Edmondo and Thérèse Morbilli (Degas), 614n.9
education, 23
    arts and, 463–64, 810
    arts and cultural management and, 5–6, 7,
        142, 151
    of authors, 8–9, 10*f*
    in Canada, 25
    diversity and, 811, 812, 813
    funding of, 534
    gamification and, 448
    music and, 309
    theories of, 146, 148*t*, 152, 153–54
Education Commission of the States, 810
effectuation, 725, 734
Electoral College (USA), 302
Elliot, Caroline, 129–30
Ellwood, Sheila, 647
Elmgreen & Dragset (artists), 511–12
Elsevier, 28
emancipation, 725, 730–31
emancipatory entrepreneurship, 730–31. *See
    also* entrepreneurship
Emanuel, Rahm, 733
EMBOK, 402
Emerson, Ralph Waldo, 264
emotions
    servicescape and, 498–99
    value and, 498–99
endowment effect, 123
England. *See also* United Kingdom
    ACOs in, 647–48
    cultural policy in, 669, 672, 675
    cultural value in, 663–64, 669–71, 672
English language, 19, 26, 27, 794–95
entrepreneurial economy, 763
entrepreneurial excellence model (EEM),
    703–4, 706–13
entrepreneurship, 17–18, 762, 763–65
    arts and, 724–29, 730–31, 732–33, 734
    cultural, 703–4, 705, 706–11, 712, 713, 714–15,
        761–62, 765–66
    culture and, 703–4
    definition of, 705–6, 761–62
    dissent and, 723–24, 735–36
    economy and, 761, 763, 770
    emancipatory, 730–31
    environment of, 762

institutional, 723–24, 725–29, 735–36
public, 725, 732–33
theories of, 148*t*
environment
of ACOs, 535, 539
arts and, 270, 274–75, 276–77
corporate impacts on, 538
COVID-19 impacts on, 785–86
cultural events and, 396–97, 397*f*
cultural heritage and, 240
cultural planning and, 203
ECoC and, 756
economics and, 121–22
emotions and, 499, 508–9
of entrepreneurship, 762
festivals and, 355–58
impacts of genocide, 302–3
in Lithuania, 251
open systems theory and, 62–103, 104–5, 110
of organizations, 101, 102, 105, 108, 109, 110–11
servicescape and, 497, 498, 500–2, 502*t*, 503–4, 506–7, 510
social, 724
theories of, 106
environmentalism, 414–15, 538, 667–68
equilibrium, 415–16
equity, 675–76
Essen, Germany, 745
Estelami, Hooman, 467–68
Estelami, Nicole N., 467–68
Estonia, 766–67
ethics
ACOs and, 269–77
arts and, 273–74
cultural leadership and, 263–64, 269–77
evaluation and, 665–66
funding and, 274–76
leadership and, 263–67, 277
ethnography, 350, 351, 354–55
of museums, 378
Eucharist, 614n.3
EU National Institutes for Culture, 196–97
EURAM Conference, 339n.1
Eurocentrism
in the arts, 204, 215, 733–34

Europe
antitrust law in, 125
arts management in, 142
arts research in, 67–68
cultural funding in, 270, 545, 703
cultural heritage of, 239–40
cultural policy in, 523, 527
cultural production in, 786–87, 788–89, 793–94
cultural promotion in, 185
cultural sector in, 713, 762
digital heritage in, 191
disability access in, 624–25
expos in, 185
festivals in, 397
Hallyu and, 789–90
legal scholarship in, 575
museums in, 606
peripheral regions and, 753*t*
philanthropy in, 526
politics in, 642
Europeana, 191
European Academy of Management, 65
European Capitals of Culture (ECoC), 393, 647, 672–73, 743, 745, 752
impacts of, 744–47, 751–53, 756–57
European Commission, 229–30, 270, 276, 580–81, 587–88, 763
European Court of Justice (ECJ), 579, 586–87, 588
European Journal of Cultural Management and Policy, 6
European Parliament, 225, 231n.7, 232n.14
European Union (EU)
art imports to, 585
art patrons in, 463–64
copyright in, 223–31
cultural heritage and, 239–40
cultural initiatives of, 743, 745
cultural production in, 788
economy of, 763, 767
heritage communities in, 243, 249
tax incentives in, 578, 579, 580–81, 582–88
evaluation, 667
aesthetics and, 650
of culture, 663–64, 665–66, 669–71, 674–76, 674*t*
definition of, 666
legitimacy of, 665–66
study of, 648–50

Evard, Yves, 6, 126–27, 141
Event Canvas methodology, 405–6
event co-creation, 349–50, 351–53, 355–61, 362, 363–64
event management studies, 393, 394–96, 399–400, 402–4, 406
　project management and, 400–2, 404–6
events. *See also* cultural events
　definition of, 393
event studies, 349–51
Ewell, Maryo Gard, 205
executive directors, 79, 84, 284, 286
existentialism, 83
experience
　start-ups and, 712
experiences, 681–83, 685–86, 796
　Of music, 683, 686, 687–90, 691–95
experiential marketing, 683, 695–96
explicit knowledge, 372

F
Faaborg Museum, 511
Facebook, 187
Fairfax, Virginia, 812
fairness doctrine, 231n.1
Falk, John H., 748
Faro Convention, 239–41, 242–44, 245–46, 247–54
　principles of, 242
Faro Convention Network (FCN), 247–48
Faro Venezia, 250–51
Fasan, Marco, 553–54
Father and Son (game), 440, 450n.1
FC Bayern Munich, 120–21
Federal Communications Commission, 179
Federal Council on the Arts and Humanities, 174–76
Federal Emergency Management Agency (FEMA), 810
Federation for the Humanities and Social Sciences (FHSS), 26
feminism
　economics and, 121–22
　theories of, 113, 152
feminist systems theory, 113
Fenko, Anna, 684

Feral File, 603, 604–5, 615n.18, 615–16n.20
Ferando, Christina, 613
Fernandez-Blanco, Victor, 129–30
Ferri, Delia, 623–24
Festival della Filosofia (Festival of Philosophy), 504–5
festivalization of culture, 350–51
festivals
　co-creation of, 349–50, 351–53, 355–61, 362, 363–64
　complexity of, 396
　culinary, 504–5
　ethnography of, 354–55
　evolution of, 349
　history of, 350–51
　leadership of, 284, 285, 294–95
　as liminal space, 350, 353–54, 361–65
　museums and, 728
　music, 681
festival studies, 349–51, 394, 808
fields, academic, 7, 25, 32, 36, 38, 143–44
　definition of, 11–12
　interdisciplinarity of, 4
　professions and, 24
Fillis, Ian, 484
films, 187
finance
　ACOs and, 597–98
　ECoC and, 755–56, 757
　entrepreneurship and, 770, 774
　ethics in, 265, 278
　NFTs and, 597f, 598, 598f, 605–7
Fine Arts Journal, 61–62
Finland, 251–52
Fire Shut Up in My Bones (opera), 308
Flavin, Dan, 587–88
"Floating Piers, The" (art installation), 396
floods, 600–1
Florence Convention, 240
Florence, Italy, 167
　floods in, 600
Florida, Richard, 49, 109, 148*t*
Florida, University of, 815, 816
Florida, USA, 192–93
　servicescapes in, 503–4
Florida State University, 5–6
Floyd, George, 299, 308

Flys, Elena SV, 625, 638n.2
Fombrun, Charles J., 530–31
Fonds de recherche du Québec science et culture (FRQSC), 35
Fontecchio, Italy, 251–53
food
    as art, 727–28
    at concerts, 689, 691
    at festivals, 504–5
Forbes (magazine), 423
Forbidden City (China), 531
Ford Foundation, 627
Foreman, Susan, 460
Foreman-Wernet, Lois, 645
Fortes, Nuno, 685–86
Fortune 500, 94
fossil fuels, 274
Foster, Kenneth, 267–68, 278
Foucault, Michel, 148t, 728–29
Fox, Hannah, 285–87, 289, 290, 295
France
    creative industries in, 44
    cultural bureaucracy of, 168–70, 170f
    cultural enterprises in, 714
    cultural heritage of, 249–50
    cultural policy of, 164–71, 180n.1, 180n.3, 523
    economy of, 766–67
    online arts in, 126
    publications in, 28–29, 29t, 31
    tax incentives in, 578, 581
Franciscan friars, 600
Franklin, Benjamin, 575
Franks, Pamela, 613
Fraser, Andrea, 727–28
Freeman, R. Edward, 653, 654–55
Freeman, Sarah, 719n.4
free riders, 413–14
French language, 26, 27
    publications in, 28, 31
French Model (cultural policy), 164–73, 179
"French Pastels: Treasures from the Vault" (exhibition), 596, 614n.8
Frey, Bruno, 131, 460
Frey, Stef, 427–28
Fribourg Declaration, 243, 255n.13
Frissen, Roel, 405–6

Friuli Doc (festival), 504–5
Frost, Nicola, 351, 363–64
FTX Trading Limited, 613n.2
Fuller, Nancy, 378–79
Fundación Caixa, 625
Fundación Once, 625
Fundación Universia, 625
funding, of arts and culture, 16, 32, 33–34, 34t
    for accessibility, 625–26, 631–32
    in Canada, 31–36, 33t
    conflict and, 538
    COVID-19 and, 539
    cultural planning and, 206–7, 211
    ethics and, 274–77
    markets and, 533
    mechanisms of, 534–35, 536f
    of performing arts, 90
    policies for, 523–24
    race and, 300
    research on, 523, 527
    sources of, 525–27, 529t, 531–32, 536–37
fundraising
    for ACOs, 458–59, 462–64, 467–68, 470–72
    ethics and, 279
    Great Recession and, 545
    marketing and, 457, 459–60, 469–72
    sources of, 552–54
    study of, 545–46, 556–60
"Fusing Arts, Culture and Social Change: High Impact Strategies for Philanthropy" (report), 810

G

Gabriel, Helen, 377
Gainer, Brenda, 460
Gallagher, B. Kathleen, 109, 468
galleries, 510, 727–28
Galloway, S., 131
Gallup, 422, 806–7
gamification, 15, 437–42, 443–45, 444f, 449–50
    impact of, 446t, 446–47, 448–50
Garcia, Beatriz, 744, 746
García Martínez, Elías, 595
Garrido, M. José, 468–69
Gates, Theaster, 723–24, 725, 729, 731–33, 734–35

gender
　arts and, 217, 309, 311–12
　of authors, 8
　of concertgoers, 689–90
　digital access and, 189
　leadership and, 271, 319–20, 322–23, 327, 337
　of museum directors, 322–23, 324, 335f
General Social Survey (GSS), 806, 809
Generation Z, 808
genius loci, 251
genocide, 302–3
Gentile, Chiara, 685
gentrification, 732
Gentry, Alastair, 626
geography
　of authors, 9–10, 19
　of cultural production, 786–90, 798
　entrepreneurship and, 109
　of festivals, 358
　fundraising and, 557
GeoParadise (nonprofit), 354–57
George Mason University, 812
Germany
　arts and cultural management in, 5–6
　arts fundraising in, 461
　copyright in, 229–30
　cultural enterprises in, 713–15, 718
　cultural policy of, 523
　culture funding in, 703
　customs laws of, 586–87
　economy of, 766–67
　music in, 133
　sports in, 133
　tax incentives in, 578
Getty Museum, 527
Getz, Donald, 351, 407n.1, 407n.2
Geursen, Gus, 483
Ghilardi, Lia, 205, 206, 208
Ghosh, Arundhati, 263, 272–73
gifts, 358, 360, 576, 577–78
Gill, Amrit, 287–88, 289, 290, 292, 293, 295
Gilmore, James H., 683, 685
Gini-Simpson Index, 327
Girard, Augustin, 164–67, 180n.3, 180n.4, 180n.6
Giustiniani, Lorenzo, 595, 614n.4
Give2Asia, 579

Giverny, France, 596
Glasgow, Scotland, 276
Global Entrepreneurship and Development Index (GEDI), 763
globalization, 18, 49
Global North, 664, 792
Global South, 19, 789, 790, 792, 796
Goetzmann, William N., 322
Gold, Becky, 636
Goldin, Nan, 723–24, 725, 729–31, 734–35
Goldratt, Eliyahu M., 404–5
Goleman, Daniel, 105–6
Gomes, Pedro, 745–46
Google, 227–29
Gordon, Christopher, 180n.2, 180n.5
Goudey, Alain, 507–8
Goulding, Christina, 503–4
governance
　of ACOs, 79–82, 84, 91–92
　democracy and, 797–98
　models of, 81
　of museums, 316, 317–18, 337–38
　shared leadership and, 292
　social, 792
governments
　cultural policy and, 170–71, 173–74, 523
　evaluation of culture, 647, 676
　funding from, 87–88, 101–2, 524, 525–26, 536
　fundraising and, 552, 554
　legitimacy and, 81
　taxes and, 575, 576–77
　unions and, 423
　violence and, 299–300
Governors State University, 812
Gracie Mansion (New York), 421
Graeae Theatre, 627, 637
graffiti, 59–60
Graham, Martha, 190
grants
　in Canada, 32–33, 35
　from the NEA, 174, 206, 536, 538, 812–13
Grappi, Silvia, 504–5
Gray, Aysa, 311
Gray, Clive, 63–64, 676
Greater London Authority (GLA), 195
Great Recession, 16, 539, 545, 560
Greece, 616n.23, 745

Green Book (UK), 676n.1
greenwashing, 275
Greenwood, Margaret, 647
Greenwood, Royston, 726
Griffero, Tonino, 507
Griffin, Des, 321–22
Griffin, Jennifer J., 320
Grincheva, Natalia, 191, 195–96
Grint, Keith, 264–65, 273
Grizzle, Cleopatra, 469–70
Gross Domestic Product (GDP), 770
Grossetête, Olivier, 396
Gross, Jonathan, 46
Grosvenor, Bendor, 601–2
Gstraunthaler, Thomas, 644–45
Guggenheim Museum of Art, 532–33, 727
Guide to the Project Management Body of Knowledge, A, 402
Gummerus, Johanna, 482
Gupta, Sachin, 461, 471

H
Haacke, Hans, 727
Haanpää, Minni, 349, 352
Haase, Janina, 684, 694–95
Habermas, Jürgen, 148t
habitats
  preservation of, 251
habitus, 143, 144, 147, 152
Hackman, J. Richard, 382–83
Hadley, Bree, 632
Hager, Mark A., 320
Hair, Joseph F., 691–93
Ha, Kyoungnam, 469–70, 471, 552–53
Hallman, Kirstin, 128–29, 130
Hall of Whispers (Viola), 587–88
Hallyu (Korean Wave), 188, 789–90
Hämäläinen, Raimo, 105–6
Hamburg University of Music and Theatre, 5–6
happiness
  cultural economics and, 131–32
happiness research, 124
Hardiman, Kaitlyn, 7
Harrison, David A. 327
Hart, 729–30
Hausmann, Andrea, 468–69

health
  art and, 814–18, 819
HEC-Montréal Business School, 27–29, 30, 35, 36
hedonic products, 683
Hekkert, Paul, 684
Helicon Collaborative, 300, 810
Hellenic Ancient Culture Institute, 616n.23
Helmefalk, Miralem, 684
Helms, Jesse, 538
Hemels, Sigrid, 579
Hemmings, Terry, 378
heritage communities, 239, 241–48, 254. *See also* cultural heritage
  definition of, 243
  participation in, 248–53
heritage sites, 594. *See also* cultural heritage
heritage walks, 249–50
Hermans, Carolien, 626
heterodox economics, 121–22. *See also* economics
Hidalgo, César A., 47, 48
high art, 44. *See also* art
Hill, Liz, 467–68
Hille, Adrian, 133
Hine, Hank, 192
hip-hop diplomacy, 185–86
Hiroshima, 731–32
Hirschman, Elizabeth C., 537, 683
Hispanic Americans
  arts participation of, 811, 812
  arts programs and, 813
historically black colleges and universities (HBCUs), 812
Hitler, Adolf, 512
Hofer, Charles W., 705
Hoffman, Robert, 122
Hokusai, Katsushika, 601–2, 614–15n.12
Holbeck, Leeds, 263
Holbrook, Morris B., 683
Holden, John, 46
Hollywood, 420–21
Hollywood diplomacy, 185–86
Holmes, Kat, 627
Holmes, Sean, 419
Holocaust memorials, 512
HoloLens (AR), 187

Holt, Douglas, 465
Höne, Katherina, 194–95
Hopwood, Anthony G., 646
Horizon (VR), 187
Hôtel du Nord, 249–50, 256n.24
hotels, 685–86
House Committee on Un-American Activities, 420–21
Howkins, John, 45
Huber, Christian, 647
Huelva, Spain, 250
Hughes, Larry, 613
Hultén, Bertil, 684
human capital, 711
   of boards, 316–18, 319
   of museum directors, 337–38
humanities, 654–55
human rights, 196
   cultural heritage and, 239–40, 253
   digital, 196–97
humans
   algorithms and, 227–29
   arts and, 807–8
   COVID-19 impacts on, 785–86
   evaluation by, 649–50
   perception of art, 186–87
   technology and, 191, 791–92, 798
   views of, 302–3, 304, 305
Hungary, 766–67
Hutter, 650
Hybe (company), 188
hybridity
   of arts organizations, 79
Hyde Park Art Center (Chicago), 731–32

I

IATSE, 430n.4
Idanha-a-Nova, Portugal, 357–58
Iglesias, Oriol, 684, 685–86
Illinois, University of, 309
imagination, 50, 443
Impact and Insight Toolkit, 669–70
Impressionism, 596
incentives theory, 222–23
India, 190–91, 270, 789, 796
India Foundation for the Arts, 263, 270, 272–73
Indianapolis, 307
Indianapolis Museum of Art at Newfields, 307–8
indigenous peoples, 241
   festivals and, 354–55
individualism, 303*b*, 305
   donations and, 550, 556–57
Indonesia, 187, 793
industrial revolution, 417
information technology. *See also* technology
   knowledge management and, 375
Inglis, Loretta, 87, 93–94
innovation, 786, 796
   authoritarianism and, 797
input-process-output model, 382–83
Instagram, 429
Institute of Contemporary Arts, 538
Institute of Museum and Library Services (IMLS), 174–76
Institut national de la recherche scientifique (INRS), 35–36, 37
institutional critique, 723–24, 725–29, 735–36
institutional entrepreneurship, 723–24, 725–29, 735–36. *See also* entrepreneurship
institutional isomorphism, 81
institutional theory, 80–81, 84–85, 91–92
institutions
   art and, 724, 725–29, 734
   definition of, 723–24
   disciplines and, 24
instrumental values, 120
integrity, 277*f*, 278
intellectual property, 221–22, 231n.4, 274, 793–95
interdisciplinarity, 4, 7, 12, 141, 152, 154–57, 393
Internal Revenue Service (IRS), 533, 537–38, 545–46
International Andong Mask Dance Festival, 504–5
International Brotherhood of Teamsters, 422–23
International Conference on Cultural Policy Research (ICCPR), 27–28
International Council of Museums (ICOM), 605–6
International Event Management Book of Knowledge Framework, 402

International Francophonie Research Chair
  on Cultural Heritage Policy, 36–37
International Journal of Arts Management, 6,
  28–29, 30, 31, 59, 60–61
International Journal of Cultural Policy, 6, 29,
  59, 60–61, 135–36n.1
*International Journal of the Inclusive Museum,
  The*, 152, 153t
internet. *See also* technology
  access to, 188–89, 194, 197
  history of, 223–25, 231n.6
  marketing and, 468–69
  NFTs and, 615n.19
Internet of Things, 194
interpretivist paradigm, 63–64
intrinsic values, 120
Ioan, Lorenzo, 402–3
Ippolito, Dennis, 414
Ireland, 580, 581, 582
Iseo Lake, 396
Italy, 166–68
  copyright in, 229–30
  creative industries in, 44
  cultural heritage of, 250–53
  cultural policy of, 180n.5, 523
  cultural preservation in, 322, 335
  economy of, 766–67
  festivals in, 397, 405, 504–5
  museums in, 127–28, 440, 503–4
  NFTs in, 615n.14
  state museums in, 316–17, 318–19, 324–26,
    335–37, 338–39, 339n.1
  tax incentives in, 581, 582

J

Jackob, Nikolaus, 530–31
Jacobs, Marc, 734
Jacobson, Barbara, 194–95
Jafari, Aliakbar, 481
James Irvine Foundation, 806–7
Jancovich, Leila, 671–72, 673
Janssen, Ruud, 405–6
Japan, 523–24, 578
  cultural production in, 789
Jaworski, Bernard J., 460
jazz, 190
jazz diplomacy, 185–86

Jeffers, Malina Simone, 307–8
Jesus Christ, 595
Jewish Museum (Berlin), 512
Jewish Museum (Stockholm), 187
Jobst, Johanna, 506
John F. Kennedy Center for the Performing
  Arts, 174–76, 815
Johnson, Steven, 215
Johnston, Kirsty, 632–33
Jones, Bernie, 206, 208–9
Jones, Bryan D., 416
Jones, Chelsea, 632–33
Jones, Kenneth, 302–3, 310–11
Journal of Arts Management, Law, and Society,
  6, 28–29, 59–61, 144, 153t
Journal of Cultural Economics, 6, 59, 60–61,
  121–22, 135–36n.1, 151, 152–53, 155
  Statistics on, 153t
journals, 28–31, 38–39, 60–61, 62, 62f
  arts management and, 142, 145–46, 147,
    152–54, 153t
  impact of, 59
  open systems theory and, 102
Joy, Annamma, 481–82, 483
Joyce, James, 580
Juliana (Queen of the Netherlands), 581
Julie's Bicycle (environmental group), 276
Julmi, Christian, 498, 508–9, 512
Jung, Yuha
  on arts and culture, 534
  background of, 9–10
  on fundraising, 461
  on interdisciplinarity, 7
  on museum management, 375
  on open systems theory, 108–9, 110–11,
    112–13, 534
  on theoretical mapping, 142, 144, 146, 151,
    152

K

Kadishman, Menashe, 512
Kangas, Anita, 167–68
Kant, Ravi, 375
Kaplan, Robert S., 380, 381, 641–42
Karababa, Eminegül, 352–53, 485
Kassel, Germany, 728
Kaszynska, Patrycja, 483

Katsur, Troy, 626
Katz, Richard S., 523
Kaufman, Bruce E., 423
Kaunas, Lithuania, 251
KBF Canada, 579
K-dramas, 794–96
KEA report, 44
Keeney, Kate Preston, 110
Keller, Anthony S., 311–12
Kelly, Christine, 625
Kennedy Center, 174–76, 815
Kentucky, University of, 7, 9–10
Kickstarter, 545–46
Kilowatt Festival, 397
Kim, Mirae, 381, 536
Kim, Sungjin, 461, 471
Kim, Youngseon, 469–70, 471, 552–53
Kinesthetic qualities, 507–8, 510, 511–12
King Baudouin Foundation United States (KBFUS), 578–79
King, Martin Luther Jr., 299–300, 312
KIVA (website), 545–46
Kjeldgaard, Dannie, 352–53, 485
Klamer, Arjo, 120, 664–65
Klein, April, 319–20
Klein, Katherine J., 327
knowledge
  ACOs and, 371–72
  acquisition of, 377, 379*t*
  of business, 710–11, 712
  cultural, 710–12
  cultural events and, 403
  of NFTs, 598–99
  organizational, 372, 373, 384
  subjectivity and, 649–50
  types of, 372, 513
  use of, 384
knowledge management, 15, 371–72, 376–80, 384
  definition of, 372–73, 377
  enablers of, 373–80, 376*t*, 382–83, 383*f*
  orientation, 373, 376–80, 379*t*, 382–83, 383*f*, 384
knowledge processes, 378–79
Koch, Alexander, 302–3
Kohli, Ajay K., 460
Kolkata, 263

Konrad, Elmar D., 708, 709, 710–11, 712
Konstruktion in Emaille I (Telefonbild) (Moholy-Nagy), 587
Korean Wave, 188, 789–90
Kotler, Neil, 461
Kotler, Philip, 458, 461, 497, 500–1
Kotler, Wendy, 461
Kottasz, Rita, 463, 503–4
Kovacs, Jason F., 207, 208
K-pop, 188, 790, 794–95
Krawczyk, Kelly, 552–53
Krebs, Anne, 126–27
Kreiser, Patrick M., 764–65
Krishna, Aradhna, 694–95
kunsthallen, 594
Kunzmann, Klaus R., 207
Kuo, Michelle, 603
Kurbalija, Jovan, 194–95
Kusama, Yayoi, 723–24, 725, 729, 733–35

L
Labaronne, Leticia, 467–68
Labenz, Franziska, 684, 694–95
Labour Economics (journal), 133
Labour Party (UK), 669–70
LaCollection, 596, 601–2, 615n.14
Lakhani, Karim R., 49–50
LaKind, Debra, 596, 613, 614n.9, 614n.11
LaMarre, Andrea, 625, 635
Lamont, Michèle, 648–49, 652
Landry, Charles, 206, 273
Lang, Siglinde, 364
Langton, Chris G., 406
language
  in Canada, 25
Larkin, Roslyn, 266
Larsen, Lotta Bjorklund, 191
LASALLE College of the Arts, 5–6
Las Reinas Magas (The Wise Women) (band), 689
Latin language, 666
Latvia, 766–67
La Valleta, Malta, 746–47
Laval, Université, 37
law
  copyright, 221–27
  creativity and, 221–22

cultural heritage and, 241–48, 249
customs, 585
theories from, 151–52
Lawrence, Thomas B., 725–26
Lazzeretti, Luciana, 44, 49, 50, 54
   on imagination, 50
leadership
   of ACOs, 13–14
   charismatic, 291
   of festivals, 285–86, 288–90, 292
   gender and, 319–20, 322–23, 324, 327, 337
   morality and, 264–67, 271–72, 277
   shared, 283, 284–85, 291–95
   values and, 291
Leahy, Ann, 623–24
Leavitt, Jacqueline, 205, 217
Leca, Bernard, 725–26
Lechner, Michael, 133
Lee, Choon-Ki 504–5
Lee, Clarence, 461, 471
Leeds, England, 263
Lee, Francis, 191
Lee, Heeseok, 374, 375–76, 380–81, 383
Lee, Hyunjung, 469–70, 471, 552–53
Lee, Jin-Soo, 504–5
Lee, Young-Joo, 468
Lefebvre, Henri, 148t, 186
legitimacy, 82–83
   of ACOs, 81, 82, 84, 87–88, 89, 90–91, 92–94
   of arts and cultural management, 60, 61–62, 64–68, 64t, 69t
   of fields, 61–62, 65
   of institutions, 723–24
   social, 108
   theories of, 80–81, 82–83
Lehman, Kim, 484
Leibenstein, Harvey, 123
"Leisure and Subjective Well-Being" (Ateca-Amestoy), 131
Leniaud, Jean-Marie, 242
Leonard-Barton, Dorothy, 374
Leonardo da Vinci Science and Technology Museum, 437–38
Le Roy, Jean-Baptiste, 575
Lerro, Antonio, 748–49, 750
Lévy-Garboua, Louis, 129
Levy, Sydney J., 485

Lewis, Jamie, 285–86, 287–88, 290, 293, 295
Liao, Mei-Na, 460
liberalism, 420–21
libraries, 594, 786–87
Librero-Cano, Alejandro, 745–46
licensing, 225–26
Lichtenstein, Nelson, 423
Lichtmann, John, 467–68
Liddell, Frances, 617n.25
Li, Feng, 748
lifestyle, 683
   arts and, 123–24
Likert scale, 717–18, 719n.2
liminal spaces, 350, 353–54, 361–65
Lincoln Castle, 503–4
Lindinger, Elisa, 196–97
Lin, Yi, 534, 537
Lin, Yi Hsin, 685–86
Lippard, Lucy, 727
Lisi, Domenico, 127–28
literary arts, 808
literature, 649–50
literature reviews, 145
Lithuania, 251, 766–67
Liverpool, England, 672–73, 745
Logic of Collective Action, The (Olson), 413–14
London, 5–6, 463
   charities in, 579
   cultural policy of, 195
   museums in, 503–4
   protests in, 275
   theatre in, 126
London VAT and Duties Tribunal, 587–88
Los Angeles, 206, 209, 421–22, 429, 813
Louis Vuitton (brand), 733
Louvre, 111–12, 126–27, 578
Love, Ann Rowson, 534
Lowry, Glenn, 603
Lucas McKay, Katherine, 774
Luhmann, Niklas, 110
Luijer, Dennis, 405–6
Luxembourg, 745

M
Macau, China, 504–5
MacDonald, Heather, 308–9
MacDowell, Lachlan, 209–10

Mach, David, 538
machine learning, 184
Macron, Emmanuel, 606
Madsen, Tina Annette, 511
Magenta Book (UK), 676n.1
Magna Carta, 503–4
Maheu, René, 163
Mahieu, Sandrine, 530–31
Mainland, Kath, 285–87, 288–89, 290, 293, 295
Making Things Valuable (book), 650
Maldives, 187
managed economy, 763
management, 141, 147–51, 154–55. *See also* arts and cultural management
   of ACOs, 15
   art and, 364–65
   boards and, 319–20, 338
   of cultural enterprises, 718
   of cultural events, 393
   ethics and, 264–67
   festival studies and, 351
   of knowledge, 371–72, 373
   of nonprofits, 106
   theories of, 148t, 151
Management Accounting Research (journal), 646–47
Manet, Edouard, 614n.8
Manhattan, 729–30, 733
Manovich, Lev, 192, 195–96
mapping
   cultural policy and, 163, 171–73, 174, 178, 179–80
   of habitus, 144
   of museums, 195–96
   of strategic planning, 596
   of theories, 144–45, 147
Mapplethorpe, Robert, 538, 587
marching bands, 812
March, James, 524
marginalization, 724, 731–32
Maribor, Slovenia, 746–47
market economy, 525. *See also* economics
market force, 533
marketing
   of ACOs, 15–16, 457, 458–59, 461, 464, 466–67
   branding and, 464–66

   of cultural enterprises, 718
   definition of, 458
   ECoC and, 754
   experiential, 683, 695–96
   fundraising and, 457, 458–60, 462, 469–72
   innovation and, 15
   journals of, 30–31
   morality and, 458–59
   multisensory, 695–96
   of nonprofits, 457
   relational, 437
   types of, 461–62
market orientation, 459–60, 462, 467, 470, 471
markets, 119–20, 122, 125–31, 136n.2, 785–86. *See also* economics
   for art, 484
   arts funding and, 523, 533
market segmentation, 464
Markovic, Stefan, 684, 686
Markusen, Anne, 46
Marseille, 249–50
Marshall, Alfred, 124–25
Martel, Frédéric, 789–90
Martin, Laurent, 164–65
Martin, Ron, 47–48
Marty, Paul F., 375
Marxian economics, 121–22
Marx, Karl, 146–47, 148t
Mashburn, Whitney, 625
Mason, Marco, 375
Mason, Michela C., 504–5
Massachusetts, 205, 320
Massachusetts Institute of technology (MIT), 186–87
Massiah, Carolyn, 501–2
Matarasso, François, 273, 666, 667, 672, 673, 675
Matera, Italy, 744, 751–54, 753t, 755–56, 757
Matera Basilicata 2019 Foundation, 751
mathematics, 668
Matlin, Marlee, 626
Maton, Karl, 144
Mauss, Marcel, 143
Mautz, R.K., 646, 648, 651–52
McClelland, David C., 713
McColl-Kennedy, Janet R., 501
McDonnell, Diarmuid, 468

McGill, Anthony, 308-9
McGill, Demarre, 308-9
McGraw, Hesse, 732
McIntyre, Charles, 510
McKay, Kieryn, 667
McKenzie, Jordi, 129
McMaster University, 37
McNulty, Robert, 206
Meamber, Laurie A., 482
measurement
   of ACO performance, 765-66
mechanisms, 534-35
mechanistic systems, 104
Mediterranean region, 753t
mega-platforms, 793-96
Mehrabian, Albert, 498-99
Meier, Stephan, 460
Meireles, Cildo, 728
Melbourne, Australia, 285, 286-87, 289-90, 291
Melbourne Festival of the Arts, 286-87
Melbourne, University of, 195-96
Melotti, Gian Carlo, 286
Menil Collection, 607
Mercer, Colin, 207, 208
Mercouri, Melina, 745
Merritt, Elizabeth, 192
metaverse, 187-89
methodologies, 59-60, 66, 67, 68-69, 70-71
methods, 59-60, 62-69, 70-71
MeToo movement, 152
Metro Arts, 287-88
Metropolitan Museum of Art, 532, 537-38, 602-3, 731
Metropolitan Opera, 308, 468
Meyrick, Julian, 645
Michigan, 422
Michigan Council for Cultural Affairs, 625
Microsoft, 187
migration, 244
Mihailova, Mihaela, 192-93
Milan, 437-38
Miles, Steven, 627
military, arts and, 814-15
Miller, Merton H., 765-66
Miller, Peter, 648
Miller, Toby, 6, 168

Ministère de la culture et des communications (Quebec), 35-36
Ministry of Culture (France), 164-65, 180n.3
Ministry of Culture (MIC) (Italy), 317, 318-19, 322, 335, 337, 338
Ministry of Economy and Finance (Italy), 318-19
Ministry of Propaganda (Nazi Germany), 173-74
Minneapolis, 299
Minnesota, University of, 426
Mintzberg, Henry, 719n.4
Mio, Chiara, 553-54
Mitacs (nonprofit), 35
Mitsufuji, Toshioa, 378-79
Modestini, Dianne, 595
Modigliani, Franco, 765-66
Modigliani-Miller theorems, 774
Moeran, Brian, 524
Moholy-Nagy, László, 587
Moments of Valuation (book), 650
Monaco Roundtable on Cultural Action and Policy, 163-64
Mona Lisa, 510-11
Monet, Claude, 596, 614n.8
Monfries, Kristi, 288, 290, 291, 295
monopolies, 417
Mons, Belgium, 745
Montague, Alan, 266
Montanari, Fabrizio, 504-5
Montgomery, John, 208
Montgomery, Sarah S., 129-30
Monti, Alberto, 85-86, 93, 320-21, 322, 327
Montmarquette, Claude, 129
Montoya, Detra Y., 501
Montréal, Université de, 37
Moore, Anne, 613
Moore, Mark H., 381
morality
   arts and, 273-74
   marketing and, 458-59
Moreau, François, 126
Moreira, António C., 685-86
Morgan, Anne, 616-17n.25
Morgan Library, 605
Morin, Edgar, 395
Morris, Charles G., 382-83

Moss-Pultz, Sean, 613
motivation, 712–13
Moussouri, Theano, 375
movies
    digitalization of, 122
movie theaters
    economics of, 125, 129–30
Mozart effect, 132–33
Mukherjee, Kamaleswar, 263, 268, 278
Mulligan, Martin, 209–10
multidisciplinarity, 7. *See also* interdisciplinarity
"Multi-Modal Understanding of Arts Participation, A" (report), 808
multipolarism, 797–98
multisensory perception, 683, 684, 686, 687–89, 687f, 690, 693–96
    measurement of, 688t, 692t
Mumbai, 263
Municipal Art Museum Association (Suzhou), 537–38
Muñiz, Christina, 130
museology, 146–47, 152, 154
Museo Mann, 450n.1
museum decolonization, 274
museum directors, 321–25, 326, 329–35, 337, 338–39
    data on, 326t, 330t, 331t, 332t, 333t, 334f, 335f
Museum from Home (app), 186–87
Museum Management and Curatorship, 378–79
Museum of Cycladic Art, 616n.23
Museum of Fine Arts, 111–12
Museum of Fine Arts Boston
    collections of, 614n.8
    NFTs and, 599–607, 614n.9, 614n.11
    strategy of, 601f
Museum of Modern Art (MOMA), 439, 531, 532–33, 603–5, 604f, 606–7
museums
    atmosphere of, 510, 512
    attendance at, 806–7
    Balanced Scorecard and, 381
    boards of, 323–25, 328t, 329–35
    business models of, 614n.6, 748
    creativity and, 531
    critiques of, 724, 730, 731, 734–35
    digital experiences and, 444f, 446t
    digitalization and, 437–39, 441, 442–43, 444–45, 446–47
    directors of, 321–25, 326, 326t, 327, 328t, 329–35 (*see also* museum directors)
    evaluation and, 644
    evolution of, 315–16
    festivals and, 728
    funding of, 527, 531, 532–33, 593, 597–98, 602–3
    fundraising of, 463–64, 553–54
    gamification and, 438–42, 443–45, 447, 449, 450
    governance of, 316–17, 321–22, 337–38
    hiring practices of, 307–8
    internet and, 126–28
    in Italy, 317, 318–19, 322, 325–26, 335–37, 339n.1
    knowledge management and, 375–76, 378–79
    laws and, 585
    mapping of, 195–96
    marketing of, 469–70
    NFTs and, 593–94, 596, 598–611
    open systems theory and, 108–9, 110–11
    patronage and, 786–87
    performance art in, 727–28
    research focus on, 66, 67
    servicescape of, 503–4, 504t
    state-owned, 316–17, 321, 325–26, 338–39, 339n.1
    stores at, 602–3
    strategic planning and, 596–97
    taxes and, 576, 582, 583., –84, 602–3
    traveling, 753t
    virtualization of, 186–87
museumscape, 503–4
music
    benefits of, 132–33
    digitalization of, 122, 126
    experience of, 686, 687–89, 691–95
    kinesthetic qualities of, 507–8
    live, 681, 684
    pricing of, 134
    in South Korea, 794–95
musicians
    unionization of, 417

Muslim world, 789–90
mutual causality, 103–4
Myerhoff, Barbara, 353–54
Myers, Michael D., 49

N
Naess, Arne, 103–4
Nahavandi, Afsaneh, 264
Naples, 440, 450n.1
Narcissus Garden (Kusama), 733–34
Narver, John C., 460
Nason, Robert W., 765–66
National Alliance of Theatrical Employees, 417, 430n.2
National Archeological Museum (Naples), 440
National Archive of Data on Arts and Culture (NADAC), 809
National Arts Participation Survey (Australia), 625–26
National Arts Statistics and Evidence Reporting Center (NASERC), 809, 810
National Association of Latino Arts and Culture (NALAC), 813
National Committee for Responsive Philanthropy, 810
National Construction Alliance, 423
National Endowment for the Arts (NEA), 174, 206, 523–24, 812–13
  censorship of, 179, 538
  DEIA and, 811
  environment and, 276
  ethics and, 270
  governance recommendations, 81
  grants from, 174, 206, 536, 538, 812–13
  office of Research and Analysis, 806
  research by, 806–7, 808, 809–10, 812–19
National Endowment for the Humanities (NEH), 174–76
National Foundation on Arts and Humanities, 174–76
National Gallery of Art (USA), 174
National Gallery of Denmark, 511–12
National Institutes of Health (NIH), 815
nationalism, 728
National Labor Relations Board (NLRB), 411–12, 423, 427

National Library of Ireland, 580
National Park Service (USA), 174–76
national projection, 185
National Studies of Cultural Policy (series), 164
National Theatre Live, 126
National Theatre (Washington, DC), 420
Native Americans, 204, 302–3, 812, 813
  in arts management, 311
"Native Arts and Culture: Resilience, Reclamation, and Relevance" (report), 812
Native Arts and Cultures Foundation, 812
Nazism, 512
  cultural policy of, 173–74
NEA Research Labs, 809, 813, 815, 817
Nemunas River, 251
neocolonialism, 798
neo-institutional theory, 106, 108
neoliberalism, 649, 654–55
  copyright and, 222–23
  culture and, 664
Netflix, 49, 50, 789, 795–96
Netherlands, 523, 578, 580, 581–82, 584
  festivals in, 355
networking
  cultural events and, 402–3
networks
  cultural entrepreneurship and, 761–62
  in entrepreneurship, 707–8, 709, 716–17
neurodiversity, 633, 636, 638n.6, 733
New Haven, Connecticut, 205, 206
New Orleans Museum of Art, 616–17n.25
New York City, 88, 421–22, 603, 734
  galleries in, 727–28
  museums in, 273, 439, 531, 603
  photography in, 727
New York Philharmonic, 88, 89
New York Post, 421
New York (state), 422
New York State Mediation Board, 421
New York Times, 424, 613n.2
New Zealand, 241
  cultural policy of, 67
Next Wave (arts festival), 285–86, 287–88, 289–90, 291, 292, 293–95
Nguyen, Godefroy Dang, 126
Nguyen, Michael, 613

Nigeria, 789
Noci, Giuliano, 685
Nolan, Yvette, 80, 91–92
Nolin, Heather R., 614–15n.12
Nolin-Whitaker Method (NWM), 596, 597–98, 611–12
Nollywood, 789
Nonaka, Ikujiro, 373, 375, 377
Nondualistic approaches, 506–8, 512–13
non-fungible tokens (NFTs), 16, 613n.1, 613n.2
    art and, 593–95
    arts and cultural management and, 611–12
    criticism of, 594–95
    funding and, 599–610, 608f, 616–17n.25
    institutions and, 609–10, 610f, 612–13
    museums and, 594, 596, 598–603
    study of, 59–60, 65, 68, 598–99
    uses of, 609–10, 611
non-governmental organizations (NGOs). See also nonprofits
    governments and, 254
nonprofit industrial complex (NPIC), 310, 311
nonprofit management, 106. See also management, arts and cultural management
nonprofits
    ACOs and, 80
    boards of, 79–80, 84, 316, 319–21
    competition among, 129
    creative ecosystem and, 46
    cultural enterprises and, 703, 706
    cultural planning and, 203, 204, 207–8, 209, 218
    diversity and, 320–21, 323–25
    evaluation of, 648
    fundraising of, 545–47, 549, 554
    marketing and, 457, 458–59, 460, 461–62, 469
    NFTs and, 594
    performance of, 381
    pricing and, 133–34, 135
    ratings of, 555
    revenue of, 467–68, 469–70
    in the USA, 111
nonstate actors
    cultural diplomacy and, 183
NORC (University of Chicago), 806–7

norms, 108
    art and, 724, 734
    of cultural policy, 168–70, 179–80, 181n.11
    of institutions, 723–24, 726
    legitimacy and, 82–83
North America
    arts management research in, 65–66, 67–68
    philanthropy in, 526
Norton, David P., 380, 381, 641–42
Not Just Money: Equity Issues in Cultural Philanthropy, 300
Novels, 807
Nutcracker (ballet), 309
Nuttall, Peter J., 470, 471
Nye, Joseph S. Jr., 664–65
Nysveen, Herbjorn, 686

O

Oakes, Helen, 647–48
Oakes, Steve, 647–48
Obama, Barack, 302
Obarzanek, Gideon, 285–87, 289, 290, 292, 293, 295
objectivity, 303b, 304
O'Brien, Dave, 483, 647, 648
Occidental College, 813
off-Broadway theatre, 421
Office of Research and Analysis (NEA), 806
O'Grady, Alice, 353–54
Oiseaux de Passage, Les (birds of passage) (website), 249–50
Okun, Tema, 302–5, 306–7, 310–11
Oldenburg, Claes, 586–87
Oliver, Richard L., 688t
Olson, Mancur, 413–15
Olympics, 393
On Justification: Economies of Worth, 527–28
online communities, 791. See also communities; internet
online content-sharing service providers (OCSSPs), 225–29, 231–32n.11
Online Etymology Dictionary, 666
Open Access (union initiative), 412, 425–29
Open Archive (Budapest), 187
open systems
    cultural events as, 396–97
open systems theory, 101, 102, 103–6, 114, 534

in arts management, 101–3, 108–10, 114, 534
DEI and, 102–3, 110–14
environment and, 104–5, 110–11
history of, 103–4
organization theory and, 106–8, 114
opera
diversity and, 327
servicescape and, 505–6
Opera del Duomo di Firenze, 605
opioids, 724, 730
orchestras, 87–89, 535
in the USA, 88, 89
Oregon Arts Commission, 625
organic systems, 104
Organisation for Economic Co-operation and Development (OECD), 576, 577
organizational ecology theory, 108, 109
organizations. *See also* arts and cultural organizations (ACOs)
business model of, 748–50
cultural enterprises as, 708–9
culture of, 374, 375
entrepreneurship and, 764–65
environment of, 101, 104, 105, 108, 109, 110–11
festivals and, 351
knowledge and, 373–74, 375–76, 377
open systems theory and, 106–8
orientation of, 376–77
performance of, 380–82, 383, 383f, 384
structure of, 374
systems thinking and, 105–6
theories of, 148t, 151, 154–55
organization theory, 107
Orsini, Michael, 625
Oscars (awards), 626, 790
Oster, Sharon, 322
Ostrower, Francie, 319–20
O'Sullivan, Carolin, 467–68
O'Sullivan, Terry, 467–68
Othello (character), 420
Ottawa, University of, 28–29, 36–37
Our Town initiative, 816
ownership
of NFTs, 595
Oxford University Press, 650

P

Padanyi, Paulette, 460
Page, Stephen J., 407n.1
Paggiaro, Adriano, 504–5
paintings
legal definition of, 587
Pak (artist), 594–95
Palau de les Arts Reina Sofía (Valencia), 505–6
Paley, William S., 613n.2
Palmer, Robert, 393
Palmyra Teatro, 637
Panama, 354–55
Pandey, Sanjay K., 381
Pandey, Sheela, 381
Paolucci, Antonio, 167
Papalia, Carmen, 625
Paquette, Jonathan, 6–7, 12, 141–42, 144, 147, 154–55
Paradiso, Livio, 404–6
Parasite (film), 790
Paris
museums in, 111–12
Partners for Livable Places (nonprofit), 206
paternalism, 303b
"Paths to Participation: Understanding How Art Forms and Activities Intersect" (report), 808
paticca samuppada (Buddhism), 103–4
patronage
of cultural sector, 786–87, 788, 793–94
Paxton, Pamela, 555–56
Peacock, Darren, 375
Pecqueur, Antoine, 789
pedagogical theory, 152, 154
Pederson, Jesper Strandgaard, 524
Pedersen, Per E., 686
Pelé effect, 132–33
Peñaloza, Lisa, 485
Pendergast, William, 165, 180n.1
Pennsylvania, 422
perfectionism, 302–3, 304
"Perfect Moment, The," (Mapplethorpe), 538
performance
of ACOs, 762
of start-ups, 717
performance evaluation
approaches to, 651–52
in the arts, 641–43, 648–50, 652–56
studies of, 643–46

performing arts
    attendance of, 806–7, 808
    audiences and, 94
    Balanced Scorecard and, 381
    decision-making in, 80, 86–88, 93–94
    disability access in, 625–27, 628–30, 637–38
    governance and, 79–82, 84, 86–88, 91–92
    NFTs and, 594
    research focus on, 66, 67
    social justice and, 623–24
    unions and, 416–20
Performing Arts: The Economic Dilemma (Baumol and Bowen), 151
Perloff, Harvey, 206, 209
Perry, Bryn, 401
Persée database, 31
personhood doctrine, 231n.1
Pervan, Simon J., 470, 471
PEST (political, economic, social, and technological) model, 535
Petrie Institute of Western American Art, 609–10
Pfeffer, Jeffrey, 108
Phamaly Theatre, 637
phenomenology, 63, 507, 510
Philadelphia, Pennsylvania, 88, 538, 812
philanthropy
    politics and, 538
    research on, 810
    venture, 526
philosophy
    cultural value and, 664
    ethics and, 266
    open systems theory and, 103–4, 114
    theories from, 148t, 151–52
photography, 727, 731, 813
Piber, Martin, 644–45, 647–48, 671–72, 673, 675
Pielichaty, Hanya, 403–4
Pine, B. Joseph, 683, 685
Piotrovsky, Mikhail, 609
Piper, Adrian, 726
piracy, digital, 122, 126
Piranesi, Giovanni Battista, 614–15n.12
Pissaro, Camille, 614n.8
Pisticci, Italy, 751
Pizzi, Alejandro, 170–71

place, 468, 796
Plakoyiannaki, Emmanuela, 466–67
plants, 104
Plate Convergence (exhibition), 731–32
Plato, 668
Plattner, Stuart, 482
play
    economics and, 120
    festivals and, 353–54
pleasure-arousal-dominance (P-A-D) model, 498–500
pluralism, 415–16, 675–76
PMBOK Guide, 402
podcasts, 441, 442, 443–44, 449
    impact of, 445, 446, 446t, 447–48
Poellmann, Lorenz, 468–69
Poetics (journal), 29, 59, 60–61
poetry, 807
Pola Museum of Art, 527
Poland, 229–30, 766–67
police, 299–300
policy
    economy and, 763
    entrepreneurship and, 775–76
    public opinion and, 415–16
    social, 668, 669
    theories of, 148t, 151
political science
    funding of, 35
politics, 414–16
    art and, 525, 727, 728–29
    of cultural value, 663–64, 675–76
Pompeii, 325–26
Ponzi schemes, 594–95
Poon, Patrick, 685–86, 694–95
Pop Art, 724, 733–34, 735
popular culture, 44, 646–47
    arts and, 129
    international, 185–86
population ecology theory, 106, 108
Portugal
    festivals in, 355, 357–58
positivism
    in studies of diplomacy, 194
positivist paradigm, 63–64
postcolonialism, 482
Postma, Jan, 603

postmodernism, 364
    open systems theory and, 113
Potenza, Italy, 751
Potts, Jason, 42–43, 47
poverty, 667–68
Powell, Walter W., 108, 724
practice, theory of, 142, 143–44, 155
pragmatism, 653–54
Pratt, Andy C., 121
Preece, Chloe, 484
Preece, Stephen B., 527, 535, 553–54
Prescription Addiction Intervention Now
    (P.A.I.N.), 730–31
preservation
    of culture, 315–16
    in Italy, 318–19, 322
President's Committee for the Arts and
    Humanities (PCAH), 174–76, 178f
prices
    arts and, 133–35
Prieto-Rodriguez, Juan, 122–23, 129–30
printing press, 223–25
private sector, 524
privatization
    of technology, 227
Producing Managers' Association (PMA), 418
product (marketing), 466–67
professions, 23–24
profit, 761–62
programmed freedom, 350
Program of Canadian Research Chairs, 36
project building, 404–5
project management, 394–96, 400–2, 404–6,
    754. *See also* management
Project Management Institute, 402
project planning, 404–5
Prolific Academic (crowdsourcing platform),
    444–45
promotion (marketing), 468–69
propaganda, 193, 797
psychology
    cognitive, 684
    economics and, 122–23, 124
    theories of, 148t, 152, 153
publications, 28–31, 29t
public domain, 221–22
public entrepreneurship, 725, 732–33

public good, 675–76
public relations (PR), 458–59
public support, of arts, 526–27. *See also*
    funding, of arts and culture
public value, 381
Pulido, Cristian, 466
punctuated equilibrium theory, 413, 415–16
Punggi Ginseng Festival, 504–5
punk, 729–30, 735
Purdue Pharma, 730

Q

qualifications, for arts jobs, 110
qualitative approach, 673
quality of life, 718
Qualls, Larry, 729–30
quantitative data, 664
quantitative studies, 67
Québec, 27, 30, 35
Québec city, 37
Queens Museum, 273

R

Race
    ACOS and, 204, 216–17
    of art donors, 463
    arts participation and, 808
    cultural planning and, 217
    DEIA and, 814
    festivals and, 358
    theatre and, 420
    theories of, 152
Race Against Time (game), 440
racial justice, 299–300, 306, 310
racism, 299–300, 301–2, 305–6
    art and, 733–34
    in theatre, 424–25
    in the USA, 299–300, 301, 306, 310, 312, 805
Rafiq, Mohammed, 377, 378
Raicovich, Laura, 273
Raimondo, Gina M., 194–95
Ramaswamy, Venkat, 352–53
Ranucci, Rebecca, 470, 471
rap diplomacy, 185–86
Rascuite, Simona, 131
rationalism
    event studies and, 349–50

Rauh, Andreas, 510–11
Raunig, Gerald, 728–29
Ravanas, Philippe, 134–35, 466
Ray, Gene, 728–29
realist paradigm, 63–64
Real-Time Diplomacy (Seib), 190
Reas, Casey, 603, 615n.18
Rebuild Foundation, 732
Redaelli, Eleonora, 141–42, 144
Regional Entrepreneurship and Development
 Index (REDI), 763–65, 764*t*, 766, 767, 769,
 770–76, 771*t*, 772*t*
regions
 entrepreneurship and, 763, 767, 775–76
regulation
 of copyright, 229–31
Relational Aesthetics, 727–28
relationship fundraising, 462
relationship marketing, 15–16, 437, 461–62,
 470, 471. *See also* marketing
relationship portfolio, 709, 710
religion
 sociology of, 148*t*
Rentschler, Ruth, 6, 320, 321–22, 461, 483
Republican Party (USA), 525
reputation, 89
reputation force, 530–31, 537–38
research
 on the arts, 806–7, 808, 809–10, 813–18, 819
 structure of, 23–24
research chairs
 in Canada, 36–37, 38–39
Research Grants in the Arts, 809, 813
resource-based theory, 319
resource dependency theory, 84–85, 90, 91–92,
 106, 108, 109–10, 319
resource diversification, 109–10
responsibility assignment matrix (RAM), 405
Ressler, Robert W., 555–56
Reynolds, Jeremy, 309
rhizomes, 105
Rialp, Josep, 684, 686
Rice, Carla, 625, 635
Richards, Greg, 393
right-to-work laws, 430n.3
Rijeka, Croatia, 746–47
Rijksmuseum (Amsterdam), 581–82
Ringle, Christian M., 691–93

Rising (arts festival), 285–87, 288–89, 290, 291,
 292, 293, 294–95
Rittel, Horst W.J., 663, 666–69, 671, 675–76
ritual, 646–47
 festivals as, 350, 351, 353
ritualization, 353–54, 361
Rius-Ulldemolins, Joaquim, 168–70
Roberge, Jonathan, 37
Robert Wood Johnson Foundation, 815
Robeson, Paul, 420
Robinson, Mark, 666
Robinson, Michael D., 129–30
Rodner, Victoria L., 485
Rodriguez, Dylan, 310
Rodríguez, José, 748
Rodriguez, Plácido, 130
Roman Catholicism, 614n.3
Romania, 250
Rome, 325–26
Rome Film Fest, 405
Rosenbaum, Mark S., 501–2
Ross, Chris, 483
Rossiter, John R., 498–99
Roswell, Ellen, 145
Rotana Group, 789
Rowe, David, 667
Royal Academy of Music (UK), 582
Royal National Theatre, 125–26
Royal Swedish Academy of Sciences, 23
Royce, Susan J., 748
Ruangrupa (artist collective), 793
Rudan, Elena, 746–47
Rudin, Scott, 424–25
Ruffa, Michela, 404–6
Ruhr (region), 647
Rushton, Michel, 133–34
Russell, Harold, 626
Russell, James A., 498–99
Rutte, Mark, 581

S

Saarinen, Esa, 105–6
Sacco, Pier Luigi 19, 791–92
Sackler family, 730–31
sacred value, 491
safe harbors (copyright), 223–25, 231n.9
safe spaces, 350, 361–62, 364–65
Salancik, Gerald R., 108

Salisbury, Robert H., 414–15
Salmela, Ulla, 252
Salvator Mundi (da Vinci), 595
San Antonio, Texas, 208
Sánchez-Guijo, Fernando, 626–27
Sanchez, Sofia Izquierdo, 129–30
Šančiai, Lithuania, 251
Sandahl, Carrie, 626–27
Sandals, Leah, 626
Sandfort, Jodi R., 381
San Jose, Rebecca, 468–69
San Pietro di Castello (basilica), 595, 614n.1
Sansepolcro, Italy, 397
Santa Croce, 600
Santiago, Ramiro, 685–86
Saren, Michael, 508
Sargeant, Adrian, 460, 461, 465–66
Sarr, Felwine, 606
Sarstedt, Marko, 691–93
Savoy, Bénédicte 606
Saxons, in Romania, 250
Scabby the Rat (union symbol), 411, 430n.1
Scherdin, Mikael, 761–62
Scherhag, Christian, 461
Scheytt, Tobias, 647
Schifferstein, Hendrik N.J., 684
Schiuma, Giovannia, 748–49, 750
Schmidt, Bryan, 363–64
Schmitt, Bernd H., 683, 685–86
Schmitz, Hermann, 507
Schrander, Florian, 748
Schroeder, Jonathan E., 465
Schultze, Ulrike, 498
Schumpeter, Joseph, 124–25
science
    in Canada, 27
    logic of, 642, 650
    policy and, 668, 669
science fiction, 187
Science Museum (London), 275
SciVal (database), 28, 31
Scopus (database), 30–31
Scotland, 488. *See also* United Kingdom
Scott, Carol A., 664–65
Scott, W. Richard, 104–5
sculpture
    legal definition of, 586–88

Seaman, Bruce A., 136n.2
Second City (comedy club), 428
Second Life (online game), 187
segregation, in theatre, 420
Seib, Philip, 190
Selden, Sally Coleman, 381
self-regulation, 107
Senegal, 167–68
Senge, Peter, 105–6
sensory experience, 683. *See also* experiences, multisensory experience
Service Employees International Union (SEIU), 422–23
servicescape
    approaches to, 497–98, 508–10, 512–13
    environment of, 497, 500–2, 502*t*, 503–4
    of museums, 503–4, 504*t*
    research on, 498–500, 503–8, 510–12
    virtual, 512–13
sexism, 734
    in theatre, 424–25
Shaheed, Farida, 242
Shah, H.G., 375
Shakespeare, William, 309
"Shalechet" (Fallen Leaves) (Kadishman), 512
Shane, Rachel, 145
Shanghai, 531
Shapolsky et al. Manhattan Real Estate Holdings, a Real-Time Social System, as of May 1, 1971 (Haacke), 727
Shavemaker, Margriet, 613
Shell (corporation), 275
Sheppard, Beverly K., 748
Sherer, Peter D., 90, 92, 109–10
Sherry, John F. Jr., 481–82
Shilbury, David, 6
Shindle, Kate, 425, 426, 429
Shin, Sunny Y., 129
Shone, Anton, 401
Shon, Jongmin, 468
Sidford, Holly, 810
Simmons, Robert, 129–30
Simon, Herbert, 524
Singapore, 5–6, 440
Singer, Marie-Noëlle, 748
Singer, Peter, 265, 267
Singh, Jatinder J., 685–86
Sirayi, Mzo, 364

Six Alternating Cool White/Warm White Fluorescent Lights Vertical and Centered (Flavin), 587–88
Skard, Siv, 686
SK Telecom, 188
Slater, Stanley F., 460
Slembeck, Tilman, 467–68
Slevin, Dennis P., 706
Slovakia, 766–67
Slovenia, 766–67
Slung Low (theatre company), 263, 278
Small Business Administration, 174
smart cities, 194
smell, 689, 694
    servicescapes and, 511–12
Smith, Adam, 124–25
Smith, Brett R., 553
Smithsonian Institution, 174–76, 469–70
Snow Crash (novel), 187
social categorization theory, 324, 415
social comparison, 415
social competence, 710–11
social identification, 415
social identity theory, 413, 415
socialism
    culture ministries and, 168
sociality, 732
social justice
    arts leadership and, 14
    performing arts and, 623–24
    unions and, 429–30
social media, 437–38, 441, 793–96
    ACOs and, 190–91
    impacts of, 193
    promotion and, 468–69
social movements
    open systems theory and, 101
social network theory, 84–85
social policy, 668, 669
Social Return on Investment, 664–65
social science
    arts management and, 69
    festival studies and, 351
Social Sciences and Humanities Research Council of Canada (SSHRC), 32–33, 33*t*, 34*t*, 35

social structure
    taxonomy of, 42
Social Theory, Politics, and the Arts (STP&A) conference, 6, 27–28
social value judgment theory, 80–82, 85–86, 87, 90, 91, 94
societal orientation, 460
Société québécoise de sciences politiques (SQSP), 27
society
    festivals and, 357
Socio-Economic Panel Study (SOEP) (Germany), 133
sociology
    arts management and, 63–64, 66
    cultural policy and, 173
    economics and, 121–22
    of festivals, 351
    theories from, 147–51
    of valuation, 648–49
Some Aspects of French Cultural Policy (Girard), 180n.3
Song, Michael C., 765–66
songs, 689
Sonke, J., 815
Sotheby's, 613n.2
Sound Health initiative, 815
South Arts (Atlanta), 625
South Australia, University of, 5–6
Southeast Asia, 290
South Korea, 188, 504–5
    cultural production in, 789–90, 793–96
Soviet Union, 190
    culture ministry of, 168
Sowa, Jessica E., 381, 468
Spain, 126–27, 129–30, 580
    copyright in, 229–30
    creative industries in, 44
    cultural heritage of, 250
    disability access in, 623–24, 625, 628–29, 634, 637
    museums in, 439
    music in, 681
Spaulding, John T., 614n.9
Spence, Charles, 508
Spicer, André, 264
Spigel, Ben, 52, 53

Spiller, Nicola, 685
Spoleto, Italy, 286
sponsorship
   of festivals, 358, 359
sports
   arts and, 123–24, 129–30, 132–33
   benefits of, 132–33
   happiness and, 131–32
Srakar, Andrej, 170–71, 745–46, 770, 774, 775
SSNIP (small but significant nontransitory increase in price), 125
Stabell, Charles, 498
stagehands
   unionization of, 417
stakeholders
   business models and, 748–49, 749f, 750, 755
   of cultural events, 397–98, 398f
stakeholder theory, 84–85, 91
Stalker, George M., 107–8
Stam, Erik, 52, 53, 54
Standard Oil, 417
standard utility theory, 123
Stanley, Christine, 275–76
Starbucks, 423–24
Star Garden (club), 411–12, 428–29
Stark, David, 650
Starry Night (van Gogh), 603–4, 606–7
start-ups, 705. *See also* cultural enterprises
State Data Infrastructure Project for Arts Education, 810
State Department (USA), 174
State Hermitage Museum (St. Petersburg), 593–94, 609
states
   diplomacy and, 183
status, 88–89, 94
Stedelijk Museum (Amsterdam), 585
Stefancic, Jean, 301–2
Steinberg, Katharina, 512
Stenslund, Anette, 511
Stephenson, Neal, 187
Sterback, Elise, 45, 46
Stern, Leonard N., 616n.23
Stevenson, David, 671–72, 673
Stevenson, Deborah, 206, 667
Stigler, George, 128–29
Still, William Grant, 308

stimulus-organism-response (S-O-R) paradigm, 498–99
Stipanović, Christian, 746–47
St. John, Graham, 354, 363–64
Stockenstrand, Anna-Karin, 535
Stockholm, 187
Stoneham, Nathan, 288, 289–90, 291, 295
Stone, Melissa M., 319–20
storytelling, 66
St. Petersburg, Russia, 593–94
Strasbourg, 167
strategy
   in entrepreneurship, 705
streaming
   Economics of, 122, 126
Streed, Odile, 462–63, 466
strikebreakers, 418, 419
strikes, 411, 418–19, 420, 421, 422
structural contingency theory, 107–8
Stutzer, Alois, 131
Suárez, Maria J., 130
subcultures, 791
Subjective Wellbeing, 664–65
subjectivity, 649–50, 652
subtitles, 794–95
Suchman, Mark C., 61–62
Suddaby, Roy, 90, 92, 109–10, 725–26
Sunley, Peter, 47–48
surrealism, 192
Survey of Public Participation in the Arts (SPPA), 806, 807, 809, 811
sustainability, 270
   arts and, 364–65
   arts and cultural management and, 5
   cultural events and, 406
   culture and, 718
   economic, 598–99, 610
   festivals and, 357–58
sustainable development, 253–54, 256n.17
Sustainable Development Goals (UN), 239–40
Suzhou, China, 531, 537–38
Swanson, Scott R., 123–24, 466–67
Sweden, 535, 766–67
   virtual embassy of, 187
Swedish Institute, 187
Switzerland, 730
   museums in, 322

SWOT (strength, weaknesses, opportunities, and threats) analysis, 403–4
Sydney, Australia, 287–88, 290
synesthetic qualities, 508, 510, 511–12
systematic literature review (SLR), 142, 145, 146–47, 155
systems
   levels of, 104
systems intelligence, 103, 105–6, 110
systems leadership, 103, 105–6, 110
systems theory, 102–4, 112, 113–14
systems thinking, 102, 103, 105–6
Szerb, László, 763

T

tacit knowledge, 372
Taheri, Babak, 481
Tajfel, Henri, 415
Tajtáková, Mária, 462–63
Takeuchi, Hirotaka, 375
Tangled Art + Disability (nonprofit), 626
Tapp, Shelley R., 469–70, 471
Tasmania, 286–87
taste, 694
Tate Modern, 190–91, 538, 587–88
Tate Museum, 440, 615n.13
tax credits, 578
taxes, 575, 576–77, 582–84
   ACOs and, 578
   art and, 580–82
   fundraising and, 463–64
   museums and, 602–3
   nonprofits and, 111
   in the USA, 176
tax incentives, 575–77, 578–79, 581–88
   for ACOs, 577–80, 583–85, 588
   art and, 523–24, 580–81
   knowledge and, 579–80
taxonomy, 42–47
Taylor, Johanna K., 112–13
Taylor, Susan, 616–17n.25
technology. *See also* digitalization
   access to, 792
   copyright and, 223, 226–29
   cultural diplomacy, 183–89, 193–98
   cultural economics and, 120–21
   impacts of, 791–94, 798

television, 794–95
   digitalization of, 122
Tennesee, 730
Tenth Man, The (play), 421
textbooks, 638n.4
Thailand
   museums in, 378–79
theatre, 417
   accessibility and, 632–33
   arts participation and, 808
   boards and, 80
   broadcasting of, 125–26
   fundraising and, 526
   integration of, 420
   market orientation and, 460, 467
   patronage and, 786–87
   race and, 309
   servicescape and, 505–6
   unionization of, 411–12, 413, 417–18, 427, 429–30
   volunteer work and, 263
TheatreDost, 263, 268, 271–72, 278
Theatre Network Australia, 287–88
thematic analysis, 486
theory
   in arts management, 144–45, 147–52, 148t
theory of practice, 142, 143–44, 155
Thepthepa, Nopparat, 378–79
Thévenot, Laurent, 524, 527–28
Thomas, Sarah R., 470, 471
Thomson, Elaine, 485
Throsby, David
   on cultural and creative industries, 43
   on cultural economics, 48, 119–20, 122, 131
   on value, 484, 485, 664–65, 670–71
Thurik, Roy, 763
Thyssen-Bornemisza Museum, 439
Tight, Malcolm, 24
TikTok, 437–38
Tinkelman, Daniel, 319–20
Tiravanija, Rirkrit, 727–28
Tischler, Rachel J., 588
Today Art Museum (TAM) (Beijing), 537
Tokyo, 734
Tombs, Alastair, 501
tour guides, 512
tourism, 250–51, 525, 673

in Italy, 167
music and, 681
Townsend, Claudia, 558–59
Traballi, Alberto, 582
transfiguration of the commonplace, 727–28
transformational festivals, 355. *See also* festivals
Transnational Giving Europe (TGE), 579
Treasury (UK), 676n.1
trees, 205, 601–2
Tribal Gathering (festival), 350, 354–57, 356*t*, 358–59, 360–61
TripAdvisor, 59–60
Troubled Island (opera), 308
Trump, Donald, 174–76, 302
trust, 530–31
Tubillejas-Andrés, Berta, 505–6
Turkey, 796
Turner, John, 415
Turner Prize, 793
Turner, Victor, 353–54, 362–63
Tuscany, 397
Twitter
fundraising and, 468

U
UCCA Center for Contemporary Art, 532
Uffizi Museum, 437–38
UNCTAD, 44
UNESCO, 44, 163
cultural policy, 163, 164, 179
France and, 164–65, 167–68, 180n.1
funding from, 190–91
sustainability and, 406
UNESCO Convention for the Safeguarding of Intangible Cultural Heritage (2003), 243, 244, 245
UNESCO Convention on the Protection of the World Cultural and Natural Heritage, 240, 241, 244
UNESCO Intergovernmental Conference on Institutional, Administrative and Financial Aspects of Cultural Policies (1970), 163
UNIDO, 47
unions, 411, 412, 416
collective action and, 413, 414, 415

cultural, 411, 415, 420, 429–30
history of, 412, 413, 422–24
performing arts and, 416–20
support for, 423–24
United Food and Commercial Workers, 422–23
United Kingdom. *See also* England; Scotland
ACOs in, 441, 524
art in, 486
arts and cultural management in, 5–6, 25
arts funding in, 525–26, 535
arts research in, 806–7
creative industries in, 43, 44
cultural bureaucracy of, 168–70, 169*f*
cultural policy of, 67, 523
cultural production in, 788
cultural sector in, 264, 269
cultural value in, 665, 669–71, 674–75
diplomacy of, 194–95
disability access in, 626, 637
diversity in, 272–73
ECoC and, 744
economy of, 766–67
environmental policy of, 276–77
festivals in, 286–87
fundraising in, 462–63
museums in, 378
protests in, 275
publications in, 29, 29*t*
servicescapes in, 503–4
tax incentives in, 578, 580, 581, 582, 583–84
theatre broadcasts in, 125–26
volunteering in, 263
United Kingdom Household Longitudinal Study, 131
United Nations (UN), 163, 623–24
cultural heritage and, 246–47
sustainability goals, 239–40
United States
ACOs in, 79, 378–79, 524, 535
activism in, 300
addiction in, 730
antitrust law in, 125
arts in, 206, 216–17
arts and cultural management in, 5–6, 25, 142
arts ecology of, 809, 812, 817

United States (cont.)
  arts research in, 806–7, 808, 809–10, 813–19
  boards in, 65–66
  copyright in, 221–22
  cultural diplomacy of, 190, 194–95
  cultural economics in, 151
  cultural funding in, 270, 545
  cultural planning in, 203, 204, 205, 206–7, 210
  cultural policy of, 173–79, 175f, 176f, 177f, 178f, 523–24, 533, 536
  cultural production in, 786–89, 793–96
  culture in, 112
  demographics of, 463–64
  disability access in, 623–24, 628–30, 634, 637
  disparities in, 805, 813
  diversity in, 214
  education in, 216
  festivals in, 355, 357
  individualism in, 305
  labor movement in, 411, 420, 430
  landscape of, 788
  legal scholarship in, 575
  museums in, 192, 375, 532
  nonprofits in, 111, 555
  politics of, 415–16, 525
  popular culture of, 185–86
  racism in, 299–300, 301, 306, 310, 312, 805
  sports in, 134
  tax incentives in, 578, 588
  unions in, 411–12, 417–20, 421–24, 427, 429–30
United States Performing Arts Research Coalition, 129–30
United Way, 320
Universal Declaration of Human Rights, 163, 623–24
Université du Québec Network, 35–36
universities, 35–36
  structure of, 23
University of California, Los Angeles, 615n.18
University of California, San Francisco, 815
University of Texas at El Paso, 813
University Park, Illinois, 812
Untitled (Free) (Tiravanija), 727–28
Urrutiaguer, Daniel, 465–66

USA Survey of Public Participation in the Arts (2012), 127
US Census Bureau, 806, 810
U.S. Congress, 179, 730–31
U.S. Constitution, 231n.2
US Customs Court, 588
U.S. Senate, 538
US Steel, 417
U.S. Supreme Court, 221–22
utilitarianism, 266, 275

V

vaccines, 815
Vaidhyanathan, Siva, 231n.5
Vakharia, Neville, 109, 112–13, 378–79, 534
Valencia, Spain, 505–6
Valencia, University of, 689
Valentin, P., 587–88
valuation studies, 648–50, 651, 652–53, 654–55
value
  ACOs and, 747, 750, 752–53, 757
  of art, 481–83, 484, 485–86, 487f, 488–89, 491–92
  co-creation and, 352–53
  creation of, 483, 485, 486–89, 491–92, 786
  cultural, 483–84, 663–66, 667–72, 675–76
  of cultural goods, 43, 44, 46
  economic, 120
  emotions and, 498–99
  forms of, 484
  instrumental, 120
  intrinsic, 120
  public, 381
  sacred, 491
  study of, 642–43
value added tax (VAT), 576, 582–85, 586–88
value boundary, 726–27
value order worlds, 527–30, 529t
values
  of art funders, 524
  colonialism and, 786–87
  economic vs. cultural, 120
Valuing Culture and Heritage Capital framework, 669–70
van den Ende, Leonore, 350, 353, 354, 360–61
Van der Ven, Andrew, 52, 53, 54
Van de veld, Willem, 581

Van Gogh, Vincent, 603–4, 606–7
Van Ryzin, Gregg G., 536
Varela, Ximena, 3
Vaujany, François-Xavier de, 512
Veblen goods, 482
Vecco, Marilena
  on cultural policy, 170–71
  on European Capitals of Culture, 745–46
  on entrepreneurship, 705, 708, 770, 774, 775
  on values, 666
Velasco, Kristopher, 555–56
Velthuis, Olav, 597–98
Venice, 167, 250–51, 595, 614n.4, 733–34
Venn diagrams, 596–97, 601, 611–12
Venkatesh, Alladi, 482, 485
venture philanthropy, 526
Vesci, Massimiliano, 504–5
veterans, 814–15
video art, 587–88
video games, 437–38, 448. *See also* gamification
  arts and, 130, 439
  in museums, 439–40, 450
Village Improvement movement, 205
Viola, Bill, 587–88
virtual embassies, 187
virtual experience, 126–27
virtualization, 184, 185–89, 197, 198
virtual reality, 15, 183–84, 186, 188–89, 197
virtual spaces, 512–13
virtual tours, 441, 442–44
  impact of, 445, 446–47, 446t
Viscri, Romania, 250
visual arts, 286–87, 808
visuals, 694
Viveros-Fauné, Christian, 730
vlogs, 59–60, 68
Vloot op de rede (painting), 581
Voelpel, Sven, 372
volunteering, 359–60
vom Lehn, Dirk, 481, 512
Von Bertalanffy, Ludwig, 101, 103, 108–9
Von Krogh, Georg, 372
Voorhees, Clay M., 501
Voss, Glenn B. 460, 467
Voss, Zannie Giraud, 460, 467

W

wages
  of actors, 421–22
Waitress: The Musical, 427
Waldfogel, Joel, 122
Walker, Darren, 627
Wallenberg, Raoul, 187
Wall, Madeleine, 426
Walmsley, Ben, 663
Walter, Achim, 709
Walter, Nadine, 686
Wang, Catherine L., 377, 378
Washington, DC, 206, 420, 538, 806–7
Washington, Marvin, 89
Web 2.0, 450
Webber, Melvin M., 663, 666–69, 671, 675–76
Weber, Max, 82
Weigand, Annie, 634
Weinstein, Stanley, 459–60
welfare, 785–86
Weltanschauung, 62
"WE-Making: How Arts and Culture Unite People to Work Toward Community Well-Being" (report), 815
Were, Wendy, 279
West (region)
  arts and, 19
Western culture, 790
Western philosophy, 103, 114
Weverse, 188
"What Is Critique?" (Foucault), 728–29
Wheatley, Daniel, 131
Whitby, Andrew, 125–26
white Americans, 301, 302–3, 304, 305–6, 307, 312
  in arts management, 311
  arts participation of, 811
White Night Festival, 286
white supremacism, 300–4, 310–11. *See also* racism
white supremacy culture, 302–7, 303b, 309–12, 425. *See also* racism
Whole Village Project (Romania), 250
"Why Everything Has Changed: The Recent Revolution in Cultural Economics" (Cowen), 120–21
wicked problems, 663, 666–69, 675

Wickham, Mark, 484
Wicks, Andrew C., 653, 654–55
Wiedmann, 684, 685–86, 694–95
Wiggins, Jennifer, 553–54
Wikipedia, 594–95
Willem-Alexander (King of the Netherlands), 581
Williams College Museum of Art, 605
Wilson, Francis, 417–18
Wilson, Fred, 727–28
Wilson, James F., 414
Winkelmann, Mike, 593–94
WIPO Copyright Treaty, 223–25
WolfBrown (company), 673
women
   arts groups and, 205
   in arts management, 311–12
   cultural planning and, 217
   leadership and, 322–23, 324
Wooddell, Michelle, 552–53
Woods, Eric, 596
Woolfe, Zachary, 308
word clouds, 7, 8f, 9f
work breakdown structure (WBS), 400, 405
worker skills, 374
Work Foundation, 44
Work of Art in the Age of Mechanical Reproduction, The (Benjamin), 186–87
Works Progress Administration (WPA), 205
World Bank, 629–30
World Book Day, 187
World Customs Organization, 586
world expos, 185
World Health Organization, 623–24, 625, 629–30
World Heritage Committee (WHC), 255n.11
World Intellectual Property Organization, 43–44

World Report on Disability, 629–30
World War II, 786–87
Wright, Michelle, 275–76
Wurth, Bernd, 52, 53
Wyatt, Danielle, 209–10
Wymer, Walter, 459
Wyszomirski, Margaret, 181n.10

X

xenophobia, 218, 735
Xie, Lishan, 685–86, 694–95

Y

Yale Collection of Western Americana, 609
Yale University, 5–6, 609
Yamaguchi, Shoji (character), 731–32
Ying, Jiang, 196
Yin, R.K. 672
Yoo, Youngjin, 49
Young, Greg, 215
YouTube, 223–25, 227–29
Yudice, George, 168

Z

Zajac, Edward J., 89
Zander, Ivo, 725, 726–27, 761–62
Zan, Luca, 644, 654
Zarantonello, Lia, 685–86
Zembla (TV program), 581
Žemieji Šančiai Bendruomenė, 251
Zhang, Wenxuan, 685–86, 694–95
Zhao, Yushan, 123–24
Zoom, 286, 596, 628–29
Zubović, Vedran, 746–47
Zuckerberg, Mark, 187
Zuckerman, Ezra W., 649–50
Zwick, Detlev, 363–64